THE COMPLETE HISTORY OF THE BRITISH LEAGUE

EDITED
BY
PETER OAKES

THE COMPLETE HISTORY OF THE BRITISH LEAGUE

■ **The Complete History of the British League was first published in Great Britain, 1991, by Front Page Books, PO Box 251, Warrington, Cheshire, WA5 5AY. Tel: 0925-59484. Fax: 0925-58047.**

■ **The Complete History of the British League was published by Front Page Books, printed by The Bath Press, Bath, England, from film prepared by Pinegen Limited, 95, Brighton Road, Surbiton, Surrey, KT6 5NF (081-399-0012) and is distributed by Front Page Books.**
■ **The dust jacket was printed by Nightingale Press (Baldock) Limited, Newark Close, Royston, Hertfordshire, SG8 5HL (0763-248393).**

British Library Cataloguing in Publication Data

Oakes, Peter, 1944-
The Complete History of the British League
I. Title.
796.75

ISBN 0948882077

ISBN 0 948882 07 7 **£14.95**

THE COMPLETE HISTORY OF THE BRITISH LEAGUE

THANKS

We would like to offer particular thanks to Philip Rising, Mike Patrick, Alf Weedon and Glyn Shailes for their help and co-operation during the production of The Complete History of the British League. Without their assistance this book would not have been possible.

Many of the photographs used in The Complete History of the British League have come from the private collections of supporters and riders and we would like to thank them all.

The continuing support of our Subscribers is always appreciated.

THE COMPLETE HISTORY OF THE BRITISH LEAGUE

I don't believe it would ever be possible to complete a book of this size and nature and be able to confidently say there are no mistakes in it.
I am sure there will be errors of fact in The Complete History of the British League but every effort has been taken to limit those errors to the barest minimum.
Wherever possible where there has been debate I have endeavoured to revert to official sources.
Fortunately during the time when Bryan Seery was manager of the British Speedway Promoters' Association he kept accurate records of all British League matches but this was not always the case before his arrival and has not been the case since his departure.
All international records have been checked with the staging nation and where matches were not deemed to be officially recognised this is stated in the accompanying text.
Unfortunately there remain two Internationals in New Zealand for which no complete records are available despite research in New Zealand and a personal approach to the Lions' manager of the time.
Unless otherwise stated any reference to the British League refers to the senior Division from 1965 until 1990 and any reference to the National League relates to the second League which operated under three distinct names, British League Division Two, the New National League and the National League variously between 1968 and 1990.
In the Club by Club averages §§ indicates a rider making his first appearance in the League and § indicates a rider making his club debut.
Guest appearances have not been included. All British League averages take into account League, Cup and, where appropriate League Cup matches while National League averages also include the one season when the First Division Knock Out Cup included teams from the National League.
Where scores are underlined in team events this indicates that team was at home.

PETER OAKES
Front Page Books

1965 Roll of Honour

World Champion
BJÖRN KNUTSSON
European Champion
OVE FUNDIN
Nordic Champion
SÖREN SJÖSTEN
Continental Champion
ANDRZEJ WYGLENDA
British Champion
BARRY BRIGGS

World Team Cup Champions
POLAND
(Andrzej Wyglenda, Andrzej Pogorzelski, Antonin Woryna, Zbigniew Podlecki, Pawel Waloszek)

THE changing face of world speedway is reflected throughout this World Championship Roll of Honour.

While The Complete History of the British League is not meant to be a review of the World Championship from 1965 until 1990, it would be wrong not to acknowledge the important part that the FIM events do play in the speedway lives of the British League fans.

So in the next few pages we recall the World Championship winners – perhaps an in depth look at some of those achievement will form the basis of another book at some future time.

The birth of the British League in 1965 coincided with the first-ever World Final win by Björn Knutsson, strangely one of the few top riders never to have raced in the British League although he had been a regular team-mate of his great friend and rival Barry Briggs while at National League Southampton.

Björn's success at Wembley probably hastened his departure from the

1966 Roll of Honour

World Champion
BARRY BRIGGS
European Champion
IVAN MAUGER
Nordic Champion
KALEVI LAHTINEN
Continental Champion
ANDRZEJ POGORZELSKI
British Champion
BARRY BRIGGS

World Team Cup Champions
POLAND
(Andrzej Wyglenda, Antonin Woryna, Marian Rose, Andrzej Pogorzelski, Edmund Migos)

1967 Roll of Honour

World Champion
OVE FUNDIN
European Champion
ANDRZEJ WYGLENDA
Nordic Champion
OVE FUNDIN
Continental Champion
ANDRZEJ WYGLENDA
British Champion
BARRY BRIGGS

World Team Cup Champions
SWEDEN
(Göte Nordin, Bengt Jansson, Ove Fundin, Torbjörn Harrysson, Per Olof Soderman)

1968 Roll of Honour

World Champion
IVAN MAUGER
European Champion
PAWEL WALOSZEK
Nordic Champion
REIDAR EIDE
Continental Champion
GENNADY KURILENKO
British Champion
IVAN MAUGER

World Team Cup Champions
GREAT BRITAIN
(Ivan Mauger, Nigel Boocock, Martin Ashby, Barry Briggs, Norman Hunter)

1969 Roll of Honour

World Champion
IVAN MAUGER
European Champion
VALERI KLEMENTIEV
Nordic Champion
TORBJÖRN HARRYSSON
Continental Champion
ANTONIN WORYNA
British Champion
BARRY BRIGGS

World Team Cup Champions
POLAND
(Andrzej Wyglenda, Edward Jancarz, Stanislaw Tkocz, Henryk Glucklich, Andrzej Pogorzelski)

World Pairs Champions
†NEW ZEALAND
(Ivan Mauger & Bob Andrews)

†The 1969 World Final is no longer recognised by the FIM even though gold medals were awarded at the time.

1970 Roll of Honour

World Champion
IVAN MAUGER
European Champion
IVAN MAUGER
Nordic Champion
GÖTE NORDIN
Continental Champion
HANS JURGEN FRITZ
British Champion
IVAN MAUGER

World Team Cup Champions
SWEDEN
(Ove Fundin, Bengt Jansson, Anders Michanek, Sören Sjösten, Bernt Persson)

World Pairs Champions
NEW ZEALAND
(Ivan Mauge & Ronnie Moore)

domestic scene as he concentrated on his own businesses once he had become World Champion.

The birth of the British League was the birth of new stars – stars like Ivan Mauger who broke his ankle in his very first meeting in 1965 but then went on to win a record six World Speedway Finals as he superceded Ronnie Moore and Barry Briggs as the King of the Kiwis.

The launch of the British League Second Division in 1968 was a far-sighted blueprint for England's future prosperity although no-one can be sure whether that was the genuine aim.

But as more and more youngsters took to the shale the day came when England could hold her head high in international racing and a first World Team Cup triumph in 1973 with a Great Britain side that didn't have to rely on any Commonwealth cousins heralded a new golden era during which Peter Collins became the first English-born rider to be crowned World Champion since the late, great Peter Craven in 1962.

But England's domination couldn't stand unchallenged and as the sport surged towards the Roaring Eighties two new nations began to make their presence felt...America and Denmark!

1971 Roll of Honour

World Champion
OLE OLSEN
European Champion
IVAN MAUGER
Nordic Champion
OLE OLSEN
Continental Champion
HENRYK GLUCKLICH
British Champion
IVAN MAUGER

World Team Cup Champions
GREAT BRITAIN
(Ray Wilson, Ivan Mauger, Jim Airey, Barry Briggs, Ronnie Moore)

World Pairs Champions
POLAND
(Jerzy Szczakiel & Andrzej Wyglenda)

World Long Track Champion
IVAN MAUGER

1972 Roll of Honour

World Champion
IVAN MAUGER
European Champion
PAWEL WALOSZEK
Nordic Champion
BENGT JANSSON
Continental Champion
VIKTOR TROFIMOV
British Champion
IVAN MAUGER

World Team Cup Champions
GREAT BRITAIN
(Ivan Mauger, John Louis, Ray Wilson, Terry Betts, Ronnie Moore)

World Pairs Champions
ENGLAND
(Ray Wilson & Terry Betts)

World Long Track Champion
IVAN MAUGER

1973 Roll of Honour

World Champion
JERZY SZCZAKIEL
European Champion
ANDERS MICHANEK
Nordic Champion
OLE OLSEN
Continental Champion
VALERI GORDEEV
British Champion
RAY WILSON

World Team Cup Champions
GREAT BRITAIN
(Peter Collins, Terry Betts, Malcolm Simmons, Ray Wilson, Dave Jessup)

World Pairs Champions
SWEDEN
(Anders Michanek & Bengt Jansson)

World Long Track Champion
OLE OLSEN

1974 Roll of Honour

World Champion
ANDERS MICHANEK
European Champion
PETER COLLINS
Nordic Champion
OLE OLSEN
Continental Champion
VLADIMIR GORDEEV
British Champion
ERIC BOOCOCK

World Team Cup Champions
ENGLAND
(Peter Collins, John Louis, Dave Jessup, Malcolm Simmons, Ray Wilson)

World Pairs Champions
SWEDEN
(Anders Michanek & Sören Sjösten)

World Long Track Champion
EGON MÜLLER

1975 Roll of Honour

World Champion
OLE OLSEN
European Champion
IVAN MAUGER
Inter Continental Final
IVAN MAUGER
Nordic Champion
OLE OLSEN
Continental Champion
EDWARD JANCARZ
British Champion
JOHN LOUIS

World Team Cup Champions
ENGLAND
(Peter Collins, Malcolm Simmons, Martin Ashby, John Louis, Dave Jessup)

World Pairs Champions
SWEDEN
(Anders Michanek &Tommy Jansson)

World Long Track Champion
EGON MÜLLER

Scott Autrey was the first of the colourful Californians to build an international reputation and Ole Olsen's World Championship exploits encouraged dozens of Danish schoolchildren to begin dreaming of a speedway career.

Forever the unpredictable, the World Championship also provided a seemingly inexhaustible fund of shocks.

Jerzy Szczakiel became Poland's first World Champion; Australia and New Zealand won the World Team Cup against all the odds; and German night-club entertainer Egon Müller won the first World Final to be held in his country.

And who would ever have envisaged a World Champion announcing his retirement as he stood on the rostrum – to go into an American soap opera TV series about a Highway Patrol motor-cycle cop?

But that's exactly what the charismatic Bruce Penhall did at the Los Angeles Coliseum in 1982. And who could have imagined that Bradford – and not Wembley – would be the British home of the World Final?

As the Nineties approached Denmark had taken a stranglehold of the major honours but for how long?

That's the tantalising question that can only

1976 Roll of Honour

World Champion
PETER COLLINS
Inter Continental Final
PETER COLLINS
Nordic Champion
OLE OLSEN
Continental Champion
EGON MÜLLER
British Champion
MALCOLM SIMMONS
Australasian Champion
JOHN BOULGER

World Team Cup Champions
AUSTRALIA
(Phil Crump, Billy Sanders, Phil Herne, John Boulger, Garry Middleton)

World Pairs Champions
ENGLAND
(John Louis & Malcolm Simmons)

World Long Track Champion
IVAN MAUGER

1977 Roll of Honour

World Champion
PETER COLLINS
Inter Continental Final
PETER COLLINS
Nordic Champion
OLE OLSEN
Continental Champion
EGON MÜLLER
British Champion
MALCOLM SIMMONS
Australasian Champion
IVAN MAUGER

World Team Cup Champions
ENGLAND
(Peter Collins, Michael Lee, Dave Jessup, John Davis, Malcolm Simmons)

World Pairs Champions
ENGLAND
(Peter Collins & Malcolm Simmons)

World Long Track Champion
ANDERS MICHANEK

1978 Roll of Honour

World Champion
OLE OLSEN
Inter Continental Final
OLE OLSEN
Nordic Champion
OLE OLSEN
Continental Champion
HANS WASSERMANN
British Champion
MICHAEL LEE
Australasian Champion
MITCH SHIRRA

World Team Cup Champions
DENMARK
(Hans Nielsen, Ole Olsen, Mike Lohmann, Finn Thomsen, Kristian Praestbro)

World Pairs Champions
ENGLAND
(Malcolm Simmons & Gordon Kennett)

World Long Track Champion
EGON MÜLLER

1979 Roll of Honour

World Champion
IVAN MAUGER
Inter Continental Final
MICHAEL LEE
Commonwealth Champion
MICHAEL LEE
Nordic Champion
JAN ANDERSSON
Continental Champion
CHRISTOPH BETZL
British Champion
PETER COLLINS
Australasian Champion
BILLY SANDERS

World Team Cup Champions
NEW ZEALAND
(Larry Ross, Mitch Shirra, Ivan Mauger, Bruce Cribb, Roger Abel)

World Pairs Champions
DENMARK
(Ole Olsen & Hans Nielsen)

World Long Track Champion
ALOIS WIESBÖCK

1980 Roll of Honour

World Champion
MICHAEL LEE
Inter Continental Final
CHRIS MORTON
Commonwealth Champion
DAVE JESSUP
Nordic Champion
HANS NIELSEN
Continental Champion
ZENON PLECH
British Champion
DAVE JESSUP
Australasian Champion
BILLY SANDERS

World Team Cup Champions
ENGLAND
(Michael Lee, Chris Morton, Peter Collins, Dave Jessup, John Davis)

World Pairs Champions
ENGLAND
(Dave Jessup & Peter Collins)

World Long Track Champion
KARL MAIER

be answered in time!

The world governing body, the FIM, have in their debateable wisdom decided to explore the real possibility of scrapping most of the major World Championships as we have known them to accommodate a World Championship Grand Prix.

It has a monetary appeal as a possible vehicle for increased television coverage and more lucrative sponsorships but will find few advocates among those who look at the accompanying annual Roll of Honour and recall and remember some of the drama and controversy that surrounded the events which produced World Champions in Individual, Pairs, Team, Long Track and Under 21 events over the years.

And what of the sudden death nature of an individual World Championship which has, almost every year, produced a hurdle too high for a world-class rider to overcome during a qualifying round when everything has gone wrong?

To so many supporters, most British-based administrators, and even some top riders that has been the very essence of the traditional one-off World Final night.

Will all that be sacrificed for a pot of gold?

1981 Roll of Honour

World Champion
BRUCE PENHALL
Inter Continental Final
BRUCE PENHALL
Overseas Champion
DAVE JESSUP
Nordic Champion
TOMMY KNUDSEN
Continental Champion
EGON MÜLLER
British Champion
STEVE BASTABLE
Australasian Champion
IVAN MAUGER

World Team Cup Champions
DENMARK
(Hans Nielsen, Erik Gundersen, Tommy Knudsen, Ole Olsen, Finn Thomsen)

World Pairs Champions
UNITED STATES OF AMERICA
(Bruce Penhall & Bobby Schwartz)

World Long Track Champion
MICHAEL LEE

1982 Roll of Honour

World Champion
BRUCE PENHALL
Inter Continental Final
LES COLLINS
Overseas Champion
DAVE JESSUP
Nordic Champion
HANS NIELSEN
Continental Champion
JIRI STANCL
British Champion
ANDY GRAHAME

World Team Cup Champions
UNITED STATES OF AMERICA
(Kelly Moran, Bruce Penhall, Bobby Schwartz, Shawn Moran, Scott Autrey)

World Pairs Champions
UNITED STATES OF AMERICA
(Dennis Sigalos & Bobby Schwartz)

World Long Track Champion
KARL MAIER

1983 Roll of Honour

World Champion
EGON MÜLLER
Inter Continental Final
HANS NIELSEN
Overseas Champion
PHIL COLLINS
Nordic Champion
HANS NIELSEN
Continental Champion
ZENON PLECH
British Champion
CHRIS MORTON

World Team Cup Champions
DENMARK
(Erik Gundersen, Hans Nielsen, Ole Olsen, Peter Ravn, Finn Thomsen)

World Pairs Champions
ENGLAND
(Kenny Carter & Peter Collins)

World Long Track Champion
SHAWN MORAN

1984 Roll of Honour

World Champion
ERIK GUNDERSEN
Inter Continental Final
SHAWN MORAN
Overseas Champion
LANCE KING
Nordic Champion
HANS NIELSEN
Continental Champion
EGON MÜLLER
British Champion
KENNY CARTER

World Team Cup Champions
DENMARK
(Erik Gundersen, Bo Petersen, Hans Nielsen, Preben Eriksen, Peter Ravn)

World Pairs Champions
ENGLAND
(Chris Morton & Peter Collins)

World Long Track Champion
ERIK GUNDERSEN

1985 Roll of Honour

World Champion
ERIK GUNDERSEN
Inter Continental Final
SHAWN MORAN
Overseas Champion
SHAWN MORAN
Nordic Champion
TOMMY KNUDSEN
Continental Champion
EGON MÜLLER
British Champion
KENNY CARTER

World Team Cup Champions
DENMARK
(Tommy Knudsen, Erik Gundersen, Hans Nielsen, Preben Eriksen, Bo Petersen)

World Pairs Champions
DENMARK
(Erik Gundersen & Tommy Knudsen)

World Long Track Champion
SIMON WIGG

1986 Roll of Honour

World Champion
HANS NIELSEN
Inter Continental Final
ERIK GUNDERSEN
Overseas Champion
SAM ERMOLENKO
Commonwealth Champion
JEREMY DONCASTER
Nordic Champion
HANS NIELSEN
Continental Champion
VIKTOR KUZNETSOV
British Champion
NEIL EVITTS

World Team Cup Champions
DENMARK
(Erik Gundersen, Hans Nielsen, Jan O. Pedersen, Tommy Knudsen, John Jorgensen)

World Pairs Champions
DENMARK
(Erik Gundersen & Hans Nielsen)

World Long Track Champion
ERIK GUNDERSEN

1987 Roll of Honour

World Champion
HANS NIELSEN
Inter Continental Final
ERIK GUNDERSEN
Overseas Champion
MITCH SHIRRA
Commonwealth Champion
KELVIN TATUM
Nordic Champion
ERIK GUNDERSEN
Continental Champion
GERD RISS
British Champion
KELVIN TATUM

World Team Cup Champions
DENMARK
(Hans Nielsen, Jan O. Pedersen, Erik Gundersen, Tommy Knudsen, John Jorgensen)

World Pairs Champions
DENMARK
(Erik Gundersen & Hans Nielsen)

World Long Track Champion
KARL MAIER

1988 Roll of Honour

World Champion
ERIK GUNDERSEN
Inter Continental Final
JAN O. PEDERSEN
Overseas Champion
SIMON CROSS
Commonwealth Champion
KELVIN TATUM
Nordic Champion
HANS NIELSEN
Continental Champion
ZENON KASPRZAK
British Champion
SIMON WIGG

World Team Cup Champions
DENMARK
(Hans Nielsen, Jan O. Pedersen, Erik Gundersen, Tommy Knudsen, John Jorgensen)

World Pairs Champions
DENMARK
(Erik Gundersen & Hans Nielsen)

World Long Track Champion
KARL MAIER

World Under 21 Champion
PETER NAHLIN

1989 Roll of Honour

World Champion
HANS NIELSEN
Inter Continental Final
KELVIN TATUM
Overseas Champion
SAM ERMOLENKO
Commonwealth Champion
SIMON WIGG
Nordic Champion
HANS NIELSEN
Continental Champion
ZOLTAN ADORJAN
British Champion
SIMON WIGG

World Team Cup Champions
ENGLAND
(Jeremy Doncaster, Paul Thorp, Kelvin Tatum, Simon Wigg, Simon Cross)

World Pairs Champions
DENMARK
(Erik Gundersen & Hans Nielsen)

World Long Track Champion
SIMON WIGG

World Under 21 Champion
GERT HANDBERG

1990 Roll of Honour

World Champion
PER JONSSON
Inter Continental Champion
SHAWN MORAN
Overseason Champion
JEREMY DONCASTER
Nordic Champion
JAN O. PEDERSEN
Continental Champion
GERD RISS
Commonwealth Champion
KELVIN TATUM
British Champion
KELVIN TATUM

World Team Cup Champions
UNITED STATES OF AMERICA
(Kelly Moran, Sam Ermolenko, Shawn Moran, Billy Hamill, Rick Miller)

World Pairs Champions
DENMARK
(Hans Nielsen & Jan O. Pedersen)

World Long Track Champion
SIMON WIGG

World Under 21 Champion
CHRIS LOUIS

From Russia with shove

ANY REAL chance the Russians had of conquering Britain ended on the last lap of heat two in the first test against Britain.

Their undisputed number two Boris Samorodov – expected to give firm backing to tour skipper Igor Plechanov – drifted wide as he headed Nigel Boocock for what would have been a morale-boosting heat victory for the tourists and clouted the Plough Lane fence.

At first he appeared to have come through the hair-raising episode without too much damage to himself (his bike was written off) but shortly after regaining his feet to the applause of a big Wimbledon crowd, he collapsed and was rushed to hospital.

There, x-rays revealed a broken shoulder and a badly bruised foot: injuries that were to keep the former World number four out of the rest of the tour.

His absence left a huge gap at the heart of the Soviet party and was one they could never overcome.

It was only the Russians' second tour of Britain – they had come for the first time 12 months earlier and raced three internationals at Wembley, Coventry and Belle Vue – and there was still some mystique about their appearance.

The Russkies had a five-Test schedule and two other meetings on their 12-day visit and while they lost all three internationals against Great Britain they did register their first Test win in the country when they outscored Scotland at Meadowbank.

Skipper Plechanov was the star visiting turn and of the meagre seven points that Barry Briggs dropped over the five matches three came when he stopped in the opening race in the final Test at Newport's Somerton Park and three others came in defeats against Plechanov.

There were countless casualties during a tour in which the Russkies mixed it at every turn – among them Oxford's Ron How (dislocated shoulder) and Sheffield's Billy Bales, who had three stitches in a badly cut right leg.

But the biggest upset of all was at Newport where the Welsh fans, impressed by the never-say-die attitude of their visitors, turned on the referee after he had excluded, initially, Vladimir Sokolov and subsequently Valentin Moiseyev after Charlie Monk had fallen.

Monk, who won the re-run, later admitted: "I stopped the race. The Russian didn't have a chance of avoiding me."

1965 Great Britain v Soviet Union Tour Results

Wimbledon, Monday, July 5
GREAT BRITAIN 71 (†Barry Briggs 17, Nigel Boocock 16, Charlie Monk 14, Ken McKinlay 10, George Hunter 6, Trevor Hedge 3, Reg Luckhurst 3, Ron How 2) **SOVIET UNION 36** (Vladimir Sokolov 13, †Igor Plechanov 10, Gabdrahman Kadirov 8, Gennady Kurilenko 3, Yuri Chekranov 2, Boris Samorodov 0, Vladimir Kornev 0, Valentin Moiseyev did not ride).

Coventry, Wednesday, July 7
GREAT BRITAIN 66 (†Barry Briggs 18, Nigel Boocock 16, Ken McKinlay 9, Jim Lightfoot 8, Charlie Monk 7, George Hunter 6, Jim Airey 2, Mike Broadbank 0) **SOVIET UNION 42** (Gennady Kurilenko 12, †Igor Plechanov 10, Valentin Moiseyev 10, Yuri Chekranov 8, Sergei Lyatosinsky 2, Vladimir Sokolov 0, Gabdrahman Kadirov 0, Vladimir Kornev, did not ride).

Sheffield, Thursday, July 8
GREAT BRITAIN 73 (†Barry Briggs 17, Nigel Boocock 17, Charlie Monk 15, Ken McKinlay 9, Cyril Maidment 6, Clive Featherby 5, Jack Kitchen 4, Billy Bales 0) **SOVIET UNION 35** (†Igor Plechanov 15, Vladimir Sokolov 9, Gabdrahman Kadirov 5, Gennady Kurilenko 3, Yuri Chekranov 3, Valentin Moiseyev 0, Vladimir Kornev 0, Sergei Lyatosinsky, did not ride).

Belle Vue, Wednesday, July 14
GREAT BRITAIN 69 (†Barry Briggs 17, Nigel Boocock 15, Dick Fisher 11, Ken McKinlay 10, Cyril Maidment 7, Jack Kitchen 6, Charlie Monk 3, George Hunter 0) **SOVIET UNION 39** (†Igor Plechanov 15, Gennady Kurilenko 8, Vladimir Sokolov 6, Yuri Chekranov 5, Gabdrahman Kadirov 3, Valentin Moiseyev 2, Vladimir Kornev, Sergei Lyatosinsky, did not ride).

Newport, Friday, July 16
GREAT BRITAIN 63 (Ken McKinlay 15, †Barry Briggs 14, Charlie Monk 11, Jimmy Gooch 8, George Hunter 7, Nigel Boocock 6, Alby Golden 1, Peter Vandenberg 1) **SOVIET UNION 45** (Gennady Kurilenko 14, †Igor Plechanov 12, Vladimir Sokolov 7, Valentin Moiseyev 5, Yuri Chekranov 5, Gabdrahman Kadirov 2, Vladimir Kornev, Sergei Lyatosinsky, did not ride).

Great Britain win the series 5-0.

Edinburgh, Saturday, July 10
SCOTLAND 51 (George Hunter 15, †Ken McKinlay 13, Charlie Monk 13, Ross Gilbertson 4, Bert Harkins 2, Colin McKee 2, Gordon McGregor 2, Willie Templeton 0) **SOVIET UNION 57** (†Igor Plechanov 14, Valdimir Sokolov 11, Valentin Moiseyev 10, Yuri Chekranov 8, Gabdrahman Kadirov 7, Gennady Kurilenko 7).

Exeter, Monday, July 12
WEST OF ENGLAND 56 (Colin Gooddy 16, Alan Cowland 11, Jimmy Squibb 11, Bill Andrew 9, Ronnie Genz 7, †Barry Briggs 2, Martin Ashby 0, Mike Broadbank 0) **SOVIET UNION 51** (†Igor Plechanov 15, Yuri Chekranov 10, Gabdrahman Kadirov 8, Valentin Moiseyev 8, Gennady Kurilenko 7, Vladimir Sokolov 3).

- *The Great Britain team managers for the series were: Trevor Redmond (Wimbledon), Charles Foot (Coventry), Charles Ochiltree (Sheffield), Mike Parker (Belle Vue) and Ronnie Greene (Newport).*
- *The Scotland team manager was Trevor Redmond and the West of England team manager was Pete Lansdale.*
- *The Soviet Union team manager was G.S. Tcherkassy.*

RED DEVILS...the 1965 Soviet Union squad on parade before the opening Test at Wimbledon

There was no doubting the Russians' pace if they got out of the gate.

Speedy Plechanov equalled the Newport track record in his opening ride; saw his team-mate Gennady Kurilenko set a new time in heat three; and then went out and equalled that time in heat seven!

And, at Exeter in a representative match, he made light work of a sawdust-strewn track (the management laid down 87 bags to get the meeting on) sliced nearly a second off Trevor Hedge's previous fastest four laps to set up a new time of 71.4 seconds as late as heat thirteen.

The crowds flocked to see the Iron Curtain invaders – there were 8,000 plus at Edinburgh – and few of those fans who turned up were disappointed.

While the Russians departed with an overall record of six defeats from seven matches they certainly won over the British public for a second successive year.

1965 Edinburgh Tour of Poland

TEENAGER Bernt Persson gave the Eastern world a glimpse of his potential – as he top-scored for his British club side Edinburgh on a late season tour of Poland.

The 19-year-old Swede had made his debut for the Monarchs a couple of weeks before the nine-rider party set out, and simply added to his already glowing reputation top scoring in three of the six matches, including a 14-point haul in one.

And, by the end of the 12-day, six match visit, he had established himself as the Scottish club's number one with a series of brilliant performance on the uncustomary Polish circuits.

Persson was top scorer in three of the six matches and at Bydgoszcz dropped only one point in five starts.

The Monarchs drafted in four guest riders for the trip – two each from Newport and Long Eaton – and one of them, Ray Wilson, provided Persson with his main backing.

The Monarchs opened their tour with a 10-point defeat in Wroclaw and then went down heavily to Polish League champions ROW Rybnik and were comprehensively beaten in all six matches, including a 60-18 hammering in their last meeting at Krakow where the local side brought in guests Antonin Woryna and Stanislaw Tkocz instead of Viktor Waloszek and Lotar Dudek, neither of whom had been impressive scorers in the Polish League.

Edinburgh promoter Ian Hoskins claimed: "All nine riders were exhausted by the programme. I will insist any future league team shall have a shortened itinerary."

Wroclaw, Sunday, October 10
SPARTA 44 (Konstanty Pociejkowicz 10, Adolf Slabon 8, Jerzy Trzeszkowski 8, Bogdan Jarowszewicz 7, Zygmunt Antos 6, Stanislaw Nowak 3, Piotr Bruzda 2) **EDINBURGH 34** (Ray Wilson 9, †Doug Templeton 6, Norman Storer 5, George Hunter 5, Bernt Persson 5, Henry Harrfeldt 4, Colin McKee 0)

Rybnik, Tuesday, October 12
ROW 52 (Stanislaw Tkocz 12, Antonin Woryna 11, Joachim Maj 10, Waldemar Motyka 9, Alojzy Norek 6, Jerzy Gryt 3, Antoni Maslowski 1) **EDINBURGH 26** (Bernt Persson 10, Ray Wilson 6, Norman Storer 6, †Doug Templeton 2, George Hunter 2, Henry Harrfeldt 0, Colin McKee 0).

Gorzow, Thursday, October 14
STAL 44 (Edmund Migos 12, Andrzej Pogorzelski 10, Bronislaw Rogal 7, Wojciech Jurasz 6, Jerzy Bartoszewicz 4, Wladislaw Opala 3 Marian Pilarczyk 2) **EDINBURGH 34** (George Hunter 10, †Doug Templeton 8, Bernt Persson 8, Jon Erskine 4, Ray Wilson 2, Norman Storer 1, Geoff Penniket 1).

Gdansk, Sunday, October 17
NA ZUZLU 45 (Zbigniew Podlecki 12, Jan Tkocz 10, Marian Kaiser 7, Zygfryd Friedek 6, Bogdan Berlinski 4, Jan Ziolkowski 3, Roman Wieczorek 3) **EDINBURGH 33** (Bernt Persson 9, Geoff Penniket 7, George Hunter 5, Colin McKee 5, †Doug Templeton 3, Jon Erskine 2, Henry Harrfeldt 2).

Bydgoszcz, Monday, October 18
POLONIA 45 (Zygfryd Friedek 11, Mieczyslaw Polukard 10, Rajmund Switala 9, Edward Kupczynski 8, Andrzej Koselski 3, Henryk Glucklich 2, Norbert Switala 2) **EDINBURGH 33** (Bernt Persson 14, Ray Wilson 10, Norman Storer 4, Colin McKee 3, †Doug Templeton 1, Jon Erskine 1, Geoff Penniket 0, George Hunter 0).

Krakow, Tuesday, October 19
SLASK 60 (Pawel Waloszek 12, Jan Mucha 12, Stanislaw Tkocz 11, Antonin Woryna 10, Zygmunt Pytka 6, Erwin Brabanski 5, Krystian Foltyn 4) **EDINBURGH 18** (Ray Wilson 7, Bernt Persson 6, †Doug Templeton 3, Norman Storer 1, Henry Harrfeldt 1, Jon Erskine 0, Colin McKee 0).

1965 Scotland v England Results

Edinburgh, Saturday, May 15
SCOTLAND 60 (Charlie Monk 18, †Ken McKinlay 17, George Hunter 16, Willie Templeton 5, Doug Templeton 3, Colin McKee 1, Bill Landels 0, Bert Harkins 0) **ENGLAND 48** (Brian Brett 12, †Ronnie Genz 10, Jimmy Gooch 10, Maurie Mattingley 8, Jack Kitchen 5, Jimmy Squibb 2, Peter Kelly 1, John Dews 0).

Newcastle, Monday, May 31
ENGLAND 55 (†Nigel Boocock 14, Mike Broadbank 11, Cyril Maidment 9, Peter Kelly 9, Pete Jarman 7, Jack Kitchen 4, Brian Craven 1, Brian Brett 0). **SCOTLAND 52** (George Hunter 18, †Ken McKinlay 17, Bluey Scott 6, Gordon McGregor 5, Doug Templeton 5, Willie Templeton 1, Colin McKee 0, Bert Harkins 0)

Glasgow, Wednesday, June 2
SCOTLAND 62 (†Ken McKinlay 18, Charlie Monk 17, George Hunter 17, Gordon McGregor 4, Doug Templeton 3, Willie Templeton 3, Bill McMillan, Bert Harkins, did not ride) **ENGLAND 46** (Colin Gooddy 13, †Nigel Boocock 12, Martin Ashby 12, Norman Hunter 5, Brian Brett 4, Malcolm Simmons 0, John Dews 0).

Scotland win the series 2-1.

● *The Scotland team managers were Ian Hoskins (Edinburgh and Newcastle) and Trevor Redmond (Glasgow).*
● *The England team managers were Mike Parker (Edinburgh) and Tom Graham (Newcastle and Glasgow).*

●Scotland's heat leaders Charlie Monk, Ken McKinlay and George Hunter dropped only six points between them throughout the 1965 series against England.

1965 Vargarna (Sweden) Club Tour of England – All the Results

ONLY Newcastle, boosted by the return of their skipper Ivan Mauger who was in peerless form with a 12-point maximum, inflicted a defeat on Vargarna, the third of the summer's overseas tourists.

Led by a brilliant top four of Göte Nordin, Leif Larsson, Bengt Jansson and teenager Bernt Persson, the Swedes began with a draw at West Ham where home fans forced the management into persuading the wily Ken McKinlay to borrow team-mate Malcolm Simmons' bike in the vital last heat.

He duly claimed the two points that brought the sides level! The Stockholm side was managed by Wimbledon's Olle Nygren in three of their matches but when he wasn't available the rôle was taken over by teenager Ronny Aman who also doubled as one of the tourists' reserves.

● *The Vargarna team managers were Olle Nygren (Newcastle, Newport and Sheffield) and Ronny Aman.*

West Ham, Tuesday, August 10
WEST HAM 39 (Sverre Harrfeldt 12, Malcolm Simmons 10, Brian Leonard 7, †Ken McKinlay 5, Reg Trott 2, Tony Ede 2, Norman Hunter 1) **VARGARNA 39** (Bengt Jansson 11, †Göte Nordin 9, Bernt Persson 7, Leif Larsson 6, Arne Carlsson 4, Runo Wedin 2, Sture Lindblom 0).

Newport, Wednesday, August 11
NEWPORT 38 (Jack Biggs 8, Peter Vandenberg 8, Jon Erskine 7, †Alby Golden 6, Geoff Pennikett 4, Vic White 3, Bob Hughes 2) **VARGARNA 39** (†Göte Nordin 11, Leif Larsson 9, Bengt Jansson 7, Arne Carlsson 7, Runo Wedin 4, Bernt Persson 1, Ronny Aman 0).

Wolverhampton, Friday, August 13
WOLVERHAMPTON 35 (†Tommy Sweetman 8, Bob Andrews 7, Gordon Guasco 6, Cyril Francis 6, Brian Maxted 3, Jim Airey 3, James Bond 2) **VARGARNA 43** (Leif Larsson 12, †Göte Nordin 10, Bengt Jansson 9, Bernt Persson 5, Runo Wedin 4, Arne Carlsson 3, Sture Lindblom 0).

Belle Vue, Saturday, August 14
BELLE VUE 35 (Cyril Maidment 11, Norman Nevitt 9, †Dick Fisher 6, Jim Yacoby 5, Sandor Levai 2, Gordon McGregor 1, Bill Powell 1) **VARGARNA 43** (†Göte Nördin 11, Bengt Jansson 10, Bernt Persson 7, Leif Larsson 7, Runo Wedin 5, Arne Carlsson 3, Sture Lindblom 0).

Newcastle, Monday, August 16
NEWCASTLE 45 (†Ivan Mauger 12, Peter Kelly 8, Brian Craven 7, Mike Watkin 6, Ken Sharples 6, Brian Brett 4, Russ Dent 2) **VARGARNA 33** (Bengt Jansson 12, †Göte Nordin 10, Leif Larsson 7, Runo Wedin 3, Bernt Persson 1, Arne Carlsson 0, Ronny Aman 0).

Sheffield, Thursday, August 19
SHEFFIELD 35 (†Jack Kitchen 10, Clive Featherby 7, John Dews 6, Alan Jay 5, Bob Paulson 4, Billy Bales 2, David Crane 1) **VARGARNA 43** (†Göte Nordin 10, Bengt Jansson 10, Leif Larsson 10, Arne Carlsson 7, Runo Wedin 3, Bernt Persson 3, Ronny Aman 0).

1965 Gornik Rybnik (Poland) Club Tour of England Results

REIGNING Polish League champions Gornik Rybnik were overshadowed on their first British League visit...but still provided plenty of entertainment.

Their tour coincided with the visit of the full-strength Soviet Union squad and British fans were spoilt for choice with the last two Russian matches on the same day as two of Rybnik's first three meetings.

Little wonder that they ended their visit with just two defeats, in their opener at Brough Park and their last match at Oxford, as their touring party included three 1965 World Finalists in Andrzej Wyglenda, Antonin Woryna and Andrzej Pogorzelski.

The thumping at Oxford – a clash of each nations 1964 League champions – was largely explained by a third heat crash in which Pogorzelski, who had been unbeaten at Poole 24 hours earlier, thumped the fence after his foot rest snapped coming out of the first turn.

He refused to go to hospital with a badly bruised hip but was forced to watch the rest of the meeting from the pits. In all the Poles had four riders who were unbeaten in a match. Besides Pogo, Woryna, Wyglenda and Stanislaw Tkocz all had maximum returns.

● *The Gornik team manager was Jerzy Kubik.*

Newcastle, Monday, July 12
NEWCASTLE 41 (Peter Kelly 9, Ken Sharples 7, Russ Dent 6, Mike Watkin 6, Brian Brett 6, †Ivan Mauger 5, Dave Gifford 2) **GORNIK 37** (†Andrzej Wyglenda 13, Antonin Woryna 6, Stanislaw Tkocz 6, Alojzy Norek 6, Andrzej Pogorzelski 5, Joachim Maj 1, Karol Peszke 0).

Long Eaton, Tuesday, July 13
LONG EATON 35 (Ray Wilson 9, Kid Bodie 9, Norman Storer 8, Ron Sharp 4, Ray Cresp 3, Clive Hitch 2, †Ken Adams 0) **GORNIK 43** (Joachim Maj 9, Andrzej Pogorzelski 9, Antonin Woryna 8, †Andrzej Wyglenda 8, Stanislaw Tkocz 5, Alojzy Norek 2, Waldemar Motyka 2).

Wolverhampton, Friday, July 16
WOLVERHAMPTON 38 (†Tommy Sweetman 9, Jim Airey 7, Cyril Francis 6, Bob Andrews 6, James Bond 5, Gordon Guasco 5, Brian Maxted 0) **GORNIK 39** (Andrzej Wyglenda 12, Antonin Woryna 11, Andrzej Pogorzelski 11, Joachim Maj 3, Stanislaw Tkocz 2, Alojzy Norek 0, Waldemar Motyka 0).

Halifax, Saturday, July 17
HALIFAX 39 (Tommy Roper 11, Eric Boocock 10, †Eric Boothroyd 8, Dave Younghusband 4, Bert Kingston 3, Ray Day 3, Dennis Gavros 0) **GORNIK 39** (Joachim Maj 9, Stanislaw Tkocz 8, †Andrzej Wyglenda 7, Antonin Woryna 7, Andrzej Pogorzelski 6, Alojzy Norek 1, Waldemar Motyka 1).

Cradley Heath, Monday, July 19
CRADLEY HEATH 36 (Nigel Boocock 14, John Hart 11, Leo McAuliffe 5, Chris Julian 2, Eric Hockaday 2, Tim Bungay 1, John Debbage 1) **GORNIK 42** (Andrzej Pogorzelski 11, Joachim Maj 9, Stanislaw Tkocz 8, †Andrzej Wyglenda 7, Antonin Woryna 3, Karol Peszke 3, Alojzy Norek 1).

Poole, Wednesday, July 21
POOLE 26 (Bill Andrew 8, Ronnie Genz 8, †Geoff Mudge 7, Ross Gilbertson 1, Pete Smith 1, Pete Munday 1, Peter Swain 0) **GORNIK 52** (Andrzej Pogorzelski 12, Stanislaw Tkocz 11, †Andrzej Wyglenda 9, Antonin Woryna 9, Joachim Maj 8, Alojzy Norek 2, Karol Peszke 2).

Oxford, Thursday, July 22
OXFORD 46 (†Jimmy Gooch 12, Arne Pander 11, John Bishop 9, Eddie Reeves 5, Ken Vale 3, Stan Stevens 3, Jimmy Heard 3) **GORNIK 32** (Stanislaw Tkocz 11, Antonin Woryna 7, Joachim Maj 6, †Andrzej Wyglenda 5, Karol Peszke 3, Alojzy Norek 0, Andrzej Pogorzelski 0).

POLEDRIVERS...the successful Gornik side that won four matches in Britain, left to right Stanislaw Tkocz, Antonin Woryna, Alojzy Norek, Joachim Maj, Andrzej Pogorzelski, Waldemar Motyka, Karol Peszke and Andrzej Wyglenda with manager Jerzy Kubik

Hammered and so sickle!

THE Soviet Union crashed to their biggest defeat of the tour in the final Test at West Ham...after a schedule that left them tired and weary.

From their opening match at Poole they travelled more than 1,000 miles almost the length and breadth of Britain before arriving at West Ham a fortnight later.

And the problems of having to fit in eight tough matches in 15 days certainly told on the touring party who were hammered out of sight on the Custom House track that should have suited their Eastern European style and engines.

They began brightly enough with a two-point win at Poole against a Southern Counties side that almost looked stronger than the England squad they were to meet in five Test matches.

Barry Briggs again relished the competition, claiming an 18-point maximum in both the opener and a later outing for the West of England at Swindon. Newcomer Viktor Trofimov began sensationally with 16 points in his first international meeting in England and looked a major find until all the travelling dulled his impact.

But, once again, the Russians relied heavily on their skipper Igor Plechanov – who continued to make friends with his cheery disposition and his penchant for collecting track badges wherever he rode – and his fellow World Finalist Boris Samorodov, obviously fully recovered from the shoulder injuries which had ruled him out of the bulk of the previous year's visit.

1966 England v Soviet Union Tour Results

Newcastle, Monday, July 4
ENGLAND 49 (†Nigel Boocock 13, Brian Brett 12, Eric Boocock 9, Ron Mountford 8, Trevor Hedge 5, Dave Younghusband 1, Peter Kelly 1, Dick Fisher 0) **SOVIET UNION 59** (Viktor Trofimov 16, †Igor Plechanov 15, Boris Samorodov 11, Vladimir Kornev 8, Yuri Chekranov 7, Gennady Kurilenko 2, Gabdrahman Kadirov and Rail Farfarov, did not ride).

Halifax, Wednesday, July 6
ENGLAND 59 (Eric Boocock 14, Eric Boothroyd 11, †Nigel Boocock 10, Ron Mountford 10, Trevor Hedge 7, Bob Paulson 6, Dave Younghusband 1) **SOVIET UNION 49** (†Igor Plechanov 14, Viktor Trofimov 11, Yuri Chekranov 10, Boris Samorodov 9, Vladimir Kornev 5, Gabdrahman Kadirov 0, Gennady Kurilenko 0, Rail Farfarov, did not ride).

Wolverhampton, Friday, July 8
ENGLAND 59 (Eric Boocock 15, †Nigel Boocock 12, Terry Betts 11, Trevor Hedge 11, Brian Brett 4, Ron Mountford 3, Bob Paulson 2, Ivor Brown 1) **SOVIET UNION 49** (†Igor Plechanov 13, Viktor Trofimov 13, Boris Samorodov 11, Yuri Chekranov 9, Gabdrahman Kadirov 2, Rail Farfarov 1, Gennady Kurilenko 0, Vladimir Volsky, did not ride).

Exeter, Monday, July 11
ENGLAND 60 (†Nigel Boocock 16, Ron Mountford 13, Trevor Hedge 11, Colin Pratt 7, Colin Gooddy 7, Tommy Sweetman 6, Chris Blewett, Jimmy Squibb, did not ride) **SOVIET UNION 48** (Boris Samorodov 16, †Igor Plechanov 14, Gennady Kurilenko 6, Viktor Trofimov 4, Yuri Chekranov 4, Gabdrahman Kadirov 4, Rail Farfarov and Vladimir Volsky, did not ride).

West Ham, Tuesday, July 12
ENGLAND 71 (Norman Hunter 18, Terry Betts 15, †Nigel Boocock 13.5, Colin Pratt 12.5, Brian Brett 6, Malcolm Simmons 4, Trevor Hedge 1, Reg Luckhurst 1) **SOVIET UNION 37** (†Igor Plechanov 11, Boris Samorodov 9, Viktor Trofimov 6, Gabdrahman Kadirov 5, Yuri Chekranov 4, Gennady Kurilenko 2, Rail Farfarov and Vladimir Volsky, did not ride).

England win the series 4-1.

Poole, Wednesday, June 29
SOUTHERN COUNTIES 53 (†Barry Briggs 18, Peter Vandenberg 9, Bill Andrew 8, Mike Broadbank 6, Geoff Mudge 5, Ronnie Genz 5, Neil Street 2) **SOVIET UNION 55** †(Igor Plechanov 14, Gennady Kurilenko 14, Boris Samorodov 13, Yuri Chekranov 6, Gabdrahman Kadirov 4, Vladimir Kornev 4).

Swindon, Saturday, July 9
WEST OF ENGLAND 59 (Barry Briggs 18, †Mike Broadbank 16, Bill Andrew 10, Martin Ashby 6, Jack Biggs 5, Colin Gooddy 3, Jon Erskine 1, Neil Street 0) **SOVIET UNION 49** (Boris Samorodov 13, †Igor Plechanov 12, Viktor Trofimov 12, Yuri Chekranov 10, Gabdrahman Kadirov 1, Rail Farfarov 1).

- *The England team managers for the series were: Bill Bridgett (Newcastle), Frank Varey (Halifax), Mike Parker (Wolverhampton), Charles Foot (Exeter) and Charles Ochiltree (West Ham).*
- *The Scotland team manager was Ian Hoskins.*
- *The Soviet Union team manager was Aleksi Ipatenko.*

1966 Scotland v Soviet Union Tour Result

BORIS SAMORODOV came, saw and conquered Scotland...even if the Russkies had to concede defeat in their second visit North of the Border.

A year earlier Boris had missed the trip to Edinburgh having been injured in the opening match at Wimbledon and he quickly made up for lost time. After losing to Charlie Monk in his opening race and finishing third second time out, he reeled off four successive wins to leave Scotland thankful that top-scorer Monk's father had been born in Dundee!

Glasgow, Monday, July 1
SCOTLAND 57 (Charlie Monk 15, George Hunter 11, Willie Templeton 9, †Ken McKinlay 9, Bluey Scott 7, Doug Templeton 6) **SOVIET UNION 51** (Boris Samorodov 15, Gennady Kurilenko 13, Yuri Chekranov 12, †Igor Plechanov 8, Vladimir Kornev 2, Rail Farfarov 1).

1966 Scotland v England Results

ENGLAND'S last Test win at Newcastle ensured them a first-ever series victory over Scotland as they came from 2-0 down to take the rubber.

The 78-30 win at Halifax was also the biggest victory ever, surpassing the previous highest scoreline of 73-35 to Scotland at Glasgow White City in 1964.

Edinburgh, Saturday, May 7
SCOTLAND 63 (Charlie Monk 17, George Hunter 15, †Ken McKinlay 11, Bluey Scott 10, Doug Templeton 8, Willie Templeton 1, Jimmy Tannock 1, Bill Landels 0) **ENGLAND 45** (†Brian Brett 14, Terry Betts 10, Ray Wilson 7, Norman Hunter 7, Maurie Mattingley 3, Roy Trigg 3, Peter Kelly 1, Mike Watkin, did not ride).

Glasgow, Friday, June 17
SCOTLAND 61 (Charlie Monk 14, †Ken McKinlay 13, Bluey Scott 13, George Hunter 10, Willie Templeton 6, Doug Templeton 5, Bill McMillan and Bert Harkins, did not ride) **ENGLAND 46** (Trevor Hedge 13, Dave Younghusband 11, Eric Boocock 10, Mike Watkin 7, Maurie Mattingley 3, Peter Kelly 2, †Mike Broadbank 0).

Halifax, Wednesday, June 22
ENGLAND 78 (Nigel Boocock 18, Dave Younghusband 17, †Eric Boothroyd 15, Eric Boocock 13, Tommy Roper 8, Ray Wilson 6, Bob Paulson 1, Cyril Maidment 0) **SCOTLAND 30** (Charlie Monk 9, †Ken McKinlay 8, Bluey Scott 8, Willie Templeton 3, Doug Templeton 2, George Hunter 0, Bill McMillan 0, Jimmy Tannock 0).

Middlesbrough, Thursday, June 23
ENGLAND 63 (†Mike Broadbank 17, Dave Younghusband 14, Eric Boocock 13, Cyril Maidment 11, Ray Wilson 5, Peter Kelly 2, Mike Watkin 1, Allan Butterfield, did not ride) **SCOTLAND 45** (Charlie Monk 16, †Ken McKinlay 12, George Hunter 11, Willie Templeton 4, Bluey Scott 2, Doug Templeton 0, Jimmy Tannock 0, Bill McMillan, did not ride).

Newcastle, Monday, October 10
ENGLAND 74 (Eric Boocock 17, Nigel Boocock 16, Dave Younghusband 13, Brian Brett 12, Mike Watkin 8, Peter Kelly 8, Allan Butterfield and Russ Dent, did not ride) **SCOTLAND 34** (Charlie Monk 15, George Hunter 10, Willie Templeton 6, Bluey Scott 2, Bill Landels 1, Bert Harkins 0, Bill McMillan 0, Doug Templeton 0).

England win series 3-2.

- *The England team managers were: Eddie Glennon (Edinburgh), Tom Graham (Glasgow), Frank Varey (Halifax) and Eric Boothroyd (Middlesbrough),*
- *The Scotland team managers were: Ian Hoskins (Edinburgh, Middlesbrough), Trevor Redmond (Glasgow) and Johnnie Hoskins (Halifax),*

- ***The fourth Test match in the England-Scotland 1966 series was staged at Middlesbrough – the first time in British League history that a non-league circuit hosted a Test.***

Ivan's left at the start

IVAN MAUGER was left kicking his heels at London's Heathrow Airport after a mix-up over numbers deprived him of a seat on the plane taking the Great Britain party to Poland.

And, like the rest of his team-mates, when he finally did arrive at Bysdgoszcz for the opening test match only 40 minutes before the parade, he was left stranded at the tapes by the swifter than lightning starts of the home stars.

Immediately before the first race all the British riders were lectured on the starting technique...and then saw the referee totally ignore everything he had said as Andrzej Pogorzelski and Edmund Migos left skipper Barry Briggs and his partner Cyril Maidment stranded at the start, hopelessly slow out from under the tapes. But that wasn't the end of the surprises.

The British riders were stunned when they found in charge at the second Test at Gdansk was Irene Nadolna, the world's only international-class woman referee.

Then, on their way to the third and what was to become the series-clinching match at Gorzow, the British party lost their trailer which had been hitched onto the back of the coach they were on being transported from venue to venue. It had become uncoupled, run off into a turnip field and was lying there a write-off with most of the bikes badly damaged.

Almost as soon as the series was over the Poles were on their way to England – and the huge gulf in standards between the two countries was illustrated with another whitewash, this time for the Brits with skipper Briggs dropping only one point to an opponent (Konstanty Pociejkowicz at Coventry) in 18 starts and equalling Colin Pratt's Hackney track record.

Trevor Hedge, too, collected a maximum at Sheffield where Mauger made a flying start, equalling Clive Featherby's two- year-old Owlerton track record.

One feature shone through the series – the keen rivalry but sportsmanship of the two sides. In the opening Test at Waterden Road Terry Betts and Andrzej Wyglenda came off on the last bend, the Pole then won the pushing race for the line by a bike's length and promptly lent Betts one of his machines for his last ride as the King's Lynn star had buckled his front wheel in the pile-up!

POWER-POLE...top scorer on the tour of Great Britain was Pawel Waloszek of Slask Swietochlowice

1966 Poland v Great Britain Tour Results

Bydgoszcz, Monday, July 18
POLAND 77 (Pawel Waloszek 18, Andrzek Pogorzelski 16, Edmund Migos 14, Mieczyslaw Polukard 11, Marian Rose 10, Henryk Glucklich 7, Marian Kaiser 1, Benedykt Kosek 0) **GREAT BRITAIN 31** (Nigel Boocock 7, Ivan Mauger 6, Barry Briggs 5, Cyril Maidment 4, Eric Boocock 3, Trevor Hedge 3, Ken McKinlay 2, Bill Andrew 1).

Gdansk, Tuesday, July 19
POLAND 62 (Pawel Waloszek 14, Antonin Woryna 14, Andrzej Wyglenda 11, Henryk Zyto 9, Stanislaw Tkocz 6, Marian Kaiser 3, Jerzy Trzeszkowski 3, Jan Tkocz 2) **GREAT BRITAIN 46** (Barry Briggs 16, Nigel Boocock 12, Ivan Mauger 9, Eric Boocock 5, Ken McKinlay 2, Cyril Maidment 2, Bill Andrew 0, Trevor Hedge 0).

Gorzow, Thursday, July 21
POLAND 74 (Edmund Migos 16, Andrzej Pogorzelski 16, Andrzej Wyglenda 13, Joachim Maj 11, Stanislaw Tkocz 10, Bronislaw Rogal 5, Jerzy Padewski 3) **GREAT BRITAIN 34** (Barry Briggs 15, Trevor Hedge 10, Nigel Boocock 6, Bill Andrew 1, Eric Boocock 1, Cyril Maidment 1, Ken McKinlay 0, Ivan Mauger 0).

Wroclaw, Friday, July 22
POLAND 77 (Pawel Waloszek 16, Konstanty Pociejkowicz 13, Antonni Woryna 13, Andrzej Pogorzelski 11, Jerzy Trzeszkowski 10, Andrzej Wyglenda 10, Bogdan Jaroszewicz 4, Joachim Maj, did not ride) **GREAT BRITAIN 31** (Barry Briggs 12, Nigel Boocock 8, Ivan Mauger 4, Trevor Hedge 2, Ken McKinlay 2, Bill Andrew 1, Eric Boocock 1, Cyril Maidment 1).

Czestochowa, Sunday, July 24
POLAND 38 (Joachim Maj 8, Marian Rose 8, Stanislaw Rurarz 8, Wiktor Jastrzebski 7, Jerzy Padewski 4, Jan Mucha 2, Jerzy Trzeszkowski 1) **GREAT BRITAIN 16** (Barry Briggs 5, Nigel Boocock 5, Eric Boocock 2, Cyril Maidment 2, Trevor Hedge 1, Ken McKinlay 1, Ivan Mauger 0, Bill Andrew, did not ride).
Match abandoned after nine races.

Poland win the series 4-0, one match abandoned.

1966 Great Britain v Poland Tour Results

Hackney, Friday, July 29
GREAT BRITAIN 61 (†Barry Briggs 18, Colin Pratt 15, Nigel Boocock 13, Trevor Hedge 7, Terry Betts 5, Ivan Mauger 3, Ken McKinlay and Norman Hunter, did not ride) **POLAND 47** (Antonin Woryna 10, Edmund Migos 8, Pawel Waloszek 8, †Andrzej Pogorzelski 7, Stanislaw Tkocz 7, Andrzej Wyglenda 5, Konstanty Pociejkowicz 2, Marian Kaiser, did not ride).

Coventry, Monday, August 1
GREAT BRITAIN 57 (†Barry Briggs 17, Nigel Boocock 14, Jim Lightfoot 10, Ken McKinlay 6, Bill Andrew 3, Eric Boocock 3, Rick France 3, Cyril Maidment 1) **POLAND 51** (Andrzej Wyglenda 12, Konstanty Pociejkowicz 11, Antonin Woryna 11, Pawel Waloszek 6, Stanislaw Tkocz 5, Edmund Migos 4, Marian Kaiser 1, †Andrzej Pogorzelski 1).

Sheffield, Thursday, August 4
GREAT BRITAIN 76 (Trevor Hedge 18, †Barry Briggs 17, Nigel Boocock 17, Ivan Mauger 11, Eric Boocock 10, Cyril Maidment 3, Bill Andrew and Billy Bales, did not ride) **POLAND 32** (Pawel Waloszek 8, Andrzej Wyglenda 6, Konstanty Pociejkowicz 6, Antonin Woryna 5, †Andrzej Pogorzelski 4, Stanislaw Tkocz 3, Edmund Migos 0, Marian Kaiser, did not ride).

Great Britain win the series 3-0.

TOUR MATCH
Newport, Friday, August 5
WALES & THE WEST 53 (†Göte Nordin 18, Barry Briggs 15, Bill Andrew 6, Alby Golden 5, Jon Erskine 3, Bob Hughes 3, Tommy Sweetman 2, Mike Broadbank 1) **POLAND 54** (Pawel Waloszek 14, Edmund Migos 11, Antonin Woryna 11, Andrzej Wyglenda 6, Konstanty Pociejkowicz 5, Stanislaw Tkocz 5, †Andrzej Pogorzelski 2).

■ ***See also Scotland v Poland.***

- *The Great Britain team manager for both the series was Vic Gooden.*
- *The Poland team manager in Great Britain was Tadeusz Trawinski.*

1966 Scotland v Poland Tour Result

SCOTLAND reeled under the Polish assault and went down to a humiliating defeat.

But Edinburgh promoter Ian Hoskins found some comfort even in this result pointing out: "England chickened out and raced the Poles as Great Britain."

Certainly the Poles, on their first-ever visit North of the Border, were far too strong for the home nation and could afford to have the normally high-scoring Andrzej Wyglenda filling a spectator's rôle in the Meadowbank pits.

Edinburgh, Saturday, July 30
SCOTLAND 29 (†Ken McKinlay 9, George Hunter 8, Charlie Monk 5, Bert Harkins 3, Willie Templeton 2, Doug Templeton 1, Maurie Mattingley 1, Jimmy Tannock 0) **POLAND 79** (Andrzej Pogorzelski 15, Edmund Migos 15, Stanislaw Tkocz 13, Pawel Waloszek 13, Antonin Woryna 12, Konstanty Pociejkowicz 11, Andrzej Wyglenda and Marian Kaiser, did not ride).

WORLD Champion Björn Knutsson, who hadn't raced in Britain since his spell with West Ham during the 1964 season, returned...and showed everyone what we were missing.

The brilliant Knuttie, who had quit the British League to concentrate on hissecond hand car sales business in his hometown of Norrkoping, top-scored in all seven matches against club sides and amassed 83 points out of a possible 90 with unbeaten performances at Newcastle, Cradley Heath and Oxford.

He opened the tour with a 12-point maximum at Belle Vue but, oddly, that was to be the Stockholm side's only victory even though, on paper, they probably had a stronger side than the so-successful 1965 touring party.

One new face who certainly wowed the English fans was the spectacular Torbjörn Harrysson who, before the tour was over, had been offered a 1967 contract by multi-track promoter Mike Parker despite missing the last match through injury.

1966 Vargarna (Sweden) Tour Results

Belle Vue, Saturday, July 30
BELLE VUE 30 (†Dick Fisher 9, Jim Yacoby 6, Norman Nevitt 5, Sandor Levai 3, Cyril Maidment 3, Bill Powell 3, Gordon McGregor 1) **VARGARNA 48** (†Björn Knutsson 12, Torbjörn Harrysson 12, Sören Sjösten 11, Runo Wedin 4, Peo Söderman 4, Sture Lindblom 4, Rino Westergren 1).

Poole, Wednesday, August 3
POOLE 43 (†Geoff Mudge 11, Ronnie Genz 9, Bill Andrew 9, Colin McKee 6, Pete Smith 4, Wayne Briggs 2, Bruce Cribb 2) **VARGARNA 35** (†Björn Knutsson 8, Torbjörn Harrysson 8, Sören Sjösten 8, Runo Wedin 4, Sture Lindblom 4, Peo Söderman 3, Rino Westergren 0).

West Ham, Thursday, August 4
WEST HAM 45 (Norman Hunter 12, Sverre Harrfeldt 10, †Ken McKinlay 10, Reg Trott 5, Brian Leonard 3, Malcolm Simmons 3, Don Smith 2) **VARGARNA 33** (†Björn Knutsson 13, Torbjörn Harrysson 10, Sören Sjösten 6, Runo Wedin 3, Peo Söderman 1, Sture Lindblom 0, Rino Westergren 0).
■ ***Original staging on Tuesday, August 2, postponed, waterlogged track.***

Newcastle, Monday, August 8
NEWCASTLE 42 (Allan Butterfield 12, †Ivan Mauger 9, Graham Coombes 8, Russ Dent 4, Mike Watkin 3, Peter Kelly 2, Dave Younghusband 2) **VARGARNA 35** (†Björn Knutsson 12, Peo Söderman 7, Torbjörn Harrysson 6, Sören Sjösten 5, Runo Wedin 2, Sture Lindblom 2, Rino Westergren 1).

Long Eaton, Tuesday, August 9
LONG EATON 38 (Ray Wilson 9, Leif Enecrona 8, Vic White 6, †Ray Cresp 5, Dennis Newton 5, Norman Storer 4, Greg Kentwell 1) **VARGARNA 39** (†Björn Knutsson 11, Torbjörn Harrysson 9, Sören Sjösten 9, Peo Söderman 5, Runo Wedin 4, Rino Westergren 1, Sture Lindblom 0).

Cradley Heath, Wednesday, August 10
CRADLEY HEATH 43 (Ivor Hughes 10, †Ivor Brown 8, Colin Pratt 8, Chum Taylor 5, Howard Cole 5, Clive Featherby 5, Chris Julian 2) **VARGARNA 34** (†Björn Knutsson 15, Peo Söderman 7, Sören Sjösten 5, Runo Wedin 4, Rino Westergren 2, Torbjörn Harrysson 1, Sture Lindblom 0).
■ ***Original staging on Saturday, August 6, postponed, waterlogged track.***

Oxford, Thursday, August 11
OXFORD 39 (†Arne Pander 12, Eddie Reeves 8, Jimmy Gooch 8, John Bishop 7, Maurie McDermott 2, Tony Clarke 2, Des Lukehurst 0) **VARGARNA 39** (†Björn Knutsson 12, Olle Nygren 10, Peo Söderman 6, Sören Sjösten 4, Runo Wedin 3, Rino Westergren 3, Sture Lindblom 1).

● *The Vargarna team manager was Charles Ringblom.*

Ron bores for Britain

RON MOUNTFORD was the most unpopular man in Scotland...when he tried to take the lead for Great Britain!

The Coventry star had already come from last to second when he launched himself past another opponent to try and grab the lead.

There was only one problem...his 'rival' was his own team-mate Charlie Monk and after both had come down the Glasgow-based Aussie was ruled out of the rest of the Test with a badly damaged machine.

Mountford's no-holds-barred insistence on racing to win (no matter who he was against) brought a storm of booing from the big White City crowd.

But at least it brought another Scot into the action with Edinburgh's George Hunter grabbing nine points from four rides as Monk's replacement.

Great Britain's 66-41 win levelled the series but the Swedes, who had looked world-beaters until Barry Briggs returned from injury for the third test, clinched the series at Belle Vue, two days later than planned as the June monsoon washed away any hopes of the Saturday night staging.

In the other summer series Poland defied a catalogue of injuries – Antonin Woryna even missed the parade at Wimbledon so that he could have a pain-killing injection for a fractured elbow and cracked toe – and pushed the hosts to a best-of-five rubber, winning courtesy of a story-book performance from reserve Geoff Mudge in the second Test.

He replaced the injured Barry Briggs after only one ride and recorded a match winning double figure score just when it looked as if Great Britain might go 2-0 down in the series. The poor old Poles never had a chance in the decider. They were without Andrzej Wyglenda for the third match in a row, had equipment and spares stolen from outside their hotel and ended up with only five fit riders after both Viktor Jastrzebski and Jerzy Trzeszkowski crashed in the first seven heats.

1967 Great Britain v Sweden Tour Results

Wimbledon, Thursday, June 15
GREAT BRITAIN 46 (Reg Luckhurst 13, Trevor Hedge 10, Ivan Mauger 6, Ray Wilson 6, Eric Boocock 4, †Nigel Boocock 4 Terry Betts 3, Norman Hunter 0) **SWEDEN 62** (Göte Nordin 17, Olle Nygren 16, †Ove Fundin 13, Bengt Jansson 9, Torbjörn Harrysson 6, Gunnar Malmqvist 1, Bernt Persson 0, Leif Söderberg 0).

Coventry, Saturday, June 17
GREAT BRITAIN 46 (Ken McKinlay 12, Rick France 11, †Nigel Boocock 9, Ray Wilson 5, Ivan Mauger 4, Jim Airey 3, Ron Mountford 2, Jim Lightfoot 0)) **SWEDEN 62** (Göte Nordin 14, Torbjörn Harrysson 14, †Ove Fundin 11, Olle Nygren 8, Gunnar Malmqvist 8, Bengt Jansson 7, Bo Josefsson 0, Nils Ringstrom, did not ride).

Newport, Wednesday, June 21
GREAT BRITAIN 62 (Eric Boocock 15, Charlie Monk 12, †Barry Briggs 11, Nigel Boocock 8, Terry Betts 7, Jimmy Gooch 5, Jon Erskine 4, Roy Trigg, did not ride) **SWEDEN 46** (Torbjörn Harrysson 15, †Ove Fundin 11, Anders Michanek 11, Bernt Persson 6, Gunnar Malmqvist 2, Bengt Jansson 1, Bo Josefsson 0, Nils Ringstrom 0).

Glasgow, Friday, June 23
GREAT BRITAIN 66 (Eric Boocock 15, Nigel Boocock 14, †Barry Briggs 12, George Hunter 9, Ivan Mauger 7, Charlie Monk 5, Ron Mountford 4, Ken McKinlay 0) **SWEDEN 41** (Göte Nordin 12, †Olle Nygren 10, Bernt Persson 10, Anders Michanek 7, Gunnar Malmqvist 1, Bo Josefsson 1, Bengt Larsson 0, Nils Ringstrom 0).

Belle Vue, Monday, June 26
GREAT BRITAIN 44 (†Barry Briggs 14, Eric Boocock 12, Ray Wilson 6, Ken McKinlay 4, Nigel Boocock 4, Cyril Maidment 3, Trevor Hedge 1, Arnold Haley 0) **SWEDEN 63** (Bernt Persson 14, Anders Michanek 12, Olle Nygren 9, †Göte Nordin 8, Torbjörn Harrysson 7, Gunnar Malmqvist 7, Bengt Jansson 6, Bengt Larsson, did not ride).
■ ***Original staging on Saturday, June 24 was postponed because of rain.***

Sweden win the series 3-2.

● *The Great Britain team managers for the series were: Charles Ochiltree (Wimbledon), Ronnie Greene (Coventry), Wally Mawdsley (Newport), Ian Hoskins (Glasgow) and Mike Parker (Belle Vue).*
● *The Sweden manager was Charles Ringblom.*

1967 Great Britain v Poland Tour Results

West Ham, Tuesday, July 18
GREAT BRITAIN 39 (Colin Pratt 13, †Nigel Boocock 8, Reg Luckhurst 7, Ken McKinlay 5, Eric Boocock 3, Terry Betts 3, Trevor Hedge 0, Norman Hunter 0) **POLAND 69** (†Antonin Woryna 17, Pawel Waloszek 15, Andrzej Wyglenda 14, Andrzej Pogorzelski 11, Edmund Migos 4, Zygmunt Pytka 4, Jerzy Trzeszkowski 4, Wiktor Jastrzebski, did not ride).

Poole, Wednesday, July 19
GREAT BRITAIN 59 (†Nigel Boocock 10, Ivan Mauger 10, Geoff Mudge 10, Eric Boocock 9, Charlie Monk 9, Ray Wilson 8, Barry Briggs 3, Jim Airey 0) **POLAND 49** (Pawel Waloszek 12, Andrzej Wyglenda 12, Andrzej Pogorzelski 10, †Antonin Woryna 10, Edmund Migos 5, Wiktor Jastrzebski 0, Zygmunt Pytka 0).

Wolverhampton, Friday, July 21
GREAT BRITAIN 66 (†Nigel Boocock 15, Roy Trigg 13, Eric Boocock 12, Jim Airey 11, Terry Betts 10, Rick France 4, Peter Vandenberg 1, Ray Wilson 0) **POLAND 42** (Edmund Migos 15, Pawel Waloszek 8, Wiktor Jastrzebski 8, Andrzej Pogorzelski 6, †Antonin Woryna 3, Jerzy Trzeszkowski 2, Zygmunt Pytka 0).

Halifax, Saturday, July 22
GREAT BRITAIN 53 (Eric Boocock 18, †Nigel Boocock 10, Dave Younghusband 8, Ivan Mauger 7, Charlie Monk 6, Eric Boothroyd 2, Colin Pratt 2, Ray Wilson 0) **POLAND 55** (Andrzej Pogorzelski 14,† Antonin Woryna 14, Zygmunt Pytka 13, Edmund Migos 6, Pawel Waloszek 6, Wiktor Jastrzebski 1, Jerzy Trzeszkowski 1).

Newcastle, Monday, July 24
GREAT BRITAIN 77 (†Nigel Boocock 17, Ivan Mauger 15, Eric Boocock 14, Charlie Monk 12, Dave Younghusband 12, George Hunter 5, Mike Watkin 2) **POLAND 30** (Andrzej Pogorzelski 10, Edmund Migos 7, Zygmunt Pytka 6, †Antonin Woryna 4, Pawel Waloszek 3, Wiktor Jastrzebski 0, Jerzy Trzeszkowski 0).

Great Britain win the series 3-2.

● *The Great Britain team managers were Wally Mawdsley (West Ham), Ronnie Greene (Poole), Charles Ochiltreee (Wolverhampton), Ron Wilson (Halifax) and Ian Hoskins (Newcastle).*
● *The Poland team manager was Jerzy Kubik.*

●*Ivan Mauger was forced to withdraw from the fifth and deciding Test against Sweden so that he could race for his club side Newcastle in a British League match against Wolverhampton.*

1967 England v Sweden

WHAT on earth would have happened to England without the Boocock brothers?

The two Yorkshire battlers totally dominated the Lions scorechart and without them the result would have been an even more devastating defeat in England's first international against Sweden since July 4, 1958!

Sweden got away to a flying start with two successive maximums and the Boococks were the only home riders to win a race.

Eric's two defeats came against an unbeaten Ove Fundin in heats seven and 16.

Exeter, Monday, June 19
ENGLAND 38 (Eric Boocock 16, †Nigel Boocock 9, Jimmy Gooch 5, Reg Luckhurst 3, Jimmy Squibb 2, Cyril Maidment 2, Bob Kilby 1, Martin Ashby 0) **SWEDEN 70** (†Ove Fundin 18, Göte Nordin 14, Torbjörn Harrysson 12, Gunnar Malmqvist 10, Olle Nygren 9, Bengt Jansson 7, Bengt Larsson and Leif Söderberg, did not ride).

● *The England team manager was Charles Foot and the Sweden team manager was Charles Ringblom.*

1967 Ruda Hvezda (Czechoslovakia) Tour of England Results

JAN HOLUB will never forget his 25th birthday.

For he recorded his first ever double figure score in England and helped the touring Red Star party to wind up their hectic six-match, nine-day tour with a four point win at Dudley Wood.

It was a remarkable end to a history-making tour that looked as if it was doomed to failure as the Czechs opened at Hackney.

They found the Waterden Road bends far too difficult to negotiate and had a faller in four of the first five races.

Only Antonin Kasper seemed at ease as he was beaten once, by the Hawks' Bengt Jansson, in five impressive British debut rides.

But he had little or no support and there were real fears that the tour could turn into a spectator nightmare.

Thankfully those fears proved groundless and the longer the tour went on the better the Czechs rode. And no-one could complain about the entertainment value.

Kasper, by far the most impressive tourist, provided a spectacular party piece in the second tour match at King's Lynn when he temporarily lost control and careered across the centre green after clouting the fence.

Referee Arthur Humphrey gave him a special public commendation for the way he regained control of his bike and avoided the usual bevy of centre green watchers!

Match number three at Exeter only went ahead after tons of sawdust soaked up some of the surface water and the following night only the absence of skipper Lubos Tomicek deprived the tourists of their first win against an injury-weakened Long Eaton side missing their own captain Jim Lightfoot.

While the rain had marred the entertainment in Devon it actually was a major asset to the Czechs as they recorded their first ever victory in Britain when Frantisek Ledecky and skipper Tomicek filled the minor placings in the last race at Oxford to give them a one-point win. The start of the meeting was held up for 20 minutes and and it was so wet that race-winning times were generally a second a lap slower than normal with home star Roy Trigg particularly ill at ease with the British Final only five nights away.

And then came Holub's birthday party on another sodden circuit, this time at Dudley Wood. Fittingly it was Jan's third place in heat 12 that ensured victory for the Czechs although Cradley's last race maximum closed the score-line.

Hackney, Friday, August 4
HACKNEY 52 (Bengt Jansson 11, †Colin Pratt 10, Colin McKee 7, Malcolm Brown 7, Brian Davies 6, Les McGillivray 6, Gary Everett 5) **RUDA HVEZDA 26** (Antonin Kasper 14, †Lubos Tomicek 6, Frantisek Ledecky 2, Antonin Svab 2, Jan Holub 1, Stanislav Kubicek 1, Miloslav Verner 0, Karel Prusa, did not ride).

King's Lynn, Saturday, August 5
KING'S LYNN 43 (†Terry Betts 12, David Crane 12, Clive Featherby 8, Terje Henriksson 4, Howard Cole 4, Ted Laessing 3, John Mills 0) **RUDA HVEZDA 35** (Antonin Svab 10, Antonin Kasper 9, Jan Holub 7, Frantisek Ledecky 3, Karel Prusa 3, †Lubos Tomicek 2, Stanislav Kubicek 1, Miloslav Verner, did not ride)

Exeter, Monday, August 7
EXETER 42 (†Jimmy Squibb 9, Gunnar Malmkvist 8, Wayne Briggs 8, Jack Geran 6, Tommy Sweetman 5, Neil Street 5, Chris Blewett 1) **RUDA HVEZDA 36** (Antonin Svab 9, Antonin Kasper 9, Karel Prusa 6, Jan Holub 5, Frantisek Ledecky 3, Stanislav Kubicek 3, †Lubos Tomicek 1, Miloslav Verner, did not ride).

Long Eaton, Tuesday, August 8
LONG EATON 41 (Anders Michanek 14, †Ray Wilson 12, Les Bentzen 5, John Boulger 3, Vic White 3, Norman Storer 2, Ian Champion 2) **RUDA HVEZDA 37** (Antonin Kasper 9, Antonin Svab 9, Jan Holub 6, Frantisek Ledecky 6, Stanislav Kubicek 4, Miloslav Verner 2, Karel Prusa 1, †Lubos Tomicek, did not ride).

Oxford, Thursday, August 10
OXFORD 38 (†Eddie Reeves 12, Des Lukehurst 10, Leo McAuliffe 7, Colin Gooddy 4, Rick Timmo 3, Roy Trigg 2, Maurie McDermott 0) **RUDA HVEZDA 39** (Karel Prusa 9, Antonin Svab 9, Jan Holub 8, Antonin Kasper 4, Frantisek Ledecky 4, †Lubos Tomicek 3, Miloslav Verner 2, Stanislav Kubicek, did not ride).

Cradley Heath, Saturday, August 12
CRADLEY HEATH 37 (†Ivor Brown 12, Graham Coombes 8, Chris Julian 7, Brian Brett 6, Ken Wakefield 3, Alan Totney 1, Peter Wrathall 0) **RUDA HVEZDA 41** (Antonin Kasper 12, Jan Holub 10, Antonin Svab 9, †Lubos Tomicek 4, Miloslav Verner 4, Frantisek Ledecky 2, Karel Prusa 0, Stanislav Kubicek, did not ride).

● *The Ruda Hvezda team manager was Pavel Kacer.*

1967 England v Scotland

GEORGE HUNTER defied medical advice and insisted on lining up as reserve for Scotland as they took on England for the 32nd time in history.

It was to be one clash that every Scot would want to forget as England won for the first time at Old Meadowbank after five straight defeats stretching back over 17 years.

Young Lion Ray Wilson – beaten only in his last race by Hunter – and Terry Betts dropped only four points between them and, in all, English riders took the chequered flag in 16 of the 18 races.

Scotland's lone heat winner was Glasgow's Charlie Monk in his first and fourth races.

Edinburgh, Saturday, May 6
SCOTLAND 34 (Charlie Monk 10, Doug Templeton 10, †Ken McKinlay 8, George Hunter 5, Bert Harkins 1, Maurie Mattingley 0, Willie Templeton 0, Bill Landels 0) **ENGLAND 74** (†Ray Wilson 16, Terry Betts 16, Roy Trigg 14, Trevor Hedge 9, Norman Hunter 8, Colin Pratt 7, Arnold Haley 2, Bob Paulson 2).

HIGHLAND FLING...Doug Templeton was joint top-scorer for the Scots as they lost to England for the first time in 17 years at Old Meadowbank. He didn't do quite so well against the Poles two months later but at least that time he finished on the winning side.

1967 Scotland v Poland

IAN HOSKINS summed up the selection to wear the Scottish colours to take on the pulverising Poles.

"Nationality means nothing. Bernt Persson and Reidar Eide rode for Edinburgh, although they weren't born in Scotland. They have never ridden for no other British team and that's good enough for us."

The two Scandinavians helped bury the memories of the 1966 hammering against the Poles with a convincing win.

Such was the victory euphoria that the huge Meadowbank crowd refused to leave until the Select had come back on the track for a victory salute.

Edinburgh, Saturday, July 15
SCOTLAND SELECT 64 (Bernt Persson 16, George Hunter 13, Charlie Monk 11, †Ken McKinlay 9, Reidar Eide 9, Doug Templeton 5, Bill Landels 1, Willie Templeton, did not ride) **POLAND 44** (Andrzej Pogorzelski 15, Edmund Migos 13, Zygmunt Pytka 6, Pawel Waloszek 4, Andrzej Wyglenda 3, Wiktor Jastrzebski 2, Jerzy Trzeszkowski 1, Antonin Woryna 0).

Worra Lorra Bottle on Tour

Betts gets it in the neck as Oz goes wild

A LONE Australian found it all too hard to take as England opened the first Ashes series in almost a decade with a tight as a drum-string one-point win at the famed Sydney Showground.

Betts, one of the English heroes, was joining his team-mates on a ceremonial lap of honour when he was knocked off his bike by a bottle hurled from the crowd by an irate Oz fan who couldn't stomach a shock Lions victory.

The King's Lynn star, who had scored seven points in the British victory, was taken to hospital for treatment and had a total of eight stitches inserted into a deep cut above his left eye and another on his scalp.

He admitted: "It smashed me in the face and knocked me clean out. I must have had a million smaller cuts on my face, boy, did I look a mess."

Betts' assailant didn't look none too good either as angry supporters turned on him and he had a broken nose, ribs and jaw by the time police arrested him.

It was an unsavoury start to the first series between speedway's traditional rivals since 1960 but, happily, both sides quickly forgot about the trouble and entertained the Down Under fans to a cliff-hanging series.

England, who had finished the opener with only five riders as both Ken McKinlay and Ray Wilson suffered insurmountable mechanical problems reached agreement with their hosts that both sides could call upon eight riders from the Third Test onwards and added a locally-based Brit for each of the remaining matches.

An unbeaten Eric Boocock helped the Lions regain the overall lead in that Third Test but a surprise maximum from his Halifax team-mate Greg Kentwell in the Fourth Test – again at the Showground – ensured the Ashes were still in dispute for the last Test at Adelaide.

After taking time out to visit former World Champion Jack Young and take in the Australian Motorcycle Grand Prix during a near three week break between the fourth and fifth Tests, the Lions did the business. And how!

Ken McKinlay and Ray Wilson set the ball rolling with a 1-2 in the opening race and even though the scores were level after eight heats, the Lions pulled away with successive maximums from Roy Trigg and Nigel Boocock and then Ray Wilson and the imported reserve Bryan Elliott.

Gretel Dunstan, wife of the South Australian Premier, presented the garland of honour to skipper Nigel Boocock after a comprehensive 16 point win and, a few days later, the party set off for a week-long successful three Test tour of neighbouring New Zealand.

1967-68 England Tour of Australia Results

Sydney, Saturday, November 11, 1967
AUSTRALIA 53 (Jim Airey 15, Gordon Guasco 14, Greg Kentwell 12, Jack White 5, Trevor Harding 4, Bill Bryden 3, Kevin Torpie 0) **ENGLAND 54** (Eric Boocock 14, Roy Trigg 13, †Nigel Boocock 8, Terry Betts 7, Ray Wilson 6, Colin Pratt 4, Ken McKinlay 2).

Brisbane, Saturday, November 25, 1967
AUSTRALIA 62 (Keith Gurtner 15, Gordon Guasco 14, Jim Airey 13, John Boulger 8, Peter Ingram 8, Jack White 3, Greg Kentwell 1) **ENGLAND 46** (Ken McKinlay 15, Eric Boocock 10, Roy Trigg 8, Ray Wilson 7, Terry Betts 4, †Nigel Boocock 2, Colin Pratt 0).

Sydney, Saturday, December 2, 1967
AUSTRALIA 43 (Jim Airey 13, Greg Kentwell 10, Chum Taylor 7, Gordon Guasco 6, John Boulger 4, Bill Bryden 3, Keith Gurtner 0, Peter Ingram 0) **ENGLAND 64** (Eric Boocock 18, †Nigel Boocock 15, Ken McKinlay 13, Ray Wilson 9, Roy Trigg 5, Terry Betts 4, Colin Pratt 0, Bill Landels, did not ride).

Sydney, Saturday, December 16, 1967
AUSTRALIA 68 (Greg Kentwell 18, Jim Airey 17, Gordon Guasco 14, Jack White 9, Kevin Torpie 6, John Boulger 4, Bill Bryden and Brian Collins, did not ride) **ENGLAND 40** (Ken McKinlay 12, Eric Boocock 11, †Nigel Boocock 9, Terry Betts 4, Ray Wilson 3, Bill Landels 1, Colin Pratt 0, Roy Trigg 0).

Adelaide, Friday, January 5, 1968
AUSTRALIA 46 (Charlie Monk 12, Greg Kentwell 11, Gordon Guasco 8, Jim Airey 6, John Boulger 6, Don Prettejohn 3, Trevor Harding 0, Garry Middleton 0) **ENGLAND 62** (Eric Boocock 18, †Nigel Boocock 15, Ray Wilson 11, Roy Trigg 6, Terry Betts 5, Bryan Elliott 4, Ken McKinlay 3, Colin Pratt 0).

England win the series 3-2.

TOUR MATCHES
Brisbane, Saturday, November 18, 1967
QUEENSLAND 24 (Keith Gurtner 6, Kevin Torpie 5, Bryan Loakes 4, Tony Hart 4, Peter Ingram 3, Jack White 2, Doug Hands 0) **ENGLAND 30** (Ken McKinlay 7, Eric Boocock 6, Ray Wilson 6, Terry Betts 6, Troy Trigg 3, †Nigel Boocock 2, Colin Pratt 0).

Rockhampton, Wednesday, November 29, 1967
AUSTRALIAN SELECT 25 (Gordon Guasco 11, Jim Airey 7, Tony Hart 4, Jack White 3) **ENGLAND 23** (†Nigel Boocock 9, Ken McKinlay 7, Eric Boocock 5, Ray Wilson 2).

Kembla Grange, Sunday, December 10, 1967
NEW SOUTH WALES 18 (Jim Airey 9, Gordon Guasco 8, Lionel Levy 1) **ENGLAND 18** (†Nigel Boocock 9, Eric Boocock 8, Bill Landels 1).

Brisbane, Wednesday, December 27, 1967
QUEENSLAND 13 (Jack White 5, Kevin Torpie 4, Peter Ingram 2, Tony Hart 2, Keith Gurtner 0) **ENGLAND 34** (†Nigel Boocock 12, Ken McKinlay 12, Ray Wilson 8, Terry Betts 2).

● *The England tour rider-manager was Ken McKinlay.*

1967-68 England Tour of New Zealand Results

Auckland, Saturday, January 20, 1968
NEW ZEALAND 39 (Bob Andrews 15, Rick Timmo 12, Gary Peterson 4, Merv Neil 4, Bryce Subritzky 3, Len Jelaca 1, Brian Carkeek, did not ride) **ENGLAND 69** (†Nigel Boocock 15, Eric Boocock 14, Roy Trigg 12, Terry Betts 11, Howard Cole 9, Colin Pratt 8, Ken McKinlay 0).

Napier, Wednesday, January 24, 1968
NEW ZEALAND 55 (Rick Timmo 16, Bob Andrews 14, Bryce Subritzky 10, Len Jelaca 5, Merv Neil 4, Dave Whitaker 4, Gary Peterson 2) **ENGLAND 53** (Roy Trigg 12, Terry Betts 10, Colin Pratt 10, Eric Boocock 7, Howard Cole 6, Ken McKinlay 5, †Nigel Boocock 3).

New Plymouth, Thursday, January 25, 1968
NEW ZEALAND 22 (Bob Andrews 8, Merv Neil 6, Rick Timmo 6, Dave Whitaker 2, Len Jelaca 0, Bruce Ovenden 0, Bryce Subritzky 0) **ENGLAND 86** (Ken McKinlay 18, †Nigel Boocock 17, Eric Boocock 16, Colin Pratt 14, Roy Trigg 13, Terry Betts 8, Howard Cole, did not ride).

Auckland, Saturday, January 27, 1968
NEW ZEALAND 29 (Rick Timmo 11, Bob Andrews 9, Ronnie Moore 6, Merv Neil 3, Len Jelaca 0, Bryce Subritzky 0, Dave Whitaker 0) **ENGLAND 79** (Eric Boocock 17, †Nigel Boocock 16, Ken McKinlay 16, Colin Pratt 12, Terry Betts 9, Roy Trigg 9, Howard Cole, did not ride).

Christchurch, Monday, February 5, 1968
NEW ZEALAND 47 (Ronnie Moore 17, Bob Andrews 10, Frank Shuter 10, Allan Brown 5, Merv Neil 3, Roger Wright 2, Bryce Subritzky 0) **ENGLAND 60** (†Nigel Boocock 20, Ken McKinlay 18, Colin Pratt 14, Howard Cole 6, Roy Trigg 2).
England win the series 4-1.

WORLD KINGS!

1968 WORLD LEAGUE FINAL TABLE

	P	W	D	L	PtsF	PtsA	Pts
GREAT BRITAIN	6	6	0	0	297	171	12
Poland	4	1	1	2	144	168	3
Soviet Union	4	0	1	3	121	191	1
Sweden	2	0	0	2	62	94	0

THE BRAINCHILD of the British Speedway Promoters' Association, it was wholly fitting that not only should the World League be launched in Britain but also that the first-ever winners of the brand new competition should be the hosts Great Britain.

With the World Team Cup restricted to basically the top five riders from each nation it was swiftly agreed between the premier speedway nations that there was room for a totally new competition which would test the overall strengths of each country.

And to make it a financially viable proposition Poland, Sweden and the Soviet Union all stayed on in Britain for further three match international series to provide British fans with a glut of summer Test action. The biggest disadvantage of the whole concept is that it was teribly weighted in favour of the host nation as the somewhat incongruous final World League table shows with Great Britain having had six matches and Sweden only two. The only World League meetings other than the initial six held in the UK were in Poland towards the end of the year when the two East European countries met although they never even managed return fixtures in the Soviet Union.

●Highlights of the opening World League match – between Great Britain and Sweden at Wimbledon – were recorded and shown on the ATV programme Sportsweek the following night.

In effect, then, the competition became a bright but still-born idea.

It was agreed that all matches would be raced over the conventional 13-heat British League formula with a five-race individual competition to follow the interval to divorce the matches from conventional international status and Barry Briggs became the first race winner while his great rival, World Champion Ove Fundin, who had been sponsored to take part in the series so that his thriving Scandinavian oil business did not suffer financially from his absence, became the first rider to fail to finish a race, suffering from a night-long ailing engine.

Great Britain's successive wins over their most powerful rivals Sweden – with Ivan Mauger recovering from German measles to take his place in the line-up at Halifax – virtually settled the competition before it had really got under way and neither Russia nor Poland could shake the Lions.

After their shattering defeat at West Ham, where Norman Hunter rattled up his second Test match maximum against the Soviets, the Russians asked for, and were given, special practice facilities on the morning of the match at Exeter but even that didn't do them any good as they went down to a second heavy defeat with former World number two Igor Plechanov, the one-time County Ground track record holder, a mere shadow of his former self.

Two defeats left Poland, impressive visitors in previous years, as the only country who could possibly dent Great Britain's 100% record but all the anticipation was quickly dispelled within the first four heats as Great Britain went into a 19-5 lead with Terry Betts, who had to fit a new magneto after spending half an hour trying to get his engine to fire during the pits preparation, leading the points charge. Betts, home star Colin Pratt and Martin Ashby were all unbeaten, leaving Poland having to salvage their pride in the final UK-based World League match at Coventry. They did that and almost won the match, seeing their victory hopes finally disappear in a dramatic last race in which Ivan Mauger, in third place, held out the repeated challenges of Jerzy Trzeszkowski to ensure Great Britain maintained their unbeaten World League record for posterity.

1968 WORLD LEAGUE

Wimbledon, Thursday, June 13
GREAT BRITAIN 43 (†Barry Briggs 12, Nigel Boocock 9, Reg Luckhurst 7, Malcolm Simmons 7, Martin Ashby 7, Eric Boocock 1, Trevor Hedge 0) **SWEDEN 35** (Bengt Jansson 10, Olle Nygren 7, Torbjörn Harrysson 6, Bernt Persson 5, †Ove Fundin 4, Anders Michanek 3, Sören Sjösten 0).

Halifax, Saturday, June 15
GREAT BRITAIN 51 (Eric Boocock 11, †Barry Briggs 11, Ivan Mauger 9, Dave Younghusband 6, Nigel Boocock 5, Ray Wilson 5, Martin Ashby 4) **SWEDEN 27** (Olle Nygren 8, Anders Michanek 7, †Ove Fundin 5, Torbjörn Harrysson 4, Bengt Jansson 3, Hasse Holmkvist 0, Gunnar Malmqvist 0).

West Ham, Saturday, June 29
GREAT BRITAIN 52 (Norman Hunter 12, Martin Ashby 11, Terry Betts 9, Ray Wilson 7, †Ken McKinlay 6, Trevor Hedge 5, Colin Pratt 2) **SOVIET UNION 26** (Gennady Kurilenko 7, †Igor Plechanov 6, Boris Ciechanowicz 3, Vladimir Smirnov 3, Boris Samorodov 3, Gabdrahman Kadirov 2, Yuri Lombotski 2).

Exeter, Monday, July 1
GREAT BRITAIN 51 (Martn Ashby 12, Bill Andrew 11, †Eric Boocock 9, Norman Hunter 5, Jimmy Squibb 5, Ray Wilson 5, Neil Street 4) **SOVIET UNION 27** (Boris Samorodov 10, Gennady Kurilenko 7, Vladimir Smirnov 4, †Igor Plechanov 3, Anatoli Piotrowski 3, Gabdrahman Kadirov 0, Yuri Lombotski 0).

Hackney, Friday, July 12
GREAT BRITAIN 60 (Terry Betts 12, Martin Ashby 11, Colin Pratt 11, Ivan Mauger 8, †Nigel Boocock 8, Norman Hunter 7, Ray Wilson 3) **POLAND 18** (†Antonin Woryna 7, Pawel Waloszek 7, Stanislaw Tkocz 3, Edward Jancarz 1, Konstanty Pociejkowicz 0, Zbigniew Podlecki 0, Jerzy Trzeszkowski 0).

Coventry, Saturday, July 13
GREAT BRITAIN 40 (†Nigel Boocock 9, Martin Ashby 7, Terry Betts 6, Norman Hunter 6, Ray Wilson 5, Ivan Mauger 4, Ken McKinlay 3) **POLAND 38** (Pawel Waloszek 14, †Antonin Woryna 8, Henrik Glucklich 6, Jerzy Padewski 6, Zbigniew Podlecki 3, Jerzy Trzeszkowski 1, Edward Jancarz 0).

Gorzow, Thursday, October 10
POLAND 39 (Edmund Migos 12, Andrzej Wyglenda 8, Edward Jancarz 7, Andrzej Pogorzelski 4, Jerzy Padewski 4, Joachim Maj 2, Stanislaw Tkocz 2) **SOVIET UNION 39** (Vladimir Kononowicz 10, Yuri Chekranov 7, Anatoli Piotrowski 7, Viktor Trofimov 6, Valeri Klementiev 5, Gennady Kurilenko 3, Gabdrahman Kadirov 1).

Rybnik, Sunday, October 13
POLAND 49 (Stanislaw Tkocz 10, Edward Jancarz 9, Jerzy Padewski 8, Joachim Maj 7, Edmund Migos 7, Andrzej Wyglenda 7, Andrzej Pogorzelski 1) **SOVIET UNION 29** (Valeri Klementiev 13, Gennady Kurilenko 7, Vladimir Kononowicz 6, Anatoli Piotrowski 1, Gabdrahman Kadirov 1, Viktor Trofimov 1, Yuri Chekranov 0).

- *The Great Britain team managers were Wally Mawdsley (v Poland and Sweden at Wimbledon),, Frank Varey (Sweden at Halifax), Ronnie Green (v Soviet Union at West Ham) and Charles Foot (v Soviet Union at Exeter).*
- *The Sweden team manager was Charles Ringblom.*
- *The Poland team manager was Wladyslaw Mazurek.*
- *The Soviet Union team manager was Alexander Ivanov.*

Briggo, Booey and the Brits battered

SWEDEN gained some revenge for their World League hammering with a Test series win over an injury-hit Great Britain.

Barry Briggs (dislocated and chipped thumb) and Nigel Boocock (broken collar bone) both crashed out in the opening match at Wolverhampton and in their absence Sweden went an unassailable 2-0 up with a thumping big win at Coatbridge where only Martin Ashby salvaged his reputation with 14 points and a new first race track record.

Booey – and the Brits – bounced back in the 'dead' Test at Swindon but before then England had met both the Soviet Union and Poland in two three-match rubbers with the five completed matches ending in comfortable home victories.

Ashby was again the dominant force with a new Somerton Park track record and an 18-point maximum against the Russkies who finished the tour in a sorry state through injuries and mechanical problems.

The Poles, with Antonin Woryna and Pawel Waloszek majestic, were far stiffer opposition in a series reduced to two matches because of a waterlogged Brough Park, although their starting procedures caused consternation in the referees' boxes, six re-runs at Sheffield and a combined total of £7 in fines!

GREAT BRITS...team-mates Nigel Boocock and Ivan Mauger plan their race campaign

1968 Great Britain v Sweden Results

Wolverhampton, Friday, June 21
GREAT BRITAIN 52 (Jim Airey 14, Martin Ashby 12, Peter Vandenberg 7, Eric Boocock 6, Ken McKinlay 6, Nigel Boocock 4, †Barry Briggs 3, Ivan Mauger 0) **SWEDEN 55** (Anders Michanek 14, Olle Nygren 12, Sören Sjösten 11, †Ove Fundin 8, Torbjörn Harrysson 6, Bernt Persson 2, Hasse Holmkvist 2, Gunnar Malmqvist, did not ride).

Coatbridge, Saturday, June 22
GREAT BRITAIN 37 (Martin Ashby 14, Jim McMillan 7, Charlie Monk 5, Eric Boocock 3, Arnold Haley 3, Ivan Mauger 3, Norman Hunter 2, Bert Harkins 0) **SWEDEN 71** (Bengt Jansson 15, †Ove Fundin 14, Bernt Persson 14, Sören Sjösten 14, Torbjörn Harrysson 10, Olle Nygren 4, Lars Jansson 0, Gunnar Malmqvist 0).

Swindon, Saturday, July 20
GREAT BRITAIN 62 (Martin Ashby 15, Mike Broadbank 14, †Nigel Boocock 11, Eric Boocock 9, Terry Betts 7, Ivan Mauger 4, Reg Luckhurst 2, Norman Hunter 0) **SWEDEN 46** (Bengt Jansson 15, Anders Michanek 14, Sören Sjösten 10, †Olle Nygren 4, Torbjörn Harrysson 3, Lars Jansson 0, Bengt Larsson 0, Bernt Persson 0).

Sweden win the series 2-1.

● *The Great Britain team managers were Charles Ochiltree (Wolverhampton), Ian Hoskins (Coatbridge) and Charles Foot (Swindon)*
● *The Sweden team managers were Charles Ringblom and Erik Karlsson (Swindon only).*

1968 England v Soviet Union Results

Coventry, Wednesday, July 3
ENGLAND 58 (Martin Ashby 13, Eric Boocock 12, Norman Hunter 11, Terry Betts 10, Col Cottrell 5, Roy Trigg 4, Ray Wilson 3, Trevor Hedge 0) **SOVIET UNION 50** (†Igor Plechanov 16, Gennady Kurilenko 15, Vladimir Smirnov 9, Boris Samorodov 8, Anatoli Piotrowski 2, Gabdrahman Kadirov 0, Yuri Lombotski 0, Boris Ciechanowicz 0).

Newport, Friday, July 5
ENGLAND 68 (Martin Ashby 17, †Eric Boocock 15, Norman Hunter 11, Terry Betts 10, Jon Erskine 6, Roy Trigg 5, Jimmy Gooch 2, Jimmy Squibb 2) **SOVIET UNION 40** (Vladimir Smirnov 13, †Igor Plechanov 11, Gennady Kurilenko 9, Boris Ciechanowicz 3, Gabdrahman Kadirov 2, Yuri Lombotski 2, Boris Samorodov 0).

Belle Vue, Saturday, July 6
ENGLAND 77 (†Eric Boocock 18, Norman Hunter 18, Martin Ashby 13, Ray Wilson 11, Terry Betts 9, Arnold Haley 4, Cyril Maidment 3, Tommy Roper 1) **SOVIET UNION 31** (†Igor Plechanov 12, Vladimir Smirnov 9, Gennady Kurilenko 6, Yuri Lombotski 3, Boris Ciechanowicz 1, Boris Samorodov 0).

England win the series 3-0.

● *The England team managers were Wally Mawdsley (Coventry and Newport) and Ronnie Greene (Belle Vue).*
● *The Soviet Union manager was Alexander Ivanov.*

1968 England v Poland Results

Newcastle, Monday, July 15
Cancelled due to heavy rain and waterlogged track.

Poole, Wednesday, July 17
ENGLAND 55 (Reg Luckhurst 10, Terry Betts 10, Norman Hunter 10, Eric Boocock 9, Martin Ashby 8, †Nigel Boocock 4, Ray Wilson 4, Jimmy Squibb, did not ride) **POLAND 53** (†Antonin Woryna 16, Pawel Waloszek 15, Henryk Glucklich 12, Stanislaw Tkocz 4, Jerzy Trzeszkowski 3, Zbigniew Podlecki 2, Konstanty Pociejkowicz 1, Jerzy Padewski 0, Edward Jancarz, did not ride).

Sheffield, Thursday, July 18
ENGLAND 61 (Martin Ashby 14, †Nigel Boocock 11, Terry Betts 10, Ray Wilson 10, Tommy Roper 5, Arnold Haley 5, Norman Hunter 4, Eric Boocock 2, Dave Younghusband, did not ride) **POLAND 47** (†Antonin Woryna 14, Pawel Waloszek 12, Edward Jancarz 9, Henryk Glucklich 8, Jerzy Padewski 2, Stanislaw Tkocz 2, Zbigniew Podlecki 0, Jerzy Trzeszkowski 0, Konstanty Pociejkowicz, did not ride).

England win the series 2-0.

● *The England team managers were Mike Parker (Newcastle), Ronnie Greene (Poole) and Charles Ochiltree (Sheffield).*
● *The Poland team manager was Wladyslaw Mazurek.*

For results of Great Britain v Poland, Soviet Union and Sweden World League matches – see separate results section.

1968 Ruda Hvezda, Prague (Czechoslovakia) Club Tour of England Results

CLUB side Ruda Hvezda (Red Star) made their second visit to Britain...but this time they went home empty-handed.

The tour coincided with a wet spell and after their opening match at Poole was called off because of the rain, conditions at Hackney were almost as atrocious.

But both sides agreed to race with Antonin Kasper and Antonin Svab teaming up for a surprise maximum over the Hawks' Swedish Test star Bengt Jansson and later repeated the performance against Jack Biggs and Les McGillivray for their only two heat advantages.

King's Lynn lost the services of their tough guy Clive Featherby with an arm injury (which needed stitches) in the opening race and his absence helped the Czechs push the home side all the way.

Hopes of a series win ended when Kasper crashed at Newcastle for club side Coventry, on the eve of the third match at Leicester and while he struggled through he had to pull out of the remaining meetings.

There were further troubles when reserve Karel Prusa crashed at Oxford but that gave British fans their first opportunity to see a 19-year-old newcomer who was, in the seasons ahead, to become the most popular visitor of all.

His name was Vaclav Verner!

The final match of the visit, at Cradley Heath where they had won the previous year, was notable for a rare maximum from Swede Lars Jansson (his only unbeaten performance in Britain in official competition) who had to ride the Dudley Wood track spare as his own machine was still in Scandinavia.

For once he had outscored his more famous brother Bengt against the same opposition!

It was also to be the last time British fans saw skipper Lubos Tomicek who was killed in a crash at the Jubilee Golden Helmet at Pardubice a few weeks later.

Poole, Wednesday, August 7
Cancelled, waterlogged track.

Hackney, Friday, August 9
HACKNEY 46 (†Colin Pratt 11, Bengt Jansson 10, Jack Biggs 8, Des Lukehurst 7, Les McGillivray 5, Malcolm Brown 3, Gary Everett 2) **RUDA HVEZDA 32** (Antonin Kasper 10, Jan Holub 5, Jaroslav Volf 5, Antonin Svab 5, Frantisek Ledecky 4, Miloslav Verner 3, †Lubos Tomicek 0).

King's Lynn, Saturday, August 10
KING'S LYNN 43 (†Terry Betts 12, Howard Cole 10, Alan Belham 7, Geoff Penniket 6, Brian Davies 6, Allan Brown 2, Clive Featherby 0) **RUDA HVEZDA 35** (†Lubos Tomicek 9, Jan Holub 8, Frantisek Ledecky 6, Jaroslav Volf 4, Miloslav Verner 4, Antonin Svab 3, Karel Prusa 1).

Leicester, Tuesday, August 13
LEICESTER 54 (†Ray Wilson 12, Anders Michanek 12, John Boulger 11, George Major 9, Norman Storer 5, John Hart 5, Roger Mills 0) **RUDA HVEZDA 24** (Jaroslav Volf 6, †Lubos Tomicek 4, Jan Holub 3, Frantisek Ledecky 3, Antonin Kasper 3, Antonin Svab 3, Miloslav Verner 2).

Oxford, Wednesday, August 14
OXFORD 43 (Leo McAuliffe 9, †Eddie Reeves 9, Colin Gooddy 9, Ronnie Genz 8, John Bishop 4, Rick Timmo 3, Godtfred Andreasen 1) **RUDA HVEZDA 35** (Jan Holub 8, Antonin Kasper 7, Antonin Svab 6, Jaroslav Volf 6, Frantisek Ledecky 4, Miloslav Vérner 3, †Lubos Tomicek 1, Karel Prusa 0).

Glasgow, Friday, August 16
GLASGOW 51 (Charlie Monk 11, Øyvind Berg 11, Jim McMillan 11, Bill McMillan 7, †Willie Templeton 7, Russ Dent 4, Brian Whaley 0) **RUDA HVEZDA 27** (Jaroslav Volf 7, Frantisek Ledecky 6, Jan Holub 4, Antonin Svab 4, Miloslav Verner 3, Vaclav Verner 2, †Lubos Tomicek 1).

Cradley Heath, Saturday, August 17
CRADLEY HEATH 51 (Lars Jansson 12, Roy Trigg 12, Bob Andrews 9, Graham Coombes 6, Chris Julian 5, †Ivor Brown 5, Alan Totney 2) **RUDA HVEZDA 27** (Jan Holub 9, Frantisek Ledecky 6, †Lubos Tomicek 5, Miloslav Verner 3, Antonin Svab 2, Jaroslav Volf 2, Vaclav Verner 0).

● *The Ruda Hvezda team manager was Pavel Kacer.*

1968 England v Scotland

SCOTLAND came from behind to clinch victory over an experimental England squad that included a blend of experience and Test rawness.

Jimmy Squibb, 46, was included along with 29-year-old James Bond and Kent-born Kiwi Dave Gifford, winning the only England caps of their careers .

Martin Ashby began with three great wins but tailed off in his later rides as the Scots, inspired by first-season rider Brian Collins, pulled back from six down after five heats to ensure victory with two 5-1s in the last three heats.

Provost James Dowdall presented the Trophy to stand-in Scottish skipper Doug Templeton.

Coatbridge, Saturday, August 31
SCOTLAND 62 (Brian Collins 14, †Doug Templeton 11, Øyvind Berg 10, Jim McMillan 10, Bert Harkins 10, George Hunter 6, Willie Templeton 1) **ENGLAND 46** (†Martin Ashby 15, Norman Hunter 12, Arnold Haley 7, Jimmy Squibb 7, James Bond 4, Dave Gifford 1, Russ Dent 0, Peter Jarman 0).

1968 Leningrad (Soviet Union) Club Tour Results

LENINGRAD NEVA became the first Russian club side to tour Britain – largely because of the relationship between Belle Vue and the Soviet Cultural Department reponsible for organising regular visits to this country by the State Circus but ostensibly to celebrate the famous Manchester club's 40th Anniversary.

It was also a reciprocal visit as Belle Vue had become the first British side to visit the Soviet Union in 1967.

The meeting at Hyde Road actually took place the day before the official birthday but, with Sunday a non-racing day, it was the closest anyone could get to the actual anniversary and no-one was counting!

The Russian party included only one rider who had been involved in the summer's World League – Yuri Lombotski – and was, in this instance, a genuine club side, based around the team that had been Soviet Champions two years earlier. The biggest disappointment was the non-availability of the highly impressive Vladimir Smirnov.

But they certainly began well enough without him. Gennady Vyonov and Anatoli Belkin claimed a maximum in heat two in the fastest time of the meeting, but Belle Vue steadily forged ahead with Cyril Maidment and Tommy Roper claiming full scores.

In their second match they were outclassed at Blackbird Road after Vyonov had fallen in heat two and been forced to withdraw after aggravating an already damaged shoulder.

Belle Vue, Saturday, July 27
BELLE VUE 48 (†Cyril Maidment 12, Tommy Roper 12, Sören Sjösten 10, Sandor Levai 5, Bill Powell 5, Norman Nevitt 3, Chris Pusey 1) **LENINGRAD 30** (Gennady Vyonov 9, Yuri Lombotski 7, †Anatoli Belkin 7, Ivan Andreev 2, Viktor Katyuzanski 2, Vladimir Kannunikov 2, Genrikh Lemberg 1).

Leicester, Tuesday, July 30
LEICESTER 60 (John Boulger 12, Anders Michanek 10, Norman Storer 10, †Ray Wilson 9, Vic White 9, George Major 6, John Hart 4) **LENINGRAD 17** (†Anatoli Belkin 8, Yuri Lombotski 3, Ivan Andreev 2, Viktor Katyuzanski 2, Genrikh Lemberg 1, Vladimir Kannunikov 1, Gennady Vyonov 0).

The impressive Belkin, the Russians' only race winner, lacked any sort of support as John Boulger, Anders Michanek and Ray Wilson were all unbeaten by an opponent and second strings Norman Storer and Vic White also had a real field day.

Lions blown away

JIM AIREY inspired Australia to their first series victory over the touring Lions since 1959 with a near perfect exhibition in the fifth and final Test at the Sydney Showground.

England had opened with a convincing win at Melbourne and forced the series into a last match decider after the Kangaroos had been hit by a double injury blow at Brisbane.

Greg Kentwell had been rushed to hospital with a broken arm even before the meeting started – he hit the fence during a practice lap when a chain snapped.

And Les Bentzen was forced to join him (head injuries) after he and Eric Boocock crashed heavily in heat two.

Boocock was also obviously feeling the effects of the spill and after taking two points in the re-run (when Kevin Torpie also threw a chain) he withdrew from later rides.

Earlier in the tour the younger Boocock had helped set up a morale-boosting opening Test win at Melbourne by lowering the track record to 52.7 seconds.

Everything was set for a showdown at Sydney, except for the weather!

Lightning illuminated the night sky and a vicious wind swirled around the Showground but the expected thunderstorm never materialised but still provided a dramatic backdrop to the Ashes decider.

Geoff Curtis, called up for his Test debut at reserve, replaced Bert Kingston in heat seven and crowned his first international appearance with a tapes-to-flag win. Partner Charlie Monk followed him home to give the Aussies a 25-17 lead which they never surrendered.

With Airey dropping his only point to Nigel Boocock in his third ride, the 'Roos had the far more solid-scoring outfit with tail-enders Curtis, Kentwell and John Boulger all grabbing vital points.

Contrastingly, England's top four scored all but one of the 48 points with Mike Broadbank, Bob Kilby and Dave Younghusband collecting only one point between them at the expense of Curtis who was cut around the eye by a mystery object flung up by a rear wheel.

He was taken to hospital and had to be told the final result by a doctor later that night.

1968-69 England Lions tour of Australia – All the Results

Melbourne, Saturday, November 23, 1968
AUSTRALIA 43 (Jim Airey 13, Geoff Mudge 12, Charlie Monk 8, John Langfield 8, John Dewhurst 2, Peter Moore 0) **ENGLAND 65** (†Nigel Boocock 16, Eric Boocock 14, Ken McKinlay 13, Jim McMillan 8, Dave Younghusband 7, Bob Kilby 7).

Adelaide, Friday, December 6, 1968
AUSTRALIA 61 (Charlie Monk 18, Jim Airey 16, John Langfield 8, John Boulger 7, Geoff Mudge 6, Greg Kentwell 4, Gordon Guasco 2) **ENGLAND 47** (Ken McKinlay 13, Eric Boocock 11, †Nigel Boocock 9, Jim McMillan 8, Dave Younghusband 3, Mike Broadbank 3, Bob Kilby 0).

Sydney, Saturday, December 14, 1968
AUSTRALIA 68 (JIm Airey 16, John Langfield 15, Charlie Monk 12, Jack White 12, Greg Kentwell 8, John Boulger 5, Geoff Mudge, did not ride) **ENGLAND 40** (Ken McKinlay 17, Jim McMillan 9, Eric Boocock 8, †Nigel Boocock 4, Mike Broadbank 1, Bob Kilby 1, Dave Younghusband 0).

Brisbane, Saturday, January 11, 1969
AUSTRALIA 51 (Jack White 12, Jim Airey 11, Charlie Monk 10, Bert Kingston 8, Bryan Loakes 6, Kevin Torpie 4, Les Bentzen 0) **ENGLAND 57** (†Nigel Boocock 16, Ken McKinlay 12, Mike Broadbank 10, Bob Kilby 8, Jim McMillan 6, Dave Younghusband 3, Eric Boocock 2).

Sydney, Saturday, January 18, 1969
AUSTRALIA 60 (Jim Airey 17, Jack White 14, Charlie Monk 12, John Langfield 7, Geoff Curtis 4, John Boulger 3, Bert Kingston 3) **ENGLAND 48** (†Nigel Boocock 13, Ken McKinlay 12, Eric Boocock 11, Jim McMillan 11, Mike Broadbank 1, Bob Kilby 0, Dave Younghusband 0).

Australia win the series 3-2.

TOUR MATCHES
Melbourne, Saturday, November 16
VICTORIA 15 (Peter Bradshaw 5, Ken McKinlay 4, John Mills 2, Peter Moore 2, John Board 1, John Dewhurst 1) **ENGLAND 39** (Bob Kilby 8, †Nigel Boocock 7, Jim McMillan 7, Dave Younghusband 6, Eric Boocock 6, Mike Broadbank 5).

Brisbane, Saturday, January 4, 1969
QUEENSLAND 24 (Les Bentzen 9, Kevin Torpie 6, Bert Kingston 5, Jack White 2, Bob Gourlay 2, Bluey Scott 0, Keith Gurtner 0) **ENGLAND 30** (Eric Boocock 8, †Nigel Boocock 7, Ken McKinlay 6, Bob Kilby 4, Jim McMillan 3, Mike Broadbank 1, Dave Younghusband 1).

1969 Lions tour of New Zealand – All the Results

■ *STRAIGHT after the tour of Australia four of the official English Lions party headed for New Zealand where local promoters billed a four match series as Test matches.*

■ *However these have never been recognised as official internationals by the British authorities and are not, therefore, included in Test match records.*

■ *As can be seen the meetings were something of a hot-potch with Howard Cole managing to ride for both nations during the series afer both Ronnie Moore and Ivan Mauger declined to race at Palmerston North! This was the meeting where the Kiwis used a total of six riders to England's four...and still managed to lose.*

■ *At Napier, in the previous Test, Bill Andrew was only drafted into the Kiwi side after winning two support races as a replacement for the mechanically struggling Colin McKee.*

Auckland, Saturday, January 25, 1969
NEW ZEALAND 24 (Ivan Mauger 9, Bob Andrews 8, Ronnie Moore 5, Bryce Subritzky 2) **ENGLAND 24** (†Nigel Boocock 10, Jim McMillan 10, Dave Younghusband 2, Bob Kilby 2).

Napier, Wednesday, January 29, 1969
NEW ZEALAND 25 (Ivan Mauger 11, Bob Andrews 6, Bill Andrew 5, Bryce Subritzky 2, Colin McKee 1) **ENGLAND 23** (†Nigel Boocock 10, Jim McMillan 9, Howard Cole 2, Dave Younghusband 1, Bob Kilby 1).

Palmerston North, Thursday, January 30, 1969
NEW ZEALAND 11 (Howard Cole 4, Bob Andrews 3, Colin McKee 2, Jack Hart 1, Merv Hodgson 1, Bryce Subritzky 0) **ENGLAND 37** (†Nigel Boocock 11, Bob Kilby 10, Jim McMillan 10, Dave Younghusband 6).

Christchurch, Saturday, February 1, 1969
NEW ZEALAND 26 (Ronnie Moore 12, Ivan Mauger 7, Bob Andrews 4, Roger Wright 2, Bill Moulin 1) **ENGLAND 22** (JIm McMillan 9, †Nigel Boocock 8, Bob Kilby 3, Dave Younghusband 2).

New Zealand win the series 2-1 with one drawn.

BRIGHT NEW SKIDS ON THE OLD BLOCK

THE MOST famous international series of all made it's re-appearance on the British calendar with the resumption of the Ashes Tests between England and Australia.

And with it came a host of fresh, new names who only knew of the competition's history from what they may have read in books.

The last time England had raced against Australia on home soil was on Saturday, August 29, 1953, at Birmingham's Alexander Sports Stadium when Split Waterman led the Lions to a 61-47 victory over a Kangaroos' side captained by Arthur Payne and including the great Jack Young, Aub Lawson and Graham Warren. All the names had changed by the time the two famous adversaries came out on parade at Poole on Wednesday, May 28, 1969, but the 15 interceding seasons had done nothing to lessen the rivalry between the two countries who staged speedway's first ever Test match at Wimbledon, way back in June, 1930.

Like that inaugural series, England were the winners and this time they never dropped a match even though they lost Norman Hunter with a groin strain after a hectic third heat in which he came down on the first turn.

Referee Peter Ryall allowed all four riders back but Hunter's meeting was over and he was replaced in all six programmed rides by reserves Pete Smith and Roy Trigg.

A second England win followed at Sheffield to clinch the series and the most comprehensive success of all was in the re-staged Test at Wolverhampton early in July when Terry Betts recorded as exciting a maximum as you could ever see.

Having revived one old Test rubber the British Speedway Promoters' Association also brought back another that had lain dormant since the early fifties...and proof was provided of the Antipodean swing in the power axis.

New Zealand roared back with a team built around the solid rock of Barry Briggs, Ivan Mauger and Ronnie Moore and astounded everyone by taking the series 2-1 despite losing Ronnie Moore with a couple of broken toes in heat eight of the second match at a time when he had scored only one point. His absence was compensated for by probably the finest performance of his entire career from partner Dave Gifford who picked up 14 points to provide the backing that Mauger and Briggs needed and the Kiwis took a winning series lead with victory at Newcastle.

Moore missed the last Test and this time he was sorely missed. Briggs and Mauger got 30 points between them – the rest just 10 as England rounded off their international summer with a victory parade at Hackney.

That, coupled with a Great Britain 5-0 series scoreline against Sweden set British promoters wondering if England was now ready to go it alone internationally....

The newly-formed Second Division, in its second season, also got in on the international act, and so did Scotland!

The first Division Two Test was at Canterbury on Saturday, August 16, when Young England's Peter Murray won the first race against Czechoslovakia and, a month later, a second series (this time between Young Britain and Young Australasia) was staged.

With 12 of the 16 Second Division tracks playing host to a Test match (and a 13th, Romford, having a club match against the barnstorming Czechs) no-one could complain that junior League fans were being ignored!

Miloslav Verner, later to become one of the major figures in the administration of world speedway, was an absolute revelation on his third trip to this country, and his cousin Vaclav made his international mark in the final deciding Test at Reading with 14 points. Norway joined the succession of new kids on the international block with their first tour of Britain.

They opened with a couple of Test matches against Scotland (who also met Australia for the first time) and then continued with matches against three English club sides.

1969 Sweden v Great Britain Result

IN THE first international betwen the two nations for nine years on home soil Sweden were held to a draw by a Great Britain side inspired by the brilliant Ivan Mauger.

The Kiwi won his first five rides but lost his chance of a remarkable maximum when he was pipped by Ove Fundin in heat 16.

The Great Britain squad included four of the World Team Cup side that had been in action in Poland two days earlier and then Mauger, Andrews, Boocock and Ashby went on to Stockholm for the World Pairs Final.

Barry Briggs was a notable absentee because of an outstanding legal case against Swedish newspapers and there can be little doubt that with the New Zealander within their ranks it would have been another great British victory.

Malmo, Tuesday, September 23
SWEDEN 54 (Ove Fundin 15, Sören Sjösten 12, Anders Michanek 12, Göte Nordin 8, Terje Henriksson 4, Bengt Jansson 3, Conny Samuelsson 0) **GREAT BRITAIN 54** (Ivan Mauger 17, Nigel Boocock 14, Jim McMillan 10, Terry Betts 7, Martin Ashby 3, Pete Smith 2, Bob Andrews 1).

1969 Great Britain v Sweden Results

Wimbledon, Thursday, June 12
GREAT BRITAIN 68 (Ivan Mauger 18, Ronnie Moore 14, †Barry Briggs 11, Nigel Boocock 11, Reg Luckhurst 10, Trevor Hedge 2, Eric Boocock 1, Ray Wilson 1) **SWEDEN 40** (Bengt Jansson 12, Olle Nygren 8, Sören Sjösten 7, Torbjörn Harrysson 7, Ove Fundin 2, Bernt Persson 2, Anders Michanek 1, †Göte Nordin 1).

Newport, Friday, June 13
GREAT BRITAIN 70 (†Barry Briggs 15, Ivan Mauger 14, Martin Ashby 12, Nigel Boocock 11, Eric Boocock 10, Reg Luckhurst 6, Jon Erskine 1, Tony Clarke 1) **SWEDEN 38** (†Torbjörn Harrysson 13, Anders Michanek 9, Bengt Jansson 7, Göte Nordin 6, Sören Sjösten 2, Olle Nygren 1, Ove Fundin 0, Bernt Persson 0).

Leicester, Tuesday, June 17
GREAT BRITAIN 79 (Ivan Mauger 18, Barry Briggs 17, †Nigel Boocock 13, Ray Wilson 13, Norman Hunter 10, Eric Boocock 8, Martin Ashby and John Boulger, did not ride) **SWEDEN 29** (†Anders Michanek 12, Torbjörn Harrysson 7, Bengt Jansson 4, Göte Nordin 4, Ove Fundin 1, Sören Sjösten 1, Bengt Larsson 0, Bernt Persson 0).

Halifax, Saturday, June 21
GREAT BRITAIN 62 (†Eric Boocock 13, Ray Wilson 11, Jim McMillan 10, Jim Airey 9, Greg Kentwell 8, Martin Ashby 6, Charlie Monk 4, Norman Hunter 1)) **SWEDEN 46** (Torbjörn Harrysson 9, Anders Michanek 9, Sören Sjösten 9, †Ove Fundin 7, Göte Nordin 5, Bengt Larsson 4, Bengt Jansson 3, Bengt Andersson 0).

Cradley Heath, Monday, June 23
GREAT BRITAIN 63 (Nigel Boocock 17, Ray Wilson 14, †Barry Briggs 12, Ivan Mauger 11, Roy Trigg 5, Jim Airey 2, Bob Andrews 2, Norman Hunter 0) **SWEDEN 45** (Anders Michanek 12, Sören Sjösten 10, †Bernt Persson 8, Ove Fundin 8, Torbjörn Harrysson 4, Bengt Jansson 2, Conny Samuelsson 1, Göte Nordin 0).

Great Britain win the series 5-0.

- *The Great Britain team managers were Reg Fearman (Wimbledon and Newport), Ronnie Greene (Leicester), Frank Varey (Halifax) and Charles Ochiltree (Cradley Heath).*
- *The Sweden team manager was Charles Ringblom.*

1969 England v Australia Results

Poole, Wednesday, May 28
ENGLAND 66 (Martin Ashby 15, Eric Boocock 12, †Nigel Boocock 12, Terry Betts 9, Pete Smith 9, Ray Wilson 6, Roy Trigg 3, Norman Hunter 0) **AUSTRALIA 42** (Geoff Mudge 13, †Jim Airey 11, Charlie Monk 10, Gordon Guasco 4, Garry Middleton 3, John Boulger 1, Dennis Gavros 0, Peter Vandenberg 0).

Wolverhampton, Friday, May 30
ENGLAND 8 *(†Nigel Boocock 3, Norman Hunter 3, Martin Ashby 1, Ray Wilson 1, Terry Betts, James Bond, Trevor Hedge and Roy Trigg, did not ride)* ***AUSTRALIA 4*** *(†Jim Airey 2, Charlie Monk 2, Gordon Guasco 0, Peter Vandenberg 0, Chris Bass, John Boulger, Peter Bradshaw and Geoff Mudge, did not ride).*
Match abandoned after two heats because of rain.

Sheffield, Thursday, June 5
ENGLAND 69 (†Nigel Boocock 17, Norman Hunter 14, Arnold Haley 12, Martin Ashby 9, Ray Wilson 8, Eric Boocock 5, Tommy Roper 4, Dave Younghusband, did not ride) **AUSTRALIA 39** †(Jim Airey 16, Charlie Monk 12, Geoff Mudge 9, Dennis Gavros 1, Greg Kentwell 1, Chris Bass 0, John Boulger 0, Gordon Guasco 0).

Wolverhampton, Friday, July 4
ENGLAND 73 (Terry Betts 18, Ray Wilson 18, †Nigel Boocock 14.5, Martin Ashby 9.5, Pete Smith 7, Roy Trigg 3, Arnold Haley 2, Tony Clarke 1) **AUSTRALIA 35** (Geoff Mudge 11, †Jim Airey 10, Greg Kentwell 7, Chris Bass 4, Gordon Guasco 3, John Boulger 0, Peter Bradshaw 0, Dennis Gavros 0).

England win the series 3-0.

- *The England team managers were Charles Foot (Poole), Mike Parker (Sheffield) and Charles Ochiltree (Wolverhampton).*
- *The Australia team manager was Peter White.*

1969 England v New Zealand Results

Swindon, Wednesday, August 6
ENGLAND 43 (†Nigel Boocock 14, Martin Ashby 12, Ray Wilson 9, Colin Pratt 3, Eric Boocock 2, Roy Trigg 2, Arnold Haley 1, Bob Kilby 0) **NEW ZEALAND 65** (†Barry Briggs 17, Ivan Mauger 17, Ronnie Moore 15, Bob Andrews 9, Dave Gifford 5, Rick Timmo 1, Dave Whitaker 1, Wayne Briggs 0).

Newcastle, Monday, August 18
ENGLAND 47 (†Nigel Boocock 14, Arnold Haley 12, Ray Wilson 9, Pete Smith 4, Howard Cole 4, Mike Watkin 3, Roy Trigg 1, Russ Dent 0) **NEW ZEALAND 61** (Ivan Mauger 15, Dave Gifford 14, †Barry Briggs 12, Bob Andrews 11, Rick Timmo 7, Bruce Cribb 1, Ronnie Moore 1, Wayne Briggs 0).

Hackney, Friday, August 29
ENGLAND 68 (†Nigel Boocock 15, Terry Betts 13, Ray Wilson 13, Martin Ashby 12, Colin Pratt 8, Tony Clarke 4, Howard Cole 2, Trevor Hedge 1) **NEW ZEALAND 40** (†Barry Briggs 16, Ivan Mauger 14, Bob Andrews 4, Dave Gifford 4, Allan Brown 1, Graham Coombes 1, Bruce Cribb 0, Roger Wright 0).

New Zealand win the series 2-1.

- *The England team managers were Reg Fearman (Swindon), Mike Parker (Newcastle) and Ronnie Greene (Hackney).*
- *The New Zealand team managers were George Allan (Swindon) and Trevor Redmond (Newcastle & Hackney).*

1969 Scotland v Norway

NORWAY joined the growing list of international opponents to Scotland during a tour of British League tracks which preceded three England club encounters at Poole, Oxford and King's Lynn. Jim McMillan led the Scots to a first international win of the season at Hampden Park and then Bert Harkins celebrated captaining his country for the first time by top-scoring at Coatbridge. The visitors built their side around their British League performers but included, for his first British visit, Edgar Stangeland.

Glasgow, Friday, September 19
SCOTLAND 62 (†Jim McMillan 16, Charlie Monk 14, Doug Templeton 13, Bert Harkins 10, Willie Templeton 8, Brian Collins 1, Bobby Beaton 0, Alistair Brady 0) **NORWAY 46** (†Reidar Eide 13, Øyvind Berg 13, Odd Fossengen 8, Ulf Lovaas 5, Per Aulie 4, Edgar Stangeland 2, Jon Odegaard 1).

Coatbridge, Saturday, September 20
SCOTLAND 56 (†Bert Harkins 16, Jim McMillan 10, Willie Templeton 10, Doug Templeton 10, George Hunter 7, Brian Collins 3, Alistair Brady 0, Alex Hughson, did not ride) **NORWAY 52** (†Reidar Eide 17, Odd Fossengen 15, Øyvind Berg 15, Ulf Lovaas 4, Per Aulie 1, Edgar Stangeland 0, Einar Egedius 0).

Scotland win the series 2-0.
- *The Scotland team managers were Neil Macfarlane (Glasgow) and Tommy Hughson (Coatbridge).*
- *The Norway team manager was Tore Kittilsen.*

1969 Scotland v Australia

ANOTHER historic international landmark for the two nations with the first ever official Test match.

It was agreed that both would restrict their choice to home-born riders only and the Aussie squad had a powerful look about it with seven seasoned Test riders in Peter White's selection.

Bert Harkins scored his first Test match maximum but owed that to referee Watson who allowed him back in a heat 16 re-run after he had fallen on the first turn when clashing with Charlie Monk, who took the brunt of the blame from the partisan Coatbridge crowd who had never rated the Glasgow star as one of their favourites!

Coatbridge, Saturday, June 28
SCOTLAND 47 (Bert Harkins 18, †Jim McMillan 11, George Hunter 10, Doug Templeton 4, Brian Collins 2, Bobby Beaton 1, Willie Templeton 1, Alex Hughson 0)
AUSTRALIA 61 (†Charlie Monk 14, Greg Kentwell 11, Jim Airey 10, Geoff Mudge 10, Peter Vandenberg 9, Gordon Guasco 7, Dennis Gavros and Geoff Curtis, did not ride).

- ***Charlie Monk, Reidar Eide and Øyvind Berg all rode FOR and AGAINST Scotland during the 1969 season even though the Scots had only four internationals all year!***

1969 Scotland v England

MISSING the solid international expertise of Ken McKinlay (racing for West Ham at Wolverhampton), Scotland took on a cosmopolitan look with Norwegians Reidar Eide and Øyvind Berg joining Charlie Monk in their squad.

England took a second race lead, were 10 points up after five races, and were never in serious danger of losing. Scotland's biggest blow was the poor form of George Hunter who missed his opening ride, took his only point off Jimmy Squibb (a late replacement for Tommy Roper) and was withdrawn from three of his last four programmed outings. Roy Trigg, Martin Ashby and Ray Wilson won 10 races between them to spearhead the Anglos win.

Glasgow, Friday, August 15
SCOTLAND 50 (†Jim McMillan 15, Charlie Monk 14, Reidar Eide 11, Bert Harkins 7, Øyvind Berg 2, George Hunter 1, Brian Collins 0, Willie Templeton 0) **ENGLAND 58** (Martin Ashby 15, Roy Trigg 15, †Ray Wilson 11, Arnold Haley 7, Eddie Reeves 7, Jimmy Squibb 2, Russ Dent 1, Chris Pusey 0).

1969 Britain v Australasia Results (Division Two)

Berwick, Friday, September 5
BRITAIN 59 (†Mark Hall 15, Eric Broadbelt 13, Peter Bailey 11, Tom Leadbitter 9, Steve Waplington 6, Mick Bell 3, Dave Schofield 2, Terry Lee, did not ride) **AUSTRALASIA 48** (Graeme Smith 17, Roger Wright 11, †Geoff Curtis 8, Paul O'Neal 5, Roy Williams 3, Dene Davies 2, Bob Tabet 2, Colin Tucker 0).

Nelson, Tuesday, September 9
BRITAIN 66 (Geoff Ambrose 17, Alan Knapkin 15, Eric Broadbelt 12, Tom Leadbitter 8, Steve Waplington 7, †Dave Schofield 5, Ian Turner 2, Terry Lee, did not ride) **AUSTRALASIA 42** (Paul O'Neal 14, †Geoff Curtis 11, Graeme Smith 10, Terry Shearer 3, Dene Davies 2, Roy Williams 1, Bob Tabet 1, Roger Wright 0).

Crayford, Wednesday, September 10
BRITAIN 62 (†Archie Wilkinson 16, Martyn Piddock 12, Dave Jessup 11, Phil Woodcock 9, Geoff Ambrose 7, Chris Harrison 6, Mick Steel 1, Richard May 0) **AUSTRALASIA 46** (Graeme Smith 11, Roy Williams 10, Terry Shearer 7, †Geoff Curtis 6, Paul O'Neal 6, Roger Wright 3, Dene Davies 3, Neville Slee, did not ride).

Eastbourne, Sunday, September 21
BRITAIN 69 (Martyn Piddock 17, Dave Jessup 14, †Geoff Ambrose 12, Mick Bell 11, Malcolm Shakespeare 7, Richard May 6, Peter Murray 2, Mac Woolford 0) **AUSTRALASIA 38** (Graeme Smith 14, †Geoff Curtis 10, Cec Platt 5, Roy Williams 3, Paul O'Neal 3, Roger Wright 3, Dene Davies 0).

Ipswich, Thursday, September 25
Britain 51 (Martyn Piddock 12, †John Harrhy 12, Mick Bell 10, Peter Bailey 7, Ian Turner 6, Geoff Ambrose 3, Archie Wilkinson 1, Geoff Maloney, did not ride) **AUSTRALASIA 57** (†Peter Bradshaw 15, Graeme Smith 14, Paul O'Neal 14, Dene Davies 7, Roger Wright 6, Cec Platt 1, Bob Tabet 0).

Britain win the series 4-1.

- ***The Britain team managers were Dent Oliver (Berwick and Nelson) and Bryan Seery (Crayford, Eastbourne and Ipswich).***
- ***The Australasia team manager was Peter White.***

1969 England v Czechoslovakia (Division Two) Results

Canterbury, Saturday, August 16
ENGLAND 47 (Geoff Ambrose 13, †Martyn Piddock 8, Graham Miles 8, Richard May 8, Peter Murray 5, Dave Jessup 4, Mick Bell 1, Colin Clark 0) **CZECHOSLOVAKIA 61** (Zdenek Majstr 15, †Frantisek Ledecky 13, Karel Prusa 12, Miloslav Verner 10, Jan Klokocka 6, Jiri Stancl 4, Josef Lid 1, Vaclav Verner, did not ride).

Doncaster, Sunday, August 17
ENGLAND 62 (Ken Eyre 16, †Geoff Ambrose 15, Eric Broadbelt 11, Terry Lee 9, Dave Baugh 3, Ian Bottomley 3, Tom Leadbitter 3, Steve Waplington 2) **CZECHOSLOVAKIA 46** (†Frantisek Ledecky 12, Miloslav Verner 10, Jiri Stancl 9, Jan Klokocka 8, Zdenek Majstr 3, Josef Lid 3, Karel Prusa 1, Vaclav Verner, did not ride).

Crewe, Monday, August 18
ENGLAND 54 (Chris Bailey 14, Tom Leadbitter 11, Terry Lee 10, Geoff Ambrose 10, Eric Broadbelt 3, Dave Parry 3, Roger Mills 3, †Ian Bottomley 0) **CZECHOSLOVAKIA 54** (Miloslav Verner 17, Karel Prusa 15, †Frantisek Ledecky 9, Jiri Stancl 8, Zdenek Majstr 4, Josef Lid 1, Jan Klokocka 0, Vaclav Verner, did not ride).

Middlesbrough, Thursday, August 21
ENGLAND 63 (Geoff Ambrose 16, Terry Lee 13, †Tom Leadbitter 12, Mick Bell 8, Martyn Piddock 7, Richard May 4, Roger Mills 3, Dave Schofield, did not ride) **CZECHOSLOVAKIA 45** (†Miloslav Verner 15, Frantisek Ledecky 11, Zdenek Majstr 11, Vaclav Verner 6, Jiri Stancl 1, Karel Prusa 1, Jan Klokocka 0, Josef Lid 0).

Rayleigh, Saturday, August 23
ENGLAND 49 (Richard May 10, Dingle Brown 10, Chris Bailey 9, †Geoff Maloney 8, Phil Woodcock 6, Mike Vernam 4, Mick Bell 2, Ian Turner 0) **CZECHOSLOVAKIA 59** (Miloslav Verner 17, †Frantisek Ledecky 14, Zdenek Majstr 12, Jiri Stancl 5, Jan Klokocka 5, Karel Prusa 4, Vaclav Verner 2, Josef Lid, did not ride).

King's Lynn, Sunday, August 24
ENGLAND 45 (Peter Murray 15, Martyn Piddock 11, Phil Woodcock 9, †Arthur Price 5, Peter Bailey 3, Geoff Maloney 1, John Harrhy 1, Dingle Brown 0) **CZECHOSLOVAKIA 62** (†Miloslav Verner 17, Frantisek Ledecky 11, Zdenek Majstr 10, Vaclav Verner 7, Jan Klokocka 6, Josef Lid 6, Jiri Stancl 5, Karel Prusa 0).

Reading, Monday, August 25
ENGLAND 51 (Martyn Piddock 10, †Richard May 10, Mick Bell 10, Geoff Maloney 9, Peter Murray 5, Eric Broadbelt 5, Mike Vernam 1, Dave Jessup 1) **CZECHOSLOVAKIA 57** (Miloslav Verner 18, Vaclav Verner 14, Zdenek Majstr 9, Jiri Stancl 7, Josef Lid 5, †Frantisek Ledecky 2, Karel Prusa 2, Jan Klokocka 0).

Czechoslovakia win the series 4-2, with one Test drawn.

CLUB MATCH
Romford, Thursday, August 14
ROMFORD 35 (Phil Woodcock 11, Frank Wendon 9, Brian Davies 6, †Ross Gilbertson 5, Ian Gills 2, Brian Foote 1, Charlie Benham 1) **CZECHOSLOVAKIA 43** (Jan Klokocka 10, Miloslav Verner 9, Jiri Stancl 8, Zdenek Majstr 8, Vaclav Verner 4, Karel Prusa 3, †Frantisek Ledecky 1, Josef Lid 0).

- *The England team managers were Lionel Hoskins (Canterbury), Derek Bridgett (Doncaster), Ken Adams (Crewe), Henry Atkinson (Middlesbrough), Charlie Mugford (Rayleigh), Cyril Crane (King's Lynn) and Dick Bailey (Reading).*
- *The Czechoslovakia team manager was Pavel Kacer.*

1969 BriSA Triangular Team Tournament

COVENTRY promoter Charles Ochiltree dreamt up the ill-fated BriSA Triangular Team Tournament while on an Inter City train journey between London and his West Midlands home.

The originator wanted to combine team competition with an element of pairs riding and individualism. Pairings were maintained throughout the 14 heats with overall victors in the team event, a parallel pairs event, and a conventional second half individual event!

The first meeting was sensational with Jim Airey smashing the track record in heat 6 and then Ivan Mauger and Ole Olsen facing a run-off in the last race after they had dead-heated in the four-rider International Speedway Trophy Final. But the Exeter round was ruined by four programmed absentees after the original staging had been rained off. It ended with American DeWayne Keeter and Czechoslovakian Jan Holub riding in Scandinavia's colours!

Coventry, Wednesday, July 2
BRITANNIA 33 (Nigel Boocock 11, Terry Betts 5 [16]; Ray Wilson 10, Norman Hunter 1 [11]; Rick France 6) **SCANDINAVIA 26** (Sören Sjösten 9, Bernt Persson 6 [15]; Ole Olsen 7, Reidar Eide 0 [7]; Conny Samuelsson 4) **AUSTRALASIA 24** (Ivan Mauger 9, Ronnie Moore 3 [12]; Jim Airey 9, John Boulger 2 [11]; Greg Kentwell 1).

Exeter, Monday, August 11
AUSTRALASIA 35 (Ivan Mauger 12, Ronnie Moore 4 [16]; Jim Airey 11, Geoff Mudge 8 [19]) **BRITANNIA 27** (Martin Ashby 8, Nigel Boocock 6 [14]; Jimmy Squibb 6, Ray Wilson 5 [11]; Alan Cowland 2) **SCANDINAVIA 22** (Reidar Eide 10, Odd Fossengen 1 [11]; Øyvind Berg 5, DeWayne Keeter 0 [5]; Jan Holub 6).

1969 Norway Tour Results

Poole, Wednesday, September 24
POOLE 42(Gordon Guasco 10, Bruce Cribb 8, †Geoff Mudge 8, Pete Smith 6, Ted Laessing 5, Mike Vernam 4, Frank Shuter 1) **NORWAY 36** (†Reidar Eide 11, Odd Fossengen 8, Øyvind Berg 7, Ulf Lovaas 6, Einar Egedius 2, Per Aulie 1, Jon Odegaard 1, Edgar Stangeland, did not ride).

Oxford, Thursday, September 25
OXFORD 48 (†Eddie Reeves 12, Colin Gooddy 11, Peter Jarman 7, Rick Timmo 7, George Major 6, Peter Seaton 5, David Crane 0) **NORWAY 30** (†Reidar Eide 10, Odd Fossengen 7, Øyvind Berg 5, Ulf Lovaas 4, Jon Odegaard 2, Einar Egedius 2, Per Aulie 0, Edgar Stangeland, did not ride).

King's Lynn, Saturday, September 27
KING'S LYNN 49 (Malcolm Simmons 12, Howard Cole 11, †Terry Betts 11, Clive Featherby 7, Peter Bradshaw 3, Allan Brown 3, Alan Belham 2) **NORWAY 29** (*Olle Nygren 9*, Øyvind Berg 8, Odd Fossengen 5, Edgar Stangeland 3, Ulf Lovaas 3, Einar Egedius 1, Per Aulie 0).

NEWLY-CROWNED 1969 British League Champions Poole undertook a whistle-stop tour of Poland during October...and returned without a win but with plenty of new friends.

The Pirates actually arrived back in Britain only a few hours before being presented with the championship trophy at the British League Riders' Championship Final.

Polish League Champions Stal Gorzow – Poole's first opponents – reinforced their side by bringing in three guests and not surprisingly were comfortable 19-point winners. The closest the Dorset club came to victory was in the second match against Second Division champions Kolejarz Opole who clawed their way back from six points down and gave British riders their first glimpse of a teenager who was, later, to rock the speedway world...19-year-old Jerzy Szczakiel who recorded a 15-point maximum in the wake of an impressive Polish Final debut where he finished fifth.

STAL GORZOW 48 POOLE 30 (Geoff Mudge 9, Gordon Guasco 6, Bruce Cribb 4, Frank Shuter 4, Odd Fossengen 3, Pete Smith 3, Ted Laessing 1).

KOLEJARZ OPOLE 43 POOLE 35 (Gordon Guasco 10, Odd Fossengen 6, Pete Smith 5, Bruce Cribb 5, Geoff Mudge 4, Ted Laessing 4, Frank Shuter 1).

WLOKNIARZ CZESTOCHOWA 47 POOLE 31 (Gordon Guasco 8, Bruce Cribb 8, Pete Smith 6, Frank Shuter 3, Geoff Mudge 3, Odd Fossengen 2, Ted Laessing 1).

UNIA TARNOW 51 POOLE 27 (Geoff Mudge 8, Bruce Cribb 5, Pete Smith 5, Gordon Guasco 3, Odd Fossengen 3, Frank Shuter 3, Ted Laessing 0).

SLASK SWIETOCHLOWICE 50 POOLE 27 (Odd Fossengen 8, Gordon Guasco 6, Bruce Cribb 6, Pete Smith 4, Geoff Mudge 3, Frank Shuter 0, Ted Laessing 0).

BELLE VUE made their second visit to the Soviet Union to further cement the happy relations between themselves and Leningrad Neva.

Around 5,00 fans filled the Neva Stadium for a challenge match that went right to the last heat. Top home rider Vladimir Smirnov shut out Tommy Roper as Ivan Mauger took first place to give the Russians a tight 40-38 victory.

The following afternoon the Belle Vue riders took part in an individual meeting with Mauger taking first place with a15 point maximum which included the fastest time of the event. Teammate Tommy Roper was third with Anatoli Belkin runner-up.

LENINGRAD 40 (Anatoli Belkin 10, Vladimir Smirnov 9, Vladimir Kannunikov 8, Giorgi Markatanov 5, Valeri Katyuzhanski 3, Genrikh Lemberg 3, Gennady Vyunov 2) **BELLE VUE 38** (Sören Sjösten 13, Ivan Mauger 10, Tommy Roper 7, Chris Pusey 5, Chris Bailey 2, Steve Waplington 1, Dave Hemus 0).

CHRIS PUSEY...thrilled the Russians at Leningrad

Brave Booey

NIGEL BOOCOCK vowed that he would lead the Lions on their tour of Australasia – even as he lay in a bed at Leicester Royal Infirmary, suffering from a hairline fracture of the skull.

And the tough battling Tyke achieved his target, passing a late fitness test on the day before the fifth and final match at Sydney Showground early in the New Year.

He had made such a remarkable recovery that the Speedway Control Board, who nominated and paid for Sheffield's Arnold Haley to go as his touring replacement, agreed to pay his air fare to Australia as a mark of respect for his past services to the England cause, a well appreciated gesture from the authorities.

Typically, Booey arrived Down Under, declared he wanted to race, and was picked at reserve instead of Howard Cole (himself a replacement for Martin Ashby who broke his ankle in the second Test).

Booey took four rides, scored six valuable points and helped the Lions take the series 3-2 in a pulsating finale.

He was then able to continue his winter's activity by accompanying the team on their three-Test tour of New Zealand where he claimed double figures in all three matches, top scoring for the Lions in the final two Tests.

Booey's younger brother Eric had taken over the captainship of the tourists and reserved his best till last, top scoring in that deciding Test at the Showground after Australia had levelled affairs with the closest victory of all, by just four points at Brisbane on Boxing Day.

The stage was set for Nigel's return....

1969-70 England Lions tour of Australia Results

Perth, Friday, November 21, 1969
AUSTRALIA 61 (†Jim Airey 17, Chum Taylor 16, John Boulger 10, Greg Kentwell 8 Terry O'Leary 7, Charlie Monk 3, Abe Schneider 0) **ENGLAND 47** (†Eric Boocock 10, Jim McMillan 10, Arnold Haley 9, Ray Wilson 6, Ken McKinlay 6, Martin Ashby 3, Tony Clarke 3).

Adelaide, Friday, December 5, 1969
AUSTRALIA 45 (†Jim Airey 15, John Boulger 9, Chum Taylor 8, Charlie Monk 7, Jack White 3, Chris Bass 3, Greg Kentwell 0) **ENGLAND 63** (Ray Wilson 16, †Eric Boocock 13, Jim McMillan 11, Tony Clarke 10, Martin Ashby 8, Ken McKinlay 5, Arnold Haley 0).

Sydney, Saturday, December 13, 1969
AUSTRALIA 50 (†Jim Airey 18, Bert Kingston 9, Jack White 9, Charlie Monk 7, John Boulger 4, John Langfield 3, Trevor Harding 0) **ENGLAND 58** (Jim McMillan 13, Tony Clarke 11, Arnold Haley 11, †Eric Boocock 9, Ray Wilson 9, Ken McKinlay 3, Howard Cole 2).

Brisbane, Friday, December 26, 1969
AUSTRALIA 56 (†Jim Airey 14, Jack White 13, Doug White 11, Bert Kingston 10, Garry Middleton 6, Charlie Monk 2, Steve Reinke 0) **ENGLAND 52** (Tony Clarke 13, Ray Wilson 11, Arnold Haley 10, Jim Mc Millan 8, †Eric Boocock 5, Ken McKinlay 3, Howard Cole 2).

Sydney, Saturday, January 3, 1970
AUSTRALIA 49 (†Jim Airey 15, Chum Taylor 9, Bert Kingston 7, Jack White 7, Greg Kentwell 7, Doug White 3, Bill Landels 1) **ENGLAND 58** (†Eric Boocock 15, Arnold Haley 14, Tony Clarke 13, Nigel Boocock 6, Jim McMillan 4, Ray Wilson 4, Ken McKinlay 2).

England win the series 3-2.

1970 Lions tour of New Zealand Results

Auckland, Saturday, January 17, 1970
NEW ZEALAND 36 (Bob Andrews 10, Ivan Mauger 9, Ronnie Moore 7, Bill Andrew 5, Colin McKee 3, Bryce Subritzky 2, Goog Allan 0) **ENGLAND 72** (Tony Clarke 17, Jim McMillan 17, Eric Boocock 11, Ray Wilson 11, Nigel Boocock 10, Arnold Haley 6, Ken McKinlay, did not ride).

Auckland, Saturday, January 24, 1970
NEW ZEALAND 43 (Ivan Mauger 17, Ronnie Moore 9, Bryce Subritzky 7, Bob Andrews 6, Bill Andrew 3, Colin McKee 1, Goog Allan 0) **ENGLAND 65** (Nigel Boocock 17, Jim McMillan 14, Eric Boocock 11, Ray Wilson 11, Arnold Haley 7, Tony Clarke 5, Ken McKinlay, did not ride).

Christchurch, Saturday, January 31, 1970
NEW ZEALAND 40 (Ronnie Moore 16, Ivan Mauger 12, Bob Andrews 4, Bill Andrew 4, Allan Brown 2, Tom Black 2, Roger Wright 0) **ENGLAND 67** (Nigel Boocock 14, Arnold Haley 14, Eric Boocock 13, Jim McMillan 10, Ray Wilson 10, Tony Clarke 6).

England win the series 3-0.

It's GREAT Britain

1970 Great Britain v Sweden Results

Glasgow, Friday, July 3
GREAT BRITAIN 66 (Ivan Mauger 17, Eric Boocock 11, Nigel Boocock 9, †Barry Briggs 8, Jim McMillan 8, Ronnie Moore 8, Charlie Monk 4, Les Sharpe 1) **SWEDEN 42** (Anders Michanek 14, Bernt Persson 10, Sören Sjösten 10, Christer Löfqvist 5, Olle Nygren 3, †Ove Fundin 0, Bengt Larsson 0).

Halifax, Saturday, July 4
GREAT BRITAIN 48 (†Barry Briggs 14, Jim Airey 8, Nigel Boocock 7, Martin Ashby 5, Ray Wilson 4, Arnold Haley 4, Eric Boocock 3, Les Sharpe 3) **SWEDEN 60** (†Anders Michanek 17, Bernt Persson 15, Sören Sjösten 11, Olle Nygren 7, Bengt Jansson 6, Bengt Larsson 2, Christer Löfqvist 2, Bengt Brannefors, did not ride).

Exeter, Monday, July 6
GREAT BRITAIN 66 (†Barry Briggs 17, Nigel Boocock 16, Ronnie Moore 11, Ray Wilson 10, Ivan Mauger 9, Martin Ashby 3, Bob Kilby 0, Bob Andrews, did not ride) **SWEDEN 42** (†Anders Michanek 14, Bengt Jansson 8, Bernt Persson 7, Christer Löfqvist 5, Olle Nygren 4, Sören Sjösten 2, Bengt Larsson 2, Bengt Brannefors 0).

West Ham, Tuesday, July 7
GREAT BRITAIN 62 (†Barry Briggs 18, Ivan Mauger 17, Ronnie Moore 15, Eric Boocock 4, Tony Clarke 3, Terry Betts 2, Bob Kilby 2, Trevor Hedge 1) **SWEDEN 46** (†Anders Michanek 15, Bengt Jansson 13, Olle Nygren 9, Sören Sjösten 6, Christer Löfqvist 2, Bengt Larsson 1, Bernt Persson 0, Bengt Brannefors 0).

Newport, Friday, July 10
GREAT BRITAIN 70 (†Barry Briggs 17, Ronnie Moore 16, Nigel Boocock 12, Bill Andrew 11, Ivan Mauger 10, Martin Ashby 2, Jim Airey 2, Ray Wilson 0) **SWEDEN 38** (Sören Sjösten 10, Bernt Persson 7, Bengt Jansson 7, †Anders Michanek 6, Olle Nygren 6, Christer Löfqvist 2, Bengt Brannefors 0, Bengt Larsson, did not ride).

Coventry, Saturday, July 11
GREAT BRITAIN 71 (Ivan Mauger 18, †Nigel Boocock 16, Rick France 13, Jim McMillan 10, Ken McKinlay 8, John Boulger 6) **SWEDEN 37** (†Anders Michanek 13, Olle Nygren 8, Sören Sjösten 8, Bernt Persson 4, Bengt Larsson 2, Bengt Jansson 1, Christer Löfqvist 1, Bengt Brannefors 0).

Great Britain win the series 5-1.

● *The Great Britain team managers were: Ian Hoskins (Glasgow), Reg Fearman (Halifax), Wally Mawdsley (Exeter), Gordon Parkins (West Ham), Pete Lansdale (Newport) and Charles Ochiltree (Coventry).*
● *The Sweden team managers were Charles Ringblom (Glasgow and Halifax) and Christer Bergstrom (Exeter, West Ham, Newport and Coventry).*

BARRY BRIGGS arrived late at Hampden Park...and then wasted no time at all in helping demolish Sweden.

Briggo was held up when his plane was delayed and missed his first three rides, not coming out until heat 10.

But he certainly made amends with eight points from his last three programmed rides to give Great Britain a flying start in a series in which Sweden had vowed to extract revenge for the previous year's whitewash.

In 1969 much of the blame in a Swedish post-mortem had been heaped on the fact that their riders weren't competing in the British League.

This time around there was no such excuse and they were able to call on a vast amount of experience.

And it looked as if the opening defeat at Hampden Park might simply have been a hang-over from 12 months earlier.

For Anders Michanek slashed a fifth of a second off the Halifax track record in the opening heat of the second international as he defeated Briggo and his Swindon team-mate Martin Ashby who finished fourth behind veteran Olle Nygren to give Sweden a flying start.

They never let up and could even overcome the absence of Christer Löfqvist who had to pull out after cracking his frame in finishing second behind Jim Airey in his opening race.

Michanek went on to win his next four

A SERIOUS injury to top Scot Jim McMillan marred Great Britain's series win in Sweden.

The Glasgow youngster broke his leg in two places during the second Test at Målilla after he had been the hero of the first international with a superb victory-enhancing 15 points.

Jimmy Mac was lying second in Heat 5 when his engine seized and Bengt Jansson, close behind, had no chance at all of avoiding him as he ground to a dramatic halt.

Great Britain collapsed following the shock of seeing McMillan taken off to hospital but vowed that they would complete their mission in the third and final international at Stockholm.

Ivan Mauger, skipper for his first tour, said: "We won the last match for him as well as the country!"

A poor crowd, less than 5,000, looked lost at Gothenburg's Ullevi Stadium and Swedish officials claimed it was previous poor performances by British teams that had accounted for the lack of interest.

If that was the case then certainly the tourists ensured that would never be the excuse again.

1970 Sweden v Great Britain Results

Gothenburg, Tuesday, September 29
SWEDEN 45 (Anders Michanek 14, Sören Sjösten 12, Göte Nordin 8, Bengt Jansson 5, Bengt Brannefors 3, Bengt Larsson 2, †Ove Fundin 1, Tommy Johansson 0) **GREAT BRITAIN 63** (†Ivan Mauger 18, Jim McMillan 15, Eric Boocock 12, Bob Kilby 6, Arnold Haley 5, Martin Ashby 4, Roy Trigg 2, Ray Wilson 1).

Målilla, Sunday, October 4
SWEDEN 73 (Sören Sjösten 18, †Ove Fundin 15, Anders Michanek 14, Tommy Johansson 12, Peo Söderman 9, Bo Wirebrand 4, Bengt Jansson 1, Bo Josefsson 0) **GREAT BRITAIN 34** (†Ivan Mauger 14, Eric Boocock 9, Bob Kilby 5, Arnold Haley 3, Martin Ashby 1, Ray Wilson 1, Jim McMillan 1, Roy Trigg 0).

Stockholm, Tuesday, October 6
SWEDEN 47 (Anders Michanek 18, Leif Enecrona 8, Sören Sjösten 8, †Ove Fundin 6, Tommy Johansson 5, Peo Söderman 1, Tommy Bergkvist 1, Börje Melin 0) **GREAT BRITAIN 61** (†Ivan Mauger 14, Martin Ashby 13, Ray Wilson 12, Roy Trigg 9, Eric Boocock 8, Bob Kilby 5, Arnold Haley 0, Mike Broadbank 0).

Great Britain win the series 2-1.

CLUB MATCH
Stockholm, Saturday, October 3
VARGARNA 34 (Anders Michanek 12, Olle Nygren 7, Peo Söderman 6, Tommy Bergkvist 4, Leif Enecrona 4, Runo Wedin 1, Lars Johansson 0) **GREAT BRITAIN 44** (Eric Boocock 11, Bob Kilby 10, Martin Ashby 7, Jim McMillan 5, Roy Trigg 5, Arnold Haley 3, Ray Wilson 3).

● *The Great Britain team managerwas Charles Foot.*
● *The Sweden team managers were Evert Andersson (Gothenburg), and Arne Bergstöm (Målilla and Stockholm)*

rides and didn't drop a point until the final result was well beyond doubt, to Nigel Boocock in his last race.

The most disappointed rider of all was Nigel's brother Eric who had wanted, desperately, to celebrate becoming a father earlier in the day when his wife Diane presented him with a new son Richie!

The entire series swung on a 'professional foul' midway through the third and vital Test at Exeter.

Sören Sjösten came down on the opening lap after trying to push past Nigel Boocock and looked to be unhurt as referee Peter Ryall allowed the race to continue.

But the tiny Swede dramatically dropped to the shale and, as the red warning lights came on, he equally as dramatically skipped to his feet and sauntered off onto the centre green.

Even though he argued that Booey should have been excluded

BRITAIN'S BROTHERS...Nigel and Eric Boocock played a major rôle in Great Britain's big series win over Sweden and then teamed up again as England had the best of a wet weather series against Australia before walloping the Kiwis despite the top-heavy scoring efforts of Ivan Mauger and Barry Briggs.

1970 England v Australia Results

Hackney, Friday, April 17
ENGLAND 30 (Colin Pratt 7, Tony Clarke 6, †Nigel Boocock 5, Trevor Hedge 5, Terry Betts 4, Martin Ashby 3, Graham Plant and Martyn Piddock, did not ride) **AUSTRALIA 24** (†Jim Airey 9, Charlie Monk 8, Garry Middleton 3, Geoff Mudge 3, Peter Bradshaw 1, Gordon Guasco 0, Neil Street 0).
Abandoned after nine heats, rain.

Newcastle, Monday, April 20
ENGLAND 29 (†Nigel Boocock 9, Ray Wilson 7, Terry Betts 7, Eric Boocock 6, Arnold Haley 0, Reg Luckhurst 0, Tommy Roper and Russ Dent, did not ride) **AUSTRALIA 31** (†Jim Airey 10, Gordon Guasco 6, Les Sharpe 4, Garry Middleton 4, John Boulger 4, Charlie Monk 3, Geoff Mudge and Peter Vandenberg did not ride).
Abandoned after 10 heats, rain.

Cradley Heath, Monday, May 11
ENGLAND 70 (Terry Betts 17, Eric Boocock 13, †Nigel Boocock 13, Ray Wilson 10, Trevor Hedge 9, Roy Trigg 8, Arnold Haley, did not ride) **AUSTRALIA 38** (Les Sharpe 14, Garry Middleton 9, John Boulger 5, †Jim Airey 4, Charlie Monk 4, Gordon Guasco 2, Peter Vandenberg 0, Geoff Mudge 0).

England win the series 1-0.

● *The England team managers were Ronnie Greene (Hackney), Dent Oliver (Newcastle) and Mike Parker (Cradley Heath).*
● *The Australia team managers were Johnnie Hoskins (Hackney and Newcastle) and Greg Kentwell (Cradley Heath).*

1970 England v New Zealand Results

Wimbledon, Thursday, July 30
ENGLAND 54 (Tony Clarke 12, Trevor Hedge 12, Martin Ashby 10, Roy Trigg 9, Ray Wilson 8, Howard Cole 2, †Nigel Boocock 1, Bob Kilby 0) **NEW ZEALAND 53** (Ivan Mauger 18, †Barry Briggs 17, Bob Andrews 7, Dave Gifford 7, Rick Timmo 3, Frank Shuter 1, Bill Andrew 0, Colin McKee 0).

Belle Vue, Wednesday, August 5
ENGLAND 66 (Martin Ashby 12, †Nigel Boocock 12, Eric Boocock 11, Arnold Haley 11, Trevor Hedge 11, Ray Wilson 9, Chris Pusey and Tommy Roper, did not ride) **NEW ZEALAND 42** (†Ivan Mauger 18, Barry Briggs 17, Rick Timmo 3, Bill Andrew 2, Bob Andrews 2, Wayne Briggs 0, Dave Gifford 0, Colin McKee 0).

Swindon, Wednesday, August 12
ENGLAND 70 (Bob Kilby 16, Terry Betts 13, Ray Wilson 13, Martin Ashby 10, Eric Boocock 9, †Nigel Boocock 9, Arnold Haley and Trevor Hedge, did not ride) **NEW ZEALAND 37** (†Barry Briggs 18, Ivan Mauger 10, Bruce Cribb 5, Rick Timmo 3, Bob Andrews 1, Bill Andrew 0, Wayne Briggs 0, Dave Gifford 0).

Sheffield, Thursday, August 27
ENGLAND 64 (Eric Boocock 14, †Nigel Boocock 13, Arnold Haley 11, Bob Kilby 10, Tommy Roper 9, Martin Ashby 7, Chris Pusey and Ray Wilson, did not ride) **NEW ZEALAND 44** (Ivan Mauger 18, †Barry Briggs 15, Bob Andrews 8, Bill Andrew 2, Colin McKee 1, Wayne Briggs 0, Frank Shuter 0, Dave Gifford 0).

England win the series 4-0.

● *The England team managers were Vic Gooden (Wimbledon), Dent Oliver (Belle Vue), Dick Bradley (Swindon) and Terry Thornhill (Sheffield).*
● *The New Zealand team manager was Trevor Redmond.*

no-one at the County Ground believed he had done anything other than win a second chance for his race partner Bengt Larsson.

It was a ploy that didn't work for two reasons. Ivan Mauger and Boocock tied up the re-run and it merely fired up the Brits who then provided all but one of the remaining nine heat winners to take a 2-1 lead with matches at West Ham, Newport and Coventry to follow.

Briggs, Mauger and the third of the great Kiwi trio Ronnie Moore revelled at Custom House winning 14 of the 18 races between. They didn't have too much support but they didn't need is at they actually outscored the Swedes 50-46 on their own!

It meant Sweden had to win in Wales but they were never at the party.

Great Britain lost the services of Ray Wilson with a broken collar bone in the opening heat and had to call on reserves Jim Airey and Martin Ashby to fill his shoes.

Briggs was, yet again, superlative and was only deprived of his second maximum in four nights in his last ride when he was pipped to the flag by Anders Michanek who had been strangely ineffective until then, picking up only three points from his first five rides.

A much-changed Great Britain side (missing Briggs, Moore, the injured Ray Wilson and Terry Betts) steamrollered their way to victory in the sixth and final Test against a Swedish side also missing two of its mainstays, Ove Fundin and Hasse Holmkvist.

Mauger was unbeaten; Nigel Boocock dropped only one point to an opponent and Rick France stormed back with 13 points.

For Sweden Bengt Jansson was taken to hopspital with a wrist injury; Christer Löfqvist blew up his engine on the stand; and they had only one finisher in almost half of the races.

So the series went 5-1 to Great Britain and with 12 wins out of the last 14 Test matches between the two countries it was time for some serious thinking about the international future.

AFTER their initial foray into providing Second Division fans with international competition promoters pressed ahead with a full programme of Test competition.

Czechoslovakia and Sweden both sent over touring parties and the Britain-Australasia matches were again part of the 1970 international calendar.

Additionally an England squad, drawn solely from Division Two, undertook a three matches in three days visit to Czechoslovakia.

The final tally of Test matches was a total of 20 (15 of them with an England side and five as Britain) with the popular Czecho-

1970 Stal Gorzow (Poland) Club Tour Results

AFTER Poole were crowned the 1969 British League champions they made a five-match tour of Poland. And while over there promoter Charles Foot suggested a reciprocal 1970 visit from the previous season's Polish League champions Stal Gorzow.

Backed by three other tracks who also offered to host a match, the tour featured in the early months of the new season with Stal Gorzow boosting the overall strength of their own line-up by including three guests from ROW Rybnik, Andrzej Wyglenda, Antonin Woryna and Jerzy Gryt.

Their tour opened painfully for both the team – beaten in a last heat decider at King's Lynn – and Edward Jancarz in particular. He was ruled out of his last two rides and three of the remaining four matches when he crashed in heat 10 and snapped his collar bone.

Despite this blow Stal went on to defeat Exeter, Poole and Halifax, losing their only other match to an Ole Olsen inspired Wolverhampton. Edmund Migos and the tall Andrzej Pogorzelski were both unbeaten at Wimborne Road as they totally outclassed the defending British League title-holders to complete a home-and-away double having beaten the Pirates 48-30 in their opening tour match a few months earlier.

After their heavy defeat at Monmore Green in a torrid encounter of shoulder-to-shoulder racing, Jancarz returned for the last match at The Shay – basically to cover for the injured Pogo – and made everyone wonder what might have happened had he been fit for the entire tour as he shrugged off the discomfort of a heavily strapped collar-bone to sail through his four programme rides undefeated.

King's Lynn, Saturday, April 11
KING'S LYNN 41 (Malcolm Simmons 12, †Terry Betts 9, Allan Brown 8, David Crane 5, Alan Belham 4, Cyril Maidment 3, Howard Cole 0) **STAL GORZOW 37** (Edmund Migos 11, Andrzej Wyglenda 9, Antonin Woryna 6, Edward Jancarz 5, †Andrzej Pogorzelski 3, Ryszard Dziatkowiak 2, Jerzy Gryt 1).

Exeter, Monday, April 13
EXETER 37 (Bruce Cribb 11, Neil Street 9, †Martin Ashby 5, Chris Julian 4, Jan Holub 4, Phil Woodcock 4, Bob Coles 0) **STAL GORZOW 41** (†Andrzej Pogorzelski 13, Edmund Migos 10, Andrzej Wyglenda 7, Antonin Woryna 6, Ryszard Dziatkowiak 4, Jerzy Gryt 1, Wojciech Jurasz 0).

Poole, Wednesday, April 15
POOLE 31 (Gordon Guasco 8, Odd Fossengen 6, Pete Smith 6, †Geoff Mudge 5, Mike Cake 3, Ted Laessing 3, Frank Shuter 0) **STAL GORZOW 47** (Edmund Migos 12, †Andrzej Pogorzelski 11, Andrzej Wyglenda 10, Wojciech Jurasz 7, Antonin Woryna 4, Ryszard Dziatkowiak 3, Jerzy Gryt 0).

Wolverhampton, Friday, April 17
WOLVERHAMPTON 46 (†Ole Olsen 12, Norman Hunter 10, Peter Vandenberg 8, James Bond 6, Geoff Ambrose 4, Peter Jackson 4, Mick Handley 2) **STAL GORZOW 32** (Andrzej Wyglenda 11, Edmund Migos 10, †Andrzej Pogorzelski 5, Antonin Woryna 3, Ryzard Dziatkowiak 2, Wojciech Jurasz 1, Jerzy Gryt 0).

Halifax, Saturday, April 18
HALIFAX 38 (†Eric Boocock 10, Les Sharpe 7, Greg Kentwell 6, Dave Younghusband 6, Colin McKee 6, Alan Jay 2, Terry Lee 1) **STAL GORZOW 40** (†Edward Jancarz 12, Edmund Migos 9, Andrzej Wyglenda 9, Wojciech Jurasz 4, Ryszard Dziatkowiak 3, Antonin Woryna 3, Jerzy Gryt 0).

● *The Stal Gorzow team manager was Witold Glowania.*

1970 Leningrad (Soviet Union) Club Tour Results

LENINGRAD brough two new faces to Britain on their second club tour – skipper Vasili Baturin and Giorgi Ivanov.

Sadly though they were without Gennady Vyunov who had been top-scorer at Hyde Road on Neva's first visit 12 months earlier.

He had died after a practice match crash a month before the tourists arrived in Britain and his death also ended Belle Vue's hopes of becoming the first English club to sign a Soviet rider.

Belle Vue general manager Jack Fearnley was ready to offer Anatoli Belkin a contract to stay in Manchester for the rest of the season but the Russian club management said they could not release him from domestic racing following Vyunov's death.

Vladimir Smirnov was again the most impressive of the Leningrad visitors while he had double figure back-up from Baturin in matches at Exeter and Poole.

Exeter called up Swindon's Bob Kilby to replace Jan Holub (ill in hospital in his native Czechoslovakia) and he would almost certainly have collected a paid maximum but for his handlebars snapping in his last ride.

Two nights later, at Poole, the Soviet speedsters had to go into action with only six riders after Viktor Katyuzanski crashed in pre-match practice and they were reduced to virtually a four-man side as neither Belkin nor Vladimir Kannunikov (who failed to score a point in three matches) were able to cope with the Wimborne Road bends.

Belle Vue, Saturday, June 13
BELLE VUE 50 (†Ivan Mauger 12, Chris Pusey 12, Sören Sjösten 9, Ken Eyre 6, Tommy Roper 5, Dave Hemus 3, Mike Hiftle 3) **LENINGRAD 28** (Vladimir Smirnov 9, Giorgi Ivanov 6, †Vasili Baturin 6, Yuri Lombotski 5, Anatoli Belkin 2, Vladimir Kannunikov 0, Viktor Katyuzanski 0).

Exeter, Monday, June 15
EXETER 47 (Bengt Andersson 9, †Martin Ashby 8, Neil Street 8, Bob Kilby 7, Chris Julian 6, Phil Woodcock 5, Bob Coles 4) **LENINGRAD 31** (Vladimir Smirnov 11, †Vasili Baturin 10, Giorgi Ivanov 8, Yuri Lombotski 2, Vladimir Kannunikov 0, Viktor Katyuzanski 0, Anatoli Belkin 0).

Poole, Wednesday, June 17
POOLE 43 (Gordon Guasco 10, Pete Smith 8, †Geoff Mudge 7, Mike Cake 7, Odd Fossengen 5, Frank Shuter 4, Ted Laessing 2) **LENINGRAD 35** (Vladimir Smirnov 12, †Vasili Baturin 11, Giorgi Ivanov 8, Yuri Lombotski 4, Anatoli Belkin 0, Vladimir Kannunikov 0, Viktor Katyuzanski, did not ride).

● *The Leningrad team manager was Yuli Podvalnyi.*

1970 England v Czechoslovakia (Division Two) Results

Romford, Thursday, August 6
ENGLAND 56 (Dave Jessup 14, Richard May 14, Barry Crowson 9, Malcolm Shakespeare 7, John Louis 5, †Phil Woodcock 4, Brian Foote 2, Geoff Maloney 1) **CZECHOSLOVAKIA 52** (†Miloslav Verner 16, Vaclav Verner 14, Jiri Stancl 12, Zdenek Majstr 7, Jan Klokocka 2, Zbynek Novotny 1, Milan Spinka 0, Josef Lid 0).

Canterbury, Saturday, August 8
ENGLAND 46 (Barry Thomas 10, †Barry Crowson 9, John Louis 7, Phil Woodcock 6, Malcolm Shakespeare 5, Richard May 5, Geoff Maloney 3, Graham Banks 1) **CZECHOSLOVAKIA 62** (Vaclav Verner 15, †Miloslav Verner 12, Jan Klokocka 11, Zdenek Majstr 10, Jiri Stancl 9, Milan Spinka 4, Josef Lid 1, Zbynek Novotny, did not ride).

Rochdale, Sunday, August 9
ENGLAND 40 (†Eric Broadbelt 11, Alan Knapkin 9, Richard May 6, John Louis 6, Tom Leadbitter 4, Alan Wilkinson 3, Ken Moss 1, John Jackson 0) **CZECHOSLOVAKIA 68** (Vaclav Verner 18, †Miloslav Verner 15, Jiri Stancl 13, Zdenek Majstr 12, Jan Klokocka 5, Milan Spinka 5, Zbynek Novotny 0).

King's Lynn, Wednesday, August 12
ENGLAND 66 (Richard May 16, John Louis 14, †Geoff Maloney 12, Malcolm Shakespeare 9, Dave Jessup 8, Phil Woodcock 5, Arthur Price 2,Peter Bailey, did not ride) **CZECHOSLOVAKIA 42** (†Miloslav Verner 16, Jiri Stancl 10, Milan Spinka 9, Josef Lid 4, Jan Klokocka 3, Zdenek Majstr 0, Vaclav Verner 0, Zbynek Novotny 0).

Ipswich, Thursday, August 13
ENGLAND 56 (John Louis 17, †John Harrhy 12, Malcolm Shakespeare 9, Peter Bailey 7, Geoff Maloney 4, Barry Crowson 3, Richard May 2, Mike Vernam 2) **CZECHOSLOVAKIA 51** (†Miloslav Verner 13, Jiri Stancl 12, Milan Spinka 12, Jan Klokocka 8, Josef Lid 5, Zbynek Novotny 1, Zdenek Majstr 0).

Rayleigh, Saturday, August 15
ENGLAND 49 (John Louis 12, Mike Vernam 11, Dave Jessup 9, Phil Woodcock 8, †Geoff Maloney 5, Richard May 4, Hugh Saunders 0, Brian Foote 0) **CZECHOSLOVAKIA 59** (†Miloslav Verner 13, Jan Klokocka 12, Milan Spinka 11, Jiri Stancl 9, Zdenek Majstr 8, Josef Lid 6, Zbynek Novotny, did not ride).

Reading, Monday, August 17
ENGLAND 53 (Barry Thomas 14, Dave Jessup 12, John Louis 11, Barry Crowson 8, †Richard May 6, Mike Vernam 2, Malcolm Shakespeare 0, Peter Bailey 0) **CZECHOSLOVAKIA 55** (†Miloslav Verner 14, Josef Lid 13, Jiri Stancl 10, Milan Spinka 9, Zdenek Majstr 4, Jan Klokocka 3, Zbynek Novotny 2).

Czechoslovakia win the series 4-3.

CLUB MATCH
Crewe, Monday, August 10
CREWE 48 (Paul O'Neal 14, Ian Bottomley 10, Barry Meeks 7, John Jackson 5, Dave Parry 5, Dai Evans 4, Warren Hawkins 3, Rob Jackson 0) **CZECHOSLOVAKIA 59** (Vaclav Verner 12, Miloslav Verner 12, Jiri Stancl 11, Zdenek Majstr 9, Milan Spinka 6, Josef Lid 6, Zbynek Novotny 3, Jan Klokocka 0).

● *The England team managers were: Maurice Morley (Romford), Russ Osbourn (Canterbury), Alan Middleton (Rochdale), Maurice Littlechild (King's Lynn), John Berry (Ipswich), Charlie Mugford (Rayleigh) and Reg Fearman (Reading).*
● *The Czechoslovakia team manager was Pavel Kacer.*

1970 Czechoslovakia v England Results (Division Two)

Koprivnice, Friday, May 1
CZECHOSLOVAKIA 60 (Zdenek Majstr 13, Jiri Stancl 12, Miloslav Verner 12, Milos Duda 9, Jan Jasa 8, Jiri Plisak 4, Karol Vallner 2) **ENGLAND 48** (Tom Leadbitter 14, Peter Bailey 11, Phil Woodcock 9, Richard May 7, Graham Miles 4, Eric Broadbelt 2, Alan Knapkin 1, Malcolm Shakespeare 0).

Brezolup, Saturday, May 2
CZECHOSLOVAKIA 66.5 (Miloslav Verner 15, Jiri Stancl 15, Zdenek Majstr 15, Jan Jasa 10, Milos Duda 8, Milan Trlicha 2.5, Jozef Toth 1) **ENGLAND 41.5** (Alan Knapkin 11, Phil Woodcock 9, Malcolm Shakespeare 8, Peter Bailey 7, Tom Leadbitter 3.5, Richard May 2, Eric Broadbelt 1, Graham Miles 0).

Zarnovice, Sunday, May 3
CZECHOSLOVAKIA 64 (Miloslav Verner 15, Jiri Stancl 15, Zdenek Majstr 15, Milos Duda 7, Jan Jasa 6, Karol Vallner 3, Jozef Toth 3, Ludovit Bartfay 0) **ENGLAND 44** (Phil Woodcock 11, Tom Leadbitter 7, Alan Knapkin 6, Eric Broadbelt 6, Richard May 6, Malcolm Shakespeare 4, Graham Miles 4, Peter Bailey 0).

Czechoslovakia win the series 3-0.

● *The Czechoslovakia team manager was Rudolf Duda.*
● *The England team manager was Reg Fearman.*

● *Czechoslovakia supplied the England touring party with machines for the tour – and manager Reg Fearman was so unhappy with the original equipment that he threatened to call off the tour.*

1970 Britain v Australasia (Division Two) Results

Middlesbrough, Thursday, August 27
BRITAIN 64 (Dave Jessup 16, Alan Knapkin 12, John Jackson 12, Roger Mills 10, Tom Leadbitter 9, †Richard May 3, Tim Swales 2) **AUSTRALASIA 44** (†Gary Peterson 14, Graeme Smith 14, Bob Valentine 8, Dene Davies 5, Malcolm Mackay 1, Paul O'Neal 1, Warren Hawkins 1, Lou Sansom 0).

Crewe, Monday, August 31
BRITAIN 55 (Alan Knapkin 13, Barry Meeks 11, Dave Jessup 9, John Jackson 8, Alan Wilkinson 6, Dave Parry 3, Tom Leadbitter 3, †Richard May 2) **AUSTRALASIA 53** (Paul O'Neal 18, †Gary Peterson 16, Bob Valentine 15, Warren Hawkins 2, Malcolm Mackay 2, Hec Haslinger 0, Lou Sansom 0, Dene Davies 0).

Berwick, Saturday, September 12
BRITAIN 59 (Eric Broadbelt 15, †Tom Leadbitter 15, Alan Wilkinson 13, Tim Swales 8, Malcolm Shakespeare 4, Alistair Brady 2, Alan Knapkin 1, Kenny Omand 1) **AUSTRALASIA 49** (†Gary Peterson 18, Hec Haslinger 11, Lou Sansom 9, Malcolm Mackay 9, Warren Hawkins 2, Dene Davies 0, Paul O'Neal 0, Bob Valentine 0).

Eastbourne, Sunday, September 20
BRITAIN 74 (Arthur Price 14, John Louis 14, †Richard May 13, Barry Crowson 13, Dave Jessup 11, Gordon Kennett 6, Laurie Sims 3, Barry Thomas 0) **AUSTRALASIA 34** (†Bob Valentine 13, Dene Davies 10, Malcolm Mackay 5, Warren Hawkins 3, Lou Sansom 3, Chris Blythe 0, Cec Platt 0).

Canterbury, Saturday, September 26
Britain 45 (Graham Banks 11, Graham Miles 8, Gordon Kennett 7, Barry Thomas 6, †Richard May 5, Malcolm Shakespeare 5, Mike Vernam 3, Barry Crowson 0) **AUSTRALASIA 62** (Paul O'Neal 14, †Gary Peterson 11, Dene Davies 11, Malcolm Mackay 9, Bob Valentine 6, Lou Sansom 6, Warren Hawkins 5, Cec Platt 0).

Britain win the series 4-1.

● *The Britain team managers were: Ron Wilson (Middlesbrough), Maurice Littlechild (Crewe and Berwick), Dave Lanning (Eastbourne) and Russ Osbourn (Canterbury).*
● *The Australasia team managers were Bob Jameson (all except Berwick) and Ken Taylor (Berwick).*

slovakians also undertaking a tough match at Crewe!

The Czechs, as usual, were marvellous entertainment winning a tight series in the last match at Reading by just two points!

Vaclav Verner set off on the right footing by lowering the Brooklands track record in a four point defeat at Romford and followed that up with an 18 point maximum as the Czechs levelled the series with a thumping 28 point win at Rochdale.

SLICK DICK...Richard May celebrated with double figures in six of England's summer internationals.

But his tour was to end prematurely when he smashed up his wrist in a traumatic night at King's Lynn which also saw Zdenek Majstr stretchered off.

While Majstr was able to continue the tour Verner's racing was over as x-rays confirmed he had broken his wrist.

Josef Lid, originally named as number eight, replaced Verner for the rest of the visit and turned out to be the Czechs' match-winner in the sixth Test at Reading when he adapted superbly to the Tilehurst track with 13 points that made all the difference.

Sweden, the summer's first overseas visitors, included Lennart Michanek – 24-year-old taxi driver younger brother of Anders – in their touring party and also gave a first overseas tour to 17-year-old Tommy Jansson who had, at the end of 1969, finished fourth in the Swedish Junior Championship, the highest ever placing for a first season rider.

Both failed to see out the tour. Michanek broke his arm in the opener at Middlesbrough and 24 hours later Jansson was ruled out for the duration after he took a tumble at Workington.

It left the Swedes reduced to only six fit riders and even though they called up Christer Löfqvist for the final Test they were still not in with a shout and managed only 37 points at Foxhall Heath.

The final Test series was a re-run of the Britain-Australasia set-to with the hosts again winning four matches against a Colonial side relying too heavily on Gary Peterson for their points inspiration.

1970 England v Sweden (Division Two) Results

Middlesbrough, Thursday, July 23
ENGLAND 68 (Richard May 16, John Louis 15, Dave Jessup 13, Roger Mills 10, †Tom Leadbitter 7, Geoff Maloney 7, Alan Knapkin and Chris Bailey, did not ride) **SWEDEN 38** (Kall Haage 12, Tommy Johansson 11, Tommy Jansson 10, Kurt Nyqvist 2, Göran Jansson 2, †Sixten Karlberg 1, Lennart Michanek 0, Roland Karlsson 0).

Workington, Friday, July 24
ENGLAND 75 (Tom Leadbitter 18, †Richard May 16, Eric Broadbelt 15, John Louis 10, Dave Jessup 8, Geoff Maloney 4, Reg Wilson 4, Alan Knapkin, did not ride) **SWEDEN 32** (Tommy Johansson 11, Roland Karlsson 6, †Kall Haage 5, Göran Jansson 5, Kurt Nyqvist 4, Sixten Karlberg 1, Tommy Jansson 0).

Berwick, Saturday, July 25
ENGLAND 54 (†Eric Broadbelt 15, Tom Leadbitter 11, Peter Bailey 11, John Louis 6, Richard May 6, Alistair Brady 3, Andy Meldrum 2, Dave Jessup 0) **SWEDEN 54** (Tommy Johansson 18, Kall Haage 17, Roland Karlsson 10, Göran Jansson 4, †Kurt Nyqvist 3, Sixten Karlberg 2).

Reading, Monday, July 27
ENGLAND 69 (Richard May 14, †Mike Vernam 14, John Louis 12, Peter Bailey 8, Dave Jessup 8, Barry Crowson 6, John Harrhy 4, Barry Thomas 3) **SWEDEN 39** (Tommy Johansson 18, Roland Karlsson 7, Sixten Karlberg 7, Göran Jansson 4, †Kurt Nyqvist 2, Kall Haage 1).

Ipswich, Thursday, July 30
ENGLAND 71 (Ian Turner 16, Richard May 12, Dave Jessup 12, Phil Woodcock 10, †John Harrhy 10, John Louis 8, Peter Bailey 3, Geoff Maloney, did not ride) **SWEDEN 37** (Christer Löfqvist 15, Tommy Johansson 11, Roland Karlsson 5, Kurt Nyqvist 4, Kall Haage 1, †Sixten Karlberg 1, Göran Jansson 0).

England win the series 4-0 with one Test drawn.

● *England team managers were: Ron Wilson (Middlesbrough), Ian Thomas (Workington), Ken Taylor (Berwick), Dick Bailey (Reading) and Howdy Byford (Ipswich).*

● *Swedish team manager was Christer Bergstrom.*

TEEN IDOL...Tommy Jansson, the youngest member of the touring Sweden party made an instant impression with British fans with his full throttle racing at Middlesbrough but was forced out of the last three Tests with back and leg injuries after crashing at Workington.

1970 Scotland v England Results

CHARLIE MONK seized his best motor at Hampden Park and then, at Brough Park, Tommy Roper's engine blew up in the opening heat and Norman Hunter joined him on the sidelines later. And, in a nutshell, that was what decided each match plus the brilliance of Ken McKinlay in the second Test.

Glasgow, Friday, June 19
SCOTLAND 47 (†Jim McMillan 14, George Hunter 14, Charlie Monk 5, Bobby Beaton 5, Bert Harkins 3, Willie Templeton 3, Ken McKinlay 2, Doug Templeton 1) **ENGLAND 61** (Eric Boocock 15, †Nigel Boocock 14, Ray Wilson 14, Chris Pusey 8, Alan Jay 6, Dave Younghusband 4, Russ Dent, did not ride).

Newcastle, Monday, June 22
ENGLAND 49 (†Terry Betts 13, Chris Pusey 10, Arnold Haley 9, Trevor Hedge 8, Norman Hunter 4, Russ Dent 3, Tommy Roper 1, Mike Watkin 1) **SCOTLAND 59** (Ken McKinlay 18, Jim McMillan 14, Charlie Monk 10, †George Hunter 7, Brian Collins 6, Bert Harkins 4, Willie Templeton 0, Bobby Beaton, did not ride).

● *The Scotland team managers were Ian Hoskins (Glasgow) and Tommy Hughson (Newcastle).*
● *The England team manager was Tom Graham.*

Aussies overcome the odds

BOSOM BUDDIES...the late Gordon Guasco and friend Jim Airey sort out a mechanical problem

AUSTRALIA was reeling from a double body blow when Nigel Boocock and his 1970-71 tourists arrived in Western Australia.

Not only had they suffered the tragic loss of former Sunderland, Wolverhampton and Poole favourite Gordon Guasco but National Champion Jim Airey ruled himself out of the entire Test series.

Guasco died a week before his 30th birthday, eight days after being involved in a three rider crash at New South Wales' Liverpool Raceway.

While he didn't use it as a reason not to race for his country against the Lions his closest friend's death must have had a bearing on Airey's decision to make himself unavailable although he was also involved in a financial wrangle with the promoters at the Sydney Showground, venue for two of the seven matches.

Without ther two mainstays Australia might have been fearing the worst but the tourists had worries of their own.

Jim McMillan was chosen ahead of Tony Clarke even though he had suffered a broken leg in the Test series in Sweden. He produced a doctor's certificate saying he would have fully recovered to race again in December and the selectors' took him at his word.

It meant the Lions went into the opening Test with only six riders, and a hastily acquired seventh rider in Peter Boston, after a last minute approach to Australian-based Scot Bill Landels failed.

Poor Landels had expected to ride for Australia and travelled to Perth a couple of days before the meeting and practised at Claremont the previous day. But that night he was told he couldn't represent Australia as he had been born in Scotland. England immediately offered him the reserve race-jacket but, sticking to his principles, he refused the opportunity to extend his international career.

Australia coped with their traumas and unearthed a brand new star in South Australian Laurie Hodgson, a 24-year-old Government electrician who became an international bright spark with a 12 point tally on his first ever visit to Perth.

His high-scoring was to play a crucial part in Australia's success although his own story was to have an unhappy ending when he crashed with Workington's Malcolm Mackay and was paralysed only a few weeks before he was due to leave for England and a British career with Exeter.

McMillan returned for the second Test at Perth but was obviously struggling and England's winter took another turn for the worse in the third Test when Arnold Haley (who had scored 26 points in the first two matches) crashed, broke his collar-bone and was invalided home.

George Hunter, based in Adelaide for the off-season, was called up as his replacement but couldn't stop the Aussie steamroller.

Finally the biggest blow of all came in the last Test in New Zealand where the exciting Chris Pusey had a torrid time.

He fell in three successive races and, in the last, hit the fence and fractured his leg.

1970-71 England Tour of Australia Results

Perth, Friday, November 20, 1970
AUSTRALIA 58 (John Langfield 13, Laurie Hodgson 12, †Chum Taylor 11, Bob O'Leary 9, Les Sharpe 8, John Boulger 5) **ENGLAND 50** (†Nigel Boocock 15, Arnold Haley 12, Chris Pusey 12, Roy Trigg 5, Bob Kilby 4, Ken McKinlay 2, Peter Boston, did not ride).

Perth, Friday, November 27, 1970
AUSTRALIA 61 (Laurie Hodgson 16, John Langfield 14, †Chum Taylor 13, Les Sharpe 6, Bob O'Leary 6, Garry Middleton 5, Les Leisk 1) **ENGLAND 46** (Arnold Haley 14, Chris Pusey 10, †Nigel Boocock 8, Bob Kilby 5, Ken McKinlay 3, Roy Trigg 3, Jim McMillan 3).

Adelaide, Friday, December 4, 1970
AUSTRALIA 55 (Laurie Hodgson 14, Charlie Monk 14, John Langfield 12, John Boulger 9, Chris Bass 4, †Chum Taylor 2, Jack White 0) **ENGLAND 53** (Roy Trigg 14, Nigel Boocock 12, George Hunter 12, Ken McKinlay 7, Chris Pusey 5, Bob Kilby 3, Arnold Haley 0).

Sydney, Saturday, December 26, 1970
AUSTRALIA 52 (John Langfield 13, John Boulger 8, Laurie Hodgson 8, Bert Kingston 8, †Chum Taylor 7, Bob Valentine 5, Garry Middleton 3) **ENGLAND 56** (†Nigel Boocock 14, Chris Pusey 13, Bob Kilby 10, Roy Trigg 8, Ken McKinlay 6, George Hunter 5).

Brisbane, Saturday, January 2, 1971
AUSTRALIA 54 (John Langfield 12, Bert Kingston 11, John Boulger 10, Jack White 9, Doug White 7, Steve Reinke 5, †Chum Taylor 0) **ENGLAND 54** (Roy Trigg 14, †Nigel Boocock 13, Bob Kilby 9, Ken McKinlay 8, Chris Pusey 6, Jim McMillan 4, George Hunter 0).

Brisbane, Saturday, January 9, 1971
AUSTRALIA 54 (†Bert Kingston 14, John Boulger 11, John Langfield 9, Jack White 9, Doug White 7, Laurie Hodgson 2, Steve Reinke 2) **ENGLAND 54** (†Nigel Boocock 16, Roy Trigg 12, George Hunter 10, Chris Pusey 7, Bob Kilby 5, Ken McKinlay 2, Jim McMillan 2).

Sydney, Saturday, January 30, 1971
AUSTRALIA 56 (†Bert Kingston 18, Laurie Hodgson 12, Jack White 10, Bob Valentine 5, Kevin Torpie 4, Bob Humphreys 4, Doug White 3) **ENGLAND 52** (Chris Pusey 16, †Nigel Boocock 10, Roy Trigg 8, Bob Kilby 7, Jim McMillan 7, George Hunter 4, Ken McKinlay, did not ride).
Australia win the series 4-1 with two Tests drawn.

● *The Australia team managers were Aub Lawson (Perth), Keith Gurtner (Brisbane) and Peter White (Sydney).*
● *The England rider-manager was Nigel Boocock and Ken McKinlay (last Test only).*

1971 England Tour of New Zealand Results

Auckland, Saturday, February 6
NEW ZEALAND 48.5 (Gary Peterson 12, †Bob Andrews 11, Rick Timmo 9.5, Bryce Subritzky 8, Jack Millen 4, Lance Gandy 3, Frank Shuter 1, Jim Wells, did not ride) **ENGLAND 59.5** (Nigel Boocock 17, Roy Trigg 15, Chris Pusey 12.5, Jim McMillan 12, Bob Kilby 1, Ken McKinlay 1, Tommy Sweetman 1, Colin Tucker, did not ride).

Auckland, Saturday, February 13
NEW ZEALAND 40 (Ivan Mauger 15, †Bob Andrews 8, Bryce Subritzky 7, Rick Timmo 7, Gary Peterson 2, Lance Gandy 1, Jack Millen 0, Frank Shuter 0) **ENGLAND 68** (Chris Pusey 15, †Nigel Boocock 13, Roy Trigg 13, Bob Kilby 12, Jim McMillan 12, Tommy Sweetman 2, Ken McKinlay 1, Colin Tucker, did not ride).

Christchurch, Saturday, February 20
NEW ZEALAND 65 (†Ivan Mauger 18, Allan Brown 13, Rick Timmo 10, Bob Andrews 9, Gary Peterson 8, Frank Shuter 7) **ENGLAND 43** (Roy Trigg 14, †Nigel Boocock 10, Chris Pusey 8, Howard Cole 4, Ken McKinlay 4, Tommy Sweetman 3).

RIDER EXCHANGE IS GREAT TEST LEVELLER

WHILE RONNIE MOORE was leading Great Britain to victory over Poland at Swindon one of the Robins' star men, Martin Ashby, was suffering half way across Europe as the Poles were gaining their revenge at Gdansk!

The World gone mad? No, it was simply an unique experiment in which the two countries met in simultaneous Test series in each other's country. Great Britain sent what was was labelled a B team to Eastern Europe for six matches while the Poles sent their first-string squad to this country for another six-match rubber.

The Poles could probably claim a moral victory as they at least snatched a win at Glasgow during their visit while our tour party returned home on the wrong end of six sound beatings against a Poland side that might have been described as a B string but still included Edward Jancarz, Henryk Glucklich and, for early matches, Andrzej Pogorzelski.

Perhaps the Poles just have more strength in depth – or maybe they split their resources a little move evenly than Great Britain whose only automatic choice on tour was Ashby.

Reading's Geoff Curtis had the unique experience of starting the reciprocal tours riding in Gdansk in the first Polish Test and then, 48 hours later, watching the second Test at Reading!

In the meantime he had spent a night in a Polish hospital where worried officials decided he would be better returning home for further treatment rather than continuing the tour on its travels behind the Iron Curtain.

Curtis claimed: "I told them I was perfectly all right but they insisted on flying me home."

It would appear that doctors misread the x-rays signs as Curtis went on: "I think they saw some fractured ribs that went back to a non-speedway accident in 1963!"

Poland were given a warning of what to expect in the first two Tests when Great Britain, without Ivan Mauger who was committed to club matches, went on the rampage.

And, once he joined up, so did Mauger who got a full maximum at Leicester and a paid one at Glasgow where the Poles salvaged some lost honour with their one win.

By the time the Poles arrived at Belle Vue for the final match the news of their severe beatings affected the attendance.

1971 Great Britain v Poland Results

Swindon, Saturday, May 22
GREAT BRITAIN 80 (†Ronnie Moore 14, Jim Airey 13, Trevor Hedge 12, Ray Wilson 12, Jim McMillan 11, Bruce Cribb 10, Norman Hunter 5, Sandor Levai 3) **POLAND 28** (Andrzej Wyglenda 8, Jerzy Szczakiel 7, Jan Mucha 5, Antonin Woryna 4, Stanislaw Bombik 2, †Pawel Waloszek 1, Zygmunt Pytka 1, Jerzy Trzeszkowski 0).

Reading, Monday, May 24
GREAT BRITAIN 78 (Ray Wilson 18, Nigel Boocock 15, Jim Airey 13, †Barry Briggs 12, Ronnie Moore 12, Eric Boocock 8, Garry Middleton and Terry Betts, did not ride) **POLAND 30** (Andrzej Wyglenda 11, †Pawel Waloszek 6, Jerzy Szczakiel 6, Antonin Woryna 4, Jan Mucha 2, Jerzy Trzeszkowski 1, Stanislaw Bombik 0, Zygmunt Pytka 0).

Leicester, Tuesday, May 25
GREAT BRITAIN 77 (†Ivan Mauger 18, Barry Briggs 15, Ray Wilson 15, Ronnie Moore 13, Eric Boocock 10, Nigel Boocock 3, Jim Airey 2, Graham Plant 1) **POLAND 30** (†Pawel Waloszek 7, Antonin Woryna 7, Jerzy Trzeszkowski 7, Jan Mucha 6, Jerzy Szczakiel 2, Andrzej Wyglenda 1, Zygmunt Pytka 0, Stanislaw Bombik 0).

Sheffield, Thursday, May 27
GREAT BRITAIN 66 (Barry Briggs 16, Jim Airey 14, †Ivan Mauger 13, Nigel Boocock 11, Ray Wilson 7, Eric Boocock 5, Bruce Cribb 0, Bert Harkins, did not ride) **POLAND 42** (Andrzej Wyglenda 12, Antonin Woryna 9, Jan Mucha 8, †Pawel Walsozek 7, Jerzy Szczakiel 4, Jerzy Trzeszkowski 2, Zygmunt Pytka 0, Stanislaw Bombik, did not ride).

Glasgow, Friday, May 28
GREAT BRITAIN 47 (†Ivan Mauger 16, Ray Wilson 10, Jim McMillan 9, Charlie Monk 6, Howard Cole 5, Terry Betts 1, Bobby Beaton 0) **POLAND 61** (Jan Mucha 14, Jerzy Trzeszkowski 11, Andrzej Wyglenda 10, †Pawel Waloszek 9, Jerzy Szczakiel 8, Antonin Woryna 8, Zygmunt Pytka 1, Stanislaw Bombik, did not ride).

Belle Vue, Saturday, May 29
GREAT BRITAIN 57 (†Ivan Mauger 18, Ronnie Moore 12, Jim McMillan 11, Jim Airey 11, Bruce Cribb 3, Dave Hemus 2, Trevor Hedge 0, Garry Middleton 0) **POLAND 51** (Andrzej Wyglenda 13, Antonin Woryna 11, Jan Mucha 9, Jerzy Szczakiel 7, Jerzy Trzeszkowski 6, †Pawel Waloszek 5, Zygmunt Pytka 0, Stanislaw Bombik, did not ride).

Great Britain win the series 5-1.

● *The Great Britain team manager was Ronnie Greene.*
● *The Poland team manager was Jozef Olejniczak.*

1971 Poland v Great Britain Results

Gdansk, Saturday, May 22
POLAND 81 (Edward Jancarz 17, Zbigniew Podlecki 16, Henryk Glucklich 14, Henryk Zyto 13, Stanislaw Kasa 7, Andrzej Pogorzelski 5, Jan Tkocz 5, Leszek Marsz 4) **GREAT BRITAIN 25** (†Martin Ashby 7, John Boulger 6, Tony Clarke 5, Bob Kilby 5, Arnold Haley 1, Roy Trigg 1, Geoff Curtis 0, George Hunter 0).

Bydgoszcz, Sunday, May 23
POLAND 71 (Henryk Glucklich 14, Stanislaw Kasa 13, Andrzej Pogorzelski 11, Henryk Zyto 10, Andrzej Koselski 9, Zbigniew Podlecki 6, Edward Jancarz 5, Marian Zaranek 3) **GREAT BRITAIN 37** (†Martin Ashby 14, Bob Kilby 7, Arnold Haley 6, Roy Trigg 4, John Boulger 3, George Hunter 2, Tony Clarke 1).

Gorzow, Tuesday, May 25
POLAND 70 (Zdzislaw Dobrucki 16, Zbigniew Marcinkowski 15, Edward Jancarz 14, Jerzy Padewski 10, Pawel Protasiewicz 10, Zbigniew Jader 3, Ryszard Dziatkowiak 2, Andrzej Pogorzelski 0) **GREAT BRITAIN 38** (†Martin Ashby 8, John Boulger 8, George Hunter 8, Arnold Haley 6, Tony Clarke 4, Bob Kilby 2, Roy Trigg 2).

Wroclaw, Thursday, May 27
POLAND 76 (Edward Jancarz 17, Pawel Bruzda 16, Jerzy Gryt 13, Zdzislaw Dobrucki 10, Stanislaw Nowak 10, Jerzy Padewski 10, Zbigniew Jader 0, Jan Chudzikowski 0) **GREAT BRITAIN 32** (Arnold Haley 8, John Boulger 7, †Martin Ashby 6, Tony Clarke 5, George Hunter 3, Bob Kilby 2, Roy Trigg 1).

Opole, Saturday, May 29
POLAND 75 (Henryk Glucklich 16, Jerzy Gryt 14, Edward Jancarz 14, Stanislaw Kasa 10, Stanislaw Skowron 8, Pawel Bruzda 6, Zygfryd Friedek 6, Henryk Golec 1) **GREAT BRITAIN 33** (John Boulger 10, †Martin Ashby 9, Tony Clarke 6, Arnold Haley 3, Roy Trigg 3, George Hunter 2, Bob Kilby 0).

Tarnow, Sunday, May 30
POLAND 76 (Edward Jancarz 17, Henryk Glucklich 14, Stanislaw Chorobik 13, Stanislaw Kasa 9, Jerzy Padewski 8, Zbigniew Podlecki 7, Jerzy Gryt 5, Czeslaw Kolman 3) **GREAT BRITAIN 31** (Tony Clarke 7, †Martin Ashby 6, John Boulger 6, Goerge Hunter 6, Roy Trigg 5, Arnold Haley 1, Bob Kilby 0).

Poland win the series 6-0.

● *The Great Britain team manager was Charles Foot.*
● *The Poland team manager was Janusz Kolek.*

But those who didn't bother to turn up at Hyde Road missed yet another superb 18-point maximum from the irrepressible Mauger.

The Kiwi then had to sit out the rest of the international schedule as the authorities dispensed with Colonial support and matched England against both Sweden and the Soviet Union.

It was a decision that looked like backfiring on the selectors as Sweden took a 10-point lead in the first Test before it was called off because of heavy rain and then they established a six point lead to win the second.

But Eric Boocock's boys bounced back, levelled the series with a big win at Halifax where Dave Younghusband, who had gone out of the World Championship in the Nordic British Final at Glasgow the previous evening, showed no signs of a hangover with an 18 point maximum. He and partner Bob Kilby showed an almost telepathic understanding and, as a partnership, scored 29 points out of 30 with Exeter's Kilby picking up five bonus points!

Younghusband must have thought that performance would win him a regular place in the England team for the next series against the Russians and it might have done had he not broken his wrist riding for Halifax at Cradley Heath on the night that Kilby, still on a high, registered a 17-point tally that allowed England to edge out the Russkies by a single point at the County Ground.

Nigel Boocock cracked a rib at Poole – where the two nations drew – and then the Russians claimed only their second-ever win over England at Halifax where their shock top scorer, for the second successive match, was first-time visitor Grigori Mironov who hadn't even been listed in the tour starters!

Gone were the Old Guard of Igor Plechanov, Boris Samorodov and Gabdrahman 'The Beatle' Kadirov and British fans were also deprived of seeing their thrilling discovery Valeri Klementiev who had died after a practice crash only a few months earlier when he looked fully capable of providing the Soviets with a genuine World Final contender.

It was planned, at one stage of the season, to wind up the international entertainment with a third successive series against New Zealand, spearheaded by their trio of World Champions Mauger, Barry Briggs and Ronnie Moore.

But the series was eventually scrapped when everyone ran into a problem over dates, trying to fit in matches when the Kiwis could be at full strength.

So England's season ended with eight Tests, four of which were won, two lost, one drawn and one, against Sweden at Wolverhampton, abandoned while the visitors held a precious 10 points lead.

GÖTE NORDIN (Sweden)

1971 England v Sweden Results

Wolverhampton, Friday, July 2
ENGLAND 22 (Ray Wilson 7, Bob Kilby 5, †Nigel Boocock 3, Roy Trigg 2, Norman Hunter 2, Terry Betts 2, Trevor Hedge 1, Howard Cole 0) **SWEDEN 32** (Bengt Jansson 8, †Anders Michanek 7, Göte Nordin 6, Bernt Persson 6, Sören Sjösten 3, Olle Nygren 2, Jan Simensen, did not ride).
Abandoned after nine heats, rain.

Wimbledon, Thursday, July 22
ENGLAND 51 (Ray Wilson 14, Eric Boocock 14, Trevor Hedge 9, Roy Trigg 4, Barry Thomas 4, Martin Ashby 3, †Nigel Boocock 2, Terry Betts 1) **SWEDEN 57** (Bengt Jansson 15, Bernt Persson 15, Sören Sjösten 12, †Anders Michanek 7, Christer Löfqvist 5, Olle Nygren 3, Göte Nordin 0, Jan Simensen 0).

Halifax, Saturday, July 31
ENGLAND 63 (Dave Younghusband 18, †Eric Boocock 14, Bob Kilby 11, Ray Wilson 8, Trevor Hedge 6, Terry Betts 4, Sandor Levai 2, Graham Plant 0) **SWEDEN 45** (†Anders Michanek 11, Bengt Jansson 10, Sören Sjösten 8, Olle Nygren 8, Bernt Persson 5, Bo Wirebrand 2, Jan Simensen 1).

Series drawn 1-1 with one Test abandoned.

● *The Great Britain team manager was Ronnie Greene.*
● *The Sweden team manager was Bengt Andersson.*

1971 England v Soviet Union Results

Exeter, Monday, August 23
ENGLAND 54 (Bob Kilby 17, Tony Lomas 9, Ray Wilson 9, †Nigel Boocock 8, Martin Ashby 6, Barry Thomas 4, Pete Smith 1, Graham Plant, did not ride) **SOVIET UNION 53** (Vladimir Gordeev 13, Vladimir Paznikov 11, Gennady Kurilenko 10, Grigori Mironov 7, Grigori Khlinovsky 6, Anatoli Kuzmin 5, Vladimir Smirnov 1, Alexander Pavlov, did not ride).

Poole, Wednesday, August 25
ENGLAND 54 (Ray Wilson 18, Martin Ashby 13, Pete Smith 10, Barry Thomas 4, Tony Lomas 4, Trevor Hedge 3, Graham Plant 2, †Nigel Boocock 0) **SOVIET UNION 54** (Gennady Kurilenko 12, Vladimir Paznikov 12, Alexander Pavlov 9, Grigori Khlinovsky 7, Vladimir Smirnov 8, Anatoli Kuzmin 5, Grigori Mironov 1, Vladimir Gordeev, did not ride).

Wimbledon, Thursday, August 26
ENGLAND 61 (Trevor Hedge 14, Roy Trigg 12, Malcolm Simmons 11, Martin Ashby 9, Ray Wilson 8, Eric Boocock 7, Barry Thomas 0) **SOVIET UNION 46** (Grigori Mironov 14, Alexander Pavlov 10, Viktor Trofimov 6, Gennady Kurilenko 6, Vladimir Paznikov 6, Vladimir Gordeev 2, Grigori Khlinovsky 2, Anatoli Kuzmin, did not ride).

Halifax, Saturday, August 28
ENGLAND 51 (Ray Wilson 15, †Eric Boocock 10, Bob Paulson 8, Alan Jay 7, Arnold Haley 6, Barry Thomas 3, Reg Luckhurst 2, Graham Plant 0) **SOVIET UNION 57** (Grigori Mironov 15, Vladimir Paznikov 11, Alexander Pavlov 10, Gennady Kurilenko 8, Grigori Khlinovsky 6, Vladimir Smirnov 4, Vladimir Gordeev 2, Anatoli Kuzmin 1).

Coventry, Monday, August 30
ENGLAND 59 (Tony Lomas 16, Ray Wilson 11, Nigel Boocock 10, Bob Kilby 9, Roy Trigg 5, Roger Hill 4, Terry Betts 4, Graham Plant 0) **SOVIET UNION 49** (Alexander Pavlov 15, Grigori Khlinovsky 11, Vladimir Gordeev 6, Vladimir Paznikov 5, Gennady Kurilenko 4, Grigori Mironov 3, Viktor Trofimov 3, Vladimir Smirnov 2).

England win the series 3-1 with one Test drawn.

● *The England team manager was Ronnie Greene.*

King Louis laps it up

■ ENGLAND'S Young Lions took speedway by storm with successive series wins over summer visitors Sweden and Czechoslovakia and then wrapped up the season with a 3-0 wipe-out of the Anzacs!

■ And the fact that for one Test the selectors actually called up 38-year-old Ross Gilbertson shouldn't take the gloss off some of the performances of the newcomers.

■ And what a summer it was for Ipswich's John Louis, a latecomer but a quick learner.

■ In all John had 76 rides and dropped just 32 points out of a maximum 228 and that includes three races when he fell and was excluded!

■ King John, Ipswich's greatest ever discovery, began like a train and continued like an express throughout the international season.

■ He was unbeaten at Foxhall Heath in the first of 15 Test matches at Division Two level and 'Tiger' Louis rode in 14 of them, scoring double figures in all but two of those Tests.

■ He came off in his third ride at Middlesbrough and was taken to hospital with a back injury and then he tangled with the 28-year-old bearded Pavel Mares in the last of the seven Tests against Czechoslovakia and was detained overnight in hospital with concussion.

■ Neither spill kept him out of racing but, on each occasion, his opponents must have been secretly relieved to see him take that ambulance ride away from the track!

■ Louis confirmed his immense talent throughout the summer – and fans had the bonus of witnessing the early dawn of another world-class career.

■ Sweden included their exciting teenage discovery Tommy Jansson in their squad.

■ Jansson, a 1970 visitor whose first trip to Britain was cut short by injury, had already qualified for his first World Final when he led the Swedes on parade at Ipswich for the first of their five matches.

■ He didn't let anyone down with five double figure performances which made him a challenger for Louis's Man of the Summer accolade.

■ It goes almost without saying, that the Czechs were tremendous value for money and it looked as if they would inflict defeat on England as they stormed into a 2-1 lead with only three Tests left (one other match was drawn).

■ But England staged a fighting comeback and finally clinched the series with a 12-point victory at Ipswich despite the aformentioned absence of skipper Louis.

■ After two storming series against Sweden and Czechoslovakia the rubber against Australasia had something to live up to and, happily, it did with Malcolm Mackay's 16-point haul at Bradford ensuring the series went to a decider at Canterbury.

■ Even that match could have gone the other way had Phil Crump not twice wrecked an engine while leading Louis!

1971 England v Sweden (Division Two) Results

Ipswich, Thursday, June 17
ENGLAND 66.5 (†John Louis 18, Malcolm Shakespeare 17, Tony Davey 10, Geoff Bouchard 8.5, Kevin Holden 8, Peter Bailey 4, Malcolm Ballard 1, Richard Greer, did not ride) **SWEDEN 40.5** (Tommy Bergkvist 11.5, †Tommy Jansson 10, Karl-Erik Claesson 9, Christer Sjösten 5, Hakan Karlsson 3, Lars-Åke Andersson 1, Terje Henriksson 1, Stefan Salomonsson 0).

Rayleigh, Saturday, June 19
ENGLAND 49 (†John Louis 13, Hugh Saunders 12, Mike Vernam 11, Dingle Brown 5, Arthur Price 4, Tony Davey 3, David Kennett 1, Geoff Maloney 0) **SWEDEN 59** (†Tommy Jansson 13, Christer Sjösten 12, Tommy Bergkvist 10, Karl-Erik Claesson 9, Hakan Karlsson 9, Lars-Åke Andersson 6, Stefan Salomonsson, did not ride).

Eastbourne, Sunday, June 20
ENGLAND 64 (Malcolm Ballard 14, †John Louis 14, Gordon Kennett 11, Kevin Holden 9, Malcolm Shakespeare 9, David Kennett 5, Hugh Saunders 2, Graham Banks 0) **SWEDEN 43** (†Tommy Jansson 12, Christer Sjösten 10, Tommy Bergkvist 8, Lars-Åke Andersson 5, Karl-Erik Claesson 4, Hakan Karlsson 4, Stefan Salomonsson, did not ride).

Crewe, Monday, June 21
ENGLAND 60 (Alan Wilkinson 17, †John Louis 15, Barry Meeks 10, Alan Knapkin 7, †John Jackson 6, Paul Tyrer 5, Geoff Bouchard 0, Arthur Price 0) **SWEDEN 48** (†Tommy Jansson 12, Tommy Bergkvist 10, Christer Sjösten 10, Hakan Karlsson 6, Lars-Åke Andersson 5, Stefan Salomonsson 5, Karl-Erik Cleasson 0).

Middlesbrough, Thursday, June 24
ENGLAND 42 (Alan Knapkin 11, Arthur Price 8, Dave Durham 7, Doug Wyer 6, Tim Swales 6, †John Louis 3, John Jackson 1, Alan Wilkinson 0) **SWEDEN 66** (†Tommy Jansson 17, Tommy Bergkvist 16, Lars-Åke Andersson 15, Bo Wirebrand 14, Hakan Karlsson 3, Stefan Salomonsson 1).

England win the series 3-2.

● *The England team managers were John Berry (Ipswich), Dave Lanning (Eastbourne) and Ken Adams (Crewe).*
● *The Sweden team manager was Christer Bergström*

1971 England v Czechoslovakia (Division Two) Results

Canterbury, Saturday, August 7
ENGLAND 47 (†John Louis 17, Tony Davey 10, Malcolm Ballard 9, Gordon Kennett 4, Graham Banks 3, Malcolm Shakespeare 3, Kevin Holden 1, Geoff Bouchard 0) **CZECHOSLOVAKIA 60** (Milan Spinka 12, Zdenek Majstr 12, †Miloslav Verner 11, Vaclav Verner 10, Jiri Stancl 8, Pavel Mares 3, Pavel Busta 3, Jaroslav Volf 1).

Crewe, Monday, August 9
ENGLAND 54 (†John Louis 15, Peter Collins 14, Carl Glover 7, Alan Knapkin 7, Reg Wilson 6, John Jackson 5, Barry Meeks 0, Arthur Price, did not ride) **CZECHOSLOVAKIA 54** (Pavel Mares 15, Zdenek Majstr 14, †Miloslav Verner 10, Jiri Stancl 9, Vaclav Verner 3, Milan Spinka 3, Jaroslav Volf 0, Pavel Busta 0).

Bradford, Wednesday, August 11
ENGLAND 64 (Doug Wyer 17, Arthur Price 15, †John Louis 14, Alan Knapkin 12, Dave Baugh 6, Tony Davey 0, Dave Kumeta 0, Paul Tyrer, did not ride) **CZECHOSLOVAKIA 44** (Jiri Stancl 11, Zdenek Majstr 10, †Miloslav Verner 6, Vaclav Verner 5, Pavel Mares 5, Milan Spinka 4, Pavel Busta 2, Jaroslav Volf 1).

Peterborough, Sunday, August 15
ENGLAND 52 (†John Louis 18, Arthur Price 11, Richard Greer 7, Tony Davey 5, Bruce Forrester 4, Alan Knapkin 4, Roy Carter 2, Malcolm Shakespeare 1) **CZECHOSLOVAKIA 56** (Jiri Stancl 12, Vaclav Verner 10, Pavel Mares 10, Zdenek Majstr 10, †Miloslav Verner 8, Milan Spinka 6, Pavel Busta 0).

Workington, Monday, August 17
ENGLAND 55 (†John Louis 15, Alan Knapkin 15, Doug Wyer 13, Reg Wilson 6, Roger Mills 4, Arthur Price 2, Malcolm Shakespeare 0, Dave Kumeta 0) **CZECHOSLOVAKIA 52** (Pavel Mares 15, †Miloslav Verner 13, Jiri Stancl 11, Zdenek Majstr 6, Milan Spinka 4, Vaclav Verner 3, Jaroslav Volf 0, Pavel Busta 0).
Original staging on Friday, August 13, was postponed because of rain.

Romford, Thursday, August 19
ENGLAND 66 (Kevin Holden 15, Bob Coles 13, Ross Gilbertson 13, †John Louis 13, Alan Knapkin 8, Reg Wilson 4, Arthur Price 0, Malcolm Shakespeare 0) **CZECHOSLOVAKIA 42** (Milan Spinka 13, †Miloslav Verner 12, Pavel Mares 11, Vaclav Verner 4, Jaroslav Volf 1, Pavel Busta 1, Zdenek Majstr 0).

Ipswich, Friday, August 20
ENGLAND 60 (Kevin Holden 14, Tony Davey 13, Alan Knapkin 12, Peter Bailey 8, Malcolm Shakespeare 7, Geoff Bouchard 6, †John Louis 0, Graham Banks, did not ride) **CZECHOSLOVAKIA 48** (Milan Spinka 18, Vaclav Verner 13, †Miloslav Verner 12, Pavel Busta 3, Pavel Mares 1, Jaroslav Volf 1).

England win the series 4-2 with one Test drawn.

● *The England team managers were Russ Osbourne (Canterbury), Ken Adams (Crewe), Stan Holey (Bradford), Alec Ford (Peterborough), Ian Thomas (Workington), Maurice Morley (Romford) and John Berry (Ipswich).*
● *The Czechoslovakia team manager was Jaroslav Bartosek.*

1971 England v Australasia (Division Two) Results

Peterborough, Friday, September 10
ENGLAND 55 (†John Louis 18, Arthur Price 15, Geoff Bouchard 6, Joe Hughes 5, John Jackson 5, Brian Clark 3, Carl Glover 2, Richard Greer 1) **AUSTRALASIA 53** (Phil Crump 15, Jim Ryman 13, †Malcolm Mackay 12, Lou Sansom 6, Graeme Smith 5, Robin Adlington 2, Bob Young 0).

Bradford, Wednesday, September 15
ENGLAND 40 (†Alan Knapkin 12, Doug Wyer 11, Kevin Holden 6, Barry Meeks 5, Peter Bailey 3, Tim Swales 2, Russ Osborne 1, Paul Tyrer 0) **AUSTRALASIA 68** (†Malcolm Mackay 16, Phil Crump 15, Robin Adlington 13, Jim Ryman 10, Jack Millen 8, Lou Sansom 6, Robin Amundson and Hec Haslinger, did not ride).

Canterbury, Saturday, September 25
ENGLAND 65 (†John Louis 17, Graham Banks 15, Richard Greer 12, Tony Davey 9, Geoff Bouchard 7, Malcolm Ballard 5, Ted Hubbard 0, Roger Johns, did not ride) **AUSTRALASIA 43** (†Graeme Smith 12, Jack Millen 10, Graeme Stapleton 8, Bob Young 6, Phil Crump 5, Robin Adlington 1, Kym Amundson 1, Jim Ryman 0).

England win the series 2-1.

● *The England team managers were Alec Ford (Peterborough), Stan Holey (Bradford) and Russ Osbourn (Canterbury).*

● *The Australasia team manager was George Allan.*

1971 Bradford v Fredericia (Denmark) Result

BRADFORD broke new ground by becoming the first British club to be involved in an Anglo-Danish club challenge.

The clash stemmed from an early season practice session at Odsal when Fredericia sent across their riders for practice.

Out of that visit the talk got round to a challenge and it was agreed that Fredericia would visit Bradford in 1971 with Northern making the return trip early in the 1972 season.

The Danish party included Nordic-British Finalist Kurt Bøgh, ranked number three in Denmark behind Ole Olsen and Bent Norregaard, former Oxford team member Godtfred Andreasen, back in two wheel action after a year's retirement.

Team manager was Egon Boisen, whose own racing career was brought to a premature end when he broke his back in a crash.

Bradford, Wednesday, September 29
BRADFORD 44 (†Alan Knapkin 11, Dave Baugh 11, Alf Wells 10, Robin Adlington 6, Mick Fielding 3, Rod Chessell 2, Sid Sheldrick 1) **FREDERICIA 34** (Erik Tilgaard 9, Kurt Bøgh 8, Godtfred Andreasen 5, Erling Rasmussen 5, Erik Greene 4, Frank Jahn 2, Finn Schelde 1).

1971 Scotland v England Result

Glasgow, Friday, June 25
SCOTLAND 60 (Bobby Beaton 15, †Jim McMillan 12, Charlie Monk 11, Bert Harkins 11, George Hunter 7, Brian Collins 2, Doug Templeton 2, Bill McMillan 0) **ENGLAND 48** (†Nigel Boocock 13, Arnold Haley 10, Tony Lomas 8, Dave Younghusband 7, Eric Boocock 5, Alan Jay 4, Roy Trigg 1, Eric Broadbelt, did not ride).

● *The Scotland team manager was Neil Macfarlane.*

● *The England team manager was Eric Boothroyd.*

Johnny McNo

SCOTLAND selector Ian Hoskins discovered that John Boulger's father had been born in the famed Gorbals in Glasgow before emigrating to Australia.

And, hey presto, the Scots had discovered a new international talent.

But Johnny B never got as far as the start-line of the only international against England as he had to pull out with strained knee ligaments only hours before the match.

Despite his absence the Scots were too powerful for a predominently Northern-based England squad captained by Nigel Boocock.

It was a memorable victory for the home side as it was the first time they had beaten the Auld Enemy in three meetings at Hampden Park and was built on a splendid display from young Bobby Beaton.

WHEEL DO IT NOW

ORANGE LEATHERED John Langfield made the English Lions see red as he top-scored for the Aussies in the opening Test of the 1971-72 tour.

For Langfield used the outlawed 22 inch rear wheel on his Jawa – and showed a clean pair of heals to the Brits as he dropped only two points.

Even though England's rider-manager Nigel Boocock didn't lodge an official protest there was no disguising the distaste of him and his team.

The 22-inch rear wheel had gone out in 1956 and been officially banned by the World governing body, the FIM, although there were no regulations expressly barring it in Australia!

After some serious discussion it was agreed that Langfield wouldn't use it in any future internationals.

After building up a two-Test lead Australia were beaten in the third match at Brisbane – and this time they got all heated up.

Manager Bert Kingston claimed that the England party were using the banned FIM additive nitro-methane but nothing further happened and there wasn't even a fuel sampling.

The Aussieshad left national champion John Boulger out of their side – claiming it was because they felt he would be too tired having ridden at Perth the previous evening or perhaps it was simply a sign of their confidence.

He returned for the next victory at Adelaide but England forced their way back into the series at Melbourne eight days later, when, for a second time, the incompetence of the Australian authorities was exposed.

For reasons best known only to themselves, they sanctioned a parallel international at Brisbane the same evening and while England were getting back in the series at Brooklyn Aussie champ Boulger, Jack White, Bill Landels and Steve Reinke were all up in Queensland beating the Swedes!

That Melbourne Test was the turning point and from a seemingly hopeless 3-1 deficit Booey's boys stormed back to record three successive wins to take the series with a 46-point last Test win at Perth.

1971 U.S.A. v U.K.

Costa Mesa, Friday, October 29
UNITED STATES OF AMERICA 48 (Larry Shaw 10, Mike Bast 8, Steve Bast 8, Sonny Nutter 8, Bill Cody 6, Mike Konle 4, Rick Woods 4)
UNITED KINGDOM 42 (Ivan Mauger 12, Barry Briggs 11, Jim Airey 8, Bert Harkins 5, Jim McMillan 3, George Hunter 2, Dave Gifford 1).

Ascot Park, Wednesday, November 3
UNITED STATES OF AMERICA 43 (Rick Woods 13, Sonny Nutter 11, Mike Bast 7, Bill Cody 5, Steve Bast 3, Mike Konle 3, Larry Shaw 1) **UNITED KINGDOM 47** (Barry Briggs 13, Ivan Mauger 12, Jim Airey 9, Bert Harkins 7, Jim McMillan 4, George Hunter 2, Dave Gifford 0).

Costa Mesa, Friday, November 5
UNITED STATES OF AMERICA 49 (Larry Shaw 10, Mike Bast 9, Rick Woods 8, Bill Cody 8, Sonny Nutter 6, Steve Bast 5, Mike Konle 3)
UNITED KINGDOM 40 (Ivan Mauger 15, Barry Briggs 14, Jim Airey 7, Bert Harkins 4, George Hunter 0, Jim McMillan 0).

<u>United States of America win the series 2-1.</u>

1971-72 England Tour of Australia Results

Sydney, Saturday, November 13, 1971
AUSTRALIA 60 (John Langfield 16, †Jim Airey 15, Jack White 12, Kevin Torpie 7, John Boulger 6, Bill Landels 3, John Bowerman 1) **ENGLAND 48** (Jim McMillan 14, †Nigel Boocock 11, Malcolm Simmons 8, George Hunter 6, Chris Pusey 5, Bert Harkins 3, Tony Lomas 1).

Brisbane, Saturday, November 20, 1971
AUSTRALIA 61 (John Boulger 15, Jack White 13, John Langfield 8, Kevin Torpie 8, †Jim Airey 6, Tony Hart 6, Steve Reinke 5) **ENGLAND 47** (†Nigel Boocock 13, Tony Lomas 10, Jim McMillan 9, Chris Pusey 8, Bert Harkins 4, Malcolm Simmons 3, George Hunter 0).

Brisbane, Saturday, November 27, 1971
AUSTRALIA 46 (Jim Airey 10, Tony Hart 10, Jack White 7, John Langfield 7, Steve Reinke 6, Kevin Torpie 6, Greg Kentwell 0) **ENGLAND 61** (Chris Pusey 18, †Nigel Boocock 13, Tony Lomas 9, Bert Harkins 7, Malcolm Simmons 7, George Hunter 5, Jim McMillan 2).

Adelaide, Friday, January 7, 1972
AUSTRALIA 57 (†Jim Airey 18, John Boulger 16, Charlie Monk 14, Jack White 6, John Langfield 2, Phil Crump 1, Chris Bass 0) **ENGLAND 51** (Jim McMillan 12, Bert Harkins 9, Chris Pusey 9, Tony Lomas 6, Malcolm Simmons 6, †Nigel Boocock 5, George Hunter 4).

Melbourne, Saturday, January 22, 1972
AUSTRALIA 44 (Phil Crump 12, John Langfield 10, Johnny Dewhurst 9, Greg Kentwell 5, Jack Biggs 3, Neil Street 3, Charlie Monk 2) **ENGLAND 64** (George Hunter 15, Chris Pusey 13, Jim McMillan 11, Tony Lomas 10, Malcolm Simmons 10, Bert Harkins 4, †Nigel Boocock 1).

Perth, Friday, January 28, 1972
AUSTRALIA 49 (†Jim Airey 16, Chum Taylor 10, Les Sharpe 10, John Boulger 8, Les Leisk 4, Bob O'Leary 1, Doug Underwood 0) **ENGLAND 59** (Chris Pusey 13, †Nigel Boocock 12, Malcolm Simmons 11, Bert Harkins 9, Jim McMillan 8, George Hunter 5, Tony Lomas 1).

Perth, Friday, February 4, 1972
AUSTRALIA 31 (John Langfield 14, Jack White 6, Les Leisk 4, Jim Ryman 3, Chum Taylor 2, Les Sharpe 1, Bob O'Leary 1) **ENGLAND 77** (Bert Harkins 17, †Nigel Boocock 16, Malcolm Simmons 16, Chris Pusey 10, George Hunter 9, Jim McMillan 9).

<u>England win the series 4-3.</u>

CLUB MATCHES

Liverpool, Wednesday, November 17, 1971
LIVERPOOL 43 (†Ole Olsen 11, John Boulger 9, Neil Cameron 8, Dave Mills 6, Barry Van Praag 4, Bill Landels 3, Helmut Schippl 2) **ENGLAND 35** (Jim McMillan 10, †Nigel Boocock 7, Bert Harkins 7, Malcolm Simmons 5, Tony Lomas 2, George Hunter 2, Chris Pusey 2).

Brisbane, Saturday, December 4, 1971
QUEENSLAND 67 (†Jack White 18, Steve Reinke 14, Tony Hart 12, Kevin Torpie 10, Bob Gourlay 10, Bryan Loakes 3, John Titman 0) **ENGLAND 41** (†Nigel Boocock 11, Tony Lomas 10, Chris Pusey 8, Malcolm Simmons 7, Jim McMillan 3, Bert Harkins 2, George Hunter 0).

Rockhampton, Monday, December 13, 1971
ROCKHAMPTON 66 (†Jim Airey 18, Ole Olsen 16, John Langfield 15, Jack White 12, Kevin Torpie 4, Tony Hart 1) **ENGLAND 42** (†Nigel Boocock 13, Tony Lomas 8, Chris Pusey 7, Jim McMillan 4, Malcolm Simmons 4, Bert Harkins 3, George Hunter 3).

Melbourne, Saturday, January 8, 1972
VICTORIA 20 (†Phil Crump 7, Jack Biggs 6, Johnny Dewhurst 6, Peter Moore 1, Dave O'Connor 0, Neil Street 0) **ENGLAND 34** (Jim McMillan 7, George Hunter 7, †Nigel Boocock 5, Malcolm Simmons 5, Chris Pusey 5, Tony Lomas 4, Bert Harkins 1).

WHILE England were touring Australia the Swedes were also in the country having their own Test series. All three nations came together just once for a triangular tournament at the Sydney Showground which was won by the England side, labelled more accurately on this occasion, as Britain.
Australia won four of the six Tests against Sweden with another abandoned while they were leading.
Sydney, Saturday, December 18, 1971

AUSTRALIA 40 (†Jim Airey 12, Bill Landels 11, John Langfield 9, Jack White 6, John Boulger 2) **BRITAIN 41** (Malcolm Simmons 15, Jim McMillan 12, Chris Pusey 10, †Nigel Boocock 2, Bert Harkins 2) **SWEDEN 26** (Bengt Larsson 8, Bernt Persson 6, Bengt Jansson 6, Anders Michanek 4, Sören Sjösten 2).

ENGLAND RULE OK!

1972 Inter Nations Championship Results

Belle Vue, Saturday, July 1
AUSTRALIA 40 (John Boulger 10, Bob Valentine 8, Geoff Mudge 8, †Garry Middleton 7, Charlie Monk 4, Geoff Curtis 3, John Langfield 0) **NEW ZEALAND 38** (†Ivan Mauger 15, Ronnie Moore 11, Dave Gifford 4, Bob Andrews 3, Rick Timmo 3, Barry Briggs 1, Frank Shuter 1).

Coventry, Saturday, July 8
ENGLAND 43 (Ray Wilson 9, Terry Betts 8, †Nigel Boocock 8, Martin Ashby 7, Eric Boocock 6, Tony Lomas 5, Bob Kilby 0) **SWEDEN 35** (Christer Löfqvist 12, Hasse Holmkvist 7, Bernt Persson 5, Tommy Jansson 4, Sören Sjösten 3, †Jan Simensen 2, Bengt Jansson 2).

Reading, Monday, July 10
NORWAY-DENMARK 38 (Dag Lovaas 12, †Ole Olsen 11, Reidar Eide 8, Øyvind Berg 5, Svein Kaasa 1, Odd Fossengen 1, Kurt Bøgh 0) **SWEDEN 40** (Christer Löfqvist 13, Bernt Persson 7, Jan Simensen 6, Bengt Jansson 5, Hasse Holmkvist 5, Olle Nygren 4, Anders Michanek 0).

Hackney, Friday, July 14
AUSTRALIA 39 (John Boulger 11, †Garry Middleton 10, Bob Humphreys 9, John Langfield 3, Geoff Curtis 3, Geoff Mudge 3, Charlie Monk 0) **SWEDEN 39** (Hasse Holmkvist 10, †Bengt Jansson 7, Göte Nordin 7, Christer Löfqvist 7, Tommy Jansson 5, Olle Nygren 3).

King's Lynn, Saturday, July 15
AUSTRALIA 39 (Phil Crump 10, John Langfield 9, Geoff Mudge 6, Garry Middleton 5, Charlie Monk 4, John Boulger 3, Geoff Curtis 2) **NORWAY-DENMARK 39** (Ole Olsen 12, Reidar Eide 9, Dag Lovaas 8, Kurt Bøgh 5, Øyvind Berg 5, Odd Fossengen 0, Svein Kaasa 0).

Swindon, Saturday, July 15
NEW ZEALAND 28 (†Ronnie Moore 9, Bob Andrews 8, Dave Gifford 6, Graeme Stapleton 3, Terry Shearer 1, Rick Timmo 1, Frank Shuter 0) **SWEDEN 50** (Christer Löfqvist 12, †Anders Michanek 11, Hasse Holmkvist 9, Bengt Jansson 6, Tommy Jansson 5, Jan Simensen 4, Olle Nygren 3).

Poole, Wednesday, July 19
ENGLAND 37 (Ray Wilson 10, Terry Betts 9, Nigel Boocock 7, Pete Smith 6, Eric Boocock 3, Bob Kilby 1, Tony Lomas 1) **NORWAY-DENMARK 41** (Ole Olsen 14, Reidar Eide 9, Dag Lovaas 7, Øyvind Berg 6, Kurt Bøgh 3, Odd Fossengen 1, Edgar Stangeland 1).

Wimbledon, Thursday, July 20
ENGLAND 51 (†Ray Wilson 12, Trevor Hedge 8, Bob Kilby 8, Terry Betts 7, Eric Boocock 6, Dave Jessup 6, Barry Thomas 4) **NEW ZEALAND 26** (†Ronnie Moore 9, Dave Gifford 7, Frank Shuter 4, Graeme Stapleton 3, Bob Andrews 2, Rick Timmo 1).

Wolverhampton, Friday, July 21
NORWAY-DENMARK 55 (†Ole Olsen 15, Øyvind Berg 10, Dag Lovaas 10, Reidar Eide 7, Odd Fossengen 5, Edgar Stangeland 4, Kurt Bøgh 4) **NEW ZEALAND 22** (†Ronnie Moore 10, Dave Gifford 5, Terry Shearer 4, Graeme Stapleton 1, Rick Timmo 1, Frank Shuter 1, Bob Andrews 0).

Halifax, Saturday, July 22
ENGLAND 48 (Ray Wilson 12, Nigel Boocock 10, †Eric Boocock 9, Peter Collins 7, Terry Betts 6, Martin Ashby 3, Arnold Haley 1) **AUSTRALIA 30** (†Garry Middleton 12, Geoff Mudge 6, John Langfield 4, Greg Kentwell 3, John Boulger 2, Phil Crump 2, Bob Valentine 1).

● *The team managers for the series were: Australia (Peter White), England (Ron Hart), New Zealand (George Allan), Norway-Denmark (Tore Kittilsen) and Sweden (Arne Bergström).*

	P	W	D	L	PtsF	PtsA	Pts
ENGLAND	4	3	0	1	179	132	6
Norway-Denmark	4	2	1	1	173	138	5
Sweden	4	2	1	1	164	148	5
Australia	4	1	2	1	148	164	4
New Zealand	4	0	0	4	114	196	0

THERE were fond hopes when Garry Middleton, Geoff Curtis, Ivan Mauger and Bob Andrews came to the tapes at Belle Vue's Hyde Road Stadium that everyone there was witnessing the birth of speedway's first World Cup.

The idea had been to invite all the sport's top nations to an international tournament, spread over three mid-summer weeks. Poland and the Soviet Union, for reasons best known to themselves, declined the invitation but Australia, New Zealand, Sweden and a combined Norway-Denmark side all agreed to compete.

With the majority of the riders already contracted to British League clubs it was an idea which had every chance of working and certainly there was enough entertainment and interest in the inaugural competition to continue the following year.

England, as hosts, scorned tradition and stepped aside to allow Australia and New Zealand take centre stage at the official opening. Phil Crump was a non-arrival (he raced for King's Lynn instead against Wolverhampton in a League match!) but all that was forgotten in a grim heat nine crash which saw both John Langfield (detained overnight) and Barry Briggs take to hospital. The Kiwis suffered more than their Colonial neighbours and were left a predominantly two-man side.

Australia were in action again six nights later and figured in the first abandoned match (against Sweden) before England took to the track amidst controversy.

Only after a 45 minute delay, during which the interminably patient fans waited and waited, did the meeting go ahead and England opened up with a win despite the heroics of Swedish reserve Christer Löfqvist who followed up his 12 points at Brandon with 13 at Reading where Sweden inched ahead of their Scandinavian rivals by just two points.

Sören Sjösten was another absentee in Sweden's third match and this time they dropped their first point to Australia who had Langfield back in their side despite that heavy fall at Belle Vue. New Zealand were rocked by a second injury, this time to Ivan Mauger who broke bones in his hand in the World Long Track Final and joined Briggo on the sidelines for the Kiwis' last three meetings which, effectively relegated them to wooden spoonists.

An England defeat by Norway-Denmark (who had Ole Olsen at reserve as a tactical ploy) meant that the Lions HAD to win the final match of the tournament against Australia to head the table. They trailed after two heats, drew level in heat three and were never headed after maximum-man Ray Wilson and partner Peter Collins registered a heat four 5-1.

MISSED...Sweden suffered from Sören Sjösten's absence

1972 England v Sweden (Division Two) Results

Workington, Sunday, June 25
ENGLAND 55 (Paul Tyrer 15, John Jackson 11, †Richard Greer 10, John Davis 10, Taffy Owen 4, Arthur Browning 2, Bob Coles 2, Frank Auffret 1) **SWEDEN 52** (Bengt Larsson 12, Lars Jansson 11, Christer Sjösten 10, Lars-Inge Hultberg 8, Tommy Jansson 5, Carl-Erik Claesson 5, Sören Karlsson 1).

Birmingham, Monday, June 26
ENGLAND 57 (Arthur Pricc 12, Gordon Kennett 11, Brian Foote 10, Arthur Browning 9, Paul Tyrer 9, †Richard Greer 5, Geoff Bouchard 1, Mick Hines 0) **SWEDEN 51** (Bengt Larsson 14, Christer Sjösten 13, Tommy Jansson 8, Lars Jansson 5, Carl-Erik Claesson 5, Sören Karlsson 5, Kall Haage 1, Lars-Inge Hultberg 0).

Bradford, Wednesday, June 28
ENGLAND 47 (Dave Baugh 15, Bob Coles 8, Arthur Browning 7, Malcolm Ballard 7, Arthur Price 5, †Richard Greer 3, Roger Mills 2, Geoff Bouchard 0) **SWEDEN 61** (Bengt Larsson 13, Christer Sjösten 13, Lars Jansson 11, Lars-Inge Hultberg 11, Tommy Jansson 9, Kall Haage 4, Carl-Erik Claesson 0, Sören Karlsson 0).

Peterborough, Friday, June 30
ENGLAND 48 (†Richard Greer 17, Brian Foote 8, John Davis 7, Russell Osborne 6, Gordon Kennett 5, Malcolm Ballard 4, Geoff Bouchard 1, Arthur Browning 0) **SWEDEN 60** (Tommy Jansson 16, Bengt Larsson 15, Lars-Inge Hultberg 12, Lars Jansson 11, Carl-Erik Claesson 3, Christer Sjösten 2, Sören Karlsson 1, Kall Haage 0).

Canterbury, Saturday, July 1
ENGLAND 55 (Graham Banks 15, Ted Hubbard 13, David Piddock 10, †Richard Greer 9, Gordon Kennett 6, Barney Kennett 2, Ross Gilbertson 0, Bobby McNeil, did not ride) **SWEDEN 53** (Tommy Jansson 18, Christer Sjösten 13, Bengt Larsson 9, Sören Karlsson 8, Lars Jansson 4, Carl-Erik Claesson 1, Lars-Inge Hultberg 0, Kall Haage 0).

England win the series 3-2.

● *The England team managers were Ian Thomas (Workington), Joe Thurley (Birmingham), Stan Holey (Bradford), Alec Ford (Peterborough) and Russ Osbourne (Canterbury)*
● *The Swedish team manager was Christer Bergström*

Cracker Crumpie is the big noise

IF THE 1971 international season at Division Two level belonged to England's John Louis then the Mildura Marvel, Australian Phil Crump, succeeded to the throne in 1972.

He may not have had as many Test match opportunities as Louis but he was the total master behind Australasia's first-ever series win in Britain.

He was unbeaten in the first Test at Middlesbrough and again in the final Test at Boston and, sandwiched in between, he dropped three points at Rayleigh. But consider the circumstances.

He was leading heat 16 and heading for another 18-point maximum when he took a tumble at The Weir and when the track doctor examined him he declared: "You've broken your wrist!"

That didn't worry the tough Aussie who immediately went out the following evening at Boston to make it 17 wins out of 18 races and to lead the Anzacs to a 3-0 series success.

Earlier England had squeezed to a best-of-five victory over Sweden – it went to the wire – for whom Tommy Jansson was again an immaculate performer without quite having the force or power of the sensational Crump.

While Jansson was the stylish supreme Christer Sjösten provided the thrills with his spectacular style.

1972 Fredericia (Denmark) Club Tour of Division Two Results

Hillerod, Sunday, May 7
FREDERICIA 48 BRADFORD 30 (Dave Baugh 12, Robin Adlington 11, Sid Sheldrick 3, Chris Roynon 2, †Alan Knapkin 2, Barry Meeks 0, Mick Fairbairn 0).

Hull, Wednesday, July 26
HULL 55 (Malcolm Mackay 12, Dave Mills 10, Peter Boston 9, †Tony Childs 8, Clark Facey 8, Dennis Wasden 5, Bryan Loakes 3) **FREDERICIA 23** (Erik Tilgaard 8, Jens Krause-Kjaer 8, †Arne Andreasen 3, Skjold Larsen 2, Jens Ring 1, Preben Pedersen 1, Erik Grön 0).

Peterborough, Friday, July 28
PETERBOROUGH 51 (†Richard Greer 11, John Davis 9, Ted Howgego 9, Roy Carter 8, Peter Saunders 7, Brian Clark 4, Alan Witt 2, John Amies 1) **FREDERICIA 27** (Nils Schelde 7, Jens Krause-Kjaer 6, †Arne Andreasen 4, John Hansen 3, Preben Pedersen 3, Erik Tilgaard 3, Skjold Larsen 1, Erik Grön 0).

Bradford, Sunday, July 30
BRADFORD 49 (Robin Adlington 12, †Alan Knapkin 11, Alan Bridgett 8, Dave Baugh 7, Sid Sheldrick 6, Colin Meredith 5, Lex Fielding 0) **FREDERICIA 27** (Nils Schelde 9, Erik Tilgaard 6, †Arne Andreasen 5, Erik Grön 3, John Hansen 2, Preben Pedersen 2, Jens Krause-Kjaer 0, Skjold Larsen 0).
● *The Fredericia team manager was Jorgen Dorscheus.*

1972 Olching (West Germany) Club Tour of Division Two Results

Canterbury, Saturday, April 29
CANTERBURY 39 (Ted Hubbard 10, Mike Vernam 8, Barney Kennett 7, Bob Hughes 7, †Ross Gilbertson 4, David Piddock 3, Trevor Barnwell 0) **OLCHING 37** (Hubert Kullman 9, †Josef Angermüller 8, Otto Barth 8, Wilhelm Reinhard 5, Dieter Dauderer 3, Georg Gilgenreiner 2, Alois Müller 2).

Boston, Sunday, April 30
BOSTON 64 (Jim Ryman 11.5, Carl Glover 11, Arthur Price 10, Russ Osborn 9.5, Jack Bywater 8, Tony Featherstone 7, Ray Bales 7) **OLCHING 12** (Otto Barth 4, Alois Müller 3, Wilhelm Reinhard 3, Hubert Kullman 1, Georg Gilgenreiner 1, Otto Weiß 0, †Josef Angermüller 0).

Birmingham, Monday, May 1
BIRMINGHAM 51 (Mike Gardner 10, Terry Shearer 10, Peter Bailey 8, Malcolm Corradine 7, Cliff Emms 6, †George Major 6, Mick Hines 4) **OLCHING 27** (†Josef Angermüller 11, Otto Barth 7, Hubert Kullman 6, Georg Gilgenreiner 1, Otto Weiß 1, Dieter Dauderer 1, Alois Müller 0).
● *The Olching team manager was Ulrich Brehmer.*

Olching, Sunday, June 18
OLCHING 49 (Hans Siegl 10, Otto Barth 10, Josef Angermüller 9, Rudi Kastl 7, Hubert Kullman 6, Georg Gilgenreiner 5, Wilhelm Reinhardt 2) **EASTBOURNE 29** (Gordon Kennett 9, Roger Johns 7, Bobby McNeil 6, John Davis 3, Simon Bruce 3, Trevor Geer 1, Paul Gachet 0).

1972 England v Australasia

Middlesbrough, Thursday, August 17
ENGLAND 51 (†Malcolm Ballard 14, Dave Durham 10, John Jackson 8, Tony Childs 5, Arthur Browning 5, Richard Greer 5, Arthur Price 3, Frank Auffret 1) **AUSTRALASIA 55** (†Phil Crump 18, Jack Millen 14, Graeme Smith 10, Lou Sansom 8, Dave Mills 3, Robin Amundson 2, Garry Flood 0, Roger Wright 0).

Rayleigh, Saturday, August 19
ENGLAND 52 (†Malcolm Ballard 15, Arthur Price 13, Allen Emmett 9, Brian Foote 6, Arthur Browning 5, Gordon Kennett 4, John Davis 0, Trevor Barnwell 0) **AUSTRALASIA 56** (†Phil Crump 15, Bob Young 14, Jack Millen 12, Graeme Smith 9, Garry Flood 3, Terry Shearer 1, Roger Wright 1, Dave Mills 1).

Boston, Sunday, August 20
ENGLAND 47 (Arthur Price 12, †Malcolm Ballard 10, Brian Foote 10, Richard Greer 7, John Jackson 5, Russ Osborne 2, John Davis 1, Tony Childs 0) **AUSTRALASIA 60** (†Phil Crump 18, Jack Millen 17, Malcolm Mackay 15, Bob Young 5, Garry Flood 3, Dave Mills 2, Lou Sansom 0).

Australasia win the series 3-0.

KINGPIN....Crewe Kings' star Phil Crump crowned a marvellous 1972 campaign by winning the first Second Division Riders' Championship Final at Wimbledon. He was also the first Australian to win the title

1972 Leningrad (USSR) Tour

Belle Vue, Saturday, May 10
BELLE VUE 41 (Sören Sjösten 10, †Alan Wilkinson 8, Chris Pusey 7, Peter Collins 7, Eric Broadbelt 4, Dave Hemus 3, Ken Eyre 2)
LENINGRAD 37 (Anatoli Kuzmin 11, †Giorgi Ivanov 8, Oleg Dobrinski 7, Vladimir Smirnov 7, Grigori Markatanov 3, Viktor Chistiakov 1).

Exeter, Tuesday, June 13
EXETER 45 (†Bob Kilby 11, Bruce Cribb 10, Edgar Stangeland 7, Dave Hemus 6, Chris Julian 5, Kevin Holden 3, Peter Ingram 3)
LENINGRAD 33 (†Giorgi Ivanov 12, Anatoli Kuzmin 12, Vladimir Smirnov 6, Grigori Markatanov 2, Oleg Dobrinski 1, Viktor Chistiakov 0).
Original staging on Monday, June 12, postponed, waterlogged track.

Poole, Wednesday, June 14
POOLE 44 (John Langfield 10, Frank Shuter 10, †Pete Smith 8, Odd Fossengen 8, Christer Löfqvist 7, Mike Cake 1, Bruce Cribb 0)
LENINGRAD 33 (Vladimir Smirnov 15, Anatoli Kuzmin 11, †Giorgi Ivanov 4, Viktor Chistiakov 2, Grigori Markatanov 1, Oleg Dobrinski 0).

Ipswich, Thursday, June 15
IPSWICH 43 (Olle Nygren 9, †John Louis 9, Sandor Levai 7, Tommy Johansson 7, Billy Sanders 6, Mick Hines 3, Alan Sage 2)
LENINGRAD 35 (Anatoli Kuzmin 16, Vladimir Smirnov 7, Grigori Markatanov 6, Viktor Chistiakov 4, †Giorgi Ivanov 2).

● *The Leningrad team manager was Ivan Ivanov.*

1972 England v Scotland

Glasgow, Friday, June 16
SCOTLAND 53 (George Hunter 15, Jim McMillan 13, Bobby Beaton 12, Bert Harkins 6, Charlie Monk 3, Andy Meldrum 2, Jim Gallacher 1, Willie Templeton 1) **ENGLAND 55** (Chris Pusey 16, Peter Collins 11, Eric Boocock 10, Ray Wilson 9, Arnold Haley 7, Malcolm Simmons 2, Dave Younghusband 0, Alan Wilkinson 0).

Halifax, Monday, September 18
ENGLAND 66 (†Eric Boocock 18, Peter Collins 13, Dave Jessup 13, Chris Pusey 12, Alan Jay 7, Arnold Haley 1, Doug Wyer 1, Eric Broadbelt 1)
SCOTLAND 42 (Bobby Beaton 14, †Jim McMillan 13, George Hunter 10, Bert Harkins 4, Jim Gallacher 1, Brian Collins 0, Charlie Monk 0, Andy Meldrum 0).

1972 Glasgow in Norway

Skien, Sunday, October 29
NORWEGIAN SELECT 39 (Ulf Lovaas 11, Reidar Eide 8, Øyvind Berg 6, Odd Fossengen 5, Helge Langli 4, Jonny Larsen 3, Tormod Langli 2)
GLASGOW 39 (†Bobby Beaton 10, Brian Collins 9, Reg Wilson 7, Doug Wyer 6, Robin Adlington 4, Paul O'Neal 2, Allan Mackie 1).
Sandnes, Saturday, November 4
SANDNES & JÆREN 44 (†Reidar Eide 12, Ulf Lovaas 11, Kjell Gimre 10, Per Hetland 6, Kjell Skjæveland 2, Odd Klinge 2, Per Andersen 1)
GLASGOW 34 (†Bobby Beaton 10, Doug Wyer 8, Reg Wilson 6, Allan Mackie 5, Robin Adlington 3, Brian Collins 2, Paul O'Neal 0).

PUSEY'S PUNCH-UP

JIM AIREY streaked to a six-ride maximum against Nigel Boocock's tourists...and then promptly handed the initiative back to the Lions by breaking his wrist when teaching youngsters how to ride a motor-bike!

He didn't return to the Test arena (at least as a rider) until the final Test at the Sydney Showground and, by then, it was all over and England were on the wrong end of a major drubbing.

Even Airey's injury was overshadowed by the events at Adelaide where, at the last minute, the Aussies replaced broken collar-bone victim Robin Amundson with his brother Kym, four years his younger. England led by six points after nine heats and the water cart was sent out which brought a torrent of protests from the Lions camp, all of which fell on apparent deaf ears.

So the effusive Chris Pusey tried to flag down the truck and had to dodge out of the way. As the cart continued, Pusey, holding his right leg, hobbled across the infield and was then involved in a brawl with the driver, stewards and ambulance men.

It took several burly Australians to restrain the Liverpudlian who was then thrown out of the remainder of the meeting by officials, prompting an initial response from skipper-manager Boocock: "No Pusey, no England."

It was announced that Australia had won by default but after two intervening stock car races the Test continued after Pusey had pleaded with his team-mates not to let down the paying public.

Pusey was a delighted as anyone when England won by eight points but that was to be their only victory in a long tour.

Any chance the Lions may have had of staging another winter comeback were ended when Peter Collins crashed into the notorious Showground wall at Sydney and was invalided home, being replaced for the rest of the series by his belle Vue team-mate Alan Wilkinson and, later, George Hunter, both of whom were free-lancing Down Under.

TEST ROOKIE...John Titman was called up at Brisbane

1972-73 England Tour of Australia Results

Perth, Friday, November 17, 1972
AUSTRALIA 60 (†Jim Airey 18, John Boulger 14, Les Sharpe 8, Chum Taylor 8, Les Leisk 6, John Langfield 4, Bob O'Leary 2) **ENGLAND 48** (Bob Kilby 13, †Nigel Boocock 11, Chris Pusey 8, Arnold Haley 7, Peter Collins 7, Barry Thomas 2, Eric Broadbelt 0).

Adelaide, Friday, November 24, 1972
AUSTRALIA 50 (†John Boulger 16, Bob Valentine 14, John Langfield 9, Phil Crump 8, Chris Bass 1, Steve Reinke 1, Kym Amundson 1) **ENGLAND 58** (Arnold Haley 14, Peter Collins 14, †Nigel Boocock 10, Barry Thomas 9, Eric Broadbelt 5, Chris Pusey 4, Bob Kilby 2).

Sydney, Saturday, December 23, 1972
AUSTRALIA 63 (†John Boulger 15, Jack White 15, Bob Valentine 13, John Langfield 7, Bill Landels 6, Kevin Torpie 6, Barry Van Praag 1) **ENGLAND 45** (Peter Collins 15, †Nigel Boocock 12, Eric Broadbelt 8, Arnold Haley 5, Barry Thomas 2, Chris Pusey 2, Bob Kilby 1).

Sydney, Saturday, December 30, 1972
AUSTRALIA 58 (†John Boulger 15, Kevin Torpie 11, Bob Valentine 11, John Langfield 11, Bill Landels 8, Barry Van Praag 2, Bob Humphreys 0) **ENGLAND 50** (†Nigel Boocock 12, Peter Collins 11, Arnold Haley 9, Bob Kilby 6, Chris Pusey 5, Barry Thomas 5, Eric Broadbelt 2).

Brisbane, Saturday, January 6, 1973
AUSTRALIA 71 (†John Boulger 17, Kevin Torpie 15, Doug White 13, Steve Reinke 12, John Titman 7, Bob Valentine 4, Jack White 3) **ENGLAND 36** (Chris Pusey 14, †Nigel Boocock 7, Barry Thomas 5, Arnold Haley 4, Eric Broadbelt 3, Alan Wilkinson 3, Bob Kilby 0).

Brisbane, Saturday, January 13, 1973
AUSTRALIA 58 (†John Boulger 15, Steve Reinke 11, Jack White 9, Doug White 8, John Titman 8, Kevin Torpie 6, Bob Gourlay 1) **ENGLAND 50** (†Nigel Boocock 10, Chris Pusey 10, Arnold Haley 10, Bob Kilby 9, Barry Thomas 7, Eric Broadbelt 4, Alan Wilkinson 0).

Sydney, Monday, January 22, 1973
AUSTRALIA 62 (John Langfield 18, John Boulger 17, †Jim Airey 14, Barry Van Praag 7, Bob Valentine 5, Bill Landels 1, Geoff Curtis 0) **ENGLAND 46** (George Hunter 11, Chris Pusey 9, †Nigel Boocock 9, Arnold Haley 9, Eric Broadbelt 5, Bob Kilby 3, Barry Thomas 0).

Australia win the series 6-1.

OTHER MATCHES

Rockhampton, Saturday, January 20, 1973
AUSTRALIAN SELECT 77 (Jack White 18, Kevin Torpie 16, Steve Reinke 12, Doug White 11, John Titman 11, Greg Kluver 8, Mal Brown 1) **ENGLAND 31** (George Hunter 8, Eric Broadbelt 7, †Nigel Boocock 5, Chris Pusey 5, Arnold Haley 4, Bob Kilby 2, Alan Wilkinson 0).

1973 England Tour of New Zealand

Auckland, Saturday, February 3
NEW ZEALAND 52 (†Ronnie Moore 14, Bob Andrews 12, Roger Wright 9, Graeme Stapleton 8, Gary Peterson 6, Bryce Subritzky 3, John Goodall 0) **ENGLAND 56** (Bob Kilby 12, Chris Pusey 12, Arnold Haley 12, George Hunter 11, Eric Broadbelt 7, †Nigel Boocock 2, Barry Thomas 0).

Christchurch, Saturday, February 10
NEW ZEALAND 77 (†Ivan Mauger 18, Barry Briggs 17, Ronnie Moore 15, Graeme Stapleton 11, Roger Wright 9, Frank Shuter 7) **ENGLAND 31** (Chris Pusey 11, Eric Broadbelt 9, †Nigel Boocock 6, Arnold Haley 3, Bob Kilby 2, George Hunter 0).

Auckland, Monday, February 19
NEW ZEALAND 53 (†Ivan Mauger 15, Graeme Stapleton 12, Ronnie Moore 11, Gary Peterson 8, Roger Wright 4, Bob Andrews 2, Bryce Subritzky 1) **ENGLAND 54** (Bob Kilby 15, Arnold Haley 14, Chris Pusey 9, Eric Broadbelt 8, George Hunter 8, Nigel Boocock 0, Tommy Sweetman 0).

Wellington, Saturday, February 24
NEW ZEALAND 67 (†Ivan Mauger 18, Barry Briggs 16, Ronnie Moore 11, Graeme Stapleton 9, Graeme Smith 9, Lance Gandy 2, Rick Timmo 2) **ENGLAND 41** (Chris Pusey 14, Eric Broadbelt 12, Nigel Boocock 8, Bob Kilby 7, Arnold Haley 0, George Hunter 0, Tommy Sweetman 0).

The series was drawn 2-2.

●*Five officials, including the meeting referee, were needed to decide Graeme Stapleton had blocked George Hunter in heat 18 of the third New Zealand-England Test, turning a 55-53 Kiwi win into a one-point England triumph.*

PC GRABS LAST-GASP GLORY

IT WAS A night that no true-blooded English fan will ever want to forget...and a evening that Anders Michanek and his Swedish team-mates won't want to remember!

For the destination of the Daily Mirror International Tournament trophy was decided in the split second it takes to blink with experienced British referee Arthur Humphrey having to make the most crucial decision there has ever been outside a World Final.

HERO...youngster Peter Collins takes Anders Michanek in the tie-breaker

The Tournament, in all but name a World Cup competition embracing eight world powers (Scandinavians Denmark and Norway again combined forces) had built up to the sort of climax that belongs in a novel.

After 13 heats England and Sweden, who had fought their way through six qualifying matches and a semi-final, were locked together 39-39 and the only way to decide the winners of a three week long championship was by a sudden death race-off.

Sweden team boss Christer Bergström had no hesitation in naming 11-point top scorer Anders Michanek as his contender.

England chief Len Silver bravely went for 19-year-old Peter Collins who had won only two of his four races and hadn't even been the Lions' top scorer.

Collins made the sort of start that you dream of and led the far more experienced Michanek for the opening lap. Then the big Swede feinted to go the long way round on the first bend of lap two and as PC, almost as if he had eyes in the back of his helmet, moved out to block the expected sweep, Mich cut inside and went for fresh air.

Did Collins realise his mistake and chop back towards the line to close the gap? Or did Michanek realise the only way he could make it

this time was by keeping the throttle open?

Referee Humphrey had to decide as Collins came down against the Wembley fence and he swiftly put on the white exclusion light which indicated that he blamed Michanek for the collision.

It brought this reaction from Swedish team boss Bergström: "That was the worst decision I have ever seen."

But Silver retorted: "Michanek made his own gap, but then he hit Collins. That's boring and the referee had to exclude him."

Referee Humphrey explained: "I have been refereeing for long enough to trust my own judgement and I am confident that the decision was right."

For the first time millions of television viewers could also be judge and jury as the final was being screened by ITV's World of Sport and their experts, commentator Dave Lanning and summariser Barry Briggs, both agreed that the action replay vindicated the referee – even though it's doubtful if the Swedish party would ever admit it.

Certainly it was a dramatic finale to a competition which caught the imagination of both the supporters and the media.

With backing from the Daily Mirror the extravangza of action received blanket coverage from not only the Mirror group but also their Fleet Street rivals.

It all began at the stroke of 7.30 p.m. at Leicester, on Tuesday, June 26.

Or, at least it should have done. Instead at the time the rain was pouring down and referee Stan Green had little alternative but to call off the first of the Tournament matches.

England skipper Ray Wilson and his New Zealand counterpart Ivan Mauger concurred with the official verdict and, in what many would claim as typical speedway weather, the grand opening was delayed.

Initially for 24 hours, but then for 48 as the second match, between Australia and the amalgamated Norway-Denmark, was also abandoned.

All four teams were awarded a point each as the organisers had, at least, considered the possibility of the British summer turning nasty!

That meant Sheffield became the first track to see International Tournament action as youngsters Collins and Reg Wilson tore into Sweden.

Reg Wilson was a surprise winner of the second heat and even though England provided nine of the 13 heat winners the Swedes so successfully packed the minor placings that it needed a last race 4-2 for England to go to the top of the table after their second scheduled match.

England stayed there for the rest of the preliminaries to head the four semi-finalists.

But before the last four were known there was a glut of other matches, each in its own way, providing headlines.

Barry Briggs made his racing comeback at Exeter as New Zealand demolished Poland with Ivan Mauger knocking .4 of a second off the County Ground track record in heat 12!

Vladimir Zapleczny was taken to the ambulance room after being struck, midships, by his team-mate Viktor Trofimov in a hecticv heat 10 at Leicester.

Poland called-up Poole's Antonin Woryna (left out of their original party) for their match on his home track against Norway-Denmark and he very nearly helped cause a major upset.

Australia claimed (wrongly) that Briggo was using the banned additive nitro-methane when they were soundly thumped at Wimbledon.

Ray Wilson, Terry Betts and reserve Malcolm Simmons were all unbeaten by an opponent as English thrashed Russia at Ipswich.

Zenon Plech marked his arrival on the British international scene with 11 points (and a fall) from five starts against England at Hackney.

STUNNER...great London display by Zenon Plech

Anders Michanek (Sweden) and Garry Middleton (Australia) missed their match at Newport after being stranded on the M4.

The Russians, despite two laps practice immediately before the meeting, went on a tapes breaking spree at Cradley Heath.

Plech caught the bug the same night at Halifax where he finished with only one point, two exclusions and a stoppage.

England came from eight points down to beat Australia who had Jim Airey, John Boulger and John Titman excluded at vital times for tape offences.

And New Zealand clinched their place in the semis in the very last qualifying match on race points difference after the impetuousity of the Russians (SIX tape exclusions in 13 races!) cost them what would have been their solitary tournament victory.

Joining the Kiwis in the last four were England, Sweden and Australia.

New Zealand suffered a psychological blow in the opening heat of their semi-final against England when Ivan Mauger was beaten by Ray Wilson and with reserve Alan Wilkinson using every ounce of his Belle Vue experience to good effect, the Lions surged to an unexpectedly comfortable victory.

In the other semi, at Coventry, Sweden had an even more comfortable victory against Australia to book their place in what was going to be a truly dramatic showdown.

Their heat leader trio of Michanek, Sören Sjosten and Christer Löfqvist, rattled up 34 out of a maximum 36 points with John Boulger the Aussies' solitary heat winner.

Neither manager made any startling changes for the final but Silver must have wondered how his young side would cope with a meeting at Wembley.

And in particular how would teenager Collins ("I've never seen the place before, not even as a spectator") cope with the pressures of a heaving Empire Stadium?

Any fears on that score were quickly dispelled. Skipper Wilson won the opening race and Malcolm Simmons took the flag in heat two. With Martin Ashby and Terry Betts filling the minor placings, England were four points ahead.

And they never went behind although Sweden pulled level through Bernie Persson and Sjösten in heat seven and the remaining six races were all shared to set up that unforgettable sudden death race off!

1973 Great Britain v Rest of the World

PETER COLLINS and Anders Michanek immediately renewed their rivalries in the Eterna Watches sponsored showpiece which followed immediately after the International Tournament Final.

Again they were on opposite sides and this time the Swede had the victory he had so desperately wanted a little earlier in the evening. He beat PC twice in the space of four heats to help the Rest of the World to an easy win.

Wembley, Saturday, July 14

GREAT BRITAIN 30 (†Ray Wilson 11, Ivan Mauger 8, Peter Collins 4, John Boulger 3, Malcolm Simmons 3, Jim McMillan 1, Terry Betts 0) **REST OF THE WORLD 48** (†Ole Olsen 11, Anders Michanek 10, Edward Jancarz 7, Dag Lovaas 6, Zenon Plech 6, Christer Löfqvist 6, Bernt Persson 2).

1973 Daily Mirror International Tournament Results

Leicester, Tuesday, June 26
ENGLAND** (†Ray Wilson, Terry Betts, John Louis, Martin Ashby, Eric Boocock, Malcolm Simmons, Peter Collins) **v NEW ZEALAND** (†Ivan Mauger, Graeme Stapleton, Ronnie Moore, Bill Andrew, Frank Shuter, Gary Peterson, Dave Gifford), **abandoned, rain.

Coventry, Wednesday, June 27
AUSTRALIA** (†John Boulger, John Titman, Jim Airey, Bob Valentine, Garry Middleton, Les Sharpe, Geoff Curtis) **v NORWAY-DENMARK** (†Ole Olsen, Dag Lovaas, Reidar Eide, Øyvind Berg, Edgar Stangeland, Ulf Lovaas, Odd Fossengen), **abandoned, rain.

Sheffield, Thursday, June 28
ENGLAND 40 (Reg Wilson 11, Peter Collins 10, †Ray Wilson 9, Eric Boocock 5, John Louis 4, Martin Ashby 1, Doug Wyer 0) **SWEDEN 38** (Bernt Persson 10, Sören Sjösten 8, †Anders Michanek 7, Tommy Jansson 5, Christer Löfqvist 5, Bengt Larsson 2, Bengt Jansson 1).

Hackney, Friday, June 29
SWEDEN 49 (†Bengt Jansson 12, Anders Michanek 12, Bernt Persson 7, Christer Sjösten 7, Tommy Jansson 5, Christer Löfqvist 5, Olle Nygren 1) **SOVIET UNION 29** (Vladimir Gordeev 13, Anatoli Kuzmin 5, Vladimir Zapleczny 5, Oleg Dzjadick 3, Grigori Khlinovsky 3, †Aleksander Pavlov 0, Giorgi Ivanov 0).

Wolverhampton, Friday, June 29
NORWAY-DENMARK 40 (†Ole Olsen 11, Dag Lovaas 9, Reidar Eide 7, Edgar Stangeland 7, Øyvind Berg 4, Odd Fossengen 2, Ulf Lovaas 0) **NEW ZEALAND 37** (Barry Briggs 9, Dave Gifford 8, †Ivan Mauger 6, Graeme Stapleton 4, Gary Peterson 4, Bill Andrew 3, Ronnie Moore 3).

Belle Vue, Saturday, June 30
ENGLAND 48 (†Ray Wilson 10, Alan Wilkinson 10, Peter Collins 9, Eric Boocock 8, Martin Ashby 5, Reg Wilson 4, Terry Betts 2) **NORWAY-DENMARK 30** (†Ole Olsen 10, Dag Lovaas 7, Øyvind Berg 4, Edgar Stangeland 4, Odd Fossengen 2, Reidar Eide 2, Ulf Lovaas 1).

Halifax, Saturday, June 30
POLAND 42 (Edward Jancarz 10, Henryk Zyto 10, Zenon Plech 10, †Pawel Waloszek 8, Jan Mucha 4, Marek Cieslak 0, Jerzy Szczakiel 0) **SOVIET UNION 36** (Vladimir Gordeev 7, Anatoli Kuzmin 7, †Aleksander Pavlov 6, Grigori Khlinovsky 6, Vladimir Zapleczny 6, Viktor Trofimov 3, Giorgi Ivanov 1).

Swindon, Saturday, June 30
NEW ZEALAND 35 (†Ivan Mauger 10, Barry Briggs 8, Rick Timmo 6, Bill Andrew 4, Frank Shuter 3, Ronnie Moore 3, Graeme Stapleton 1) **SWEDEN 42** (Christer Löfqvist 11, †Anders Michanek 9, Bernt Persson 7, Bengt Jansson 6, Hasse Holmkvist 4, Tommy Jansson 3, Sören Sjösten 2).

Oxford, Sunday, July 1
AUSTRALIA 54 (†John Boulger 11, Geoff Curtis 11, Jim Airey 10, John Titman 7, Bob Valentine 6, Bob Humphreys 5, Charlie Monk 4) **POLAND 23** (Jan Mucha 11, Edward Jancarz 4, †Pawel Waloszek 3, Henryk Zyto 3, Zenon Plech 2, Jerzy Szczakiel 0, Zbigniew Marcinkowski 0).

Cradley Heath, Monday, July 2
NORWAY-DENMARK 33 (†Ole Olsen 13, Reidar Eide 6, Øyvind Berg 4, Ulf Lovaas 4, Edgar Stangeland 3, Dag Lovaas 2, Odd Fossengen 1) **SWEDEN 45** (Anders Michanek 11, Christer Löfqvist 9, Bernt Persson 9, Bengt Jansson 6, Tommy Jansson 6, Sören Sjösten 4, Hasse Holmkvist 0).

Exeter, Monday, July 2
NEW ZEALAND 53 (†Ivan Mauger 12, Ronnie Moore 9, Barry Briggs 8, Gary Peterson 7, Bill Andrew 7, Dave Gifford 5, Frank Shuter 5) **POLAND 25** (Zenon Plech 9, Jan Mucha 6, †Pawel Waloszek 4, Henryk Zyto 3, Edward Jancarz 2, Zbigniew Marcinkowski 1, Marek Cieslak 0).

Leicester, Tuesday, July 3
AUSTRALIA 45 (†John Boulger 11, John Titman 10, Bob Valentine 8, Garry Middleton 8, Jim Airey 4, Charlie Monk 4, Bob Humphreys 0) **SOVIET UNION 33** (Vladimir Gordeev 9, Vladimir Zapleczny 6, †Aleksander Pavlov 6, Anatoli Kuzmin 6, Grigori Khlinovsky 3, Giorgi Ivanov 2, Viktor Trofimov 1).

Poole, Wednesday, July 4
NORWAY-DENMARK 43 (Dag Lovaas 11, †Ole Olsen 9, Kurt Bøgh 7, Odd Fossengen 5, Reidar Eide 5, Øyvind Berg 5, Edgar Stangeland 1) **POLAND 35** (Zenon Plech 12, Edward Jancarz 10, Antonni Woryna 8, Marek Cieslak 2, Jan Mucha 1, †Pawel Waloszek 1, Zbigniew Marcinkowski 1).

Ipswich, Thursday, July 5
ENGLAND 56 (†Ray Wilson 12, John Louis 11, Terry Betts 9, Malcolm Simmons 8, Martin Ashby 7, Barry Thomas 5, Eric Boocock 4) **SOVIET UNION 21** (†Aleksander Pavlov 4, Anatoli Kuzmin 4, Grigori Khlinovsky 4, Vladimir Zapleczny 3, Viktor Trofimov 3, Vladimir Gordeev 2, Giorgi Ivanov 1).

Wimbledon, Thursday, July 5
AUSTRALIA 28 (Bob Valentine 7, †John Boulger 6, Charlie Monk 6, Geoff Curtis 3, Jim Airey 2, Garry Middleton 2, John Titman 2) **NEW ZEALAND 50** (†Ivan Mauger 12, Barry Briggs 10, Ronnie Moore 10, Gary Peterson 10, Graeme Stapleton 6, Frank Shuter 2, Dave Gifford 0).

Hackney, Friday, July 6
ENGLAND 45 (John Louis 12, †Ray Wilson 10, Malcolm Simmons 7, Barry Thomas 6, Eric Boocock 5, Martin Ashby 3, Terry Betts 2) **POLAND 32** (Zenon Plech 11, Jan Mucha 6, †Pawel Waloszek 6, Edward Jancarz 4, Antonin Woryna 4, Zbigniew Marcinkowski 1, Marek Cieslak 0).

Newport, Friday, July 6
SWEDEN 38 (Christer Löfqvist 10, Bernt Persson 8, Bengt Jansson 7, Hasse Holmkvist 6, Tommy Jansson 4, Bo Wirebrand 3, Sören Sjösten 0) **AUSTRALIA 40** (Jim Airey 8, John Boulger 7, Neil Street 7, Geoff Curtis 6, Charlie Monk 5, Bob Valentine 4, John Titman 3).

Cradley Heath, Saturday, July 7
NORWAY-DENMARK 47 (Dag Lovaas 12, †Ole Olsen 11, Øyvind Berg 10, Reidar Eide 7, Odd Fossengen 4, Edgar Stangeland 2, Kurt Bøgh 1) **SOVIET UNION 31** (Vladimir Gordeev 12, Grigori Khlinovsky 10, Anatoli Kuzmin 3, †Aleksander Pavlov 2, Giorgi Ivanov 2, Vladimir Zapleczny 2).

Halifax, Saturday, July 7
SWEDEN 53 (†Sören Sjösten 12, Anders Michanek 11, Bernt Persson 11, Christer Löfqvist 10, Olle Nygren 5, Christer Sjösten 2, Bengt Larsson 2) **POLAND 25** (†Pawel Waloszek 10, Edward Jancarz 8, Henryk Zyto 2, Zbigniew Marcinkowski 2, Antonin Woryna 2, Zenon Plech 1, Jan Mucha 0).

King's Lynn, Sunday, July 8
ENGLAND 44 (Eric Boocock 12, Malcolm Simmons 9, Peter Collins 6, †Ray Wilson 6, John Louis 6, Terry Betts 4, Barry Thomas 1) **AUSTRALIA 34** (†John Boulger 11, Bob Valentine 7, Garry Middleton 6, Billy Sanders 5, Jim Airey 3, John Titman 2, Bob Humphreys 0).

Reading, Monday, July 9
NEW ZEALAND 43 (†Ivan Mauger 12, Ronnie Moore 11, Barry Briggs 9, Gary Peterson 4, Graeme Stapleton 4, Bill Andrew 3, Dave Gifford 0) **SOVIET UNION 34** (Vladimir Gordeev 10, Grigori Khlinovsky 9, Viktor Trofimov 6, Vladimir Zapleczny 3, Anatoli Kuzmin 3, †Aleksander Pavlov 2, Giorgi Ivanov 1).

Daily Mirror International Tournament League Table

	P	W	D	L	A	PtsF	PtsA	Pts
ENGLAND	6	5	0	0	1	233	155	11
Sweden	6	4	0	2	0	265	202	8
New Zealand	6	3	0	2	1	218	169	7
Australia	6	3	0	2	1	201	188	7
Norway-Denmark	6	3	0	2	1	193	196	7
Poland	6	1	0	5	0	182	284	2
Soviet Union	6	0	0	6	0	184	282	0

SEMI FINAL

Belle Vue, Wednesday, July 11
ENGLAND 48 (†Ray Wilson 11, Peter Collins 10, Alan Wikinson 8, John Louis 7, Malcolm Simmons 6, Martin Ashby 5, Eric Boocock 1) **NEW ZEALAND 30** (†Ivan Mauger 13, Barry Briggs 7, Ronnie Moore 6, Graeme Stapleton 1, Bill Andrew 1, Gary Peterson 1, Dave Gifford 1).

Coventry, Wednesday, July 11
SWEDEN 51 (Christer Löfqvist 12, Anders Michanek 12, †Sören Sjösten 10, Bernt Persson 9, Tommy Jansson 4, Bengt Jansson 2, Olle Nygren 2) **AUSTRALIA 27** (†John Boulger 7, Jim Airey 4, Charlie Monk 4, Garry Middleton 4, John Titman 3, Bob Valentine 3, Geoff Curtis 2).

FINAL

Wembley, Saturday, July 14
ENGLAND 39 (Malcolm Simmons 10, Terry Betts 10, Peter Collins 9, †Ray Wilson 6, Martin Ashby 2, John Louis 2, Eric Boocock 0) **SWEDEN 39** (Anders Michanek 11, Christer Löfqvist 10, Bernt Persson 8, Tommy Jansson 5, Hasse Holmkvist 3, Sören Sjösten 2, †Olle Nygren 0).

■ ***Peter Collins (England) defeated Anders Michanek (Sweden) in a run-off for the championship.***

● *Team Managers were: Australia (Sam Bass), England (Len Silver), New Zealand (Trevor Redmond), Norway-Denmark (Tore Kittilsen), Poland (Zbigniew Puzio), Soviet Union (Fedor Karabanov) and Sweden (Christer Bergström).*

1973 Poland v Great Britain Results

Wroclaw, Saturday, May 6
POLAND 76 (Jan Mucha 15, Zenon Plech 14, Zbigniew Marcinkowski 14, Edward Jancarz 13, Henryk Glucklich 12, Zdzislaw Dobrucki 4, Jerzy Trzeszkowski 2, †Pawel Waloszek 2) **GREAT BRITAIN 31** (John Louis 11, John Boulger 6, †Ray Wilson 6, Terry Betts 5, Malcolm Simmons 2, Martin Ashby 1, Eric Boocock 0, Jim McMillan 0).

Rybnik, Saturday, May 13
POLAND 53 (†Pawel Waloszek 13, Edward Jancarz 12, Jan Mucha 10, Zbigniew Marcinkowski 8, Andrzej Wyglenda 7, Zygmunt Golebiowski 3, Zdzislaw Dobrucki 0, Jerzy Szczakiel 0) **GREAT BRITAIN 55** (†Ray Wilson 13, Jim McMillan 12, John Louis 11, Reg Wilson 10, John Boulger 5, Terry Betts 4, Pete Smith 0).

Gorzow, Saturday, June 17
POLAND 75 (Zenon Plech 18, Edward Jancarz 14, Jerzy Szczakiel 14, Marek Cieslak 12, †Pawel Waloszek 11, Henryk Zyto 4, Zbigniew Marcinkowski 2, Jerzy Kowalski 0) **GREAT BRITAIN 33** (†Ivan Mauger 9, Jim McMillan 8, Terry Betts 8, John Louis 4, John Boulger 3, Ray Wilson 1, Reg Wilson 0, Malcolm Simmons 0).

Poland win the series 2-1.

- *The Polish team managers were Jerzy Salabun (Wroclaw), Jerzy Kubik (Rybnik) and Witold Glowania (Gorzow).*
- *The Great Britain team managers were Dent Oliver (Wroclaw and Rybnik) and Reg Fearman (Gorzow).*

1973 Poland Under 23 v Great Britain Under 23 Results

Leszno, Saturday, May 6
POLAND U23 66 (Ryszard Fabiszewski 15, Boguslaw Nowak 13, Marek Cieslak 12, Bernard Jader 12, Andrzej Tkocz 12, Piotr Pyszny 1, Andrzej Jurczynski 1, Jan Gagolewicz 0) **GREAT BRITAIN U23 41** (†Chris Pusey 10, Bobby Beaton 9, Barry Thomas 9, Peter Collins 6, Doug Wyer 5, Graham Plant 2, Reg Wilson 0, Gordon Kennett 0).

Czestochowa, Saturday, May 13
POLAND U23 63 (Boguslaw Nowak 15, Marek Cieslak 9, Bernard Jader 9, Jerzy Bozyk 8, Ryszard Fabiszewski 8, Marian Wardzala 7, Andrzej Jurczynski 4, Franciszek Stach 3) **GREAT BRITAIN U23 45** (†Chris Pusey 12, Peter Collins 10, Doug Wyer 8, Reg Wilson 6, Bobby Beaton 3, Graham Plant 3, Barry Thomas 2, Gordon Kennett 1).

Gniezno, Wednesday, May 17
POLAND U23 70 (Zbigniew Filipiak 17, Boguslaw Nowak 16, Bernard Jader 14, Ryszard Fabiszewski 11, Andrzej Tkocz 5, Jerzy Bozyk 4, Franciszek Stach 3, Marian Wardzala 0) **GREAT BRITAIN U23 36** (Doug Wyer 10, John Titman 10, Bobby Beaton 7, †Chris Pusey 4, Peter Collins 3, Alan Wilkinson 2, Barry Thomas 0, Graham Plant 0).

Poland win the series 3-0.

- *The Great Britain Under-23 team manager was Len Silver.*

A look at the rest of the 1973 International scene

WHILE most of the country was caught up by the uephoria of the Daily Mirror International Tournament, Second Division fans had Continental excitement of their own with a full programme of Test matches.

Poland – who had also entertained a British senior side and an Under-23 squad on their own tracks during May and June – despatched some of their most promising young riders to England at the end of June for an eight-match rubber on Division Two tracks. Their party included 1972 Polish Junior Champion Bernard Jader and fourth-placed Boguslaw Nowak who had top-scored in the Under-23 series immediately before setting off for Britain.

They certainly had conflicting tours!

Nowak began by winning his first race at Canterbury (after coming into the main body of the team as a replacement for Marian Wardzala who suffered internal injuries after a pre-meeting practice crash) but Jader never looked remotely confortable on strange tracks and scored only 13 points on the entire tour.

Nowak struggled the more he rode and the Poles ended up with Ryszard Fabiszewski, Andzrej Tkocz and Zbigniew Filipiak as their major scorers as they won at Kingsmead, Hull and Peterborough but lost the overall rubber 4-3, with the last Test at Workington a victim of heavy rain and a schedule which made it impossible to re-stage 24 hours later as had happened earlier in the tour at the Alwalton.

Sweden were the second full-scale international opponents (West German undertook a three match club tour) on Division Two tracks and, like the Poles, pulled in huge crowds.

But, unlike, the Poles, they were over-run after a one-point defeat in the opening Test at Eastbourne where England lost Roger Johns with a badly cut eye.

In all it couldn't have been a happy series for Johns as he was also an early departee in the final Test at Peterborough where he had to pull out on medical advice after a heavy fall in his fourth ride.

The only real bright spots for the visitors were at Cleveland Park, where tour leader Leif Enecrona equalled the track record in his opening ride, and a double figure performance from Richard Hellsén at Bradford which was to win him a King's Lynn contract.

Scotland had the rarity of five international matches against the Auld Enemy – but at two different levels!

In two matches on British League tracks the Scots won at home and lost away while they went down in the Second Division rubber, losing all three Tests, all of which were raced on English tracks although they were afforded the status of the home team at Berwick!

1973 England v Scotland Results

Coatbridge, Friday, September 14
SCOTLAND 57 (†Jim McMillan 18, Bert Harkins 13, Bobby Beaton 12, Jim Gallacher 6, Charlie Monk 6, Andy Meldrum 2, Alistair Brady and Wattie Robertson, did not ride) **ENGLAND 51** (Tony Davey 15, †Dave Jessup 14, Reg Wilson 8, Mike Hiftle 6, Doug Wyer 5, Arnold Haley 1, Dave Gatenby 1, Tom Owen 1).

Halifax, Monday, September 17
ENGLAND 68 (†Peter Collins 15, Alan Wilkinson 14, Reg Wilson 12, Arnold Haley 9, Tony Davey 8, Mike Hiftle 5, Doug Wyer 5, Dave Gatenby, did not ride) **SCOTLAND 40** (Bobby Beaton 11, †Jim McMillan 11, Bert Harkins 7, George Hunter 6, Charlie Monk 4, Alistair Brady 1, Jim Gallacher 0, Andy Meldrum 0).

England and Scotland draw the series 1-1.

- *The Scotland team manager was Neil Macfarlane.*
- *The England team manager was Eric Boothroyd.*

1973 England v Scotland (Division Two) Results

Berwick, Saturday, June 5
ENGLAND 48 (Peter Reading 14, Frank Auffret 10, Dave Gatenby 8, †Bruce Forrester 8, Graham Jones 6, Mitch Graham 2, Geoff Davies 0, John Jackson, did not arrive) **SCOTLAND 60** (†Doug Templeton 17, Willie Templeton 16, Jim Gallacher 10, Andy Meldrum 9, Wattie Robertson 6, John Wilson 2, Ken McKinlay 0, Mick Beaton 0).

Sunderland, Friday, June 15
ENGLAND 70 (Frank Auffret 15, Terry Kelly 14, †Bruce Forrester 13, Dave Gatenby 12, Peter Reading 9, Russ Dent 3, John Jackson 2, Tim Swales 2) **SCOTLAND 38** (†Doug Templeton 12, Ken McKinlay 11, Willie Templeton 11, John Wilson 3, Andy Meldrum 1, Wattie Robertson 0, Mick Beaton 0).

Middlesbrough, Thursday, August 16
ENGLAND 66 (Bruce Forrester 17, Peter Reading 17, Dave Gatenby 10, Frank Auffret 9, Carl Glover 7, Arthur Browning 6, Mitch Graham 0) **SCOTLAND 42** (Doug Templeton 15, Jim Gallacher 12, Ken McKinlay 6, Ross Gilbertson 6, Willie Templeton 3, John Wilson 0, Wattie Robertson 0, Andy Meldrum 0).

England win the series 2-1.

1973 England v Poland (Division Two) Results

Canterbury, Saturday, June 30
ENGLAND 47 (John Davis 14, †Arthur Price 10, Roger Mills 8, Roger Johns 5, Barney Kennett 4, Bobby McNeil 4, Ted Hubbard 1, David Beech 1) **POLAND 61** (Boguslaw Nowak 15, Zbigniew Filipiak 15, Andrzej Tkocz 10, Ryszard Fabiszewski 8, Franciszek Stach 6, Andrzej Jurczynski 5, Bernard Jader 2).

Boston, Sunday, July 1
ENGLAND 55 (Carl Glover 13, Richard Greer 13, †Arthur Price 12, John Davis 9, Bruce Forrester 5, Roger Mills 2, Mitch Graham 1, Roger Johns 0) **POLAND 52** (Andrzej Tkocz 15, Franciszek Stach 14, Boguslaw Nowak 9, Ryszard Fabiszewski 7, Zbigniew Filipiak 4, Andrzej Jurczynski 2, Bernard Jader 1).

Hull, Wednesday, July 4
ENGLAND 53 (Bobby McNeil 14, †Arthur Price 12, Tony Childs 9, Carl Glover 7, John Davis 6, Arthur Browning 5, Bruce Forrester 0, Mitch Graham 0) **POLAND 55** (Ryszard Fabiszewski 12, Zbigniew Filipiak 11, Franciszek Stach 11, Andrzej Tkocz 10, Boguslaw Nowak 8, Bernard Jader 3, Andrzej Jurczynski, did not ride).

Peterborough, Saturday, July 7
ENGLAND 52 (John Davis 17, Richard Greer 10, Bruce Forrester 10, Brian Clark 5, †Arthur Price 5, Arthur Browning 3, John Jackson 1, Roger Mills 1) **POLAND 56** (Ryszard Fabiszewski 15, Andrzej Tkocz 12, Zbigniew Filipiak 12, Franciszek Stach 6, Andrzej Jurczynski 5, Boguslaw Nowak 4, Bernard Jader 2).

Eastbourne, Sunday, July 8
ENGLAND 67 (John Davis 14, Roger Johns 13, †Arthur Price 13, Arthur Browning 11, Bobby McNeil 9, Ted Hubbard 4, David Beech 3) **POLAND 41** (Andrzej Tkocz 17, Ryszard Fabiszewski 11, Franciszek Stach 7, Andrzej Jurczynski 3, Boguslaw Nowak 2, Bernard Jader 1, Zbigniew Filipiak 0).

Birmingham, Monday, July 9
ENGLAND 64 (†Arthur Price 14, Arthur Browning 13, Richard Greer 11, Bruce Forrester 11, Mike Lanham 7, Frank Auffret 7, John Jackson 1, Roger Mills 0) **POLAND 43** (Andrzej Tkocz 15, Ryszard Fabiszewski 11, Franciszek Stach 8, Andrzej Jurczynski 4, Boguslaw Nowak 3, Bernard Jader 2, Zbigniew Filipiak 0).

Middlesbrough, Thursday, July 12
ENGLAND 49 (Roger Johns 13, Bruce Forrester 12, Arthur Browning 8, Frank Auffret 7, Richard Greer 6, Roger Mills 2, †Arthur Price 1, Tim Swales 0) **POLAND 59** (Ryszard Fabiszewski 18, Andrzej Tkocz 12, Franciszek Stach 9, Zbigniew Filipiak 8, Andrzej Jurczynski 7, Boguslaw Nowak 3, Bernard Jader 2).

Workington, Friday, July 13
ENGLAND v POLAND, cancelled, waterlogged track.

Poland win the series 4-3.

● *The Polish team manager was Jerzy Olejniczak.*

1973 England v Australasia (Division Two) Results

Canterbury, Saturday, September 8
ENGLAND 55 (Carl Glover 15, Arthur Price 12, Bobby McNeil 11, Roger Johns 8, John Davis 6, Richard Greer 3, David Beech 0, †Barney Kennett 0) **AUSTRALASIA 53** (†Lou Sansom 16, Dave Mills 16, Phil Herne 10, Bob Young 5, Malcolm Mackay 3, Paul O'Neal 2, Glyn Taylor 1, Peter Moore 0).

Workington, Sunday, September 9
ENGLAND 44 (Mitch Graham 10, Richard Greer 10, Dave Baugh 8, Carl Glover 7, Tom Owen 5, John Davis 2, Roger Johns 1, †Arthur Browning 1) **AUSTRALASIA 64** (†Lou Sansom 18, Dave Mills 12, Roger Wright 10, Malcolm Mackay 9, Paul O'Neal 6, Kym Amundson 5, Phil Herne 4, Robin Adlington, did not ride).

Hull, Wednesday, September 12
ENGLAND 44 (Arthur Price 12, Carl Glover 12, †Bobby McNeil 11, Dave Morton 4, John Davis 3, Roger Johns 2, Richard Greer 0, Alan Cowland 0) **AUSTRALASIA 64** (†Lou Sansom 17, Jim Wells 15, Dave Mills 11, Malcolm Mackay 9, Jack Millen 7, Dennis Gavros 3, Phil Herne 2, Roger Wright 0).

Australasia win the series 2-1.

● *The England team managers were: Wally Mawdsley (Canterbury) and Joe Thurley (Workington and Hull).*

● *The Australasia team manager was Colin Tucker.*

1973 England v Sweden (Division Two) Results

Eastbourne, Sunday, September 30
ENGLAND 54 (Frank Auffret 13, John Davis 11, Bobby McNeil 10, Arthur Browning 7, Carl Glover 7, Paul Gachet 3, †Roger Johns 2, Dave Morton 1) **SWEDEN 53** (†Leif Enecrona 15, Kennet Selmosson 14, Tommy Nilsson 14, Sven Nilsson 5, Stefan Salomonsson 3, Peter Smith 2, Richard Hellsén 0, Karl-Erik Claesson 0).

Crewe, Monday, October 1
ENGLAND 77 (John Davis 16, †Dave Morton 15, Geoff Ambrose 13, John Jackson 12, Ray Bales 12, Mitch Graham 7, Graham Drury 2, Geoff Pusey, did not ride) **SWEDEN 31** (Tommy Nilsson 12, Richard Hellsén 4, Peter Smith 4, Karl-Erik Claesson 4, †Leif Enecrona 3, Sven Nilsson 2, Stefan Salomonsson 1, Kennet Selmosson 1).

Bradford, Wednesday, October 3
ENGLAND 73 (Carl Glover 16, Mitch Graham 14, Arthur Price 12, Tony Featherstone 12, †Dave Baugh 10, Roger Johns 9, Frank Auffret and Graham Drury, did not ride) **SWEDEN 35** (Richard Hellsén 11, †Leif Enecrona 6, Tommy Nilsson 6, Peter Smith 6, Stefan Salomonsson 4, Karl-Erik Claesson 1, Kennet Selmosson 1, Sven Nilsson 0).

Middlesbrough, Thursday, October 4
ENGLAND 62 (†Bruce Forrester 15, Arthur Price 15, Roger Johns 11, Frank Auffret 9, Carl Glover 6, Dave Baugh 4, Peter Reading 2, Dave Morton, did not ride) **SWEDEN 46** (†Leif Enecrona 16, Sven Nilsson 13, Kennet Selmosson 11, Peter Smith 3, Stefan Salomonsson 2, Karl-Erik Claesson 1, Richard Hellsén 0, Börje Klingberg 0).

Peterborough, Friday, October 5
ENGLAND 75 (†John Davis 18, Richard Greer 16, Graham Drury 14, Carl Glover 14, Arthur Price 9, Roger Johns 3, Arthur Browning 1, Brian Clark 0) **SWEDEN 33** (Peter Smith 10, †Leif Enecrona 6, Richard Hellsén 6, Stefan Salomonsson 6, Börje Klingberg 4, Kennet Selmosson 1, Karl-Erik Claesson 0, Sven Nilsson 0).

England win the series 5-0.

● *The England team managers were: Wally Mawdsley (Eastbourne), Ian Thomas (Crewe and Middlesbrough),Joe Thurley (Bradford) and Ron Wilson (Peterborough).*

● *The Sweden team manager was Kim Malmberg.*

1973 West Germany Tour of Division Two Results

Barrow, Tuesday, August 14
BARROW 38 (Sid Sheldrick 11, Tom Owen 11, †Mike Sampson 6, Joe Owen 5, Craig Pendlebury 3, Terry Kelly 2, Chris Roynon 0) **WEST GERMANY 40** (†Josef Angermüller 11, Christoph Betzl 11, Hans Siegl 9, Otto Barth 3, Hubert Kullman 3, Albert Strasser 3, Albert Stickl 0).

Berwick, Wednesday, August 15
BERWICK 38 (Willie Templeton 9, Andy Meldrum 8, Robert Hollingworth 7, Doug Templeton 5, Denny Morter 4, Graham Jones 3, Chris Quigley 2) **WEST GERMANY 40** (Hans Siegl 12, †Josef Angermüller 11, Christoph Betzl 7, Albert Strasser 5, Otto Barth 3, Albert Stickl 2, Hubert Kullman 0).

Stoke, Thursday, August 16
STOKE 42 (Alan Bridgett 10, †Mike Broadbank 10, Mick Handley 8, Nigel Wasley 6, Geoff Pusey 6, Brian Woodward 2, Martin Yeates 0) **WEST GERMANY 36** (Albert Strasser 9, Hans Siegl 8, Christoph Betzl 7, Otto Barth 5, †Josef Angermüller 5, Albert Stickl 2, Hubert Kullman 0).

● *The West German team manager was Ulrich Brehmer.*

"I wouldn't like to give impression tour was all trouble but it did get naughty"

THOSE were the words of Great Britain tour manager Reg Fearman within days of arriving back in England after one of the most successful tours of all time.

The Lions lost only once during a three-month stay in Australia and that was the sixth Test when they already held a 5-0 lead in the series.

But, once again, it was a visit that was enveloped by controversy, dubious refereeing decisions and a series of ugly protests, including a sit-in by irate Aussie fans!

The series began badly for the home nation with John Boulger declaring himself unavailable (he later rescinded that decision) and a two-point defeat at Perth where the tourists overcame an eight-point deficit after only two races to take the lead in heat 14 and maintain it for the remaining four races. The Lions raced into a 3-0 lead and there was even more gloom in the Aussie camp when long-serving international John Langfield announced his retirement from Test racing on the night the Aussies went down at Adelaide.

Boulger, who had undergone surgery for a cartilage injury, came back to top score at Sydney in the Fourth Test – where Great Britain made sure of the Ashes – but was ruled out again after twisting his damaged knee at Brisbane a week later.

Then Australia won their only Test in the stormiest scenes of all as the referee had to warn the two sides to cut out the rough stuff and the meeting was held up as police had to remove 200 protesters disputing a decision to exclude Jack White after a heat 17 crash with Eric Broadbelt. As the riders lined up for the re-run a fan jumped over the fence and aimed a blow at the Belle Vue rider who fell from his machine and, ironically, his bike then crashed down on the spectator and broke his leg!

1973-74 Great Britain Tour of Australia Results

Perth, Friday, November 23, 1973
AUSTRALIA 53 (†Bob O'Leary 15, Billy Sanders 11, Bob Valentine 9, Bob Humphreys 6, Les Leisk 6, Peter Thompson 5, Glyn Taylor 1) **GREAT BRITAIN 55** (Peter Collins 15, †Nigel Boocock 10, Reg Wilson 10, Jim McMillan 6, Eric Broadbelt 6, Doug Wyer 5, Geoge Hunter 3).

Perth, Friday, December 7, 1973
AUSTRALIA 33 (Billy Sanders 8, †Bob O'Leary 7, Chum Taylor 6, Les Leisk 4, Bob Humphreys 4, Phil Crump 3, Peter Thompson 1) **GREAT BRITAIN 75** (Jim McMillan 15, George Hunter 15, Reg Wilson 14, †Nigel Boocock 14, Peter Collins 12, Eric Broadbelt 4, Doug Wyer 1).

Adelaide, Saturday, December 15, 1973
AUSTRALIA 44 (Lou Sansom 13, Steve Reinke 12, Billy Sanders 7.5, †John Langfield 7.5, Phil Crump 2, Robin Amundson 1, Kym Amundson 1) **GREAT BRITAIN 64** (Peter Collins 15, Jim McMillan 13, George Hunter 11, †Nigel Boocock 10, Eric Broadbelt 6, Doug Wyer 5, Reg Wilson 4).

Sydney, Saturday, January 5, 1974
AUSTRALIA 50 (Steve Reinke 13, †John Boulger 11, Billy Sanders 11, Greg Kentwell 5, Ricky Day 5, Phil Herne 4, Bill Landels 1) **GREAT BRITAIN 58** (Reg Wilson 14, Peter Collins 12, George Hunter 10, Eric Broadbelt 9, Jim McMillan 6, †Nigel Boocock 5, Doug Wyer 2).

Brisbane, Saturday, January 12, 1974
AUSTRALIA 46 (Steve Reinke 11, John Titman 9, †John Boulger 8, Jack White 7, Kevin Torpie 6, Bryan Loakes 3, Billy Sanders 2) **GREAT BRITAIN 62** (Reg Wilson 17, Peter Collins 12, †Nigel Boocock 11, George Hunter 11, Eric Broadbelt 7, Doug Wyer 4, Jim McMillan 0).

Brisbane, Saturday, January 19, 1974
AUSTRALIA 60 (†Steve Reinke 15, John Titman 13, Jack White 10, Phil Crump 9, Kevin Torpie 8, Lou Sansom 3, Bryan Loakes 2) **GREAT BRITAIN 47** (Reg Wilson 14, †Nigel Boocock 9, Eric Broadbelt 9, Jim McMillan 6, Peter Collins 5, George Hunter 3, Doug Wyer 1).

Sydney, Saturday, January 26, 1974
AUSTRALIA 53 (†John Langfield 16, Billy Sanders 14, Ricky Day 11, Phil Herne 8, Greg Kentwell 2, Paul Johnstone 2, Robbie Blackadder 0) **GREAT BRITAIN 55** (Peter Collins 14, Reg Wilson 13, Eric Broadbelt 10, Doug Wyer 6, George Hunter 5, Jim McMillan 4, †Nigel Boocock 3).

<u>Great Britain win the series 6-1.</u>

Whyalla, Sunday, December 9, 1973
SOUTH AUSTRALIA 46 (Lou Sansom 14, Helmut Schippl 11, Robin Amundson 8, Kym Amundson 7, Dene Davies 4, Brenton Langlois 2) **GREAT BRITAIN 62** (Peter Collins 13, George Hunter 11, Jim McMillan 11, †Nigel Boocock 11, Doug Wyer 8, Reg Wilson 8, Eric Broadbelt, did not ride).
Liverpool
OLE OLSEN'S SEVEN 50 (†Ole Olsen 18, John Titman 11, Billy Sanders 10, Dave Mills 6, Steve Reinke 5, Bill Landels 0, Greg Kentwell 0) **GREAT BRITAIN 58** (Reg Wilson 15, Peter Collins 11, George Hunter 11, Jim McMillan 9, Eric Broadbelt 6, Doug Wyer 4, †Nigel Boocock 2).
Newcastle, Friday, January 4, 1974
AUSTRALIAN SELECT 31 (Bob Valentine 9, Billy Sanders 9, Greg Kentwell 4, Phil Herne 4, Brian Shields 3, Don Howison 1, Robbie Blackadder 1) **GREAT BRITAIN 77** (George Hunter 18, Eric Broadbelt 13, Peter Collins 12, †Nigel Boocock 12, Jim McMillan 11, Reg Wilson 11).
Newcastle, Sunday, Janury 27, 1974
JERILDERIE PARK SELECT 36 (Bob Valentine 10, John Langfield 10, Billy Sanders 8, Dave Mills 4, Phil Herne 3, Robbie Blackadder 1, Bill Landels 0) **GREAT BRITAIN 72** (Eric Broadbelt 15, Peter Collins 14, George Hunter 14, Jim McMillan 12, Reg Wilson 10, Doug Wyer 4, †Nigel Boocock 3).

● *The Great Britain team manager was Reg Fearman.*

1974 New Zealand v Rest of the World Results

Christchurch, Saturday, February 23
NEW ZEALAND 48 (Ivan Mauger 14, Barry Briggs 13, Ronnie Moore 11, Graeme Stapleton 7, Robin Adlington 2, Allan Brown 1, Roger Wright 0) **REST OF THE WORLD 59** (Edward Jancarz 16, Zenon Plech 12, Chris Pusey 12, Scott Autrey 9, Bert Harkins 7, Howard Cole 3, Richard May 0).

1974 Rest of the World v Great Britain Results

Auckland, Saturday, February 9
REST OF THE WORLD 53 (Jim Airey 15, John Titman 12, John Boulger 8, Steve Reinke 7, Mike Hiftle 6, Antonin Woryna 3, Mike Fullerton 2) **GREAT BRITAIN 55** (Peter Collins 17, Jim McMillan 13, Eric Broadbelt 11, †Nigel Boocock 7, George Hunter 4, Reg Wilson 2, Doug Wyer 1).

1974 U.S.A. v Rest of the World Results

Costa Mesa, Friday, March 15
UNITED STATES OF AMERICA 53 (Billy Cody 16, Mike Bast 12, Steve Bast 8, Scott Autrey 6, Sonny Nutter 6, Mike Curoso 3, Danny Becker 1) **REST OF THE WORLD 55** (Ivan Mauger 15, Barry Briggs 15, Zenon Plech 11, Chris Pusey 6, Bert Harkins 5, Edward Jancarz 3).

Costa Mesa, Saturday, March 16,
UNITED STATES OF AMERICA 59 (Mike Bast 15, Bioll Cody 13, Steve Bast 10, Danny Becker 9, Sonny Nutter 6, Mike Curoso 4, Scott Autrey 2) **REST OF THE WORLD 49** (Ivan Mauger 14, Barry Briggs 13, Zenon Plech 10, Bert Harkins 6, Edwards Jancarz 2, Martin Ashby 2, Chris Pusey 2).

Costa Mesa, Sunday, March 17
UNITED STATES OF AMERICA 52 (Mike Bast 11, Mike Curoso 11, Bill Cody 9, Steve Bast 9, Scott Autrey 6, Sonny Nutter 5, Danny Becker 1) **REST OF THE WORLD 56** (Ivan Mauger 15, Chris Pusey 12, Barry Briggs 11, Bert Harkins 9, Zenon Plech 6, Martin Ashby 3).

WILLIE'S WONDERS

TEAM-MATE John Louis summed up the worth of Ray Wilson: "The work he has done for England cannot be faulted in any way, both as a rider and as a captain."

"I would liken him to Ray Illingworth, the former England cricket captain, who was so good at leading his side that he was selected even when he wasn't in the best of form himself. That has been the case with Ray this season. He struggled in the early part of the year, had to overcome niggling injuries and mechanical worries and this had, as it would have done any rider, an unsettling effect on his confidence.

"Even so his contribution to England's efforts have been as important as ever before, perhaps not in terms of points scored out on the track, but certainly in the way he carried out his responsibilities as team captain.

"Skippering a team may appear to most people to be merely a question of tossing up at the start and choosing gate positions. That may have been true years ago but not now, and one of the men who has changed all that is Ray Wilson.

"He takes it upon himself to get the team keyed up and organised before the start of the meeting, fully informed as to what is required of them once the racing gets under way, and is always available for help and advice."

That was a glowing tribute from a colleague who was also a World Championship rival and there is no doubt that the combination of skipper Willie and manager Len Silver led England through a golden era.

Just look at their 1974 international record. Played 17. Won 17. And that apart from achievements elsewhere in the World Team Cup.

The Test summer began against Sweden at King's Lynn on Saturday, June 15, three days after Eric Boocock, overlooked for the international so he could lead his club side Halifax against Hull, won the British Final. But the biggest shock at Brandon had been the elimination of the England captain who must have arrived at the Test feeling as low as any rider with World title aspirations could have been.

But Willie rallied his troops and despite a one-man super show from Sören Sjösten, England totally dominated. And that was the story in all the remaining internationals that summer.

Sjösten was a one-man band and one dreads to think what the scorelines might have been without him. He got 71 points in five matches and his nearest challenger in the score-charts was Tommy Jansson with 30!

The Swedes dismissed, the Poles were the next lambs to the slaughter.

Any hopes of a competitive series were destroyed by the chatter of the teleprinters as the Press Association tapped out the result of the opening international: ENGLAND 88 POLAND 19.

They were spared the embarrassment of a total whitewash in the penultimate race when referee Graham Brodie, quite rightly, excluded Wilson after a first bend fall!

That score remains the most one-sided international in history and England only twice failed to reach 70 points in the seven encounters.

At Exeter the calculating brain of the captain was working overtime and he ensured that he grabbed the pits place normally occupied by Falcons' skipper Ivan Mauger in another example of his willingness to look beyond the norm in his quest to make England the world's top speedway nation.

Edward Jancarz and Zenon Plech tried manfully to stem the red and white tide but they had precious little back up and it was with some relief that Peter Collins took the chequered flag at Leicester to end a totally one-sided series.

Could the Russians do any better? We would soon find out the answer as within a day of the Poles heading back behind the Iron Curtain the

WHITEWASH WILLIE...Ray Wilson led England to 13 successive Test wins in 1974

1974 England v Sweden Results

King's Lynn, Saturday, June 15
ENGLAND 71 (Dave Jessup 15, Terry Betts 15, Bob Kilby 13, †Ray Wilson 10, Malcolm Simmons 10, Tony Davey 4, Richard Greer 3, Kevin Holden 1) **SWEDEN 37** (†Sören Sjösten 17, Bengt Jansson 9, Olle Nygren 5, Tommy Jansson 4, Tommy Nilsson 2, Sören Karlsson 0, Thomas Petterson 0, Kennet Selmosson 0).

Poole, Wednesday, June 19
ENGLAND 66 (Terry Betts 13, John Louis 13, Dave Jessup 13, Peter Collins 10, †Ray Wilson 10, Malcolm Simmons 7, Martin Ashby 0, Pete Smith 0) **SWEDEN 42** (†Sören Sjösten 16, Tommy Jansson 11, Bengt Jansson 5, Tommy Nilsson 4, Olle Nygren 3, Kennet Selmosson 2, Sören Karlsson 1, Thomas Pettersson, did not ride).

Sheffield, Thursday, June 20
ENGLAND 83 (Peter Collins 18, Terry Betts 17, Doug Wyer 14, Reg Wilson 13, Chris Pusey 12, Martin Ashby 9) **SWEDEN 25** (†Sören Sjösten 10, Tommy Jansson 5, Bengt Jansson 5, Tommy Nilsson 2, Thomas Pettersson 2, Kennet Selmosson 1, Sören Karlsson 0, Olle Nygren 0).

Hackney, Friday, June 21
ENGLAND 73 (Dave Jessup 15, John Louis 15, Chris Pusey 14, Peter Collins 14, Barry Thomas 9, †Ray Wilson 6) **SWEDEN 35** (†Sören Sjösten 15, Thomas Pettersson 6, Bengt Jansson 5, Tommy Jansson 5, Tommy Nilsson 3, Kennet Selmosson 1, Sören Karlsson 0, Olle Nygren 0).

Coventry, Saturday, June 22
ENGLAND 71 (John Louis 15, Dave Jessup 15, Doug Wyer 15, †Ray Wilson 12, Reg Wilson 7, Nigel Boocock 5, Tony Davey 2, Barry Thomas, did not ride) **SWEDEN 37** (†Sören Sjösten 13, Tommy Nilsson 8, Tommy Jansson 5, Thomas Pettersson 4, Sören Karlsson 4, Olle Nygren 2, Bengt Jansson 1, Kennet Selmosson, did not ride)

England win the series 5-0.

- *The England team manager was Len Silver.*
- *The Sweden team manager was Christer Bergström.*

Russians were racing at Swindon.

Len Silver took the opportunity to rest some of his first-string stars and to bring in a host of new faces while the Russians tracked both Valeri and Vladimir Gordeev, thus destroying the growing myth that they were, in fact, one and the same rider!

They put paid to that mistaken belief as early as the opening race at Blunsdon when they came out wearing the white and yellow helmet colours!

Chris Pusey (severe bruising) and Anatoli Kuzmin (broken leg) were rushed to hospital after separate spills at Wolverhampton and, for six mud-splattered heats it did look as though England might lose that unbeaten tag at Newport's Somerton Park.

The Russians led from an opening heat 4-2 and had provided all six heat winners when continous rain made it impossible to continue.

Maybe, on this one occasion, the Rain Gods were on England's side as it saved the Lions from what looked almost certain defeat.

There was one other major attraction throughout the seven match series – the fifth Test at Oxford was scrubbed without a race being run.

At Wimbledon fans were entertained to an extra treat as Ronnie Moore and Barry Briggs were given a thunderous reception as they went out for a best-of-three match race series.

And that was the only time all summer that England were upstaged!

There had been plans for a return visit to Poland – Terry Betts, Peter Collins, Dave Jessup, John Louis, Chris Pusey, Malcolm Simmons, Ray Wilson and Reg Wilson actually applied for visas – but the the trip was called off by the Poles, because of a date clash.

1974 England v Poland Results

Hackney, Friday, July 12
ENGLAND 88 (John Louis 18, Peter Collins 16, Barry Thomas 15, Dave Jessup 14, †Ray Wilson 13, Terry Betts 12, Martin Ashby and Tony Davey, did not ride) **POLAND 19** (†Edward Jancarz 6, Henryk Glucklich 4, Jan Mucha 4, Zenon Plech 3, Ryszard Fabiszewski 2, Zbigniew Filipiak 0, Pawel Waloszek 0).

King's Lynn, Sunday, July 14
ENGLAND 78 (†Ray Wilson 16, Terry Betts 15, John Louis 14, Malcolm Simmons 13, Chris Pusey 11, Dave Jessup 9, Martin Ashby and Barry Thomas, did not ride) **POLAND 30** (†Edward Jancarz 11, Ryszard Fabiszewski 8, Zenon Plech 5, Henryk Glucklich 3, Pawel Waloszek 2, Jan Mucha 1, Zbigniew Filipiak, did not ride).

Exeter, Monday, July 15
ENGLAND 73 (Malcolm Simmons 16, Peter Collins 14, Terry Betts 14, Dave Jessup 11, Kevin Holden 6, John Louis 5, Tony Lomas 4, †Ray Wilson 3) **POLAND 35** (Ryszard Fabiszewski 13, Zenon Plech 11, †Edward Jancarz 10, Henryk Glucklich 1, Zbigniew Filipiak 0, Jan Mucha 0, Pawel Waloszek 0).

Hull, Wednesday, July 17
ENGLAND 69 (Martin Ashby 18, Malcolm Simmons 13, Dave Jessup 12, Terry Betts 10, Tony Davey 8, †Ray Wilson 8) **POLAND 39** (Zenon Plech 13, †Edward Jancarz 9, Jan Mucha 6, Ryszard Fabiszewski 5, Henryk Glucklich 3, Pawel Waloszek 3, Zbigniew Filipiak 0).

Ipswich, Thursday, July 18
ENGLAND 78 (John Louis 18, Dave Jessup 18, †Ray Wilson 13, Malcolm Simmons 12, Terry Betts 9, Peter Collins 4, Tony Davey 4, Barry Thomas, did not ride) **POLAND 30** (Zenon Plech 9, †Edward Jancarz 8, Jan Mucha 7, Henryk Glucklich 5, Ryszard Fabiszewski 1, Pawel Waloszek 0).

Halifax, Saturday, July 20
ENGLAND 65 (Reg Wilson 16, Doug Wyer 14, †Ray Wilson 13, John Louis 10, Dave Jessup 7, Barry Thomas 3, Graham Plant 2) **POLAND 42** (†Edward Jancarz 16, Jan Mucha 10, Zenon Plech 8, Ryszard Fabiszewski 4, Pawel Waloszek 2, Henrik Glucklich 2).

Leicester, Tuesday, July 23
ENGLAND 76 (Peter Collins 15, Malcolm Simmons 14, †Ray Wilson 13, Terry Betts 13, John Louis 12, Dave Jessup 9) **POLAND 32** (Zenon Plech 14, †Edward Jancarz 11, Jan Mucha 4, Ryszard Fabiszewski 2, Pawel Waloszek 1, Henrik Glucklich 0).

England win the series 7-0.

- *The England team manager was Len Silver.*
- *The Poland team manager was Ryszard Szymanski.*

1974 England v Soviet Union Results

Swindon, Saturday, July 27
ENGLAND 66 (†Martin Ashby 17, Tony Davey 16, Dave Jessup 16, John Louis 6, Barry Thomas 5, Frank Auffret 4, Bob Coles 2, Tom Leadbitter 0) **SOVIET UNION 42** (Vladimir Gordeev 13, Grigori Khlinovsky 11, Anatoli Kuzmin 10, Nikolai Kornev 5, Vladimir Nesterov 3, Valeri Gordeev 0).

Wolverhampton, Sunday, July 28
ENGLAND 61 (Kevin Holden 15, Peter Collins 10, †Ray Wilson 9, Chris Pusey 9, Alan Wilkinson 7, Richard Greer 6, Terry Betts 3, Tom Leadbitter 2) **SOVIET UNION 47** (Grigori Khlinovsky 14, Valeri Gordeev 12, Anatoli Kuzmin 10, Viktor Kuznetsov 5, Vladimir Gordeev 3, Sergei Douzhenko 3, Nikolai Kornev 0).

Wimbledon, Thursday, August 1
ENGLAND 71 (Barry Thomas 16, Trevor Hedge 15, †Martin Ashby 12, Kevin Holden 10, Eric Broadbelt 8, Roger Johns 5, Malcolm Simmons 3, Laurie Etheridge 2) **SOVIET UNION 37** (Grigori Khlinovsky 10, Vladimir Gordeev 9, Valeri Gordeev 8, Nikolai Kornev 5, Vladimir Nesterov 2, Viktor Kuznetsov 2, Sergei Douzhenko 1).

Cradley Heath, Saturday, August 3
ENGLAND 65 (†Barry Thomas 14, Tony Davey 13, Eric Broadbelt 12, Howard Cole 10, Kevin Holden 9, Richard Greer 5, Arthur Price 2, Frank Auffret, did not ride) **SOVIET UNION 43** (Valeri Gordeev 10, Vladimir Gordeev 10, Grigori Khlinovsky 10, Nikolai Kornev 5, Vladimir Nesterov 4, Sergei Douzhenko 2, Viktor Trofimov 2).

Oxford, Sunday, August 4
ENGLAND v SOVIET UNION, cancelled, waterlogged track.

Belle Vue, Wednesday, August 7
ENGLAND 75 (Peter Collins 18, Chris Pusey 15, Richard Greer 12, †Ray Wilson 11, Doug Wyer 9, Reg Wilson 8, Paul Tyrer 2, Alan Wilkinson, did not ride) **SOVIET UNION 33** (Grigori Khlinovsky 14, Vladimir Gordeev 8, Valeri Gordeev 6, Nikolai Kornev 3, Vladimir Nesterov 1, Sergei Douzhenko 1, Viktor Kuznetsov 0).

Newport, Friday, August 9
***ENGLAND 17** (†John Louis 4, Doug Wyer 4, Dave Jessup 3, Chris Pusey 3, Terry Betts 2, Kevin Holden 1, Bob Coles and Frank Auffret, did not ride) **SOVIET UNION 19** (Grigori Khlinovsky 6, Valeri Gordeev 6, Nikolai Kornev 4, Vladimir Gordeev 3, Vladimir Nesterov 0, Viktor Kuznetsov 0, Sergei Douzhenko 0).*
Meeting abandoned after six heats, track waterlogged.

England win the series 5-0 with one Test cancelled.

- *The England team manager was Len Silver.*
- *The Soviet Union manager was Nikolai Konstantinovich.*

Bruce kicks over traces of old career

BRUCE FORRESTER always wanted to be an international....

But he and his family thought it was more likely to be at soccer than speedway as he played alongside England defender-to-be Jack Charlton in Leeds United's A team.

Eventually a series of knee injuries forced him to hang up his kicking boots. After a career of grass track racing, he turned to speedway in 1968.

Within three years he had made his international debut – against Czechoslovakia – and when Joe Thurley began to look around for someone to skipper the England squad in 1974 he opted for the Teesside leader who was appointed his country's captain at the ripe old age of 33!

He admitted: "I wish I'd started when I was 15 or 16 instead of when I was 28. But football was the only thing I thought about and I trained four nights a week and had no time for anything else."

Forrester justified his surprise selection as captain by leading England to an early season series win against Czechoslovakia and another, later in the year, when Poland were the opposition.

He was certainly the hero of the hour in the second Test at Eastbourne where he was beaten only once, by Petr Ondrasik, as England took advantage of the absence of World Ice Speedway Champion Milan Spinka who was racing in a Long Track event in Germany which forced him to miss the two opening matches, both of which England won.

He arrived in time for the third match at Barrow's Holker Street, scored 11 poinst and helped the Czechs to draw!

And he could easily have led the Eastern Europeans to their first win at Bradford the following night until Thurley introduced reserve Sid Sheldrick at heat 12. He won that and two subsequent heats to put England 2-1 up!

Another reserve, Mike Lanham, was the match-winner at Peterborough while at Workington skipper Forrester grabbed the two points England needed to clinch victory in the last race after Bradford hero Sheldrick (another with a soccer background having been on Sheffield United's books as a goalkeeper!) had fallen.

The Czechs went home with a consolation victory at Birmingham after John Jackson had been forced out with a finger injury in his second ride.

Poland began with an astonishing win at Peterborough even though Carl Glover broke the track recorded and they finished the last eight heats sharing just three working machines and followed that up with a second success at Workington in a hair-raising scrap of bloody proportions with three riders being taken to hospital!

The series was level after four Tests and as injuries took their toll Poland finished the fifth set-to at Barrow with only five fit riders but managed to patch everyone up for the last match at Canterbury.

They didn't win but they certainly left some heart-stopping memories!

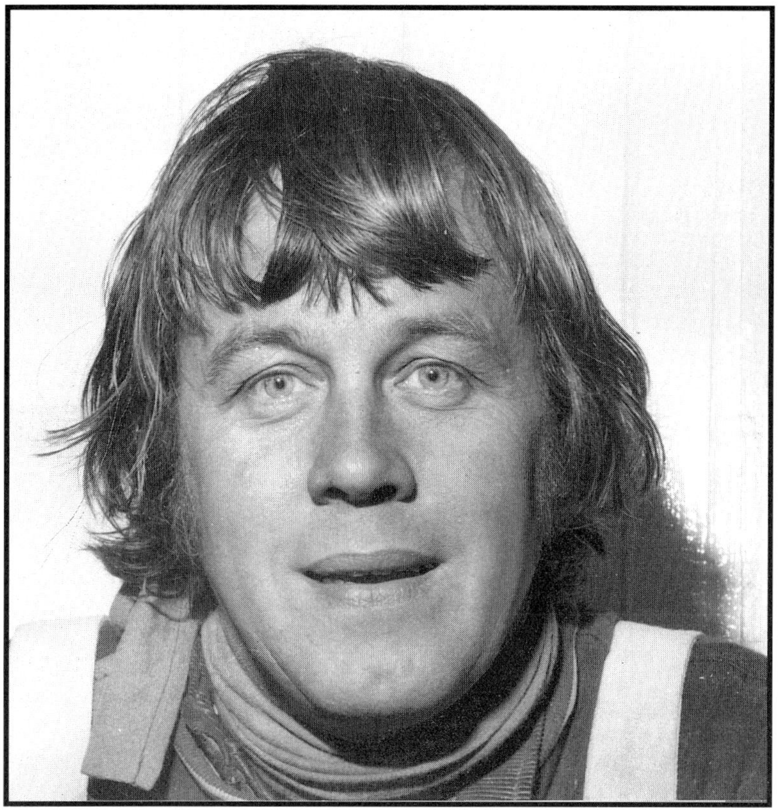

BY GOLLY...Olle Nygren was a surprise late guest for Kaparna on their Division Two tour

1974 England v Czechoslovakia (Division Two) Results

Canterbury, Saturday April 13
ENGLAND 63 (Bobby McNeil 14, Carl Glover 13, Graham Drury 10, †Bruce Forrester 9, Mike Sampson 8, Trevor Jones 5, Ted Hubbard 4, Brian Foote, did not ride) **CZECHOSLOVAKIA 45** (Jiri Stancl 12, Jan Verner 10, Petr Ondrasik 9, Vaclav Verner 7, Emil Sova 6, Zdenek Kudrna 1, Jindrich Dominic 0).

Eastbourne, Sunday, April 14
ENGLAND 72 (†Bruce Forrester 17, Mike Sampson 16, Bobby McNeil 14, John Jackson 9, Carl Glover 8, Arthur Browning 8) **CZECHOSLOVAKIA 36** (Jiri Stancl 14, Petr Ondrasik 13, Vaclav Verner 8, Jindrich Dominic 1, Jan Verner 0, Emil Sova 0, Zdenek Kudrna 0).

Barrow, Tuesday, April 16
ENGLAND 54 (†Bruce Forrester 15, Mike Sampson 12, Carl Glover 11, Graham Drury 6, Sid Sheldrick 6, Arthur Browning 3, Tom Owen 1, Mitch Graham 0) **CZECHOSLOVAKIA 54** (Vaclav Verner 15, Milan Spinka 11, Jiri Stancl 9, Petr Ondrasik 9, Jan Verner 5, Jindrich Dominic 3, Emil Sova 2).

Bradford, Wednesday, April 17
ENGLAND 58 (Carl Glover 16, †Bruce Forrester 15, Sid Sheldrick 9, Tom Owen 9, Tony Featherstone 6, John Jackson 2, Colin Meredith 1, Mitch Graham 0) **CZECHOSLOVAKIA 50** (Petr Ondrasik 12, Vaclav Verner 12, Jan Verner 10, Jiri Stancl 8, Milan Spinka 7, Jindrich Dominic 1, Emil Sova 0, Zdenek Kudrna, did not ride).

Peterborough, Friday, April 19
ENGLAND 57 (Brian Clark 11, Carl Glover 11, †Bruce Forrester 9, Bobby McNeil 9, Mike Sampson 9, Mike Lanham 6, Graham Drury 2) **CZECHOSLOVAKIA 51** (Jiri Stancl 13, Milan Spinka 11, Vaclav Verner 11, Petr Ondrasik 9, Jan Verner 7, Jindrich Dominic 0, Zdenek Kudrna 0, Emil Sova 0).

Workington, Sunday, April 21
ENGLAND 55 (Mitch Graham 14, Carl Glover 11, †Bruce Forrester 7, John Jackson 7, Graham Drury 6, Dave Morton 5, Sid Sheldrick 4, Tom Owen 1) **CZECHOSLOVAKIA 53** (Vaclav Verner 12, Milan Spinka 11, Petr Ondsrasik 10, Jan Verner 9, Jiri Stancl 7, Emil Sova 4, Zdenek Kudrna 0, Jindrich Dominic, did not ride).

Birmingham, Monday, April 22
ENGLAND 52 (Arthur Browning 12, †Bruce Forrester 12, Keith White 8, Mike Lanham 8, Brian Woodward 6, Paul Gachet 4, John Jackson 2) **CZECHOSLOVAKIA 56** (Milan Spinka 17, Jiri Stancl 16, Vaclav Verner 13, Petr Ondrasik 8, Emil Sova 1, Jindrich Dominic 1, Jan Verner 0, Zdenek Kudrna, did not ride).

England win the series 5-1, with one Test drawn.

- *The England team manager was Joe Thurley.*
- *The Czechoslovakia team manager was Rudolf Jaros.*

1974 England v Scotland (Division Two) Results

Sunderland, Sunday, June 9
ENGLAND 57 (Bruce Forrester 12, Geoff Bouchard 12, Tony Featherstone 12, Brian Havelock 10, Graham Drury 6, Russ Dent 4, John Robson 1, Vic Harding 0) **SCOTLAND 50** (Jim Gallacher 16, Ken McKinlay 12, Doug Templeton 9, John Wilson 8, Andy Meldrum 3, Ian Wilson 2, Willie Templeton 0, Wattie Robertson 0).

Berwick, Saturday, July 27
ENGLAND 64 (Mitch Graham 18, Tom Owen 16, Graham Jones 10, Bruce Forrester 9, Denny Morter 7, Brian Havelock 3, Dave Trownson 1, Vic Harding 0) **SCOTLAND 44** (Andy Meldrum 11, Brian Collins 11, Willie Templeton 9, Jim Gallacher 7, John Wilson 2, Ken McKinlay 2, Wattie Robertson 2, Ian Wilson 0).

1974 Kaparna (Sweden) Club Tour of Division Two Results

GLOUCESTERSHIRE pig farmer Roger Jones, a former mechanic to five-time World Champion Ove Fundin, took charge of the touring Gothenburg club side Kaparna on an early season visit to England.

The team, which raced its home matches at the seaport's Ullevi Stadium, was headed by the veteran Bengt Brannefors but ran into all sorts of troubles before recuiting a series of guests to bolster their squad.

Stand-ins include Eastbourne's Trevor Geer and young Danish prospect Finn Thomsen while veteran Olle Nygren also helped out in the later stages of their visit.

Berwick, Saturday, April 6
BERWICK 49 (Denny Morter 11, †Doug Templeton 9, Graham Jones 8, Willie Templeton 8, Ian Wilson 5, Robin Dixon 4, Colin Farquharson 4) **KAPARNA 29** (Kennet Selmosson 11, Roy Dantanus 6, Stefan Hjort 6, Sören Karlsson 3, Tommy Strauss 2, Svante Sand 1, †Bengt Brannefors 0).

Scunthorpe, Monday, April 8
SCUNTHORPE 41 (†Ken McKinlay 12, Jack Bywater 9, Rex Garrod 6, Doug Underwood 6, Dingle Brown 5, Roger Pascall 3, Peter Wrathall 0) **KAPARNA 37** (Sören Karlsson 9, Stefan Hjort 9, Roy Dantanus 7, Kennet Selmosson 6, †Bengt Brannefors 4, Tommy Strauss 2, Svante Sand 0).

Ellesmere Port, Tuesday, April 9
ELLESMERE PORT 43 (†Graham Drury 11, Colin Goad 10, Steve Taylor 8, Wayne Hughes 6, Duncan Meredith 5, Gerald Smitherman 3, Steve Casey 0) **KAPARNA 35** (Kennet Selmosson 12, Roy Dantanus 9, Stefan Hjort 7, Sören Karlsson 6, Svante Sand 1, Tommy Strauss 0, †Bengt Brannefors 0).

Long Eaton, Friday, April 12
LONG EATON 37 (†Geoff Bouchard 13, Alan Molyneux 8, Dave Harvey 6, James Bond 5, Pip Austen 3, Alan Witt 1, Dave Patten 1) **KAPARNA 41** (Kennet Selmosson 14, Stefan Hjort 12, †Sören Karlsso 10, *Trevor Geer 4,* Tommy Strauss 1, Svante Sand 0).
Original staging on Thursday, April 11, postponed, waterlogged track.

Boston, Sunday, April 14
BOSTON 43 (Jim Ryman 9, David Piddock 8, Robert Hollingworth 7, David Gagen 7, Russ Osborne 5, Jack Millen 4, Rob Mouncer 3) **KAPARNA 35** (Sören Sjösten 11, †Olle Nygren 11, Sören Karlsson 7, Stefan Hjort 5, Tommy Strauss 1, Svante Sand 0, †Bengt Brannefors 0).

Weymouth, Tuesday, April 16
WEYMOUTH 43 (Geoff Swindells 9, Kelvin Mullarkey 9, Nigel Couzens 9, Clark Facey 7, †Bob Hughes 5, Russell Foote 3, Steve Lomas 1) **KAPARNA 35** (†Olle Nygren 11, Sören Karlsson 10, *Finn Thomsen 7,* Stefan Hjort 6, Tommy Strauss 1, Kennet Selmosson 0, Svante Sand 0).

Stoke, Thursday, April 18
STOKE 36 (†Mike Broadbank 12, Brian Woodward 10, Geoff Pusey 7, Alan Bridgett 6, Steve Holden 1, Roger Parker 0, Barry Duke 0) **KAPARNA 42** (Kennet Selmosson 10, †Olle Nygren 9, *Finn Thomsen 8,* Sören Karlsson 6, Stefan Hjort 4, Tommy Strauss 3, Svante Sand 2).

- *The Kaparna team manager was Roger Jones.*

1974 England v Poland (Division Two) Results

Peterborough, Friday, July 5
ENGLAND 48 (Carl Glover 12, Trevor Jones 12, Brian Clark 9, Bobby McNeil 8, Geoff Bouchard 4, †Bruce Forrester 2, Mike Lanham 1, Graham Drury 0) **POLAND 60** (Franciszek Stach 15, Boguslaw Nowak 11, Marek Cieslak 10, Jerzy Rembas 9, Mieczyslaw Wozniak 8, Jacek Goerlitz 6, Zenon Urbaniec 1, Gerard Stach 0).

Workington, Sunday, July 7
ENGLAND 53 (Carl Glover 14, Sid Sheldrick 8, Bobby McNeil 8, Brian Clark 7, †Bruce Forrester 7, Tom Owen 7, Mitch Graham 2, Steve Watson 0) **POLAND 54** (Marek Cieslak 17, Boguslaw Nowak 14, Franciszek Stach 10, Jerzy Rembas 8, Mieczyslaw Wozniak 3, Jacek Goerlitz 1, Zenon Urbaniec 1).

Crewe, Monday, July 8
ENGLAND 74 (Dave Morton 13, Graham Drury 12, Carl Glover 12, John Jackson 11, Mitch Graham 11, Keith White 10, †Bruce Forrester 4, Geoff Pusey 1) **POLAND 34** (Marek Cieslak 11, Boguslaw Nowak 11, Franciszek Stach 7, Jerzy Rembas 3, Mieczyslaw Wozniak 1, Jacek Goerlitz 1, Gerard Stach, did not ride).

Middlesbrough, Thursday, July 11
ENGLAND 66 (Carl Glover 15, Arthur Browning 14, †Bruce Forrester 11, Bobby McNeil 10, Dave Durham 9, Graham Drury 7) **POLAND 42** (Marek Cieslak 13, Jerzy Rembas 11, Franciszek Stach 7, Boguslaw Nowak 4, Mieczyslaw Wozniak 4, Jacek Goerlitz 2, Gerard Stach 1).

Birmingham, Monday, July 15
ENGLAND 61 (Arthur Browning 15, Carl Glover 11, †Bruce Forrester 9, Graham Drury 8, Bobby McNeil 7, David Gagen 5, Geoff Bouchard 4, Colin Meredith 2) **POLAND 47** (Marek Cieslak 15, Jerzy Rembas 13, Boguslaw Nowak 9, Mieczyslaw Wozniak 5, Jacek Goerlitz 4, Franciszek Stach 1).

Barrow, Tuesday, July 16
ENGLAND 61 (Carl Glover 15, Tom Owen 12, Joe Owen 9, Graham Drury 8, Sid Sheldrick 7, †Bruce Forrester 5, Arthur Browning 4, Colin Meredith 1) **POLAND 46** (Marek Cieslak 15, Jerzy Rembas 11, Jacek Goerlitz 11, Gerard Stach 5, Mieczyslaw Wozniak 4, Boguslaw Nowak 0).

Canterbury, Saturday, July 20
ENGLAND 57 (Carl Glover 13, Bobby McNeil 11, †Bruce Forrester 10, Trevor Geer 9, Dave Gooderham 7, Mike Lanham 3, Brian Clark 2, Neil Middleditch 2) **POLAND 50** (Jerzy Rembas 14, Marek Cieslak 11, Mieczyslaw Wozniak 9, Boguslaw Nowak 8, Franciszek Stach 4, Jacek Goerlitz 4, Gerard Stach 0).

England win the series 5-2.

CLUB MATCH
Eastbourne, Sunday, July 21
EASTBOURNE 58 (Paul Gachet 15, Trevor Geer 10, †Peter Jarman 9, Neil Middleditch 7, Bobby McNeil 7, Martin Yeates 6, Steve Weatherley 4, Alan Johns 0) **POLAND 50** (Jerzy Rembas 16, Marek Cieslak 15, Boguslaw Nowak 7, Gerard Stach 6, Jacek Goerlitz 4, Mieczyslaw Wozniak 2).

- *The England team manager was Joe Thurley.*
- *The Poland team manager was Jozef Olejeczak.*

1974 England v Australasia (Division Two) Results

AUSTRALASIA should have been buried without trace as they had to take on England without three of their big-scoring stars.

Jack Millen, Phil Herne and Malcolm Mackay were all missing but the BSPA gave special dispensation to allow First Division Bob Humphreys (and later Bruce Cribb) to be included in the Anzacs squad.

Humphreys wasted no time at all in stamping his mark on the series by beating home star Tom Owen in the opening race at Barrow to help his side to a surprise win.

England hit back at Middlesbrough and then the series went to a race off at Boston where Carl Glover defeated Boston team-mate Jim Ryman after the two teams had finished level in the final Test.

Barrow, Tuesday, September 10
ENGLAND 53 (†Bruce Forrester 13, Carl Glover 12, Tom Owen 11, Joe Owen 8, Mike Sampson 4, Russ Hodgson 4, Colin Goad 1) **AUSTRALASIA 55** (Bob Humphreys 14, Robin Adlington 13, Dave Gifford 10, Jim Wells 7, †Jim Ryman 6, Phil Bass 3, Roger Wright 2).

Middlesbrough, Thursday, September 12
ENGLAND 61 (Dave Durham 16, Carl Glover 11, Arthur Browning 9, Graham Drury 8, Trevor Geer 7, Brian Havelock 7, Mitch Graham 3, †Bruce Forrester 0) **AUSTRALASIA 45** (Bruce Cribb 12, Roger Wright 10, Dave Gifford 10, Bob Humphreys 6, †Jim Ryman 4, Merv Salt 3, Jim Wells 0, Robin Adlington 0).

Boston, Sunday, September 15
ENGLAND 54 (Carl Glover 16, †Bruce Forrester 12, Arthur Browning 12, David Gagen 9, Tony Featherstone 3, Mike Lanham 2, Brian Clark 0, Graham Drury 0) **AUSTRALASIA 54** (†Jim Ryman 16, Bob Humphreys 11, Phil Bass 9, Bruce Cribb 8, Doug Underwood 6, Dave Gifford 3, Jim Wells 1, Ricky Day 0).

Carl Glover (England) defeated Jim Ryman (Australasia) in a race-off to decide the series.

England win the series in a race-off after a 1-1 draw with one Test drawn.

- *The England team manager was Joe Thurley.*
- *The Australasia team manager was Dennis Gavros.*

1975 U.S.A. v Rest of the World

THE first-ever officially sanctioned indoor international – in the splendour of the Houston Astrodome – ended in a comfortable win for a strong Rest of the World squad that included four former World Champions (Ivan Mauger, Barry Briggs, Ole Olsen and Anders Michanek) and heir-apparent Peter Collins.

Houston Astrodome, Sunday, February 2
UNITED STATES OF AMERICA 44 (Mike Bast 12, Jeff Sexton 11, Sonny Nutter 8, Bill Cody 6, Rick Woods 5, Scott Sivadge 2) **REST OF THE WORLD 64** (Ivan Mauger 17, Anders Michanek 12, Barry Briggs 11, Ole Olsen 8, Peter Collins 8, Ray Wilson 8, Terry Betts, did not ride).

WALLABIED!

TOUR manager Wally Mawdsley called for an emergency meeting with the Australian Speedway Control Council after an opening Test defeat at Brisbane Exhibition Grounds

He later explained: "The starts were dreadful and the referee didn't seem to care what happened going into the first bend. There was no such thing as first bend bunching as far as he was concerned. I asked for the meeting to try and lay down the guidelines for the rest of the series."

It would appear that the hard-line approach by Mawdsley reaped immediate dividends as he and his squad were far happier with what went on in the second Test at Brisbane the following Saturday night as the Lions levelled the series on the 402 metre track where Eric Broadbelt made up for his disappointing first Test with a double figure return against an Aussie side led by the out-of-sorts Steve Reinke who returned his lowest-ever Test score on his own home circuit.

Australia regained the Ashes with a third-in-a-row win at new Test venue Liverpool – a suburb of Sydney – which prompted Mawdsley to advocate the introduction of two linesmen at the fenceless track so that they could watch for riders going outside the non-existent fence.

He insisted that both Phil Crump and John Titman used an outside and illegal line without falling foul of the meeting steward who wasn't perched in a box above the track but conducted the entire meeting from the centre green!

Phil Crump had destroyed Great Britain's chance of holding onto the Ashes in the space of seven days over the Christmas holiday. He had scored successive 18 point maximums in wins at Newcastle and Sydney Showground and weighed in with another 14 at Liverpool in the first official international at the smart 310 metre circuit. With the series dead the Lions still hoped to make it a respectable looking scoreline but ran into another example of Australian inefficiency, even at the highest level.

At Adelaide all races were started by an elastic band and the Test match was interspersed with the more traditional bill of fare so after each three heats there were two other events.

The worst example of all was between heats 12 and 13 when riders not only had to endure an interval but also a four-lap Reubens Outdoor Centre Sidecar Handicap and the 4-lap Topline Paint Solo Handicap!

Even had they kept strictly to schedule then there would have still been a 25 minute gap between the end of heat 12 and the next Test heat!

The final Test brought a second win for the Lions, a best-ever international performance from Chris Morton which capped a splendid weekend for the family as elder brother Dave, racing in Auckland, became the New Zealand Champion.

That 14-point haul by Morton, who had been a doubt for the tour because of a late season shoulder injury which cut short his 1974 campaign, increased the pressures on Mawdsley who came under fire from afar for keeping Morton at reserve and his own Exeter rider Kevin Holden in the main body of the side for most of the tour.

But Mawdsley defended his decision: "Unlike the British international match formula only one reserve is available to each team in Australian Ashes fixtures. It's essential that that one reserve is a very strong rider capable of coming into any match at any time to replace any rider and Chris was capable of doing just that. In fact, he had 30 starts to Kevin's 19!"

While the tour ended disappointingly on the results front it was one of the best organised with, for the first time, riders staying together as a touring party in motels rather than seeking their own accommodation with old friends.

1974-75 Great Britain Tour of Australia Results

Brisbane, Saturday, November 30, 1974
AUSTRALIA 62 (John Titman 16, Phil Crump 12, Billy Sanders 11, Bryan Loakes 10, †Steve Reinke 8, John Langfield 5, Steve Koppe 0) **GREAT BRITAIN 45** (Doug Wyer 17, Reg Wilson 11, †Nigel Boocock 9, Jim McMillan 3, Chris Morton 3, Eric Broadbelt 2, Kevin Holden 0).

Brisbane, Saturday, December 7, 1974
AUSTRALIA 50 (Phil Crump 12, John Titman 11, John Langfield 8, Billy Sanders 7, Bryan Loakes 6, Steve Koppe 4, †Steve Reinke 2) **GREAT BRITAIN 58** (Doug Wyer 14, Reg Wilson 13, Eric Broadbelt 12, †Nigel Boocock 6, Jim McMillan 5, Kevin Holden 4, Chris Morton 4).

Newcastle, Friday, December 20, 1974
AUSTRALIA 63 (Phil Crump 18, Billy Sanders 15, Phil Herne 10, Bob Valentine 9, †John Langfield 7, John Titman 2, Robbie Blackadder 2) **GREAT BRITAIN 45** (Doug Wyer 10, Reg Wilson 9, Jim McMillan 8, Eric Broadbelt 8, Chris Morton 5, †Nigel Boocock 5, Kevin Holden 0).

Sydney, Saturday, December 21, 1974
AUSTRALIA 55 (Phil Crump 18, Billy Sanders 15, †John Langfield 9, Phil Herne 6, John Titman 4, Ricky Day 2, Paul Johnstone 1) **GREAT BRITAIN 53** (Doug Wyer 12, Eric Broadbelt 11, Jim McMillan 9, Reg Wilson 9, †Nigel Boocock 8, Chris Morton 4, Kevin Holden 0).

Liverpool, Thursday, December 26, 1974
AUSTRALIA 57 (Billy Sanders 14, Phil Crump 14, Bob Valentine 13, John Titman 8, Phil Herne 5, †John Langfield 2, Bob Humphreys 1) **GREAT BRITAIN 51** (Jim McMillan 11, Eric Broadbelt 8, Reg Wilson 8, Doug Wyer 8, Kevin Holden 7, †Nigel Boocock 7, Chris Morton 2).

Adelaide, Friday, January 3, 1975
AUSTRALIA 59 (Phil Crump 17, Billy Sanders 16, John Titman 9, †John Langfield 8, Kym Amundson 4, Lou Sansom 4, Peter Thompson 1) **GREAT BRITAIN 49** (Jim McMillan 10, Reg Wilson 9, Doug Wyer 9, Eric Broadbelt 7, Chris Morton 6, †Nigel Boocock 6, Kevin Holden 2).

Perth, Friday, January 17, 1975
AUSTRALIA 46 (John Titman 15, Phil Crump 12, †John Langfield 11, Billy Sanders 6, Peter Thompson 2, Doug Underwood 0) **GREAT BRITAIN 61** (Chris Morton 14, Doug Wyer 12, Reg Wilson 10, Eric Broadbelt 10, Jim McMillan 8, †Nigel Boocock 6, Kevin Holden 1).

Australia win the series 5-2.

Ayr, Wednesday, December 11, 1974
NORTH QUEENSLAND 41 (Mike Farrell 13, †Steve Koppe 12, Malcolm Bedkober 7, Kim Crocker 4, Ray Garvey 3, Brian Hodder 2) **GREAT BRITAIN 67** (Eric Broadbelt 18, Doug Wyer 15, Jim McMillan 14, Reg Wilson 9, †Nigel Boocock 7, Kevin Holden 4, Chris Morton 0).

Rockhampton, Saturday, December 14, 1974
ROCKHAMPTON 43 (†Steve Koppe 9, John Titman 8, Bryan Loakes 8, Greg Kluver 8, Jack White 5, Ron Henderson 5) **GREAT BRITAIN 65** (Jim McMillan 15, †Nigel Boocock 12, Eric Broadbelt 12, Reg Wilson 12, Doug Wyer 11, Chris Morton 3, Kevin Holden 0).

● *The Great Britain team manager was Wally Mawdsley.*
● *The Australia team managers were Keith Poultney (Brisbane), Jim Airey (Newcastle, Sydney, Liverpool) and Chum Taylor (Perth)*

World-beaters

THE 1975 Daily Mirror International Tournament could hardly have got off to a more inauspicious opening...with Sweden going into the first match of the series with only FIVE riders!

Anders Michanek and Christer Löfqvist failed to arrive at Sheffield's Owlerton Stadium and it was only after a long, heated discussion between Sweden manager Charles Ringblom, his English counterpart John Berry, England skipper Ray Wilson and referee Colin Tirrell that it was agreed that the match could start with the Swedes operating rider replacement for Michanek and using their two programmed reserves to cover for the absent Löfqvist.

That meant a busy night for Sören Karlsson and Tommy Nilsson who took 10 rides between them in the 13 heats! Little wonder that England, who had won the previous season's tournament, got off to a flying start! If England's win was predictable then Australia pulled off the first major shock beating a powerful-looking Rest of the World side at Exeter despite coming up against County Ground track specialists Ivan Mauger and Scott Autrey from the home club.

The star of the show was not so much a rider – but an engine! Both Phil Crump and father-in-law Neil Street had wins over Mauger on the Street 4-valve conversion unit which was ideally suited to the flat-out Devon track.

England then blitzed the Aussies at Leicester and a 7,131 crowd packed The Boulevard at Hull for the match that would decide the overall outcome as the Lions needed to beat the Rest of the World – by now reinforced by both Ole Olsen and Barry Briggs – to maintain their 100% record. Mauger got a maximum but it wasn't enough and even though England suffered a 5-1 reverse in the final heat they already had a match and tournament winning lead.

In addition to the international competition the Daily Mirror also sponsored an individual championship at Wimbledon which was won by Olsen with 15 points ahead of Peter Collins and Anders Michanek who partly atoned for his absence at Sheffield by getting 11 points in Sweden's win over the Rest of the World.

Earlier in July, England had given themselves a big pyschological boost for the International Tournament by an overwhelming 5-0 victory over their chief rivals Sweden with John Louis the star turn.

Louis was beaten only once by an opponent (Sören Karlsson, pictured) in the first Test, got 18 point maximums in the next two, dropped one point to Bernie Persson at King's Lynn and wrapped up the series with a paid maximum at Belle Vue to finish the five Tests with an astonishing 17.50 average!

England also travelled abroad in search of even more success. A combined party of 16 riders visited Poland on a June week-end, were split into two teams for a total of four matches on which the Lions won three and lost only one.

1975 Daily Mirror International Tournament Results

Sheffield, Monday, July 21
ENGLAND 54 (Peter Collins 12, Dave Jessup 10, Doug Wyer 9, John Louis 8, Malcolm Simmons 7, †Ray Wilson 4, Carl Glover 4) **SWEDEN 24** (Tommy Jansson 9, †Sören Sjösten 7, Tommy Nilsson 5, Bernt Persson 2, Sören Karlsson 1).

Exeter, Monday, July 21
AUSTRALIA 42 (Phil Crump 11, Neil Street 10, Billy Sanders 6, †John Boulger 5, Steve Reinke 5, Phil Herne 4, John Titman 1) **REST OF THE WORLD 36** (†Ivan Mauger 13, Jim McMillan 10, Edgar Stangeland 5, Scott Autrey 5, Dag Lovaas 2, Reidar Eide 1, Bruce Cribb 0).

Leicester, Tuesday, July 22
ENGLAND 50 (John Louis 12, †Ray Wilson 8, Peter Collins 8, Malcolm Simmons 8, Dave Jessup 7, Martin Ashby 5, Terry Betts 2) **AUSTRALIA 28** (Phil Crump 13, Billy Sanders 6, Bob Valentine 4, †John Boulger 4, Bob Humphreys 1, Phil Herne 0, Garry Middleton 0).

Hackney, Tuesday, July 22
SWEDEN 41 (†Anders Michanek 11, Tommy Jansson 9, Bernt Persson 8, Sören Sjösten 4, Bengt Jansson 4, Sören Karlsson 3, Tommy Nilsson 2) **REST OF THE WORLD 37** (†Ivan Mauger 13, Reidar Eide 8, Scott Autrey 7, Jim McMIllan 5, Edgar Stangeland 4, Gary Peterson 0, Dag Lovaas 0).

Hull, Wednesday, July 23
ENGLAND 41 (Doug Wyer 11, Peter Collins 8, Chris Pusey 8, John Louis 7, Dave Jessup 6, Martin Ashby 1, †Ray Wilson 0) **REST OF THE WORLD 37** (†Ivan Mauger 15, Scott Autrey 8, Bobby Beaton 5, Ole Olsen 5, Dag Lovaas 2, Jim McMillan 1, Barry Briggs 1).

Poole, Wednesday, July 23
AUSTRALIA 41 (Phil Crump 9, Phil Herne 9, Billy Sanders 7, †John Boulger 7, Bob Valentine 6, Neil Street 3, Garry Middleton 0) **SWEDEN 37** (Tommy Jansson 11, †Anders Michanek 7, Bernt Persson 6, Sören Sjösten 5, Tommy Nilsson 4, Bengt Jansson 3, Sören Karlsson 1).

	P	W	D	L	PtsF	PtsA	Pts
ENGLAND	3	3	0	0	145	89	6
Australia	3	2	0	1	111	123	4
Sweden	3	1	0	2	102	132	2
Rest of the World	3	0	0	3	110	124	0

● *The team managers were: Peter Moore (Australia), John Berry and Len Silver (England), Charles Ringblom (Sweden) and Trevor Redmond (Rest of the World).*

1975 England v Rest of the World

PLANS for a five-match series between England and the Rest of the World were scrapped but one match – at Ipswich – did get off the ground.

The Management Committee mapped out a five match rubber and even agreed financial terms with four-time World Champion Ivan Mauger.

But at the final analysis it was decided to run only one meeting and that was marred by a combination of the absence of new World Champion Ole Olsen and former title-holder Anders Michanek and heavy pre-meeting rain which ruined the Foxhall Heath track. Only Mauger, Scott Autrey and Billy Sanders offered anything other than token opposition to a powerhouse England team.

Ipswich, Thursday, October 2
ENGLAND 63 (John Louis 14, Peter Collins 13, Malcolm Simmons 11, Martin Ashby 9, Dave Jessup 9, Ray Wilson 6, Tony Davey 1) **REST OF THE WORLD 45** (Scott Autrey 11, Ivan Mauger 11, Billy Sanders 11, Bengt Jansson 5, Phil Crump 5, Jim McMillan 2).

But those victories were achieved at a price. Arnold Haley (fractured collar bone), Terry Betts (two cracked ribs and damaged knee ligaments) and Ray Wilson (damaged shoulder) all came back nursing injuries.

Fortunately none were seriously hurt and Betts was included in a party that undertook a five-Test visit to Sweden shortly before the World Final.

Skipper Ray Wilson was allowed to stay at home and help his club Leicester but they hardly missed their inspirational leader with five spanking wins against a Swedish side denuded of their major asset Anders Michanek for the first four meetings because of 'flu'.

In the re-named New National League, Swedish club side Kaparna opened the international season but failed to excite too many folk and then West Germany were dispatched with equal ceremony, claiming one draw (at Scunthorpe) in eight matches. What they did prove though was their toughness with Peter Lempenauer refusing to quit even though he broke three toes in his left foot in the first match.

England licked Australasia (who were forced to track rookie and former road racer John Howell at Peterborough even though he hadn't ridden a competitive meeting in Britain) and the Anzacs also took on Scotland at Paisley where Jim Gallacher broke his leg after he and Mike Fullerton had been unable to avoid a fallen Doug Templeton.

1975 England v Sweden Results

Poole, Wednesday, July 2
ENGLAND 77 (Peter Collins 15, John Louis 14, Dave Jessup 13, Martin Ashby 12, †Ray Wilson 10, Malcolm Simmons 10, Eric Broadbelt 2, John Davis 1) **SWEDEN 29** (Tommy Jansson 6, Sören Sjösten 6, †Anders Michanek 5, Sören Karlsson 5, Bernt Persson 3, Christer Löfqvist 3, Bengt Jansson 1, Tommy Johansson 0).

Leicester, Tuesday, July 8
ENGLAND 66 (John Louis 18, †Ray Wilson 15, Peter Collins 13, Dave Jessup 10, Doug Wyer 6, Martin Ashby 4, Frank Auffret 0) **SWEDEN 42** (Tommy Jansson 10, Sören Sjösten 9, Bernt Persson 7, Tommy Johansson 7, Christer Löfqvist 4, †Anders Michanek 3, Bengt Jansson 2, Sören Karlsson 0).

Hackney, Friday, July 11
ENGLAND 62 (John Louis 18, Dave Jessup 16, †Ray Wilson 10, Peter Collins 10, Dave Morton 5, Barry Thomas 1, Terry Betts 1, Malcolm Simmons 1) **SWEDEN 46** (Christer Löfqvist 11, Tommy Jansson 9, Anders Michanek 9, Bernt Persson 8, †Bengt Jansson 6, Tommy Johansson 2, Tommy Nilsson 1).

King's Lynn, Sunday, July 13
ENGLAND 70 (John Louis 17, Dave Jessup 14, †Ray Wilson 11, Martin Ashby 10, Malcolm Simmons 10, Terry Betts 7, Doug Wyer 1, Chris Pusey, did not ride) **SWEDEN 38** (Bernt Persson 16, Tommy Jansson 10, †Sören Sjösten 6, Christer Löfqvist 3, Bengt Jansson 2, Christer Sjösten 1, Sören Karlsson 0, Tommy Nilsson 0).

Belle Vue, Wednesday, July 16
ENGLAND 79 (John Louis 17, Peter Collins 16, †Ray Wilson 14, Dave Jessup 12, Chris Morton 11, Chris Pusey 9, Doug Wyer and Rick France, did not ride) **SWEDEN 29** (Tommy Jansson 13, †Sören Sjösten 7, Bengt Jansson 6, Sören Karlsson 2, Bernt Persson 1, Christer Löfqvist 0, Eddie Davidsson 0, Olle Nygren, did not ride).

England win the series 5-0.

● *The England team manager was Len Silver.*
● *The Sweden team manager was Kim Malmberg.*

1975 Poland v England Results

Bydgoszcz, Saturday, June 7
POLAND 71 (Henryk Glucklich 18, Zenon Plech 18, Edward Jancarz 12, Boguslaw Nowak 7, Jerzy Rembas 7, Andrzej Koselski 6, Janusz Plewinski 2, Jan Zabik 1) **ENGLAND 37** (Malcolm Simmons 10, Dave Jessup 8, Doug Wyer 7, †Ray Wilson 5, Jim McMillan 4, John Louis 2, Arthur Price 1, Barry Thomas 0).

Chorzow, Saturday, June 7
POLAND 46 (Andrzej Jurczynski 10, Pawel Waloszek 8, Jozef Jarmula 9, Antoni Fojcik 7, Piotr Pyszny 6, Jerzy Wilim 5, Andrzej Wyglenda 1, Andrzej Tkocz 0) **ENGLAND 62** (Peter Collins 17, John Davis 12, Chris Pusey 11, †Martin Ashby 8, Eric Broadbelt 7, Frank Auffret 5, Terry Betts 2, Arnold Haley 0).

Gorzow, Sunday, June 8
POLAND 50 (Zenon Plech 12, Jerzy Rembas 11, Henryk Glucklich 8, Ryszard Fabiszewski 8, Edward Jancarz 6, Mieczyslaw Wozniak 3, Janusz Koselski 2, Boguslaw Nowak 0) **ENGLAND 58** (Dave Jessup 15, Doug Wyer 13, Malcolm Simmons 13, Jim McMillan 5, †Ray Wilson 5, John Louis 3, Arthur Price 3, Barry Thomas 1).

Poznan, Sunday, June 8
POLAND 52 (Jozef Jarmula 15, Zygfryd Kostka 11, Jerzy Szczakiel 11, Piotr Bruzda 7, Andrzej Jurczynski 5, Piotr Pyszny 2, Zygmunt Slowinski 1) **ENGLAND 56** (Peter Collins 18, John Davis 12, Chris Pusey 9, Eric Broadbelt 7, Frank Auffret 7, Martin Ashby 3, Terry Betts and Arnold Haley, did not ride).

England win the series 3-1.

● *The England team manager was Len Silver.*

1975 Sweden v England Results

Kumla, Tuesday, August 26
SWEDEN 53 (Tommy Jansson 15, Bernt Persson 14, Sören Karlsson 10, Tommy Johansson 8, Hasse Holmkvist 4, Tommy Nilsson 1, Bengt Jansson 1, Per-Åke Gerhardsson 0) **ENGLAND 55** (Peter Collins 16, †Martin Ashby 13, Chris Pusey 8, John Davis 5, Dave Morton 5, Terry Betts 5, Chris Morton 3, Doug Wyer 0).

Eskilstuna, Wednesday, August 27
SWEDEN 51 (Tommy Jansson 16, Bengt Jansson 10, Tommy Johansson 10, Bernt Persson 9, Sören Karlsson 4, Sören Sjösten 2, Stefan Salomonsson 0, Hasse Holmkvist 0) **ENGLAND 57** (Peter Collins 14, †Martin Ashby 14, Dave Morton 10, Chris Morton 7, John Davis 6, Chris Pusey 5, Terry Betts 1, Doug Wyer 0).

Stockholm, Thursday, August 28
SWEDEN 44 (Bernt Persson 12, Tommy Johansson 11, Bengt Jansson 11, Tommy Jansson 6, Tommy Nilsson 4, Sören Karlsson 0, Sören Sjösten 0) **ENGLAND 64** (†Martin Ashby 18, Peter Collins 15, Dave Jessup 12, Chris Pusey 7, Chris Morton 6, Terry Betts 4, John Davis 2, Doug Wyer, did not ride).

Vetlanda, Friday, August 29
SWEDEN 40 (Tommy Jansson 16, Bernt Persson 14, Sören Karlsson 3, Tommy Johansson 3, Bo Wirebrand 2, Sören Sjösten 1, Gunnar Malmqvist 1, Bo Josefsson 0) **ENGLAND 68** (†Martin Ashby 14, Dave Morton 12, Malcolm Simmons 11, Peter Collins 11, Dave Jessup 9, Chris Pusey 8, John Davis 3).

Mariestad, Sunday, August 31
SWEDEN 50 (Anders Michanek 18, Sören Sjösten 14, Tommy Jansson 11, Bernt Persson 2, Börje Klingberg 2, Bengt Jansson 2, Sören Karlsson 1, Karl-Erik Claesson 0) **ENGLAND 58** (John Davis 11, Gordon Kennett 11, Dave Morton 10, †Malcolm Simmons 10, Dave Jessup 10, Eric Broadbelt 6, Barry Thomas 0).

England win the series 5-0.

● *The England team manager was Len Silver.*

●*Polish riders and officials were puzzled by a sticker on the handlebars of Peter Collins' bikes when he raced at Chorzow and Poznan in England B's two tests. The sticker was to remind him always to turn on his fuel taps after forgetting on several occasions. Collins claimed: "I forget at Sheffield and decided to put the sticker on to remind me because I had so many important World Championship events coming up. It seemed a sensible idea to be wise rather than sorry!"*

1975 England v Australasia (Division Two) Results

Birmingham, Monday, June 9
ENGLAND 76 (Arthur Browning 17, Paul Gachet 14, Steve Bastable 12.5, Keith White 12, Keith Anderson 11, Neil Middleditch 6, John Jackson 3.5) **AUSTRALASIA 32** (Jack Millen 9.5, Jim Wells 9, Kym Amundson 5.5, Lou Sansom 5, Doug Underwood 3, Dave Gifford 0, Roger Wright 0, Ricky Day 0).

Middlesbrough, Thursday, June 12
ENGLAND 47 (Joe Owen 15, Alan Emerson 9, Michael Lee 8, Brian Havelock 5, Graham Jones 5, John Jackson 4, Peter Reading 1) **AUSTRALASIA 60** (Lou Sansom 14, Roger Wright 10, Colin Farquharson 10, Doug Underwood 10, Ron Henderson 8, Jack Millen 5, Kym Amundson 3).

Peterborough, Friday, June 13
ENGLAND 66 (Barney Kennett 15, Brian Clark 11, Paul Gachet 10, Dave Gooderham 10, Keith White 10, Ken Matthews 8, Michael Lee 2) **AUSTRALASIA 42** (Lou Sansom 16, Phil Bass 13, Colin Farquharson 6, Kym Amundson 5, Jack Millen 2, Doug Underwood 0, Andrew Cowan 0, John Howell 0).

Workington, Friday, June 20
ENGLAND 58 (Tom Owen 13, Joe Owen 11, John Jackson 10, Sid Sheldrick 10, Alan Emerson 6, Brian Woodward 4, Michael Lee 4) **AUSTRALASIA 50** (Kym Amundson 16, Lou Sansom 12, Jack Millen 10, Robbie Blackadder 6, Colin Farquharson 2, Ron Henderson 2, Mike Fullerton 2, Jim Wells 0).

Eastbourne, Sunday, June 22
ENGLAND 78 (Les Rumsey 18, Neil Middleditch 14, Barney Kennett 13, Paul Gachet 11, Arthur Browning 11, Steve Weatherley 10, Dave Gooderham 1) **AUSTRALASIA 30** (Lou Sansom 10, Ron Henderson 8, Jim Wells 5, Phil Bass 2, Robbie Blackadder 2, Kym Amundson 2, Carl Askew 1).

England win the series 4-1.

1975 West German Club Tour (Division Two) Results

Birmingham, Monday, August 4
BIRMINGHAM 58 (John Hart 11, Arthur Browning 11, Alan Grahame 11, Carl Askew 10, Ricky Day 6, †George Major 5, Keith White 4) **WEST GERMANY 20** (Waldemar Bacik 10, Leonhard Oswald 4, Otto Barth 2, Albert Stickl 2, Peter Lempenauer 1, Franz Lang 1, Günther Kern 0).

Ellesmere Port, Tuesday, August 5
ELLESMERE PORT 59 (†Colin Goad 10, Wayne Hughes 9, John Jackson 9, Mick McKeon 9, Duncan Meredith 8, Andy Reid 8, Nicky Allott 6) **WEST GERMANY 19** (Leonhard Oswald 6, Waldemar Bacik 5, Otto Barth 2, Albert Stickl 2, Peter Lempenaur 2, Franz Lang 1, Günther Kern 1).

Scunthorpe, Wednesday, August 6
SCUNTHORPE 39 (Tony Childs 11, Colin Cook 10, Andy Hines 9, Tony Gillias 6, Ray Watkins 3, Andy Sims 0, †Ken McKinlay 0) **WEST GERMANY 39** (Waldemar Bacik 10, Otto Barth 10, Peter Lempenauer 6, Leonhard Oswald 5, Franz Lang 4, Albert Stickl 2, Günther Kern 2).

Workington, Friday, August 8
WORKINGTON 53 (†Lou Sansom 13, Robbie Gardner 12, Terry Kelly 11, Taffy Owen 10, Mick Newton 5, Roger Wright 2) **WEST GERMANY 25** (Waldemar Bacik 12, Leonhard Oswald 7, Franz Lang 4, Albert Stickl 2, Otto Barth 0, Günther Kern 0).

Paisley, Saturday, August 9
PAISLEY 55 (Mick Sheldrick 10, †Sid Sheldrick 10, Mike Fullerton 10, Chris Roynon 9, Alan Bridgett 8, Bernie Foot 5, Stuart Mountford 3) **WEST GERMANY 22** (Otto Barth 7, Franz Lang 6, Peter Lempenauer 4, Leonhard Oswald 2, Albert Stickl 2, Günther Kern 1).

Newcastle, Monday, August 11
NEWCASTLE 54 (Joe Owen 12, Tom Owen 11, Robbie Blackadder 9, †Brian Havelock 7, Ron Henderson 7, Phil Michelides 6, Tim Swales 2) **WEST GERMANY 24** (Leonhard Oswald 8, Otto Barth 7, Peter Lempenauer 6, Günther Kern 2, Franz Lang 1, Albert Stickl 0).

Weymouth, Tuesday, August 12
WEYMOUTH 58 (Martin Yeates 11, †Brian Woodward 10, Chris Robins 10, Vic Harding 10, Melvyn Soffe 9, Nigel Couzens 5, Roger Stratton 3) **WEST GERMANY 20** (Otto Barth 10, Leonhard Oswald 4. Franz Lang 2, Albert Stickl 2, Peter Lempenauer 2, Günther Kern 0).

Canterbury, Saturday, August 16
CANTERBURY 60 (Graham Clifton 10, Brian Kennett 10, †Les Rumsey 10, Dave Gooderham 10, Terry Casserly 9, Gerald Purkiss 9, Bob Spelta 2) **WEST GERMANY 18** (Franz Lang 5, Leonhard Oswald 5, Otto Barth 4, Albert Stickl 3, Peter Lempenauer 1, Günther Kern 0).

● *The West German team manager was Ulrich Brehmer.*

1975 England v Scotland

Newcastle, Monday, October 13
ENGLAND 59 (Alan Molyneux 14, †Tom Owen 13, Joe Owen 12, Colin Meredith 9, Tom Leadbitter 6, Tim Swales 4, Robbie Gardner 1) **SCOTLAND 48** (†Jim McMillan 14, Bobby Beaton 13, Bert Harkins 9, Brian Collins 5, Ken McKinlay 4, Willie Templeton 2, Doug Templeton 1, Peter Waite 0).

1975 Scotland v Australasia

Paisley, Friday, July 19
SCOTLAND 58 (†Brian Collins 13, Tom Davie 12, Willie Templeton 12, Harry MacLean 9, Jim Gallacher 5, Willie Templeton 4, Fred Caffrey 3, John Wilson 0) **AUSTRALASIA 50** (Mike Fullerton 13, Mitch Shirra 13, Roger Wright 12, Robbie Blackadder 6, Bernie Foot 3, Phil Michelides 1, Geoff Snyder 1, Stuart Mountford 1).

1975 Kaparna (Sweden) Tour of Division Two Results

KAPARNA'S problems began early...when Swindon's Sören Karlsson failed to arrive for the opening match of a six-match tour at Boston.

Veteran Olle Nygren stepped into the breach as a late, late replacement and topped the scorechart.

But their heavy defeat against the 'Cudas was the prelude to a singularly unsuccessful tour in which they lost all their matches quite heavily.

The major saving grace from the visit was the British discovery of 17-year-old Jan Andersson who impressed everywhere but, particularly at Perry Barr where he took one race to weigh up the track, had another five rides and was beaten only once, by Arthur Browning on the last turn of his last race.

Roy Dantanus rode in the first match and then was ruled out of the remaining fixtures with concussion.

Boston, Sunday, April 6
BOSTON 47 (Robert Hollingworth 11, David Piddock 10, †David Gagen 9, Trevor Whiting 6, Billy Burton 5, Michael Lee 4, Rob Mouncer 2) **KAPARNA 31** (Olle Nygren 10, †Kennet Selmosson 9, Jan Andersson 8, Billy Syren 2, Roy Dantanus 1, Göran Jonsson 1, Tommy Strauss 0).

Birmingham, Monday, April 7
BIRMINGHAM 49 (John Hart 12, Arthur Browning 9, Keith White 8, Keith Anderson 7, †George Major 6, Carl Askew 4, Ricky Day 3) **KAPARNA 29** (Jan Andersson 14, Sören Karlsson 12, Billy Syren 2, Tommy Strauss 1, †Kennet Selmosson 0, Göran Jonsson 0).

Ellesmere Port, Tuesday, April 8
ELLESMERE PORT 46 (†Colin Goad 9, Steve Taylor 9, John Jackson 8, Wayne Hughes 6, Duncan Meredith 6, Gerald Smitherman 5, Barry Booth 3) **KAPARNA 32** (Tommy Nilsson 14, Jan Andersson 13, Billy Syren 3, Tommy Strauss 1, Göran Jonsson 1, †Kennet Selmosson 0).

Canterbury, Saturday, April 12
CANTERBURY 51 (Dave Gooderham 12, †Les Rumsey 11, Graham Clifton 8, Barney Kennett 7, Gerald Purkiss 6, Bob Spelta 4, Alan Johns 3) **KAPARNA 27** (Jan Andersson 12, Billy Syren 6, Sören Karlsson 5, †Kennet Selmosson 3, Göran Jonsson 1, Tommy Strauss 0).

Eastbourne, Sunday, April 13
EASTBOURNE 47 (Paul Gachet 12, †Peter Jarman 10, Neil Middleditch 9, Steve Weatherley 6, Eric Dugard 5, Colin Richardson 5, Mike Bessent 0) **KAPARNA 28** (Olle Nygren 9, †Kennet Selmosson 5, Jan Andersson 5, Sören Karlsson 3, Göran Jonsson 3, Billy Syren 2, Tommy Strauss 1).

Weymouth, Tuesday, April 15
WEYMOUTH 51 (Martin Yeates 12, Brian Woodward 12, Vic Harding 8, †Geoff Swindells 6, Tony Freegard 5, Glyn Facey 4, Chris Robins 4) **KAPARNA 27** (Jan Andersson 14, Olle Nygren 9, Billy Syren 3, Tommy Strauss 1, †Kennet Selmosson 0, Göran Jonsson 0).

● *The Kaparna team manager was Bengt Brannefors.*

"I was not willing to have a death on my conscience" – Berry

MANAGER John Berry led a walk-out of the England riders after Lions' skipper Chris Pusey was taken to hospital with a suspected broken leg after crashing during the Sixth Test at the Sydney Showground.

Berry, who had joined the touring party as a replacement for Reg Fearman, led a pre-meeting protest at the condition of the track, covered with a four inch layer of newly laid dirt that hadn't been watered or rolled until immediately before the start of the match.

England had grave doubts about riding with skipper Pusey claiming: "Somebody is going to be badly injured if we are not careful."

Little did he realise at the time that he would shortly be on his way to hospital after being involved in a frightening spill with Aussies John Langfield and Billy Sanders.

Langfield locked up with Pusey immediately behind him and when the Brit went into the fence the closely following Sanders was unable to avoid him.

That prompted a major protest by Berry and his team with the England boss insisting: "There are dangers in speedway but the conditions exceeded the normal danger limit."

It was only after considerable aregument that the England men agreed to unload their bikes again and continue the meeting but even then Berry warned them: "Don't take any risks and don't even attempt to pass from the back."

That direction was followed to the letter and it helped Australia to their only win in seven Tests.

Fortunately the injuries to Pusey were not as serious as first feared and it was later diagnosed as knee ligament damage and a chipped knee-bone.

Pusey missed the following and final Test at Brisbane but was back in action a fortnight later when England began the New Zealand leg of the winter tour.

All seven tourists were to come together again two months after they'd completed an Australasian trip that had brought nine Test wins out of ten.

The occasion was a special one-off Test between the Tour party and the 1975 World Team Cup winning side – the only home international activity at British League level.

After a run of 35 successive home wins – England's last defeat had been against the might of Denmark and Norway in July, 1972 – it was becoming increasingly difficult to find legitimate opponents for the England Test team.

So instead both Poland and Russia faced club sides...and didn't fare that well either!

1975-76 England Tour of Australia Results

Perth, Friday, November 14, 1975
AUSTRALIA 41 (Phil Crump 17, Glyn Taylor 9, Mick McKeon 5, Peter Thompson 4, Les Leisk 4, Rod Chessell 2, Bob O'Leary 0) **ENGLAND 67** (Peter Collins 14, John Davis 12, Chris Morton 12, †Chris Pusey 9, Doug Wyer 9, Dave Morton 9, Gordon Kennett 2).

Perth, Friday, November 28, 1975
AUSTRALIA 34 (Phil Crump 17, †John Langfield 5, Phil Herne 5, Billy Sanders 2, Peter Thompson 2, Glyn Taylor 2, Les Leisk 1) **ENGLAND 74** (Peter Collins 17, †Chris Pusey 15, Doug Wyer 13, John Davis 12, Chris Morton 9, Dave Morton 7, Gordon Kennett 1).

Newcastle, Friday, December 5, 1975
AUSTRALIA 32 (Phil Crump 7, John Titman 7, Billy Sanders 6, Phil Herne 4, Bob Valentine 3, John Langfield 3, Garry Middleton 2) **ENGLAND 76** (Peter Collins 18, John Davis 15, Chris Morton 13, Doug Wyer 12, Gordon Kennett 9, †Chris Pusey 6, Dave Morton 3).

Sydney, Saturday, December 6, 1975
AUSTRALIA 38 (Phil Crump 15, Phil Herne 9, John Langfield 8, Ricky Day 3, John Titman 2, Billy Sanders 1, Mitch Shirra 0) **ENGLAND 70** (Doug Wyer 18, Peter Collins 14, John Davis 11, Dave Morton 8, Chris Morton 8, †Chris Pusey 7, Gordon Kennett 4).

Liverpool, Friday, December 26, 1975
AUSTRALIA 47 (Phil Crump 17, Billy Sanders 11, Phil Herne 7, Terry Sutherland 4, Garry Middleton 3, Mitch Shirra 3, John Langfield 2) **ENGLAND 61** (Peter Collins 17, Doug Wyer 13, Chris Morton 9, John Davis 7, Gordon Kennett 7, †Chris Pusey 5, Dave Morton 3).

Sydney, Saturday, December 27, 1975
AUSTRALIA 62 (Phil Herne 16, Phil Crump 15, Billy Sanders 11, Ricky Day 7, John Langfield 6, Terry Sutherland 4, Stuart Mountford 3) **ENGLAND 45** (John Davis 15, Doug Wyer 10, Dave Morton 9, Chris Morton 5, Gordon Kennett 3, Peter Collins 2, †Chris Pusey 1).

Brisbane, Saturday, January 10, 1976
AUSTRALIA 50 (Phil Crump 17, Billy Sanders 8, John Titman 7, Phil Herne 7, Ron Henderson 6, Mike Farrell 4, Neil Coddington 1) **ENGLAND 57** (Peter Collins 15, †Doug Wyer 13, John Davis 10, Malcolm Simmons 7, Dave Morton 7, Chris Morton 5, Gordon Kennett 0).

England win the series 6-1.

● *The England team managers were Reg Fearman (first three Tests), Charlie Mugford (Fourth Test at Sydney) and John Berry (Sixth and Seventh Tests)*

1976 England Tour of New Zealand Results

Auckland, Saturday, January 24, 1976
NEW ZEALAND 23 (Colin Farquharson 7, Larry Ross 5, Graeme Stapleton 4, Mike Fullerton 3, Colin Tucker 2, John Goodall 2, Paul Church 0) **ENGLAND 85** (Peter Collins 18, John Davis 16, Chris Morton 14, Dave Morton 12, †Chris Pusey 12, Doug Wyer 11, Gordon Kennett 2).

Christchurch, Friday, January 30, 1976
NEW ZEALAND 24 ENGLAND 84 (Chris Morton 17, John Davis 17, Peter Collins 15, †Chris Pusey 13, Doug Wyer 12, Dave Morton 10, Gordon Kennett, did not ride).

Auckland, Monday, February 9, 1976
NEW ZEALAND 25 ENGLAND 83

● *The England team manager was John Berry.*

Further evidence of the staggeringly high standard of competition in the British League was provided as neither the Poles nor the Russkies could record a single victory in a combined total of a dozen matches!

The closest the Soviets came to a celebratory drink was by scoring 32 points at Reading while their fellow Eastern Europeans got to within nine points of Poole after showing they had sufferd no long term hangover after a 60-17 hiding at Newport.

No-one knew it at the time but that meeting was to be a watershed for the Iron Curtain nations as they came up against, for the first time, Neil Street's revolutionary four-valve conversion....

It was to be the beginning of the end of the Eastern European challenge at the highest level as they lagged further and further behind mechanically.

1976 Soviet Union Tour Results

Wolverhampton, Friday, June 4
WOLVERHAMPTON 56 (Finn Thomsen 12, Alan Molyneux 11, †George Hunter 10, Bruce Cribb 9, Jim McMillan 6, Leif Berlin 4, John Jackson 4) **SOVIET UNION 22** (Vladimir Gordeev 6, Grigori Khlinovsky 5, Viktor Trofimov 5, Valeri Gordeev 4, Nikolai Kornev 2, Viktor Kuznetsov 0, Vladimir Paznikov 0).

Reading, Monday, June 7
READING 46 (John Davis 11, Boleslaw Proch 8, Mick Bell 8, †Dave Jessup 6, Bob Humphreys 6, Ian Gledhill 4, Bernie Leigh 3) **SOVIET UNION 32** (Grigori Khlinovsky 10, Vladimir Gordeev 7, Mikhail Starostin 5, Viktor Trofimov 4, Valeri Gordeev 3, Viktor Kuznetsov 3, Nikolai Kornev 0).

Belle Vue, Wednesday, June 9
BELLE VUE 53 (Peter Collins 12, Chris Morton 9, Kristian Praestbro 9, Paul Tyrer 8, †Alan Wilkinson 6, Russ Hodgson 5, Geoff Pusey 4) **SOVIET UNION 25** (Valeri Gordeev 7, Grigori Khlinovsky 7, Viktor Trofimov 4, Vladimir Gordeev 2, Viktor Kuznetsov 2, Nikolai Kornev 1, Valdimir Paznikov 1, Mikhail Starostin 1).

Sheffield, Thursday, June 10
SHEFFIELD 51 (Craig Pendlebury 12, †Reg Wilson 11, Nicky Allott 9, Keith Evans 8, Alan Wilkinson 6, Ernst Bøgh 3, Tony Boyle 2) **SOVIET UNION 27** (Grigori Khlinovsky 8, Vladimir Paznikov 5, Valeri Gordeev 4, Mikhail Starostin 4, Vladimir Gordeev 3, Viktor Kuznetsov 2, Viktor Trofimov 1).

Swindon, Saturday, June 12
SWINDON 47 (Bob Kilby 12, †Martin Ashby 10, Geoff Bouchard 9, Bobby McNeil 6, David Ashby 6, Norman Hunter 4, Kevin Pope 0) **SOVIET UNION 31** (Grigori Khlinovsky 8, Mikhail Starostin 4, Valeri Gordeev 4, Viktor Kuznetsov 4, Vladimir Paznikov 4, Viktor Trofimov 4, Vladimir Gordeev 3).

Exeter, Monday, June 14
EXETER 53 (†Ivan Mauger 12, Scott Autrey 12, John Titman 9, Les Rumsey 7, Peter Prinsloo 5, Kevin Holden 5, Kazimierz Adamczak 3) **SOVIET UNION 25** (Grigori Khlinovsky 8, Mikhail Starostin 7, Valeri Gordeev 3, Vladimir Paznikov 3, Viktor Kuznetsov 2, Vladimir Gordeev 2, Nikolai Kornev 0).

1976 Poland Tour Results

Newport, Friday, April 16
NEWPORT 60 (Phil Crump 12, Phil Herne 12, Tormod Langli 8, Steve Gresham 8, Preben Rosenkilde 8, Brian Woodward 7, †Neil Street 5) **POLAND 17** (Piotr Bruzda 5, Edward Jancarz 4, Boguslaw Nowak 4, Marek Cieslak 2, Andrzej Tkocz 1, Henryk Glucklich 1, Jerzy Szczakiel 0).

King's Lynn, Monday, April 19
KING'S LYNN 54 (Michael Lee 11, Ray Bales 10, †Terry Betts 7, Ian Turner 7, Adi Funk 7, David Gagen 7, Jan Henningsen 5) **POLAND 24** (Edward Jancarz 10, Marek Cieslak 6, Henryk Glucklich 3, Ryszard Jany 2, Andrzej Tkocz 2, Piotr Bruzda 1, Boguslaw Nowak 0).

Poole, Wednesday, April 21
POOLE 43 (†Malcolm Simmons 12, Eric Broadbelt 12, Pete Smith 5, Christer Sjösten 4, Richard May 4, Neil Middleditch 4, Colin Gooddy 2) **POLAND 34** (Edward Jancarz 11, Zenon Plech 9, Ryszard Jany 6, Jerzy Szczakiel 4, Piotr Bruzda 3, Marek Cieslak 1, Henryk Glucklich 0).

Hackney, Friday, April 23
HACKNEY 45 (Dave Morton 12, †Barry Thomas 9, Keith White 9, Zenon Plech 5, Alan Sage 5, Steve Lomas 3, David Kennett 2) **POLAND 33** (Edward Jancarz 13, Andrzej Tkocz 6, Piotr Bruzda 5, Jerzy Szczakiel 4, Boguslaw Nowak 3, Marek Cieslak 1, Ryszard Jany 1).

Halifax, Saturday, April 24
HALIFAX 46 (Graham Plant 12, Henny Kroeze 10, Steve Finch 9, Ian Cartwright 8, †Chris Pusey 7, Adam Olkiewicz 0, Andy Cusworth 0) **POLAND 32** (Edward Jancarz 7, Zenon Plech 6, Andrzej Tkocz 6, Henryk Glucklich 5, Eugeniusz Blaszak 5, Boguslaw Nowak 2, Piotr Bruzda 1).

Coventry, Wednesday, April 28
COVENTRY 52 (Ole Olsen 12, Alan Molyneux 9, Mitch Shirra 9, †Nigel Boocock 8, Jiri Stancl 8, John Harrhy 3, Frank Smith 3) **POLAND 26** (Zenon Plech 9, Edward Jancarz 7, Piotr Bruzda 5, Henryk Glucklich 2, Andrzej Tkocz 2, Jerzy Szczakiel 1, Boguslaw Nowak 0).

1976 England World Team Cup v England Lions

ENGLAND's overall supremacy in world speedway left British promoters with a tricky problem going into the 1976 season...who could they meet?

After discounting foreign opposition – including a full-blown series against Australia – it was agreed to pitch the 1975 World Team Cup winning side against a team based around the winter Australian tourists, augmented and obviously considerably strengthened by WTC star Peter Collins.

The surprise defeat for the World Champions was largely accounted for by Collins' 'defection' and a first race fall which saw skipper Ray Wilson, in front of his home fans, ruled out of the rest of the meeting.

Leicester, Tuesday, April 6
ENGLAND WORLD TEAM CUP 36 (Malcolm Simmons 9, Dave Jessup 9, Martin Ashby 8, John Louis 6, Reg Wilson 3, Terry Betts 1, †Ray Wilson 0) **ENGLAND LIONS 42** (†Peter Collins 12, Gordon Kennett 8, Chris Morton 6, Chris Pusey 5, Doug Wyer 5, John Davis 3, Dave Morton 3).

1976 Rest of the World v England

IT TOOK probably the strongest Rest of the World side ever assembled to inflict a rare defeat on England.

With no worthwhile competition likely to have taxed the Lions on a British track it was agreed they would travel to Denmark to face a powerful Rest squad.

Five World Champions, with a combined total of 15 individual titles between them at that time, were included in the opposition but even so England took them to a last heat decider.

Peter Collins, who lowered the Vojens track record, charged to the front but try as he might team-mate Malcolm Simmons couldn't split the superb team riding of rivals Ole Olsen and Ivan Mauger to provide a dramatic finale to the meeting. England manager John Berry was without three 1976 World Finalists. Chris Morton was getting married while Doug Wyer and John Louis were both on the injured list.

Vojens, Denmark, Sunday, July 25
REST OF THE WORLD 43 (†Ole Olsen 12, Ivan Mauger 7, Anders Michanek 7, Phil Crump 5, Egon Müller 5, Barry Briggs 5, Jiri Stancl 2) **ENGLAND 41** (Peter Collins 14, Gordon Kennett 7, †Malcolm Simmons 6, Dave Jessup 4, Martin Ashby 4, John Davis 3, Dave Morton 3).

SWEDISH Second Division champions Njudungarna warmed up for their first season back in the top flight with a tour of National League tracks.

It could hardly have done anything for their morale as they lost all six matches and only twice topped 30 points.

And that was with the boost of two guests in their travelling party, Ornarna's internationals Karl-Erik Claesson and Börje Klingberg who were their two top-scorers and major threats until they also called up Christer Löfqvist as a further reinforcement.

Unfortunately for most British fans Löfqvist didn't turn up in the colours of the Vetlanda club until the fifth match, at Peterborough where he grabbed an entertaining 12 point maximum and he had another dozen (this time from five rides) in the final match at Rye House where there was a bonus point in each of the 13 heats!

The only pukka international series of the summer saw an eight match England-Australasia rubber, the eighth annual clash between the Lions and the hybrid nation.

The Anzacs, with only two previous series victories behind them, were virtually down and out before they even set wheel on track at Newcastle for the first match.

Tony Boyle, Ron Hendersen, Jack Millen and Lou Sansom were all absentees because of injury which left manager Dennis Gavros with serious heat leader problems.

There were even more worries for the former rider when Robbie Blackadder joined the lengthening casualty list after crashing twice at Brough Park.

He missed the second Test at Workington but at least home star Sansom was back although he was upstaged by the brilliant Steve Lawson who, upset at having been overlooked for the opening match, roared out a defiant ignore me if you dare message to the selectors with a six ride maximum.

Such was England's superiority that the series was in danger of dying on its feet and to give the remaining matches fresh appeal it was agreed that Australasia would bring in Division One riders.

The introduction of Cradley Heath's Kiwi Bruce Cribb and Aussie Doug Underwood (Leicester) at Scunthorpe worked according to plan as England lost their first match but the Lions hit back and won the remaining five matches despite the spasmodic but liberal use of Division One riders like John Titman, Phil Herne, Billy Sanders and Mitch Shirra.

1976 England v Australasia (Division Two) Results

Newcastle, Monday, August 9
ENGLAND 77 (Joe Owen 18, John Jackson 18, Les Collins 14, †Tom Owen 13, Robert Hollingworth 8, Chris Turner 6, Alan Emerson and Steve Lawson, did not ride) **AUSTRALASIA 30** (Colin Farquharson 8, Phil Michelides 6, Roger Wright 6, Eddie Argall 3, Robbie Blackadder 3, Mick McKeon 2, Andrew Cowan 1, Robin Adlington 1).

Workington, Friday, August 13
ENGLAND 66 (Steve Lawson 18, Les Collins 13, Joe Owen 11, Brian Havelock 10, Colin Goad 7, Tom Owen 6, Graham Jones 1) **AUSTRALASIA 42** (Lou Sansom 12, Roger Wright 7, Phil Michelides 7, Dave Gifford 5, Mick McKeon 5, Stuart Mountford 4, Colin Farquharson 2, Eddie Argall 0).

Scunthorpe, Monday, August 16
ENGLAND 44 (Steve Lawson 16, Keith Evans 14, Les Collins 7, Tony Featherstone 4, Robert Hollingworth 2, Andy Hines 1, Phil Kynman 0, Brian Havelock 0) **AUSTRALASIA 63** (Bruce Cribb 18, Doug Underwood 11, Colin Farquharson 9, Phil Bass 9, Carl Askew 8, Robin Adlington 6, Stuart Mountford 2, Mick McKeon 0).

Middlesbrough, Thursday, August 19
ENGLAND 60 (Tom Owen 17, Joe Owen 17, Steve Wilcock 11, Tom Leadbitter 5, Robert Hollingworth 4, Peter E. Smith 4, John Jackson 2, Andy Cusworth 0) **AUSTRALASIA 48** (Bruce Cribb 15, Doug Underwood 14, Bob Humphreys 12, Phil Michelides 4, Mick McKeon 1, Andrew Cowan 1, Stuart Mountford 1, Robbie Blackadder 0).

Boston, Sunday, August 22
ENGLAND 65 (Joe Owen 16, Keith Evans 16, Tom Owen 14, Tony Featherstone 10, Robert Hollingworth 7, Martin Yeates 1, Stuart Cope 1, Ken Matthews 0) **AUSTRALASIA 43** (Bob Humphreys 13, John Titman 11, Doug Underwood 10, Phil Bass 4, Phil Michelides 2, Robin Adlington 2, Carl Askew 1, Robbie Blackadder 0).

Ellesmere Port, Tuesday, August 24
ENGLAND 80 (Joe Owen 18, John Jackson 17, Tom Owen 14, Les Collins 12, Steve Lawson 10, Chris Turner 9, Steve Finch and Colin Goad, did not ride) **AUSTRALASIA 28** (Bruce Cribb 10, Bob Humphreys 8, Phil Bass 7, Robin Adlington 3, Stuart Mountford 0, Mick McKeon 0, Carl Askew 0, Mike Fullerton 0).

Stoke, Thursday, August 26
ENGLAND 63 (Joe Owen 16, Les Collins 15, Steve Finch 11, Tom Owen 10, Keith Evans 7, Malcolm Shakespeare 4, Mick Newton 0) **AUSTRALASIA 45** (Mitch Shirra 15, Doug Underwood 12, Ricky Day 10, Phil Bass 6, Phil Michelides 2, John Titman 0, Robin Adlington 0).

Canterbury, Saturday, August 28
ENGLAND 60 (†Joe Owen 15, Ted Hubbard 14, Steve Weatherley 12, Les Rumsey 8, Hugh Saunders 6, Graham Clifton 4, Barney Kennett 1, Martin Yeates 0) **AUSTRALASIA 48** (Phil Herne 15, John Titman 10, †Steve Koppe 7,Phil Bass 6, Bob Spelta 4, Danny Kennedy 2, Billy Sanders 2, Terry Casserly 2).

England win the series 7-1.

● *The Australasia team managers were Dennis Gavros and Peter Moore (Canterbury only)*

1976 Njudungarna (Sweden) Tour of Division Two Results

Oxford, Thursday, March 25
OXFORD 57 (†Mick Handley 10, Malcolm Corradine 9, Kevin Young 9, Brian Leonard 8, Carl Askew 8, Harry MacLean 7, Phil Bass 6) **NJUDUNGARNA 21** (†Bo Wirebrand 7, Lars-Åke Andersson 7, Karl-Erik Claesson 3, Börje Klingberg 2, Willy Karlsson 1, Stefan Johansson 1, Göran Waltersson 0).

Canterbury, Saturday, March 27
CANTERBURY 52 (Reg Luckhurst 12, †Barney Kennett 9, Graham Banks 9, Bob Spelta 8, Graham Clifton 5, Terry Casserly 5, Alan Diprose 4) **NJUDUNGARNA 26** (Lars-Åke Andersson 7, Willy Karlsson 6, Börje Klingberg 5, Stefan Johansson 4, Karl-Erik Claesson 3, Göran Waltersson 1, †Bo Wirebrand 0).

Mildenhall, Sunday, March 28
MILDENHALL 53 (Kevin Jolly 12, Fred Mills 11, †Bob Coles 10, John Gibbons 7, Stan Stevens 7, Paul Clipstone 6, Neil Leeks 0) **NJUDUNGARNA 25** (Karl-Erik Claesson 9, †Bo Wirebrand 5, Lars-Åke Andersson 5, Börje Klingberg 4, Willy Karlsson 2, Göran Waltersson 0, Leif Bergqvist 0).

Weymouth, Tuesday, March 30
WEYMOUTH 54 (Martin Yeates 12, †Vic Harding 12, Roger Stratton 11, Derek Cook 5, Ricky Owen 5, Garry May 5, Chris Robins 4) **NJUDUNGARNA 24** (Lars-Åke Andersson 9, †Bo Wirebrand 5, Karl-Erik Claesson 5, Willy Karlsson 2, Göran Waltersson 2, Börje Klingberg 1, Leif Bergqvist 0).

Peterborough, Friday, April 2
PETERBOROUGH 43 (Tony Featherstone 11, †Brian Clark 10, Ken Matthews 6, Roy Carter 5, Alan Cowland 4, Ian Clark 4, Russ Osborne 3) **NJUDUNGARNA 35** (Christer Löfqvist 12, Karl-Erik Claesson 7, †Bo Wirebrand 5, Lars-Åke Andersson 5, Willy Karlsson 4, Börje Klingberg 2, Göran Waltersson 0).

Rye House, Sunday, April 4
RYE HOUSE 45 (Ted Hubbard 10, Karl Fiala 8, Bob Cooper 7, David Beech 6, †Brian Foote 6, Kelvin Mullarkey 5, Hugh Saunders 3) **NJUDUNGARNA 33** (Karl-Erik Claesson 13, Christer Löfqvist 12, †Bo Wirebrand 6, Willy Karlsson 1, Börje Klingberg 1, Lars-Åke Andersson 0, Göran Waltersson 0).

● *The Njudungarna team manager was Henry Stein.*

1976 Holland Tour (Division Two) Results

THE Dutch tourists, managed by Jos Vaessen, spent two days at Ivan Mauger's Training School before facing two National League clubs where Henny Kroeze showed his class and had solid backing from Henk Steman, who was later to join British League Bristol.

Peterborough, Friday, March 26
PETERBOROUGH 47 (Russ Osborne 10, Tony Featherstone 9, Roy Carter 7, Ken Matthews 7, †Brian Clark 6, Ian Clark 4, Alan Cowland 4) **HOLLAND 31** (†Henny Kroeze 13, Frits Koning 8, Henk Steman 6, Frits Koppe 2, Toni Egges 1, Piet Seur [senior] 1, Ab de Groot 0).

Eastbourne, Sunday, March 28
EASTBOURNE 76 (Steve Weatherley 15, Colin Richardson 13, †Peter Jarman 12, Mike Sampson 11, Eric Dugard 10, Ian Fletcher 6, Roger Abel 6, Steve Naylor 3) **HOLLAND 32** (†Henny Kroeze 12, Henk Steman 6, Ab de Groot 4, Frits Koppe 4, Frits Koning 3, Toni Egges 1, Piet Seur [senior] 1, Freddy Dost 1).

ENGLAND'S successful run of international victories brought it's own problems for British promoters.

Fast running out of opponents who could challenge the Lions, they turned to World Champions Speedway Series (CI) Limited, a company run jointly by Ivan Mauger and Barry Briggs.

Their brief was simple: Provide a Rest of the World side that can give England competition.

They did exactly that to clinch what turned out to be a five-match rubber in the fourth Test at Reading.

Originally it had been planned to have six Tests, all sponsored by Bulmers under their Strongbow brand, but the sixth and final Test at Bristol was eventually called off amidst political problems after England team-mates Malcolm Simmons and Dave Jessup said they would refuse to ride on the controversial Eastville track.

England began well enough, with 18-year-old Michael Lee winning his first senior cap and finishing with 11 points on his full England debut, with a victory at London White City but the Rest of the World gave notice of their intentions when they levelled the series at Ipswich even though they were without skipper Mauger who, curiously for someone so well prepared, announced he couldn't ride because he did not have an engine!

Reading promoter Reg Fearman lashed into the England riders after the series-decider claiming they didn't have the professional approach of the World stars, pointing out that most of the Lions' had been riding on the Continent 24 hours earlier!

1977 England v Rest of the World Results

White City, Wednesday, May 11
ENGLAND 63 (†John Louis 13, Michael Lee 11, Peter Collins 10, Dave Jessup 10, Gordon Kennett 8, Malcolm Simmons 8, Chris Morton 3) **REST OF THE WORLD 45** (Billy Sanders 13, Ole Olsen 12, †Ivan Mauger 8, Anders Michanek 7, Phil Crump 3, Egon Müller 2, Jim McMillan 0).

Ipswich, Thursday, May 12
ENGLAND 51 (Dave Jessup 14, Peter Collins 12, †John Louis 9, Malcolm Simmons 7, Gordon Kennett 5, Michael Lee 3, Terry Betts 1) **REST OF THE WORLD 57** (Phil Crump 13, †Ole Olsen 11, Billy Sanders 11, Jim McMillan 7, Anders Michanek 6, Phil Herne 5, Egon Müller 4).

Coventry, Saturday, May 21
ENGLAND 48 (Michael Lee 12, Dave Jessup 10, Peter Collins 8, Malcolm Simmons 8, Gordon Kennett 6, †John Louis 4, Alan Molyneux 0) **REST OF THE WORLD 59** (Ole Olsen 14, †Ivan Mauger 12, Billy Sanders 11, Phil Crump 9, Mitch Shirra 7, Scott Autrey 6, Barry Briggs 0).

Reading, Monday, May 23
ENGLAND 46 (Malcolm Simmons 11, Peter Collins 10, Gordon Kennett 8, Michael Lee 8, John Davis 6, †John Louis 3, Dave Jessup 0) **REST OF THE WORLD 62** (Ole Olsen 15, Billy Sanders 13, John Boulger 12, Phil Crump 11, †Ivan Mauger 7, Edward Jancarz 4, Egon Müller 0).

Hull, Tuesday, May 24
ENGLAND 55 (Malcolm Simmons 10, Michael Lee 10, Terry Betts 9, Peter Collins 9, Dave Jessup 8, Chris Morton 7, Doug Wyer 2) **REST OF THE WORLD 53** (†Ivan Mauger 16, Ole Olsen 15, Billy Sanders 9, Phil Crump 6, Bobby Beaton 4, Egon Müller 2, Barry Briggs 1).

Bristol, Friday, May 27
Cancelled after protests about the Eastville track.

Rest of the World win the series 3-2.

- *The England team manager was John Berry.*
- *The Rest of the World team managers were Barry Briggs (White City, Ipswich and Reading) and Philip Rising (Ipswich and Hull).*

- *BARRY BRIGGS began the Strongbow series as the Rest of the World team manager – and ended up riding in two of the five Tests.*

Briggs, who had announced his retirement from League racing at the end of the previous season although he still competed on the Continent, was plagued by mechanical problems and managed only one third place in six rides.

1977 Young England v Young Overseas

SPONSORS Bulmers, deprived of a sixth and final Test between England and the Rest of the World looked elsewhere to complete their support package.

And they agreed to back an Under-23 England-Overseas Test in which each team had the option of picking one over age rider.

Both opted for home-based riders – England tracking Mick Hines and Overseas his Wimbledon team-mate Edward Jancarz.

Even though the meeting was called off by referee Graham Brodie after 12 heats because of heavy rain the result was to stand.

Chances of an Overseas victory were hit by the late arrival of Mitch Shirra (who missed his first ride) and the early departure of Finn Thomsen who walked out after falling in the first race and being left half underneath the fence while the race continued for two full laps!

Wimbledon, Thursday, October 20
YOUNG ENGLAND 39 (Michael Lee 10, John Davis 10, Gordon Kennett 8, Keith White 7, Colin Richardson 4, †Mick Hines 0, Steve Weatherley 0, Steve Bastable 0) **YOUNG OVERSEAS 33** (Scott Autrey 11, †Edward Jancarz 7, Mitch Shirra 5, Ila Teromaa 3, Phil Herne 3, Larry Ross 2, Hans Nielsen 2, Finn Thomsen 0).
Abandoned after 12 heats rain.

1977 Stal Gorzow (Poland) Tour Results

CHAMPIONS of Poland in 1976 when they finished four points ahead of their nearest rivals Wlokniarz Czestochowa, Stal Gorzow were expected to provide a tough pipe-opener to the 1977 British League season.

Unfortunately, the Poles were sadly outclassed in all five tour matches and had only one double figure scorer throughout the tour, guest Marek Cieslak who stayed on for his first British League season with White City at the end of the visit.

Interestingly, they returned home to win the 1977 Polish League with Jerzy Rembas and Boguslaw Nowak (a palpable failure in Britain) finishing in the top four of the national averages! Missing from their title winning side were Zenon Plech (on army duty at Gdansk after asking for a winter transfer!), Ryszard Fabiszewski and the veteran Jerzy Padewski but they were adequately replaced by Wlokniarz number one Cieslak and Unia Leszno's number two Mariusz Okoniewski who had a singularly unsuccessful first visit, scoring just two points from three matches.

King's Lynn, Saturday, March 19
KING'S LYNN 50 (Ian Turner 11, Michael Lee 10, †Terry Betts 8, Billy Burton 7, David Gagen 7, William Spiers 4, Richard Hellsén 3) **STAL GORZOW 28** (†Edward Jancarz 7, Marek Cieslak 7, Boguslaw Nowak 5, Mieczyslaw Wozniak 5, Jerzy Rembas 3, Marek Towalski 1, Boleslaw Rzewinski 0, Mariusz Okoniewski 0).

Reading, Monday, March 21
READING 47 (†Dave Jessup 12, John Davis 11, Bob Humphreys 8, Bengt Jansson 6, Bernie Leigh 5, Glyn Taylor 4, Bo Jansson 1) **STAL GORZOW 31** (†Edward Jancarz 8, Jerzy Rembas 8, Marek Cieslak 7, Boguslaw Nowak 5, Marek Towalski 1, Mieczyslaw Wozniak 1, Boleslaw Rzewinski 1).

Leicester, Tuesday, March 22
LEICESTER 59 (Dave Jessup 12, Ila Teromaa 11, Garry Middleton 10, Doug Underwood 8, Ray Bales 7, Adi Funk 6, Les Leisk 5) **STAL GORZOW 19** (Marek Cieslak 10, †Edward Jancarz 5, Jerzy Rembas 2, Boguslaw Nowak 1, Mieczyslaw Wozniak 1, Boleslaw Rzewinski 0, Marek Towalski 0, Mariusz Okoniewski 0).

Hackney, Friday, March 25
HACKNEY 56 (Dave Morton 12, Keith White 9, †Barry Thomas 9, Laurie Etheridge 8, Trevor Hedge 8, Steve Lomas 8, Tony Featherstone 2) **STAL GORZOW 22** (Jerzy Rembas 9, †Edward Jancarz 5, Mieczyslaw Wozniak 3, Boguslaw Nowak 3, Mariusz Okoniewski 2, Boleslaw Rzewinski 0, Marek Towalski 0).

Exeter, Monday, March 28
EXETER 57 (Mike Farrell 12, Peter Prinsloo 11, Scott Autrey 11, Walter Grubmüller 7, †Ivan Mauger 6, Steve Koppe 5, John Titman 5) **STAL GORZOW 21** (†Edward Jancarz 7, Marek Cieslak 6, Jerzy Rembas 5, Marek Towalski 1, Mieczyslaw Wozniak 1, Boguslaw Nowak 1, Boleslaw Rzewinski 0).

- *The Stal Gorzow team manager was Witold Glowania.*

1977 Ruda Hvezda, Prague (Czechoslovakia) Division Two Tour Results

Newport, Thursday, April 14
NEWPORT 37 (John Goodall 11, Jim Brett 7, Malcolm Bedkober 6, Cliff Anderson 4, Tony Childs 4, Rob Hamman 3, Dave Shepherd 2) **RUDA HVEZDA 40** (Vaclav Verner 8, Petr Ondrasik 8, †Jiri Stancl 8, Jan Verner 7, Jiri Svoboda 5, Zdenek Kudrna 4, Lubos Tomicek [junior] 0).

Peterborough, Friday, April 15
PETERBOROUGH 43 (Andy Hines 12, †Brian Clark 10, Ken Matthews 8, Ian Clark 6, Nigel Couzens 3, Kevin Hawkins 3, Roy Carter 1) **RUDA HVEZDA 34** (†Jiri Stancl 10, Vaclav Verner 7, Jan Verner 6, Zdenek Kudrna 5, Jiri Svoboda 3, Lubos Tomicek 3).

Canterbury, Saturday, April 16
CANTERBURY 36 (Steve Koppe 10, †Barney Kennett 9, Bob Spelta 4, Brendan Shilleto 4, Terry Casserly 4, Brian Canning 4, Graham Clifton 1) **RUDA HVEZDA 41** (†Jiri Stancl 11, Vaclav Verner 10, Jan Verner 10, Zdenek Kudrna 4, Lubos Tomicek 3, Jiri Svoboda 3).

Newcastle, Monday, April 18
NEWCASTLE 44 (†Tom Owen 14, Phil Kynman 9, Phil Michelides 8, Robbie Blackadder 8, Robbie Gardner 5, Robin Dixon 0, Nigel Crabtree, did not ride) **RUDA HVEZDA 34** (Jan Verner 8, †Jiri Stancl 8, Vaclav Verner 7, Lubos Tomicek 6, Jiri Svoboda 5, Zdenek Kudrna 0).

Middlesbrough, Thursday, April 21
MIDDLESBROUGH 40 (Peter E. Smith 12, Steve Wilcock 11, Andrew Cowan 4, Peter Reading 4, Martin Cusworth 4, †Alan Emerson 3, Harry MacLean 2) **RUDA HVEZDA 37** (†Vaclav Verner 16, Jan Verner 10, Lubos Tomicek 7, Zdenek Kudrna 4, Jiri Svoboda 0, Petr Ondrasik 0).

Workington, Friday, April 22
WORKINGTON 40 (Steve Lawson 11, †Brian Havelock 9, Colin Goad 7, Chris Bevan 5, Mick Newton 4, Terry Kelly 4, Ian Hindle 0) **RUDA HVEZDA 38** (†Vaclav Verner 10, Jan Verner 9, Zdenek Kudrna 9, Lubos Tomicek 7, Jiri Svoboda 3, Petr Ondrasik 0).

Rye House, Sunday, April 24
RYE HOUSE 49 (Bob Garrad 11, †Hugh Saunders 8, Kelvin Mullarkey 8, Ted Hubbard 7, Karl Fiala 7, Bob Cooper 4, Ashley Pullen 4) **RUDA HVEZDA 29** (Lubos Tomicek 14, †Vaclav Verner 10, Jan Verner 3, Petr Ondrasik 1, Jiri Svoboda 1, Zdenek Kudrna 0).

● *The Ruda Hvezda team manager was Dr. Zednicek.*

PANIC set in when there was no sign of the Czechoslovakia tourists at Dover customs only hours before the scheduled opening match of another tour by the national champions.

They were nowhere to be seen and worried officials swiftly prepared an emergency plan to replace the Newport meeting with a challenge against a British League Select, drawn from riders living within easy travelling distance of Somerton Park.

Three hours before the first race a series of frantic telephone calls finally elicited the recollection from a toll operator on the Severn Bridge that he had seen a foreign coach travel into Wales earlier in the day.

A search party was dispatched and finally found the Red Star team catching a few hours sleep in their coach, parked in a side street within a stone's throw of the stadium.

Apparently the Czechs had changed their travel arrangements, arrived at Folkestone instead of Dover and, not finding a welcoming party awaiting them, consulted a road map and found their own way to Newport!

That was the first trauma – more were to follow when the visitors were reduced to only six fit riders when Petr Ondrasik was sidelined with a broken foot in the opening match of their seven-meeting tour, sustained, ironically, in the second half individual event that was to be a feature of all the meetings.

One new face, the teenage son of former World Finalist Lubos Tomicek, was included in the touring party and he got better and better as the visit progressed, rounding off with 14 points at Rye House which immediately prompted promoter Len Silver to offer him a 1978 contract.

Sadly the youngster was never able to take up that offer as he was to be seriously injured in a high-speed long-track accident later in the summer, his blossoming career cut short at the stem.

Ondrasik returned prematurely at Middlesbrough after Jiri Stancl had been forced to return home to prepare for his World Championship qualifer in Italy, but lasted only two races before having to pull out and even though he rode in the two remaining matches he was obviously still suffering and didn't score a point.

Highlight of the tour for the entire party was a night of 'home cooking' at Mirek Markl's bistro on Teesside and, for top-scoring Vaclav Verner, his Saturday night debut for Exeter at Swindon, sandwiched between visits to Workington and Rye House!

Two victories from seven meetings was scant reward for another thrilling visit.

1977 Smederna (Sweden) v Wimbledon Result

WIMBLEDON undertook an emotion-charged trip to Sweden – in honour of their former skipper Tommy Jansson.

A full strength Dons' line-up took on his Swedish club side Smederna and to add even more poignancy to the occasion his elder brother Bo rode in the meeting.

Eskilstuna, Monday, May 16
SMEDERNA 34 (Bernt Persson 15, Stefan Salomonsson 6, Bo Jansson 5, Åke Dovhed 3, Gert Carlsson 3, Bengt Jansson 2, Lennart Bengtsson 0) **WIMBLEDON 44** (Edward Jancarz 12, Larry Ross 11, Mick Hines 9, Roger Johns 5, Rob Jones 4, Colin Richardson 3).

1977 Rodenbach (Germany) v Peterborough Result

Rodenbach, West Germany
RODENBACH 30 (Franz Kreimoser 12, Helmut Ziller 10, Jurgen Hehlert 4, Rob Mouncer 2, Karl-Heinz Wanke 1, Wilhelm Kall 1, Erich Domanics 0) **PETERBOROUGH 47** (Kevin Hawkins 10, Andy Hines 10, Nigel Flatman 9, Brian Clark 7, Ken Matthews 5, Nigel Couzens 3, Ian Clark 3).

1977 England v Australasia (Division Two) Results

Middlesbrough, Thursday, July 7
ENGLAND 76 (Tom Owen 16, Colin Richardson 15, Laurie Etheridge 15, John Jackson 11, Alan Emerson 11, Steve Wilcock 8, Peter E. Smith and Graham Jones, did not ride) **AUSTRALASIA 32** (Steve Koppe 9, Doug Underwood 8, John McNeill 7, Colin Farquharson 3, Mick McKeon 2, Robbie Blackadder 2, Robin Adlington 1).

Weymouth, Tuesday, July 12
ENGLAND 67 (Colin Richardson 18, Martin Yeates 12, Vic Harding 11, †Malcolm Corradine 11, Mike Sampson 10, Robert Hollingworth 4, Kevin Young 1, Geoff Swindells 0) **AUSTRALASIA 41** (Roger Abel 10, †Danny Kennedy 9, Steve Koppe 9, Stuart Mountford 9, Bob Spelta 3, Colin Farquharson 1, Phil Baker 0).

Newport, Friday, July 15
ENGLAND 58 (Colin Meredith 16, Brian Woodward 13, Bob Coles 10, Barney Kennett 6, Jim Brett 6, Robert Henry 5, Chris Robins 2) **AUSTRALASIA 50** (Steve Koppe 12, Bob Spelta 9, Tim Nunan 9, John Goodall 9, Stuart Mountford 9, Colin Farquharson 2, Robbie Blackadder 0, Cliff Anderson 0).

Canterbury,Saturday, July 16
ENGLAND 44 (Ted Hubbard 13, David Kennett 8, Les Rumsey 6, Graham Banks 5, Alan Sage 5, Bob Coles 4, Barney Kennett 3) **AUSTRALASIA 63** (Mike Farrell 18, †Steve Koppe 15, Roger Abel 14, John McNeill 7, Bob Spelta 6, Phil Bass 2, Terry Casserly 1).

Mildenhall, Sunday, July 17
ENGLAND 57 (Martin Yeates 13, Bob Coles 11, Neil Leeks 10, Tom Owen 9, Robert Henry 6, Steve Lawson 4, Vic Harding 3, Trevor Jones 1) **AUSTRALASIA 51** (Doug Underwood 11, Mike Farrell 11, Steve Koppe 10, Danny Kennedy 10, Tim Nunan 5, John McNeill 3, Bob Spelta 1).

England win the series 4-1.

● *The England team managers were: Tony Coupland (Middlesbrough), Richard Murphy (Weymouth), Maurice Morley (Canterbury and Newport) and Terry Waters (Mildenhall).*
● *The Australasia team manager was Peter Moore.*

Fearman's fliers

REG FEARMAN and Peter Collins helped bring some pride back into the Lions' touring team...but the Australian selectors did their utmost to make it easier for the tourists!

For they banned in-form John Boulger for six weeks – a suspension that saw him miss the vital opening Test at Newcastle – and they failed to agree financial terms with their other potential big-scorer Billy Sanders so he, too, sat out the opener.

And as the series progressed the three Australian selectors Bill Bates-Brownsword, Owen Bateman and Phil Tolley gave a passable impression of having been lost in Hampton Court maze for a year or two as they ignored some of their classier riders for patently below par political choices.

Fearman, a two-time tourist as a rider and manager of the successful 1973-74 tourists made no bones about his aims: "The big job is to bring back the Ashes."

But he added: "We want success, but against the very best opposition available."

His party of riders, led by Collins, included new boys Keith White and Neil Middleditch to augment a selection based on big-track expertise.

The tourists left London's Heathrow Airport on Boxing Day and faced a heavy itinerary which included seven Tests, at least five open meetings and would end in February, a curtailed visit with a large concentration of tough team meetings.

Australia had hoped to include Mitch Shirra in their plans but, on the eve of the series, he announced that he wanted to continue representing New Zealand, the country of his birth, in international events and that ruled him out.

So they went into the first Test at Newcastle denuded of the banned Boulger, the unavailable Shirra, the striking Sanders and the still unfit Phil Crump who had yet to recover from the broken leg he had sustained at Sheffield towards the end of the previous British season.

MISSING...mainstay Billy Sanders missed the first two 1978 Tests because of a pay dispute but returned in the Third Test to lead the Kangaroos to their first victory of the series with a 17 out of 18 point tally at Brisbane

1978 England Lions Tour of Australia Results

Newcastle, Monday, January 2
AUSTRALIA 38 (John Titman 12, Phil Herne 11, Ricky Day 7, Terry Sutherland 3, John Langfield 3, Robbie Blackadder 2, Wayne Forrest 0) **ENGLAND 70** (†Peter Collins 18, John Davis 17, Doug Wyer 11, Gordon Kennett 10, Alan Wilkinson 6, Keith White 5, Neil Middleditch 3).

Brisbane, Saturday, January 7
AUSTRALIA 51 (John Titman 14, †John Boulger 13, Steve Koppe 9, Mick McKeon 9, Mike Farrell 5, Neil Coddington 1, Ken Murray 0) **ENGLAND 57** (†Peter Collins 14, Alan Wilkinson 12, John Davis 12, Gordon Kennett 7, Doug Wyer 6, Keith White 5, Neil Middleditch 1).

Brisbane, Saturday, January 14
AUSTRALIA 61 (Billy Sanders 17, John Titman 15, †John Boulger 10, Mick McKeon 10, Steve Koppe 5, Mike Farrell 2, Phil Herne 2) **ENGLAND 47** (†Peter Collins 16, John Davis 11, Gordon Kennett 10, Alan Wilkinson 4, Keith White 4, Doug Wyer 2, Neil Middleditch 0).

Sydney, Friday, January 20
AUSTRALIA 53 (Billy Sanders 15, John Titman 11, Phil Herne 7, Mick McKeon 7, Mike Farrell 7, Ricky Day 5, Wayne Forrest 1) **ENGLAND 55** (†Peter Collins 14, John Davis 10, Alan Wilkinson 9, Doug Wyer 8, Keith White 7, Gordon Kennett 7, Neil Middleditch 0).

Adelaide, Friday, February 3
AUSTRALIA 56 (†John Boulger 14, Billy Sanders 14, John Titman 13, Mick McKeon 6, Tony Boyle 5, Phil Herne 4, Mike Farrell 0) **ENGLAND 52** (Doug Wyer 11, †Peter Collins 11, Alan Wilkinson 10, Gordon Kennett 9, Neil Middleditch 6, Keith White 5, John Davis 0).

Sydney, Saturday, February 11
AUSTRALIA 47 (Billy Sanders 13, John Titman 13, Mick McKeon 6, John Boulger 5, Lloyd Cross 5, Mike Farrell 4, Phil Herne 1)) **ENGLAND 61** (†Peter Collins 17, Gordon Kennett 15, John Davis 11, Doug Wyer 9, Alan Wilkinson 7, Keith White 2, Neil Middleditch 0).

Perth, Friday, February 24
AUSTRALIA 38 (Mick McKeon 12, Billy Sanders 10, John Titman 6, Phil Herne 5, Glyn Taylor 3, Mick Moores 1, Lloyd Cross 1) **ENGLAND 70** (†Peter Collins 18, Gordon Kennett 14, John Davis 14, Doug Wyer 12, Keith White 8, Alan Wilkinson 4, Neil Middleditch, did not ride).

England win the series 5-2.

Sydney, Saturday, December 30, 1977
NEW SOUTH WALES 34 (Billy Sanders 11, Wayne Forrest 6, Paul O'Neal 4, David Shields 4, Glenn McDonald 4, Ricky Day 3, Phil Herne 2) **ENGLAND 43** (†Peter Collins 10, John Davis 10, Doug Wyer 9, Alan Wilkinson 7, Gordon Kennett 4, Keith White 2, Neil Middleditch 1).

Mildura, Sunday, February 5
PHIL CRUMP SELECT 57 (John Boulger 16, Phil Crump 13, Billy Sanders 11, John McNeill 9, Tony Boyle 5, Tim Nunan 3) **ENGLAND 50** (Neil Middleditch 15, Doug Wyer 14, Alan Wilkinson 12, †Peter Collins 7, Keith White 2, John Davis 0, Gordon Kennett 0).

● *England team manager was Reg Fearman.*

There was further bewilderment in some of the Australian tactics as England went on a points-spree. John Titman was axed from his third ride despite having scored four points while Wayne Forrest took all his SIX programme rides even though he finished last in every one!

Boulger was reprieved for the first of two Tests in eight days at Brisbane and for the second of them Billy Sanders had also made his peace and their dual return inspired the Kangaroos to their first win.

Sanders also smashed the Exhibition Grounds three-lap track record but the euphoria of victory was quickly blown away by Boulger's announcement that he was quitting the Test arena and a subsequent two-point defeat at Sydney six days later.

England's joy at opening up a 3-1 lead was also muted as Doug Wyer crashed in the last heat and was taken to hospital with a dislocated shoulder.

He was soon back but replaced on the injured list by John Davis (a total of 46 stitches in leg and heel gashes), Keith White (bruised spine and kidneys) and Alan Wilkinson who was struck by a snapping chain.

All were back in action for the sixth Test where a Lions victory ensured the Ashes stayed in Britain.

And gave the 1978 England international programme the ideal launching pad....

Tourists Collins, Davis, Middleditch, White, Wilkinson and Wyer were joined by Reg Wilson (replacing Gordon Kennett) for a Test trial (see panel) before England began a five-match series against the cream of the Colonies.

But before the first Test at Bristol the British Speedway Promoters' Association spent many sleepless nights debating whether to accept a lucrative but controversial sponsorship offer.

In those pre-Aids days safe sex was a taboo subject and there were some track bosses who felt it was morally wrong to link a family sport like speedway with the London Rubber Company of London whose best known product was contraceptives!

EVERPRESENT...Larry Ross rode in all five Tests

Finally those who advocated taking the money and presenting the sponsorship in as tasteful a way as possible won the day.

Bob Hall, Marketing Director, LRC Products Limited said: "Our success in motor racing and cricket encouraged us to do even more in the area of sport so we looked for a sport with a fine image, a strong and active governing body and with good spectator facilities.

"Speedway fitted the bill on all counts and we are delighted with the co-operation we have received from the speedway authorities."

The series got underway in front of a massive crowd at Bristol's Eastville Stadium and with recognised heat leaders Peter Collins and Michael Lee struggling, the Anzacs certainly ended any fears that the rubber would not be box office.

They won by four points and that one result probably added an extra thousand or two on all subsequent attendances.

Gordon Kennett, who missed the first match with a heavy cold, came back at Birmingham and Dave Morton replaced Alan Grahame to provide a winning combination.

It looked as if England would build on that victory as they went into a 10-point lead at Ipswich but an Australasian fightback – aided by their decision to use new tyres after an interval watering – ensured the series would go to the fifth match if England were to win at Hull.

They didn't after tracking a shadow squad with three new caps, Frank Auffret, Ian Cartwright and Kevin Jolly, and Tom Owen whose only previous senior international experience had been five years earlier against Scotland!

The England selectors had no option for it had been agreed that the twice postponed British Final *HAD* to be held on the same night as the Fourth Test!

Denmark (without DMU approval) toured five National League tracks, never lost a match but did little for the sport's image as Finland's Ari Koponen rode for the Danes at Edinburgh and Andy Hibbs, god-son to former international Geoff Pymar, collected his first international cap even though he was still waiting to make his National League debut with Boston.

1978 England v Australasia Results

Bristol, Friday, July 21
ENGLAND 52 (†Malcolm Simmons 15, Tony Davey 10, Chris Morton 10, Alan Grahame 7, Peter Collins 4, Michael Lee 3, Steve Bastable 3, Les Collins 0) **AUSTRALASIA 56** (Phil Crump 17, John Titman 13, Larry Ross 12, Billy Sanders 10, John Boulger 2, †Ivan Mauger 1, Mitch Shirra 1, Bruce Cribb 0).

Birmingham, Monday, July 24
ENGLAND 59 (Michael Lee 15, †Malcolm Simmons 12, Gordon Kennett 9, Dave Morton 8, Peter Collins 7, Tony Davey 5, Chris Morton 2, Steve Bastable 1) **AUSTRALASIA 49** (Billy Sanders 11, Larry Ross 11, Phil Crump 11, John Titman 9, †Ivan Mauger 3, Bruce Cribb 3, Phil Herne 1, John Boulger 0).

Ipswich, Thursday, August 10
ENGLAND 51 (Tony Davey 14, Michael Lee 11, John Louis 10, †Malcolm Simmons 7, Peter Collins 5, Gordon Kennett 4, Dave Jessup 0, Terry Betts, did not ride) **AUSTRALASIA 57** (Billy Sanders 14, John Titman 14, †Ivan Mauger 10, Larry Ross 10, Phil Crump 6, Mitch Shirra 2, Phil Herne 1, John Boulger 0).

Hull, Wednesday, August 16
ENGLAND 36 (Tom Owen 10, Ian Cartwright 7, Frank Auffret 7, Kevin Jolly 6, Neil Middleditch 3, Chris Pusey 2, Terry Betts 1, Graham Drury 0) **AUSTRALASIA 70** (Phil Crump 16, Billy Sanders 15, Larry Ross 13, John Titman 9, Mitch Shirra 7, †Ivan Mauger 7, John Boulger 3, Bruce Cribb, did not ride).

Hackney, Friday, August 18
ENGLAND 56 (Michael Lee 12, †Malcolm Simmons 10, Dave Jessup 10, Peter Collins 9, John Louis 9, Tony Davey 3, Gordon Kennett 3, Barry Thomas, did not ride) **AUSTRALASIA 52** (Billy Sanders 12, †Ivan Mauger 12, Mitch Shirra 11, John Titman 7, Phil Crump 5, Larry Ross 5, John Boulger and Bruce Cribb, did not ride).

Australasia win the series 3-2.

- *The England team manager was John Berry.*
- *The Australasia team manager was Wayne Wattie.*

1978 England World Team Cup v England Lions

AFTER a season's absence the early season 'Test trial' matching the winter's touring side against the previous year's World Team Cup squad was revived.

Once again the tourists had first call on riders with Peter Collins and John Davis stepping out of the '77 Team Cup squad to be replaced by two World Team Cup stalwarts in Terry Betts and John Louis.

England boss John Berry also handed out a first senior cap to 21-year-old Steve Bastable.

Gordon Kennett was the one major absentee from the Lions – he was on holiday – and that caused bitter resentment between Leicester co-promoter Vic White and Kennett's White City boss Danny Dunton. He was replaced by Reg Wilson.

It turned into a relatively easy win for Malcolm Simmons' squad!

Leicester, Tuesday, April 18
ENGLAND WORLD TEAM CUP 63 (†Malcolm Simmons 16, Michael Lee 15, Steve Bastable 10, Terry Betts 10, Dave Jessup 7, John Louis 4, Chris Morton 1) **ENGLAND LIONS 45** (†Peter Collins 14, Doug Wyer 8, Alan Wilkinson 7, John Davis 6, Reg Wilson 6, Keith White 4, Neil Middleditch 0).

1978 Great Britain v Denmark (Division Two) Results

Stoke, Sunday, September 3
GREAT BRITAIN 41 (Malcolm Shakespeare 9, George Hunter 8, Ted Hubbard 7, Laurie Etheridge 7, Les Rumsey 5, Kelvin Mullarkey 3, Karl Fiala 2, Bob Garrad 0) **DENMARK 67** (Hans Nielsen 18, †Finn Thomsen 16, Alf Busk 16, Finn Jensen 10, Steen Mastrup 5, Knud Ellegaard 2).

Eastbourne, Sunday, September 17
GREAT BRITAIN 53 (Mike Sampson 13, Phil Collins 12, Eric Dugard 10, David Kennett 7, Andy Hines 7, Steve Finch 4, Laurie Etheridge 0, Steve Naylor 0) **DENMARK 55** (†Finn Thomsen 15, Bo Petersen 14, Mike Lohmann 9, Bent Rasmussen 9, Alf Busk 7, Steen Mastrup 1, Klaus Lohmann 0).

Edinburgh, Wednesday, September 27
GREAT BRITAIN 54 (Nicky Allott 13, Mike Sampson 11, Phil Collins 10, Steve Lomas 9, George Hunter 6, Steve Lawson 3, Dave Trownson 2) **DENMARK 54** (Hans Nielsen 18, Kristian Praestbro 16, *Ari Koponen 14,* Bo Petersen 4, Bent Rasmussen 2, Klaus Lohmann 0).

Boston, Sunday, October 1
GREAT BRITAIN 45 (Dave Allen 11, Robert Hollingworth 11, Tony Lomas 10, Nicky Allott 7, Steve Lomas 4, Steve Wilcock 2, Andy Hibbs 0, Stuart Cope 0) **DENMARK 63** (Bo Petersen 13, †Finn Thomsen 12, Kristian Praestbro 11, Hans Nielsen 10, Finn Jensen 9, Bent Rasmussen 7, Steen Mastrup 1).

Middlesbrough, Thursday, October 19
GREAT BRITAIN 42 (Steve Wilcock 11, Phil Collins 11, †Tom Owen 9, Mike Sampson 8, Peter E. Smith 3, Steve Finch 0, Brian Havelock 0) **DENMARK 66** (Hans Nielsen 14, Bo Petersen 14, Mike Lohmann 12, †Finn Thomsen 11, Kristian Praestbro 6, Bent Rasmussen 5, Klaus Lohmann 4).

Denmark win the series 4-0 with one Test drawn.

- *The Great Britain team manager was Colin Pratt.*

While the Test series was given official international status by the British authorities it was NOT authorised by the Danish Motor Union and Denmark did not award caps for the series.

1978 England Under 23 v Ruda Hvezda (Prague)

SEAN WILLMOTT became the third youngest rider ever to win an England cap when he was still a month short of his 17th birthday when he made his debut in the first-ever England Under 23 match.

He was one of two National League riders – Rye House's Bob Garrad was the other – brought into the line-up for the first speedway international to be held at Bristol's Eastville Stadium.

Making it an even more memorable occasion for the Weymouth youngster was the fact that he was celebrating his first Test experience in his own home-town and he didn't let anyone down with half a dozen points as England got off to a winning start, mainly thanks to the imperious form of Michael Lee.

The match came during Red Star's five-meeting tour of National League tracks.

Bristol, Friday, April 21
ENGLAND U23 42 (†Michael Lee 12, Joe Owen 9, Sean Willmott 6, Steve Bastable 5, Les Collins 4, Neil Middleditch 4, Bob Garrad 2) **RUDA HVEZDA 36** (Jiri Stancl 12, †Vaclav Verner 11, Zdenek Kudrna 6, Jan Verner 5, Jiri Svoboda 2, Milan Spinka 0, Petr Ondrasik 0).

See also Club Tour of National League tracks.

1978 England v Australasia (Division Two) Results

Milton Keynes, Tuesday, August 1
ENGLAND 54 (Bob Garrad 14, Phil Collins 9, Derek Harrison 9, Ted Hubbard 8, Andy Hines 7, Melvyn Taylor 7, Mike Sampson 0) **AUSTRALASIA 54** (David Shields 14, Roger Abel 13, †Steve Koppe 11, Doug Underwood 8, Carl Askew 6, Phil Bass 2, Tony Boyle 0).

Boston, Sunday, August 6
ENGLAND 53 (Dave Allen 13, Nicky Allott 12, Laurie Etheridge 8, Les Rumsey 6, Steve Finch 5, Stuart Cope 5, Phil White 4) **AUSTRALASIA 55** (Gary Guglielmi 14, David Shields 12, Bob Humphreys 11, †Steve Koppe 9, John McNeill 5, Tony Boyle 3, Carl Askew 1).

Crayford, Tuesday, October 3
ENGLAND 84 (Alan Sage 18, Tom Owen 16, Les Rumsey 16, Laurie Etheridge 12, Eric Dugard 12, Kelvin Mullarkey 8, Ted Hubbard 2) **AUSTRALASIA 24** (Roger Abel 7, Bruce Cribb 6, Stuart Mountford 5, Colin Farquharson 3, Rod Hunter 2, Tony Garard 1).

Stoke, Saturday, October 7
ENGLAND 69.5 (Nicky Allott 17, Ray Bales 14, Tony Lomas 12.5, Tom Owen 9, Dave Gooderham 8, Ian Gledhill 6, Derek Harrison 2, Ian Robertson 1) **AUSTRALASIA 38.5** (Tim Nunan 12.5, Robbie Blackadder 9, John McNeill 9, David Shields 5, Colin Farquharson 2, Stuart Mountford 1, Bob Humphreys 0, Rod Hunter 0).

Berwick, Sunday, October 15
Cancelled because Australasia did not field a full side.
ENGLAND (Dave Trownson, Mike Hiftle, Steve Wilcock, Andy Reid, Derek Richardson, Graham Jones, Peter E. Smith and Ivan Blacka) **AUSTRALASIA** (David Shields, †Steve Koppe, John McNeill, Carl Askew, Colin Farquharson, Dave Gifford, Merv Janke, James Moore.).

England win the series 2-1 with one Test drawn and one abandoned.

- *The England team manager was Colin Pratt.*
- *The Australasia team manager was Wayne Wattie.*

■ ***Following the decision to cancel the Fifth Test at Berwick a substitute National League Select v Overseas Select match was raced but abandoned after 12 heats because of rain.***
■ ***The scorers at the time were:***

NATIONAL LEAGUE SELECT 23(Graham Jones 6, Andy Reid 6, Derek Richardson 3, Mike Hiftle 3, Mike Caroline 2, Steve Wilcock 2, Peter E. Smith 1) OVERSEAS SELECT 44 (Colin Farquharson 11, Merv Janke 8, Carl Askew 8, Ivan Blacka 6, James Moore 5, Rob Grant 3, Dave Trownson 3).

IT IS doubtful if there has ever been a more disorganised or chaotic Test series in Britain than this!

It was bad enough when Ladbroke General Manager Gordon Linton had to publicily apologise to Crayford fans after the Third Test in which only Eastbourne's Roger Abel, late substitute Bruce Cribb and Stuart Mountford, beat an opponent in a totally one-sided match.

But worse, much worse, was to follow....

Australasia's team problems had been highlighted at the Kent track when skipper Steve Koppe withdrew because of 'flu' and then both Gary Guglielmi and John McNeill were pulled out because of what appeared to be a relatively unimportant Midland Cup match between Leicester and Coventry.

Koppe and Merv Janke were also missing from the Fourth Test at Stoke (a clash of Saturday night race-days) but the entire series crumbled into unspeakable chaos in the fifth and final Test at Berwick.

Thirty minutes before the parade was due to start Australasia had only four riders at Shielfield Park – and all three heat leaders, Koppe, David Shields and McNeill were missing.

It was apparent they weren't going to turn up so the Berwick public had to suffer a swiftly arranged challenge match (see panel alongside) that did nothing whatever for the sport's credibility.

It was a tragedy the series should have sunk to such abysmal depths as it had begun with all the promise of a rich and entertaining series with the two sides drawing at Milton Keynes (Groveway's first-ever international) and then Australasia winning for the third time in four matches at Boston where, controversially, the Anzacs called up Tony Boyle only a week after he had walked out on the Barracudas' management!

1978 Ruda Hvezda (Czechoslovakia) Division Two Tour Results

Canterbury, Saturday, April 15
CANTERBURY 41 (Les Rumsey 11, Graham Banks 8, Brendan Shilleto 7, Steve Koppe 6, †Barney Kennett 5, Graham Clifton 3, Bob Spelta 1) **RUDA HVEZDA 37** (Jan Verner 9, Zdenek Kudrna 8, Vaclav Verner 8, Jiri Stancl 8, Jiri Svoboda 3, Milan Spinka 1, Petr Ondrasik 0).

Mildenhall, Sunday, April 16
MILDENHALL 38 (Neil Leeks 12, Ray Bales 9, †Bob Coles 7, Mick Bates 4, Robert Henry 3, Melvyn Taylor 2, Mike Spink 1) **RUDA HVEZDA 40** (Vaclav Verner 10, Jiri Stancl 9, Zdenek Kudrna 8, Jan Verner 5, Milan Spinka 4, Petr Ondrasik 4, Jiri Svoboda 0).

Stoke, Saturday, April 22
STOKE 23 (John Harrhy 7, Tony Lomas 5, Ian Robertson 5, Ian Gledhill 4, †Tim Nunan 1, Ian Jeffcoate 1, Stuart Mountford 0) **RUDA HVEZDA 55** (Jan Verner 11, Jiri Stancl 10, Vaclav Verner 10, Milan Spinka 8, Petr Ondrasik 8, Zdenek Kudrna 6, Jiri Svoboda 2).

Newcastle, Sunday, April 23
NEWCASTLE 34 (†Tom Owen 10, Kevin MacDonald 8, Graeme Stapleton 5, Robbie Gardner 5, Kenny Carter 2, Neil Coddington 2, Robbie Blackadder 2) **RUDA HVEZDA 43** (Vaclav Verner 11, Jiri Stancl 10, Petr Ondrasik 8, Zdenek Kudrna 7, Milan Spinka 3, Jan Verner 3, Jiri Svoboda 1).

Weymouth, Tuesday, April 18
Cancelled, waterlogged track.

Milton Keynes, Tuesday, April 25
MILTON KEYNES 30 (Cliff Anderson 7, Andy Grahame 7, †Phil Bass 6, Kevin Cox 3, Harry MacLean 3, Derek Harrison 3, Alan MacLean 1) **RUDA HVEZDA 47** (Petr Ondrasik 10, Vaclav Verner 10, Jan Verner 8, Jiri Stancl 7, Milan Spinka 5, Ladislav Hradecky 4, Zdenek Kudrna 3).

● *The Ruda Hvezda team manager was Miroslav Zlatnik.*

● *1977 Czechoslovakian Junior Champion Ladislav Hradecky made his first tour of Great Britain but had to wait for the final match of the visit to make his debut.*

1978 Scottish Select v English Select

NOT OFFICIALLY recognised as an International (hence the Select) but a meeting that was given the blessing of the British Speedway Promoters' Association.

And it was also the success of this meeting that was to prompt promoters to launch a pukka England-Scotland series again the following year.

Blantyre, Saturday, October 7
SCOTTISH SELECT 51 (George Hunter 15, Merv Janke 14, Benny Rourke 9, Brian Collins 9, Jim Beaton 3, Colin Caffrey 1, Charlie McKinna 0) **ENGLISH SELECT 57** (Steve Lawson 17, Derek Richardson 16, Dave Trownson 14, Keith Bloxsome 6, Andy Reid 3, Graham Jones 1, Ivan Blacka 0).

1978 Bristol in Holland Result

BRISTOL's visit to Geleen was the first team meeting to be screened by Dutch television.

THE NETHERLANDS 38 (Henny Kroeze 11, Frits Koning 9, G. Meyer 6, Henk Steman 5, Frits Koppe 5, Rudy Muts 2, Rainer Van Gulick 0) **BRISTOL 40** (Reidar Eide 10, Steve Gresham 10, Mike Ferreira 7, Derek Hole 5, Bruce Cribb 5, Neil Farnish 3, Nigel Boocock 0).

LIONS IN 7-UP TOAST

MICHAEL LEE demonstrated what all the fuss was about on his first international appearance in Australia...and set up the most devastating string of performances ever seen Down Under.

The 20-year-old hot-shot had time to weigh up the big Perth track when he won the King of Claremont Championship a week before the opening Test...and then streaked to an 18-point maximum that got an England side, hand-picked by Nigel Boocock but given official status by the Speedway Control Board, off to a flying start with a 30-point win.

It was the beginning of a memorable series in which the Lions won all seven matches for the first time in Ashes history and completed the first clean sweep since Ken McKinlay's 5-0 victory in the 1959-60 series.

Boocock, the most popular of all the English tourists, could even afford the luxury of naming himself as reserve for most of the meetings as England decimated the opposition in every speedway state.

Mick McKeon was ruled out of the scenesetter with a broken wrist and the Aussies' three National Leaguers Steve Koppe, Danny Kennedy and David Shields all struggled after being hampered by a fuel strike which made it difficult for them to travel across from the Eastern seaboard.

Within a week of that win at Claremont the series was all but over as the Lions raced to successive wins in 24 hours at Adelaide and Liverpool.

John Boulger, missing at Perth, was called up at Rowley Park – where Gordon Kennett equalled the 4-year old track record – and at Liverpool Raceway Gary Guglielmi collected his first cap with a fine 7-point debut.

England won by 13 points but it could so easily have been more as Lee, who had dropped only one point in the first two matches, broke a con-rod in his first ride, borrowed bikes for the rest of the meeting and still ended up with a dozen points.

Within three weeks of touching down in Western Australia the Lions were celebrating a series victory with another double within 24 hours at Newcastle and Sydney Showground.

Any fears that the Christmas festivities and a month-long break from Test racing would lessen the resolve of the tourists to complete their clean sweep were dispelled by skipper Doug Wyer in the sixth and penultimate match at Brisbane on New Year's Day.

Australia had brought in Phil Crump but when the original staging was washed out on the last Saturday of 1978 he returned home to Mildura and had to be replaced by local reserve Ken Murray.

All that was left was Test number seven and Australia tried everything to avoid the indignity of failing to win a match.

Billy Sanders was named at reserve, the Brisbane Exhibition Ground had a three inch layer of deep dirt and Crump was again brought across from Victoria, this time actually riding for his country!

But there was no-stopping Booey's battlers and they completed what had seemed impossible when they first set out from Britain even though celebrations were muted because of a crash which left the popular Alan Grahame in the Royal Brisbane Hospital having an operation on a dislocated shoulder and fractured collar bone.

Tourist Steve Bastable said: "We are justifiably proud of ourselves."

Everything looked fine and dandy on the England front...but how things were to change in the following nine months or so!

1978-79 England Tour of Australia Results

Perth, Friday, November 17, 1978
AUSTRALIA 39 (†John Titman 14, Billy Sanders 9, Steve Koppe 5, Danny Kennedy 4, Mick Moores 4, Mike Farrell 3, David Shields 0) **ENGLAND 69** (Michael Lee 18, †Doug Wyer 11, Steve Bastable 10, Alan Grahame 10, Phil Collins 10, Gordon Kennett 9, Nigel Boocock 1).

Adelaide, Friday, November 24, 1978
AUSTRALIA 45 (Billy Sanders 13, Phil Herne 8, John Boulger 8, †John Titman 7, Steve Koppe 5, Robert Maxfield 4, Kym Amundson 0) **ENGLAND 63** (Michael Lee 17, Gordon Kennett 16, †Doug Wyer 13, Alan Grahame 7, Steve Bastable 6, Phil Collins 4, Nigel Boocock, did not ride).

Liverpool, Saturday, November 25, 1978
AUSTRALIA 47 (Billy Sanders 16, †John Titman 10, Gary Guglielmi 7, Ricky Day 7, Phil Herne 6, Glenn McDonald 1, Phil Cain 0) **ENGLAND 60** (Gordon Kennett 14, Michael Lee 12, †Doug Wyer 12, Alan Grahame 9, Steve Bastable 9, Phil Collins 3, Nigel Boocock 1).

Newcastle, Friday, December 1, 1978
AUSTRALIA 50 (Billy Sanders 15, †John Titman 14, Phil Herne 9, Ricky Day 6, Glenn McDonald 3, Gary Guglielmi 2, Mick Moores 1) **ENGLAND 58** (†Doug Wyer 11, Gordon Kennett 11, Steve Bastable 9, Michael Lee 8, Phil Collins 8, Alan Grahame 7, Nigel Boocock 4).

Sydney, Saturday, December 2, 1978
AUSTRALIA 51.5 (Billy Sanders 16, †John Titman 15, Phil Herne 8.5, Ricky Day 7, Glenn McDonald 5, Gary Guglielmi 0, Mick Moores 0) **ENGLAND 56.5** (†Doug Wyer 16, Michael Lee 15, Gordon Kennett 11, Alan Grahame 8, Phil Collins 4.5, Steve Bastable 2, Nigel Boocock, did not ride).

Brisbane, Monday, January 1, 1979
AUSTRALIA 50 (Billy Sanders 13, Mike Farrell 13, Mick McKeon 10, †John Titman 7, Steve Koppe 6, Neil Coddington 1, Ken Murray 0) **ENGLAND 58** (†Doug Wyer 18, Gordon Kennett 14, Michael Lee 14, Steve Bastable 5, Phil Collins 4, Alan Grahame 3, Nigel Boocock, did not ride).

Brisbane, Saturday, January 6, 1979
AUSTRALIA 43 (†John Titman 14, Phil Crump 11, Steve Koppe 7, Mike Farrell 6, Billy Sanders 4, Danny Kennedy 1, Robbie Blackadder 0) **ENGLAND 65** (†Doug Wyer 14, Michael Lee 14, Gordon Kennett 13, Phil Collins 9, Steve Bastable 7, Alan Grahame 5, Nigel Boocock 3).

England win the series 7-0

OTHER MATCHES

Rockhampton, Sunday, December 10, 1978
ROCKHAMPTON 47 (†Steve Koppe 13, Mike Lohmann 12, John Titman 11, Mike Farrell 10, Neil Coddington 1, M. Shepherd 0, Greg Kluver 0) **ENGLAND 61** (Michael Lee 17, Gordon Kennett 14, †Doug Wyer 12, Phil Collins 8, Steve Bastable 6, Alan Grahame 4).

Ayr, Tuesday, December 12, 1978
PIONEER PARK 25 (Terry Keyse 6, Dennis Cavill 5, Tony Constantinides 5, Ray Garvey 4, Brian Hodder 4, David Christopher 1, Dennis Garvey 0) **ENGLAND 82** (Michael Lee 18, Gordon Kennett 18, Alan Grahame 12, †Doug Wyer 12, Steve Bastable 11, Phil Collins 11).

Brisbane, Tuesday, December 26, 1978
QUEENSLAND SELECT 47 (†John Titman 13, Steve Koppe 12, Mike Farrell 9, Neil Coddington 7, Mike Lohmann 5, Ken Murray 1, Mark Stewart 0) **ENGLAND 48** (†Doug Wyer 17, Gordon Kennett 13, Michael Lee 6, Alan Grahame 5, Nigel Boocock 3, Steve Bastable 2, Phil Collins 2).
Abandoned after 16 heats, rain.

Avalon, Saturday, January 13, 1979
AVALON 25 (†Phil Crump 11, Rod North 4, Kevin McNeill 3, Glen McNeill 2, Danny Kennedy 2, Owen Hall 1, Roger Lambert 1, I. Smith 1, Danny Young 0) **ENGLAND 58** (Phil Collins 14, Michael Lee 13, †Doug Wyer 11, Steve Bastable 8, Gordon Kennett 6, Nigel Boocock 6).

- *The Australia team manager was Jim Airey.*
- *England team manager was Phil Mountford.*

John Berry began the domestic season running the England team and ended the year as an ex-manager.

No-one could complain about the one full-scale international series – England won all five Tests against an Ivan Mauger-less Australasia – but elimination from the World Team Cup in a preliminary round at Reading where the Lions trailed in third behind eventual gold-medal winners New Zealand and an American squad that was without number one Scott Autrey who had refused to ride for his country following the American Motorcycle Association's decision not to seed him through as one of their World Championship contenders, a ludicrous ruling considering he was top of the entire British League averages!

Berry quit after the Australasian series but not before axing skipper Malcolm Simmons to make way for a wave of new faces.

KENNY CARTER would have become the youngest rider ever to represent England in an official Test match when he was chosen to make his debut against Denmark at Halifax on Monday, June 18.

But the meeting was cancelled at short notice when the Danes made fresh financial demands which the British Speedway Promoters' Association refused to yield to. Carter had to wait another 19 days before making his England bow against Poland and, by then, he was two days older than Peter Collins had been when he rode against Scotland in 1972.

1979 England World Team Cup v England Lions

THE THIRD staging of this early season meeting brought another victory for the successful winter tourists.

And their win would have been even more comprehensive had it not been for the form of the World Team Cup reserves Chris Morton and Ian Cartwright who revelled in the extra rides they were given by troubled manager John Berry as he wrestled with pressing selection problems.

Yet the World Cup squad had started off in bristling style with an opening race 5-1 from Dave Jessup and Malcolm Simmons. Mechanical problems didn't help – with Tony Davey, John Davis and Peter Collins all experiencing setbacks of one sort or another.

The result certainly did little to help England settle on the best squad with the World Team Cup qualifying round at Reading on the horizon.

Leicester, Tuesday, April 17
ENGLAND WORLD TEAM CUP 51 (Ian Cartwright 13, Dave Jessup 12, Dave Morton 8, Chris Morton 7, Peter Collins 6, John Davis 3, Malcolm Simmons 2, Tony Davey 0)
ENGLAND LIONS 57 (Doug Wyer 14, Gordon Kennett 12, Michael Lee 11, Alan Grahame 9, Steve Bastable 6, Phil Collins 5).

1979 Denmark v England

ONE match hardly qualifies for the tag series – but this should have been the start of the first ever rubber between the two nations.

England had agreed to send a team to Vojens and, in return, the Danes would give official sanction to a four-Test series in England.

It never got off the ground as, less than two weeks before the scheduled first match at Halifax, the Danish Motor Union asked for a further £1,000 and after a series telexes between the respective governing bodies the series was called off a week before the scheduled opening match. Nonetheless, England fulfilled their part of the bargain and the Danes scraped a three-point win in the first official international between the two countries with a sell-out 16,000 crowd.

Ole Olsen and Hans Nielsen were unbeaten while England's top scorer was reserve Ian Cartwright who was given five rides by manager John Berry.

Vojens, Friday, May 18
DENMARK 40 (Ole Olsen 12, Hans Nielsen 12, Mike Lohmann 5, Bo Petersen 5, Bent Rasmussen 4, Alf Busk 2, Erik Gundersen 0) **ENGLAND 37** (Ian Cartwright 10, Malcolm Simmons 9, Chris Morton 7, Peter Collins 6, Gordon Kennett 5, Dave Jessup 0, Michael Lee 0).

1979 England v Australasia Results

Wimbledon, Thursday, July 12
ENGLAND 61 (John Davis 13, Dave Jessup 12, Michael Lee 11, Peter Collins 9, †Malcolm Simmons 9, Gordon Kennett 7, Roger Johns 0, Chris Morton, did not ride) **AUSTRALASIA 47** (†Phil Crump 13, Larry Ross 12, Billy Sanders 11, Bruce Cribb 5, John Titman 4, Mitch Shirra 2, Gary Guglielmi 0, Steve Koppe 0).

Swindon, Friday, July 27
ENGLAND 67 (Michael Lee 16, Dave Jessup 15, Chris Morton 11, Peter Collins 9, †Malcolm Simmons 8, John Davis 4, Kenny Carter 4) **AUSTRALASIA 41** (Ivan Mauger 12, †Phil Crump 10, Billy Sanders 10, Larry Ross 8, John Titman 1, Phil Herne 0, John Boulger 0, Bruce Cribb 0).

Ipswich, Thursday, August 2
ENGLAND 60 (Michael Lee 16, Dave Jessup 11, Peter Collins 9, John Louis 7, Kevin Jolly 7, Joe Owen 7, Gordon Kennett 2, †Malcolm Simmons 1) **AUSTRALASIA 48** (†Phil Crump 17, Billy Sanders 15, Larry Ross 9, Danny Kennedy 6, Steve Koppe 1, Bruce Cribb 0, Gary Guglielmi 0).

Cradley Heath, Wednesday, August 22
ENGLAND 72 (†Peter Collins 17, Dave Jessup 16, Phil Collins 11, John Davis 10, Alan Grahame 8, Michael Lee 8, Chris Morton 2) **AUSTRALASIA 36** (†Phil Crump 12, Larry Ross 6, John Boulger 6, John Titman 6, Bruce Cribb 5, John McNeill 1, Mitch Shirra 0, Phil Herne 0).

Halifax, Sunday, October 14
ENGLAND 68 (†John Davis 15, Reg Wilson 14, Kenny Carter 14, Ian Cartwright 10, Steve Bastable 9, Phil Collins 6, Joe Owen, did not ride) **AUSTRALASIA 40** (Mitch Shirra 15, Larry Ross 8, Mike Farrell 8, Mick McKeon 7, John Boulger 1, Gary Guglielmi 1).
Originally postponed on Sunday, August 13.

England win the series 5-0.

- *The England team managers were John Berry and Wally Mawdsley (Wimbledon only).*
- *The Australasia team managers were Wayne Wattie and Dennis Gavros (Halifax only).*

1979 Poland v England

MALCOLM SIMMONS took on the rôle of rider coach as England undertook a weekend visit to Poland.

But it was newly-crowned Commonwealth Champion Michael Lee who was the star of the show.

He dropped just one point in the opening match and then went on to record a six-ride maximum at Gdansk where he shattered Zenon Plech's track record by two fifths of a second to establish a new time of 68.8 seconds on the 349 metre circuit, a time that stood for nearly two years.

Bydgoszcz, Saturday, July 7
POLAND 64 (Robert Slabon 14, Jerzy Rembas 14, Marek Ziarnik 12, Henryk Glucklich 11, Andrzej Huszcza 6, Jan Zabik 4, Andrzej Marynowski 3, Boleslaw Proch 0) **ENGLAND 44** (Michael Lee 17, Malcolm Simmons 9, Kenny Carter 6, Joe Owen 6, Kevin Jolly 3, Chris Morton 3, Phil Collins 0).
Gdansk, Sunday, July 8
POLAND 44 (Andrzej Huszcza 14, Zenon Plech 10, Andrzej Marynowski 8, Robert Slabon 5, Miroslaw Berlinski 5, Marek Ziarnik 1, Jerzy Rembas 1, Jan Zabik 0) **ENGLAND 64** (Michael Lee 18, Malcolm Simmons 17, Chris Morton 12, Kenny Carter 7, Joe Owen 5, Kevin Jolly 3, Phil Collins 2).

1979 Young Sweden Club Tour (Division Two)

VETERAN Olle Nygren put his Swedish proteges under the microscope when he acted as coach for a condensed tour of five National League tracks.

Unfortunately the tourists suffered cruelly from injuries but 21-year-old Lillebror Johansson looked a sensational prospect at Boston yet was to wait another three years before being offered a British League contract.

Boston, Sunday April 8
BOSTON 42 (Tony Featherstone 9, Robert Hollingworth 6, Andy Hibbs 6, Colin Ackroyd 6, †Dave Allen 5, Andy Fisher 5, Dave Mortiboys 5, Dennis Mallett 0) **YOUNG SWEDEN 36** (Lillebror Johansson 15, †Lars Ericsson 9, Börje Ring 7, Ingemar Andersson 4, Lennart Bengtsson 1, Thomas Hydling 0, Lars Rosberg 0, Uno Johansson 0).

Crayford, Tuesday, April 10
CRAYFORD 32 (Richard Davey 6, †Laurie Etheridge 6, John Hooper 6, Alan Sage 6, Steve Naylor 5, Peter Wigley 2, Paul Gilbert 1) **YOUNG SWEDEN 45** (†Lars Ericsson 10, Thomas Hydling 10, Tommy Steen 9, Ingemar Johansson 5, Lillebror Johansson 5, Jan Eriksson 5, Börje Ring 1).

Oxford, Thursday, April 12
OXFORD 49 (†George Hunter 12, Les Rumsey 8, Carl Askew 7, John Hack 7, Pip Lamb 7, John Barker 5, Glenn McDonald 3) **YOUNG SWEDEN 29** (Thomas Hydling 9, †Lars Ericsson 7, Lillebror Johansson 5, Tommy Steen 4, Börje Ring 2, Uno Johansson 2, Jan Eriksson 0, Lars Rosberg 0).

Edinburgh, Friday, April 13
EDINBURGH 41 (Dave Trownson 10, Steve Lomas 9, Ivan Blacka 7, †Brian Collins 4, Rob Mouncer 4, Tim Curnock 4, Alan Bridgett 3) **YOUNG SWEDEN 34** (Börje Ring 12, Tommy Steen 8, Uno Johansson 5, Lillebror Johansson 5, Ingemar Johansson 2, Lennart Bengtsson 2, †Lars Eriksson 0, Thomas Hydling 0).

Newcastle, Sunday, April 15
NEWCASTLE 40 (†Tom Owen 12, Robbie Blackadder 9, David Bargh 9, Neil Coddington 6, Graeme Stapleton 3, Robbie Gardner 1, Rod Hunter 0) **YOUNG SWEDEN 38** (Tommy Steen 10, † Lennart Bengtsson 10, Thomas Hydling 7, Ingemar Andersson 6, Lillebror Johansson 5, Lars Rosberg 0, Börje Ring 0).

- *The Young Sweden team manager was Lars Lantz.*

1979 Getingarna (Sweden) Club Tour Results

Reading, Monday, April 16
READING 52 (John Davis 12, Terry Betts 12, Jan Andersson 10, Reidar Eide 7, Bernie Leigh 6, Sigvart Pedersen 4, Andy Campbell 1) **GETINGARNA 26** (Anders Michanek 8, Christer Sjösten 7, Tommy Nilsson 5, Frederick Lindqvist 2, Kent Eriksson 2, Per Ove Gudmundsson 2, Thomas Hydling 0).
Weymouth, Tuesday, April 17
WEYMOUTH 37.5 (Bob Coles 9, Doug Underwood 8.5, Brian Woodward 7, Kevin Bowen 5, Terry Tulloch 5, Nigel Davis 2, Geoff Swindells 1) **GETINGARNA 40.5** (Tommy Nilsson 11, Anders Michanek 10.5, Frederick Lindqvist 5, Lars Lundgren 4, Kent Eriksson 4, Per Ove Gudmundsson 3, Thomas Hydling 3).

INTERNATIONAL racing returned to Scotland – after an absence of nearly four years with a five-match National League series against England.

And how the Scots celebrated as Jimmy McMillan (left), brought in from the British League, led them to victory with three straight wins and a sole defeat against Tom Owen when he won the first race after the interval.

In a towering display Jimmy Mac also set up a new Powderhall track record in his opening ride and he helped the Scots complete a home soil double with another win in the second Test at Glasgow.

Despite their fond hopes of a series win the Scots finally went down in a best of five thriller when they lost the last Test at Middlesbrough...but they could point to two broken chains at Berwick as their downfall.

McMillan and Beaton both failed to finish a race at Shielfield Park where England scraped through to a one-point win when reserve Nig Close got the better of his opposite number in the last heat.

It left the two nations all square going into the final Test at Middlesbrough and this time the Lions began badly but came from behind to have the match sewn up with four races left thanks to double figure scores from skipper Tom Owen, Mike Sampson, Malcolm Corradine and home star Steve Wilcock.

1979 England v Scotland (Division Two) Results

Edinburgh, Friday May 11
SCOTLAND 60 (†Jim McMillan 15, Bobby Beaton 15, Bert Harkins 8, Brian Collins 8, Andy Reid 8, Harry MacLean 4, Charlie McKinna 2, Colin Caffrey, did not ride) **ENGLAND 48** (†Tom Owen 14, Dave Trownson 9, Derek Harrison 8, Derek Richardson 7, Steve Lawson 7, Steve Lomas 3, Graham Jones 0, Ivan Blacka 0).

Glasgow, Sunday, May 13
SCOTLAND 60 (George Hunter 17, †Jim McMillan 16, Bobby Beaton 16, Andy Reid 4, Charlie McKinna 3, Brian Collins 2, Bert Harkins 1, Jim Beaton 1) **ENGLAND 48** (Dave Trownson 14, Steve Lawson 12, Steve McDermott 8, †Derek Richardson 5, Nigel Close 5, Derek Harrison 4, Sid Sheldrick 0, Keith Bloxsome 0).

Workington, Sunday, May 20
ENGLAND 70 (†Tom Owen 16, John Jackson 13, Steve Finch 11, Steve Lawson 11, Alan Emerson 10, Brian Havelock 7, Steve Wilcock 2, Mark Dickinson, did not ride) **SCOTLAND 38** (†Jim McMillan 17, Bobby Beaton 11, Brian Collins 6, Charlie McKinna 2, Bert Harkins 1, Jim Beaton 1, Andy Reid 0, George Hunter 0).

Berwick, Saturday, June 2
ENGLAND 54 (†Tom Owen 15, Steve Finch 14, Dave Trownson 8, Graham Jones 7, Les Rumsey 7, Steve McDermott 2, Nigel Close 1, Ivan Blacka 0) **SCOTLAND 53** (†Jim McMillan 15, George Hunter 15, Bobby Beaton 14, Colin Caffrey 4, Jim Beaton 3, Harry MacLean 1, Andy Reid 1, Charlie McKinna 0).

Middlesbrough, Thursday, June 7
ENGLAND 66 (†Tom Owen 15, Mike Sampson 13, Malcolm Corradine 12, Steve Wilcock 12, Steve Finch 8, Geoff Pusey 6, Brian Havelock 0) **SCOTLAND 42** (†Jim McMillan 15, Bobby Beaton 15, Harry MacLean 5, Benny Rourke 4, Andy Reid 2, Bert Harkins 1, Ian Darling 0, Colin Caffrey 0).

England win the series 3-2.

- *The England team manager was Dave Younghusband.*
- *The Scotland team managers were Dick Barrie and George Cummings (Edinburgh only).*

1979 England v Australasia (Division Two) Results

Oxford. Thursday, September 20
ENGLAND 73 (Andy Grahame 18, Melvyn Taylor 14, †Ashley Pullen 14, Steve Finch 9, John Hack 9, Les Rumsey 6, Malcolm Holloway 3) **AUSTRALASIA 35** (†Bob Humphreys 14, Wayne Brown 14, Rod Hunter 7, Greg McNeill 0, Terry Tulloch 0, Roger Lambert 0, Robert Dole 0, Frank England 0).

Boston, Sunday, September 23
ENGLAND 72 (†Robert Hollingworth 18, Les Rumsey 13, Andy Hines 12, Nigel Flatman 11, Ian Clark 10, Andy Grahame 6, Dave Allen 2) **AUSTRALASIA 36** (†Bob Humphreys 12, Wayne Brown 10, Robbie Blackadder 6, Rod Hunter 4, Terry Tulloch 3, Greg McNeill 1, Doug Underwood 0).

Milton Keynes, Tuesday, September 25
ENGLAND 69 (Melvyn Taylor 14, Steve Finch 14, †Andy Grahame 12, Nigel Flatman 10, Derek Harrison 10, Steve Wilcock 7, Malcolm Holloway 2, Kevin Hawkins 0) **AUSTRALASIA 39** (Wayne Brown 11, Danny Kennedy 11, †Bob Humphreys 9, Greg McNeill 3, Stuart Mountford 3, Carl Askew 2, Glenn McDonald 0).

England win the series 3-0.

SECOND TIMER...Ladislav Hradecky made his second tour of National League tracks with his Czech club side Ruda Hvezda but had to sit out most of the matches, making only three appearances in 7 matches.

1979 Ruda Hvezda (Czechoslovakia) Division Two Tour Results

Ellesmere Port, Friday, April 6
ELLESMERE PORT 32 (†John Jackson 12, Paul Tyrer 8, Steve Finch 6, Louis Carr 3, Paul Embley 2, John Williams 1, Peter Ellams 0) **RUDA HVEZDA 46** (†Jiri Stancl 10, Vaclav Verner 10, Jan Verner 8, Zdenek Kudrna 7, Jiri Svoboda 5, Petr Ondrasik 4, Milan Spinka 2).

Canterbury, Saturday, April 7
CANTERBURY 33 (Tim Hunt 8, Barney Kennett 6, †Nigel Boocock 6, Mike Ferreira 6, Graham Clifton 4, Paul Woods 2, David Piddock 1) **RUDA HVEZDA 45** (†Jiri Stancl 12, Petr Ondrasik 9, Jan Verner 6, Zdenek Kudrna 5, Milan Spinka 5, Jiri Svoboda 3, Vaclav Verner 3, Ladislav Hradecky 2).

Newcastle, Sunday, April 8
NEWCASTLE 33 (Robbie Blackadder 13, †Tom Owen 10, David Bargh 4, Rod Hunter 3, Graeme Stapleton 3, Neil Coddington 0) **RUDA HVEZDA 45** (Vaclav Verner 10, Petr Ondrasik 8, †Jiri Stancl 7, Zdenek Kudrna 7, Milan Spinka 6, Jan Verner 4, Jiri Svoboda 3).

Milton Keynes, Tuesday, April 10
MILTON KEYNES 31 (†Bob Humphreys 12, Andy Grahame 7, Derek Harrison 5, Malcolm Holloway 3, Harry MacLean 2, Chris Robins 2) **RUDA HVEZDA 47** (Jiri Stancl 10, †Jan Verner 10, Vaclav Verner 10, Zdenek Kudrna 5, Milan Spinka 5, Petr Ondrasik 4, Ladislav Hradecky 3).

Long Eaton, Wednesday, April 11
Cancelled, waterlogged track.

Oxford, Friday, April 13
OXFORD & NOTTINGHAM 37 (†George Hunter 12, Dave Perks 7, Mike Sampson 6, Carl Askew 6, Pip Lamb 5, Glenn McDonald 1, Les Rumsey 0) **RUDA HVEZDA 41** (Vaclav Verner 9, Jan Verner 9, Zdenek Kudrna 8, †Jiri Stancl 7, Milan Spinka 7, Petr Ondrasik 1, Jiri Svoboda 0).

Stoke, Saturday, April 14
Cancelled, waterlogged track.

Boston, Sunday, April 15
BOSTON 25 (Andy Fisher 7, †Dave Allen 4, Tony Featherstone 4, Colin Ackroyd 3, Dave Mortiboys 3, Robert Hollingworth 3, Phil Cain 1, Andy Hibbs 0) **RUDA HVEZDA 53** (†Jiri Stancl 11, Vaclav Verner 10, Zdenek Kudrna 8, Milan Spinka 8, Jan Verner 7, Petr Ondrasik 6, Ladislav Hradecky 3).

Weymouth, Monday, April 16
WEYMOUTH 26 (Doug Underwood 8, Geoff Swindells 7, †Bob Coles 4, Terry Tulloch 4, Brian Woodward 2, Kevin Bowen 1, George Hunter 0) **RUDA HVEZDA 52** (Vaclav Verner 12, Zdenek Kudrna 12, †Jiri Stancl 9, Milan Spinka 8, Petr Ondrasik 5, Jan Verner 4, Jiri Svoboda 2).

● *The Ruda Hvezda team manager was Alexander Zvolenski.*

1979 Poland Under 23 Tour of Division Two

THE TOUR by Poland was officially billed as being at Under 23 level.

In reality only four of the tourists qualified under the age limit and, to boost, their entertainment value, 32-year-old Edward Jancarz was drafted in before the Poles returned home to their own domestic racing!

An interesting newcomer to Britain was Jan Szydlik who had finished top of the Polish Second Division averages but he crashed out of the tour in only the second match at Mildenhall.

And there were further injury problems for the Poles as the match at Long Eaton was abandoned in the second half when Boleslaw Proch was rushed to hospital with chest injuries although he recovered quickly and was back on his bike at Stoke three days later!

In all the Poles won two matches and lost another by a single point but their most remarkable display was at the aforementioned Station Road where they went into action with only five fit riders and still outpointed the home side with plenty to spare.

At Middlesbrough, beaten by a single point, they were also reduced to five men, one of whom, Jozef Kafel, had four last places.

Peterborough, Friday, May 11
PETERBOROUGH 45.5 (Nigel Flatman 11, Andy Hines 9, Nigel Couzens 8, Ian Clark 7.5, †Brian Clark 7, Peter Spink 2, Dave Gooderham 1) **POLAND U23 32.5** (Boleslaw Proch 9, Mariusz Okoniewski 8, Piotr Pyszny 7, Jozef Kafel 3.5, Jan Szydlik 2, Andrzej Jurczynski 2, Stanislaw Kepowicz 1).

Mildenhall, Sunday, May 13
MILDENHALL 43 (†Robert Henry 10, Melvyn Taylor 10, Mick Hines 9, Mike Spink 8, Mick Bates 4, Mark Baldwin 2, Ray Bales 0) **POLAND U23 35** (Edward Jancarz 12, Piotr Pyszny 8, Boleslaw Proch 7, Andrzej Jurczynski 6, Mariusz Okoniewski 1, Jozef Kafel 1, Jan Szydlik 0).

Newcastle, Monday, May 14
NEWCASTLE 49 (Robbie Blackadder 12, †Tom Owen 11, Rod Hunter 8, Graeme Stapleton 6, Neil Coddington 5, David Bargh 4, Nigel Crabtree 3) **POLAND U23 29** (Edward Jancarz 12, Piotr Pyszny 9, Mariusz Okoniewski 4, Andrzej Jurczynski 2, Boleslaw Proch 1, Jozef Kafel 1, Stanislaw Kepowicz 0).

Long Eaton, Wednesday, May 16
NOTTINGHAM 31 (Dave Perks 10, Mike Sampson 8, Kevin Hawkins 7, Glenn McDonald 4, Craig Featherby 1, Tony Garard 1, Nigel Wasley 0) **POLAND U23 47** (Boleslaw Proch 15, Piotr Pyszny 11, Mariusz Okoniewski 8, Jozef Kafel 6, *Les Sawyer 4*, Stanislaw Kepowicz 3).

Middlesbrough, Thursday, May 17
MIDDLESBROUGH 39 (Steve Wilcock 10, Mark Courtney 10, Martin Dixon 5, Geoff Pusey 5, Malcolm Corradine 4, Paul Stead 4, Martin Cusworth 1) **POLAND U23 38** (Andrzej Tkocz 15, Piotr Pyszny 11, Mariusz Okoniewski 8, Stanislaw Kepowicz 4, Jozef Kafel 0, *Mick Conroy 0*).

Stoke, Saturday, May 19
STOKE 38 (Billy Burton 10, Ian Robertson 7, Stuart Mountford 6, Ian Gledhill 5, Tony Lomas 5, Frank Smith 5, Mitch Graham 0) **POLAND U23 40** (Edward Jancarz 12, Boleslaw Proch 11, Piotr Pyszny 7, Mariusz Okoniewski 6, Stanislaw Kepowicz 2, Jozef Kafel 1, *Ian Jeffcoate 1*).

Stars and strife for new bosses

WHAT'S THE SCORE...Steve Gresham checks up with American manager John Scott

AMERICAN skipper Scott Autrey took a leaf out of his team-mate Ivan Mauger's pyschological warfare book...to send England to defeat in the first series between the two countries for three decades.

He organised a War Cabinet with his Californian team-mates and plotted ways and means they could upset the Lions.

And as soon as the England riders began arriving at The Boulevard for the vital Third Test they knew that they had been upstaged for the Americans were staking claim to the superior home side of the pits.

Protests, led by the new England management team of Ian Thomas and Eric Boocock, were in vain as the Yanks refused to budge and went into the opening heat on a high, having convinced themselves, if not their rivals, that they had won an important mental victory.

They went on to claim their first win of the series and never lost another match!

The two countries had never met since a tour of Third Division tracks in 1950 and after a pulsating opener at Wimbledon the future of the series was guaranteed for years to come.

One of the first decisions of the new men in charge was to recall Ipswich's 38-year-old John Louis to the side and they made him captain for all five Tests.

That was one ploy that met with considerable success but another backfired horrendously on England and eventually cost them overall victory.

A few days before the fourth Test at Poole – a match England had to win if they were to take the rubber – Eric Boocock telephoned the Pirates management and asked them to arrange for a liberal supply of dirt on the track.

Boocock thought it would blunt the gating edge that the Americans appeared to have but skipper Louis and Michael Lee were hopelessly at sea on a deep, wet surface and managed only a couple of points between them to hand America their biggest-ever win against the Lions.

What made it even more meritorious was the fact that the Americans lost the services of Ron Preston by the interval when he was taken to hospital with torn knee ligaments which were, eventually, to force his early retirement from the sport.

America could not lose the series but there was still optimism in the English camp, so much so that the British League Management Committee discussed what they should do if England levelled the series at Swindon.

They needn't have bothered....

For the second time in the summer they commandeered the home pits and certainly had the crowd on their side with a recalled John Davis admitting: "You would have thought we were racing in America rather than England!"

There were backstage murmurings that Boocock and Thomas should go on the strength of a 3-1 defeat.

Fortunately for England they survived and went on to show they had learnt lessons out of defeat by leading England back to the top of the speedway world with a tremendous triumph in the 1980 World Team Cup Final.

A performance which deserved, and got, an honourable mention in the B.B.C.'s Sports Personality of the Year programme.

1980 England v United States of America Results

Wimbledon, Thursday, May 1
ENGLAND 54 (Chris Morton 12, †John Louis 11, Peter Collins 11, Michael Lee 9, John Davis 7, Malcolm Simmons 4, Kenny Carter 0, Les Collins 0) **UNITED STATES OF AMERICA 54** (†Scott Autrey 15, Bruce Penhall 13, Bobby Schwartz 8, Ron Preston 8, Dennis Sigalos 7, Steve Gresham 3, John Cook and Larry Kosta, did not ride).

Cradley Heath, Saturday, May 3
ENGLAN D 62 (Dave Jessup 17, Michael Lee 12, Peter Collins 9, Phil Collins 9, †John Louis 8, Chris Morton 7, John Davis 0, Les Collins 0) **UNITED STATES OF AMERICA 46** (Bruce Penhall 15, Dennis Sigalos 12, †Scott Autrey 8, Bobby Schwartz 4, Steve Gresham 4, Ron Preston 3, John Cook 0, Larry Kosta, did not ride).

Hull, Wednesday, May 7
ENGLAND 47 (John Davis 11, †John Louis 11, Michael Lee 10, Kenny Carter 7, Chris Morton 3, Frank Auffret 3, Phil Collins 2, Peter Collins 0) **UNITED STATES OF AMERICA 61** (Dennis Sigalos 15, †Scott Autrey 14, Bruce Penhall 14, Bobby Schwartz 9, Steve Gresham 7, Ron Preston 1, Shawn Moran 1, John Cook 0).

Poole, Wednesday, May 14
ENGLAND 44 (Dave Jessup 13, Peter Collins 11, Les Collins 7, Malcolm Simmons 7, Chris Morton 4, Michael Lee 2, †John Louis 0, Phil Collins 0) **UNITED STATES OF AMERICA 63** (Bruce Penhall 16, †Scott Autrey 12, Bobby Schwartz 10, Steve Gresham 10, Dennis Sigalos 9, Shawn Moran 4, Ron Preston 2, John Cook, did not ride).

Swindon, Saturday, May 24
ENGLAND 49 (Dave Jessup 12, Michael Lee 12, †John Louis 10, Peter Collins 8, Kenny Carter 4, John Davis 2, Chris Morton 1, Les Collins 0) **UNITED STATES OF AMERICA 59** (†Scott Autrey 15, Dennis Sigalos 15, Bruce Penhall 14, Shawn Moran 6, Steve Gresham 5, Bobby Schwartz 4, John Cook and Larry Kosta, did not ride).

United States of America win the series 3-1 with one Test drawn.

- *The England team manager was Ian Thomas with coach Eric Boocock.*
- *The United States of America team managers were John Scott and Harry Oxley.*

THE DAWN of a new decade marked something of a watershed in international competition for National League tracks.

After the lukewarm reception from fans to the traditional England-Australasia clashes it was decided to drop the series and the calendar was, for once, devoid of any international series.

Czechoslovakian champions Ruda Hvezda were invited for a fourth successive tour but asked to send over a predominantly youthful squad without any of their renowned international performers.

Italy became new visitors with a five-match itinerary and Sweden were once again restricted to a series against club sides.

The Swedes and the Latins began brightly enough – Sweden won convincingly at Middlesbrough and the Italians snatched a draw at Canterbury – but both finished up with a losing record.

And Red Star, such powerful visitors in previous years, were so hopelessly outclassed that they were eventually forced to draft in King's Lynn's Ladislav Hradecky, Wolverhampton's Petr Ondrasik and finally Poole's fiery Vaclav Verner before they attained respectability.

The Italians, however, made friends with their all-action effort and were invited back to open the 1981 season at National League level.

1980 Italy Division Two Tour Results

Canterbury, Saturday, March 29
CANTERBURY 39 (Ted Hubbard 11, Mike Ferreira 11, David Piddock 7, †Barney Kennett 7, Kevin Howland 2, Tony Reynolds 1, Ray Griffiths 0) **ITALY 39** (Francesco Biginato 9, Mario Andrioli 8, Gianni Famari 7, Mauro Ferracciolí 7, Fausto Birbini 4, Mario Zanin 3, Ottaviano Righetto 1).

Mildenhall, Sunday, March 30
MILDENHALL 59 (Ian Gledhill 11, †Robert Henry 10, Mark Baldwin 9, Ray Bales 8, Mick Bates 8, Richard Knight 7, Mark Bilner 6) **ITALY 19** (Francesco Biginato 6, Fausto Birbini 5, Mauro Ferracciolí 4, Mario Andrioli 3, Mario Zanin 1, Gianni Famari 0, Ottaviano Righetto 0).

Crayford, Tuesday, April 1
Cancelled, waterlogged track.

Long Eaton, Wednesday, April 2
NOTTINGHAM 48 (†Mike Sampson 12, Glenn McDonald 11, Arthur Price 7, Craig Featherby 7, Mark Collins 7, John Homer 3, Mark Williams 1) **ITALY 30** (Mauro Feracciolí 10, Ottaviano Righetto 8, Mario Andrioli 5, Fausto Birbini 3, Francesco Biginato 3, Mario Zanin 1, Gianni Famari 0).

Oxford, Friday, April 4
OXFORD 43 (†Dave Perks 12, John Hack 12, Mick Handley 9, Colin Ackroyd 8, Chris Sully 1, William Spiers 1, John Grahame 0) **ITALY 34** (Mauro Ferracciolí 9, Fausto Birbini 6, Mario Andrioli 6, Francesco Biginato 6, Mario Zanin 3, Ottaviano Righetto 2 Gianni Famari 2).

1980 Young Sweden Division Two Tour Results

Middlesbrough, Thursday, April 17
MIDDLESBROUGH 32 (Mark Courtney 11, †Steve Wilcock 7, Brian Havelock 6, Geoff Pusey 5, Martin Dixon 2, Bernie Collier 1, Peter Reading 0) **YOUNG SWEDEN 45** (Åke Fridell 12, Börje Ring 10, Hans Danielsson 8, †Tommy Nilsson 6, Thomas Hydling 5, Lennart Bengtsson 4, Jerry Karlsson 0).

Peterborough, Friday, April 18
PETERBOROUGH 45 (Andy Hines 11, Nigel Flatman 10, †Richard Greer 9, Dave Gooderham 6, Andy Buck 4, Ian Barney 4, Nigel Couzens 1) **YOUNG SWEDEN 33** (†Tommy Nilsson 13, Hans Danielsson 9, Börje Ring 8, Åke Fridell 2, Jerry Karlsson 1, Thomas Hydling 0, Jan Eriksson 0).

Boston, Sunday, April 20
BOSTON 57 (†David Gagen 15, Dennis Mallett 11, Robert Hollingworth 11, Steve Lomas 9, Chris Turner 7, Tony Featherstone 3, Michael Holding 1) **YOUNG SWEDEN 20** (†Tommy Nilsson 5, Åke Fridell 4, Thomas Hydling 4, Lennart Bengtsson 3, Hans Danielsson 2, Börje Ring 1, Ingemar Andersson 1).

Scunthorpe, Monday, April 21
SCUNTHORPE 37 (Kevin Teager 12, Phil White 9, †Arthur Browning 8, Ian Jeffcoate 5, Rob Woffinden 2, John Priest 1, Mike Beaumont 0) **YOUNG SWEDEN 41** (Thomas Hydling 12, Börje Ring 9, †Tommy Nilsson 7, Hans Danielsson 6, Lennart Bengtsson 5, Tommy Steen 1, Åke Fridell 1).

Crayford, Tuesday, April 22
CRAYFORD 44 (Alan Sage 10, Steve Naylor 9, Paul Woods 9, Les Rumsey 7, Alan Johns 3, Jack Bibby 3, Paul Gilbert 3) **YOUNG SWEDEN 33** (†Tommy Nilsson 12, Tommy Steen 8, Börje Ring 7, Hans Danielsson 2, Thomas Hydling 2, Lennart Bengtsson 1, Åke Fridell 1).

Exeter, Thursday, April 24
EXETER 50 (Robert Maxfield 12, †Nigel Boocock 11, John Barker 11, Martin Hewlett 9, Tony Sanford 5, Alan Leaver 2, Mike Sanderson 0) **YOUNG SWEDEN 27** (Hans Danielsson 9, †Tommy Nilsson 5, Åke Fridell 5, Börje Ring 3, Jan Eriksson 2, Ingemar Andersson 2, Tommy Steen 1).

1980 Ruda Hvezda (Czechoslovakia) Division Two Tour Results

Mildenhall, Wednesday, August 20
MILDENHALL 51 (†Robert Henry 12, Ian Gledhill 11, Ray Bales 10, Mick Bates 7, Carl Baldwin 5, Richard Knight 3, Andy Warne 3) **RUDA HVEZDA 27** (Antonin Kasper [junior] 6, †Jan Verner 5, Petr Kucera 5, Jiri Svoboda 5, Zbysec Holy 4, Stanislav Urban 2, Jiri Hnidak 0).

Edinburgh, Friday, August 22
EDINBURGH 50 (George Hunter 12, Neil Collins 11, Dave Trownson 10, Roger Lambert 8, Benny Rourke 6, Harry MacLean 2, †Brian Collins 1) **RUDA HVEZDA 28** (†Jan Verner 10, Jiri Svoboda 5, Zbysec Holy 4, Petr Kucera 4, Stanislav Urban 4, Antonin Kasper 1, Jiri Hnidak 0).

Glasgow, Saturday, August 23
GLASGOW 54 (Steve Lawson 12, †Andy Reid 12, Alan Emerson 10, Kenny McKinna 8, Charlie McKinna 6, Jim Beaton 5, Adrian Pepper 1) **RUDA HVEZDA 24** (†Jan Verner 6, Petr Kucera 6, Jiri Svoboda 5, Antonin Kasper 2, Stanislav Urban 2, *Ken Hall 2*, Zbysec Holy 1).

Ellesmere Port, Sunday, August 24
ELLESMERE PORT 49 (Louis Carr 10, Peter Carr 9, †Steve Finch 9, John Jackson 7, Eric Monaghan 7, Phil Alderman 4, Paul Embley 3) **RUDA HVEZDA 29** (†Jan Verner 10, Ladislav Hradecky 9, Petr Kucera 6, Jiri Svoboda 3, Zbysec Holy 1, Stanislav Urban 0, Antonin Kasper 0).

Newcastle, Monday, August 25
NEWCASTLE 44 (David Bargh 14, Rod Hunter 9, †Robbie Blackadder 9, Keith Bloxsome 5, Derek Richardson 4, Nigel Crabtree 2, Michael Easton 1) **RUDA HVEZDA 34** (Petr Ondrasik 11, †Jan Verner 10, Petr Kucera 6, Jiri Svoboda 5, Antonin Kasper 2, Zbysec Holy 0, Stanislav Urban 0).

Milton Keynes, Tuesday, August 26
MILTON KEYNES 38 (Bert Harkins 9, †Bob Humphreys 8, Graham Plant 8, Andy Hibbs 7, Barry Allaway 4, Nigel Davis 1, Mick Blaynee 1) **RUDA HVEZDA 40** (Ladislav Hradecky 9, †Jan Verner 8, Petr Kucera 8, Petr Ondrasik 8, Jiri Svoboda 5, Stanislav Urban 2, Antonin Kasper 0).

Oxford, Wednesday, August 28
OXFORD 36 (George Hunter 11, Steve Crockett 6, Derek Harrison 6, Colin Ackroyd 6, Mick Fletcher 3, Kevin Bowen 2, John Grahame 2) **RUDA HVEZDA 42** (Petr Ondrasik 13, †Jan Verner 8, Petr Kucera 7, Jiri Svoboda 7, Antonin Kasper 4, Stanislav Urban 3, Zbysec Holy 0).

Peterborough, Friday, August 29
Cancelled, waterlogged track.

Canterbury, Saturday, August 30
CANTERBURY 40 (Mike Ferreira 12, Ted Hubbard 10, Denzil Kent 7, †Barney Kennett 6, Kevin Brice 3, Duncan Tolhurst 2, Rob Dolman 0) **RUDA HVEZDA 38** (Vaclav Verner 10, Ladislav Hradecky 9, †Jan Verner 6, Jiri Svoboda 4, Antonin Kasper 4, Petr Kucera 3, Stanislav Urban 2).

● *The Ruda Hvezda team manager was Jiri Santrucek.*

GOLDEN SILVER

LEN SILVER had all the incentive in the world to lead England back to the pinnacle of international success.

For he had been handed a second chance to return in charge of the Lions after being axed following World Team Cup elimination in 1976.

And it wrankled that Ian Thomas and Eric Boocock had basked and bathed in the glory of regaining the World Team Cup in 1980 and milked the publicity of the occasion for all it was worth.

As Silver pointed out: "The one thing they hadn't managed was to win the Test series against America and it became a matter of personal pride to make sure we began with revenge.

"I was sick of people telling me how much Ian Thomas and Eric Boocock had done as the England management team."

The two men who had struck gold with the Lions – and written a book *Speedway Grand Slam* about their 1980 season in charge of the national squad, had quit for differing reasons.

Eric Boocock tendered his resignation because of the added pressures of being elected to the Management Committee and his job at Belle Vue and then Thomas quit after being seriously hurt in a car crash.

They handed over at a time of rare bouyancy and Silver, in conjunction with the Management Committee, adopted a defined course of selection.

He divided the English riders into three distinct groups: cast iron choices, international class, and horses for courses who could come in on a particular track.

Four riders figured in the rarest group – World Champion Michael Lee, Inter Continental Champion Chris Morton, British Champion Dave Jessup and Halifax's exciting young prospect Kenny Carter.

Jessup succeeded John Louis as England captain and Silver set about picking his first team for five years!

One of his automatic choices Carter was ruled out three weeks before the first Test of the summer when he shattered his jaw against Birmingham, ruling himself out of the series.

IT'S ALL YOURS...one of Len Silver's first decisions was to make Dave Jessup the new England skipper

It reduced the elite group of riders to three with Lee, Jessup and Morton justifying Silver's faith in their ability by filling three of the top four places in the England averages.

England opened with a 12-point win at Belle Vue where the trio scored 39 points between them and took advantage of the foul weather conditions everywhere but the North West as America had to begin without Scott Autrey, who had passed on the captaincy to Bruce Penhall, and his Poole team-mate Ron Preston who had taken seven hours to fight their way to Manchester.

Silver gambled on naming Gordon Kennett as reserve for the second Test – he was still not convinced that the former world number two had overcome his diabetes problem – and he proved a match-winner with a dozen points that tipped the balance and won him the Daily Mirror Man of the Match as he raced in six out of the last 10 heats.

Victory at Swindon gave England a winning series lead and Silver could then afford the luxury of experimentation in the last two matches...with an eye on the forthcoming rubber against Denmark!

Carter had recovered in time for the opening Test at Hackney as England quickly wrapped up the series with successive wins

1981 Denmark v England

IN A CURIOUS piece of fixture planning England travelled to Denmark only 48 hours before the Inter Continental Final of the World Team Cup – hardly, one would have thought, ideal preparation.

The Danes maintained their record in front of their own fans but at least the defeat didn't demoralise the Lions as they went on to win the WTC round with Steve Bastable the only squad member who had not figured in the Vojens defeat.

Vojens, Friday, June 26
DENMARK 60 (Tommy Knudsen 13, Finn Thomsen 11, Erik Gundersen 11, †Ole Olsen 11, Hans Nielsen 11, Bo Petersen 3, Preben Eriksen 0) **ENGLAND 48** (Michael Lee 12, Chris Morton 12, Kenny Carter 8, Les Collins 8, Gordon Kennett 7, †Dave Jessup 1, John Davis 0).

1981 England v Denmark Results

Hackney, Friday, June 12
ENGLAND 62 (†Dave Jessup 17, Les Collins 13, Kenny Carter 11, Michael Lee 8, Gordon Kennett 7, Chris Morton 6, Kevin Smith and Sean Willmott, did not ride) **DENMARK 46** (Tommy Knudsen 12, Finn Thomsen 10, Erik Gundersen 8, †Ole Olsen 7, Bo Petersen 6, Hans Nielsen 3, Preben Eriksen and Bent Rasmussen, did not ride).

Reading, Monday June 22
ENGLAND 58 (Kenny Carter 14, Michael Lee 13, †Dave Jessup 12, Chris Morton 9, Steve Bastable 6, Gordon Kennett 2, John Davis 2, Kevin Jolly, did not ride) **DENMARK 50** (Erik Gundersen 15, Tommy Knudsen 11, †Ole Olsen 10, Finn Thomsen 6, Preben Eriksen 5, Hans Nielsen 3, Bo Petersen 0, Mike Lohmann, did not ride).

Coventry, Wednesday, July 1
ENGLAND 46 (†Dave Jessup 12, Michael Lee 11, Kenny Carter 8, Steve Bastable 7, Les Collins 6, Dave Morton 1, Alan Grahame 1, Ian Cartwright 0) **DENMARK 62** (Erik Gundersen 16, Tommy Knudsen 14, Finn Thomsen 12, †Ole Olsen 9, Alf Busk 7, Finn Jensen 2, Hans Nielsen 1, Preben Eriksen 1).

England win the series 2-1.

- *The England team manager was Len Silver.*
- *The Denmark team managers were Olaf Frimodt Pedersen and Hardy Jensen.*

NEW BOY...Poole's new signing Kevin Smith (right) made his full England debut against America with Pirates' team-mate John Davis and close friend Michael Lee

1981 England v United States of America Results

Belle Vue, Sunday, April 26
ENGLAND 60 (Michael Lee 14, Chris Morton 13, †Dave Jessup 12, Les Collins 8, Ian Cartwright 6, Alan Grahame 5, Phil Collins 2, Steve Bastable 0) **UNITED STATES OF AMERICA 48** (†Bruce Penhall 15, Steve Gresham 10, Dennis Sigalos 8, Bobby Schwartz 6, Scott Autrey 5, Ron Preston 3, Shawn Moran 1, Larry Kosta 0).

Poole, Wednesday, April 29
ENGLAND 55 (Gordon Kennett 12, †Dave Jessup 11, Chris Morton 10, Michael Lee 9, Les Collins 8, John Davis 5, Kevin Smith 0, Malcolm Simmons 0) **UNITED STATES OF AMERICA 53** (Dennis Sigalos 15, †Bruce Penhall 14, Scott Autrey 9, Ron Preston 6, Bobby Schwartz 6, Kelly Moran 3, Steve Gresham 0, Shawn Moran, did not ride).

Swindon, Saturday, May 2
ENGLAND 64 (Michael Lee 16, Steve Bastable 13, †Dave Jessup 13, Chris Morton 9, Gordon Kennett 7, Les Collins 6, John Davis 0, Malcolm Simmons, did not ride) **UNITED STATES OF AMERICA 43** (†Bruce Penhall 11, Steve Gresham 10, Kelly Moran 9, Bobby Schwartz 8, Scott Autrey 5, Dennis Sigalos 0, Shawn Moran 0, John Cook 0).

Ipswich, Thursday, May 7
ENGLAND 44 (†Dave Jessup 11, Gordon Kennett 11, Chris Morton 10, Michael Lee 6, John Davis 4, Kevin Jolly 1, Alan Grahame 1, Melvyn Taylor, did not ride) **UNITED STATES OF AMERICA 52** (†Bruce Penhall 12, Dennis Sigalos 11, Scott Autrey 9, Bobby Schwartz 9, John Cook 8, Steve Gresham 3, Larry Kosta, did not ride).
Abandoned after 16 heats because of rain, result to stand.

Cradley Heath, Sunday, May 10
ENGLAND 69 (†Dave Jessup 17, Chris Morton 14, Michael Lee 13, Alan Grahame 10, Gordon Kennett 9, Phil Collins 6, Les Collins and Ian Cartwright, did not ride) **UNITED STATES OF AMERICA 38** (Bobby Schwartz 10, †Bruce Penhall 9, Shawn Moran 7, Kelly Moran 5, Scott Autrey 3, John Cook 3, Dennis Sigalos 1, Keith Chrisco 0).

England win the series 4-1.

- *The England team manager was Len Silver.*
- *The United States of America team manager was John Scott.*

1981 Young Poland Division Two Tour Results

Canterbury, Saturday, June 13
CANTERBURY 41 (Denzil Kent 11, †Mike Ferreira 9, Barney Kennett 7, Kevin Brice 6, Rob Dolman 5, Jamie Luckhurst 3, Darryl Simpson 0) **YOUNG POLAND 37** (Wojciech Zabialowicz 13, Jerzy Kochman 9, Wlodzimierz Helinski 8, Leon Kujawski 6, Antoni Skupien 1, Miroslaw Berlinski 0, Herbert Karwat 0).

Mildenhall, Sunday, June 14
MILDENHALL 57 (†Robert Henry 11, Richard Knight 11, Ray Bales 9, Mick Bates 7, Ian Gledhill 7, Carl Baldwin 6, Mark Bilner 6) **YOUNG POLAND 21** (Wojciech Zabialowicz 9, Jerzy Kochman 6, Leon Kujawksi 4,† Andrzej Tkocz 1, Miroslaw Berlinski 1, Wlodzimierz Helinski 0, Antoni Skupien 0).

Scunthorpe, Monday, June 15
SCUNTHORPE 44 (†Nicky Allott 10, Kevin Teager 9, Rob Woffinden 7, Mark DeKok 6, Tony Featherstone 5, Graeme Beardsley 5, Julian Parr 2) **YOUNG POLAND 34** (Wojciech Zabialowicz 11, †Andrzej Tkocz 10, Jerzy Kochman 7, Wlodzimierz Helinski 4, Antoni Skupien 2, Leon Kujawski 0, Miroslaw Berlinski 0).

Oxford, Thursday, June 18
OXFORD 45 (Colin Ackroyd 12, †Dave Perks 12, Derek Harrison 10, Alan MacLean 5, Mick Fletcher 3, John Grahame 2, Paul Evitts 1) **YOUNG POLAND 33** (Wojciech Zabialowicz 9, Jerzy Kochman 9, Leon Kujawski 6, Wlodzimierz Helinski 6, †Andrzej Tkocz 2, Herbert Karwat 1, Antoni Skupien 0).

Ellesmere Port, Friday, June 19
ELLESMERE PORT 56 (John Jackson 11, Rob Ashton 10, Peter Carr 9, Eric Monaghan 9, †Steve Finch 9, Paul Embley 5, Phil Alderman 3) **YOUNG POLAND 22** (Antoni Skupien 10, Wojciech Zabialowicz 7, Jerzy Kochman 3, Leon Kujawski 1, Miroslaw Berlinski 1, †Andrzej Tkocz 0, Wlodzimierz Helinski 0).

Boston, Sunday, June 21
BOSTON 53 (Robert Hollingworth 10, †David Gagen 9, Steve Regeling 9, Dennis Mallett 9, Steve Lomas 8, Michael Holding 5, Keven Dye 3) **YOUNG POLAND 25** (Wojciech Zabialowicz 11, Jerzy Kochman 5, Leon Kujawski 4, Wlodzimierz Helinski 4, Antoni Skupien 1, Miroslaw Berlinski 0, †Andrzej Tkocz 0).

Newcastle, Monday, June 22
NEWCASTLE 61 (Rod Hunter 12, †Robbie Blackadder 11, Glenn McDonald 10, David Bargh 8, Alan Emerson 8, Keith Bloxsome 8, Kym Mauger 4) **YOUNG POLAND 17** (Wojciech Zabialowicz 6, Miroslaw Berlinski 4, Wlodzimierz Helinski 3, Jerzy Kochman 3, Leon Kujawski 1, Herbert Karwat 0, Antoni Skupien 0).

- *The Young Poland team manager was Jozef Olejniczak.*

and everyone could gloss over a third Test defeat at Coventry where Morton was an absentee after asking to be excused duty because of a hectic schedule which, he feared, might lead to a nervous breakdown.

Italy, Norway and Young Poland toured the National League but undertook club matches only in a season without a full-scale international series.

Italy, after their bright showing the previous year, proved a disastrous drawcard; Poland were outclassed with only Wojciech Zabialowicz looking even National League standard; and Norway's biggest plus was the re-appearance of the much travelled Reidar Eide who acted as tour manager, having taken over responsibility to rebuilding Norway into a prominent speedway nation.

Their national champion Dag Haaland was topscorer in the first two meeting (the first, fittingly, at one of Eide's old clubs Edinburgh) but it was only when Leicester's Rolf Gramstad was allowed to join the team for the final match at Scunthorpe that they managed to avoid defeat.

Maybe we are being a little harsh on overseas teams finding it difficult to adjust to British conditions as often our own club sides struggle overseas.

When First Division Eastbourne undertook a four match tour of Poland they failed to win a match and were on the wrong end of a 71-18 hiding in their last meeting at Leszno!

1981 Italy Division Two Tour Results

Canterbury, Saturday, April 11
CANTERBURY 53 (†Mike Ferreira 12, Denzil Kent 12, Brendan Shilleto 11, Barney Kennett 7, Rob Dolman 7, Kevin Brice 4, Graham Knowler 0) **ITALY 24** (Francesco Biginato 8, Mauro Ferraccioli 4, Ottaviano Righetto 4, Armando dal Chiele 4, Giorgio Zaramella 2, Roberto Incao 2, Lorenzo Franchetti 0, Paolo Castagna 0).

Wolverhampton, Sunday, April 12
WOLVERHAMPTON 52 (Bruce Cribb 11, Billy Burton 10, Tony Boyle 10, †Les Rumsey 9, Mike Wilding 4, Neil Evitts 4, Steve Crockett 4) **ITALY 25** (Francesco Biginato 8, Mauro Ferraccioli 6, Giorgio Zaramella 3, Armando dal Chiele 3, Roberto Incao 3, Paolo Castagna 2, Ottaviano Righetto 0).

Exeter, Monday, April 13
EXETER 55 (John Williams 11, John Barker 10, †Robert Maxfield 10, Les Sawyer 8, Martin Hewlett 7, Dave Brewer 7, Andy Campbell 2) **ITALY 23** (Mauro Ferraccioli 10, Francesco Biginato 6, Roberto Incao 3, Armando dal Chiele 3, Paolo Castagna 1, Giorgio Zaramella 0).

Milton Keynes, Tuesday, April 14
MILTON KEYNES 55 (Andy Hibbs 12, †Bob Humphreys 8, Mark Baldwin 8, Brett Alderton 8, Barry Allaway 7, Graham Plant 7, Steve Payne 5) **ITALY 22** (Francesco Biginato 10, Armando dal Chiele 7, Giorgio Zaramella 2, Mauro Ferraccioli 1, Roberto Incao 1, Paolo Castagna 1).

Oxford, Friday, April 17
OXFORD 46 (†Dave Perks 12, Derek Harrison 11, Colin Ackroyd 7, Alan MacLean 5, Mick Handley 5, Mick Fletcher 4, John Grahame 2) **ITALY 32** (Mauro Ferraccioli 10, Armando dal Chiele 7, Ottaviano Righetto 5, Francesco Biginato 4, Giorgio Zaramella 3, Roberto Incao 2, Paolo Castagna 1).

● *The Italy team manager was Vito Artosin.*

1981 Norway Division Two Tour Results

Edinburgh, Friday, August 7
EDINBURGH 47 (Neil Collins 12, †George Hunter 12, Dave Trownson 9, Guy Robson 6, Peter Erskine 3, Roger Lambert 3, Benny Rourke 2) **NORWAY 29** (†Dag Haaland 10, Asgeir Bjerga 8, Jorn Haugvaldstad 5, Roy Otto 3, Terje Tollefsen 1, Dagfinn Jorgensen 1, Per Hansen 1).

Stoke, Saturday, August 8
STOKE 50 (Mark Collins 12, Rod North 9, Robert Lightfoot 7, †Arthur Browning 6, Mike Sampson 6, Steve Sant 5, Ian Robertson 5) **NORWAY 27** (†Dag Haaland 9, Asgeir Bjerga 8, Roy Otto 5, Jorn Haugvaldstad 3, Terje Tollefsen 1, Dagfinn Jorgensen 1, Rolf Havirstad 0).

Workington, Sunday, August 9
WORKINGTON 44 (†Terry Kelly 12, Wayne Jackson 11, David Blackburn 7, Derek Wilson 7, David Price 3, John Frankland 3, John Walmsley 1) **NORWAY 34** (Roy Otto 11, †Dag Haaland 6, Asgeir Bjerga 5, Jorn Haugvaldstad 4, Terje Tollefsen 4, Dagfinn Jorgensen 3, Rolf Havirstad 1).

Scunthorpe, Monday, August 10
SCUNTHORPE 39 (†Kevin Teager 15, Rob Woffinden 10, Tony Childs 6, Mark DeKok 5, Tony Featherstone 2, Phil Kynman 1, Julian Parr, did not ride) **NORWAY 39** (Rolf Gramstad 10, †Dag Haaland 10, Asgeir Bjerga 8, Roy Otto 7, Dagfinn Jorgensen 3, Terje Tollefsen 1, Per Hansen 0).

● *The Norway team manager was Reidar Eide.*

1981 Eastbourne in Poland Tour Results

Wroclaw, Saturday, June 27
KADRA PZM 49 (Alfred Siekierka 11, Ryszard Buskiewicz 9, Henryk Jasek 8, Roman Jankowski 8, Leonard Raba 7, Robert Slabon 5, Bernard Jader 1, Henryk Piekarski 0) **EASTBOURNE 29** (Edward Jancarz 12, Paul Woods 5, Jan Davidsson 5, Malcolm Simmons 3, David Kennett 2, Olli Tyrvainen 1, Trevor Geer 1).

Gdansk, Sunday, June 28
WYBRZEZE 47 (Boguslaw Nowak 12, Marek Towalski 12, Andrzej Marynowski 12, Bogdan Skrobisz 6, Grzegorz Dzikowski 5, Krzysztof Fede 0, Grzegorz Szymko 0, Piotr Zyto 0) **EASTBOURNE 43** (Malcolm Simmons 14, Paul Woods 8, Robert Slabon 7, Jan Davidsson 5, Trevor Geer 4, Olli Tyrvainen 3, David Kennett 2).

Gniezno, Wednesday, July 1
START GNIEZNO 55 (Eugeniusz Blaszak 14, Wojciech Kaczmarek 11, Piotr Podrzycki 10, Marek Mierkiewicz 7, Kazimierz Wojcik 5, Leon Kujawski 4, Jan Puk 2, Tadeusz Brillowski 2) **EASTBOURNE 35** (Kelly Moran 13, †Gordon Kennett 10, Paul Woods 7, Robert Slabon 2, Trevor Geer 1, Olli Tyrvainen 1, David Kennett 1).

Leszno, Friday, July 3
UNIA LESZNO 71 (Bernard Jader 13, Stanislaw Turek 11, Wlodzimierz Helinski 10, Ryszard Buskiewicz 10, Marek Okoniewski 9, Roman Jankowski 8, Andrzej Cichy 7, Grzegorz Sterna 3) **EASTBOURNE 18** (Robert Slabon 5, Paul Woods 5, †Gordon Kennett 3, Trevor Geer 3, Kelly Moran 1, David Kennett 1, Olli Tyrvainen, did not ride).

● *The Eastbourne team manager was Bob Dugard.*

1981 Leicester in Norway

Elgane, Sunday, August 16
SANDNES & JÆREN 22 (Trond Skretting 9, Dag Haaland 5, Roy Otto 3, Kurt Ueland 2, Audun Ove Olsen 1, Asgeir Bjerga 1, Terje Tollefsen 1, Geir Aasland 0) **LEICESTER 56** (Rolf Gramstad 10, †John Titman 9, Les Collins 9, Finn Jensen 9, Colin Cook 8, Peter E. Smith 6, Phil Herne 5).

1981 Scotland v England

AN engine failure in the last heat robbed England skipper Dave Trownson of an 18-point maximum.

Edinburgh, Wednesday, June 17
SCOTLAND 43 (George Hunter 13, †Jim McMillan 13, Benny Rourke 7, Charlie McKinna 7, Brian Collins 2, Harry MacLean 1, Kenny McKinna 0, Colin Caffrey 0)
ENGLAND 64 (†Dave Trownson 15, Steve Lawson 11, Ivan Blacka 11, Chris Turner 10, Neil Collins 9, Alan Emerson 8, Martin Dixon 0, Rob Grant 0).

● *The Scotland team manager was John Doherty.*

● *The England team manager was Dave Younghusband.*

1981 Canterbury v Holland

Canterbury, Saturday, April 18, First leg
CANTERBURY 48 (†Mike Ferreira 11, Denzil Kent 7, Kevin Brice 7, Barney Kennett 7, Rob Dolman 6, Graham Knowler 5, Brendan Shilleto 5) **HOLLAND 30** (Frits Koppe 14, Rudy Muts 6, Henk Steman 5, Willi Stroes 3, Hilke Dijkema 1, Leo Bathoorn 1, Reiner van Gulik 0).

Amsterdam, Monday, April 20, Second leg
HOLLAND 30 (Henny Kroeze 13, Henk Steman 8, Hilke Dijkema 3, Piet Seur 3, Frits Koppe 3, Reiner van Gulik 0, Leo Bathoorn 0)
CANTERBURY 48 (†Mike Ferreira 12, Denzil Kent 10, Brendan Shilleto 8, Barney Kennett 7, Rob Dolman 6, Kevin Brice 3, Graham Knowler 2).

Carter's the new King Lion!

KENNY CARTER roared to an 18-point maximum in his first Test match of 1982... and never stopped making a meal of international opponents throughout the year.

Len Silver had made him an automatic England choice in 1981 and Nigel Boocock asked him to lead a Young England squad to Australia during the winter, a tour which was given the official stamp of approval by the Speedway Control Board.

The 20-year-old was an absolute sensation Down Under, scoring THREE 18-point maximums in five Test matches as Young England won the series.

And when he returned there was little doubt that the international experience had done him a power of good as he maintained that streak of double figure scoring virtually throughout the 1982 international campaign.

He led the England charge in the opening Test against the United States at Wimbledon – where heavy rain, the Capital's first for three weeks, turned the track into a skating rink – and after finshing second to Dennis Sigalos in his first race won his next five as England overcame the absence, with a reported stomach complaint, of Michael Lee.

Lee had a furious row in the Plough Lane pits with Eric Boocock, working in tandem with John Berry, and Booey was so incensed that he advocated dropping Lee from the rest of the series but failed to get the backing of the Management Committee who overruled him and insisted that the 1980 World Champion would keep his England place.

It was to turn out to be a demoralising decision for Boocock as Lee managed only two points in the second Test at Swindon (where he arrived with only one bike), seven at Ipswich (where he twice finished last) and just a single point at Poole in the vital deciding Test.

Peter Collins (pictured left with team-mate Kenny) was recalled to Test match action at his

1981-82 Young England tour of Australia Results

Perth, Friday, November 27, 1981
AUSTRALIA 54 (Billy Sanders 14, Glyn Taylor 12, Phil Crump 9, Gary Guglielmi 9, Les Sawyer 8, John Titman 2, Clayton Isbel 0) **YOUNG ENGLAND 54** (Kenny Carter 18, †John Davis 12, Andy Grahame 10, Alan Grahame 9, Phil Collins 3, Kevin Smith 1, Neil Collins 1).

Mildura, Sunday, December 13, 1981
AUSTRALIA 54 (Phil Crump 18, Danny Kennedy 16, Billy Sanders 11, John Titman 5, Rod North 3, Terry Tulloch 1, John Boulger 0) **YOUNG ENGLAND 54** (Phil Collins 13, Kenny Carter 11, Alan Grahame 11, Andy Grahame 6, Neil Collins 6, †John Davis 4, Kevin Smith 3).

Liverpool, Saturday, December 19, 1981
AUSTRALIA 41 (Billy Sanders 10, Gary Guglielmi 10, Phil Herne 7, John Titman 7, Phil Crump 6, Dave Mills 1, Danny Kennedy 0) **YOUNG ENGLAND 66** (Kenny Carter 18, †John Davis 15, Andy Grahame 11, Alan Grahame 9, Phil Collins 8, Neil Collins 4, Kevin Smith 1).

Newcastle, Sunday, December 20, 1981
AUSTRALIA 59 (Phil Crump 13, Billy Sanders 11, John Titman 11, Gary Guglielmi 11, Phil Herne 7, Danny Kennedy 5, Robbie Blackadder 1) **YOUNG ENGLAND 49** (Kenny Carter 12, Andy Grahame 12, Alan Grahame 8, Phil Collins 8, †John Davis 6, Neil Collins 2, Kevin Smith 1).

Brisbane, Saturday, January 9, 1982
AUSTRALIA 46 (Gary Guglielmi 15, Billy Sanders 11, Phil Crump 7, Danny Kennedy 5, Neil Coddington 5, John Titman 3, Steve Koppe 0) **YOUNG ENGLAND 62** (Kenny Carter 18, Alan Grahame 15, Andy Grahame 11, †John Davis 9, Phil Collins 6, Kevin Smith 2, Neil Collins 1).

England win 2-1 with two Tests drawn.

TOUR MATCH

Brisbane, Saturday, January 2, 1982
AUSTRALASIAN SELECT 38 (John Titman 14, Peter Carswell 7, Steve Koppe 6, Stan Bear 5, Neil Coddington 2, Steve Regeling 2, Mitch Shirra 2) **YOUNG ENGLAND 70** (Alan Grahame 16, Kenny Carter 14, Andy Grahame 14, John Davis 11, Phil Collins 10, Kevin Smith 4, Neil Collins 1).

● *England rider-team manager was Nigel Boocock.*

1982 England v Denmark

Halifax, Sunday, June 13
ENGLAND 60 (Kenny Carter 17, Chris Morton 10, Alan Grahame 10, †Peter Collins 8, John Louis 6, Ian Cartwright 5, Andy Grahame 4, Phil Collins, did not ride) **DENMARK 48** (Hans Nielsen 12, Erik Gundersen 9, †Ole Olsen 8, Tommy Knudsen 8, Bo Petersen 6, Finn Thomsen 3, Preben Eriksen 2, Peter Ravn, did not ride).

Leicester, Tuesday, June 15
ENGLAND 66 (Kenny Carter 15, Andy Grahame 12, Alan Grahame 12, Chris Morton 10, Phil Collins 7, Les Collins 4, Neil Collins 4, †Peter Collins 2) **DENMARK 42** (Tommy Knudsen 13, Preben Eriksen 10, Erik Gundersen 6, Bo Petersen 6, †Ole Olsen 3, Hans Nielsen 3, Finn Thomsen 1, Finn Jensen, did not ride).

Hackney, Friday, August 6
ENGLAND 40 (†Malcolm Simmons 13, Andy Grahame 8, Les Collins 6, Chris Morton 5, John Davis 3, John Louis 3, Alan Grahame 2, Peter Collins, did not arrive) **DENMARK 68** (Tommy Knudsen 16, Erik Gundersen 15, Hans Nielsen 14, Bo Petersen 8, Finn Thomsen 7, †Ole Olsen 4, Preben Eriksen 4, Jens Rasmussen 0).
■ ***Original staging on Friday, June 18, was postponed, waterlogged track.***

England win 2-1.

Vojens, Friday, August 20
DENMARK 73 (Tommy Knudsen 14, Hans Nielsen 14, Erik Gundersen 14, Preben Eriksen 12, Ole Olsen 11, Bo Petersen 8) **ENGLAND 35** (Alan Grahame 12, Andy Grahame 7, Chris Morton 6, Les Collins 5, Phil Collins 4, Peter Collins 1, Neil Collins 0).

● *England team managers were Eric Boocock and John Berry.*
● *The Denmark team manager was Jorgen L. Jensen.*

own home track Belle Vue and must have provided inspiration to his England colleagues as he rolled back the years in a vintage PC performance that brought him four match-turning race wins.

Any temptation to keep Collins in the squad for the final Test at Poole was ignored by the England management duo and despite a quite brilliant one-man show from Carter (a last first time out then five wins in a row) America were comprehensive victors by an astonishing 30 points with Lee being replaced for all three second half rides after just one third place (ahead of partner Malcolm Simmons) in the first eight heats!

Somehow Carter also found time in a busy schedule to captain Young England in four Tests on National League tracks and he never dropped a single point.

He missed the first match at Rye House – he was partnering Peter Collins to first place in the World Pairs semi-final in Czechoslovakia – cracked the Middlesbrough track record and then returned to senior fare as England opened their second summer series, this time against Denmark.

He maintained his superb form with 17 points against the Danes, got 15 in the second Test which clinched the series and then went back to entertaining National League fans with another maximum at Newcastle to complete a June international record of six Tests and a massive 86 points out of a possible 90!

His form slipped a little later in the year when the BSPA launched another of those competitions that looked attractive in principle but turned into a real turkey in reality.

Their own advertising hailed it as "an exciting new international series" and it should have been as it brought together England, America, Denmark and Australasia.

A heavy Cradley Heath track detracted from the racing in the opening round – won by America – and after England finished third in the last meeting at Eastbourne (where Mark Martin scored Australasia's only point!) Eric Boocock resigned.

He complained: "All I want at the moment is to have a long rest from speedway and, after giving 100% to the sport for 21 years, to get back to living a normal life again.

"I've had enough and I'm getting out. I just want to forget all about speedway.

"I've got no enthusiasm left for the sport in any shape or form. Maybe when I've had six months off to get it all out of my system I'll be back."

AMERICAN HEROES...Reading's Bobby Schwartz and new Eastbourne capture Kelly Moran

1982 England v United States of America Results

Wimbledon, Thursday, April 29
ENGLAND 63 (Kenny Carter 17, Malcolm Simmons 12, Andy Grahame 9, John Davis 8, †Dave Jessup 6, Alan Grahame 6, Chris Morton 5, Gordon Kennett 0) **UNITED STATES OF AMERICA 45** (Dennis Sigalos 13, Shawn Moran 13, †Bruce Penhall 9, Bobby Schwartz 6, Kelly Moran 3, Scott Autrey 1, Brad Oxley 0, John Cook 0).

Swindon, Sunday, May 2
ENGLAND 47 (†Dave Jessup 12, Kenny Carter 11, Chris Morton 10, Malcolm Simmons 6, Alan Grahame 3, Steve Bastable 3, Michael Lee 2, John Davis 0) **UNITED STATES OF AMERICA 60** (Shawn Moran 12, †Bruce Penhall 12, Scott Autrey 11, Dennis Sigalos 10, Kelly Moran 9, John Cook 5, Bobby Schwartz 1, Ron Preston, did not ride).

Ipswich, Thursday, May 6
ENGLAND 42 (Kenny Carter 15, †Dave Jessup 8, Chris Morton 7, Michael Lee 7, Gordon Kennett 4, Kevin Jolly 1, Andy Grahame 0, Alan Grahame 0) **UNITED STATES OF AMERICA 66** (Shawn Moran 14, †Bruce Penhall 14, Dennis Sigalos 13, Kelly Moran 11, Bobby Schwartz 8, Scott Autrey 5, John Cook 1, Ron Preston, did not ride).

Belle Vue, Sunday, May 9
ENGLAND 61 (Chris Morton 15, Peter Collins 14, Kenny Carter 11, Alan Grahame 8, Andy Grahame 5, Les Collins 3, Malcolm Simmons 3, †Dave Jessup 2) **UNITED STATES OF AMERICA 47** (Dennis Sigalos 14, †Bruce Penhall 13, Shawn Moran 13, Kelly Moran 5, Scott Autrey 1, Bobby Schwartz 1, Lance King 0, Steve Gresham 0).

Poole, Wednesday, May 19
ENGLAND 39 (Kenny Carter 15, Alan Grahame 7, Malcolm Simmons 6, Les Collins 4, Chris Morton 3, John Davis 2, Michael Lee 1, †Dave Jessup 1) **UNITED STATES OF AMERICA 69** (Dennis Sigalos 15, Shawn Moran 15, †Bruce Penhall 14, Kelly Moran 12, Bobby Schwartz 8, Scott Autrey 5, John Cook and Ron Preston, did not ride).

United States of America win the series 3-2.

- *The England team managers were John Berry and Eric Boocock.*
- *The United States of America team managers were John Scott and John Smith.*

1982 International Fours Results

Cradley Heath, Sunday, September 26
UNITED STATES OF AMERICA 35 (†Dennis Sigalos 10, Bobby Schwartz 8, Shawn Moran 8, Lance King 8, Brad Oxley 1) **ENGLAND 28** (Peter Collins 9, †Kenny Carter 7, Phil Collins 5, Chris Morton 4, Alan Grahame 3) **DENMARK 27** (Tommy Knudsen 9, Erik Gundersen 6, Preben Eriksen 5, †Ole Olsen 4, Peter Ravn 3) **AUSTRALASIA 17** (Billy Sanders 6, Steve Regeling 4, Larry Ross 3, Steve Baker 3, Bruce Cribb 1).

Reading, Monday, September 27
UNITED STATES OF AMERICA 46 (Bobby Schwartz 11, †Dennis Sigalos 11, Shawn Moran 9, Ron Preston 9, Brad Oxley 6) **ENGLAND 29** (†Kenny Carter 11, Alan Grahame 5, Gordon Kennett 5, Malcolm Simmons 5, Tim Hunt 3) **DENMARK 23** (Erik Gundersen 8, Tommy Knudsen 6, Preben Eriksen 4, Peter Ravn 3, Finn Thomsen 2) **AUSTRALASIA 10** (Steve Baker 3, Steve Regeling 2, Billy Sanders 2, John Titman 2, Larry Ross 1).

Sheffield, Thursday, September 30
DENMARK 35 (Hans Nielsen 11, Tommy Knudsen 10, Erik Gundersen 7, Bo Petersen 4, Alf Busk 3) **ENGLAND 30** (†Kenny Carter 10, Chris Morton 7, Andy Grahame 6, Peter Collins 5, Alan Grahame 2) **UNITED STATES OF AMERICA 23** (Brad Oxley 10, †Shawn Moran 8, Scott Autrey 3, Ron Preston 2, Steve Gresham, did not arrive) **AUSTRALASIA 20** (Larry Ross 5, Mitch Shirra 5, Billy Sanders 5, David Bargh 3, Gary Guglielmi 2).

Eastbourne, Sunday, October 3
UNITED STATES OF AMERICA 46 (Shawn Moran 12, Bobby Schwartz 11, †Dennis Sigalos 11, Ron Preston 7, Brad Oxley 5) **DENMARK 36** (Erik Gundersen 10, Bo Petersen 9, Hans Nielsen 8, Tommy Knudsen 7, Preben Eriksen 2) **ENGLAND 25** (Gordon Kennett 7, Paul Woods 7, †Kenny Carter 6, Malcolm Simmons 3, Dave Jessup 2) **AUSTRALASIA 1** (Mark Martin 1, †Mitch Shirra 0, Gary Guglielmi 0, Steve Baker 0, Danny Kennedy 0).

Overall scores:

1 UNITED STATES OF AMERICA 150
2 DENMARK 121
3 ENGLAND 112
4 AUSTRALASIA 48

● *The team managers were Eric Boocock (England), John Scott and John Smith (United States of America), Mikael Lohmann (Denmark) and Trevor Redmond (Australasia).*

1982 Ruda Hvezda (Czechoslovakia) Division Two Tour Results

Exeter, Monday, October 4
EXETER 38 (Keith Wright 10, Keith Millard 9, Mike Semmonds 8, †Bob Coles 6, Andy Campbell 3, Michael Coles 2, Steve Bishop 0) **RUDA HVEZDA 39** (†Vaclav Verner 12, Jan Verner 10, Petr Ondrasik 6, Milan Spinka 6, Ladislav Hradecky 2, Petr Kubicek 2, Jiri Hnidak 1).

Birmingham, Wednesday, October 6
BIRMINGHAM 40 (†Hans Nielsen 11, Alan Grahame 11, Ari Koponen 6, Neil Evitts 4, Bruce Cribb 4, John Eskildsen 3, John Jørgensen 1) **RUDA HVEZDA 38** (Petr Ondrasik 9, Jan Verner 8, †Jiri Stancl 7, Ales Dryml 6, Milan Spinka 4, Ladislav Hradecky 3, Jiri Hnidak 1).

Swindon, Saturday, October 9
SWINDON 45 (†Steve Bastable 9, Steen Mastrup 9, Björn Andersson 8, Malcolm Holloway 7, Keith Millard 6, Mike Ferreira 6, Steve Bishop 0) **RUDA HVEZDA 33** (Milan Spinka 8, Jan Verner 7, Ladislav Hradecky 7, Petr Ondrasik 6, Petr Kubicek 2, †Jiri Stancl 2, Jiri Hnidak 1).

Rye House, Sunday, October 10
RYE HOUSE 54 (Peter Johns 15, Marvyn Cox 12, Bob Garrad 11, †Kelvin Mullarkey 7, Steve Naylor 5, Steve Bryenton 2, John Barclay 2) **RUDA HVEZDA 41** (†Jiri Stancl 12, Jan Verner 9, Milan Spinka 7, Ladislav Hradecky 5, Petr Ondrasik 5, Petr Kubicek 2, Jiri Hnidak 1).

Reading, Monday, October 11
READING 48 (Steve Gresham 12, †Jan Andersson 10, Bobby Schwartz 10, Dave Trownson 7, John Grahame 5, Uno Johansson 4, Martin Satchell 0) **RUDA HVEZDA 30** (†Jiri Stancl 11, Petr Ondrasik 8, Milan Spinka 5, Petr Kubicek 3, Jan Verner 2, Ladislav Hradecky 1, Jiri Hnidak 0).

● *The Ruda Hvezda team manager was Jiri Santrucek.*

1982 National League v Young England Results

Rye House, Sunday, June 6
NATIONAL LEAGUE 45 (Bob Garrad 13, Steve Naylor 11, Andy Hines 10, Kelvin Mullarkey 4, Marvyn Cox 4, †Joe Owen 3, Keith White 0, Barry Thomas 0) **YOUNG ENGLAND 63** (†Phil Collins 16, Mark Courtney 9, Neil Collins 9, Nigel Flatman 9, Tim Hunt 9, Kevin Smith 7, John Grahame 2, Paul Woods 2).

Exeter, Monday, June 7
NATIONAL LEAGUE 47 (Andy Campbell 12, Dave Trownson 11, Keith Millard 9, †Joe Owen 7, John Barker 7, Bob Garrad 1, Derek Harrison 0, Simon Wigg, did not arrive) **YOUNG ENGLAND 61** (†Kenny Carter 18, Neil Collins 14, Phil Collins 12, Kevin Smith 8, Martin Hewlett 4, Neil Evitts 4, Sean Willmott 1, Nigel Flatman 0).

Middlesbrough, Thursday, June 10
NATIONAL LEAGUE 37 (†Joe Owen 13, Martin Dixon 11, Mike Spink 7, Steve Wilcock 3, Steve Lawson 2, David Gagen 1, Alan Emerson 0, Geoff Pusey 0) **YOUNG ENGLAND 71** (†Kenny Carter 18, Mark Courtney 13, Louis Carr 11, Phil Collins 11, Neil Collins 9, Paul Woods 9, Peter Carr and John Grahame, did not ride).

Newcastle, Monday, June 28
NATIONAL LEAGUE 48 (Rod Hunter 12, †Joe Owen 10, Paul Stead 9, Simon Wigg 7, Steve Lawson 3, Martin Dixon 3, Steve Wilcock 3, Bobby Beaton 1) **YOUNG ENGLAND 60** (†Kenny Carter 18, Neil Collins 13, Mark Courtney 12, Paul Woods 7, Nigel Flatman 5, Kevin Hawkins 4, Martin Hewlett 1, Phil White 0).

Edinburgh, Friday, July 9
NATIONAL LEAGUE 51 (†Joe Owen 12, Simon Wigg 10, Dave Trownson 10, Bobby Beaton 8, Steve Lawson 7, Martin Dixon 3, Steve Wilcock 1) **YOUNG ENGLAND 57** (†Kenny Carter 18, Louis Carr 11, Nigel Flatman 11, Paul Woods 7, Phil White 4, Tim Hunt 3, Peter Carr 3).

Young England win the series 5-0.

● *The National League team managers were Len Silver and Ian Thomas.*
● *The Young England team managers were John Berry and Eric Boocock.*

1982 Scotland v England Results

Edinburgh, Friday, May 14
SCOTLAND 62 (Charlie McKinna 14, Andy Campbell 14, †Jim McMillan 10, Bobby Beaton 9, Brian Collins 8, George Hunter 7, Jim Beaton and Pete Erskine, did not ride) **ENGLAND 46** (†Dave Trownson 10, Eric Broadbelt 10, Steve Wilcock 9, Steve McDermott 9, Chris Turner 4, Ivan Blacka 4, Mike Caroline 0, Ian Westwell 0).

● *The Scotland team manager was Willie Templeton.*
● *The England team manager was Dave Younghusband.*

SPEEDWAY returned to Northern Ireland with a one-off meeting at Ballymena Showgrounds, organised by stock-car promoter Robert Mathers and Cradley Heath's Peter Adams. The venture involved erecting a wooden fence around the quarter mile circuit and covering the tarmac track with a shale and sand surface. A crowd of several thousand turned up for a challenge match between Cradley Heath and an Ivan Mauger Select that went to the last race where Erik Gundersen and Lance King held out the Mauger challenge to give the Heathens a two point win. The venture was not a financial success and plans to stage a subsequent Irish Championship were dropped and the roar of speedway engines in full flight has never been heard since in Northern Ireland.

Ballymena, Tuesday, July 13
CRADLEY HEATH 40 (Alan Grahame 12, Bruce Penhall 9, Erik Gundersen 7, Phil Collins 6, Lance King 3, Andy Reid 3, Bill Barrett 0) **IVAN MAUGER SELECT 40** (Kenny Carter 10, Ivan Mauger 8, Shawn Moran 6, David Bargh 5, Reg Wilson 4, Dave Morton 3, Steve Bastable 2).

OLD TIME'S SAKE

PC answers Test SOS

WALLY MAWDSLEY became England's fifth manager in as many years when he was asked to take charge of the national squad following his defeat in a vote to stay on as British League chairman.

The post had initially been offered to Peter Adams who, in 1982, had led injury-hit Cradley Heath to a Speedway Star Knock Out Cup Final win, but he turned it down.

And it then became a straight fight between Sheffield's Carl Glover and multi-track supremo Mawdsley who won on a 12-2 vote of members.

Everyone had to wait nearly five months to see Mawdsley pick his first squad of riders and he certainly didn't disappoint those who felt he would be his own man.

He controversially recalled Michael Lee – who had been axed almost a year previously after scoring only one point in the last Test against America – and also brought back 101-cap Peter Collins who had flitted across the international scene for a couple of years.

He also handed the England captaincy to the Belle Vue skipper and named only one uncapped rider in a squad of 12 from which he would pick the five teams to take on the United States although he left the door open: "Any rider who springs to prominence in the next week or so could still be brought in for the series.

"At the moment I expect to choose my sides from these 12 but the England door isn't closed to anyone."

He was a man of his word as both Poole's Kevin Smith and Coventry's Steve Bastable had won their international spurs in the five-match series that went England's way in a decider at Sheffield after the results had see-sawed one way and the other.

America led 1-0, then 1-1, then 1-2, then 2-2, and finally 3-2 to PC and his boys.

The Yanks got a flying start when they opted to use Carlisle tyres at Wimbledon where Dave Jessup went from first to last in the opening heat and they overcame their limited options (they only had seven riders available to them) accentuated by an AMA ban on Steve Gresham.

Peter Collins had a nightmare at Ipswich – last in his four rides – but then made amends when it really mattered at Sheffield thanks to the boldness of manager Mawdsley.

He gambled on bringing in reserve Neil Collins in the penultimate heat and he teamed up with Kenny Carter for a 5-1 which gave the Lions a four point lead going into the last race.

Mawdsley's first home series in charge – he had previously been to Australia – was not without it's backstage dramas though.

He didn't arrive at Swindon until five minutes before the start of the second Test and once there he had a head-to-head with Kenny Carter when he wanted to pull the youngster out of a race.

Carter, in full hearing of the pits staff, gave his manager a blunt four letter response and the pair of them were seen hustling off to the dressing rooms for a private heart-to-heart!

Harmony in the camp was hardly helped by a 16-point defeat in the first

ENGLAND 1983: The team that won the [illegible] Test against Den[illegible] to clinch the series at [illegible]. Standing, left to right, Kenny Carter, Peter Collins, Malcolm Simmons, manager Wally Mawdsley, Michael Lee and Les Collins. [illegible] Jessup, Chris Morton and John Davis.

of three Tests against Denmark even though the Danes went into the clash without their inspiration Ole Olsen.

Not that they missed him for replacement Peter Ravn came out for the first heat on a sodden Brandon racetrack and knocked a fifth of a second off the track record!

Olsen also missed the second match at Halifax and this time his points were missed by the Danes who ran up against another vintage Collins performance. PC finished third behind his team-mate Alan Grahame and Hans Nielsen in heat two but wasn't going to be beaten again!

For the second time in his short reign Mawdsley went into the last match of a series with the result still in doubt and this time he gambled on bringing back Michael Lee who, like PC before him, rewarded his manager's faith.

Michael looked like the Lee of old as England capitalised on Olsen's shakiness (he had only just come back after injury) and a heat 16 crash in which Tommy Knudsen suffered concussion and a broken wrist.

By then, though, the series was over with England claiming their third successive series wins against the nation who were beginning to make their indelible mark in world speedway....

1983 England v United States of America Results

Wimbledon, Thursday, April 21
ENGLAND 43 (Chris Morton 10, Malcolm Simmons 9, †Peter Collins 6, John Davis 6, Kenny Carter 4, Michael Lee 4, Dave Jessup 4, Les Collins 0) **UNITED STATES OF AMERICA 64** (Dennis Sigalos 18, †Bobby Schwartz 16, Shawn Moran 14, Lance King 9, Mike Faria 4, Kelly Moran 3, Rick Miller, did not ride).

Swindon, Sunday, April 24
ENGLAND 57 (Chris Morton 16, Dave Jessup 12, Simon Wigg 10, †Peter Collins 8, Kenny Carter 5, John Davis 4, Gordon Kennett 2, Malcolm Simmons 0) **UNITED STATES OF AMERICA 51** (†Bobby Schwartz 11, Dennis Sigalos 11, Lance King 10, Kelly Moran 10, Shawn Moran 6, Mike Faria 3, Rick Miller, did not ride).

Poole, Wednesday, May 4
ENGLAND 63 (Kenny Carter 16, Michael Lee 12, Simon Wigg 12, †Peter Collins 10, Dave Jessup 6, Chris Morton 3, John Davis 3, Kevin Smith 1) **UNITED STATES OF AMERICA 45** (Dennis Sigalos 11, Kelly Moran 11, Shawn Moran 8, †Bobby Schwartz 7, Lance King 6, John Cook 2, Rick Miller, did not ride).

Ipswich, Thursday, May 5
ENGLAND 42 (Kenny Carter 13, Chris Morton 9, Simon Wigg 9, Dave Jessup 7, Michael Lee 3, Neil Collins 1, †Peter Collins 0, John Davis 0) **UNITED STATES OF AMERICA 66** (Shawn Moran 18, †Bobby Schwartz 16, Dennis Sigalos 15, Kelly Moran 6, John Cook 6, Lance King 4, Rick Miller 1, Steve Gresham, did not ride).

Sheffield, Sunday, May 8
ENGLAND 58 (†Peter Collins 16, Chris Morton 14, Kenny Carter 13, Les Collins 5, Michael Lee 4, Neil Collins 4, Steve Bastable 2, Andy Grahame 0) **UNITED STATES OF AMERICA 50** (Dennis Sigalos 13, Shawn Moran 12, †Bobby Schwartz 11, John Cook 6, Kelly Moran 5, Lance King 3, Steve Gresham 0, Rick Miller, did not ride).

England win the series 3-2.

● *The England team manager was Wally Mawdsley.*
● *The United States of America team manager was John Scott.*

1983 Inter Nations Tournament Results

Cradley Heath, Monday, September 12
ENGLAND 45 (†Kenny Carter 10, Alan Grahame 9, Simon Wigg 7, Phil Collins 7, Les Collins 6, Dave Jessp 4, Mark Courtney 2) **REST OF THE WORLD 34** (Dennis Sigalos 10, Billy Sanders 10, Bobby Schwartz 6, Lance King 6, Rick Miller 2, Kai Niemi 0, Larry Ross 0) **DENMARK 29** (Erik Gundersen 8, Hans Nielsen 7, †Ole Olsen 5, Peter Ravn 5, Bo Petersen 2, Jens Rasmussen 2, Sam Nikolajsen, did not ride).

King's Lynn, Wednesday, September 14
REST OF THE WORLD 39 (Dennis Sigalos 10, Mitch Shirra 8, Lance King 7, Billy Sanders 5, Richard Hellsén 5, Bobby Schwartz 4) **DENMARK 38** (Hans Nielsen 12, Erik Gundersen 12, Sam Nikolajsen 5, Preben Eriksen 4, Peter Ravn 3, †Ole Olsen 2, Jens Rasmussen 0) **ENGLAND 31** (†Kenny Carter 11, John Louis 7, Phil Collins 6, Dave Jessup 5, Gordon Kennett 2, Peter Collins 0, Mark Courtney 0).

Birmingham, Friday, September 23
REST OF THE WORLD 41 (Dennis Sigalos 11, Mitch Shirra 11, Bobby Schwartz 8, Richard Hellsén 5, Rick Miller 4, Gary Guglielmi 2, Shawn Moran 0) **ENGLAND 37** (†Kenny Carter 11, Alan Grahame 9, Simon Wigg 8, Dave Jessup 4, Andy Grahame 3, Michael Lee 2, Steve Bastable 0) **DENMARK 30** (Hans Nielsen 12, Erik Gundersen 9, Bo Petersen 5, Peter Ravn 2, Kent Noer 1, Sam Nikolajsen 1, Jan O. Pedersen 0).

OVERALL SCORES
REST OF THE WORLD 114 ENGLAND 113 DENMARK 97

● *The team managers were Wally Mawdsley (England), John Scott (Rest of the World) and Tommy Knudsen (Denmark).*

1983 England v Denmark Results

Coventry, Wednesday, June 29
ENGLAND 46 (†Peter Collins 9, Kenny Carter 8, Chris Morton 8, Andy Grahame 7, Simon Wigg 6, Les Collins 6, Mark Courtney 1, Phil Collins 1) **DENMARK 62** (Tommy Knudsen 16, †Hans Nielsen 13, Erik Gundersen 13, Peter Ravn 8, Sam Nikolajsen 7, Finn Thomsen 4, Preben Eriksen 1, Alf Busk, did not ride).

Halifax, Sunday, July 3
ENGLAND 65 (†Peter Collins 14, Kenny Carter 14, Alan Grahame 13, Chris Morton 12, Andy Grahame 6, Mark Courtney 4, Les Collins 2) **DENMARK 43** (†Hans Nielsen 15, Erik Gundersen 14, Tommy Knudsen 12, Peter Ravn 2, Finn Thomsen 0, Preben Eriksen 0, Kent Noer 0).

Hackney, Friday, July 8
ENGLAND 65 (Michael Lee 16, Kenny Carter 14, Chris Morton 13, Dave Jessup 10, †Peter Collins 7, Les Collins 5, Kevin Smith and Paul Woods, did not ride) **DENMARK 43** (†Ole Olsen 11, Erik Gundersen 9, Hans Nielsen 8, Peter Ravn 6, Finn Thomsen 6, Tommy Knudsen 1, Preben Eriksen 1, Jens Rasmussen 1).

England win the series 2-1.

● *The England team manager was Wally Mawdsley.*
● *The Denmark team manager was Jorgen Jensen.*

1983 Four Team Test (Denmark) Results

Selskov, Thursday, May 12
DENMARK 41 (Erik Gundersen 12, Hans Nielsen 11, Tommy Knudsen 9, Preben Eriksen 6, Per Sørensen 3) **SWEDEN 24** (Jan Andersson 9, Björn Andersson 8, Tommy Nilsson 4, Lennart Bengtsson 3, Hasse Danielsson 0) **ENGLAND 23** (John Davis 7, Kenny Carter 5, Neil Collins 5, Michael Lee 4, Simon Wigg 2) **POLAND 20** (Andrzej Huszcza 9, Leonard Raba 5, Miroslaw Berlinski 3, Marek Kepa 2, Jerzy Rembas 1).

1983 Canterbury v Rijswijk (Holland) Results

Canterbury, Saturday, March 26
CANTERBURY 62 (†Barney Kennett 14, Laurie Etheridge 10, Keith Pritchard 9, Les Rumsey 9, Jamie Luckhurst 8, Denzil Kent 8, Terry Broadbank 4) **RIJSWIJK 34** (†Frits Koppe 10, Hylke Dijkema 10, Ralph Geurtz 6, Wil Stroes 6, Koos Noordman 2, Anne Elzinga 0, Lillebror Johansson 0).

Amsterdam, Monday, May 30
RIJSWIJK 45 (Scorers not available) **CANTERBURY 50** (†Barney Kennett 13, Kelvin Mullarkey 10, Laurie Etheridge 9, Keith Pritchard 8, Jamie Luckhurst 5, Kevin Brice 3, David Mullett 2).

Canterbury win 112-79 on aggregate.

1983 National League v Young England Results

A NEW NAME wore the famous Lion of England race-jacket for the first time in the second series between Young England and the pick of the National League.

Wimbledon's 18-year-old former public schoolboy Kelvin Tatum was originally ignored when manager Wally Mawdsley sat down to pick his teams.

But he was finally given his chance at Crayford as a late, late replacement for the unavailable Neil Evitts...and certainly let down no-one.

Tatum won his first race, fell off but remounted for the third place in his second and then added three more wins to score 14 points on his international debut and help England make it eight wins out of eight in successive encounters with the cream of the lower league.

Young England could have done with that sort of performance two nights later at Middlesbrough where the luckless Mark Courtney experienced the rather rare distinction of finishing on the losing side despite scoring a six-ride maximum!

For the first time the National League enjoyed a victory but even that was tainted following a last race in which it looked as if Young England were going to save their proud record as Neil Collins and Paul Woods headed for what would have been a match-winning maximum.

Then Bobby Beaton fell off when under no real pressure and could hardly suppress a smile when the race was stopped and re-run.

At the second time of asking Steve Wilcock split the Collins-Woods pairing for the two points that brought Young England's winning run to a temporary halt.

By now Courtney was on song and he turned in another unbeaten performance at Long Eaton where Young England confirmed their overall superiority after something of a tongue-lashing from their disgruntled manager, unhappy at seeing a 100% record go.

Courtney and Neil Collins (beaten only once by Dave Perks) also got their names on the track record file, jointly sharing the fastest-ever four laps around Station Road on a night in which the old record, held by Alan Molyneux, was beaten or equalled five times in 18 races!

No-one knew at the time but after two years of crowd-pulling competition the Long Eaton match would be the last time that the two representative sides would meet before the amalgamation of the old National and British Leagues at the end of 1990.

It may have had its detractors but it had served its purpose by blooding a handful of riders who later went on to stake a claim to a place in England's senior squad and it was a launch pad for Courtney's elevation as he was picked for two of the season's three remaining Tests.

Exeter, Monday, May 23
NATIONAL LEAGUE 38 (†Robert Henry 13, Jim McMillan 11, Keith Millard 6, Nigel Sparshott 2, Robert Maxfield 2, Simon Cross 2, Steve Bishop 1, Steve Schofield 1) **YOUNG ENGLAND 70** (Kevin Jolly 16, Paul Woods 12, Kevin Smith 11, Colin Richardson 11,† Melvyn Taylor 10, Andy Campbell 6, Sean Willmott 4).

Weymouth, Tuesday, May 24
NATIONAL LEAGUE 52 (Jim McMillan 12, Joe Owen 12, Steve Schofield 11, †Robert Henry 9, Nigel Sparshott 5, Martin Yeates 2, Bob Garrad 1, Simon Cross 0) **YOUNG ENGLAND 56** (Kevin Smith 18, Kevin Jolly 11, Paul Woods 9, Neil Evitts 8, †Melvyn Taylor 8, Andy Campbell 2, Sean Willmott 0, Martin Hagon 0).

Crayford, Tuesday, May 31
NATIONAL LEAGUE 44 (Barry Thomas 14, Marvyn Cox 10, Joe Owen 7, Bob Garrad 6, †Robert Henry 4, Alan Mogridge 2, Richard Knight 1, Denzil Kent 0) **YOUNG ENGLAND 63** (†Paul Woods 16, Kevin Smith 15, Kelvin Tatum 14, Kevin Jolly 7, Nigel Flatman 4, Colin Richardson 3, Andy Campbell 2, Martin Hagon 2).

Middlesbrough, Thursday, June 2
NATIONAL LEAGUE 55 (Joe Owen 14, Steve Wilcock 11, Bobby Beaton 11, Barry Thomas 9, Steve Lawson 6, Rod Hunter 3, Mike Spink 1, †Robert Henry 0) **YOUNG ENGLAND 53** (†Mark Courtney 18, Paul Woods 11, Neil Collins 10, Kevin Hawkins 9, Martin Dixon 4, Colin Richardson 1, Andy Smith 0).

Long Eaton, Wednesday, June 8
NATIONAL LEAGUE 33 (†Dave Perks 10, Rod Hunter 10, Joe Owen 10, Barry Thomas 2, Charlie McKinna 1, Tom Owen 0, Nigel Sparshott 0, David Gagen 0) **YOUNG ENGLAND 75** (Mark Courtney 18, Neil Collins 16, †Melvyn Taylor 13, Kevin Jolly 10, Colin Richardson 9, Kevin Hawkins 9).

Young England win the series 4-1.

● *The National League manager was Dave Younghusband.*

● *The Young England manager was Wally Mawdsley.*

1983 Frederiksborg (Denmark) Tour Results

Oxford, Thursday, March 24
Original staging, postponed, waterlogged track.

Stoke, Saturday, March 26
STOKE 65 (†Tom Owen 14, Ian Robertson 12, John Jackson 12, Peter E. Smith 11, Steve Sant 7, Jim Burdfield 6, Garry Johnson 3) **FREDERISKBORG 31** (Peter Glanz 12, Frank Andersen 11, Lars Jensen 4, Per Sørensen 2, Egon Jensen 1, Rene Mortensen 1, Benny Thøgersen 0).

Scunthorpe, Monday, March 28
SCUNTHORPE 74 (Andy Fisher 14, Julian Parr 13, †Nigel Crabtree 12, Ian Gibson 11, Robert Hollingworth 9, Mark DeKok 8, Kevin Armitage 7) **FREDERIKSBORG 22** (Peter Glanz 5, Per Sørensen 5, Lars Jensen 4, Frank Andersen 4, Egon Jensen 2, Benny Thøgersen 1, Rene Mortensen 1).

1983 Getingarna (Sweden) Tour Results

King's Lynn, Saturday, March 19
KING'S LYNN 41 (†John Louis 12, Gordon Kennett 9, Kevin Jolly 7, Melvyn Taylor 6, Keith Bloxsome 5, Colin Richardson 2, Paul Clarke 0) **GETINGARNA 37** (Tommy Nilsson 10, †Anders Michanek 9, Erik Stenlund 6, Richard Hellsén 5, Per Jonsson 4, Jimmy Nilsen 2, Per Ove Gudmundsson 1).

Newcastle, Monday, March 21
NEWCASTLE 37 (Rod Hunter 14, Bobby Beaton 10, †Joe Owen 9, Alan Emerson 2, David Wild 2, Neil Barnsley 0, Steve Duckworth 0) **GETINGARNA 41** (Tommy Nilsson10, †Anders Michanek 8, Erik Stenlund 5, Per Jonsson 5, Jimmy Nilsen 5, Per Ove Gudmundsson 5, Richard Hellsén 3).

Poole, Friday, March 25
POOLE 52 (†John Davis 12, Neil Middleditch 12, Kevin Smith 9, Michael Lee 7, Brian Jacobsen 7, Keith Millard 4, Andy Campbell 1) **GETINGARNA 26** (Erik Stenlund 6, †Anders Michanek 5, Tommy Nilsson 5, Per Jonsson 3, Per Ove Gudmundsson 3, Anders Eriksson 3, Jimmy Nilsen 1).
Original staging on Wednesday, March 23, postponed, waterlogged track.

Eastbourne, Sunday, March 27
Cancelled, waterlogged track.

Reading, Monday, March 28
READING 40 (†Jan Andersson 12, Mitch Shirra 11, Bobby Schwartz 7, Tim Hunt 4, John Grahame 3, Glyn Taylor 2, Dave Trownson 1) **GETINGARNA 38** (†Anders Michanek 8, Tommy Nilsson 7, Per Ove Gudmundsson 6, Erik Stenlund 6, Richard Hellsén 6, Per Jonsson 4, Jimmy Nilsen 1).

Leicester, Tuesday, March 29
LEICESTER 43 (Finn Jensen 9, Phil Herne 8, Neil Collins 6, Colin Cook 6, †Les Collins 5, Steve Regeling 5, Mark Courtney 4) **GETINGARNA 35** (†Anders Michanek 10, Jimmy Nilsen 8, Tommy Nilsson 6, Per Ove Gudmundsson 4, Erik Stenlund 3, Richard Hellsén 3, Per Jonsson 1).

1983 Indianerna (Sweden) Tour Results

Boston, Sunday, March 27
BOSTON 50 (†David Gagen 13, Robert Hollingworth 13, David Blackburn 8, Peter Framingham 6, Phil Alderman 4, Guy Wilson 3, Billy Burton 3) **INDIANERNA 46** (†Åke Fridell13, Kjell Nielsen 12, Hasse Holmkvist 10, Stefan Karlsson 7, Ove Österberg 2, Håkan Andersson 2, Leif Andersson 0).

Crayford, Tuesday, March 29
CRAYFORD 63 (†Barry Thomas 12, Kevin Teager 11, Alan Mogridge 10, Paul Bosley 10, Trevor Banks 9, Alan Sage 6, Andy Galvin 5) **INDIANERNA 33** (†Åke Fridell 13, Stefan Karlsson 10, Ove Österberg 4, Kjell Nielsen 4, Hasse Holmqvist 2, Leif Andersson 0, Håkan Andersson 0).

Edinburgh, Friday, April 1
Cancelled, Indianerna were unable to book a ferry home over the Easter period.

1-2-3-4-FIVE

PETER COLLINS began the year as England's Test captain – and his Belle Vue team-mate Chris Morton led out the Lions in the last international of 1984.

But in between England had three other skippers – Kenny Carter, Dave Jessup and Michael Lee – and that just about summed up a season that was wrecked by internal rows and bust-ups, most of which centred around the individualistic style of one Kenneth Malcolm Carter!

When Carl Glover, former National League Riders' Champion and son of Sheffield promoter Ray, was elected to take over from Wally Mawdsley as the England team chief one of his first actions was to take the captaincy away from PC and hand it, on a platter, to fellow Yorkshireman Carter.

Glover explained: "He is very, very patriotic and his credentials on the track are exceptional. I think he will do a good job and lead England magnificently. He will be a good motivator!"

Little did Glover know but that one action was to have bitter repercussions throughout the summer although the big showdown was delayed because the Halifax hero had hardly had time to get used to tossing for gate positions than disaster struck.

Michael Lee, in trouble a few weeks earlier when referee John Eglese banned him from the remainder of a meeting after he had dangerously parked his bike across the track in protest at a start, pulled out on the eve of the first Test at Swindon claiming he didn't have a suitable bike for international racing, and without him England went down by eight points.

Seven days later Carter fell in the first heat of the Dukes' League Cup match at Cradley Heath, was hit by partner Craig Pendlebury and carted off to hospital with a compound fracture of his right leg.

Jessup took over the captaincy, Lee returned and England levelled matters at Sheffield where Simon Wigg defied three broken ribs for his country.

No-one knew the drama just around the corner....

At Cradley Heath Jessup had only two rides, excluded for breaking the tapes in heat three and last in his only other ride two races later.

At Ipswich Michael Lee was thrown out of the opening race for a starting offence, threw off his England race-jacket and stormed into the dressing room spitting blood: "If you cannot go out there and race, why go out there at all? Referees – and Frank Ebdon in particular – are ruining the sport. There is so much pressure on the riders in these meetings but referees don't understand."

Glover didn't share his rider's views and hit out: "Michael has got to turn round and face it and not run away. He must change, speedway will not change."

Lee: "They just won't give me a chance. After my efforts last season, they continually kick me in the face."

America went on their own sweet way, taking advantage of the discord within the England camp by winning both matches to seal the series with one Test to go.

Glover called up Kevin Smith as the 18th rider to face the cock-a-hoop Californians but it didn't make any difference to the final result as England went down again to lose a stormy series 4-1.

Malcolm Simmons, ex-British Champion and, at that time, the holder of 76 England caps, joined the debate asking: "Have the boys got any respect for Carl Glover? Carl is a nice bloke but he has never really been a promoter and he wasn't a top-class rider."

In the three weeks or so between the last Test against America and the first against Denmark, Glover had time to assemble his thoughts.

He sacked Jessup as captain and installed Chris Morton as the Lions' leader, talked about giving youngsters their head and immediately recalled 38-year-old Simmons!

SUPER SIGGY...Dennis Sigalos led America to a 4-1 series win over England with a 15 point plus average

1984 England v United States of America Results

Swindon, Saturday, April 14
ENGLAND 50 (Chris Morton 13, Dave Jessup 12, †Kenny Carter 10, Simon Wigg 7, Peter Collins 6, Phil Collins 2, Kelvin Tatum 0, John Davis 0) **UNITED STATES OF AMERICA 58** (Dennis Sigalos 17, John Cook 13, Shawn Moran 12, †Bobby Schwartz 6, Lance King 6, Sam Ermolenko 4, Rick Miller 0, Steve Lucero, did not ride).

Sheffield, Sunday, April 29
ENGLAND 58 (Michael Lee 16, Simon Wigg 10, Peter Collins 10, †Dave Jessup 10, Chris Morton 9, Neil Collins 2, Les Collins 1, Alan Grahame, did not ride) **UNITED STATES OF AMERICA 50** (Shawn Moran 15, Dennis Sigalos 14, John Cook 9, Lance King 7, †Bobby Schwartz 5, Sam Ermolenko 0, Rick Miller 0, Eddie Ingels, did not ride).

Cradley Heath, Saturday, May 5
ENGLAND 49 (Michael Lee 12, Phil Collins 10, Simon Wigg 10, Peter Collins 8, Alan Grahame 5, Chris Morton 2, Andy Grahame 2, †Dave Jessup 0) **UNITED STATES OF AMERICA 59** (Dennis Sigalos 14, Shawn Moran 13, John Cook 12, †Bobby Schwartz 7, Sam Ermolenko 7, Lance King 6, Rick Miller, did not ride).

Ipswich, Monday, May 7
ENGLAND 36 (Chris Morton 9, Richard Knight 8, Kelvin Tatum 6, Jeremy Doncaster 5, Paul Woods 4, †Dave Jessup 3, John Louis 1, Michael Lee 0) **UNITED STATES OF AMERICA 72** (Shawn Moran 18, Dennis Sigalos 15, John Cook 13, Lance King 11, †Bobby Schwartz 9, Sam Ermolenko 5, Rick Miller 1, Robert Pfetzing 0).

Poole, Wednesday, May 9
ENGLAND 50 (Alan Grahame 10, Simon Wigg 9, Phil Collins 9, †Michael Lee 7, Peter Collins 7, Chris Morton 4, John Davis 3, Kevin Smith 1) **UNITED STATES OF AMERICA 58** (Shawn Moran 15, †Bobby Schwartz 13, Lance King 12, Rick Miller 8, John Cook 8, Sam Ermolenko 1, Steve Lucero 1).

The United States of America win the series 4-1.

- *The England team manager was Carl Glover.*
- *The United States of America team manager was John Scott.*

Jessup refused to sulk and actually top-scored in the first Test at Reading although the saviour was reserve John Davis.

Denmark were six points in front when Glover made his first programme change bringing in the former Smallmead favourite for Phil Collins in heat 12.

Davis became England's second heat winner, went on to score a further five, paid seven points, and rescued the Lions from another humiliating defeat.

The final match at Halifax was the decider with the two nations tied on one win, one draw and one defeat.

That, and a scintillating World Pairs Final victory for Morton and Collins, seemed to have put England to rights again – but then came the biggest blow-up of all as Carter, battling back from his broken leg, was stripped of the England captaincy and left out of the World Team Cup squad after an explosive row at the British Final where Carter led a virtual one-man campaign to have the meeting go ahead in atrocious conditions.

He went on to win the title but there were ugly dressing room scenes that had Glover admitting: "If I were to put him in England's team I wouldn't get the best out of them. He doesn't fit in. When I select an England team I cannot get a rider who wants to ride with Kenny!"

1984 4 Team Tournament

Vojens, Friday, April 27
DENMARK 44 (†Erik Gundersen 12, Hans Nielsen 12, Bo Petersen 11, Preben Eriksen 9) **UNITED STATES OF AMERICA 30** (Lance King 10, Dennis Sigalos 8, Shawn Moran 7, †Bobby Schwartz 5) **ENGLAND 17** (†Chris Morton 5, Phil Collins 4, Les Collins 4, Alan Grahame 3, Peter Collins 1) **WEST GERMANY 5** (†Egon Müller 3, Klaus Lausch 1, Hans-Otto Pingel 1, Georg Hack 0).

1984 England v Denmark Results

Reading, Monday, June 4
ENGLAND 54 (Dave Jessup 11, Peter Collins 11, John Louis 10, †Chris Morton 10, John Davis 8, Malcolm Simmons 3, Phil Collins 1, Mark Courtney, did not ride) **DENMARK 54** (†Erik Gundersen 15, Hans Nielsen 15, Bo Petersen 13, Peter Ravn 5, John Eskildsen 3, John Jørgensen 2, Jens Rasmussen 1, Preben Eriksen 0).

Wimbledon, Thursday, June 7
ENGLAND 45 (Dave Jessup 9, Peter Collins 8, John Davis 8, †Chris Morton 7, Phil Collins 7, Malcolm Simmons 3, John Louis 3, Colin Richardson 0) **DENMARK 63** (Hans Nielsen 17, †Erik Gundersen 14, Bo Petersen 13, John Eskildsen 11, Jens Rasmussen 5, John Jørgensen 2, Peter Ravn 1, Preben Eriksen 0).

Wolverhampton, Friday, June 8
ENGLAND 59 (Phil Collins 16, †Chris Morton 13, Andy Grahame 9, John Louis 8, Peter Collins 7, Alan Grahame 6, Les Collins, did not ride) **DENMARK 48** (Preben Eriksen 14, †Erik Gundersen 11, Hans Nielsen 11, Bo Petersen 5, Peter Ravn 3, John Jørgensen 2, Jens Rasmussen 1, John Eskildsen 1).

Halifax, Sunday, June 10
ENGLAND 59 (Alan Grahame 13, Phil Collins 11, Chris Morton 11, John Louis 10, Neil Evitts 9, Andy Grahame 3, Peter Collins 1, Andy Smith 1) **DENMARK 49** (Hans Nielsen 15, †Erik Gundersen 13, Bo Petersen 8, Preben Eriksen 8, Jan O. Pedersen 4, Jens Rasmussen 1, Sam Nikolajsen 0).

England win the series 2-1 with one Test drawn.

● *The England team manager was Carl Glover.*
● *The Denmark team manager was Jorgen Jensen.*

Fredericia, Sunday, July 1
DENMARK 59 (Erik Gundersen 17, Hans Nielsen 14, Preben Eriksen 11, Peter Ravn 11, John Jørgensen 4, Flemming Pedersen 1, Bo Petersen 1, Tommy Knudsen 0) **ENGLAND 49** (Chris Morton 10, Neil Evitts 10, Phil Collins 9, Neil Collins 8, Alan Grahame 7, Peter Collins 3, Mark Courtney 1, Peter Carr 1).

● *The Denmark team manager was Ole Olsen.* ● *The England team manager was Carl Glover.*

DENMARK 1984: The Danish squad for the opening Test at Reading which ended in a nerve-tingling 54-54 draw. Left to right: Preben Eriksen, Bo Petersen, Hans Nielsen, skipper Erik Gundersen, John Eskildsen, Jens Rasmussen, Peter Ravn (kneeling) and John Jørgensen

Carter WAS left out of the next England team but the diplomatic Morton, who had been confirmed as national captain, tried to heal the breach.

He said: "England needs the bloke the way he is riding and when he is fit. But some of the things he has said he shouldn't have said and that is part of the problem.

"Like insisting that he is the only one who should be England captain and he is England's only hope of winning the World title. We want the bloke to ride with us but we've got to work together as a team.

"The bloke wants to win but we all want to win. Somewhere Kenny gets crossed up when he rides for England. He is very patriotic."

Carter hit back: "I wasn't asking for any favours at Coventry and certainly didn't get any. All I got was a load of stick from some of the other riders, including some of my so-called England team-mates.

"The things they said to me were disgusting and one threatened to punch me in the face after the meeting.

"I couldn't really believe the way some of the riders ganged up on me. I want to come back and captain England when I'm fully fit but I'm a bit disgusted about certain things that happened at Coventry."

The final word was with Glover: "For speedway's sake we have got to come together. Unfortunately there are 260 one way and Kenny Carter the other way"

Time was given the opportunity to be the healer as, after going out of the World Championship at the Inter Continental Final when he still needed to be helped on and off his bike, Carter accepted medical advice to rest his broken leg.

And Glover was left with no alternative but to leave him out of the Lions World Team Cup squad....

CZECHOSLOVAKIA provided the principal international entertainment in the National League with a six match clash with club sides.

Their visit came in August but, earlier in the year, the Swedish Elite League side Örnarna opened the season for several tracks.

They had finished comfortably mid-table in Sweden the previous year but imported several riders from Vargarna to bring their squad up to full strength, including Mikael Blixt.

Veteran Olle Nygren took over the team management of the Mariestad side but all they could salvage from the visit was a draw at Stoke where Mats Olsson, who had ridden for Halifax in both 1982 and 1983, made Loomer Road fans wonder why he hadn't established himself in the British League.

He was beaten twice by Tom Owen who, along with Nigel Crabtree, won the last four races to snatch a draw after the Swedes led by eight points at one stage.

Blixt missed the last match at Middlesbrough which reduced the visitors to six fit men and rider replacement and it was just as well they tracked Olsson at reserve as he scored another dozen points to be the outstanding success.

If Örnarna were easy meat for at least four of their five opponents (a further scheduled match at Hackney had been called off because of rain) then everyone thought the Czechs would be far tougher opposition.

Unusually that didn't turn out to be the case as the Prague administrators decided to send an experimental team to England.

Vaclav Verner and ex-Belle Vue rider Emil Sova were the only two riders well known to all but the most knowledgeable of Eastern European shale action, and the squad included five riders with little or no Western pedigree at all.

It was only some years later, when he joined Hackney, that the name Pavel Karnas, one of the tourists, meant anything to British fans.

Verner had an uncomfortable night at the Groveway in the opener and in the farewell meeting at Arena Essex but other than that was the exciting performer he had always been.

Exeter, who had hoped to include him in their 1984 British League side, could only stand and think of what might have been as he got double figure scores at Long Eaton and one of his all-time favourite tracks Canterbury.

There was one major scare on the visit when they failed to get to Hackney by start-time having ridden at Middlesbrough the previous evening.

So the London management put on a sponsored second half first and the international challenge itself didn't get underway until nine o'clock.

After another heavy defeat, one of six, the Czechs must have wondered if it was worth getting there at all....

1984 Czechoslovakia Tour of Division Two Results

Milton Keynes, Tuesday, August 21
MILTON KEYNES 54 (†Keith White 14, Steve Payne 10, David Blackburn 8, Nigel De'ath 8, Rob Wall 8, Peter Framingham 5, Chris Hunt 1) **CZECHOSLOVAKIA 24** (Lubomir Jedek 8, Zdenek Schneiderwind 6, Emil Sova 3, Pavel Karnas 3, Karel Kadlec 2, †Vaclav Verner 2, Miroslav Prager 0).

Long Eaton, Wednesday, August 22
LONG EATON 50 (Graham Drury 10, †Dave Perks 9, Miles Evans 8, Mark Stevenson 7, Paul Stead 6, John Frankland 5, Chris Pidcock 5) **CZECHOSLOVAKIA 28** (†Vaclav Verner 10, Emil Sova 6, Lubomir Jedek 5, Pavel Karnas 5, Karel Kadlec 1, Zdenek Schneiderwind 1, Miroslav Prager 0).

Middlesbrough, Thursday, August 23
MIDDLESBROUGH 46 (Steve Wilcock 11, †Geoff Pusey 11, Mike Spink 9, Paul Price 8, Jim Burdfield 4, Ashley Norton 2, Rob Carter 1) **CZECHOSLOVAKIA 32** (Emil Sova 9, †Vaclav Verner 9, Zdenek Schneiderwind 5, Lubomir Jedek 4, Pavel Karnas 4, Miroslav Prager 1, Karel Kadlec 0).

Hackney, Friday, August 24
HACKNEY 54 (Paul Bosley 12, Kevin Teager 12, Trevor Banks 11, †Barry Thomas 7, Andy Galvin 5, Paul Whittaker 5, Linden Warner 2) **CZECHOSLOVAKIA 24** (†Vaclav Verner 7, Zdenek Schneiderwind 7, Emil Sova 4, Pavel Karnas 3, Lubomir Jedek 2, Miroslav Prager 1, Karel Kadlec 0).

Canterbury, Saturday, August 25
CANTERBURY 50 (Alan Mogridge 12, Kevin Brice 9, David Mullett 9, †Barney Kennett 7, Neville Tatum 6, Rob Tilbury 4, Jeremy Luckhurst 3) **CZECHOSLOVAKIA 28** (†Vaclav Verner 13, Emil Sova 5, Pavel Karnas 4, Zdenek Schneiderwind 4, Lubomir Jedek 2, Karel Kadlec 0, Miroslav Prager 0).

Arena Essex, Monday, August 27
ARENA ESSEX 46 (Martin Goodwin 10, Alan Sage 8, David Smart 7, Bill Barrett 6, †Bob Humphreys 6, David Cheshire 6, Peter Johns 3) **CZECHOSLOVAKIA 32** (Antonin Kasper [junior] 14, Lubomir Jedek 9, †Vaclav Verner 4, Zdenek Schneiderwind 3, Pavel Karnas 1, Emil Sova 1, Miroslav Prager 0).

● *The Czechoslovakia team manager was Josef Janeba.*

1984 Örnarna (Sweden) Tour Results

Milton Keynes, Tuesday, March 27
MILTON KEYNES 55 (Paul Clarke 10, †Keith White 10, Kevin Smart 9, David Blackburn 9, Nigel De'ath 8, Peter Framingham 8, Steve Payne 1) **ÖRNARNA 23** (Mats Olsson 9, Mikael Blixt 5, †Börje Ring 4, Kenneth Nyström 4, Raymond Forsberg 1, Peter Karlsson 0, Rolf Sundberg 0).

Hackney, Friday, March 30
Cancelled, waterlogged track.

Stoke, Saturday, March 31
STOKE 39 (†Tom Owen 15, Nigel Crabtree 11, Ashley Pullen 7, Steve Bishop 3, Russell Birks 3, Gary O'Hare 0, Ian Stead 0) **ÖRNARNA 39** (Mats Olsson 13, Mikael Blixt 10, †Börje Ring 6, Kenneth Nyström 4, Rolf Sundberg 4, Raymond Forsberg 1 Peter Karlsson 1).

Boston, Sunday, April 1
BOSTON 49 (†David Gagen 12, Steve Lomas 11, Robert Hollingworth 11, Dennis Mallett 7, Peter Chapman 7, Colin Cook 1, Guy Wilson 0)
ÖRNARNA 28 (†Börje Ring 8, Jan Davidsson 6, Kenneth Nyström 5, Peter Karlsson 4, Mats Olsson 2, Mikael Blixt 2, Raymond Forsberg 1).

Long Eaton, Wednesday, April 4
LONG EATON 43 (†Dave Perks 12, Graham Drury 9, John Frankland 8, Paul Stead 6, Miles Evans 4, Chris Pidcock 2, David Tyler 2) **ÖRNARNA 35** (Kenneth Nyström 9, Jan Davidsson 9, Mats Olsson 8, †Börje Ring 7, Mikael Blixt 1, Raymond Forsberg 1, Peter Karlsson 0).

Middlesbrough, Thursday, April 5
MIDDLESBROUGH 49 (†Geoff Pusey 12, Steve Wilcock 12, Peter E. Smith 9, Mike Spink 7, Paul Price 4, John Place 3, Mark Crang 2) **ÖRNARNA 29** (Mats Olsson 12, Jan Davidsson 7, Kenneth Nyström 6, †Börje Ring 3, Raymond Forsberg 1, Peter Karlsson 0).

● *The Örnarna team manager was Olle Nygren.*

1984 England v Scotland (Division Two) Results

NOT a series to be remembered and one look at the scorers will tell why! Sean Courtney rode for both England and Scotland; Colonials Brett Saunders and Bruce Cribb also represented the Scots – but Jim McMillan was overlooked for the second match.

Edinburgh, Friday, May 4
SCOTLAND 61 (Bobby Beaton 17, Charlie McKinna 13, †Jim McMillan 8, Steve McDermott 8, Roger Lambert 6, Steve Lawson 6, Dave Trownson 3)
ENGLAND 47 (†Dave Perks 14, Steve Wilcock 12, Tom Owen 8, Keith White 6, Chris Pidcock 4, Kevin Smart 3, Paul Stead 0, Sean Courtney 0).

Long Eaton, Wednesday, May 16
ENGLAND 64 (†Dave Perks 14, Kevin Smart 11, Paul Stead 10, Keith White 9, Nigel Crabtree 8, Chris Pidcock 6, Tom Owen 5, Steve Wilcock 1) **SCOTLAND 44** (†Bobby Beaton 16, Steve Lawson 12, Steve McDermott 8, Andy Reid 4, Bruce Cribb 4, Roger Lambert 0, Sean Courtney 0, Martin Johnson 0).

Mickey–takers

ENGLAND suffered the final international indignity at Swindon on Sunday, September 8th, 1985.

America had already made certain of the series and skipper Bobby Schwartz and Test partner John Cook turned to manager John Scott and told him: "Let the reserves take our place."

So America went into that 16th heat with Belle Vue's Eddie Ingels lining up alongside 24-year-old Mickey Rooney, in England for the season as Cookie's mechanic!

He had been pressed into service as a figurehead reserve only as Scott was confined to seven experienced riders to wear the Stars and Stripes.

Rooney, who hadn't ridden competitively for several years, had actually had an outing in the first Test at Belle Vue but that was because of a tape-breaking and the lack of any alternative.

This time it was by choice as the Americans decided to take the Mickey out of their outclassed opponents.

The American victory, following as it did a 2-1 defeat against Denmark, relegated England to the Second Division of international speedway...and there was nothing new manager John Berry could do about it.

Berry had replaced Carl Glover during the winter and had high hopes that he could translate his hard-nosed style of management to the international arena with similar success to that he enjoyed at his club Ipswich.

It didn't work that way as England were outgunned and outwitted.

Berry began his reign in unorthodox manner by revealing that he wouldn't appoint an England captain but instead would choose whoever he fancied on the day of the meeting.

Kelvin Tatum was the first to get the honour on his home track at Coventry but it was another famous Bee Ole Olsen who won through in the end despite an unbelievable row with one of his big stars.

Hans Nielsen, at loggerheads with Olsen, was named at reserve as a disciplinary measure, sat in the pits place normally reserved for visiting juniors, and then refused to go out when asked by his manager.

He threatened to do the same at Oxford before his Cheetahs promoter Bernard Crapper persuaded him to take the place of the excluded Bo Petersen in heat 14!

But he refused to race in the third Test and was banned for three days while the Danes staged a tremendous comeback to overcome a six point deficit with two heats to go with successive maximums that gave them the series.

In the third of the summer's rubbers England enjoyed success at last, defeating an Australasian side denuded of one of it's stars by Billy Sanders' suicide.

THRILL-PHIL...*Phil Collins, the one-off England skipper*

1985 England v Denmark Results

Coventry, Saturday, April 20
ENGLAND 47 (Kenny Carter 11, Chris Morton 10, †Kelvin Tatum 8, Phil Collins 6, Jeremy Doncaster 6, Andy Smith 6, Simon Wigg 0, Simon Cross 0) **DENMARK 61** (Peter Ravn 15, Tommy Knudsen 12, Preben Eriksen 11, Bo Petersen 10, John Jørgensen 5, †Erik Gundersen 5, John Eskildsen 3, Hans Nielsen, did not ride).

Oxford, Sunday, April 28
ENGLAND 58 (Kelvin Tatum 15, Phil Collins 13, Chris Morton 11, †Simon Wigg 9, Jeremy Doncaster 5, Richard Knight 3, Andy Smith 1, Kenny Carter 1) **DENMARK 50** (Tommy Knudsen 12, John Eskildsen 10, Peter Ravn 8, Bo Petersen 7, †Erik Gundersen 4, Hans Nielsen 4, Preben Eriksen 3, Jens Rasmussen 2).

Cradley Heath, Saturday, May 4
ENGLAND 53 (Simon Wigg 13, †Phil Collins 12, Chris Morton 9, Kenny Carter 8, Kelvin Tatum 6, Simon Cross 3, Neil Evitts 1, Andy Smith 1) **DENMARK 55** (†Erik Gundersen 15, Tommy Knudsen 13, Bo Petersen 11, Jan O. Pedersen 7, Preben Eriksen 4, Peter Ravn 3, John Jørgensen 2, John Eskildsen 0).

Denmark win the series 2-1.

- *The England team manager was John Berry.*
- *The Denmark team manager was Ole Olsen.*

1985 England v Australasia Results

King's Lynn, Tuesday, July 23
ENGLAND 71 (Kelvin Tatum 17, Jeremy Doncaster 17, Dave Jessup 15, Simon Cross 9, Andy Smith 7, Richard Knight 5, Neil Collins 1) **AUSTRALASIA 37** (Phil Crump 9, †Steve Regeling 8, Larry Ross 6, Rod Hunter 6, Mitch Shirra 5, David Bargh 2, David Cheshire 1, Steve Baker 0).

Oxford, Friday, July 26
ENGLAND 69 (Kelvin Tatum 17, †Simon Wigg 15, Andy Smith 10, Richard Knight 10, Neil Collins 9, John Davis 5, Simon Cross 2, Marvyn Cox 1) **AUSTRALASIA 38** (†Phil Crump 9, Mitch Shirra 9, Rod Hunter 9, David Bargh 7, Steve Regeling 3, Ray Dole 1, Larry Ross 0, Stan Bear 0).

Halifax, Sunday, September 15
ENGLAND 53 (Kelvin Tatum 17, Andy Smith 12, John Davis 8, Neil Colllins 7, Peter Carr 4, Richard Knight 3, Neil Evitts 2, Carl Blackbird 0) **AUSTRALASIA 55** (Larry Ross 13, David Bargh 13, Rod Hunter 10, Mitch Shirra 10, Steve Regeling 4, Steve Baker 3, †Phil Crump 2).

England win the series 2-1.

- *The England team manager was John Berry.*
- *The Australasia team managers were James Easter and Trevor Redmond.*

1985 England v United States of America Results

Belle Vue, Sunday, September 1
ENGLAND 48 (Simon Wigg 9, Phil Collins 7, Jeremy Doncaster 7, Neil Collins 7, Kelvin Tatum 6, Richard Knight 6, †John Davis 3, Andy Smith 3) **UNITED STATES OF AMERICA 58** (John Cook 14, Shawn Moran 10, Rick Miller 10, †Bobby Schwartz 9, Sam Ermolenko 6, Lance King 6, Eddie Ingels 3, Michael Rooney 0).

Ipswich, Thursday, September 5
ENGLAND 50 (Jeremy Doncaster 12, Dave Jessup 12, Richard Knight 10, Simon Wigg 7, Phil Collins 5, John Davis 3, Kelvin Tatum 1, Carl Blackbird 0) **UNITED STATES OF AMERICA 58** (Shawn Moran 17, John Cook 10, Sam Ermolenko 10, Lance King 8, †Bobby Schwartz 7, Rick Miller 5, Eddie Ingels 1, Kelly Moran 0).

Swindon, Sunday, September 8
ENGLAND 42 (Kelvin Tatum 12, John Davis 9, Jeremy Doncaster 8, Richard Knight 6, Phil Collins 4, Malcolm Simmons 3, Neil Evitts 0, Andy Smith 0) **UNITED STATES OF AMERICA 66** (Lance King 17, Shawn Moran 13, †Bobby Schwartz 10, John Cook 9, Rick Miller 9, Sam Ermolenko 6, Eddie Ingels 2, Michael Rooney 0).

United States of America win the series 3-0.

- *The England team manager was John Berry.*
- *The United States of America team manager was John Scott.*

1985 Ipswich in Germany

Landshut, Sunday, April 16
LANDSHUT 94 (Klaus Lausch 27, Gerd Riss 21, Georg Hack 16, Karl Maier 14, Peter Nieder 10, Franz Kreimoser 6) **IPSWICH 91** (John Davis 25, Kai Niemi 23, Malcolm Simmons 16, Richard Knight 13, Nigel Flatman 10, Alan Farmer 4) **LONIGO [ITALY] 39** (Valentino Furlanetto 16, Francesco Biginato 7, Armando dal Chiele 7, Ottaviano Righetto 6, Guiseppe Scalcolaro 3, Davide Guarise 0).
Scorers: 5-4-3-2-1-0.

SPOILSPORTS

YOU CAN search through this book and you won't find the name of Sean Diiullo anywhere other than on this page.

Yet the 19-year-old kid from California's Newport Beach has his own place in British League history....

For holidaying Sean was called up to help out the injury hit Americans in the 1986 Sunbrite series.

It was Lance King who alerted manager John Scott to Sean's availability and, with Kelly Moran out injured and selection options down to the bare minimum of six riders, Diiullo was handed the number seven race jacket for the three match series.

He even got a ride at Oxford in the second Test after Lance King had been excluded for a tapes offence but never managed to finish his one and only international race!

While Diiullo's presence in the American squad was one of those odd talking points the biggest controversy of all was the ruling that spectacular celebratory wheelies would be banned.

Referee Paul Ackroyd was the first to enforce the order from above when he spoilt Simon Wigg's day at Oxford.

The England skipper had won his first five rides and was heading for his first full maximum for his country when he lifted his front wheel 30 yards from the chequered flag...and was as stunned as everyone in the 5,000 crowd when he was excluded.

Wigg claimed: "It was a diabolical decision. We are here to entertain the public but we have no chance with decisions like that."

It was a view echoed by fans at Ipswich – and the American riders who became victims of the clampdown.

Sam Ermolenko and John Cook were initially excluded in heat three to hand England, already 10-2 up, a 5-0 and to show their contempt for the hardline approach wheelied their way around Foxhall Heath in the last race.

COWBOY COOKIE...John Cook's wheelie exciting antics upset referee Paul Ackroyd and saw him thrown out

1986 England v United States of America Results

Sheffield, Sunday, August 10
ENGLAND 60 (†Simon Wigg 16, Chris Morton 12, Neil Collins 9, Jeremy Doncaster 7, Marvyn Cox 5, Neil Evitts 5, Peter Carr 5, Phil Collins 1) **UNITED STATES OF AMERICA 48** (Shawn Moran 14, Lance King 13, Sam Ermolenko 8, Rick Miller 5, †Bobby Schwartz 4, John Cook 4, Sean Diiullo, did not ride).

Oxford, Wednesday, August 13
ENGLAND 60 (†Simon Wigg 15, Kelvin Tatum 13, Marvyn Cox 12, Jeremy Doncaster 12, Andrew Silver 3, Neil Evitts 3, Chris Morton 2, Richard Knight 0) **UNITED STATES OF AMERICA 47** (Rick Miller 11, John Cook 10, Shawn Moran 10, Lance King 7, Sam Ermolenko 6, †Bobby Schwartz 3, Sean Diiullo 0).

Ipswich, Thursday, August 14
ENGLAND 62 (Jeremy Doncaster 15, †Simon Wigg 9, Chris Morton 8, Richard Knight 8, Andrew Silver 7, Marvyn Cox 6, Carl Blackbird 5, Neil Evitts 4) **UNITED STATES OF AMERICA 43** (Shawn Moran 14, Sam Ermolenko 11, Lance King 7, Rick Miller 4, John Cook 4, †Bobby Schwartz 3, Sean Diiullo, did not ride).

England win the series 3-0.

- *The England team managers were Eric Boocock and Colin Pratt.*
- *The United States of America team manager was John Scott.*

The whitewash against the Yanks helped make up for earlier international disappointment when the Sunbrite Lions were outclassed by Denmark who went into the first Test without Tommy Knudsen, locked in a bitter argument with the Danish Motor Union.

Knudsen had expected to be seeded through to the Nordic Final as their sixth qualifier after finishing way down the order at the Danish Final.

Instead they went for Sam Nikolajsen with a furious Knudsen claiming: "I've taken it as a great insult after what I've done for Denmark in the past."

Even without him the Danes snatched a two point win in the opener at Dudley Wood where Chris Morton became the third rider to win 100 England caps.

National League star Andrew Silver was called up for the Third Test at Wolverhampton and by then Knudsen had been reinstated in the World Championship, made his peace, and scored 15 points in the Danes victory over England at Belle Vue.

But Silver was far from overawed by the occasion and it looked, for all the world, that he was in at the birth of a burgeoning international career.

Sadly, that match was also to be the last international appearance of Kenny Carter who won his last ever race for England in heat nine against Hans Nielsen and John Jørgensen.

Four days later he and his wife Pam were dead – and England, still reeling from his loss, pulled back one of the Tests on his old home track at Bradford.

As Neil Evitts, the man who was to succeed him as both British Champion and Bradford captain, said: "Kenny would have liked us to have won!"

For what seemed like the umpteenth year in a row (it was actually the seventh) there was another change of name and face as England manager.

John Berry, after an unhappy second stint in charge, gave way to another dual appointment.

Eric Boocock, who had previously worked with both Berry and Ian Thomas, was joined in tandem by former World Finalist Colin Pratt, the first time that two ex-riders had been put in charge of England affairs.

They were also boosted by the news that Coal Products Limited were to extend their speedway involvement in 1986 as far as backing the national team who became the Sunbrite Lions.

They also broke with tradition by calling riders together for a special briefing at Coventry.

Their initial selection was hampered by a rain-ruined weekend which prevented them looking at the current form of several candidates and they played relatively safe by naming a 10 rider squad.

The only mild surprises were the inclusion of Belle Vue's two-cap Carl Blackbird and an international recall for Alan Grahame who hadn't represented his country for nearly two years.

The other big announcement was that they would revert to the customary policy of having a permanent England captain.

Their choice was Oxford's Simon Wigg who accepted the rôle with grace: "I'm honoured to captain England."

To avoid any nastiness with Kenny Carter Boocock added: "We want Kenny to ride at number one, to go out and win the first race and all his others."

He didn't manage to do that at Dudley Wood but he did get 10 points as England went down by only two points in the first Test.

One major innovation by the new England incumbents was to revive the Young England team.

Boocock and Pratt, firm believers in giving youth its fling, again chose to send them around the National League circuits but this time they matched them up against Australia.

It was a one-sided series from which little was learnt other than the fact that Middlesbrough's 17-year-old former Youth Division Grass Track Champion Gary Havelock was a gilt-edged prospect.

Havvy, who was already impressing while doubling up for Bradford in the British League, got 18 out of 18 at Cleveland Park and followed that up with 17 at Birmingham.

Australia manager James Easter was moved to claim: "Year for year, England have got the best side in the world at the moment."

Another to impress was National League Riders' Champion Paul Thorp who actually outpaced Havelock with two 18-point maximums and a top-scoring 16 points at Crayford where his only dropped points were at the expense of New Zealand's World Finalist Mitch Shirra who adopted the nationality of his family's domicile once again....

1986 England v Denmark Results

Cradley Heath, Saturday, May 3
ENGLAND 53 (†Simon Wigg 14, Chris Morton 10, Kenny Carter 10, Phil Collins 9, Jeremy Doncaster 7, Carl Blackbird 3, Kelvin Tatum 0, Simon Cross 0) **DENMARK 55** (Hans Nielsen 13, Jan O. Pedersen 12, †Erik Gundersen 12, Preben Eriksen 8, John Jørgensen 6, Peter Ravn 4, Sam Nikolajsen 0, John Eskildsen 0).

Belle Vue, Friday, May 16
ENGLAND 45 (†Simon Wigg 10, Chris Morton 10, Kenny Carter 8, Jeremy Doncaster 8, Neil Evitts 4, Neil Collins 4, Kelvin Tatum 1, Carl Blackbird 0) **DENMARK 63** (†Erik Gundersen 15, Tommy Knudsen 15, Hans Nielsen 15, Jan O. Pedersen 8, John Jørgensen 7, Jens Rasmussen 3, Bo Petersen 0, John Eskildsen, did not ride).

Wolverhampton, Friday, May 23
ENGLAND 41 (Chris Morton 10, Neil Collins 9, Jeremy Doncaster 9, Andrew Silver 7, †Simon Wigg 4, Neil Evitts 2, Phil Collins 0, Carl Blackbird 0) **DENMARK 66** (†Erik Gundersen 17, Hans Nielsen 14, Bo Petersen 10, Jan O. Pedersen 9, Tommy Knudsen 9, John Jørgensen 6, John Eskildsen 1, Jan Stæchmann 0).

Bradford, Sunday, May 25
ENGLAND 57 (Jeremy Doncaster 14, Chris Morton 12, †Simon Wigg 11, Neil Evitts 8, Kelvin Tatum 5, Simon Cross 5, John Davis 1, Richard Knight 1) **DENMARK 51** (†Erik Gundersen 15, Bo Petersen 10, Hans Nielsen 8, Jan O. Pedersen 8, Tommy Knudsen 5, John Jørgensen 3, Jens Rasmussen 2, John Eskildsen, did not ride).

Oxford, Friday, May 30
ENGLAND 49 (†Simon Wigg 12, Chris Morton 9, Jeremy Doncaster 8, Kelvin Tatum 8, Andrew Silver 5, Phil Collins 4, Marvyn Cox 2, Simon Cross 1) **DENMARK 59** (Hans Nielsen 17, †Erik Gundersen 13, Jan O. Pedersen 13, Bo Petersen 13, John Jørgensen 2, Sam Nikolajsen 1, Jens Rasmussen 0, John Eskildsen 0).

Denmark win the series 4-1.

- *The England team managers were Eric Boocock and Colin Pratt.*
- *The Denmark team manager was Hardy Jensen.*

●Peter Ravn was back in international action a day short of a year since he fractured both his ankles during his last Test appearance for Denmark at Cradley Heath.

1986 Young England v Australia (Division Two) Results

Middlesbrough, Thursday, September 11
YOUNG ENGLAND 75 (Gary Havelock 18, Paul Thorp 18, †Andrew Silver 17, Martin Dugard 10, Darren Sumner 4, Jamie Luckhurst 4, David Blackburn 2, Alastair Stevens 2) **AUSTRALIA 33** (†Mark Fiora 11, Stephen Davies 7, Alan Rivett 6, Steve Regeling 3, David Jackson 3, Jim Burdfield 2, Mark Carlson 1).

Hackney, Friday, September 12
YOUNG ENGLAND 74 (Paul Thorp 16, Andy Galvin 14, †Andrew Silver 14, Martin Dugard 10, Gary Havelock 8, Jamie Luckhurst 6, Neville Tatum 6, Alastair Stevens 0) **AUSTRALIA 33** (Mitch Shirra 12, Mark Fiora 6, Stephen Davies 6, †Steve Regeling 5, David Jackson 2, Alan Rivett 2, Jim Burdfield 0, Mark Carlson 0).

Birmingham, Sunday, September 14
YOUNG ENGLAND 78 (Paul Thorp 18, Gary Havelock 17, †Andrew Silver 15, Martin Dugard 12, Andy Galvin 11, Kevin Smart 4, Ian M. Stead 1) **AUSTRALIA 30** (†Stephen Davies 9, David Jackson 9, Mark Fiora 5, Jim Burdfield 3, Steve Regeling 2, Alan Rivett 2, Mark Carlson 0).
Young England win the series 3-0.

- *The Young England team managers were Colin Pratt (all Tests) and Eric Boocock (Hackney and Birmingham).*
- *The Australia team managers were James Easter (Middlesbrough and Hackney) and Phil Crump.*

1986 Young Czechoslovakia Tour Results

Exeter, Monday, October 6
EXETER 59 (Bruce Cribb 13, Steve Bishop 11, Kevin Smart 11, †Colin Cook 10, Michael Coles 8, Andy Sell 4, Alan Mason 2, Jon Gould 0) **YOUNG CZECHOSLOVAKIA 49** (Roman Matousek 15, Lubomir Jedek 12, Stanislav Urban 11, Pavel Karnas 6, Josef Fejfar 4, Petr Vandirek 1, Jan Holub [junior] 0, Borivoj Hadek 0).

Middlesbrough, Thursday, October 9
MIDDLESBROUGH 74 (†Martin Dixon 18, Mark Courtney 15, Gary Havelock 13, Steve Wilcock 13, Jim Burdfield 10, Roland Tebbs 5) **YOUNG CZECHOSLOVAKIA 34** (Stanislav Urban 13, Josef Fejfar 6, Borivoj Hadek 5, Lubomir Jedek 5, Pavel Karnas 3, Emil Sova 2, Jan Holub 0).

Canterbury, Saturday, October 11
CANTERBURY KENT SELECT 37 (†Malcolm Simmons 11, Jamie Luckhurst 7, Paul Woods 6, Jeremy Luckhurst 5, Martin Goodwin 4, Andy Galvin 4, Steve Hone 0) **YOUNG CZECHOSLOVAKIA 41** (Lubomir Jedek 12, Stanislav Urban 10, Pavel Karnas 6, Petr Vandirek 5, Borivoj Hadek 4, Jan Holub 4, Josef Fejfar 0).

Reading, Monday, October 13
READING 46 (Mitch Shirra 12, Tony Olsson 10, †Jan Andersson 8, Malcolm Holloway 8, Peter Glanz 6, Gary Tagg 1, Trevor Williams 1) **YOUNG CZECHOSLOVAKIA 32** (Petr Vandirek 8, Roman Matousek 7, Stanislav Urban 6, Borivoj Hadek 5, Lubomir Jedek 5, Pavel Karnas 1, Josef Fejfar 0).

Poole, Wednesday, October 15
POOLE 51 (†Sam Ermolenko 18, Martin Yeates 15, Steve Schofield 14, Will James 2, Wayne Barrett 1, Gordon Humphreys 1, Peter Read 0) **YOUNG CZECHOSLOVAKIA 57** (Petr Vandirek 16, Lubomir Jedek 13, Stanislav Urban 8, Pavel Karnas 7, Josef Fejfar 6, Jan Holub 4, Borivoj Hadek 3).
■ ***Original staging on Tuesday, October 14, postponed, waterlogged track.***

- *The Young Czechoslovakia team manager was Vaclav Verner.*

TRACK WARS

THERE has never been any great love between England and Denmark.

But much of the respect that there has always been between two of speedway's great nations disappeared during the last heat of the the third Test at Cradley Heath.

Everyone in the England camp was ready to rush onto the Dudley Wood track when the chequered flag came down on a match-winning 5-1 to the Sunbrite Lions from Kelvin Tatum and partner Marvyn Cox.

But then referee David Hughes switched on the red light as Coventry's John Jørgensen, trailing behind his team-mate Tommy Knudsen, slipped off.

England's Eric Boocock claimed: "He deliberately fell. It's cheating, what else can you call it?"

Jørgensen countered: "A lot of people said I had fallen off on purpose but that wasn't true, I had nowhere to go. I wasn't hurt but I couldn't get up quickly because the bike was on top of me."

The stopped and re-run race – with Jørgensen rightly excluded – gave the Danes a second chance and Knudsen took full advantage of his opportunity to take the three points that saw the two countries tied, in both the match and the series.

Earlier there had been another explosive incident when Danish skipper Erik Gundersen (pictured left) lashed out verbally at his own Cradley promoter and joint England boss Colin Pratt over the interval watering of the dusty circuit.

Gundersen, who had finished stone last in the first race after the

1987 England v Denmark Results

King's Lynn, Sunday May 3
ENGLAND 58 (Kelvin Tatum 14, †Simon Wigg 14, Jeremy Doncaster 11, Chris Morton 7, Paul Thorp 6, Simon Cross 5, Richard Knight 1, Carl Blackbird, did not ride) **DENMARK 50** (Hans Nielsen 15, Tommy Knudsen 13, Jan O. Pedersen 10, †Erik Gundersen 6, John Jørgensen 5, Peter Ravn 1, Allan Johansen 0, Jens Rasmussen 0).

Oxford, Friday, May 8
ENGLAND 49 (Marvyn Cox 14, †Simon Wigg 12, Kelvin Tatum 6, Simon Cross 6, Jeremy Doncaster 5, Chris Morton 3, Andrew Silver 2, Martin Dugard 1) **DENMARK 59** (Hans Nielsen 17, †Erik Gundersen 16, Tommy Knudsen 12, Jan O. Pedersen 6, John Jørgensen 6, Jens Rasmussen 1, Peter Glanz 1, Peter Ravn 0).

Cradley Heath, Sunday, May 10
ENGLAND 54 (Kelvin Tatum 14, Andy Grahame 13, Simon Cross 8, Marvyn Cox 6, †Simon Wigg 6, Chris Morton 4, Paul Thorp 3, Martin Dugard, did not ride) **DENMARK 54** (Hans Nielsen 12, †Erik Gundersen 12, John Jørgensen 9, Peter Ravn 8, Tommy Knudsen 7, Peter Glanz 3, Jens Rasmussen 3, Brian Karger, did not ride).

Belle Vue, Saturday, May 16
ENGLAND 56 ((Kelvin Tatum 12, Paul Thorp 11, †Simon Wigg 9, Jeremy Doncaster 8, Chris Morton 8, Simon Cross 4, Marvyn Cox 3, Alun Rossiter 1) **DENMARK 52** (Hans Nielsen 15, †Erik Gundersen 13, Tommy Knudsen 12, Peter Ravn 8, John Jørgensen 4, Jens Rasmussen 0, Peter Glanz 0, Jan Stæchmann 0).

Wolverhampton, Monday, May 18
ENGLAND 53 (Simon Cross 12, Jeremy Doncaster 9, †Simon Wigg 7, Andrew Silver 7, Chris Morton 6, Gary Havelock 5, Kelvin Tatum 4, Neil Evitts 3) **DENMARK 55** (Hans Nielsen 18, †Erik Gundersen 16, Tommy Knudsen 10, John Jørgensen 9, Preben Eriksen 1, Allan Johansen 1, Peter Ravn 0, Jan Stæchmann 0).

Series drawn 2-2 with one Test drawn.

- *The England team managers were Eric Boocock and Colin Pratt.*
- *The Denmark team manager was Preben Knudsen.*

1987 Denmark v England Results

Outrup, Sunday, April 19
DENMARK 68 (Jan O. Pedersen 14, †Erik Gundersen 13, Hans Nielsen 11, Peter Ravn 11, John Jørgensen 11, Tommy Knudsen 7, John Eskildsen 1, Frank Andersen, did not ride) **ENGLAND 40** (†Simon Wigg 11, Jeremy Doncaster 11, Chris Morton 8, Carl Blackbird 5, Kelvin Tatum 2, Marvyn Cox 2, Richard Knight 1, Neil Evitts 0).

Brovst, Sunday, April 26
DENMARK 67 (Hans Nielsen 15, †Erik Gundersen 13, Tommy Knudsen 11, John Jørgensen 11, Peter Ravn 8, Jan O. Pedersen 5, Sam Nikolajsen 4, John Eskildsen, did not ride) **ENGLAND 41** (†Simon Wigg 13, Jeremy Doncaster 9, Kelvin Tatum 6, Chris Morton 6, Gary Havelock 4, Richard Knight 2, Carl Blackbird 1, Marvyn Cox 0).

Denmark win the series 2-0.

- *The England team manager was Colin Pratt.*
- *The Denmark team manager was Preben Knudsen.*

- ***King's Lynn fanssaw an England-Denmark Test match eight years late! The track should have staged the first between the two countries in 1979 but that series was called off at a few days' notice.***

interval, exploded on his return to the pits to ignite an already smouldering atmosphere.

Tempers had cooled by the time the two teams met at Belle Vue in the fourth Test but the track action was still red-hot with Paul Thorp, in his first season in the British League, the England match-winner.

He beat Hans Nielsen in the penultimate race to ensure victory for his team and even though the Danish pairing of Knudsen and Jørgensen – at the centre of the third Test brouhaha – collected maximum points it was too late for the Danes to save their bacon.

Hans Nielsen gave Denmark a flying start by lowering the Monmore Green track record in the first heat and he made it a triumphant return to the track where he started his British career in 1977, with an 18 point full score, the first in the summer's seven Tests between the two countries.

Even though the Danes were carrying four virtual passengers (Preben Eriksen, Allan Johansen, Peter Ravn and Jan Stæchmann scored only two points between them) they had too much top-end power for an England side that lost the gutsy Andrew Silver for his last ride when he suffered facial injuries in a heat 15 tumble.

That was the race that all but sealed it for the Danes as that Knudsen-Jørgensen pairing grabbed a five-one over Simon Wigg.

With a drawn series against the Danes – two matches in Scandinavia earlier in the year had resulted in a couple of Danish victories – England looked to America as their summer salvation.

American manager John Scott faced his usual problem of finding eight fit riders and had to go into combat with only six team members in the Foxhall Heath pits.

The injured Kelly Moran was there offering help wherever he could but the Yanks went out for every race knowing a starting offence would leave them a rider short in the re-run.

They lost by only three points with Shawn Moran immaculate, were ahead by two points when the second Test at Hackney was abandoned, and then went down by 10 points at Sheffield.

Following the calling off of the Waterden Road clash Sam Ermolenko was ordered to take a drugs test but forgot to do so and was subsequently suspended from British League competition pending a Tribunal.

1987 England v United States of America Results

Ipswich, Thursday, August 13
ENGLAND 55 (Jeremy Doncaster 16, Simon Cross 12, Marvyn Cox 8, Kelvin Tatum 6, †Simon Wigg 6, Andrew Silver 4, Chris Morton 3, Richard Knight 0) **UNITED STATES OF AMERICA 52** (†Shawn Moran 18, Rick Miller 11, Sam Ermolenko 11, Lance King 6, Robert Pfetzing 3, Ronnie Correy 3).

Hackney, Friday, August 21
ENGLAND 34 *(Kelvin Tatum 11, Jeremy Doncaster 7, Simon Cross 5, Andrew Silver 5, †Simon Wigg 3, Martin Dugard 2, Paul Thorp 1, Marvyn Cox 0)* ***UNITED STATES OF AMERICA 36*** *(Sam Ermolenko 10, Rick Miller 7, Ronnie Correy 5, Kelly Moran 5, †Shawn Moran 4, Lance King 3, Robert Pfetzing 2).*
Abandoned after 12 heats, rain.

Sheffield, Sunday, August 30
ENGLAND 59 (Simon Cross 14, Kelvin Tatum 11, Peter Carr 9, Chris Morton 8, Jeremy Doncaster 7, †Simon Wigg 6, Marvyn Cox 4, Paul Thorp 0) **UNITED STATES OF AMERICA 49** (Sam Ermolenko 12, Shawn Moran 10, Kelly Moran 9, Rick Miller 9, Lance King 8, Randy Green 1, Ronnie Correy 0).

England win the series 2-0 with one Test abandoned.

- *The England team managers were Eric Boocock and Colin Pratt.*
- *The United States of America team manager was John Scott.*

A fortnight later Ermolenko was banned for 15 months (meaning he couldn't ride in England until 1989) but this was subsequently overturned with Speedway Control Board manager Dick Bracher explaining: "He was cleared because his suspension was an unsound decision. The regulations governing these offence are badly worded."

Ermolenko said: "My solicitor presented the facts and the fact is that I am not guilty. I'm glad it's all over, now I can plan for the future."

MAGICAL MORT...Only his former Belle Vue team-mate Peter Collins won more England caps during the British League era than Chris Morton whose all-action style thrilled fans all over the World. During his Test career Mort appeared in 128 internationals for his country, one of only three riders to reach the magic century mark

1987 Czechoslovakia Tour of Division Two Results

ROMAN MATOUSEK, missing from the British League after his five official matches for Ipswich the previous year, handed out a timely reminder to any interested promoter that he was one of the most exciting – but injury-prone – riders in the world.

The strong-man of Czechoslovakia held his country together in their first two matches but was badly missed when he had to sit out the visit to Exeter's County Ground where tour manager and former Falcons' favourite Vaclav Verner made a comeback as a fill-in reserve.

Matousek tried to race again at Poole but his injured back gave out and he had to pull off onto the centre green after his first lap and had similar painful problems when he took just one ride at Middlesbrough.

Peterborough, Friday, October 2
PETERBOROUGH 50 (Ian Barney 9, †Kevin Hawkins 8, Jamie Habbin 8, Peter Chapman 8, Carl Baldwin 7, Craig Hodgson 5, Nigel Flatman 5) **CZECHOSLOVAKIA 28** (†Roman Matousek 14, Borivoj Hadek 4, Bohumil Brhel 4, Josef Fejfar 2, Pavel Karnas 2, Vladimir Kalina 2, Jan Schinagl 0)

Canterbury, Saturday, October 3
CANTERBURY 54 (Paul Whittaker 11, Paul Evitts 10, †Mike Spink 9, Rob Tilbury 8, David Mullett 6, Carl Chalcraft 6, Mark Lyndon 4) **CZECHOSLOVAKIA 24** (†Roman Matousek 10, Bohumil Brhel 6, Josef Fejfar 2, Borivoj Hadek 2, Jan Schinagl 2, Zdenek Tesar 2, Vladimir Kalina 0).

Exeter, Monday, October 5
EXETER 39 (Alan Rivett 9, Kevin Price 7, Michael Coles 7, Andy Sell 6, †Colin Cook 5, David Smart 5, Tony Mattingley 0) **CZECHOSLOVAKIA 39** (Bohumil Brhel 11, Borivoj Hadek 10, Jan Schinagl 5, Zdenek Tesar 4, Vladimir Kalina 4, †Vaclav Verner 3, Pavel Karnas 2).

Poole, Tuesday, October 6
POOLE 46 (Kevin Smith 12, Steve Schofield 11, †Martin Yeates 8, David Biles 8, Wayne Barrett 3, Will James 3, Peter Read 1) **CZECHOSLOVAKIA 32** (Zdenek Tesar 11, Bohumil Brhel 9, Borivoj Hadek 7, Jan Schinagl 3, Vladimir Kalina 2, Pavel Karnas 0, †Roman Matousek 0).

Long Eaton, Wednesday, October 7
LONG EATON v CZECHOSLOVAKIA
Cancelled, track waterlogged.

Middlesbrough, Thursday, October 8
MIDDLESBROUGH 45 (†Martin Dixon 15, Steve Wilcock 9, Peter McNamara 7, Ashley Norton 6, Andrew Buck 4, Geoff Pusey 4)) **CZECHOSLOVAKIA 32** (Pavel Karnas 9, Borivoj Hadek 8, Bohumil Brhel 8, Zdenek Tesar 5, Jan Schinagl 2, †Roman Matousek 0, Vladimir Kalina 0).

● *The Czechoslovakia team manager was Vaclav Verner.*

1987 Poole v Australia Result

Poole, Tuesday, September 1
POOLE 52 (†Martin Yeates 13, Steve Schofield 12, David Biles 12, Kevin Smith 7, Wayne Barrett 6, Will James 1, Peter Read 1) **AUSTRALIA 44** (Brett Saunders 10, Glen Baxter 9, †Stephen Davies 8, Glenn Doyle 8, David Jackson 7, Craig Hodgson 2, Alan Rivett 0).

1987 National League v Poland Results

JOHN BERRY was typically blunt and forthright in his condemnation of the Polish tour: "I would have put them straight back on the boat."

Berry suffered in two capacities – as National League team manager and one of the administrative team at Wimbledon, their first port of call and the track that suffered more than most from the inadequacies of the visiting party.

The Poles didn't arrive at Plough Lane until 35 minutes after the first race had been due to start and then they were totally at sea as the National League rattled up a massive score, dropping only four points in 18 heats – two when Roger Johns fell in the opening race and the other two in the last race when Ryszard Franczyszyn beat Martin Dugard and David Biles in the race to the line. Not surprisingly after their 36 hour marathon overland journey from Warsaw, the Poles were ill prepared and ill equipped for competition and Berry added: "Their riders were understrength in quality and quantity."

And Alan Hodder, Director of Operations at the National League, hit out: "The initial request was for the full national team and we assumed that is what it would be but while three of the riders were possibly National League standard, the rest weren't."

The second Test at Powderhall was called off at four o'clock in the afternoon and the Poles wound up their disastrous whistle-stop visit with another heavy defeat at Stoke where they again had only one heat winner – Piotr Swist in his second ride!

Wimbledon, Wednesday, May 27
NATIONAL LEAGUE 86 (Kevin Jolly 18, Melvyn Taylor 16, Martin Dugard 16, David Mullett 14, David Biles 12, †Roger Johns 10) **POLAND 22** (†Ryszard Franczyszyn 10, Jan Krzystniak 6, Miroslaw Korbel 3, Piotr Swist 2, Zbigniew Blazejczak 1, Ryszard Dolomisiewicz 0, Marek Kepa, did not ride).

Edinburgh, Friday, May 29
***NATIONAL LEAGUE** (†Les Collins, Charlie McKinna, Andrew Silver, Martin Dixon, Steve Lawson, Martin Dugard, Neville Tatum, Dean Standing) v **POLAND** (†Ryszard Franczyszyn, Zbigniew Blazejczak, Ryszard Dolomisiewicz, Miroslaw Korbel, Piotr Swist, Marek Kepa, Jan Krzystniak).*
Cancelled, waterlogged track.

Stoke, Saturday, May 30
NATIONAL LEAGUE 80 (Les Collins 18, Neville Tatum 16, †Nigel Crabtree 16, Darren Sumner 9, Martin Dugard 9, David Biles 8, Graham Jones 4) **POLAND 28** (Piotr Swist 10, †Ryszard Franczyszyn 8, Ryszard Dolomisiewicz 3, Jan Krzystniak 3, Miroslaw Korbel 2, Zbigniew Blazejczak 1, Marek Kepa 1).

National League win the series 2-0 with one Test abandoned.

● *The National League team manager was John Berry.*
● *The Poland team manager was Edward Jancarz.*

1987 Smederna (Sweden) Club Tour of Division Two Results

NEWLY-PROMOTED Smederna, the team from Eskilstuna, opened the National League season at Stoke, provided early opposition at Exeter and Poole and shared in the dubious distinction of being involved in Arena Essex's first cancellation of the year!

They never looked like winning any of their three completed matches and were heading for a heavy defeat at Loomer Road before referee David Hughes called off the splashing action after 14 heats with the rain giving Stoke more problems than the visitors!

Stoke, Saturday, April 4
STOKE 60 (Darren Sumner 14, †Nigel Crabtree 10, Mike Wilding 10, Graham Jones 10, Derek Richardson 8, Bobby Duncan 5, Paul Stead 3) **SMEDERNA 24** (†Olli Tyrvainen 8, Mikael Blixt 5, Peter Nahlin 3, Patrik Nystedt 2, Lennart Bengtsson 2, Jan Bergqvist 2, Marko Kunelius 1, Claes Johansson 1).
Abandoned after 14 heats, rain.

Exeter, Monday, April 6
EXETER 60 (David Gibbs 13, †Colin Cook 12, Bruce Cribb 9, David Smart 9, Michael Coles 7, Andy Sell 7, Tony Mattingley 3, Jon Gould 0) **SMEDERNA 48** (Mikael Blixt 15, Peter Nahlin 15, †Olli Tyrvainen 13, Lennart Bengtsson 2, Patrik Nystedt 1, Claes Johansson 1, Jan Bergqvist 1, Marko Kunelius 0).

Poole, Tuesday, April 7
POOLE 72 (Steve Schofield 18, †Martin Yeates 17, Kevin Smith 12, David Biles 11, Nigel Newman 5, Will James 4, Wayne Barrett 3, Nigel Tremelling 2) **SMEDERNA 36** (†Olli Tyrvainen 12, Mikael Blixt 10, Peter Nahlin 7, Lennart Bengtsson 4, Claes Johansson 2, Patrik Nystedt 1, Marko Kunelius 0, Jan Bergqvist 0).

Wimbledon, Wednesday, April 8
WIMBLEDON 48 (†Roger Johns 12, Kevin Jolly 11, Neville Tatum 10, Jeremy Luckhurst 5, Terry Mussett 5, Alan Farmer 5, Mark Lyndon 0) **SMEDERNA 30** (Tony Olsson 9, †Olli Tyrvainen 9, Mikael Blixt 5, Peter Nahlin 3, Lennart Bengtsson 3, Jan Bergqvist 1, Patrik Nystedt 0).

Arena Essex, Thursday, April 9
ARENA ESSEX v SMEDERNA,
Cancelled, track waterlogged.

● *The Sweden team manager was Bo Jansson.*

DIAMOND JEWELS

BRITISH SPEEDWAY PROMOTERS' ASSOCIATION Director of Operations Peter York heralded the sport's sixtieth birthday with the announcement of the Diamond Jubilee Tournament.

And then one of the glittering gems in England's international history turned back the clock with a vintage performance that must have left a red-faced King's Lynn programme compiler for he wrote: "His international days may be nearing the end."

Whether it was reading that apparent epitaph to a Test career in which he had represented his country more than a hundred times, or simply that everything went right on the night Chris Morton was the England star, scoring a paid maximum against the first of three opponents, old foes America.

Co-manager Eric Boocock was moved to point out: "We've never said it was time he packed up or suggested that his international career was over."

Despite that claim the Belle Vue racer had been left out of the Sunbrite Lions squad to take on Sweden at Reading (the team had been named before the King's Lynn meeting) and he was then recalled for the final group match against Denmark at Ipswich.

By then it was simply a rehearsal of the final to come as the fixture planners ensured it was the last of the six preliminariy matches and both were undefeated as they headed for Foxhall Heath.

England had suffered so much at the hands of the Danes in recent times that the four-point win looked as if it might herald a new era.

Teenage buddies Gary Havelock and Andrew Silver had spent a couple of days staying with each other in the build-up to the meeting and displayed an uncanny understanding of each other's racing line as they stormed to a 5-1 in the reserves' race (the entire tournament was run under the British League formula).

Silver was used for two extra races as he top-scored but Ipswich fans were bemused when he was left out of the nominated riders' heat.

Instead Simon Wigg and Kelvin Tatum were chosen and they responded with a 4-2 that secured what should have been a morale-boosting victory for their side.

Had the final been held there and then England could have capitalised on their performance but they then had to wait for nearly two months.

During that time Denmark brooded on their shock defeat at Ipswich with their captain Erik Gundersen admitting: "We had a few things happening at Ipswich which we wanted to put right."

Team-mate Hans Nielsen added: "We were a bit down and disappointed after Ipswich. We are determined to win today."

By the start of heat four the Danes led 14-4 and it was all over as a contest with reserve Peter Ravn being unbeaten in four of his five rides.

England were also handicapped by the loss of skipper Simon Wigg when he fell heavily in his second outing and reserves Richard Knight – on his home track – and earlier hero Silver failed to win a race between them.

Only Tatum and Simon Cross were able to live with the powerhouse Danes as they added another trophy to their seemingly inexhaustible collection of silverware.

1988 Diamond Jubilee Series Results

Bradford, Sunday, April 17
ENGLAND 57 (Chris Morton 14, Kelvin Tatum 10, Neil Evitts 10, Jeremy Doncaster 7, Gary Havelock 7, †Simon Wigg 5, Simon Cross 4) **UNITED STATES OF AMERICA 33** (Shawn Moran 10, Lance King 10, Rick Miller 6, Robert Pfetzing 4, Kelly Moran 2, Randy Green 1, Mike Faria 0).

Wolverhampton, Wednesday, April 20
DENMARK 62 (Hans Nielsen 15, †Erik Gundersen 13, John Jørgensen 11, Jan O. Pedersen 8, Tommy Knudsen 6, Peter Ravn 5, Preben Eriksen 4) **SWEDEN 28** (†Per Jonsson 12, Tony Olsson 4, Peter Nahlin 3, Henrik Gustafsson 3, Erik Stenlund 3, Conny Ivarsson 2, Roland Dannö 1).

Swindon, Sunday, April 24
UNITED STATES OF AMERICA 47 (Lance King 10, Mike Faria 9, Kelly Moran 8, Shawn Moran 7, Sam Ermolenko 5, Robert Pfetzing 5, Randy Green 3) **SWEDEN 43** (Per Jonsson 13, Erik Stenlund 12, Tony Olsson 10, Peter Nahlin 6, Roland Dannö 2, Conny Ivarsson 0, Henrik Gustafsson 0).

Reading, Monday, April 25
ENGLAND 58 (†Simon Wigg 14, Marvyn Cox 11, Jeremy Doncaster 9, Kelvin Tatum 8, Simon Cross 7, Neil Evitts 5, Andrew Silver 4) **SWEDEN 32** (Per Jonsson 17, Tony Olsson 6, Henrik Gustafsson 6, Erik Stenlund 2, Roland Dannö 1, Conny Ivarsson 0, Peter Nahlin 0).

Coventry, Wednesday, April 27
DENMARK 60 (Tommy Knudsen 15, Hans Nielsen 14, Jan O. Pedersen 8, Peter Ravn 8, John Jørgensen 7, †Erik Gundersen 5, Bo Petersen 3) **UNITED STATES OF AMERICA 30** (Lance King 12, Shawn Moran 6, Rick Miller 4, Kelly Moran 3, Sam Ermolenko 2, Mike Faria 2, Ronnie Correy 1).

Ipswich, Sunday, May 1
ENGLAND 47 (Andrew Silver 10, †Simon Wigg 10, Kelvin Tatum 7, Chris Morton 7, Gary Havelock 5, Simon Cross 4, Jeremy Doncaster 4) **DENMARK 43** (Hans Nielsen 9, Tommy Knudsen 9, Peter Ravn 8, Jan O. Pedersen 6, †Erik Gundersen 6, John Jørgensen 3, Lars Munkedal 2).

	P	W	D	L	PtsF	PtsA	Pts
ENGLAND	3	3	0	0	162	108	6
Denmark	3	2	0	1	165	105	4
USA	3	1	0	2	110	160	2
Sweden	3	0	0	3	103	167	0

FINAL

King's Lynn, Sunday, June 26
ENGLAND 38 (Kelvin Tatum 14, Simon Cross 10, Chris Morton 5, Richard Knight 4, Jeremy Doncaster 3, Andrew Silver 1, †Simon Wigg 1) **DENMARK 52** (Hans Nielsen 13, Peter Ravn 11, Jan O. Pedersen 9, †Erik Gundersen 7, Bo Petersen 6, Tommy Knudsen 5, John Jørgensen 1).

● *The team managers for the series were: Denmark (Kjeld Lund), England (Eric Boocock and Colin Pratt), Sweden (Bo Wirebrand) and United States of America (John Scott).*

Danes cook Lions' bacon

EVERPRESENT...Coventry's John Jørgensen rode in all seven internationals against the England Lions

ERIC BOOCOCK returned from a chastening trip to Denmark with a depressing verdict: "We have to accept that the Danes are still the best and that's the way it's going to be until we can match their consistency."

A few months later that consistency was still missing as England lost another home series to the World Champions and defeat had Boocock admitting: "The blunt truth is that we couldn't beat the Danes at the moment if we had 10 team managers.

"Maybe it's time Colin Pratt and I stepped down and let someone else have a go. Plenty of people think they could do a better job but there's more to it than wearing a blazer and filling in a programme. The results have been very disappointingf over the past three years and I feel I've given my best. I can't motivate the riders any more than I have done up to now."

Boocock had started the international year seeing the Sunbrite Lions crushed in successive matches at Brovst and Slangerup where only Simon Wigg and Kelvin Tatum had won a heat against a rampant Denmark providing 30 of the 36 race winners!

And then he had to suffer again as they lost the first Test at Cradley Heath, saw the rain win the second at Oxford, and then lost the next match (and the series) at Sheffield even though reserve Peter Carr came in to bludgeon his way to a race win and five more valuable points to save the Sunbrite Lions from complete annihilation.

The rained-off Oxford Test was re-arranged for the end of October but a furious row erupted between the British Speedway Promoters' Association and the Auto-Cycle Union over priorities. The Test clashed with the annual Ace of Aces grass track spectacular and as a result the ACU withdrew the international permit which allowed Wigg to race at the grass-track event, a decision which was to have far-reaching repercussions. England won to give hope for the future.

1988 England v Denmark Results

Cradley Heath, Sunday, September 25
ENGLAND 48 (Chris Morton 13, Simon Cross 10, Kelvin Tatum 9, Martin Dugard 6, Jeremy Doncaster 5, Gary Havelock 2, Andrew Silver 2, †Simon Wigg 1) **DENMARK 60** (Hans Nielsen 17, Erik Gundersen 14, Tommy Knudsen 10, Jan O. Pedersen 10, Brian Karger 5, Peter Ravn 3, John Jørgensen 1, Jan Stæchmann 0).

Sheffield, Sunday, October 2
ENGLAND 46 (Simon Cross 15, †Simon Wigg 11, Chris Morton 7, Peter Carr 7, Gary Havelock 5, Kelvin Tatum 1, Neil Collins 0, Martin Dugard 0) **DENMARK 62** (Erik Gundersen 16, Hans Nielsen 13, Peter Ravn 11, Jan O. Pedersen 9, Brian Karger 9, John Jørgensen 4, Jan Stæchmann 0, Gert Handberg 0).

Oxford, Sunday, October 30
ENGLAND 55 (†Kelvin Tatum 16, Simon Cross 10, Martin Dugard 8, Gary Havelock 8, Jeremy Doncaster 6, Andrew Silver 3, Richard Knight 2, Paul Thorp 2) **DENMARK 53** (Hans Nielsen 17, Tommy Knudsen 15, Erik Gundersen 10, Brian Karger 6, Peter Ravn 3, Jan O. Pedersen 2, John Jørgensen 0).

Denmark win the series 2-1.

- *The England team managers were Eric Boocock and Colin Pratt.*
- *The Denmark team manager was Kjeld Lund.*

1988 Denmark v England

Brovst, Wednesday, May 11
DENMARK 74 (Hans Nielsen 17, Jan O. Pedersen 14, Tommy Knudsen 14, Erik Gundersen 13, Peter Ravn 7, Jan Stæchmann 6, John Jørgensen 3, Kurt Hansen, did not ride) **ENGLAND 34** (Kelvin Tatum 11, Simon Wigg 9, Gary Havelock 6, Jeremy Doncaster 5, Neil Evitts 1, Chris Morton 1, Andrew Silver 1, Simon Cross 0).

Slangerup, Thursday, May 12
DENMARK 71 (Hans Nielsen 15, Tommy Knudsen 15, Jan O. Pedersen 15, Peter Ravn 12, Per Sørensen 7, Erik Gundersen 6, Jan Stæchmann 1, Kurt Hansen, did not ride) **ENGLAND 37** (Kelvin Tatum 10, Simon Wigg 10, Jeremy Doncaster 6, Chris Morton 4, Simon Cross 3, Andrew Silver 3, Gary Havelock 1, Neil Evitts 0).

- *The England team managers were Eric Boocock and Colin Pratt.*
- *The Denmark team manager was Kjeld Lund.*

1988 Getingarna (Sweden) Club Tour Results

Oxford, Thursday, March 17
OXFORD 53 (†Hans Nielsen 12, Simon Wigg 10, Alastair Stevens 8, Martin Dugard 7, Marvyn Cox 7, Nigel De'ath 5, Peter Lloyd 4) **GETINGARNA 37** (Per Jonsson 17, †Jimmy Nilsen 12, Bo Ahren 7, Kent Rickardsson 1, Tony Rickardsson 0, Erik Stenlund 0, Tommy Nilsson 0, Sören Brolin 0).

King's Lynn, Saturday, March 19
KING'S LYNN 52 (Adrian Stevens 12, Lance King 12, †Richard Knight 11, Stephen Davies 9, Bo Petersen 5, Allan Johansen 3, John Davis 0) **GETINGARNA 37** (Jimmy Nilsen 14, Erik Stenlund 10, Bo Ahren 8, Kent Rickardsson 3, Tony Rickardsson 1, Per Jonsson 1, Tommy Nilsson 0).

Reading, Monday, March 21
READING 57 (Per Jonsson 11, †Jan Andersson 11, David Mullett 10, Tony Olsson 9, Mitch Shirra 8, Malcolm Holloway 5, Rodney Payne 3) **GETINGARNA 33** (Jimmy Nilsen 17, Bo Ahren 7, Erik Stenlund 5, Sören Brolin 2, Anders Nilsson 1, Tommy Nilsson 1, Tony Rickardsson 0).

Swindon, Saturday, March 26
SWINDON 47 (Brian Karger 12, †Richard Hellsén 9, Andrew Silver 7, Alun Rossiter 6, Gary Chessell 5, Jimmy Nilsen 4, Kevin Smart 4) **GETINGARNA 42** (Tommy Nilsson 13, Bo Ahren 9, Erik Stenlund 8, †Per Jonsson 4, Jan Andersson 4, Tony Rickardsson 3, Sören Brolin 1).

- *The Getingarna team manager was Torbjörn Harrysson.*

CAP'N KENNY...Glasgow's Kenny McKinna led the National League against Australia but had been chosen for only one of the internationals against Sweden, what should have been the fifth and final Test at Edinburgh's prestigious Powderhall Stadium

1988 National League v Sweden Results

Mildenhall, Sunday, July 17
NATIONAL LEAGUE 52 (Mark Loram 12, †Andy Galvin 10, Ian Barney 8, Andy Hines 7, Melvyn Taylor 6, Eric Monaghan 4, Chris Louis 3, Kevin Jolly 2) **SWEDEN 55** (†Tony Olsson 13, Peter Nahlin 12, Roland Dannö 11, Bo Ahren 7, Niklas Karlsson 6, Conny Ivarsson 6, Krister Karlsson 0).

Exeter, Monday, July 18
NATIONAL LEAGUE 53 (Mark Loram 13, David Biles 10, Ian Barney 8, †Andy Galvin 7, Richard Green 6, Colin Cook 4, Dean Standing 4, Peter Jeffery 1) **SWEDEN 55** (Peter Nahlin 14, †Jimmy Nilsen 12, Conny Ivarsson 10, Krister Karlsson 8, Bo Ahren 7, Niklas Karlsson 4, *Jon Gould* 0, Roland Dannö, did not arrive).

Wimbledon, Wednesday, July 20
NATIONAL LEAGUE 45 (†Andy Galvin 10, Kevin Jolly 10, Martin Goodwin 7, Alastair Stevens 6, Chris Louis 6, Mark Loram 5, Melvyn Taylor 1, Nathan Simpson 0) **SWEDEN 63** (†Per Jonsson 17, Jimmy Nilsen 15, Tony Olsson 11, Conny Ivarsson 8, Peter Nahlin 6, Niklas Karlsson 3, Bo Ahren 3, Krister Karlsson 0).

Middlesbrough, Thursday, July 21
NATIONAL LEAGUE 48 (Mark Courtney 15, Martin Dixon 8, Darren Sumner 7, Nigel Crabtree 7, Peter McNamara 5, Graham Jones 4, †Les Collins 1, Louis Carr 1) **SWEDEN 59** (Tony Olsson 13, †Per Jonsson 10, Krister Karlsson 10, Roland Dannö 8, Conny Ivarsson 8, Peter Nahlin 4, Niklas Karlsson 3, Bo Ahren 3).

Edinburgh, Friday, July 22
NATIONAL LEAGUE 10 (Mark Courtney 3, Kenny McKinna 2, Darren Sumner 2, Steve Lawson 1, Nigel Crabtree 1, Jamie Luckhurst 1, Sean Courtney, did not ride) **SWEDEN 8** (†Per Jonsson 3, Tony Olsson 3, Bo Ahren 2, Conny Ivarsson 0, Niklas Karlsson 0, Peter Nahlin 0, Krister Karlsson, did not ride).
Abandoned after three heats, rain.

Sweden win the series 4-0 with one Test abandoned.

● *The National League team managers were John Louis and Tim Swales (Edinburgh only).* ● *The Sweden team manager was Bo Wirebrand.*

1988 National League v Australia Results

Stoke, Saturday, October 1
NATIONAL LEAGUE 54 (Nigel Crabtree 13, Ian Barney 12, Melvyn Taylor 8, Louis Carr 7, Steve Schofield 7, †Kenny McKinna 6, Ray Morton 1) **AUSTRALIA 41** (Todd Wiltshire 12, Troy Butler 10, †Steve Regeling 7, Mick Poole 6, Mark Fiora 3, Glenn Doyle 2, Craig Boyce 1).

Eastbourne, Sunday, October 2
NATIONAL LEAGUE 51 (Andy Buck 14, †Kenny McKinna 10, Dean Standing 9, Gordon Kennett 8, Kevin Jolly 6, Ray Morton 4, Alastair Stevens 0) **AUSTRALIA 45** (Mick Poole 13, Troy Butler 10, Craig Boyce 9, †Steve Regeling 5, Mark Carlson 5, Gary Allan 2, Todd Wiltshire 1).

Poole, Tuesday, October 4
NATIONAL LEAGUE *(†Kenny McKinna, Steve Schofield, Mark Loram, Melvyn Taylor, David Biles, Peter Jeffery, Ray Morton)* ***AUSTRALIA*** *(Mick Poole, Craig Boyce, Todd Wiltshire, Glenn Doyle, Troy Butler, Craig Hodgson, †Steve Regeling).*
Cancelled, waterlogged track.

Long Eaton, Wednesday, October 5
NATIONAL LEAGUE 44 (†Kenny McKinna 13, Steve Schofield 11, Keith White 11, Melvyn Taylor 8, Martin Dixon 1, Ian Barney 0, Gary O'Hare 0) **AUSTRALIA 52** (Craig Boyce 11, Mark Fiora 11, Mick Poole 9, Glenn Doyle 7, †Steve Regeling 5, Troy Butler 5, Craig Hodgson 4).

Peterborough, Friday, October 7
NATIONAL LEAGUE 46 (Ian Barney 15, †Kenny McKinna 9, Kevin Hawkins 8, Steve Schofield 7, Richard Green 3, Dean Barker 2, Melvyn Taylor 2) **AUSTRALIA 50** (†Mick Poole 12, Mark Fiora 12, Troy Butler 8, Craig Hodgson 7, Craig Boyce 6, Glenn Doyle 5, Glen Baxter 0).

Series drawn 2-2 with one Test abandoned.

● *The National League team manager was Martin Rogers.*
● *The Australia team manager was James Easter.*

THE GROWING improvement of Australia's new breed of riders in the international market place was emphasised by the re-introduction of Test matches.

And New South Walian Todd Wiltshire, only 19, translaterdhis Wimbledon form to the more competitve Test arena in the opening match at Stoke where he won his first four rides before being excluded on two minutes when he was within reach of a first maximum for his country.

But just to show how hard life can be at times he was replaced for his last ride at Eastbourne the followiong afternoon after a struggling third place, a fall and an exclusion and two lasts!

Australia recorded their first victory of the season at Station Road even though their skipper and driving force Steve Regeling ended the night in hospital with a foot injury which kept him out of the final Test at Peterborough where replacement captain Mick Poole top-scored in front of his own fans to lead the Kangaroos to a second series-saving victory.

Poole's heat 16 win over the National League leader Kenny McKinna and his partner Melvyn Taylor was enough to give the Aussies a four-point win which meant the series had finished all square, two matches a piece with what might have been a vital third Test at Poole called off only 15 minutes before the scheduled start-time.

1988 Club Matches v Australia Results

EVEN though not classed as official international appearances the Australian Select was chosen by national team manager James Easter who used the meetings as Test trials.

Poole, Tuesday, May 31
POOLE 51 (Craig Boyce 10, David Biles 9, *Mark Loram 9, Colin Cook 8,* Robbie Fuller 8, Kevin Smart 5, Steve Bishop 2) **AUSTRALIAN SELECT 45** (Mark Fiora 15, †Mick Poole 10, Craig Hodgson 7, David Jackson 7, Glen Baxter 6, Alan Rivett 0, Steve Langdon 0).

Exeter, Monday, June 27
EXETER 45 (Alan Rivett 11, Richard Green 8, †Colin Cook 7, Tony Mattingley 6, Peter Jeffery 5, David Smart 4, Andy Sell 4,) **AUSTRALIAN SELECT 51** (Craig Boyce 14, Troy Butler 12, †Mick Poole 12, Craig Hodgson 9, Tony Primmer 3, *Steve Brennan 1,* Mark Carlson 0).

Won and dusted...

KEV THE REV...England's last regular skipper of the Eighties – dashing Kelvin Tatum

BART BAST had bitter-sweet thoughts as he lined up for the deciding Test against England.

For his call-up came within days of being sacked by Sunbrite League Swindon and he was asked to go back to Blunsdon as the American's reserve.

There was no fairy-tale ending for Bast as he bit the dust, coming down heavily in each of his first two rides on a track that resembled the Sahara desert on a windy day!

England managers Colin Pratt and Eric Boocock took the law into their own hands as they applied the hosepipes in a vain bid to quell the dust – but at least had the satisfaction of seeing their team zip to the biggest win during their time in charge.

England were every bit as superior as the 75-32 scoreline but the victory was soured by track preparation with Boocock claiming: "I would have had to have backed the riders if they had walked out and so would Colin. The track preparation was a disgrace."

The Sunbrite Lions had started the series with a 20-point win to maintain the proud record of the Boocock-Pratt partnership who had never lost a Test against the United States since taking over from John Berry at the beginning of 1986.

England had decided on an unashamed horses for courses policy to get back on the winning international track. Alan Grahame was the first to benefit, brought in for his first Test in five years.

He relished the unexpected extension of his international career on his home Dudley Wood track, scoring a paid dozen.

But the Americans hit back immediately in the second match at Belle Vue where England skipper Kelvin Tatum – appointed on a permanent basis to succeed Simon Wigg following his absence from the last international of 1988 and his request to be left out of the Cradley Heath match because of a conflicting continental commitment – had to pull out at the last minute.

While England were delighted to win the series – Tatum admitted: "It was important for us to go into a Test series and to win it having been beaten consistently by the Danes at that level for a few years. It was a tremendous boost for us before the World Team Cup Final." – the Americans could not have been in worse shape.

Already down to bare numbers they lost Kelly Moran when he broke his finger in brother Shawn's testimonial meeting and then Ronnie Correy broke his wrist, also at Belle Vue, during the one-point win.

Finally his Wolverhampton colleague Sam Ermolenko was sidelined after breaking his thigh in the World Long Track Championship leaving the Yanks missing three big scorers for the decider.

1989 England v United States of America Results

Cradley Heath, Sunday, July 2
ENGLAND 64 (Jeremy Doncaster 13, †Kelvin Tatum 12, Simon Cross 11, Alan Grahame 10, Paul Thorp 10, Richard Knight 8, Martin Dugard 0, Andrew Silver, did not ride) **UNITED STATES OF AMERICA 44** (Lance King 12, Sam Ermolenko 11, †Shawn Moran 7, Ronnie Correy 6, Robert Pfetzing 4, Rick Miller 4, Greg Hancock 0, Bart Bast 0).

Belle Vue, Friday, July 14
ENGLAND 53 (†Chris Morton 14, Simon Cross 11, Andrew Silver 10, Paul Thorp 7, Martin Dugard 6, Jeremy Doncaster 4, Neil Collins 1, Andy Smith 0) **UNITED STATES OF AMERICA 54** (Lance King 13, Sam Ermolenko 13, †Shawn Moran 12, Robert Pfetzing 11, Ronnie Correy 3, Greg Hancock 2, Rick Miller 0, Bart Bast 0).

Swindon, Sunday, July 30
ENGLAND 75 (†Kelvin Tatum 15, Neil Evitts 15, Jeremy Doncaster 14, Martin Dugard 11, Andrew Silver 10, Richard Knight 8, Sean Wilson 2, Paul Thorp 0) **UNITED STATES OF AMERICA 32** (Lance King 12, †Shawn Moran 9, Rick Miller 6, Robert Pfetzing 5, Greg Hancock 0, Bart Bast 0, Kelly Moran and Gary Hicks, did not ride.

England win the series 2-1.

- *The England team managers were Eric Boocock and Colin Pratt.*
- *The United States of America team manager was John Scott.*

1989 Denmark v Rest of the World

ENGLAND star Simon Cross was ruled out of the World Pairs Final with a fractured shoulder and torn ligaments. He came off after clashing with team-mate Simon Wigg as the powerful Danes maintained their position as the strongest national in the world.

Vojens, Friday, July 28
DENMARK 48 (Erik Gundersen 14, Brian Karger 8, Hans Nielsen 8, John Jørgensen 6, Allan Johansen 6, Bo Petersen 5, Ole Hansen 1) **REST OF THE WORLD 42** (Kelvin Tatum 13, Per Jonsson 10, Jimmy Nilsen 8, Simon Wigg 7, Simon Cross 2, Mitch Shirra 2, Roman Matousek 0).

1989 National League v Australia Results

A CRAZY mix-up over bookings and then a clash of dates helped to undermine the importance of the series.

Fans at Edinburgh suffered the worst as four of the programmed riders withdrew for various reasons and then Mark Courtney and David Blackburn appeared to put in so little effort that the National League subsequently announced that they would never be picked for any future representative matches.

Australia took full advantage of the lackadaisical approach and also the refusal of Eastbourne's Dean Barker to travel to Scotland (he rode instead in a challenge match at Oxford) to go into a series lead.

But then they saw that lead wiped out when they had to go into the televised third Test at Ipswich without their three top riders – on duty 200 miles away at Belle Vue in the World Championship Commonwealth Final.

Not surprisingly the Kangaroos were soundly beaten at Foxhall Heath where Chris Louis (right) was watched by his proud father as he made what seems certain to be the first of a long, long string of international appearances.

Wimbledon, Wednesday, May 31
NATIONAL LEAGUE 47 (Steve Schofield 14, †Andy Galvin 11, Martin Goodwin 9, Alun Rossiter 4, Neville Tatum 4, Dean Barker 3, Chris Louis 2) **AUSTRALIA 47** (Craig Boyce 10, Mick Poole 9, Craig Hodgson 7, Todd Wiltshire 7, Leigh Adams 6, †Troy Butler 6, Glen Baxter 2).

Edinburgh, Friday, June 2
NATIONAL LEAGUE 30 (Scott Lamb 9, Neville Tatum 8, Darren Sumner 4, Sean Courtney 4, Dean Standing 4, Mark Courtney 1, David Blackburn 0) **AUSTRALIA 66** (Craig Boyce 15, †Brett Saunders 13, Rod Hunter 12, Todd Wiltshire 9, Leigh Adams 8, Mick Poole 5, Mick Powell 4).

Ipswich, Sunday, June 4
NATIONAL LEAGUE 60 (Mark Loram 14, Chris Louis 13, Alun Rossiter 12, Alan Mogridge 7, Steve Schofield 6, †Andy Galvin 5, Dean Standing 3) **AUSTRALIA 36** (Craig Boyce 10, Todd Wiltshire 7, Leigh Adams 6, Craig Hodgson 5, †Steve Regeling 4, Mick Poole 3, Glen Baxter 1).

Poole, Tuesday, June 6
NATIONAL LEAGUE 53 (Alun Rossiter 12, Steve Schofield 11, Chris Louis 9, Alastair Stevens 9, Mark Loram 7, †Andy Galvin 5, Neville Tatum 0) **AUSTRALIA 43** (Craig Boyce 14, Leigh Adams 14, Mick Poole 8, Rod Hunter 7, Craig Hodgson 0, Tony Langdon 0, †Steve Regeling 0).

Hackney, Friday, June 9
NATIONAL LEAGUE 64 (†Andy Galvin 15, Mark Loram 13, Steve Schofield 11, Martin Goodwin 10, Chris Louis 5, Alan Mogridge 5, Alun Rossiter 5) **AUSTRALIA 32** (Rod Hunter 9, †Stephen Davies 7, Craig Boyce 5, Leigh Adams 5, Steve Regeling 3, Todd Wiltshire 3, Mick Poole 0).

National League win the series 3-1 with one Test drawn.

- *The National League team manager was John Louis.*
- *The Australia team manager was James Easter.*

- ***Eastbourne promoter Gareth Rogers was fined £500 by the National League for letting Dean Barker race in the challenge at Oxford instead of the Edinburgh Test.***

◆ *AUSTRALIA staged a series of matches during the 1989-1990 winter which was described as a Test rubber in Down Under newspaper and television advertising.*
◆ *However the touring team, selected by Australian promoter Vic Butler, was never given official sanction by the British authorities and was, in fact, frowned upon by both the British Speedway Promoters' Association and the Speedway Control Board.*
◆ *The tourists were Andy Galvin, Mark Loram, Ray Morton, Steve Schofield, Paul Thorp, Sean Wilson, and Jeremy Doncaster who returned home after three matches to be replaced, for the sixth and seventh matches, by Kelvin Tatum.*
◆ *As none of the matches were official Tests they are not included in this section.*

1989 Slangerup (Denmark) Division Two Tour Results

Hackney, Friday, April 14
HACKNEY 62 (Steve Schofield 15, Gary Rolls 15, †Andy Galvin 10, Paul Whittaker 7, Barry Thomas 6, Gary Tagg 5, Lee Pavitt 4) **SLANGERUP 34** (Kenneth Nystrom 10, †Kurt Hansen 8, Per Sørensen 7, Jesper Olsen 4, Bo Sørensen 4, Rene Mortensen 1, Peter Olsen 0).

Arena Essex, Saturday, April 15
ARENA ESSEX 54 (†Martin Goodwin 13, Rob Tilbury 11, Ian Humphreys 7, Troy Pratt 6, Wayne Garratt 6, Malcolm Simmons 6, Simon Wolstenholme 5) **SLANGERUP 41** (†Kurt Hansen 16, Per Sørensen 12, Kenneth Nystrom 8, Rene Mortensen 3, Bo Sørensen 2, Jesper Olsen 0, Peter Olsen 0).

Eastbourne, Sunday, April 16
EASTBOURNE 63 (Andy Buck 12, †Gordon Kennett 12, David Norris 11, Dean Barker 10, Keith Pritchard 9, Jon Surman 5, Darren Standing 4) **SLANGERUP 33** (Per Sørensen 10, Kenneth Nystrom 7, Jesper Olsen 7, Rene Mortensen 3, Bo Sørensen 2, Kurt Hansen 2, Peter Olsen 2).

Exeter, Monday, April 17
EXETER 65 (Frank Andersen 14, Alan Rivett 13, Richard Green 11, Colin Cook 10, †Steve Regeling 7, Peter Jeffery 6, Andy Sell 4) **SLANGERUP 31** (Per Sørensen 10, †Kurt Hansen 8, Lars Munkedal 7, Kenneth Nystrom 5, Jesper Olsen 1, Peter Olsen 0, Rene Mortensen 0).

Poole, Tuesday, April 18
POOLE 58 (Craig Boyce 14, Leigh Adams 12, †Alun Rossiter 10, Kevin Smart 9, Tony Langdon 6, Alastair Stevens 5, Gary Allan 2) **SLANGERUP 38** (Per Sørensen 11, †Kurt Hansen 10, Lars Munkedal 8, Bo Sørensen 5, Jesper Olsen 2, Peter Olsen 1, Kenneth Nystrom 1).

- *The Slangerup team manager was Klaus Lohmann.*

SIMPLE FOR SIMON...Cradley Heath's Simon Cross was in devastating international form against Denmark

Simon tames Danes

ENGLAND roared into a new decade with hope for the future...

It was all based on a summer whitewash against former World Champions Denmark who, for the first time since the series was inaugurated in 1981, failed to win a single Test in England.

For the second successive season Simon Wigg was overlooked by the England selectors Eric Boocock and Colin Pratt, in their fifth season as the national team bosses.

A year earlier the reason given was that he had opted to race overseas rather than for his country but this time around the management team insisted that he was being omitted from the squad because of his poor Sunbrite League performances.

A damning verdict on his form as the first Test against the Danes was at his home Oxford track.

England didn't appear to miss him as Denmark struggled to compensate for the premature retirement through injury of two of their outstanding riders Erik Gundersen and Tommy Knudsen.

It was almost as if their absence had affected Hans Nielsen as he was beaten twice at Sandy Lane and actually went through a series without scoring at least one maximum although he extended his lead as the highest scorer in Tests between the two countries!

England found a new hero in Simon Cross, a member of the Test team for several years but, until now, looked upon as a dependable scorer rather than an out-and-out spearhead.

He formed a devastating first Test partnership with Bradford's on-loan Marvyn Cox (a paid 34 points out of 36), dropped just two points at Odsal and then was beaten only once in the final Test at Wolverhampton.

It was a long time since an England rider had gone through an entire series dropping only four points and the best-ever sequence of scores by any Sunbrite Lion against Denmark.

How sad then that a few weeks later Simon should be lying in a German hospital with serious back injuries after what seemed like a fairly innocent fall in the World Pairs Final at Landshut.

Both countries had their injury problems.

Denmark had Peter Ravn (dislocated collar bone) and Jan Stæchmann ruled out

England lost the services of Martin Dugard for the clash at Cowley when he broke his ankle at King's Lynn – in an accident that also forced Richard Knight to withdraw but overcame those problems with three straight wins.

The victories came in the wake of England's superb World Team Cup Final triumph at Bradford at the end of 1989 and Boocock, who had reconsidered his decision to resign during the winter, said: "We've beaten the Danes three times out of three in Test matches. We won the World Team Cup last September. Who can deny us our right to be called World Champions now?"

1990 England v Denmark Results

Oxford, Wednesday, April 18
ENGLAND 63 (Simon Cross 14, Marvyn Cox 14, Andrew Silver 12, †Kelvin Tatum 9, Gary Havelock 9, Jeremy Doncaster 4, Dean Barker 1, Mark Loram 0) **DENMARK 45** (†Hans Nielsen 15, Jan O. Pedersen 9, Brian Karger 8, Bo Petersen 6, John Jørgensen 4, Lars Munkedal 3, Gert Handberg 0).

Bradford, Sunday, April 22
ENGLAND 62 (Simon Cross 13, Gary Havelock 13, Jeremy Doncaster 12, †Kelvin Tatum 11, Andy Smith 10, Sean Wilson 2, Paul Thorp 1, Marvyn Cox 0) **DENMARK 46** (†Hans Nielsen 12, Jan O. Pedersen 11, Brian Karger 8, Bo Petersen 5, Gert Handberg 5, John Jørgensen 4, Lars Munkedal 1).

Wolverhampton, Monday, April 30
ENGLAND 60 (Simon Cross 16, †Kelvin Tatum 14, Gary Havelock 10, Andrew Silver 8, Jeremy Doncaster 7, Marvyn Cox 4, Martin Dugard 1, Graham Jones 0) **DENMARK 47** (†Hans Nielsen 15, Jan O. Pedersen 15, John Jørgensen 5, Lars Munkedal 4, Peter Ravn 3, Brian Karger 3, Bo Petersen 2, Gert Handberg 0).

England win the series 3-0.

- *The England team managers were Eric Boocock and Colin Pratt.*
- *The Denmark team manager was Kjeld Lund.*

1990 Soviet Union Division Two Tour Results

Exeter, Monday, April 23
EXETER 78 (†Steve Regeling 14, Steve Bishop 13, Richard Green 13, Colin Cook 12, Peter Jeffery 10, Andy Sell 9, Mark Simmonds 7) **SOVIET UNION 18** (Viktor Gaidym 7, Nikolai Kornev [junior] 5, Igor Marko 3, †Vladimir Trofimov 3, Mikhail Starostin 0, Sergei Tershak 0).

Poole, Tuesday, April 24
POOLE 59 (†Alun Rossiter 15, Craig Boyce 15, Gary Chessell 10, Gary Allan 8, Steve Leigh 6, Rod Colquhoun 5, Steve Langdon 0) **SOVIET UNION 37** (†Vladimir Trofimov 12, Igor Zverev 9, Grigori Harchenko 9, Viktor Gaidym 4, Igor Marko 1, Mikhail Starostin 1, Nikolai Kornev 1).

Ipswich, Thursday, April 26
IPSWICH 66 (Chris Louis 15, David Norris 12, †Alan Mogridge 10, Robbie Fuller 9, Shane Parker 7, Dean Standing 7, Colin White 6) **SOVIET UNION 30** (†Vladimir Trofimov 11, Mikhail Starostin 8, Viktor Gaidym 5, Grigori Harchenko 2, Nikolai Kornev 2, Igor Zverev 1, Igor Marko 1).

Peterborough, Friday, April 27
PETERBOROUGH 67 (Frank Andersen 15, †Mick Poole 13, Craig Hodgson 10, Ian Barney 9, Scott Norman 9, Nigel Flatman 8, Sean Barker 3) **SOVIET UNION 27** (†Vladimir Trofimov 8, Igor Marko 5, Nikolai Kornev 5, Mikhail Starostin 3, Igor Zverev 3, Viktor Gaidym 2, Grigori Harchenko 1).

Newcastle, Sunday, April 29
NEWCASTLE 45 (Martin Dixon 14, †Peter Carr 13, Paul Smith 6, Mark Thorpe 5, John Wainwright 4, Simon Green 2, Spencer Timmo 1) **SOVIET UNION 51** (Grigori Harchenko 14, Mikhail Starostin 10, †Vladimir Trofimov 7, Igor Marko 7, Viktor Gaidym 6, Nikolai Kornev 6, Igor Zverev 1).

● *The Soviet Union team managers were Boris Judin and Grigori Khlinovski.*

◆ ***RUSSIA'S first British tour since 1976 began where it had finished...and with the same end results!***
◆ ***Viktor Gaidym (above) top-scored on his first trip to England at Exeter's County Ground track 14 years after Grigori Khlinovsky – back as tour manager – had done exactly the same thing as the Soviets said their farewells after losing all six tour matches.***
◆ ***Times have changed – but the Russians found it as hard in 1990 as they had done in 1976 even though their opposition was now confined to National League tracks.***
◆ ***It looked as if the Russians would return to the Soviet Union with a similar losing record but they saved any red blushes with an extraordinary win at Newcastle in their last match when Grigori Harchenko swept to a paid maximum in what was only his fourth tour match.***

EX-WORLD Finalist Bo Petersen helped to prove that one man can work wonders....
For it was the prematurely balding Danish international who turned Slangerup from merely attractive visitors to the National League into a match-winning squad.
And no doubt his performances on the tour were noted and stored for another day by his mechanic and sponsor Ivan Henry who was already having thoughts of turning his vast financial investment in the sport into promoting his own track.
Bo the Go went...and rattled the opposition with a paid maximum at Eastbourne and a full maximum at Poole a couple of days later.
After that flying start he tailed off slightly in the remaining matches but scored another 45 points from three meetings as the Danes ended the visit with a tour record that read far more impressively than in 1989.
Then they had ridden five matches and lost the lot. This time that record showed an improvement to played five, won two.
And Petersen wasn't the only visitor to impress and shine. Jesper Olsen got a paid dozen at Glasgow's Shawfield Park and did enough to attract instant contract offers from the Radio Clyde Tigers and their League rivals Exeter and Milton Keynes.
He turned them all down but returned home to Denmark with plenty on his mind!

● *The Slangerup team managers were Klaus Lohmann and Sven Mortensen.*

1990 Slangerup (Denmark) Division Two Tour Results

Eastbourne, Sunday, April 8
EASTBOURNE 39 (Andy Buck 11, †Keith Pritchard 9, Paul Woods 9, Tony Primmer 6, Steve Masters 4, Darren Grayling 0, John Cook, did not ride) **SLANGERUP 57** (†Bo Petersen 14, Lars Munkedal 11, Jan Stæchmann 9, Bo Sørensen 7, Jesper Olsen 6, Peter Glanz 6, Per Sørensen 4).

Poole, Tuesday, April 10
POOLE 43 (†Craig Boyce 14, Gary Allan 8, Gary Chessell 8, Rod Colquhoun 6, Tony Langdon 5, Steve Langdon 2, Steve Leigh, did not ride) **SLANGERUP 53** (†Bo Petersen 18, Lars Munkedal 11, Jan Stæchmann 10, Tim Korneliussen 6, Jesper Olsen 5, Bo Sørensen 3).

Glasgow, Wednesday, April 11
GLASGOW 51 (Charlie McKinna 11, Kenny McKinna 11, Shane Bowes 10, †Steve Lawson 6, Sean Courtney 5, Martin McKinna 4, Jason Lyons 4) **SLANGERUP 45** (†Bo Petersen 16, Jeper Olsen 10, Bo Sørensen 8, Jan Stæchmann 5, Peter Glanz 3, Lars Munkedal 2, Tim Korneliussen 1).

Middlesbrough, Thursday, April 12
MIDDLESBROUGH 55 (David Cheshire 12, Steve Wilcock 11, Darren Sumner 9, Rod Hunter 8, †Jamie Luckhurst 7, Paul Bentley 6, Paul Smith 2) **SLANGERUP 41** (†Bo Petersen 13, Peter Glanz 8, Lars Munkedal 7, Jan Stæchmann 7, Jesper Olsen 5, Bo Sørensen 1, Tim Korneliussen 0).

Edinburgh, Sunday, April 15
EDINBURGH 53 (Les Collins 14, Carl Blackbird 10, Michael Coles 8, Frede Schøtt 8, Mark Blackbird 6, †Brett Saunders 6, Nigel Alderton 1) **SLANGERUP 41** (†Bo Petersen 16, Lars Munkedal 15, Jesper Olsen 8, Jan Stæchmann 2, Bo Sørensen 0, Per Sørensen 0).

1990 Club Tours of Poland – Ipswich and Exeter Results

Rzeszow, Saturday, July 7
STAL RZESZOW 54 (Janusz Stachyra 13, Jacek Rempala 11, Piotr Podrzycki 7, Robert Kuzdzal 7, Romuald Janusz 6, Janusz Staczka 5, Giorgi Petranov 3, Krzystof Nurzynski 2) **IPSWICH 36** (Chris Louis 11, †Alan Mogridge 9, Craig Hyde 5, Robbie Fuller 4, Shane Parker 4, Dean Standing 2, Colin White 1).

Tarnow, Sunday, July 8
UNIA TARNOW 48 (Robert Kuzdzal 12, Jacek Rempala 10, Janus Stachyra 8, Piotr Styczynski 5, Romuald Janusz 5, Slawomir Tronina 3, Piotr Lesniowski 3, Piotr Zieba 2) **IPSWICH 42** (Chris Louis 14, †Alan Mogridge 14, Craig Hyde 6, Colin White 4, Dean Standing 3, Shane Parker 1, Robbie Fuller 0).

Leszno, Sunday, October 6
UNIA LESZNO 57 (Piotr Pawlicki 14, Roman Jankowski 13, Zenon Kasprzak 12, Zbigniew Krakowski 11, Dairusz Lowicki 4, Piotr Grycha 2, Roman Mitura 1, Slawomir Rypien 0) **EXETER 32** (†Steve Regeling 11, Richard Green 10, Mark Simmonds 5, Steve Bishop 3, Deon Prinsloo 2, Rob Woffinden 1, Frank Smart 0).

INTERNATIONAL RESULTS GUIDE

AUSTRALIA v ENGLAND

1967-68	
Sydney	Australia 53 England 54
Brisbane	Australia 62 England 46
Sydney	Australia 43 England 64
Sydney	Australia 68 England 40
Adelaide	Australia 46 England 62
1969-69	
Melbourne	Australia 43 England 65
Adelaide	Australia 61 England 47
Sydney	Australia 68 England 40
Brisbane	Australia 51 England 57
Sydney	Australia 60 England 48
1969	
Poole	England 66 Australia 42
Sheffield	England 69 Australia 39
Wolverhampton	England 73 Australia 35
1969-70	
Perth	Australia 61 England 47
Adelaide	Australia 45 England 63
Sydney	Australia 50 England 58
Brisbane	Australia 56 England 52
Sydney	Australia 49 England 58
1970	
Cradley Heath	England 70 Australia 38
1970-71	
Perth	Australia 58 England 50
Perth	Australia 61 England 46
Adelaide	Australia 55 England 53
Sydney	Australia 52 England 56
Brisbane	Australia 54 England 54
Brisbane	Australia 54 England 54
Sydney	Australia 56 England 52
1971-72	
Sydney	Australia 60 England 48
Brisbane	Australia 61 England 47
Brisbane	Australia 46 England 61
Adelaide	Australia 57 England 51
Melbourne	Australia 44 England 64
Perth	Australia 49 England 69
Perth	Australia 31 England 77
1972	
IN Halifax	England 48 Australia 30
1972-73	
Perth	Australia 60 England 48
Adelaide	Australia 50 England 58
Sydney	Australia 63 England 45
Sydney	Australia 58 England 50
Brisbane	Australia 71 England 36
Brisbane	Australia 58 England 50
Sydney	Australia 62 England 46
1973	
DMI King's Lynn	England 44 Australia 34
1975	
Leicester	England 50 Australia 28
1975-76	
Perth	Australia 41 England 67
Perth	Australia 34 England 74
Newcastle	Australia 32 England 76
Sydney	Australia 38 England 70
Liverpool	Australia 47 England 61
Sydney	Australia 62 England 45
Brisbane	Australia 50 England 57
1978	
Newcastle	Australia 38 England 70
Brisbane	Australia 51 England 57
Brisbane	Australia 61 England 47
Sydney	Australia 53 England 55
Adelaide	Australia 56 England 52
Sydney	Australia 47 England 61
Perth	Australia 38 England 70
1978-79	
Perth	Australia 39 England 69
Adelaide	Australia 45 England 63
Liverpool	Australia 47 England 60
Newcastle	Australia 50 England 58
Sydney	Australia 51.5 England 56.5
Brtisbane	Australia 50 England 58
Brtisbane	Australia 43 England 65

AUSTRALIA v GREAT BRITAIN

1973-74	
Perth	Australia 53 Great Britain 55
Perth	Australia 33 Great Britain 75
Adelaide	Australia 44 Great Britain 64
Sydney	Australia 50 Great Britain 58
Brtisbane	Australia 46 Great Britain 62
Brisbane	Australia 46 Great Britain 62
Brisbane	Australia 60 Great Britain 47
Sydney	Australia 53 Great Britain 55
1974-75	
Brisbane	Australia 62 Great Britain 45
Brisbane	Australia 50 Great Britain 58
Newcastle	Australia 63 Great Britain 45
Sydney	Australia 55 Great Britain 53
Liverpool	Australia 57 Great Britain 51
Adelaide	Australia 59 Great Britain 49
Perth	Australia 46 Great Britain 61

AUSTRALIA v YOUNG ENGLAND

1981-82	
Perth	Australia 54 Young England 54
Mildura	Australia 54 Young England 54
Liverpool	Australia 41 Young England 66
Newcastle	Australia 59 Young England 49
Brisbane	Australia 46 Young England 62

The internationals listed on these pages, unless otherwise stated, are officially recognised as Test matches by both the competing nations.
WL = *1968 World League*
IN = *1972 Inter Nations Championship*
DMI = *Daily Mirror International Tournament*
◆ = *1988 Diamond Jubilee Series*

ENGLAND v AUSTRALASIA

1978	
Bristol	England 52 Australasia 56
Birmingham	England 59 Australasia 49
Ipswich	England 51 Australasia 57
Hull	England 36 Australasia 70
Hackney	England 56 Australasia 52
1979	
Wimbledon	England 61 Australasia 47
Swindon	England 67 Australasia 41
Ipswich	England 60 Australasia 48
Cradley Heath	England 72 Australasia 36
Halifax	England 68 Australasia 40
1985	
King's Lynn	England 71 Australasia 37
Oxford	England 69 Australasia 38
Halifax	England 53 Australasia 55

DENMARK v ENGLAND v USA v WEST GERMANY

1984	
Vojens	Denmark 44 England 17 USA 30 West Germany 5

DENMARK v ENGLAND v POLAND v SWEDEN

1983	
Selskov	Denmark 41 England 23 Poland 20 Sweden 24

ENGLAND v AUSTRALASIA v DENMARK v USA

1982	
Cradley Heath	England 28 Australasia 17 Denmark 27 USA 35
Reading	England 29 Australasia 10 Denmark 23 USA 46
Sheffield	England 30 Australasia 20 Denmark 35 USA 23
Eastbourne	England 25 Australasia 1 Denmark 36 USA 46

ENGLAND v DENMARK

1979	
Vojens	Denmark 40 England 37
1981	
Vojens	Denmark 60 England 48
Hackney	England 62 Denmark 46
Reading	England 58 Denmark 50
Coventry	England 46 Denmark 62
1982	
Halifax	England 60 Denmark 48
Leicester	England 66 Denmark 42
Hackney	England 40 Denmark 68
Vojens	Denmark 73 England 35
1983	
Coventry	England 46 Denmark 62
Halifax	England 65 Denmark 43
Hackney	England 65 Denmark 43
1984	
Reading	England 54 Denmark 54
Wimbledon	England 45 Denmark 63

INTERNATIONAL RESULTS GUIDE

Wolverhampton	England 59 Denmark 48
Halifax	England 59 Denmark 49
1985	
Coventry	England 47 Denmark 61
Oxford	England 58 Denmark 50
Cradley Heath	England 53 Denmark 55
1986	
Cradley Heath	England 53 Denmark 55
Belle Vue	EnglAnd 45 Denmark 63
Wolverhampton	England 41 Denmark 66
Bradford	England 57 Denmark 51
Oxford	England 49 Denmark 59
1987	
King's Lynn	England 58 Denmark 50
Oxford	England 49 Denmark 59
Cradley Heath	England 54 Denmark 54
Belle Vue	EnglAnd 56 Denmark 52
Wolverhampton	England 53 Denmark 55
Outrup	Denmark 68 England 40
Brovst	Denmark 67 England 41
1988	
◆ Ipswich	England 47 Denmark 43
◆ King's Lynn	England 38 Denmark 52
Cradley Heath	England 48 Denmark 60
Sheffield	England 46 Denmark 62
Oxford	England 55 Denmark 53
Brovst	Denmark 74 England 34
Slangerup	Denmark 71 England 37
1990	
Oxford	England 63 Denmark 45
Bradford	England 62 Denmark 46
Wolverhampton	England 60 Denmark 47

ENGLAND v DENMARK v REST OF THE WORLD

1983	
Cradley Heath	England 45 Denmark 29 Rest of the World 34
King's Lynn	England 31 Denmark 38 Rest of the World 39
Birmingham	England 37 Denmark 30 Rest of the World 41

ENGLAND v NORWAY-DENMARK

1972	
IN Poole	England 37 Norway-Denmark 41
1973	
DMI Belle Vue	England 48 Norway-Denmark 30

ENGLAND v NEW ZEALAND

1968	
Auckland	New Zealand 39 England 69
Napier	New Zealand 55 England 53
New Plymouth	New Zealand 22 England 86
Auckland	New Zealand 29 England 79
Christchurch	New Zealand 47 England 60
1969	
Auckland	New Zealand 24 England 24
Napier	New Zealand 25 England 23
Palmerston Nth	New Zealand 11 England 37
Christchurch	New Zealand 26 England 22
1969	
Swindon	England 43 New Zealand 65
Newcastle	England 47 New Zealand 61
Hackney	England 68 New Zealand 40
1970	
Auckland	New Zealand 36 England 72
Auckland	New Zealand 43 England 65
Christchurch	New Zealand 40 England 67
Wimbledon	England 54 New Zealand 53
Belle Vue	England 66 New Zealand 42
Swindon	England 70 New Zealand 37
Sheffield	England 64 New Zealand 44
1971	
Auckland	New Zealand 48.5 England 59.5
Auckland	New Zealand 40 England 68
Christchurch	New Zealand 65 England 43
1972	
IN Wimbledon	England 51 New Zealand 26
1973	
Auckland	New Zealand 52 England 56
Christchurch	New Zealand 77 England 31
Auckland	New Zealand 53 England 54
Wellington	New Zealand 67 England 41
DMI Belle Vue	England 48 New Zealand 30
1976	
Auckland	New Zealand 23 England 85
Christchurch	New Zealand 24 England 84
Auckland	New Zealand 25 England 83

ENGLAND v POLAND

1968	
Poole	England 55 Poland 53
Sheffield	England 61 Poland 47
1973	
DMI Hackney	England 45 Poland 33
1974	
Hackney	England 88 Poland 19
King's Lynn	England 78 Poland 30
Exeter	England 73 Poland 35
Hull	England 69 Poland 39
Ipswich	England 78 Poland 30
Halifax	England 65 Poland 42
Leicester	England 76 Poland 32
1975	
Bydgoszcz	Poland 71 England 37
Chorzow	Poland 46 England 62
Gorzow	Poland 50 England 58
Poznan	Poland 52 England 56
1979	
Bydgoszcz	Poland 64 England 44
Gdansk	Poland 44 England 64

ENGLAND v REST OF THE WORLD

1975	
Hull	England 41 Rest of the World 37
Ipswich	England 63 Rest of the World 45
1976	
Vojens	Rest of the World 43 England 41
1977	
White City	England 63 Rest of the World 45
Ipswich	England 51 Rest of the World 57
Coventry	England 48 Rest of the World 59
Reading	England 46 Rest of the World 62
Hull	England 55 Rest of the World 53

ENGLAND v SCOTLAND

1965	
Ediinburgh	Scotland 60 England 48
Newcastle	England 55 Scotland 52
Glasgow	Scotland 62 England 46
1966	
Edinburgh	Scotland 63 England 45
Glasgow	Scotland 61 England 46
Halifax	England 78 Scotland 30
Middlesbrough	England 63 Scotland 45
Newcastle	England 74 Scotland 34
1967	
Edinburgh	Scotland 34 England 74
1968	
Coatbridge	Scotland 62 England 46
1969	
Glasgow	Scotland 50 England 58
1970	
Glasgow	Scotland 47 England 61
Newcastle	England 49 Scotland 59
1971	
Glasgow	Scotland 60 England 48
1972	
Glasgow	Scotland 53 England 55
Halifax	England 66 Scotland 42
1973	
Coatbridge	Scotland 57 England 51
Halifax	England 68 Scotland 40

ENGLAND v SOVIET UNION

1966	
Newcastle	England 49 Soviet Union 59
Halifax	England 59 Soviet Union 49
Wolverhampton	England 59 Soviet Union 49
Exeter	England 60 Soviet Union 48
West Ham	England 71 Soviet Union 37
1968	
Coventry	England 58 Soviet Union 50
Newport	England 68 Soviet Union 40
Belle Vue	England 77 Soviet Union 31
1971	
Exeter	England 54 Soviet Union 53
Poole	England 54 Soviet Union 54
Wimbledon	England 61 Soviet Union 46
Halifax	England 51 Soviet Union 57
Coventry	England 59 Soviet Union 49
1973	
DMI Ipswich	England 56 Soviet Union 21
1974	
Swindon	England 66 Soviet Union 42
Wolverhampton	England 61 Soviet Union 47
Wimbledon	England 71 Soviet Union 37
Cradley Heath	England 65 Soviet Union 43
Belle Vue	England 75 Soviet Union 33

ENGLAND v SWEDEN

1967	
Exeter	England 38 Sweden 70
1971	
Wimbledon	England 51 Sweden 57
Halifax	England 63 Sweden 45
1972	
IN Coventry	England 43 Sweden 35
1973	
DMI Sheffield	England 40 Sweden 38
DMI Wembley	England 39 Sweden 39†
† England won the Final on a run-off.	
1974	
King's Lynn	England 71 Sweden 37
Poole	England 66 Sweden 42
Sheffield	England 83 Sweden 25
Hackney	England 73 Sweden 35
Coventry	England 71 Sweden 37
1975	
Sheffield	England 54 Sweden 24
Poole	England 77 Sweden 29
Leicester	England 66 Sweden 42
Hackney	England 62 Sweden 46
King's Lynn	England 70 Sweden 38
Belle Vue	England 79 Sweden 29
Kumla	Sweden 53 England 55
Eskilstuna	Sweden 51 England 57
Stockholm	Sweden 44 England 64
Vetlanda	Sweden 40 England 68
Mariestad	Sweden 50 England 58
1988	
◆ Reading	England 58 Sweden 32

INTERNATIONAL RESULTS GUIDE

ENGLAND v UNITED STATES OF AMERICA

1980	
Wimbledon	England 54 USA 54
Cradley Heath	England 62 USA 46
Hull	England 47 USA 61
Poole	England 44 USA 63
Swindon	England 49 USA 59
1981	
Belle Vue	England 60 USA 48
Poole	England 55 USA 53
Swindon	England 64 USA 43
Ipswich	England 44 USA 52
Cradley Heath	England 69 USA 38
1982	
Wimbledon	England 63 USA 45
Swindon	England 47 USA 60
Ipswich	England 42 USA 66
Belle Vue	England 61 USA 47
Poole	England 39 USA 69
1983	
Wimbledon	England 43 USA 64
Swindon	England 57 USA 51
Poole	England 63 USA 45
Ipswich	England 42 USA 66
Sheffield	England 58 USA 50
1984	
Swindon	England 50 USA 58
Sheffield	England 58 USA 50
Cradley Heath	England 49 USA 59
Ipswich	England 36 USA 72
Poole	England 50 USA 58
1985	
Belle Vue	England 48 USA 58
Ipswich	England 50 USA 58
Swindon	England 42 USA 66
1986	
Sheffield	England 60 USA 48
Oxford	England 60 USA 47
Ipswich	England 62 USA 43
1987	
Ipswich	England 55 USA 52
Sheffield	England 59 USA 49
1988	
◆ Bradford	England 57 USA 33
1989	
Cradley Heath	England 64 USA 44
Belle Vue	England 53 USA 54
Swindon	England 75 USA 32

ENGLAND WORLD TEAM CUP v ENGLAND LIONS

1976	
Leicester	England WTC 36 England Lions 42
1978	
Leicester	England WTC 63 England Lions 45
1979	
Leicester	England WTC 51 England Lions 57

ENGLAND UNDER 23 v RUDA HVEZDA (Prague)

1978	
Bristol	England 42 Ruda Hvezda 36

The internationals listed on these pages, unless otherwise stated, are officially recognised as Test matches by both the competing nations.
WL = *1968 World League*
IN = *1972 Inter Nations Championship*
DMI = *Daily Mirror International Tournament*
◆ = *1988 Diamond Jubilee Series*

GREAT BRITAIN v POLAND

1966	
Hackney	Great Britain 61 Poland 47
Coventry	Great Britain 57 Poland 51
Sheffield	Great Britain 76 Poland 32
Bydgoszcz	Poland 77 Great Britain 31
Gdansk	Poland 62 Great Britain 46
Gorzow	Poland 74 Great Britain 34
Wroclaw	Poland 77 Great Britain 31
1967	
West Ham	Great Britain 39 Poland 69
Poole	Great Britain 59 Poland 49
Wolverhampton	Great Britain 66 Poland 42
Halifax	Great Britain 53 Poland 55
Newcastle	Great Britain 77 Poland 30
1968	
WL Hackney	Great Britain 60 Poland 18
WL Coventry	Great Britain 40 Poland 38
1971	
Swindon	Great Britain 80 Poland 28
Reading	Great Britain 78 Poland 30
Leicester	Great Britain 77 Poland 30
Sheffield	Great Britain 66 Poland 42
Glasgow	Great Britain 47 Poland 61
Belle Vue	Great Britain 57 Poland 51
Gdansk	Poland 81 Great Britain 25
Bydgoszcz	Poland 71 Great Britain 37
Gorzow	Poland 70 Great Britain 38
Wroclaw	Poland 76 Great Britain 32
Opole	Poland 75 Great Britain 33
Tarnow	Poland 76 Great Britain 31
1973	
Wroclaw	Poland 76 Great Britain 31
Rybnik	Poland 53 Great Britain 55
Gorzow	Poland 75 Great Britain 33

GREAT BRITAIN v REST OF THE WORLD

1973	
Wembley	Great Britain 30 Rest of the World 48

GREAT BRITAIN v SOVIET UNION

1965	
Wimbledon	Great Britain 71 Soviet Union 36
Coventry	Great Britain 66 Soviet Union 42
Sheffield	Great Britain 73 Soviet Union 35
Belle Vue	Great Britain 69 Soviet Union 39
Newport	Great Britain 63 Soviet Union 45
1968	
WL West Ham	Great Britain 52 Soviet Union 26
WL Exeter	Great Britain 51 Soviet Union 27

GREAT BRITAIN v SWEDEN

1967	
Wimbledon	Great Britain 46 Sweden 62
Coventry	Great Britain 46 Sweden 62
Newport	Great Britain 62 Sweden 46
Glasgow	Great Britain 66 Sweden 41
Belle Vue	Great Britain 44 Sweden 63
1968	
WL Wimbledon	Great Britain 43 Sweden 35
WL Halifax	Great Britain 51 Sweden 27
Wolverhampton	Great Britain 52 Sweden 55
Coatbridge	Great Britain 37 Sweden 71
Swindon	Great Britain 62 Sweden 46
1969	
Wimbledon	Great Britain 68 Sweden 40
Newport	Great Britain 70 Sweden 38
Leicester	Great Britain 79 Sweden 29
Halifax	Great Britain 62 Sweden 46
Cradley Heath	Great Britain 63 Sweden 45
Malmo	Sweden 54 Great Britain 54
1970	
Glasgow	Great Britain 66 Sweden 42
Halifax	Great Britain 48 Sweden 60
Exeter	Great Britain 66 Sweden 42
West Ham	Great Britain 62 Sweden 46
Newport	Great Britain 70 Sweden 38
Coventry	Great Britain 71 Sweden 37
Gothenburg	Sweden 45 Great Britain 63
Målilla	Sweden 73 Great Britain 34
Stockholm	Sweden 47 Great Britain 61

GREAT BRITAIN UNDER 23 v POLAND UNDER 23

1973	
Leszno	Poland 66 Great Britain 41
Czestochowa	Poland 63 Great Britain 45
Gniezno	Poland 70 Great Britain 36

SCOTLAND v AUSTRALIA

1969	
Coatbridge	Scotland 47 Australia 61

SCOTLAND v NORWAY

1969	
Glasgow	Scotland 62 Norway 46
Coatbridge	Scotland 56 Norway 52

SCOTLAND v POLAND

1967	
Edinburgh	Scotland 64 Poland 44

SCOTLAND v SOVIET UNION

1965	
Edinburgh	Scotland 51 Soviet Union 57
1966	
Glasgow	Scotland 57 Soviet Union 51

UNITED STATES OF AMERICA v UNITED KINGDOM

1971	
Costa Mesa	USA 48 United Kingdom 42
Ascot Park	USA 43 United Kingdom 47
Costa Mesa	USA 49 United Kingdom 40

COWBOY...regular American teamster John Cook

INTERNATIONAL RESULTS GUIDE

ENGLAND v AUSTRALASIA (Division Two)

1971	
Peterborough	England 55 Australasia 53
Bradford	England 40 Australasia 68
Canterbury	England 65 Australasia 43
1972	
Middlesbrough	England 51 Australasia 55
Rayleigh	England 52 Australasia 56
Boston	England 47 Australasia 60
1973	
Canterbury	England 55 Australasia 53
Workington	England 44 Australasia 64
Hull	England 44 Australasia 64
1974	
Barrow	England 53 Australasia 55
Middlesbrough	England 61 Australasia 45
Boston	England 54 Austraslaia 54
1975	
Birmingham	England 76 Australasia 32
Middlesbrough	England 47 Australasia 60
Peterborough	England 66 Australasia 42
Workington	England 58 Australsia 50
Eastbourne	England 78 Australsia 30
1976	
Newcastle	England 77 Australasia 30
Workington	England 66 Australasia 42
Scuinthorpe	England 44 Australasia 63
Middlesbrough	England 60 Australasia 48
Boston	England 65 Australasia 43
Ellesmere Port	England 80 Australasia 28
Stoke	England 63 Australasia 45
Canterbury	England 60 Australasia 48
1977	
Middlesbrough	England 76 Australasia 32
Weymouth	England 67 Australasia 41
Newport	England 58 Australasia 50
Canterbury	England 44 Australasia 63
Mildenhall	England 57 Australasia 51
1978	
Milton Keynes	England 54 Australasia 54
Boston	England 53 Australasia 55
Crayford	England 84 Australasia 24
Stoke	England 69.5 Australasia 38.5
1979	
Oxford	England 73 Australasia 35
Boston	England 72 Australasia 36
Milton Keynes	England 69 Australasia 39

ENGLAND v CZECHOSLOVAKIA (Division Two)

1969	
Canterbury	England 47 Czechoslovakia 61
Doncaster	England 62 Czechoslovakia 46
Crewe	England 54 Czechoslovakia 54
Middlesbrough	England 63 Czechoslovakia 45
Rayleigh	England 49 Czechoslovakia 59
King's Lynn	England 45 Czechoslovakia 62
Reading	England 51 Czechoslovakia 43
1970	
Koprivnice	Czechoslovakia 60 England 48
Brezolup	Czechoslovakia 66.5 England 41.5
Zarnovice	Czechoslovakia 64 England 44
Romford	England 56 Czechoslovakia 52
Canterbury	England 46 Czechoslovakia 62
Rochdale	England 40 Czechoslovakia 68
King's Lynn	England 66 Czechoslovakia 42
Ipswich	England 56 Czechoslovakia 51
Rayleigh	England 49 Czechoslovakia 59
Reading	England 53 Czechoslovakia 55
1971	
Canterbury	England 47 Czechoslovakia 60
Crewe	England 54 Czechoslovakia 54
Bradford	England 54 Czechoslovakia 54
Peterborough	England 52 Czechoslovakia 56
Workington	England 55 Czechoslovakia 52
Romford	England 66 Czechoslovakia 42
Ipswich	England 60 Czechoslovakia 48
1974	
Canterbury	England 63 Czechoslovakia 45
Eastbourne	England 72 Czechoslovakia 36
Barrow	England 54 Czechoslovakia 54
Bradford	England 58 Czechoslovkaia 50
Peterborough	England 57 Czechoslovakai 51
Workington	England 55 Czechoslovakia 53
Birmingham	England 52 Czechoslovakia 56

ENGLAND v POLAND (Division Two)

1973	
Canterbury	England 47 Poland 61
Boston	England 55 Poland 52
Hull	England 53 Poland 55
Peterborough	England 52 Poland 56
Eastbourne	England 67 Poland 41
Birmingham	England 64 Poland 43
Middlesbrough	England 49 Poland 59
1***974***	
Peterborough	England 48 Poland 60
Workington	England 53 Poland 54
Crewe	England 73 Poland 34
Middlesbrough	England 66 POland 42
Birmingham	England 61 Poland 47
Barrow	England 61 Poland 46
Canterbury	England 57 Poland 50

ENGLAND v SCOTLAND (Division Two)

1973	
Berwick	England 48 Scotland 60
Sunderland	England 70 Scotland 38
Middlesbrough	England 66 Scotland 42
1974	
Sunderland	England 57 Scotland 50
Berwick	England 64 Scotland 44
1975	
Newcastle	England 59 Scotland 48
1979	
Edinburgh	Scotland 60 England 48
Glasgow	Scotland 60 England 48
Workington	England 70 Scotland 38
Berwick	England 54 Scotland 53
Middlesbrough	England 66 Scotland 42
1981	
Edinburgh	Scotland 43 England 64
1982	
Edinburgh	Scotland 62 England 46
1984	
Edinburgh	Scotland 61 England 47
Long Eaton	England 64 Scotland 44

ENGLAND v SWEDEN (Division Two)

1970	
Middlesbrough	England 68 Sweden 38
Workington	England 75 Sweden 32
Berwick	England 54 Sweden 54
Reading	England 69 Sweden 39
Ipswich	England 71 Sweden 37
1971	
Ipswich	England 66.5 Sweden 40.5
Rayleigh	England 49 Sweden 59
Eastbourne	England 64 Sweden 43
Crewe	England 60 Sweden 48
Middlesbrough	England 42 Sweden 66
1972	
Workington	England 55 Sweden 52
Birmingham	England 57 Sweeden 51
Bradford	England 47 Sweden 61
Peterborough	England 48 Sweden 60
Canterbury	England 55 Sweden 53
1973	
Eastbourne	England 54 Sweden 53
Crewe	England 77 Sweden 31
Bradford	England 73 Sweden 35
Middlesbrough	England 62 Sweden 46
Peterborough	England 75 Sweden 33

▼ CZECH-MATE...regular tourist Toni Kasper

INTERNATIONAL RESULTS GUIDE

GREAT BRITAIN v AUSTRALASIA (Division Two)

1969

Berwick	Great Britain 59 Australasia 48
Nelson	Great Britain 66 Australasia 42
Crayford	Great Britain 62 Australasia 46
Eastbourne	Great Britain 69 Australasia 38
Ipswich	Great Britain 51 Australasia 57

1970

Middlesbrough	Great Britain 64 Australasia 44
Crewe	Great Britain 55 Australasia 53
Berwick	Great Britain 59 Australasia 49
Eastbourne	Great Britain 74 Australasia 34
Canterbury	Great Britain 45 Australasia 62

GREAT BRITAIN v DENMARK (Division Two)

1978

Stoke	Great Britain 41 Denmark 67
Eastbourne	Great Britain 53 Denmark 55
Edinburgh	Great Britain 54 Denmark 54
Boston	Great Britain 45 Denmark 63
Middlesbrough	Great Britain 42 Denmark 66

(The above series is listed an official international series by the Great Britain authorities but was not authoried by the Danish Motor Union).

NATIONAL LEAGUE v AUSTRALIA

1988

Stoke	National League 54 Australia 41
Eastbourne	National League 51 Australia 45
Long Eaton	National League 44 Australia 52
Peterborough	National League 46 Australia 50

1989

Wimbledon	National League 47 Australia 47
Edinburgh	National League 30 Australia 66
Ipswich	National League 60 Australia 36
Poole	National League 53 Australia 43
Hackney	National League 64 Australia 32

NATIONAL LEAGUE v POLAND

1987

Wimbledon	National League 86 Poland 22
Stoke	National League 80 Poland 28

NATIONAL LEAGUE v SWEDEN

1988

Mildfenhall	National League 52 Sweden 55
Exeter	National League 53 Sweden 55
Wimbledon	National League 45 Sweden 63
Middlesbrough	National League 48 Sweden 59

NATIONAL LEAGUE v YOUNG ENGLAND

1982

Rye House	National League 45 Y. England 63
Exeter	National League 47 Y. England 61
Middlesbrough	National League 37 Y. England 71
Newcastle	National League 48 Y. England 60
Edinburgh	National League 51 Y. England 57

1983

Exeter	National League 38 Y. England 70
Weymouth	National League 52 Y. England 56
Crayford	National League 44 Y. England 63
Middlesbrough	National League 55 Y. England 53
Long Eaton	National League 33 Y. England 75

SCOTLAND v AUSTRALASIA (Division Two)

1975

Paisley	Scotland 58 Australasia 50

YOUNG ENGLAND v AUSTRALIA (Division Two)

1986

Middlesbrough	Young England 75 Australia 33
Hackney	Young England 74 Australia 33
Birmingham	Young England 78 Australia 30

ANZACS AHOY...the late Billy Sanders (Australia) and New Zealander David Bargh provided plenty of Colonial cheer in the British League international arena

THE COMPLETE HISTORY OF THE BRITISH LEAGUE

BRITISH LEAGUE SECTION

1965 BRITISH LEAGUE TABLE

	P	W	D	L	PtsF	PtsA	W	D	L	PtsF	PtsA	Pts
1 WEST HAM	**34**	**16**	**0**	**1**	**781**	**542**	**7**	**1**	**9**	**649**	**673**	**47**
2 Wimbledon	34	15	1	1	767	553	7	1	9	629	692	46
3 Coventry	34	16	0	1	769	549	4	0	13	615	709	40
4 Oxford	34	14	0	3	717	607	5	2	10	591	733	40
5 Halifax	33	13	3	1	754	564	5	0	11	568	676	39
6 Newport	34	17	0	0	802	523	2	0	15	558	765	38
7 Wolverhampton	34	15	1	1	819	506	3	0	14	610	710	37
8 Hackney	34	16	0	1	783.5	537.5	2	1	14	544	782	37
9 Exeter	34	16	0	1	787	539	2	0	15	538.5	784.5	36
10 Poole	34	14	0	3	780	540	3	1	13	598	726	35
11 Sheffield	34	14	1	2	761	564	2	1	14	539	782	34
12 Newcastle	34	14	1	2	782	543	2	0	15	581	739	33
13 Glasgow	34	13	0	4	784	540	2	1	14	531	789	31
14 Belle Vue	34	15	0	2	792	532	0	0	17	536	780	30
15 Swindon	34	12	1	4	744	577	1	1	15	601	723	28
16 Cradley Heath	33	10	1	5	621	626	1	0	16	511	812	23
17 Edinburgh	34	11	0	6	680	641	0	0	17	493	830	22
18 Long Eaton	34	5	0	12	631	685	2	0	15	476	849	14

■ **WEST HAM were confirmed as the first British League champions on Saturday, October 23, 1965, when they won at Cradley Heath.**

1965 British League Riders' Championship Final

Saturday, October 16, Belle Vue:
1 Barry Briggs 15, 2 Jimmy Gooch 13, 3 Cyril Maidment 12, 4 Olle Nygren 11, 5 Nigel Boocock 11, 6 Charlie Monk 9, 7 Ivan Mauger 8, 8 Pete Jarman 8, 9 Eric Boocock 7, 10 Colin Goody 6, 11 Ken McKinlay 5, 12 Jack Kitchen 5, 13 Gerald Jackson 3, 14 George Major 3, 15 Ronnie Genz 2, 16 Alby Golden 2. *Reserves: Alf Wells 0, †Kid Bodie 0.*
†Kid Bodie later qualified under his real name Howard Cole.

1965 KNOCK OUT CUP

Round 1
Long Eaton 51 Halifax 45
Edinburgh 49 Hackney 46
Round 2
Exeter 63 Belle Vue 33
Newcastle 46 Swindon 51
WEST HAM 56 Newport 40
Long Eaton 50 Coventry 45
Glasgow 64 Sheffield 32
†Oxford 35 Wimbledon 43
Poole 51 Edinburgh 45
Cradley Heath 43 Wolverhampton 53
Round 3
WEST HAM 48 Wimbledon 48
Exeter 68 Long Eaton 28
Poole 45 Wolverhampton 51
Glasgow 49 Swindon 46
Round 3 Replay
Wimbledon 47 WEST HAM 49
Semi Finals
Exeter 59 Wolverhampton 37
Glasgow 43 WEST HAM 50

FINAL
First leg, October 5:
WEST HAM 63 (Sverre Harrfeldt 15, Norman Hunter 12, Reg Trott 12, Ken McKinlay 11, Malcolm Simmons 9, Brian Leonard 4, Tony Clarke 0) *Exeter 33* (Jack Geran 10, Ivor Hughes 7, Colin Gooddy 5, Des Lukehurst 5, Jimmy Squibb 4, Chris Blewett 1, Alan Cowland 1)
Second leg, October 11:
Exeter 45 (Gooddy 10, Squibb 8, Geran 7, Lukehurst 6, Cowland 6, Hughes 4, Blewett 4) WEST HAM 51 (Harrfeldt 14, McKinlay 13, Hunter 9, Simmons 7, Leonard 3, Trott 3, Clarke 2).
❑ WEST HAM win 114-78 on aggregate.
†By mistake the Oxford tie was staged over 13 heats instead of 16 but the result was allowed to stand.

1965 ALL THE RESULTS

	BELLE VUE	COVENTRY	CRADLEY HEATH	EDINBURGH	EXETER	GLASGOW	HACKNEY	HALIFAX	LONG EATON	NEWCASTLE	NEWPORT	OXFORD	POOLE	SHEFFIELD	SWINDON	WEST HAM	WIMBLEDON	WOLVERHAMPTON
BELLE VUE		44-34	55-23	47-30	43-35	36-42	51-27	45-33	53-25	41-37	55-23	60-18	43-35	52-26	43-35	30-47	44-34	50-28
COVENTRY	45-31		47-31	58-20	52-26	51-26	42-36	47-30	42-36	45-33	41-36	37-41	47-30	47-30	48-30	39-38	40-38	41-37
CRADLEY HEATH	42-35	27-51		43-35	42-36	43-35	49-29	Not Raced	43-35	40-38	35-43	36-42	41-37	39-39	40-38	31-47	29-49	41-37
EDINBURGH	47-30	31-46	40-38		45-33	36-42	40-38	35-42	38-40	36-41	43-35	47-31	39-38	47-31	40-38	34-44	40-38	42-36
EXETER	54-24	41-37	51-27	52-26		46-32	54-24	40-38	45-33	44-34	51-27	52-26	42-36	50-28	48-30	46-32	41-37	30-48
GLASGOW	46-32	56-22	53-25	48-30	54-24		59-19	33-44	60-18	42-36	43-35	38-40	49-29	37-41	40-38	46-32	37-41	43-34
HACKNEY	48-29	44-34	45-32	50-28	41.5-36.5	54-24		45-33	48-30	59-18	47-31	46-32	43-35	54-24	40-38	40-37	35-43	44-33
HALIFAX	50-28	40-38	62-16	48-30	50-27	39-39	44-34		36-41	44-32	42-35	41-36	50-28	43-34	39-39	39-38	39-39	48-30
LONG EATON	41-36	29-49	45-32	52-26	32-44	41-37	38-40	36-41		36-41	32-46	38-39	31-47	37-40	40-37	37-41	34-44	32-45
NEWCASTLE	45-33	51-27	42-36	46-32	57-21	48-30	50-28	49-29	50-28		51-27	39-39	41-37	48-30	43-35	46-32	38-40	38-39
NEWPORT	53-25	47-31	56-22	51-27	45-33	50-28	56-22	46-32	52-26	44-34		44-34	41-37	44-33	41-37	42-36	49-29	41-37
OXFORD	41-37	42-36	41-37	48-30	44-34	48-30	42-36	42-36	50-28	40-38	45-32		34-44	41-36	41-37	33-45	38-40	47-31
POOLE	47-29	47-31	52-26	46-32	37-41	49-26	48-30	36-42	59-19	45-33	44-34	42-36		50-28	37-40	51-27	45-33	45-33
SHEFFIELD	41-37	35-42	40-38	53-25	54-24	42-36	39-39	45-33	53-25	48-30	41-37	47-31	55-23		40-38	37-41	49-29	42-36
SWINDON	41-37	45-33	38-40	49-29	46-32	54-24	46-32	38-40	44-34	43-35	48-30	38-40	39-39	52-26		45-33	36-37	42-36
WEST HAM	44-34	42-36	40-37	49-29	51-27	47-30	36-42	45-33	60-18	44-34	43-35	43-35	48-30	51-27	48-30		48-30	42-35
WIMBLEDON	44-32	42-36	52-26	46-30	46-32	49-29	44-34	45-33	63-15	41-36	40-38	39-39	45-33	50-28	41-37	38-40		42-35
WOLVERHAMPTON	51-27	46-32	53-25	44-34	45-33	56-21	44-34	49-29	53-25	47-31	64-14	46-32	38-40	40-38	54-24	39-39	50-28	

1966 BRITISH LEAGUE TABLE

	P	W	D	L	PtsF	PtsA	W	D	L	PtsF	PtsA	Pts
1 HALIFAX	**36**	**17**	**0**	**1**	**877**	**527**	**10**	**0**	**8**	**697**	**702**	**54**
2 Coventry	36	18	0	0	866	537	7	1	10	682	718	51
3 Swindon	36	18	0	0	891	509	5	0	13	662	739	46
4 Wimbledon	36	17	0	1	835	566	5	0	13	650	748	44
5 Newcastle	36	17	0	1	857.5	541.5	3	0	15	634	763	40
6 Poole	36	16	0	2	822.5	576.5	3	2	13	620.5	779.5	40
7 West Ham	36	15	0	3	830	573	4	1	13	669.5	731.5	39
8 Glasgow	36	17	0	1	819	567	1	0	17	576	827	36
9 Wolverhampton	36	16	0	2	773	626	1	2	15	567.5	835.5	36
10 Exeter	36	15	1	2	810	589	2	0	16	582.5	814.5	35
11 Sheffield	36	17	0	1	848	555	0	0	18	562	839	34
12 Edinburgh	35	16	0	2	796.5	605.5	1	0	16	514	808	34
13 Belle Vue	36	16	0	2	817	586	0	0	18	545	857	32
14 Hackney	36	14	1	3	759.5	643.5	1	0	17	588	813	31
15 Oxford	36	13	2	3	743	656	1	0	17	548	854	30
16 King's Lynn	36	14	0	4	746	652	1	0	17	529	872	30
17 Newport	36	12	1	5	774	630	0	0	18	545	856	25
18 Long Eaton	36	12	1	5	750	648	0	0	18	536	868	25
19 Cradley Heath	35	10	0	7	659	657	0	0	18	537	849	20

■ *HALIFAX became the first club to tie up the British League championship in front of their own fans when they beat Belle Vue at The Shay on Saturday, October 8, 1966.*

1966 British League Riders' Championship Final

Saturday, October 22, Belle Vue:
1 Barry Briggs 15, 2 Olle Nygren 14, 3 Norman Hunter 12, 4 Ivan Mauger 11, 5 Ray Wilson 10, 6 Nigel Boocock 8, 7 George Hunter 7, 8 Bill Andrew 6, 9 Jimmy Gooch 6, 10 Cyril Maidment 5, Terry Betts 5, Charlie Monk 5, 13 Peter Vandenberg 5, 14 Tommy Sweetman 4, 15 Eric Boocock 3, 16 Colin Pratt 2. *Reserves: John Dews, Jack Biggs, Clive Featherby, did not ride.*

1966 KNOCK OUT CUP

Round 1
King's Lynn 43 *Wimbledon 53*
Newcastle 54 Oxford 42
West Ham 59 Exeter 37

Round 2
Belle Vue 60 Newport 36
Coventry 55 Sheffield 41
Hackney 48.5 Cradley Heath 47.5
HALIFAX 57 Glasgow 39
Long Eaton 54 Edinburgh 40
Poole 53 Newcastle 43
West Ham 61 Wolverhampton 35
Wimbledon 50 Swindon 46

Round 3
Belle Vue 53 Long Eaton 43
Hackney 47 *Wimbledon 49*
HALIFAX 52 West Ham 44
†Poole 50 Coventry 46

Round 3 Restaging
Poole 47 Coventry 49

Semi Finals
HALIFAX 60 Belle Vue 36
Wimbledon 54 Coventry 42

FINAL
First leg, October 12:
HALIFAX 69 (Dave Younghusband 15, Eric Boocock 14, Eric Boothroyd 12, Tommy Roper 11, Dennis Gavros 9, Bob Jameson 6, Maurie Robinson 2) *Wimbledon 27* (Olle Nygren 11, Trevor Hedge 6, Reg Luckhurst 4, Bob Dugard 4, Jim Tebby 2, Peter Jackson 0, Tony Childs 0)
Second leg, October 17:
Wimbledon 52 (Nygren 15, Hedge 10, Luckhurst 10, Dugard 9, Tebby 6, Jackson 2, Childs 0) HALIFAX 44 (Boocock 12, Boothroyd 10, Younghusband 10, Gavros 5, Jameson 3, Robinson 2, Roper 2).
❏ HALIFAX win 113-79 on aggregate.
†Match re-run as Poole wrongly objected to Coventry using rider replacement for Jim Lightfoot, ruled to have been withholding his services.

1966 ALL THE RESULTS

	BELLE VUE	COVENTRY	CRADLEY HEATH	EDINBURGH	EXETER	GLASGOW	HACKNEY	HALIFAX	KING'S LYNN	LONG EATON	NEWCASTLE	NEWPORT	OXFORD	POOLE	SHEFFIELD	SWINDON	WEST HAM	WIMBLEDON	WOLVES
BELLE VUE		44-34	43-35	43-35	55-23	42-36	49-29	34-44	47-31	51-27	41-37	53-24	51-27	35-43	43-35	43-35	50-28	40-38	53-25
COVENTRY	46-32		50-28	49-29	53-25	42-36	46-32	52-25	53-25	48-30	45-33	55-23	47-31	44-34	53-25	54-24	42-36	42-36	45-33
CRADLEY HEATH	48-30	28-50		Not Raced	33-39	41-37	45-33	27-51	34-43	42-36	44-34	41-37	46-31	31-47	46-32	39-38	33-44	37-41	44-34
EDINBURGH	42-35	44-34	49-29		42-36	46-31	43-35	37-41	51-27	50-28	50-28	47-31	43-35	42-36	45-33	45-33	42-36	43-35	35.5 42.5
EXETER	48-30	39-39	49-29	37-41		46-32	45-32	36-41	50-28	42-36	45-33	47-31	53-25	44-33	43-35	48-30	41-37	46-30	51-27
GLASGOW	54-24	41-37	36-29	43-35	45-32		52-26	42-36	53-25	50-28	45-33	46-32	45-33	60-17	42-35	38-40	39-38	48-29	40-38
HACKNEY	41-37	38-40	44-34	46-32	43-35	41-37		37-41	42-36	51-27	40-38	43-35	42-36	42.5 34.5	47-31	41-37	39-39	36-42	46-32
HALIFAX	52-26	45-33	51-27	54-24	43-35	60-18	44-34		53-25	50-28	38-40	57-21	55-23	41-37	52-26	42-36	41-37	46-32	53-25
KING'S LYNN	40-38	41-36	40-38	43-32	41-37	45-33	41-37	42-36		43-35	48-29	49-29	37-40	37-41	41-37	33-45	43-35	35-43	47-31
LONG EATON	40-38	32-46	50-27	48-29	48-30	48-30	41-37	35-42	44-33		42-36	43-35	50-28	41-37	40-38	38-39	37-40	34-44	39-39
NEWCASTLE	57-21	38-39	53-25	54-24	46.5 31.5	52-26	48-30	43-35	50-28	53-25		45-32	48-30	48-30	41-36	40-38	44-34	47-30	50-27
NEWPORT	53-25	34-44	45-33	43-35	38-40	38-40	47-31	36-42	43-35	57-21	31-47		44-34	39-39	54-24	44-34	42-36	43-35	43-35
OXFORD	40-37	36-42	50-27	42-36	42-36	40-38	50-27	35-42	42-36	51-27	42-36	40-38		39-39	40-38	40-38	35-43	40-37	39-39
POOLE	48-30	49-29	42-35	56-22	48-30	48-30	41-36	40-38	54-23	45-33	35-42	41-37	51-27		55-23	38-40	42.5 35.5	49-28	40-38
SHEFFIELD	50-28	42-36	54-24	56-22	47-31	49-29	47-31	34-44	55-23	47-31	41-36	58-20	44-34	55-23		40-38	40-38	41-37	48-30
SWINDON	53-25	45-33	54-24	52-26	52-26	53-25	46-32	49-29	53-25	44-34	42-33	52-25	60-18	45-33	45-33		45-33	43-35	58-20
WEST HAM	44-34	36-42	48-29	50-28	50-28	43-35	45-33	37-41	51-27	52-26	48-30	48-30	51-27	43-35	54-24	41-37		36-42	53-25
WIMBLEDON	48-30	44-34	45-32	52-26	44-34	48-30	45-33	46-32	56-22	51-27	47-31	46-32	43-35	44-33	49-28	36-42	40-38		51-27
WOLVERHAMPTON	53-25	42-34	46-32	40-38	44-34	45-33	38-40	40-37	41-37	41-37	39-38	45-33	44-34	49-29	49-29	39-38	36-42	42-36	

1967 BRITISH LEAGUE TABLE

	P	W	D	L	PtsF	PtsA	W	D	L	PtsF	PtsA	Pts
1 SWINDON	**36**	**18**	**0**	**0**	**887**	**514**	**6**	**0**	**12**	**649**	**752**	**48**
2 Coventry	36	17	0	1	882	517	5	2	11	642	758	46
3 West Ham	36	17	0	1	862	540	4	3	11	652	748	45
4 Edinburgh	36	16	1	1	861	540	4	1	13	624	778	42
5 Hackney	36	17	1	0	824	578	3	0	15	578	822	41
6 Poole	26	16	1	1	829	572	1	2	15	633	767	37
7 Halifax	36	16	1	1	857	545	2	0	16	599	804	37
8 Wolverhampton	36	17	0	1	824	573	1	1	16	599	803	37
9 Sheffield	36	16	1	1	795.5	604.5	2	0	16	538	866	37
10 Newcastle	36	16	0	2	807	595	2	0	16	579	822	36
11 Wimbledon	36	15	1	2	775	623	1	2	15	617	786	35
12 Newport	36	14	1	3	819	584	3	0	15	568	829	35
13 Glasgow	36	13	1	4	771	628	3	1	14	572	829	34
14 Oxford	36	15	1	2	810.5	591.5	1	0	17	558	841	33
15 Exeter	36	16	0	2	843	560	0	0	18	541.5	858.5	32
16 Belle Vue	36	14	0	4	756	643	2	0	16	577.5	820.5	32
17 Long Eaton	36	13	3	2	749	654	1	0	17	573	827	31
18 Cradley Heath	36	11	0	7	739	658	1	0	17	523	875	24
19 King's Lynn	36	11	0	7	759	641	0	0	18	538	864	22

■ ***FOR THE** first time every single British League match was completed in the 1967 British League season.*

1967 KNOCK OUT CUP

Round 1
Belle Vue 50 Wimbledon 46
Cradley Heath 45 Long Eaton 51
Edinburgh 56 Sheffield 40

Round 2
COVENTRY 50 Newcastle 46
Edinburgh 54 Wolverhampton 42
Hackney 53 Oxford 43
King's Lynn 51 Belle Vue 44
Long Eaton 54 Newport 42
Poole 60 Halifax 36
Swindon 61 Exeter 35
West Ham 67 Glasgow 29

Round 3
COVENTRY 58.5 King's Lynn 37.5
Hackney 53 Poole 42
Long Eaton 44 Edinburgh 52
West Ham 51 Swindon 45

Semi Finals
COVENTRY 58 Edinburgh 38
West Ham 51 Hackney 45

FINAL
First leg, September 23:
COVENTRY 57 (Ron Mountford 13, Nigel Boocock 12, Les Owen 9, Col Cottrell 8, Rick France 8, Roger Hill 4, Clive Hitch 3) *West Ham 39* (Ken McKinlay 15, Norman Hunter 9, Sverre Harrfeldt 8, Tony Clarke 3, Brian Leonard 3, George Barclay 1, Malcolm Simmons 0)
Second leg, September 26:
West Ham 49 (Leonard 11, Simmons 11, McKinlay 9, Hunter 9, Clarke 5, Stan Stevens 4, Harrfeldt 0) COVENTRY 47 (Boocock 14, France 12, Mountford 9, Owen 4, Cottrell 4, Hitch 2, Hill 2).
❑ COVENTRY win 104-88 on aggregate.

1967 British League Riders' Championship Final

Saturday, October 21, Belle Vue:
1 Barry Briggs 15, 2 Nigel Boocock 14, 3 Ray Wilson 12, 4 Eric Boocock 10, 5 Torbjörn Harrysson 10, 6 Ivan Mauger 10, 7 Olle Nygren 9, 8 Bengt Jansson 8, 9 Ove Fundin 6, 10 Charlie Monk 6, Göte Nordin 6, 12 Jim Airey 5, 13 Ken McKinlay 4, 14 Terry Betts 4, 15 Wayne Briggs 1, 16 Roy Trigg 0. *Reserves: Brian Brett 0, John Hart, did not ride.*

1967 ALL THE RESULTS

	BELLE VUE	COVENTRY	CRADLEY HEATH	EDINBURGH	EXETER	GLASGOW	HACKNEY	HALIFAX	KING'S LYNN	LONG EATON	NEWCASTLE	NEWPORT	OXFORD	POOLE	SHEFFIELD	SWINDON	WEST HAM	WIMBLEDON	WOLVES
BELLE VUE		43-35	48-30	35-43	43-35	47-31	46-31	45-33	46-32	34-44	47-31	44-32	39-38	40-38	37-41	43-35	34-43	40-38	45-33
COVENTRY	44-31		56-22	48-30	46-32	56-22	51-27	56-22	57-21	44-34	54-24	41-36	57-21	46-32	54-24	37-41	47-31	44-34	44-33
CRADLEY HEATH	54-24	36-41		34-44	47-30	37-41	44-34	36-42	39-38	45-33	37-41	35-43	38-39	40-37	42-36	46-31	42-35	46-32	41-37
EDINBURGH	56-22	49-29	59-19		55-23	38-40	45-33	45-33	49-28	46-32	47-31	50-28	47-31	45-32	50-28	50-28	39-39	46-31	45-33
EXETER	41-36	36-42	54-24	51-27		50-28	49-29	43-35	50-28	46-32	51-27	38-40	50-28	47-31	61-17	48-30	42-36	42-36	44-34
GLASGOW	36-41	42-35	46-32	41-37	42-34		48-30	43-35	48-30	50-28	36-42	43-34	44-34	39-39	49-29	35-43	32-46	40-38	57-21
HACKNEY	45-33	42-36	48-30	42-35	50-28	39-39		43-35	54-24	42-36	46-31	44-34	40-38	44-34	49-29	45-33	41-37	57-21	53-25
HALIFAX	47-31	39-39	30-39	42-36	49-29	46-33	43-35		61-17	43-35	54-24	60-18	52-26	52-26	46-32	42-36	48-29	52-26	44-34
KING'S LYNN	53-24	47-31	47-31	36-42	48-29	42-35	35-43	45-33		55-23	43-35	35-42	44-34	44-34	36-42	34-44	34-44	43-35	38-40
LONG EATON	42-36	32-46	50-28	40-38	52-26	38-40	44-34	40-38	40-38		40-38	41-36	45-33	40-38	47-31	41-37	39-39	39-39	39-39
NEWCASTLE	43-35	51-27	40-38	45-32	45-33	56-22	58-20	34-44	43-36	40-38		47-31	44-33	40-38	49-29	32-46	54-24	46-32	40-38
NEWPORT	42-36	39-39	55-22	38-40	43-35	44-34	56-22	41-37	49-29	50-28	45-33		50-28	37-41	53-25	38-40	41-37	46-32	52-26
OXFORD	44-34	38-39	51-27	45-33	47.5 30.5	41-36	42-36	55-23	47-31	46-32	49-29	56-22		39-39	44-34	46-32	44-34	36-42	40-38
POOLE	38-40	48-30	45-33	39-39	42-36	48-30	43-34	47-31	57-21	57-21	45-33	45-33	52-25		48-30	48-30	46-31	40-38	41-37
SHEFFIELD	43.5 34.5	41-37	48-27	59-19	53-25	44-34	46-32	43-35	45-33	47-31	41-37	47-31	42-36	41-37		43-35	33-45	39-39	40-37
SWINDON	51-27	47-31	44-33	46-32	56-22	52-26	55-23	52-26	44-34	47-31	53-24	52-26	53-25	42-35	51-27		50-28	47-31	45-33
WEST HAM	53-25	48-30	52-26	51-27	48-30	51-27	37-40	46-32	42-36	45-33	49-28	60-18	52-26	44-34	54-24	44-34		43-35	43-35
WIMBLEDON	41-37	35-42	43-35	46-32	45-33	43-34	42-36	44-33	42-36	42-35	43-35	48-29	43-35	42-36	47-31	38-39	39-39		52-26
WOLVERHAMPTON	47-31	45-33	51-27	40-38	47-31	58-20	†38-39	46-32	51-27	48-27	42-36	43-35	49-28	45-32	49-29	42-35	43-35	40-38	

†Amended result. On track score was 43-35.

1968 BRITISH LEAGUE TABLE

	P	*W*	*D*	*L*	*PtsF*	*PtsA*	*W*	*D*	*L*	*PtsF*	*PtsA*	*Pts*
1 COVENTRY	**36**	**17**	**0**	**1**	**825**	**578**	**5**	**0**	**13**	**611**	**791**	**44**
2 Hackney	36	18	0	0	801	600	3	2	13	620	783	44
3 Exeter	36	18	0	0	927	474	2	1	15	629.5	774.5	41
4 Sheffield	36	18	0	0	866.5	536.5	2	1	15	597	801	41
5 Newcastle	36	18	0	0	837	566	2	0	16	617	784	40
6 West Ham	36	16	0	2	794	604	3	1	14	660	744	39
7 Halifax	36	17	1	0	846	557	2	0	16	578	822	39
8 Coatbridge	36	16	1	1	838	563	2	0	16	566	834	37
9 Wimbledon	36	17	0	1	837	562	1	0	17	574	822	36
10 Belle Vue	36	16	0	2	819	585	2	0	16	568	832	36
11 Swindon	36	14	0	4	839	560	3	1	14	609	793	35
12 Leicester	36	16	1	1	770	631	1	0	17	603	799	35
13 Newport	36	17	1	0	823	579	0	0	18	525	878	35
14 Cradley Heath	36	13	1	4	783	620	2	3	13	590	810	34
15 Oxford	36	16	0	2	774	628	1	0	17	545	859	34
16 Wolverhampton	36	16	0	2	800	600	0	0	18	588	813	32
17 Poole	36	13	2	3	755	648	0	0	18	572	830	28
18 King's Lynn	36	13	1	4	763	636	0	0	18	567	837	27
19 Glasgow	36	11	1	6	757	647	2	0	16	555	848	27

■ ***COVENTRY'S championship win is the only time in British League Division One history that the title has been decided on race points.***

1968 British League Riders' Championship Final

Saturday, October 19, Belle Vue:
1 Barry Briggs 14, 2 Eric Boocock 14, 3 Ivan Mauger 13, 4 Torbjörn Harrysson 11, 5 Martin Ashby 11, 6 Terry Betts 8, Anders Michanek 8, Sören Sjösten 8, 9 Hasse Holmkvist 7, Bernt Persson 7, 11 Norman Hunter 5, 12 Charlie Monk 5, Nigel Boocock 5, 14 Colin Pratt 2, Olle Nygren 2, 16 Roy Trigg 0. ***Reserves: Jim McMillan, Geoff Mudge and Colin Gooddy did not ride.***

1968 KNOCK OUT CUP

Round 1
Coatbridge 66 Glasgow 42
Halifax 57 Exeter 51
West Ham 55 Hackney 52
Round 2
Belle Vue 64 West Ham 44
Leicester 52 Coventry 56
Newcastle 77 Coatbridge 30
Poole 56 Newport 52
Sheffield 71 Cradley Heath 37
Swindon 58 Oxford 50
WIMBLEDON 60 King's Lynn 48
Wolverhampton 60 **Halifax 47**
Round 3
Belle Vue 65 Sheffield 42
Poole 54 Swindon 54
WIMBLEDON 64 Newcastle 44
Wolverhampton 58 **Coventry 50**
Round 3 Replay
Swindon 60 Poole 47
Semi Finals
WIMBLEDON 80 Swindon 28
Wolverhampton 67 **Belle Vue 40**
FINAL
First leg, October 18:
Wolverhampton 53 **(Hasse Holmkvist 15, Jim Airey 14, Peter Vandenberg 8, James Bond 6, Dave Hemus 6, Doug White 3, Mick Handley 1, Pete Jarman 0) WIMBLEDON 55 (Olle Nygren 14, Trevor Hedge 12, Reg Luckhurst 10, Bob Dugard 9, Alan Cowland 4, Peter Murray 3, Jim Tebby 3, Garry Middleton 0)**
Second leg, October 31:
WIMBLEDON 63 (Hedge 17, Nygren 14, Luckhurst 12, Middleton 8, Cowland 6, Murray 2, Dugard 2, Tebby 2) ***Wolverhampton 45*** **(Holmkvist 12, Bond 10, Vandenberg 8, Airey 7, Handley 5, Jarman 3, White 0, Hemus 0).**

❑ **WIMBLEDON win 118-98 on aggregate.**

1968 ALL THE RESULTS

	BELLE VUE	COATBRIDGE	COVENTRY	CRADLEY HEATH	EXETER	GLASGOW	HACKNEY	HALIFAX	KING'S LYNN	LEICESTER	NEWCASTLE	NEWPORT	OXFORD	POOLE	SHEFFIELD	SWINDON	WEST HAM	WIMBLEDON	WOLVES
BELLE VUE		41-37	55-23	47-31	34-44	50-28	45-33	49-29	40-38	40-38	41-37	51-27	52-26	45-33	37-41	55-23	44-34	52-26	41-37
COATBRIDGE	41-36		38-40	51-27	39-39	48-30	53-25	52-26	49-29	43-35	46-32	48-30	54-24	44-34	42-36	43-35	48-30	46-32	53-23
COVENTRY	37-41	47-31		53-25	43-35	48-30	41-36	46-32	47-31	45-33	43-35	46-32	56-22	49-29	44-34	43-35	42-36	50-28	45-33
CRADLEY HEATH	45-33	54-24	37-41		42-36	53-25	46-32	37-41	46-32	36-42	38-40	42-36	50-28	43-35	42-35	39-39	40-38	44-34	49-29
EXETER	46-31	53-25	51-27	61-16		50-28	51-27	58-19	59-19	56-22	47-31	53-25	50-28	52-26	50-28	49-29	41-37	49-29	51-27
GLASGOW	44-34	38-40	47-31	39-39	36-42		36-42	34-44	44-34	47-31	41-37	55-23	49-29	46-32	38-40	43-35	31-47	40-38	49-29
HACKNEY	48-30	40-36	42-36	43-35	43-35	47-31		46-32	41-37	43-35	42-36	48-30	46-32	47-31	42-35	47-31	42-36	52-26	42-36
HALIFAX	52-26	51-27	42-36	56-22	43-35	50-27	54-24		44-34	47-31	40-38	47-31	52-26	42-36	39-39	45-33	43-35	50-28	49-29
KING'S LYNN	41-37	50-28	37-41	39-39	45-33	36-42	36-42	43-35		41-37	41-37	40-38	48-30	50-28	49-29	42-36	38-40	47-26	40-38
LEICESTER	44-34	40-38	37-41	50-27	40-38	43-35	39-39	41-37	48-30		44-34	51-27	44-34	41-37	39-37	45-33	41-37	43-35	40-38
NEWCASTLE	59-19	48-30	52-26	40-38	50-28	45-33	46-32	50-28	40-38	40-38		53-25	41-37	43-35	46-32	46-32	49-29	49-28	40-38
NEWPORT	46-32	43-35	42-36	47-31	41-37	49-29	46-32	45-33	42-36	44-33	51-27		53-25	48-29	49-29	47-31	39-39	46-32	45-33
OXFORD	43-35	43-35	41-37	30-47	43-35	42-36	45-33	51-26	43-35	43-35	41-37	54-24		42-36	42-36	38-40	46-32	43-35	44-34
POOLE	36-42	38-40	43-35	39-39	40-38	45-33	39-39	42-36	45-33	43-35	44-34	43-35	49-29		43-35	38-40	41-37	45-32	42-36
SHEFFIELD	54-24	46-32	51-27	53-25	44.5 33.5	51-27	43-35	42-36	51-27	45-33	50-27	51-27	49-29	51-27		50-28	41-37	50-28	44-34
SWINDON	56-22	57-20	43-34	36-42	50-28	61-17	36-42	48-30	51-27	43-35	38-39	54-24	45-33	53-24	47-31		36-42	39-38	46-32
WEST HAM	41-36	43-35	46-32	39-38	48-30	36-42	41-37	42-35	48-30	50-28	44-34	50-28	41-37	45-33	48-29	37-40		43-35	52-25
WIMBLEDON	54-24	51-26	54-24	42-36	50-28	49-29	46-32	42-35	49-29	47-31	46-31	49-29	37-41	41-37	55-22	43-34	41-37		41-37
WOLVERHAMPTON	45-32	51-27	33-44	45-33	43-35	45-33	40-38	54-24	50-28	46-31	47-31	43-34	43-35	48-30	49-29	43-35	41-37	34-44	

1969 BRITISH LEAGUE TABLE

	P	W	D	L	PtsF	PtsA	W	D	L	PtsF	PtsA	Pts
1 POOLE	**36**	**18**	**0**	**0**	**850.5**	**550.5**	**8**	**1**	**9**	**668**	**734**	**53**
2 Belle Vue	36	18	0	0	865	536	5	1	12	668	732	47
3 Wimbledon	36	18	0	0	908.5	493.5	4	2	12	647	755	46
4 Halifax	36	18	0	0	889	515	4	2	12	594	729	46
5 Leicester	36	16	0	2	833	570	5	2	11	660	742	44
6 Sheffield	36	18	0	0	848	554	1	1	16	619.5	782.5	39
7 Cradley Heath	36	16	1	1	778	621	2	1	15	598	805	38
8 Glasgow	36	15	2	1	818	583	2	1	15	605	797	37
9 King's Lynn	36	16	0	2	799	601	2	0	16	614	789	36
10 Swindon	36	15	0	3	770	627	3	0	15	621	781	36
11 Coatbridge	36	15	1	2	788	616	2	0	16	602	802	35
12 Exeter	36	15	0	3	790	611	1	0	17	588	814	32
13 Newcastle	36	14	1	3	783	615	1	1	16	565	835	32
14 Coventry	36	13	3	2	799	603	1	0	17	620.5	780.5	31
15 Oxford	36	13	1	4	754	571	2	0	16	536	865	31
16 Wolverhampton	36	12	0	6	739	664	1	1	16	572	830	27
17 Newport	36	13	1	4	760	641	0	0	18	496	905	27
18 West Ham	36	10	2	6	711	693	1	1	16	565	834	25
19 Hackney	36	10	2	6	720	682	0	0	18	509	891	22

■ ***POOLE'S six point title winning margin was the biggest to date in the history of the British League.***

1969 British League Riders' Championship Final

Saturday, October 18, Belle Vue:
1 Barry Briggs 14, 2 Ivan Mauger 12, 3 Jim Airey 12, 4 Martin Ashby 11, 5 Eric Boocock 10, 6 Roy Trigg 9, 7 Ray Wilson 8, 8 Trevor Hedge 8, 9 Sandor Levai 7, 10 Ole Olsen 6, 11 Tony Clarke 6, 12 Terry Betts 5, 13 Reidar Eide 5, 14 Jim McMillan 3, 15 Pete Smith 2, Colin Goody 2. *Reserves: James Bond 0, Colin Pratt, Col Cottrell, did not ride.*

1969 KNOCK OUT CUP

Round 1
Coatbridge 53 Hackney 25
Leicester 54 Newport 24
West Ham 39 King's Lynn 39
Round 1, Replay
King's Lynn 39 West Ham 39
Round 1, 2nd Replay
West Ham 36 King's Lynn 42
Round 2
Belle Vue 38 Sheffield 40
Coventry 46 Oxford 32
Cradley Heath 41 Glasgow 37
Exeter 36 WIMBLEDON 42
Halifax 43 Wolverhampton 35
Newcastle 36 Belle Vue 42
Poole 43 Coatbridge 33
Sheffield 52 King's Lynn 26
Swindon 47 Leicester 31
Round 3
Belle Vue 38 *Sheffield 40*
Cradley Heath 41 Swindon 37
Halifax 47 Coventry 31
WIMBLEDON 49 Poole 29
Semi Finals
Cradley Heath 36 WIMBLEDON 42
Sheffield 43.5 Halifax 34.5
FINAL
First leg, October 8:
Sheffield 40 (Arnold Haley 11, Jim Airey 9, Billy Bales 9, John Dews 5, Dave Baugh 3, Bengt Larsson 2, Reg Wilson 1) WIMBLEDON 38 (Trevor Hedge 12, Cyril Maidment 10, Reg Luckhurst 8, Ronnie Moore 4, Jim Tebby 3, Bob Dugard 1, Gary Everett 0)
Second leg, October 9:
WIMBLEDON 56 (Hedge 12, Moore 12, Luckhurst 9, Tebby 7, Dugard 6, Maidment 6, Everett 4)
Sheffield 22 (Airey 9, Haley 9, Larsson 3, Bales 1, Baugh 0, Dews 0, Wilson 0).
❑ WIMBLEDON win 94-62 on aggregate.

1969 ALL THE RESULTS

	BELLE VUE	COATBRIDGE	COVENTRY	CRADLEY HEATH	EXETER	GLASGOW	HACKNEY	HALIFAX	KING'S LYNN	LEICESTER	NEWCASTLE	NEWPORT	OXFORD	POOLE	SHEFFIELD	SWINDON	WEST HAM	WIMBLEDON	WOLVES
BELLE VUE		52-26	44-33	40-38	50-28	43-35	56-22	50-28	54-24	52-26	47-30	53-25	44-33	47-31	44-34	47-31	47-31	55-23	40-38
COATBRIDGE	33-45		46-32	42-36	40-38	49-29	50-28	37-41	43-35	41-37	39-39	53-25	49-29	40-38	44-34	40-38	43-35	47-31	52-26
COVENTRY	39-39	48-30		41-37	46-32	43-35	51-27	40-38	38-40	40-37	42-36	56-22	60-18	43-35	39-39	38-39	48-30	39-39	48-30
CRADLEY HEATH	37-41	49-29	45-33		41-37	46-32	49-28	45-32	41-37	39-39	50-28	42-35	41-37	44-33	42-36	45-33	40-38	40-37	42-36
EXETER	40-38	50-28	44-34	51-27		51-27	§51-27	43-35	45-33	38-40	40-38	43-35	48-30	38-40	40-38	38-39	44-33	42-36	44-33
GLASGOW	45-33	46-32	42-36	39-39	46-32		52-25	37-41	49-29	44-34	54-24	52-26	42-35	39-39	44-33	42-36	52-26	45-33	48-30
HACKNEY	32-46	44-34	41-37	47-31	40-38	39-38		44-34	37-41	38-40	36-42	47-30	40-38	37-41	42-36	36-42	39-39	42-36	39-39
HALIFAX	40-38	49-29	41-37	40-20	47-31	47-31	54-24		48-30	44-34	58-20	58-20	58-20	48-30	46-32	50-28	60-18	47-31	45-33
KING'S LYNN	44-34	43-35	41-37	42-36	49-29	43-34	48-29	41-37		44-34	39-38	49-29	52-26	50-28	35-42	44-34	40-38	38-40	57-21
LEICESTER	43-35	44-34	42-35	40-38	46-32	47-31	53-25	49-29	40-38		49-29	52-26	54-24	47-31	46-32	48-30	38-40	37-41	58-20
NEWCASTLE	38-39	41-37	51-26	53-25	47-31	41-37	44-34	39-39	46-32	36-42		44-33	56-21	36-41	43-35	44-34	42-36	41-37	41-36
NEWPORT	42-36	35-43	43-35	46-32	36-42	43-35	45-33	48-30	41-36	39-39	51-26		51-27	32-46	47-31	41-37	40-37	36-42	44-34
OXFORD	44-34	48-30	46-32	33-45	46-32	46-32	50-28	†Lost	50-28	38-39	52-26	47-31		38-40	47-31	45-33	43-35	39-39	42-36
POOLE	48-29	42-36	41.5 36.5	58-20	43-34	46-32	57-21	44-34	40-38	46-32	44-34	49-29	51-27		51-27	48-29	55-23	43-35	44-34
SHEFFIELD	42-36	42-36	48-30	52-26	47-31	53-25	48-30	40-38	42-36	46-32	53-25	46-32	46-32	50-28		46-32	44-32	45-33	58-20
SWINDON	40-36	38-40	40-38	42-35	46-32	35-43	40-38	43-34	41-37	40-38	45-32	54-24	49-29	37-41	40-38		57-20	40-37	43-35
WEST HAM	38-40	40-38	32-46	44-34	47-31	39-39	41-37	39-39	41-37	41-37	43-35	43-35	38-40	37-41	41-37	40-38		38-40	29-49
WIMBLEDON	44-34	47-31	48-30	54-24	47-30	48-30	57-20	54-24	52-26	45-33	46-32	62-16	52-26	42-36	49.5 28.5	46-32	59-19		56-22
WOLVERHAMPTON	43-35	44-34	45-33	32-46	50-28	38-40	45-33	36-41	41-37	31-47	47-31	55-23	34-44	29-49	42-36	43-35	43-35	41-37	

† Oxford defeated Halifax 41-37 on April 17, 1969, but in September the Speedway Control Board declared the result void and awarded the match points to Halifax. §Result was amended from 50-28 to 51-27 by the referee after the end of the meeting.

1970 BRITISH LEAGUE TABLE

	P	W	D	L	PtsF	PtsA	W	D	L	PtsF	PtsA	Pts
1 BELLE VUE	**36**	**18**	**0**	**0**	**882.5**	**517.5**	**9**	**2**	**7**	**713**	**688**	**56**
2 Wimbledon	36	18	0	0	859	541	4	2	12	647	756	46
3 Coventry	36	17	1	0	880	521	5	0	13	637.5	766.5	45
4 Leicester	36	16	0	2	771	631	5	0	13	652	750	42
5 Poole	36	16	0	2	785	615	4	0	14	607	794	40
6 Halifax	36	17	0	1	855.5	547.5	2	1	15	637	766	39
7 Sheffield	36	14	2	2	797.5	606.5	4	1	13	617	785	39
8 Glasgow	36	17	1	0	832	570	1	0	17	606	797	37
9 Wolverhampton	36	15	1	2	791	612	1	1	16	580	821	34
10 Exeter	36	16	1	1	821	583	0	0	18	548.5	851.5	33
11 Hackney	36	15	1	2	778	625	0	1	17	591.5	810.5	32
12 King's Lynn	36	14	0	4	774	629	2	0	16	585	814	32
13 Oxford	36	14	0	4	772.5	631.5	2	0	16	588	814	32
14 Wembley	36	13	2	3	738	665	2	0	16	589.5	809.5	32
15 Cradley Heath	36	12	0	6	746.5	648.5	3	1	14	605	797	31
16 Swindon	36	13	1	4	778	623	1	1	16	608	795	30
17 Newcastle	36	15	0	3	794	610	0	0	18	570	834	30
18 West Ham	36	13	1	4	773	629	1	1	16	568.5	834.5	30
19 Newport	36	10	0	8	718	685	2	0	16	540	863	24

■ ***BELLE VUE broke Poole's record for the biggest winning points margin in the British League Division One.***

1970 British League Riders' Championship Final

Saturday, October 17, Belle Vue:
1 Barry Briggs 13, 2 Anders Michanek 13, 3 Eric Boocock 13, 4 Ronnie Moore 12, 5 Ivan Mauger 10, 6 Nigel Boocock 10, 7 Jim Airey 9, 8 Martin Ashby 7, 9 Reidar Eide 7, 10 Ole Olsen 5, Ray Wilson 5, 12 Bernt Persson 5, 13 Charlie Monk 4, 14 Terry Betts 4, 15 Hasse Holmkvist 1, Olle Nygren 1. *Reserves: Sandor Levai 1, Garry Middleton, Gordon Guasco, did not ride.*

1970 KNOCK OUT CUP

Round 1

Exeter 51 King's Lynn 27
West Ham 29 *Belle Vue 49*
WIMBLEDON 44 Hackney 34

Round 2

Belle Vue 49 Exeter 29
Halifax 43 Coventry 35
Newcastle 41 Wembley 37
Newport 35 Leicester 43
Oxford 38 Poole 40
Sheffield 44 Glasgow 34
Swindon 44 Wolverhampton 34
WIMBLEDON 49 Cradley Heath 29

Round 3

Belle Vue 56 Poole 22
Sheffield 41 Halifax 37
Swindon 46 Leicester 32
WIMBLEDON 46 Newcastle 32

Semi Finals

WIMBLEDON 44 Swindon 34
Belle Vue 40 Sheffield 38

FINAL

First leg, October 15:
WIMBLEDON 46 (Trevor Hedge 12, Ronnie Moore 11, Cyril Maidment 6, Jim Tebby 6, Reg Luckhurst 5, Bob Dugard 4, Peter Murray 2) *Belle Vue 31* (Tommy Roper 10, Ivan Mauger 8, Chris Pusey 6, Sören Sjösten 4, Ken Eyre 2, Steve Waplington 1, Mike Hiftle 0)
Second leg, October 24:
Belle Vue 44 (Mauger 12, Sjösten 10, Roper 6, Hiftle 6, Dave Hemus 4, Pusey 3, Eyre 3)
WIMBLEDON 34 (Moore 13, Hedge 10, Luckhurst 5, Tebby 2, Maidment 2, Dugard 1, Murray 1).

❑ WIMBLEDON win 80-75 on aggregate.

1970 ALL THE RESULTS

	BELLE VUE	COVENTRY	CRADLEY HEATH	EXETER	GLASGOW	HACKNEY	HALIFAX	KING'S LYNN	LEICESTER	NEWCASTLE	NEWPORT	OXFORD	POOLE	SHEFFIELD	SWINDON	WEMBLEY	WEST HAM	WIMBLEDON	WOLVES
BELLE VUE		49-29	54-23	50-28	48-30	44.5 33.5	51-27	41-37	40-38	54-24	55-22	49-29	53-25	44-34	43-35	48-28	54-24	54-24	51-27
COVENTRY	40-37		51-27	54-24	53-25	44-33	39-39	59-19	45-33	47-31	52-26	50-28	41-37	53-25	46-32	47-31	55-23	48-29	56-22
CRADLEY HEATH	34-44	40.5 37.5		42-35	47-31	47-31	37-40	41-36	33-44	40-38	42-36	49-29	46-31	37-41	51-27	37-40	42-36	44-34	37-38
EXETER	39-39	54-24	42-36		44-34	54-24	45-33	57-21	51-27	41-37	42-36	37-41	43-35	43-35	46-32	47-31	46-32	41-37	49-29
GLASGOW	43-34	45-33	44-34	43-35		53-24	45-33	47-31	41-37	48-30	59-19	44-34	48-30	44-34	39-39	45-33	43-35	43-35	58-20
HACKNEY	44-34	52-26	48-30	48-30	47-30		40-38	40-38	40-38	42-36	47-31	40-38	36-42	42-36	42-36	52-26	38-40	39-39	41-37
HALIFAX	37-41	49-29	45-33	52-26	42-36	43-35		46-32	42-36	47-31	55-23	54-24	56-22	46-32	49-28	47.5 30.5	51-27	44-34	50-28
KING'S LYNN	35-43	34-44	43-35	46-32	46-32	46-32	40-38		37-41	40-38	51-27	48-30	42-35	41-37	42-36	49-29	56-22	37-41	41-37
LEICESTER	41-37	38-40	44-34	42-35	41-37	47-31	40-38	34-43		48-30	52-26	40-38	42-36	46-32	40-38	45-33	48-30	43-35	40-38
NEWCASTLE	32-46	40-38	40-38	52-26	55-23	40-38	38-40	56-22	44-34		45-33	37-41	40-38	48-30	42-36	42-36	50-28	48-30	45-33
NEWPORT	37-41	34-44	34-44	41-37	37-41	41-37	42-36	40-38	35-43	43-35		49-28	37-41	38-40	44-34	45-33	45-33	34-44	42-36
OXFORD	37-41	41-37	38-40	46-32	43-35	50-28	40-38	42-36	48-30	46-32	36-42		50-28	51-27	49-29	42-36	39.5 38.5	32-46	42-36
POOLE	40-38	42-36	49-29	44-33	41-37	51-27	43-35	39-38	45-32	48-30	35-43	51-27		43-34	48-30	37-41	44-34	41-37	44-34
SHEFFIELD	40-38	34-44	39-39	44.5 33.5	44-34	47-31	47-31	46-32	45-33	51-27	51-27	50-28	38-40		46-32	43-35	39-39	48-30	45-33
SWINDON	38-40	42-36	33-43	57-21	40-38	41-37	41-37	40-37	43-35	51-27	56-22	43-34	37-41	39-39		48-29	43-35	38-40	48-30
WEMBLEY	39-39	41-37	42-36	45-33	42-36	41-37	40-38	38-40	37-41	40-38	45-33	42-36	40-38	38-39	41-37		47-31	41-37	39-39
WEST HAM	35-43	37-41	55-23	41-36	41-31	42-36	41-37	48-30	44-34	51-27	46-32	40-38	47-30	37-41	37-41	47-31		39-39	45-33
WIMBLEDON	44-33	51-27	44-33	61-17	45-33	40-38	48-30	48-29	42-36	50-28	54-24	49-29	50-28	50-28	44-34	43-34	48-30		48-30
WOLVERHAMPTON	33-45	43-35	52-26	43-35	41-37	39-39	49-29	52-26	38-40	47-31	40-38	42-36	48-30	45-33	46-32	45-33	46-31	42-36	

1971 BRITISH LEAGUE TABLE

	P	W	D	L	PtsF	PtsA	W	D	L	PtsF	PtsA	Pts
1 BELLE VUE	**36**	**17**	**0**	**1**	**879**	**519**	**8**	**1**	**9**	**704**	**698**	**51**
2 Leicester	36	13	1	4	795	607	9	2	7	695	702	47
3 Coventry	36	17	0	1	860	543	6	0	12	635	767	46
4 Sheffield	36	18	0	0	827.5	576.5	3	1	14	622.5	780.5	43
5 Swindon	36	13	1	4	766	636	6	2	10	647	756	41
6 Reading	36	15	2	1	810.5	589.5	3	2	13	627.5	771.5	40
7 Hackney	36	13	0	5	762	641	4	4	10	648	752	38
8 Newport	36	17	0	1	793	611	2	0	16	597	805	38
9 Wembley	36	14	1	3	810	594	3	2	13	623	778	37
10 Wimbledon	36	16	1	1	796.5	604.5	2	0	16	592.5	810.5	37
11 Poole	36	14	1	3	802	600	3	1	14	605	799	36
12 Wolverhampton	36	13	1	4	757	639	4	0	14	625	773	35
13 King's Lynn	36	12	2	4	746.5	654.5	4	0	14	650	752	34
14 Halifax	36	16	1	1	803	600	0	1	17	571	830	34
15 Exeter	36	14	0	4	793	607	2	0	16	586	817	32
16 Glasgow	36	14	1	3	804	599	1	0	17	599	802	31
17 Oxford	36	12	0	6	740	658	0	1	17	523.5	879.5	25
18 Cradley Heath	36	8	4	6	717	685	0	0	18	581	822	20
19 West Ham	36	9	1	8	708	696	0	0	18	528	875	19

■ ***BELLE VUE were the first club to successfully defend the title.***

1971 British League Riders' Championship Final

Saturday, October 16, Belle Vue:
1 Ivan Mauger 14, 2 Barry Briggs 12, 3 Jim McMillan 12, 4 Bob Kilby 10, 5 Nigel Boocock 9, 6 Eric Boocock 9, 7 Ole Olsen 8, 8 Christer Löfqvist 8, 9 Jim Airey 7, 10 Reidar Eide 6, 11 Ray Wilson 6, 12 Ronnie Moore 5, 13 Anders Michanek 5, 14 Sandor Levai 4, 15 Terry Betts 2, 16 Bengt Jansson 1. *Reserves: Bert Harkins, 2, Øyvind Berg, Roy Trigg, did not ride.*

1971 KNOCK OUT CUP

Round 1
Halifax 49 West Ham 29
Oxford 46 Poole 32
Swindon 43 Wimbledon 35

Round 2
Glasgow 43 Leicester 34
Halifax 42 Coventry 36
King's Lynn 46 Newport 32
Oxford 39 Exeter 38
Reading 38 *Cradley Heath 40*
Sheffield 48 Wembley 30
Swindon 36 HACKNEY 42
Wolverhampton 43 Belle Vue 35

Round 3
Cradley Heath 40 Glasgow 38
Halifax 43 Sheffield 35
King's Lynn 39 HACKNEY 39
Wolverhampton 45 Oxford 32

Round 3 Replay
HACKNEY 49 King's Lynn 29

Semi Finals
Cradley Heath 50 Wolverhampton 28
HACKNEY 50 Halifax 27

FINAL
First leg, October 4:
Cradley Heath 41 (Bernt Persson 11, Bob Andrews 9, Mick Handley 7, Pete Jarman 6, John Hart 5, Roy Trigg 3, Cyril Francis 0) HACKNEY 37 (Bengt Jansson 10, Barry Thomas 8, Hughie Saunders 8, Garry Middleton 7, Laurie Etheridge 2, Geoff Maloney 1, Eddie Reeves 1).
Second leg, October 8:
HACKNEY 51 (Jansson 12, Middleton 10, Thomas 9, Dave Kennett 9, Etheridge 4, Saunders 4, Reeves 3) *Cradley Heath 27* (Howard Cole 10, Hart 6, Andrews 5, Trigg 3, Jarman 2, Handley 1, Ralph Waller 0).

❑ HACKNEY win 88-68 on aggregate.

1971 ALL THE RESULTS

	BELLE VUE	COVENTRY	CRADLEY HEATH	EXETER	GLASGOW	HACKNEY	HALIFAX	KING'S LYNN	LEICESTER	NEWPORT	OXFORD	POOLE	READING	SHEFFIELD	SWINDON	WEMBLEY	WEST HAM	WIMBLEDON	WOLVES
BELLE VUE		43-35	46-32	51-27	46-32	42-36	48-30	42-36	35-37	48-30	61-17	46-32	46-32	48-30	55-23	59-19	55-23	59-19	49-29
COVENTRY	41-37		52-26	62-16	48-30	47-31	43-35	47-30	43-35	55-23	52-26	41-37	52-26	49-29	49-29	45-33	51-27	47-31	36-42
CRADLEY HEATH	33-45	44-34		39-38	38-40	39-39	49-29	34-44	39-39	40-37	39-39	41-37	38-40	41-37	36-42	39-39	49-29	37-41	42-36
EXETER	40-38	38-40	55-23		52-25	42-36	41-37	42-36	36-41	40-38	52-26	49-29	45-33	43-35	36-42	47-31	52-26	46-32	37-39
GLASGOW	32-46	49-29	47-30	40-38		52-26	39-39	35-43	47-31	41-37	54-24	37-41	51-27	41-37	50-28	45-33	54-24	49-29	41-37
HACKNEY	36-42	42-36	48-30	40-38	41-37		46-32	39-38	38-40	46-32	41-37	52-26	43-35	46-32	33-45	38-40	56-22	41-37	36-42
HALIFAX	41-37	43-35	42-36	44-34	41-37	49-29		49-29	34-44	46-31	50-28	55-23	46-32	39-39	40-38	48-30	42-36	50-28	44-34
KING'S LYNN	42-36	38-40	47-31	40-38	41-37	39-39	53-25		36-42	34-44	42-36	39-39	41-37	41.5 36.5	44-34	48-30	42-36	42-36	37-39
LEICESTER	38-40	44-33	43-35	48-30	47-31	47-30	57-21	42-36		49-29	47-31	38-40	37-41	38-40	47-31	39-39	48-30	41-37	45-33
NEWPORT	40-38	40-38	43-35	59-19	40-38	37-41	48-30	51-27	46-32		43-35	44-34	43-35	40-38	47-31	40-38	48-30	42-36	42-36
OXFORD	42-36	38-40	40-38	37-41	40-38	41-37	45-31	42-36	33-45	42-36		44-34	37-40	48-30	36-41	38-40	45-33	39-38	53-24
POOLE	52-26	50-28	52-26	43-35	56-20	38-40	43-35	42-36	41-37	48-30	49-29		39-39	38-40	40-38	44-34	46-32	36-42	45-33
READING	38-39	49-29	42-36	42-36	49-29	38-38	45-33	48-30	44-34	41-37	48.5 28.5	57-21		52-26	39-39	40-38	46-32	51-27	41-37
SHEFFIELD	41-37	43-35	43-35	42-36	46-32	44-34	46-32	40-38	44-34	44-34	61-17	48-30	43-35		47-31	44-34	56-22	45.5 32.5	50-28
SWINDON	36-41	48-30	42-36	37-41	43-35	39-39	42-36	35-43	38-40	47-31	49-29	42-36	45-33	41-37		43-34	47-31	50-28	42-36
WEMBLEY	30-48	37-41	51-27	54-24	44-34	50-28	52-26	47-31	39-39	45-33	44-34	37-41	46-32	45-33	43-35		49-29	49-29	48-30
WEST HAM	34-44	36-42	46-32	40-38	40-38	32-46	42-36	41-37	37-41	38-40	52-26	40-38	39-39	38-40	37-41	32-46		41-37	43-35
WIMBLEDON	43-35	50-28	40-38	46-32	47-31	33-44	48-30	41-37	40-38	52-26	52-26	47-31	40.5 37.5	48-30	39-39	45-33	43-34		42-35
WOLVERHAMPTON	39-39	35-42	43-35	53-25	43-35	43-35	43-34	35-43	32-46	49-29	43-35	42-36	40-34	44-34	38-40	44-32	46-32	45-33	

1972 BRITISH LEAGUE TABLE

	P	W	D	L	PtsF	PtsA	W	D	L	PtsF	PtsA	Pts
1 BELLE VUE	**34**	**17**	**0**	**0**	**873.5**	**449.5**	**14**	**1**	**2**	**719**	**602**	**63**
2 Reading	34	17	0	0	806	518	8	1	8	648	676	51
3 King's Lynn	34	16	0	1	769	556	8	3	6	663	663	51
4 Sheffield	34	13	1	3	804	521	10	2	5	684	642	49
5 Leicester	34	14	1	2	748	578	3	4	10	617	709	39
6 Ipswich	34	11	1	5	728	594	6	0	11	604	719	35
7 Poole	34	13	1	3	746	579	2	1	14	561	763	32
8 Hackney	34	14	0	3	754	569	2	0	15	552	772	32
9 Wolverhampton	34	14	0	3	729	595	2	0	15	573	753	32
10 Coventry	34	12	2	3	756	568	2	0	15	571	749	30
11 Exeter	34	12	1	4	735.5	590.5	1	1	15	556	767	28
12 Halifax	34	12	2	3	713	612	1	0	16	548	776	28
13 Wimbledon	34	14	0	3	724	597	0	0	17	501	824	28
14 Glasgow	34	11	2	4	730	595	1	0	16	533	790	26
15 Swindon	34	12	1	4	736	589	0	0	17	578	748	25
16 Cradley Heath	34	10	2	5	679	646	1	1	15	555.5	770.5	25
17 Oxford	34	10	0	7	697	625	0	0	17	503.5	818.5	20
18 Newport	34	9	0	8	658	666	0	0	17	481	844	18

■ ***BELLE VUE are the only club in British League history to have won the First Division championship three years in succession.***

1972 British League Riders' Championship Final

Saturday, October 18, Belle Vue:
1 Ole Olsen 15, 2 Martin Ashby 14, 3 Ronnie Moore 13, 4 John Louis 11, 5 Anders Michanek 9, 6 Terry Betts 9, 7 Ivan Mauger 8, 8 Garry Middleton 8, 9 Christer Löfqvist 7, 10 Bernt Persson 6, 11 Ray Wilson 5, 12 Bengt Jansson 4, 13 Bob Kilby 3, 14 Eric Boocock 3, 15 Nigel Boocock 2, 16 Arnold Haley 1. *Reserves: Jim McMillan 2, Tony Clarke, did not ride.*

1972 KNOCK OUT CUP

Round 1
Exeter 48 Swindon 30
Halifax 42 Leicester 36
Ipswich 46 Sheffield 32

Round 2
BELLE VUE 41 Glasgow 37
Cradley Heath 39 *Hackney 39*
Exeter 50 Wimbledon 28
Newport 42 Coventry 35
Oxford 35 King's Lynn 42
Poole 52 Halifax 26
Wolverhampton 38 Reading 40
Ipswich – bye

Round 2 Replay
Hackney 52 Cradley Heath 26

Round 3
BELLE VUE 58 Newport 20
Hackney 45 Poole 33
Ipswich 38 Reading 40
King's Lynn 56 Exeter 22

Semi Finals
Hackney 40 Reading 38
King's Lynn 38 BELLE VUE 40

FINAL
First leg, October 20:
Hackney 40 (Bengt Jansson 12, Barry Thomas 9, Geoff Maloney 7, David Kennett 6, Eddie Reeves 4, Laurie Etheridge 2, Hugh Saunders 0) BELLE VUE 37 (Alan Wilkinson 11, Ivan Mauger 10, Peter Collins 6, Sören Sjösten 6, Chris Pusey 3, Eric Broadbelt 1, Ken Eyre 0).
Second leg, October 25:
BELLE VUE 45 (Sjösten 10, Pusey 9, Mauger 8, Eyre 7, Collins 5, Wilkinson 4, Broadbelt 2) *Hackney 33* (Jansson 12, Maloney 10, Thomas 6, Kennett 3, Saunders 2, Etheridge 0, Reeves 0)

❑ BELLE VUE win 82-73 on aggregate.

1972 ALL THE RESULTS

	BELLE VUE	COVENTRY	CRADLEY HEATH	EXETER	GLASGOW	HACKNEY	HALIFAX	IPSWICH	KING'S LYNN	LEICESTER	NEWPORT	OXFORD	POOLE	READING	SHEFFIELD	SWINDON	WIMBLEDON	WOLVERHAMPTON
BELLE VUE		47-30	47.5-30.5	59-19	46-32	53-25	56-21	57-21	43-35	52-26	56-22	55-22	51-27	53-25	48-30	45-33	55-23	50-28
COVENTRY	32-45		49-29	42-36	50-28	47-31	48-30	38-39	49-29	39-39	50-28	59-19	39-39	40-38	38-40	45-33	48-30	43-35
CRADLEY HEATH	29-49	43-34		39-39	40-38	37-41	41-37	35-43	41-37	39-39	60-18	43-35	41-37	33-45	29-49	41-37	46-32	42-36
EXETER	38-40	49-29	51-27		41-37	52-26	35-43	51-27	39-39	38-40	44-34	46.5-31.5	40-38	41-37	35-43	46-32	47-31	42-36
GLASGOW	34-44	45-33	39-39	42-35		43-35	45-33	43-35	38-40	39-39	56-22	43-35	51-27	37-41	28-50	43-35	51-27	53-25
HACKNEY	35-43	48-29	51-27	45-32	51-27		50-28	41-37	37-41	46-32	40-38	60-18	40-37	41-37	38-40	40-38	46-32	45-33
HALIFAX	39-39	41-37	49-29	42-36	47-30	44-34		37-41	37-41	44-34	40-38	47-31	40-38	41-37	39-39	44-34	44-34	38-40
IPSWICH	36-42	44-34	51-27	38-40	45-32	41-36	45-33		39-39	38-40	52-26	43-34	41-36	38-40	31-47	49-29	56-22	41-37
KING'S LYNN	35-43	42-36	44-34	49-29	46-32	41-37	42-36	44-34		40-38	59-19	50-28	57-21	40-38	42-36	51-27	44-33	43-35
LEICESTER	38-40	47-31	41-37	44-34	44-34	48-30	46-32	50-28	42-36		42-36	44-34	49-29	39-39	38-40	45-33	47-31	44-34
NEWPORT	31-46	38-40	36-42	40-38	46-32	43-35	41-37	37-41	24-54	41-37		48-29	37-41	32-46	30-48	42-36	42-36	50-28
OXFORD	35-43	36-41	45-33	43-35	50-27	47-30	45-33	40-38	33-45	38-40	51-27		36-42	35-42	36-42	43-35	43-35	41-37
POOLE	33-44	40-38	53-25	54-24	44-34	51-27	46-32	47-31	35-43	40-38	42-36	49-29		36-42	39-39	45-33	51-27	41-37
READING	40-37	55-23	45-33	47-31	51-27	48-30	44-34	41-36	49-29	49-29	53-25	43-35	50-28		47-31	44-34	49-29	51-27
SHEFFIELD	37-41	41-37	41-37	52-26	58-20	48-30	45-33	38-39	39-39	40-38	54-24	58-20	56-22	56-22		45-33	58-20	38-40
SWINDON	36-42	47-30	42-36	48-30	45-33	38-40	54-24	41-37	44-34	39-39	46-32	43-35	50-28	34-44	38-40		45-33	46-32
WIMBLEDON	43-34	44-34	46-32	40-37	38-40	40-38	44-33	41-37	37-41	45-33	55-22	41-36	44-34	38-40	43-35	40-38		45-33
WOLVERHAMPTON	31-47	42-35	40-38	43-35	48-30	51-27	49-29	38-40	37-41	42-36	44-34	46-32	41-37	42-36	43-35	40-38	52-26	

1973 BRITISH LEAGUE TABLE

	P	W	D	L	PtsF	PtsA	W	D	L	PtsF	PtsA	Pts
1 READING	**34**	**15**	**1**	**1**	**815**	**510**	**10**	**0**	**7**	**679**	**646**	**51**
2 Sheffield	34	16	1	0	861	463	6	2	9	628	694	47
3 King's Lynn	34	15	0	2	763	560	5	3	9	632	693	43
4 Leicester	34	16	0	1	788	536	5	0	12	606	718	42
5 Ipswich	34	17	0	0	800	523	2	3	12	593	732	41
6 Belle Vue	34	16	0	1	842	477	3	1	13	609	711	39
7 Wolverhampton	34	14	1	2	720	605	4	0	13	599	726	37
8 Exeter	34	14	1	2	780	544	2	2	13	564.5	759.5	35
9 Halifax	34	14	1	2	722	603	2	1	14	533	791	34
10 Newport	34	16	0	1	807.5	516.5	0	0	17	543	779	32
11 Oxford	34	13	1	3	749	574	1	1	15	518	807	30
12 Wimbledon	34	12	1	4	725	600	2	0	15	538	783	29
13 Swindon	34	10	3	4	675	650	3	0	14	569	757	29
14 Poole	34	9	1	7	711	615	4	1	12	589	736	28
15 Coventry	34	13	0	4	713	611	0	0	17	520	804	26
16 Hackney	34	10	3	4	700	625	1	1	15	527	796	26
17 Coatbridge	34	11	1	5	710	608	1	0	16	509	813	25
18 Cradley United	34	6	2	9	651	672	1	2	14	536	787	18

■ ***READING became the first former Division Two side to be elevated to the British League First Division and to go on to win the championship.***

1973 British League Riders' Championship Final

Saturday, November 3, Belle Vue:
1 Ivan Mauger 14, 2 Ray Wilson 11, 3 Anders Michanek 11, 4 Ole Olsen 11, 5 Arnold Haley 11, 6 Martin Ashby 10, 7 Jim McMillan 10,8 John Louis 8, 9 Sören Sjösten 7, 10 Trevor Hedge 6, 11 Barry Thomas 5, 12 Garry Middleton 5, 13 Malcolm Simmons 5, 14 Reidar Eide 3, 15 Howard Cole 3, 16 Pete Smith 0. *Reserves: Bill Andrew 0, Gordon Kennett 0.*
Sponsors: Players No 10.

1973 KNOCK OUT CUP

Round 1
Coventry 73 (44 29) Reading 83 (34 49)
Oxford 71 (41 30) BELLE VUE 85 (37 48)

Round 2
BELLE VUE 92 (43 49) Sheffield 64 (35 29)
Coatbridge 63 (41 22) *Reading 93 (37 56)*
Cradley United 75 (37 38) Poole 81 (41 40)
Exeter 72 (37 35) Wolverhampton 84 (41 43)
Hackney 78 (43 35) Swindon 78 (35 43)
Ipswich 74 (41 33) Newport 82 (37 45)
King's Lynn 84 (42 42) Leicester 72 (36 36)
Wimbledon 66 (37 29) Halifax 90 (41 49)

Round 2 Replay
Hackney 68 (43 25) Swindon 87 (35 52)

Round 3
BELLE VUE 94 (57 37) Halifax 62 (21 41)
King's Lynn 86 (47 39) Poole 70 (31 39)
Reading 88 (55 33) Newport 68 (23 45)
Wolverhampton 82 (43 39) Swindon 74 (35 39)

Semi Finals
Reading 90 (52 38) King's Lynn 66 (26 40)
Wolverhampton 72 (42 30) BELLE VUE 84 (36 48)

FINAL
First leg, October 1:
Reading 47 (Anders Michanek 11, Dag Lovaas 11, Geoff Curtis 9, Mick Bell 7, Bobby McNeil 4, Richard May 4, Bernie Leigh 1) BELLE VUE 31 (Peter Collins 12, Paul Tyrer 7, Eric Broadbelt 6, John Louis 3, Alan Wilkinson 2, Sören Sjösten 1, Chris Morton 0).
Second leg, October 24:
BELLE VUE 47 (Collins 10, Jim McMillan 8, Sjösten 8, Wilkinson 8, Broadbelt 7, Tyrer 6, Morton 0) *Reading 31* (Michanek 12, Lovaas 8, Bell 6, Mitch Graham 5, Leigh 0, Trevor Geer 0, Paul Gachet, did not ride).
❑ BELLE VUE win 78-78 on aggregate. Collins defeated Michanek in a run-off at the second leg.
†For the first time all rounds were run over two legs.

1973 ALL THE RESULTS

	BELLE VUE	COATBRIDGE	COVENTRY	CRADLEY UNITED	EXETER	HACKNEY	HALIFAX	IPSWICH	KING'S LYNN	LEICESTER	NEWPORT	OXFORD	POOLE	READING	SHEFFIELD	SWINDON	WIMBLEDON	WOLVERHAMPTON
BELLE VUE		38-37	59-19	50-27	42-36	55-23	51-27	51-27	51-27	54-22	52-26	53-25	48-30	55-23	38-40	46-32	55-22	44-33
COATBRIDGE	34-40		42-35	47-31	40-37	52-26	38-40	46-32	41-37	42-36	46-31	49-29	36-42	40-37	39-39	37-41	43-35	38-40
COVENTRY	42-35	52-26		32-46	46-32	41-37	58-20	36-42	42-36	43-35	40-38	50-28	41-36	30-48	40-38	41-37	42-36	37-41
CRADLEY UNITED	39-39	37-41	45-33		36-42	41-37	42-35	39-39	40-38	33-45	44-34	38-40	35-43	30-48	36-41	48-30	32-45	36-42
EXETER	28-50	59-19	55-23	45-32		56-22	42-36	39-39	39-38	35-43	56-22	49-29	45-33	46-32	49-29	50-28	46-32	41-37
HACKNEY	41-37	43-35	46-31	39-39	44-34		43-35	39-39	30-48	41-37	45-33	48-30	36-42	28-50	39-39	48-30	38-40	52-26
HALIFAX	44-34	47-31	42-36	44-34	40-38	49-29		46-32	39-39	43-35	40-38	46-32	36-42	41-37	37-40	45-33	43-35	40-38
IPSWICH	45-33	49-29	48-30	48-30	46-32	40-37	53-25		51-27	42-36	48-30	51-27	47-31	44-34	42-34	47-31	55-23	44-34
KING'S LYNN	45-33	47-31	47-31	47-31	58-20	40-36	37-41	40-38		48-30	39-38	55-23	43-35	36-42	41-37	41-37	54-24	45-33
LEICESTER	46-32	50-28	47-31	52-25	52-26	49-29	49-29	42-36	36-42		44-33	49-29	51-27	46-32	45-33	42-36	45-33	43-35
NEWPORT	41-37	43-35	56-22	54-24	42.5 34.5	51-27	56-22	49-29	45-33	53-25		43-34	57-21	33-45	44-34	48-30	52-26	40-38
OXFORD	40-38	50-28	40-38	59-19	45-33	43-35	48-29	37-41	39-39	44-34	51-26		42-36	30-48	38-40	44-34	47-30	52-26
POOLE	29-49	47-31	54-24	42-36	37-41	54-24	48-30	43-35	36-42	38-40	45-33	39-39		36-42	38-40	38-40	44-34	43-35
READING	46-32	55-22	52-26	53-25	58-20	47-31	59-19	50-28	39-39	44-34	47-31	45-33	41-37		37-41	47-31	54-24	41-37
SHEFFIELD	48-30	59-19	46-32	47-31	53-25	57-21	39-39	56-22	52-26	45-33	57-21	56-22	50-28	43-35		51-27	51-26	51-26
SWINDON	42-35	43-35	44-34	39-39	39-39	37-41	42-36	40-38	33-45	35-43	40-38	40-38	39-39	35-43	44-34		42-36	41-37
WIMBLEDON	46-32	52-26	41-37	46-32	42-36	39-39	41-37	39-38	35-43	35-43	45-33	55-23	45-33	35-43	45-33	46-32		38-40
WOLVERHAMPTON	55-23	42-36	40-38	43-35	39-39	45-33	45-33	40-38	45-33	43-35	40-38	41-37	44-34	38-40	42-36	38-40	40-37	

1974 BRITISH LEAGUE TABLE

	P	W	D	L	PtsF	PtsA	W	D	L	PtsF	PtsA	Pts
1 EXETER	**32**	**16**	**0**	**0**	**760**	**485**	**9**	**1**	**6**	**615**	**632**	**51**
2 Belle Vue	32	16	0	0	795	453	7	0	9	585	653	46
3 Ipswich	32	15	0	1	741	505	7	1	8	623	623	45
4 Sheffield	32	16	0	0	824	424	5	0	11	602	643	42
5 King's Lynn	32	14	1	1	713	535	6	0	10	568	675	41
6 Newport	32	15	0	1	742	506	2	3	11	557	691	37
7 Halifax	32	13	1	2	694	554	1	2	13	515	732	31
8 Wimbledon	32	13	1	2	731	509	1	0	15	469	778	29
9 Hackney	32	10	1	5	670	574	3	1	12	548	699	28
10 Leicester	32	11	1	4	676	572	2	0	14	534	710	27
11 Wolverhampton	32	9	1	6	633.5	609.5	4	0	12	524	723	27
12 Swindon	32	11	2	3	674	574	1	0	15	505	742	26
13 Cradley United	32	8	1	7	648	598	4	0	12	523	724	25
14 Poole	32	12	0	4	665	580	0	1	15	482	764	25
15 Coventry	32	10	0	6	636	607	2	0	14	511	735	24
16 Hull	32	10	0	6	708	530	0	0	16	504	739	20
17 Oxford	32	8	0	8	651.5	594.5	2	0	14	545	699	20

■ *EXETER are the only club to have literally won the British League championship as a result of a protest. They were declared champions on Monday, October 21, when the Speedway Control Board upheld their protest which turned a 40-38 defeat at Wolverhampton into a 41-37 title clinching victory!*

1974 British League Riders' Championship Final

Saturday, October 19, Belle Vue:
1 Peter Collins 15, 2 Ivan Mauger 12, 3 Phil Crump 12, 4 John Louis 11, 5 Bob Valentine 11, 6 Dave Jessup 10, 7 Martin Ashby 8, 8 Barry Briggs 7, 9 George Hunter 7, 10 Jim McMillan 6, 11 John Boulger 6, 12 Eric Boocock 5, 13 Bob Kilby 4, 14 Dag Lovaas 13, 15 Terry Betts 2, 16 Nigel Boocock 1. *Reserves: Eric Broadbelt, Sören Sjösten and Reidar Eide did not ride.*

1974 KNOCK OUT CUP

Preliminary Round

Oxford 68 (40 28) *Ipswich 87 (37 50)*
Wolverhampton 86 (48 38) Cradley United 70 (30 40)

Round 1

Halifax 60 (35 25) Belle Vue 96 (43 53)
Ipswich 92 (52 40) Wimbledon 64 (26 38)
King's Lynn 87 (45 42) Wolverhampton 69 (33 36)
Leicester 79 (43 36) Coventry 77 (35 42)
Newport 80 (42 38) Swindon 76 (36 40)
Poole 80 (42 38) Hackney 76 (36 40)
SHEFFIELD 92 (52 40) Hull 64 (26 38)
Exeter - bye, after Reading withdrew from the League.

Round 2

Exeter 78 (46 32) Belle Vue 76 (32 44)
Ipswich 82 (42 40) Leicester 74 (36 38)
King's Lynn 78 (38 40) Poole 78 (40 38)
Newport 67 (35 32) SHEFFIELD 89 (43 46)

Round 2 Replay

Poole 81 (45 36) King's Lynn 74 (32 42)

Semi Finals

Exeter 70 (42 28) *Ipswich 86 (36 50)*
Poole 69 (37 32) SHEFFIELD 86 (40 46)

FINAL

First leg, October 6:
Ipswich 37 (John Louis 11, Billy Sanders 10, Tony Davey 6, Mick Hines 5, Ted Howgego 3, Alan Sage 2, Trevor Jones 0) SHEFFIELD 41 (Arnold Haley 13, Bob Valentine 11, Doug Wyer 8, Reg Wilson 6, Craig Pendlebury 2, Bob Paulson 1, Carl Glover 0).
Second leg, October 7:
SHEFFIELD 49 (Valentine 11, Wyer 8, Haley 8, Pendlebury 8, Wilson 7, Glover 6, Paulson 1) *Ipswich 29* (Louis 13, Davey 9, Sanders 3, Hines 2, Mike Lanham 1, Howgego 1, Sage 0).

❑ SHEFFIELD win 90-66.

1974 ALL THE RESULTS

	BELLE VUE	COVENTRY	CRADLEY UNITED	EXETER	HACKNEY	HALIFAX	HULL	IPSWICH	KING'S LYNN	LEICESTER	NEWPORT	OXFORD	POOLE	SHEFFIELD	SWINDON	WIMBLEDON	WOLVERHAMPTON
BELLE VUE		59-19	50-28	46-32	49-29	54-24	52-26	48-30	56-22	51-27	45-33	42-36	48-30	46-32	53-25	53-25	43-35
COVENTRY	45-32		43-35	40-38	36-42	44-34	48-30	36-42	35-43	28-50	42-36	40-35	43-35	34-43	42-36	42-36	38-40
CRADLEY UNITED	35-43	43-35		37-41	29-49	44-34	42-36	35-43	38-40	38-40	39-39	38-40	49-29	41-37	44-33	49-29	47-30
EXETER	44-34	50-28	43-35		49-29	56-22	51-24	42-36	44-34	49-29	43-35	50-28	53-25	45-33	46-32	50-28	45-33
HACKNEY	37-41	43-35	42-36	38-40		39-39	48-30	30-47	38-40	47-28	40-38	41-37	43-35	37-41	49-29	49-29	49-29
HALIFAX	31-47	40-38	43-35	40-38	46-32		42-36	42-36	47-31	42-36	39-39	42-36	50-28	35-43	49-29	52-26	54-24
HULL	60-9	58-20	37-41	34-44	44-34	49-29		31-46	36-42	42-36	51-27	40-38	58-20	45-33	48-30	38-40	37-41
IPSWICH	54-24	41-37	53-25	36-41	48-30	48-30	44-34		44-33	44-34	51-27	48-30	50-28	40-38	40-38	56-22	44-34
KING'S LYNN	41-37	49-29	38-40	40-38	42-36	51-27	42-36	39-39		46-32	51-27	42-36	41-37	43-35	44-34	55-23	49-29
LEICESTER	40-38	47-31	48-30	39-39	42-36	35-43	51-27	37-41	43-35		41-37	46-32	44-34	23-55	53-25	51-27	36-42
NEWPORT	41-37	52-26	51-27	37-41	45-33	40-38	45-33	51-27	47-31	50-28		41-37	57-21	44-34	42-36	51-27	48-30
OXFORD	32-46	48-29	36.5 41.5	38-40	34-44	41-37	50-28	30-48	48-30	47-31	34-44		52-26	35-43	36-42	43-34	47-31
POOLE	37-41	36-42	45-33	38-40	44-34	41-37	43-34	42-36	42-36	43-34	40-38	45-32		45-33	43-35	43-35	38-40
SHEFFIELD	40-38	44-34	62-16	51-27	61-17	51-27	42-36	43-35	47-31	56-22	52-26	58-20	52-26		55-23	57-21	53-25
SWINDON	38-40	45-33	49-29	38-40	41-37	39-39	49-29	40-38	41-37	44-34	39-39	32-46	46-32	44-34		45-33	44-34
WIMBLEDON	35-43	49-29	45-32	43-35	50-27	55-23	50-27	41-37	33-41	40-38	51-27	48-30	39-39	46-31	55-23		51-27
WOLVERHAMPTON	43-35	31-46	38.5 39.5	†37-41	39-39	45-32	40-38	36-42	36-42	43-35	33-45	46-32	39-37	40-37	43-35	44-34	

†The result was amended on protest after finishing 40-38 on track as Wolverhampton illegally used Ricky Day.

1975 BRITISH LEAGUE TABLE

	P	W	D	L	PtsF	PtsA	W	D	L	PtsF	PtsA	Pts
1 IPSWICH	**34**	**17**	**0**	**0**	**802**	**522**	**9**	**1**	**7**	**656**	**670**	**53**
2 Belle Vue	34	17	0	0	819	507	8	2	7	669	657	52
3 Newport	34	17	0	0	883	442	7	1	9	655	670	49
4 Exeter	34	14	0	3	762	564	6	3	8	648	676	43
5 Sheffield	34	15	0	2	760	564	6	0	11	608	717	42
6 Reading	34	16	0	1	754	571	5	0	12	588	737	42
7 Oxford	34	14	0	3	757	563	4	0	13	613	711	36
8 Leicester	34	14	1	2	733	593	2	3	12	615	710	36
9 Wimbledon	34	13	1	3	728	596	3	1	13	589	735	34
10 Halifax	34	12	2	3	707	618	3	1	13	582	744	33
11 Cradley United	34	12	2	3	736	588	3	0	14	552	768	32
12 King's Lynn	34	10	2	5	716	609	4	1	12	579	746	31
13 Wolverhampton	34	11	1	5	691	635	2	0	15	546	779	27
14 Hull	34	9	2	6	691	634	1	2	14	567	759	24
15 Poole	34	9	2	6	691	635	1	1	15	549	776	23
16 Coventry	34	8	2	7	673.5	651.5	1	0	16	503	822	20
17 Hackney	34	8	1	8	685	641	1	0	16	536.5	788.5	19
18 Swindon	34	8	0	9	652	672	0	0	17	550	775	16

1975 British League Riders' Championship Final

Saturday, October 18, Belle Vue:
1 Peter Collins 15, 2 Phil Crump 12, 3 Martin Ashby 11, 4 John Louis 11, 5 Doug Wyer 10, 6 Chris Pusey 9, 7 Malcolm Simmons 9, 8 Dave Jessup 8, 9 Anders Michanek 8, 10 Ivan Mauger 6, 11 Tommy Jansson 6, 12 Terry Betts 5, 13 Jim McMillan 4, 14 Dag Lovaas 3, 15 Bob Valentine 3, 16 John Boulger 0.
Reserve: Dave Morton, did not ride.
Sponsor: Skol.

1975 KNOCK OUT CUP

Preliminary Round
Exeter 81 (47 34) Sheffield 75 (31 44)
Wolverhampton 66 (37 29) BELLE VUE 90 (41 49)

Round 1
BELLE VUE 85 (49 36) Ipswich 70 (28 42)
Coventry 51 (33 18) Oxford 105 (45 60)
Hackney 71 (40 31) *Leicester 85 (38 47)*
Hull 77 (46 31) Swindon 79 (32 47)
King's Lynn 74 (42 32) Cradley United 82 (36 46)
Newport 86 (46 40) Reading 70 (32 38)
Poole 76 (41 35) Exeter 80 (37 43)
Wimbledon 69 (49 20) Halifax 87 (29 58)

Round 2
BELLE VUE 87 (45 42) Oxford 69 (33 36)
Cradley United 80 (51 29) Newport 76 (27 49)
Halifax 82 (47 35) Exeter 74 (31 43)
Leicester 85 (42 43) Swindon 71 (36 35)

Semi Finals
Cradley United 66 (32 34) BELLE VUE 89 (45 44)
Leicester 87 (47 40) Halifax 68 (31 37)

FINAL
First leg, October 7:
Leicester 38 (Dave Jessup 11, Ila Teromaa 10, Ray Wilson 9, Frank Auffret 6, Doug Underwood 2, Tony Lomas 0, Keith White 0) BELLE VUE 40 (Peter Collins 12, Chris Morton 9, Sören Sjösten 7, Alan Wilkinson 4, Geoff Pusey 4, Russ Hodgson 3, Paul Tyrer 1).
Second leg, October 22:
BELLE VUE 46 (Collins 12, Sjösten 8, Tyrer 8, Wilkinson 8, Morton 7, Hodgson 2, Pusey 1) *Leicester 32* (Jessup 8, Wilson 7, Underwood 6, Auffret 6, Lomas 3, Teromaa 1, White 1).

❑ BELLE VUE win 86-70 on aggregate.

1975 ALL THE RESULTS

	BELLE VUE	COVENTRY	CRADLEY UNITED	EXETER	HACKNEY	HALIFAX	HULL	IPSWICH	KING'S LYNN	LEICESTER	NEWPORT	OXFORD	POOLE	READING	SHEFFIELD	SWINDON	WIMBLEDON	WOLVERHAMPTON
BELLE VUE		49-29	42-36	55-23	49-29	42-36	46-32	50-28	46-32	47-31	49-29	42-36	45-33	50-28	51-27	48-30	53-25	55-23
COVENTRY	30-48		44-34	42-36	44.5 33.5	35-43	39-39	41-37	39-39	38-40	33-45	52-26	41-37	38-40	37-41	44-34	41-37	35-42
CRADLEY UNITED	39-39	58-20		39-39	42-36	47-31	51-27	38-40	45-33	42-35	45-32	40-38	44-34	35-43	43-35	43-35	35-43	50-28
EXETER	41-37	58-20	30-48		55-23	41-37	51-27	45-33	46-32	45-33	36-42	†43-35	46-32	43-35	42-36	47-31	43-35	50-28
HACKNEY	35-43	43-35	58-20	39-39		52-26	41-37	31-47	38-40	30-48	43-35	37-41	36-42	35-43	42-36	49-29	34-44	42-36
HALIFAX	34-44	40-38	45-33	43-35	43-35		39-39	35-43	42-36	39-39	47-31	44-34	49-29	44-34	33-44	42-36	47-31	41-37
HULL	39-39	42-36	47-31	36-42	42-36	39-39		37-41	36-41	43-35	35-43	40-38	49-29	36-42	38-40	43-35	42-36	47-31
IPSWICH	42-36	53-25	45-33	42-36	46-32	59-19	50-28		50-28	42-36	42-36	40-38	43-34	50-27	55-23	47-31	50-28	46-32
KING'S LYNN	36-42	52-25	36-42	35-43	52-26	41-37	37-41	33-45		39-39	40-38	41-37	39-39	48-30	41-37	41-37	51-27	54-24
LEICESTER	40-38	45-33	49-29	37-41	43-35	34-44	43-35	39-39	47-31		43-35	43-35	43-35	45-33	43-35	46-32	48-30	45-33
NEWPORT	55-23	58-20	49-29	40-38	58-20	53-25	46-32	56-22	52-26	52-26		52-26	56-22	51-27	61-17	47-31	47-30	50-28
OXFORD	34-44	58-20	58-14	35-43	44-34	49-29	49-29	40-38	49-29	40-38	36-42		44-34	46-32	44-34	44-34	44-34	43-35
POOLE	37-41	42-36	48-30	42-36	46-32	46-32	42-36	36-42	43-35	39-39	39-39	45-33		37-41	31-47	45-33	36-42	37-41
READING	41-37	48-30	40-38	43-34	53-25	42-36	48-30	36-42	46-32	41-37	42-36	41-37	50-28		41-37	50-28	40-38	52-26
SHEFFIELD	38-40	47-31	46-32	41-37	51-27	40-38	48-30	42-36	50-28	45-33	34-44	41-36	51-27	42-36		51-27	44-34	49-29
SWINDON	40-38	37-41	33-45	36-41	46-31	32-46	42-36	36-42	36-42	42-36	29-49	37-41	44-34	48-30	33-45		41-37	40-38
WIMBLEDON	36-42	45-33	53-25	39-39	40-38	52-26	45-33	44-34	35-43	43-35	40-38	42-35	50-28	42-36	37-41	42-36		43-35
WOLVERHAMPTON	40-38	47-31	45-33	32-46	34-44	40-38	42-36	31-47	46-32	43-35	37-41	31-47	46-32	47-31	45-33	46-32	39-39	

† Exeter lost the meeting on protest although the scoreline remains 43-35!

1976 BRITISH LEAGUE TABLE

	P	W	D	L	PtsF	PtsA	W	D	L	PtsF	PtsA	Pts
1 IPSWICH	**36**	**18**	**0**	**0**	**853**	**550**	**9**	**1**	**8**	**702**	**702**	**55**
2 Belle Vue	36	15	1	2	833	570	8	1	9	682	719	48
3 Exeter	36	18	0	0	792	607	5	2	11	668	731	48
4 Coventry	36	18	0	0	829.5	573.5	3	2	13	616.5	784.5	44
5 Swindon	36	15	3	0	828	574	4	1	13	634	769	42
6 Reading	36	14	2	2	795	609	5	1	12	682	716	41
7 Hackney	36	16	0	2	761	636	4	0	14	631	768	40
8 Newport	36	18	0	0	841.5	559.5	1	1	16	595	807	39
9 Cradley United	36	16	1	1	772	631	3	0	15	625	777	39
10 Poole	36	15	0	3	808	593	3	1	14	583	819	37
11 Wolverhampton	36	12	0	6	738	663	6	1	11	609	793	37
12 Hull	36	14	0	4	797	602	4	0	14	672.5	729.5	36
13 White City	36	13	1	4	794.5	609.5	3	2	13	643	758	35
14 King's Lynn	36	14	2	2	798	602	2	1	15	628	773	35
15 Halifax	36	14	1	3	771.5	630.5	0	0	18	533	870	29
16 Wimbledon	36	11	2	5	756	645	1	1	16	604.5	798.5	27
17 Sheffield	36	13	1	4	745	658	0	0	18	576	825	27
18 Birmingham	36	7	0	11	658	741	0	0	18	538.5	862.5	14
19 Leicester	36	5	1	12	683	719	0	0	18	550	852	11

1976 British League Riders' Championship Final

Saturday, October 16, Belle Vue:
1 Ole Olsen 14, 2 Peter Collins 14, 3 John Louis 13, 4 Martin Ashby 12, 5 Dave Jessup 11, 6 Phil Crump 8, 7 Chris Pusey 6, 8 Barry Briggs 6, 9 Ivan Mauger 5, 10 Doug Wyer 5, 11 Gordon Kennett 5, 12 Dave Morton 4, 13 Malcolm Simmons 2, 14 Terry Betts 2, 15 Jim McMillan 1, 16 John Boulger 0. *Reserves: Ila Teromaa 6, Mick Hines 3.*
Sponsor: Skol.

1976 KNOCK OUT CUP

Preliminary Round
Birmingham 68 (38 30) Wimbledon 88 (40 48)
Halifax 80 (41 39) Leicester 76 (37 39)
Wolverhampton 68 (38 30) Coventry 87 (39 48)

Round 1
Belle Vue 92 (49 43) Wimbledon 64 (29 35)
Hull 76 (44 32) Halifax 79 (33 46)
IPSWICH 83 (39 44) Cradley United 72 (38 34)
King's Lynn 84 (42 42) Sheffield 72 (36 36)
Newport 79 (47 32) Exeter 77 (31 46)
Reading 75 (37 38) Hackney 81 (41 40)
Swindon 90 (54 36) Poole 66 (24 42)
White City 81 (49 32) Coventry 75 (29 46)

Round 2
Hackney 74 (43 31) Halifax 82 (35 47)
King's Lynn 84 (44 40) White City 72 (34 38)
Newport 73 (40 33) Belle Vue 83 (38 45)
Swindon 77 (44 33) IPSWICH 79 (34 45)

Semi Final
IPSWICH 80 (43 37) Belle Vue 76 (35 41)
King's Lynn 81 (46 35) Halifax 74 (32 42)

FINAL
First leg, October 17:
King's Lynn 36 (Michael Lee 12, Ian Turner 11, Terry Betts 7, David Gagen 3, Ray Bales 2, Richard Hellsén 1, Adi Funk 0) IPSWICH 41 (John Louis 11, Dave Gooderham 8, Tony Davey 7, Billy Sanders 6, Mike Lanham 4, Ted Howgego 3, Kevin Jolly 2).
Second leg, October 18:
IPSWICH 50 (Louis 12, Sanders 10, Davey 8, Lanham 7, Gooderham 7, Howgego 3, Jolly 3)
King's Lynn 27 (Betts 10, Lee 9, Turner 5, Hellsén 2, Billy Spiers 1, Peter Smith 0, Gagen 0).

❑ IPSWICH win 91-63 on aggregate.

1976 ALL THE RESULTS

	BELLE VUE	BIRMINGHAM	COVENTRY	CRADLEY UNITED	EXETER	HACKNEY	HALIFAX	HULL	IPSWICH	KING'S LYNN	LEICESTER	NEWPORT	POOLE	READING	SHEFFIELD	SWINDON	WHITE CITY	WIMBLEDON	WOLVES
BELLE VUE		45-33	47-31	48-30	36-42	48-29	44-34	41-37	38-40	47-31	54-24	55-23	43-35	39-39	50-28	47-31	48-30	54-24	49-29
BIRMINGHAM	35-43		35-43	33-45	31-47	39-37	39-38	34-44	41-37	34-44	41-37	41-37	37-39	27-51	44-34	42-36	34-44	34-44	37-41
COVENTRY	40-38	45-33		47-31	41-37	41-37	47-31	41-37	41-37	44-34	50-28	52-26	52-26	46-32	42-35	54-24	47-31	46.5 31.5	53-25
CRADLEY UTD	48-30	52-26	39-39		40-38	42-36	41-37	39-38	45-33	43-35	44-34	43-35	47-31	40-38	43-35	40-38	41-37	48-30	37-41
EXETER	46-31	45-33	40-36	41-37		45-33	41-37	43-35	45-33	46-32	43-35	45-33	50-28	40-38	47-30	40-38	44-33	45-33	46-32
HACKNEY	38-40	50-28	41-37	43-35	45-33		44-34	42-35	29-49	41-36	40-38	42-36	46-32	45-30	45-32	41-37	41-36	45-33	43-35
HALIFAX	35-43	51-27	41.5 35.5	47-31	39-39	48-30		40-38	38-40	44-33	44-34	40-38	45-33	45-33	40-38	47-31	38-40	43-35	46-32
HULL	36-42	52-26	51-27	37-41	45-33	46-32	45-33		36-42	40-38	45-32	40-36	53-25	44-33	43-35	38-40	43-34	46-32	57-21
IPSWICH	41-37	45-33	54-24	47-30	46-32	49-29	56-22	49-29		47-31	48-30	46-32	48-30	50-28	46-32	53-25	42-36	42-36	44-34
KING'S LYNN	39-39	54-24	49-29	47-31	36-39	49-29	43-35	41-37	44-34		50-27	46-32	51-27	40-38	52-26	39-39	42-36	41-37	35-43
LEICESTER	38-40	42-36	38-40	35-43	38-40	36-42	44-34	32-46	36-42	39-39		50-28	35-43	30-47	41-37	35-43	35-43	43-35	36-41
NEWPORT	45-33	52.5 24.5	44-34	43-35	41-37	44-34	59-19	42-36	47-31	49-29	48-30		50-28	41-36	46-32	45-323	46-32	45-33	54-24
POOLE	38-39	42-36	49-29	41-37	43-34	43-35	58-20	41-37	37-41	55-23	59-19	41-37		38-40	44-34	42-36	41-37	46-32	50-27
READING	40-38	47-31	42-36	48-30	43-35	35-43	56-22	42-36	38-40	41-37	52-26	39-39	52-26		50-28	47-31	39-39	42-36	42-36
SHEFFIELD	48-30	43-35	46-32	42-35	42-36	43-35	45-33	36-42	40-38	40-38	43-35	31-47	43-35	37-41		45-33	44-34	39-39	38-40
SWINDON	40-38	52-26	39-39	45-33	39-39	42-35	51-27	45-33	39-39	45-33	44-34	54-24	48-30	41-37	53-25		47-31	52-25	52-26
WHITE CITY	46-32	51-27	45-33	53-25	46-32	42-36	60-18	33.5 44.5	42-36	38-40	51-27	49-29	39-39	41-37	43-35	35-43		45-33	35-43
WIMBLEDON	35-43	44-34	38-40	40-38	42-35	38-39	48-30	45-33	34-44	40-37	54-24	47-31	43-35	40-38	52-26	38-40	39-39		39-39
WOLVERHAMPTON	31-46	50-26	46-32	40-38	38-40	38-40	49-29	43-35	32-46	40-38	42-36	46-32	37-41	32-46	44-34	41-37	47-31	42-36	

1977 BRITISH LEAGUE TABLE

	P	W	D	L	PtsF	PtsA	W	D	L	PtsF	PtsA	Pts
1 WHITE CITY	**36**	**16**	**0**	**2**	**840**	**558**	**11**	**1**	**6**	**703**	**700**	**55**
2 Exeter	36	17	0	1	913	489	8	3	7	712	689	53
3 Reading	36	16	2	0	807	597	9	1	8	675	726	53
4 Ipswich	36	18	0	0	838	564	7	1	10	669	729	51
5 Belle Vue	36	12	2	4	782.5	619.5	7	1	10	691	711	41
6 King's Lynn	36	14	1	3	789	611	5	1	12	659	739	40
7 Cradley Heath	36	13	0	5	792.5	602.5	7	0	11	645	755	40
8 Coventry	36	16	1	1	837	561	3	0	15	617.5	779.5	39
9 Wimbledon	36	16	1	1	789	612	1	1	16	624	775	36
10 Poole	36	14	1	3	802	595	3	1	14	580	821	36
11 Swindon	36	16	1	1	832.5	569.5	1	0	17	591	810	35
12 Bristol	36	16	0	2	817	583	1	0	17	564	834	34
13 Sheffield	36	15	2	1	805.5	595.5	1	0	17	569	835	34
14 Hull	36	13	0	5	776	627	2	0	16	573.5	827.5	30
15 Wolverhampton	36	10	0	8	709	689	4	0	14	625	779	28
16 Hackney	36	13	0	5	733.5	659.5	0	1	17	523	878	27
17 Halifax	36	12	0	6	777	625	0	0	18	511	879	24
18 Birmingham	36	8	0	10	675	725	0	0	18	545	856	16
19 Leicester	36	6	0	12	678	723	0	0	18	528.5	807.5	12

1977 British League Riders' Championship Final

Saturday, October 15, Belle Vue:
1 Ole Olsen 14, 2 Peter Collins 14, 3 Michael Lee 13, 4 Ivan Mauger 12, 5 Ila Teromaa 11, 6 Edward Jancarz 9, 7 Jim McMillan 8, 8 Bob Kilby 7, 9 Doug Wyer 7, 10 Phil Herne 5, 11 Dave Jessup 5, 12 Chris Pusey 4, 13 Gordon Kennett 4, 14 Ray Wilson 3, 15 Graham Drury 2, 16 Billy Sanders 1.
Reserves: Steve Bastable, Keith White, did not ride.
Sponsor: Leyland.

1977 KNOCK OUT CUP

Preliminary Round
Leicester 67 (40 27) Wolverhampton 89 (38 51)
Reading 80 (43 37) Poole 76 (35 41)
Swindon 71 (43 28) Exeter 85 (35 50)

Round 1
Birmingham 61 (34 27) White City 95 (44 51)
Exeter 59 (38 21) Coventry 97 (40 57)
Hackney 81 (49 32) Sheffield 75 (29 46)
Hull 82 (46 36) Cradley Heath 74 (32 42)
Ipswich 57 (38 19) Belle Vue 99 (40 59)
KING'S LYNN 92 (55 37) Wolverhampton 64 (23 41)
Reading 93 (53 40) Halifax 63 (25 38)
Wimbledon 70 (48 22) Bristol 86 (30 56)

Round 2
Coventry 71 (43 28) White City 85 (35 50)
Hackney 70 (34 36) KING'S LYNN 86 (44 42)
Hull 75 (49 26) Bristol 81 (29 52)
Reading 81 (51 30) Belle Vue 75 (27 48)

Semi Finals
Reading 83 (47 36) Bristol 73 (31 42)
White City 76 (42 34) KING'S LYNN 78 (34 44)

FINAL
First leg, October 24:
Reading 40 (John Davis 10, Dave Jessup 8, Hans Wassermann 7, Bengt Jansson 6, Doug Underwood 4, Bob Humphreys 3, Ian Gledhill 2) KING'S LYNN 38 (Michael Lee 15, Terry Betts 12, Ian Turner 5, Carl Glover 5, Richard Hellsén 1, David Gagen 0, Billy Spiers 0).
Second leg, October 26
KING'S LYNN 41 (Betts 10, Hellsén 7, Lee 7, Turner 6, Gagen 6, Spiers 3, Glover 2) *Reading 37* (Jessup 15, Davis 8, Jansson 6, Underwood 4, Humphreys 3, Wassermann 1, Gledhill 0).

❑ KING'S LYNN win 79-77 on aggregate.

1977 ALL THE RESULTS

	BELLE VUE	BIRMINGHAM	BRISTOL	COVENTRY	CRADLEY HEATH	EXETER	HACKNEY	HALIFAX	HULL	IPSWICH	KING'S LYNN	LEICESTER	POOLE	READING	SHEFFIELD	SWINDON	WHITE CITY	WIMBLEDON	WOLVES
BELLE VUE		44-34	41-37	47-31	54-23	25-53	51-27	51-27	38-39	26-52	45-33	56.5 21.5	47-31	39-39	46-32	46-32	37-41	39-39	50-28
BIRMINGHAM	33-45		43-35	41-37	38-40	35-42	40-38	43-32	38-40	31-47	36-42	44-34	35-43	37-41	40-38	41-37	34-44	41-37	25-53
BRISTOL	40-38	47-31		59-19	48-30	35-42	48-30	43-35	47-31	44-33	43-34	58-20	45-33	57-21	43-35	42-36	40-38	36-41	42-36
COVENTRY	39-39	46-31	48-30		42-36	42-36	57-21	44-34	58-20	45-32	45-33	57-20	47-30	45-32	54-24	43-35	31-47	48-29	46-32
CRADLEY HEATH	36-42	49-29	51-26	40-38		43-35	55-23	52-26	44-33	37-41	41-33	48-29	50-27	41-37	50-28	36-42	33.5 44.5	48-30	38-40
EXETER	32-46	58-20	54-23	52-26	57-21		52-26	48-30	53-25	53-25	47-31	52-26	56-21	59-19	42-36	56-22	46-32	42-36	54-24
HACKNEY	42-36	44-34	43-35	35-39	53-25	41-37		39-32	42-36	48-30	33-45	47-31	42-36	33-45	46-32	50-28	37.5 40.5	45-33	41-37
HALIFAX	32-46	52-26	45-33	48-30	36-42	34-44	54-24		48-30	44-34	40-38	49-29	48-30	36-42	46-32	49-28	38-40	41-36	37-41
HULL	36-42	51-27	42-36	44-33	44-34	36-42	48-30	48-30		44-34	38-40	41-37	47-31	31-47	52-26	41-37	38-40	43-35	52-26
IPSWICH	41-37	49-28	44-34	46-32	43-35	41-37	47-30	44-34	44-34		45-33	54-24	58-20	49-29	46-32	47-31	41-37	44-34	55-23
KING'S LYNN	42-35	43-35	45-33	43-34	37-41	38-40	49-28	52-26	52-26	38-40		44-33	47-31	42-36	48-30	47-31	39-39	41-37	42-36
LEICESTER	36-42	44-34	35-42	27-51	38-40	33-45	42-36	45-33	43-35	36-42	42-36		38-40	37-41	36-42	41-37	37-40	40-37	34-44
POOLE	41-36	44-33	55-23	48-30	36-42	50-28	50-27	53-25	48-30	33-41	39-39	54-24		42-36	48-30	42-36	35-43	44-34	40-38
READING	42-36	52-26	49-29	40-38	40-38	39-39	47-31	57-21	42-36	42-36	43-35	49-29	39-39		49-29	44-34	43-35	47-31	43-35
SHEFFIELD	49-29	46-32	49-29	43-35	42-36	39-39	39-39	43-35	44.5 33.5	49-29	43-35	42-35	46-32	37-40		54-23	51-27	44-34	45-33
SWINDON	50-28	47-31	51-27	44.5 33.5	41-37	39-39	51-27	62-15	46-32	41-37	40-38	43-35	47-31	32-46	52-26		46-32	50-27	50-28
WHITE CITY	43-35	49-29	49-26	40-37	51-27	47-31	61-17	53-24	54-24	42-36	37-41	50-28	46-32	36-41	46-32	52-26		42-36	42-36
WIMBLEDON	40-38	48-30	43-35	47-31	48-30	41-36	47-31	50-27	47-31	39-39	44-34	43-35	47-31	42-36	43-35	39-38	38-40		43-35
WOLVERHAMPTON	37-41	43-35	47-31	35-43	40-35	47-31	40-38	52-26	39-38	37-41	44-33	39-38	36-42	31-47	48-30	40-38	35-43	40-38	

1978 BRITISH LEAGUE TABLE

	P	W	D	L	PtsF	PtsA	W	D	L	PtsF	PtsA	Pts
1 COVENTRY	**36**	**18**	**0**	**0**	**840**	**560**	**9**	**0**	**9**	**702**	**697**	**54**
2 Belle Vue	36	16	0	2	809	595	10	0	8	682.5	720.5	52
3 Hull	36	18	0	0	867	533	4	2	12	610	792	46
4 Wimbledon	36	16	0	2	826	572	6	1	11	676	728	45
5 Cradley Heath	36	17	0	1	829	573	4	1	13	648	749	43
6 Ipswich	36	17	0	1	816	583	4	1	13	655	747	43
7 Exeter	36	17	0	1	902	501	3	1	14	630	768	41
8 Sheffield	36	17	1	0	793.5	608.5	2	1	15	573	831	40
9 Bristol	36	17	0	1	823	579	2	0	16	609	788	38
10 Poole	36	15	1	2	804	599	2	2	14	622	780	37
11 Leicester	36	15	0	3	781	621	2	0	16	587	813	34
12 Halifax	36	14	1	3	810.5	589.5	0	2	16	561	842	31
13 King's Lynn	36	12	2	4	786	616	2	0	16	605	796	30
14 Reading	36	11	2	5	739	659	2	1	15	599	803	29
15 White City	36	9	2	7	709	686	3	1	14	610.5	788.5	27
16 Swindon	36	11	2	5	714	688	1	1	16	541	856	27
17 Wolverhampton	36	10	1	7	707	693	1	0	17	605	798	23
18 Birmingham	36	11	1	6	743	660	0	0	18	537	865	23
19 Hackney	36	9	1	8	724	677	1	0	17	540	861	21

1978 British League Riders' Championship Final

Saturday, October 21, Belle Vue:
1 Ole Olsen 13, 2 Peter Collins 12, 3 Steve Bastable 12, 4 Larry Ross 11, 5 Malcolm Simmons 10, 6 Scott Autrey 10, 7 John Titman 9, 8 Billy Sanders 9, 9 Doug Wyer 7, 10 Ian Cartwright 7, 11 Phil Crump 7, 12 Ivan Mauger 5, 13 Phil Herne 3, 14 Hans Nielsen 1, 15 Michael Lee 1, 16 Dave Jessup 0. *Reserve: Finn Thomsen, did not ride. Track reserve: Andy Heyes 2.*
Sponsor: Leyland.

1978 KNOCK OUT CUP

Preliminary Round

Coventry 78 (44 34) Exeter 78 (34 44)
King's Lynn 79 (39 40) Hull 77 (39 38)
Poole 89 (48 41) Birmingham 67 (30 37)

Preliminary Round replay

Exeter 88.5 (48 40.5) Coventry 67.5 (3037.5)

Round 1

Belle Vue 81 (44 37) Wimbledon 75 (34 41)
Bristol 74 (39 35) Leicester 82 (39 43)
Exeter 85 (52 33) Sheffield 71 (26 45)
Hackney 97 (46 51) King's Lynn 57 (31 26)
Halifax 69 (43 26) White City 86 (34 52)
Poole 78 (42 36) Swindon 78 (36 42)
Reading 77 (37 40) Cradley Heath 79 (41 38)
Wolverhampton 74 (34 40) Ipswich 81 (43 38)

Round 1 Replay

Swindon 66 (37 29) Poole 90 (41 49)

Round 2

Belle Vue 87 (43 44) Poole 68 (34 34)
Exeter 102 (58 44) Hackney 54 (20 34)
Leicester 69 (39 30) Cradley Heath 87 (39 48)
White City 49 (26 23) Ipswich 106 (52 54)

Semi Final

Belle Vue 84 (27 57) Exeter 72 (51 21)
Cradley Heath 78 (40 34) Ipswich 82 (38 44)

FINAL

First leg, October 14:
Belle Vue 39 (Peter Collins 15, Chris Morton 14, Les Collins 5, Chris Turner 2, Jim Brett 1, Steve Finch 1, Uno Johansson 1) IPSWICH 39 (Mike Lanham 9, John Louis 8, Tony Davey 7, Colin Cook 6, Kevin Jolly 5, Billy Sanders 4, Tim Hunt 0).
Second leg, October 19:
IPSWICH 53 (Georg Hack 10, Louis 9, Davey 9, Sanders 9, Lanham 7, Jolly 6, Cook 3)*Belle Vue 25* (Peter Collins 10, Morton 8, Les Collins 4, Turner 1, Derek Richardson 1, Eric Dugard 1, Johansson 0).

❑ IPSWICH win 92-64 on aggregate.

1978 ALL THE RESULTS

	BELLE VUE	BIRMINGHAM	BRISTOL	COVENTRY	CRADLEY HEATH	EXETER	HACKNEY	HALIFAX	HULL	IPSWICH	KING'S LYNN	LEICESTER	POOLE	READING	SHEFFIELD	SWINDON	WHITE CITY	WIMBLEDON	WOLVES
BELLE VUE		49-29	36-42	42-36	40-38	52-26	51-27	48-30	47-31	38-40	42-36	43-35	47-31	46-32	42-36	47-31	44-34	43-35	52-26
BIRMINGHAM	37-41		46-32	41-37	38-40	45-33	37-41	57-21	40-38	30-48	50-28	43-35	39-39	41-37	48-30	47-31	34-43	29-49	41-37
BRISTOL	52-26	42-36		43-35	46-31	41-37	45-33	47-31	44-34	45-33	40-38	54-24	51-27	55-23	49-29	47-31	41-37	37-41	44-33
COVENTRY	43-35	48-30	39-38		40-37	45-33	56-22	48-30	48-30	41-37	48-30	45-31	53-25	54-24	45-33	53-25	47-31	46-32	41-37
CRADLEY HEATH	43-35	57-20	50-28	40-38		51-27	45-33	48-30	53-25	41-37	34.5 43.5	50-28	42-36	40-38	50-28	52-26	45.5 32.5	43-35	44-34
EXETER	40-38	52-26	46-32	37-41	47-31		56-22	61-17	56-22	45-33	56-21	52-26	47-31	53-25	53-25	53-25	52-26	49-29	47-31
HACKNEY	38-40	45-33	44-34	36-42	38-40	39-39		47-31	38-40	35-43	37-41	40-38	40-38	35-43	41-37	51-27	39-36	38-40	43-35
HALIFAX	41.5 36.5	41-37	44-34	36-42	43-35	41-36	48-29		45-33	39-39	50-28	51-27	49-27	58-20	37-41	50-28	46-32	37-41	54-24
HULL	54-24	57-21	48-30	55-22	46-32	44-33	52-26	41-37		42-36	52-26	48-29	41-37	44-33	49-29	49-29	47-31	50-28	48-30
IPSWICH	46-32	48-30	56-22	35-42	44-31	42-36	43-35	51-27	46-32		42-36	50-28	41-37	39-38	51-27	50-28	48-30	43-35	41-37
KING'S LYNN	36-42	54-24	49-29	42-35	42-36	43-35	49-29	46-32	36-41	55-23		37-41	39-39	39-39	36-42	47-31	52-26	40-38	44-34
LEICESTER	32-46	43-35	39-38	37-41	37-41	41-36	48-30	48-30	55-23	46-32	42-36		43-35	40-38	51-27	46-32	42-36	43-35	48-30
POOLE	35-43	53-25	46-32	38-40	44-34	45-33	49-29	46-32	48-30	42-36	43-34	45-33		41-37	51-27	43-35	53-25	39-39	43-35
READING	35-43	45-33	44-33	38-40	37-40	40-37	53-24	46-32	39-39	39-37	43-35	43-35	38-40		42-36	39-39	34-43	40-38	43-35
SHEFFIELD	40-37	41-37	42-35	40-38	43-35	50-28	53-25	42-36	44-34	40-38	46.5 31.5	44-34	43-35	44-34		54-24	39-39	46-32	42-36
SWINDON	37-41	44-34	41-36	26-52	40-37	35-43	42-36	39-39	34-44	42-36	47-31	48-30	42-36	40-38	39-39		36-42	41-37	41-37
WHITE CITY	35-43	45-33	41-37	43-34	39-39	36-42	40-38	39-39	36-42	31-47	40-37	29-49	38-40	42-36	51-27	42-29		36-42	46-32
WIMBLEDON	38-40	61-17	39-38	41-37	44-33	40-37	53-24	47-30	44-33	43-35	42-36	51-27	42-36	56-22	52-26	50-28	47-31		36-42
WOLVERHAMPTON	38-40	40-37	38-39	27-51	40-38	38-39	41-37	41-37	39-39	53-25	41-37	40-37	45-33	36-42	44-34	36-42	42-36	28-50	

1979 BRITISH LEAGUE TABLE

	P	W	D	L	PtsF	PtsA	W	D	L	PtsF	PtsA	Pts
1 COVENTRY	**34**	**17**	**0**	**0**	**780**	**545**	**9**	**0**	**8**	**638**	**686**	**52**
2 Hull	34	17	0	0	878	447	7	2	8	668	652	50
3 Cradley Heath	34	17	0	0	849	473	7	0	10	651	673	48
4 King's Lynn	34	16	0	1	783	543	6	1	10	613	713	45
5 Exeter	34	16	0	1	800	523	5	0	12	613	707	42
6 Halifax	34	15	0	2	768.5	556.5	3	0	14	568	755	36
7 Reading	34	14	0	3	738	586	3	0	14	607	719	34
8 Swindon	34	12	1	4	738	585	3	2	12	612	714	33
9 Wimbledon	34	14	0	3	750	573	2	1	14	577	747	33
10 Belle Vue	34	10	4	3	700	625	4	0	13	623	701	32
11 Wolverhampton	34	12	0	5	703	620	3	1	13	603	722	31
12 Poole	34	13	2	2	745	579	1	1	15	552	773	31
13 Sheffield	34	13	1	3	716	608	1	1	15	512	812	30
14 Birmingham	34	10	0	7	689	635	3	2	12	568	757	28
15 Ipswich	34	10	1	6	689	631	2	1	14	575	750	26
16 Eastbourne	34	8	2	7	700	623	2	0	15	542	783	22
17 Leicester	34	9	0	8	648	677	1	0	16	502.5	820.5	20
18 Hackney	34	9	1	7	655	670	0	0	17	475	845	19

■ ***COVENTRY and Hull met in their respective last matches of the season at Brandon on Saturday, October 13 – with the winners assured of taking the championship!***

1979 British League Riders' Championship Final

Saturday, October 20, Belle Vue:
1 John Louis 14, 2 Bruce Penhall 13, 3 Michael Lee 12, 4 Peter Collins 11, 5 Larry Ross 10, 6 Phil Crump 9, 7 Hans Nielsen 9, 8 Scott Autrey 8, 9 Ole Olsen 7, 10 Ivan Mauger 6, 11 Malcolm Simmons 5, 12 John Titman 5, 13 Ian Cartwright 5, 14 John Davis 4, 15 Andy Grahame 1, 16 Gordon Kennett 1. *Reserves: Reg Wilson, Finn Thomsen, did not ride.*
Sponsor: Gauntlet.

1979 KNOCK OUT CUP

Preliminary Round
Ipswich 96 (53 43) Eastbourne 119 (54 65)
Leicester 82 (40 42) Cradley Heath 134 (68 66)

Round 1
Cradley Heath 131 (53 78) Wimbledon 83 (54 29)
Exeter 117 (70 47) Belle Vue 99 (38 61)
†Hackney lost to Halifax, walk-over
Poole 93 (59 34) Coventry 122 (48 74)
Reading 120 (77 43) Eastbourne 96 (31 65)
Sheffield 85 (60 25) Hull 129 (48 81)
Swindon 111 (62 49) Birmingham 105 (46 59)
Wolverhampton 111 (56 55) King's Lynn 105 (52 53)

Round 2
Coventry 93 (60 33) Hull 123 (48 75)
Cradley Heath 127 (56 71) Wolverhampton 89 (52 37)
Exeter 118 (62 56) Swindon 98 (46 52)
Reading 82 (29 53) Halifax 134 (79 55)

Semi Finals
Cradley Heath 102 (59 43) Halifax 72 (49 23)
Exeter 98 (60 38) Hull 118 (48 70)

FINAL
First leg, October 13:
CRADLEY HEATH 62 (Bruce Penhall 11, Alan Grahame 11, Erik Gundersen 9, Dave Perks 9, Phil Collins 9, Bobby Schwartz 6, Kristian Praestbro 4, John Hack 3) *Hull 46* (Ivan Mauger 14, Bobby Beaton 13, Joe Owen 6, Dennis Sigalos 6, Frank Auffret 6, Nigel Close 1, Brian Havelock 0, Graham Drury 0).
Second leg, October 31:
Hull 50 (Sigalos 13, Kelly Moran 8, Louis Carr 7, Beaton 6, Owen 5, Auffret 4, Close 4, Mauger 3) CRADLEY HEATH 58 (Penhall 13, Schwartz 11, Collins 9, Praestbro 9, Grahame 6, Hack 5, Gundersen 5, Perks 0).

❑ CRADLEY HEATH win 120-96 on aggregate.
†Hackney withdrew following the death of Vic Harding.
Matches staged over 18 heats with 8 riders per team.

1979 ALL THE RESULTS

	BELLE VUE	BIRMINGHAM	COVENTRY	CRADLEY HEATH	EASTBOURNE	EXETER	HACKNEY	HALIFAX	HULL	IPSWICH	KING'S LYNN	LEICESTER	POOLE	READING	SHEFFIELD	SWINDON	WIMBLEDON	WOLVERHAMPTON
BELLE VUE		39-39	42-36	42-36	46-32	38-40	46-32	42-36	29-49	47-31	40-38	44-33	47-31	43-35	38-40	39-39	39-39	39-39
BIRMINGHAM	28-50		38-40	37-39	38-40	40-38	46-32	59-19	38-40	32-45	40-38	41-37	39-38	42-36	49-29	38-40	43-35	41-37
COVENTRY	42-36	43-35		42-36	54-24	40-38	48-30	43-34	42-36	42-36	45-33	52-26	48-30	43-35	51-27	43-35	54-24	48-30
CRADLEY HEATH	46-32	51-27	49-29		51-27	57-21	50-25	64-14	41-37	52-26	49-29	53-24	47-31	40-38	45-33	50-28	57-21	47-31
EASTBOURNE	38-40	36-42	43-35	36-41		49-28	51-27	44-34	50-27	39-39	35-43	48-30	39-39	37-41	50-28	31-47	42-36	32-46
EXETER	41-37	53-25	40-38	45-33	50-28		50-27	42-35	45-33	55-23	38-40	57-21	51-27	40-38	42-35	44-34	52-26	55-23
HACKNEY	41-37	46-31	43-35	37-41	38-40	43-35		34-44	33-45	41-37	36-42	42-36	37-41	46-32	39-39	29-49	22-56	44-34
HALIFAX	49-29	44-34	38-40	46-31	42-36	41-37	55-23		38-40	43-35	49-29	44.5 33.5	53-25	46-32	47-31	45-33	45-33	43-35
HULL	42-36	58-20	51-27	41-37	50-28	45-33	56-22	43-34		57-21	56-22	60-18	62-16	51-27	57-21	55-23	51-27	43-35
IPSWICH	47-31	39-39	36-41	33-45	41-37	41-37	52-26	44-34	42-33		37-41	35-42	44-34	33-45	45-33	43-35	42-36	35-42
KING'S LYNN	43-35	41-37	50-28	47-31	53-25	45-33	55-23	38-40	40-38	42-36		40-38	42-36	49-29	58-20	44-34	52-26	44-34
LEICESTER	28-50	30-40	30-48	41-37	44-33	32-46	44-34	35-43	38-40	36-42	34-44		40-38	40-38	44-34	41-37	46-32	45-33
POOLE	51-26	43-35	55-23	41-37	44-34	33-45	59-19	44-34	39-39	44-34	44-34	50-28		33-45	45-33	39-39	40-37	41-37
READING	37-41	44-34	35-42	32-46	49-29	46-32	48-30	48-30	42-35	42-36	46-32	56-22	43-35		45-33	43-35	41-37	45-33
SHEFFIELD	41-36	42-36	34-44	44-34	49-29	36-42	48-30	44-34	29-49	47-31	39-39	44-34	46-32	41-37		46-32	45-32	41-37
SWINDON	41-37	49-29	37-41	40-38	48-30	38-39	46-31	40-38	39-39	46-32	38-40	59-19	36-42	45-33	50-27		40-38	46-32
WIMBLEDON	44-34	63-15	37-41	36-42	42-36	41-36	45-32	48-30	41-36	41-37	43-35	50-28	41-37	45-33	56-22	44-34		33-45
WOLVERHAMPTON	42-36	36-42	28-50	33-45	44-34	42-33	46-32	43-35	26-52	44-34	44-34	49-29	54-24	45-33	51-27	40-38	36-42	

1980 BRITISH LEAGUE TABLE

	P	W	D	L	PtsF	PtsA	W	D	L	PtsF	PtsA	Pts
1 READING	**32**	**15**	**0**	**1**	**767**	**481**	**9**	**1**	**6**	**667**	**581**	**49**
2 Hackney	32	15	0	1	719	526	8	0	8	581	662	46
3 Belle Vue	32	16	0	0	711	534	5	1	10	587	659	43
4 Coventry	32	15	0	1	724.5	523.5	5	2	9	601.5	646.5	42
5 Cradley Heath	32	16	0	0	732.5	514.5	4	0	12	569.5	674.5	40
6 King's Lynn	32	15	0	1	759	487	2	0	14	594	654	34
7 Ipswich	32	14	0	2	739	506	2	2	12	559	688	34
8 Swindon	32	11	2	3	686	562	5	0	11	578	669	34
9 Poole	32	31	1	2	699	545	2	1	13	555	692	32
10 Halifax	32	13	1	2	697	550	2	0	14	522	721	31
11 Leicester	32	12	0	4	676	572	2	0	14	577	669	28
12 Hull	32	10	3	3	674	572	1	2	13	533	714	27
13 Wimbledon	32	12	1	3	682	562	0	1	15	513	732	26
14 Birmingham	32	9	0	7	627	621	2	1	13	531	717	23
15 Wolverhampton	32	7	2	7	643	602	2	0	14	549	695	20
16 Eastbourne	32	8	1	7	615	630	1	0	15	478	769	19
17 Sheffield	32	8	0	8	618	628	0	0	16	421	826	16

■ *READING became the first British League club to win the championship at two different home tracks. In their previous title season in 1973 they had been racing at Tilehurst and in 1980 they were at a new base at Smallmead.*

1980 British League Riders' Championship Final

Saturday, October 18, Belle Vue:
1 Les Collins 14, 2 Bruce Penhall 12, 3 Larry Ross 11, 4 Jan Andersson 10, 5 Hans Nielsen 10, 6 Peter Collins 10, 7 Kenny Carter 9, 8 Scott Autrey 8, 9 Ole Olsen 7, 10 Dennis Sigalos 6, 11 John Louis 5, 12 Steve Bastable 5, 13 Bo Petersen 4, 14 Michael Lee 3, Malcolm Simmons 3, 16 Gordon Kennett 1. *Reserve: Doug Wyer, did not ride. Track reserves: Bernie Collier 2, Mike Wilding 0.*
Sponsor: Gauntlet.

1980 KNOCK OUT CUP

Preliminary Round

Poole 102 (53 49) Leicester 111 (55 59)

Round 1

Birmingham 110 (56 54) Coventry 105 (51 54)
Hackney 86 (45 41) Hull 130 (63 67)
King's Lynn 106 (58 48) CRADLEY HEATH 110 (50 60)
Leicester 96 (54 42) Ipswich 120 (54 66)
Reading 112 (62 50) Halifax 103 (46 57)
Sheffield 111 (56 55) Wolverhampton 105 (52 53)
Swindon 117.5 (62 55.5) Eastbourne 98.5 (46 52.5)
Wimbledon 105 (57 48) *Belle Vue 111 (51 60)*

Round 2

Hull 106 (66 40) *Belle Vue 110 (42 68)*
Ipswich 100 (55 45) Swindon 116 (53 63)
Reading 107 (53 54) CRADLEY HEATH 109 (55 54)
Sheffield 79 (49 30) Birmingham 134 (58 76)

Semi Finals

Birmingham 97 (56 41) CRADLEY HEATH 119 (52 67)
Swindon 105 (56 49) *Belle Vue 111 (52 59)*

FINAL

First leg, October 11:
Belle Vue 67 (Chris Morton 14, Robert Maxfield 14, Peter Collins 13, Pekka Hautamaki 10, Louis Carr 5, Steve Wilcock 5, Dave Allen 4, Derek Richardson 2) CRADLEY HEATH 41 (Alan Grahame 13, Phil Collins 13, Erik Gundersen 7, Ila Teromaa 6, John Hack 1, *Steve Lawson 1*, Craig Featherby 0).
Second leg, October 29:
CRADLEY HEATH 75 (Bruce Penhall 15, Gundersen 13, Collins 12, Grahame 11, *Andy Reid 9*, Teromaa 8, *Lawson 5*, Featherby 2)) *Belle Vue 33* (Carr 10, Hautamaki 10, *Tony Boyle 6, John Williams 4*, Morton 2, Collins 1, Allen 0).

❑ CRADLEY HEATH win 116-100.

1980 ALL THE RESULTS

	BELLE VUE	BIRMINGHAM	COVENTRY	CRADLEY HEATH	EASTBOURNE	HACKNEY	HALIFAX	HULL	IPSWICH	KING'S LYNN	LEICESTER	POOLE	READING	SHEFFIELD	SWINDON	WIMBLEDON	WOLVERHAMPTON
BELLE VUE		41-37	40-38	42-36	53-25	49-29	44-34	43-35	44-34	40-38	41-37	45-33	43-35	47-30	52-25	46-31	41-37
BIRMINGHAM	37-41		35-43	45-33	33-45	44-34	41-37	44-34	42-36	34-44	41-37	41-37	32-46	41-37	35-43	46-32	36-42
COVENTRY	44-34	45-33		36.5 41.5	47-31	52-26	47-31	52-26	42-36	43-35	43-35	47-31	40-38	48-30	44-34	49-29	45-33
CRADLEY HEATH	42-36	49-29	44.5 33.5		57-21	44-34	40-38	45-33	53-25	40-38	39-38	42-36	46-32	50-28	46-32	51-27	44-34
EASTBOURNE	45-33	37-41	47-31	45-31		34-43	41-37	37-41	40-38	42-36	31-47	34-44	26-52	46-32	30-48	39-39	41-37
HACKNEY	45-33	41-37	44-34	37-40	44-34		45-32	46-31	46-32	40-38	43-35	44-34	40-38	53-25	43-35	56-22	52-26
HALIFAX	46-32	44-34	37-41	40-38	52-26	38-39		48-30	44-34	42-36	43-35	42-36	39-39	49-29	42-36	40-38	51-27
HULL	38-40	51-27	39-39	42-36	46-32	38-40	32-46		39-39	41-37	42-36	39-39	40-38	60-18	42-36	44-33	41-36
IPSWICH	41-36	54-24	43-35	46-32	48-30	49-28	56-22	43-35		40-38	48-30	45-33	31-47	59-19	48-30	50-27	38-40
KING'S LYNN	43-34	49-29	46-32	52-26	63-15	43-35	48-30	56-22	40-38		44-33	50-28	38-40	58-20	44-34	44-34	41-37
LEICESTER	37-41	46-32	42-36	40-38	49-29	38-40	51-27	43-35	42-36	40-38		42-36	32-46	48-30	38-40	45-33	43-35
POOLE	43-35	43-35	37-41	48-30	46-32	45-32	57-21	39-39	47-31	41-37	41-37		38-40	44-34	44-34	43-35	43-32
READING	47-31	45-33	43-35	40-38	52-26	47-31	48-30	43-35	56-22	52-26	53-25	47-31		54-24	38-40	53-25	49-29
SHEFFIELD	27-51	38-40	31-47	48-30	46-32	38-40	34-43	43-35	37-41	43-35	28-50	34-43	41-37		45-33	41-37	44-34
SWINDON	39-39	52-26	43-35	35-43	43-35	32-46	44-34	46-32	39-39	40-38	45-33	49-29	33-45	59-19		41-37	46-32
WIMBLEDON	36-42	43-35	39-39	44-34	47-31	37-41	51-24	47-31	40-37	40-38	44-34	47-31	35-43	49-29	43-35		40-38
WOLVERHAMPTON	49-29	39-39	36-42	34-43	43-34	34-43	42-36	39-39	37-41	36-42	43-35	44-34	27-51	61-17	35-43	44-34	

1981 BRITISH LEAGUE TABLE

	P	W	D	L	PtsF	PtsA	W	D	L	PtsF	PtsA	Pts
1 CRADLEY	**30**	**15**	**0**	**0**	**710**	**445**	**11**	**1**	**3**	**629**	**538**	**53**
2 Ipswich	30	14	1	0	683	483	7	3	5	567	602	46
3 Swindon	30	12	1	2	641	503	7	2	6	581	586	41
4 Belle Vue	30	13	0	2	671	498	6	1	8	568	588	39
5 Coventry	30	13	0	2	659	510	5	0	10	573	593	36
6 Birmingham	30	12	1	2	654	515	1	0	14	509	659	27
7 Halifax	30	13	0	2	658	509	0	1	14	491	679	27
8 Hackney	30	10	0	5	639	530	2	2	11	543	627	26
9 Poole	30	9	1	5	616.5	551.5	3	1	11	512	657	26
10 Sheffield	30	11	0	4	656	513	2	0	13	464	701	26
11 Reading	30	7	4	4	601	568	2	3	10	528	640	25
12 Hull	30	10	4	1	634	535	0	0	15	434	710	24
13 Eastbourne	30	9	2	4	627	542	1	1	13	467	702	23
14 King's Lynn	30	7	1	7	622	548	3	1	11	560	610	22
15 Leicester	30	9	0	6	602	568	2	0	13	515.5	653.5	22
16 Wimbledon	30	6	2	7	578	587	1	1	13	464	706	17

■ ***PETER ADAMS established a new record by becoming the first manager to take two DIFFERENT clubs to the British League Division One title. Having already been in charge at Coventry when they won the crown in 1978 and 1979, he guided Cradley Heath to their first ever championship victory.***

1981 British League Riders' Championship Final

Saturday, October 27, Belle Vue:
1 Kenny Carter 15, 2 Chris Morton 13, 3 Shawn Moran 13, 4 Phil Crump 10, 5 Dave Jessup 9, 6 Hans Nielsen 8, 7 Dennis Sigalos 8, 8 Bruce Penhall 8, 9 Les Collins 7, Malcolm Simmons 7, 11 Gordon Kennett 6, 12 Scott Autrey 5, 13 Jan Andersson 5, 14 Bo Petersen 4, 15 Ole Olsen 2, 16 Joe Owen 0. *Reserves:*
Sponsor: Daily Mirror.

1981 KNOCK OUT CUP

Preliminary Round

Berwick 39 Wimbledon 57
Boston 47 Hull 48
Edinburgh 49 Sheffield 47
Middlesbrough 43 Eastbourne 53
Mildenhall 38 Poole 58
Newcastle 40 Leicester 56
Peterborough 50 Halifax 46
Rye House 34 *Birmingham 62*

Round 1

Belle Vue 95 (53 42) Hull 97 (43 54)
Birmingham 121 (63 58) Peterborough 71 (33 38)
Eastbourne 85 (49 36) Cradley Heath 107 (47 60)
Hackney 70 (37 33) Coventry 122 (59 63)
King's Lynn 90 (47 43) IPSWICH 102 (49 53)
Leicester 98 (51 47) Poole 94 (45 49)
Reading 111 (55 56) Wimbledon 81 (41 40)
Swindon 118 (69 49) Edinburgh 74 (27 47)

Round 2

Birmingham 99 (52 47) Hull 93 (44 49)
Coventry 94 (49 45) Reading 96 (45 51)
Cradley Heath 90 (48 42) IPSWICH 102 (48 54)
Leicester 67 (45 22) Swindon 125 (51 74)

Semi Finals

Birmingham 101 (54 47) Reading 91 (42 49)
IPSWICH 107 (57 50) Swindon 85 (39 46)

FINAL

First leg, October 16:
Birmingham 47 (Hans Nielsen 14, Kai Niemi 13, Andy Grahame 8, Bruce Cribb 8, Neil Evitts 4, Paul Thorp 0, Simon Wigg 0) IPSWICH 49 (Preben Eriksen 12, John Cook 11, Kevin Jolly 7, Tim Hunt 6, Dennis Sigalos 6, Mike Lanham 5, Nigel Flatman 2).

Second leg, October 25:
IPSWICH 51 (Sigalos 11, Cook 10, Eriksen 8, Jolly 7, Lanham 7, Hunt 6, Flatman 2) *Birmingham 45* (Nielsen 17, Grahame 17, Niemi 8, Cribb 1, Evitts 1, Mike Wilding 1, Thorp 0).

❑ IPSWICH win 100-92.

† *Following the scrapping of the Inter League KO Cup the top eight National League tracks were drawn at home in a preliminary round.*

1981 ALL THE RESULTS

	BELLE VUE	BIRMINGHAM	COVENTRY	CRADLEY HEATH	EASTBOURNE	HACKNEY	HALIFAX	HULL	IPSWICH	KING'S LYNN	LEICESTER	POOLE	READING	SHEFFIELD	SWINDON	WIMBLEDON
BELLE VUE		51-27	43-35	29-49	52-26	41-37	40-38	44-33	50-28	46-32	44-34	47-31	45-33	43-35	38-40	58-20
BIRMINGHAM	44-34		42-36	34-44	44-34	46-32	51-27	47-30	38-40	40-38	44-34	42-36	39-39	53-25	42-36	48-30
COVENTRY	47-31	53-25		26-52	45-33	45-33	48-30	51-27	42-36	42-36	44-34	44-34	42-35	50-28	37-41	43-35
CRADLEY HEATH	40-26	47-31	44-33		58-20	40-38	48-30	52-26	47-30	46-32	49-29	52-26	50-28	47-30	43-35	47-31
EASTBOURNE	39-39	40-38	38-40	35-43		43-35	50-28	48-30	39-39	38-40	40-38	41-37	44-34	46-32	38-39	48-30
HACKNEY	43-34	47-31	41-37	38-40	42-36		43-35	55-23	38-40	43-35	38-40	36-42	46-32	49-29	38-40	42-36
HALIFAX	37-41	45-33	41-36	41-37	47-30	42-36		46-32	48-30	42-36	41-37	46-32	37-41	54-24	42-35	49-29
HULL	42-36	42-36	43-35	34-44	46-32	45-33	39-39		39-39	42-36	47-31	45-33	45-33	47-30	39-39	39-39
IPSWICH	41-37	39-38	42-35	44-34	54-24	44-34	51-27	52-26		40-38	48-30	53-25	41-37	52-24	39-39	43-35
KING'S LYNN	29-49	47-31	34-44	37-41	36-42	42-36	46-32	49-29	38-40		35-43	53-25	39-39	49-29	34-44	54-24
LEICESTER	40-38	40-38	35-43	37-41	43-35	44-34	41-37	41-37	35-43	37-41		45-33	47-31	33-45	38-40	46-32
POOLE	38-40	45-33	29-49	36-41	44-34	37-41	46-32	45-33	34-44	41-37	44.5 33.5		39-39	46-32	42-35	50-28
READING	38-40	40-37	40-38	38-40	39-39	39-39	40-38	47-31	37-41	39-39	40-38	39-39		48-30	34-44	43-35
SHEFFIELD	38-40	43-35	49-29	29-49	56-22	42-36	50-28	49-29	41-37	40-38	47-31	35-42	38-40		41-37	58-20
SWINDON	41-37	46-32	42-36	42-36	51-27	38-40	42-36	40-14	39-39	43-35	49-29	42-36	41-36	47-30		38-40
WIMBLEDON	31-46	34-44	30-47	38-38	45-33	39-39	44-34	44-34	37-41	31-47	43-34	37-41	47-31	37-41	41-37	

1981 LEAGUE CUP FINAL

First leg, October 10:
COVENTRY 68 (Tommy Knudsen 15, Mitch Shirra 14, Ole Olsen 11, Kevin Hawkins 10, Gary Guglielmi 8, Keith White 5, Rob Hollingworth 5) **King's Lynn 28** (Richard Hellsén 16, Dave Jessup 5, Melvyn Taylor 4, Hasse Danielsson 3, David Gagen 0, Nigel Sparshott 0, Dennis Mallett 0. Rider replacement for Michael Lee).
Second leg, October 11:
King's Lynn 42 (Jessup 16, Hellsén 9, Taylor 7, Danielsson 5, Nigel Sparshott 3, Gagen 2, Robbie McGregor, did not ride. Rider replacement for Lee.) **COVENTRY 54** (Olsen 15, Knudsen 13, Shirra 10, Hollingworth 7, Guglielmi 4, White 3, Hawkins 2).
❏ ***COVENTRY win 122-70 on aggregate.***

1982 LEAGUE CUP FINAL

First leg, June 19:
CRADLEY HEATH 42 (Bruce Penhall 11, Erik Gundersen 9, Alan Grahame 8, Phil Collins 5, Simon Cross 5, Steve Lawson 2, Andy Reid 2) ***Ipswich 36*** (Dennis Sigalos 14, Jeremy Doncaster 6, Preben Eriksen 6, John Cook 6, Kevin Jolly 2, Nigel Flatman 2, Mike Lanham 0).
Second leg, June 24:
Ipswich 37 (Cook 9, Sigalos 7, Eriksen 6, Jolly 5, Doncaster 5, Lanham 4, Flatman 1)
CRADLEY HEATH 41 (Penhall 13, Gundersen 10, Grahame 9, Simon Wigg 6, Collins 3, Jan Verner 0, Reid 0).
❏ ***CRADLEY HEATH win 83-73 on aggregate.***

1981 ALL THE RESULTS SECTION A

	BELLE VUE	BIRMINGHAM	COVENTRY	CRADLEY HEATH	HALIFAX	HULL	LEICESTER	SHEFFIELD
BELLE VUE		54-47	47-49	51-45	50-45	51-45	51-45	46.5 49.5
BIRMINGHAM	51-45		42-54	35-61	66-30	51-45	49-47	68-28
COVENTRY	69-27	59-36		65-31	59-37	53-43	50-46	53-43
CRADLEY HEATH	55-41	58-38	57-39		65-31	63-33	53-43	54-42
HALIFAX	47-48	50-46	32-64	43-54		60-36	52-42	58-38
HULL	50-46	55-41	43-53	44-52	54-42		68-28	53-43
LEICESTER	54-42	42-54	47-49	42-54	60-36	59-37		54-42
SHEFFIELD	47-49	49-47	57-39	51-45	50-46	49-47	53-43	

1 COVENTRY	14	12	0	2	755	588	24
2 Cradley Heath	14	11	0	3	747	597	22
3 Belle Vue	14	7	0	7	648.5	693.5	14
4 Sheffield	14	7	0	7	641.5	702.5	14
5 Birmingham	14	6	0	8	666	677	12
6 Hull	14	5	0	9	653	691	10
7 Leicester	14	4	0	10	652	690	8
8 Halifax	14	4	0	10	608	732	8

1982 ALL THE RESULTS SOUTHERN SECTION

	EASTBOURNE	HACKNEY	IPSWICH	KING'S LYNN	POOLE	READING	SWINDON	WIMBLEDON
EASTBOURNE		40-38	33-45	51-27	46-32	44-34	49-29	39-39
HACKNEY	36-42		42-35	44-34	45-32	46-32	48-30	38-40
IPSWICH	44-32	54-24		46-32	44-34	40-38	46-32	48-29
KING'S LYNN	38-40	45-33	38-40		44-34	42-36	42-36	36-42
POOLE	53-25	42-36	41-37	44-34		46-30	37-41	45-33
READING	37-41	43-35	38-40	40-38	44-34		40-38	43-35
SWINDON	39-39	37-41	35-43	38-40	46-32	39-38		36-42
WIMBLEDON	44-34	43-35	38-40	47-31	44-34	38-40	46-32	

1 IPSWICH	14	12	0	2	602	486	24
2 Eastbourne	14	8	2	4	555	535	18
3 Wimbledon	14	8	1	5	560	531	17
4 Poole	14	6	0	8	542	549	12
5 Hackney	14	6	0	8	541	549	12
6 Reading	14	6	0	8	533	558	12
7 King's Lynn	14	5	0	9	521	571	10
8 Swindon	14	3	1	10	508	583	7

1981 ALL THE RESULTS SECTION B

	EASTBOURNE	HACKNEY	IPSWICH	KING'S LYNN	POOLE	READING	SWINDON	WIMBLEDON
EASTBOURNE		50-45	39-56	38-57	55-41	47-49	50-46	59-37
HACKNEY	52-44		51-45	48-48	51-43	48-47	41-55	59-37
IPSWICH	61-35	63-33		65-31	53-42	47-49	59-37	71-24
KING'S LYNN	53-43	52-44	58-38		50-46	50-46	55-40	66-29
POOLE	55-41	64-32	53-43	48.5 47.5		56-40	54-42	62-34
READING	55-40	59-37	57-38	54.5 41.5	63-33		64-32	55-41
SWINDON	57-39	62-34	42-54	47-49	51-44	50-46		52-44
WIMBLEDON	40-56	49.5 46.5	44-52	46-50	52-44	40-56	46-49	

1 KING'S LYNN	14	10	1	3	708	633	21
2 Reading	14	10	0	4	740.5	600.5	20
3 Ipswich	14	9	0	5	745	595	18
4 Poole	14	7	0	7	685.5	654.5	14
5 Swindon	14	7	0	7	662	679	14
6 Hackney	14	5	1	8	621.5	718.5	11
7 Eastbourne	14	5	0	9	636	704	10
8 Wimbledon	14	2	0	12	563.5	777.5	4

1982 ALL THE RESULTS NORTHERN SECTION

	BELLE VUE	BIRMINGHAM	COVENTRY	CRADLEY HEATH	HALIFAX	LEICESTER	SHEFFIELD
BELLE VUE		45-33	49-29	37-41	46-32	43-35	44-34
BIRMINGHAM	38-40		36-42	39-39	42-36	42-35	54-24
COVENTRY	44-34	46-32		44-34	44-34	47-31	41-35
CRADLEY HEATH	42-36	41-37	34.5 43.5		46-32	48-30	49-28
HALIFAX	45-33	51-26	46-32	39-39		45-33	50-28
LEICESTER	39-39	41-37	40-38	35-43	d.n.r.		46-32
SHEFFIELD	39-39	40-37	38-40	24-54	35-43	43-35	

1 CRADLEY HEATH	14	8	2	2	510.5	424.5	18
2 Coventry	12	9	0	3	490.5	443.5	18
3 Belle Vue	12	6	2	4	485	451	14
4 Halifax	11	6	1	4	453	404	13
5 Birmingham	12	3	1	8	453	480	7
6 Leicester	11	3	1	7	400	457	7
7 Sheffield	12	2	1	9	400	532	5

1982 BRITISH LEAGUE TABLE

	P	W	D	L	PtsF	PtsA	W	D	L	PtsF	PtsA	Pts
1 BELLE VUE	**28**	**13**	**0**	**1**	**676**	**415**	**10**	**0**	**4**	**548**	**542**	**46**
2 Cradley Heath	28	14	0	0	644	445	6	0	8	564	527	40
3 Ipswich	28	10	1	3	609.5	418.5	6	1	7	550	541	34
4 Coventry	28	12	0	2	605	487	4	2	8	515	574	34
5 Sheffield	28	13	1	0	643	448	1	2	11	481	611	31
6 Birmingham	28	11	0	3	595	495	2	1	11	501	589	27
7 Hackney	28	10	1	3	582.5	506.5	2	2	10	476	615	27
8 Swindon	28	9	1	4	556	536	4	0	10	486	604	27
9 Reading	28	11	0	3	594	497	1	2	11	484	606	26
10 Leicester	28	11	0	3	596	495	2	0	12	465	627	26
11 Wimbledon	28	10	1	3	566	525	2	1	11	444.5	646.5	26
12 Eastbourne	28	10	2	2	617	474	1	1	12	482	608	25
13 Halifax	28	9	1	4	625	463	1	0	13	451	641	21
14 King's Lynn	28	9	2	3	571	520	0	1	13	454	636	21
15 Poole	28	3	3	8	541	551	0	0	14	437.5	653.5	9

■ *BELLE VUE'S victory was, at that time, a record-breaking fourth British League Division One title. It saw them move two ahead of nearest rivals Coventry, Ipswich and Reading, all of whom had won the title twice.*

■ *HULL dropped out of the British League after a dispute between the promoters Ian Thomas and Brian Larner and the landlords of The Boulevard, Hull Rugby League Football Club. Their decision reduced membership of Division One to a new all-time low of only 15 tracks.*

1982 British League Riders' Championship Final

Saturday, October 16, Belle Vue:
1 Kenny Carter 15, 2 Shawn Moran 14, 3 Hans Nielsen 13, 4 Erik Gundersen 10, 5 Les Collins 9, 6 Bobby Schwartz 9, 7 Jan Andersson 8, 8 Steve Bastable 7, 9 Billy Sanders 7, 10 Ole Olsen 6, 11 Chris Morton 6, 12 Finn Thomsen 5, 13 Dennis Sigalos 4, 14 Gordon Kennett 3, 15 Dave Jessup 3, 16 John Davis 0. *Track Reserves:* *Andy Smith 1, Lee Edwards 0.*

1982 KNOCK OUT CUP

Round 1

Belle Vue 97 (57 40) Reading 56 (18 38)
Birmingham 82 (48 34) Poole 74 (30 44)
Coventry 71 (40 31) Ipswich 84 (38 46)
CRADLEY HEATH 79 (43 36) Sheffield 77 (35 42)
Hackney 71 (38 33) Halifax 85 (40 45)
King's Lynn 81 (48 33) Leicester 75 (30 45)
Swindon 70 (38 32) Eastbourne 86 (49 46)
Bye: Wimbledon

Round 2

Belle Vue 81 (44 37) Halifax 75 (34 41)
Eastbourne 81 (43 38) Wimbledson 75 (35 40)
Ipswich 75.5 (38.4 37) CRADLEY HEATH 80.5 (39.5 41)
King's Lynn 78 (43 35) Birmingham 78 (35 43)

Round 2 Replay

Birmingham 76 (40 36) King's Lynn 80 (38 42)

Semi Finals

Belle Vue 91 (49 42) King's Lynn 65 (29 36)
CRADLEY HEATH 84 (48 36) Eastbourne 721 (30 41)

FINAL

First leg, October 23:
CRADLEY HEATH 46 (Erik Gundersen 15, Lance King 13, Phil Collins 7, Simon Wigg 5, Andy Reid 3, Alan Grahame 3, rider replacement for the retired Bruce Penhall) *Belle Vue 32* (Chris Morton 12, Peter Collins 6, Peter Ravn 6, Larry Ross 4, Louis Carr 2, Jim McMillan 1, Peter Carr 1).

Second leg, October 30:
Belle Vue 43 (Morton 10, Peter Collins 7, Ravn 7, Rod Hunter 6, Ross 6, Louis Carr 5, Andy Smith 2) CRADLEY HEATH 35 (Gundersen 15, King 8, Grahame 8, Wigg 2, Phil Collins 1, Reid 1, rider replacement for Penhall).

❑ CRADLEY HEATH win 81-75 on aggregate.

1982 ALL THE RESULTS

	BELLE VUE	BIRMINGHAM	COVENTRY	CRADLEY HEATH	EASTBOURNE	HACKNEY	HALIFAX	IPSWICH	KING'S LYNN	LEICESTER	POOLE	READING	SHEFFIELD	SWINDON	WIMBLEDON
BELLE VUE		45-33	45-33	48-30	48-30	53-25	52-26	37-41	50-28	53-25	44-34	52-26	40-38	56-21	53-25
BIRMINGHAM	38-40		37-41	35-43	41-37	42-36	48-30	41-37	49-29	47-31	46-31	45-32	42-36	43-35	41-37
COVENTRY	38-40	33-45		40-38	46-32	42-36	46-32	40-38	43-35	47-31	49-29	45-33	46-32	41-37	49-29
CRADLEY HEATH	46-32	45-32	45-33		49-29	48-30	46-32	40-37	46-32	47-31	45-33	40-38	50-28	49-29	48-29
EASTBOURNE	35-43	46-32	49-29	39-38		38-40	43-35	39-39	45-33	50-28	54-24	45-33	39-39	44-34	51-27
HACKNEY	35-43	36-41	34-43	40-38	43-34		49-29	42-36	45-33	41-37	42.5 35.5	42-36	47-31	47-31	39-39
HALIFAX	38-39	40-38	37-40	42-36	54-24	49-28		38-40	51-27	54-24	45-33	46-32	39-39	36-41	56-22
IPSWICH	36-42	42-36	37-41	40-38	40-38	38-40	46-32		47-30	43-35	47-31	39-39	49-29	54-24	51.5 26.5
KING'S LYNN	35-42	44-34	39-39	30-48	42-36	39-39	44-34	41-37		40-38	43-35	45-33	46-32	37-41	46-32
LEICESTER	41-37	49-29	42-36	41-37	48-30	43-35	38-40	38-40	45-32		43-35	40-38	40-38	38-40	50-28
POOLE	36-42	39-39	41-37	32-46	39-39	39-39	50-28	36-42	43-35	38-40		38-40	38-40	35-43	37-41
READING	38-40	42-36	47-30	32-46	41-37	43-34	49-29	37-41	44-34	41-37	56-22		42-36	40-38	42-36
SHEFFIELD	50-28	44-34	39-39	43-35	46-31	52-26	48-30	40-38	45-33	47-31	51-27	50-28		41-37	47-31
SWINDON	36-42	41-37	42-36	33-45	30-48	41-37	41-37	41-37	44-34	42-36	46-32	39-39	44-34		36-42
WIMBLEDON	40-38	43-35	40-38	32-46	41-37	48-30	41-37	31-47	39-39	37-41	42-36	40-37	49-29	43-35	

1983 BRITISH LEAGUE TABLE

	P	W	D	L	PtsF	PtsA	W	D	L	PtsF	PtsA	Pts
1 CRADLEY	**28**	**14**	**0**	**0**	**747**	**345**	**12**	**0**	**2**	**642**	**450**	**52**
2 Ipswich	28	13	1	0	622	470	9	0	5	555	537	45
3 Coventry	28	13	0	1	667	424	6	0	8	522	568	38
4 Reading	28	13	0	1	620	470	4	0	10	517	574	34
5 Belle Vue	28	13	0	1	599	491	2	3	9	493	598	33
6 Wimbledon	28	11	0	3	630	459	4	1	9	492	600	31
7 Hackney	28	10	0	4	590	501	4	0	10	482	605	28
8 King's Lynn	28	12	0	2	622	469	0	1	13	466	626	25
9 Birmingham	28	10	0	4	618	472	2	0	12	496	594	24
10 Sheffield	28	9	2	3	583	508	1	0	13	403	689	22
11 Halifax	28	10	0	4	601	491	0	1	13	432	659	21
12 Leicester	28	8	2	4	579	513	1	0	13	461	629	20
13 Poole	28	8	0	6	571	519	1	0	13	446	645	18
14 Eastbourne	28	6	1	7	524	567	1	0	13	409	682	15
15 Swindon	28	6	0	8	523	568	1	0	13	451	640	15

■ *CRADLEY HEATH set a new record by going through the entire British League season dropping only four points – beating the previous best set by Belle Vue in 1972 when they dropped only five points.*

■ *Cradley's two away defeats were by a mere two points at Coventry and by 14 points at runners-up Ipswich. The Heathens also won the Knock Out Cup without losing a tie although they were held to a draw by Final opponents Coventry.*

■ *Swindon, founder members of the British League, finished bottom of the table for the second time, the previous occasion being 1975.*

1983 British League Riders' Championship Final

Saturday, October 15, Belle Vue:
1 Erik Gundersen 14, 2 Michael Lee 12, 3 Hans Nielsen 12, 4 Kenny Carter 10, 5 John Louis 9, 6 Billy Sanders 9, 7 Phil Crump 8, Bo Petersen 8, Mitch Shirra 8, 10 Ole Olsen 7, 11 Jan Andersson 7, 12 Chris Morton 5, 13 Paul Woods 5, 14 David Bargh 5, 15 Mark Courtney 1, 16 Kai Niemi 0. *Track reserves: Martin Scarisbrick 0, Dave Wild 0.*

1983 KNOCK OUT CUP

Round 1

Hackney 67 (35 32) CRADLEY HEATH 89 (43 46)
Halifax 63 (41 22) Belle Vue 93 (37 56)
Ipswich 81 (43 38) Leicester 74 (34 40)
King's Lynn 90 (47 43) Eastbourne 65 (31 34)
Reading 79 (44 35) Birmingham 77 (34 43)
Sheffield 70 (37 33) *Coventry 86 (41 45)*
Swindon 66 (34 32) Wimbledon 90 (44 46)
Bye: Poole

Round 2

Belle Vue 91 (58 33) King's Lynn 65 (20 45)
CRADLEY HEATH 96 (53 43) Poole 60 (25 35)
Ipswich 77 (39 38) Reading 79 (39 40)
Wimbledon 72 (38 34) *Coventry 84 (40 44)*

Semi finals

Coventry 84 (44 40) Belle Vue 72 (34 38)
Reading 63 (32 31) CRADLEY HEATH 93 (46 47)

FINAL

First leg, October 12:
Coventry 39 (Ole Olsen 10, Gary Guglielmi 8, Sam Nikolajsen 7, Steve Bastable 5, Rick Miller 4, *Finn Thomsen 3,* Kevin Hawkins 2) CRADLEY HEATH 39 (Erik Gundersen 13, Simon Wigg 11, Phil Collins 8, Alan Grahame 3, Peter Ravn 2, Jan O. Pedersen 2, Simon Cross, did not ride, rider replacement for Lane King).

Second leg, October 17:
CRADLEY HEATH 47 (Gundersen 13, Grahame 9, Wigg 7, Ravn 7, Collins 6, Pedersen 5, Cross, did not ride, rider replacement for King) *Coventry 31* (Olsen 10, Guglielmi 10, *Bo Petersen 7,* Bastable 2, Hawkins 1, Miller 1, Nikolajsen 0).

❑ CRADLEY HEATH win 86-70 on aggregate.

1983 ALL THE RESULTS

	BELLE VUE	BIRMINGHAM	COVENTRY	CRADLEY HEATH	EASTBOURNE	HACKNEY	HALIFAX	IPSWICH	KING'S LYNN	LEICESTER	POOLE	READING	SHEFFIELD	SWINDON	WIMBLEDON
BELLE VUE		42-36	42-36	29-49	45-33	46-31	45-33	41-37	46-32	41-37	49-29	42-36	42-36	47-31	42-36
BIRMINGHAM	40-38		38-40	36-42	55-23	38-39	53-25	40-38	48-30	45-33	52-26	44-33	50-28	43-35	36-42
COVENTRY	55-23	46-32		40-38	58-20	43-34	54-24	36-42	47-31	45-33	47-31	48-30	52-26	53-25	43-35
CRADLEY HEATH	55-23	42-36	49-29		56-22	55-23	56-22	49-29	59-19	56-22	57-21	45-33	56-22	53-25	59-19
EASTBOURNE	40-38	†41-36	36-42	22-56		31-47	42-36	35-43	40-38	43-35	38-40	32-46	45-33	40-38	39-39
HACKNEY	41-37	42-36	38-39	29-49	45-33		41-37	35-43	40-38	60-18	41-37	43-35	54-24	49-29	32-46
HALIFAX	38-40	44-34	36-42	37-41	51-27	43-35		38-40	47-31	46-32	47-31	40-38	48-30	43-35	43-35
IPSWICH	39-39	50-28	41-37	46-32	45-33	47-31	50-28		42-36	42-36	47-31	42-36	43-35	41-37	47-31
KING'S LYNN	40-38	43-35	53-25	31-47	51-27	43-35	43-34	31-47		45-33	47-31	43-35	53-25	49-29	50-28
LEICESTER	39-39	42-36	40-38	22-56	50-28	48-30	40-38	35-43	39-39		44-34	37-41	55-23	38-40	50-28
POOLE	41-36	42-36	36-42	27-51	38-40	49-28	56-22	37-41	45-33	43-35		36-42	38-40	41-37	42-36
READING	45-33	41-37	43-35	35-43	43-34	43-35	50-28	45-33	46-32	40-37	46-32		51-27	48-30	44-34
SHEFFIELD	39-39	44-34	41-37	32-46	54-24	44-34	39-39	41-37	40-38	37-41	45-33	42-36		47-30	38-40
SWINDON	34-44	30-47	28-50	29-49	46-32	38-40	45-33	37-41	44-34	40-38	43-35	34-44	40-38		35-43
WIMBLEDON	52-26	45-33	47-30	35-43	45-33	37-40	45-33	37-41	43-35	46-31	42-36	46-32	62-16	48-30	

†Birmingham were awarded the match after Eastbourne illegally used a guest rider. The result was NOT changed but it is recorded as a defeat for Eastbourne.

1983 LEAGUE CUP PLAY-OFFS

First leg, June 25:
Coventry 41 (Tommy Knudsen 10, Ole Olsen 9, Gary Guglielmi 6, Steve Bastable 5, Sam Nikolajsen 4, Kevin Hawkins 4, Rick Miller 3) **Ipswich 37** (Dennis Sigalos 10, Billy Sanders 9, Andy Hibbs 6, Jeremy Doncaster 5, Preben Eriksen 3, Andy Hines 3, Nigel Flatman 1).
Second leg, July 14:
Ipswich 38 (Sigalos 11, Sanders 9, Eriksen 5, Flatman 5, Doncaster 4, Hines 3, Hibbs 1) ***Coventry 40*** (Olsen 11, Guglielmi 8, *Erik Gundersen 6*, Miller 6, Bastable 5, Hawkins 4, Nikolajsen 0).

❑ ***COVENTRY win 81-75 on aggregate.***

First leg, July 2:
BELLE VUE 50 (Chris Morton 12, Peter Collins 10, Louis Carr 8, Larry Ross 7, Andy Smith 7, Kenny McKinna 5, Rod Hunter 1) **Wimbledon 28** (Malcolm Simmons 10, Kai Niemi 6, Dave Jessup 5, Ari Koponen 5, Mike Ferreira 1, Kelvin Tatum 1, Roger Johns 0).
Second leg, July 7:
Wimbledon 42.5 (Jessup 11, Niemi 7, Johns 7, Simmons 6, Ferreira 5.5, Koponen 3, Tatum 3) **BELLE VUE 35.5** (Collins 11, Morton 10, Ross 8.5, McKinna 2, Smith 2, Louis Carr 1, Peter Carr 1).

❑ ***BELLE VUE win 85.5-70.5 on aggregate***

LEAGUE CUP FINAL

First leg, October 22:
Coventry 39 (Olsen 7, Nikolajsen 7, Bastable 7, Guglielmi 6, Hawkins 5, Miller 4, *Andy Grahame 3*) **BELLE VUE 39** (Morton 11, Collins 10, Ross 10, Louis Carr 3, McKinna 2, Smith 2, Peter Carr 1).
Second leg, October 23:
BELLE VUE 47 (Collins 12, Ross 10, Morton 10, Peter Carr 8, Smith 6, Louis Carr 1, McKinna 0) **Coventry 31** (Olsen 11, Miller 7, Guglielmi 5, *David Bargh 4*, Hawkins 4, Nikolajsen 0, Bastable 0).

❑ ***BELLE VUE win 86-70 on aggregate.***

1983 ALL THE RESULTS SOUTHERN SECTION

	EASTBOURNE	HACKNEY	IPSWICH	KING'S LYNN	POOLE	READING	SWINDON	WIMBLEDON
EASTBOURNE		37-41	43-35	39-39	32-46	32-46	43-35	31-47
HACKNEY	48-30		41-36	41-36	48-30	40-38	50-28	33-45
IPSWICH	47-31	37-41		43-35	41-37	40-38	42-36	42-36
KING'S LYNN	54-24	46-32	34-44		44-34	42-36	d.n.r.	46-32
POOLE	45-33	48-30	40-37	42-26		38-40	42-36	47-31
READING	47-31	47-31	35-43	46-32	41-37		42-36	33-45
SWINDON	43-35	43-35	34-44	31-47	36-42	32-46		37-41
WIMBLEDON	40-38	45-33	51-27	43-35	42-36	40-38	44-34	

1 Wimbledon	14	11	0	3	582	510	22
2 Hackney	14	8	0	6	544	546	16
3 Poole	14	8	0	6	564	527	16
4 Ipswich	14	9	0	5	558	532	18
5 King's Lynn	13	6	1	6	526	487	13
6 Reading	14	8	0	6	573	519	16
7 Eastbourne	14	2	1	11	479	613	5
8 Swindon	13	2	0	11	461	553	4

1983 ALL THE RESULTS NORTHERN SECTION

	BELLE VUE	BIRMINGHAM	COVENTRY	CRADLEY HEATH	HALIFAX	LEICESTER	SHEFFIELD
BELLE VUE		48-30	48-30	41-37	45-33	41-37	52-26
BIRMINGHAM	42-36		36-42	35-40	48-30	42-36	40-38
COVENTRY	40-38	40-38		39-39	37-40	53-25	49-29
CRADLEY HEATH	52-26	56-22	35-43		43-35	45-33	50-28
HALIFAX	38-40	44-34	36-42	41-37		43-35	43-35
LEICESTER	42-36	43-35	38-40	37-41	47-31		43-35
SHEFFIELD	31-47	44-34	37-41	43-35	45-33	42-36	

1 COVENTRY	12	9	1	2	496	439	19
2 Belle Vue	12	8	0	4	498	438	16
3 Cradley Heath	12	7	1	4	510	423	15
4 Halifax	12	5	0	7	447	488	10
5 Leicester	12	4	0	8	452	484	8
6 Sheffield	12	4	0	8	433	503	8
7 Birmingham	12	4	0	8	436	497	8

ACES HIGH...the League Cup winning Belle Vue squad – Peter Carr, Andy Smith, Louis Carr, Chris Morton, Kenny McKinna, Peter Collins and Larry Ross.

WONDER WITCHES...the 1984 British League champions Ipswich. Back row: Richard Knight, Billy Sanders, Carl Blackbird, Nigel Flatmasn. Front: Kai Niemi, Jeremy Doncaster and John Cook.

1984 LEAGUE CUP PLAY-OFFS

First leg, July 21:
Belle Vue 55 (Peter Collins 12, Chris Morton 10, Larry Ross 8, Mark Courtney 7, Andy Smith 6, Peter Carr 6, Kenny McKinna 6) **Wimbledon 23** (Malcolm Simmons 9, John Davis 7, John Titman 3, Gordon Kennett 2, Roger Johns 1, Mike Ferreira 1, Andy Galvin 0).
Second leg, August 9:
Wimbledon 38 (Davis 15, Ferreira 8, Simmons 5, Johns 5, Kennett 4, Titman 1) ***Belle Vue 40*** (Collins 11, Morton 11, Courtney 7, Ross 6, Carr 3, Smith 2, McKinna 0).
❏ ***BELLE VUE win 95-61 on aggregate.***

First leg, August 4:
CRADLEY HEATH 52 (Lance King 12, Phil Collins 12, Erik Gundersen 11, Alan Grahame 7, Simon Cross 6, Finn Jensen 4, Steve Collins 0) **Reading 26** (Mitch Shirra 8, Jan Andersson 7, Peter Glanz 5, Malcolm Holloway 2, Per Jonsson 2, Pierre Brannefors 1, Tim Hunt 1).

1984 ALL THE RESULTS SOUTHERN SECTION	EASTBOURNE	EXETER	IPSWICH	KING'S LYNN	OXFORD	POOLE	READING	SWINDON	WIMBLEDON
EASTBOURNE		52-26	42-36	42-36	42-36	51.5 26.5	37-41	40-30	45-33
EXETER	39-39		38-40	35-43	37-41	35-42	30-47	28-50	34-44
IPSWICH	49-29	51-27		40-38	36-42	54-24	40-38	47-31	48-30
KING'S LYNN	44-33	53-25	42-36		32-46	42-36	43-34	41-37	25-53
OXFORD	35-43	59-19	29-49	43-35		42-35	3741	4335	38-40
POOLE	37-41	52-26	39-38	41-37	40-38		32-46	40-38	40-38
READING	47-31	45-33	37-41	44-34	37-41	44-34		47-31	41-37
SWINDON	44-34	55-23	39-39	40-38	41-37	37-41	29-49		36-42
WIMBLEDON	46-32	52-26	43-35	42-36	37-41	45-33	40-38	42-36	

1 Reading	16	11	0	5	676	570	22
2 Wimbledon	16	11	0	5	664	584	22
3 Ipswich	16	10	1	5	679	568	21
4 Eastbourne	16	9	1	6	633.5	613.5	19
5 Oxford	16	9	0	7	648	599	18
6 Poole	16	8	0	8	592.5	652.5	16
7 King's Lynn	16	7	0	9	619	627	14
8 Swindon	16	5	1	10	617	631	11
9 Exeter	16	0	1	15	481	765	1

Second leg, August 13:
Reading 42 (Shirra 10, Jonsson 7, Andersson 7, Brannefors 5, Hunt 5, Glanz 5, Holloway 3) **CRADLEY HEATH 36** (Gundersen 15, Grahame 7, Phil Collins 7, Jensen 3, King 2, Cross 2, Collins 0).
❏ ***CRADLEY HEATH win 88-68 on aggregate.***

FINAL

First leg, October 7:
CRADLEY HEATH 44 (Phil Collins 12, Gundersen 11, King 10, Grahame 4, Jensen 3, Cross 3, Brett Saunders 1) ***Belle Vue 34*** (Morton 11, Collins 5, Carr 5, Smith 5, Ross 4, McKinna 3, Courtney 1).
Second leg, October 14:
Belle Vue 42 (Smith 9, Courtney 8, Morton 7, Collins 7, Carr 6, Ross 3, McKinna 2) **CRADLEY HEATH 36** (King 11, Gundersen 11, Phil Collins 7, Grahame 5, Cross 1, Steve Collins 1, Jensen 0).
❏ ***CRADLEY HEATH win 80-76 on aggregate.***

1984 ALL THE RESULTS NORTHERN SECTION	BELLE VUE	COVENTRY	CRADLEY HEATH	HALIFAX	NEWCASTLE	SHEFFIELD	WOLVERHAMPTON
BELLE VUE		54-24	51-27	54-24	60-18	53-25	48-30
COVENTRY	32-46		40-38	43-35	37-41	52-26	42-35
CRADLEY HEATH	40-38	41-37		50-28	42-36	43-35	44-34
HALIFAX	27-51	43-35	41-37		48-30	44-34	46-31
NEWCASTLE	33-44	41-37	45-33	45-32		41-37	38-39
SHEFFIELD	36-42	41-37	43-35	49-29	42-36		43-35
WOLVERHAMPTON	44-34	37-41	39-38	42-36	30-47	40-38	

1 Belle Vue	12	10	0	2	575	360	20
2 Cradley Heath	12	6	0	6	468	467	12
3 Newcastle	12	6	0	6	451	481	12
4 Coventry	12	5	0	7	457	478	10
5 Sheffield	12	5	0	7	449	487	10
6 Wolverhampton	12	5	0	7	436	495	10
7 Halifax	12	5	0	7	433	501	10

1984 BRITISH LEAGUE TABLE

	P	W	D	L	PtsF	PtsA	W	D	L	PtsF	PtsA	Pts
1 IPSWICH	**30**	**15**	**0**	**0**	**732**	**436**	**10**	**2**	**3**	**611**	**558**	**52**
2 Belle Vue	29	14	0	0	724	368	9	3	3	598	570	49
3 Cradley Heath	30	13	1	1	701	469	8	1	6	607	562	44
4 Reading	30	14	0	1	666	502	3	1	11	536.5	624.5	35
5 Sheffield	30	11	0	4	663	507	4	0	11	528	641	30
6 King's Lynn	30	11	0	4	635	535	4	0	11	508	661	30
7 Wimbledon	30	13	0	2	645	524	2	0	13	494	674	30
8 Oxford	30	11	1	3	640	530	3	0	12	534	636	29
9 Swindon	29	11	2	2	646.5	523.5	1	0	13	496	596	26
10 Wolverhampton	30	9	0	6	609	556	4	0	11	532.5	637.5	26
11 Eastbourne	30	11	0	4	652.5	514.5	1	1	13	504.5	663.5	25
12 Coventry	30	10	1	4	662	508	1	1	13	507	660	24
13 Poole	30	10	1	4	603	560	0	0	15	472	698	21
14 Halifax	30	9	2	4	605	565	0	1	14	424	746	21
15 Exeter	30	8	2	5	622	547	0	0	15	423	746	18
16 Newcastle	30	9	0	6	609	558	0	0	15	427.5	741.5	18

■ ***A FLURRY of winter action saw Exeter, Newcastle and Oxford return to the British League Division One while Birmingham closed down and Hackney dropped into the National League under a new promotion.***

■ *THREE attempts were made to stage the Belle Vue-Swindon British League match but on each occasion heavy rain forced the meeting to be postponed and eventually it was cancelled.*

1984 British League Riders' Championship Final

Saturday, October 20, Belle Vue:
1 Chris Morton 13, 2 Hans Nielsen 13, 3 Erik Gundersen 13, 4 Peter Ravn 12, 5 Shawn Moran 11, 6 Tommy Knudsen 10, 7 Billy Sanders 8, 8 Malcolm Simmons 7, 9 Sam Ermolenko 6, 10 Jan Andersson 6, 11 Bobby Schwartz 5, 12 Phil Crump 5, 13 Neil Evitts 4, 14 Martin Scarisbrick 4, 15 Andy Campbell 2, 16 John Louis 1.
Track reserves: Glenn Hornby 0, Lee Edwards 0.

1984 KNOCK OUT CUP

Round 1

Coventry 84 (52 32) Wimbledon 72 (26 46)
Cradley Heath 82 (46 36) Reading 73 (32 41)
IPSWICH 87 (45 42) Swindon 69 (33 36)
King's Lynn 94 (49 45) Newcastle 61 (29 32)
Oxford 66 (38 28) *Belle Vue 90 (40 50)*
Poole 73 (37 36) Eastbourne 82 (41 41)
Sheffield 90 (49 41) Halifax 66 (29 37)
Wolverhampton 91 (45 46) Exeter 65 (33 32)

Round 2

Coventry 70 (42 28) *Belle Vue 86 (36 50)*
Cradley Heath 72 (40 32) IPSWICH 91 (34 57)
Eastbourne 78 (57 21) King's Lynn 78 (21 57)
Wolverhampton 80 (42 38) Sheffield 76 (36 40)

Round 2 Replay

King's Lynn 85 (51 34) Eastbourne 69 (27 42)

Semi finals

King's Lynn 65 (44 21) IPSWICH 91 (34 57)
Wolverhampton 62 (40 22) *Belle Vue 94 (38 56)*

FINAL

First leg, October 27:
Belle Vue 33 (Kenny McKinna 9, Peter Collins 8, Chris Morton 6, Andy Smith 6, Larry Ross 2, Peter Carr 2, Mark Courtney 0) IPSWICH 45 (Billy Sanders 12, John Cook 10, Richard Knight 8, Jeremy Doncaster 7, Kai Niemi 6, Nigel Flatman 2, Carl Blackbird 0).
Second leg, October 28:
IPSWICH 47 (Sanders 9, Doncaster 8, Cook 8, Blackbird 8, Niemi 6, Knight 5, Flatman 3) *Belle Vue 31* (Ross 9, Smith 9, Morton 6, McKinna 4, Carr 2, Collins 1, Courtney 0).

❑ IPSWICH win 92-64 on aggregate.

1984 ALL THE RESULTS

	BELLE VUE	COVENTRY	CRADLEY HEATH	EASTBOURNE	EXETER	HALIFAX	IPSWICH	KING'S LYNN	NEWCASTLE	OXFORD	POOLE	READING	SHEFFIELD	SWINDON	WIMBLEDON	WOLVES
BELLE VUE		44-34	44-34	64-14	50-28	54-24	55-23	48-30	47-31	49-29	57-21	53-25	49-29	Not raced	61-17	49-29
COVENTRY	39-39		37-41	48-30	59-19	53-25	50-38	50-28	51-27	36-42	42-36	42-36	47-31	38-40	43-35	37-41
CRADLEY HEATH	48-30	46-32		44-34	52-26	44-34	39-39	51-27	56-22	46-32	44-34	48-30	49-29	51-27	36-42	47-31
EASTBOURNE	36-42	43-35	42-35		49-28	52-26	38-40	36-42	54-24	45-33	40-38	35.5 42.5	48-30	40-38	47-30	47-31
EXETER	38-40	42-35	36-42	41-37		51-27	39-39	33-45	47-31	43-35	46-32	39-39	38-40	44-34	48-30	37-41
HALIFAX	36-42	39-39	39-39	41-37	44-34		31-47	45-33	41-37	46-32	44-34	42-36	35-43	42-36	45-33	35-43
IPSWICH	42-36	52-26	46-32	51-27	51-27	58-30		46-32	60-17	46-32	51-27	41-37	48-29	40-38	48-30	52-26
KING'S LYNN	31-47	43-35	29-49	44-34	50-28	57-21	34-44		47-31	37-41	48-30	45-33	44-34	45-33	41-37	40-38
NEWCASTLE	37-41	42-35	29-49	37-40	48-30	45-33	28-50	35-43		44-34	50-28	44-34	38-40	46-32	46-31	40-38
OXFORD	39-39	43-35	45-33	40.5 37.5	56-22	57-21	35-43	37-41	41-37		43-35	42-36	34-44	41-37	46-32	40.5 37.5
POOLE	38-40	41-37	35-43	41-37	41-37	39-39	37-41	44-34	43-35	46-32		31-40	40-38	41-37	41-37	45-33
READING	40-37	47-30	40-38	43-35	54-24	49-29	32-46	50-28	49-29	41-37	45-33		42-36	46-32	47-31	41-37
SHEFFIELD	37-41	51-27	32-46	47-31	55-23	48-30	43-35	48-30	55-23	40-38	50-28	38-40		41-37	43-35	35-43
SWINDON	39-39	47-31	32-46	39-39	53-25	49-29	32-46	48-30	51.5 26.5	40-38	44-34	41-37	40-38		46-32	45-33
WIMBLEDON	33-44	45-33	43-35	42-36	43-35	47-31	37-41	44-34	42-36	40-38	52-26	44-34	46-32	40-38		47-31
WOLVERHAMPTON	37-41	35-43	33-45	41-36	41-37	43-35	38-39	46-31	57-21	37-41	42-36	39-37	43-35	41-37	36-42	

1985 BRITISH LEAGUE TABLE

	P	W	D	L	PtsF	PtsA	W	D	L	PtsF	PtsA	BP	Pts
1 OXFORD	**20**	**9**	**1**	**0**	**446**	**333**	**7**	**0**	**3**	**403**	**375**	**10**	**43**
2 Sheffield	20	9	0	1	449	330	4	1	5	367	411	6	33
3 Coventry	20	9	0	1	442	335	2	2	6	375	405	7	31
4 Halifax	20	9	0	1	452	326	0	1	9	331	448	5	24
5 Ipswich	20	8	1	1	424	355	1	1	8	357	423	4	24
6 Belle Vue	20	9	0	1	443	334	1	0	9	335	443	4	24
7 Cradley Heath	19	8	0	2	422	358	2	0	7	318	382	4	24
8 Swindon	20	6	1	3	446	333	2	0	8	350	429	6	23
9 Reading	19	5	2	2	383	316	1	2	7	351	427	6	22
10 Wolverhampton	20	4	2	4	397	382	1	0	9	318	461	2	14
11 King's Lynn	20	5	0	5	387	393	0	0	10	290	487	0	10

1985 LEAGUE CUP TABLE

	P	W	D	L	PtsF	PtsA	W	D	L	PtsF	PtsA	BP	Pts
1 CRADLEY	**20**	**9**	**0**	**1**	**440**	**340**	**4**	**1**	**5**	**382**	**397**	**7**	**34**
2 Oxford	20	7	1	2	432	347	4	1	5	388	391	8	32
3 Ipswich	20	9	0	1	438	342	3	1	6	370	410	7	32
4 Coventry	20	7	2	1	419	360	3	1	6	378	402	7	30
5 Wolverhampton	20	8	1	1	436	343	2	0	8	369	411	6	27
6 Swindon	20	7	0	3	419	361	4	0	6	348	432	4	26
7 Belle Vue	20	7	2	1	423	357	2	0	8	354	426	4	24
8 Reading	20	8	1	1	421	359	0	1	9	349	430	3	21
9 Halifax	20	7	0	3	408	372	1	0	9	332	447	4	20
10 Sheffield	20	6	0	4	428	352	1	1	8	339	441	4	19
11 King's Lynn	20	4	0	6	392	387	0	1	9	311	469	1	10

LEAGUE CUP PLAY OFFS

First leg, August 15:
Ipswich 37 (John Cook 14, Jeremy Doncaster 8, Richard Knight 8, Kai Niemi 3, Nigel Flatman 3, Alan Farmer 1) ***Oxford 41*** (Hans Nielsen 12, Jens Rasmussen 7, Melvyn Taylor 7, Simon Wigg 6, Marvyn Cox 5, Andy Grahame 4, Troy Butler 0).
Second leg, September 27:
Oxford 39 (Nielsen 15, Wigg 11, Cox 5, Rasmussen 4, Klaus Lausch 2, Taylor 2, Butler 0) **Ipswich 39** (Cook 9, Doncaster 8, Knight 7, Flatman 6, Farmer 5, Niemi 3, Andy Hines 1).

❑ ***OXFORD win 80-76 on aggregate.***

First leg, September 25
Cradley Heath 40 (Erik Gundersen 10, Phil Collins 9, Finn Jensen 9, *Preben Eriksen 8*, Simon Cross 3, Nigel Leaver 1, Paul Taylor 0) **COVENTRY 38** (*Jan Andersson 12*, Kelvin Tatum 10, David Bargh 5, Steve Bastable 5, Rick Miller 3, John Jørgensen 2, Frank Andersen 1)
Second leg, October 2:
COVENTRY 46 (Tatum 12, Tommy Knudsen 11, Jørgensen 9, Bastable 5, Bargh 4, Andersen 3, Miller 2) **Cradley Heath 32** (Jan O. Pedersen 9, Gundersen 9, Jensen 7, Collins 4, Cross 2, Kevin Smith 1, Leaver 0)

❑ ***COVENTRY win 84-72 on aggregate.***

LEAGUE CUP FINAL

First leg, October 25:
Oxford 42 (Wigg 14, Nielsen 13, Cox 9, Nigel De'ath 3, Rasmussen 2, Butler 1) **COVENTRY 36** (Knudsen 11, Tatum 9, Miller 5, Bargh 4, Andersen 3, Steve Bastable 3, Jørgensen 1).
Second leg, October 26:
COVENTRY 50 (Tatum 12, Miller 10, Knudsen 9, Jørgensen 6, Bastable 5, Andersen 4, Bargh 4) **Oxford 28** (Nielsen 14, Wigg 6, Rasmussen 4, Butler 2, Cox 1, Melvyn Taylor 1)

❑ ***COVENTRY win 86-70 on aggregate.***

1985 KNOCK OUT CUP

Round 1
Coventry 70 (35 35) OXFORD 86 (43 43)
Halifax 77 (48 29) Wolverhampton 79 (30 49)
Ipswich 87 (45 42) **Swindon 69 (33 36)**

Round 2
Belle Vue 74 (40 34) OXFORD 82 (38 44)
King's Lynn 64 (39 25) Cradley Heath 92 (39 53)
Reading 78 (46 32) Sheffield 78 (32 46)
Wolverhampton 71 (40 31) ***Ipswich 85 (38 47)***

Round 2 Replay
Sheffield 73 (39 34) Reading 82 (39 43)

Semi Finals
Cradley Heath 71 (36 35) ***Ipswich 85 (42 43)***
OXFORD 81 (41 40) Reading 74 (36 38)

FINAL
First leg, October 27:
Ipswich 41 **(John Cook 10, Jeremy Doncaster 10, Richard Knight 9, Dennis Sigalos 5, Alan Farmer 4, Kai Niemi 2, Robbie Fuller 1) OXFORD 37 (Hans Nielsen 14, Simon Wigg 10, Melvyn Taylor 5, Marvyn Cox 4, Jens Rasmussen 3, Troy Butler 1).**
Second leg, October 30:
OXFORD 42 (Nielsen 15, Wigg 12, Cox 7, Alastair Stevens 4, Butler 4, Rasmussen 0) ***Ipswich 35*** **(Cook 12, Knight 9, Sigalos 4, Farmer 4, Doncaster 3, Niemi 2, Fuller 1).**

❑ **OXFORD win 79-76 on aggregate.**

1985 British League Riders' Championship Final

Saunday, October 20, Belle Vue:
1 Erik Gundersen 14, 2 Peter Collins 12, 3 Chris Morton 12, 4 Tommy Knudsen 11, 5 Shawn Moran 11, Hans Nielsen 11, Kelvin Tatum 11, 8 Neil Evitts 8, 9 John Cook 6, 10 Bo Petersen 5, 11 Jan Andersson 5, 12 Simon Wigg 5, 13 Dave Jessup 13, 14 Les Collins 2, Jeremy Doncaster 2, 16 Peter Ravn 2. ***Track reserves: Barry Ayres and Declan Eccles, did not ride. Sponsor: TNT Sameday.***

1985 ALL THE RESULTS

▼ Figures in italics relate to 1985 League Cup. ▼

	BELLE VUE	COVENTRY	CRADLEY HEATH	HALIFAX	IPSWICH	KING'S LYNN	OXFORD	READING	SHEFFIELD	SWINDON	WOLVES
BELLE VUE		45-33 *41-37*	43-35 *35-43*	47-31 *40-38*	41-37 *39-39*	51-27 *49-29*	37-40 *44-34*	42-35 *43-35*	40-37 *39-39*	50-28 *51-27*	47-31 *42-36*
COVENTRY	43-34 *41-37*		41-36 *45-32*	43-35 *38-40*	45-33 *42-36*	47-31 *48-30*	37-41 *39-39*	45-33 *39-39*	49-29 *44-34*	39-38 *42-36*	53-25 *41-37*
CRADLEY HEATH	41-37 *45-33*	34-44 *41-37*		48-30 *45-33*	42-36 *45-33*	48-30 *50-28*	41-37 *38-40*	41-37 *46-32*	38-40 *42-36*	40-38 *47-31*	49-29 *41-37*
HALIFAX	49-29 *41-37*	47-31 *37-41*	47-30 *36-42*		44-34 *44-34*	47-30 *46-32*	40-38 *40-38*	49-29 *43-35*	33-45 *36-42*	44-34 *44-34*	52-26 *41-37*
IPSWICH	42-36 *44-34*	43-35 *44-34*	42-36 *40-38*	43-35 *52-26*		40-38 *43-35*	36-42 *43-35*	39-39 *52-26*	47-30 *44-34*	43-35 *36-42*	49-29 *42-36*
KING'S LYNN	37-41 *35-43*	40-38 *37-41*	32-46 *44-34*	42-36 *43-35*	34-44 *36-42*		32-46 *30-47*	41-37 *42-36*	52-26 *51-27*	36-42 *38-40*	41-37 *36-42*
OXFORD	44-34 *52-26*	43-35 *40-38*	47-31 *39-39*	47-30 *51-27*	39-39 *36-42*	47-31 *42-36*		50-28 *41-36*	43-35 *48-30*	45-33 *38-40*	41-37 *45-33*
READING	43-35 *42-36*	39-39 *39-39*	d.n.r. *45-33*	51-27 *45-33*	42-36 *43-35*	54-22 *41-37*	35-42 *42-36*		39-39 *41-37*	46-32 *37-41*	34-44 *46-32*
SHEFFIELD	42-36 *33-45*	40-38 *36-42*	49-29 *34-44*	41-37 *51-27*	41-37 *34-44*	63-15 *61-17*	41-37 *42-36*	38-40 *41-37*		48-30 *52-26*	46-31 *44-34*
SWINDON	61-16 *43-35*	35-43 *47-31*	45-33 *35-43*	47-31 *42-36*	49-29 *48-30*	46-32 *50-28*	38-40 *37-41*	39-39 *43-35*	37-41 *41-37*		49-29 *33-45*
WOLVERHAMPTON	41-37 *50-28*	39-39 *40-38*	36-42 *44-34*	39-39 *40-37*	46-32 *43-35*	44-34 *39-39*	38-40 *36-42*	43-34 *40-38*	33-45 *57-21*	38-40 *47-31*	

1986 BRITISH LEAGUE TABLE

	P	W	D	L	PtsF	PtsA	W	D	L	PtsF	PtsA	BP	Pts
1 OXFORD	**18**	**8**	**0**	**0**	**404**	**220**	**10**	**0**	**0**	**459**	**320**	**8**	**44**
2 Cradley Heath	20	9	0	1	443	337	4	3	3	411	369	9	38
3 Wolverhampton	19	8	0	2	435	345	5	0	4	336	365	6	32
4 Sheffield	19	7	1	2	440	339	3	1	5	343	358	6	28
5 Coventry	20	7	0	3	438	342	3	1	6	391	389	6	27
6 Bradford	20	7	1	2	443	335	1	0	9	315	464	4	21
7 Reading	20	4	3	3	409	371	3	0	7	348	430	4	21
8 Swindon	19	5	1	4	386	389	3	0	6	307	395	4	21
9 Ipswich	20	5	0	5	391	389	2	1	7	338	442	3	18
10 Belle Vue	19	4	0	5	346	356	1	0	9	329	449	2	12
11 King's Lynn	20	0	0	10	327	453	2	0	8	299	481	0	4

1986 LEAGUE CUP TABLE

	P	W	D	L	PtsF	PtsA	W	D	L	PtsF	PtsA	BP	Pts
1 COVENTRY	**20**	**10**	**0**	**0**	**446**	**333**	**4**	**1**	**5**	**369**	**410**	**8**	**37**
2 Oxford	20	8	0	2	414	362	5	1	4	396	383	9	36
3 Ipswich	20	10	0	0	425	351	2	1	7	376	404	5	30
4 Cradley Heath	20	9	0	1	433	346	1	2	7	375	404	7	29
5 Swindon	20	8	2	0	449	331	1	1	8	365	415	6	27
6 Sheffield	20	7	0	3	425	355	3	2	5	366	407	5	27
7 Bradford	20	6	2	2	432	348	3	1	6	366	412	5	26
8 Reading	20	9	0	1	430	343	1	0	9	342	435	4	24
9 Belle Vue	20	4	2	4	407	372	2	0	8	330	449	3	17
10 Wolverhampton	20	6	1	3	416	364	0	0	10	328	452	3	16
11 King's Lynn	20	2	2	6	381	399	0	0	10	291	487	0	6

1986 KNOCK OUT CUP

Round 1

Belle Vue 77 (45 32) CRADLEY HEATH 79 (33 46)
Ipswich 69 (38 31) Swindon 87 (40 47)
King's Lynn 68 (43 25) Reading 88 (35 53)

Round 2

CRADLEY HEATH 83 (50 33) Reading 73 (28 45)
Sheffield 78 (44 34) Coventry 77 (34 43)
Swindon 67 (37 30) OXFORD 89 (41 48)
Wolverhampton 71 (38 33) Bradford 85 (40 45)

Semi finals

†CRADLEY HEATH 50 (50) Bradford 28 (28)
OXFORD 90 (45 45) Sheffield 66 (33 33)

FINAL

First leg, Novemb er 1:
CRADLEY HEATH 39 (Jan O. Pedersen 9, Phil Collins 8, Erik Gundersen 7, Nigel Leaver 6, Steve Bastable 4, Paul Fry 3, Simon Cross 2)
OXFORD 39 (Hans Nielsen 14, Marvyn Cox 9, Simon Wigg 9, Nigel De'ath 4, Per Sørensen 1, Jon Surman 1, Andy Grahame 1).

Two attempts were made to stage the tie at Oxford, on October 31 and November 3, but on both occasions the meeting was called off because of rain.

It was agreed the trophy would be shared between the two clubs.

❏ CRADLEY HEATH and OXFORD draw 39-39 on aggregate.

†The second leg of the Cradley Heath-Bradford tie was twice postponed and the BSPA ruled that Bradford should concede the tie.

LEAGUE CUP PLAY OFFS

First leg, September 3:
Coventry 39 (Kelvin Tatum 12, Tommy Knudsen 8, John Jørgensen 8, Rick Miller 4, David Clarke 3, Alun Rossiter 3, David Bargh 1) **CRADLEY HEATH 39** (Erik Gundersen 11, Jan O. Pedersen 8, Steve Bastable 8, Simon Cross 4, Phil Collins 4, Paul Fry 3, Nigel Leaver 1)
Second leg, September 10:
CRADLEY HEATH 41 (Gundersen 10, Cross 8, Collins 6, Pedersen 6, Bastable 4, Fry 4, Leaver 3) **Coventry 37** (Tatum 13, Jørgensen 9, Knudsen 8, Rossiter 4, Miller 1, Bargh 1, Clarke 1)

❏ ***CRADLEY HEATH win 80-76 on aggregate.***

First leg, September 3:
OXFORD 40 (Hans Nielsen 15, Marvyn Cox 11, Simon Wigg 10, Per Sørensen 2, Nigel De'ath 1, Jon Surman 1, Andy Grahame 0) **Ipswich 38** (Kai Niemi 8, Jeremy Doncaster 6, Jens Rasmussen 6, Richard Knight 6, Robbie Fuller 5, Alan Mogridge 4, Louis Carr 3)
Second leg, September 21:
Ipswich 34 (Doncaster 11, Niemi 9, Fuller 6, Rasmussen 4, Knight 3, Carr 1, Alan Farmer 0) **OXFORD 42** (Wigg 11, Nielsen 10, Cox 9, Sørensen 6, De'ath 3, Surman 2, Grahame 1).

❏ ***OXFORD win 82-72 on aggregate.***

LEAGUE CUP FINAL

First leg, October 18:
CRADLEY HEATH 38 (Erik Gundersen 11, Phil Collins 7, Simon Cross 6, Jan O. Pedersen 5, Steve Bastable 5, Nigel Leaver 2, Paul Fry 2) **OXFORD 40** (Hans Nielsen 11, Marvyn Cox 10, Simon Wigg 9, Nigel De'ath 4, Per Sørensen 4, Andy Grahame 2, Jon Surman 0).

Two attempts were made to stage the tie at Oxford, on October 24 and November 3, but on both occasions the meeting was called off because of rain.

It was agreed the trophy would be shared between the two clubs.

OXFORD became the first team in British League history to go through their League campaign with a 100% record although two matches were never raced because of the weather.

1986 British League Riders' Championship Final

Sunday, October 12, Belle Vue:
1 Hans Nielsen 15, 2 Erik Gundersen 11, 3 Shawn Moran 11, 4 Jan Andersson 11, 5 Chris Morton 11, 6 Simon Wigg 9, 7 Jeremy Doncaster 8, John Jørgensen 8, Tommy Knudsen 8, Jan O. Pedersen 8, 11 Alan Grahame 6, 12 John Davis 5, 13 Neil Evitts 3, 14 Andy Campbell 3, Preben Eriksen 3, 16 Kai Niemi 0. *Track reserve: Lee Edwards 0. Sponsor: TNT Sameday.*

1986 ALL THE RESULTS

†1986 League Cup scores in italics

	BELLE VUE	BRADFORD	COVENTRY	CRADLEY HEATH	IPSWICH	KING'S LYNN	OXFORD	READING	SHEFFIELD	SWINDON	WOLVES
BELLE VUE		49-29 *38-40*	40-38 *38-39*	35-43 *46-32*	37-41 *32-46*	44-34 *47-31*	33-45 *33-45*	31-47 *46-32*	32-46 *39-39*	Not Raced *39-39*	45-33 *49-29*
BRADFORD	40-37 *41-37*		33-45 *35-43*	39-39 *39-39*	56-22 *39-39*	53-25 *49-29*	35-43 *36-40*	48-29 *50-28*	43-35 *44-34*	46-32 *47-31*	50-28 *52-26*
COVENTRY	52-26 *44-33*	42-36 *45-33*		40-38 *43-35*	55-23 *44-34*	54-24 *46-32*	32-46 *42-36*	51-27 *46-32*	40-38 *46-32*	34-44 *46-32*	38-40 *44-34*
CRADLEY HEATH	47-31 *44-34*	42-36 *41-37*	43-35 *41-37*		47-31 *41-37*	46-32 *57-20*	33-45 *38-40*	55-23 *42-36*	45-33 *43-35*	42-36 *42-36*	43-35 *44-34*
IPSWICH	42-36 *43-35*	47-31 *39-37*	35-43 *44-34*	32-46 *40-38*		46-32 *46-31*	36-42 *39-38*	40-38 *43-35*	44-34 *47-31*	32-46 *40-38*	37-41 *44-34*
KING'S LYNN	35-43 *47-31*	32-46 *39-39*	35-43 *38-40*	23-55 *39-39*	36-42 *32-46*		33-45 *38-40*	29-49 *37-41*	35-43 *36-42*	36-42 *35-43*	33-45 *40-38*
OXFORD	53-25 *36-42*	58-20 *43-35*	42-36 *35-43*	43-35 *40-37*	46-32 *41-34*	60-18 *45-33*		44-34 *42-33*	Not Raced *46-32*	58-20 *40-38*	Not Raced *44-34*
READING	40-38 *54-24*	54-24 *41-37*	39-39 *47-31*	46-32 *42-36*	39-39 *40-38*	38-40 *49-29*	35-43 *40-38*		39-39 *31-40*	43-35 *40-38*	36-42 *46-32*
SHEFFIELD	47-30 *35-43*	49-29 *36-42*	40-38 *48-30*	39-39 *40-38*	44-34 *45-33*	53-25 *56-22*	29-49 *38-40*	37-41 *43-35*		55-23 *43-35*	47-31 *41-37*
SWINDON	44-34 *52-26*	42-35 *53-25*	42-36 *45-33*	39-39 *41-37*	41-37 *41-37*	36-42 *44-34*	21-56 *39-39*	49-28 *46-32*	36-41 *39-39*		36-41 *49-29*
WOLVERHAMPTON	49-29 *53-25*	49-29 *37-41*	40-38 *39-39*	33-45 *34-44*	41-37 *46-32*	51-27 *48-30*	33-45 *40-38*	46-32 *40-38*	44-34 *36-42*	49-29 *43-35*	

1987 BRITISH LEAGUE TABLE

	P	W	D	L	PtsF	PtsA	W	D	L	PtsF	PtsA	BP	Pts
1 COVENTRY	**22**	**11**	**0**	**0**	**508**	**350**	**8**	**3**	**0**	**462**	**396**	**11**	**52**
2 Cradley Heath	22	9	1	1	485	371	4	0	7	432	425	9	36
3 Swindon	22	7	2	2	458	399	5	0	6	426.5	429.5	7	33
4 Sheffield	22	10	0	1	475	382	3	0	8	396	458	6	32
5 Bradford	22	9	1	1	501	356	1	2	8	381	476	7	30
6 Ipswich	22	7	1	3	461	396	3	2	6	413	443	6	29
7 Reading	22	9	1	1	470.5	387.5	2	1	8	404	453	4	28
8 Belle Vue	22	8	1	2	458	399	2	0	9	385	473	5	26
9 Hackney	22	6	2	3	432	422	1	1	9	363	495	3	20
10 Wolverhampton	22	5	1	5	431	425	1	1	9	359	498	3	17
11 Oxford	22	6	0	5	437	421	0	1	10	388	470	3	16
12 King's Lynn	22	4	1	6	405	453	0	0	11	352	505	2	11

1987 LEAGUE CUP TABLE

	P	W	D	L	PtsF	PtsA	W	D	L	PtsF	PtsA	BP	Pts
1 COVENTRY	**22**	**11**	**0**	**0**	**520**	**338**	**5**	**1**	**5**	**423**	**434**	**10**	**43**
2 Oxford	22	10	0	1	468	390	4	2	5	416	442	9	39
3 Belle Vue	22	10	1	0	513	344	4	0	7	408	448	9	38
4 Cradley Heath	22	9	0	2	474	384	5	0	6	414	444	8	36
5 Sheffield	22	9	0	2	471	383	4	2	5	418	439	5	33
6 Reading	22	8	0	3	466	390	4	1	6	401	457	6	31
7 Swindon	22	8	2	1	465	393	1	0	10	413	445	6	26
8 Wolverhampton	22	9	0	2	483	374	0	1	10	345	512	4	23
9 Bradford	22	6	1	4	454	404	2	1	8	375	481	4	22
10 Hackney	22	5	2	4	438	419	1	0	10	363	494	3	17
11 King's Lynn	22	4	1	6	421	435	1	0	10	344	512	1	12
12 Ipswich	22	4	1	6	440	416	0	0	11	350	505	1	10

LEAGUE CUP PLAY OFFS

First leg, August 14:
Oxford 42 (Hans Nielsen 12, Marvyn Cox 11, Andy Grahame 7, Nigel De'ath 6, Jon Surman 3, Alastair Stevens 2, Jens Rasmussen 1) ***Belle Vue 36*** (Chris Morton 9, Peter Ravn 9, Paul Thorp 8, Carl Blackbird 6, Kenny McKinna 2, David Blackburn 2, Glenn Hornby 0).
Second leg, August 22:
Belle Vue 44 (Blackbird 11, Thorp 10, Morton 9, Ravn 5, McKinna 5, Hornby 3, Whittaker 1) **Oxford 34** (Cox 13, Nielsen 12, Grahame 6, De'ath 2, Surman 1, Rasmussen 0, Stevens 0).
❑ ***BELLE VUE win 80-76 on aggregate.***

First leg, August 31:
Cradley Heath 36 (Erik Gundersen 12, Simon Cross 9, Jan O. Pedersen 7, Alan Grahame 6, Jan Jakobsen 2, David Walsh 0, Paul Fry 0) **COVENTRY 42** (Tommy Knudsen 10, Kelvin Tatum 10, Rick Miller 6, David Bargh 6, John Jørgensen 6, Andy Hackett 3, Wayne Broadhurst 1)
Second leg, August 31:
COVENTRY 45 (Knudsen 12, Tatum 10, Bargh 8, Miller 6, Jørgensen 5, Hackett 4, Broadhurst 0) **Cradley Heath 33** (Cross 11, Gundersen 7, Grahame 5, Pedersen 4, Walsh 3, Jakobsen 2, Fry 1,)
❑ ***COVENTRY win 87-69 on aggregate.***

FINAL

First leg, September 15:
COVENTRY 41 (Knudsen 9, Bargh 9, Tatum 7, Miller 6, Jørgensen 5, David Clarke 4, Broadhurst 1) ***Belle Vue 37*** (Ravn 12, Morton 10, Thorp 9, Blackbird 5, Andy Smith 1, McKinna 0, Hornby 0).
Second leg, October 18:
Belle Vue 41 (Ravn 12, Thorp 9, Morton 8, McKinna 6, Smith 2, Blackbird 2, Hornby 2) **COVENTRY 37** (Knudsen 9, Tatum 9, Miller 7, Jørgensen 6, Bargh 4, Clarke 2, Broadhurst 0)
❑ ***Match tied 78-78.***

FINAL REPLAY

First leg, October 24:
COVENTRY 46 (Knudsen 11, Tatum 11, Miller 8, Bargh 7, Jørgensen 6, Clarke 3, Broadhurst 0) ***Belle Vue 32*** (Ravn 11, Thorp 7, Smith 5, McKinna 4, Morton 4, Hornby 1, Bernie Collier 0)
Second leg, November 1:
Belle Vue 40 (Morton 14, Ravn 11, McKinna 8, Richard Knight 4, Hornby 2, Blackburn 1, Bernie Collier 0) **COVENTRY 38** (Bargh 10, Knudsen 8, Tatum 8, Miller 5, Jørgensen 4, Clarke 3, Broadhurst 0)
❑ ***COVENTRY win 84-72.***

1987 KNOCK OUT CUP

Round 1
Belle Vue 86 (47 39) Oxford 94 (43 51)
Bradford 91 (49 42) Hackney 89 (41 48)
Sheffield 100 (51 49) King's Lynn 80 (39 41)
Wolverhampton 87 (44 43) Swindon 93 (46 47)

Round 2
Coventry 93 (51 42) **Sheffield 86 (38 48)**
CRADLEY HEATH 104 (55 49) Bradford 76 (35 41)
Ipswich 89 (47 42) Oxford 91 (43 48)
Reading 95 (48 47) Swindon 84 (41 43)

Semi Finals
CRADLEY HEATH 82 (39 43) Oxford 80 (33 47)
Reading 89 (47 42) ***Coventry 91 (43 48)***

FINAL
First leg, October 20:
Coventry 45 **(Tommy Knudsen 17, David Bargh 8, John Jørgensen 8, David Clarke 6, Wayne Broadhurst 3, Rick Miller 3, Kelvin Tatum 0)**
CRADLEY HEATH 45 (David Walsh 12, Jan O. Pedersen 11, Erik Gundersen 11, Simon Cross 8, Jan Jakobsen 2, Paul Fry 1, Nigel Leaver 0).
Second leg, Octonber 21:
CRADLEY HEATH 49 (Pedersen 11, Gundersen 11, Walsh 11, Cross 9, Fry 4, Jakobsen 2, Leaver 1)
Coventry 41 **(Knudsen 16, Bargh 7,** ***Kelly Moran 7,*** **Jørgensen 5, Clarke 3, Miller 3, Broadhurst 0).**
❑ **CRADLEY HEATH win 94-86 on aggregate.**

1987 British League Riders' Championship Final

– See 1988 Statistics –

1987 ALL THE RESULTS

▼ Figures in italics relate to 1987 League Cup results. ▼

	BELLE VUE	BRADFORD	COVENTRY	CRADLEY HEATH	HACKNEY	IPSWICH	KING'S LYNN	OXFORD	READING	SHEFFIELD	SWINDON	WOLVES
BELLE VUE		46-32 *51-27*	39-39 *43-34*	37-41 *41-37*	45-33 *49-29*	43-35 *44-34*	42-36 *50-28*	42-36 *41-37*	41-37 *50-28*	44-34 *39-39*	41-36 *45-33*	38-40 *60-18*
BRADFORD	53-25 *38-40*		29-49 *41-37*	42-36 *37-41*	49-29 *38-40*	39-39 *48-30*	46-32 *44-34*	52-26 *48-30*	47-31 *37-41*	47-31 *39-39*	44-34 *42-36*	53-24 *42-36*
COVENTRY	46-32 *43-35*	53-25 *50-28*		44-34 *52-26*	50-28 *47-31*	44-34 *54-24*	50-28 *53-25*	44-34 *44-34*	42-36 *43-35*	48-30 *47-31*	42-36 *40-38*	45-33 *47-31*
CRADLEY HEATH	47-31 *40-38*	39-39 *43-35*	38-40 *38-40*		43-35 *52-26*	44-34 *47-31*	43-35 *44-34*	43-35 *37-41*	41-37 *41-37*	45-32 *44-34*	50-27 *40-38*	52-26 *48-30*
HACKNEY	35-43 *33-45*	39-39 *39-39*	34-44 *39-39*	41-36 *43-35*		38-38 *39-38*	43-35 *51-27*	40-38 *38-40*	40-38 *38-40*	37-40 *35-43*	40-38 *40-38*	45-33 *43-35*
IPSWICH	38-40 *38-40*	42-36 *38-39*	39-39 *40-38*	41-37 *38-40*	50-28 *50-28*		50-27 *38-39*	42-36 *43-35*	46-32 *37-41*	33-45 *38-40*	37-41 *41-37*	43-35 *39-39*
KING'S LYNN	46-32 *37-41*	42-36 *42-36*	34-44 *36-42*	29-49 *37-41*	44-34 *41-37*	36-42 *43-34*		43-35 *39-39*	35-43 *36-42*	34-44 *27-50*	23-55 *33-45*	39-39 *50-28*
OXFORD	43-35 *45-33*	41-37 *42-36*	35-43 *37-41*	40-38 *40-38*	35-43 *43-35*	38-40 *48-30*	44-34 *43-35*		36-42 *44-34*	40-38 *42-36*	38-40 *40-38*	47-31 *44-34*
READING	40-38 *45-33*	49-29 *45-32*	39-39 *34-44*	40-38 *41-37*	51-27 *43-35*	41-37 *48-30*	53-25 *47-30*	40-38 *33-45*		40-38 *38-40*	36.5 41.5 *41-37*	41-37 *51-27*
SHEFFIELD	42-36 *45-31*	42-36 *38-40*	36-42 *44-34*	41-37 *38-40*	46-32 *45-33*	46-32 *45-32*	42-36 *45-33*	43-35 *42-36*	40-37 *43-35*		42-36 *43-35*	55-23 *43-34*
SWINDON	41-37 *42-36*	48-30 *45-33*	36-42 *36-42*	36-42 *40-38*	39-39 *44-34*	41-37 *44-34*	48-30 *46-32*	42-36 *39-39*	39-39 *39-39*	48-29 *45-33*		40-38 *45-33*
WOLVERHAMPTON	42-36 *42-36*	35-42 *48-30*	37-41 *46-32*	34-44 *37-41*	43-35 *42-35*	33-45 *45-33*	44-34 *51-27*	39-39 *38-40*	46-32 *49-29*	42-35 *45-33*	36-42 *40-38*	

1988 BRITISH LEAGUE TABLE

	P	W	D	L	PtsF	PtsA	W	D	L	PtsF	PtsA	BP	Pts
1 COVENTRY	**40**	**17**	**2**	**1**	**1034**	**766**	**14**	**0**	**6**	**944.5**	**852.5**	**18**	**82**
2 Belle Vue	40	19	0	1	1049	749	7	1	12	863	937	13	66
3 Cradley Heath	39	16	0	4	997	802	6	1	12	834	873	15	60
4 Oxford	40	13	3	4	958.5	835.5	7	3	10	891.5	907.5	13	59
5 Reading	40	15	0	5	993	805	5	3	12	864	931	12	55
6 Sheffield	39	13	2	4	913	795	6	0	14	818.5	981.5	8	48
7 Swindon	40	12	0	8	917.5	879.5	5	1	14	789	1009	8	43
8 Wolverhampton	40	13	2	5	964	836	2	1	17	817	981	8	41
9 King's Lynn	40	12	2	6	942	857	2	1	17	776.5	1021.5	7	38
10 Ipswich	39	11	0	9	893	902	2	0	17	758	952	4	30
11 Bradford	39	10	0	9	881	828	0	0	20	699	1096	2	22

■ *COVENTRY won the League championship for a record-breaking fifth time and also became the only team in history to have retained the title for a second time. They had previously won back-to-back pennants in 1978 and 1979.*
Team manager Mick Bell also became the first person to have won First Division League titles for two different clubs as both a rider and manager, having previously guided Reading to the championship in 1980.

■ *HACKNEY returned to the National League after one financially disastrous season back in Division One.*

1988 British League Riders' Championship Final

Sunday, October 9, Belle Vue:
1 Jan O. Pedersen 14, 2 Erik Gundersen 13, 3 Hans Nielsen 12, 4 Chris Morton 12, 5 Shawn Moran 10, 6 Richard Knight 9, 7 Ronnie Correy 9, 8 Simon Wigg 8, 9 Kelvin Tatum 7, 10 Per Jonsson 5, 11 Brian Karger 5, 12 Kelly Moran 5, *†13 Gary Havelock 5,* 14 Jan Andersson 5, 15 Tommy Knudsen 1, 16 Jeremy Doncaster 0. *Track reserves: Paul Smith 0, Carl Stonehewer 0.*

†Gary Havelock was subsequently convicted of giving a positive drugs sample at the meeting.
Sponsor: TNT Sameday.

1988 KNOCK OUT CUP

Round 1

Bradford 73 (36 37) Belle Vue 107 (54 53)
CRADLEY HEATH 98 (51 47) Sheffield 82 (39 43)
Ipswich 77 (34 43) King's Lynn 102 (55 47)

Round 2

CRADLEY HEATH 103 (53 50) King's Lynn 77 (37 40)
Reading 86 (49 37) *Coventry 94 (41 53)*
Swindon 89 (47 42) Oxford 91 (43 48)
Wolverhampton 82 (45 37) Belle Vue 98 (45 53)

Semi Finals

Coventry 93 (44 49) Oxford 84 (46 38)
CRADLEY HEATH 91 (49 42) Belle Vue 89 (41 48)

FINAL

First leg, October 22:
Coventry 40 (Tommy Knudsen 11, Kelvin Tatum 11, Rick Miller 6, Andy Hackett 5, John Jørgensen 5, David Clarke 2, Neville Tatum 0) CRADLEY HEATH 50 (Alan Grahame 10, Gert Handberg 9, Jan O. Pedersen 8, Erik Gundersen 8, Simon Cross 8, David Walsh 5, Wayne Garratt 2)
Second leg, October 23:
CRADLEY HEATH 50 (Grahame 13, Pedersen 11, Cross 9, Gundersen 8, Walsh 7, Handberg 1, Garratt 1) *Coventry 40* (Knudsen 13, Jørgensen 9, Hackett 6, Clarke 6, Kelvin Tatum 5, Miller 1, Neville Tatum 0).

❑ CRADLEY HEATH win 100-80 on aggregate.

1987 British League Riders' Championship

Sunday, October 11, Belle Vue:
1 Hans Nielsen 14, 2 Chris Morton 13, 3 Kelly Moran 11, 4 Kelvin Tatum 11, 5 Tommy Knudsen 10, 6 Jan Andersson 10, Richard Knight 10, 8 Mitch Shirra 8, 9 Simon Wigg 7, 10 Jan O. Pedersen 6, 11 Sean Willmott 6, 12 Erik Gundersen 4, 13 Jimmy Nilsen 4, 14 Preben Eriksen 4, 15 Louis Carr 0, Shawn Moran 0.
Track reserve: Bernie Collier 2.
Sponsor: TNT Sameday.

◆ *HANS NIELSEN became the first and only rider to win the World Final and the British League Riders' Championship in the same season TWICE. The only other World Champions who have also won the BLRC in the same season have been Barry Briggs (1966), Ole Olsen (1978) and Erik Gundersen (1985). Nielsen's first double was in 1986.*

1988 ALL THE RESULTS

	BELLE VUE	BRADFORD	COVENTRY	CRADLEY HEATH	IPSWICH	KING'S LYNN	OXFORD	READING	SHEFFIELD	SWINDON	WOLVES
BELLE VUE		61-29 61-29	42.5 46.5 53-37	47-42 48-42	50-40 58-32	48-42 58-32	47-43 49-41	54-36 51-39	55-35 51.5 38.5	53-37 65-25	51-39 46-44
BRADFORD	42-48 40-50		46-44 40-50	50-40 43-47	49-41 Not Raced	50-40 62-28	44-46 46-44	43-47 41-49	43-47 49-41	48-42 42-48	46-43 57-33
COVENTRY	48-42 46-44	61-29 57-33		55-35 46-44	46-44 50-40	56-34 55-35	51-39 45-45	45-45 56-34	47-43 59-31	50-40 65-25	52-38 44-46
CRADLEY HEATH	48-42 50-40	57-33 48-41	43-47 42-40		42-48 57-33	53-37 55-35	39-51 40-42	47-43 47 43	52-38 62 28	51-39 56 36	48-42 63 37
IPSWICH	52-38 40-50	46-44 50-40	36-54 40-50	40-50 48-41		47-43 46-44	44-46 42-48	47-43 49-38	37-53 42-48	52-38 42-47	46-44 47-43
KING'S LYNN	51-39 56-34	56-34 51-39	36-54 40-50	49-41 44-46	48-42 46-44		45-45 53-37	42-48 42-48	48-42 41-49	45-45 50-39	53-37 46-44
OXFORD	45-45 50-40	49-41 53-33	46-44 38-51	49-41 43-47	54-36 53-37	53-37 53.5 36.5		45-45 47-42	49-41 54-36	49-41 41-49	45-45 42-48
READING	48-42 43-47	52-38 63-27	43-47 48-42	46-44 49-41	53-37 48-42	42-48 56-33	46-44 42-48		53-37 43-47	56-34 53-37	60-29 49-41
SHEFFIELD	53-37 44-46	48-42 53-37	35-55 42-48	45-45 Not Raced	53-37 51-39	46-44 58-32	45-45 46-43	41-49 48-41		48-42 60-30	49-41 48-42
SWINDON	39-51 44-46	57-33 46-44	44-46 40-49	39-50 46-44	41-49 51-39	48-42 40-49	43-47 47.5 42.5	48-42 46-44	53-37 46-44		53-37 46-44
WOLVERHAMPTON	47-43 51-39	63-27 64-26	47-43 51-39	39-51 47-43	50-40 52-38	50-40 45-45	48-42 37-53	45-45 47-43	53-37 44-46	42-48 42-48	

1989 BRITISH LEAGUE TABLE

	P	W	D	L	PtsF	PtsA	W	D	L	PtsF	PtsA	BP	Pts
1 OXFORD	**32**	**14**	**0**	**2**	**845**	**592**	**8**	**1**	**7**	**735**	**701**	**13**	**58**
2 Wolverhampton	32	13	1	2	830	607	6	1	9	681	759	12	52
3 Cradley Heath	32	13	2	1	834.5	605.5	6	1	9	716	722	10	51
4 Belle Vue	32	13	0	3	798	639	6	2	8	698	739	10	50
5 Coventry	32	10	2	4	741	696	5	1	10	648	790	8	41
6 Swindon	32	10	0	6	762	677	2	1	13	633.5	806.5	8	33
7 Reading	32	9	1	6	735	705	4	0	12	621	816	5	32
8 Bradford	32	8	1	7	760	678	1	1	14	587	851	3	23
9 King's Lynn	32	7	1	8	718	721	1	0	15	601	839	3	20

1989 ALL THE RESULTS

	BELLE VUE	BRADFORD	COVENTRY	CRADLEY HEATH	KING'S LYNN	OXFORD	READING	SWINDON	WOLVES
BELLE VUE		49-41 59-31	57-32 49-41	49-41 49-41	54-36 53-37	42-48 48-41	42-48 57-32	48-42 49-41	39-51 47-43
BRADFORD	39-51 45-45		48-42 44-46	44-46 43-46	55-35 56-34	49-40 49-41	44-46 42-48	50-40 51-39	44-46 57-33
COVENTRY	46-44 46-44	48-40 45-45		37-53 53-37	39-51 51-39	40-50 46-43	42-48 57-33	45-45 46-44	50-40 50-40
CRADLEY HEATH	45-45 48-42	57-33 61-29	57-33 52-38		49-41 56-34	45-45 46-44	53-37 56-34	58-32 58.5-31.5	52-38 41-49
KING'S LYNN	33-57 42-47	54-36 53-37	44-46 48-42	38-52 47-43		38-52 34-56	62-28 49-41	48-42 44-46	39-51 45-45
OXFORD	63-27 42-47	52-38 60-30	60-30 49-41	51-38 48-42	54-36 58-32		46-43 54-36	53-37 41-49	60-30 54-36
READING	42-48 41-49	43-47 50-40	51-39 45-45	49-41 34-56	55-35 49-41	47-43 38-52		49-41 51-39	40-50 51-39
SWINDON	52-38 56-33	50-40 55-35	43-47 42-48	33-57 54-36	52-38 54-36	39-51 44-46	47-43 51-39		43-47 47-43
WOLVERHAMPTON	48-42 51-39	55-35 60-30	44-46 57-32	45-45 48-42	58-32 46-44	53-37 43-46	53-36 61-29	59-31 49-41	

1989 KNOCK OUT CUP

Round 1

King's Lynn 71 (38 33) Belle Vue 109 (52 57)
Wolverhampton 94 (49 45) Swindon 86 (41 45)

Round 2

Belle Vue 84.5 (45.5 39) Reading 95.5 (44.551)
Bradford 91 (46 45) Coventry 89 (44 45)
Oxford 85 (45 40) CRADLEY HEATH 95 (45 50)
Bye: Wolverhampton

Semi Finals

Reading 88 (40 48) CRADLEY HEATH 92 (50 42)
Wolverhampton 93 (60 33) Bradford 87 (30 57)

FINAL

First leg, October 16:
Wolverhampton 41 (Ronnie Correy 9, Robert Pfetzing 8, Graham Jones 7, Andy Phillips 7, *Brian Karger 5*, Neil Collins 3, Jan Staechmann 2) CRADLEY HEATH 49 (*Kelvin Tatum 13*, Greg Hancock 11, *Jimmy Nilsen 10*, Gert Handberg 6, Alan Grahame 6, Simon Cross 2, John Bostin 1)

Second leg, October 26:
CRADLEY HEATH 46 (*Shawn Moran 14*, Cross 12, *Tatum 7*, Handberg 5, Hancock 5, Grahame 3, Bostin 0) *Wolverhampton 44* (*Jimmy Nilsen 10*, Jones 9, Pfetzing 6, Phillips 6, Correy 5, Collins 4, Staechmann 4)

❑ CRADLEY HEATH win 95-85 on aggregate.

■ *Cradley Heath's victory was their fourth in a row and their eighth in 11 years.*

1989 British League Riders' Championship Final

Sunday, October 1, Belle Vue:
1 Shawn Moran 15, 2 Hans Nielsen 14, 3 Brian Karger 12, 4 Martin Dugard 9, 5 Ronnie Correy 8, 6 Jimmy Nilsen 8, 7 Kelvin Tatum 8, 8 Alan Grahame 8, 9 Simon Wigg 7, 10 Rick Miller 7, 11 Richard Knight 7, 12 Lance King 5, 13 Peter Ravn 5, 14 Jeremy Doncaster 5, 15 Paul Thorp 2, 16 Mitch Shirra 0. *Track reserves: Glenn Hornby 0, Scott Smith 0.*
Sponsor: TNT Sameday.

1989 GOLD CUP

THE GOLD CUP was re-introduced to the British League calendar following the closure of Sheffield and Ipswich's move into the National League to provide as early season tournament.

The nine remaining British League teams were split into two regional groups and they met each other in as mini-league on a home and away basis with the two group winners qualifying for a place in the Gold Cup Final.

SOUTHERN GROUP RESULTS

	COVENTRY	KING'S LYNN	OXFORD	READING	SWINDON
COVENTRY		41-49	49-40	50-39	45-45
KING'S LYNN	45-45		45-45	42-48	51-39
OXFORD	58-32	59-31		53-36	56-34
READING	46-44	49-41	41-49		46-43
SWINDON	46-44	48-42	41-49	44-46	

1 OXFORD	8	6	1	1	409	309	4	17
2 Reading	8	5	0	3	351	366	2	12
3 King's Lynn	8	2	2	4	346	374	2	8
4 Coventry	8	2	2	4	350	368	1	7
5 Swindon	8	2	1	5	340	379	1	6

NORTHERN GROUP RESULTS

	BELLE VUE	BRADFORD	CRADLEY HEATH	WOLVES
BELLE VUE		43-47	55-35	49-41
BRADFORD	51-39		55-35	43-47
CRADLEY HEATH	47-43	46-44		49-41
WOLVERHAMPTON	42-47	51-39	39-51	

1 CRADLEY	6	4	0	2	263	277	1	9
2 Bradford	6	3	0	3	279	261	2	8
3 Belle Vue	6	3	0	3	276	263	2	8
4 Wolverhampton	6	2	0	4	261	278	1	5

SOUTHERN clubs had competed in a Gold Cup tournament – mainly sponsored by Gauntlet – for nine years between 1972 and 1980. The winners of each competition are listed alongside.

Roll of Honour

1972 Reading
1973 King's Lynn
1974 Newport
1975 Newport
1976 Ipswich
1977 Reading
1978 Exeter
1979 Wimbledon
1980 King's Lynn

1989 GOLD CUP FINAL

First leg, August 26
Cradley Heath 42 (Erik Gundersen 13, Alan Grahame 8, Jan O. Pedersen 6, Simon Cross 5, Greg Hancock 4, Gert Handberg 4, Mark Robinson 2) OXFORD 48 (Hans Nielsen 14, Troy Butler 11, Simon Wigg 8, Marvyn Cox 7, Martin Dugard 6, Paul Dugard 2, Andy Grahame 0).

Second leg, September 15
OXFORD 54 (Nielsen 14, Martin Dugard 11, Butler 8, *Neil Evitts 7*, Wigg 6, Grahame 5, Paul Dugard 3) *Cradley Heath 36* (Gundersen 10, *Kelvin Tatum 9*, Hancock 9, Cross 5, John Bostin 2, Handberg 1, Grahame 0).

❑ OXFORD win 102-78 on aggregate.

■ *See alongside for previous British League regional Gold Cup tournament.*

1990 BRITISH LEAGUE TABLE

	P	W	D	L	PtsF	PtsA	W	D	L	PtsF	PtsA	BP	Pts
1 READING	**32**	**13**	**1**	**2**	**827**	**609**	**6**	**2**	**8**	**686.5**	**751.5**	**13**	**54**
2 Wolverhampton	32	14	1	1	794	644	3	4	9	652	787	10	49
3 Belle Vue	32	12	1	3	794	644	7	1	8	660	774	7	47
4 Oxford	32	9	1	6	764	672	8	1	7	703	733	10	46
5 Bradford	32	14	1	1	834	603	2	0	14	636	804	8	41
6 Swindon	32	11	1	4	812	626	4	1	11	650	790	8	41
7 Cradley Heath	32	10	0	6	756.5	683.5	2	1	13	669	771	7	32
8 Coventry	32	6	2	8	727	709	4	1	11	659	778	7	30
9 King's Lynn	32	6	4	6	734	706	1	1	14	581	854	2	21

1990 ALL THE RESULTS

	BELLE VUE	BRADFORD	COVENTRY	CRADLEY HEATH	KING'S LYNN	OXFORD	READING	SWINDON	WOLVES
BELLE VUE		48-42 59-31	56-34 51-39	47-43 55-35	43-46 55-35	41-49 40-49	50-40 51-39	48-42 54-36	51-39 45-45
BRADFORD	58-32 59-31		44-46 47-41	47-43 50-40	57-33 46-43	46-44 57-33	53-37 49-41	49-41 58-32	69-21 45-45
COVENTRY	34-56 43-35	44-46 46-44		46-44 45-45	52-38 58-32	43-46 48-42	42-48 43-47	45-45 44-46	52-38 42-47
CRADLEY HEATH	53-37 38-52	58-32 48-42	43-47 41-49		53-37 47-43	41-49 39-51	52-38 42.5 47.5	53-37 48-42	47-43 53-37
KING'S LYNN	45-45 43-47	52-38 42-48	45-45 50-40	48-42 47-43		45-45 43-47	46-44 61-29	44-46 35-55	45-45 43-47
OXFORD	44-45 50-40	49-41 51-39	42-48 51-38	52-38 48-42	66-24 45-45		41-48 43-46	44-46 49-41	40-50 49-41
READING	44-45 61-29	56-34 54-36	46-44 49-41	57-33 44-46	57-33 57-30	51-39 47-43		59-31 53-37	47-43 45-45
SWINDON	55-35 42-48	50-40 46-44	64-26 54-36	46-44 38-52	59-31 59-31	57-31 43-47	40-50 45-45		57-33 57-33
WOLVERHAMPTON	53-36 52-37	53-37 48-42	49-41 46-44	47-43 54-36	51-39 49-41	48-42 44-46	45-45 48-42	49-41 58-32	

1990 KNOCK OUT CUP

Round 1

Coventry 91 (45 46) Oxford 89 (45 46)

Round 2

Cradley Heath 81 (45 36) *Bradford 99 (45 54)*
King's Lynn 83 (47 36) READING 96 (42 54)
Swindon 109 (56 53) Coventry 71 (34 37)
Wolverhampton 63 (34 29) Belle Vue 117 (56 61)

Semi Finals

Bradford 91 (51 40) Swindon 89 (39 50)
READING 91 (53 38) Belle Vue 87 (36 51)

FINAL

First leg, October 8:
READING 51 (Todd Wiltshire 15, Per Jonsson 12, Jan Andersson 6, Jeremy Doncaster 6, David Mullett 5, Armando Castagna 5, David Steen 2)
Bradford 39 (Marvyn Cox 11, Gary Havelock 11, Glenn Doyle 10, Paul Thorp 3, Andy Smith 2, Neil Evitts 1, Bryan Larner 1).
Second leg, October 13:
Bradford 43 (Havelock 11, Cox 9, Smith 7, Thorp 7, Evitts 5, Larner 2, Stuart Parnaby 2, Doyle 0)
READING 47 (Wiltshire 13, Mullett 11, Castagna 6, Doncaster 6, Andersson 5, Jonsson 4, Steen 2).

❑ READING win 98-82.

1989 British League Riders' Championship Final

Sunday, October 14, Belle Vue:
1 Hans Nielsen 15, 2 Kelly Moran 12, 3 Ronnie Correy 12, 4 Marvyn Cox 12, 5 Sam Ermolenko 11, 6 John Jørgensen 8, 7 Andrew Silver 8, 8 Jeremy Doncaster 8, 9 Shawn Moran 7, 10 Gary Havelock 7, 11 Mark Loram 6, 12 Todd Wiltshire 5, 13 Jimmy Nilsen 3, 14 Kelvin Tatum 3, 15 Greg Hancock 1, 16 Martin Dugard 0. *Track reserves: Bobby Ott 2, Richard Musson 0.*
Sponsors: Dunlop and Groundwork Landscapes Limited.

■ *BARRY BRIGGS holds the record for British League Riders' Championship Final victories with six wins – in the first six years of the competition.*

1990 GOLD CUP

BRADFORD'S victory over Oxford in the second Gold Cup Final was their first national trophy in the club's long history.

Even though there had been speedway in the Yorkshire city since the sport was first introduced to Odsal Stadium on an Open Licence basis in 1945.

Bradford had competed in League racing from 1946 to 1957, from 1970 to 1975 and from 1986 to 1990.

But in all those years they had never even reached a national Cup Final until their appearance in the 1990 Gold Cup decider. Ironically the Coalite Dukes followed that up with a place in the 1990 Speedway Star Knock Out Cup Final although, on that occasion, they were beaten by Reading.

NORTHERN GROUP RESULTS

	BELLE VUE	BRADFORD	COVENTRY	CRADLEY HEATH	WOLVES
BELLE VUE		48-42	46-44	44-43	42-48
BRADFORD	47-43		51-39	63-27	67-23
COVENTRY	46-44	46-44		40-50	53-37
CRADLEY HEATH	52-38	41-49	52-38		55-35
WOLVERHAMPTON	47-43	61-29	47-43	45-45	

1 BRADFORD	8	5	0	3	392	328	3	13
2 Cradley Heath	8	4	1	3	365	352	3	12
3 Wolverhampton	8	4	1	3	343	377	1	10
4 Belle Vue	8	3	0	5	348	369	2	8
5 Coventry	8	3	0	5	349	371	1	7

SOUTHERN GROUP RESULTS

	KING'S LYNN	OXFORD	READING	SWINDON
KING'S LYNN		39-51	44-46	47-43
OXFORD	46-44		53-37	39-51
READING	46-44	47-43		51-39
SWINDON	51-39	38-51	47-42	

1 OXFORD	6	4	0	2	283	256	3	11
2 Reading	6	4	0	2	269	270	2	10
3 Swindon	6	3	0	3	269	269	1	7
4 King's Lynn	6	1	0	5	257	283	0	2

1990 GOLD CUP FINAL

First leg, June 22
Oxford 47 (Hans Nielsen 15, Martin Dugard 14, Dean Barker 6, Paul Dugard 5, Troy Butler 5, Alastair Stevens 2, Kevin Pitts, did not ride)
BRADFORD 43 (Neil Evitts 13, Marvyn Cox 12, Paul Thorp 7, Andy Smith 6, Glenn Doyle 3, Gary Havelock 2, Bryan Larner 0).

Second leg, June 23
BRADFORD 63 (Evitts 15, Thorp 12, Smith 12, Havelock 10, Doyle 7, Cox 5, Stuart Parnaby 2, Larner 0)
Oxford 27 (Nielsen 11, Martin Dugard 9, Paul Dugard 3, Butler 3, Barker 1, Stevens 0, Kevin Pitts, did not ride).

❑ BRADFORD win 106-74 on aggregate.

■ *See 1989 for details of the regional Gold Cup competition.*

Alan's the Premier

1982 PREMIERSHIP

First leg, March 20:
CRADLEY HEATH 43 (Phil Collins 10, Bruce Penhall 10, Lance King 7, Alan Grahame 7, Erik Gundersen 5, Andy Reid 4, Ian Gledhill 0) IPSWICH 35 (John Cook 14, Jeremy Doncaster 5, Preben Eriksen 4, Nigel Flatman 4, Kevin Jolly 4, Dennis Sigalos 3, Mike Lanham 1).
Second leg, March 25:
IPSWICH 37 (Cook 9, Jolly 9, Sigalos 6, Lanham 5, Flatman 4, Doncaster 3, Eriksen 1) CRADLEY HEATH 41 (Collins 11, King 10, Penhall 8, Gundersen 8, Grahame 3, Gledhill 1, Reid 0).
❑ CRADLEY HEATH win 84-72 on aggregate.
♣ *Cradley were 1981 British League Champions and Ipswich 1981 Speedway Star Knock Out Cup winners.*
Meeting sponsors: Avco Trust.

1983 PREMIERSHIP

First leg, March 19:
CRADLEY HEATH 36 (Erik Gundersen 12, Simon Wigg 11, Jan O. Pedersen 4, Alan Grahame 4, Lance King 3, Andy Reid 2, Phil Collins unable to ride bercause of appendicitis) BELLE VUE 42 (Chris Morton 13, Larry Ross 9, Peter Collins 8, Louis Carr 5, Peter Ravn 4, Peter Carr 2, Andy Smith 1).
Second leg, March 20:
BELLE VUE 37 (Morton 15, Collins 9, Ross 6, Louis Carr 4, Ravn 1, Smith 1, Peter Carr 1) CRADLEY HEATH 41 (Grahame 11, Wigg 9, Gundersen 8, King 8, Pedersen 3, Reid 2, Phil Collins, did not ride).
❑ BELLE VUE win 79-77 on aggregate.
♣ *Belle Vue were 1982 British League champions and Cradley Heath 1982 Speedway Star Knock Out Cup winners.*

1984 PREMIERSHIP

First leg, March 17:
BELLE VUE 38 (Chris Morton 11, Larry Ross 10, Andy Smith 5, Peter Collins 4, Peter Carr 4, Kenny McKinna 3, Mark Courtney 1) CRADLEY HEATH 40 (Finn Jensen 10, Lance King 8, Erik Gundersen 7, Phil Collins 7, Alan Grahame 5, Mike Wilding 3, Steve Collins 0).
Second leg, March 21:
CRADLEY HEATH 42 (Gundersen 11, Phil Collins 10, Grahame 8, King 6, Jensen 6, Wilding 1, Steve Collins 0) BELLE VUE 36 (Collins 11, Morton 10, Courtney 7, Ross 3, McKinna 3, Smith 2, Carr 0).
❑ CRADLEY HEATH win 82-74 on aggregate.
♣ *Cradley Heath were the 1983 British League champions and Belle Vue 1983 League Cup winners.*

1985 PREMIERSHIP

First leg, March 28:
IPSWICH 38 (Richard Knight 9, Jeremy Doncaster 9, John Cook 8, Billy Sanders 6, Andy Hines 4, Nigel Flatman 2, Alan Farmer 0) CRADLEY HEATH 40 (Erik Gundersen 12, Phil Collins 10, Simon Cross 6, Jan O. Pedersen 4, Finn Jensen 4, Alan Grahame 3, Steve Collins 1).
Second leg, March 30:
CRADLEY HEATH 41 (Gundersen 11, Phil Collins 10, Cross 6, Pedersen 5, Grahame 5, Steve Collins 4, Jensen 0) IPSWICH 37 (Sanders 14, Cook 8, Knight 6, Doncaster 4, Flatman 2, Hines 2, Farmer 1).
❑ CRADLEY HEATH win 81-75 on aggregate.
♣ *Ipswich were the 1984 British League champions and Cradley Heath 1984 League Cup winners.*

THE PREMIERSHIP was made for Cradley Heath.

For no club has dominated a competition as completely as the Black Country side in the annual pre-season opener.

In the nine years that the Premiership was contested in the British League the Heathens won it six times and were beaten finalists in two of the other three!

And one rider spanned the Cradley team that went into the first Premiership as defending British League champions in 1982 and the 1990 competition when the Dudley Wood side were the previous year's Speedway Star Knock Out Cup winners.

He was Alan Grahame, the quiet but inwardly tough Midlander who fought against a form of cancer to save his career.

Alan made a record EIGHT appearances in the Premiership, a remarkable achievement for anyone but truly amazing considering the handicap that he has raced under for the latter years of his speedway life.

1986 PREMIERSHIP

First leg, March 15:
COVENTRY 41 (Alun Rossiter 11, Tommy Knudsen 10, Rick Miller 9, John Jørgensen 6, David Bargh 3, Mike Bacon 2, Kelvin Tatum 0) OXFORD 37 (Hans Nielsen 12, Simon Wigg 8, Andy Grahame 6, Marvyn Cox 5, Mark Carlson 4, Nigel De'ath 2, Jon Surman 0).
Second leg, March 21:
OXFORD 33 (Nielsen 12, Wigg 7, Grahame 7, Kevin Smart 3, Cox 2, De'ath 1, Surman 1) COVENTRY 45 (Knudsen 11, Miller 9, Jørgensen 9, Tatum 6, Bargh 5, Rossiter 4, Bacon 1).
❑ COVENTRY win 86-70 on aggregate.
♣ *Oxford were 1985 British League champions and Coventry 1985 League Cup winners.*

1987 PREMIERSHIP

First leg, March 21:
CRADLEY HEATH 37 (Erik Gundersen 12, Simon Cross 10, Jan O. Pedersen 7, Alan Grahame 3, David Walsh 3, Paul Fry 2, Dean Barker 0) OXFORD 41 (Hans Nielsen 11, Nigel De'ath 8, Marvyn Cox 6, Jens Rasmussen 5, Andy Grahame 5, Alastair Stevens 3, Jon Surman 3).
Second leg, April 3:
OXFORD 41 (Cox 9, Nielsen 9, Grahame 8, Rasmussen 5, Surman 4, De'ath 3, Stevens 3) CRADLEY HEATH 36 (Gundersen 12, Pedersen 12, Cross 8, Walsh 3, Barker 1, Fry 0, Grahame 0).
❑ OXFORD win 82-73 on aggregate.
♣ *Oxford were 1986 British League champions and Cradley Heath 1986 Speedway Star Knock Out Cup winners.*

1988 PREMIERSHIP

First leg, April 4:
CRADLEY HEATH 43 (Jan O. Pedersen 14, Erik Gundersen 11, Simon Cross 8, Alan Grahame 4, Gert Handberg 3, David Walsh 3, Wayne Garratt 0) COVENTRY 47 (Tommy Knudsen 14, Kelvin Tatum 8, Andy Hackett 7, John Jørgensen 6, Rick Miller 5, David Clarke 5, Neville Tatum 2).
❑ CRADLEY HEATH were awarded the trophy when Coventry failed to stage the return leg.
♣ *Coventry were 1987 British League champions and Cradley Heath 1987 Speedway Star Knock Out Cup winners.*

1989 PREMIERSHIP

First leg, March 27:
CRADLEY HEATH 55 (Simon Cross 15, Jan O. Pedersen 13, Erik Gundersen 7, Alan Grahame 7, Gert Handberg 6, Justin Walker 5, John Bostin 2) COVENTRY 34 (Kelvin Tatum 10, John Jørgensen 5, Kai Niemi 5, Andy Hackett 5, Sean Wilson 4, Rick Miller 4, Wayne Broadhurst 1).
Second leg, March 27:
COVENTRY 33 (Hackett 11, Wilson 5, Tatum 4, Jørgensen 4, Broadhurst 4, Miller 3, Niemi 2) CRADLEY HEATH 57 (Cross 14, Pedersen 14, Gundersen 10, Grahame 9, Handberg 6, Bostin 3, Walker 1).
❑ CRADLEY HEATH win 112-67 on aggregate.
♣ *Coventry were 1988 British League champions and Cradley Heath 1988 Speedway Star Knock Out Cup winners.*

1990 PREMIERSHIP

First leg, March 30:
OXFORD 45 (Hans Nielsen 13, Martin Dugard 8, Dean Barker 7, Alastair Stevens 7, Simon Wigg 5, Troy Butler 4, Paul Dugard 1) CRADLEY HEATH 45 (Simon Cross 14, Jan O. Pedersen 11, *Mark Loram 10*, Billy Hamill 4, Greg Hancock 3, Alan Grahame 2, Mark Robinson 1).
Second leg, March 31:
CRADLEY HEATH 50 (Cross 14, Pedersen 12, Hancock 10, Hamill 9, Grahame 5, *rider replacement for Handberg*, Robinson 0, *David Haynes, did not ride*) OXFORD 40 (Nielsen 12, Martin Dugard 12, Butler 7, Stevens 4, Paul Dugard 3, Barker 2, Wigg 0).
❑ CRADLEY HEATH win 95-85 on aggregate.
♣ *Oxford were 1989 British League champions and Cradley Heath 1989 Speedway Star Knock Out Cup winners.*

A LOOK AT THE GIANT KILLING ACTS IN THE INTER LEAGUE CUP

ROBERT HOLLINGWORTH and David Piddock went out for the last race – knowing they were on the threshold of speedway's biggest ever Cup upset.

For they needed three points to put Boston through to the quarter finals of the first-ever Inter League Knock Out Cup – with a giant-killing victory over First Division rivals Hackney.

Heavy rain had improved the odds on a major upset and a series of problems afflicted the Hawks with Barry Thomas and Dave Morton, in particular, suffering.

They scored only nine points between them, each suffering a tapes exclusion, a fall, and, at crucial times, an engine failure.

And once Thomas stopped in the last race the celebrations could begin as Hollingworth and Piddock said a silent prayer as they finished in the minor placings behind race winner Ted Hubbard.

The records show that the Cudas then reached the semi-final but only after Swindon refused to put on a meeting against them, claiming it was insulting the intelligence of their fans to stage a home match against Second Division opposition!

Workington became the 1976 giant-killers with an East Anglian double over Ipswich and King's Lynn – coincidentally the two teams who fought out the Speedway Star Cup Final the same season!

The Comets' win over King's Lynn was the more remarkable as they did it without leading scorer and first round hero Lou Sansom (13 against the Witches but a quarter final flu victim) and operating rider replacement with Brian Havelock scoring double figures, including a last race third place when he and Steve Lawson claimed the points that took the Cumbrians into the semi final.

The closest any other club came to conquering a First Division giant was Oxford in the last year of the competition in 1980 when they were deprived of a win in a sensational last race.

Leicester, for whom Colin Cook arrived late and John Titman broke his collar bone in heat 11, had to go into the last race needing to share the points but tracking debutant Robert Lightfoot (scoreless) and Polish international Andrzej Huszcza who had picked up just one point from his first three outings.

The Pole's vast experience paid off as he won from the tapes to force a replay at Blackbird Road three weeks later.

The following year eight National League tracks were invited to compete in the Speedway Star Knock Out Cup and once again there was delight on the minnows' terraces with Edinburgh beating Sheffield by two points and Peterborough having a four point victory against Halifax despite an 18-point maximum from the Dukes' international John Louis.

1975 INTER LEAGUE KNOCK OUT CUP

Round 1

Birmingham 38 Belle Vue 40
Boston 40 Hackney 38
Bradford 34 Oxford 44
Crewe 20 Newport 58
Eastbourne 28 Halifax 50
Peterborough 28 Ipswich 49
Teesside 26 Cradley Heath 52
Workington 38 Swindon 39

Round 2

Belle Vue 50 Newport 28
Boston walkover, Swindon withdrew
Halifax 48 Ipswich 30
Oxford 43 Cradley Heath 35

Semi Finals

Halifax 46 Oxford 32
Belle Vue 58 *Boston* 20

FINAL

First leg, October 6:
Halifax 38 (Chris Pusey 11, Rick France 8, Ian Cartwright 6, Charlie Monk 5, Henny Kroeze 4, Mike Hioftle 3, Graham Plant 1) BELLE VUE 40 (Sören Sjösten 10, Peter Collins 8, Chris Morton 7, Russ Hodgson 7, Alan Wilkinson 6, Paul Tyrer 2, Geoff Pusey 0).

Second leg, October 15:
BELLE VUE 50 (Sjösten 12, Collins 12, Morton 10, Wilkinson 8, G. Pusey 4, Tyrer 2, Chris Turner 2) Halifax 27 (France 7, C. Pusey 6, Monk 4, Plant 4, Kroeze 3, Andy Cusworth 3, Cartwright 0).

❑ BELLE VUE win 90-65 on aggregate.

■ *Boston became the first Division Two club to beat senior opposition.*

1976 INTER LEAGUE KNOCK OUT CUP

Round 1

Berwick 35 HULL 43
Boston 30 King's Lynn 48
Crayford 38 Leicester 40
Eastbourne 32 Hackney 46
Ellesmere Port 39 Birmingham 39
Newcastle 37 Newport 41
Stoke 34 Wolverhampton 43
Workington 40 Ipswich 38

Round 1 Replay

Birmingham 44 *Ellesmere Port 33*

Round 2

Hackney 46 Birmingham 31
HULL 50 Newport 27
Leicester 38 Wolverhampton 40
Workington 40 King's Lynn 38

Semi Finals

HULL 54 *Workington 23*
Wolverhampton 43 Hackney 35

FINAL

First leg, October 20:
HULL 57 (Bobby Beaton 18, Graham Drury 10, Mike Curoso 10, Barry Briggs 7, Frank Auffret 7, Mitch Graham 5) Wolverhampton 21 (Jim McMillan 8, John Jackson 7, *Bruce Cribb 5, Robert Hollingworth* 1, Leif Berlin 0, *Bernie Leigh* 0, Kenneth Hall 0)

Second leg, October 22:
Wolverhampton 39 (George Hunter 10, Jackson 10, *Cribb* 8, McMillan 7, Berlin 2, *Steve Bastable* 2, *Hollingworth* 0) HULL 39 (Drury 10, Curoso 8, Beaton 7, Briggs 7, Auffret 6, Graham 1).

❑ HULL win 96-60 on aggregate.

1977 INTER LEAGUE KNOCK OUT CUP

Round 1

Berwick 34 Bristol 41
Canterbury 20 White City 57
Coatbridge 38 Halifax 40
Crayford 25 King's Lynn 52
Eastbourne 28 Wolverhampton 49
Ellesmere Port 33 IPSWICH 45
Newcastle 34 Cradley Heath 44
Peterborough 24 Belle Vue 54
Rye House 38 Hackney 39
Workington 28 Hull 50

Round 2

IPSWICH walk-over, Halifax withdrew
White City 46 Hackney 32

Round 3

Belle Vue 49 Wolverhampton 29
Cradley Heath 53 White City 25
IPSWICH 43 King's Lynn 35
Hull 48 Bristol 30

Semi Finals

Cradley Heath 41 Hull 37
IPSWICH 39 Belle Vue 38

FINAL

First leg, October 27:
IPSWICH 49 (John Louis 12, Tony Davey 12, Billy Sanders 10, Ted Howgego 6, Mike Lanham 5, Kevin Jolly 4, Dave Gooderham 0) Cradley Heath 29 (Bob Valentine 10, Steve Bastable 6, Bruce Cribb 4, Arthur Price 3, Dave Perks 3, *Trevor Geer* 3).

Second leg, October 29:
Cradley Heath 46 (*Larry Ross* 11, Cribb 10, Perks 8, Valentine 7, Bastable 7, Price 3) IPSWICH 32 (Sanders 11, Louis 9, Davey 5, Lanham 2, Howgego 2, Jolly 2, Andy Hines 1).

❑ IPSWICH win 81-75 on aggregate.

1978 INTER LEAGUE KNOCK OUT CUP

Round 1

Boston 28 Bristol 50
Canterbury 36 Sheffield 42
Eastbourne 32 Hull 45
Ellesmere Port 33 Cradley Heath 43
Mildenhall 38 White City 39
Newcastle 26 KING'S LYNN 52
Peterborough 26 Exeter 52
Rye House 25 Hackney 51

Round 2

Bristol 40 Cradley Heath 38
Hackney 41 Hull 37
KING'S LYNN 51 Sheffield 27
White City 30 Exeter 48

Semi Finals

Exeter 49 Hackney 29
KING'S LYNN 46 Bristol 32

FINAL

First leg, October 6:
Exeter 39 (Scott Autrey 11, Vaclav Verner 10, Steve Koppe 7, Reidar Eide 6, Mike Farrell 4, Peter Prinsloo 1, Bob Watts 0) KING'S LYNN 39 (Michael Lee 12, Terry Betts 8, Ian Turner 7, Richard Hellsén 6, Peter E. Smith 4, Bent Rasmussen 2).

Second leg, October 7
KING'S LYNN 55 (Lee 12, Gagen 9, Turner 9, Betts 8, Rasmussen 7, Hellsén 7, Smith 3) Exeter 23 (Autrey 9, Verner 6, Eide 3, Farrell 3, *Mike Spink* 2, Prinsloo 0, Bob Garrad 0).

❑ KING'S LYNN win 94-62 on aggregate.

■ *For the second successive year First Division clubs won their ties.*

1979 INTER LEAGUE KNOCK OUT CUP

Round 1

Canterbury 36 Sheffield 42
Ellesmere Port 36 King's Lynn 42
Glasgow 20 Hull 58
Newcastle 32 Eastbourne 46
Oxford 35 Hackney 43
Peterborough 27 CRADLEY HEATH 51
Rye House 37 Exeter 41
Stoke 32 Swindon 46

Round 2

CRADLEY HEATH 49 Exeter 29
Eastbourne 37 Hull 41
Hackney 44 Swindon 34
King's Lynn 41 Sheffield 37

Semi Finals

CRADLEY HEATH 50 Hull 27
Hackney 38 King's Lynn 40

FINAL

First leg, October 22:
CRADLEY HEATH 43 (Bruce Penhall 9, Alan Grahame 9, Erik Gundersen 8, Phil Collins 7, Bobby Schwartz 5, Dave Perks 3, Kristian Praestbro 2) King's Lynn 35 (Michael Lee 11, Bent Rasmussen 11, Dave Jessup 7, Richard Hellsén 4, Peter E. Smith 1, Derek Harrison 1, Ian Turner 0).

Second leg, October 24:
King's Lynn 36 (Lee 13, Jessup 10, Hellsén 6, Rasmussen 4, Smith 2, Turner 1, Harrison 0) CRADLEY HEATH 42 (Collins 12, Penhall 9, Grahame 6, Perks 6, Gundersen 4, Praestbro 3, Schwartz 2).

❑ CRADLEY HEATH win 85-71 on aggregate.

1980 INTER LEAGUE KNOCK OUT CUP

Round 1

Berwick 24 Eastbourne 54
Glasgow 33 Cradley Heath 43
Mildenhall 28 Hull 50
Milton Keynes 21 Sheffield 56
Newcastle 38 Hackney 40
Oxford 39 Leicester 39
Peterborough 31 Swindon 47
Rye House 31 KING'S LYNN 47

Round 1 Replay

Leicester 47 *Oxford 31*

Round 2

Cradley Heath 52 Sheffield 26
KING'S LYNN 49 Hull 29
Leicester 42 Hackney 36
Swindon 42 Eastbourne 36

Semi Finals

KING'S LYNN 49 Cradley Heath 29
Leicester 38 Swindon 40

FINAL

First leg, September 25:
Swindon 37 (Scott Autrey 11, Phil Crump 10, Steve Gresham 8, Malcolm Holloway 5, Bob Humphreys 2, Mike Ferreira 1, Milan Spinka 0) KING'S LYNN 41 (Dave Jessup 11, Michael Lee 10, Nigel Sparshott 9, Richard Hellsén 6, Melvyn Taylor 3, Bent Rasmussen 1, Peter E. Smith 1).

Second leg, September 29:
KING'S LYNN 42 (Jessup 11, Hellsén 10, Taylor 9, Rasmussen 8, Sparshott 2, Smith 2, Dennis Mallett 0) Swindon 36 (Autrey 11, Holloway 9, Steen Mastrup 6, Ferreira 5, Jan Verner 3, Spinka 2, Humphreys 0).

❑ KING'S LYNN win 83-73 on aggregate.

BELLE VUE

FOUNDER members of the British League having been in the National League Division One in 1964.

1965...1965...1965...1965...1965...1965

	M	R	Pts	BP	TPts	Ave	F	P	Total
§§Cyril Maidment	32	128	328.0	5.0	333.0	10.406	7	2	9
§§Dick Fisher	31	124	244.0	22.0	266.0	8.581	1	5	6
§§Gordon McGregor	**35**	**140**	**248.0**	**17.0**	**265.0**	**7.571**	**1**	**1**	**2**
§§Sandor Levai	29	116	158.0	30.0	188.0	6.483		1	1
§§Norman Nevitt	**35**	**140**	**167.0**	**35.0**	**202.0**	**5.771**			
§§Dent Oliver	8	32	35.0	7.0	42.0	5.250			
§§Bill Powell	13	52	57.0	9.0	66.0	5.077			
§§Fred Collier	1	4	2.0	1.0	3.0	3.000			
§§Jim Yacoby	34	136	81.0	19.0	100.0	2.941			
§Vic White	14	56	33.0	8.0	41.0	2.929			
§Taffy Owen	2	8	2.0	0.0	2.0	1.000			
§§Leo McAuliffe	1	4	1.0	0.0	1.0	1.000			
§§Dave Schofield	6	24	5.0	0.0	5.0	0.833			
§John Ellis	1	3	0.0	0.0	0.0	0.000			
§§Len Kirkham	3	7	0.0	0.0	0.0	0.000			

1966...1966...1966...1966...1966...1966

	M	R	Pts	BP	TPts	Ave	F	P	Total
Cyril Maidment	37	165	383.0	11.0	394.0	9.552	9	3	12
Sandor Levai	**39**	**170**	**291.0**	**40.0**	**331.0**	**7.788**	**1**		**1**
Dick Fisher	33	132	223.0	26.0	249.0	7.545	1	2	3
§§David Baybutt	3	6	7.0	2.0	9.0	6.000			
Norman Nevitt	37	148	197.0	20.0	217.0	5.865	1		1
Gordon McGregor	30	104	123.0	16.0	139.0	5.346		1	1
Bill Powell	35	138	138.0	35.0	173.0	5.014		1	1
Jim Yacoby	39	132	119.0	22.0	141.0	4.273			
Dave Schofield	6	10	6.0	0.0	6.0	2.400			
§§Laszlo Munkasci	3	6	1.0	0.0	1.0	0.667			
Taffy Owen	6	11	1.0	0.0	1.0	0.364			

BELLE VUE are the only team in British League history to have had TWO Hungarian riders on their books in the same season when Sandor Levai and Laszlo Munkacsi both rode for the club in 1965.

1967...1967...1967...1967...1967...1967

	M	R	Pts	BP	TPts	Ave	F	P	Total
§Ove Fundin	12	51	122.0	1.0	123.0	9.647	2		2
§§Sören Sjösten	13	58	123.0	8.0	131.0	9.034	2		2
Cyril Maidment	37	166	329.5	16.0	345.5	8.325	2	1	3
§Tommy Roper	**38**	**169**	**310.0**	**21.0**	**331.0**	**7.834**	**2**		**2**
Norman Nevitt	30	127	179.0	25.0	204.0	6.425		1	1
Sandor Levai	37	152	188.0	36.0	224.0	5.895			
Taffy Owen	4	11	9.0	2.0	11.0	4.000			
§§Eric Broadbelt	16	45	32.0	8.0	40.0	3.556			
§§Peter Thompson	4	8	6.0	1.0	7.0	3.500			
Jim Yacoby	12	35	23.0	6.0	29.0	3.314			
§§Paul O'Neal	13	32	19.0	3.0	22.0	2.750			
§John Woodcock	14	47	25.0	7.0	32.0	2.723			
§Garry Middleton	6	20	11.0	2.0	13.0	2.600			
§§Dave Hardy	19	58	34.0	3.0	37.0	2.552			
§§Chris Pusey	1	2	1.0	0.0	1.0	2.000			

EVEN though he was making his British League debut Sören Sjösten had ridden for the Aces in the old National League First Division.

1968...1968...1968...1968...1968...1968

	M	R	Pts	BP	TPts	Ave	F	P	Total
Sören Sjösten	35	159	356.0	7.0	363.0	9.132	7	1	8
Tommy Roper	28	119	246.0	7.0	253.0	8.504	2		2
Sandor Levai	37	154	246.0	39.0	285.0	7.403		2	2
Cyril Maidment	37	157	256.0	32.0	288.0	7.338	1	2	3
Bill Powell	24	96	118.0	17.0	135.0	5.625			
Norman Nevitt	30	115	144.0	16.0	160.0	5.565			
Taffy Owen	13	33	30.0	7.0	37.0	4.485			
§§Ken Eyre	9	28	24.0	6.0	30.0	4.286			
§§Brian Bentley	1	2	2.0	0.0	2.0	4.000			
Chris Pusey	38	137	104.0	21.0	125.0	3.650			
§§Chris Bailey	3	8	6.0	0.0	6.0	3.000			
Eric Broadbelt	11	23	13.0	3.0	16.0	2.783			
John Woodcock	3	6	4.0	0.0	4.0	2.667			
§§Ken Moss	1	1	0.0	0.0	0.0	0.000			

1969...1969...1969...1969...1969...1969

	M	R	Pts	BP	TPts	Ave	F	P	Total
§Ivan Mauger	37	158	456.0	5.0	461.0	11.671	22	3	25
Sören Sjösten	34	140	338.0	15.0	353.0	10.086	6	6	12
Tommy Roper	33	131	271.0	10.0	281.0	8.580	5	4	9
Chris Pusey	33	133	173.0	40.0	213.0	6.406		2	2
§§Steve Waplington	5	25	37.0	0.0	37.0	5.920			
§Dave Hemus	19	60	55.0	14.0	69.0	4.600			
Norman Nevitt	18	60	55.0	10.0	65.0	4.333			
Bill Powell	17	53	49.0	8.0	57.0	4.302			
Ken Eyre	23	84	78.0	9.0	87.0	4.143			
Peter Thompson	1	3	2.0	1.0	3.0	4.000			
Eric Broadbelt	25	76	61.0	12.0	73.0	3.842			
Ken Moss	5	18	11.0	5.0	16.0	3.556			
§Mike Hiftle	2	8	7.0	0.0	7.0	3.500			
§§Bill Moulin	6	21	14.0	3.0	17.0	3.238			
Taffy Owen	3	7	5.0	0.0	5.0	2.857			
Chris Bailey	1	3	1.0	1.0	2.0	2.667			
§§Phil Whittaker	1	2	0.0	0.0	0.0	0.000			

IVAN MAUGER became the third Belle Vue rider to win the World Final when he took the 1969 title.
The two others were Peter Craven (1955 and 1962) and Ove Fundin in 1967.
Mauger had joined Belle Vue from Newcastle at the beginning of the season after he had made a written transfer request, as reigning World Champion and successfully defended the crown.

1970...1970...1970...1970...1970...1970

	M	R	Pts	BP	TPts	Ave	F	P	Total
Ivan Mauger	40	170	471.0	4.0	475.0	11.176	19	2	21
Sören Sjösten	37	154	356.0	16.0	372.0	9.662	6	3	9
Tommy Roper	40	160	289.5	27.0	316.5	7.913	3	4	7
Chris Pusey	41	173	266.0	50.0	316.0	7.306	2	3	5
Dave Hemus	40	141	167.0	37.0	204.0	5.787		1	1
Ken Eyre	32	114	128.0	24.0	152.0	5.333			
Eric Broadbelt	5	24	30.0	2.0	32.0	5.333			
Mike Hiftle	42	129	106.0	31.0	137.0	4.248			
Steve Waplington	9	25	18.0	4.0	22.0	3.520			
Chris Bailey	1	4	3.0	0.0	3.0	3.000			
§§Colin Goad	1	3	1.0	0.0	1.0	1.333			

1971...1971...1971...1971...1971...1971

	M	R	Pts	BP	TPts	Ave	F	P	Total
Ivan Mauger	31	137	381.0	7.0	388.0	11.328	15	3	18
Sören Sjösten	33	141	305.0	16.0	321.0	9.106	6	1	7
Tommy Roper	20	79	130.0	11.0	141.0	7.139	1	1	2
Eric Broadbelt	36	145	222.0	32.0	254.0	7.007	1		1
Dave Hemus	27	105	159.0	24.0	183.0	6.971		1	1
§§Peter Collins	11	44	55.0	15.0	70.0	6.364			
Chris Pusey	12	47	62.0	12.0	74.0	6.298			
Ken Eyre	34	128	145.0	27.0	172.0	5.375		1	1
§Alan Wilkinson	25	81	74.0	22.0	96.0	4.741		1	1
Mike Hiftle	16	48	39.0	15.0	54.0	4.500			
§George Major	1	4	4.0	0.0	4.0	4.000			
§Paul Tyrer	1	1	0.0	0.0	0.0	0.000			

1972...1972...1972...1972...1972...1972

	M	R	Pts	BP	TPts	Ave	F	P	Total
Ivan Mauger	31	126	350.0	8.0	358.0	11.365	15	4	19
Sören Sjösten	38	150	304.5	30.0	334.5	8.920	3	3	6
Peter Collins	38	153	286.0	37.0	323.0	8.444	2	1	3
Chris Pusey	**39**	**156**	**272.0**	**48.0**	**320.0**	**8.205**	**1**	**3**	**4**
Eric Broadbelt	38	144	207.0	35.0	242.0	6.722		1	1
Alan Wilkinson	38	146	211.0	33.0	244.0	6.685	1	1	2
§Graham Banks	1	3	4.0	1.0	5.0	6.667			
Ken Eyre	28	82	87.0	27.0	114.0	5.561		1	1
Paul Tyrer	6	18	21.0	2.0	23.0	5.111			
§Lou Sansom	1	2	1.0	1.0	2.0	4.000			
§§Ian Hindle	3	9	3.0	0.0	3.0	1.333			
§§Geoff Pusey	2	5	0.0	0.0	0.0	0.000			
§David Beech	1	2	0.0	0.0	0.0	0.000			
§§Terry Kelly	1	2	0.0	0.0	0.0	0.000			

BELLE VUE

1973...1973...1973...1973...1973...1973

	M	R	Pts	BP	TPts	Ave	F	P	Total
Chris Pusey	14	58	146.0	7.0	153.0	10.552	5	1	6
Peter Collins	36	156	339.0	15.0	354.0	9.077	5	2	7
Sören Sjösten	41	176	358.0	26.0	384.0	8.727	6	1	7
Eric Broadbelt	**44**	**172**	**267.0**	**34.0**	**301.0**	**7.000**		**1**	**1**
Alan Wilkinson	**44**	**177**	**255.0**	**52.0**	**307.0**	**6.938**	**2**	**3**	**5**
Paul Tyrer	**44**	**170**	**231.0**	**33.0**	**264.0**	**6.212**	**1**	**2**	**3**
§§Chris Morton	16	55	67.0	11.0	78.0	5.673		1	1
Ian Hindle	17	45	50.0	8.0	58.0	5.156			
Terry Kelly	9	25	17.0	5.0	22.0	3.520			
Dave Hemus	3	9	5.0	2.0	7.0	3.111			
Geoff Pusey	13	42	28.0	4.0	32.0	3.048			

1974...1974...1974...1974...1974...1974

	M	R	Pts	BP	TPts	Ave	F	P	Total
Peter Collins	33	134	352.0	16.0	368.0	10.985	13	6	19
Sören Sjösten	33	135	300.0	28.0	328.0	9.719	4	3	7
Chris Pusey	35	142	280.0	28.0	308.0	8.676	2	1	3
Paul Tyrer	26	99	149.0	36.0	185.0	7.475		1	1
Chris Morton	26	95	152.0	20.0	172.0	7.242		1	1
Alan Wilkinson	**36**	**127**	**175.0**	**31.0**	**206.0**	**6.488**	**2**		**2**
§§Wayne Hughes	1	3	3.0	1.0	4.0	5.333			
§Nicky Allott	1	5	5.0	1.0	6.0	4.800			
Geoff Pusey	15	52	45.0	9.0	54.0	4.154			
§§Joe Owen	1	3	2.0	1.0	3.0	4.000			
Terry Kelly	7	21	13.0	4.0	17.0	3.238			
Ian Hindle	30	85	52.0	6.0	58.0	2.729			
Brian Bentley	1	3	0.0	0.0	0.0	0.000			
§§Alan Grimshaw	1	3	0.0	0.0	0.0	0.000			
§§Steve Holden	1	2	0.0	0.0	0.0	0.000			
§§Duncan Meredith	1	2	0.0	0.0	0.0	0.000			

1975...1975...1975...1975...1975...1975

	M	R	Pts	BP	TPts	Ave	F	P	Total
Peter Collins	39	157	434.0	3.0	437.0	11.134	21	2	23
Chris Morton	**44**	**180**	**380.0**	**37.0**	**417.0**	**9.267**	**2**	**6**	**8**
Sören Sjösten	40	162	331.0	24.0	355.0	8.765	1	4	5
Alan Wilkinson	41	163	233.0	58.0	291.0	7.141	1	1	2
Paul Tyrer	**44**	**170**	**227.0**	**37.0**	**264.0**	**6.212**			
§§Russ Hodgson	39	117	121.0	26.0	147.0	5.026			
Ian Hindle	7	23	21.0	2.0	23.0	4.000			
§§Les Collins	1	3	2.0	1.0	3.0	4.000			
Alan Grimshaw	1	2	1.0	1.0	2.0	4.000			
Geoff Pusey	41	133	98.0	20.0	118.0	3.549			
§§Chris Turner	2	5	2.0	0.0	2.0	1.600			

1976...1976...1976...1976...1976...1976

	M	R	Pts	BP	TPts	Ave	F	P	Total
Peter Collins	40	166	449.0	10.0	459.0	11.060	21	4	25
Chris Morton	42	178	406.0	18.0	424.0	9.528	3	6	9
§§Jim Brett	1	3	5.0	1.0	6.0	8.000			
Alan Wilkinson	40	162	277.0	29.0	306.0	7.556	1	2	3
Les Collins	10	41	58.0	7.0	65.0	6.341			
§Steve Lawson	3	10	14.0	1.0	15.0	6.000			
Paul Tyrer	41	153	187.0	33.0	220.0	5.752		1	1
§§Kristian Praestbro	28	96	111.0	18.0	129.0	5.375			
Chris Turner	8	27	30.0	5.0	35.0	5.185			
Russ Hodgson	38	135	122.0	27.0	149.0	4.415			
§§Derek Richardson	1	3	3.0	0.0	3.0	4.000			
Geoff Pusey	38	115	94.0	16.0	110.0	3.826		1	1
§§Phil Kynman	1	3	2.0	0.0	2.0	2.667			

PETER COLLINS became the fourth Belle Vue rider to be crowned World Champion (see 1969) but was the first who was a genuine discovery of the club as he had never ridden for any other team. He had been unearthed by Dent Oliver and was nursed through the Aces Division Two side.

He was to become the titular head of a speedway dynasty as his younger brothers Les, Neil, Phil and Steven were all to ride in the British League.

1977...1977...1977...1977...1977...1977

	M	R	Pts	BP	TPts	Ave	F	P	Total
Peter Collins	32	140	360.0	6.0	366.0	10.457	9	3	12
Chris Morton	39	179	386.0	15.0	401.0	8.961	6	4	10
Alan Wilkinson	36	154	305.5	24.0	329.5	8.558	3	1	4
Les Collins	36	149	242.0	51.0	293.0	7.866		3	3
Russ Hodgson	6	21	28.0	3.0	31.0	5.905			
Derek Richardson	4	15	14.0	5.0	19.0	5.067			
Chris Turner	**40**	**154**	**131.0**	**30.0**	**161.0**	**4.182**			
§Robert Henry	2	6	6.0	0.0	6.0	4.000			
§Robbie Gardner	1	3	2.0	1.0	3.0	4.000			
Kristian Praestbro	26	85	71.0	8.0	79.0	3.718			
Jim Brett	20	61	47.0	8.0	55.0	3.607			
§§Robert Maxfield	3	6	3.0	2.0	5.0	3.333			
§Phil Collins	1	4	3.0	0.0	3.0	3.000			
§Alan Emerson	1	3	1.0	1.0	2.0	2.667			
Steve Lawson	14	33	17.0	2.0	19.0	2.303			
§§Carl Clarke	2	5	1.0	0.0	1.0	0.800			
§§Andy Heyes	3	6	0.0	0.0	0.0	0.000			

1978...1978...1978...1978...1978...1978

	M	R	Pts	BP	TPts	Ave	F	P	Total
§Steve Wilcock	1	3	5.0	3.0	8.0	10.667			
Peter Collins	41	169	427.0	13.0	440.0	10.414	8	6	14
Chris Morton	**44**	**183**	**445.5**	**17.0**	**462.5**	**10.109**	**7**	**6**	**13**
Les Collins	**44**	**181**	**317.0**	**45.0**	**362.0**	**8.000**	**2**	**1**	**3**
Alan Wilkinson	19	75	130.0	15.0	145.0	7.733			
§John Barker	1	4	5.0	0.0	5.0	5.000			
§Steve Finch	14	49	50.0	10.0	60.0	4.898			
Jim Brett	42	123	114.0	25.0	139.0	4.520			
Chris Turner	40	152	134.0	35.0	169.0	4.447		1	1
Robert Maxfield	29	101	90.0	20.0	110.0	4.356			
Derek Richardson	16	53	48.0	9.0	57.0	4.302			
§Eric Dugard	2	8	8.0	0.0	8.0	4.000			
§Mike Ferreira	1	3	2.0	0.0	2.0	2.667			
§§Mike Spink	1	3	1.0	0.0	1.0	1.333			
§§Keith Bloxsome	5	14	3.0	1.0	4.0	1.143			
§Uno Johansson	2	6	1.0	0.0	1.0	0.667			
§Sean Willmott	2	6	0.0	0.0	0.0	0.000			
§Paul Woods	1	2	0.0	0.0	0.0	0.000			

1979...1979...1979...1979...1979...1979

	M	R	Pts	BP	TPts	Ave	F	P	Total
Peter Collins	34	150	356.0	10.0	366.0	9.760	5		5
§Barney Kennett	1	3	6.0	1.0	7.0	9.333			
Chris Morton	34	147	318.0	15.0	333.0	9.061	1	2	3
Les Collins	35	152	264.0	25.0	289.0	7.605		1	1
§Dave Allen	6	20	28.0	2.0	30.0	6.000			
§§Karl Maier	5	18	20.0	5.0	25.0	5.556			
§Pekka Hautamaki	31	113	122.0	24.0	146.0	5.168			
§§Emil Sova	24	89	97.0	10.0	107.0	4.809			
Robert Maxfield	30	97	83.0	20.0	103.0	4.247			
Derek Richardson	11	38	33.0	7.0	40.0	4.211			
§Dave Piddock	1	2	1.0	1.0	2.0	4.000			
Arnold Haley	27	78	51.0	9.0	60.0	3.077			
Keith Bloxsome	5	14	3.0	0.0	3.0	0.857			
§Rod Hunter	1	3	0.0	0.0	0.0	0.000			
§§Paul Stead	1	2	0.0	0.0	0.0	0.000			

1980...1980...1980...1980...1980...1980

	M	R	Pts	BP	TPts	Ave	F	P	Total
Peter Collins	31	147	383.0	9.0	392.0	10.667	11		11
Chris Morton	36	178	435.0	14.0	449.0	10.090	5	5	10
Robert Maxfield	16	64	105.0	18.0	123.0	7.688		2	2
Mike Lohmann	6	24	32.0	6.0	38.0	6.333			
Derek Richardson	21	75	104.0	13.0	117.0	6.240			
§Peter Carr	2	6	7.0	2.0	9.0	6.000			
Pekka Hautamaki	35	133	150.0	28.0	178.0	5.353			
§Louis Carr	22	82	91.0	15.0	106.0	5.171			
§§Larry Kosta	32	114	117.0	23.0	140.0	4.912			
§Tony Boyle	1	6	6.0	1.0	7.0	4.667			
Dave Allen	**40**	**146**	**128.0**	**27.0**	**155.0**	**4.247**			
Steve Wilcock	18	73	70.0	7.0	77.0	4.219			
Keith Bloxsome	4	12	7.0	2.0	9.0	3.000			
§John J. Williams	1	7	4.0	1.0	5.0	2.857			
Emil Sova	4	12	4.0	1.0	5.0	1.667			
Steve Finch	1	3	0.0	0.0	0.0	0.000			

BELLE VUE

1981...1981...1981...1981...1981...1981

	M	R	Pts	BP	TPts	Ave	F	P	Total
Chris Morton	42	199	466.0	19.0	485.0	9.749	11	3	14
Larry Ross	45	215	464.0	24.0	488.0	9.079	5		5
Peter Collins	3	12	21.0	1.0	22.0	7.333			
§Neil Collins	4	16	23.0	5.0	28.0	7.000			
Robert Maxfield	11	42	63.0	10.0	73.0	6.952			
Jim McMillan	44	190	255.0	31.0	286.0	6.021			
Louis Carr	42	161	183.5	42.0	225.5	5.602			
Mike Lohmann	42	164	185.0	44.0	229.0	5.585			
Larry Kosta	39	135	156.0	30.0	186.0	5.511		1	1
§§Peter Ravn	33	108	112.0	16.0	128.0	4.741			
Dave Allen	3	11	7.0	2.0	9.0	3.273			
§Paul Embley	3	7	4.0	0.0	4.0	2.286			
Peter Carr	3	9	4.0	1.0	5.0	2.222			
Keith Bloxsome	1	3	1.0	0.0	1.0	1.333			

1982...1982...1982...1982...1982...1982

	M	R	Pts	BP	TPts	Ave	F	P	Total
Chris Morton	47	196	476.0	23.0	499.0	10.184	8	5	13
Larry Ross	45	187	419.0	19.0	438.0	9.369	3	1	4
Peter Collins	**48**	**196**	**394.0**	**36.0**	**430.0**	**8.776**	**1**	**4**	**5**
Louis Carr	47	173	218.0	42.0	260.0	6.012			
Peter Ravn	42	153	183.0	33.0	216.0	5.647			
JIm McMillan	47	164	186.0	37.0	223.0	5.439			
Peter Carr	43	134	140.0	27.0	167.0	4.985			
Rod Hunter	3	9	10.0	1.0	11.0	4.889			
§Bobby Beaton	3	11	9.0	4.0	13.0	4.727			
§§Andy Smith	4	10	8.0	3.0	11.0	4.400			
Keith Bloxsome	1	2	1.0	1.0	2.0	4.000			
Robert Maxfield	2	5	1.0	1.0	2.0	1.600			

1983...1983...1983...1983...1983...1983

	M	R	Pts	BP	TPts	Ave	F	P	Total
Chris Morton	48	205	508.0	20.0	528.0	10.302	10	7	17
Peter Collins	48	202	443.0	18.0	461.0	9.129	4	3	7
Bobby Beaton	1	4	7.0	1.0	8.0	8.000			
Larry Ross	**50**	**205**	**352.5**	**25.0**	**377.5**	**7.366**	**1**		**1**
Peter Carr	45	163	187.0	42.0	229.0	5.620		1	1
Louis Carr	**50**	**186**	**212.0**	**38.0**	**250.0**	**5.376**			
Peter Ravn	11	42	39.0	13.0	52.0	4.952			
Andy Smith	**50**	**149**	**137.0**	**30.0**	**167.0**	**4.483**			
§Kenny McKinna	37	121	113.0	17.0	130.0	4.298			
Rod Hunter	3	9	5.0	2.0	7.0	3.111			
§§Martin Scarisbrick	5	11	3.0	0.0	3.0	1.091			

1984...1984...1984...1984...1984...1984

	M	R	Pts	BP	TPts	Ave	F	P	Total
Chris Morton	49	206	502.0	29.0	531.0	10.311	11	8	19
Peter Collins	49	203	422.0	40.0	462.0	9.103	5	8	13
Larry Ross	**53**	**209**	**352.0**	**53.0**	**405.0**	**7.751**	**2**	**3**	**5**
Andy Smith	50	187	302.0	37.0	339.0	7.251	2	1	3
§Mark Courtney	**53**	**201**	**303.0**	**56.0**	**359.0**	**7.144**	**1**	**3**	**4**
Peter Carr	**53**	**194**	**267.0**	**56.0**	**323.0**	**6.660**		**1**	**1**
Kenny McKinna	**53**	**174**	**232.0**	**46.0**	**278.0**	**6.391**			
§Barry Ayres	3	8	3.0	1.0	4.0	2.000			

1985...1985...1985...1985...1985...1985

	M	R	Pts	BP	TPts	Ave	F	P	Total
Chris Morton	39	169	393.0	20.0	413.0	9.775	5	3	8
Peter Collins	39	161	334.0	25.0	359.0	8.919	2	4	6
Andy Smith	38	156	267.0	29.0	296.0	7.590	4		4
§Carl Blackbird	29	113	149.0	25.0	174.0	6.159			
Kenny McKinna	**42**	**151**	**190.0**	**30.0**	**220.0**	**5.828**			
§Andy Campbell	**42**	**137**	**133.0**	**35.0**	**168.0**	**4.905**			
Martin Scarisbrick	20	67	63.0	10.0	73.0	4.358			
§Eddie Ingels	20	66	48.0	7.0	55.0	3.333			
Bernie Collier	5	15	4.0	1.0	5.0	1.333			
§§Mark Crang	10	29	5.0	3.0	8.0	1.103			
§§Declan Eccles	1	4	1.0	0.0	1.0	1.000			
Barry Ayres	2	6	1.0	0.0	1.0	0.667			

PROMOTER Stuart Bamforth plunged into the transfer market after finishing runners-up in the 1984 British League, signing Carl Blackbird from Mildenhall (£20,000), Andy Campbell from Exeter (£15,000) and Mark Crang from Middlesbrough (£6,000).

1986...1986...1986...1986...1986...1986

	M	R	Pts	BP	TPts	Ave	F	P	Total
Chris Morton	39	173	380.0	24.0	404.0	9.341	3	3	6
§Paul Thorp	3	13	23.0	3.0	26.0	8.000			
§Martin Dixon	2	7	11.0	3.0	14.0	8.000			
Carl Blackbird	**41**	**172**	**287.0**	**30.0**	**317.0**	**7.372**	**1**		**1**
Peter Collins	40	157	246.0	26.0	272.0	6.930	2	1	3
Kenny McKinna	40	155	226.0	25.0	251.0	6.477			
Andy Smith	16	61	84.0	9.0	93.0	6.098			
Mark Courtney	15	56	59.0	17.0	76.0	5.429			
Declan Eccles	27	87	84.0	9.0	93.0	4.276			
§§Glenn Hornby	2	6	5.0	0.0	5.0	3.333			
Mark Crang	4	12	6.0	2.0	8.0	2.667			
Barry Ayres	34	101	53.0	14.0	67.0	2.653			
Bernie Collier	6	20	8.0	0.0	8.0	1.600			
§§Steve Newsham	2	6	1.0	1.0	2.0	1.333			
§§Lee Edwards	11	34	7.0	2.0	9.0	1.059			
§§Jon Roberts	1	4	0.0	0.0	0.0	0.000			

1987...1987...1987...1987...1987...1987

	M	R	Pts	BP	TPts	Ave	F	P	Total
Chris Morton	49	212	440.0	33.0	473.0	8.925	3	1	4
Paul Thorp	47	212	421.0	25.0	446.0	8.415	1	3	4
Peter Ravn	50	212	420.0	24.0	444.0	8.377	3	3	6
Andy Smith	35	136	194.0	22.0	216.0	6.353	1	1	2
Kenny McKinna	51	187	230.0	42.0	272.0	5.818			
Carl Blackbird	44	170	199.0	37.0	236.0	5.553		1	1
§Gordon Whitaker	2	7	6.0	1.0	7.0	4.000			
§David Blackburn	14	50	38.0	11.0	49.0	3.920			
Glenn Hornby	51	119	63.0	16.0	79.0	2.655			
Steve Lawson	1	3	1.0	0.0	1.0	1.333			
Bernie Collier	2	4	0.0	0.0	0.0	0.000			
§§Glenn Doyle	1	3	0.0	0.0	0.0	0.000			
Jon Roberts	1	2	0.0	0.0	0.0	0.000			

1988...1988...1988...1988...1988...1988

	M	R	Pts	BP	TPts	Ave	F	P	Total
Chris Morton	44	211	429.5	46.0	475.5	9.014		2	2
Louis Carr	1	4	9.0	0.0	9.0	9.000			
§§Mike Faria	36	165	298.5	39.0	337.5	8.182			
Peter Ravn	43	189	325.0	39.0	364.0	7.704			
Paul Thorp	43	194	324.0	26.0	350.0	7.216	2		2
§Roland Dannö	43	193	292.0	42.0	334.0	6.922		1	1
Andy Smith	41	171	257.0	35.0	292.0	6.830	1	1	2
§Graham Jones	2	9	13.0	1.0	14.0	6.222			
§§Paul Smith	31	107	111.0	22.0	133.0	4.972		1	1
§§Carl Stonehewer	2	5	4.0	2.0	6.0	4.800			
Les Collins	1	4	3.0	1.0	4.0	4.000			
§Jens Rasmussen	1	4	3.0	1.0	4.0	4.000			
§Gordon Kennett	1	3	3.0	0.0	3.0	4.000			
Glenn Hornby	15	50	28.0	11.0	39.0	3.120			
§Darren Sumner	3	11	7.0	0.0	7.0	2.545			
Bernie Collier	1	3	1.0	0.0	1.0	1.333			
§Mark Loram	1	3	1.0	0.0	1.0	1.333			

1989...1989...1989...1989...1989...1989

	M	R	Pts	BP	TPts	Ave	F	P	Total
§Shawn Moran	30	143	319.0	27.0	346.0	9.678	3	5	8
§Kelly Moran	18	82	156.0	14.0	170.0	8.293	2		2
Peter Ravn	33	149	252.0	29.0	281.0	7.544			
§§Gary Hicks	20	82	126.0	21.0	147.0	7.171			
Chris Morton	34	150	235.0	18.0	253.0	6.747	1	2	3
§§Joe Screen	**36**	**161**	**232.5**	**25.0**	**257.5**	**6.398**		**1**	**1**
Carl Stonehewer	30	117	130.0	31.0	161.0	5.504			
Gordon Whitaker	9	34	22.0	7.0	29.0	3.412			
Paul Smith	6	23	11.0	1.0	12.0	2.087			
§§Mike Lewthwaite	4	13	6.0	0.0	6.0	1.846			
Glenn Hornby	1	4	1.0	0.0	1.0	1.000			

1990...19890...1990...1990...1990...1990

	M	R	Pts	BP	TPts	Ave	F	P	Total
Kelly Moran	32	151	289.0	29.0	318.0	8.424			
Shawn Moran	28	134	238.0	30.0	268.0	8.000	1	2	3
§Bobby Ott	35	157	245.0	37.0	282.0	7.185		1	1
Chris Morton	31	134	216.0	19.0	235.0	7.015	1	1	2
Joe Screen	32	141	208.0	28.0	236.0	6.695			
Peter Ravn	25	100	128.0	16.0	144.0	5.760		1	1
§§Richard Musson	33	126	118.0	31.0	149.0	4.730			
§§Max Schofield	5	13	8.0	2.0	10.0	3.077			
Mike Lewthwaite	3	10	1.0	0.0	1.0	0.400			

BELLE VUE

IT WAS the most famous speedway stadium in the world...as the brightly painted sign above the entrance to the main stand proclaimed: Home of the Aces.

Hyde Road, Manchester, the track specially built for the sport in 1929 and home of the most revered team in the country and host to riders like Jack Parker, Peter Craven, Ove Fundin, Ivan Mauger and Peter Collins.

All of a sudden the dramatic past meant nothing as the auctioneer began the bidding as, item by item, speedway's relics were sold off.

Many of the glittering trophies that had adorned the small manager's office at Belle Vue were up for grabs.

So, too, was the starting gate that had seen goodness knows how many thousands of races over the years at the only track which managed to run weekly throughout the Second World War.

Scrap metal dealer Stuart Bamforth had been hailed as the club's saviour when he bought the stadium and speedway rights from former owners Trust House Forté as the once famous landmark of Belle Vue Zoological Gardens and Entertainment Park began to be sold off piecemeal.

Most of the other entertainment had gone, along with the elephants, but Bamforth, the 1976 World Stock Car Champion, spoke of a bright future when he first took over in February, 1982.

For six years he spent heavily on riders in search of further trophies to add to that gleaming cabinet but early in October, 1987, British Car Auctions put in a planning application to completely redevelop the Belle Vue site, including the stadium.

Less than a month later it was revealed that Bamforth had sold out for £10,000,000 – and, on Tuesday, December 2, Belle Vue's heritage went under the hammer with 371 separate items being sold off to businessmen, investors and fans who wanted a simple souvenir of the Aces.

A few weeks later Peter Collins, who bought the team off Bamforth, and superfan John Perrin were given planning approval to move the club back to what had been its original home in 1928 – the Belle Vue Greyhound Stadium half a mile or so along Hyde Road!

	PETER CRAVEN MEMORIAL TROPHY		
1967	1 Ivan Mauger	2 Ove Fundin	3 Cyril Maidment
1969	1 Ole Olsen	2 Martin Ashby	3 Jim McMillan
1970	1 Jim Airey	2 Charlie Monk	3 Ray Wilson
1971	1 Ole Olsen	2 Ivan Mauger	3 Bruce Cribb
1974	1 Chris Morton	2 Sören Sjösten	3 Peter Collins
1975	1 Chris Morton	2 Tommy Jansson	3 Alan Wilkinson and Mitch Graham
1978	1 Peter Collins	2 John Titman	3 Steve Bastable
1980	1 Dennis Sigalos		
1985	1 Andy Smith	2 Shawn Moran	3 Phil Crump
1986	1 Chris Morton	2 Sam Ermolenko	3 Shawn Moran
1988	1 Kelly Moran	2 Kelvin Tatum	3 Sam Ermolenko
1989	1 Shawn Moran	2 Ronnie Correy	3 Sam Ermolenko
1990	1 Billy Hamill	2 Shawn Moran	3 Neil Collins
	DEREK WARBURTON TROPHY		
1971	1 Eric Boocock	2 Sandor Levai	3 Alan Wilkinson
1972	1 Ivan Mauger	2 Peter Collins	3 Eric Broadbelt
	JOHN PLAYER NUMBER 6 CLASSIC		
1972	1 Ole Olsen	2 Anders Michanek	2 Alan Wilkinson
1973	1 Sören Sjösten	2 Alan Wilkinson	3 Peter Collins
1974	1 Peter Collins	2 Ole Olsen	3 Paul Tyrer
1975	1 Peter Collins	2 George Hunter	3 Sören Sösten
1976	1 Peter Collins	2 Doug Wyer	3 Chris Morton
	GOLDEN APPLE		
1976	1 Chris Morton	2 Phil Collins	3 Dave Jessup
1977	1 Les Collins	2 Peter Collins	3 Jim Brett
	MARLBORO RACE OF CHAMPIONS		
1977	1 Peter Collins	2 Edward Jancarz	3 Chris Morton
	LEVIS FOR FEET NORTHERN INTERNATIONAL		
1978	1 Peter Collins	2 Chris Morton	3 Ole Olsen
	GOLDEN JUBILEE TROPHY		
1978	1 Peter Collins	2 Chris Morton	3 Dave Jessup
	JUNIOR CHAMPIONSHIP		
1982	1 Lee Edwards	2 Geoff Wilson	3 Michael Irving
1988	1 Paul Smith	2 Carl Stonehewer	3 Mike Lewthwaite
	PETER COLLINS FAREWELL		
1987	1 Shawn Moran	2 Simon Wigg	3 Chris Morton
	DIAMOND JUBILEE		
1988	1 Erik Gundersen	2 Chris Morton	3 Jan O. Pedersen
	PETER RAVN TESTIMONIAL		
1990	1 Hans Nielsen	2 John Jørgensen	3 Simon Cross

UNDER THE HAMMER....Bernie Collier takes one last look at the most famous stadium in speedway before it all comes down – and the family silverware is auctioned off to the highest bidder

BIRMINGHAM

BIRMINGHAM joined the British League after five seasons of bumper crowds in the Second Division.

1976...1976...1976...1976...1976...1976

	M	R	Pts	BP	TPts	Ave	F	P	Total
§Alan Grahame	6	30	57.0	3.0	60.0	8.000			
§Garry Middleton	19	99	150.0	16.0	166.0	6.707			
§Sören Sjösten	31	128	201.0	13.0	214.0	6.688			
§Lou Sansom	10	56	75.0	10.0	85.0	6.071			
§Jan Gravningen	35	132	144.5	28.0	172.5	5.227			
§Arthur Browning	35	138	154.0	18.0	172.0	4.986			
§Bob Valentine	21	67	72.0	7.0	79.0	4.716			
§§Ove Olsen	27	97	93.0	13.0	106.0	4.371			
§§Mike Fishwick	5	14	7.0	4.0	11.0	3.143			
§Carl Askew	7	18	5.0	3.0	8.0	1.778			
§Ricky Day	8	20	5.0	0.0	5.0	1.000			
§Keith Anderson	3	8	1.0	0.0	1.0	0.500			
§§Steve Davenport	1	2	0.0	0.0	0.0	0.000			
§§Andy Grahame	1	1	0.0	0.0	0.0	0.000			

1977...1977...1977...1977...1977...1977

	M	R	Pts	BP	TPts	Ave	F	P	Total
§Ray Wilson	**38**	**173**	**364.0**	**14.0**	**378.0**	**8.740**	**2**		**2**
§Phil Collins	1	5	7.0	1.0	8.0	6.400			
Alan Grahame	36	178	264.0	19.0	283.0	6.360			
§Richard Greer	20	76	94.0	12.0	106.0	5.579			
Lou Sansom	**38**	**156**	**171.0**	**24.0**	**195.0**	**5.000**			
Jan Gravningen	33	135	144.0	23.0	167.0	4.948			
§Malcolm Shakespeare	34	118	122.0	18.0	140.0	4.746			
Carl Askew	14	43	41.0	8.0	49.0	4.558			
§§Stuart Mountford	12	39	32.0	8.0	40.0	4.103			
§§Robert Dole	1	2	1.0	1.0	2.0	4.000			
§§Finn Jensen	13	36	24.0	7.0	31.0	3.444			
§§Kevin Hawkins	2	6	5.0	0.0	5.0	3.333			
Michael Fishwick	3	8	6.0	0.0	6.0	3.000			
§Tim Nunan	1	2	0.0	0.0	0.0	0.000			
§Ian Clark	1	2	0.0	0.0	0.0	0.000			
Andy Grahame	1	2	0.0	0.0	0.0	0.000			

1978...1978...1978...1978...1978...1978

	M	R	Pts	BP	TPts	Ave	F	P	Total
Phil Collins	1	5	11.0	0.0	11.0	8.800			
Phil Herne	37	156	321.0	13.0	334.0	8.564	2		2
Ray Wilson	23	92	182.0	9.0	191.0	8.304	5		5
§Ted Howgego	15	60	91.0	11.0	102.0	6.800			
§Mick Newton	1	3	3.0	2.0	5.0	6.667			
Richard Greer	**38**	**173**	**263.0**	**25.0**	**288.0**	**6.659**	**1**	**1**	**2**
§§Ari Koponen	33	137	132.0	41.0	173.0	5.051		1	1
§Bengt Jansson	20	72	74.0	15.0	89.0	4.944			
§Alan Emerson	36	130	118.0	22.0	140.0	4.308			
Finn Jensen	31	94	87.0	11.0	98.0	4.170			
Malcolm Shakespeare	1	4	2.0	0.0	2.0	2.000			
§Tim Nunan	1	3	1.0	0.0	1.0	1.333			
Stuart Mountford	3	8	2.0	0.0	2.0	1.000			
Andy Grahame	3	6	0.0	0.0	0.0	0.000			
§§Bobby Baker	1	2	0.0	0.0	0.0	0.000			

1979...1979...1979...1979...1979...1979

	M	R	Pts	BP	TPts	Ave	F	P	Total
Steve Bastable	5	22	51.0	1.0	52.0	9.455	2		2
Richard Greer	1	3	7.0	0.0	7.0	9.333			
Billy Sanders	28	122	266.0	13.0	279.0	9.148	3	1	4
§Dave Allen	1	5	8.0	2.0	10.0	8.000			
Phil Herne	35	134	252.0	13.0	265.0	7.910	2		2
Andy Grahame	27	110	191.0	18.0	209.0	7.600			
Finn Jensen	28	99	136.0	16.0	152.0	6.141	1		1
Alan Emerson	16	63	77.0	16.0	93.0	5.905			
Ari Koponen	26	99	105.0	20.0	125.0	5.051			
Ray Wilson	29	107	120.0	15.0	135.0	5.047			
§Steve Lawson	5	16	17.0	2.0	19.0	4.750			
Ted Howgego	19	72	65.0	13.0	78.0	4.333			
§Terry Tulloch	1	4	3.0	1.0	4.0	4.000			
§Mick Blaynee	5	16	10.0	5.0	15.0	3.750			
§§Steve Columbo	4	13	10.0	1.0	11.0	3.385			
§Robbie Blackadder	1	5	4.0	0.0	4.0	3.200			
Stuart Mountford	8	25	13.0	4.0	17.0	2.720			
§Ian Gledhill	3	7	2.0	1.0	3.0	1.714			
Ian Clark	2	4	1.0	0.0	1.0	1.000			
§Louis Carr	1	2	0.0	0.0	0.0	0.000			

1980...1980...1980...1980...1980...1980

	M	R	Pts	BP	TPts	Ave	F	P	Total
Steve Bastable	35	161	331.0	14.0	345.0	8.571	2	1	3
§Kelly Moran	22	101	192.0	16.0	208.0	8.238		2	2
Andy Grahame	**38**	**171**	**297.0**	**19.0**	**316.0**	**7.392**			
§§Neil Evitts	2	5	6.0	2.0	8.0	6.400			
§Zdenek Kudrna	22	90	122.0	18.0	140.0	6.222			
Phil Herne	7	23	27.0	8.0	35.0	6.087			
Ari Koponen	19	77	93.0	22.0	115.0	5.974			
Finn Jensen	34	135	180.0	20.0	200.0	5.926	1	1	2
Alan Emerson	22	90	107.0	18.0	125.0	5.556		1	1
§Tony Boyle	1	5	6.0	0.0	6.0	4.800			
Ove Olsen	2	7	8.0	0.0	8.0	4.571			
§§Mark Warren	2	6	4.0	2.0	6.0	4.000			
§Alan Sage	1	2	1.0	1.0	2.0	4.000			
§§Ladislaw Hradecky	22	67	53.0	9.0	62.0	3.701			
§§Paul Thorp	3	8	5.0	1.0	6.0	3.000			
Mick Blaynee	13	37	17.0	8.0	25.0	2.703			
§Peter Carr	1	3	2.0	0.0	2.0	2.667			
§Mike Spink	2	5	2.0	1.0	3.0	2.400			
§§John Eskildsen	3	4	1.0	1.0	2.0	2.000			
§Mark Bilner	1	2	1.0	0.0	1.0	2.000			
§Geoff Pusey	1	2	1.0	0.0	1.0	2.000			
§Brian Woodward	2	7	2.0	0.0	2.0	1.143			
§Rod North	1	2	0.0	0.0	0.0	0.000			

1981...1981...1981...1981...1981...1981

	M	R	Pts	BP	TPts	Ave	F	P	Total
§Billy Burton	1	5	14.0	0.0	14.0	11.200			
§Hans Nielsen	45	216	505.0	24.0	529.0	9.796	6	4	10
Andy Grahame	**53**	**249**	**511.0**	**27.0**	**538.0**	**8.643**	**4**	**3**	**7**
Kai Niemi	48	222	367.0	46.0	413.0	7.441		1	1
Ian Gledhill	1	3	4.0	1.0	5.0	6.667			
Ari Koponen	43	186	267.0	31.0	298.0	6.409	1		1
Finn Jensen	15	53	69.0	9.0	78.0	5.887			
§Les Rumsey	6	24	34.0	1.0	35.0	5.833	1		1
§§Keith Chrisco	42	173	183.0	39.0	222.0	5.133		1	1
Bruce Cribb	23	98	105.0	19.0	124.0	5.061			
Neil Evitts	22	82	86.0	15.0	101.0	4.927			
§Hasse Danielsson	17	62	63.0	13.0	76.0	4.903			
John Eskildsen	3	6	3.0	2.0	5.0	3.333			
§§Gene Woods	5	19	10.0	3.0	13.0	2.737			
Paul Thorp	27	69	28.0	9.0	37.0	2.145			
§Simon Wigg	2	6	2.0	1.0	3.0	2.000			
Arthur Browning	1	2	1.0	0.0	1.0	2.000			
§§Martin Dixon	1	2	1.0	0.0	1.0	2.000			
§Andy Passey	1	2	1.0	0.0	1.0	2.000			
§§Derek Cooper	6	14	5.0	1.0	6.0	1.714			
§§Mike Wilding	2	5	1.0	0.0	1.0	0.800			
§Peter Bacon	1	3	0.0	0.0	0.0	0.000			

HANS NIELSEN soared to the top of the Birmingham averages in his first season with the Brummies after a winter transfer from Wolverhampton.
He was to remain with the Midlanders until asking for a move at the end of the 1983 season.

1982...1982...1982...1982...1982...1982

	M	R	Pts	BP	TPts	Ave	F	P	Total
Hans Nielsen	43	190	457.0	13.0	470.0	9.895	9	2	11
Andy Grahame	41	171	377.0	9.0	386.0	9.029	8	2	10
Ari Koponen	44	173	246.0	22.0	268.0	6.197			
§Ales Dryml	14	57	76.0	10.0	86.0	6.035		1	1
John Eskildsen	44	181	230.0	43.0	273.0	6.033			
§§John Jørgensen	7	29	33.0	8.0	41.0	5.655			
Zdenek Kudrna	10	39	47.0	4.0	51.0	5.231			
Neil Evitts	43	140	142.0	34.0	176.0	5.029			
§Karl Maier	19	72	73.0	12.0	85.0	4.722			
Bruce Cribb	16	46	34.0	7.0	41.0	3.565			
§Alan Molyneux	3	6	3.0	2.0	5.0	3.333			
§Nigel Sparshott	2	5	4.0	0.0	4.0	3.200			
Mike Wilding	5	12	4.0	2.0	6.0	2.000			
§§Armando dal Chiele	7	15	3.0	0.0	3.0	0.800			
Paul Thorp	6	14	2.0	0.0	2.0	0.571			
§§Paul Evitts	1	2	0.0	0.0	0.0	0.000			
§§Paul Symonds	1	2	0.0	0.0	0.0	0.000			

BIRMINGHAM

1983...1983...1983...1983...1983...1983

	M	R	Pts	BP	TPts	Ave	F	P	Total
Hans Nielsen	39	179	478.0	6.0	484.0	10.816	11	2	13
Andy Grahame	41	179	351.0	20.0	371.0	8.291	2	1	3
Neil Evitts	34	146	222.0	29.0	251.0	6.877			0
§§Shawn McConnell	16	63	70.0	20.0	90.0	5.714			
Karl Maier	16	59	74.0	9.0	83.0	5.627			
§Derek Harrison	2	8	8.0	3.0	11.0	5.500			
§Petr Ondrasik	18	56	62.0	13.0	75.0	5.357			
John Jørgensen	35	127	136.0	23.0	159.0	5.008		1	1
§§Kent Noer	37	132	129.0	31.0	160.0	4.848			
§Nigel Crabtree	1	2	2.0	0.0	2.0	4.000			
Paul Thorp	9	23	12.0	6.0	18.0	3.130			
§Mark Fiora	1	3	1.0	1.0	2.0	2.667			
Bruce Cribb	5	14	7.0	2.0	9.0	2.571			
Mike Wilding	20	58	23.0	7.0	30.0	2.069			
Nigel Sparshott	3	8	3.0	1.0	4.0	2.000			
§§Phil Alderman	1	2	1.0	0.0	1.0	2.000			
§§Linden Warner	3	5	1.0	0.0	1.0	0.800			
§Steve Wilcock	2	4	0.0	0.0	0.0	0.000			

SECOND CITY TROPHY

1976	1 Martin Ashby	2 Mitch Shirra	3 Ole Olsen
1977	1 Steve Bastable	2 Keith White	3 Michael Lee
1978	1 John Louis	2 Mike Lohmann	3 Richard Hellsén
1979	1 John Louis	2 Ole Olsen	3 Chris Mortan
1981	1 Kenny Carter	2 Hans Nielsen	3 Ole Olsen
1983	1 Erik Gundersen	2 Mitch Shirra	3 Hans Nielsen

See also Birmingham Second Division Averages

SKOL MASTERS

1977	1 Peter Collins	2 Phil Crump	3 Arnie Haley
1978	1 Bruce Penhall	2 Ole Olsen	3 Chris Morton

EVEN though Birmingham knew that their Perry Barr track was being redeveloped at the end of the 1983 season there was still optimism among the Brummies when the season ended.

But that was to be quickly destroyed.

Promoter Dan McCormick announced plans to move the side to a new motorsport complex being built at Bordesley Green promising: "When completed it will be the first of its kind in Europe and the envy of the world."

Within a few weeks the club had been rocked by a transfer request from Hans Nielsen who claimed: "I want to be part of a successful line-up. I have been in a losing team for seven years at Wolverhampton and Birmingham."

He subsequently joined British League newcomers Oxford for a world record £30,000 fee and then, only a few weeks before the start of the new season, it was revealed that the new venue would not be sufficiently ready for Division One racing although new promoters came in and gambled on fans supporting National League action despite the spartan amenities at Bordesley Green.

The old British League side was split up – Andy Grahame joined Nielsen at Cowley, Neil Evitts went to Halifax and John Jørgensen moved to Coventry,

LOCKED UP...Australian Test star Phil Herne powers into the Perry Barr turn in the style that made him a big favourite during his time as a Brummie

BRADFORD

1986...1986...1986...1986...1986...1986

	M	R	Pts	BP	TPts	Ave	F	P	Total
§Kenny Carter	10	41	102.0	1.0	103.0	10.049	1		1
§Neil Evitts	37	154	345.0	14.0	359.0	9.325	7		7
§Lance King	27	118	234.0	8.0	242.0	8.203	1		1
§Gary Havelock	15	65	98.0	20.0	118.0	7.262		1	1
§Sean Willmott	41	160	199.0	53.0	252.0	6.300			
§Larry Ross	39	151	197.0	30.0	227.0	6.013		1	1
§Eric Monaghan	4	13	12.0	2.0	14.0	4.308			
§Gordon Whitaker	41	125	114.0	16.0	130.0	4.160			
§Paul Stead	1	4	3.0	1.0	4.0	4.000			
§Paul Evitts	1	3	2.0	1.0	3.0	4.000			
§§Michael Graves	**43**	**134**	**108.0**	**22.0**	**130.0**	**3.881**			
§§Anthony Hulme	2	6	1.0	0.0	1.0	0.667			
§§Robin Archer	1	3	0.0	0.0	0.0	0.000			
§§David Clay	1	3	0.0	0.0	0.0	0.000			
§§Jim Graham	1	3	0.0	0.0	0.0	0.000			
§Paul Whittaker	1	3	0.0	0.0	0.0	0.000			
§Bruce Cribb	1	1	0.0	0.0	0.0	0.000			

1987...1987...1987...1987...1987...1987

	M	R	Pts	BP	TPts	Ave	F	P	Total
Neil Evitts	41	185	378.0	19.0	397.0	8.584	4	1	5
Lance King	38	169	337.0	21.0	358.0	8.473	3	1	4
§Mark Fiora	1	4	7.0	1.0	8.0	8.000			
Sean Willmott	**48**	**209**	**320.0**	**64.0**	**384.0**	**7.349**	**1**	**1**	**2**
Gary Havelock	41	174	289.0	29.0	318.0	7.310	3	1	4
§Steve Bastable	**48**	**187**	**217.0**	**51.0**	**268.0**	**5.733**			
§Randy Green	37	117	139.0	28.0	167.0	5.709			
Michael Graves	47	152	146.0	43.0	189.0	4.974		2	2
Jim Graham	1	2	1.0	1.0	2.0	4.000			
Anthony Hulme	19	46	16.0	1.0	17.0	1.478			
David Clay	5	8	1.0	0.0	1.0	0.500			

1988...1988...1988...1988...1988...1988

	M	R	Pts	BP	TPts	Ave	F	P	Total
Steve Bastable	1	4	9.0	0.0	9.0	9.000			
Gary Havelock	33	174	338.0	23.0	361.0	8.299	2	1	3
§Glenn Doyle	2	9	15.0	2.0	17.0	7.556			
Neil Evitts	37	179	315.0	18.0	333.0	7.441			
Sean Willmott	39	176	239.0	26.0	265.0	6.023			
§Alan Mogridge	1	4	5.0	1.0	6.0	6.000			
§Robert Pfetzing	33	151	184.0	30.0	214.0	5.669			
§§Bryan Larner	1	3	4.0	0.0	4.0	5.333			
Michael Graves	37	149	171.0	26.0	197.0	5.289		1	1
Randy Green	18	73	82.0	12.0	94.0	5.151			
§Steve Regeling	1	6	7.0	0.0	7.0	4.667			
§Olli Tyrvainen	33	118	116.0	21.0	137.0	4.644			
§§Henrik Kristensen	4	16	12.0	4.0	16.0	4.000			
Anthony Hulme	31	112	76.0	24.0	100.0	3.571			
§§Simon Green	5	15	7.0	1.0	8.0	2.133			
Mark Fiora	1	3	1.0	0.0	1.0	1.333			
§Darren Sumner	1	4	0.0	0.0	0.0	0.000			
§Alan Rivett	1	2	0.0	0.0	0.0	0.000			

1989...1989...1989...1989...1989...1989

	M	R	Pts	BP	TPts	Ave	F	P	Total
Paul Thorp	**36**	**189**	**352.0**	**16.0**	**368.0**	**7.788**	**2**		**2**
Neil Evitts	35	154	274.0	15.0	289.0	7.506			
§Andy Smith	**30**	**109**	**275.0**	**32.0**	**307.0**	**7.266**		**2**	**2**
Bryan Larner	6	20	22.0	5.0	27.0	5.400			
Henrik Kristensen	30	111	123.0	14.0	137.0	4.937		1	1
Glenn Doyle	23	95	96.0	17.0	113.0	4.758			
§§Antal Kocso	29	113	111.0	19.0	130.0	4.602			
Michael Graves	31	116	103.0	18.0	121.0	4.172		1	1
§§Stuart Parnaby	2	6	0.0	0.0	0.0	0.000			
§§Derek Green	1	3	0.0	0.0	0.0	0.000			

1990...19890...1990...1990...1990...1990

	M	R	Pts	BP	TPts	Ave	F	P	Total
§Marvyn Cox	36	179	361.0	25.0	386.0	8.626	2	2	4
Gary Havelock	**38**	**193**	**380.0**	**30.0**	**410.0**	**8.497**	**2**	**1**	**3**
Andy Smith	27	117	191.0	34.0	225.0	7.692		3	3
Paul Thorp	**38**	**171**	**264.0**	**31.0**	**295.0**	**6.901**		**2**	**2**
Glenn Doyle	33	154	218.0	19.0	237.0	6.156			
Neil Evitts	28	105	135.0	26.0	161.0	6.133		2	2
Stuart Parnaby	8	25	12.0	1.0	13.0	2.080			
Bryan Larner	27	87	31.0	13.0	44.0	2.023			
§§Phil Disney	6	16	6.0	2.0	8.0	2.000			

BRADFORD'S Odsal Stadium re-opened for speedway at the beginning of 1986 and quickly became Britain's premier venue.

Disagreements with the landlords at The Shay forced the Halifax management to look around for a new home base and they swiftly reached agreement with Bradford City Council.

Long-time Dukes' promoter Reg Fearman sold out his interests in the company to brothers Allan and Bobby Ham, two former professional footballers running their own construction firm, and they teamed up with long-serving promoter Eric Boothroyd and his wife Bonnie to bring a new image to the club in their new surroundings.

After a financial struggle in the early days Bradford ended the British League era by winning the 1990 Gold Cup – the first national trophy success in the club's long history.

And Bradford was accepted as the British World Final venue, having staged both the 1985 and 1990 Finals.

COALITE CLASSIC

1986	1 Jan O Pedersen	2 Kelvin Tatum	3 Hans Nielsen
1988	1 Sam Ermolenko	2 Chris Morton	3 Kelly Moran
1989	1 Sam Ermolenko	2 Peter Ravn	3 Shawn Moran
1990	1 Jan O. Pedersen	2 Simon Cross	3 Marvyn Cox

GAZZA-MANIA....Gary Havelock became the controversial idol of Odsal

BRISTOL

■ *OPENING night at Bristol's Eastville Stadium – Friday, April 29, 1977 – was an evening no-one who was there could ever forget.*
■ *For 14,596 fans packed into the home of Bristol Rovers' Football Club to witness the first speedway meeting in the city since 1960.*
■ *The local council had tried to stop speedway taking place at the stadium and even after opening there were problems with protests from riders about the track surface, a sandy base to allow greyhounds to continue to use the same circuit.*
■ *Eventually after two highly successful years in which crowds rarely dropped below 5,000, the track was forced to close after continuing objections about noise.*
■ *Stadium managing director Ian Stevens gave an undertaking in closed session in the High Court that he would not allow any more meetings at Eastville on Thursday, December 14, 1878...and one of the most colourful eras in British League history was over!*

1977...1977...1977...1977...1977...1977

	M	R	Pts	BP	TPts	Ave	F	P	Total
§Phil Crump	28	131	312.0	8.0	320.0	9.771	6	2	8
§Phil Herne	**40**	**175**	**390.0**	**14.0**	**404.0**	**9.234**	**7**	**2**	**9**
§Phil Collins	2	9	14.0	3.0	17.0	7.556			
§Steve Gresham	30	127	205.0	21.0	226.0	7.118		6	6
§Bob Coles	1	4	7.0	0.0	7.0	7.000			
§Tormod Langli	39	172	244.0	31.0	275.0	6.395		1	1
§Nigel Boocock	36	159	207.0	34.0	241.0	6.063		1	1
§Phil Bass	16	46	44.0	9.0	53.0	4.609			
§Danny Kennedy	13	36	31.0	10.0	41.0	4.556			
§Edgar Stangeland	13	41	29.0	9.0	38.0	3.707			
§Tom Leadbitter	22	64	40.0	11.0	51.0	3.188			
§§Tony Garard	10	29	21.0	2.0	23.0	3.172			
§§Richard Evans	6	16	10.0	2.0	12.0	3.000			
§§Thomas Pettersson	4	11	5.0	3.0	8.0	2.909			
§§John Goodall	1	3	1.0	1.0	2.0	2.667			
§Brian Woodward	11	32	15.0	1.0	16.0	2.000			
§§Derek Hole	3	4	1.0	1.0	2.0	2.000			
§Sean Willmott	3	7	0.0	0.0	0.0	0.000			
§Alan Sage	1	4	0.0	0.0	0.0	0.000			
§§Stein Roar Pedersen	1	1	0.0	0.0	0.0	0.000			

1978...1978...1978...1978...1978...1978

	M	R	Pts	BP	TPts	Ave	F	P	Total
Phil Crump	37	175	420.0	14.0	434.0	9.920	4	2	6
Steve Gresham	32	139	306.0	12.0	318.0	9.151	4		4
Tormod Langli	35	152	251.0	26.0	277.0	7.289		2	2
Phil Collins	1	5	8.0	0.0	8.0	6.400			
Nigel Boocock	**38**	**156**	**193.0**	**37.0**	**230.0**	**5.897**			
Bruce Cribb	20	79	86.0	19.0	105.0	5.316		1	1
§Henny Kroeze	19	68	70.0	17.0	87.0	5.118			
§Henk Steman	11	35	34.0	7.0	41.0	4.686			
§Sören Sjösten	20	57	55.0	9.0	64.0	4.491			
Tony Garard	7	23	16.0	5.0	21.0	3.652			
§Paul Tyrer	12	31	20.0	7.0	27.0	3.484			
Bob Coles	9	21	10.0	2.0	12.0	2.286			
Phil Bass	1	2	1.0	0.0	1.0	2.000			
Derek Hole	5	9	2.0	0.0	2.0	0.889			
§Robert Dole	1	2	0.0	0.0	0.0	0.000			
§Mike Ferreira	1	2	0.0	0.0	0.0	0.000			
§Alan Johns	1	2	0.0	0.0	0.0	0.000			

DAILY MIRROR OPEN TOURNAMENT

1977	1 Ole Olsen	2 Ivan Mauger and Scott Autrey	
1978	1 Ole Olsen	2 Gordon Kennett	3 Chris Morton

COATBRIDGE

COATBRIDGE has a rare place in speedway history – having been the home of two of Scotland's fiercest on-track rivals!

The Clifton Hill Park Stadium – home of Scottish soccer club Albion Rovers – was first used by Edinburgh when they were forced out of their Old Meadowbank Stadium at the end of the 1967 season.

And then Glasgow set up their home base at the site in 1973 after they had been given notice to quit Hampden Park at the end of 1972!

Even though the Coatbridge track was big and fast it never flourished as a Division One venue. The Monarchs' franchise was moved to Wembley in 1970 and the Tigers' eventually moved onto Blantyre after dropping down into Division Two.

1968...1968...1968...1968...1968...1968

	M	R	Pts	BP	TPts	Ave	F	P	Total
§Bernt Persson	32	147	335.0	6.0	341.0	9.279	9		9
§Reidar Eide	29	125	273.0	9.0	282.0	9.024	5	3	
§George Hunter	31	113	163.0	20.0	183.0	6.478		3	
§Bert Harkins	**38**	**163**	**226.0**	**33.0**	**259.0**	**6.356**		**1**	
§Doug Templeton	36	150	208.0	19.0	227.0	6.053		1	
§Brian Collins	**38**	**124**	**115.0**	**21.0**	**136.0**	**4.387**			
§Alec Hughson	35	116	90.0	15.0	105.0	3.621			
§Brian Black	2	4	2.0	0.0	2.0	2.000			
§§Lex Milloy	6	12	3.0	0.0	3.0	1.000			
§§Ken Omand	3	8	2.0	0.0	2.0	1.000			
§Jimmy Tannock	1	4	1.0	0.0	1.0	1.000			

1969...1969...1969...1969...1969...1969

	M	R	Pts	BP	TPts	Ave	F	P	Total
Reidar Eide	34	145	353.0	10.0	363.0	10.014	5	3	13
Bert Harkins	36	143	255.0	29.0	284.0	7.944	3	2	8
George Hunter	**38**	**140**	**238.0**	**12.0**	**250.0**	**7.143**	**2**	**1**	**5**
§Wayne Briggs	33	132	176.0	35.0	211.0	6.394			
Brian Collins	**38**	**153**	**197.0**	**30.0**	**227.0**	**5.935**		**1**	**1**
Doug Templeton	33	116	131.0	19.0	150.0	5.172			
Alex Hughson	33	100	86.0	20.0	106.0	4.240			
§§Alistair Brady	15	45	38.0	5.0	43.0	3.822			
§Brian Murray	2	6	2.0	0.0	2.0	1.333			

1973...1973...1973...1973...1973...1973

	M	R	Pts	BP	TPts	Ave	F	P	Total
§Jim McMillan	**36**	**163**	**360.0**	**7.0**	**367.0**	**9.006**	**4**	**1**	**5**
§Bobby Beaton	35	147	281.0	13.0	294.0	8.000	1	1	2
§Christer Sjösten	32	131	195.0	14.0	209.0	6.382	4		4
§Dave Gifford	22	85	91.0	16.0	107.0	5.035			
§Jim Gallacher	33	126	126.0	26.0	152.0	4.825			
§Robin Adlington	21	73	69.0	14.0	83.0	4.548			
§Kjell Gimre	34	122	103.0	23.0	126.0	4.131		1	1
§Paul O'Neal	2	7	6.0	1.0	7.0	4.000			
§Roger Johns	2	8	7.0	0.0	7.0	3.500			
§Willie Templeton	1	4	2.0	1.0	3.0	3.000			
§Norman Strachan	3	10	5.0	1.0	6.0	2.400			
§Paul Gachet	1	2	1.0	0.0	1.0	2.000			
Alistair Brady	11	29	12.0	1.0	13.0	1.793			
§David Beech	1	3	1.0	0.0	1.0	1.333			
§Ken McKinlay	1	3	1.0	0.0	1.0	1.333			
§§Neil Middleditch	2	3	1.0	0.0	1.0	1.333			
§§Egon Müller	2	7	1.0	0.0	1.0	0.571			
§John Wilson	5	13	1.0	0.0	1.0	0.308			
§§Ettiene Olivier	1	1	0.0	0.0	0.0	0.000			

COATBRIDGE created another record of sorts – when they became the first club to stage a meeting without an official programme. That was on September 28, 1973, against Halifax when an industrial dispute preventedfthe printing of the match magazine.

BRITISH LEAGUE AVERAGES...BRITISH LEAGUE AVERAGES...BRITISH LEAGUE AVERAGES

COVENTRY

COVENTRY were founder members of the British League having competed in the 1964 National League (Division One) and they are the only one of the original clubs to have been promoted by the same person – Charles Ochiltree – every season since 1965!

1965...1965...1965...1965...1965...1965

	M	R	Pts	BP	TPts	Ave	F	P	Total
§§Nigel Boocock	**35**	**140**	**395.0**	**22.0**	**417.0**	**11.914**	**10**	**8**	**18**
§§Jim Lightfoot	33	132	279.0	13.0	292.0	8.848	4	6	10
§§Ron Mountford	32	128	249.0	24.0	273.0	8.531	1	3	4
§§Rick France	34	136	200.0	19.0	219.0	6.441	2		2
§§Col Cottrell	**35**	**140**	**176.0**	**25.0**	**201.0**	**5.743**		**4**	**4**
§§Les Owen	16	64	58.0	5.0	63.0	3.938			
§Chris Harrison	26	104	49.0	11.0	60.0	2.308			
§§Ron Bagley	5	20	6.0	1.0	7.0	1.400			
§§Fred Hodder	7	28	7.0	2.0	9.0	1.286			
§§Col Smith	4	16	3.0	0.0	3.0	0.750			
§§Peter Gay	4	16	2.0	0.0	2.0	0.500			
§§Howie Booton	11	44	5.0	0.0	5.0	0.455			
§§Roger Hill	2	4	0.0	0.0	0.0	0.000			

■ ***COVENTRY staged the first British League match in history when they defeated Midlands rivals Cradley Heath 47-31 on Saturday, March 27, 1965.***
The first race winner was the Bees' captain Nigel Boocock ahead of rival skipper Ivor Brown, Eric Hockaday and Col Cottrell.
Nigel went on to be unbeaten by an opponent but his team-mate Rick France scored the first maximum, completing his 12 point tally with his fourth win in heat 10.
The full scores were: Coventry 47 (Rick France 12, Nigel Boocock 11, Jim Lighfoot 9, Col Cottrell 7, Ron Mountford 6, Howie Booton 2, Fred Hodder 0) Cradley Heath 31 (Ivor Brown 10, George Major 9, Eric Hockaday 5, Harry Bastable 4, Alan Totney 2, John Edwards 1, John Hart 0).

1966...1966...1966...1966...1966...1966

	M	R	Pts	BP	TPts	Ave	F	P	Total
Nigel Boocock	36	159	395.0	24.0	419.0	10.541	6	6	12
Ron Mountford	29	124	262.0	26.0	288.0	9.290	6	1	7
Rick France	**39**	**170**	**363.0**	**29.0**	**392.0**	**9.224**	**3**	**3**	**6**
Jim Lightfoot	32	134	279.0	16.0	295.0	8.806	6	1	7
Col Cottrell	**39**	**155**	**189.0**	**25.0**	**214.0**	**5.523**	**2**		**2**
Les Owen	14	52	43.0	13.0	56.0	4.308			
Chris Harrison	**39**	**123**	**76.0**	**18.0**	**94.0**	**3.057**			
Roger Hill	30	76	42.0	10.0	52.0	2.737			
§§Tom Ridley	10	17	7.0	2.0	9.0	2.118			

1967...1967...1967...1967...1967...1967

	M	R	Pts	BP	TPts	Ave	F	P	Total
Nigel Boocock	40	178	455.0	13.0	468.0	10.517	8	4	12
Rick France	37	160	342.0	17.0	359.0	8.975	7		7
Ron Mountford	**41**	**170**	**341.0**	**27.0**	**368.0**	**8.659**	**5**	**3**	**8**
Col Cottrell	38	146	198.0	33.0	231.0	6.329			
Les Owen	40	165	216.0	42.0	258.0	6.255		2	2
§Clive Hitch	**41**	**142**	**142.5**	**31.0**	**173.5**	**4.887**			
Roger Hill	33	99	78.0	23.0	101.0	4.081			
Chris Harrison	13	31	19.0	6.0	25.0	3.226			
Tom Ridley	2	5	3.0	0.0	3.0	2.400			

1968...1968...1968...1968...1968...1968

	M	R	Pts	BP	TPts	Ave	F	P	Total
Nigel Boocock	31	152	392.0	16.0	408.0	10.737	3	4	7
Ron Mountford	7	32	71.0	6.0	77.0	9.625	1	1	2
§§Antonin Kasper	19	74	136.0	3.0	139.0	7.514	2		2
Col Cottrell	**38**	**167**	**265.0**	**31.0**	**296.0**	**7.090**	**1**		**1**
Les Owen	30	130	186.0	24.0	210.0	6.462			
Rick France	16	62	80.0	15.0	95.0	6.129		1	1
Roger Hill	**38**	**148**	**168.0**	**34.0**	**202.0**	**5.459**		**1**	**1**
Tom Ridley	31	93	96.0	14.0	110.0	4.731			
Chris Harrison	29	73	45.0	17.0	62.0	3.397			
§§Dave Callington	7	17	7.0	1.0	8.0	1.882			
§§Tony Lomas	1	4	1.0	0.0	1.0	1.000			

1969...1969...1969...1969...1969...1969

	M	R	Pts	BP	TPts	Ave	F	P	Total
Nigel Boocock	37	171	451.0	10.0	461.0	10.784	9	5	14
§Göte Nordin	3	13	25.0	3.0	28.0	8.615			
Antonin Kasper	15	62	108.0	9.0	117.0	7.548		1	1
Col Cottrell	37	153	252.5	29.0	281.5	7.359	3	2	5
Roger Hill	21	84	123.0	20.0	143.0	6.810		1	1
Rick France	20	78	116.0	14.0	130.0	6.667	2	2	4
Tom Ridley	7	26	31.0	5.0	36.0	5.538	1		1
Les Owen	37	133	154.0	26.0	180.0	5.414			
§§John Harrhy	15	48	47.0	11.0	58.0	4.833			
Tony Lomas	28	87	87.0	16.0	103.0	4.736			
Dave Callington	25	78	51.0	13.0	64.0	3.282			
§§Roy Carter	1	2	1.0	0.0	1.0	2.000			
§§Tony Peasland	1	4	1.0	0.0	1.0	1.000			
§David Crane	4	11	2.0	0.0	2.0	0.727			

1970...1970...1970...1970...1970...1970

	M	R	Pts	BP	TPts	Ave	F	P	Total
Nigel Boocock	34	146	377.5	11.5	389.0	10.658	12	2	14
Ken McKinlay	**37**	**143**	**282.0**	**22.0**	**304.0**	**8.503**	**3**	**1**	**4**
Rick France	**37**	**149**	**268.0**	**22.0**	**290.0**	**7.785**	**3**	**1**	**4**
Les Owen	27	100	126.0	26.0	152.0	6.080			
Tony Lomas	**37**	**130**	**168.0**	**24.0**	**192.0**	**5.908**			
Roger Hill	**37**	**135**	**157.0**	**42.0**	**199.0**	**5.896**		**1**	**1**
Col Cottrell	35	128	146.5	34.5	181.0	5.656	1		1
John Harrhy	4	14	15.0	4.0	19.0	5.429			
§§Peter Bailey	3	11	7.0	2.0	9.0	3.273			
Ron Mountford	8	19	5.5	2.0	7.5	1.579			

1971...1971...1971...1971...1971...1971

	M	R	Pts	BP	TPts	Ave	F	P	Total
Nigel Boocock	36	160	381.0	17.0	398.0	9.950	4	3	7
Tony Lomas	36	146	265.0	20.0	285.0	7.808	1	1	2
§Jan Simensen	29	118	207.0	19.0	226.0	7.661			
Roger Hill	**37**	**137**	**178.0**	**33.0**	**211.0**	**6.161**		**1**	**1**
Rick France	1	2	2.0	1.0	3.0	6.000			
Les Owen	**37**	**149**	**188.0**	**32.0**	**220.0**	**5.906**			
Ron Mountford	36	123	152.0	20.0	172.0	5.593		2	2
John Harrhy	32	112	114.0	28.0	142.0	5.071			
Col Cottrell	5	20	23.0	2.0	25.0	5.000			
Peter Bailey	2	4	3.0	1.0	4.0	4.000			
§§Brian James	1	2	1.0	0.0	1.0	2.000			
Roy Carter	2	2	0.0	0.0	0.0	0.000			

1972...1972...1972...1972...1972...1972

	M	R	Pts	BP	TPts	Ave	F	P	Total
Nigel Boocock	32	146	326.0	11.0	337.0	9.233	4	2	6
Tony Lomas	**35**	**153**	**296.0**	**14.0**	**310.0**	**8.105**	**1**		**1**
John Harrhy	28	116	177.0	28.0	205.0	7.069	1	1	2
Jan Simensen	14	52	78.0	11.0	89.0	6.846			
Rick France	**35**	**132**	**160.0**	**25.0**	**185.0**	**5.606**			
Roy Carter	9	24	25.0	7.0	32.0	5.333			
Roger Hill	24	87	93.0	20.0	113.0	5.195			
§Cliff Emms	5	16	16.0	3.0	19.0	4.750			
Les Owen	24	85	85.0	11.0	96.0	4.518			
Peter Bailey	24	84	68.0	19.0	87.0	4.143			
§§Frank Smith	2	5	3.0	0.0	3.0	2.400			
Ron Mountford	5	14	6.0	0.0	6.0	1.714			

1973...1973...1973...1973...1973...1973

	M	R	Pts	BP	TPts	Ave	F	P	Total
Nigel Boocock	**36**	**184**	**377.0**	**18.0**	**395.0**	**8.587**	**3**	**1**	**4**
§Garry Middleton	30	145	294.0	8.0	302.0	8.331	2	1	3
John Harrhy	9	38	76.0	3.0	79.0	8.316	1		1
§Alan Jay	22	109	141.0	31.0	172.0	6.312			
Les Owen	10	31	33.0	10.0	43.0	5.548			
Peter Bailey	**36**	**144**	**150.0**	**24.0**	**174.0**	**4.833**			
§§Sören Karlsson	24	86	78.0	22.0	100.0	4.651			
Roger Hill	11	36	24.0	7.0	31.0	3.444			
Cliff Emms	15	38	22.0	9.0	31.0	3.263			
Frank Smith	11	35	26.0	2.0	28.0	3.200			
§George Major	1	5	4.0	0.0	4.0	3.200			
§Roger Johns	1	3	2.0	0.0	2.0	2.667			
§§Gerhard Uhlenbrock	13	38	20.0	4.0	24.0	2.526			
Roy Carter	5	12	4.0	1.0	5.0	1.667			
§§Bob Old	1	3	1.0	0.0	1.0	1.333			
§§Jeff Shirley	2	7	1.0	0.0	1.0	0.571			
§§Roy Sizmore	1	1	0.0	0.0	0.0	0.000			

COVENTRY

1974...1974...1974...1974...1974...1974

	M	R	Pts	BP	TPts	Ave	F	P	Total
Nigel Boocock	26	113	228.0	12.0	240.0	8.496			
John Harrhy	**34**	**135**	**203.0**	**23.0**	**226.0**	**6.696**	**1**		**1**
Alan Jay	33	135	177.0	24.0	201.0	5.956			
§§Matti Olin	21	74	92.0	15.0	107.0	5.784			
§Olle Nygren	9	33	28.0	13.0	41.0	4.970			
Roy Carter	9	24	24.0	3.0	27.0	4.500			
§Ronnie Moore	2	10	11.0	0.0	11.0	4.400			
Frank Smith	33	107	95.0	21.0	116.0	4.336			
Peter Bailey	4	15	14.0	2.0	16.0	4.267			
§Robin Adlington	10	30	13.0	3.0	16.0	2.133			
§§Tony Gillias	1	2	1.0	0.0	1.0	2.000			
Jeff Shirley	7	16	6.0	1.0	7.0	1.750			
Roger Hill	4	9	3.0	0.0	3.0	1.333			
§§Krause Kjaer	2	6	1.0	0.0	1.0	0.667			

1975...1975...1975...1975...1975...1975

	M	R	Pts	BP	TPts	Ave	F	P	Total
§Bob Valentine	**36**	**155**	**326.5**	**9.0**	**335.5**	**8.658**	**2**		**2**
Nigel Boocock	**36**	**162**	**310.0**	**15.0**	**325.0**	**8.025**	**1**	**1**	**2**
§Tommy Nilsson	18	73	84.0	14.0	98.0	5.370			
John Harrhy	**36**	**147**	**167.0**	**22.0**	**189.0**	**5.143**	**1**	**2**	**3**
§Ian Hindle	22	78	83.0	11.0	94.0	4.821			
§Alan Molyneux	15	56	54.0	8.0	62.0	4.429			
Alan Jay	14	45	43.0	6.0	49.0	4.356			
Frank Smith	33	103	81.0	18.0	99.0	3.845			
§§Mitch Shirra	14	43	22.0	2.0	24.0	2.233			
§§Pepe Teromaa	1	2	1.0	0.0	1.0	2.000			
Roger Hill	12	28	9.0	3.0	12.0	1.714			
Tony Gillias	3	7	2.0	1.0	3.0	1.714			
§§Stefan Johansson	1	2	0.0	0.0	0.0	0.000			

1976...1976...1976...1976...1976...1976

	M	R	Pts	BP	TPts	Ave	F	P	Total
§Ole Olsen	34	148	395.0	14.0	409.0	11.054	12	5	17
Mitch Shirra	35	151	297.0	15.0	312.0	8.265	2	1	3
§§Jiri Stancl	25	111	164.0	25.0	189.0	6.811		1	1
Alan Molyneux	37	165	227.0	48.0	275.0	6.667		2	2
Nigel Boocock	36	146	214.5	24.0	238.5	6.534			
John Harrhy	35	107	110.0	14.0	124.0	4.636			
Frank Smith	34	110	101.5	25.0	126.5	4.600			
§Ian Hindle	18	40	17.0	4.0	21.0	2.100			
Tony Gillias	4	12	3.0	0.0	3.0	1.000			
§Dave Mortiboys	2	5	1.0	0.0	1.0	0.800			

1977...1977...1977...1977...1977...1977

	M	R	Pts	BP	TPts	Ave	F	P	Total
Ole Olsen	36	158	412.5	3.0	415.5	10.519	14	2	16
Mitch Shirra	40	165	322.0	17.0	339.0	8.218	4	1	5
Alan Molyneux	37	145	262.0	25.0	287.0	7.917	2	6	8
§§Alf Busk	35	153	203.0	41.0	244.0	6.379		2	2
Tommy Nilsson	30	122	165.0	25.0	190.0	6.230		2	2
§Mick Bell	29	100	108.0	21.0	129.0	5.160			
Frank Smith	39	104	80.0	20.0	100.0	3.846			
Tony Gillias	3	9	5.0	0.0	5.0	2.222			
David Mortiboys	12	30	13.0	2.0	15.0	2.000			
§§Gary Guglielmi	1	3	0.0	0.0	0.0	0.000			

AUSTRALIAN Gary Guglielmi began his British career racing for homeless Paisley in the Scottish Junior League racing under the name of Gary Williams.

1978...1978...1978...1978...1978...1978

	M	R	Pts	BP	TPts	Ave	F	P	Total
Ole Olsen	36	160	407.5	15.0	422.5	10.563	9	4	13
Mitch Shirra	38	161	365.0	17.0	382.0	9.491	6	2	8
Alan Molyneux	36	137	242.0	27.0	269.0	7.854		3	3
Alf Busk	36	145	190.0	36.0	226.0	6.234		1	1
Jiri Stancl	23	90	110.5	26.0	136.5	6.067			
Gary Guglielmi	18	60	71.0	13.0	84.0	5.600			
Mick Bell	**40**	**145**	**152.5**	**26.5**	**179.0**	**4.938**	**1**	**1**	**2**
Frank Smith	18	50	42.0	11.0	53.0	4.240			
§Kevin Hawkins	1	3	3.0	0.0	3.0	4.000			
Dave Mortiboys	7	14	8.0	2.0	10.0	2.857			
§Stuart Cope	4	10	2.0	1.0	3.0	1.200			
§Pip Lamb	2	5	1.0	0.0	1.0	0.800			

1979...1979...1979...1979...1979...1979

	M	R	Pts	BP	TPts	Ave	F	P	Total
Ole Olsen	34	158	378.0	14.0	392.0	9.924	5	1	6
Mitch Shirra	31	134	293.0	13.0	306.0	9.134	4	2	6
Alan Molyneux	18	72	138.0	6.0	144.0	8.000		1	1
Alf Busk	32	139	192.0	38.0	230.0	6.619	1		1
§§Tommy Knudsen	32	136	189.0	29.0	218.0	6.412		1	1
Gary Guglielmi	35	149	196.0	25.0	221.0	5.933			
Kevin Hawkins	21	74	81.0	25.0	106.0	5.730			
Mick Bell	**38**	**126**	**130.0**	**26.0**	**156.0**	**4.952**			
§Louis Carr	1	3	2.0	1.0	3.0	4.000			
§Barney Kennett	1	3	2.0	0.0	2.0	2.667			
§§Paul Embley	1	2	1.0	0.0	1.0	2.000			
§Phil Kynman	1	2	1.0	0.0	1.0	2.000			
§§Phil Cain	3	6	1.0	0.0	1.0	0.667			
§Tony Featherstone	2	8	0.0	0.0	0.0	0.000			

1980...1980...1980...1980...1980...1980

	M	R	Pts	BP	TPts	Ave	F	P	Total
Ole Olsen	28	122	276.5	14.0	290.5	9.525	3	1	4
§Rod Hunter	1	3	6.0	1.0	7.0	9.333			
Mitch Shirra	**34**	**140**	**280.0**	**19.0**	**299.0**	**8.543**	**2**	**3**	**5**
Tommy Knudsen	27	116	209.0	26.0	235.0	8.103		1	1
Alan Molyneux	31	123	193.0	17.0	210.0	6.829	2		2
Kevin Hawkins	**34**	**134**	**178.0**	**32.0**	**210.0**	**6.269**		**1**	**1**
§Mark de Kok	1	2	2.0	1.0	3.0	6.000			
Gary Guglielmi	10	35	44.0	7.0	51.0	5.829			
Alf Busk	22	78	97.5	12.0	109.5	5.615			
§Steve McDermott	1	3	4.0	0.0	4.0	5.333			
§Steve Lomas	1	4	4.0	1.0	5.0	5.000			
§David Gagen	3	10	12.0	0.0	12.0	4.800			
§Robert Hollingworth	22	59	47.0	12.0	59.0	4.000			
§Nigel Couzens	1	2	1.0	1.0	2.0	4.000			
§Mike Spink	1	3	2.0	0.0	2.0	2.667			
§Alan Sage	1	5	2.0	1.0	3.0	2.400			
Phil Cain	5	14	4.0	4.0	8.0	2.286			
§Laurie Etheridge	1	4	1.0	0.0	1.0	1.000			
§Kris Berrigan	1	2	0.0	0.0	0.0	0.000			
§Tony Boyle	1	2	0.0	0.0	0.0	0.000			
§Peter Tarrant	1	2	0.0	0.0	0.0	0.000			
§Terry Tulloch	1	2	0.0	0.0	0.0	0.000			

1981...1981...1981...1981...1981...1981

	M	R	Pts	BP	TPts	Ave	F	P	Total
Ole Olsen	41	191	431.0	19.0	450.0	9.424	3	1	4
Tommy Knudsen	47	219	467.0	48.0	515.0	9.406	2	7	9
Mitch Shirra	49	214	409.0	26.0	435.0	8.131	4	2	6
Gary Guglielmi	39	176	238.0	53.0	291.0	6.614			
Kevin Hawkins	**50**	**200**	**282.0**	**47.0**	**329.0**	**6.580**			
Alf Busk	37	155	197.0	42.0	239.0	6.168		1	1
Keith White	48	147	165.0	39.0	204.0	5.551			
Robert Hollingworth	14	41	48.0	8.0	56.0	5.463			
§Brian Havelock	1	4	5.0	0.0	5.0	5.000			
Alan Sage	1	4	5.0	0.0	5.0	5.000			
Laurie Etheridge	1	3	2.0	1.0	3.0	4.000			
§Steve Wilcock	9	28	21.0	2.0	23.0	3.286			
§§Charlie McKinna	2	5	1.0	0.0	1.0	0.800			
§Paul Bosley	1	2	0.0	0.0	0.0	0.000			

1982...1982...1982...1982...1982...1982

	M	R	Pts	BP	TPts	Ave	F	P	Total
Tommy Knudsen	39	174	378.0	23.0	401.0	9.218	3		3
Ole Olsen	37	161	347.0	19.0	366.0	9.093	2		2
Mitch Shirra	28	110	187.0	16.0	203.0	7.382		1	1
Gary Guglielmi	39	159	225.0	41.0	266.0	6.692			
Steve Wilcock	3	11	14.0	4.0	18.0	6.545			
Kevin Hawkins	**42**	**166**	**204.5**	**36.0**	**240.5**	**5.795**			
David Gagen	5	17	20.0	3.0	23.0	5.412			
Alf Busk	26	87	92.0	21.0	113.0	5.195			
Keith White	4	12	9.0	5.0	14.0	4.667			
§§Sam Nikolajsen	10	31	24.0	3.0	27.0	3.484			
Charlie McKinna	38	102	67.0	16.0	83.0	3.255			
§§Mark Reeve	3	6	2.0	0.0	2.0	1.333			

BRITISH AIRWAYS SILVER JUBILEE

1974 1 John Boulger 2 John Louis 3 Jim McMillan

TOMMY KNUDSEN TESTIMONIAL

1988 1 Hans Nielson 2 Tommy Knudsen 3 John Jørgensen

COVENTRY

1983...1983...1983...1983...1983...1983

	M	R	Pts	BP	TPts	Ave	F	P	Total
Tommy Knudsen	24	107	251.0	13.0	264.0	9.869	4	1	5
Ole Olsen	49	208	464.0	33.0	497.0	9.558	7	2	9
Gary Guglielmi	46	183	334.0	35.0	369.0	8.066	2	1	3
§Steve Bastable	**52**	**208**	**314.0**	**39.0**	**353.0**	**6.788**		**1**	**1**
Kevin Hawkins	51	175	199.0	39.0	238.0	5.440			
Sam Nikolajsen	**52**	**175**	**200.0**	**29.0**	**229.0**	**5.234**			
§§Rick Miller	50	161	170.0	26.0	196.0	4.870			
Keith White	4	11	13.0	0.0	13.0	4.727			
David Gagen	1	2	0.0	0.0	0.0	0.000			

1984...1984...1984...1984...1984...1984

	M	R	Pts	BP	TPts	Ave	F	P	Total
Tommy Knudsen	27	119	212.0	22.0	234.0	7.866	2		2
Gary Guglielmi	40	170	309.0	22.0	331.0	7.788	2		2
Steve Bastable	**46**	**184**	**292.0**	**25.0**	**317.0**	**6.891**			
Rick Miller	41	171	254.0	30.0	284.0	6.643		2	2
§John Jørgensen	42	163	216.0	36.0	252.0	6.184			
Sam Nikolajsen	45	149	177.0	21.0	198.0	5.315	1	1	2
Kevin Hawkins	40	124	131.0	30.0	161.0	5.194			
Keith White	3	7	5.0	1.0	6.0	3.429			
§Steve Payne	11	29	15.0	4.0	19.0	2.621			
§§Bob Kinning	2	4	2.0	0.0	2.0	2.000			

GARY GUGLIELMI and Steve Payne were banned from racing in Britain by the Speedway Control Board after they had both pleaded guilty to drugs charges in an Auistrlaian court. Guglielmi was subsaequerntly jailed.

1985...1985...1985...1985...1985...1985

	M	R	Pts	BP	TPts	Ave	F	P	Total
Tommy Knudsen	40	169	409.0	19.0	428.0	10.130	7	4	11
§Kelvin Tatum	43	179	388.0	19.0	407.0	9.095	3		3
John Jørgensen	42	158	216.0	48.0	264.0	6.684			
Rick Miller	44	164	222.0	29.0	251.0	6.122	1		1
Steve Bastable	45	176	226.0	35.0	261.0	5.932			
§David Bargh	40	136	163.0	33.0	196.0	5.765			
§Frank Andersen	**46**	**141**	**123.0**	**22.0**	**145.0**	**4.113**			
Kevin Hawkins	8	27	20.0	3.0	23.0	3.407			
§§Mick Bacon	2	6	1.0	1.0	2.0	1.333			

1986...1986...1986...1986...1986...1986

	M	R	Pts	BP	TPts	Ave	F	P	Total
§Malcolm Simmons	1	4	10.0	1.0	11.0	11.000			
Tommy Knudsen	36	148	343.0	15.0	358.0	9.676	5	4	9
John Jørgensen	42	167	318.0	47.0	365.0	8.743	2	2	4
Kelvin Tatum	43	174	366.0	12.0	378.0	8.690	7	2	9
Rick Miller	43	171	230.0	44.0	274.0	6.409		1	1
David Bargh	38	133	169.0	20.0	189.0	5.684			
§Alun Rossiter	**44**	**152**	**182.0**	**31.0**	**213.0**	**5.605**			
§Martin Goodwin	2	7	7.0	0.0	7.0	4.000			
§Steve Schofield	1	4	4.0	0.0	4.0	4.000			
§§David Clarke	40	128	87.0	25.0	112.0	3.500			
Mike Bacon	9	28	12.0	0.0	12.0	1.714			

1987...1987...1987...1987...1987...1987

	M	R	Pts	BP	TPts	Ave	F	P	Total
Tommy Knudsen	**54**	**229**	**559.0**	**28.0**	**587.0**	**10.253**	**12**	**5**	**17**
Kelvin Tatum	52	210	521.0	7.0	528.0	10.057	10	3	13
Rick Miller	53	216	386.0	57.0	443.0	8.204	2	3	5
John Jørgensen	51	200	317.0	73.0	390.0	7.800		7	7
David Bargh	50	201	320.0	55.0	375.0	7.463	1	1	2
§§Neville Tatum	4	14	14.0	2.0	16.0	4.571			
David Clarke	51	187	138.0	23.0	161.0	3.444			
§§Andy Hackett	30	93	52.0	8.0	60.0	2.581			
§§Wayne Broadhurst	26	66	32.0	4.0	36.0	2.182			
§§Darren Slater	6	15	6.0	2.0	8.0	2.133			
§§Miles Evans	1	4	1.0	0.0	1.0	1.000			

1988...1988...1988...1988...1988...1988

	M	R	Pts	BP	TPts	Ave	F	P	Total
Tommy Knudsen	45	235	568.5	24.0	592.5	10.085	5	4	9
Kelvin Tatum	**46**	**233**	**559.0**	**26.0**	**585.0**	**10.043**	**8**	**5**	**13**
John Jørgensen	43	182	293.0	48.0	341.0	7.495		2	2
Rick Miller	43	176	254.0	55.0	309.0	7.023		2	2
Steve Schofield	1	4	4.0	2.0	6.0	6.000			
Neville Tatum	**46**	**183**	**196.0**	**33.0**	**229.0**	**5.005**			
David Clarke	44	178	192.0	24.0	216.0	4.854			
Andy Hackett	44	172	164.0	42.0	206.0	4.791			
Kevin Hawkins	1	4	2.0	0.0	2.0	2.000			
Mike Bacon	2	7	2.0	1.0	3.0	1.714			
Wayne Broadhurst	2	5	1.0	0.0	1.0	0.800			

BUZZING...the 1980 Coventry side as they defended the British League crown. Left to right, Alf Busk, Tommy Knudsen, Alan Molyneux, Ole Olsen, manager Peter Adams, Robert Hollingworth, Kevin Hawkins and Mitch Shirra

BRITISH LEAGUE AVERAGES...BRITISH LEAGUE AVERAGES...BRITISH LEAGUE AVERAGES

COVENTRY

GREAT DANE...Coventry's three time World Champion Ole Olsen who led the club to so many victories

BRANDONAPOLIS

1965	1 Ken McKinlay
	2 Nigel Boocock
	3 Arne Pander
1966	1 Nigel Boocock
	2 Göte Nordin
	3 Ivan Mauger
1967	1 Anders Michanek
	2 Ken McKinlay
	3 Ron Mountford
1968	1 Nigel Boocock
	2 Ivan Mauger
	3 Anders Michanek
1969	1 Ray Wilson
	2 Nigel Boocock
	3 Barry Briggs
1970	1 Ole Olsen
	2 Jim McMillan
	3 John Boulger
1971	1 Nigel Boocock
	2 Ray Wilson
	3 Martin Ashby
1972	1 Ole Olsen
	2 Terry Betts
	3 Bernt Persson
1973	1 Anders Michanek
	2 John Boulger
	3 John Louis
1974	1 Ivan Mauger
	2 John Boulger
	3 Ole Olsen
1975	1 Phil Crump
	2 Dave Jessup
	3 John Louis
1976	1 Phil Crump
	2 Ole Olsen
	3 Ila Teromaa
1977	1 Ole Olsen
	2 Malcolm Simmons
	3 Alf Busk
1978	1 Ole Olsen
	2 Michael Lee
	3 Peter Collins
1979	1 Dave Jessup
	2 Billy Sanders
	3 Mitch Shirra
1980	1 Mitch Shirra
	2 Ole Olsen
	3 Les Collins
1981	1 Bruce Penhall
	2 Mitch Shirra
	3 Erik Gundersen
1982	1 Tommy Knudsen
	2 Hans Nielson
	3 Kenny Carter
1983	1 Kenny Carter
	2 Erik Gundersen
	3 Ole Olsen
1984	1 Tommy Knudsen
	2 Lance King
	3 Phil Collins
1985	1 Hans Nielsen
	2 Erik Gundersen
	3 Mitch Shirra

1989...1989...1989...1989...1989...1989

	M	R	Pts	BP	TPts	Ave	F	P	Total
Kelvin Tatum	33	177	408.0	12.0	420.0	9.492	2	1	3
Rick Miller	33	153	238.0	27.0	265.0	6.928			
§Sean Wilson	**34**	**157**	**230.0**	**26.0**	**256.0**	**6.522**			
John Jørgensen	33	156	223.0	26.0	249.0	6.385			
Andy Hackett	32	132	151.0	30.0	181.0	5.485			
§Roman Matousek	16	60	69.0	10.0	79.0	5.267			
§Kai Niemi	30	105	104.0	19.0	123.0	4.686			
Mike Bacon	6	19	10.0	4.0	14.0	2.947			
§Paul Smith	7	22	13.0	1.0	14.0	2.545			
§§Lee Coleman	1	4	1.0	0.0	1.0	1.000			
§§Rob Homer	1	4	1.0	0.0	1.0	1.000			
Wayne Broadhurst	4	12	0.0	0.0	0.0	0.000			

1990...1990...1990...1990...1990...1990

	M	R	Pts	BP	TPts	Ave	F	P	Total
Kelvin Tatum	33	177	377.0	18.0	395.0	8.927	2	1	3
John Jørgensen	**36**	**174**	**324.0**	**16.0**	**340.0**	**7.816**	**1**		**1**
Rick Miller	30	143	220.0	22.0	242.0	6.769		1	1
Roman Matousek	30	130	165.0	25.0	190.0	5.846		1	1
Tommy Knudsen	6	23	32.0	1.0	33.0	5.739			
Sean Wilson	31	137	166.0	24.0	190.0	5.547			
Andy Hackett	25	102	120.0	16.0	136.0	5.333			
§Andy Phillips	23	77	44.0	11.0	55.0	2.857			
§§Andy Meredith	14	43	18.0	3.0	21.0	1.953			
Lee Coleman	7	18	3.0	0.0	3.0	0.667			
§§Paul Bromwich	2	5	0.0	0.0	0.0	0.000			

CRADLEY HEATH

CRADLEY HEATH were founder members of the British League having raced in the 1964 Provincial League.

1965...1965...1965...1965...1965...1965

	M	R	Pts	BP	TPts	Ave	F	P	Total
§§Ivor Brown	19	76	185.0	5.0	190.0	10.000	2	1	3
§§John Hart	**34**	**136**	**265.0**	**19.0**	**284.0**	**8.353**	**2**	**1**	**3**
§§George Major	22	88	148.0	16.0	164.0	7.455		1	1
§Leo McAuliffe	19	76	101.0	9.0	110.0	5.789			
§§Eric Hockaday	31	124	146.0	26.0	172.0	5.548			
§Chris Julian	33	132	151.0	17.0	168.0	5.091			
§§Harry Bastable	16	64	59.0	14.0	73.0	4.563			
§Goog Allan	9	36	31.0	6.0	37.0	4.111			
§§Alan Totney	4	16	13.0	3.0	16.0	4.000			
§Tim Bungay	8	32	22.0	4.0	26.0	3.250			
§§John Debbage	11	44	21.0	8.0	29.0	2.636			
§§Ivor Hughes	12	48	19.0	7.0	26.0	2.167			
§§John Edwards	1	4	1.0	1.0	2.0	2.000			
§§Matt Mattocks	5	20	5.0	1.0	6.0	1.200			
§§Ron Cooper	14	56	8.0	4.0	12.0	0.857			

1966...1966...1966...1966...1966...1966

	M	R	Pts	BP	TPts	Ave	F	P	Total
Ivor Brown	32	137	254.0	16.0	270.0	7.883			
Chris Julian	**36**	**145**	**216.0**	**20.0**	**236.0**	**6.510**	**1**	**1**	**2**
§§Chum Taylor	34	136	191.0	24.0	215.0	6.324		1	1
§Clive Featherby	31	118	156.0	24.0	180.0	6.102			
Ivor Hughes	29	115	149.5	13.0	162.5	5.652	1		1
§Howard Cole	20	81	95.0	16.0	111.0	5.481			
§§Tommy Bergqvist	2	9	11.0	1.0	12.0	5.333			
John Hart	1	3	2.0	1.0	3.0	4.000			
Eric Hockaday	7	22	17.0	3.0	20.0	3.636			
Ron Cooper	9	19	11.0	6.0	17.0	3.579			
§§Joe Weichlbauer	14	30	12.0	6.0	18.0	2.400			
Matt Mattocks	11	24	11.0	3.0	14.0	2.333			
§§Ken Wakefield	8	20	8.0	2.0	10.0	2.000			

1967...1967...1967...1967...1967...1967

	M	R	Pts	BP	TPts	Ave	F	P	Total
Ivor Brown	35	157	281.0	15.0	296.0	7.541	1		1
§Brian Brett	20	85	145.0	11.0	156.0	7.341			
Tommy Bergqvist	23	94	151.0	21.0	172.0	7.319			
Chris Julian	**37**	**158**	**262.0**	**16.0**	**278.0**	**7.038**	**2**		**2**
§§Jack Scott	16	59	91.0	3.0	94.0	6.373			
Graham Coombes	32	133	169.0	32.0	201.0	6.045			
§Jack Biggs	12	48	62.0	6.0	68.0	5.667			
Alan Totney	11	33	27.0	4.0	31.0	3.758			
Ken Wakefield	35	112	75.0	20.0	95.0	3.393			
§Peter Wrathall	7	19	11.0	4.0	15.0	3.158			
§Dave Schofield	8	20	10.0	3.0	13.0	2.600			
§Ken Vale	1	4	1.0	1.0	2.0	2.000			
Eric Hockaday	5	14	5.0	1.0	6.0	1.714			
§§Archie Wilkinson	2	5	2.0	0.0	2.0	1.600			
§John Woodcock	3	8	2.0	0.0	2.0	1.000			
Joe Weichlbauer	1	2	0.0	0.0	0.0	0.000			

1968...1968...1968...1968...1968...1968

	M	R	Pts	BP	TPts	Ave	F	P	Total
Roy Trigg	**37**	**163**	**357.0**	**6.0**	**363.0**	**8.908**	**6**		**6**
§Bob Andrews	32	132	228.0	26.0	254.0	7.697	1	1	
Graham Coombes	36	143	213.0	27.0	240.0	6.713	2		
Chris Julian	**37**	**145**	**204.0**	**25.0**	**229.0**	**6.317**			
§Lars Jansson	11	40	55.0	7.0	62.0	6.200			
Ivor Brown	23	93	114.0	18.0	132.0	5.677			
Ken Wakefield	31	106	109.0	24.0	133.0	5.019			
Tommy Bergqvist	18	59	69.0	5.0	74.0	5.017			
Archie Wilkinson	7	21	14.0	8.0	22.0	4.190			
Peter Wrathall	14	42	32.0	6.0	38.0	3.619			
Alan Totney	6	19	13.0	2.0	15.0	3.158			
§§Chris Hawkins	4	8	2.0	0.0	2.0	1.000			

1969...1969...1969...1969...1969...1969

	M	R	Pts	BP	TPts	Ave	F	P	Total
Roy Trigg	38	167	380.0	7.0	387.0	9.269	6	2	8
§Bernt Persson	32	137	307.0	5.0	312.0	9.109	4		4
Bob Andrews	38	165	306.0	21.0	327.0	7.927	2		2
§Chris Bass	38	149	164.0	33.0	197.0	5.289			
Graham Coombes	38	134	133.0	31.0	164.0	4.896			
§§Mike Gardner	24	77	71.0	12.0	83.0	4.312			
Ken Wakefield	**39**	**134**	**113.0**	**26.0**	**139.0**	**4.149**			
Peter Wrathall	3	8	4.0	1.0	5.0	2.500			
§§Mike Holmes	1	2	1.0	0.0	1.0	2.000			
§Geoff Penniket	3	7	3.0	0.0	3.0	1.714			
Chris Hawkins	13	31	9.0	1.0	10.0	1.290			

1970...1970...1970...1970...1970...1970

	M	R	Pts	BP	TPts	Ave	F	P	Total
§Paul O'Neal	1	4	8.0	2.0	10.0	10.000			
Bernt Persson	30	143	323.0	9.0	332.0	9.287	1	1	2
Roy Trigg	36	170	346.0	13.0	359.0	8.447	2	1	3
Colin Pratt	20	88	165.5	5.0	170.5	7.750			
§§Jan Simensen	16	74	119.0	20.0	139.0	7.514		1	1
Chris Bass	34	116	106.0	21.0	127.0	4.379			
§Jimmy Squibb	**37**	**137**	**113.0**	**27.0**	**140.0**	**4.088**			
Mike Gardner	36	128	100.0	12.0	112.0	3.500			
Ken Wakefield	22	68	39.0	6.0	45.0	2.647			
§Glyn Chandler	4	8	3.0	1.0	4.0	2.000			
§Malcolm Shakespeare	1	2	1.0	0.0	1.0	2.000			
Mike Holmes	3	5	1.0	1.0	2.0	1.600			

1971...1971...1971...1971...1971...1971

	M	R	PTs	BP	TPts	Ave	F	P	Total
Bernt Persson	33	148	344.0	14.0	358.0	9.676	4	1	5
Bob Andrews	38	161	286.0	25.0	311.0	7.727	1		1
Roy Trigg	39	165	286.0	13.0	299.0	7.248	1		1
§Mick Handley	9	30	41.0	4.0	45.0	6.000			
Peter Jarman	27	97	118.0	17.0	135.0	5.567			
Jimmy Squibb	35	122	121.0	21.0	142.0	4.656			
§§Malcolm Ballard	2	7	7.0	1.0	8.0	4.571			
John Hart	39	158	141.0	27.0	168.0	4.253			
§John Jackson	1	3	3.0	0.0	3.0	4.000			
§Barry Duke	13	40	30.0	6.0	36.0	3.600			
§§Geoff Bouchard	3	11	6.0	2.0	8.0	2.909			
§Gordon Kennett	1	3	2.0	0.0	2.0	2.667			
§Bengt Andersson	15	38	16.0	4.0	20.0	2.105			
Mike Holmes	1	2	1.0	0.0	1.0	2.000			
§§Richard Eslick	6	13	3.0	2.0	5.0	1.538			
§Laurie Sims	1	3	1.0	0.0	1.0	1.333			
§Cyril Francis	4	10	2.0	1.0	3.0	1.200			
§§Andy Bearne	4	11	2.0	0.0	2.0	0.727			
§Ralph Waller	2	6	1.0	0.0	1.0	0.667			
§Mac Woolford	1	2	0.0	0.0	0.0	0.000			

■ *CRADLEY HEATH reached their first Cup Final since the 1963 Provincial League but lost to Hackney.*

1972...1972...1972...1972...1972...1972

	M	R	Pts	BP	TPts	Ave	F	P	Total
Bernt Persson	29	131	331.5	5.0	336.5	10.275	6	1	7
Bob Andrews	32	132	224.0	17.0	241.0	7.303		1	1
Roy Trigg	36	157	253.0	20.0	273.0	6.955	1		1
Peter Jarman	34	124	126.0	26.0	152.0	4.903			
John Hart	26	92	88.0	18.0	106.0	4.609			
Mick Handley	33	112	106.0	22.0	128.0	4.571			
Jimmy Squibb	28	88	66.0	16.0	82.0	3.727			
Bengt Andersson	2	4	2.0	1.0	3.0	3.000			
§§Ian Ross	7	20	8.0	2.0	10.0	2.000			
§§Dave Perks	10	35	7.0	1.0	8.0	0.914			
§§Dave Harvey	4	9	0.0	0.0	0.0	0.000			
§Gerald Smitherman	1	2	0.0	0.0	0.0	0.000			

1973...1973...1973...1973...1973...1973

	M	R	Pts	BP	TPts	Ave	F	P	Total
Bernt Persson	23	110	251.0	7.0	258.0	9.382	4	1	5
Howard Cole	19	75	162.0	9.0	171.0	9.120	1		1
§Roger Johns	2	7	12.0	1.0	13.0	7.429			
§§Ulf Lovaas	6	29	45.0	3.0	48.0	6.621			
§Bruce Cribb	15	61	74.0	14.0	88.0	5.770			
§Brian Clark	4	18	19.0	4.0	23.0	5.111			
§Colin Gooddy	30	118	131.0	12.0	143.0	4.847			
Peter Jarman	35	131	125.0	22.0	147.0	4.489			
Dave Perks	**36**	**139**	**130.0**	**25.0**	**155.0**	**4.460**			
§Malcolm Corradine	11	40	38.0	6.0	44.0	4.400			
Ken McKinlay	1	3	3.0	0.0	3.0	4.000			
§§Graham Drury	1	2	2.0	0.0	2.0	4.000			
Paul O'Neal	1	2	2.0	0.0	2.0	4.000			
§§Lars Hultberg	19	72	53.0	9.0	62.0	3.444			
§Geoff Ambrose	1	4	3.0	0.0	3.0	3.000			
Dave Harvey	9	24	11.0	4.0	15.0	2.500			
George Major	1	6	3.0	0.0	3.0	2.000			
§Dave Durham	1	2	1.0	0.0	1.0	2.000			
§Jim Wells	1	2	0.0	0.0	0.0	0.000			

CRADLEY HEATH

1974...1974...1974...1974...1974...1974

	M	R	Pts	BP	TPts	Ave	F	P	Total
John Boulger	32	142	350.0	7.0	357.0	10.056	6	3	9
Howard Cole	29	106	194.0	10.0	204.0	7.698	2		2
Bruce Cribb	**34**	**146**	**195.0**	**31.0**	**226.0**	**6.192**			
Sandor Levai	21	85	108.0	15.0	123.0	5.788	1		1
§§Alan Molyneux	4	14	13.0	7.0	20.0	5.714			
§Arthur Price	**34**	**144**	**170.0**	**30.0**	**200.0**	**5.556**			
§Russell Osborne	26	92	91.0	17.0	108.0	4.696			
Malcolm Corradine	19	58	53.0	7.0	60.0	4.138			
Dave Perks	11	36	31.0	5.0	36.0	4.000			
§Malcolm Mackay	1	3	2.0	1.0	3.0	4.000			
§Dave Younghusband	6	12	8.0	2.0	10.0	3.333			
§§Phil Bass	2	7	4.0	0.0	4.0	2.286			
§§Steve Bastable	10	23	9.0	3.0	12.0	2.087			
Brian Clark	1	3	0.0	0.0	0.0	0.000			
§§Andy Cusworth	1	2	0.0	0.0	0.0	0.000			
§§Eric Dugard	1	2	0.0	0.0	0.0	0.000			

1975...1975...1975...1975...1975...1975

	M	R	Pts	BP	TPts	Ave	F	P	Total
John Boulger	38	159	337.0	10.0	347.0	8.730	2	1	3
Bernt Persson	32	132	263.0	20.0	283.0	8.576	3	1	4
Arthur Price	37	148	235.0	49.0	284.0	7.676	1	3	4
Bruce Cribb	39	162	275.0	30.0	305.0	7.531		1	1
§Steve Weatherley	2	5	6.0	3.0	9.0	7.200			
Brian Clark	1	3	3.0	1.0	4.0	5.333			
§Nigel Wasley	1	3	3.0	1.0	4.0	5.333			
Sandor Levai	26	92	94.0	18.0	112.0	4.870		1	1
Steve Bastable	22	81	81.0	17.0	98.0	4.840			
§Wayne Hughes	2	6	6.0	1.0	7.0	4.667			
Dave Perks	33	107	107.0	15.0	122.0	4.561			
Graham Drury	2	6	5.0	1.0	6.0	4.000			
Phil Bass	1	3	3.0	0.0	3.0	4.000			
§Alan Sage	1	3	3.0	0.0	3.0	4.000			
§Chris Turner	1	3	2.0	1.0	3.0	4.000			
§Colin Goad	1	2	2.0	0.0	2.0	4.000			
Russell Osborne	8	26	16.0	4.0	20.0	3.077			
§Kelvin Mullarkey	5	13	9.0	1.0	10.0	3.077			
§Carl Askew	1	3	2.0	0.0	2.0	2.667			
§Keith Evans	1	3	2.0	0.0	2.0	2.667			
§Steve Holden	2	5	2.0	1.0	3.0	2.400			
§Colin Farquharson	1	2	1.0	0.0	1.0	2.000			
§§Paul Share	1	2	1.0	0.0	1.0	2.000			
§Ken Matthews	2	6	2.0	0.0	2.0	1.333			
§§Keith Anderson	1	5	1.0	0.0	1.0	0.800			
§Bob Young	2	4	0.0	0.0	0.0	0.000			
§Ricky Day	1	2	0.0	0.0	0.0	0.000			
§Pete Wigley	1	2	0.0	0.0	0.0	0.000			

1976...1976...1976...1976...1976...1976

	M	R	Pts	BP	TPts	Ave	F	P	Total
John Boulger	35	156	376.0	6.0	382.0	9.795	8		8
Bernt Persson	9	38	79.0	8.0	87.0	9.158			
§§Ian Clark	1	5	9.0	1.0	10.0	8.000			
Bruce Cribb	**38**	**170**	**304.0**	**24.0**	**328.0**	**7.718**	**1**		**1**
Phil Bass	1	3	3.0	2.0	5.0	6.667			
Arthur Price	**38**	**145**	**179.0**	**28.0**	**207.0**	**5.710**	**1**	**1**	**2**
Dave Perks	**38**	**142**	**157.0**	**28.0**	**185.0**	**5.211**			
Steve Bastable	**38**	**137**	**152.0**	**26.0**	**178.0**	**5.197**		**2**	**2**
Malcolm Corradine	1	5	6.0	0.0	6.0	4.800			
§Nigel Wasley	33	91	55.0	17.0	72.0	3.165			
§§Kevin Young	1	4	2.0	0.0	2.0	2.000			
§§Paul Church	4	9	0.0	0.0	0.0	0.000			

1977...1977...1977...1977...1977...1977

	M	R	Pts	BP	TPts	Ave	F	P	Total
§Anders Michanek	11	51	127.0	5.0	132.0	10.353	1	3	4
Bernt Persson	22	105	210.0	9.0	219.0	8.343	1	1	2
Steve Bastable	37	173	311.0	29.0	340.0	7.861	1	1	2
Bruce Cribb	**38**	**169**	**241.5**	**35.0**	**276.5**	**6.544**			
§Bob Valentine	36	141	200.0	29.0	229.0	6.496		1	1
Dave Perks	28	96	125.0	19.0	144.0	6.000		2	2
Arthur Price	37	137	157.0	35.0	192.0	5.606		1	1
§§John Hack	1	4	5.0	0.0	5.0	5.000			
§§Phil Collins	2	7	6.0	2.0	8.0	4.571			
§§John Williams	1	2	1.0	0.0	1.0	2.000			
Ken Matthews	1	2	1.0	0.0	1.0	2.000			
Phil Michelides	1	3	1.0	0.0	1.0	1.333			
§§Richie Caulwell	2	4	1.0	0.0	1.0	1.000			
§Nigel Wasley	3	7	1.0	0.0	1.0	0.571			
§§ Doug Poole	1	3	0.0	0.0	0.0	0.000			
§§James Moore	2	4	0.0	0.0	0.0	0.000			
§Kevin Hawkins	1	2	0.0	0.0	0.0	0.000			

1978...1978...1978...1978...1978...1978

	M	R	Pts	BP	TPts	Ave	F	P	Total
Steve Bastable	40	165	371.5	21.0	392.5	9.515	6	3	9
§§Bruce Penhall	35	146	307.0	31.0	338.0	9.260	3	4	7
Alan Grahame	41	172	325.0	28.0	353.0	8.209	2	1	3
Alan Sage	1	3	4.0	1.0	5.0	6.667			
§Kristian Praestbro	37	144	202.0	34.0	236.0	6.556			
Bruce Cribb	20	82	114.5	13.0	127.5	6.220			
Phil Collins	18	75	87.0	15.0	102.0	5.440		1	1
Dave Perks	28	94	107.0	16.0	123.0	5.234			
§§Pekka Hautamaki	32	102	105.0	28.0	133.0	5.216			
§§David Shields	12	38	42.0	6.0	48.0	5.053			
John Hack	3	8	5.0	4.0	9.0	4.500			
Arthur Price	9	25	17.0	6.0	23.0	3.680			
James Moore	3	6	5.0	0.0	5.0	3.333			
§§Les Sawyer	3	7	4.0	0.0	4.0	2.286			
Carl Askew	1	2	1.0	0.0	1.0	2.000			
§Pip Lamb	3	7	0.0	0.0	0.0	0.000			
JohnJ. Williams	1	2	0.0	0.0	0.0	0.000			

1979...1979...1979...1979...1979...1979

	M	R	Pts	BP	TPts	Ave	F	P	Total
Bruce Penhall	40	179	416.0	26.0	442.0	9.877	5	5	10
Alan Grahame	**44**	**189**	**354.0**	**40.0**	**394.0**	**8.339**	**2**	**2**	**4**
Phil Collins	**44**	**189**	**325.0**	**46.0**	**371.0**	**7.852**	**1**	**1**	**2**
§§Bobby Schwartz	38	170	291.0	42.0	333.0	7.835		4	4
Steve Bastable	15	56	102.0	6.0	108.0	7.714			
Kristian Praestbro	31	123	200.0	32.0	232.0	7.545		1	1
§§Erik Gundersen	29	117	192.0	23.0	215.0	7.350			
Dave Perks	25	83	116.0	26.0	142.0	6.843			
§Ila Teromaa	2	8	11.0	2.0	13.0	6.500			
Carl Askew	1	3	4.0	0.0	4.0	5.333			
§Louis Carr	1	3	2.0	2.0	4.0	5.333			
John Hack	10	31	27.0	10.0	37.0	4.774			
§Les Rumsey	13	42	44.0	6.0	50.0	4.762			
§Mike Sampson	5	17	16.0	4.0	20.0	4.706			
JohnJ. Williams	2	6	6.0	0.0	6.0	4.000			
§Ian Gledhill	2	6	2.0	1.0	3.0	2.000			
§Bob Coles	1	2	1.0	0.0	1.0	2.000			
Nigel Couzens	1	2	0.0	0.0	0.0	0.000			
Pip Lamb	1	2	0.0	0.0	0.0	0.000			

1980...1980...1980...1980...1980...1980

	M	R	Pts	BP	TPts	Ave	F	P	Total
Bruce Penhall	30	139	354.0	7.0	361.0	10.388	6	1	7
Alan Grahame	**40**	**180**	**319.5**	**55.0**	**374.5**	**8.322**		**5**	**5**
Phil Collins	35	161	299.0	30.0	329.0	8.174	2	1	3
Dave Perks	8	30	51.0	10.0	61.0	8.133		1	1
Erik Gundersen	38	176	338.0	18.0	356.0	8.091	1	1	2
Ila Teromaa	33	130	142.0	31.0	173.0	5.323		1	1
§Steve Lawson	9	31	38.0	2.0	40.0	5.161			
§Andy Reid	5	21	21.0	5.0	26.0	4.952			
Mike Sampson	10	38	38.0	8.0	46.0	4.842			
John Hack	27	88	75.0	18.0	93.0	4.227			
§Derek Harrison	12	38	32.5	6.0	38.5	4.053			
§Robert Henry	1	3	1.0	1.0	2.0	2.667			
§Craig Featherby	10	27	10.0	2.0	12.0	1.778			
§§Glen McDonald	4	10	3.0	0.0	3.0	1.200			
§§Paul Bosley	10	22	3.0	1.0	4.0	0.727			
§§Hans Klinge	3	7	1.0	0.0	1.0	0.571			
§§Mark Collins	1	3	0.0	0.0	0.0	0.000			
§§Mark Stevenson	1	2	0.0	0.0	0.0	0.000			

1981...1981...1981...1981...1981...1981

	M	R	Pts	BP	TPts	Ave	F	P	Total
Bruce Penhall	37	169	452.0	13.0	465.0	11.006	12	3	15
Erik Gundersen	45	200	474.0	12.0	486.0	9.720	12	1	13
Alan Grahame	**48**	**216**	**434.0**	**58.0**	**492.0**	**9.111**	**2**	**6**	**8**
Phil Collins	47	212	344.0	58.0	402.0	7.585		1	1
§Simon Wigg	1	5	4.0	3.0	7.0	5.600			
David Shields	**48**	**189**	**218.0**	**29.0**	**247.0**	**5.228**		**1**	**1**
§Bent Rasmussen	47	183	184.0	45.0	229.0	5.005			
Dave Perks	3	8	6.0	2.0	8.0	4.000			
§John McNeill	39	115	96.0	15.0	111.0	3.861		1	1
§Nicky Allott	1	2	1.0	0.0	1.0	2.000			
Arnold Haley	9	23	4.0	0.0	4.0	0.696			

AMERICAN Bruce Penhall was the first Cradley Heath rider to become World Champion when he took the crown in an unforgettable display in the last ever World Final at Wembley in 1981.

CRADLEY HEATH

1982...1982...1982...1982...1982...1982

	M	R	Pts	BP	TPts	Ave	F	P	Total
Bruce Penhall	30	127	325.0	16.0	341.0	10.740	8	4	12
Erik Gundersen	46	197	495.5	6.0	501.5	10.183	10	1	11
§Joe Owen	1	4	9.0	1.0	10.0	10.000			
Alan Grahame	50	213	445.0	46.0	491.0	9.221	5	5	10
§John Barker	1	4	6.0	2.0	8.0	8.000			
Phil Collins	47	193	284.0	68.0	352.0	7.295		2	2
§Kenny McKinna	1	4	6.0	1.0	7.0	7.000			
Simon Wigg	7	30	42.0	8.0	50.0	6.667			
§§Lance King	42	171	229.5	40.0	269.5	6.304			
Steve Lawson	5	17	16.0	3.0	19.0	4.471			
§Ashley Pullen	4	12	11.0	0.0	11.0	3.667			
Ian Gledhill	18	51	39.0	5.0	44.0	3.451			
§§Simon Cross	5	19	13.0	3.0	16.0	3.368			
Andy Reid	34	98	60.0	14.0	74.0	3.020			
Wayne Jackson	7	20	14.0	1.0	15.0	3.000			
§Steve Schofield	2	8	5.0	1.0	6.0	3.000			
§Jan Verner	20	58	34.0	5.0	39.0	2.690			
§§Bill Barrett	8	27	9.0	3.0	12.0	1.778			
§Graham Drury	2	4	1.0	0.0	1.0	1.000			

1983...1983...1983...1983...1983...1983

	M	R	Pts	BP	TPts	Ave	F	P	Total
Erik Gundersen	44	181	435.0	28.0	463.0	10.232	6	8	14
Simon Wigg	46	196	391.0	43.0	434.0	8.857	4	4	8
Lance King	38	125	238.0	35.0	273.0	8.736	3	1	4
Alan Grahame	**48**	**202**	**375.0**	**64.0**	**439.0**	**8.693**	**3**	**6**	**9**
Phil Collins	43	177	311.0	42.0	353.0	7.977	3	5	8
§Peter Ravn	38	126	218.0	33.0	251.0	7.968			
§§Jan O. Pedersen	36	118	163.0	37.0	200.0	6.780			
Simon Cross	14	44	51.0	15.0	66.0	6.000			
§Stan Bear	2	7	7.0	2.0	9.0	5.143			
§Ian Barney	1	3	2.0	0.0	2.0	2.667			
Andy Reid	8	22	11.0	3.0	14.0	2.545			
§§David Cheshire	5	12	5.0	2.0	7.0	2.333			
§Andy Buck	1	3	1.0	0.0	1.0	1.333			

***FORMER** Cradley Heath skipper Colin Pratt, who had spent 1973 as King's Lynn manager, took over at Dudley Wood when Peter Adams left to run Wolverhampton at the beginning of the 1984 campaign.*

1984...1984...1984...1984...1984...1984

	M	R	Pts	BP	TPts	Ave	F	P	Total
Erik Gundersen	43	184	427.0	12.0	439.0	9.543	7	2	9
Lance King	47	196	397.0	27.0	424.0	8.653	3	5	8
Phil Collins	47	198	379.0	37.0	416.0	8.404	6	4	10
Alan Grahame	**50**	**211**	**345.0**	**70.0**	**415.0**	**7.867**	**1**	**2**	**3**
Simon Cross	36	142	229.0	29.0	258.0	7.268		1	1
§Finn Jensen	47	166	191.0	20.0	211.0	5.084			
§Kerry Gray	3	12	10.0	2.0	12.0	4.000			
§Jamie Luckhurst	1	2	2.0	0.0	2.0	4.000			
Andy Reid	1	2	1.0	1.0	2.0	4.000			
§§Chris Chaplin	1	2	1.0	0.0	1.0	2.000			
§Brett Saunders	1	2	1.0	0.0	1.0	2.000			
§John Walmsley	1	2	1.0	0.0	1.0	2.000			
§Mike Wilding	18	51	21.0	4.0	25.0	1.961			
Bill Barrett	5	14	6.0	0.0	6.0	1.714			
§§Steve Collins	35	99	32.0	5.0	37.0	1.495			
§Billy Burton	2	4	0.0	0.0	0.0	0.000			
§Paul Fry	1	2	0.0	0.0	0.0	0.000			
§John Grahame	1	2	0.0	0.0	0.0	0.000			

1985...1985...1985...1985...1985...1985

	M	R	Pts	BP	TPts	Ave	F	P	Total
Erik Gundersen	39	173	447.0	2.0	449.0	10.382	18		18
Phil Collins	43	174	307.0	38.0	345.0	7.931	1	2	3
Jan O. Pedersen	42	172	291.0	49.0	340.0	7.907	1	1	2
Alan Grahame	37	146	231.0	38.0	269.0	7.370	1		1
Simon Cross	40	150	202.0	31.0	233.0	6.213	1		1
Finn Jensen	41	136	167.0	17.0	184.0	5.412			
§Kevin Smith	9	31	28.0	5.0	33.0	4.258			
Brett Saunders	1	3	3.0	0.0	3.0	4.000			
§Andrew Silver	4	13	7.0	0.0	7.0	2.154			
Steve Collins	33	101	28.0	3.0	31.0	1.228			
§§Nigel Leaver	13	40	11.0	1.0	12.0	1.200			
§Paul Taylor	1	3	0.0	0.0	0.0	0.000			

1986...1986...1986...1986...1986...1986

	M	R	Pts	BP	TPts	Ave	F	P	Total
Erik Gundersen	47	202	542.0	15.0	557.0	11.030	18	4	22
Jan O. Pedersen	48	199	382.0	45.0	427.0	8.583		8	8
Phil Collins	**49**	**196**	**348.0**	**34.0**	**382.0**	**7.796**	**2**	**1**	**3**
Simon Cross	48	184	286.0	44.0	330.0	7.174	2	1	3
Steve Bastable	48	183	247.0	31.0	278.0	6.077			
Andrew Silver	1	4	5.0	1.0	6.0	6.000			
Nigel Leaver	**49**	**154**	**126.0**	**18.0**	**144.0**	**3.740**			
Paul Fry	34	104	71.0	13.0	84.0	3.231			
Paul Taylor	11	33	14.0	3.0	17.0	2.061			
§§John Bostin	1	3	1.0	0.0	1.0	1.333			
§§Wayne Garratt	2	6	1.0	0.0	1.0	0.667			
§§John Proctor	1	4	0.0	0.0	0.0	0.000			
§§Nigel Newman	1	3	0.0	0.0	0.0	0.000			

1987...1987...1987...1987...1987...1987

	M	R	Pts	BP	TPts	Ave	F	P	Total
Erik Gundersen	50	211	541.0	10.0	551.0	10.445	11	4	15
Jan O. Pedersen	47	193	446.0	17.0	463.0	9.596	5	4	9
Simon Cross	51	217	484.0	22.0	506.0	9.327	6	2	8
§§Martin Dugard	2	9	12.0	1.0	13.0	5.778			
§David Walsh	46	181	195.0	36.0	231.0	5.105			
Alan Grahame	35	128	129.0	29.0	158.0	4.938		2	2
John Bostin	1	4	2.0	2.0	4.0	4.000			
§Rob Tilbury	1	2	1.0	1.0	2.0	4.000			
§§Jan Jakobsen	34	126	105.0	19.0	124.0	3.937			
§§Dean Barker	24	78	61.0	13.0	74.0	3.795			
Paul Fry	51	159	113.0	25.0	138.0	3.472			
Nigel Leaver	4	11	5.0	1.0	6.0	2.182			
§Darren Sumner	1	4	2.0	0.0	2.0	2.000			
Wayne Garratt	8	17	4.0	1.0	5.0	1.176			
§Alan Rivett	2	5	1.0	0.0	1.0	0.800			

1988...1988...1988...1988...1988...1988

	M	R	Pts	BP	TPts	Ave	F	P	Total
Erik Gundersen	45	216	529.0	14.0	543.0	10.056	7	3	10
Jan O. Pedersen	45	223	511.0	40.0	551.0	9.883	3	5	8
Simon Cross	**47**	**215**	**393.0**	**49.0**	**442.0**	**8.223**			
Alan Grahame	39	167	251.0	38.0	289.0	6.922		2	2
Gordon Kennett	1	4	5.0	1.0	6.0	6.000			
§Andy Galvin	1	5	6.0	1.0	7.0	5.600			
§§Gert Handberg	46	181	198.0	33.0	231.0	5.105			
David Walsh	**47**	**199**	**193.0**	**31.0**	**224.0**	**4.503**			
§§Justin Walker	3	5	4.0	1.0	5.0	4.000			
Dean Barker	1	4	4.0	0.0	4.0	4.000			
Kenny McKinna	1	4	4.0	0.0	4.0	4.000			
Wayne Garratt	46	161	109.0	30.0	139.0	3.453			
Steve Bastable	1	4	2.0	1.0	3.0	3.000			
§Mark Fiora	2	8	5.0	0.0	5.0	2.500			
Steve Schofield	1	3	1.0	0.0	1.0	1.333			
§Alastair Stevens	1	3	0.0	0.0	0.0	0.000			

1989...1989...1989...1989...1989...1989

	M	R	Pts	BP	TPts	Ave	F	P	Total
Jan O. Pedersen	17	88	211.0	14.0	225.0	10.227	2	2	4
Erik Gundersen	24	120	288.0	11.0	299.0	9.967	4	2	6
Simon Cross	34	149	303.0	37.0	340.0	9.128		3	3
Gert Handberg	35	146	198.0	40.0	238.0	6.521			
§§Greg Hancock	35	168	236.5	18.0	254.5	6.060		1	1
Alan Grahame	**38**	**148**	**180.0**	**34.0**	**214.0**	**5.784**			
John Bostin	**38**	**132**	**82.0**	**17.0**	**99.0**	**3.000**			
Justin Walker	3	11	6.0	2.0	8.0	2.909			

1990...1990...1990...1990...1990...1990

	M	R	Pts	BP	TPts	Ave	F	P	Total
Jan O. Pedersen	15	79	177.0	8.0	185.0	9.367			
Simon Cross	16	82	166.0	13.0	179.0	8.732			
§§Billy Hamill	28	133	206.0	20.0	226.0	6.797			
Alan Grahame	**34**	**151**	**201.5**	**33.0**	**234.5**	**6.212**	**2**		**2**
Gert Handberg	30	145	201.0	23.0	224.0	6.179			
Greg Hancock	18	77	102.0	4.0	106.0	5.506			
§§Mark Robinson	29	100	50.0	12.0	62.0	2.480			
§§David Haynes	6	17	1.0	1.0	2.0	0.471			
§§Scott Smith	1	3	0.0	0.0	0.0	0.000			
§§Gary Frankum	1	2	0.0	0.0	0.0	0.000			

CRADLEY HEATH

ALAN HUNT MEMORIAL TROPHY

1965	1 Nigel Boocock	2 Jimmy Gooch	3 Reg Luckhurst
1966	1 Barry Briggs	2 Ron Mountford	3 Ken McKinlay
1968	1 Hasse Holmkvist	2 Nigel Boocock	3 Colin Gooddy
1969	1 Bernt Persson	2 Ivan Mauger	3 Bob Andrews
1970	1 Ole Olsen	2 Colin Pratt	3 Ivan Mauger and Barry Briggs
1971	1 Ole Olsen	2 Ivan Mauger	3 Barry Briggs
1972	1 Peter Jarman	2 Terry Betts	3 Ray Wilson

WATNEY MANN TROPHY

1970	1 Bernt Persson	2 Bob Kilby	3 Ray Wilson
1972	1 Ole Olsen	2 Ray Wilson	3 Terry Betts
1973	1 Sören Sjösten	2 Alan Wilkinson	3 Garry Middleton
1974	1 Sören Sjösten	2 Ray Wilson	3 Bob Valentine

LP TRANSPORT TROPHY

1971	1 Ivan Mauger	2 Bernt Persson	3 Bengt Jonsson
1975	1 Malcolm Simmons	2 John Boulger	3 Bernt Persson
1976	1 Malcolm Simmons	2 Bruce Cribb	3 Zenon Plech

GOLDEN HAMMER

1977	1 Ole Olsen	2 John Boulger	3 Finn Thomsen
1978	1 Scott Autrey	2 Michael Lee	3 Peter Collins
1979	1 Bobby Schwartz	2 Hans Nielsen	3 Phil Collins
1980	1 Chris Morton	2 Scott Autrey	3 Kelly Moran
1982	1 Kenny Carter	2 Phil Crump	3 Phil Collins
1983	1 Lance King	2 Erik Gundersen	3 Dennis Sigalos
1984	1 Alan Grahame	2 Phil Collins	3 Billy Sanders
1985	1 Kenny Carter	2 Hans Nielsen	3 Erik Gundersen
1986	1 Erik Gundersen	2 Simon Cross	3 Paul Evitts
1987	1 Erik Gundersen	2 Hans Nielsen	3 Simon Cross
1988	1 Hans Nielson	2 Jan O. Pedersen	3 Chris Morton
1989	1 Jan O. Pedersen	2 Erik Gundersen	3 Hans Nielsen
1990	1 Simon Cross	2 Ronnie Correy	3 Kelvin Tatum
1991	1 Sam Ermolenko	2 Gert Handberg	3 Jan O. Pedersen

DAILY MIRROR MIDLANDS JUBILEE CLASSIC

1978	1 Steve Bastable	2 Alan Grahame	3 Kristian Praestbro

ERIK GUNDERSEN TESTIMONIAL

1988	1 Simon Cross	2 Simon Wigg	3 Jan O. Pedersen

JUICEY BRUCEY...Bruce Penhall (above), the first of Cradley Heath's trio of World Champions and (below) one of the last team pictures before his successor Erik Gundersen was seriously injured in the 1989 World Team Cup Final. Left to right: Jan O. Pedersen, Simon Cross, Greg Hancock, Erik Gundersen, Colin Pratt, John Bostin, Gert Handberg and Alan Grahame

BRITISH LEAGUE AVERAGES...BRITISH LEAGUE AVERAGES...BRITISH LEAGUE AVERAGES

EASTBOURNE

EASTBOURNE, run by the Dugard family had been members of the Second Division until 1978 but provided a new home base for the White City Rebels after their decision to quit their Shepherds Bush, London, venue.

1979...1979...1979...1979...1979...1979

	M	R	Pts	BP	TPts	Ave	F	P	Total
§Gordon Kennett	34	172	416.0	10.0	426.0	9.907	9		9
§Kai Niemi	34	164	348.0	11.0	359.0	8.756	4	1	5
§Steve Weatherley	13	59	97.0	6.0	103.0	6.983			
§David Kennett	15	58	67.0	14.0	81.0	5.586			
§Trevor Geer	34	150	172.0	19.0	191.0	5.093			
§Eric Dugard	35	119	109.0	18.0	127.0	4.269			
§Brian Clark	1	4	3.0	1.0	4.0	4.000			
§Roger Abel	28	91	73.0	16.0	89.0	3.912			
§Steve Naylor	18	48	40.0	5.0	45.0	3.750			
§Paul Woods	12	41	28.0	7.0	35.0	3.415			
§John Barker	7	22	15.0	2.0	17.0	3.091			
§§Veijo Tuoriniemi	14	50	32.0	5.0	37.0	2.960			
§Ian Fletcher	4	13	5.0	1.0	6.0	1.846			

1980...1980...1980...1980...1980...1980

	M	R	Pts	BP	TPts	Ave	F	P	Total
Gordon Kennett	24	116	281.5	0.0	281.5	9.707	4		4
Kai Niemi	23	113	228.0	8.0	236.0	8.354	2		2
Paul Woods	22	107	151.0	17.0	168.0	6.280			
Veijo Tuoriniemi	13	49	64.0	11.0	75.0	6.122			
David Kennett	33	125	151.0	23.0	174.0	5.568	1		1
Treovr Geer	16	60	64.0	9.0	73.0	4.867			
§Barney Kennett	1	5	5.0	1.0	6.0	4.800			
Eric Dugard	23	87	83.0	18.0	101.0	4.644			
§Richard Greer	9	33	27.0	8.0	35.0	4.242			
§Mick Hines	1	3	3.0	0.0	3.0	4.000			
Steve Naylor	9	30	24.0	5.0	29.0	3.867			
§Les Rumsey	4	11	9.0	1.0	10.0	3.636			
§§Jan Davidsson	24	72	47.0	18.0	65.0	3.611			
§§Borje Klingberg	3	11	7.0	2.0	9.0	3.273			
§Reidar Eide	1	3	2.0	0.0	2.0	2.667			
§Ted Hubbard	1	3	1.0	1.0	2.0	2.667			
§Sigvart Pedersen	12	42	15.0	4.0	19.0	1.810			
§Kelvin Mullarkey	1	3	1.0	0.0	1.0	1.333			
§Alan Sage	1	3	1.0	0.0	1.0	1.333			
§§Jozef Kafel	5	13	3.0	0.0	3.0	0.923			
§§Jan Puk	2	2	0.0	0.0	0.0	0.000			

1981...1981...1981...1981...1981...1981

	M	R	Pts	BP	TPts	Ave	F	P	Total
Gordon Kennett	42	203	483.0	8.0	491.0	9.675	8		8
§Kelly Moran	41	193	438.0	10.0	448.0	9.285	11		11
Mick Hines	1	5	8.0	1.0	9.0	7.200			
Paul Woods	**47**	**226**	**358.0**	**35.0**	**393.0**	**6.956**	**1**	**2**	**3**
Kai Niemi	1	5	6.0	1.0	7.0	5.600			
Richard Greer	6	18	16.0	4.0	20.0	4.444			
Trevor Geer	**47**	**180**	**171.0**	**20.0**	**191.0**	**4.244**			
Barney Kennett	3	10	10.0	0.0	10.0	4.000			
David Kennett	45	147	117.0	27.0	144.0	3.918			
§§Olli Tyrvainen	37	146	114.0	23.0	137.0	3.753			
§Keith Pritchard	4	12	8.0	2.0	10.0	3.333			
§§Mick Pither	1	4	3.0	0.0	3.0	3.000			
§§Robert Slabon	26	76	45.0	10.0	55.0	2.895			
Eric Dugard	15	50	28.0	7.0	35.0	2.800			
§§Marek Kepa	3	8	1.0	1.0	2.0	1.000			
§§Peter Lloyd	1	3	0.0	0.0	0.0	0.000			

	DAILY MIRROR GOLDEN JUBILEE TROPHY		
1978	1 John Davis	2 Gordon Kennett	3 Billy Sanders
	HARRY WESLAKE MEMORIAL TROPHY		
1979	1 Gordon Kennett	2 Dave Jessup	3 Scott Autrey
1980	1 John Louis	2 Finn Thomsen	3 Kenny Carter
	EVENING ARGUS TROPHY		
1979	1 Gordon Kennett	2 Scott Autrey	3 Kai Niemi
1980	1 Bo Petersen	2 Kai Niemi	3 Gordon Kennett
	TREVOR GEER TESTIMONIAL		
1981	1 Shawn Moran	2 John Cook	3 Kelly Moran and John Davis
	RIDER OF THE SOUTH		
1983	1 Paul Woods	2 Colin Richardson	3 Gordon Kennett

See also Eastbourne, Division Two Averages

1982...1982...1982...1982...1982...1982

	M	R	Pts	BP	TPts	Ave	F	P	Total
Gordon Kennett	**48**	**212**	**493.0**	**22.0**	**515.0**	**9.717**	**7**	**3**	**10**
Kelly Moran	35	146	322.0	29.0	351.0	9.616	7	2	9
§Ron Preston	38	162	354.0	18.0	372.0	9.185	5	3	8
Barney Kennett	3	12	18.0	5.0	23.0	7.667			
Paul Woods	45	194	289.0	32.0	321.0	6.619		3	3
§Rod Hunter	1	6	9.0	0.0	9.0	6.000			
§§Andy Buck	3	9	9.0	3.0	12.0	5.333			
§§Kenny McKinna	1	5	4.0	2.0	6.0	4.800			
§Dave Allen	1	3	2.0	1.0	3.0	4.000			
David Kennett	29	89	71.0	8.0	79.0	3.551			
§§Lillebror Johansson	18	71	55.0	8.0	63.0	3.549			
§§Lars Hammarberg	44	134	90.0	23.0	113.0	3.373			
§§Börje Ring	39	125	91.0	14.0	105.0	3.360			
Keith Pritchard	9	22	14.0	4.0	18.0	3.273			
Mick Hines	5	13	10.0	0.0	10.0	3.077			
Barry Thomas	1	4	3.0	0.0	3.0	3.000			
§§Ian Barney	1	2	0.0	0.0	0.0	0.000			
§Kenny Young	1	1	0.0	0.0	0.0	0.000			

1983...1983...1983...1983...1983...1983

	M	R	Pts	BP	TPts	Ave	F	P	Total
§Nigel Sparshott	1	5	9.0	2.0	11.0	8.800			
Paul Woods	**44**	**209**	**436.0**	**20.0**	**456.0**	**8.727**	**3**	**1**	**4**
§John Eskildsen	37	161	242.0	21.0	263.0	6.534			
Keith Pritchard	2	6	6.0	2.0	8.0	5.333			
§Ashley Pullen	6	18	20.0	0.0	20.0	4.444			
§Mike Lanham	23	89	80.0	13.0	93.0	4.180			
David Kennett	11	32	24.0	7.0	31.0	3.875			
Lillebror Johansson	22	78	63.0	11.0	74.0	3.795			
§Anders Eriksson	25	95	78.0	12.0	90.0	3.789			
§Piotr Pyszny	13	48	38.0	7.0	45.0	3.750			
Brian Kennett	5	16	12.0	3.0	15.0	3.750			
§Denzil Kent	9	34	28.0	3.0	31.0	3.647			
Trevor Geer	14	36	24.0	8.0	32.0	3.556			
§§Ottaviano Righetto	20	58	31.0	6.0	37.0	2.552			
§§Julian Parr	3	8	3.0	1.0	4.0	2.000			
§Petr Ondrasik	1	4	1.0	1.0	2.0	2.000			
Dave Allen	1	2	1.0	0.0	1.0	2.000			
Ian Barney	1	2	1.0	0.0	1.0	2.000			
§§Rene Christiansen	10	29	10.0	4.0	14.0	1.931			
§Max Schöllhorn	2	5	1.0	0.0	1.0	0.800			
Andy Buck	3	8	1.0	0.0	1.0	0.500			
§§Peter Schroeck	7	15	1.0	0.0	1.0	0.267			
§Finn Jensen	2	6	0.0	0.0	0.0	0.000			

THE details above for Paul Woods include five rides he took at Ipswich in the League Cup. It was subsequently found that he had used an illegal silencer and the seven points he scored were deducted from the final total. But his rides are still included in the statistics listed.

1984...1984...1984...1984...1984...1984

	M	R	Pts	BP	TPts	Ave	F	P	Total
§Bobby Schwartz	40	179	412.5	9.0	421.5	9.419	10	1	11
John Eskildsen	45	193	354.5	35.0	389.5	8.073	1	2	3
Paul Woods	38	159	294.0	26.0	320.0	8.050	2	1	3
§Antonin Kasper [jun]	22	81	124.0	13.0	137.0	6.765		1	1
§Colin Richardson	41	155	198.0	35.0	233.0	6.013		1	1
Olli Tyrvainen	44	156	171.5	20.0	191.5	4.910		1	1
Denzil Kent	**52**	**173**	**160.0**	**29.0**	**189.0**	**4.370**		**1**	**1**
§§Steve Lucero	31	110	97.0	18.0	115.0	4.182			
§§Martin Goodwin	10	33	26.0	7.0	33.0	4.000			
§Paul Bosley	8	21	16.0	4.0	20.0	3.810			
Keith Pritchard	2	6	3.0	0.0	3.0	2.000			
§§Erik Knudsen	2	5	2.0	0.0	2.0	1.600			
§Guy Wilson	1	3	0.0	0.0	0.0	0.000			
Ian Barney	1	2	0.0	0.0	0.0	0.000			
§§Barry Ayres	1	1	0.0	0.0	0.0	0.000			

■ *EASTBOURNE reverted to the National League in 1985. See Eastbourne, Division Two Averages.*

EDINBURGH

1965...1965...1965...1965...1965...1965

	M	R	Pts	BP	TPts	Ave	F	P	Total
§§George Hunter	31	124	309.0	2.0	311.0	10.032	7		7
§§Doug Templeton	29	116	218.0	15.0	233.0	8.034	1		1
§§Bernt Persson	3	13	25.0	1.0	26.0	8.000			
§§Colin McKee	33	132	209.0	19.0	228.0	6.909	2		2
§§Henry Harrfeldt	35	140	171.0	24.0	195.0	5.571			
§§Wayne Briggs	6	19	16.0	5.0	21.0	4.421			
§§Alf Wells	15	60	57.0	7.0	64.0	4.267			
§§Bill Landels	25	100	87.0	18.0	105.0	4.200			
§§Jimmy Tannock	3	9	7.0	1.0	8.0	3.556			
§§Bert Harkins	21	84	59.0	15.0	74.0	3.524			
§§Kevin Torpie	21	84	55.0	12.0	67.0	3.190			
§§Alfred Sitzwohl	1	4	1.0	1.0	2.0	2.000			
§§Ross Nickisson	20	80	26.0	9.0	35.0	1.750			
§§Brian Black	2	8	2.0	1.0	3.0	1.500			
§John Ellis	1	4	1.0	0.0	1.0	1.000			
§§Preben Andreasen	1	3	0.0	0.0	0.0	0.000			
§§Fred Priest	1	2	0.0	0.0	0.0	0.000			

1966...1966...1966...1966...1966...1966

	M	R	Pts	BP	TPTs	Ave	F	P	Total
George Hunter	35	142	278.0	12.0	290.0	8.169	6	1	7
§§Bengt Jansson	22	91	164.0	10.0	174.0	7.648		1	1
Doug Templeton	**36**	**151**	**270.0**	**10.0**	**280.0**	**7.417**	**1**	**1**	**2**
Reidar Eide	20	83	102.0	19.0	121.0	5.831	1		1
Kevin Torpie	2	7	8.0	2.0	10.0	5.714			
§§Brian Collins	2	5	6.0	1.0	7.0	5.600			
§§Dudley McKean	30	101	115.0	18.0	133.0	5.267			
Bill Landels	22	75	77.5	20.0	97.5	5.200		1	1
Bert Harkins	34	113	119.0	17.0	136.0	4.814			
Jimmy Tannock	30	101	92.0	23.0	115.0	4.554			
§§Runo Wedin	4	16	15.0	2.0	17.0	4.250			
Henry Harrfeldt	2	4	4.0	0.0	4.0	4.000			
§§Knut Syrrest	1	3	1.0	1.0	2.0	2.667			

1967...1967...1967...1967...1967...1967

	M	R	Pts	BP	TPts	Ave	F	P	Total
Bernt Persson	30	128	284	10	294	9.188	5	2	7
Reidar Eide	38	166	355	18	373	8.988	7	1	8
George Hunter	36	151	292	15	307	8.132	1	3	4
§§Øyvind Berg	38	147	193	46	239	6.503		1	1
Doug Templeton	**40**	**166**	**236**	**32**	**268**	**6.458**	**1**		**1**
Bill Landels	32	124	149	32	181	5.839		1	1
§§Alec Hughson	4	13	12	6	18	5.538			
Bert Harkins	34	110	121	25	146	5.309	1		1
Brian Black	7	14	15	3	18	5.143			
Brian Collins	7	18	11	5	16	3.556			
Jimmy Tannock	3	6	2	0	2	1.333			

▲ EDINBURGH were given notice to quit their Old Meadowbank Stadium during 1967 by the landlords, the City Council, who wanted to refurbish and develop the site as the major athletics venue for the 1968 Commonwealth Games. It brought an end to speedway in the Scottish capital after a run of eight consecutive seasons, initially in the Provincial League and then, from 1965, as found members of the British League.

▲ The team moved en bloc to Coatbridge – see Coatbridge for further details.

▲ Edinburgh was also the early stage for the Scottish Open Championship full details of which are at the end of this chapter.

EXETER

EXETER, possessor of the fastest home track in speedway for much of the British League era (only Second Division Crewe was faster!), were one of the founder members of the merged 1965 League and retained their top flight status until financial problems forced them to apply to join the National League in 1980.

During those years they built up a reputation for being almost unbeatable on their own County Ground track but poor travellers. However all that changed with one signing – the arrival of Ivan Mauger early in 1973 when his mere presence to sign a contract attracted a record 10,000 plus gate to the Devon circuit.

WESTERNAPOLIS

1967	1 Eric Boocock	2 Göte Nordin	3 Wayne Briggs
1968	1 Eric Boocock	2 Martin Ashby	3 Anders Michanek
1969	1 Nigel Boocock	2 Eric Boocock	3 Odd Fossengen
1970	1 Nigel Boocock	2 Bengt Jansson	3 Sören Sjösten
1971	1 Ivan Mauger	2 Jim Airey	3 Bob Kilby
1972	1 Ivan Mauger	2 Ole Olsen	3 Bob Kilby
1973	1 Ivan Mauger	2 Martin Ashby	3 Nigel Boocock and Ray Wilson
1974	1 Phil Crump	2 Peter Collins	3 Martin Ashby
1975	1 Ivan Mauger	2 Phil Crump	3 Kevin Holden and Martin Ashby
1976	1 Peter Collins	2 Malcolm Simmons	3 Dave Morton
1977	1 Michael Lee	2 Phil Crump	3 Scott Autrey
1978	1 Phil Crump	2 Scott Autrey	3 Tormod Langli
1979	1 Zdenek Kudrna	2 Phil Crump	3 Vaclav Verner
1980	1 John Williams	2 Robert Maxfield	3 John Barker
1984	1 Phil Crump	2 Gary Guglielmi	3 Mitch Shirra

JACK UNSTEAD MEMORIAL TROPHY

1965	1 Colin Gooddy	2 Chris Julian	3 Bill Andrew
1966	1 Norman Hunter	2 Maury Mattingley	3 Tommy Sweetman
1967	1 Neil Street	2 Martin Ashby	3 Gunnar Malmkvist
1968	1 Martin Ashby	2 Jim Airey	3 Alan Cowland
1969	1 Martin Ashby	2 Ray Wilson	3 Malcolm Brown
1970	1 Martin Ashby	2 Ole Olsen	3 Nigel Boocock
1971	1 Eric Boocock	2 Jim Airey	3 Bruce Cribb
1972	1 Bob Kilby	2 Pete Smith	3 Graham Plant

WESTWARD TV TROPHY

1965	1 Cyril Maidment	2 Roy Trigg	3 Colin Goody
1966	1 Jack Geran	2 Bill Andrew	3 Cyril Maidment
1967	1 Wayne Briggs	2 Göte Nordin	3 Ronnie Genz
1968	1 John Boulger	2 Martin Ashby	3 Tommy Sweetman
1971	1 Ivan Mauger	2 Bob Kilby	3 Martin Ashby
1972	1 Ivan Mauger	2 Ole Olsen	3 Anders Michanek
1973	1 Ivan Mauger	2 Ole Olsen	3 Scott Autrey
1974	1 Ivan Mauger	2 Chris Pusey	3 Chris Julian

WEST OF ENGLAND CHAMPIONSHIP

1966	1 Geoff Mudge	2 Martin Ashby	3 Chris Blewett

EXPRESS AND ECHO SPRING CLASSIC

1974	1 Kevin Holden	2 Malcolm Simmons	3 John Boulger
1975	1 Ivan Mauger	2 Scott Autrey	3 Nigel Boocock

DIY MOTOR SPARES TROPHY

1974	1 Phil Crump	2 Ivan Mauger	3 Scott Autrey

SPEEDWAY MAIL TROPHY

1975	1 Scott Autrey	2 Phil Crump	3 Neil Street and Martin Ashby

SUPPORTERS TROPHY

1975	1 Phil Crump	2 Malcolm Simmons	3 Ivan Mauger and Scott Autrey

DAIRY CREST K O TROPHY

1977	1 Scott Autrey	2 Joe Owen	3 Jim McMillan

EXETER

1965...1965...1965...1965...1965...1965

	M	R	Pts	BP	TPts	Ave	F	P	Total
§§Colin Gooddy	39	156	377.0	11.0	388.0	9.949	5	1	6
§§Jimmy Squibb	39	156	292.0	40.0	332.0	8.513		4	4
§§Jack Geran	31	124	229.0	15.0	244.0	7.871	2	1	3
§§Alan Cowland	38	152	254.5	44.0	298.5	7.855		2	2
§§Tim Bungay	7	28	37.0	5.0	42.0	6.000			
§§Des Lukehurst	28	112	127.0	32.0	159.0	5.679			
§§Chris Blewett	36	144	139.0	29.0	168.0	4.667			
§§Cliff Cox	4	16	13.0	2.0	15.0	3.750			
§§Maury McDermott	27	108	78.0	19.0	97.0	3.593			
§Ivor Hughes	6	24	16.0	5.0	21.0	3.500			
§§Pat Flanagan	2	8	4.0	2.0	6.0	3.000			
§Doug Dearden	13	52	25.0	3.0	28.0	2.154			
§§Ray Wickett	1	4	2.0	0.0	2.0	2.000			
§§Glyn Chandler	1	2	0.0	0.0	0.0	0.000			
§Tony Lewis	1	3	0.0	0.0	0.0	0.000			

1966...1966...1966...1966...1966...1966

	M	R	Pts	BP	TPts	Ave	F	P	Total
§Tommy Sweetman	37	159	343.0	19.0	362.0	9.107	6	1	7
§§Neil Street	30	124	248.0	7.0	255.0	8.226	2		2
Colin Gooddy	37	155	255.5	28.0	283.5	7.316			
Jimmy Squibb	37	156	218.0	40.0	258.0	6.615	1	1	2
Jack Geran	32	124	168.0	25.0	193.0	6.226	2	2	4
Chris Blewett	30	105	111.0	30.0	141.0	5.371	1		1
§Ted Laessing	7	15	11.0	7.0	18.0	4.800			
§Alan Smith	17	47	47.0	9.0	56.0	4.766			
§§Eric Howe	1	1	1.0	0.0	1.0	4.000			
Doug Dearden	16	40	18.0	6.0	24.0	2.400			
§Nils Paulsen	4	15	6.0	3.0	9.0	2.400			
§§Vic Ridgeon	4	11	3.0	0.0	3.0	1.091			
§§Dave Whitaker	3	8	0.0	0.0	0.0	0.000			
§Ken Vale	1	3	0.0	0.0	0.0	0.000			
§John Ellis	1	2	0.0	0.0	0.0	0.000			

1967...1967...1967...1967...1967...1967

	M	R	Pts	BP	TPts	Ave	F	P	Total
§§Gunnar Malmkvist	18	77	147.0	11.0	158.0	8.208	1		1
§Wayne Briggs	17	70	131.0	6.0	137.0	7.829		1	1
Jimmy Squibb	37	155	246.0	40.0	286.0	7.381	1	1	2
Neil Street	37	152	246.5	29.0	275.5	7.250	3	2	5
Colin Gooddy	13	49	77.0	6.0	83.0	6.776			
Jack Geran	32	122	188.0	15.0	203.0	6.656	1	1	2
§§Per Gerhardsson	6	14	17.0	6.0	23.0	6.571			
Tommy Sweetman	37	149	205.0	34.0	239.0	6.416			
Chris Blewett	28	93	104.0	25.0	129.0	5.548			
§§Mike Cake	17	41	29.0	11.0	40.0	3.902			
Tim Bungay	13	39	26.0	6.0	32.0	3.282			
§§Laurie Etheridge	3	5	3.0	0.0	3.0	2.400			
§§Phil Woodcock	1	2	0.0	0.0	0.0	0.000			

1968...1968...1968...1968...1968...1968

	M	R	Pts	BP	TPts	Ave	F	P	Total
§Martin Ashby	32	138	355.0	15.0	370.0	10.725	11	2	13
Wayne Briggs	36	148	261.0	24.0	285.0	7.703	1		1
Neil Street	37	146	245.0	29.0	274.0	7.507	3	2	5
Jimmy Squibb	37	149	242.0	36.0	278.0	7.463	1	4	5
Tommy Sweetman	37	150	229.0	45.0	274.0	7.307	1	1	2
Mike Cake	28	103	147.0	17.0	164.0	6.369		1	1
Chris Blewett	18	55	58.5	20.0	78.5	5.709			
Phil Woodcock	6	13	11.0	6.0	17.0	5.231			
§§Chris Bass	26	62	58.0	14.0	72.0	4.645			
§§Tony George	3	7	1.0	1.0	2.0	1.143			

▲ TOMMY SWEETMAN joined Exeter from Wolverhampton, scored a maximum against Wimbledon on his debut on April 4, 1966, and never missed a match in three seasons at the County Ground.
His last appearance was at Wolverhampton on October 4, 1968, a total of 111 consecutive matches.

1969...1969...1969...1969...1969...1969

	M	R	Pts	BP	TPts	Ave	F	P	Total
Martin Ashby	34	152	367.0	12.0	379.0	9.974	7	2	9
Des Lukehurst	1	3	5.0	2.0	7.0	9.333			
§§Jan Holub	31	133	255.0	15.0	270.0	8.120	1		1
Jimmy Squibb	37	157	263.0	24.0	287.0	7.312		1	1
Alan Cowland	35	125	135.0	28.0	163.0	5.216			
Mike Cake	37	139	143.0	36.0	179.0	5.151			
Chris Blewett	11	42	44.0	8.0	52.0	4.952			
Tim Bungay	36	106	106.0	20.0	126.0	4.755			
§Ross Gilbertson	9	29	29.0	4.0	33.0	4.552			
Phil Woodcock	24	74	66.0	13.0	79.0	4.270			
§§Ian Gills	1	2	1.0	0.0	1.0	2.000			

MARTIN ASHBY protested about the Rider Control Committee decision to move him from Swindon to Exeter...and then had his two best-ever seasons in the Falcons' colours!

1970...1970...1970...1970...1970...1970

	M	R	Pts	BP	TPts	Ave	F	P	Total
Martin Ashby	33	149	360.0	16.0	376.0	10.094	6	2	8
§Bruce Cribb	16	68	147.0	14.0	161.0	9.471	1	1	2
Jan Holub	28	114	170.0	24.0	194.0	6.807			
Chris Julian	38	157	209.0	30.0	239.0	6.089		1	1
Neil Street	38	138	158.0	25.0	183.0	5.304		2	2
§Bengt Andersson	18	63	74.0	8.0	82.0	5.206			
§§Bob Coles	36	121	126.5	19.0	145.5	4.810			
Phil Woodcock	31	96	89.0	22.0	111.0	4.625			
Des Lukehurst	2	5	4.0	1.0	5.0	4.000			
§George Barclay	1	3	1.0	1.0	2.0	2.667			
§Dave O'Connor	5	14	8.0	1.0	9.0	2.571			
§Stan Stevens	2	6	2.0	0.0	2.0	1.333			
§§Mike Holt	1	3	1.0	0.0	1.0	1.333			
§§Judd Drew	1	2	0.0	0.0	0.0	0.000			
Ian Gills	1	2	0.0	0.0	0.0	0.000			

1971...1971...1971...1971...1971...1971

	M	R	Pts	BP	TPts	Ave	F	P	Total
Bruce Cribb	37	170	358.0	21.0	379.0	8.918	1	1	2
§Bob Kilby	33	151	328.0	7.0	335.0	8.874	5	2	7
Ross Gilbertson	1	3	4.0	2.0	6.0	8.000			
§§Peter Ingram	37	154	211.0	36.0	247.0	6.416		2	2
Wayne Briggs	20	70	86.0	18.0	104.0	5.943			
§§Kjell Gimre	1	3	2.0	2.0	4.0	5.333			
Chris Julian	37	147	163.0	31.0	194.0	5.279			
§Tommy Bergqvist	13	51	53.0	12.0	65.0	5.098			
Stan Stevens	1	5	5.0	1.0	6.0	4.800			
Phil Woodcock	34	104	93.0	22.0	115.0	4.423			
Bob Coles	24	80	71.0	11.0	82.0	4.100			
§Kevin Holden	3	8	6.0	0.0	6.0	3.000			
§Tony Childs	1	4	3.0	0.0	3.0	3.000			
§Taffy Owen	1	4	2.0	1.0	3.0	3.000			
§§Colin Tucker	1	2	0.0	0.0	0.0	0.000			
§§Paul Palfrey	1	1	0.0	0.0	0.0	0.000			

1972...1972...1972...1972...1972...1972

	M	R	Pts	BP	TPts	AVE	F	P	Total
Bob Kilby	33	140	343.0	3.0	346.0	9.886	14		14
§Edgar Stangeland	31	130	246.5	21.0	267.5	8.231		2	2
Bob Coles	16	61	80.0	16.0	96.0	6.295			
§Christer Sjösten	4	13	16.0	4.0	20.0	6.154			
Kevin Holden	23	93	122.0	19.0	141.0	6.065		1	1
Peter Ingram	37	147	180.0	35.0	215.0	5.850			
Bruce Cribb	15	57	75.0	7.0	82.0	5.754			
§Dave Hemus	36	134	153.0	24.0	177.0	5.284		1	1
Chris Julian	27	94	96.0	19.0	115.0	4.894			
Phil Woodcock	14	44	37.0	7.0	44.0	4.000			
§§Robin Amundson	2	8	8.0	0.0	8.0	4.000			
Kjell Gimre	1	3	2.0	1.0	3.0	4.000			
§John Davis	1	2	1.0	1.0	2.0	4.000			
§Dave Mills	2	7	3.0	2.0	5.0	2.857			
§Clark Facey	7	17	5.0	0.0	5.0	1.176			
JImmy Squibb	2	4	1.0	0.0	1.0	1.000			
§Bryan Loakes	1	3	0.0	0.0	0.0	0.000			
§Mike Sampson	1	2	0.0	0.0	0.0	0.000			

EXETER

1973...1973...1973...1973...1973...1973

	M	R	Pts	BP	TPts	Ave	F	P	Total
§Ivan Mauger	26	107	295.0	7.0	302.0	11.290	13	4	17
§Tony Lomas	28	113	202.0	12.0	214.0	7.575	2	2	4
Bob Kilby	6	18	34.0	0.0	34.0	7.556	1		1
§§Scott Autrey	35	149	213.5	24.0	237.5	6.376	1	2	3
Kevin Holden	**36**	**144**	**186.0**	**30.0**	**216.0**	**6.000**			
§Neil Middleditch	2	6	7.0	2.0	9.0	6.000			
§Frank Shuter	35	129	167.0	20.0	187.0	5.798	1		1
Peter Ingram	4	11	11.0	4.0	15.0	5.455			
Chris Julian	33	119	137.0	22.0	159.0	5.345			
Mike Sampson	13	43	46.0	5.0	51.0	4.744			
Bob Coles	27	91	91.0	11.0	102.0	4.484			
§Mitch Graham	2	6	3.0	3.0	6.0	4.000			

WHEN Ivan Mauger agreed to join Exeter after being ordered to leave Belle Vue by the Rider Control Committee he insisted on several unusual clauses in his contract.

He had to be flown from London to Devon if he had been racing on the Continent the previous day; he was to be paid royalties on personal souvenirs sold in the Exeter track shop; and his photograph was to be on the front cover of the programme to help satisfy his sponsors.

He could point to justification for his stand as he didn't drop a single point at the County Ground in official competition in his debut season went on to lead the Falcons to the British League championship in 1974 before eventually joining Hull in 1978 for a record £12,000.

1974...1974...1974...1974...1974...1974

	M	R	Pts	BP	TPts	Ave	F	P	Total
Ivan Mauger	33	139	372.0	6.0	378.0	10.878	13	3	16
Scott Autrey	**36**	**152**	**277.0**	**39.0**	**316.0**	**8.316**		**2**	**2**
Tony Lomas	**36**	**146**	**242.0**	**24.0**	**266.0**	**7.288**		**1**	**1**
Kevin Holden	**36**	**152**	**232.0**	**44.0**	**276.0**	**7.263**		**3**	**3**
§§Steve Reinke	19	56	66.0	12.0	78.0	5.571			
Mike Sampson	9	31	35.0	8.0	43.0	5.548			
Chris Julian	35	121	145.0	22.0	167.0	5.521			
Neil Middleditch	1	3	2.0	2.0	4.0	5.333			
§Alan Molyneux	1	4	3.0	2.0	5.0	5.000			
Frank Shuter	30	100	103.0	16.0	119.0	4.760			
§§Peter Thompson	13	35	30.0	7.0	37.0	4.229			
§Dave Gooderham	1	2	1.0	0.0	1.0	2.000			

1975...1975...1975...1975...1975...1975

	M	R	Pts	BP	TPts	Ave	F	P	Total
Ivan Mauger	35	149	424.0	5.0	429.0	11.517	23	3	26
Scott Autrey	37	155	337.0	19.0	356.0	9.187	5	2	7
Kevin Holden	26	97	152.0	30.0	182.0	7.505	1	3	4
Steve Reinke	28	106	139.0	22.0	161.0	6.075			
§John Titman	32	127	165.0	22.0	187.0	5.890		1	1
§§Les Rumsey	9	28	34.0	6.0	40.0	5.714			
§Geoff Mudge	39	141	148.0	27.0	175.0	4.965			
§§Mike Farrell	36	134	130.0	28.0	158.0	4.716			
§Graham Drury	1	3	3.0	0.0	3.0	4.000			
Chris Julian	12	36	24.0	7.0	31.0	3.444			
§Vic Harding	4	14	8.0	3.0	11.0	3.143			
§§Gerald Purkiss	2	5	3.0	0.0	3.0	2.400			
Mike Sampson	3	9	4.0	0.0	4.0	1.778			

1976...1976...1976...1976...1976...1976

	M	R	Pts	BP	TPts	Ave	F	P	Total
Ivan Mauger	33	140	373.0	7.0	380.0	10.857	17	1	18
Scott Autrey	34	148	320.0	22.0	342.0	9.243	6	1	7
John Titman	37	155	251.0	20.0	271.0	6.994			
Mike Farrell	2	7	9.0	3.0	12.0	6.857			
Kevin Holden	37	155	214.0	36.0	250.0	6.452			
§Chris Robins	1	3	4.0	0.0	4.0	5.333			
§§Steve Koppe	22	83	86.0	21.0	107.0	5.157			
Geoff Mudge	10	37	42.0	3.0	45.0	4.865			
§§Bob Spelta	4	13	13.0	2.0	15.0	4.615			
§Tony Featherstone	3	11	8.0	3.0	11.0	4.000			
§Keith Evans	1	3	3.0	0.0	3.0	4.000			
§Peter Prinsloo	**38**	**121**	**86.0**	**21.0**	**107.0**	**3.537**			
Les Rumsey	16	46	37.0	3.0	40.0	3.478			
§Brian Havelock	2	7	5.0	1.0	6.0	3.429			
§Kazimerz Adamczak	13	34	14.0	5.0	19.0	2.235			
§Alan Johns	2	4	2.0	0.0	2.0	2.000			
§Kelvin Mullarkey	1	3	1.0	1.0	2.0	2.667			

1977...1977...1977...1977...1977...1977

	M	R	Pts	BP	TPts	Ave	F	P	Total
Ivan Mauger	32	128	324.0	12.0	336.0	10.500	10	3	13
Scott Autrey	37	163	343.0	29.0	372.0	9.129	2	4	6
§§Vaclav Verner	30	122	225.0	37.0	262.0	8.590	2	4	6
John Titman	**40**	**177**	**327.0**	**38.0**	**365.0**	**8.249**	**1**	**4**	**5**
Mike Farrell	38	142	196.0	34.0	230.0	6.479			
Steve Koppe	25	86	108.0	28.0	136.0	6.326		1	1
Peter Prinsloo	39	134	173.0	35.0	208.0	6.209			
§§Malcolm Bedkober	3	7	6.0	2.0	8.0	4.571			
§§Walter Grumbuller	13	36	30.0	6.0	36.0	4.000			
§Robert Henry	1	2	1.0	1.0	2.0	4.000			
Bob Coles	5	15	10.0	4.0	14.0	3.733			
Bob Spelta	2	4	1.0	1.0	2.0	2.000			
§Phil Collins	1	4	1.0	0.0	1.0	1.000			
§§Bob Watts	3	5	1.0	0.0	1.0	0.800			

1978...1978...1978...1978...1978...1978

	M	R	Pts	BP	TPts	Ave	F	P	Total
Scott Autrey	45	183	457.0	19.0	476.0	10.404	8	7	15
§§Ales Dryml	2	8	15.0	2.0	17.0	8.500			
§Reidar Eide	41	155	305.0	22.0	327.0	8.439	5	1	6
Vaclav Verner	43	177	338.5	31.0	369.5	8.350	3	3	6
Peter Prinsloo	32	125	189.0	30.0	219.0	7.008		1	1
Mike Farrell	33	131	188.0	33.0	2213.0	6.748	2	1	3
§Steve Finch	1	3	4.0	1.0	5.0	6.667			
Steve Koppe	30	113	134.0	38.0	172.0	6.088			
Les Rumsey	27	93	123.0	18.0	141.0	6.065	1		1
§§Jan Verner	32	114	137.0	30.0	167.0	5.860		2	2
§Dave Allen	1	3	3.0	1.0	4.0	5.333			
§John Barker	1	3	4.0	0.0	4.0	5.333			
Bob Watts	2	5	4.0	2.0	6.0	4.800			
Phil Collins	2	9	7.0	3.0	10.0	4.444			
§Sean Willmott	2	5	3.0	2.0	5.0	4.000			
§Geoff Pusey	1	3	2.0	1.0	3.0	4.000			
§§Tim Curnock	1	3	2.0	1.0	3.0	4.000			
§Pip Lamb	1	2	1.0	1.0	2.0	4.000			
§Paul Woods	1	2	1.0	1.0	2.0	4.000			
§Mike Ferreira	5	15	11.0	3.0	14.0	3.733			
§Alan Sage	2	5	3.0	1.0	4.0	3.200			
§§Ian Robertson	2	5	3.0	0.0	3.0	2.400			
§Steve Lawson	1	4	1.0	0.0	1.0	1.000			
§Ian Clark	1	2	0.0	0.0	0.0	0.000			
§§Graham Jones	1	2	0.0	0.0	0.0	0.000			
§Danny Kennedy	1	2	0.0	0.0	0.0	0.000			

1979...1979...1979...1979...1979...1979

	M	R	Pts	BP	TPts	Ave	F	P	Total
Scott Autrey	36	158	421.0	7.0	428.0	10.835	11	5	16
Vaclav Verner	35	140	272.0	25.0	297.0	8.486	1	2	3
Peter Prinsloo	**40**	**170**	**255.0**	**40.0**	**295.0**	**6.941**			
§Louis Carr	3	13	21.0	1.0	22.0	6.769			
Ales Dryml	27	97	133.0	24.0	157.0	6.474			
Jan Verner	33	120	157.0	35.0	192.0	6.400			
Steve Koppe	39	164	208.0	45.0	253.0	6.171			
Nigel Boocock	19	62	81.0	13.0	94.0	6.065			
§§Zdenek Kudrna	32	121	155.0	28.0	183.0	6.050		1	1
§§Tony Sanford	1	3	1.0	1.0	2.0	2.667			
Bob Watts	6	13	5.0	2.0	7.0	2.154			
§John J. Williams	1	4	1.0	1.0	2.0	2.000			
§§David Brown	1	2	0.0	0.0	0.0	0.000			

1984...1984...1984...1984...1984...1984

	M	R	Pts	BP	TPts	Ave	F	P	Total
Ivan Mauger	23	96	183.0	11.0	194.0	8.083	2		2
§Andy Campbell	47	215	339.0	32.0	371.0	6.902			
§Sean Willmott	42	183	241.0	34.0	275.0	6.011			
§Leif Wahlmann	10	34	42.0	3.0	45.0	5.294			
§§Buddy Robinson	18	79	89.0	15.0	104.0	5.266			
§Robert Maxfield	39	137	145.0	28.0	173.0	5.051			
§§Frank Andersen	42	143	152.0	26.0	178.0	4.979			
§Martin Goodwin	2	7	7.0	1.0	8.0	4.571			
§Louis Carr	25	81	73.0	11.0	84.0	4.148			
Bob Coles	1	3	3.0	0.0	3.0	4.000			
§§Kevin Price	7	17	9.0	2.0	11.0	2.588			
§Steve Bishop	9	25	10.0	3.0	13.0	2.080			
§Keith Millard	12	26	10.0	3.0	13.0	2.000			
§Kent Noer	2	6	3.0	0.0	3.0	2.000			
§§Stefan Deser	2	5	2.0	0.0	2.0	1.600			
§§Michael Coles	8	16	3.0	1.0	4.0	1.000			
§Andy Buck	1	3	0.0	0.0	0.0	0.000			
§§David Biles	1	2	0.0	0.0	0.0	0.000			
§§Patrice Blondy	1	2	0.0	0.0	0.0	0.000			
§§Paul Taylor	1	2	0.0	0.0	0.0	0.000			

GLASGOW

FOUNDER members of the British League in 1965, the Tigers were owned by Ian Hoskins who played very much a background rôle as he also owned rivals Edinburgh!

White City was the original home of the club but when the Stadium had to be demolished to make way for a new road, everyone was stunned when the promotion moved into Hampden Park, the biggest stadium in Britain.

One restriction at the home of Scotland's national soccer team – they weren't allowed to play music during meetings.

1965...1965...1965...1965...1965...1965

	M	R	Pts	BP	TPts	Ave	F	P	Total
§§Charlie Monk	**37**	**163**	**415.0**	**4.0**	**419.0**	**10.282**	**9**	**1**	**10**
§§Chris Julian	1	4	7.0	2.0	9.0	9.000			
§§Bluey Scott	**37**	**155**	**271.0**	**24.0**	**295.0**	**7.613**	**2**	**2**	**4**
§§Willie Templeton	31	124	200.0	22.0	222.0	7.161	1	1	2
§§Nils Paulsen	24	90	135.0	13.0	148.0	6.578		1	1
§§Morrie Mattingley	30	115	154.0	22.0	176.0	6.122		2	2
§§Graham Coombes	**37**	**130**	**130.0**	**40.0**	**170.0**	**5.231**		**1**	**1**
§§Bruce Ovenden	30	100	95.0	24.0	119.0	4.760		1	1
§§Bill McMillan	20	68	53.0	17.0	70.0	4.118			
§Red Monteith	2	8	6.0	0.0	6.0	3.000			
§Joe Hicks	4	16	4.0	2.0	6.0	1.500			
§§Bernie Lagrosse	4	16	1.0	0.0	1.0	0.250			
§Trevor Chamberlain	1	2	0.0	0.0	0.0	0.000			

NEW ZEALANDER Bernie Lagrosse later rode for Berwick in the British League Division Two...under the assumed name of Roy Williams.

1966...1966...1966...1966...1966...1966

	M	R	Pts	BP	TPts	Ave	F	P	Total
Charlie Monk	**37**	**158**	**362.0**	**4.0**	**366.0**	**9.266**	**6**	**1**	**7**
§Alf Wells	35	144	241.0	28.0	269.0	7.472	1	1	2
Bluey Scott	22	85	134.0	16.0	150.0	7.059			
Willie Templeton	**37**	**150**	**217.0**	**36.0**	**253.0**	**6.747**		**2**	**2**
Maurie Mattingley	**37**	**143**	**206.0**	**21.0**	**227.0**	**6.350**	**1**		**1**
§§Jonny Faafeng	28	89	97.0	21.0	118.0	5.303			
Bill McMillan	**37**	**135**	**130.0**	**37.0**	**167.0**	**4.948**		**1**	**1**
§§Jim McMillan	13	26	17.0	6.0	23.0	3.538			
Joe Hicks	2	4	0.0	0.0	0.0	0.000			
Red Monteith	1	2	0.0	0.0	0.0	0.000			

1967...1967...1967...1967...1967...1967

	M	R	Pts	BP	TPts	Ave	F	P	Total
Charlie Monk	36	152	396.0	3.0	399.0	10.500	14		14
§§Bo Josefsson	17	73	111.0	15.0	126.0	6.904	1		1
Alf Wells	31	115	173.0	13.0	186.0	6.470			
Maury Mattingley	22	78	105.0	20.0	125.0	6.410			
Willie Templeton	37	151	218.0	22.0	240.0	6.358	1	1	2
Jonny Faafeng	10	40	48.0	6.0	54.0	5.400			
§Russ Dent	8	31	32.0	8.0	40.0	5.161			
Jim McMillan	29	111	113.0	17.0	130.0	4.685			
§Gordon McGregor	3	12	11.0	3.0	14.0	4.667			
Bill McMillan	14	45	40.0	5.0	45.0	4.000	1		1
§Nils Ringstrom	27	98	75.0	18.0	93.0	3.796			
§§Brian Whaley	17	43	26.0	7.0	33.0	3.070			

CHARLIE MONK filed an official written transfer request during the winter insisting he wanted a move to a track nearer his adopted home at Wakefield, Yorkshire.

1968...1968...1968...1968...1968...1968

	M	R	Pts	BP	TPts	Ave	F	P	Total
Jim McMillan	**37**	**168**	**333.0**	**16.0**	**349.0**	**8.310**	**3**		**3**
Øyvind Berg	33	140	265.0	12.0	277.0	7.914	3		3
Alf Wells	8	28	42.0	10.0	52.0	7.429			
Bo Josefsson	20	73	114.0	10.0	124.0	6.795	1	1	2
Russ Dent	32	128	149.0	36.0	185.0	5.781		2	2
§§Lars Jansson	17	76	97.0	11.0	108.0	5.684			
Willie Templeton	**37**	**148**	**159.0**	**23.0**	**182.0**	**4.919**			
Bill McMillan	30	106	107.0	20.0	127.0	4.792			
§§Åke Andersson	7	23	19.0	5.0	24.0	4.174			
Brian Whaley	23	54	26.0	6.0	32.0	2.370			
§§Bobby Beaton	3	8	3.0	0.0	3.0	1.500			

1969...1969...1969...1969...1969...1969

	M	R	Pts	BP	TPts	Ave	F	P	Total
Jim McMillan	**37**	**161**	**392.0**	**11.0**	**403.0**	**10.012**	**8**	**2**	**10**
Charlie Monk	36	156	367.0	6.0	373.0	9.564	7	1	8
Øyvind Berg	36	138	244.0	35.0	279.0	8.087		2	2
Russ Dent	**37**	**132**	**153.0**	**32.0**	**185.0**	**5.606**		**1**	**1**
§Ken Vale	1	3	2.0	2.0	4.0	5.333			
Willie Templeton	**37**	**135**	**141.0**	**28.0**	**169.0**	**5.007**		**1**	**1**
§Maurie Robinson	5	19	16.0	5.0	21.0	4.421			
Alf Wells	16	48	42.0	9.0	51.0	4.250			
§Mike Hiftle	12	34	24.0	5.0	29.0	3.412			
Bobby Beaton	36	117	69.0	16.0	85.0	2.906			
§§Jim Crowhurst	2	5	1.0	1.0	2.0	1.600			
§§Jim Gallacher	1	3	1.0	0.0	1.0	1.333			
§§Brian Murray	1	2	0.0	0.0	0.0	0.000			

1970...1970...1970...1970...1970...1970

	R	Pts	BP	TPts	Ave	F	PTotal		
Jim McMillan	34	150	376.0	9.0	385.0	10.267	11	2	13
Charie Monk	36	159	326.0	13.0	339.0	8.528	4	3	7
Øyvind Berg	31	132	227.0	30.0	257.0	7.788	2	2	4
Doug Templeton	**37**	**138**	**150.0**	**35.0**	**185.0**	**5.362**		**1**	**1**
Bobby Beaton	**37**	**135**	**153.0**	**27.0**	**180.0**	**5.333**		**1**	**1**
Willie Templeton	**37**	**135**	**143.0**	**37.0**	**180.0**	**5.333**		**1**	**1**
§Alan Knapkin	1	2	1.0	1.0	2.0	4.000			
Bill McMillan	18	55	41.0	9.0	50.0	3.636			
§Alistair Brady	6	13	4.0	2.0	6.0	1.846			
Brian Murray	9	22	7.0	2.0	9.0	1.636			
§§Peter Baldock	5	11	2.0	0.0	2.0	0.727			

1971...1971...1971...1971...1971...1971

	M	R	Pts	BP	TPts	Ave	F	P	Total
Jim McMillan	35	149	329.0	13.0	342.0	9.181	4	4	8
George Hunter	36	153	298.0	19.0	317.0	8.288	3	1	4
Bobby Beaton	**38**	**158**	**254.0**	**33.0**	**287.0**	**7.266**	**1**		**1**
Charlie Monk	**38**	**147**	**226.0**	**31.0**	**257.0**	**6.993**		**1**	**1**
Willie Templeton	35	110	107.0	25.0	132.0	4.800			
Doug Templeton	**38**	**140**	**144.0**	**20.0**	**164.0**	**4.686**			
Bill McMillan	30	96	72.0	11.0	83.0	3.458			
§§Jim Beaton	2	8	4.0	2.0	6.0	3.000			
Brian Murray	3	10	5.0	0.0	5.0	2.000			
§§Allan Mackie	6	13	1.0	0.0	1.0	0.308			

1972...1972...1972...1972...1972...1972

	M	R	Pts	BP	TPts	Ave	F	P	Total
Jim McMillan	**35**	**149**	**315.0**	**15.0**	**330.0**	**8.859**	**3**	**2**	**5**
Bobby Beaton	**35**	**151**	**303.0**	**21.0**	**324.0**	**8.583**	**3**	**1**	**4**
George Hunter	25	108	218.0	9.0	227.0	8.407	3		3
Charlie Monk	32	128	202.0	19.0	221.0	6.906	3	2	5
§Svein Kaasa	6	17	17.0	4.0	21.0	4.941			
§Robin Adlington	23	83	69.0	14.0	83.0	4.000			
Doug Templeton	1	4	3.0	1.0	4.0	4.000			
§George Major	1	3	3.0	0.0	3.0	4.000			
Jim Gallacher	21	72	53.0	14.0	67.0	3.722		1	1
§§Andy Meldrum	4	11	8.0	2.0	10.0	3.636			
§Paul O'Neal	27	90	66.0	12.0	78.0	3.467			
§Arthur Browning	1	3	1.0	1.0	2.0	2.667			
§Kjell Gimre	14	46	22.0	2.0	24.0	2.087			
Willie Templeton	1	4	2.0	0.0	2.0	2.000			
Jim Beaton	7	22	7.0	3.0	10.0	1.818			
§§Dave Gatenby	2	7	3.0	0.0	3.0	1.714			
§Dave Beech	1	5	2.0	0.0	2.0	1.600			
§§John Wilson	3	9	2.0	1.0	3.0	1.333			
§Preben Rosenkilde	1	4	0.0	0.0	0.0	0.000			
§§Robin Amundson	1	3	0.0	0.0	0.0	0.000			

IT WAS a tragic season for Glasgow with two deaths. Young Norwegian Svein Kaasa was killed at Hampden Park while junior George Beaton, son of promoter Jim Beaton and elder brother of Bobby, died in a car crash.

GLASGOW OPEN CHAMPIONSHIP

1965	1 Barry Briggs	2 Sverre Harrfeldt	3 Olle Nygren
1966	1 Olle Nygren	2 Ivan Mauger	3 Bill McMillan
1968	1 Nigel Boocock	2 Ole Olsen	3 Charlie Monk

SCOTTISH WESTERN CHAMPIONSHIP

1969	1 Ivan Mauger	2 Nigel Boocock	3 Arnie Haley

HACKNEY

PROVINCIAL LEAGUE members in 1963 and 1964, the Hawks were founder members of the British League and remained at that level until promoter Len Silver sold his licence to Oxford late in 1983.

1965...1965...1965...1965...1965...1965

	M	R	Pts	BP	TPts	Ave	F	P	Total
§§Gerald Jackson	31	124	272.0	4.0	276.0	8.903	6	1	7
§§Colin Pratt	33	132	268.0	13.0	281.0	8.515	6	1	7
§§Roy Trigg	34	136	247.5	23.0	270.5	7.956	2	1	3
§§Les McGillivray	**35**	**140**	**186.0**	**45.0**	**231.0**	**6.600**		**2**	**2**
§§John Poyser	10	40	49.0	7.0	56.0	5.600			
§§Howdy Byford	34	136	139.0	34.0	173.0	5.088			
§§Brian Davies	33	132	122.0	28.0	150.0	4.545			
§§Malcolm Brown	19	76	60.0	16.0	76.0	4.000			
§§Reg Reeves	2	8	5.0	3.0	8.0	4.000			
§Maury McDermott	1	4	4.0	0.0	4.0	4.000			
§§Sandy McGillivray	12	48	21.0	4.0	25.0	2.083			
§§Joe Hicks	1	1	0.0	0.0	0.0	0.000			

1966...1966...1966...1966...1966...1966

	M	R	Pts	BP	TPts	Ave	F	P	Total
Colin Pratt	34	152	367.0	13.0	380.0	10.000	9	3	12
Roy Trigg	**38**	**166**	**340.0**	**18.0**	**358.0**	**8.627**	**3**	**3**	**6**
Gerald Jackson	31	128	211.0	7.0	218.0	6.813	1		1
Les McGillivray	**38**	**154**	**176.0**	**32.0**	**208.0**	**5.403**		**1**	**1**
Brian Davies	9	32	36.0	6.0	42.0	5.250			
Malcolm Brown	**38**	**145**	**147.0**	**19.0**	**166.0**	**4.579**			
§§Ernie Baker	33	100	75.0	11.0	86.0	3.440			
Sandy McGillivray	13	35	20.0	5.0	25.0	2.857			
§§Gary Everett	6	17	8.0	4.0	12.0	2.824			
John Poyser	18	42	16.0	5.0	21.0	2.000			
§Alan Jackson	4	9	1.0	0.0	1.0	0.444			

COLIN PRATT became the first guest rider to score a maximum when his 12 points helped West Ham win at Cradley Heath on April 30, 1966.

1967...1967...1967...1967...1967...1967

	M	R	Pts	BP	TPts	Ave	F	P	Total
§Bengt Jansson	35	150	359.0	11.0	370.0	9.867	8	4	12
Colin Pratt	**39**	**168**	**362.0**	**14.0**	**376.0**	**8.952**	**7**	**4**	**11**
§Jack Biggs	3	12	18.0	1.0	19.0	6.333			
§Colin McKee	**39**	**151**	**209.0**	**27.0**	**236.0**	**6.252**		**1**	**1**
Les McGillivray	**39**	**154**	**185.0**	**39.0**	**224.0**	**5.818**	**1**		**1**
Gerald Jackson	26	90	108.0	12.0	120.0	5.333			
Malcolm Brown	**39**	**141**	**158.0**	**20.0**	**178.0**	**5.050**		**1**	**1**
Gary Everett	13	33	33.0	8.0	41.0	4.970			
Brian Davies	37	127	120.0	28.0	148.0	4.661			
Alan Jackson	2	4	1.0	0.0	1.0	1.000			

1968...1968...1968...1968...1968...1968

	M	R	Pts	BP	TPts	Ave	F	P	Total
Colin Pratt	36	152	350.0	14.0	364.0	9.579	3	2	5
Bengt Jansson	32	137	291.0	17.0	308.0	8.993	4	1	5
Les McGillivray	**37**	**146**	**203.0**	**43.0**	**246.0**	**6.740**			
§Des Lukehurst	34	127	175.0	23.0	198.0	6.236			
Jack Biggs	33	127	169.0	24.0	193.0	6.079			
§§Graeme Smith	2	5	5.0	2.0	7.0	5.600			
Malcolm Brown	**37**	**134**	**158.0**	**20.0**	**178.0**	**5.313**	**1**		**1**
Alan Jackson	8	20	19.0	3.0	22.0	4.400			
Gary Everett	33	99	90.0	11.0	101.0	4.081			
§Laurie Etheridge	8	24	13.0	6.0	19.0	3.167			

1969...1969...1969...1969...1969...1969

	M	R	Pts	BP	TPts	Ave	F	P	Total
Colin Pratt	36	147	255.0	15.0	270.0	7.347	2	1	3
§Garry Middleton	28	118	199.0	9.0	208.0	7.051	1		1
Jack Biggs	**37**	**144**	**206.0**	**22.0**	**228.0**	**6.333**			
§Jimmy Gooch	31	120	165.0	20.0	185.0	6.167			
Les McGillivray	**37**	**135**	**155.0**	**29.0**	**184.0**	**5.452**		**1**	**1**
Laurie Etheridge	19	73	74.0	19.0	93.0	5.096			
§Brian Leonard	19	66	71.0	12.0	83.0	5.030			
Des Lukehurst	18	59	64.0	8.0	72.0	4.881			
§Tommy Sweetman	7	24	23.0	4.0	27.0	4.500			
Graeme Smith	25	71	41.0	14.0	55.0	3.099			

1970...1970...1970...1970...1970...1970

	M	R	Pts	BP	TPts	Ave	F	P	Total
Bengt Jansson	26	117	268.5	9.0	277.5	9.487	6	1	7
Garry Middleton	35	160	317.0	11.0	328.0	8.200	1	1	2
Jack Biggs	19	77	103.0	14.0	117.0	6.078			
§Bob Andrews	33	137	171.0	35.0	206.0	6.015			
Jimmy Gooch	**37**	**135**	**177.0**	**24.0**	**201.0**	**5.956**		**1**	**1**
Laurie Etheridge	35	120	121.0	24.0	145.0	4.833			
Les McGillivray	**37**	**124**	**116.0**	**30.0**	**146.0**	**4.710**			
§§Barry Thomas	14	49	37.0	7.0	44.0	3.592			
§§Hugh Saunders	1	3	1.0	1.0	2.0	2.667			
§§Geoff Maloney	1	3	1.0	0.0	1.0	1.333			
§§Frank Auffret	1	2	0.0	0.0	0.0	0.000			
§Tim Swales	1	2	0.0	0.0	0.0	0.000			
Allan Emmett	1	0	0.0	0.0	0.0	n.a.			

LES McGILLIVRAY set an all-time record for consecutive appearances in the British League Division One.

He made his debut for the Hawks in their first ever match at Glasgow on April 2nd, 1965, and never missed an official meeting until his retirement from racing at the end of the 1970 season.His last match was at Waterden Road against Leicester on October 9.

In all he rode in a total of 223 successive matches – 214 in the British League and the remaining nine in the Knock-Out Cup.

By way of contrast the Hawks programmed Allen Emmett at number two for their British League match at Wembley for his official debut.

But he was withdrawn from all his programmed rides so never actually started a race and had to wait until 1972 for his first rides in the British League even though, for officialy purposes, he had been a member of the Hackney team!

1971...1971...1971...1971...1971...1971

	M	R	Pts	BP	TPts	Ave	F	P	Total
Bengt Jansson	36	159	393.0	15.0	408.0	10.264	8	2	10
Garry Middleton	**42**	**181**	**398.0**	**8.0**	**406.0**	**8.972**	**6**		**6**
§Phil Crump	1	3	5.0	1.0	6.0	8.000			
Barry Thomas	40	172	279.0	34.0	313.0	7.279		3	3
Laurie Etheridge	**42**	**169**	**192.0**	**38.0**	**230.0**	**5.444**			
Hugh Saunders	23	73	79.0	10.0	89.0	4.877			
§Eddie Reeves	30	99	97.0	22.0	119.0	4.808			
§§David Kennett	18	55	54.0	10.0	64.0	4.655			
Geoff Maloney	16	49	45.0	10.0	55.0	4.490			
Graham Miles	13	45	44.0	5.0	49.0	4.356			
§§Preben Rosenkilde	7	24	20.0	4.0	24.0	4.000			
§Malcolm Ballard	1	2	2.0	0.0	2.0	4.000			
§Gordon Kennett	3	10	6.0	3.0	9.0	3.600			
§George Barclay	1	2	1.0	0.0	1.0	2.000			
§Taffy Owen	1	2	1.0	0.0	1.0	2.000			
§Alan Knapkin	1	3	1.0	0.0	1.0	1.333			
§§Laurie Guilfoyle	5	14	4.0	0.0	4.0	1.143			
§§Bob Young	2	4	0.0	0.0	0.0	0.000			
§Roger Mills	1	2	0.0	0.0	0.0	0.000			

1972...1972...1972...1972...1972...1972

	M	R	Pts	BP	TPts	Ave	F	P	Total
Bengt Jansson	31	139	316.0	10.0	326.0	9.381	3	1	7
Barry Thomas	35	153	278.0	20.0	298.0	7.791	1	2	4
David Kennett	**40**	**151**	**195.0**	**46.0**	**241.0**	**6.384**		**1**	**1**
Geoff Maloney	34	133	187.0	23.0	210.0	6.316		2	2
Hugh Saunders	37	139	192.0	26.0	218.0	6.273	1		2
Laurie Etheridge	**40**	**152**	**195.0**	**42.0**	**237.0**	**6.237**		**1**	**1**
Eddie Reeves	29	101	125.0	21.0	146.0	5.782			
§Jack Millen	1	5	7.0	0.0	7.0	5.600			
Roger Wright	14	42	36.0	6.0	42.0	4.000			
Allen Emmett	10	25	15.0	5.0	20.0	3.200			

HACKNEY

1973...1973...1973...1973...1973...1973

	M	R	Pts	BP	TPts	Ave	F	P	Total
Allen Emmett	1	2	6.0	0.0	6.0	12.000			
Bengt Jansson	32	121	263.0	5.0	268.0	8.860	5	2	7
Barry Thomas	**38**	**170**	**317.0**	**16.0**	**333.0**	**7.835**	**1**	**1**	**2**
§§Tommy Nilsson	16	63	87.0	14.0	101.0	6.413			
§Mike Broadbank	1	4	5.0	1.0	6.0	6.000			
David Kennett	**38**	**142**	**173.0**	**24.0**	**197.0**	**5.549**			
Geoff Maloney	36	144	162.0	34.0	196.0	5.444	1		1
Hugh Saunders	37	134	154.0	27.0	181.0	5.403			
§§Dave Morton	4	15	17.0	3.0	20.0	5.333			
§§Mitch Graham	1	3	4.0	0.0	4.0	5.333			
Laurie Etheridge	30	112	125.0	23.0	148.0	5.286			
§§Barney Kennett	17	52	48.0	8.0	56.0	4.308			
§Bobby McNeil	1	3	3.0	0.0	3.0	4.000			
§§Terry Barclay	1	2	1.0	0.0	1.0	2.000			
§Roger Johns	1	2	1.0	0.0	1.0	2.000			
§Peter Moore	5	13	5.0	1.0	6.0	1.846			
§§Glyn Taylor	1	5	1.0	1.0	2.0	1.600			
§David Beech	2	6	1.0	1.0	2.0	1.333			
§§Les Ott	1	2	0.0	0.0	0.0	0.000			

1974...1974...1974...1974...1974...1974

	M	R	Pts	BP	TPts	Ave	F	P	Total
§Dag Lovaas	29	127	321.0	2.0	323.0	10.173	6		6
Barry Thomas	33	145	265.0	17.0	282.0	7.779	2		2
Dave Morton	26	99	147.0	10.0	157.0	6.343	1	1	2
§Ted Hubbard	1	4	6.0	0.0	6.0	6.000			
§Steve Lomas	9	34	40.0	9.0	49.0	5.765			
Hugh Saunders	**34**	**131**	**144.0**	**32.0**	**176.0**	**5.374**			
Laurie Etheridge	**34**	**131**	**144.0**	**32.0**	**176.0**	**5.374**			
David Kennett	25	84	93.0	19.0	112.0	5.333			
Les Ott	3	8	7.0	3.0	10.0	5.000			
Geoff Maloney	32	99	82.0	29.0	111.0	4.485			
Barney Kennett	4	12	8.0	0.0	8.0	2.667			
Allen Emmett	2	4	0.0	0.0	0.0	0.000			

1975...1975...1975...1975...1975...1975

	M	R	Pts	BP	TPts	Ave	F	P	Total
Dave Morton	32	141	297.0	4.0	301.0	8.539	4		4
Barry Thomas	**36**	**169**	**317.0**	**13.0**	**330.0**	**7.811**	**1**	**1**	**2**
§Christer Löfqvist	12	51	84.0	13.0	97.0	7.608		1	1
§§Zenon Plech	4	18	29.0	3.0	32.0	7.111			
Laurie Etheridge	14	50	60.0	13.0	73.0	5.840		1	1
David Kennett	**36**	**130**	**128.0**	**24.0**	**152.0**	**4.677**			
Steve Lomas	34	120	113.0	25.0	138.0	4.600			
Mike Broadbank	**36**	**114**	**106.0**	**21.0**	**127.0**	**4.456**			
Ted Hubbard	28	85	72.0	10.0	82.0	3.859			
Les Ott	2	5	2.0	1.0	3.0	2.400			
§Kelvin Mullarkey	1	2	1.0	0.0	1.0	2.000			
§Trevor Barnwell	1	3	0.0	0.0	0.0	0.000			
Barney Kennett	1	3	0.0	0.0	0.0	0.000			
§§Timmy Joe Shepherd	1	2	0.0	0.0	0.0	0.000			

1976...1976...1976...1976...1976...1976

	M	R	Pts	BP	TPts	Ave	F	P	Total
Dave Morton	36	154	386.0	6.0	392.0	10.182	6	1	7
Zenon Plech	36	147	268.0	23.0	291.0	7.918	1	1	2
§Tony Featherstone	1	5	9.0	0.0	9.0	7.200			
Barry Thomas	39	165	239.0	36.0	275.0	6.667			
§Keith White	**40**	**165**	**231.0**	**30.0**	**261.0**	**6.327**		**1**	**1**
Jack Millen	1	2	2.0	1.0	3.0	6.000			
Laurie Etheridge	14	53	58.0	15.0	73.0	5.509			
§Trevor Hedge	24	82	83.0	27.0	110.0	5.366			
Steve Lomas	34	97	99.0	21.0	120.0	4.948			
Ted Hubbard	7	25	25.0	5.0	30.0	4.800			
David Kennett	**40**	**130**	**114.0**	**22.0**	**136.0**	**4.185**			
§Karl Fiala	2	4	2.0	1.0	3.0	3.000			

HACKNEY had two spells in the British League First Division. They dropped down into the National League in 1984 but then returned for one disastrous top flight season in 1987 when they blooded a promising teenager in Mark Loram.

1977...1977...1977...1977...1977...1977

	M	R	Pts	BP	TPts	Ave	F	P	Total
Dave Morton	5	24	49.0	3.0	52.0	8.667			
Keith White	**40**	**211**	**379.0**	**14.0**	**393.0**	**7.450**	**4**		**4**
Barry Thomas	39	209	295.0	45.0	340.0	6.507			
Ted Hubbard	8	29	37.0	9.0	46.0	6.345			
Karl Fiala	3	9	9.0	2.0	11.0	4.889			
§§Bent Rasmussen	29	117	123.0	14.0	137.0	4.684			
§§Bob Garrad	2	7	7.0	1.0	8.0	4.571			
§Vic Harding	19	63	55.0	11.0	66.0	4.190			
Tony Featherstone	38	114	95.0	21.0	116.0	4.070			
Laurie Etheridge	11	33	27.0	5.0	32.0	3.879			
§Alan Sage	1	4	3.0	0.0	3.0	3.000			
Steve Lomas	14	44	25.0	6.0	31.0	2.818			
§Robert Henry	1	2	1.0	0.0	1.0	2.000			
Trevor Hedge	2	5	1.0	1.0	2.0	1.600			

1978...1978...1978...1978...1978...1978

	M	R	Pts	BP	TPts	Ave	F	P	Total
§Finn Thomsen	30	135	246.0	14.0	260.0	7.704	1		1
Keith White	39	154	238.0	20.0	258.0	6.701		1	1
Barry Thomas	**40**	**176**	**246.0**	**42.0**	**288.0**	**6.545**		**1**	**1**
Vic Harding	39	163	223.0	33.0	256.0	6.282		1	1
§§Bo Petersen	34	142	190.0	28.0	218.0	6.141			
Bobby McNeil	27	91	100.0	20.0	120.0	5.275			
Ted Hubbard	15	55	63.0	9.0	72.0	5.236			
Laurie Etheridge	5	16	12.0	4.0	16.0	4.000			
§Malcolm Shakespeare	6	15	13.0	2.0	15.0	4.000			
Bent Rasmussen	10	34	24.0	7.0	31.0	3.647			
Bob Garrad	2	6	3.0	0.0	3.0	2.000			
§Billy Spiers	8	20	7.0	1.0	8.0	1.600			
Karl Fiala	2	5	2.0	0.0	2.0	1.600			
§Sean Willmott	2	8	3.0	0.0	3.0	1.500			

1979...1979...1979...1979...1979...1979

	M	R	Pts	BP	TPts	Ave	F	P	Total
Zenon Plech	20	90	170.0	5.0	175.0	7.778	2		2
Bo Petersen	32	141	252.0	21.0	273.0	7.745	2		2
Finn Thomsen	32	135	244.0	16.0	260.0	7.704	2	3	5
Barry Thomas	29	114	128.0	17.0	145.0	5.088			
§Ian Gledhill	1	4	4.0	1.0	5.0	5.000			
§Dave Gooderham	1	4	4.0	1.0	5.0	5.000			
§Kevin Smith	5	15	18.0	0.0	18.0	4.800			
Vic Harding	9	36	34.0	5.0	39.0	4.333			
Bobby McNeil	26	80	67.0	13.0	80.0	4.000			
§§Peter Carr	1	2	2.0	0.0	2.0	4.000			
Laurie Etheridge	1	2	2.0	0.0	2.0	4.000			
Sean Willmott	**34**	**122**	**96.0**	**20.0**	**116.0**	**3.803**			
Keith White	21	65	51.0	8.0	59.0	3.631			
§Bob Coles	1	5	4.0	0.0	4.0	3.200			
Karl Fiala	5	17	13.0	0.0	13.0	3.059			
Ted Hubbard	5	15	8.0	3.0	11.0	2.933			
§§Mark Bilner	2	4	1.0	0.0	1.0	1.000			
§§Simon Aindow	1	2	0.0	0.0	0.0	0.000			

VIC HARDING died after a horrifying crash with Eastbourne's Steve Weatherley during the final round of the Four Team Tournament at Waterden Road. As a mark of respect the Hawks withdrew from the following day's Speedway Star Cup match at Halifax.

1980...1980...1980...1980...1980...1980

	M	R	Pts	BP	TPts	Ave	F	P	Total
Bo Petersen	**34**	**148**	**365.0**	**15.0**	**380.0**	**10.270**	**10**	**2**	**12**
Ted Hubbard	1	4	6.0	3.0	9.0	9.000			
Zenon Plech	24	101	189.0	16.0	205.0	8.119		3	3
Finn Thomsen	32	135	244.0	18.0	262.0	7.763	1	1	2
Sean Willmott	29	105	122.0	22.0	144.0	5.486			
Barry Thomas	**34**	**121**	**137.0**	**23.0**	**160.0**	**5.289**			
§§Roman Jankowski	32	118	126.0	27.0	153.0	5.186		1	1
Keith White	33	98	106.0	15.0	121.0	4.939		1	1
Kelvin Mullarkey	1	5	5.0	0.0	5.0	4.000			
§§Andy Fines	1	2	1.0	1.0	2.0	4.000			
Kevin Smith	6	24	17.0	5.0	22.0	3.667			
§§Barry King	2	6	2.0	1.0	3.0	2.000			
Karl Fiala	1	2	1.0	0.0	1.0	2.000			

HACKNEY

1981...1981...1981...1981...1981...1981

	M	R	Pts	BP	TPts	Ave	F	P	Total
Bo Petersen	42	205	477.0	14.0	491.0	9.580	4		4
§Kevin Bowen	1	2	2.0	2.0	4.0	8.000			
Finn Thomsen	41	189	347.0	23.0	370.0	7.831			
Sean Willmott	**46**	**216**	**345.0**	**35.0**	**380.0**	**7.037**			
Zenon Plech	39	163	224.0	32.0	256.0	6.282			
Barry Thomas	20	79	88.0	21.0	109.0	5.519			
Kelvin Mullarkey	1	3	4.0	0.0	4.0	5.333			
Roman Jankowski	19	67	72.0	15.0	87.0	5.194			
§§Jens Rasmussen	3	8	6.0	4.0	10.0	5.000			
Bob Garrad	31	134	145.5	20.0	165.5	4.940			
§Andrzej Huszcza	13	49	42.0	10.0	52.0	4.245			
§Robbie Blackadder	1	2	2.0	0.0	2.0	4.000			
Ted Hubbard	19	57	43.0	8.0	51.0	3.579			
§Ian Clark	9	23	12.0	6.0	18.0	3.130			
Barry King	5	15	6.0	2.0	8.0	2.133			
Simon Aindow	13	34	9.0	0.0	9.0	1.059			
§§Martin Hagon	2	6	0.0	0.0	0.0	0.000			
Paul Hilton	1	2	0.0	0.0	0.0	0.000			
§§Cliff Ottewell	2	4	0.0	0.0	0.0	0.000			
§§Dale Rook	1	2	0.0	0.0	0.0	0.000			

1982...1982...1982...1982...1982...1982

	M	R	Pts	BP	TPts	Ave	F	P	Total
Bo Petersen	37	162	365.0	15.0	380.0	9.383	2	1	3
Barry Thomas	6	22	40.0	6.0	46.0	8.364			
Finn Thomsen	41	167	282.5	22.0	304.5	7.293	1	1	2
§John Titman	36	145	215.0	24.0	239.0	6.593			
§§Antonin Kasper [jun]	31	120	181.0	15.0	196.0	6.533			
Sean Willmott	40	169	204.0	48.0	252.0	5.964			
Jens Rasmussen	**44**	**162**	**191.0**	**33.0**	**224.0**	**5.531**			
Ian Clark	3	8	7.0	3.0	10.0	5.000			
Bob Garrad	10	31	26.0	5.0	31.0	4.000			
Martin Hagon	43	124	90.0	19.0	109.0	3.516			
§Paul Stead	1	2	1.0	0.0	1.0	2.000			
§§Marvyn Cox	1	3	0.0	0.0	0.0	0.000			

1983...1983...1983...1983...1983...1983

	M	R	Pts	BP	TPts	Ave	F	P	Total
§Paul Bosley	1	2	4.0	1.0	5.0	10.000			
Bo Petersen	30	128	254.0	17.0	271.0	8.469			
Finn Thomsen	42	189	340.0	35.0	375.0	7.937		2	2
Barry Thomas	6	13	18.0	6.0	24.0	7.385			
Jens Rasmussen	43	162	239.0	34.0	273.0	6.741			
Sean Willmott	43	191	252.0	49.0	301.0	6.304	1	1	2
John Titman	41	167	233.0	28.0	261.0	6.251			
Martin Hagon	**44**	**125**	**131.0**	**20.0**	**151.0**	**4.832**		**1**	**1**
Antonin Kasper [jun]	18	62	61.0	7.0	68.0	4.387			
Bob Garrad	12	27	21.0	8.0	29.0	4.296			
Marvyn Cox	4	14	11.0	2.0	13.0	3.714			
Ian Clark	2	5	2.0	2.0	4.0	3.200			

1987...1987...1987...1987...1987...1987

	M	R	Pts	BP	TPts	Ave	F	P	Total
§Simon Wigg	45	211	476.0	19.0	495.0	9.384	5	1	6
§§Roland Dannö	35	148	239.0	21.0	260.0	7.027			
§Andy Galvin	42	177	231.0	39.0	270.0	6.102			
§Martin Dugard	1	4	5.0	1.0	6.0	6.000			
§§Allan Johansen	42	165	207.0	24.0	231.0	5.600			
§Malcolm Simmons	25	97	121.0	10.0	131.0	5.402			
§Alan Mogridge	42	154	168.0	33.0	201.0	5.221			
Barry Thomas	15	50	54.0	11.0	65.0	5.200			
§§Mark Loram	45	129	133.0	31.0	164.0	5.085			
§Paul Whittaker	3	10	6.0	4.0	10.0	4.000			
§Trevor Banks	5	15	9.0	3.0	12.0	3.200			
§Glenn Doyle	1	3	2.0	0.0	2.0	2.667			
§§Randy Green	6	19	10.0	2.0	12.0	2.526			
§Keith Pritchard	1	2	1.0	0.0	1.0	2.000			
§§David Jackson	1	3	1.0	0.0	1.0	1.333			
§§Mike Fitzpatrick	3	6	1.0	0.0	1.0	0.667			
§§Jamie White	1	2	0.0	0.0	0.0	0.000			

SUPERAMA

1967	1 Barry Briggs	2 Bob Kilby	3 Nigel Boocock
1968	1 Anders Michanek	2 Reidar Eide	3 Terry Betts
1969	1 Barry Briggs	2 Ivan Mauger	3 Martin Ashby
1970	1 Ronnie Moore	2 Ivan Mauger	3 Sören Sjösten
1971	1 Ray Wilson	2 Barry Briggs	3 Ivan Mauger
1972	1 Ivan Mauger	2 Barry Briggs	3 Christer Löfqvist
1973	1 Anders Michanek	2 John Louis	3 Ivan Mauger
1974	1 John Louis	2 Terry Betts	3 Ivan Mauger
1975	1 Martin Ashby	2 Peter Collins	3 Ray Wilson
1976	1 Dave Jessup	2 John Louis	3 Ole Olsen
1977	1 Malcolm Simmons	2 Ole Olsen	3 Michael Lee
1978	1 Peter Collins	2 Mitch Shirra	3 Ole Olsen
1979	1 Ole Olsen	2 Alan Grahame	3 John Louis
1980	1 Dave Jessup	2 Erik Gundersen	3 Alan Grahame
1981	1 Phil Crump	2 Ole Olsen	3 Bruce Penhall

AUTUMN EXTRA TROPHY

1969	1 Trevor Hedge	2 Terry Betts	3 Jimmy Gooch

WARNERS HOLIDAY CHASE–CHAMPIONS CHASE

1973	1 Bengt Jansson	2 Martin Ashby	3 Anders Michanek
1974	1 John Louis	2 Dave Jessup	3 Tony Lomas
1975	1 Ole Olsen	2 Dave Jessup	3 Martin Ashby
1976	1 Ole Olsen	2 Dave Morton	3 Malcolm Simmons
1977	1 Ole Olsen	2 John Davis	3 Keith White
1978	1 Dave Jessup	2 Malcolm Simmons	3 Michael Lee
1979	1 Barry Thomas	2 Finn Thomsen	3 Gordon Kennett

GOLDEN JUBILEE OF BRITISH SPEEDWAY

1978	1 Michael Lee	2 Kelvin Mullarkey	3 Eric Broadbelt

VIC HARDING MEMORIAL TROPHY

1980	1 Bo Petersen	2 Erik Gundersen	3 Gordon Kennett
1981	1 Dave Jessup	2 John Louis	3 John Davis
1983	1 Finn Thomsen	2 Kenny Carter	3 Jens Rasmussen

LEN'S LONDON PRIDE...the 1982 Hawks, left to right, promoter Len Silver, Antonin Kasper, Jens Rasmussen, Finn Thomsen (on bike), Bob Garrad, Bo Petersen, John Titman and Sean Willmott

HALIFAX

1965...1965...1965...1965...1965...1965

	M	R	Pts	BP	TPts	Ave	F	P	Total
§§Eric Boocock	**34**	**136**	**327.0**	**15.0**	**342.0**	**10.059**	**6**	**2**	**8**
§§Dave Younghusband	33	132	309.0	15.0	324.0	9.818	4	1	5
§§Eric Boothroyd	**34**	**136**	**249.0**	**25.0**	**274.0**	**8.059**	**1**		**1**
§Tommy Roper	15	60	83.0	19.0	102.0	6.800		1	1
§§Bryan Elliott	33	132	158.0	39.0	197.0	5.970		2	2
§§Dennis Gavros	23	92	71.0	21.0	92.0	4.000			
§§Clive Hitch	18	72	46.0	14.0	60.0	3.333			
§§Bert Kingston	**34**	**136**	**99.0**	**14.0**	**113.0**	**3.324**			
§§Ray Day	7	28	16.0	3.0	19.0	2.714			
§Bob Jameson	7	28	9.0	2.0	11.0	1.571			

1966...1966...1966...1966...1966...1966

	M	R	Pts	BP	TPts	Ave	F	P	Total
Eric Boocock	38	161	402.0	19.0	421.0	10.460	11	6	17
Eric Boothroyd	38	164	345.0	36.0	381.0	9.293	3	3	6
Dave Younghusband	38	160	348.0	5.0	353.0	8.825	9	1	10
Tommy Roper	39	158	255.0	43.0	298.0	7.544		3	3
Bert Kingston	32	120	151.0	29.0	180.0	6.000			
Bob Jameson	**41**	**151**	**165.0**	**38.0**	**203.0**	**5.377**			
Dennis Gavros	40	134	136.0	31.0	167.0	4.985			
§§Greg Kentwell	6	14	11.0	3.0	14.0	4.000			
§§Maurie Robinson	6	12	6.0	1.0	7.0	2.333			
§§Ian Wilson	1	2	0.0	0.0	0.0	0.000			

1967...1967...1967...1967...1967...1967

	M	R	Pts	BP	TPts	Ave	F	P	Total
Eric Boocock	36	159	395.0	14.0	409.0	10.289	8	3	11
Dav e Younghusband	31	128	286.0	6.0	292.0	9.125	8	2	10
Eric Boothroyd	**37**	**153**	**299.0**	**23.0**	**322.0**	**8.418**	**1**		**1**
Dennis Gavros	36	136	168.0	36.0	204.0	6.000		1	1
§§John Woodcock	1	2	3.0	0.0	3.0	6.000			
Bert Kingston	23	77	77.0	15.0	92.0	4.779		1	1
Greg Kentwell	35	131	129.0	27.0	156.0	4.763			
Maurie Robinson	18	59	49.0	15.0	64.0	4.339			
Bob Jameson	26	84	69.0	18.0	87.0	4.143			
§§Les Bentzen	13	32	17.0	5.0	22.0	2.750			
§§Terry Lee	1	2	0.0	0.0	0.0	0.000			

1968...1968...1968...1968...1968...1968

	M	R	Pts	BP	TPts	Ave	F	P	Total
Eric Boocock	32	140	336.0	20.0	356.0	10.171	5	3	8
Dave Younghusband	33	145	304.0	16.0	320.0	8.828	3	5	8
Eric Boothroyd	**38**	**160**	**293.0**	**25.0**	**318.0**	**7.950**		**4**	**4**
§Alan Jay	16	60	84.0	10.0	94.0	6.267			
Greg Kentwell	**38**	**134**	**176.0**	**23.0**	**199.0**	**5.940**	**2**		**2**
Dennis Gavros	21	84	99.0	15.0	114.0	5.429	1	2	3
§§Les Sharpe	29	97	75.0	19.0	94.0	3.876			
Bob Jameson	**38**	**128**	**104.0**	**16.0**	**120.0**	**3.750**			
Maurie Robinson	15	39	30.0	6.0	36.0	3.692			
§§Ian Bottomley	3	7	2.0	0.0	2.0	1.143			
Terry Lee	1	2	0.0	0.0	0.0	0.000			

1969...1969...1969...1969...1969...1969

	M	R	Pts	BP	TPts	Ave	F	P	Total
Eric Boocock	**39**	**165**	**445.0**	**12.0**	**457.0**	**11.079**	**17**	**5**	**22**
Dave Younghusband	32	120	260.5	21.0	281.5	9.383	2	4	6
Greg Kentwell	34	122	225.0	9.0	234.0	7.672	4		4
Alan Jay	36	143	220.0	36.0	256.0	7.161	1	1	2
Dennis Gavros	38	145	191.0	35.0	226.0	6.234		1	1
Les Sharpe	35	123	133.0	31.0	164.0	5.333			
Terry Lee	9	27	22.0	5.0	27.0	4.000			
Bob Jameson	36	117	99.0	11.0	110.0	3.761			
§Arne Pander	3	7	4.0	1.0	5.0	2.857			
Ian Bottomley	2	6	1.0	0.0	1.0	0.667			
§Bob Tabet	1	2	0.0	0.0	0.0	0.000			

†Halifax's match at Oxford was declared void and the match points awarded to Halifax. Riders are credited with an appearance.

1970...1970...1970...1970...1970...1970

	M	R	Pts	BP	TPts	Ave	F	P	Total
Eric Boocock	36	154	392.0	14.0	406.0	10.545	11	4	15
Les Sharpe	18	77	145.0	13.0	158.0	8.208	1	4	5
Dave Younghusband	35	139	256.0	15.0	271.0	7.799	1	1	2
Alan Jay	**38**	**154**	**246.0**	**25.0**	**271.0**	**7.039**	**1**		**1**
§Colin McKee	36	131	161.0	34.0	195.0	5.954		1	1
Greg Kentwell	37	142	175.0	31.0	206.0	5.803			
§Paul O'Neal	3	11	11.0	4.0	15.0	5.455			
Terry Lee	**38**	**127**	**110.5**	**25.0**	**135.5**	**4.268**			
§§Dave Durham	2	6	3.0	1.0	4.0	2.667			
Bob Jameson	2	6	4.0	0.0	4.0	2.667			
§§Malcolm Mackay	5	14	5.0	0.0	5.0	1.429			

1971...1971...1971...1971...1971...1971

	M	R	Pts	BP	TPts	Ave	F	P	Total
Eric Boocock	38	175	431.0	15.0	446.0	10.194	7	1	8
Dave Younghusband	27	110	237.0	5.0	242.0	8.800	2		2
§Alan Knapkin	1	2	3.0	1.0	4.0	8.000			
Alan Jay	39	169	229.0	29.0	258.0	6.107	1		1
Greg Kentwell	36	147	197.0	27.0	224.0	6.095			
Paul O'Neal	**40**	**158**	**171.0**	**27.0**	**198.0**	**5.013**			
Malcolm Mackay	20	50	44.0	13.0	57.0	4.560			
§Mike Hiftle	19	61	52.0	16.0	68.0	4.459			
§Chris Bailey	28	83	73.0	15.0	88.0	4.241			
Terry Lee	21	65	55.0	6.0	61.0	3.754			
§Russ Dent	2	7	5.0	1.0	6.0	3.429			
Dave Durham	2	4	2.0	0.0	2.0	2.000			
§§John Lynch	1	2	1.0	0.0	1.0	2.000			
§Reg Wilson	1	3	1.0	0.0	1.0	1.333			

1972...1972...1972...1972...1972...1972

	M	R	Pts	BP	TPts	Ave	F	P	Total
Eric Boocock	34	154	389.0	10.0	399.0	10.364	8	1	9
§Göte Nordin	12	51	97.0	7.0	104.0	8.157			
§George Major	1	4	8.0	0.0	8.0	8.000			
Dave Younghusband	18	72	123.0	10.0	133.0	7.389	2	1	3
§Preben Rosenkilde	4	15	23.0	1.0	24.0	6.400			
Alan Jay	**36**	**150**	**200.0**	**20.0**	**220.0**	**5.867**			
Greg Kentwell	35	134	165.0	26.0	191.0	5.701			
Tommy Roper	14	53	63.0	8.0	71.0	5.358		1	1
§§John Titman	34	119	101.0	19.0	120.0	4.034			
§§Dave Kitchen	1	3	3.0	0.0	3.0	4.000			
§Robin Amundson	1	2	1.0	1.0	2.0	4.000			
Dennis Gavros	1	2	2.0	0.0	2.0	4.000			
Mike Hiftle	**36**	**129**	**97.0**	**18.0**	**115.0**	**3.566**			
Malcolm Mackay	15	51	39.0	6.0	45.0	3.529			
§Bobby McNeil	1	5	2.0	1.0	3.0	2.400			
Chris Bailey	1	3	1.0	0.0	1.0	1.333			
§§Alan Davison	1	2	0.0	0.0	0.0	0.000			

1973...1973...1973...1973...1973...1973

	M	R	Pts	BP	TPts	Ave	F	P	Total
Eric Boocock	21	95	239.0	6.0	245.0	10.316	3	2	5
§Frank Auffret	1	5	6.0	4.0	10.0	8.000			
John Titman	**38**	**167**	**274.0**	**15.0**	**289.0**	**6.922**			
§Charlie Monk	**38**	**154**	**222.0**	**21.0**	**243.0**	**6.312**			
§Bill Andrew	36	149	190.0	43.0	233.0	6.255		2	2
Mike Hiftle	26	103	124.0	21.0	145.0	5.631			
Les Sharpe	25	91	102.0	15.0	117.0	5.143			
§Carl Glover	1	5	6.0	0.0	6.0	4.800			
§Dave Gatenby	18	63	57.0	9.0	66.0	4.190			
Dennis Gavros	1	1	1.0	0.0	1.0	4.000			
§John Jackson	13	39	28.0	4.0	32.0	3.282			
§Per Hansen	13	36	16.0	5.0	21.0	2.333			
§§Jan Gravningen	10	23	5.0	2.0	7.0	1.217			
§§Jim Wells	1	2	0.0	0.0	0.0	0.000			

1974...1974...1974...1974...1974...1974

	M	R	Pts	BP	TPts	Ave	F	P	Total
Eric Boocock	26	112	251.0	18.0	269.0	9.607	2	1	3
§Rick France	26	104	183.0	12.0	195.0	7.500	1		1
Charlie Monk	20	80	130.0	14.0	144.0	7.200			
Graham Plant	30	121	197.0	15.0	212.0	7.008			
§§Henny Kroeze	31	134	155.0	27.0	182.0	5.433			
§§Ian Cartwright	4	14	17.0	2.0	19.0	5.429			
Dave Gatenby	32	119	119.0	24.0	143.0	4.807			
Mlke Hiftle	25	91	91.0	17.0	108.0	4.747			
§§Eddie Argall	3	8	6.0	2.0	8.0	4.000			
§Graham Drury	9	26	13.0	5.0	18.0	2.769			
John Jackson	7	26	16.0	1.0	17.0	2.615			
§Andy Cusworth	2	8	5.0	0.0	5.0	2.500			
§§Brian Havelock	1	4	2.0	0.0	2.0	2.000			

1975...1975...1975...1975...1975...1975

	M	R	Pts	BP	TPts	Ave	F	P	Total
§Chris Pusey	32	135	272.0	24.0	296.0	8.770			
Rick France	33	127	230.0	25.0	255.0	8.031	1	1	2
Graham Plant	36	142	248.0	21.0	269.0	7.577	3	1	4
Charlie Monk	39	157	248.0	31.0	279.0	7.108	2		2
Ian Cartwright	32	127	149.0	39.0	188.0	5.921			
Henny Kroeze	33	129	166.0	19.0	185.0	5.736	1		1
Dave Gatenby	22	72	69.0	19.0	88.0	4.889			
Mike Hiftle	21	63	56.0	12.0	68.0	4.317			
Andy Cusworth	7	23	17.0	5.0	22.0	3.826			
§Mick Newton	1	6	5.0	0.0	5.0	3.333			
John Jackson	4	10	7.0	1.0	8.0	3.200			
§Steve Finch	5	25	12.0	0.0	12.0	1.920			

HALIFAX

1976...1976...1976...1976...1976...1976

	M	R	Pts	BP	TPts	Ave	F	P	Total
Chris Pusey	**44**	**206**	**424.0**	**26.0**	**450.0**	**8.738**	**2**	**2**	**4**
Henny Kroeze	34	182	326.0	24.0	350.0	7.692	1		1
Graham Plant	22	91	166.5	4.0	170.5	7.495	2		2
§Keith Evans	1	2	3.0	0.0	3.0	6.000			
Charlie Monk	27	100	126.5	23.0	149.5	5.980			
Ian Cartwright	32	135	166.0	32.0	198.0	5.867		1	1
§§Mike Lohmann	39	147	152.0	30.0	182.0	4.952			
Andy Cusworth	31	104	95.0	21.0	116.0	4.462			
§Grahame Dawson	2	5	3.0	2.0	5.0	4.000			
Mick Newton	9	28	18.0	5.0	23.0	3.286			
Steve Finch	28	79	50.0	12.0	62.0	3.139			
§§Adam Olkiewicz	4	12	7.0	0.0	7.0	2.333			
§§Peter Adams	1	2	0.0	0.0	0.0	0.000			

1977...1977...1977...1977...1977...1977

	M	R	Pts	BP	TPts	Ave	F	P	Total
Chris Pusey	34	149	269.0	33.0	302.0	8.107	1	2	3
Henny Kroeze	11	51	91.0	3.0	94.0	7.373			
Mike Lohmann	31	135	210.0	31.0	241.0	7.141			
Ian Cartwright	**38**	**169**	**236.0**	**23.0**	**259.0**	**6.130**			
Graham Plant	33	122	176.0	10.0	186.0	6.098	3		3
§§Mick McKeon	20	77	72.0	21.0	93.0	4.831			
Steve Finch	17	59	61.0	10.0	71.0	4.814			
§§Tom Godal	33	101	78.0	18.0	96.0	3.802			
§§Sean Willmott	2	5	3.0	1.0	4.0	3.200			
§Geoff Pusey	10	27	14.0	5.0	19.0	2.815			
Mick Newton	2	6	2.0	1.0	3.0	2.000			
§Grahame Dawson	1	5	2.0	0.0	2.0	1.600			
§Geoff Swindells	2	5	1.0	0.0	1.0	0.800			

1978...1978...1978...1978...1978...1978

	M	R	Pts	BP	TPts	Ave	F	P	Total
Ian Cartwright	37	162	315.0	23.0	338.0	8.346	2	1	5
Mike Lohmann	36	154	292.5	18.0	310.5	8.065	1	2	4
Mitch Graham	27	95	158.0	19.0	177.0	7.453		1	1
Mick McKeon	33	133	179.0	27.0	206.0	6.195			
Eric Broadbelt	31	115	153.0	19.0	172.0	5.983			
Chris Pusey	33	118	144.0	28.0	172.0	5.831	1		2
§§Kenny Carter	16	60	68.0	13.0	81.0	5.400			
§Phil Collins	1	4	5.0	0.0	5.0	5.000			
§§Klaus Lohmann	32	114	112.0	25.0	137.0	4.807			
Tom Godal	1	3	2.0	1.0	3.0	4.000			
§Ian Robertson	1	6	3.0	1.0	4.0	2.667			
§Colin Ackroyd	1	3	1.0	0.0	1.0	1.333			
§§Alan Stansfield	2	4	1.0	0.0	1.0	1.000			
§§Mick Blaynee	1	3	0.0	0.0	0.0	0.000			
§§Martyn Cusworth	1	2	0.0	0.0	0.0	0.000			
§§Peter Wilson	1	2	0.0	0.0	0.0	0.000			
§Dave Allen	1	1	0.0	0.0	0.0	0.000			

1979...1979...1979...1979...1979...1979

	M	R	Pts	BP	TPts	Ave	F	P	Total
Ian Cartwright	36	148	320.0	11.0	331.0	8.946	4	2	6
Kenny Carter	35	150	272.0	33.0	305.0	8.133	3	1	4
Mike Lohmann	33	138	222.0	40.0	262.0	7.594	1	1	2
Tormod Langli	35	142	221.0	25.0	246.0	6.930			
Mick McKeon	38	149	225.0	31.0	256.0	6.872			
Klaus Lohmann	28	88	101.0	13.0	114.0	5.182			
§§Merv Janke	17	57	54.0	15.0	69.0	4.842			
§Steve Wilcock	28	90	77.5	18.0	95.5	4.244			
Alan Stansfield	3	9	6.0	1.0	7.0	3.111			
§§Paul Sheard	6	16	8.0	0.0	8.0	2.000			
Graham Plant	1	2	0.0	0.0	0.0	0.000			
Ian Robertson	1	2	0.0	0.0	0.0	0.000			

1980...1980...1980...1980...1980...1980

	M	R	Pts	BP	TPts	Ave	F	P	Total
Tormod Langli	1	4	8.0	1.0	9.0	9.000			
Kenny Carter	33	157	338.0	12.0	350.0	8.917	7		7
Ian Cartwright	32	154	284.0	21.0	305.0	7.922	1		1
Mick McKeon	29	126	172.0	34.0	206.0	6.540	1		1
Merv Janke	**34**	**142**	**187.0**	**28.0**	**215.0**	**6.056**	**1**		**1**
§Piotr Pyszny	28	109	133.0	25.0	158.0	5.798			
Craig Pendlebury	31	121	146.0	17.0	163.0	5.388			
§Les Sawyer	13	40	28.0	7.0	35.0	3.500			
§§Ian Westwell	4	14	12.0	0.0	12.0	3.429			
ALan Stansfield	8	21	12.0	3.0	15.0	2.857			
Paul Sheard	3	6	2.0	1.0	3.0	2.000			
§§Jorn Haugvaldstad	4	8	0.0	0.0	0.0	0.000			

1981...1981...1981...1981...1981...1981

	M	R	Pts	BP	TPts	Ave	F	P	Total
Kenny Carter	31	142	352.0	9.0	361.0	10.169	6	2	8
John Louis	**45**	**222**	**418.0**	**16.0**	**434.0**	**7.820**	**2**	**1**	**3**
Ian Cartwright	**45**	**220**	**405.0**	**24.0**	**429.0**	**7.800**	**2**		**2**
Craig Pendlebury	22	79	103.0	23.0	126.0	6.380			
Piotr Pyszny	21	80	83.0	23.0	106.0	5.300			
Doug Wyer	**45**	**193**	**232.0**	**17.0**	**249.0**	**5.161**			
§Dave Trownson	12	49	49.0	8.0	57.0	4.653			
§Martin Dixon	1	6	6.0	0.0	6.0	4.000			
§§Steve Baker	**45**	**151**	**110.0**	**24.0**	**134.0**	**3.550**			
§Billy Burton	2	6	4.0	1.0	5.0	3.333			
§§Rob Ashton	11	43	24.0	8.0	32.0	2.977			
§§Rob Woffinden	1	2	1.0	0.0	1.0	2.000			
§Trond Skretting	13	42	12.0	4.0	16.0	1.524			
§§Guy Wilson	3	10	2.0	1.0	3.0	1.200			
Ian Westwell	7	13	2.0	1.0	3.0	0.923			

1982...1982...1982...1982...1982...1982

	M	R	Pts	BP	TPts	Ave	F	P	Total
Kenny Carter	38	169	465.0	1.0	466.0	11.030	15		15
John Louis	42	176	315.0	16.0	331.0	7.523			
Ian Cartwright	37	145	237.0	27.0	264.0	7.283			
Merv Janke	20	72	100.0	15.0	115.0	6.389	1	1	2
§Martin Dixon	12	53	63.0	10.0	73.0	5.509			
Doug Wyer	**43**	**162**	**188.0**	**29.0**	**217.0**	**5.358**			
Steve Baker	**43**	**151**	**153.0**	**35.0**	**188.0**	**4.980**		**1**	**1**
Rob Ashton	**43**	**130**	**120.0**	**33.0**	**153.0**	**4.708**			
§§Mats Olsson	5	16	12.0	4.0	16.0	4.000			
§§Kenny Young	2	5	2.0	0.0	2.0	1.600			
§§Rob Tate	8	20	3.0	1.0	4.0	0.800			
§§Eric Monaghan	1	2	0.0	0.0	0.0	0.000			

1983...1983...1983...1983...1983...1983

	M	R	Pts	BP	TPts	Ave	F	P	Total
Kenny Carter	41	184	464.0	9.0	473.0	10.283	11	1	12
Steve Baker	38	154	222.0	32.0	254.0	6.597		1	1
Doug Wyer	**42**	**168**	**244.0**	**15.0**	**259.0**	**6.167**	**1**		**1**
Steve Finch	**42**	**165**	**209.0**	**29.0**	**238.0**	**5.770**			
Martin Dixon	40	163	189.0	39.0	228.0	5.595			
Craig Pendlebury	31	102	117.0	21.0	138.0	5.412			
§§Gianni Famari	19	59	43.0	9.0	52.0	3.525			
Eric Boocock	23	65	37.0	2.0	39.0	2.400			
§§Glen Parrott	2	7	4.0	0.0	4.0	2.286			
Mats Olsson	5	13	5.0	2.0	7.0	2.154			
§§Mark Gallagher	4	7	1.0	1.0	2.0	1.143			
§Peter Nightingale	1	3	0.0	0.0	0.0	0.000			

1984...1984...1984...1984...1984...1984

	M	R	Pts	BP	TPts	Ave	F	P	Total
Kenny Carter	8	33	75.0	1.0	76.0	9.212			
§Neil Evitts	37	173	293.0	29.0	322.0	7.445	1		1
Steve Baker	39	169	220.0	37.0	257.0	6.083	1		1
Eric Monaghan	**44**	**173**	**190.0**	**33.0**	**223.0**	**5.156**			
Doug Wyer	38	155	177.0	15.0	192.0	4.955			
Steve Finch	39	138	139.0	21.0	160.0	4.638			
Craig Pendlebury	18	55	51.0	12.0	63.0	4.582			
§§Kurt Hansen	25	84	64.0	10.0	74.0	3.524			
§§Gordon Whitaker	5	12	3.0	1.0	4.0	1.333			
§§Erik Knudsen	4	11	2.0	1.0	3.0	1.091			
§§Peter Clegg	2	5	0.0	0.0	0.0	0.000			

1985...1985...1985...1985...1985...1985

	M	R	Pts	BP	TPts	Ave	F	P	Total
Kenny Carter	27	120	301.0	3.0	304.0	10.133	8		8
Neil Evitts	41	168	277.0	28.0	305.0	7.262	2		2
§Larry Ross	**42**	**165**	**223.0**	**50.0**	**273.0**	**6.618**			
§Rod Hunter	**42**	**149**	**208.0**	**22.0**	**230.0**	**6.174**			
§Sean Willmott	40	142	164.0	28.0	192.0	5.408			
Eric Monaghan	**42**	**149**	**165.0**	**36.0**	**201.0**	**5.396**			
Kurt Hansen	33	107	107.0	31.0	138.0	5.159			
Doug Wyer	13	43	40.0	5.0	45.0	4.186			
Gordon Whitaker	1	3	0.0	0.0	0.0	0.000			

■ ***KENNY CARTER** broke his leg for a second time in little more than a year in the World Championship Inter Continental Final at Vetlanda, Sweden, to put him out of the 1985 title hunt. He was to ride in only one further World Championship meeting – a 1986 semi final – before he shot his wife Pam and then committed suicide in a tragedy that rocked speedway.*

HALIFAX

CHAMPIONS TROPHY

1965	1 Dave Younghusband	2 Eric Boocock	3 Barry Briggs

WHITAKER BREWERY TROPHY

1965	1 Eric Boocock	2 Dave Younghusband	3 Bob Andrews

DEWS TROPHY

1967	1 Jim Airey	2 Eric Boothroyd	3 Eric Boocock
1969	1 Jim Airey	2 Eric Boocock	3 Charlie Monk
1970	1 Eric Boocock	2 Anders Michanek	3 Ole Olsen
1971	1 Ole Olsen	2 Eric Boocock	3 Ronnie Moore
1972	1 Ole Olsen	2 Eric Boocock	3 Dave Younghusband
1973	1 Eric Boocock	2 Ray Wilson	3 John Boulger
1974	1 Ole Olsen	2 Chris Morton	3 Barry Thomas
1975	1 Phil Crump	2 Ole Olsen	3 Chris Pusey
1976	1 Graham Plant	2 Doug Wyer	3 Ray Wilson
1977	1 Dave Jessup	2 Chris Pusey	3 Bobby Beaton
1978	1 Alan Wilkinson	2 Ian Cartwright	3 John Titman
1979	1 Ian Cartwright	2 Craig Pendlebury	3 Hans Nielsen
1980	1 Kenny Carter	2 Zenon Plech	3 Finn Thomsen
1981	1 Kenny Carter	2 John Louis	3 Ian Cartwright

HALIFAX OPEN CHAMPIONSHIP

1968	1 Eric Boocock	2 Jim Airey	3 Dave Younghusband

DAIRY FESTIVAL TROPHY

1968	1 Dave Younghusband	2 Ole Olsen	3 Ivan Mauger
1969	1 Eric Boocock	2 Arnie Haley	3 Ole Olsen

AUTUMN CLASSIC

1971	1 Eric Boocock	2 Ray Wilson	3 George Hunter
1972	1 Reidar Eide	2 Ray Wilson	3 Eric Boocock
1973	1 Anders Michanek	2 Ray Wilson	3 John Boulger
1974	1 Rick France	2 Phil Crump	3 Tony Davey
1976	1 Reg Wilson	2 Mitch Graham	3 Bobby Beaton
1978	1 Reg Wilson	2 Ian Cartwright	3 Jim McMillan
1980	1 Kenny Carter	2 Les Collins	3 Ian Cartwright

SHAYTONA TROPHY

1972	1 John Jackson	2 Dave Morton	3 Arthur Browning
1975	1 Charlie Monk	2 Chris Pusey	3 John Davis
1979	1 Ian Cartwright	2 Reg Wilson	3 Kenny Carter

NORTHERN RIDERS' KNOCK-OUT TROPHY

1980	1 Kenny Carter	2 Ian Cartwright	3 Merv Janke

DUSTY HAIGH MEMORIAL TROPHY

1983	1 Shawn Moran	2 Doug Wyer	3 Steve Baker

HALIFAXOPOLIS

1984	1 Kenny Carter	2 Doug Wyer	3 Eric Monaghan

YORKSHIRE STAR TROPHY

1984	1 Neil Collins	2 Andy Campbell	3 Neil Evitts

Halifax moved to Bradford's Odsal Stadium at the beginning of the 1986 season after being founder members of the British League at The Shay, home ground of local Football League club.

HULL

HULL, who had spent three seasons in the Second Division, bought Coatbridge's First Division licence in the 1973-74 winter to bring senior League racing to their track at The Boulevard where they shared facilities with Hull Rugby League Football Club.

1974...1974...1974...1974...1974...1974

	M	R	Pts	BP	TPts	Ave	F	P	Total
§Jim McMillan	33	147	341.0	16.0	357.0	9.714	3	3	6
§Bobby Beaton	33	142	255.0	21.0	276.0	7.775	3		3
§Ricky Day	1	5	7.0	2.0	9.0	7.200			
§Mitch Graham	24	90	111.0	18.0	129.0	5.733			
§Tommy Roper	32	121	156.0	11.0	167.0	5.521	1	1	2
§§Tom Owen	16	49	52.0	11.0	63.0	5.143			
§Josef Angermuller	20	72	75.0	17.0	92.0	5.111		1	1
§§Robbie Gardner	**34**	**117**	**121.0**	**28.0**	**149.0**	**5.094**		**1**	**1**
§Tony Childs	2	9	9.0	1.0	10.0	4.444			
§§Steve Gresham	6	23	19.0	5.0	24.0	4.174			
§Dave Gifford	19	57	49.0	10.0	59.0	4.140			
§Alan Cowland	2	7	6.0	0.0	6.0	3.429			
§Paul Gachet	1	3	1.0	1.0	2.0	2.667			

1975...1975...1975...1975...1975...1975

	M	R	Pts	BP	TPts	Ave	F	P	Total
Jim McMillan	**36**	**168**	**395.0**	**12.0**	**407.0**	**9.690**	**2**		**2**
Joe Owen	13	62	100.0	13.0	113.0	7.290			
Bobby Beaton	**36**	**150**	**245.0**	**25.0**	**270.0**	**7.200**	**1**	**1**	**2**
§Tommy Johansson	11	44	61.0	12.0	73.0	6.636			
Mitch Graham	35	152	233.0	15.0	248.0	6.526			
§Dave Baugh	1	2	2.0	1.0	3.0	6.000			
§Graham Drury	4	20	25.0	2.0	27.0	5.400			
§Lou Sansom	9	36	38.0	9.0	47.0	5.222			
§Brian Havelock	9	28	27.0	9.0	36.0	5.143			
§Kym Amundson	13	40	43.0	8.0	51.0	5.100			
§Arthur Browning	1	5	4.0	1.0	5.0	4.000			
§§Ron Hendersen	1	5	3.0	2.0	5.0	4.000			
§Mike Sampson	1	3	3.0	0.0	3.0	4.000			
Alan Cowland	35	111	75.0	22.0	97.0	3.495			
§Robin Amundson	18	51	36.0	8.0	44.0	3.451			
§Colin Richardson	1	4	2.0	1.0	3.0	3.000			
§Steve Weatherley	1	3	2.0	0.0	2.0	2.667			
§Nigel Wasley	2	6	1.0	0.0	1.0	0.667			
§Sid Sheldrick	3	6	0.0	0.0	0.0	0.000			
§Alan Grahame	1	3	0.0	0.0	0.0	0.000			
§Pete Wigley	1	3	0.0	0.0	0.0	0.000			
§Keith Anderson	1	2	0.0	0.0	0.0	0.000			
§Phil Bass	1	2	0.0	0.0	0.0	0.000			
§Brian Clark	1	2	0.0	0.0	0.0	0.000			
Robbie Gardner	1	2	0.0	0.0	0.0	0.000			
§§Vic Harding	1	2	0.0	0.0	0.0	0.000			
§Robert Hollingworth	1	2	0.0	0.0	0.0	0.000			

1976...1976...1976...1976...1976...1976

	M	R	Pts	BP	TPts	Ave	F	P	Total
§Barry Briggs	34	136	293.0	11.0	304.0	8.941	1	1	2
Joe Owen	10	42	86.0	7.0	93.0	8.857	2		2
§Egon Müller	8	32	66.0	4.0	70.0	8.750			
Bobby Beaton	36	152	264.0	23.0	287.0	7.553			
Mitch Graham	**38**	**149**	**263.5**	**16.0**	**279.5**	**7.503**	**3**		**3**
§Frank Auffret	37	145	175.5	48.0	223.5	6.166			
§§Mike Curoso	33	116	136.0	40.0	176.0	6.069			
Graham Drury	37	134	154.0	43.0	197.0	5.881		1	1
§Tom Owen	6	26	32.0	5.0	37.0	5.692			
Brian Havelock	3	13	15.0	2.0	17.0	5.231			
§§Grahame Dawson	1	4	5.0	0.0	5.0	5.000			
§Phil Michelides	2	8	6.0	0.0	6.0	3.000			
§Colin Farquharson	1	3	1.0	1.0	2.0	2.667			
Ron Henderson	2	8	2.0	0.0	2.0	1.000			
§§Kazimierz Adamczak	1	2	0.0	0.0	0.0	0.000			

1977...1977...1977...1977...1977...1977

	M	R	Pts	BP	TPts	Ave	F	P	Total
Graham Drury	38	189	377.0	31.0	408.0	8.635	2	2	4
Bobby Beaton	36	184	346.5	22.0	368.5	8.011	2	2	4
Joe Owen	**40**	**190**	**281.0**	**33.0**	**314.0**	**6.611**			
Tom Owen	11	44	61.0	5.0	66.0	6.000			
Mike Curoso	33	125	139.0	31.0	170.0	5.440			
Frank Auffret	38	140	139.0	44.0	183.0	5.229			
Mitch Graham	37	133	130.0	26.0	156.0	4.692		1	1
§Alan Johns	1	3	2.0	1.0	3.0	4.000			
§Phil Kynman	9	21	11.0	5.0	16.0	3.048			
§§Paul Clements	1	3	1.0	0.0	1.0	1.333			
§§Neil Coddington	1	1	0.0	0.0	0.0	0.000			

1978...1978...1978...1978...1978...1978

	M	R	Pts	BP	TPts	Ave	F	P	Total
§Ivan Mauger	32	145	343.0	11.0	354.0	9.766	8	2	10
Joe Owen	16	64	125.0	20.0	145.0	9.063		3	3
Bobby Beaton	37	157	260.0	25.0	285.0	7.261	1		1
§§Kelly Moran	26	109	154.0	37.0	191.0	7.009			
Tom Owen	25	102	151.0	21.0	172.0	6.745			
§Robbie Blackadder	2	6	8.0	2.0	10.0	6.667			
Graham Drury	37	155	230.0	27.0	257.0	6.632			
Frank Auffret	**38**	**138**	**176.0**	**48.0**	**224.0**	**6.493**	**1**		**1**
§Phil Collins	2	9	10.0	4.0	14.0	6.222			
Phil Kynman	9	27	29.0	5.0	34.0	5.037			
§John Jackson	2	7	4.0	2.0	6.0	3.429			
§§Rod Hunter	8	24	10.0	4.0	14.0	2.333			
§§Pete Ellams	1	2	1.0	0.0	1.0	2.000			
§Ian Fletcher	1	3	0.0	0.0	0.0	0.000			
§§Mick Pither	1	3	0.0	0.0	0.0	0.000			
§John Barker	1	2	0.0	0.0	0.0	0.000			

HULL

1979...1979...1979...1979...1979...1979

	M	R	Pts	BP	TPts	Ave	F	P	Total
Ivan Mauger	36	148	372.0	12.0	384.0	10.378	9	2	11
Bobby Beaton	41	173	321.0	52.0	373.0	8.624		7	7
Kelly Moran	39	153	295.0	29.0	324.0	8.471	2	7	9
Joe Owen	41	170	319.0	38.0	357.0	8.400	4	2	6
Tom Owen	6	28	43.0	10.0	53.0	7.571			
§§Dennis Sigalos	40	163	271.0	33.0	304.0	7.460	2		2
Graham Drury	38	138	196.0	37.0	233.0	6.754		1	1
Frank Auffret	40	147	177.0	44.0	221.0	6.014			
§Louis Carr	2	7	7.0	1.0	8.0	4.571			
Robbie Blackadder	1	2	1.0	1.0	2.0	4.000			
Neil Coddington	2	5	3.0	1.0	4.0	3.200			
Nigel Close	2	11	5.0	1.0	6.0	2.182			
Rod Hunter	2	5	1.0	0.0	1.0	0.800			
Graeme Stapleton	2	6	1.0	0.0	1.0	0.667			
Brian Havelock	1	6	0.0	0.0	0.0	0.000			
John Williams	1	4	0.0	0.0	0.0	0.000			
§§Benny Rourke	1	3	0.0	0.0	0.0	0.000			
§§Graham Clifton	1	2	0.0	0.0	0.0	0.000			

For details of the Yorkshire TV Trophy see end of this section

1980...1980...1980...1980...1980...1980

	M	R	Pts	BP	TPts	Ave	F	P	Total
Dennis Sigalos	31	142	323.0	8.0	331.0	9.324	3		3
Ivan Mauger	25	96	210.0	6.0	216.0	9.000	5		5
Joe Owen	29	121	204.0	25.0	229.0	7.570	1	1	2
Bobby Beaton	25	103	153.0	19.0	172.0	6.680			
§§Shawn Moran	29	128	179.0	28.0	207.0	6.469		1	1
§Peter Carr	1	3	3.0	1.0	4.0	5.333			
Frank Auffret	35	140	152.0	29.0	181.0	5.171			
§John McNeill	6	19	19.0	4.0	23.0	4.842			
§§David Bargh	9	24	22.0	6.0	28.0	4.667			
Rod Hunter	10	37	37.0	6.0	43.0	4.649			
§§John Cook	35	118	107.0	16.0	123.0	4.169			
§Ian Gledhill	1	5	5.0	0.0	5.0	4.000			
Tom Owen	1	3	2.0	1.0	3.0	4.000			
§Robert Henry	1	2	2.0	0.0	2.0	4.000			
Robbie Blackadder	3	7	4.0	1.0	5.0	2.857			
§Nigel Crabtree	3	7	3.0	1.0	4.0	2.286			
Peter Ellams	1	2	1.0	0.0	1.0	2.000			
§Mike Fullerton	1	2	1.0	0.0	1.0	2.000			
§§Denzil Kent	1	3	0.0	0.0	0.0	0.000			
§§Carl Baldwin	1	2	0.0	0.0	0.0	0.000			
§Paul Embley	1	1	0.0	0.0	0.0	0.000			

1981...1981...1981...1981...1981...1981

	M	R	Pts	BP	TPts	Ave	F	P	Total
§Billy Sanders	38	183	404.0	16.0	420.0	9.180	4		4
Ivan Mauger	33	150	314.0	11.0	325.0	8.667	2	3	5
Joe Owen	47	222	376.0	28.0	404.0	7.279			
Bobby Beaton	**49**	**226**	**273.0**	**41.0**	**314.0**	**5.558**			
Graham Drury	40	170	186.0	42.0	228.0	5.365			
Frank Auffret	45	168	170.0	33.0	203.0	4.833			
Rod Hunter	5	18	18.0	3.0	21.0	4.667			
§John Eskildsen	39	136	124.0	33.0	157.0	4.618			
David Bargh	11	35	27.0	9.0	36.0	4.114			
§Alan Emerson	4	11	4.0	1.0	5.0	1.818			
§§Barry Simpson	2	7	2.0	0.0	2.0	1.143			
Paul McHale	4	8	1.0	0.0	1.0	0.500			
§Mark Collins	1	3	0.0	0.0	0.0	0.000			
§Andy Elliott	1	2	0.0	0.0	0.0	0.000			
§Mike Spink	1	2	0.0	0.0	0.0	0.000			

HEY BIG SPENDERS...Hull set a new transfer record when they paid Exeter £12,000 to sign Ivan Mauger shortly after he had won the fifth of his six World titles in 1977

IPSWICH

IPSWICH joined the First Division at the beginning of 1972 after successfully negotiating to take over the licence of West Ham who had been forced to withdraw because of doubts about the future of Custom House.

1972...1972...1972...1972...1972...1972

	M	R	Pts	BP	TPts	Ave	F	P	Total
§John Louis	**36**	**158**	**358.0**	**13.0**	**371.0**	**9.392**	**5**	**1**	**6**
§Olle Nygren	**36**	**144**	**262.0**	**18.0**	**280.0**	**7.778**	**2**	**1**	**3**
§Tommy Johansson	30	122	215.0	19.0	234.0	7.672		2	2
§Sandor Levai	33	138	213.0	27.0	240.0	6.957			
§Phil Crump	1	6	8.0	1.0	9.0	6.000			
§§Mick Hines	2	6	6.0	2.0	8.0	5.333			
§Peter Bailey	5	15	16.0	3.0	19.0	5.067			
§Alan Sage	**36**	**131**	**124.0**	**27.0**	**151.0**	**4.611**			
§§Billy Sanders	**36**	**122**	**116.0**	**20.0**	**136.0**	**4.459**			
§Tony Davey	22	69	63.0	12.0	75.0	4.348			
§Alan Bellham	1	2	2.0	0.0	2.0	4.000			
§Mike Lanham	3	8	2.0	1.0	3.0	1.500			
§Brian Foote	1	2	0.0	0.0	0.0	0.000			
§Ted Howgego	1	2	0.0	0.0	0.0	0.000			
§Clive Noy	1	2	0.0	0.0	0.0	0.000			

1973...1973...1973...1973...1973...1973

	M	R	Pts	BP	TPts	Ave	F	P	Total
John Louis	**36**	**155**	**373.0**	**17.0**	**390.0**	**10.065**	**5**	**5**	**10**
Tony Davey	**36**	**149**	**252.0**	**26.0**	**278.0**	**7.463**	**2**	**4**	**6**
Billy Sanders	28	106	172.0	25.0	197.0	7.434		2	2
Sandor Levai	31	127	179.0	20.0	199.0	6.268			
Mick Hines	33	113	143.0	29.0	172.0	6.088		1	1
Tommy Johansson	2	8	10.0	2.0	12.0	6.000			
Olle Nygren	35	128	171.0	17.0	188.0	5.875		1	1
Alan Sage	**36**	**131**	**147.0**	**39.0**	**186.0**	**5.679**			
Mike Lanham	2	5	3.0	2.0	5.0	4.000			
§Trevor Jones	1	3	3.0	0.0	3.0	4.000			
Ted Howgego	7	20	14.0	2.0	16.0	3.200			

1974...1974...1974...1974...1974...1974

	M	R	Pts	BP	TPts	Ave	F	P	Total
John Louis	40	172	448.0	16.0	464.0	10.791	10	3	13
Billy Sanders	**42**	**176**	**396.0**	**15.0**	**411.0**	**9.341**	**8**	**3**	**11**
§Phil Herne	1	5	9.0	2.0	11.0	8.800			
Tony Davey	41	176	349.0	16.0	365.0	8.295	1		1
Olle Nygren	26	97	120.0	30.0	150.0	6.186			
Mick Hines	40	146	171.0	31.0	202.0	5.534			
Mike Lanham	20	61	61.0	18.0	79.0	5.180			
Ted Howgego	16	50	54.0	6.0	60.0	4.800			
Trevor Jones	15	40	35.0	10.0	45.0	4.500			
Alan Sage	**42**	**151**	**130.0**	**32.0**	**162.0**	**4.291**			
§§Dave Gooderham	5	13	3.0	1.0	4.0	1.231			
§Ricky Day	1	3	0.0	0.0	0.0	0.000			
§Neil Middleditch	1	2	0.0	0.0	0.0	0.000			

1975...1975...1975...1975...1975...1975

	M	R	Pts	BP	TPts	Ave	F	P	Total
John Louis	**36**	**152**	**398.0**	**4.0**	**402.0**	**10.579**	**16**	**1**	**17**
Billy Sanders	**36**	**147**	**334.0**	**10.0**	**352.0**	**9.570**	**6**		**6**
Tony Davey	35	144	266.0	13.0	279.0	7.750			
Mike Lanham	**36**	**144**	**181.0**	**51.0**	**232.0**	**6.444**			
Mick Hines	**36**	**131**	**133.0**	**35.0**	**168.0**	**5.130**		**1**	**1**
Trevor Jones	**36**	**113**	**113.0**	**28.0**	**141.0**	**4.991**			
Ted Howgego	32	97	95.0	21.0	116.0	4.784			
Dave Gooderham	5	11	8.0	3.0	11.0	4.000			

1976...1976...1976...1976...1976...1976

	M	R	Pts	BP	TPts	Ave	F	P	Total
John Louis	35	144	389.0	10.0	399.0	11.083	12	6	18
Billy Sanders	43	183	413.0	19.0	432.0	9.443	1	1	2
Tony Davey	**44**	**186**	**377.0**	**12.0**	**389.0**	**8.366**	**5**	**1**	**6**
Mike Lanham	**44**	**181**	**223.0**	**58.0**	**281.0**	**6.210**			
Ted Howgego	43	154	180.0	46.0	226.0	5.870		1	1
Dave Gooderham	**44**	**159**	**195.0**	**32.0**	**227.0**	**5.711**			
§§Kevin Jolly	25	76	66.0	14.0	80.0	4.211			
Trevor Jones	13	32	23.0	8.0	31.0	3.875			
§§Andy Hines	9	27	20.0	5.0	25.0	3.704			
§§Colin Cook	1	3	2.0	0.0	2.0	2.667			

1977...1977...1977...1977...1977...1977

	M	R	Pts	BP	TPts	Ave	F	P	Total
Billy Sanders	37	152	372.0	15.0	387.0	10.184	8	3	11
John Louis	37	157	361.0	12.0	373.0	9.503	6	1	7
Tony Davey	37	148	277.0	18.0	295.0	7.973	5	1	6
Andy Hines	6	20	22.0	5.0	27.0	5.400			
Kevin Jolly	**38**	**132**	**137.0**	**36.0**	**173.0**	**5.242**			
Ted Howgego	**38**	**131**	**136.0**	**32.0**	**168.0**	**5.130**			
Mike Lanham	**38**	**142**	**149.0**	**31.0**	**180.0**	**5.070**			
Colin Cook	5	15	15.0	3.0	18.0	4.800			
Dave Gooderham	29	90	95.0	9.0	104.0	4.622			
§§Nigel Flatman	1	1	0.0	0.0	0.0	0.000			

1978...1978...1978...1978...1978...1978

	M	R	Pts	BP	TPts	Ave	F	P	Total
Billy Sanders	38	157	380.0	10.0	390.0	9.936	10	3	13
Tony Davey	**44**	**187**	**432.0**	**17.0**	**449.0**	**9.604**	**10**	**3**	**13**
John Louis	**44**	**183**	**389.0**	**24.0**	**413.0**	**9.027**	**6**	**3**	**9**
Kevin Jolly	43	179	254.0	51.0	305.0	6.816		1	1
§§Georg Hack	5	20	21.0	3.0	24.0	4.800			
Colin Cook	42	136	132.0	31.0	163.0	4.794			
Ted Howgego	27	89	78.0	20.0	98.0	4.404			
Mike Lanham	42	141	118.0	21.0	139.0	3.943			
Andy Hines	4	11	8.0	1.0	9.0	3.273			
§§Tim Hunt	7	22	14.0	3.0	17.0	3.091			
Nigel Flatman	2	6	4.0	0.0	4.0	2.667			
§§Kevin Teager	2	4	1.0	1.0	2.0	2.000			
§§Andy Hibbs	2	4	1.0	0.0	1.0	1.000			
§§Carl Squirrell	1	1	0.0	0.0	0.0	0.000			

1979...1979...1979...1979...1979...1979

	M	R	Pts	BP	TPts	Ave	F	P	Total
Ted Howgego	1	4	9.0	1.0	10.0	10.000			
John Louis	**36**	**169**	**383.0**	**11.0**	**394.0**	**9.325**	**1**	**2**	**3**
Billy Sanders	9	43	92.0	7.0	99.0	9.209		2	2
Tony Davey	9	33	57.0	5.0	62.0	7.515			
Kevin Jolly	25	112	196.0	12.0	208.0	7.429			
§Anders Michanek	8	36	54.0	12.0	66.0	7.333			
Mike Lanham	**36**	**171**	**238.0**	**37.0**	**275.0**	**6.433**			
Tim Hunt	21	80	85.0	14.0	99.0	4.950			
§Preben Eriksen	31	116	106.0	23.0	129.0	4.448			
Georg Hack	5	20	18.0	4.0	22.0	4.400			
Colin Cook	7	26	23.0	3.0	26.0	4.000			
§§Milan Spinka	13	50	40.0	7.0	47.0	3.760			
Andy Hines	13	41	27.0	8.0	35.0	3.415			
Nigel Flatman	11	33	24.0	3.0	27.0	3.273			
Kevin Teager	7	19	7.0	3.0	10.0	2.105			
§§Steve Bryenton	1	2	1.0	0.0	1.0	2.000			

1980...1980...1980...1980...1980...1980

	M	R	Pts	BP	TPts	Ave	F	P	Total
Kevin Jolly	11	44	85.0	15.0	100.0	9.091		2	2
John Louis	35	160	335.0	17.0	352.0	8.800	2	4	6
Billy Sanders	33	151	299.0	16.0	315.0	8.344	3	1	4
Mike Lanham	**36**	**156**	**243.0**	**38.0**	**281.0**	**7.205**		**2**	**2**
Preben Eriksen	34	142	199.0	27.0	226.0	6.366	1	2	3
Nigel Flatman	22	68	74.0	25.0	99.0	5.824			
Tim Hunt	**36**	**140**	**159.0**	**43.0**	**202.0**	**5.771**			
Tony Davey	17	54	66.0	6.0	72.0	5.333	1		1
Kevin Teager	6	15	13.0	5.0	18.0	4.800			
Andy Hines	13	39	40.0	6.0	46.0	4.718			
Andy Hibbs	2	5	5.0	0.0	5.0	4.000			

1981...1981...1981...1981...1981...1981

	M	R	Pts	BP	TPts	Ave	F	P	Total
§Dennis Sigalos	48	214	451.0	26.0	477.0	8.916	3		3
§John Cook	**52**	**227**	**445.0**	**45.0**	**490.0**	**8.634**	**3**	**1**	**4**
Kevin Jolly	**52**	**233**	**416.0**	**54.0**	**470.0**	**8.069**		**3**	**3**
Andy Hines	4	10	14.0	4.0	18.0	7.200			
Preben Eriksen	50	200	303.0	46.0	349.0	6.980		1	1
Mike Lanham	**52**	**224**	**325.0**	**46.0**	**371.0**	**6.625**		**1**	**1**
Nigel Flatman	**52**	**178**	**212.0**	**62.0**	**274.0**	**6.157**			
Tim Hunt	50	196	239.0	61.0	300.0	6.122			
Kevin Teager	1	2	1.0	0.0	1.0	2.000			

IPSWICH

WHEN Ipswich beat Birmingham in the 1981 Cup Final it was the first such meeting of two former Division Two clubs.

1982...1982...1982...1982...1982...1982

	M	R	Pts	BP	TPts	Ave	F	P	Total
Dennis Sigalos	39	166	403.0	16.0	419.0	10.096	6		6
Preben Eriksen	**48**	**211**	**402.0**	**48.0**	**450.0**	**8.531**		**3**	**3**
John Cook	26	106	188.0	18.0	206.0	7.774		1	1
Kevin Jolly	**48**	**196**	**303.0**	**39.0**	**342.0**	**6.980**			
§§Jeremy Doncaster	44	162	215.0	31.0	246.0	6.074		1	1
Nigel Flatman	**48**	**179**	**205.0**	**54.0**	**259.0**	**5.788**		**1**	**1**
Andy Hines	17	55	66.0	12.0	78.0	5.673			
Mike Lanham	37	114	125.0	22.0	147.0	5.158			
§Carl Baldwin	8	20	20.0	2.0	22.0	4.400			
Kevin Teager	5	12	6.0	3.0	9.0	3.000			
§§Roger Dickerson	1	2	0.0	0.0	0.0	0.000			

1983...1983...1983...1983...1983...1983

	M	R	Pts	BP	TPts	Ave	F	P	Total
Dennis Sigalos	46	198	522.0	10.0	532.0	10.747	17	1	18
Billy Sanders	47	195	461.0	12.0	473.0	9.703	7	3	10
Jeremy Doncaster	47	192	287.0	39.0	326.0	6.792			
Preben Eriksen	44	182	257.0	49.0	306.0	6.725		1	1
Georg Hack	4	17	21.0	4.0	25.0	5.882			
Nigel Flatman	45	165	158.0	41.0	199.0	4.824			
Andy Hines	45	164	165.0	20.0	185.0	4.512			
Carl Baldwin	16	48	40.0	9.0	49.0	4.083			
Andy Hibbs	24	68	56.0	13.0	69.0	4.059			
§§Andy Nightingale	11	23	1.0	1.0	2.0	0.348			
§§Lawrie Bloomfield	1	2	0.0	0.0	0.0	0.000			
Kevin Teager	1	2	0.0	0.0	0.0	0.000			

1984...1984...1984...1984...1984...1984

	M	R	Pts	BP	TPts	Ave	F	P	Total
Billy Sanders	50	208	460.0	44.0	504.0	9.692	4	5	9
John Cook	49	202	418.0	28.0	446.0	8.832	4	5	9
Jeremy Doncaster	**53**	**218**	**371.0**	**74.0**	**445.0**	**8.165**	**2**	**4**	**6**
§Kai Niemi	50	201	371.0	30.0	401.0	7.980	3	1	4
§Richard Knight	**53**	**216**	**337.0**	**64.0**	**401.0**	**7.426**	**1**	**2**	**3**
Nigel Flatman	**53**	**174**	**202.0**	**28.0**	**230.0**	**5.287**		**1**	**1**
§§Carl Blackbird	41	140	139.0	35.0	174.0	4.971			
§David Jackson	1	2	1.0	1.0	2.0	4.000			
Carl Baldwin	6	17	13.0	2.0	15.0	3.529			
§§Nick Doncaster	2	4	1.0	1.0	2.0	2.000			
§§Robbie Fuller	1	2	1.0	0.0	1.0	2.000			
Andy Nightingale	2	5	1.0	1.0	2.0	1.600			
Kevin Teager	1	3	1.0	0.0	1.0	1.333			
Lawrie Bloomfield	3	7	0.0	0.0	0.0	0.000			
§§Alan Farmer	1	2	0.0	0.0	0.0	0.000			

1985...1985...1985...1985...1985...1985

	M	R	Pts	BP	TPts	Ave	F	P	Total
Billy Sanders	4	17	48.0	1.0	49.0	11.529	3		3
John Cook	45	207	469.0	14.0	483.0	9.333	6	2	8
Jeremy Doncaster	49	229	475.0	47.0	522.0	9.118	1	3	4
Richard Knight	**50**	**226**	**410.0**	**49.0**	**459.0**	**8.124**	**1**	**1**	**2**
Kai Niemi	39	161	201.0	46.0	247.0	6.137			
§Louis Carr	10	38	49.0	3.0	52.0	5.474			
Dennis Sigalos	8	31	36.0	4.0	40.0	5.161			
Nigel Flatman	43	149	160.0	30.0	190.0	5.101			
Alan Farmer	**50**	**160**	**101.0**	**22.0**	**123.0**	**3.075**			
Andy Hines	15	47	24.0	4.0	28.0	2.383			
Robbie Fuller	3	9	2.0	2.0	4.0	1.778			
Kevin Teager	1	3	1.0	0.0	1.0	1.333			
Lawrie Bloomfield	5	15	4.0	0.0	4.0	1.067			
§Jamie Luckhurst	4	8	2.0	0.0	2.0	1.000			
§§Tony Hansford	1	3	0.0	0.0	0.0	0.000			

1986...1986...1986...1986...1986...1986

	M	R	Pts	BP	TPts	Ave	F	P	Total
Jeremy Doncaster	42	183	463.0	12.0	475.0	10.383	12	2	14
John Cook	4	16	34.0	0.0	34.0	8.500			
Kai Niemi	16	67	130.0	4.0	134.0	8.000			
§Dave Jessup	1	4	6.0	2.0	8.0	8.000			
Richard Knight	43	176	328.0	15.0	343.0	7.795	5	1	6
§Jens Rasmussen	39	149	170.0	42.0	212.0	5.691			
Colin Cook	1	3	3.0	1.0	4.0	5.333			
§Paul Stead	1	3	3.0	1.0	4.0	5.333			
§Alan Mogridge	5	16	15.0	6.0	21.0	5.250			
Nigel Flatman	2	7	6.0	3.0	9.0	5.143			
Louis Carr	**44**	**164**	**176.0**	**25.0**	**201.0**	**4.902**			
§Paul Woods	14	51	46.0	14.0	60.0	4.706			
§§Roman Matousek	5	21	22.0	2.0	24.0	4.571			
Robbie Fuller	**44**	**140**	**127.0**	**19.0**	**146.0**	**4.171**			
Alan Farmer	36	112	90.0	16.0	106.0	3.786			
§§Lee Potter	2	5	0.0	0.0	0.0	0.000			
§Ian Clark	1	3	0.0	0.0	0.0	0.000			

1987...1987...1987...1987...1987...1987

	M	R	Pts	BP	TPts	Ave	F	P	Total
Jeremy Doncaster	**46**	**204**	**477.0**	**16.0**	**493.0**	**9.667**	**8**	**4**	**12**
§Armando Castagna	41	177	321.0	33.0	354.0	8.000	1	1	2
Kai Niemi	45	186	328.0	26.0	354.0	7.613			
§Gerd Riss	38	152	203.0	40.0	243.0	6.395	1	1	2
Nigel Flatman	2	9	11.0	2.0	13.0	5.778			
David Blackburn	3	11	14.0	1.0	15.0	5.455			
Andy Hines	9	35	37.0	7.0	44.0	5.029			
Louis Carr	**46**	**158**	**146.0**	**35.0**	**181.0**	**4.582**			
§Martin Hagon	22	77	64.0	14.0	78.0	4.052			
§§Mark Blackbird	1	2	1.0	1.0	2.0	4.000			
Robbie Fuller	45	127	109.0	17.0	126.0	3.969			
Jamie Luckhurst	12	40	17.0	5.0	22.0	2.200			
Alan Farmer	2	6	2.0	0.0	2.0	1.333			
§§Mark Woods	2	3	0.0	0.0	0.0	0.000			
Lee Potter	1	2	0.0	0.0	0.0	0.000			

1988...1988...1988...1988...1988...1988

	M	R	Pts	BP	TPts	Ave	F	P	Total
Jeremy Doncaster	39	215	484.0	18.0	502.0	9.340	4	1	
§§Graham Jones	2	10	17.0	3.0	20.0	8.000			
§§Todd Wiltshire	1	1	1.0	1.0	2.0	8.000			
Kai Niemi	38	180	278.0	31.0	309.0	6.867			
Armando Castagna	31	151	237.0	18.0	255.0	6.755			
Kevin Jolly	2	7	10.0	1.0	11.0	6.286			
Carl Blackbird	37	179	246.0	31.0	277.0	6.190		1	
Gerd Riss	21	85	112.0	17.0	129.0	6.071			
§Gordon Kennett	1	4	4.0	2.0	6.0	6.000			
§Mick Poole	1	4	6.0	0.0	6.0	6.000			
§§Chris Louis	4	15	18.0	4.0	22.0	5.867			
§Kenny McKinna	4	20	25.0	4.0	29.0	5.800			
§Steve Regeling	15	60	71.0	10.0	81.0	5.400			
§Andy Galvin	5	24	27.0	4.0	31.0	5.167			
§Glenn Doyle	1	4	5.0	0.0	5.0	5.000			
§§Paolo Salvatelli	8	33	36.0	5.0	41.0	4.970			
§Melvyn Taylor	1	5	6.0	0.0	6.0	4.800			
Jens Rasmussen	1	4	3.0	0.0	3.0	3.000			
§Dean Standing	1	3	1.0	1.0	2.0	2.667			
Robbie Fuller	10	32	15.0	5.0	20.0	2.500			
Nigel Flatman	8	20	8.0	4.0	12.0	2.400			
§Mark Fiora	1	2	1.0	0.0	1.0	2.000			
Andy Hines	1	2	1.0	0.0	1.0	2.000			
§§Jon Cooper	32	102	28.0	9.0	37.0	1.451			
Lawrie Bloomfield	2	5	0.0	0.0	0.0	0.000			
§§Mark Jolly	2	4	0.0	0.0	0.0	0.000			
§§Mark Lindup	2	4	0.0	0.0	0.0	0.000			
§Troy Butler	1	2	0.0	0.0	0.0	0.000			
§§Shaun Nicholls	1	2	0.0	0.0	0.0	0.000			
§§Peter Simmons	1	2	0.0	0.0	0.0	0.000			

BILLY SANDERS first came to England from his native Sydney, Australia, as a 16-year-old to join them in their debut season in the British League. He made tremendous progress to become one of Australia's greatest ever riders, finishing third in the 1980 World Final and then, three years later, runner up to Egon Müller at Norden, Germany.

He was still at his peak when his body was found in his car, parked in woodland near Ipswich, on the morning of Tuesday, April 23, 1985. It later transpired he had been suffering from personal family problems.

IPSWICH

SEE YA...Billy Sanders looks back as he shows a clean pair of wheels to his rivals

GOLDEN SOVEREIGN

1973	1 Ole Olsen	2 Anders Michanek	3 John Louis
1974	1 Peter Collins	2 Billy Sanders	3 John Louis
1975	1 John Louis	2 Dave Jessup	3 Martin Ashby
1976	1 Billy Sanders	2 John Louis	3 Peter Collins
1977	1 Peter Collins	2 Gordon Kennett	3 John Davis
1978	1 Billy Sanders	2 John Louis	3 Kevin Jolly
1979	1 Billy Sanders	2 John Louis	3 Scott Autrey
1982	1 Melvyn Taylor	2 Preben Eriksen	3 Kenny Carter
1983	1 Hans Nielsen	2 Kenny Carter	3 Dennis Sigalos

WESLAKE CLASSIC (Marathon)

1979	1 Joe Owen	2 Phil Collins	3 Gary Guglielmi
1980	1 Billy Sanders	2 Bobby Schwartz	3 John Davis
1981	1 Phil Crump	2 Mike Lee	3 Dennis Sigalos
1982	1 Phil Crump	2 Bobby Schwartz	3 John Louis
1983	1 Kenny Carter	2 Dennis Sigalos	3 Phil Crump
1984	1 Phil Crump	2 Hans Nielsen	3 Melvyn Taylor
1985	1 Kenny Carter	2 Simon Wigg	3 Phil Crump
1986	1 Hans Nielsen	2 Lance King	3 Sam Ermolenko
1987	1 Jan O. Pedersen	2 Jeremy Doncaster	3 Paul Thorp
1989	1 Andy Galvin	2 Mark Loram	3 David Norris
1990	1 Craig Boyce	2 Alan Mogridge	3 Paul Whittaker

STAR OF ANGLIA

1979	1 John Louis	2 Ole Olsen	3 Hans Nielsen
1980	1 Ole Olsen	2 Hans Nielsen	3 Bruce Penhall

BRITISH SUPERSTARS TROPHY

1976	1 John Louis	2 Peter Collins	3 Phil Crump
1977	1 Ole Olsen	2 Michael Lee	3 Billy Sanders

METRO STADIUM TROPHY

1980	1 Bobby Schwartz	2 Bo Petersen	3 John Davis
1981	1 Kenny Carter	2 Bruce Penhall	3 Hans Nielsen, Bobby Schwartz
1982	1 Hans Nielsen	2 Bo Petersen	3 Preben Eriksen
1983	1 Dennis Sigalos	2 Bobby Schwartz	3 Hans Nielsen
1984	1 Hans Nielsen	2 Chris Morton	3 John Louis
1985	1 Hans Nielsen	2 Jeremy Doncaster	3 John Cook
1986	1 Hans Nielsen	2 Simon Wigg	3 Richard Knight
1987	1 Hans Nielsen	2 Jeremy Doncaster	3 Kai Niemi
1989	1 Chris Louis	2 Kenny McKinna	3 Mark Loram
1990	1 Chris Louis	2 Dean Standing	3 Steve Schofield

BILLY SANDERS MEMORIAL TROPHY

1988	1 Armando Castagna	2 Neil Evitts	3 Kevin Jolly

KING'S LYNN

KING'S LYNN entered the British League after running a series of open licence meetings throughoput 1965 and have been members of the First Division ever since.

1966...1966...1966...1966...1966...1966

	M	R	Pts	BP	Tpts	Ave	F	P	Total
§Terry Betts	36	159	369.0	5.0	374.0	9.409	5	1	6
§Peter Moore	34	152	343.0	6.0	349.0	9.184	9		9
§David Crane	36	153	225.0	12.0	237.0	6.196	1		1
§Alan Jay	10	40	43.0	6.0	49.0	4.900			
§Stan Stevens	36	132	130.0	26.0	156.0	4.727			
§§Alan Smith	10	32	24.0	6.0	30.0	3.750			
§Howdy Byford	35	115	81.0	21.0	102.0	3.548			
§John Mills	7	26	11.0	6.0	17.0	2.615			
§Ken Adams	21	66	35.0	8.0	43.0	2.606			
§§Vic Lonsdale	4	9	5.0	0.0	5.0	2.222			
§Cyril Crane	14	35	14.0	5.0	19.0	2.171			
§Ray Day	5	14	5.0	1.0	6.0	1.714			
§Doug Dearden	4	11	2.0	0.0	2.0	0.727			

ONLY four King's Lynn riders, turned up for their British League match at Edinburgh on Saturday, July 16, 1966, and they were forced to borrow three riders from the home track, including Glasgow's 1965 contracted rider Nils Paulsen who was in Scotland preparing for the British-Nordic Final of the World Championship. Ken Adams, David Crane and Cyril Crane were the missing riders.

1967...1967...1967...1967...1967...1967

	M	R	Pts	BP	TPts	Ave	F	P	Total
Terry Betts	37	185	441.5	9.0	450.5	9.741	8		8
Cyril Crane	1	2	3.0	1.0	4.0	8.000			
David Crane	32	150	287.0	11.0	298.0	7.947	3		3
§Clive Featherby	37	157	225.0	21.0	246.0	6.268			
Peter Moore	9	37	53.0	3.0	56.0	6.054			
§Howard Cole	21	86	94.0	29.0	123.0	5.721		1	1
§§Terje Henriksson	2	10	14.0	0.0	14.0	5.600			
§Ted Laessing	23	82	76.0	14.0	90.0	4.390			
§Stan Stevens	10	39	32.0	7.0	39.0	4.000			
John Mills	23	86	59.0	14.0	73.0	3.395			
§§Alan Bellham	3	6	4.0	1.0	5.0	3.333			
§§Doug White	24	66	35.0	10.0	45.0	2.727			
§John Poyser	8	22	12.0	3.0	15.0	2.727			
Howdy Byford	6	20	9.0	2.0	11.0	2.200			
§§Garry Middleton	5	15	6.0	1.0	7.0	1.867			
§§Graham Edmunds	6	18	4.0	2.0	6.0	1.333			

1968...1968...1968...1968...1968...1968

	M	R	Pts	BP	TPts	Ave	F	P	Total
Terry Betts	33	152	354.0	5.0	359.0	9.447	7		7
§Malcolm Simmons	18	80	179.0	9.0	188.0	9.400	4		4
Clive Featherby	31	123	167.0	21.0	188.0	6.114			0
Howard Cole	36	146	191.0	26.0	217.0	5.945			0
§Brian Davies	8	29	30.0	8.0	38.0	5.241			0
David Crane	33	124	140.0	18.0	158.0	5.097	1		1
§Geoff Penniket	35	117	106.0	21.0	127.0	4.342			0
Alan Bellham	36	110	102.0	16.0	118.0	4.291			0
§§Allan Brown	17	50	42.0	8.0	50.0	4.000			0

MALCOLM SIMMONS missed the last few months of the season after being sentenced to a six month prison sentence for motoring offences.
He initially appealed against the custodial sentence but this was dismissed.

1969...1969...1969...1969...1969...1969

	M	R	Pts	BP	TPts	Ave	F	P	Total
Terry Betts	**40**	**163**	**374.0**	**7.0**	**381.0**	**9.350**	**6**		**6**
Malcolm Simmons	**40**	**167**	**322.0**	**18.0**	**340.0**	**8.144**	**4**	**3**	**7**
Howard Cole	**40**	**159**	**275.0**	**32.0**	**307.0**	**7.723**	**1**	**3**	**4**
Clive Featherby	**40**	**156**	**219.0**	**32.0**	**251.0**	**6.436**			
Allan Brown	**40**	**131**	**126.0**	**36.0**	**162.0**	**4.947**			
Alan Bellham	**40**	**135**	**138.0**	**27.0**	**165.0**	**4.889**		**1**	**1**
§Peter Bradshaw	39	124	105.0	25.0	130.0	4.194			
Geoff Penniket	1	2	0.0	0.0	0.0	0.000			

1970...1970...1970...1970...1970...1970

	M	R	Pts	BP	TPts	Ave	F	P	Total
Terry Betts	32	141	321.0	4.0	325.0	9.220	4	1	5
Howard Cole	35	146	287.0	23.0	310.0	8.493	1	1	2
Malcolm Simmons	**37**	**162**	**291.0**	**16.0**	**307.0**	**7.580**	**1**	**1**	**2**
Allan Brown	24	91	94.0	21.0	115.0	5.055			
§Paul O'Neal	1	4	4.0	1.0	5.0	5.000			
Alan Bellham	**37**	**136**	**144.0**	**25.0**	**169.0**	**4.971**		**2**	**2**
Clive Featherby	29	90	77.0	23.0	100.0	4.444			
§§Ian Turner	23	78	67.0	18.0	85.0	4.359			
§§Arthur Price	9	25	22.0	5.0	27.0	4.320			
§§John Jackson	1	3	2.0	1.0	3.0	4.000			
David Crane	21	70	49.0	9.0	58.0	3.314			
§§Russell Osborne	2	4	2.0	1.0	3.0	3.000			

1971...1971...1971...1971...1971...1971

	M	R	Pts	BP	Tpts	Ave	F	P	Total
Terry Betts	37	170	399.0	10.0	409.0	9.624	2	1	3
Malcolm Simmons	38	174	389.5	11.5	401.0	9.218	1		1
Howard Cole	26	107	199.0	18.0	217.0	8.112	2		2
§Phil Crump	1	4	5.0	1.0	6.0	6.000			
Clive Featherby	33	113	117.0	38.0	155.0	5.487			
Ian Turner	19	75	76.5	20.0	96.5	5.147			
§Barry Crowson	27	95	96.0	21.0	117.0	4.926			
§§Bob Humphreys	**39**	**136**	**120.5**	**28.5**	**149.0**	**4.382**			
§§Jim Ryman	17	45	34.0	10.0	44.0	3.911			
Arthur Price	16	57	43.0	11.0	54.0	3.789			
§Ross Gilbertson	1	4	2.0	0.0	2.0	2.000			
§§Tony Featherstone	3	7	2.0	1.0	3.0	1.714			
§Gordon Kennett	1	4	1.0	0.0	1.0	1.000			
§Dai Evans	4	9	1.0	0.0	1.0	0.444			
§§Kelvin Mullarkey	2	3	0.0	0.0	0.0	0.000			
§Bruce Forrester	1	2	0.0	0.0	0.0	0.000			
§George Major	1	2	0.0	0.0	0.0	0.000			

1972...1972...1972...1972...1972...1972

	M	R	Pts	BP	TPts	Ave	F	P	Total
Terry Betts	35	158	402.0	13.0	415.0	10.506	7	2	9
Howard Cole	14	51	105.0	9.0	114.0	8.941	3	1	4
Malcolm Simmons	**37**	**167**	**329.0**	**20.0**	**349.0**	**8.359**	**2**	**2**	**4**
Phil Crump	19	80	128.0	18.0	146.0	7.300	1	2	3
Bob Humphreys	**37**	**152**	**204.0**	**32.0**	**236.0**	**6.211**			
Ian Turner	**37**	**142**	**162.0**	**41.0**	**203.0**	**5.718**			
Barry Crowson	36	128	153.0	22.0	175.0	5.469		1	1
Arthur Price	6	16	15.0	4.0	19.0	4.750			
Clive Featherby	8	24	19.0	7.0	26.0	4.333			
§Garry Flood	2	4	3.0	0.0	3.0	3.000			
John Jackson	2	5	3.0	0.0	3.0	2.400			
§§Ray Bales	1	3	1.0	0.0	1.0	1.333			
Tony Featherstone	2	4	1.0	0.0	1.0	1.000			
§§David Gagen	2	4	0.0	0.0	0.0	0.000			
§Jack Millen	1	3	0.0	0.0	0.0	0.000			
§Roger Mills	1	2	0.0	0.0	0.0	0.000			
§Bob Young	1	2	0.0	0.0	0.0	0.000			

1973...1973...1973...1973...1973...1973

	M	R	Pts	BP	TPts	Ave	F	P	Total
Malcolm Simmons	39	189	470.0	15.0	485.0	10.265	9	2	11
Terry Betts	35	168	407.0	11.0	418.0	9.952	6	1	7
Ian Turner	19	72	84.0	29.0	113.0	6.278		1	1
Bob Humphreys	**40**	**174**	**233.0**	**31.0**	**264.0**	**6.069**			
§§Brian Paddington	1	4	5.0	1.0	6.0	6.000			
§Dave Mills	2	10	11.0	3.0	14.0	5.600			
Barry Crowson	23	78	87.0	19.0	106.0	5.436			
§Eddie Reeves	32	124	125.0	41.0	166.0	5.355			
Arthur Price	31	117	118.0	23.0	141.0	4.821			
Ray Bales	17	51	57.0	3.0	60.0	4.706			
§§Richard Hellsén	4	16	11.0	7.0	18.0	4.500			
David Gagen	7	18	16.0	3.0	19.0	4.222			
Phil Crump	1	4	3.0	1.0	4.0	4.000			
§Ken McKinlay	2	5	4.0	0.0	4.0	3.200			
§§Dave Piddock	2	5	0.0	0.0	0.0	0.000			
§Mike Broadbank	1	2	0.0	0.0	0.0	0.000			
§§Brian Emery	1	2	0.0	0.0	0.0	0.000			
§§Wayne Forrest	1	2	0.0	0.0	0.0	0.000			
Kelvin Mullarkey	1	2	0.0	0.0	0.0	0.000			
§§Peter Taylor	1	1	0.0	0.0	0.0	0.000			

KING'S LYNN

1974...1974...1974...1974...1974...1974

	M	R	Pts	BP	TPts	Ave	F	P	Total
Terry Betts	32	133	334.0	9.0	343.0	10.316	3	3	6
Malcolm Simmons	**38**	**164**	**383.0**	**18.0**	**401.0**	**9.780**	**9**	**2**	**11**
§§Andy Sims	1	3	4.0	2.0	6.0	8.000			
Ian Turner	**38**	**146**	**207.0**	**25.0**	**232.0**	**6.356**	**1**		**1**
Barry Crowson	**38**	**144**	**175.0**	**34.0**	**209.0**	**5.806**			
Ray Bales	37	125	147.0	17.0	164.0	5.248			
Bob Humphreys	36	129	137.0	20.0	157.0	4.868			
Eddie Reeves	**38**	**130**	**123.0**	**32.0**	**155.0**	**4.769**			
David Gagen	5	12	9.0	1.0	10.0	3.333			
Kelvin Mullarkey	1	2	1.0	0.0	1.0	2.000			

1975...1975...1975...1975...1975...1975

	M	R	Pts	BP	TPts	Ave	F	P	Total
Terry Betts	32	143	306.0	11.0	317.0	8.867	2	1	3
Ian Turner	**36**	**153**	**255.0**	**31.0**	**286.0**	**7.477**			
§§Michael Lee	27	98	169.0	13.0	182.0	7.429	1	2	3
Trevor Hedge	**36**	**131**	**183.0**	**20.0**	**203.0**	**6.198**	**1**		**1**
Ray Bales	**36**	**140**	**175.0**	**27.0**	**202.0**	**5.771**			
Garry Middleton	23	82	110.0	8.0	118.0	5.756			
Olle Nygren	9	32	27.0	11.0	38.0	4.750			
David Gagen	14	43	37.0	12.0	49.0	4.558			
§§Jan Henningsen	15	54	42.0	13.0	55.0	4.074			
§§Billy Burton	6	16	14.0	2.0	16.0	4.000			
Eddie Reeves	6	13	11.0	2.0	13.0	4.000			
Andy Sims	3	7	6.0	1.0	7.0	4.000			
§Graham Drury	1	3	2.0	0.0	2.0	2.667			
§§Robert Hollingworth	1	5	2.0	1.0	3.0	2.400			
§§Peter E. Smith	1	2	0.0	0.0	0.0	0.000			

SIZZLING...Michael Lee had a tremendous debut season for the Stars as he doubled up with his Second Division career at Boston

1976...1976...1976...1976...1976...1976

	M	R	Pts	BP	TPts	Ave	F	P	Total
Terry Betts	**44**	**194**	**450.0**	**21.0**	**471.0**	**9.711**	**3**	**1**	**4**
Michael Lee	42	179	406.0	16.0	422.0	9.430	10		10
Ian Turner	**44**	**184**	**332.0**	**28.0**	**360.0**	**7.826**		**2**	**2**
David Gagen	43	162	191.0	39.0	230.0	5.679			
Ray Bales	43	160	165.0	51.0	216.0	5.400			
Richard Hellsén	25	85	79.0	18.0	97.0	4.565			
§§Billy Spiers	4	12	10.0	3.0	13.0	4.333			
Billy Burton	8	26	22.0	3.0	25.0	3.846			
Jan Henningsen	12	32	22.0	6.0	28.0	3.500			
§Adi Funk	34	90	53.0	10.0	63.0	2.800			
§§Stuart Cope	1	3	2.0	0.0	2.0	2.667			
Peter E. Smith	5	13	6.0	2.0	8.0	2.462			

1977...1977...1977...1977...1977...1977

	M	R	Pts	BP	TPts	Ave	F	P	Total
Michael Lee	44	196	511.0	8.0	5.0	129.0	13	2	15
Terry Betts	41	173	409.0	14.0	423.0	9.780	3	2	5
Ian Turner	**44**	**176**	**292.0**	**32.0**	**324.0**	**7.364**		**3**	**3**
David Gagen	**44**	**173**	**202.0**	**55.0**	**257.0**	**5.942**		**1**	**1**
Richard Hellsén	36	137	145.0	32.0	177.0	5.168		2	2
§Carl Glover	7	25	26.0	2.0	28.0	4.480			
§Paul Tyrer	34	113	98.0	17.0	115.0	4.071			
William Spiers	40	112	80.0	11.0	91.0	3.250			
Billy Burton	12	35	19.0	0.0	19.0	2.171			
Peter E. Smith	1	4	1.0	0.0	1.0	1.000			
§§Paul Gilbert	1	1	0.0	0.0	0.0	0.000			

1978...1978...1978...1978...1978...1978

	M	R	Pts	BP	TPts	Ave	F	P	Total
Michael Lee	38	165	414.0	8.0	422.0	10.230	9		9
Terry Betts	37	164	318.0	14.0	332.0	8.098	1	1	2
Ian Turner	**40**	**170**	**271.0**	**27.0**	**298.0**	**7.012**	**1**	**1**	**2**
Richard Hellsén	32	122	153.0	28.0	181.0	5.934			
David Gagen	26	105	126.0	26.0	152.0	5.790		1	1
Carl Glover	23	82	73.0	18.0	91.0	4.439			
Peter E . Smith	17	57	52.0	10.0	62.0	4.351			
Billy Spiers	8	28	19.0	6.0	25.0	3.571			
§§Frits Koppe	7	19	12.0	4.0	16.0	3.368			
§Bent Rasmussen	24	74	50.0	11.0	61.0	3.297			
§Melvyn Taylor	2	5	2.0	1.0	3.0	2.400			
§Derek Harrison	9	21	8.0	3.0	11.0	2.095			
§Phil Collins	1	4	2.0	0.0	2.0	2.000			
§§Piet Seur	2	3	1.0	0.0	1.0	1.333			
§§Andy Margarson	2	4	0.0	0.0	0.0	0.000			

TERRY BETTS, who won the first ever meeting at King's Lynn, finally left the club at the end of 1978 to join First Division rivals Reading.
He rode in nearly 500 official matches for the Stars, scoring more than 5,000 points and was, by far, the most popular rider in the club's history.

1979...1979...1979...1979...1979...1979

	M	R	Pts	BP	TPts	Ave	F	P	Total
Michael Lee	31	134	333.0	9.0	342.0	10.209	4	4	8
§Dave Jessup	33	137	325.0	8.0	333.0	9.723	8		8
Richard Hellsén	26	104	205.0	18.0	223.0	8.577		1	1
Ian Turner	34	137	170.0	35.0	205.0	5.985		1	1
§§Kevin Smith	1	6	7.0	1.0	8.0	5.333			
Bent Rasmussen	30	113	126.0	22.0	148.0	5.239			
§§Craig Featherby	3	10	12.0	1.0	13.0	5.200			
David Gagen	6	16	17.0	3.0	20.0	5.000			
Peter E. Smith	**36**	**136**	**139.0**	**30.0**	**169.0**	**4.971**		**1**	**1**
Derek Harrison	11	31	27.0	6.0	33.0	4.258			
§Bob Garrad	19	61	51.0	8.0	59.0	3.869			
§Dave Allen	3	10	9.0	0.0	9.0	3.600			
Robert Hollingworth	9	30	13.0	4.0	17.0	2.267			
§§Peter Wordingham	2	4	0.0	0.0	0.0	0.000			

1980...1980...1980...1980...1980...1980

	M	R	Pts	BP	TPts	Ave	F	P	Total
Dave Jessup	31	129	330.0	5.0	335.0	10.388	12	1	13
Michael Lee	30	129	318.0	9.0	327.0	10.140	9	3	12
Richard Hellsén	30	130	273.0	18.0	291.0	8.954	2	6	8
Melvyn Taylor	**34**	**141**	**186.0**	**44.0**	**230.0**	**6.525**		**1**	**1**
Bent Rasmussen	29	111	113.0	32.0	145.0	5.225		1	1
Peter E. Smith	33	106	92.0	21.0	113.0	4.264			
Derek Harrison	5	15	13.0	2.0	15.0	4.000			
§§Nigel Sparshott	29	89	74.0	11.0	85.0	3.820			
§§Dennis Mallett	5	15	12.0	1.0	13.0	3.467			
§Chris Turner	5	13	6.0	2.0	8.0	2.462			
§Peter Framingham	1	2	1.0	0.0	1.0	2.000			
Ian Turner	1	2	0.0	0.0	0.0	0.000			

1981...1981...1981...1981...1981...1981

	M	R	Pts	BP	TPts	Ave	F	P	Total
Michael Lee	37	181	459.0	7.0	466.0	10.298	11	1	12
Dave Jessup	44	216	496.5	20.0	516.5	9.565	9	2	11
Richard Hellsén	35	164	279.0	22.0	301.0	7.341		1	1
§Wayne Brown	1	5	8.0	1.0	9.0	7.200			
Melvyn Taylor	**48**	**221**	**323.0**	**60.0**	**383.0**	**6.932**		**2**	**2**
§Arthur Browning	1	3	5.0	0.0	5.0	6.667			
David Gagen	20	70	65.0	14.0	79.0	4.514			
Craig Featherby	42	148	129.0	24.0	153.0	4.135			
§§Robbie McGregor	1	2	1.0	1.0	2.0	4.000			
Nigel Sparshott	40	139	107.0	20.0	127.0	3.655			
§§Pierre Brannefors	21	74	50.5	8.0	58.5	3.162			
§Hasse Danielsson	13	50	32.0	5.0	37.0	2.960			
Dennis Mallett	12	33	16.0	4.0	20.0	2.424			
Peter Framingham	2	5	3.0	0.0	3.0	2.400			
§§Keven Dye	3	9	4.0	0.0	4.0	1.778			
Steve Lomas	2	6	2.0	0.0	2.0	1.333			
§§Chris Cole	1	2	0.0	0.0	0.0	0.000			

KING'S LYNN

1982...1982...1982...1982...1982...1982

	M	R	Pts	BP	TPts	Ave	F	P	Total
Michael Lee	35	155	364.0	10.0	374.0	9.652	6	1	7
§Billy Sanders	48	201	444.0	13.0	457.0	9.095	6	1	7
Richard Hellsén	44	193	296.0	42.0	338.0	7.005			
Melvyn Taylor	**50**	**204**	**265.0**	**30.0**	**295.0**	**5.784**			
§Colin Richardson	47	191	197.0	37.0	234.0	4.901			
Ron Hollingworth	31	96	83.0	14.0	97.0	4.042			
§§Mike Hintz	1	2	1.0	1.0	2.0	4.000			
§§Per Ove Gudmundsson	20	68	41.0	10.0	51.0	3.000			
Craig Featherby	3	11	8.0	0.0	8.0	2.909			
Keven Dye	11	25	9.0	2.0	11.0	1.760			
§§Jiri Hnidak	17	38	12.0	3.0	15.0	1.579			
Dennis Mallett	3	8	3.0	0.0	3.0	1.500			
Peter Framingham	8	18	2.0	0.0	2.0	0.444			
§§Paul Clarke	4	9	0.0	0.0	0.0	0.000			
Robbie MacGregor	2	4	0.0	0.0	0.0	0.000			
§§Ian Gutteridge	1	2	0.0	0.0	0.0	0.000			
§§Steve Payne	1	2	0.0	0.0	0.0	0.000			

MARTIN ROGERS, who spent seven years with the club as general manager before moving to Leicester in 1980, returned to King's Lynn as the new promoter. His first major signing was Gordon Kennett from Eastbourne (£15,000) and then he turned his attention to Halifax's John Louis who had asked for a move back to a track nearer his Ipswich home. He also brought in ex- World Finalist Colin Pratt as manager of a team that would go into action without the Poole-bound Michael Lee.

1983...1983...1983...1983...1983...1983

	M	R	Pts	BP	TPts	Ave	F	P	Total
§John Louis	**45**	**187**	**371.0**	**24.0**	**395.0**	**8.449**	**6**		**6**
§Gordon Kennett	**45**	**193**	**383.0**	**22.0**	**405.0**	**8.394**			
Richard Hellsén	**45**	**180**	**277.0**	**39.0**	**316.0**	**7.022**			
Colin Richardson	43	136	168.0	46.0	214.0	6.294		1	1
§Kevin Jolly	**45**	**168**	**208.0**	**53.0**	**261.0**	**6.214**		**1**	**1**
Melvyn Taylor	**45**	**168**	**219.0**	**31.0**	**250.0**	**5.952**			
§Keith Bloxsome	**45**	**134**	**141.0**	**35.0**	**176.0**	**5.254**			
Paul Clarke	2	6	2.0	1.0	3.0	2.000			

1984...1984...1984...1984...1984...1984

	M	R	Pts	BP	TPts	Ave	F	P	Total
John Louis	52	222	433.0	27.0	460.0	8.288	5	2	7
Dave Jessup	50	200	342.0	29.0	371.0	7.420	2	1	3
Richard Hellsén	**54**	**218**	**324.0**	**42.0**	**366.0**	**6.716**	**1**		**1**
Paul Clarke	1	3	3.0	2.0	5.0	6.667			
§Steve Regeling	**54**	**221**	**334.0**	**31.0**	**365.0**	**6.606**		**2**	**2**
Kevin Jolly	53	200	264.0	55.0	319.0	6.380		2	2
§Martin Dixon	52	193	234.0	58.0	292.0	6.052			
§Eric Monaghan	2	7	7.0	2.0	9.0	5.143			
Keith Bloxsome	**54**	**158**	**143.0**	**15.0**	**158.0**	**4.000**			
§Steve Bishop	1	3	0.0	0.0	0.0	0.000			

1985...1985...1985...1985...1985...1985

	M	R	Pts	BP	TPts	Ave	F	P	Total
Dave Jessup	**42**	**180**	**329.0**	**22.0**	**351.0**	**7.800**			
Michael Lee	19	80	140.0	4.0	144.0	7.200	2		2
Steve Regeling	38	148	198.0	31.0	229.0	6.189			
Kevin Jolly	38	149	190.0	38.0	228.0	6.121		1	1
§Mark Courtney	39	155	212.0	17.0	229.0	5.910			
Richard Hellsén	39	152	185.0	34.0	219.0	5.763			
§Steve Baker	6	19	16.0	7.0	23.0	4.842			
§Paul Woods	37	134	124.0	28.0	152.0	4.537			
Martin Dixon	4	12	7.0	5.0	12.0	4.000			
§§Armando Castagna	3	11	10.0	1.0	11.0	4.000			
§Ian Clark	2	7	6.0	0.0	6.0	3.429			
§§Mick Poole	10	30	20.0	3.0	23.0	3.067			
§§Gary Havelock	3	8	5.0	0.0	5.0	2.500			
§Ian Barney	1	3	1.0	0.0	1.0	1.333			
§Mike Spink	1	4	1.0	0.0	1.0	1.000			
Paul Clarke	1	4	0.0	0.0	0.0	0.000			
Keith Bloxsome	1	3	0.0	0.0	0.0	0.000			
§§Ray Morton	1	3	0.0	0.0	0.0	0.000			

1986...1986...1986...1986...1986...1986

	M	R	Pts	BP	TPts	Ave	F	P	Total
§Bobby Schwartz	36	173	377.0	15.0	392.0	9.064	1		1
Kevin Jolly	1	4	8.0	0.0	8.0	8.000			
Michael Lee	15	62	114.0	6.0	120.0	7.742	1		1
Malcolm Simmons	10	41	68.0	1.0	69.0	6.732	1		1
§Jamie Luckhurst	1	5	8.0	0.0	8.0	6.400			
§Andy Campbell	**42**	**171**	**203.0**	**27.0**	**230.0**	**5.380**			
§Einar Kyllingstad	32	114	114.0	26.0	140.0	4.912	1		1
Steve Regeling	37	137	136.0	25.0	161.0	4.701			
§Martin Goodwin	2	6	5.0	2.0	7.0	4.667			
§§Stephen Davies	40	134	134.0	20.0	154.0	4.597			
§Jens Rasmussen	4	15	13.0	4.0	17.0	4.533			
Ray Morton	18	58	47.0	14.0	61.0	4.207			
§Carl Baldwin	8	26	26.0	1.0	27.0	4.154			
§Les Collins	2	8	4.0	1.0	5.0	2.500			
§Kevin Hawkins	2	8	5.0	0.0	5.0	2.500			
§§Tony Pilotto	3	12	6.0	1.0	7.0	2.333			
§§Adrian Stevens	18	58	28.0	5.0	33.0	2.276			
§§John Stokes	6	18	4.0	1.0	5.0	1.111			
§§Alan Rivett	1	4	0.0	0.0	0.0	0.000			

MICHAEL LEE failed to turn up for a League Cup match at Sheffield on Thursday, June 12 – to begin a chain of events which saw him out of speedway until the beginning of 1991. He was initially suspended by the club, later transfer-listed and then announced that he did not want to ride speedway again, Because he never paid the statutory £50 Speedway Control Board fine he was subsequently suspended until 1993 although this was suspended at the end of 1990.

1987...1987...1987...1987...1987...1987

	M	R	Pts	BP	TPts	Ave	F	P	Total
§Richard Knight	45	206	417.0	13.0	430.0	8.350	3	1	4
§Bobby Schwartz	3	12	21.0	3.0	24.0	8.000			
§John Cook	8	36	55.0	5.0	60.0	6.667			
Steve Regeling	40	165	240.0	25.0	265.0	6.424			
Ian Barney	11	48	68.0	7.0	75.0	6.250			
Adrian Stevens	1	2	2.0	1.0	3.0	6.000			
Andy Campbell	45	179	220.0	19.0	239.0	5.341			
Stephen Davies	44	167	184.0	36.0	220.0	5.269			
Einar Kyllingstad	42	132	137.0	26.0	163.0	4.939			
Mick Poole	26	99	101.0	21.0	122.0	4.929		1	1
Ray Morton	43	124	116.0	20.0	136.0	4.387			
John Stokes	1	2	1.0	1.0	2.0	4.000			
§Glyn Taylor	1	2	1.0	1.0	2.0	4.000			
§§Jamie Habbin	1	4	2.0	1.0	3.0	3.000			
§§Stuart Thompson	2	4	1.0	0.0	1.0	1.000			
§Brett Saunders	1	3	0.0	0.0	0.0	0.000			
Martin Goodwin	1	2	0.0	0.0	0.0	0.000			

1988...1988...1988...1988...1988...1988

	M	R	Pts	BP	TPts	Ave	F	P	Total
§Lance King	38	186	328.5	32.0	360.5	7.753	2	1	3
§John Davis	39	192	354.0	15.0	369.0	7.688	2	1	3
Richard Knight	**44**	**210**	**356.0**	**35.0**	**391.0**	**7.448**			
§Bo Petersen	30	136	227.0	20.0	247.0	7.265		1	1
§Andy Hines	1	4	6.0	1.0	7.0	7.000			
§Steve Schofield	1	4	5.0	2.0	7.0	7.000			
§Armando dal Chiele	5	21	28.0	8.0	36.0	6.857			
Allan Johansen	38	161	219.0	36.0	255.0	6.335		1	1
Stephen Davies	27	116	153.0	28.0	181.0	6.241			
Gordon Kennett	6	24	32.0	4.0	36.0	6.000			
Steve Regeling	1	4	4.0	2.0	6.0	6.000			
Melvyn Taylor	3	13	15.0	1.0	16.0	4.923			
§Graham Jones	1	4	3.0	1.0	4.0	4.000			
Kevin Jolly	1	4	4.0	0.0	4.0	4.000			
Ray Morton	1	4	4.0	0.0	4.0	4.000			
Adrian Stevens	43	154	117.0	33.0	150.0	3.896			
§Kenny McKinna	2	6	4.0	1.0	5.0	3.333			
Les Collins	1	4	3.0	0.0	3.0	3.000			
Mick Poole	5	17	11.0	1.0	12.0	2.824			
§Mike Fitzpatrick	4	9	4.0	2.0	6.0	2.667			
Ian Barney	1	3	1.0	1.0	2.0	2.667			
§Bruce Cribb	1	3	1.0	1.0	2.0	2.667			
§Chris Louis	1	3	2.0	0.0	2.0	2.667			
§§Roger Horspool	9	25	6.0	2.0	8.0	1.280			
§Mark Loram	1	4	1.0	0.0	1.0	1.000			
§Dean Standing	1	3	0.0	0.0	0.0	0.000			
§Craig Hodgson	1	2	0.0	0.0	0.0	0.000			

KING'S LYNN

1989...1989...1989...1989...1989...1989

	M	R	Pts	BP	TPts	Ave	F	P	Total
Richard Knight	**34**	**180**	**326.0**	**26.0**	**352.0**	**7.822**			
Lance King	28	145	249.0	29.0	278.0	7.669			
John Davis	12	54	84.0	7.0	91.0	6.741	1		1
Allan Johansen	**34**	**165**	**240.0**	**34.0**	**274.0**	**6.642**			
Armando dal Chiele	20	74	79.0	14.0	93.0	5.027			
Stephen Davies	23	91	95.0	17.0	112.0	4.923			
§§Dennis Löfqvist	17	73	75.0	13.0	88.0	4.822			
Adrian Stevens	20	73	51.0	14.0	65.0	3.562			
§Paul Smith	14	51	36.0	4.0	40.0	3.137			
§§Tom Grinstead	1	2	1.0	0.0	1.0	2.000			
Roger Horspool	4	8	2.0	1.0	3.0	1.500			
§§Richard Pettman	1	3	0.0	0.0	0.0	0.000			

1990...19890...1990...1990...1990...1990

	M	R	Pts	BP	TPts	Ave	F	P	Total
Mark Loram	31	172	310.0	24.0	334.0	7.767			
Richard Knight	**34**	**175**	**301.0**	**22.0**	**323.0**	**7.383**		**1**	**1**
§§Henrik Gustafsson	5	22	36.0	3.0	39.0	7.091			
§Sean Wilson	4	17	25.0	4.0	29.0	6.824			
§Gary Hicks	17	61	78.0	12.0	90.0	5.902			
Dennis Löfqvist	**34**	**152**	**183.0**	**31.0**	**214.0**	**5.632**			
Stephen Davies	31	140	161.0	34.0	195.0	5.571			
§§Bohumil Brhel	32	141	172.0	16.0	188.0	5.333			
Tom Grinstead	3	8	2.0	1.0	3.0	1.500			
Roger Horspool	11	27	6.0	0.0	6.0	0.889			

PRIDE OF THE EAST

1966	1 Colin Pratt	2 Peter Moore	3 Mike Broadbank
1967	1 Bengt Larsson	2 Wayne Briggs	3 David Crane
1968	1 Terry Betts	2 Ken McKinlay	3 Martin Ashby
1969	1 Howard Cole	2 Ole Olsen	3 Terry Betts
1970	1 Ole Olsen	2 Nigel Boocock	3 Garry Middleton
1971	1 Ole Olsen	2 Christer Löfqvist	3 Terry Betts
1972	1 Ole Olsen	2 Ray Wilson	3 John Louis
1973	1 Anders Michanek	2 Ole Olsen	3 Zenon Plech
1974	1 Ivan Mauger	2 John Louis	3 Bob Valentine
1975	1 John Louis	2 Malcolm Simmons	3 Ivan Mauger
1976	1 Peter Collins	2 Michael Lee	3 Martin Ashby
1977	1 Ole Olsen	2 John Davis	3 Peter Collins
1978	1 Ole Olsen	2 Scott Autrey	3 Richard Hellsén
1979	1 Dave Jessup	2 Michael Lee	3 John Louis
1980	1 Dave Jessup	2 Larry Ross	3 Hans Nielsen
1981	1 Michael Lee	2 Dave Jessup	3 Malcolm Simmons
1982	1 Tommy Knudsen	2 Bobby Schwartz	3 Hans Nielsen
1983	1 Michael Lee	2 Hans Nielsen	3 John Louis
1984	1 Hans Nielsen	2 Kelvin Tatum	3 John Louis
1985	1 Jan Andersson	2 Kelvin Tatum	3 Dave Jessup
1986	1 Sam Ermolenko	2 Tommy Knudsen	3 Lance King
1987	1 Kelvin Tatum	2 Jimmy Nilsen	3 Erik Gundersen
1989	1 Martin Dugard	2 Hans Nielsen	3 Jimmy Nilsen
1990	1 Kelvin Tatum	2 Henrik Gustafsson	3 Ronnie Correy

KNIGHT-RIDER...one King's Lynn favourite, Michael Lee, presents a trophy to another, Richard Knight

LYNN TROPHY

1965	1 Terry Betts	2 David Crane	3 Geoff Pennikett

MALCOLM FLOOD MEMORIAL TROPHY

1965	1 Nigel Boocock	2 Mike Broadbank	3 Olle Nygren
1966	1 Ray Wilson	2 Norman Hunter	3 Nigel Boocock

NORFOLK CHAMPIONSHIP

1965	1 Barry Briggs	2 Olle Nygren	3 Clive Featherby
1967	1 Terry Betts	2 Trevor Hedge	3 Charlie Monk

SUPPORTERS CLUB TROPHY

1968	1 Ken McKinlay	2 Bengt Jansson	3 Howard Cole
1969	1 Ivan Mauger	2 Terry Betts	3 Bengt Larsson
1970	1 Barry Briggs	2 Terry Betts	3 John Boulger
1971	1 Terry Betts	2 Jim Airey	3 Howard Cole
1973	1 Ivan Mauger	2 Terry Betts	3 Bob Humphreys
1974	1 John Louis	2 Ivan Mauger	3 Terry Betts
1975	1 Dave Morton	2 Malcolm Simmons	3 John Louis
1976	1 Michael Lee	2 John Louis	3 Ray Wilson
1977	1 Malcolm Simmons	2 Billy Sanders	3 Dave Jessup
1978	1 Scott Autrey	2 Michael Lee	3 Gordon Kennett
1979	1 Scott Autrey	2 Jens Rasmussen	3 John Davis
1980	1 Bo Petersen	2 Dave Jessup	3 Gordon Kennett
1983	1 Dennis Sigalos	2 Kenny Carter	3 Neil Collins

CTS TROPHY

1968	1 Ken McKinlay	2 Sverre Harrfeldt	3 Terry Betts

DISCOTHEQUE TROPHY

1968	1 Ken McKinlay	2 Terry Betts	3 Olle Nygren

LITTLECHILD TROPHY

1972	1 Terry Betts	2 Ole Olsen	3 Dag Lovaas
1973	1 Ivan Mauger	2 Terry Betts	3 Barry Thomas
1974	1 Dave Jessup	2 Terry Betts	3 Jim McMillan
1975	1 Ole Olsen	2 Malcolm Simmons	3 Ray Wilson
1976	1 Malcolm Simmons	2 Michael Lee	3 Dave Jessup
1977	1 Terry Betts	2 Phil Crump	3 Michael Lee
1978	1 Ole Olsen	2 Michael Lee	3 Steve Bastable
1979	1 Bo Petersen	2 Gordon Kennett	3 Pete Smith
1980	1 Dave Jessup	2 Richard Hellsén	3 Mitch Shirra
1981	1 Jan Andersson	2 Dave Jessup	3 Steve Bastable
1982	1 Dennis Sigalos	2 Billy Sanders	3 Andy Grahame
1983	1 Les Collins	2 Michael Lee	3 Kevin Jolly
1985	1 Bobby Schwartz	2 Steve Regeling	3 Dave Jessup
1988	1 Hans Nielsen	2 Jeremy Doncaster	3 Kelly Moran

DOW DIAMOND TROPHY

1974	1 Peter Collins	2 Ole Olsen	3 Jim McMillan and Malcolm Simmons
1975	1 John Louis	2 Peter Collins	3 Reidar Eide

ESSO INVITATION TROPHY

1974	1 Phil Crump	2 Malcolm Simmons	3 Gordon Kennett
1975	1 Jim McMillan	2 Ole Olsen	3 Dag Lovaas

TERRY BETTS TESTIMONIAL

1975	1 Terry Betts	2 Malcolm Simmons	3 Dave Jessup and Peter Collins

DAILY MIRROR 500

1979	1 Michael Lee	2 Richard Hellsén	3 Billy Sanders

CHAMBER OF TRADE GALA

1985	1 Tommy Knudsen	2 Erik Gundersen	3 Bo Petersen

SIMMO SPECTACULAR

1987	1 Hans Nielsen	2 Kelvin Tatum	3 Jeremy Doncaster

BARUM TROPHY

1989	1 Hans Nielsen	2 Jeremy Doncaster	3 Erik Gundersen
1990	1 Jan O. Pedersen	2 Hans Nielsen	3 Richard Knight

GOLFERS WORLD CHALLENGE

1989	1 Hans Nielsen	2 Allan Johansen	3 Kelvin Tatum

LEICESTER

PROMOTERS Ron Wilson – who lived in the city – and Reg Fearman gambled on moving a highly-promising Long Eaton side that included new Great Britain star Ray Wilson, a talented young Swede Anders Michanek and Australian sensation John Boulger the short hop to Leicester. And it was an inspired move as the Leicester public, deprived of League racing since 1962, responded to the new look side and made the track one of the most successful in the country until its eventual closure – for all time – at the end of the 1983 season.

1968...1968...1968...1968...1968...1968

	M	R	Pts	BP	Tpts	Ave	F	P	Total
§Anders Michanek	28	117	292.0	6.0	298.0	10.188	2	1	3
§Ray Wilson	33	146	328.0	14.0	342.0	9.370	7	1	8
§John Boulger	35	148	226.0	19.0	245.0	6.622			
§George Major	35	135	167.0	19.0	186.0	5.511			
§John Hart	36	145	171.0	26.0	197.0	5.434			
§Norman Storer	36	132	148.0	25.0	173.0	5.242			
§Vic White	21	68	58.0	11.0	69.0	4.059			
§§Graham Plant	10	30	15.0	6.0	21.0	2.800			
§Roger Mills	17	45	20.0	9.0	29.0	2.578			
§§Dene Davies	1	2	0.0	0.0	0.0	0.000			
§Tom Leadbitter	1	2	0.0	0.0	0.0	0.000			

1969...1969...1969...1969...1969...1969

	M	R	Pts	BP	TPts	Ave	F	P	Total
Ray Wilson	**38**	**164**	**412.0**	**21.0**	**433.0**	**10.561**	**11**	**3**	**14**
John Boulger	**38**	**158**	**332.0**	**14.0**	**346.0**	**8.759**	**3**	**4**	**7**
John Hart	**38**	**139**	**195.0**	**30.0**	**225.0**	**6.475**			
Norman Storer	**38**	**133**	**181.0**	**33.0**	**214.0**	**6.436**	**1**		**1**
Graham Plant	**38**	**150**	**206.0**	**27.0**	**233.0**	**6.213**	**1**		**1**
§Malcolm Brown	**38**	**117**	**127.0**	**24.0**	**151.0**	**5.162**			
§§DeWayne Keeter	**38**	**127**	**125.0**	**30.0**	**155.0**	**4.882**		**1**	**1**

▲ *LEICESTER became the first team to go through an entire season without making a change with all seven riders being everpresent in each of the 36 British League matches and two Knock Out Cup clashes.*

1970...1970...1970...1970...1970...1970

	M	R	Pts	BP	TPts	Ave	F	P	Total
Ray Wilson	28	120	318.0	6.0	324.0	10.800	10	2	12
John Boulger	34	146	319.0	22.0	341.0	9.342	1	2	3
Graham Plant	37	156	246.0	16.0	262.0	6.718			
Norman Storer	**38**	**143**	**162.0**	**42.0**	**204.0**	**5.706**		**1**	**1**
John Hart	**38**	**146**	**149.0**	**35.0**	**184.0**	**5.041**			
Malcolm Brown	**38**	**127**	**129.0**	**22.0**	**151.0**	**4.756**	**1**		**1**
§Alan Cowland	**38**	**125**	**114.0**	**27.0**	**141.0**	**4.512**			
Tom Leadbitter	7	14	10.0	2.0	12.0	3.429			
§§Bruce Forrester	1	2	0.0	0.0	0.0	0.000			

1971...1971...1971...1971...1971...1971

	M	R	Pts	BP	TPts	Ave	F	P	Total
Ray Wilson	34	144	388.0	6.0	394.0	10.944	14	2	16
John Boulger	35	145	308.0	18.0	326.0	8.993	7	1	8
Graham Plant	36	138	287.0	16.0	303.0	8.783	2	2	4
§Gordon Kennett	1	5	6.0	1.0	7.0	5.600			
Alan Cowland	**37**	**136**	**157.0**	**29.0**	**186.0**	**5.471**			
Norman Storer	33	122	131.0	24.0	155.0	5.082			
Malcolm Brown	36	118	122.0	22.0	144.0	4.881			
§Malcolm Shakespeare	7	27	24.0	6.0	30.0	4.444			
Tom Leadbitter	34	114	78.0	17.0	95.0	3.333			
Bruce Forrester	1	4	1.0	1.0	2.0	2.000			
Tim Swales	1	2	0.0	0.0	0.0	0.000			

1972...1972...1972...1972...1972...1972

	M	R	Pts	BP	TPts	Ave	F	P	Total
Ray Wilson	33	142	350.0	10.0	360.0	10.141	8	1	9
John Boulger	33	134	306.0	11.0	317.0	9.463	5	2	7
§Dave Jessup	34	146	297.0	20.0	317.0	8.685		1	1
Norman Storer	31	114	120.0	22.0	142.0	4.982			
Malcolm Shakespeare	**35**	**134**	**127.0**	**34.0**	**161.0**	**4.806**			
§Geoff Ambrose	10	34	30.0	8.0	38.0	4.471			
Malcolm Brown	**35**	**116**	**96.0**	**18.0**	**114.0**	**3.931**			
Alan Cowland	25	75	50.0	11.0	61.0	3.253			
Bruce Forrester	1	3	1.0	0.0	1.0	1.333			
§Geoff Bouchard	2	4	1.0	0.0	1.0	1.000			
§Brian Foote	1	2	0.0	0.0	0.0	0.000			

1973...1973...1973...1973...1973...1973

	M	R	Pts	BP	TPts	Ave	F	P	Total
John Boulger	**36**	**155**	**384.0**	**13.0**	**397.0**	**10.245**	**9**	**3**	**12**
Ray Wilson	**36**	**155**	**352.0**	**14.0**	**366.0**	**9.445**	**4**	**3**	**7**
Dave Jessup	25	100	212.0	19.0	231.0	9.240	5	2	7
§Frank Auffret	5	20	31.0	3.0	34.0	6.800			
Malcolm Shakespeare	**36**	**147**	**180.0**	**33.0**	**213.0**	**5.796**			
Malcolm Brown	**36**	**125**	**125.0**	**21.0**	**146.0**	**4.672**		**1**	**1**
Norman Storer	35	119	109.0	21.0	130.0	4.370			
Bruce Forrester	8	19	16.0	4.0	20.0	4.211			
Geoff Ambrose	4	12	9.0	2.0	11.0	3.667			
Brian Foote	21	66	43.0	8.0	51.0	3.091			
§§Keith White	6	17	3.0	0.0	3.0	0.706			

KEITH WHITE retained the family link with the Lions – by making his debut and riding under the team managership of his father Vic who had been one of the old Leicester Hunters during their Provincial League days.

1974...1974...1974...1974...1974...1974

	M	R	Pts	BP	TPts	Ave	F	P	Total
Dave Jessup	32	142	336.0	7.0	343.0	9.662	6	1	7
Ray Wilson	32	137	307.0	13.0	320.0	9.343	6		6
Frank Auffret	32	125	176.0	26.0	202.0	6.464	1		1
§Mick Bell	**36**	**145**	**183.0**	**26.0**	**209.0**	**5.766**			
Norman Storer	35	130	145.0	31.0	176.0	5.415			
§Malcolm Ballard	6	22	16.0	7.0	23.0	4.182			
§§Tom Black	8	22	12.0	7.0	19.0	3.455			
Keith White	9	34	21.0	7.0	28.0	3.294			
§Alan Molyneux	1	3	1.0	1.0	2.0	2.667			
Malcolm Brown	29	87	49.0	8.0	57.0	2.621			
Bruce Forrester	1	3	1.0	0.0	1.0	1.333			
§§Bob Cooper	1	3	0.0	0.0	0.0	0.000			

1975...1975...1975...1975...1975...1975

	M	R	Pts	BP	TPts	Ave	F	P	Total
Dave Jessup	38	166	431.0	1.0	432.0	10.410	14		14
Ray Wilson	40	166	396.0	15.0	411.0	9.904	8	4	12
§§Ila Teromaa	34	132	154.0	41.0	195.0	5.909			
Frank Auffret	40	161	193.0	42.0	235.0	5.839			
§Tony Lomas	40	153	197.0	21.0	218.0	5.699			
Keith White	30	99	109.0	13.0	122.0	4.929			
§Doug Underwood	15	46	39.0	9.0	48.0	4.174			
Norman Storer	36	111	92.0	12.0	104.0	3.748			
Bob Cooper	2	4	1.0	1.0	2.0	2.000			
§Brian Leonard	5	16	2.0	0.0	2.0	0.500			
§§Andy Cowan	2	4	0.0	0.0	0.0	0.000			
§Phil Bass	1	3	0.0	0.0	0.0	0.000			
§§Alan Emerson	1	2	0.0	0.0	0.0	0.000			
§David Levings	1	2	0.0	0.0	0.0	0.000			

1976...1976...1976...1976...1976...1976

	M	R	Pts	BP	TPts	Ave	F	P	Total
Ray Wilson	18	78	180.0	1.0	181.0	9.282	2		2
§Eric Dugard	1	2	3.0	1.0	4.0	8.000			
§Reidar Eide	25	105	199.0	8.0	207.0	7.886	1		1
Ila Teromaa	34	144	266.0	17.0	283.0	7.861	1		1
§Tony Featherstone	4	12	15.0	2.0	17.0	5.667			
Tony Lomas	29	118	133.0	17.0	150.0	5.085		1	1
Doug Underwood	34	137	125.0	30.0	155.0	4.526			
Phil Bass	2	8	7.0	1.0	8.0	4.000			
Alan Emerson	10	28	20.0	7.0	27.0	3.857			
§Veli-Pekka Teromaa	21	48	33.0	4.0	37.0	3.083			
§§Ernst Bøgh	7	21	4.0	0.0	4.0	3.048			
§Vic Harding	2	4	2.0	1.0	3.0	3.000			
Brian Leonard	1	3	2.0	0.0	2.0	2.667			
§Hugh Saunders	1	3	1.0	1.0	2.0	2.667			
Grzegorz Szczepanik	28	86	40.0	11.0	51.0	2.372			
§John McNeill	1	4	0.0	0.0	0.0	0.000			
§§Mike Beaumont	1	3	0.0	0.0	0.0	0.000			
§Roy Carter	1	3	0.0	0.0	0.0	0.000			
Kevin Young	1	1	2.0	1.0	3.0	12.000			

LEICESTER

1977...1977...1977...1977...1977...1977

	M	R	Pts	BP	TPts	Ave	F	P	Total
Ila Teromaa	29	135	281.0	20.0	301.0	8.919			
John Boulger	32	143	286.0	15.0	301.0	8.420	2	1	3
§Garry Middleton	32	133	214.0	8.0	222.0	6.677	2		2
§Boleslaw Proch	10	48	56.0	6.0	62.0	5.167			
Pepe Teromaa	8	27	24.0	8.0	32.0	4.741			
Doug Underwood	27	98	81.0	18.0	99.0	4.041			
§Thomas Pettersson	13	48	42.0	6.0	48.0	4.000			
Ray Bales	**38**	**146**	**121.0**	**21.0**	**142.0**	**3.890**			
§Markku Helminen	18	60	43.0	7.0	50.0	3.333			
Reidar Eide	6	21	16.0	1.0	17.0	3.238			
§Chris Robins	8	27	16.0	4.0	20.0	2.963			
§Adi Funk	9	23	14.0	3.0	17.0	2.957			
§§Nigel Couzens	2	5	3.0	0.0	3.0	2.400			
John McNeill	10	28	14.0	2.0	16.0	2.286			
§§David Coles	3	8	2.0	1.0	3.0	1.500			
§§Les Leisk	3	8	2.0	0.0	2.0	1.000			

1978...1978...1978...1978...1978...1978

	M	R	Pts	BP	TPts	Ave	F	P	Total
John Titman	**40**	**175**	**375.0**	**16.0**	**391.0**	**8.937**	**6**	**2**	**8**
Ila Teromaa	37	159	324.0	22.0	346.0	8.704	4	1	5
John Boulger	39	164	326.0	19.0	345.0	8.415		1	1
§Phil Collins	3	13	21.0	5.0	26.0	8.000			
§Steve Wilcock	1	2	2.0	1.0	3.0	6.000			
§Tom Godal	36	132	139.0	24.0	163.0	4.939			
§§Jerzy Rembas	30	124	126.0	24.0	150.0	4.839			
John McNeill	30	101	94.0	19.0	113.0	4.475			
§Colin Meredith	8	24	21.0	5.0	26.0	4.333			
Ray Bales	4	12	12.0	1.0	13.0	4.333			
§§Neil Leeks	6	17	9.0	4.0	13.0	3.059			
Steve Finch	1	4	3.0	0.0	3.0	3.000			
David Coles	1	3	2.0	0.0	2.0	2.667			
§§Chris Sully	19	49	22.0	4.0	26.0	2.122			
§§Lars Ericsson	6	16	5.0	3.0	8.0	2.000			
Phil Bass	3	9	4.0	0.0	4.0	1.778			
Malcolm Shakespeare	1	3	0.0	0.0	0.0	0.000			
Nigel Couzens	1	2	0.0	0.0	0.0	0.000			
§Kevin Hawkins	1	2	0.0	0.0	0.0	0.000			

1979...1979...1979...1979...1979...1979

	M	R	Pts	BP	TPts	Ave	F	P	Total
John Titman	35	163	326	19	345.0	8.466	1	1	2
Ila Teromaa	20	79	115	9	124.0	6.278			
§Mike Farrell	33	144	190.5	25	215.5	5.986			
John Boulger	35	138	190	13	203.0	5.884			
§Colin Cook	30	126	149	21	170.0	5.397			
Tom Godal	29	101	106	14	120.0	4.752			
John McNeill	26	87	74	16	90.0	4.138			
§Chris Turner	12	39	28	6	34.0	3.487			
§Robert Henry	19	61	44	9	53.0	3.475			
Dave Gooderham	1	3	1	0	1.0	1.333			
David Coles	2	5	0	0	0.0	0.000			
Chris Sully	2	4	0	0	0.0	0.000			
§Terry Tulloch	1	2	0	0	0.0	0.000			

FORMER Speedway Star staff journalist Martin Rogers moves into Leicester as the new promoter after quitting as King's Lynn general manager. He says. "I'm going to have a go and see what can be done to re-establish the whole set-up. I will be looking for young, ambitious riders with the ability to improve."

1980...1980...1980...1980...1980...1980

	M	R	Pts	BP	TPts	Ave	F	P	Total
Les Collins	**36**	**168**	**350.0**	**25.0**	**375.0**	**8.929**	**3**	**2**	**5**
John Titman	31	129	227.0	21.0	248.0	7.690		1	1
§Rolf Gramstad	34	144	246.0	21.0	267.0	7.417	3		3
§§Andrzej Huszcza	23	89	127.0	15.0	142.0	6.382			
§§Mark Courtney	15	51	68.0	11.0	79.0	6.196			
§Bob Garrad	29	111	145.0	19.0	164.0	5.910			
Colin Cook	34	125	150.0	25.0	175.0	5.600			
§Ian Clark	**36**	**130**	**134.0**	**36.0**	**170.0**	**5.231**			
§§Steve Regeling	6	13	11.0	2.0	13.0	4.000			
§§Bernd Odermatt	6	14	5.0	1.0	6.0	1.714			
Chris Sully	1	2	0.0	0.0	0.0	0.000			
§§Phil Vance	1	2	0.0	0.0	0.0	0.000			

1981...1981...1981...1981...1981...1981

	M	R	Pts	BP	TPts	Ave	F	P	Total
Les Collins	47	233	476.0	22.0	498.0	8.549	1		1
John Titman	47	227	376.0	46.0	422.0	7.436	1	1	2
Rolf Gramstad	32	152	242.0	25.0	267.0	7.026			
Andrzej Huszcza	5	22	34.0	1.0	35.0	6.364			
§Phil Herne	43	173	232.0	26.0	258.0	5.965			
Colin Cook	46	200	247.5	44.0	291.5	5.830			
§Finn Jensen	32	134	170.0	23.0	193.0	5.761			
§Peter E. Smith	42	124	112.0	40.0	152.0	4.903			
Ian Clark	22	84	75.0	20.0	95.0	4.524			
Steve Regeling	12	30	20.0	5.0	25.0	3.333			
§Ian Gledhill	1	3	2.0	0.0	2.0	2.667			
§§Rob Lightfoot	1	4	1.0	1.0	2.0	2.000			
§§Mike Wilding	1	2	1.0	0.0	1.0	2.000			
Mark Courtney	2	5	2.0	0.0	2.0	1.600			

1982...1982...1982...1982...1982...1982

	M	R	Pts	BP	TPts	Ave	F	P	Total
Les Collins	**41**	**191**	**396.0**	**23.0**	**419.0**	**8.775**	**1**		**1**
§Neil Collins	38	172	277.0	27.0	304.0	7.070			
Phil Herne	36	139	199.0	24.0	223.0	6.417			
§Joe Owen	7	29	41.0	2.0	43.0	5.931			
Colin Cook	24	92	119.0	16.0	135.0	5.870			
Mark Courtney	**41**	**155**	**184.0**	**32.0**	**216.0**	**5.574**			
Finn Jensen	40	125	152.0	17.0	169.0	5.408			
Steve Regeling	39	147	154.0	33.0	187.0	5.088			
§Derek Harrison	4	12	14.0	1.0	15.0	5.000			
§§Mark Summerfield	2	6	0.0	0.0	0.0	0.000			

1983...1983...1983...1983...1983...1983

	M	R	Pts	BP	TPts	Ave	F	P	Total
Mark Courtney	35	152	311.0	18.0	329.0	8.658	1	2	3
Les Collins	41	180	353.0	18.0	371.0	8.244	5		5
Neil Collins	41	178	287.0	32.0	319.0	7.169		1	1
Joe Owen	6	20	26.0	5.0	31.0	6.200			
Steve Regeling	**42**	**168**	**208.0**	**42.0**	**250.0**	**5.952**		**1**	**1**
Finn Jensen	33	108	122.0	16.0	138.0	5.111			
Colin Cook	16	58	65.0	9.0	74.0	5.103			
§Mike Lanham	23	86	90.0	17.0	107.0	4.977			
§Eric Monaghan	7	21	18.0	7.0	25.0	4.762			
§§David Blackburn	1	2	1.0	1.0	2.0	4.000			
§Steen Mastrup	17	53	42.0	9.0	51.0	3.849			
Phil Herne	13	43	37.0	4.0	41.0	3.814			
Rob Lightfoot	6	15	5.0	1.0	6.0	1.600			
§Mark Fiora	2	4	1.0	0.0	1.0	1.000			
§§Chris Pidcock	1	3	0.0	0.0	0.0	0.000			
§Billy Burton	1	2	0.0	0.0	0.0	0.000			
§Paul Evitts	1	2	0.0	0.0	0.0	0.000			

LEICESTER were faced with a shock closure when their Blackbird Road Stadium was sold for housing redevelopment. The Leicester licence and rider assets were sold to Jackcity Limited, the company planning to bring British League First Division racing back to Exeter.

JUBILEE TROPHY

1977	1 Peter Collins	2 Ole Olsen	3 Finn Thomsen
1978	1 Scott Autrey	2 Malcolm Simmons	3 Peter Collins

FAREWELL TROPHY

1972	1 Ray Wilson	2 Terry Betts	3 Ronnie Moore
1973	1 John Boulger	2 Dave Jessup	3 John Titman

GOLDEN GAUNTLETS

1972	1 Ole Olsen	2 Dave Jessup	3 John Louis
1973	1 Anders Michanek	2 Terry Betts	3 John Boulger
1974	1 John Boulger	2 Sören Sjösten	3 Dave Jessup
1975	1 John Louis	2 Phil Crump	3 Dave Jessup
1976	1 Peter Collins	2 Michael Lee	3 Malcolm Simmons
1978	1 Scott Autrey	2 Dave Morton	3 Michael Lee
1979	1 Scott Autrey	2 Chris Morton	3 Bruce Penhall
1980	1 Scott Autrey	2 Peter Collins	3 Chris Morton
1981	1 Phil Crump	2 Kenny Carter	3 Les Collins
1982	1 Tommy Knudsen	2 Kenny Carter	3 Dennis Sigalos
1983	1 Kenny Carter	2 Hans Nielsen	3 Michael Lee

HOLIDAY CUP

1974	1 John Boulger	2 Terry Betts	3 Norman Hunter and Dave Jessup

LONG EATON

1965...1965...1965...1965...1965...1965

	M	R	Pts	BP	TPts	Ave	F	P	Total
§§Ray Cresp	22	88	180.0	13.0	193.0	8.773	3	1	
4§§Peter Moore	2	8	15.0	1.0	16.0	8.000			
§§Norman Storer	**37**	**148**	**261.0**	**13.0**	**274.0**	**7.405**	**2**		**2**
§§Ray Wilson	29	116	183.0	20.0	203.0	7.000			
§§Kid Bodie	33	132	200.0	29.0	229.0	6.939			
§Tommy Roper	2	8	9.0	2.0	11.0	5.500			
§§Ken Adams	**37**	**148**	**169.0**	**27.0**	**196.0**	**5.297**			
§§John Mills	13	52	52.0	10.0	62.0	4.769			
§§Terry Betts	2	8	9.0	0.0	9.0	4.500			
§Clive Hitch	18	72	60.0	15.0	75.0	4.167			
§Alan Jones	1	4	3.0	1.0	4.0	4.000			
§§Ron Sharp	13	52	30.0	8.0	38.0	2.923			
§§Bob Jameson	6	24	12.0	5.0	17.0	2.833			
§§Tich Read	1	4	2.0	0.0	2.0	2.000			
§§Rim Malskaitis	26	104	37.0	8.0	45.0	1.731			
§John Ellis	1	4	1.0	0.0	1.0	1.000			
§§Dai Evans	1	4	1.0	0.0	1.0	1.000			
§§Peter Wrathall	4	16	2.0	1.0	3.0	0.750			
§§Ian Champion	1	2	0.0	0.0	0.0	0.000			
§§Peter Harris	1	2	0.0	0.0	0.0	0.000			
§§Eric Minall	3	6	0.0	0.0	0.0	0.000			
§§Red Monteith	1	2	0.0	0.0	0.0	0.000			

1966...1966...1966...1966...1966...1966

	M	R	Pts	BP	TPts	Ave	F	P	Total
§§Ove Fundin	5	22	53.0	0.0	53.0	9.636	2		2
Ray Wilson	**38**	**170**	**358.0**	**9.0**	**367.0**	**8.635**	**5**		**5**
§§Leif Enecrona	9	37	65.0	6.0	71.0	7.676			
Ray Cresp	**38**	**162**	**245.0**	**27.0**	**272.0**	**6.716**			
Norman Storer	35	133	141.0	30.0	171.0	5.143			
§Vic White	**38**	**140**	**156.0**	**18.0**	**174.0**	**4.971**			
§§Dennis Newton	**38**	**142**	**151.0**	**25.0**	**176.0**	**4.958**			
John Mills	17	45	37.0	13.0	50.0	4.444			
§§Nils Ringstrom	9	33	32.0	2.0	34.0	4.121			
§Greg Kentwell	21	56	42.0	14.0	56.0	4.000			
§§Barry Bostock	1	2	1.0	0.0	1.0	2.000			
Ian Champion	5	9	3.0	0.0	3.0	1.333			
Peter Wrathall	2	4	0.0	0.0	0.0	0.000			

AN ODD feature of the 1966 Long Eaton side – that no-one could have known at the time – was that it included a World Champion Ove Fundin (photo below in the Archers' colours); a future World Final referee Nils Ringstrom; and a World Final announcer-to-be in a third Swede at Station Road, Leif Enecrona!

WHEN South Australian John Boulger first arrived at Station Road at the beginning of 1967 he was left out of the side for the opening home match.

But he quickly proved his worth – with a paid maximum in his home debut against Exeter on Tuesday, April 11, one of the rare occasions when a debutant celebrated his first appearance with an unbeaten performance!

That first night paid maximum was, oddly enough, the only one of his first season in the British League.

1967...1967...1967...1967...1967...1967

	M	R	Pts	BP	TPts	Ave	F	P	Total
Ray Wilson	38	176	455.0	4.0	459.0	10.432	9	2	11
§§Anders Michanek	31	140	298.0	8.0	306.0	8.743	4	1	5
§Jim Lightfoot	20	80	129.0	13.0	142.0	7.100	1	2	3
§§John Boulger	36	158	198.0	30.0	228.0	5.772		1	1
Norman Storer	**39**	**160**	**164.0**	**29.0**	**193.0**	**4.825**			
Vic White	37	142	119.0	22.0	141.0	3.972			
§John Poyser	26	74	42.0	12.0	54.0	2.919			
Ian Champion	23	50	28.0	6.0	34.0	2.720			
§Les Bentzen	5	16	7.0	2.0	9.0	2.250			
§Gordon McGregor	4	13	4.0	0.0	4.0	1.231			
§Tom Leadbitter	4	8	0.0	0.0	0.0	0.000			
§§Roger Mills	1	1	0.0	0.0	0.0	0.000			

NEWCASTLE

NEWCASTLE retained their 1964 National League winning side – with the exception of Bill Andrew – for their first season in the British League but suffered a mortal blow when Ivan Mauger broke his ankle at Wolverhampton in the opening match of the new era.

1965...1965...1965...1965...1965...1965

	M	R	Pts	BP	TPts	Ave	F	P	Total
§§Brian Brett	33	132	280.0	11.0	291.0	8.818	6		6
§§Ivan Mauger	20	80	161.0	12.0	173.0	8.650		2	2
§§Peter Kelly	**35**	**140**	**249.0**	**23.0**	**272.0**	**7.771**	**2**	**1**	**3**
§§Brian Craven	34	136	223.0	19.0	242.0	7.118	3		3
§§Mike Watkin	**35**	**140**	**174.0**	**30.0**	**204.0**	**5.829**	**2**		**2**
§§Ken Sharples	25	100	104.0	23.0	127.0	5.080			
§§Russ Dent	30	120	124.0	24.0	148.0	4.933			
§§Goog Allan	11	44	46.0	7.0	53.0	4.818			
§§Jack Winstanley	2	8	7.0	1.0	8.0	4.000			
§§Allan Butterfield	1	4	3.0	1.0	4.0	4.000			
§§Maurie Robinson	1	4	2.0	1.0	3.0	3.000			
§§Dave Gifford	18	72	35.0	3.0	38.0	2.111			

1966...1966...1966...1966...1966...1966

	M	R	Pts	BP	TPts	Ave	F	P	Total
Ivan Mauger	36	158	375.0	13.0	388.0	9.823	9	2	11
Peter Kelly	36	147	274.0	22.0	296.0	8.054	1	2	3
Brian Brett	35	140	258.0	13.0	271.0	7.743	1	1	2
§Graham Coombes	36	144	192.5	37.0	229.5	6.375		2	2
Mike Watkin	**38**	**146**	**176.0**	**47.0**	**223.0**	**6.110**			
Russ Dent	34	125	157.0	25.0	182.0	5.824			
Alan Butterfield	35	97	103.0	23.0	126.0	5.196			
Dave Gifford	12	28	26.0	6.0	32.0	4.571			
Brian Craven	2	6	4.0	0.0	4.0	2.667			

1967...1967...1967...1967...1967...1967

	M	R	Pts	BP	TPts	Ave	F	P	Total
Ivan Mauger	36	166	377.0	10.0	387.0	9.325	7	1	8
§§Ole Olsen	28	121	219.0	9.0	228.0	7.537	3		3
Mike Watkin	21	82	113.0	12.0	125.0	6.098			
Alan Butterfield	34	133	164.0	37.0	201.0	6.045		1	1
Russ Dent	17	68	90.0	12.0	102.0	6.000			
Peter Kelly	29	99	125.0	23.0	148.0	5.980			
Goog Allan	**37**	**147**	**191.0**	**27.0**	**218.0**	**5.932**			
Dave Gifford	34	115	141.0	21.0	162.0	5.635	1	1	2
§Murray Burt	6	18	6.0	2.0	8.0	1.778			
§Alan Paynter	8	17	6.0	1.0	7.0	1.647			
§Grieves Davidson	1	2	0.0	0.0	0.0	0.000			

1968...1968...1968...1968...1968...1968

	M	R	Pts	BP	TPts	Ave	F	P	Total
Ivan Mauger	36	158	447.0	2.0	449.0	11.367	23		23
Ole Olsen	37	153	346.0	13.0	359.0	9.386	4	1	5
Dave Gifford	**38**	**148**	**227.0**	**27.0**	**254.0**	**6.865**		**2**	**2**
Allan Butterfield	25	96	128.0	18.0	146.0	6.083		1	1
Goog Allan	10	34	37.0	12.0	49.0	5.765			
Mike Watkin	33	124	136.0	34.0	170.0	5.484			
§Alf Wells	20	70	77.0	12.0	89.0	5.086		1	1
§Alan Jay	24	91	101.0	14.0	115.0	5.055			
Alan Paynter	13	36	25.0	8.0	33.0	3.667			
§§Gary Peterson	10	27	21.0	3.0	24.0	3.556			
Murray Burt	19	59	28.0	5.0	33.0	2.237			

NORTHUMBRIAN OPEN CHAMPIONSHIP

1970	1 Ole Olsen	2 Anders Michanek	3 Ivan Mauger

MARLBORO CLASSIC

1984	1 Phil Crump	2 Joe Owen	3 Martin Scarisbrick and Alan Grahame

FAREWELL TROPHY

1984	1 Hans Nielsen	2 Phil Crump	3 Marvyn Cox, Peter Ravn and Alan Mason

300TH MEETING TROPHY

1984	1 Gary Guglielmi	2 Doug Wyer	3 Joe Owen

1969...1969...1969...1969...1969...1969

	M	R	Pts	BP	TPts	Ave	F	P	Total
Ole Olsen	34	152	386.0	9.0	395.0	10.395	7	1	8
§Tom Leadbitter	4	11	18.0	3.0	21.0	7.636			
Dave Gifford	**37**	**163**	**275.0**	**24.0**	**299.0**	**7.337**	**1**	**1**	**2**
§Garry Middleton	5	21	31.0	3.0	34.0	6.476			
Gary Peterson	8	35	37.0	5.0	42.0	4.800			
Mike Watkin	29	120	128.0	11.0	139.0	4.633			
§§Hilge Langli	4	15	12.0	4.0	16.0	4.267			
§§Alan Knapkin	19	61	48.0	13.0	61.0	4.000			
Alan Butterfield	5	20	17.0	1.0	18.0	3.600			
§Dave Schofield	36	121	89.0	16.0	105.0	3.471			
Murray Burt	13	47	34.0	4.0	38.0	3.234			
§§Sid Sheldrick	4	8	4.0	2.0	6.0	3.000			
§§Erik Tilgaard	3	8	4.0	0.0	4.0	2.000			
Peter Kelly	2	5	2.0	0.0	2.0	1.600			
§§Alan Bridgett	1	2	0.0	0.0	0.0	0.000			

1970...1970...1970...1970...1970...1970

	M	R	Pts	BP	TPts	Ave	F	P	Total
§Anders Michanek	28	122	330.0	2.0	332.0	10.885	9	1	10
George Hunter	**38**	**161**	**300.0**	**17.0**	**317.0**	**7.876**	**4**	**3**	**7**
Dave Gifford	37	151	230.0	20.0	250.0	6.623	2	1	3
§§Geoff Curtis	**38**	**153**	**160.0**	**37.0**	**197.0**	**5.150**		**1**	**1**
Mike Watkin	**38**	**131**	**118.0**	**23.0**	**141.0**	**4.305**			
Russ Dent	37	127	110.0	19.0	129.0	4.063			
§§Dag Lovaas	36	127	100.0	24.0	124.0	3.906			
Peter Kelly	2	7	5.0	0.0	5.0	2.857			
§§Tim Swales	1	3	1.0	0.0	1.0	1.333			

NEW PROMOTERS Allied Presentations, who installed Ian Hoskins as their front man after buying out Mike Parker announced they were transferring the Diamonds' First Division licence to Reading for the 1971 season and Brough Park fans had to wait until 1984 for their next taste of big league racing.

1984...1984...1984...1984...1984...1984

	M	R	Pts	BP	TPts	Ave	F	P	Total
§Joe Owen	42	181	349.0	15.0	364.0	8.044		2	2
§Rod Hunter	39	173	285.0	18.0	303.0	7.006	1		1
§David Bargh	39	170	267.0	17.0	284.0	6.682		1	1
§§Eddie Ingels	41	173	216.5	36.0	252.5	5.838			
§Mark Fiora	1	3	3.0	1.0	4.0	5.333			
§Steve McDermott	8	27	30.0	5.0	35.0	5.185			
§Phil White	**44**	**156**	**140.0**	**48.0**	**188.0**	**4.821**			
§Martin Scarisbrick	43	128	113.0	35.0	148.0	4.625			
§Reg Wilson	19	60	54.0	8.0	62.0	4.133			
§Bobby Beaton	1	4	4.0	0.0	4.0	4.000			
§Graham Drury	1	2	2.0	0.0	2.0	4.000			
§Alan Mason	13	50	46.0	3.0	49.0	3.920			
§Paul Stead	2	5	3.0	1.0	4.0	3.200			
§§Roger Lambert	1	4	2.0	0.0	2.0	2.000			
§§Paul McHale	1	2	0.0	0.0	0.0	0.000			
§§Paul Fry	1	1	0.0	0.0	0.0	0.000			

A REAL DIAMOND...Ole Olsen was Newcastle's first British League discovery and passes on some advice to brief team-mate Garry Middleton

NEWPORT

NEWPORT were the only Welsh team to compete in the British League and were founder members having spent just one season in the Provincial League. Their home track was shared with Newport County Football Club.

1965...1965...1965...1965...1965...1965

	M	R	Pts	BP	TPts	Ave	F	P	Total
§§Jack Biggs	34	136	292.0	14.0	306.0	9.000	4	2	6
§§Peter Vandenberg	**35**	**140**	**257.0**	**25.0**	**282.0**	**8.057**	**3**	**1**	**4**
§§Dick Bradley	21	84	145.0	21.0	166.0	7.905			
§§Alby Golden	**35**	**140**	**240.0**	**33.0**	**273.0**	**7.800**		**1**	**1**
§§Geoff Penniket	**35**	**140**	**163.0**	**34.0**	**197.0**	**5.629**	**1**		**1**
§§Jon Erskine	32	128	142.0	31.0	173.0	5.406		3	3
§§Vic White	16	64	52.0	17.0	69.0	4.313			
§§Bob Hughes	33	132	99.0	17.0	116.0	3.515			
§Ray Harris	4	16	10.0	1.0	11.0	2.750			

1966...1966...1966...1966...1966...1966

	M	R	Pts	BP	TPts	Ave	F	P	Tota
§§Göte Nordin	32	146	367.0	14.0	381.0	10.438	10	3	13
Jack Biggs	23	94	159.0	11.0	170.0	7.234	1	1	2
Jon Erskine	35	146	203.0	17.0	220.0	6.027			
§Tim Bungay	5	13	16.0	2.0	18.0	5.538			
Geoff Penniket	**37**	**154**	**186.0**	**23.0**	**209.0**	**5.429**			
Alby Golden	33	137	153.0	30.0	183.0	5.343		2	2
Bob Hughes	**37**	**139**	**152.0**	**13.0**	**165.0**	**4.748**	**2**		**2**
§Ken Vale	28	76	52.0	18.0	70.0	3.684			
§Alan Jones	2	3	1.0	1.0	2.0	2.667			
§§Fred Powell	1	3	1.0	1.0	2.0	2.667			
§§Ted Laessing	4	10	5.0	0.0	5.0	2.000			
§Peter Harris	2	4	2.0	0.0	2.0	2.000			

SWEDISH star Göte Nordin was the first rider to win the Silver Sash Match Race Championship away from home when he defeated holder Colin Pratt at Hackney on April 1, 1966. While other riders had successfully defended the title on an away track no-one had ever taken it off the holder in front of his own fans!

1967...1967...1967...1967...1967...1967

	M	R	Pts	BP	TPts	Ave	F	P	Total
§§Torbjörn Harrysson	28	123	300.0	9.0	309.0	10.049	7	3	10
§Jimmy Gooch	**37**	**162**	**310.0**	**25.0**	**335.0**	**8.272**	**1**	**1**	**2**
Jon Erskine	28	111	170.0	14.0	184.0	6.631	2		2
Alby Golden	**37**	**150**	**200.0**	**36.0**	**236.0**	**6.293**		**1**	**1**
§Cyril Francis	35	144	188.0	31.0	219.0	6.083			
Bob Hughes	20	58	60.0	9.0	69.0	4.759			
§John Bishop	**37**	**148**	**142.0**	**15.0**	**157.0**	**4.243**			
Fred Powell	6	11	5.0	0.0	5.0	1.818			
§§Roger White	3	9	2.0	0.0	2.0	0.889			
§John Ellis	6	11	2.0	0.0	2.0	0.727			
§§Alan Paynter	7	12	0.0	0.0	0.0	0.000			
§§Bob Stevens	2	3	0.0	0.0	0.0	0.000			
§§Terry Shearer	1	2	0.0	0.0	0.0	0.000			

1968...1968...1968...1968...1968...1968

	M	R	Pts	BP	TPts	Ave	F	P	Total
Torbjörn Harrysson	22	95	219.5	11.5	231.0	9.726	2	2	4
§Dave Schofield	1	2	2.0	2.0	4.0	8.000			
Jimmy Gooch	30	130	243.0	16.0	259.0	7.969	2		2
Jon Erskine	**37**	**170**	**247.0**	**32.0**	**279.0**	**6.565**		**1**	**1**
§Norman Strachan	24	94	146.0	6.0	152.0	6.468	1		1
Bob Hughes	35	138	196.5	19.5	216.0	6.261	1	1	2
Alby Golden	**37**	**121**	**137.0**	**36.0**	**173.0**	**5.719**			
Cyril Francis	31	128	161.0	21.0	182.0	5.688	1		1
Terry Shearer	29	66	28.0	5.0	33.0	2.000			
§Dai Evans	3	7	2.0	0.0	2.0	1.143			
Bob Stevens	1	2	0.0	0.0	0.0	0.000			
§§Ian Terrar	1	2	0.0	0.0	0.0	0.000			

1969...1969...1969...1969...1969...1969

	M	R	Pts	BP	TPts	Ave	F	P	Total
§Sandor Levai	**37**	**175**	**346.0**	**19.0**	**365.0**	**8.343**	**1**		**1**
Norman Strachan	35	129	184.0	19.0	203.0	6.295			
§Chris Julian	**37**	**157**	**215.0**	**23.0**	**238.0**	**6.064**			
Alby Golden	12	37	46.0	9.0	55.0	5.946	1		1
Bob Hughes	27	104	139.0	15.0	154.0	5.923	1	2	3
Jon Erskine	**37**	**151**	**188.0**	**32.0**	**220.0**	**5.828**			
Cyril Francis	23	84	82.0	16.0	98.0	4.667			
Terry Shearer	27	78	62.0	11.0	73.0	3.744			
§§Einar Egedius	7	22	14.0	1.0	15.0	2.727			
§Brian Davies	2	6	3.0	1.0	4.0	2.667			
Ian Terrar	4	8	1.0	0.0	1.0	0.500			
§§Adrian Baker	1	3	0.0	0.0	0.0	0.000			
§§Neil Glover	2	3	0.0	0.0	0.0	0.000			
§Chris Harrison	1	2	0.0	0.0	0.0	0.000			

1970...1970...1970...1970...1970...1970

	M	R	Pts	BP	TPts	Ave	F	P	Total
Sandor Levai	36	169	339.0	18.0	357.0	8.450			
§§John Louis	6	30	57.0	3.0	60.0	8.000	1		1
§Bill Andrew	35	149	273.0	17.0	290.0	7.785		1	1
§Alan Knapkin	1	6	8.0	2.0	10.0	6.667			
§§Edgar Stangeland	34	151	207.0	34.0	241.0	6.384			
§Des Lukehurst	2	10	12.0	1.0	13.0	5.200			
§§Bengt Brannefors	12	42	41.0	7.0	48.0	4.571			
Bob Hughes	36	131	124.0	18.0	142.0	4.336			
Jon Erskine	14	44	37.0	8.0	45.0	4.091			
§§Colin Sanders	1	2	2.0	0.0	2.0	4.000			
Norman Strachan	**37**	**128**	**111.0**	**14.0**	**125.0**	**3.906**	**1**		**1**
§Brian Leonard	10	35	25.0	8.0	33.0	3.771			
§George Major	3	11	9.0	1.0	10.0	3.636			
§§Dave O'Connor	3	8	6.0	1.0	7.0	3.500			
Cyril Francis	6	19	15.0	1.0	16.0	3.368			
§Ross Gilbertson	8	25	13.0	1.0	14.0	2.240			
§§Kevin Holden	2	5	2.0	0.0	2.0	1.600			
§Ian Gills	1	3	1.0	0.0	1.0	1.333			
§§Malcolm Shakespeare	1	3	0.0	0.0	0.0	0.000			
Ian Terrar	1	1	0.0	0.0	0.0	0.000			

WASPISH...Jon Erskine, son of Old Etonian Mike, was a tower of strength with Newport in the first few years of the British League

NEWPORT

1971...1971...1971...1971...1971...1971

	M	R	Pts	BP	TPts	Ave	F	P	Total
Sandor Levai	36	158	330.0	16.0	346.0	8.759	3	1	4
§§Tommy Johansson	32	136	251.0	22.0	273.0	8.029	1	2	3
Edgar Stangeland	**37**	**155**	**267.0**	**38.0**	**305.0**	**7.871**		**2**	**2**
Bill Andrew	36	153	255.0	22.0	277.0	7.242	1		1
Ted Laessing	17	57	58.0	11.0	69.0	4.842			
Bob Hughes	**37**	**121**	**112.0**	**25.0**	**137.0**	**4.529**			
Bengt Brannefors	13	48	50.0	3.0	53.0	4.417			
§Ronnie Genz	13	42	37.0	9.0	46.0	4.381			
Dave O'Connor	21	55	25.0	4.0	29.0	2.109			
§§Phil Crump	2	6	2.0	1.0	3.0	2.000			
§Malcolm Ballard	1	4	1.0	0.0	1.0	1.000			
Ian Gills	1	4	1.0	0.0	1.0	1.000			
Terry Shearer	3	8	1.0	0.0	1.0	0.500			
§Dave Kennett	1	2	0.0	0.0	0.0	0.000			

1972...1972...1972...1972...1972...1972

	M	R	Pts	BP	TPts	Ave	F	P	Total
Ronnie Genz	14	51	81.0	14.0	95.0	7.451			
§Tony Clarke	35	146	251.0	10.0	261.0	7.151	1		1
Graham Plant	35	146	219.0	15.0	234.0	6.411	1	1	2
§Neil Street	35	137	164.0	17.0	181.0	5.285	1		1
§Mike Sampson	2	8	8.0	2.0	10.0	5.000			
§Doug Templeton	1	5	6.0	0.0	6.0	4.800			
§Phil Woodcock	22	82	79.0	13.0	92.0	4.488			
§Bo Wirebrand	18	66	66.0	6.0	72.0	4.364			
§§David Beech	2	7	7.0	0.0	7.0	4.000			
Ted Laessing	16	48	41.0	4.0	45.0	3.750			
§Barry Duke	35	109	81.0	14.0	95.0	3.486			
§§Arthur Browning	1	4	2.0	1.0	3.0	3.000			
Terry Shearer	2	7	3.0	1.0	4.0	2.286			
§Stan Stevens	1	3	1.0	0.0	1.0	1.333			
§§Brian Woodward	5	15	3.0	1.0	4.0	1.067			

NEWPORT won their first ever Cup match against Coventry on Friday, June 16, 1972 – after first match defeats in each of their previous seven seasons! The star of their breakthrough was Londoner Tony Clarke who smashed the Somerton Park track record in his opening ride and became the first Wasp to score a maximum. In six of the seven previous seasons Newport had been drawn away in their opening Cup round and even when they did get a home draw – against Leicester in 1970 – they lost 35-43!

1973...1973...1973...1973...1973...1973

	M	R	Pts	BP	TPts	Ave	F	P	Total
§Reidar Eide	31	133	306.0	19.0	325.0	9.774	3	6	9
Graham Plant	36	141	250.5	10.0	260.5	7.390	2	2	4
§Roy Trigg	37	158	266.0	25.0	291.0	7.367	1	1	2
Neil Street	**38**	**151**	**248.0**	**27.0**	**275.0**	**7.285**	**3**	**3**	**6**
§Peter Ingram	34	137	166.0	40.0	206.0	6.015		1	1
§§Rick Woods	6	25	28.0	5.0	33.0	5.280			
§Geoff Mudge	19	66	69.0	10.0	79.0	4.788			
§Jim Tebby	37	114	90.0	22.0	112.0	3.930			
§Alan Cowland	11	32	27.0	2.0	29.0	3.625			
§§Peter Smith (Sw)	3	8	5.0	2.0	7.0	3.500			
Jimmy Squibb	1	3	2.0	0.0	2.0	2.667			
Brian Woodward	1	5	3.0	0.0	3.0	2.400			

1974...1974...1974...1974...1974...1974

	M	R	Pts	BP	TPts	Ave	F	P	Total
Phil Crump	35	156	414.0	7.0	421.0	10.795	14	2	16
Reidar Eide	34	149	336.0	15.0	351.0	9.423	2	1	3
Neil Street	29	119	205.0	24.0	229.0	7.697	2	3	5
§Alan Molyneux	1	3	3.0	1.0	4.0	5.333			
§Tom Owen	5	19	24.0	1.0	25.0	5.263			
§Bob Coles	35	137	146.0	28.0	174.0	5.080			
Roy Trigg	31	115	114.0	23.0	137.0	4.765			
Geoff Mudge	34	112	99.0	23.0	122.0	4.357			
Jim Tebby	**36**	**107**	**86.0**	**25.0**	**111.0**	**4.150**			
§§Roger Austin	2	5	3.0	0.0	3.0	2.400			
Brian Woodward	2	3	0.0	0.0	0.0	0.000			

1975...1975...1975...1975...1975...1975

	M	R	Pts	BP	TPts	Ave	F	P	Total
Phil Crump	37	156	433.0	2.0	435.0	11.154	25	1	26
Reidar Eide	34	134	280.0	21.0	301.0	8.985		2	2
§Phil Herne	33	131	257.0	28.0	285.0	8.702	2	1	3
Neil Street	36	136	224.0	25.0	249.0	7.324	5	5	10
Bob Coles	13	46	68.0	14.0	82.0	7.130			
§Keith Evans	2	9	13.0	3.0	16.0	7.111			
Steve Gresham	33	123	154.0	41.0	195.0	6.341			
Tom Owen	24	91	111.0	28.0	139.0	6.110			
Mike Sampson	1	2	2.0	1.0	3.0	6.000			
Arthur Browning	2	8	10.0	1.0	11.0	5.500			
§Brian Kennett	1	4	4.0	1.0	5.0	5.000			
§Ricky Day	1	3	2.0	1.0	3.0	4.000			
Jim Tebby	21	65	43.0	10.0	53.0	3.262			
§Graham Drury	1	3	2.0	0.0	2.0	2.667			
§Russell Osborne	1	3	1.0	1.0	2.0	2.667			
§Joe Owen	1	3	2.0	0.0	2.0	2.667			
§§John McNeill	2	6	2.0	1.0	3.0	2.000			
§Tony Boyle	1	3	1.0	0.0	1.0	1.333			
§§Mike Powell	1	3	1.0	0.0	1.0	1.333			
Tony Featherstone	1	4	1.0	0.0	1.0	1.000			
§Phil Bass	1	4	0.0	0.0	0.0	0.000			
§Alan Grahame	1	3	0.0	0.0	0.0	0.000			
§§Pete Rogers	1	2	0.0	0.0	0.0	0.000			

1976...1976...1976...1976...1976...1976

	M	R	Pts	BP	TPts	Ave	F	P	Total
§Kevin Young	1	1	2.0	1.0	3.0	12.000			
Phil Crump	39	183	483.0	5.0	488.0	10.667	15	1	16
Phil Herne	27	101	229.0	16.0	245.0	9.703	2	2	4
Steve Gresham	34	157	268.0	23.0	291.0	7.414			
Brian Woodward	30	123	161.0	28.0	189.0	6.146		3	3
Bob Coles	25	104	105.0	25.0	130.0	5.000			
Neil Street	21	67	67.0	15.0	82.0	4.896			
§§Tormod Langli	27	102	100.0	20.0	120.0	4.706			
§§Danny Kennedy	10	32	33.0	4.0	37.0	4.625			
§Kazimierz Adamczak	9	35	30.5	6.0	36.5	4.171			
Phil Bass	6	22	19.0	3.0	22.0	4.000			
Brian Kennett	16	51	41.0	9.0	50.0	3.922			
§§Robert Henry	4	10	7.0	0.0	7.0	2.800			
§Preben Rosenkilde	3	8	5.0	0.0	5.0	2.500			
§Kelvin Mullarkey	1	4	2.0	0.0	2.0	2.000			
§Graham Banks	3	10	3.0	1.0	4.0	1.600			
Tony Featherstone	2	8	3.0	0.0	3.0	1.500			
§§Graham Clifton	1	5	0.0	0.0	0.0	0.000			
John McNeill	1	2	0.0	0.0	0.0	0.000			
§Jack Millen	1	2	0.0	0.0	0.0	0.000			
§§Tim Nunan	1	2	0.0	0.0	0.0	0.000			
§Neil Cameron	1	1	0.0	0.0	0.0	0.000			

WELSH CHAMPIONSHIP

1965	1 Barry Briggs	2 Nigel Boocock	3 Alby Golden
1968	1 Nigel Boocock	2 Jimmy Gooch	3 Chris Julian
1970	1 Nigel Boocock	2 Sandor Levai	3 Ronnie Moore
1973	1 Ivan Mauger	2 Dave Jessup	3 Sören Sjösten
1974	1 Martin Ashby	2 Phil Crump	3 Bob Kilby
1975	1 Phil Crump	2 Reidar Eide	3 Ian Turner

SEVERN BRIDGE TROPHY

1966	1 Alby Golden	2 Nigel Boocock	3 Bob Hughes
1967	1 Reg Luckhurst	2 Sverre Harrfeldt	3 Mike Broadbank

TWW SPORTS PREVIEW TROPHY

1967	1 Alby Golden	2 Nigel Boocock	3 Barry Briggs

NEWPORT TROPHY

1968	1 Norman Hunter	2 Jimmy Gooch	3 Jon Erskine

EDDIE GLENNON MEMORIAL TROPHY

1969	1 Barry Briggs	2 Martin Ashby	3 Nigel Boocock

PRINCE OF WALES TROPHY

1969	1 Barry Briggs	2 Reg Luckhurst	3 Jim Airey
1970	1 Barry Briggs	2 Christer Löfqvist	3 Bill Andrew
1971	1 Jim Airey	2 Barry Briggs	3 Anders Michanek and Sandor Levai
1972	1 Ole Olsen	2 Ivan Mauger, Sandor Levai and Dag Lovaas	
1973	1 Anders Michanek	2 Martin Ashby	3 Nigel Boocock
1974	1 Phil Crump	2 Neil Street	3 Reidar Eide
1975	1 Reidar Eide	2 Phil Crump	3 Ole Olsen
1976	1 Phil Crump	2 Gordon Kennett	3 Bob Kilby

SOUTHERN PROMOTIONS TROPHY

1971	1 Sandor Levai	2 Pete Smith	3 Ronnie Genz

WELSHANAPOLIS

1972	1 John Boulger	2 Peter Collins	3 Sandor Levai and Ray Wilson

SOMERTON PARK ROSEBOWL

1973	1 Ivan Mauger	2 Nigel Boocock	3 Dag Lovaas

BRITISH LEAGUE AVERAGES...BRITISH LEAGUE AVERAGES...BRITISH LEAGUE AVERAGES

OXFORD

OXFORD, who won the 1964 National League (First Division) were able to retain their three top scorers Arne Pander, Ron How and Jimmy Gooch for their first season of British League racing. Of their title winning side they released Jack Geran, Colin Gooddy and Ronnie Genz.

1965...1965...1965...1965...1965...1965

	M	R	Pts	BP	TPts	Ave	F	P	Total
§§Arne Pander	**35**	**140**	**366.0**	**5.0**	**371.0**	**10.600**	**12**		**12**
§§Jimmy Gooch	32	128	336.0	3.0	339.0	10.594	7	1	8
§§Ron How	18	72	176.0	12.0	188.0	10.444	2	4	6
§§John Belcher	1	4	5.0	0.0	5.0	5.000			
§Maurie McDermott	4	16	15.0	2.0	17.0	4.250			
§§John Bishop	28	112	104.0	12.0	116.0	4.143			
§§Ken Vale	30	120	106.0	17.0	123.0	4.100			
§§Eddie Reeves	34	136	116.0	22.0	138.0	4.059			
§§Danny Dunton	1	4	4.0	0.0	4.0	4.000			
§§Jimmy Heard	16	64	37.0	8.0	45.0	2.813			
§Stan Stevens	16	64	36.0	8.0	44.0	2.750			
§§John Leader	2	8	3.0	2.0	5.0	2.500			
§Glyn Chandler	11	44	26.0	1.0	27.0	2.455			
§§Wayne Barry	1	4	1.0	1.0	2.0	2.000			
§§John Hook	8	32	8.0	1.0	9.0	1.125			
§§John Hensley	4	16	4.0	0.0	4.0	1.000			
§§Bill Finch	1	2	0.0	0.0	0.0	0.000			
§§Tyburn Gallows	2	4	0.0	0.0	0.0	0.000			

1966...1966...1966...1966...1966...1966

	M	R	Pts	BP	TPts	Ave	F	P	Total
Arne Pander	36	149	348.0	7.0	355.0	9.530	7	1	8
Jimmy Gooch	32	138	255.0	26.0	281.0	8.145	1		1
Eddie Reeves	36	139	171.0	36.0	207.0	5.957			
John Bishop	36	148	199.0	18.0	217.0	5.865			
Maurie McDermott	36	127	136.0	24.0	160.0	5.039			
§Des Lukehurst	36	115	96.0	22.0	118.0	4.104			
§Tony Clarke	32	110	92.0	16.0	108.0	3.927			
§§Pete Seaton	10	24	5.0	1.0	6.0	1.000			

BELLE VUE junior Taffy Owen rode for Oxford in the second race of their match at Hyde Road on Saturday, October 1...as the Cheetahs became the first British League team to use EIGHT riders in a meeting. Late arriving Maurie McDermott was able to complete his last three programmed outings!

1967...1967...1967...1967...1967...1967

	M	R	Pts	BP	TPts	Ave	F	P	Total
Arne Pander	13	51	121.0	1.0	122.0	9.569	4		4
§Roy Trigg	37	163	373.0	9.0	382.0	9.374	9	1	10
§Colin Gooddy	20	84	156.0	18.0	174.0	8.286		1	1
Eddie Reeves	37	154	259.0	30.0	289.0	7.506	2	1	3
Des Lukehurst	33	126	168.0	23.0	191.0	6.063		1	1
Leo McAuliffe	35	133	142.5	22.0	164.5	4.947		1	1
§§Rick Timmo	34	118	111.0	27.0	138.0	4.678			
Maurie McDermott	26	77	60.0	17.0	77.0	4.000			
§Tim Bungay	2	7	4.0	1.0	5.0	2.857			
Pete Seaton	10	25	12.0	3.0	15.0	2.400			
Ken Vale	3	10	4.0	1.0	5.0	2.000			
§§Ted Spittles	5	14	1.0	1.0	2.0	0.571			

1968...1968...1968...1968...1968...1968

	M	R	Pts	BP	TPts	Ave	F	P	Total
Ronnie Genz	28	121	243.0	15.0	258.0	8.529	1	3	4
Eddie Reeves	35	152	255.0	23.0	278.0	7.316			
Colin Gooddy	36	152	237.0	24.0	261.0	6.868	1		1
Leo McAuliffe	**37**	**163**	**244.0**	**24.0**	**268.0**	**6.577**	**1**	**1**	**2**
Rick Timmo	**37**	**153**	**173.0**	**38.0**	**211.0**	**5.516**		**1**	**1**
Arne Pander	4	10	11.0	0.0	11.0	4.400			
John Bishop	34	115	98.0	28.0	126.0	4.383			
§§Mick Bell	5	9	7.0	2.0	9.0	4.000			
Pete Seaton	15	39	22.0	5.0	27.0	2.769			
§John Poyser	1	3	1.0	1.0	2.0	2.667			
§§Godtfred Andreasen	3	11	6.0	1.0	7.0	2.545			
§§Peter Saunders	1	2	0.0	0.0	0.0	0.000			
Ted Spittles	1	1	0.0	0.0	0.0	0.000			

1969...1969...1969...1969...1969...1969

	M	R	Pts	BP	TPts	Ave	F	P	Total
Eddie Reeves	**37**	**157**	**291.0**	**26.0**	**317.0**	**8.076**	**1**	**3**	**4**
Colin Gooddy	36	147	265.0	30.0	295.0	8.027		1	1
Leo McAuliffe	9	37	66.0	1.0	67.0	7.243	1		1
§Peter Jarman	36	152	227.0	39.0	266.0	7.000	1	1	2
Rick Timmo	34	139	209.0	22.0	231.0	6.647	1		1
§George Major	16	66	76.0	11.0	87.0	5.273			
§§Conny Samulesson	13	48	43.0	7.0	50.0	4.167			
Mick Bell	12	40	35.0	5.0	40.0	4.000			
§David Crane	12	39	33.0	6.0	39.0	4.000			
John Bishop	21	62	50.0	6.0	56.0	3.613			
Pete Seaton	4	10	6.0	1.0	7.0	2.800			
Peter Saunders	4	7	3.0	0.0	3.0	1.714			
Ken Vale	1	3	0.0	0.0	0.0	0.000			

†The match v Halifax was declared void and the match points awarded to Halifax. Riders are credited with an appearance.

1970...1970...1970...1970...1970...1970

	M	R	Pts	BP	TPts	Ave	F	P	Total
§Hasse Holmkvist	23	98	212.0	11.0	223.0	9.102	3	3	6
Ronnie Genz	36	157	245.0	31.0	276.0	7.032	1		1
Colin Gooddy	35	124	184.5	22.0	206.5	6.661	1		1
Peter Jarman	**37**	**145**	**203.0**	**32.0**	**235.0**	**6.483**			
Rick Timmo	34	141	200.0	25.0	225.0	6.383		2	2
Eddie Reeves	30	108	142.0	17.0	159.0	5.889			
Mick Bell	36	127	125.0	26.0	151.0	4.756			
Peter Seaton	6	17	9.0	3.0	12.0	2.824			
Pete Saunders	2	4	1.0	1.0	2.0	2.000			
George Major	3	7	2.0	1.0	3.0	1.714			
§§Andy Ross	1	3	1.0	0.0	1.0	1.333			
§Pat Johnson	1	2	0.0	0.0	0.0	0.000			
§Paul O'Neal	1	1	0.0	0.0	0.0	0.000			

1971...1971...1971...1971...1971...1971

	M	R	Pts	BP	TPts	Ave	F	P	Total
§Øyvind Berg	**39**	**170**	**290.0**	**33.0**	**323.0**	**7.600**		**1**	**1**
§Arthur Price	2	8	12.0	3.0	15.0	7.500			
Ken McKinlay	36	129	203.0	22.0	225.0	6.977	1	1	2
Colin Gooddy	**39**	**141**	**225.0**	**17.0**	**242.0**	**6.865**	**2**	**1**	**3**
Ronnie Genz	22	91	121.0	33.0	154.0	6.769		2	2
Rick Timmo	33	134	204.5	20.0	224.5	6.701			
Tommy Roper	16	69	102.0	11.0	113.0	6.551			
§John Louis	1	5	7.0	0.0	7.0	5.600			
Pete Seaton	1	5	6.0	0.0	6.0	4.800			
§Norman Strachan	35	124	119.0	23.0	142.0	4.581			
Col Cottrell	21	73	55.0	16.0	71.0	3.890			
§John Jackson	9	28	18.0	0.0	18.0	2.571			
Peter Saunders	2	5	2.0	1.0	3.0	2.400			
§§Laurie Sims	2	6	2.0	1.0	3.0	2.000			
§Phil Crump	1	4	1.0	0.0	1.0	1.000			
§John Davis	3	9	1.0	1.0	2.0	0.889			
§§Richard Greer	3	6	0.0	0.0	0.0	0.000			
§§Brian Clark	2	5	0.0	0.0	0.0	0.000			
§Dingle Brown	1	2	0.0	0.0	0.0	0.000			

1972...1972...1972...1972...1972...1972

	M	R	Pts	BP	TPts	Ave	F	P	Total
Garry Middleton	30	140	315.5	8.0	323.5	9.243	3	1	4
Øyvind Berg	28	129	239.0	18.0	257.0	7.969		1	1
Colin Gooddy	30	111	164.0	16.0	180.0	6.486	1		1
§Malcolm Ballard	13	55	65.0	21.0	86.0	6.255			
Rick Timmo	31	130	142.0	25.0	167.0	5.138			
Ken McKinlay	28	89	89.0	18.0	107.0	4.809			
§Roger Johns	3	10	8.0	4.0	12.0	4.800			
Norman Strachan	30	109	107.0	12.0	119.0	4.367			
§§Julian Wigg	1	2	1.0	1.0	2.0	4.000			
§Gordon Kennett	5	15	11.0	3.0	14.0	3.733			
§Preben Rosenkilde	9	33	22.0	8.0	30.0	3.636			
John Davis	11	32	22.0	2.0	24.0	3.000			
§Bobby McNeil	2	7	4.0	1.0	5.0	2.857			
§§Ted Hubbard	1	3	2.0	0.0	2.0	2.667			
§Bob Hughes	1	3	2.0	0.0	2.0	2.667			
§§Svein Kaasa	6	21	7.0	2.0	9.0	1.714			
§§Lou Sansom	1	3	1.0	0.0	1.0	1.333			
George Major	1	4	0.0	0.0	0.0	0.000			
§§Paul Gachet	1	3	0.0	0.0	0.0	0.000			
Laurie Sims	1	1	0.0	0.0	0.0	0.000			

OXFORD

1973...1973...1973...1973...1973...1973

	M	R	Pts	BP	TPts	Ave	F	P	Total
§Mike Broadbank	1	3	6.0	0.0	6.0	8.000			
Hasse Holmkvist	28	120	226.0	7.0	233.0	7.767	2	1	3
§Bob Kilby	12	47	78.0	8.0	86.0	7.319	1		1
Gordon Kennett	35	139	184.0	39.0	223.0	6.417		1	1
John Davis	17	53	69.0	13.0	82.0	6.189		1	1
Malcolm Ballard	**36**	**138**	**180.0**	**30.0**	**210.0**	**6.087**	**1**		**1**
Brian Clark	1	2	2.0	1.0	3.0	6.000			
§Tony Lomas	7	31	41.0	4.0	45.0	5.806			
§John Dews	35	137	171.0	25.0	196.0	5.723		1	1
Rick Timmo	35	125	142.0	26.0	168.0	5.376	1		1
Bobby McNeil	2	6	7.0	1.0	8.0	5.333			
Roger Johns	7	25	26.0	4.0	30.0	4.800			
Eddie Reeves	8	21	14.0	3.0	17.0	3.238			
Paul Gachet	2	5	3.0	0.0	3.0	2.400			

1974...1974...1974...1974...1974...1974

	M	R	Pts	BP	TPts	Ave	F	P	Total
Bob Kilby	33	139	280.0	9.0	289.0	8.317	2	1	3
Paul Gachet	2	6	10.0	2.0	12.0	8.000			
Gordon Kennett	27	106	176.0	18.0	194.0	7.321	1	1	2
§Ulf Lovaas	28	103	164.5	13.0	177.5	6.893			
John Davis	33	133	203.0	25.0	228.0	6.857		1	1
Richard Greer	**34**	**136**	**194.0**	**36.0**	**230.0**	**6.765**	**1**		**1**
John Dews	28	98	105.0	22.0	127.0	5.184			
Bobby McNeil	9	26	19.0	8.0	27.0	4.154			
§Trevor Geer	12	32	29.0	3.0	32.0	4.000			
§Ricky Day	1	4	3.0	1.0	4.0	4.000			
§David Gagen	1	3	2.0	1.0	3.0	4.000			
§§Alan Johns	1	2	2.0	0.0	2.0	4.000			
Rick Timmo	10	29	19.0	8.0	27.0	3.724			
Peter Jarman	3	8	4.0	3.0	7.0	3.500			
§Neil Middleditch	2	4	2.0	1.0	3.0	3.000			
§§Henk Steman	8	20	7.0	1.0	8.0	1.600			
Brian Clark	1	2	0.0	0.0	0.0	0.000			
§Martin Yeates	1	2	0.0	0.0	0.0	0.000			

1975...1975...1975...1975...1975...1975

	M	R	Pts	BP	TPts	Ave	F	P	Total
§Dag Lovaas	35	165	396.0	18.0	414.0	10.036	10	2	12
Gordon Kennett	**38**	**175**	**340.0**	**28.0**	**368.0**	**8.411**	**1**	**2**	**3**
Hasse Holmkvist	1	4	7.0	1.0	8.0	8.000			
Richard Greer	**38**	**170**	**270.0**	**48.0**	**318.0**	**7.482**		**2**	**2**
John Dews	**38**	**151**	**207.0**	**41.0**	**248.0**	**6.570**			
Brian Clark	6	17	21.0	6.0	27.0	6.353			
Trevor Geer	**38**	**134**	**156.0**	**36.0**	**192.0**	**5.731**		**1**	**1**
§Richard Hellsén	14	48	45.0	12.0	57.0	4.750			
Paul Gachet	25	53	44.0	11.0	55.0	4.151			
§Helge Langli	9	26	13.0	3.0	16.0	2.462			
§§Eddie Davidsson	6	17	6.0	0.0	6.0	1.412			
§Barney Kennett	1	2	0.0	0.0	0.0	0.000			
§Steve Weatherley	2	2	0.0	0.0	0.0	0.000			

COWLEY STADIUM accept a £230,000 offer from the City Council to develop their site to spell an end to speedway at Sandy Lane. But a campaign by supporters persuades the Council to review the situation although the Rebels are on the move to London White City. As they go Stoke promoter Harry Bastable moves into Cowley with National League racing and that's the weekly fare until the re-named Cheetahs apply to join the 1984 British League..

1984...1984...1984...1984...1984...1984

	M	R	Pts	BP	TPts	Ave	F	P	Total
§Hans Nielsen	41	181	463.0	24.0	487.0	10.762	10	9	19
§Simon Wigg	40	168	383.0	24.0	407.0	9.690	4	6	10
§Marvyn Cox	45	185	262.0	29.0	291.0	6.292	1	1	2
§Melvyn Taylor	35	135	180.5	24.0	204.5	6.059	1	1	2
§Jens Rasmussen	27	102	120.0	22.0	142.0	5.569		2	2
§Steve Wilcock	1	3	4.0	0.0	4.0	5.333			
§Ian Clark	45	148	148.0	22.0	170.0	4.595			
§Nigel Sparshott	39	136	130.5	22.0	152.5	4.485			
§§Klaus Lausch	13	53	47.0	8.0	55.0	4.151			
§§Andrew Silver	3	12	6.0	4.0	10.0	3.333			
§Kevin Smart	6	18	10.0	4.0	14.0	3.111			
§Jim McMillan	1	3	1.0	1.0	2.0	2.667			
§Martin Yeates	9	24	10.0	2.0	12.0	2.000			
§Dave Perks	9	27	10.0	3.0	13.0	1.926			
§§Nigel De'ath	4	8	1.0	0.0	1.0	0.500			
§§Mark Chessell	2	5	0.0	0.0	0.0	0.000			
§§David Tyler	1	2	0.0	0.0	0.0	0.000			

1985...1985...1985...1985...1985...1985

	M	R	Pts	BP	TPts	Ave	F	P	Total
Hans Nielsen	50	221	603.0	24.0	627.0	11.348	17	11	28
Simon Wigg	**52**	**228**	**504.0**	**15.0**	**519.0**	**9.105**	**4**	**2**	**6**
§Andy Grahame	33	131	211.0	24.0	235.0	7.176			
Marvyn Cox	**52**	**212**	**295.0**	**27.0**	**322.0**	**6.075**			
Jens Rasmussen	50	193	241.0	52.0	293.0	6.073	1		1
§§Alastair Stevens	4	14	13.0	5.0	18.0	5.143			
Melvyn Taylor	35	124	127.0	24.0	151.0	4.871			
Klaus Lausch	10	36	37.0	6.0	43.0	4.778			
Nigel De'ath	4	15	11.0	5.0	16.0	4.267			
§§Troy Butler	51	164	81.0	10.0	91.0	2.220			
Nigel Sparshott	3	9	1.0	1.0	2.0	0.889			
§§Jon Surman	3	9	1.0	0.0	1.0	0.444			

1986...1986...1986...1986...1986...1986

	M	R	Pts	BP	TPts	Ave	F	P	Total
Hans Nielsen	45	187	523.0	18.0	541.0	11.572	22	9	31
Simon Wigg	45	182	449.0	15.0	464.0	10.198	6	5	11
Marvyn Cox	**46**	**180**	**333.0**	**32.0**	**365.0**	**8.111**	**4**	**3**	**7**
Andy Grahame	**46**	**179**	**234.0**	**41.0**	**275.0**	**6.145**			
§Per Sørensen	33	129	176.0	19.0	195.0	6.047		1	1
Nigel De'ath	45	149	176.0	23.0	199.0	5.342			
Kevin Smart	12	36	35.0	4.0	39.0	4.333			
§§Jeremy Luckhurst	2	7	6.0	1.0	7.0	4.000			
Alastair Stevens	1	4	2.0	1.0	3.0	3.000			
Jon Surman	**46**	**138**	**67.0**	**17.0**	**84.0**	**2.435**			

1987...1987...1987...1987...1987...1987

	M	R	Pts	BP	TPts	Ave	F	P	Total
Hans Nielsen	49	219	602.0	21.0	623.0	11.379	21	9	30
Marvyn Cox	49	219	454.0	13.0	467.0	8.530	2	2	4
Andy Grahame	46	189	356.0	16.0	372.0	7.873	2		2
Jens Rasmussen	34	131	161.0	25.0	186.0	5.679			
Nigel De'ath	46	175	165.0	27.0	192.0	4.389			
Troy Butler	4	13	10.0	3.0	13.0	4.000			
Mark Carlson	2	5	4.0	1.0	5.0	4.000			
§§Neil McCarthy	1	2	1.0	1.0	2.0	4.000			
Kevin Smart	19	71	55.0	11.0	66.0	3.718			
Alastair Stevens	38	131	95.0	24.0	119.0	3.634			
Jon Surman	**52**	**155**	**94.0**	**24.0**	**118.0**	**3.045**			
§Nigel Crabtree	2	7	4.0	1.0	5.0	2.857			
Andy Buck	1	2	1.0	0.0	1.0	2.000			
Nigel Sparshott	4	15	7.0	0.0	7.0	1.867			
§Peter Lloyd	4	12	2.0	0.0	2.0	0.667			
§§Nigel Greenhalgh	1	2	0.0	0.0	0.0	0.000			
§§Wayne Ross	1	2	0.0	0.0	0.0	0.000			

SKOL MASTERS TROPHY

1990	1 Simon Wigg	2 Sam Ermolenko	3 Kelly Moran

SPEEDWAY CHAMPIONS TROPHY

1968	1 Ivan Mauger	2 Nigel Boocock	3 Roy Trigg
1969	1 Barry Briggs	2 Ole Olsen	3 Bernt Persson
1970	1 Anders Michanek	2 Barry Briggs	3 Ole Olsen
1973	1 Terry Betts	2 Ole Olsen	3 Hasse Holmkvist and Anders Michanek
1975	1 Phil Crump	2 Reidar Eide	3 Scott Autrey

OXFORD STADIUM TROPHY

1978	1 Steve Koppe	2 Melvyn Taylor	3 James Moore

SUPPORTERS TROPHY

1980	1 Martin Yeates	2 Bob Humphreys	3 Bob Garrad
1981	1 Dave Perks	2 Les Rumsey	3 Bob Humphreys
1982	1 Martin Yeates	2 Keith White	3 Derek Harrison
1983	1 Martin Yeates	2 Keith White	3 Bob Garrad
1984	1 Jan Andersson	2 Gordon Kennett	3 Hans Nielsen
1985	1 Simon Wigg	2 Kelvin Tatum	3 Andy Grahame
1986	1 Erik Gundersen	2 Hans Nielsen	3 Jan O. Pedersen
1988	1 Jan O. Pedersen	2 Hans Nielsen	3 Kelvin Tatum
1989	1 Hans Nielsen	2 Martin Dugard	3 Lance King
1977	1 Martin Yeates	2 Phil Collins	3 Laurie Etheridge

DOUBLE DIAMOND TROPHY

1965	1 Ken McKinlay	2 Nigel Boocock	3 Jimmy Gooch

OXFORDSHIRE BRITISH LEAGUE TWO CHAMPIONSHIP

1990	1 Paul Dugard	2 David Steen	3 Matthew Cross

OXFORD

1988...1988...1988...1988...1988...1988

	M	R	Pts	BP	TPts	Ave	F	P	Total
Hans Nielsen	44	232	625.0	15.0	640.0	11.034	15	4	19
Simon Wigg	41	194	400.0	19.0	419.0	8.639	2	2	4
Marvyn Cox	44	185	286.0	49.0	335.0	7.243		1	1
§Martin Dugard	44	198	311.0	34.0	345.0	6.970			
§Glenn Doyle	1	4	4.0	2.0	6.0	6.000			
Nigel De'ath	44	189	182.0	22.0	204.0	4.317			
Alastair Stevens	10	43	37.0	5.0	42.0	3.907			
Jon Surman	11	42	34.0	6.0	40.0	3.810			
§Lars Munkedal	25	79	49.0	9.0	58.0	2.937			
§§Spencer Timmo	4	10	6.0	1.0	7.0	2.800			
Peter Lloyd	32	110	58.0	15.0	73.0	2.655			
§Einar Kyllingstad	6	19	3.0	0.0	3.0	0.632			
§§Paul Muchene	1	4	0.0	0.0	0.0	0.000			

1989...1989...1989...1989...1989...1989

	M	R	Pts	BP	TPts	Ave	F	P	Total
Hans Nielsen	**34**	**173**	**460.0**	**12.0**	**472.0**	**10.913**	**9**	**5**	**14**
Simon Wigg	32	142	247.0	26.0	273.0	7.690			
Martin Dugard	**34**	**152**	**263.0**	**26.0**	**289.0**	**7.605**		**2**	**2**
Andy Grahame	33	139	222.0	18.0	240.0	6.906		2	2
Marvyn Cox	28	113	160.0	32.0	192.0	6.796			
Troy Butler	26	112	143.0	24.0	167.0	5.964			
§§Paul Dugard	29	100	56.0	8.0	64.0	2.560			
§§Kevin Pitts	8	22	9.0	0.0	9.0	1.636			
Paul Muchene	1	4	1.0	0.0	1.0	1.000			
§§Colin White	1	1	0.0	0.0	0.0	0.000			

1990...19890...1990...1990...1990...1990

	M	R	Pts	BP	TPts	Ave	F	P	Total
Hans Nielsen	**34**	**181**	**439.0**	**30.0**	**469.0**	**10.365**	**1**	**4**	**5**
Martin Dugard	32	151	301.0	11.0	312.0	8.265	2		2
Simon Wigg	26	116	204.0	14.0	218.0	7.517			
§Dean Barker	33	135	165.0	31.0	196.0	5.807			
Alastair Stevens	33	145	181.0	20.0	201.0	5.545			
Troy Butler	31	126	133.0	26.0	159.0	5.048			
Paul Dugard	14	45	29.0	10.0	39.0	3.467			
Jon Surman	1	4	3.0	0.0	3.0	3.000			
Kevin Pitts	1	4	2.0	0.0	2.0	2.000			
§§Sean McCullagh	1	2	1.0	0.0	1.0	2.000			
§John Bostin	16	50	19.0	4.0	23.0	1.840			
§§Kieran McCullagh	4	10	1.0	0.0	1.0	0.400			
§§Wayne Parker	1	3	0.0	0.0	0.0	0.000			

▼ TITLE-WINNERS...skipper Hans Nielsen proudly shows off the 1985 British League championship trophy won in the Cheetahs second season back in the top flight

BRITISH LEAGUE AVERAGES...BRITISH LEAGUE AVERAGES...BRITISH LEAGUE AVERAGES

POOLE

POOLE, under the control of the Knott family, were one of the major movers in the formation of the British League in 1965 and worked tirelessly towards bringing to an end the animosity between the 1964 National League (First Division) and Provincial League.
They had finished mid-table in 1964 but strengthened up by signing Ronnie Genz from Oxford – the 1964 National League champions – and Bill Andrew from Provincial League title-winners Newcastle.

1965...1965...1965...1965...1965...1965

	M	R	Pts	BP	TPts	Ave	F	P	Total
§§Ronnie Genz	**36**	**152**	**351.0**	**8.0**	**359.0**	**9.447**	**6**	**2**	**8**
§§Bill Andrew	**36**	**157**	**344.0**	**12.0**	**356.0**	**9.070**	**6**	**1**	**7**
§§Ross Gilbertson	33	135	224.0	38.0	262.0	7.763			
§§Geoff Mudge	30	127	212.0	24.0	236.0	7.433			
§§Alf Hagon	4	15	22.0	4.0	26.0	6.933			
§§Norman Strachan	20	73	89.0	23.0	112.0	6.137			
§§Pete Smith	34	121	136.0	31.0	167.0	5.521			
§§Brian Leonard	2	6	6.0	0.0	6.0	4.000			
§§Pete Munday	**36**	**114**	**70.0**	**22.0**	**92.0**	**3.228**			
§§Bruce Cribb	11	25	15.0	4.0	19.0	3.040			
§§Terry Stone	3	9	3.0	1.0	4.0	1.778			
§§Peter Swain	7	13	2.0	0.0	2.0	0.615			

1966...1966...1966...1966...1966...1966

	M	R	Pts	BP	TPts	Ave	F	P	Total
Bill Andrew	35	143	314.0	12.0	326.0	9.119	3	1	4
Ronnie Genz	37	149	319.0	10.0	329.0	8.832	4	2	6
Geoff Mudge	**38**	**153**	**288.5**	**26.0**	**314.5**	**8.222**	**2**	**1**	**3**
§Colin McKee	**38**	**154**	**193.0**	**45.0**	**238.0**	**6.182**	**1**		**1**
Pete Smith	32	123	139.0	38.0	177.0	5.756		1	1
§Wayne Briggs	25	85	98.5	18.0	116.5	5.482			
Norman Strachan	33	109	123.0	25.0	148.0	5.431			
Bruce Cribb	27	80	66.0	18.0	84.0	4.200			

NEW ZEALANDER Colin McKee went through the entire 1966 season taking every single programmed ride! He was never pulled out of a race – and never given an extra outing all year.

1967...1967...1967...1967...1967...1967

	M	R	Pts	BP	TPts	Ave	F	P	Total
§Gote Nordin	34	147	356.0	11.0	367.0	9.986	8		8
Geoff Mudge	**38**	**162**	**309.0**	**25.0**	**334.0**	**8.247**		**3**	**3**
Ronnie Genz	37	154	280.0	28.0	308.0	8.000		2	2
§Tony Lewis	6	13	18.0	4.0	22.0	6.769			
Peter Smith	**38**	**138**	**181.0**	**36.0**	**217.0**	**6.290**		**1**	**1**
Norman Strachan	37	142	183.0	27.0	210.0	5.915		1	1
Bruce Cribb	37	115	117.0	25.0	142.0	4.939			
§Geoff Penniket	**38**	**129**	**120.0**	**31.0**	**151.0**	**4.682**			

1968...1968...1968...1968...1968...1968

	M	R	Pts	BP	TPts	Ave	F	P	Total
Göte Nordin	1	4	11.0	1.0	12.0	12.000		1	1
Bill Andrew	20	88	176.0	7.0	183.0	8.318			
Geoff Mudge	**39**	**181**	**319.0**	**28.0**	**347.0**	**7.669**			
Pete Smith	**39**	**172**	**294.0**	**27.0**	**321.0**	**7.465**		**1**	**1**
§§Odd Fossengen	37	162	253.0	28.0	281.0	6.938			
Bruce Cribb	32	119	146.0	24.0	170.0	5.714			
§Ted Laessing	33	122	133.0	27.0	160.0	5.246			
§Maurie Mattingley	2	7	8.0	1.0	9.0	5.143			
§Tim Bungay	36	120	101.0	35.0	136.0	4.533			
Tony Lewis	12	33	32.0	4.0	36.0	4.364			
§§Mike Vernam	8	13	8.0	2.0	10.0	3.077			
§Arne Pander	6	10	2.0	0.0	2.0	0.800			
§§Tony Hall	4	8	1.0	0.0	1.0	0.500			

GÖTE NORDIN, top scorer in 1967, was unbeaten in the first match of the season against Wimbledon – and then walked out on the Pirates to return home to Sweden to look after his business interests. He was eventually replaced by new Norwegian capture Odd Fossengen.

1969...1969...1969...1969...1969...1969

	M	R	Pts	BP	TPts	Ave	F	P	Total
Pete Smith	34	136	293.5	24.0	317.5	9.338	4	4	8
Geoff Mudge	37	152	314.0	30.0	344.0	9.053	3		3
Odd Fossengen	36	149	263.0	25.0	288.0	7.732	1		1
Bruce Cribb	**38**	**156**	**241.0**	**44.0**	**285.0**	**7.308**	**1**	**2**	**3**
§Gordon Guasco	**38**	**140**	**221.0**	**33.0**	**254.0**	**7.257**	**2**		**2**
§Frank Shuter	37	129	147.0	32.0	179.0	5.550			
Ted Laessing	**38**	**112**	**105.0**	**21.0**	**126.0**	**4.500**			
Ross Gilbertson	1	3	2.0	1.0	3.0	4.000			
Mike Vernam	4	9	4.0	1.0	5.0	2.222			

▲ *ONE OF THE great myths of the British League was that when Poole won the 1969 title they did it with a team of riders who all averaged seven points a match. As the above statistics show the Pirates actually had TWO nine-point riders in their side. However, when the season began not one of the Poole seven had an average above eight points a match. The 1968 averages of the championship winning squad were: Mudge 7.67, Smith 7.47, Fossengen 6.94, Cribb 5.71, Laessing 5.25. Shuter, allocated from Swindon, had a 5.25 average and Guasco, who hadn't ridden in Britain since 1966 had a 7.77 average at Wolverhampton.*

1970...1970...1970...1970...1970...1970

	M	R	Pts	BP	TPts	Ave	F	P	Total
Geoff Mudge	**38**	**164**	**303.0**	**22.0**	**325.0**	**7.927**			
Gordon Guasco	35	145	244.0	36.0	280.0	7.724	1	1	2
Odd Fossengen	**38**	**157**	**250.0**	**40.0**	**290.0**	**7.389**		**1**	**1**
Pete Smith	**38**	**157**	**269.0**	**17.0**	**286.0**	**7.287**	**2**	**1**	**3**
§Mike Cake	**38**	**152**	**194.0**	**28.0**	**222.0**	**5.842**		**1**	**1**
Ted Laessing	19	63	63.0	12.0	75.0	4.762			
Frank Shuter	33	103	109.0	12.0	121.0	4.699			
Mike Vernam	18	39	19.0	4.0	23.0	2.359			
§Derek Cook	6	12	3.0	0.0	3.0	1.000			

1971...1971...1971...1971...1971...1971

	M	R	Pts	BP	TPts	Ave	F	P	Total
§Reidar Eide	36	156	341.0	14.0	355.0	9.103	2	4	6
Odd Fossengen	36	151	269.0	24.0	293.0	7.762	1		1
Pete Smith	36	151	264.0	29.0	293.0	7.762	1		1
§§Bo Wirebrand	31	120	154.0	27.0	181.0	6.033		1	1
§John Langfield	36	145	191.0	27.0	218.0	6.014			
Mike Cake	35	129	133.0	26.0	159.0	4.930			
Derek Cook	33	88	51.0	18.0	69.0	3.136			
§§John Davis	4	7	2.0	1.0	3.0	1.714			
Mike Vernam	3	7	3.0	0.0	3.0	1.714			

1972...1972...1972...1972...1972...1972

	M	R	Pts	BP	TPts	Ave	F	P	Total
Christer Löfqvist	29	125	257.0	21.0	278.0	8.896	1	2	3
Pete Smith	35	148	276.0	20.0	296.0	8.000		1	1
Odd Fossengen	34	137	192.0	38.0	230.0	6.715			
John Langfield	29	118	178.0	13.0	191.0	6.475	1	1	2
Brian Collins	31	121	147.0	27.0	174.0	5.752			
Frank Shuter	**36**	**135**	**159.0**	**24.0**	**183.0**	**5.422**		**1**	**1**
Mike Cake	23	79	74.0	18.0	92.0	4.658			
§Jim Ryman	7	28	28.0	2.0	30.0	4.286			
§§Trevor Barnwell	1	2	1.0	1.0	2.0	4.000			
§Dai Evans	1	2	1.0	1.0	2.0	4.000			
§Stan Stevens	2	5	3.0	1.0	4.0	3.200			
§Lou Sansom	1	2	1.0	0.0	1.0	2.000			
§§Len Davis	6	14	4.0	1.0	5.0	1.429			
§§Martin Yeates	3	7	0.0	0.0	0.0	0.000			
§Phil Cole	1	2	0.0	0.0	0.0	0.000			
§§Bryan Loakes	1	2	0.0	0.0	0.0	0.000			

POOLE were the main beneficiaries from West Ham's closure as a British League track as they were able to sign Swedish international Christer Löfqvist who made an instant impression with the Pirates's fans.

POOLE

1973...1973...1973...1973...1973...1973

	M	R	Pts	BP	TPts	Ave	F	P	Total
Christer Löfqvist	20	86	196.0	10.0	206.0	9.581	3		3
Pete Smith	34	133	265.0	11.0	276.0	8.301	3		3
Odd Fossengen	36	152	228.0	45.0	273.0	7.184		1	1
§§Antonin Woryna	29	111	164.0	16.0	180.0	6.486	2	1	3
Brian Collins	37	147	183.0	35.0	218.0	5.932	1		1
Bo Wirebrand	31	106	127.0	15.0	142.0	5.358		1	1
§Arthur Browning	1	3	3.0	1.0	4.0	5.333			
§Roger Johns	2	6	7.0	0.0	7.0	4.667			
JIm Ryman	16	59	55.0	9.0	64.0	4.339			
§Miike Broadbank	1	2	2.0	0.0	2.0	4.000			
Norman Strachan	9	27	20.0	5.0	25.0	3.704			
§Russell Osborne	2	7	5.0	0.0	5.0	2.857			
Martin Yeates	9	25	11.0	4.0	15.0	2.400			
§§Dave Buttigieg	8	21	10.0	1.0	11.0	2.095			
§Dave Mills	1	2	1.0	0.0	1.0	2.000			
§Jimmy Squibb	1	3	1.0	0.0	1.0	1.333			
§Dingle Brown	1	4	0.0	0.0	0.0	0.000			
Trevor Barnwell	1	2	0.0	0.0	0.0	0.000			
§Brian Clark	1	2	0.0	0.0	0.0	0.000			
§Geoff Swindells	1	2	0.0	0.0	0.0	0.000			

1974...1974...1974...1974...1974...1974

	M	R	Pts	BP	TPts	Ave	F	P	Total
§Eric Broadbelt	28	123	247.0	17.0	264.0	8.585	1	1	2
§Malcolm Ballard	3	11	19.0	4.0	23.0	8.364			
Pete Smith	35	156	266.0	18.0	284.0	7.282	1		1
§Phil Herne	1	5	7.0	2.0	9.0	7.200			
§Richard May	39	175	238.0	38.0	276.0	6.309	1		1
§Colin Gooddy	37	143	203.0	22.0	225.0	6.294			
Odd Fossengen	5	21	30.0	2.0	32.0	6.095			
§Øyvind Berg	4	17	19.0	4.0	23.0	5.412			
Antonin Woryna	36	151	177.0	22.0	199.0	5.272			
§Neil Middleditch	3	10	10.0	1.0	11.0	4.400			
Jim Ryman	6	20	11.0	3.0	14.0	2.800			
Mike Cake	20	63	29.0	11.0	40.0	2.540			
Martin Yeates	12	42	22.0	2.0	24.0	2.286			
Brian Clark	1	2	1.0	0.0	1.0	2.000			
§§Russell Foot	5	15	4.0	2.0	6.0	1.600			
§Keith White	1	3	1.0	0.0	1.0	1.333			
Dingle Brown	1	2	0.0	0.0	0.0	0.000			

1975...1975...1975...1975...1975...1975

	M	R	Pts	BP	TPts	Ave	F	P	Total
§Malcolm Simmons	33	143	368.0	4.0	372.0	10.406	15	1	16
Eric Broadbelt	**36**	**153**	**273.0**	**14.0**	**287.0**	**7.503**			
§Christer Sjösten	29	120	163.0	24.0	187.0	6.233			
Colin Gooddy	27	101	121.0	15.0	136.0	5.386	1		1
Pete Smith	25	96	103.0	24.0	127.0	5.292			
Neil Middleditch	29	100	89.0	23.0	112.0	4.480			
§Steve Weatherley	1	5	3.0	2.0	5.0	4.000			
§Keith Anderson	1	3	2.0	1.0	3.0	4.000			
§Robert Hollingworth	1	2	2.0	0.0	2.0	4.000			
§Neil Cameron	35	103	83.0	14.0	97.0	3.767			
§Alan Grahame	2	10	8.0	1.0	9.0	3.600			
Martin Yeates	18	60	30.0	8.0	38.0	2.533			
§Dave Piddock	1	2	1.0	0.0	1.0	2.000			
§§Keith Evans	1	3	1.0	0.0	1.0	1.333			
§§Christoph Betzl	2	7	1.0	0.0	1.0	0.571			
Brian Clark	1	2	0.0	0.0	0.0	0.000			

MALCOLM SIMMONS, signed from King's Lynn, became the first Poole rider to finish the season with an average above 10 points a meeting.

1976...1976...1976...1976...1976...1976

	M	R	Pts	BP	TPts	Ave	F	P	Total
Malcolm Simmons	35	164	409.0	8.0	417.0	10.171	8	3	11
Eric Broadbelt	21	84	143.0	7.0	150.0	7.143	2	1	3
Christer Sjösten	32	141	210.0	25.0	235.0	6.667	2		2
Pete Smith	36	148	201.0	27.0	228.0	6.162			
Neil Middleditch	**38**	**149**	**159.0**	**29.0**	**188.0**	**5.047**			
Richard May	33	119	135.0	15.0	150.0	5.042			
Colin Gooddy	35	116	117.0	28.0	145.0	5.000			
Martin Yeates	12	37	33.0	7.0	40.0	4.324			
§Vic Harding	2	8	3.0	2.0	5.0	2.500			
§Tony Featherstone	1	3	0.0	0.0	0.0	0.000			

1977...1977...1977...1977...1977...1977

	M	R	Pts	BP	TPts	Ave	F	P	Total
Malcolm Simmons	28	127	321.0	5.0	326.0	10.268	9	1	10
Kevin Holden	3	13	27.0	4.0	31.0	9.538			
Christer Sjösten	17	60	101.0	11.0	112.0	7.467		1	1
Eric Broadbelt	29	123	201.0	15.0	216.0	7.024	1	2	3
Neil Middleditch	**38**	**160**	**213.0**	**39.0**	**252.0**	**6.300**	**1**		**1**
Colin Gooddy	30	109	130.0	21.0	151.0	5.541			
Richard May	30	102	106.0	21.0	127.0	4.980		1	1
Pete Smith	36	128	124.0	22.0	146.0	4.563			
Martin Yeates	14	46	46.0	6.0	52.0	4.522			
§Alan Sage	1	2	1.0	1.0	2.0	4.000			
§§Nigel Davis	1	1	0.0	0.0	0.0	0.000			
§§Roger Abel	1	2	0.0	0.0	0.0	0.000			

1978...1978...1978...1978...1978...1978

	M	R	Pts	BP	TPts	Ave	F	P	Total
Malcolm Simmons	39	163	436.0	3.0	439.0	10.773	12	1	13
Neil Middleditch	39	160	283.0	24.0	307.0	7.675			
Christer Sjösten	37	149	249.0	21.0	270.0	7.248			
§Mike Curoso	43	156	214.0	38.0	252.0	6.462		1	1
§Steve Finch	2	7	9.0	2.0	11.0	6.286			
Danny Kennedy	18	71	96.0	11.0	107.0	6.028			
Martin Yeates	42	160	205.0	35.0	240.0	6.000		1	1
§Kelvin Mullarkey	25	96	107.0	28.0	135.0	5.625			
§§Andrzej Tkocz	22	71	62.0	18.0	80.0	4.507			
Colin Gooddy	22	63	40.0	13.0	53.0	3.365			
§Alan Johns	1	4	2.0	1.0	3.0	3.000			
§Sean Willmott	4	11	5.0	2.0	7.0	2.545			
§§Gary Ford	1	2	1.0	0.0	1.0	2.000			
§David Shields	1	2	0.0	0.0	0.0	0.000			

1979...1979...1979...1979...1979...1979

	M	R	Pts	BP	TPts	Ave	F	P	Total
Malcolm Simmons	32	135	299	6	305.0	9.037	4		4
§§Ron Preston	32	139	277	21	298.0	8.576	4	2	6
Christer Sjösten	26	101	144.0	20.0	164.0	6.495			
Neil Middleditch	**36**	**147**	**209.0**	**29.0**	**238.0**	**6.476**	**1**	**1**	**2**
Danny Kennedy	31	124	157.0	31.0	188.0	6.065			
Andrzej Tkocz	21	66	82.0	14.0	96.0	5.818		2	2
§Pip Lamb	2	7	8.0	1.0	9.0	5.143			
Martin Yeates	**36**	**121**	**113.0**	**18.0**	**131.0**	**4.331**			
Alan Sage	1	4	3.0	1.0	4.0	4.000			
§§Piotr Pyszny	1	2	2.0	0.0	2.0	4.000			
§Louis Carr	1	3	2.0	0.0	2.0	2.667			
Kelvin Mullarkey	8	28	15.0	3.0	18.0	2.571			
§Nigel Crabtree	1	5	2.0	0.0	2.0	1.600			
Nigel Davis	2	6	1.0	0.0	1.0	0.667			
§Barney Kennett	1	3	0.0	0.0	0.0	0.000			
§Bob Coles	1	1	0.0	0.0	0.0	0.000			
§§Peter Spink	1	1	0.0	0.0	0.0	0.000			

1979 ended tragically for Poole when their popular Swedish international Christer Sjösten, younger brother of Belle Vue's Sören, was killed in a track crash at Brisbane, Australia, shortly before Christmas. Sjösten was the third British League rider to die during the year – Vic Harding had been killed at Hackney and Long Eaton's Nigel Wasley died from a blood infection after fracturing his leg.

1980...1980...1980...1980...1980...1980

	M	R	Pts	BP	TPts	Ave	F	P	Total
Malcolm Simmons	28	123	274.0	15.0	289.0	9.398	3	1	4
Ron Preston	23	101	214.0	16.0	230.0	9.109	1	1	2
Peter Prinsloo	33	146	234.0	31.0	265.0	7.260			
Neil Middleditch	**34**	**142**	**212.0**	**35.0**	**247.0**	**6.958**			
§Vaclav Verner	27	113	165.0	26.0	191.0	6.761			
§Benny Rourke	1	3	4.0	1.0	5.0	6.667			
Danny Kennedy	33	130	135.0	26.0	161.0	4.954			
Martin Yeates	10	31	32.0	5.0	37.0	4.774			
§John McNeill	26	73	60.0	13.0	73.0	4.000			
§§Mark De Kok	1	2	2.0	0.0	2.0	4.000			
§Kevin Bowen	8	18	3.0	2.0	5.0	1.111			
§§Garry May	1	2	0.0	0.0	0.0	0.000			

POOLE

1981...1981...1981...1981...1981...1981

	M	R	Pts	BP	TPts	Ave	F	P	Total
John Davis	15	61	144.0	4.0	148.0	9.705	5		5
§Scott Autrey	45	215	417.5	35.0	452.5	8.419	2	1	3
Ron Preston	12	62	110.0	9.0	119.0	7.677	1		1
§Kevin Smith	44	187	319.0	31.0	350.0	7.487		1	1
Danny Kennedy	**47**	**223**	**371.0**	**42.0**	**413.0**	**7.408**	**1**		**1**
Peter Prinsloo	**47**	**216**	**305.0**	**49.0**	**354.0**	**6.556**			
Neil Middleditch	46	188	229.5	57.0	286.5	6.096		1	1
§Les Sawyer	13	35	23.0	4.0	27.0	3.086			
§Nicky Allott	1	3	1.0	1.0	2.0	2.667			
§Pete Ellams	18	46	22.0	7.0	29.0	2.522			
§Andy Campbell	4	11	6.0	0.0	6.0	2.182			
§§Keith Wright	6	13	4.0	1.0	5.0	1.538			
§Malcolm Bedkober	12	25	6.0	2.0	8.0	1.280			
§John Barker	1	4	1.0	0.0	1.0	1.000			
§§Claes Jensen	13	29	1.0	0.0	1.0	0.138			
§§Michael Holding	1	2	0.0	0.0	0.0	0.000			

1982...1982...1982...1982...1982...1982

	M	R	Pts	BP	TPts	Ave	F	P	Total
John Davis	37	156	325.5	13.0	338.5	8.679			
Scott Autrey	42	189	354.0	30.0	384.0	8.127			
Neil Middleditch	44	165	205.0	43.0	248.0	6.012			
§Dave Allen	1	2	2.0	1.0	3.0	6.000			
Vaclav Verner	34	127	159.0	27.0	186.0	5.858			
Kevin Smith	43	173	214.0	38.0	252.0	5.827			
Danny Kennedy	29	111	125.0	22.0	147.0	5.297			
John McNeill	1	4	5.0	0.0	5.0	5.000			
Peter Prinsloo	31	82	71.0	21.0	92.0	4.488			
Les Sawyer	7	20	17.0	4.0	21.0	4.200			
§§Rod North	2	7	7.0	0.0	7.0	4.000			
§§Chris Barnes	1	2	1.0	1.0	2.0	4.000			
Pete Ellams	17	45	27.0	10.0	37.0	3.289			
Andy Campbell	6	16	5.0	1.0	6.0	1.500			
§§Mikael Blixt	4	9	2.0	1.0	3.0	1.333			

1983...1983...1983...1983...1983...1983

	M	R	Pts	BP	TPts	Ave	F	P	Total
§Michael Lee	42	191	471.0	14.0	485.0	10.157	7	1	
John Davis	33	130	246.0	5.0	251.0	7.723	2		
Kevin Smith	42	176	287.0	19.0	306.0	6.955	2		
Vaclav Verner	25	93	125.0	16.0	141.0	6.065			
§Andy Buck	1	2	2.0	1.0	3.0	6.000			
Neil Middleditch	43	171	167.0	63.0	230.0	5.380			
Andy Campbell	43	161	154.0	37.0	191.0	4.745			
§§Stan Bear	12	39	35.0	8.0	43.0	4.410			
§Richard Knight	2	10	11.0	0.0	11.0	4.400			
§§Sam Ermolenko	4	16	15.0	2.0	17.0	4.250			
§§Brian Jakobsen	17	53	47.0	9.0	56.0	4.226			
§§Erik Stenlund	15	46	36.0	5.0	41.0	3.565			
§Keith Millard	9	23	15.0	2.0	17.0	2.957			
§Robert Maxfield	6	14	7.0	1.0	8.0	2.286			
§Robert Henry	1	2	0.0	0.0	0.0	0.000			
§Nigel Sparshott	1	2	0.0	0.0	0.0	0.000			

1984...1984...1984...1984...1984...1984

	M	R	Pts	BP	TPts	Ave	F	P	Total
Michael Lee	11	42	97.0	0.0	97.0	9.238	4		4
Sam Ermolenko	41	177	268.0	29.0	297.0	6.712			
§Finn Thomsen	34	138	196.0	22.0	218.0	6.319			
Stan Bear	45	175	220.0	49.0	269.0	6.149			
Brian Jakobsen	35	121	160.0	17.0	177.0	5.851			
Neil Middleditch	48	181	223.0	38.0	261.0	5.768			
Kevin Smith	40	147	179.5	27.0	206.5	5.619			
Colin Cook	3	8	8.0	2.0	10.0	5.000			
§Alun Rossiter	1	4	4.0	1.0	5.0	5.000			
§§Gerd Riss	6	21	21.0	3.0	24.0	4.571			
§Bob Garrad	6	18	16.0	2.0	18.0	4.000			
§Mike Spink	1	3	3.0	0.0	3.0	4.000			
§§Leif Wahlmann	8	26	19.0	4.0	23.0	3.538			
§§Bobby Ott	2	7	5.0	1.0	6.0	3.429			
§David Mullett	2	4	3.0	0.0	3.0	3.000			
§Andy Fines	5	9	2.0	2.0	4.0	1.778			
§Robert Holllingworth	2	6	1.0	0.0	1.0	0.667			
§§Marcus Bisson	1	2	0.0	0.0	0.0	0.000			
§Ashley Pullen	1	2	0.0	0.0	0.0	0.000			
§Andrew Silver	1	2	0.0	0.0	0.0	0.000			

JOHNNIE THOMSON TROPHY

1967	1 Reidar Eide	2 Ronnie Genz	3 Geoff Mudge
1970	1 Trevor Hedge	2 Barry Briggs	3 Martin Ashby

HIGH SPEED GAS TROPHY

1967	1 Reidar Eide	2 Colin Pratt	3 Ivan Mauger

BLUE RIBAND

1970	1 Barry Briggs	2 Martin Ashby	3 Jim McMillan
1971	1 Ole Olsen	2 Anders Michanek	3 Barry Briggs
1972	1 Ray Wilson	2 Nigel Boocock	3 Barry Briggs
1973	1 Anders Michanek	2 Peter Collins	3 Christer Löfqvist
1974	1 Ole Olsen	2 John Louis	3 Ivan Mauger
1975	1 Malcolm Simmons	2 Scott Autrey	3 John Louis
1976	1 Malcolm Simmons	2 Eric Broadbelt	3 Phil Crump
1977	1 Malcolm Simmons	2 Dave Jessup	3 Phil Herne
1978	1 Malcolm Simmons	2 Ole Olsen	3 Scott Autrey
1979	1 Bobby Schwartz	2 Jim McMillan	3 Larry Ross
1980	1 Dave Jessup	2 Scott Autrey	3 Bobby Schwartz
1981	1 Bruce Penhall	2 Peter Prinsloo	3 Dennis Sigalos
1982	1 Bobby Schwartz	2 Phil Crump	3 Simon Wigg
1983	1 Erik Gundersen	2 Simon Wigg	3 Lance King
1984	1 Mitch Shirra	2 Erik Gundersen	3 Bobby Schwartz
1985	1 Stan Bear	2 Kevin Smith	3 Bruce Cribb
1986	1 Kevin Smith	2 Les Collins	3 Nigel Crabtree
1987	1 Melvyn Taylor	2 Neville Tatum	3 Steve Schofield
1988	1 Steve Schofield	2 Melvyn Taylor	3 Jens Rasmussen
1989	1 Steve Schofield	2 Alastair Stevens	3 Mick Poole
1990	1 Chris Louis	2 Alun Rossiter	3 Steve Regeling
1991	1 Marvyn Cox	2 Gary Havelock	3 Jan O. Pedersen

GORDON GUASCO TROPHY

1971	1 John Langfield	2 Bruce Cribb	3 Reidar Eide

SKOL MASTERS SOUTHERN FINAL

1977	1 Malcolm Simmons	2 John Davis	3 Eric Broadbelt

CHRISTER SJÖSTEN MEMORIAL TROPHY

1980	1 Bob Kilby	2 John Davis	3 Scott Autrey

RINGS PANASONIC KO TROPHY

1980	1 Billy Sanders	2 Bo Petersen	3 Bobby Schwartz

POOLE TRADERS GALA NIGHT

1983	1 Dennis Sigalos	2 Kevin Smith	3 Hans Nielsen
1983	1 Dennis Sigalos	2 Michael Lee	3 Chris Morton
1984	1 Mitch Shirra	2 Stan Bear	3 Phil Crump
1984	1 Mitch Shirra	2 Simon Cross	3 Stan Bear
1984	1 John Davis	2 Malcolm Simmons	3 Finn Thomsen

POOLE GALA FAIR

1983	1 Michael Lee	2 Bo Petersen	3 Simon Wigg
1984	1 Simon Wigg	2 Lance King	3 Phil Crump

LEIF WAHLMAN MEMORIAL TROPHY

1984	1 Stan Bear	2 Finn Thomsen	3 Neil Middleditch

AMERICAN STYLE SPEEDWAY

1984	1 Stan Bear	2 Neil Middleditch	3 Sean Willmott

READING

1971...1971...1971...1971...1971...1971

	M	R	Pts	BP	TPts	Ave	F	P	Total
§Anders Michanek	29	119	294.0	5.0	299.0	10.050	8	2	10
§Dag Lovaas	35	140	235.0	36.0	271.0	7.743	1	1	2
§Geoff Mudge	19	73	119.0	13.0	132.0	7.233			
§Geoff Curtis	36	140	214.0	22.0	236.0	6.743			
§Richard May	36	137	183.0	27.0	210.0	6.131	1	2	3
§Mick Bell	**37**	**125**	**132.0**	**32.0**	**164.0**	**5.248**			
§§Bernie Leigh	**37**	**117**	**114.0**	**25.0**	**139.0**	**4.752**			
§§Terry Chandler	2	5	3.0	2.0	5.0	4.000			
§§Josef Angermuller	8	23	14.0	5.0	19.0	3.304			
§§Max Amor	1	2	0.0	0.0	0.0	0.000			

DAG LOVAAS was involved in two dead heats during his first season with the Racers...in successive matches at home to Oxford and then away to Wimbledon!

1972...1972...1972...1972...1972...1972

	M	R	Pts	BP	TPts	Ave	F	P	Total
Anders Michanek	26	105	270.0	6.0	276.0	10.514	8	2	10
Dag Lovaas	35	143	287.0	27.0	314.0	8.783	4	1	5
Geoff Curtis	**37**	**146**	**243.0**	**39.0**	**282.0**	**7.726**		**3**	**3**
Geoff Mudge	35	134	206.0	31.0	237.0	7.075			
Richard May	35	138	187.0	33.0	220.0	6.377		2	2
Mick Bell	**37**	**134**	**180.0**	**29.0**	**209.0**	**6.239**			
Bernie Leigh	29	82	81.0	22.0	103.0	5.024			
§Graeme Smith	11	35	28.0	5.0	33.0	3.771			
§Roger Johns	1	3	1.0	1.0	2.0	2.667			
§Arthur Browning	1	2	0.0	0.0	0.0	0.000			

1973...1973...1973...1973...1973...1973

	M	R	Pts	BP	TPts	Ave	F	P	Total
Anders Michanek	37	156	439.0	4.0	443.0	11.359	22	4	26
Dag Lovaas	42	175	430.0	10.0	440.0	10.057	11	1	12
§Carl Glover	1	3	6.0	1.0	7.0	9.333			
Geoff Curtis	43	172	323.0	31.0	354.0	8.233	2	7	9
§Alan Knapkin	1	4	6.0	1.0	7.0	7.000			
Richard May	43	162	212.0	33.0	245.0	6.049		2	2
Mick Bell	**44**	**170**	**203.0**	**45.0**	**248.0**	**5.835**		**1**	**1**
§Bobby McNeil	7	25	27.0	6.0	33.0	5.280			
§Richard Greer	3	10	9.0	4.0	13.0	5.200			
§Peter Murray	3	7	6.0	3.0	9.0	5.143			
§Mike Broadbank	2	6	4.0	3.0	7.0	4.667			
Bernie Leigh	**44**	**139**	**129.0**	**26.0**	**155.0**	**4.460**			
Roger Johns	3	9	9.0	1.0	10.0	4.444			
§Mitch Graham	1	5	5.0	0.0	5.0	4.000			
§Jack Millen	12	40	28.0	4.0	32.0	3.200			
§Geoff Bouchard	1	3	1.0	1.0	2.0	2.667			
§Graham Drury	1	3	1.0	1.0	2.0	2.667			
§§Jack Walker	5	13	6.0	2.0	8.0	2.462			
§Trevor Geer	2	5	2.0	1.0	3.0	2.400			
§Doug Templeton	1	2	1.0	0.0	1.0	2.000			
§Dave Morton	1	3	0.0	0.0	0.0	0.000			
§Roy Sizmore	1	2	0.0	0.0	0.0	0.000			

READING had hoped to celebrate winning the 1973 British League championship by opening the new season in the newly-built Smallmead Stadium. But the three-day week caused by industrial unrest delayed work at the site – a former Council rubbish tip – and the Reading managemd to loan their riders out for the 1974 campaign..

1975...1975...1975...1975...1975...1975

	M	R	Pts	BP	TPts	Ave	F	P	Total
Anders Michanek	24	95	255.0	4.0	259.0	10.905	9	2	11
§John Davis	33	140	243.0	15.0	258.0	7.371	2		2
§Bengt Jansson	**36**	**149**	**240.0**	**23.0**	**263.0**	**7.060**	**1**		**1**
§§Colin Richardson	3	9	10.0	3.0	13.0	5.778			
Bernie Leigh	**36**	**141**	**170.0**	**27.0**	**197.0**	**5.589**			
§Bob Humphreys	**36**	**146**	**175.0**	**28.0**	**203.0**	**5.562**		**1**	**1**
Mick Bell	34	112	119.0	27.0	146.0	5.214			
Richard May	**36**	**109**	**117.0**	**19.0**	**136.0**	**4.991**			
§Andy Cowan	1	2	1.0	0.0	1.0	2.000			
§Eddie Argall	1	2	0.0	0.0	0.0	0.000			
§Ricky Day	1	2	0.0	0.0	0.0	0.000			

1976...1976...1976...1976...1976...1976

	M	R	Pts	BP	TPts	Ave	F	P	Total
§Dave Jessup	**38**	**158**	**398.0**	**11.0**	**409.0**	**10.354**	**9**	**4**	**13**
John Davis	36	144	324.0	12.0	336.0	9.333	3	2	5
Bernie Leigh	37	150	218.0	35.0	253.0	6.747			
Bob Humphreys	**38**	**149**	**201.0**	**38.0**	**239.0**	**6.416**		**1**	**1**
Bengt Jansson	10	39	52.0	10.0	62.0	6.359			
§§Boleslaw Proch	29	108	121.0	24.0	145.0	5.370			
Mick Bell	37	124	130.0	30.0	160.0	5.161		1	1
§§Eugeniusz Blaszak	8	24	18.0	4.0	22.0	3.667			
§§Ian Gledhill	8	19	11.0	0.0	11.0	2.316			
§§Gary Spencer	1	3	0.0	0.0	0.0	0.000			

1977...1977...1977...1977...1977...1977

	M	R	Pts	BP	TPts	Ave	F	P	Total
Dave Jessup	45	193	489.0	9.0	498.0	10.321	12	3	15
Bengt Jansson	41	163	234.0	43.0	277.0	6.798	1	2	3
Bob Humphreys	**46**	**174**	**215.0**	**48.0**	**263.0**	**6.046**		**2**	**2**
Bernie Leigh	39	153	198.0	27.0	225.0	5.882			
§§Hans Wassermann	36	129	148.0	32.0	180.0	5.581			
Boleslaw Proch	13	47	48.0	9.0	57.0	4.851			
§Doug Underwood	22	65	62.0	9.0	71.0	4.369		1	1
Ian Gledhill	16	49	33.0	7.0	40.0	3.265			
§Glyn Taylor	8	19	11.0	1.0	12.0	2.526			
Roy Sizmore	1	2	0.0	0.0	0.0	0.000			
§§Bo Jansson	1	1	0.0	0.0	0.0	0.000			
§§Merv Janke	1	2	0.0	0.0	0.0	0.000			

1978...1978...1978...1978...1978...1978

	M	R	Pts	BP	TPts	Ave	F	P	Total
Dave Jessup	33	151	374.0	11.0	385.0	10.199	6	2	8
§Phil Collins	1	5	11.0	1.0	12.0	9.600			
John Davis	37	168	368.0	7.0	375.0	8.929	3	1	4
Hans Wassermann	16	65	75.0	21.0	96.0	5.908			
Bernie Leigh	**38**	**162**	**222.0**	**17.0**	**239.0**	**5.901**		**1**	**1**
Doug Underwood	35	130	128.0	25.0	153.0	4.708			
§Melvyn Taylor	15	53	47.0	13.0	60.0	4.528			
Ian Gledhill	7	23	21.0	4.0	25.0	4.348			
§Roger Abel	14	45	37.0	8.0	45.0	4.000			
Bob Humphreys	21	65	51.0	9.0	60.0	3.692			
§§Dave Allen	1	4	3.0	0.0	3.0	3.000			
§§Henryk Glucklich	20	64	41.0	6.0	47.0	2.938			
§§Kevin Bowen	10	25	13.0	3.0	16.0	2.560			
§§Ashley Pullen	5	15	9.0	0.0	9.0	2.400			
§Steve Clarke	2	3	1.0	0.0	1.0	1.333			

1979...1979...1979...1979...1979...1979

	M	R	Pts	BP	TPts	Ave	F	P	Total
John Davis	32	133	335.0	8.0	343.0	10.316	5	2	7
Jan Andersson	32	143	294.0	15.0	309.0	8.643	3	1	4
Terry Betts	34	143	256.0	21.0	277.0	7.748			
Bernie Leigh	**38**	**154**	**195.0**	**48.0**	**243.0**	**6.312**			
Melvyn Taylor	30	114	129.0	32.0	161.0	5.649			
§Nigel Couzens	2	5	7.0	0.0	7.0	5.600			
§Reidar Eide	17	62	67.0	14.0	81.0	5.226			
Bob Humphreys	27	103	121.0	12.0	133.0	5.165			
§Jiri Stancl	14	50	52.0	12.0	64.0	5.120			
Ashley Pullen	17	48	40.0	5.0	45.0	3.750		1	1
§§Sigvart Pedersen	3	8	3.0	1.0	4.0	2.000			
§§Alois Wiesböck	1	3	1.0	0.0	1.0	1.333			
Doug Underwood	4	8	2.0	0.0	2.0	1.000			
Kevin Bowen	2	5	1.0	0.0	1.0	0.800			
§Brian Woodward	4	16	2.0	0.0	2.0	0.500			
§§Garry May	1	3	0.0	0.0	0.0	0.000			
Malcolm Shakespeare	1	2	0.0	0.0	0.0	0.000			

THE WINTER brought sweeping changes at Reading – the most radical in the club's entire history.
Dave Lanning, a staff writer at TV Times but a long-time speedway buff, was engaged as Speedway Executive with former Racer Mick Bell as team manager.
Lanning took out an insurance policy which guaranteed the club £50,000 if they won the British League and his first major signing was Tony Briggs, son of four-time World Champion Barry. Reading were hardly out of the new all season and finally clinched that super pay-off by winning the title although the whole affair ended in uproar with Lanning eventually successfully suing Reading for a share of the pay-out.

BRITISH LEAGUE AVERAGES...BRITISH LEAGUE AVERAGES...BRITISH LEAGUE AVERAGES

READING

1980...1980...1980...1980...1980...1980

	M	R	Pts	BP	TPts	Ave	F	P	Total
Jan Andersson	33	139	321.0	28.0	349.0	10.043	6	2	8
§Bobby Schwartz	**36**	**156**	**363.0**	**27.0**	**390.0**	**10.000**	**8**	**3**	**11**
John Davis	34	138	325.0	6.0	331.0	9.594	5	2	7
Jiri Stancl	31	128	200.0	36.0	236.0	7.375	1	1	2
§Dave Trownson	6	17	23.0	8.0	31.0	7.294			
Reidar Eide	2	7	9.0	2.0	11.0	6.286			
Bernie Leigh	**36**	**143**	**169.0**	**41.0**	**210.0**	**5.874**			
§Steve McDermott	4	10	12.0	2.0	14.0	5.600			
§Barney Kennett	1	3	3.0	1.0	4.0	5.333			
Martin Ashby	24	80	81.0	25.0	106.0	5.300			
§§Tony Briggs	34	114	113.0	29.0	142.0	4.982			
§§Andy Campbell	1	2	1.0	0.0	1.0	2.000			
Ashley Pullen	7	20	7.0	2.0	9.0	1.800			
§§Mark Leslie	1	2	0.0	0.0	0.0	0.000			

1981...1981...1981...1981...1981...1981

	M	R	Pts	BP	TPts	Ave	F	P	Total
Jan Andersson	48	235	594.0	9.0	603.0	10.264	9		9
John Davis	26	111	254.0	14.0	268.0	9.658	1	1	2
Bobby Schwartz	45	219	487.0	23.0	510.0	9.315	1	5	6
Anders Michanek	5	22	34.0	3.0	37.0	6.727		1	1
Bernie Leigh	46	201	229.5	37.0	266.5	5.303			
Tony Briggs	26	108	105.0	30.0	135.0	5.000			
§§Denny Pyeatt	**50**	**204**	**203.0**	**45.0**	**248.0**	**4.863**			
Ashley Pullen	47	153	139.0	35.0	174.0	4.549			
§Colin Ackroyd	5	19	18.0	2.0	20.0	4.211			
Ian Gledhill	8	22	18.0	3.0	21.0	3.818			
§Andrzej Huszcza	5	18	10.0	5.0	15.0	3.333			
§Kelvin Mullarkey	1	4	3.0	0.0	3.0	3.000			
Steve McDermott	6	16	8.0	3.0	11.0	2.750			
§§Mark Leslie	5	10	3.0	3.0	6.0	2.400			
§§Barry Allaway	1	2	1.0	0.0	1.0	2.000			
§Charlie McKinna	1	2	1.0	0.0	1.0	2.000			
§§Peter Weurterle	8	21	6.0	2.0	8.0	1.524			
§§Max Schöllhorn	3	6	1.0	1.0	2.0	1.333			
§Richard Knight	1	2	0.0	0.0	0.0	0.000			

1982...1982...1982...1982...1982...1982

	M	R	Pts	BP	TPts	Ave	F	P	Total
Jan Andersson	38	163	395.0	11.0	406.0	9.963	3	4	7
Bobby Schwartz	33	144	351.0	3.0	354.0	9.833	7	1	8
§Steve Gresham	36	140	186.0	9.0	195.0	5.571			
Ashley Pullen	1	3	3.0	1.0	4.0	5.333			
Denny Pyeatt	29	103	111.0	25.0	136.0	5.282			
Jiri Stancl	23	88	101.0	14.0	115.0	5.227			
§Tim Hunt	41	155	156.0	41.0	197.0	5.084			
Dave Trownson	15	61	61.0	10.0	71.0	4.656			
Colin Ackroyd	7	22	19.0	3.0	22.0	4.000			
§§John Grahame	43	120	94.0	22.0	116.0	3.867			
§Dave Perks	2	7	4.0	1.0	5.0	2.857			
§Uno Johansson	7	23	12.0	4.0	16.0	2.783			
§Derek Harrison	2	5	2.0	1.0	3.0	2.400			
§Brett Saunders	1	2	1.0	0.0	1.0	2.000			
§§Steve Schofield	1	3	0.0	0.0	0.0	0.000			
Mark Leslie	1	2	0.0	0.0	0.0	0.000			

1983...1983...1983...1983...1983...1983

	M	R	Pts	BP	TPts	Ave	F	P	Total
§Mitch Shirra	47	196	478.0	13.0	491.0	10.020	10	2	12
Jan Andersson	46	190	437.0	13.0	450.0	9.474	6		6
Bobby Schwartz	43	176	372.0	25.0	397.0	9.023	3		3
§Pierre Brannefors	40	162	239.0	56.0	295.0	7.284		1	1
Steve McDermott	4	15	15.0	2.0	17.0	4.533			
Tim Hunt	38	142	122.0	31.0	153.0	4.310			
§Nigel Sparshott	1	4	3.0	1.0	4.0	4.000			
§§Peter Glanz	35	110	86.0	20.0	106.0	3.855			
Dave Trownson	6	20	13.0	4.0	17.0	3.400			
§§Stanislav Urban	25	84	57.0	11.0	68.0	3.238			
John Grahame	27	76	44.0	8.0	52.0	2.737			
§§Michael Warren	1	2	1.0	0.0	1.0	2.000			
§Glyn Taylor	5	13	6.0	0.0	6.0	1.846			
§Richard Knight	2	7	3.0	0.0	3.0	1.714			
Dave Perks	2	7	3.0	0.0	3.0	1.714			
Derek Harrison	1	3	1.0	0.0	1.0	1.333			
Steve Schofield	3	10	3.0	0.0	3.0	1.200			
§Finn Jensen	2	6	0.0	0.0	0.0	0.000			

1984...1984...1984...1984...1984...1984

	M	R	Pts	BP	TPts	Ave	F	P	Total
Jan Andersson	44	187	455.0	15.0	470.0	10.053	9	1	10
Mitch Shirra	47	196	449.0	5.0	454.0	9.265	5		5
§§Per Jonsson	47	184	275.0	25.0	300.0	6.522			
§Bruce Cribb	2	8	9.0	4.0	13.0	6.500			
\Tim Hunt	50	190	217.0	56.0	273.0	5.747			
Malcolm Holloway	50	182	203.0	44.0	247.0	5.429			
Pierre Brannefors	47	162	183.0	36.0	219.0	5.407			
Peter Glanz	47	156	155.0	35.0	190.0	4.872			
Michael Warren	2	3	1.0	0.0	1.0	1.333			
§Robert Henry	1	3	1.0	0.0	1.0	1.333			
§Jamie Luckhurst	1	2	0.0	0.0	0.0	0.000			
§Peter Nightingale	1	3	0.0	0.0	0.0	0.000			
§Barry Thomas	1	2	0.0	0.0	0.0	0.000			

1985...1985...1985...1985...1985...1985

	M	R	Pts	BP	TPts	Ave	F	P	Total
Jan Andersson	40	179	401.0	21.0	422.0	9.430	4	3	7
John Davis	32	143	311.0	11.0	322.0	9.007	2		2
Mitch Shirra	32	126	196.0	18.0	214.0	6.794		1	1
Per Jonsson	37	153	219.0	23.0	242.0	6.327	1		1
Tim Hunt	32	118	129.0	36.0	165.0	5.593			
Peter Glanz	28	107	120.0	29.0	149.0	5.570			
§David Mullett	5	15	16.0	3.0	19.0	5.067			
Malcolm Holloway	42	139	136.0	28.0	164.0	4.719		1	1
§Neil Middleditch	12	42	38.0	11.0	49.0	4.667			
§Martin Goodwin	1	3	2.0	1.0	3.0	4.000			
§David Blackburn	3	9	6.0	2.0	8.0	3.556			
§Mark Fiora	2	9	6.0	0.0	6.0	2.667			
§Carl Baldwin	1	3	1.0	1.0	2.0	2.667			
§Mark Chessell	12	39	16.0	4.0	20.0	2.051			
§§Einar Kyllingstad	5	16	5.0	2.0	7.0	1.750			
§§Stuart Williams	1	3	0.0	0.0	0.0	0.000			

BRIGGO MARK 2...Reading's big 1980 capture youngster Tony Briggs

READING

1986...1986...1986...1986...1986...1986

	M	R	Pts	BP	TPts	Ave	F	P	Total
Jan Andersson	42	185	400.0	32.0	432.0	9.341	3	1	4
John Davis	26	106	223.0	8.0	231.0	8.717	3		3
Mitch Shirra	37	154	287.0	17.0	304.0	7.896	2	1	3
Per Jonsson	38	157	243.0	46.0	289.0	7.363	1	2	3
Peter Glanz	43	163	211.0	29.0	240.0	5.890			
Malcolm Holloway	31	106	129.0	16.0	145.0	5.472			
David Mullett	14	48	54.0	10.0	64.0	5.333			
§Andy Galvin	6	18	18.0	2.0	20.0	4.444			
§§Tony Olsson	5	21	19.0	3.0	22.0	4.190			
Neil Middleditch	2	7	4.0	3.0	7.0	4.000			
Bruce Cribb	2	7	4.0	1.0	5.0	2.857			
§§Gary Tagg	22	68	17.0	6.0	23.0	1.353			
§§Trevor Williams	3	9	3.0	0.0	3.0	1.333			
§§Billy Pinder	22	66	18.0	3.0	21.0	1.273			

1987...1987...1987...1987...1987...1987

	M	R	Pts	BP	TPts	Ave	F	P	Total
Per Jonsson	43	188	421.0	18.0	439.0	9.340	5	1	6
Jan Andersson	46	198	425.0	20.0	445.0	8.990	2	3	5
David Mullett	2	9	14.0	3.0	17.0	7.556			
John Davis	31	118	191.0	14.0	205.0	6.949			
Tony Olsson	45	191	271.0	44.0	315.0	6.597		1	1
Peter Glanz	**48**	**188**	**234.0**	**69.0**	**303.0**	**6.447**			
Malcolm Holloway	45	166	200.0	50.0	250.0	6.024			
§Miles Evans	2	6	8.0	1.0	9.0	6.000			
§§Gary O'Hare	2	7	4.0	2.0	6.0	3.429			
Gary Tagg	39	94	46.5	14.0	60.5	2.574			
§§Rodney Payne	10	24	6.0	2.0	8.0	1.333			
§Nigel Crabtree	1	3	1.0	0.0	1.0	1.333			
§David Jackson	1	4	1.0	0.0	1.0	1.000			

1988...1988...1988...1988...1988...1988

	M	R	Pts	BP	TPts	Ave	F	P	Total
Per Jonsson	38	183	385.0	26.0	411.0	8.984	4	2	6
Jan Andersson	37	177	371.0	24.0	395.0	8.927	1	3	4
§Mick Poole	1	5	11.0	0.0	11.0	8.800			
Mitch Shirra	39	184	359.0	18.0	377.0	8.196	2	1	3
Tony Olsson	40	175	260.0	44.0	304.0	6.949		1	1
§Graham Jones	1	4	6.0	0.0	6.0	6.000			
Malcolm Holloway	38	155	188.0	30.0	218.0	5.626			
David Mullett	41	173	194.0	32.0	226.0	5.225			
Gary Tagg	21	75	48.0	10.0	58.0	3.093			
§Dean Standing	1	4	3.0	0.0	3.0	3.000			
Rodney Payne	20	64	33.0	12.0	45.0	2.813			
§Craig Hodgson	1	3	2.0	0.0	2.0	2.667			
§§Steve Chambers	3	8	2.0	1.0	3.0	1.500			
§Glenn Doyle	1	3	1.0	0.0	1.0	1.333			
§Mark Loram	1	4	1.0	0.0	1.0	1.000			
Andy Campbell	1	3	0.0	0.0	0.0	0.000			
§§Troy Smith	2	3	0.0	0.0	0.0	0.000			

IN THE MONEY...the 1980 Reading British League winning side that picked up a £40,000 bonus. Bobby Schwartz, Jan Andersson, Bernie Leigh, Jiri Stancl, John Davis, manager Mick Bell, Tony Briggs and Martin Ashby

1989...1989...1989...1989...1989...1989

	M	R	Pts	BP	TPts	Ave	F	P	Total
Jeremy Doncaster	**36**	**196**	**391.0**	**31.0**	**422.0**	**8.612**		**2**	**2**
Mitch Shirra	**36**	**186**	**339.5**	**15.0**	**354.5**	**7.624**	**1**		**1**
Tony Olsson	32	146	207.0	30.0	237.0	6.493			
§Carl Blackbird	35	153	186.0	25.0	211.0	5.516			
§Armando Castagna	9	38	48.0	4.0	52.0	5.474			
David Mullett	33	132	139.0	29.0	168.0	5.091			
Malcolm Holloway	20	73	63.0	17.0	80.0	4.384			
§§David Steen	8	25	10.0	6.0	16.0	2.560			
Steve Chambers	5	11	3.0	1.0	4.0	1.455			
§§Scott Pulleyn	4	12	3.0	0.0	3.0	1.000			
Troy Smith	1	3	0.0	0.0	0.0	0.000			

1990...1990...1990...1990...1990...1990

	M	R	Pts	BP	TPts	Ave	F	P	Total
Jeremy Doncaster	36	168	371.0	11.0	382.0	9.095	2		2
§Todd Wiltshire	29	141	286.0	23.0	309.0	8.766	1		1
Per Jonsson	37	174	331.0	34.0	365.0	8.391		1	1
Jan Andersson	37	167	258.5	43.0	301.5	7.222		1	1
Armando Castagna	8	33	41.0	12.0	53.0	6.424			
David Mullett	33	147	193.0	39.0	232.0	6.313			
Tony Olsson	27	112	146.0	29.0	175.0	6.250			
Troy Smith	3	8	5.0	1.0	6.0	3.000			
§§Nathan Murray	14	43	19.0	8.0	27.0	2.512			
David Steen	23	76	35.0	6.0	41.0	2.158			
§§Christian Howell	2	4	1.0	0.0	1.0	1.000			

READING OPEN CHAMPIONSHIP

1968	1 Graham Plant	2 John Poyser	3 Allan Brown
1970	1 Richard May	2 John Louis	3 Bernie Leigh

STADIUM TROPHY

1968	1 Graham Plant	2 Dene Davies	3 Mick Handley
1969	1 Barry Crowson	2 Pete Bradshaw	3 Dene Davies
1970	1 Richard May	2 Mike Vernam	3 Alan Knapkin

PETER ARNOLD MEMORIAL TROPHY

1969	1 John Harrhy	2 Martyn Piddock	3 Mick Bell
1970	1 Richard May	2 Arthur Price	3 John Harrhy
1971	1 Ray Wilson	2 Geoff Curtis	3 John Louis
1972	1 Reidar Eide	2 Ray Wilson	3 Ronnie Moore, Dag Lovaas, Richard May

MANPOWER TROPHY

1971	1 Barry Briggs	2 Anders Michanek	3 Reidar Eide
1972	1 Ivan Mauger	2 Anders Michanek	3 Ray Wilson
1973	1 Anders Michanek	2 Ole Olsen	3 Reidar Eide
1975	1 Phil Crump	2 Malcolm Simmons	3 Ole Olsen
1976	1 Peter Collins	2 Anders Michanek	3 John Louis
1977	1 Finn Thomsen	2 Gordon Kennett	3 Ole Olsen
1978	1 John Davis	2 Billy Sanders	3 Peter Collins
1979	1 Peter Collins	2 Bruce Penhall	3 Dave Jessup
1980	1 Chris Morton	2 Michael Lee	3 Bobby Schwartz

GEOFF CURTIS TROPHY

1975	1 John Davis	2 Tommy Jansson	3 Dag Lovaas
1976	1 Dave Jessup	2 John Davis	3 John Boulger
1979	1 Jan Andersson	2 Preben Eriksen	3 Bernie Leigh
1980	1 Bobby Schwartz	2 Preben Eriksen	3 Bernie Leigh
1984	1 Mitch Shirra	2 Jan Andersson	3 John Davis

JUBILEE TROPHY

1976	1 Ole Olsen	2 Peter Collins	3 Dave Jessup
1977	1 Michael Lee	2 Peter Collins	3 Dave Jessup
1978	1 Michael Lee	2 Malcolm Simmons	3 Ila Teromaa

TRADERS' TROPHY

1979	1 Dave Jessup	2 Bruce Penhall	3 John Davis

RADIO 210 GALA NIGHT

1980	1 Mitch Shirra	2 Bobby Schwartz	3 Zenon Plech

DENNY PYEATT MEMORIAL TROPHY

1988	1 Shawn Moran	2 Martin Dugard and Kelly Moran	
1989	1 Troy Butler	2 Martin Dugard	3 David Mullett
1990	1 Per Jonsson	2 Todd Wiltshire and Armanda Castagna	

DICK BAILEY MEMORIAL TROPHY

1989	1 Steve Chambers	2 David Steen	3 Kevin Pitts

SHEFFIELD

1965...1965...1965...1965...1965...1965

	M	R	Pts	BP	TPts	Ave	F	P	Total
§§Jack Kitchen	34	136	291.0	22.0	313.0	9.206	3	1	4
§§Clive Featherby	**35**	**140**	**255.0**	**15.0**	**270.0**	**7.714**	**3**	**1**	**4**
§§Billy Bales	30	120	206.0	15.0	221.0	7.367	2	3	5
§§Tommy Roper	5	20	34.0	1.0	35.0	7.000	1		1
§§John Dews	**35**	**140**	**185.0**	**36.0**	**221.0**	**6.314**		**1**	**1**
§§David Crane	26	104	110.0	21.0	131.0	5.038			
§§Alan Jay	**35**	**140**	**141.0**	**33.0**	**174.0**	**4.971**			
§§Cyril Crane	2	8	7.0	0.0	7.0	3.500			
§§Bob Paulson	33	132	92.0	18.0	110.0	3.333			
§Eric Minall	1	4	2.0	1.0	3.0	3.000			
§§Arnie Haley	4	16	6.0	1.0	7.0	1.750			
§§Derek Jay	1	4	1.0	0.0	1.0	1.000			
§§Stan Holey	1	2	0.0	0.0	0.0	0.000			
§Len Kirkham	1	2	0.0	0.0	0.0	0.000			
§§Taffy Owen	1	2	0.0	0.0	0.0	0.000			

1966...1966...1966...1966...1966...1966

	M	R	Pts	BP	TPts	Ave	F	P	Total
John Dews	**37**	**161**	**305.0**	**22.0**	**327.0**	**8.124**	**2**	**2**	**4**
Bob Paulson	25	105	187.0	18.0	205.0	7.810	2	3	5
Billy Bales	36	138	224.0	27.0	251.0	7.275	5	1	6
Jack Kitchen	24	105	165.0	23.0	188.0	7.162	1		1
§George Major	8	28	43.0	5.0	48.0	6.857		1	1
§John Hart	**37**	**151**	**199.0**	**25.0**	**224.0**	**5.934**			
§Eric Hockaday	23	66	79.0	15.0	94.0	5.697			
Arnold Haley	34	124	140.0	36.0	176.0	5.677			
Alan Jay	18	63	70.0	6.0	76.0	4.825			
Derek Jay	2	4	2.0	1.0	3.0	3.000			
§§Dennis Wasden	4	5	2.0	0.0	2.0	1.600			

1967...1967...1967...1967...1967...1967

	M	R	Pts	BP	TPts	Ave	F	P	Total
§§Bengt Larsson	23	98	152.5	21.0	173.5	7.082	1		1
Arnold Haley	**37**	**158**	**250.0**	**28.0**	**278.0**	**7.038**			
John Hart	**37**	**151**	**236.0**	**27.0**	**263.0**	**6.967**		**3**	**3**
Bob Paulson	25	98	149.0	14.0	163.0	6.653	1	1	2
Alan Jay	36	142	185.0	36.0	221.0	6.225			
John Dews	31	109	148.0	16.0	164.0	6.018		1	1
Billy Bales	34	112	146.0	17.0	163.0	5.821		1	1
George Major	24	77	92.0	13.0	105.0	5.455			
Eric Hockaday	8	18	15.0	2.0	17.0	3.778			
Dennis Wasden	2	4	0.0	0.0	0.0	0.000			

SWEDISH Test star Bengt Larsson couldn't have made a better start to his British League career – he scored a 15-point maximum in his first away match at King's Lynn on April 7. It turned out to be the only full maximum of his career and was partly explained by the fact that he had spent a week practising at the Norfolk track under the eagle eye of veteran Olle Nygren!

1968...1968...1968...1968...1968...1968

	M	R	Pts	BP	TPts	Ave	F	P	Total
§Charlie Monk	37	160	391.0	12.0	403.0	10.075	10	4	14
Bengt Larsson	30	131	225.0	36.0	261.0	7.969		1	1
Arnold Haley	**38**	**167**	**279.0**	**36.0**	**315.0**	**7.545**	**1**		**1**
Bob Paulson	20	83	123.0	18.0	141.0	6.795			
John Dews	**38**	**139**	**203.0**	**19.0**	**222.0**	**6.388**	**2**	**1**	**3**
§Brian Maxted	**38**	**155**	**209.5**	**28.0**	**237.5**	**6.129**	**1**		**1**
Billy Bales	37	116	120.0	18.0	138.0	4.759	1		1
§§Guy Hawkes	7	16	13.0	3.0	16.0	4.000			
Dennis Wasden	1	2	2.0	0.0	2.0	4.000			
§§Dave Baugh	16	35	11.0	2.0	13.0	1.486			
§§Peter Maxted	1	2	0.0	0.0	0.0	0.000			

1969...1969...1969...1969...1969...1969

	M	R	Pts	BP	TPts	Ave	F	P	Total
§Jim Airey	40	175	425.0	8.0	433.0	9.897	7	3	10
Arnold Haley	**41**	**175**	**351.0**	**26.0**	**377.0**	**8.617**	**4**	**2**	**6**
Bengt Larsson	30	129	235.0	37.0	272.0	8.434		1	1
Bob Paulson	22	80	104.0	16.0	120.0	6.000	1		1
Brian Maxted	39	151	184.0	37.0	221.0	5.854			
John Dews	**41**	**146**	**175.0**	**29.0**	**204.0**	**5.589**	**1**		**1**
Billy Bales	39	124	141.0	27.0	168.0	5.419			
Dave Baugh	21	60	45.0	12.0	57.0	3.800			
§§Doug Wyer	1	3	1.0	0.0	1.0	1.333			
Guy Hawkes	5	11	3.0	0.0	3.0	1.091			
§§Reg Wilson	4	8	1.0	0.0	1.0	0.500			

1970...1970...1970...1970...1970...1970

	M	R	Pts	BP	TPts	Ave	F	P	Total
Jim Airey	37	162	436.0	4.0	440.0	10.864	13	2	15
Arnold Haley	38	155	335.0	9.0	344.0	8.877	4	1	5
Bengt Larsson	33	140	221.0	25.0	246.0	7.029			
Bob Paulson	38	145	162.0	31.0	193.0	5.324			
John Dews	38	142	160.5	24.0	184.5	5.197			
Brian Maxted	**39**	**135**	**121.0**	**23.0**	**144.0**	**4.267**			
Dave Baugh	32	99	69.0	11.0	80.0	3.232			
Reg Wilson	3	5	3.0	1.0	4.0	3.200			
Doug Wyer	8	22	11.0	3.0	14.0	2.545			
§§Stuart Ulph	2	5	2.0	1.0	3.0	2.400			
§§Bob Valentine	1	4	2.0	0.0	2.0	2.000			

1971...1971...1971...1971...1971...1971

	M	R	Pts	BP	TPts	Ave	F	P	Total
Jim Airey	35	155	411.0	5.0	416.0	10.735	14	1	15
Arnold Haley	31	129	224.5	20.0	244.5	7.581			
Bengt Larsson	30	123	186.5	30.0	216.5	7.041		2	2
Bob Paulson	**38**	**151**	**209.0**	**40.0**	**249.0**	**6.596**		**1**	**1**
Bob Valentine	**38**	**152**	**191.0**	**38.0**	**229.0**	**6.026**		**1**	**1**
Doug Wyer	23	77	94.0	20.0	114.0	5.922			
Reg Wilson	19	54	57.0	12.0	69.0	5.111			
Brian Maxted	**38**	**114**	**109.0**	**22.0**	**131.0**	**4.596**			
George Major	1	3	1.0	0.0	1.0	1.333			
Taffy Owen	1	3	0.0	0.0	0.0	0.000			
§§Bernie Hornby	1	2	0.0	0.0	0.0	0.000			

JIM AIREY stunned Sheffield – and the rest of speedway – when he announced his retirement after his best-ever season in the sport in which he averaged nearly 11 points a meeting and finished seventh on his World Final debut. Despite many overtures he stuck to his vow not to race in England again explaining: "I always wanted to be World Champion – and I realised at Gothenburg that I was never going to make it." Airey continued to race in his native Australia but concentrated on building up his motor-cycle business in Sydney. He now lives, in retirement, on Queensland's Gold Coast.

1972...1972...1972...1972...1972...1972

	M	R	Pts	BP	TPts	Ave	F	P	Total
§Reidar Eide	33	145	295.0	26.0	321.0	8.855		1	1
Arnold Haley	32	129	260.0	24.0	284.0	8.806		4	4
Doug Wyer	28	111	180.0	27.0	207.0	7.459		2	2
Reg Wilson	26	97	157.0	21.0	178.0	7.340	1	1	2
§Bert Harkins	**35**	**142**	**221.0**	**33.0**	**254.0**	**7.155**			
Bob Valentine	**35**	**127**	**189.0**	**38.0**	**227.0**	**7.150**	**1**	**2**	**3**
Bob Paulson	**35**	**134**	**185.0**	**27.0**	**212.0**	**6.328**	**1**	**1**	**2**
Brian Maxted	7	22	12.0	1.0	13.0	2.364			
Bernie Hornby	1	2	0.0	0.0	0.0	0.000			

1973...1973...1973...1973...1973...1973

	M	R	Pts	BP	TPts	Ave	F	P	Total
Bob Valentine	35	141	308.0	20.0	328.0	9.305	8	1	9
Arnold Haley	34	129	232.0	19.0	251.0	7.783	1	2	3
Reg Wilson	**36**	**142**	**234.0**	**40.0**	**274.0**	**7.718**		**2**	**2**
Doug Wyer	35	137	230.0	22.0	252.0	7.358		1	1
Bengt Larsson	34	124	173.0	46.0	219.0	7.065		2	2
Bob Paulson	**36**	**126**	**182.0**	**36.0**	**218.0**	**6.921**			
§Rick France	32	118	167.0	35.0	202.0	6.847			
§§Rod Haynes	3	9	5.0	1.0	6.0	2.667			
§§Craig Pendlebury	2	4	0.0	0.0	0.0	0.000			

1974...1974...1974...1974...1974...1974

	M	R	Pts	BP	TPts	Ave	F	P	Total
Bob Valentine	39	156	367.0	20.0	387.0	9.923	7	3	10
Taffy Owen	1	3	6.0	1.0	7.0	9.333			
Reg Wilson	**40**	**166**	**361.0**	**22.0**	**383.0**	**9.229**	**3**	**4**	**7**
Doug Wyer	39	159	334.0	29.0	363.0	9.132	4	3	7
Bob Paulson	32	126	181.0	47.0	228.0	7.238		2	2
Arnold Haley	**40**	**161**	**226.0**	**55.0**	**281.0**	**6.981**		**4**	**4**
§Carl Glover	11	35	51.0	5.0	56.0	6.400			
Craig Pendlebury	**40**	**130**	**160.0**	**32.0**	**192.0**	**5.908**			
Rod Haynes	38	109	97.0	31.0	128.0	4.697			

SHEFFIELD

1975...1975...1975...1975...1975...1975

	M	R	Pts	BP	TPts	Ave	F	P	Total
Reg Wilson	9	38	86.0	7.0	93.0	9.789		4	4
Doug Wyer	**36**	**160**	**367.0**	**8.0**	**375.0**	**9.375**	**7**	**1**	**8**
§Phil Bass	1	4	8.0	1.0	9.0	9.000			
Arnold Haley	20	86	157.0	13.0	170.0	7.907	1		1
Carl Glover	35	146	197.0	37.0	234.0	6.411			
§Sören Karlsson	27	88	108.0	26.0	134.0	6.091			
Rod Haynes	4	14	14.0	7.0	21.0	6.000			
§Carl Askew	1	2	3.0	0.0	3.0	6.000			
§Ricky Day	1	2	2.0	1.0	3.0	6.000			
Craig Pendlebury	31	121	153.0	25.0	178.0	5.884			
§§Tony Boyle	1	3	3.0	1.0	4.0	5.333			
§§Les Glover	5	11	11.0	2.0	13.0	4.727			
Taffy Owen	23	67	71.0	7.0	78.0	4.657			
§Nicky Allott	18	53	37.0	5.0	42.0	3.170			
§Ken Matthews	1	3	1.0	1.0	2.0	2.667			
§Tony Featherstone	1	3	1.0	0.0	1.0	1.333			
§§Kym Amundson	1	3	0.0	0.0	0.0	0.000			
Bernie Hornby	1	3	0.0	0.0	0.0	0.000			

1976...1976...1976...1976...1976...1976

	M	R	Pts	BP	TPTs	Ave	F	P	Total
Doug Wyer	35	165	394.0	3.0	397.0	9.624	9		9
Reg Wilson	**38**	**195**	**390.0**	**25.0**	**415.0**	**8.513**	**2**	**1**	**3**
§Keith Evans	15	51	59.0	15.0	74.0	5.804			
Craig Pendlebury	34	147	166.0	31.0	197.0	5.361			
Carl Glover	36	169	192.0	29.0	221.0	5.231			
§Ernst Bøgh	2	6	5.0	1.0	6.0	4.000			
Bengt Larsson	13	43	32.0	8.0	40.0	3.721			
Les Glover	21	61	39.0	10.0	49.0	3.213			
Tony Boyle	14	48	34.0	3.0	37.0	3.083			
Nicky Allott	24	66	42.0	8.0	50.0	3.030			
Arnold Haley	1	5	2.0	1.0	3.0	2.400			
Taffy Owen	2	8	4.0	0.0	4.0	2.000			
Colin Goad	1	2	1.0	0.0	1.0	2.000			
§§Ian Jeffcoate	2	5	1.0	1.0	2.0	1.600			
§§Chris Bevan	4	8	1.0	0.0	1.0	0.500			
§§Louis Carr	1	2	0.0	0.0	0.0	0.000			

1977...1977...1977...1977..1977...1977

	M	R	Pts	BP	TPts	Ave	F	P	Total
Doug Wyer	**38**	**163**	**370.0**	**3.0**	**373.0**	**9.153**	**9**		**9**
Reg Wilson	**38**	**161**	**346.0**	**10.0**	**356.0**	**8.845**	**7**		**7**
Craig Pendlebury	**38**	**146**	**206.5**	**33.0**	**239.5**	**6.562**		**2**	**2**
§§Phil White	5	14	13.0	6.0	19.0	5.429			
Arnold Haley	**38**	**143**	**165.0**	**29.0**	**194.0**	**5.427**		**2**	**2**
Keith Evans	**38**	**130**	**140.0**	**24.0**	**164.0**	**5.046**			
Tony Boyle	34	115	108.0	16.0	124.0	4.313			
Carl Glover	23	81	71.0	9.0	80.0	3.951			
§Billy Burton	10	32	23.0	3.0	26.0	3.250			
Chris Bevan	1	2	1.0	0.0	1.0	2.000			
§§Trevor Oldham	1	2	0.0	0.0	0.0	0.000			

JOHN DEWS, a former Tigers' favourite took over as speedway manager following the resignation of Terry Thornhill who had been at Owlerton since 1964.

1978...1978...1978...1978...1978...1978

	M	R	Pts	BP	TPts	Ave	F	P	Total
Doug Wyer	37	159	364.5	7.0	371.5	9.346	8		8
Reg Wilson	37	155	320.0	13.0	333.0	8.594	4	2	6
§Bernt Persson	30	124	188.0	27.0	215.0	6.935		2	2
Nicky Allott	23	89	142.0	6.0	148.0	6.652	1	1	2
Craig Pendlebury	**38**	**150**	**206.0**	**36.0**	**242.0**	**6.453**		**1**	**1**
§Sean Willmott	1	4	4.0	2.0	6.0	6.000			
Keith Evans	5	16	12.0	3.0	15.0	3.750			
§Bo Wirebrand	12	37	28.0	3.0	31.0	3.351			
§Ian Clark	3	12	8.0	2.0	10.0	3.333			
Tony Boyle	10	30	21.0	3.0	24.0	3.200			
Billy Burton	37	113	71.0	12.0	83.0	2.938			
Arnold Haley	1	3	1.0	1.0	2.0	2.667			
Phil White	14	38	20.0	4.0	24.0	2.526			
Ian Jeffcoate	3	8	5.0	0.0	5.0	2.500			
§§Rauli Makinen	5	16	7.0	0.0	7.0	1.750			
Phil Bass	1	3	0.0	0.0	0.0	0.000			
§§Mike Ferreira	1	3	0.0	0.0	0.0	0.000			
§Barney Kennett	1	2	0.0	0.0	0.0	0.000			

1979...1979...1979...1979...1979...1979

	M	R	Pts	BP	TPts	Ave	F	P	Total
Reg Wilson	**36**	**162**	**341.0**	**13.0**	**354.0**	**8.741**	**4**	**1**	**5**
Doug Wyer	25	102	189.0	4.0	193.0	7.569	4		4
§Laurie Etheridge	1	5	9.0	0.0	9.0	7.200			
Craig Pendlebury	34	139	203.0	22.0	225.0	6.475			
Eric Broadbelt	**36**	**142**	**192.0**	**22.0**	**214.0**	**6.028**			
§Henny Kroeze	14	48	50.0	9.0	59.0	4.917			
Nicky Allott	21	76	83.0	9.0	92.0	4.842	1	1	2
§Steve Finch	16	61	64.0	5.0	69.0	4.525			
Phil White	19	64	60.0	10.0	70.0	4.375			
Keith Evans	8	23	20.0	4.0	24.0	4.174			
§§Tommy Morley	17	61	46.0	9.0	55.0	3.607			
§§Neil Collins	15	48	35.0	5.0	40.0	3.333			
§Terry Tulloch	1	5	4.0	0.0	4.0	3.200			
§Arthur Browning	1	3	1.0	0.0	1.0	1.333			
Ian Jeffcoate	2	8	1.0	0.0	1.0	0.500			

1980...1980...1980...1980...1980...1980

	M	R	Pts	BP	TPts	Ave	F	P	Total
Reg Wilson	24	107	198.0	16.0	214.0	8.000	2		2
Doug Wyer	24	104	175.0	10.0	185.0	7.115	1		1
§Shawn Moran	6	21	33.0	3.0	36.0	6.857		1	1
Eric Broadbelt	21	81	116.0	13.0	129.0	6.370			
Phil White	23	98	127.0	25.0	152.0	6.204			
§Steve Lomas	2	8	11.0	1.0	12.0	6.000			
Arnold Haley	1	5	7.0	0.0	7.0	5.600			
§Ales Dryml	6	23	28.0	4.0	32.0	5.565			
Neil Collins	23	92	103.0	14.0	117.0	5.087			
Nicky Allott	19	73	84.0	8.0	92.0	5.041			
§Klaus Lohmann	19	74	75.0	15.0	90.0	4.865			
Steve Finch	8	31	32.0	4.0	36.0	4.645			
§§Jan Zabik	26	97	92.0	14.0	106.0	4.371		1	1
Henny Kroeze	16	48	38.0	6.0	44.0	3.667			
§Paul Stead	20	62	45.0	5.0	50.0	3.226			
Carl Glover	1	5	1.0	1.0	2.0	1.600			
Brett Saunders	1	3	1.0	0.0	1.0	1.333			
§§Wieslaw Patynek	1	2	0.0	0.0	0.0	0.000			
§§Guy Robson	1	1	0.0	0.0	0.0	0.000			

1981...1981...1981...1981...1981...1981

	M	R	Pts	BP	TPts	Ave	F	P	Total
Shawn Moran	38	179	351.0	19.0	370.0	8.268	5	1	6
Dave Morton	**45**	**210**	**405.0**	**16.0**	**421.0**	**8.019**	**2**	**2**	**4**
Eric Broadbelt	40	177	259.0	35.0	294.0	6.644		2	2
§§John Frankland	1	2	2.0	1.0	3.0	6.000			
Phil White	**45**	**189**	**233.0**	**40.0**	**273.0**	**5.778**			
§Alan Molyneux	38	142	185.0	17.0	202.0	5.690			
Reg Wilson	**45**	**177**	**212.5**	**36.0**	**248.5**	**5.616**			
§Wayne Brown	7	20	24.0	2.0	26.0	5.200			
§§Mark Fiora	31	104	99.0	19.0	118.0	4.538			
Paul Stead	9	24	11.0	3.0	14.0	2.333			
§§Rob Carter	11	28	8.0	1.0	9.0	1.286			
§§Brett Saunders	1	1	0.0	0.0	0.0	0.000			

ONE familiar face was missing from the Sheffield team line-up when the 1981 season got underway.
England international Doug Wyer who had left Owlerton to join Halifax after 12 seasons with the Tigers.
Only Reg Wilson made more first team appearances for the club during the British League era. Wyer was to enjoy a further four full-time seasons in the First Division before joining Birmingham and later Edinburgh where his career ended when he badly fractured his thigh in a crash early in 1988.

1982...1982...1982...1982...1982...1982

	M	R	Pts	BP	TPts	Ave	F	P	Total
Shawn Moran	34	155	352.0	18.0	370.0	9.548	3		
§David Bargh	33	134	201.0	28.0	229.0	6.836			
Dave Morton	**42**	**168**	**249.0**	**24.0**	**273.0**	**6.500**			
Reg Wilson	41	161	234.0	27.0	261.0	6.484	1	1	
Wayne Brown	**42**	**161**	**235.0**	**25.0**	**260.0**	**6.460**			
Phil White	**42**	**145**	**169.0**	**33.0**	**202.0**	**5.572**		**1**	
§Zenon Plech	11	38	39.0	8.0	47.0	4.947			
Mark Fiora	23	66	52.0	11.0	63.0	3.818			
§§Robbie Foy	8	21	8.0	1.0	9.0	1.714			
Rob Carter	3	7	1.0	1.0	2.0	1.143			

SHEFFIELD

1983...1983...1983...1983...1983...1983

	M	R	Pts	BP	TPts	Ave	F	P	Total
Shawn Moran	26	120	262.0	21.0	283.0	9.433	1	2	3
§John Davis	6	25	52.0	4.0	56.0	8.960	1	1	2
David Bargh	40	174	290.0	16.0	306.0	7.034	2		2
Phil White	41	170	240.0	26.0	266.0	6.259			
Dave Morton	37	139	187.0	16.0	203.0	5.842		2	2
Reg Wilson	41	150	159.0	32.0	191.0	5.093			
Paul Stead	1	3	3.0	0.0	3.0	4.000			
§Eric Monaghan	33	119	104.0	14.0	118.0	3.966			
§§Alan Mason	33	97	69.0	10.0	79.0	3.258			
§§John Walmsley	3	9	3.0	2.0	5.0	2.222			
§§Gerald Short	9	30	14.0	2.0	16.0	2.133			
§§David Walsh	3	9	2.0	0.0	2.0	0.889			
§§Kerry Gray	1	2	0.0	0.0	0.0	0.000			
§§Andy Steward	1	1	0.0	0.0	0.0	0.000			

1984...1984...1984...1984...1984...1984

	M	R	Pts	BP	TPts	Ave	F	P	Total
Shawn Moran	39	173	404.0	22.0	426.0	9.850	6	5	11
§Neil Collins	37	153	278.0	29.0	307.0	8.026	3	2	5
§Les Collins	45	191	347.0	27.0	374.0	7.832	1	1	2
Dave Morton	42	154	203.0	28.0	231.0	6.000		2	2
§Jan O. Pedersen	25	96	130.0	14.0	144.0	6.000			
§Martin Hagon	45	163	193.0	18.0	211.0	5.178	1		1
Reg Wilson	30	109	108.0	22.0	130.0	4.771			
§Nigel Crabtree	8	29	21.0	5.0	26.0	3.586			
John Walmsley	2	4	2.0	1.0	3.0	3.000			
Alan Mason	23	72	43.0	10.0	53.0	2.944			
Gerald Short	4	8	4.0	0.0	4.0	2.000			
§Julian Parr	7	19	7.0	1.0	8.0	1.684			
David Walsh	4	15	5.0	1.0	6.0	1.600			
§Colin Cook	1	3	1.0	0.0	1.0	1.333			
Paul Stead	1	2	0.0	0.0	0.0	0.000			
§Guy Wilson	1	2	0.0	0.0	0.0	0.000			

1985...1985...1985...1985...1985...1985

	M	R	Pts	BP	TPts	Ave	F	P	Total
Shawn Moran	38	166	405.0	26.0	431.0	10.386	4	9	13
Dave Morton	4	12	20.0	4.0	24.0	8.000			
Neil Collins	**44**	**184**	**313.0**	**24.0**	**337.0**	**7.326**	**1**	**1**	**2**
Les Collins	**44**	**180**	**289.0**	**22.0**	**311.0**	**6.911**	**2**		**2**
§Peter Carr	43	172	234.0	59.0	293.0	6.814		3	3
§Sam Nikolajsen	23	84	118.0	15.0	133.0	6.333	1		1
Martin Hagon	41	143	181.0	28.0	209.0	5.846			
§Alf Busk	16	48	53.0	13.0	66.0	5.500			
Reg Wilson	1	3	3.0	1.0	4.0	5.333			
§Steve Baker	23	73	59.0	18.0	77.0	4.219			
Gerald Short	18	55	40.0	6.0	46.0	3.345			
§§Flemming Rasmussen	4	13	2.0	0.0	2.0	0.615			
David Walsh	1	2	0.0	0.0	0.0	0.000			

1986...1986...1986...1986...1986...1986

	M	R	Pts	BP	TPts	Ave	F	P	Total
Shawn Moran	35	153	337.0	32.0	369.0	9.647	4	4	8
Kelly Moran	21	90	187.0	10.0	197.0	8.756	1	1	2
Neil Collins	42	178	332.0	19.0	351.0	7.888	4		4
Peter Carr	39	153	256.0	32.0	288.0	7.529		5	5
Les Collins	11	42	65.0	11.0	76.0	7.238		1	1
§§Sean Wilson	18	59	77.0	9.0	86.0	5.831			
Doug Wyer	3	11	13.0	3.0	16.0	5.818			
Martin Hagon	30	112	129.0	24.0	153.0	5.464		1	1
§David Cheshire	3	12	13.0	2.0	15.0	5.000			
David Walsh	37	123	116.0	26.0	142.0	4.618		1	1
§Paul Thorp	2	8	7.0	0.0	7.0	3.500			
§§Peter McNamara	28	88	60.0	12.0	72.0	3.273			
§Paul Whittaker	1	3	2.0	0.0	2.0	2.667			
Reg Wilson	1	3	1.0	1.0	2.0	2.667			
§§Tony Forward	5	17	9.0	1.0	10.0	2.353			
§Paul Evitts	1	3	1.0	0.0	1.0	1.333			
§§Derrol Keats	1	3	0.0	0.0	0.0	0.000			

SHEFFIELD closed down at the beginning of 1989 when safety requirements at Owlerton Greyhound Stadium reduced the crowd capacity to less than 2,000 and promoter Maurice Ducker could not agree on a suitable rental figure for the forthcoming season with the Stadium owners.

1987...1987...1987...1987...1987...1987

1987	M	R	Pts	BP	TPts	Ave	F	P	Total
Shawn Moran	43	180	400.0	26.0	426.0	9.467	4	5	9
Kelly Moran	38	159	339.0	28.0	367.0	9.233	6	3	9
Neil Collins	47	194	342.0	26.0	368.0	7.588			
Peter Carr	47	189	285.0	58.0	343.0	7.259		2	2
Sean Wilson	43	171	206.0	29.0	235.0	5.497			
§Rob Woffinden	3	12	10.0	5.0	15.0	5.000			
§§Ian M. Stead	47	150	144.0	33.0	177.0	4.720			
§Adrian Stevens	44	132	96.0	32.0	128.0	3.879			
David Blackburn	1	2	1.0	0.0	1.0	2.000			
Derrol Keats	4	11	4.0	1.0	5.0	1.818			
§§Rob Tilbury	1	3	1.0	0.0	1.0	1.333			
§§Glenn Doyle	1	2	0.0	0.0	0.0	0.000			
§§Wayne Elliott	2	2	0.0	0.0	0.0	0.000			

1988...1988...1988...1988...1988...1988

	M	R	Pts	BP	TPts	Ave	F	P	Total
Shawn Moran	39	199	449.0	24.0	473.0	9.508	3	3	6
Kelly Moran	**41**	**207**	**424.5**	**24.0**	**448.5**	**8.667**	**2**	**4**	**6**
Neil Collins	31	138	233.0	14.0	247.0	7.159			
Glenn Doyle	2	9	13.0	2.0	15.0	6.667			
§Dean Standing	3	14	21.0	1.0	22.0	6.286			
§Andy Galvin	1	4	6.0	0.0	6.0	6.000			
Peter Carr	29	121	148.0	27.0	175.0	5.785			
Olli Tyrvainen	3	13	16.0	2.0	18.0	5.538			
Sean Wilson	33	145	168.0	24.0	192.0	5.297			
§Steve Regeling	3	13	16.0	1.0	17.0	5.231			
§Darren Sumner	2	6	6.0	1.0	7.0	4.667			
Ian M. Stead	38	158	156.0	25.0	181.0	4.582			
§Randy Green	6	19	16.0	3.0	19.0	4.000			
§§Valentino Furlanetto	11	40	28.0	8.0	36.0	3.600			
Gordon Whitaker	8	30	23.0	4.0	27.0	3.600			
Einar Kyllingstad	7	26	16.0	6.0	22.0	3.385			
§Gary O'Hare	2	6	5.0	0.0	5.0	3.333			
Nigel Crabtree	1	4	2.0	1.0	3.0	3.000			
Les Collins	1	5	3.0	0.0	3.0	2.400			
§Trevor Banks	1	4	2.0	0.0	2.0	2.000			
§Graham Jones	1	4	2.0	0.0	2.0	2.000			
Derrol Keats	4	10	3.0	1.0	4.0	1.600			
§§Mike Long	6	11	0.0	0.0	0.0	0.000			
§Craig Hodgson	1	3	0.0	0.0	0.0	0.000			
§Alan Mogridge	1	3	0.0	0.0	0.0	0.000			
§Steve Bastable	1	2	0.0	0.0	0.0	0.000			

APOLLO CUP

1967	1 Billy Bales	2 Ivan Mauger	3 John Dews

HANDICAP TROPHY

1970	1 Bob Valentine	2 Reg Wilson	3 Dave Baugh

FRANK VAREY TROPHY

1971	1 George Hunter	2 Doug Wyer	3 Terry Betts

YORKSHIRE BANK TROPHY

1973	1 Bob Valentine	2 Ole Olsen	3 Anders Michanek
1974	1 John Boulger	2 Dave Jessup	3 Peter Collins
1975	1 Peter Collins	2 Phil Crump	3 Martin Ashby
1976	1 Peter Collins	2 Gordon Kennett	3 Chris Morton
1977	1 Alan Wilkinson	2 Doug Wyer	3 John Boulger
1978	1 Gordon Kennett	2 Steve Bastable	3 Craig Pendlebury
1979	1 Doug Wyer	2 Reg Wilson	3 Scott Autrey

SKOL NORTHERN MASTERS FINAL

1977	1 Doug Wyer	2 Alan Molyneux	3 Arnie Haley

JUBILEE TROPHY

1979	1 Reg Wilson	2 Ivan Mauger	3 Scott Autrey

DOUG WYER TESTIMONIAL

1980	1 Ivan Mauger	2 Doug Wyer	3 Hans Nielsen

BLUEY WILKINSON MEMORIAL TROPHY

1981	1 Dave Morton	2 Tommy Knudsen	3 Phil Crump
1983	1 John Davis	2 Neil Evitts	3 David Bargh

OWLERTON OPEN HANDICAP

1981	1 Kenny Carter	2 Les Collins	3 Shawn Moran

STONES OPEN CHAMPIONSHIP

1984	1 Dave Morton	2 Shawn Moran	3 Steve Bastable

MARLBORO INVITATION CHALLENGE

1985	1 Simon Wigg	2 Andy Smith	3 Shawn Moran

DIAMOND JUBILEE OPEN CHAMPIONSHIP

1988	1 Kelly Moran	2 Chris Morton	3 Mitch Shirra

SWINDON

1965...1965...1965...1965...1965...1965

	M	R	Pts	BP	TPts	Ave	F	P	Total
§§Barry Briggs	34	149	406.0	1.0	407.0	10.926	21	1	22
§§Mike Broadbank	**36**	**150**	**382.0**	**11.0**	**393.0**	**10.480**	**9**	**6**	**15**
§§Martin Ashby	35	149	306.0	23.0	329.0	8.832	6	2	8
§Doug Dearden	1	3	4.0	0.0	4.0	5.333			
§§Roy Bowers	7	28	29.0	1.0	30.0	4.286			
§§Bob Kilby	32	117	95.0	22.0	117.0	4.000			
§§Mike Keen	32	118	98.0	18.0	116.0	3.932			
§§Peter Sampson	32	111	81.0	9.0	90.0	3.243			
§§Tony Eadon	1	4	2.0	1.0	3.0	3.000			
§§Alan Stapleton	2	6	4.0	0.0	4.0	2.667			
§§Alan Jackson	18	52	20.0	6.0	26.0	2.000			
§§Ray Harris	1	2	1.0	0.0	1.0	2.000			
§§Frank Shuter	19	49	14.0	4.0	18.0	1.469			
§§Trevor Chamberlain	1	2	0.0	0.0	0.0	0.000			

1966...1966...1966...1966...1966...1966

	M	R	Pts	BP	TPts	Ave	F	P	Total
Barry Briggs	32	137	378.0	3.0	381.0	11.124	19		19
Mike Broadbank	36	153	353.0	13.0	366.0	9.569	8	2	10
Martin Ashby	32	131	271.0	24.0	295.0	9.008	3		3
§John Ellis	1	2	2.0	1.0	3.0	6.000			
§Clive Hitch	35	136	167.0	33.0	200.0	5.882		3	3
Bob Kilby	**37**	**141**	**172.0**	**28.0**	**200.0**	**5.674**	**2**	**1**	**3**
Mike Keen	24	93	101.0	22.0	123.0	5.290		1	1
Frank Shuter	33	108	101.0	20.0	121.0	4.481			
§Pete Munday	19	42	21.0	5.0	26.0	2.476			
Alan Stapleton	4	9	4.0	1.0	5.0	2.222			

MIKE BROADBANK was the first rider to have seven rides in an official meeting when he took the extra outings in the Knock Out Cup at Wimbledon on July 25.

1967...1967...1967...1967...1967...1967

	M	R	Pts	BP	TPts	Ave	F	P	Total
Barry Briggs	32	131	361.0	1.0	362.0	11.053	17	1	18
Martin Ashby	**38**	**163**	**334.0**	**26.0**	**360.0**	**8.834**	**1**	**5**	**6**
Bob Kilby	**38**	**158**	**310.0**	**30.0**	**340.0**	**8.608**	**7**	**3**	**10**
Mike Broadbank	**38**	**152**	**285.0**	**40.0**	**325.0**	**8.553**	**4**	**4**	**8**
Frank Shuter	**38**	**130**	**111.0**	**34.0**	**145.0**	**4.462**			
Mike Keen	**38**	**128**	**116.0**	**25.0**	**141.0**	**4.406**			
Pete Munday	37	129	120.0	17.0	137.0	4.248			
§Peter Jackson	5	8	5.0	1.0	6.0	3.000			

1968...1968...1968...1968...1968...1968

	M	R	Pts	BP	TPts	Ave	F	P	Total
Barry Briggs	21	92	248.0	2.0	250.0	10.870	10	1	11
Mike Broadbank	**40**	**180**	**353.0**	**30.0**	**383.0**	**8.511**		**4**	**4**
Bob Kilby	35	139	269.0	16.0	285.0	8.201	5		5
Mike Keen	**40**	**156**	**197.0**	**44.0**	**241.0**	**6.179**		**2**	**2**
Clive Hitch	**40**	**159**	**197.0**	**41.0**	**238.0**	**5.987**		**1**	**1**
Frank Shuter	38	134	160.0	16.0	176.0	5.254			
Pete Munday	**40**	**149**	**153.0**	**31.0**	**184.0**	**4.940**	**1**		**1**
Peter Jackson	20	42	34.0	11.0	45.0	4.286			
Mac Woolford	3	5	1.0	1.0	2.0	1.600			

■ *BARRY BRIGGS failed to win a race at Wimbledon on Tuesday, April 25, bringing to an end a run of 102 successive matches in which he was first past the flag at least once a meeting.*

■ *PETE MUNDAY was the first reserve to score a four ride maximum in the British League. He achieved the feat against Poole on a waterlogged track on May 4 – and then went on to win his second half heat and Final!*

1969...1969...1969...1969...1969...1969

	M	R	Pts	BP	TPts	Ave	F	P	Total
Barry Briggs	35	164	454.0	2.0	456.0	11.122	18		18
Bob Kilby	32	127	229.0	18.0	247.0	7.780	3		3
Mike Keen	31	115	175.0	18.0	193.0	6.713	1		1
Mike Broadbank	24	92	125.0	16.0	141.0	6.130			
§Des Lukehurst	1	4	6.0	0.0	6.0	6.000			
Clive Hitch	**38**	**159**	**178.0**	**38.0**	**216.0**	**5.434**			
Pete Munday	37	143	147.0	27.0	174.0	4.867		1	1
§§Barry Duke	34	115	113.0	24.0	137.0	4.765			
§§Jon Odegaard	2	8	9.0	0.0	9.0	4.500			
Mac Woolford	19	49	20.0	5.0	25.0	2.041			
§§Bob Tabet	2	4	0.0	0.0	0.0	0.000			

1970...1970...1970...1970...1970...1970

	M	R	Pts	BP	TPts	Ave	F	P	Total
Barry Briggs	34	147	385.0	2.0	387.0	10.531	13		13
Bob Kilby	**39**	**164**	**392.0**	**5.0**	**397.0**	**9.683**	**11**	**1**	**12**
Mike Broadbank	2	7	9.0	1.0	10.0	5.714			
Clive Hitch	**39**	**152**	**181.0**	**31.0**	**212.0**	**5.579**		**1**	**1**
Barry Duke	**39**	**152**	**166.0**	**34.0**	**200.0**	**5.263**		**1**	**1**
Pete Munday	**39**	**148**	**147.0**	**22.0**	**169.0**	**4.568**			
Mike Keen	38	128	122.0	17.0	139.0	4.344			
§§Pat Johnson	1	1	1.0	0.0	1.0	4.000			
§John Bishop	34	101	73.0	14.0	87.0	3.446			
Mac Woolford	4	11	9.0	0.0	9.0	3.273			

1971...1971...1971...1971...1971...1971

	M	R	Pts	BP	TPts	Ave	F	P	Total
Barry Briggs	35	153	407.0	1.0	408.0	10.667	12		12
Martin Ashby	37	161	382.0	11.0	393.0	9.764	9		9
Mike Keen	**38**	**143**	**219.0**	**18.0**	**237.0**	**6.629**		**1**	**1**
Mike Broadbank	37	131	131.0	32.0	163.0	4.977			
Clive Hitch	32	118	120.0	21.0	141.0	4.780			
§Jim Gallacher	18	60	53.0	4.0	57.0	3.800			
Pete Munday	36	134	110.0	17.0	127.0	3.791		1	1
§James Bond	17	49	33.0	9.0	42.0	3.429			
Barry Duke	3	10	5.0	1.0	6.0	2.400			
§§Clark Facey	5	13	5.0	2.0	7.0	2.154			
§§Ralph Waller	1	2	1.0	0.0	1.0	2.000			
§Bob Coles	1	2	0.0	0.0	0.0	0.000			

1972...1972...1972...1972...1972...1972

	M	R	Pts	BP	TPts	Ave	F	P	Total
Barry Briggs	24	109	281.0	2.0	283.0	10.385	7		7
Martin Ashby	34	154	380.0	8.0	388.0	10.078	5		5
§Norman Hunter	13	50	69.0	7.0	76.0	6.080			
Mike Broadbank	33	118	122.0	22.0	144.0	4.881			
§Brian Leonard	34	135	129.0	27.0	156.0	4.622			
Clive Hitch	34	132	115.0	24.0	139.0	4.212			
§§Billy Wall	1	3	2.0	1.0	3.0	4.000			
Mike Keen	33	102	85.0	14.0	99.0	3.882			
James Bond	13	36	24.0	8.0	32.0	3.556			
§§David Ashby	9	18	7.0	2.0	9.0	2.000			
§§Garry Flood	2	4	1.0	0.0	1.0	1.000			
§§Bobo Valentine	2	6	1.0	0.0	1.0	0.667			

1973...1973...1973...1973...1973...1973

	M	R	Pts	BP	TPts	Ave	F	P	Total
Martin Ashby	**40**	**187**	**463.0**	**13.0**	**476.0**	**10.182**	**10**	**1**	**11**
Norman Hunter	**40**	**171**	**302.0**	**12.0**	**314.0**	**7.345**	**2**		**2**
Edgar Stangeland	38	171	256.0	35.0	291.0	6.807	2	1	3
Mike Keen	20	78	115.0	15.0	130.0	6.667	1		1
§Arthur Browning	1	3	3.0	1.0	4.0	5.333			
§Paul Gachet	1	3	3.0	1.0	4.0	5.333			
§Geoff Bouchard	9	31	33.0	5.0	38.0	4.903			
§Carl Glover	1	5	6.0	0.0	6.0	4.800			
Brian Leonard	39	144	125.0	28.0	153.0	4.250			
Clive Hitch	26	89	73.0	20.0	93.0	4.180			
§George Barclay	1	3	3.0	0.0	3.0	4.000			
§Russell Osborne	1	2	1.0	1.0	2.0	4.000			
Mick Handley	17	57	46.0	5.0	51.0	3.579			
§§Doug Underwood	1	3	2.0	0.0	2.0	2.667			
David Ashby	17	50	26.0	5.0	31.0	2.480			
§§Martin Hitch	1	2	1.0	0.0	1.0	2.000			
§Roger Johns	1	2	1.0	0.0	1.0	2.000			
§§Sumner McKnight	8	17	4.0	0.0	4.0	0.941			
Billy Wall	8	16	1.0	1.0	2.0	0.500			
§Peter Murray	1	3	0.0	0.0	0.0	0.000			

1974...1974...1974...1974...1974...1974

	M	R	Pts	BP	TPts	Ave	F	P	Total
Martin Ashby	**34**	**149**	**371.0**	**5.0**	**376.0**	**10.094**	**10**	**1**	**11**
§Phil Herne	1	5	11.0	1.0	12.0	9.600			
Edgar Stangeland	30	130	246.0	13.0	259.0	7.969	1		1
Norman Hunter	32	130	189.0	18.0	207.0	6.369			
§Bernie Leigh	**34**	**131**	**133.0**	**34.0**	**167.0**	**5.099**			
Mike Keen	29	95	90.0	18.0	108.0	4.547			
David Ashby	15	47	43.0	10.0	53.0	4.511			
Mick Handley	21	70	69.0	2.0	71.0	4.057			
Brian Leonard	26	85	61.0	15.0	76.0	3.576			
Geoff Bouchard	9	32	17.0	3.0	20.0	2.500			
§§Alan Sorensen	1	2	1.0	0.0	1.0	2.000			

BRITISH LEAGUE AVERAGES...BRITISH LEAGUE AVERAGES...BRITISH LEAGUE AVERAGES

SWINDON

1975...1975...1975...1975...1975...1975

	M	R	Pts	BP	TPts	Ave	F	P	Total
Martin Ashby	37	175	432.0	11.0	443.0	10.126	6	1	7
Bob Kilby	34	156	311.0	11.0	322.0	8.256	2		2
Edgar Stangeland	5	22	34.0	1.0	35.0	6.364			
Norman Hunter	33	115	132.0	24.0	156.0	5.426			
§Alan Grahame	11	42	44.0	8.0	52.0	4.952			
§§Jan Andersson	18	71	70.0	11.0	81.0	4.563			
Geoff Bouchard	**38**	**153**	**143.0**	**26.0**	**169.0**	**4.418**			
§Bobby McNeil	33	119	104.0	23.0	127.0	4.269			
§Pete Wigley	1	4	4.0	0.0	4.0	4.000			
§§Steve Wilcock	1	3	2.0	1.0	3.0	4.000			
Mike Keen	13	34	23.0	4.0	27.0	3.176			
David Ashby	18	56	30.0	9.0	39.0	2.786			
§Ron Henderson	2	6	3.0	0.0	3.0	2.000			
Mick Handley	1	3	1.0	0.0	1.0	1.333			
Barry Duke	6	10	3.0	0.0	3.0	1.200			
§§Melvin Soffe	2	4	0.0	0.0	0.0	0.000			
§§Graham Crook	1	3	0.0	0.0	0.0	0.000			
§Colin Richardson	1	3	0.0	0.0	0.0	0.000			
§Wayne Hughes	1	2	0.0	0.0	0.0	0.000			
§Ken Matthews	1	2	0.0	0.0	0.0	0.000			
§§Dave Patten	1	2	0.0	0.0	0.0	0.000			

1976...1976...1976...1976...1976...1976

	M	R	Pts	BP	TPts	Ave	F	P	Total
Martin Ashby	**40**	**177**	**415.0**	**22.0**	**437.0**	**9.876**	**5**		**5**
Bob Kilby	37	160	353.0	16.0	369.0	9.225	4	1	5
Bobby McNeil	31	116	193.0	28.0	221.0	7.621	1		1
Jan Andersson	21	83	118.0	16.0	134.0	6.458			
§Sören Karlsson	22	84	117.0	17.0	134.0	6.381			
Geoff Bouchard	39	168	207.0	46.0	253.0	6.024			
§§Chris Robins	1	2	2.0	1.0	3.0	6.000			
Norman Hunter	25	87	97.0	23.0	120.0	5.517			
§Ian Clark	1	4	3.0	1.0	4.0	4.000			
David Ashby	26	73	58.0	13.0	71.0	3.890			
§§Pete Reading	1	3	2.0	0.0	2.0	2.667			
§§Cliff Anderson	11	26	12.0	1.0	13.0	2.000			
§§Kevin Pope	4	12	2.0	1.0	3.0	1.000			
§Phil Bass	1	2	0.0	0.0	0.0	0.000			
Brian Leonard	1	2	0.0	0.0	0.0	0.000			
§Karl Fiala	1	3	0.0	0.0	0.0	0.000			
§Kelvin Mullarkey	1	3	0.0	0.0	0.0	0.000			

1977...1977...1977...1977...1977...1977

	M	R	Pts	BP	TPts	Ave	F	P	Total
Martin Ashby	29	122	287.5	9.0	296.5	9.721	7	1	8
Bob Kilby	36	163	347.0	9.0	356.0	8.736	2	1	3
Jan Andersson	25	114	191.0	26.0	217.0	7.614		2	2
Bobby McNeil	31	120	164.0	36.0	200.0	6.667		1	1
Geoff Bouchard	**38**	**175**	**199.0**	**41.0**	**240.0**	**5.486**			
Sören Karlsson	29	100	112.0	25.0	137.0	5.480		1	1
David Ashby	31	99	101.0	17.0	118.0	4.768			
§Kevin Young	10	25	17.0	2.0	19.0	3.040			
§§Richard Evans	6	16	10.0	2.0	12.0	3.000			
Kevin Pope	3	4	2.0	1.0	3.0	3.000			
§§Malcolm Holloway	7	18	4.0	1.0	5.0	1.111			

1978...1978...1978...1978...1978...1978

	M	R	Pts	BP	TPts	Ave	F	P	Total
Bob Kilby	37	153	314.0	9.0	323.0	8.444	4	1	5
Jan Andersson	31	145	282.0	10.0	292.0	8.055	2		2
Martin Ashby	31	136	245.0	16.0	261.0	7.676	1		1
Geoff Bouchard	**40**	**177**	**251.0**	**39.0**	**290.0**	**6.554**	**1**		**1**
David Ashby	35	132	123.0	22.0	145.0	4.394			
§§Rolf Gramstad	11	40	30.0	10.0	40.0	4.000			
§Robert Henry	17	58	38.0	8.0	46.0	3.172			
§§Jerzy Trzeszkowski	11	33	17.0	3.0	20.0	2.424			
Malcolm Holloway	15	42	20.0	4.0	24.0	2.286			
§Tim Nunan	1	2	1.0	0.0	1.0	2.000			
§§Steen Mastrup	13	34	12.0	4.0	16.0	1.882			
Richard Evans	8	16	4.0	2.0	6.0	1.500			
Sören Karlsson	6	19	1.0	1.0	2.0	0.421			
§§Leonard Raba	5	11	0.0	0.0	0.0	0.000			

1979...1979...1979...1979...1979...1979

	M	R	Pts	BP	TPts	Ave	F	P	Total
Phil Crump	35	154	390.0	8.0	398.0	10.338	11	1	12
Bob Kilby	37	149	270.0	15.0	285.0	7.651	3		3
§Steve Gresham	33	129	211.0	14.0	225.0	6.977			
Geoff Bouchard	28	113	144.0	34.0	178.0	6.301	1		1
Martin Ashby	38	155	199.0	36.0	235.0	6.064		1	1
Steen Mastrup	29	100	121.0	27.0	148.0	5.920			
§Milan Spinka	5	20	24.0	3.0	27.0	5.400			
Rolf Gramstad	37	127	134.0	14.0	148.0	4.661			
Malcolm Holloway	13	50	37.0	7.0	44.0	3.520			
David Ashby	6	22	15.0	3.0	18.0	3.273			
§§Martin Hewlett	1	3	2.0	0.0	2.0	2.667			
§Louis Carr	1	4	0.0	0.0	0.0	0.000			

1980...1980...1980...1980...1980...1980

	M	R	Pts	BP	TPts	Ave	F	P	Total
§Scott Autrey	36	170	406.5	15.0	421.5	9.918	6		6
Phil Crump	20	93	211.0	12.0	223.0	9.591	2	3	5
Martin Hewlett	1	3	4.0	2.0	6.0	8.000			
Bob Kilby	21	81	140.0	10.0	150.0	7.407	1		1
Steve Gresham	36	152	250.0	25.0	275.0	7.237		1	1
Milan Spinka	19	71	95.0	21.0	116.0	6.535			
Reidar Eide	6	26	34.0	8.0	42.0	6.462			
§Jan Verner	3	11	15.0	2.0	17.0	6.182			
Steen Mastrup	31	117	131.0	31.0	162.0	5.538			
§Mike Ferreira	9	31	38.0	4.0	42.0	5.419			
§Mike Spink	1	3	3.0	1.0	4.0	5.333			
Malcolm Holloway	36	134	144.0	34.0	178.0	5.313			
Bob Humphreys	11	48	50.0	10.0	60.0	5.000			
§John Barker	9	25	15.0	2.0	17.0	2.720			
§Steve Koppe	2	8	5.0	0.0	5.0	2.500			
§Nigel Boocock	10	30	13.0	2.0	15.0	2.000			
Louis Carr	1	3	0.0	0.0	0.0	0.000			
§John J. Williams	1	3	0.0	0.0	0.0	0.000			

BOSOM BUDDIES...World champions, ex-Southampton team-mates Barry Briggs and Björn Knutsson talk over old rivalries

SWINDON

1981...1981...1981...1981...1981...1981

	M	R	Pts	BP	TPts	Ave	F	P	Total
Phil Crump	49	236	591.0	17.0	608.0	10.305	8	2	10
§Steve Bastable	44	204	408.0	28.0	436.0	8.549	2	3	5
Steve Gresham	41	182	304.0	38.0	342.0	7.516	1		1
Mike Ferreira	15	63	101.0	10.0	111.0	7.048			
Malcolm Holloway	49	217	329.0	44.0	373.0	6.876	1	1	2
Steen Mastrup	45	173	222.0	39.0	261.0	6.035		2	2
§Steve Lawson	1	4	4.0	2.0	6.0	6.000			
Martin Yeates	13	49	51.0	10.0	61.0	4.980			
§§Björn Andersson	37	142	145.0	22.0	167.0	4.704			
Bob Humphreys	1	3	2.0	1.0	3.0	4.000			
§§Henry Nielsen	5	17	9.0	5.0	14.0	3.294			
§§Lennart Bengtsson	6	20	11.0	5.0	16.0	3.200			
§§Steve Bishop	2	4	2.0	1.0	3.0	3.000			
John McNeill	4	15	10.0	1.0	11.0	2.933			
§Denzil Kent	3	9	6.0	0.0	6.0	2.667			
Martin Hewlett	6	12	5.0	2.0	7.0	2.333			
§§Martin Satchell	7	18	6.0	2.0	8.0	1.778			
§Veijo Tuoriniemi	7	19	2.0	0.0	2.0	0.421			
§§Kevin Smart	2	6	0.0	0.0	0.0	0.000			
§§Chris Hunt	1	3	0.0	0.0	0.0	0.000			
§§Darryl Simpson	3	7	0.0	0.0	0.0	0.000			
§§Terry Broadbank	1	2	0.0	0.0	0.0	0.000			

1982...1982...1982...1982...1982...1982

	M	R	Pts	BP	TPts	Ave	F	P	Total
Phil Crump	43	191	445.0	7.0	452.0	9.466	7	1	8
Steve Bastable	41	173	313.0	15.0	328.0	7.584	2		2
Björn Andersson	21	91	135.0	12.0	147.0	6.462			
§Steve Finch	1	2	2.0	1.0	3.0	6.000			
Malcolm Holloway	40	160	201.0	38.0	239.0	5.975	1		1
Mike Ferreira	40	159	181.0	28.0	209.0	5.258			
Steen Mastrup	27	84	91.0	18.0	109.0	5.190			
§§Keith Millard	2	6	6.0	1.0	7.0	4.667			
Martin Yeates	15	45	37.0	10.0	47.0	4.178			
Martin Hewlett	39	123	105.0	22.0	127.0	4.130			
§Steve Schofield	1	2	1.0	1.0	2.0	4.000			
§Eric Broadbelt	4	12	9.0	2.0	11.0	3.667			
Jan Verner	15	43	32.0	3.0	35.0	3.256			
Denzil Kent	1	3	2.0	0.0	2.0	2.667			
Kevin Smart	4	8	2.0	2.0	4.0	2.000			
Steve Bishop	1	2	0.0	0.0	0.0	0.000			

1983...1983...1983...1983...1983...1983

	M	R	Pts	BP	TPts	Ave	F	P	Total
Phil Crump	**43**	**207**	**512.0**	**7.0**	**519.0**	**10.029**	**5**	**1**	**6**
Björn Andersson	18	81	133.0	9.0	142.0	7.012	1		1
§Phil Herne	24	87	105.0	18.0	123.0	5.655			
Martin Yeates	17	62	65.0	16.0	81.0	5.226			
Steve Gresham	18	70	81.0	9.0	90.0	5.143			
Malcolm Holloway	32	125	141.0	15.0	156.0	4.992			
§Alf Busk	40	144	135.0	20.0	155.0	4.306			
§Tim Hunt	5	20	18.0	3.0	21.0	4.200			
Steen Mastrup	20	65	50.0	8.0	58.0	3.569			
§§Per Sørensen	23	75	43.0	11.0	54.0	2.880			
Terry Broadbank	3	7	3.0	2.0	5.0	2.857			
Steve Bishop	7	15	7.0	3.0	10.0	2.667			
Bob Kilby	4	10	5.0	0.0	5.0	2.000			
Milan Spinka	11	27	13.0	0.0	13.0	1.926			
§Paul Bosley	3	7	2.0	1.0	3.0	1.714			
§§Alun Rossiter	5	10	4.0	0.0	4.0	1.600			
§§David Smart	1	2	0.0	0.0	0.0	0.000			

1984...1984...1984...1984...1984...1984

	M	R	Pts	BP	TPts	Ave	F	P	Total
Phil Crump	46	218	533.0	9.0	542.0	9.945	5		5
§Bo Petersen	41	191	378.0	20.0	398.0	8.335	1	4	5
§Ari Koponen	43	173	241.0	25.0	266.0	6.150	1	1	2
Björn Andersson	12	44	55.0	8.0	63.0	5.727		1	1
§Shawn McConnell	34	135	146.0	34.0	180.0	5.333			
Alun Rossiter	28	75	67.0	27.0	94.0	5.013			
Alf Busk	42	137	142.5	27.0	169.5	4.949			
Per Sørensen	42	153	158.0	20.0	178.0	4.654			
Martin Yeates	11	36	29.0	5.0	34.0	3.778			
§Kevin Smith	3	11	9.0	1.0	10.0	3.636			
Colin Cook	2	8	6.0	0.0	6.0	3.000			
§Steve Lawson	2	8	3.0	0.0	3.0	1.500			
David Smart	3	7	2.0	0.0	2.0	1.143			
Bob Humphreys	2	4	0.0	0.0	0.0	0.000			

▼ ***ROCKIN' ROBINS...**the 1982 Swindon squad, Phil Crump, Steen Mastrup, Steve Bastable, Malcolm Holloway, manager Henry Hitch, Martin Hewlett, Jan Verner and Mike Ferreira*

BRITISH LEAGUE AVERAGES...BRITISH LEAGUE AVERAGES...BRITISH LEAGUE AVERAGES

SWINDON

1985...1985...1985...1985...1985...1985

	M	R	Pts	BP	TPts	Ave	F	P	Total
Bo Petersen	39	166	369.0	19.0	388.0	9.349	4	3	7
Phil Crump	31	135	283.0	18.0	301.0	8.919		3	3
§Malcolm Simmons	40	167	306.0	24.0	330.0	7.904	3		3
§§Jimmy Nilsen	16	63	91.0	12.0	103.0	6.540		1	1
§Gordon Kennett	12	45	56.0	15.0	71.0	6.311			
Per Sørensen	41	153	167.0	45.0	212.0	5.542		1	1
Alf Busk	12	40	47.0	7.0	54.0	5.400			
Ari Koponen	35	125	134.0	23.0	157.0	5.024			
Alun Rossiter	36	116	82.0	25.0	107.0	3.690			
§§Gary Chessell	1	4	1.0	1.0	2.0	2.000			
Martin Yeates	9	28	10.0	2.0	12.0	1.714			
David Smart	5	15	5.0	1.0	6.0	1.600			
§§Steve Goodwin	2	6	0.0	0.0	0.0	0.000			
Colin Cook	1	3	0.0	0.0	0.0	0.000			

1986...1986...1986...1986...1986...1986

	M	R	Pts	BP	TPts	Ave	F	P	Total
Phil Crump	35	151	307.0	24.0	331.0	8.768	1		1
§Kai Niemi	23	98	203.0	4.0	207.0	8.449	1		1
Jimmy Nilsen	33	135	233.0	31.0	264.0	7.822			
§Richard Hellsén	42	172	245.0	47.0	292.0	6.791			
Alan Grahame	26	103	152.0	19.0	171.0	6.641			
§Finn Thomsen	33	122	163.0	22.0	185.0	6.066			
§Dave Jessup	3	12	15.0	2.0	17.0	5.667			
§Kevin Jolly	1	3	4.0	0.0	4.0	5.333			
Per Sørensen	10	31	35.0	5.0	40.0	5.161			
Kevin Smith	2	7	7.0	2.0	9.0	5.143			
§§Brian Karger	15	48	51.0	4.0	55.0	4.583			
§§Rob Fortune	**43**	**134**	**81.0**	**25.0**	**106.0**	**3.164**			
Steve Bishop	1	3	0.0	0.0	0.0	0.000			
Gordon Kennett	1	3	0.0	0.0	0.0	0.000			

1987...1987...1987...1987...1987...1987

	M	R	Pts	BP	TPts	Ave	F	P	Total
Jimmy Nilsen	41	176	406.0	17.0	423.0	9.614	3	6	9
§Mitch Shirra	42	179	409.0	10.0	419.0	9.363	4	1	5
§Andrew Silver	10	43	71.0	8.0	79.0	7.349		1	1
Richard Hellsén	**48**	**192**	**278.0**	**45.0**	**323.0**	**6.729**		**1**	**1**
Brian Karger	47	201	282.0	47.0	329.0	6.547			
Alun Rossiter	44	174	232.0	45.0	277.0	6.368			
§§Conny Ivarsson	28	113	148.0	14.0	162.0	5.735			
§Gary Chessell	6	21	18.0	3.0	21.0	4.000			
§§Andy Sell	1	2	1.0	1.0	2.0	4.000			
David Smart	4	11	5.0	1.0	6.0	2.182			
§§Nick Bates	1	2	1.0	0.0	1.0	2.000			
§§Matthew Cross	23	52	16.0	4.0	20.0	1.538			
§§Darren Knapman	2	4	1.0	0.0	1.0	1.000			
§§Stephen Rose	21	54	7.5	1.0	8.5	0.630			
§Martin Chessell	6	12	1.0	0.0	1.0	0.333			
§Miles Evans	1	0	0.0	0.0	0.0	n.a.			

1988...1988...1988...1988...1988...1988

	M	R	Pts	BP	TPts	Ave	F	P	Total
§Andy Galvin	1	4	8.0	2.0	10.0	10.000			
Peter Nahlin	6	25	42.0	6.0	48.0	7.680			
§Mark Loram	3	12	20.0	3.0	23.0	7.667			
Brian Karger	38	176	302.0	27.0	329.0	7.477			
Andrew Silver	41	204	349.0	20.0	369.0	7.235	1		1
Jimmy Nilsson	28	129	216.0	17.0	233.0	7.225			
§Erik Stenlund	15	64	85.0	20.0	105.0	6.563		1	1
Gordon Kennett	1	4	4.0	2.0	6.0	6.000			
Richard Hellsén	**42**	**172**	**223.5**	**32.0**	**255.5**	**5.942**			
Alun Rossiter	40	173	208.0	46.0	254.0	5.873			
§Martin Goodwin	2	8	9.0	2.0	11.0	5.500			
Gary Chessell	**42**	**164**	**177.0**	**45.0**	**222.0**	**5.415**			
§Troy Butler	2	6	6.0	2.0	8.0	5.333			
§Kenny McKinna	1	4	4.0	1.0	5.0	5.000			
§Craig Hodgson	2	8	6.0	1.0	7.0	3.500			
§Dean Standing	1	6	4.0	1.0	5.0	3.333			
David Smart	3	9	5.0	2.0	7.0	3.111			
§Ian Barney	1	3	2.0	0.0	2.0	2.667			
§Glenn Doyle	1	3	1.0	1.0	2.0	2.667			
Kevin Jolly	1	3	1.0	0.0	1.0	1.333			
Louis Carr	1	4	0.0	0.0	0.0	0.000			
§Andy Campbell	1	3	0.0	0.0	0.0	0.000			
§Mark Chessell	1	3	0.0	0.0	0.0	0.000			
§Steve Regeling	1	3	0.0	0.0	0.0	0.000			
§Nigel Sparshott	1	2	0.0	0.0	0.0	0.000			

WILLS WOODBINE TROPHY

1965	1 Barry Briggs	2 Mike Broadbank	3 Jimmy Gooch

TEODOROWICZ MEMORIAL TROPHY

1965	1 Barry Briggs	2 Sverre Harrfeldt	3 Mike Broadbank
1967	1 Ray Wilson	2 Sverre Harrfeldt	3 Mike Broadbank

SILVER PLUME

1972	1 Ray Wilson	2 Barry Briggs	3 Bob Kilby
1973	1 Bengt Jansson	2 Martin Ashby	3 Jim McMillan
1974	1 Martin Ashby	2 John Louis	3 Eric Boocock
1975	1 Peter Collins	2 Martin Ashby	3 Ray Wilson
1976	1 Peter Collins	2 Dave Jessup	3 Martin Ashby
1978	1 Jim McMillan	2 Bob Kilby	3 Reidar Eide
1979	1 Peter Collins	2 Scott Autrey	3 Phil Crump
1980	1 Michael Lee	2 Dave Jessup	3 Dennis Sigalos

ARTDEANS TROPHY

1975	1 Phil Crump	2 Bob Kilby	3 Martin Ashby
1978	1 Dave Morton	2 Hans Nielsen	3 John Boulger
1979	1 John Davis	2 Phil Crump	3 Scott Autrey
1980	1 Larry Ross	2 Gordon Kennett	3 Phil Crump

JUBILEE TROPHY

1977	1 Martin Ashby	2 Geoff Bouchard	3 John Titman

MIRRORSPORT TROPHY

1979	1 Ole Olsen	2 Phil Crump	3 Bob Kilby

DUPLEX LITHO PRESS TROPHY

1979	1 Dave Jessup	2 Ole Olsen	3 Peter Collins

MARTIN ASHBY TESTIMONIAL

1979	1 Michael Lee	2 Scott Autrey	3 Dave Jessup

JUNIOR MASTER OF SPEEDWAY

1979	1 Barry Allaway	2 Neil Marnish	3 Peter Wordingham
1980	1 David Blackburn	2 Steve Bryenton	3 Steve Payne

GODDEN ENGINE NEWTON OILS 16 LAP SUPER

1981	1 Phil Crump	2 John Cook	3 John Davis
1982	1 Alan Grahame	2 Larry Ross	3 Steve Bastable

EVENING ADVERTISER SUPERSTAR

1981	1 Bo Petersen	2 Phil Crump	3 Bobby Schwartz
1982	1 Phil Crump	2 Bruce Penhall	3 Shawn Moran
1983	1 Michael Lee	2 Jan Andersson	3 Billy Sanders
1984	1 Phil Crump	2 Hans Nielsen	3 Mitch Shirra
1985	1 Bo Petersen	2 Hans Nielsen	3 Kai Niemi

BRITISH CAR AUCTIONS CLASSIC

1988	1 Mitch Shirra	2 Shawn Moran	3 Kelly Moran

BIKE FOR LIFE

1989	1 John Davis	2 Jimmy Nilsen	3 Alan Grahame

SOFT WATER CLASSIC

1990	1 Jan O. Pedersen	2 Kelvin Tatum	3 Andrew Silver

1989...1989...1989...1989...1989...1989

	M	R	Pts	BP	TPts	Ave	F	P	Total
Jimmy Nilsen	30	155	304.0	22.0	326.0	8.413	1	3	4
Brian Karger	**34**	**170**	**316.0**	**28.0**	**344.0**	**8.094**		**1**	**1**
Matthew Cross	1	1	1.0	1.0	2.0	8.000			
Andrew Silver	32	148	245.0	28.0	273.0	7.378			
§John Davis	16	63	90.0	15.0	105.0	6.667			
Peter Nahlin	32	133	172.5	35.0	207.5	6.241			
§§Bart Bast	18	76	75.0	21.0	96.0	5.053			
Gary Chessell	27	96	105.0	12.0	117.0	4.875			
§§Tom Knudsen	2	6	5.0	1.0	6.0	4.000			
David Smart	**34**	**127**	**97.0**	**21.0**	**118.0**	**3.717**			
Martin Chessell	1	2	0.0	0.0	0.0	0.000			
§Derrol Keats	1	1	0.0	0.0	0.0	0.000			

1990...19890...1990...1990...1990...1990

	M	R	Pts	BP	TPts	Ave	F	P	Total
Jimmy Nilsen	31	153	316.0	12.0	328.0	8.575	1	1	2
Brian Karger	11	47	89.0	4.0	93.0	7.915		1	1
Andrew Silver	**36**	**163**	**273.0**	**34.0**	**307.0**	**7.534**		**2**	**2**
Peter Nahlin	35	162	242.0	54.0	296.0	7.309	1	1	2
John Davis	29	103	163.0	21.0	184.0	7.146	1	1	2
§§Leigh Adams	31	153	245.0	23.0	268.0	7.007		1	1
Phil Crump	18	67	70.0	25.0	95.0	5.672			
David Smart	33	130	127.0	38.0	165.0	5.077			
Matthew Cross	1	2	0.0	0.0	0.0	0.000			

WEMBLEY

MILLIONAIRE businessman Bernard Cottrell found it hard to stop thinking about bringing speedway back to Wembley Stadium.

After all he had been steeped in the Lions and could still, so long after, recall the day when Sir Arthur Elvin, the father of Wembley and the man who introduced dirt-track racing to the world's most famous stadium, stopped his Daimler and bought a copy of the old London Star from him as he sold papers outside the Empire Stadium. Cottrell had come a long way and now presided over a six-storey office building which housed his business empire...but the best view was still from his suite and it overlooked the stadium!

Cottrell decided he wanted speedway back after a long, long gap of 13 years and began talks with former Lion Trevor Redmond.

The outcome was that they took over the Coatbridge First Division licence and riders Reidar Eide, Bert Harkins and Brian Collins (photo below). They then revealed their plans to move the team into Wembley to give the sport it's biggest boost for years. Everything was done on the grand scale.

Radio disc-jockey Ed Stewart was employed to provide between race entertainment and the announcer was one of Britain's most famous voices, Bob Danvers Walker.

Even Ove Fundin was tempted back to ride in Britain once more.

The Lions roared again at their home base on Saturday, May 30, when they had already completed half a dozen League matches away from home.

A published crowd of near 20,000 saw that first match against Hackney and, fittingly, it ended in a home win for the Lions with the evergreen Fundin topping the scorechart. Wembley's return wasn't an unqualified success though.

Some of the presentation left much to be desired and Fundin only managed 14 matches before doing his disappearing act.

That didn't matter as Wembley were not only staging British League racing but Redmond and Cottrell were pleased enough with their financial investment that they quickly confirmed that they would again be coming to the starting tapes in 1971.

This time they signed another of the Swedish giants Göte Nordin but he, like Fundin, found it difficult to commit himself fully to British speedway but Sverre Harrfeldt became a popular signing as he successfully battled against dreadful injuries he had received in the World Championship when he looked to be on the verge of mounting a genuine challenge for the title.

A second season over, plans went ahead for 1972 and everything was in full swing when Trevor Redmond was told: "There'll be no more speedway here."

The stadium authorities said: "We cannot guarantee regular speedway because of the possible extension of the football season and other events that may be held at the Stadium."

So Wembley's short life in the British League was over and Redmond began searching for a new life for his Lions.

1970...1970...1970...1970...1970...1970

	M	R	Pts	BP	TPts	Ave	F	P	Tota
§Reidar Eide	**37**	**163**	**354.0**	**17.0**	**371.0**	**9.104**	**3**	**1**	**4**
§Tony Hall	1	1	1.0	1.0	2.0	8.000			
§Ove Fundin	14	59	115.0	2.0	117.0	7.932			
§Bert Harkins	**37**	**157**	**262.0**	**25.0**	**287.0**	**7.312**	**1**		**1**
§§Richard May	1	5	9.0	0.0	9.0	7.200			
§Brian Collins	36	149	200.0	31.0	231.0	6.201			
§§Graham Banks	1	2	3.0	0.0	3.0	6.000			
§Wayne Briggs	32	117	146.0	25.0	171.0	5.846			
§§Brian Foote	2	5	5.0	1.0	6.0	4.800			
§Dave Jessup	19	71	73.5	11.0	84.5	4.761			
§Brian Leonard	20	71	66.0	8.0	74.0	4.169			
§Des Lukehurst	8	22	17.0	4.0	21.0	3.818			
§Tim Bungay	28	86	61.0	9.0	70.0	3.256			
§Bengt Andersson	9	28	14.0	3.0	17.0	2.429			
§§Steve Bast	2	5	2.0	1.0	3.0	2.400			
§Brian Davies	2	6	3.0	0.0	3.0	2.000			
§Stan Stevens	2	7	3.0	0.0	3.0	1.714			
§George Barclay	1	2	0.0	0.0	0.0	0.000			
§Cec Platt	1	2	0.0	0.0	0.0	0.000			

1971...1971...1971...1971...1971...1971

	M	R	Pts	BP	TPts	Ave	F	P	Total
§Göte Nordin	11	46	101.0	3.0	104.0	9.043			
Bert Harkins	30	130	238.0	31.0	269.0	8.277	1	3	4
§Sverre Harrfeldt	33	121	216.0	20.0	236.0	7.802	2		2
Dave Jessup	28	120	202.0	21.0	223.0	7.433			
§Tony Clarke	35	146	234.0	30.0	264.0	7.233	1		1
§John Louis	1	4	6.0	0.0	6.0	6.000			
Brian Collins	35	143	181.0	33.0	214.0	5.986			
Brian Leonard	**37**	**135**	**164.0**	**29.0**	**193.0**	**5.719**			
§§Christer Sjösten	6	19	16.0	4.0	20.0	4.211			
§§Tommy Jansson	3	11	11.0	0.0	11.0	4.000			
Tim Bungay	3	7	2.0	1.0	3.0	1.714			
§§Peter Prinsloo	11	24	7.0	1.0	8.0	1.333			
§§Roger Johns	1	3	1.0	0.0	1.0	1.333			
§§Bobby McNeil	1	3	0.0	0.0	0.0	0.000			
§§Trevor Geer	1	1	0.0	0.0	0.0	0.000			
§Norman Strachan	1	1	0.0	0.0	0.0	0.000			
§Reg Trott	1	1	0.0	0.0	0.0	0.000			

WEST HAM

GLORIOUS West Ham were the team of 1965....
They began the British League era by sweeping all before them to complete the Cup and League double – to set the standards for all to follow.
Their success was built around the bulkhead of a tremendous top three in Ken McKinlay, Sverre Harrfeldt and Norman Hunter, who scored more than 1,000 points between them as they stormed their way through what might have been a worrying season. And they had another trump card in Kent teenager Malcolm Simmons who had scored just 13 points in the 1964 National League but grabbed nearly 300 in the British League!

1965...1965...1965...1965...1965...1965

	M	R	Pts	BP	TPts	Ave	F	P	Total
§§Ken McKinlay	**40**	**160**	**439.0**	**16.0**	**455.0**	**11.375**	**15**	**5**	**20**
§§Sverre Harrfeldt	38	152	409.0	12.0	421.0	11.079	11	3	14
§§Norman Hunter	39	156	352.0	25.0	377.0	9.667	5	3	8
§§Malcolm Simmons	**40**	**160**	**227.0**	**47.0**	**274.0**	**6.850**	**1**		**1**
§Reg Trott	29	116	113.0	16.0	129.0	4.448		1	1
§Brian Leonard	38	152	121.0	14.0	135.0	3.553			
§§Bob Dugard	2	8	6.0	1.0	7.0	3.500			
§§Tony Clarke	13	52	29.0	8.0	37.0	2.846			
§§Ted Ede	17	68	26.0	9.0	35.0	2.059			
§Geoff Hughes	1	4	1.0	1.0	2.0	2.000			
§Ray Wickett	8	32	11.0	4.0	15.0	1.875			
§Stan Stevens	5	20	7.0	1.0	8.0	1.600			
§Alf Hagon	1	4	1.0	0.0	1.0	1.000			
§§Kevin Russell	1	4	1.0	0.0	1.0	1.000			
§§Dave Wills	6	24	4.0	0.0	4.0	0.667			
§§John Ellis	1	3	0.0	0.0	0.0	0.000			
§§Tony Lewis	1	2	0.0	0.0	0.0	0.000			

1966...1966...1966...1966...1966...1966

	M	R	Pts	BP	TPts	Ave	F	P	Total
Sverre Harrfeldt	28	126	298.5	13.0	311.5	9.889	6	2	8
Ken McKinlay	34	144	325.0	23.0	348.0	9.667	2	5	7
Norman Hunter	**39**	**172**	**382.0**	**23.0**	**405.0**	**9.419**	**8**	**3**	**11**
Malcolm Simmons	37	153	188.0	47.0	235.0	6.144	1		1
Brian Leonard	37	146	180.0	35.0	215.0	5.890		1	1
Ray Wickett	3	6	6.0	2.0	8.0	5.333			
Reg Trott	36	134	125.0	19.0	144.0	4.299			
Ted Ede	18	43	27.0	11.0	38.0	3.535			
§§Don Smith	17	40	25.0	5.0	30.0	3.000			
§Terry Stone	8	19	8.0	3.0	11.0	2.316			

1967...1967...1967...1967...1967...1967

	M	R	Pts	BP	TPts	Ave	F	P	Total
Sverre Harrfeldt	37	153	383.0	9.0	392.0	10.248	14	1	15
Ken McKinlay	40	172	368.0	42.0	410.0	9.535	2	7	9
Norman Hunter	40	165	293.5	17.5	311.0	7.539	4	2	6
Malcolm Simmons	**41**	**172**	**266.5**	**38.5**	**305.0**	**7.093**	**1**	**1**	**2**
Brian Leonard	37	156	229.0	45.0	274.0	7.026		1	1
§§George Barclay	8	21	19.0	6.0	25.0	4.762			
Stan Stevens	28	87	81.0	16.0	97.0	4.460			
Tony Clarke	39	134	125.0	21.0	146.0	4.358			
§§Barry Crowson	2	4	2.0	0.0	2.0	2.000			
Don Smith	3	9	2.0	0.0	2.0	0.889			
§Dai Evans	6	15	2.0	1.0	3.0	0.800			
§Tyburn Gallows	2	3	0.0	0.0	0.0	0.000			
Reg Trott	1	2	0.0	0.0	0.0	0.000			

1968...1968...1968...1968...1968...1968

	M	R	Pts	BP	TPts	Ave	F	P	Total
Sverre Harrfeldt	30	130	313.0	5.0	318.0	9.785	7		7
Norman Hunter	35	150	349.0	15.0	364.0	9.707	6	3	9
Ken McKinlay	33	137	301.0	11.0	312.0	9.109	6	2	8
Brian Leonard	**38**	**147**	**172.0**	**25.0**	**197.0**	**5.361**		**1**	**1**
Tony Clarke	37	148	169.0	14.0	183.0	4.946			
Stan Stevens	34	122	110.0	26.0	136.0	4.459			
George Barclay	31	95	63.0	16.0	79.0	3.326			
§§Martyn Piddock	4	12	6.0	3.0	9.0	3.000			
Barry Crowson	15	42	22.0	5.0	27.0	2.571			
Tyburn Gallows	1	2	1.0	0.0	1.0	2.000			

1969...1969...1969...1969...1969...1969

	M	R	Pts	BP	TPts	Ave	F	P	Total
Tony Clarke	**39**	**186**	**372.0**	**23.0**	**395.0**	**8.495**	**3**		**3**
Olle Nygren	21	94	180.0	6.0	186.0	7.915	2		
Ken McKinlay	33	142	247.0	26.0	273.0	7.690			
Stan Stevens	35	145	170.0	22.0	192.0	5.297			
§§John Langfield	21	85	95.0	12.0	107.0	5.035			
Barry Crowson	33	122	103.0	21.0	124.0	4.066			
§§Ken Coleman	1	2	2.0	0.0	2.0	4.000			
Martyn Piddock	19	54	41.0	8.0	49.0	3.630			
§§Bent Norregaard	8	32	24.0	5.0	29.0	3.625			
George Barclay	8	20	9.0	2.0	11.0	2.200			
Brian Leonard	10	32	12.0	3.0	15.0	1.875			
§Brian Davies	6	20	8.0	1.0	9.0	1.800			
§Dave Jessup	3	12	4.0	1.0	5.0	1.667			
§§Graham Miles	1	3	1.0	0.0	1.0	1.333			
§Tony Childs	1	2	0.0	0.0	0.0	0.000			
§§Cec Platt	1	2	0.0	0.0	0.0	0.000			

1970...1970...1970...1970...1970...1970

	M	R	Pts	BP	TPts	Ave	F	P	Total
Olle Nygren	34	150	332.0	19.0	351.0	9.360	1	1	2
§John Louis	1	4	8.0	0.0	8.0	8.000			
§§Christer Löfqvist	27	112	204.0	15.0	219.0	7.821	3	3	6
Tony Clarke	**37**	**155**	**278.0**	**12.0**	**290.0**	**7.484**	**1**		**1**
§Peter Bradshaw	17	64	81.0	9.0	90.0	5.625			
Stan Stevens	15	61	72.0	10.0	82.0	5.377			
Sverre Harrfeldt	12	38	39.0	5.0	44.0	4.632			
Martyn Piddock	20	69	72.5	7.0	79.5	4.609			
§§Garry Hay	22	80	70.0	15.0	85.0	4.250			
§Antonin Kasper	25	81	75.0	9.0	84.0	4.148			
Barry Crowson	9	27	20.0	4.0	24.0	3.556			
Brian Leonard	3	11	6.0	1.0	7.0	2.545			
§§Alan Sage	3	5	1.0	0.0	1.0	0.800			
§Des Lukehurst	1	2	0.0	0.0	0.0	0.000			

THE HEART was torn out of the West Ham side at Lokeren (see separate section) but the Hammers bravely carried on despite their sad losses. And if there was a bonus to come out of a truly tragic season it was that Sverre Harrfeldt, who returned as team manager to replace Phil Bishop, decided to make a racing comeback before the end of the season.

1971...1971...1971...1971...1971...1971

	M	R	Pts	BP	TPts	Ave	F	P	Total
Christer Löfqvist	34	153	323.0	11.0	334.0	8.732	2		2
Olle Nygren	36	170	333.0	13.0	346.0	8.141	1	1	2
Reg Luckhurst	30	129	191.0	19.0	210.0	6.512		1	1
§Preben Rosenkilde	24	86	91.0	15.0	106.0	4.930			
Barry Duke	10	36	35.0	5.0	40.0	4.444			
Mick Handley	23	88	68.0	16.0	84.0	3.818			
§Alan Bellham	**37**	**130**	**99.0**	**20.0**	**119.0**	**3.662**			
Alan Sage	**37**	**115**	**73.0**	**17.0**	**90.0**	**3.130**			
Stan Stevens	13	43	28.0	4.0	32.0	2.977			
§§Carl Glover	1	2	1.0	0.0	1.0	2.000			
§Mike Gardner	2	3	0.0	0.0	0.0	0.000			
§§Dingle Brown	1	2	0.0	0.0	0.0	0.000			
§John Davis	1	2	0.0	0.0	0.0	0.000			

PLEAS for the Hammers to carry on racing at Custom House following the sale of the stadium for housing were turned down although Romford did move in for a truncated season before they were turfed out.

Now the old Custom House track – one of speedway's most famous – is no more but at least the memory of the club lives on in the new neighbourhood estate.

For several of the roads were named after some of the famous riders who wore the red and blue and crossed hammers of West Ham Speedway.

West Ham's licence and riders were sold to John Berry and Joe Thurley to allow Ipswich's elevation.

WHITE CITY

WINNING the 1977 British League championship came expensive to White City promoters Danny Dunton and Bob Dugard.

For they later admitted that they made losses of around £30,000 in their most successful season at the Shepherds Bush venue.

White City was adopted by the British Speedway Promoters' Association as a small-scale alternative to Wembley for World Team Cup Finals and intermediate rounds of the World Championship.

But it was always a difficult venue to fill – and that's exactly what Dugard and Dunton found when they moved their Oxford franchise there at the end of 1975 when it looked as if speedway was doomed at Cowley. They won the immediate backing of London Broadcasting Company – one of two commercial stations operating in the Capital – and also provided a more than competitive side but after three seasons of poor crowds they moved on again – this time down to Eastbourne!

RELIABLE...Trevor Geer only missed one of 122 official fixtures for the White City Rebels during their three year stay at Shepherds Bush

1976...1976...1976...1976...1976...1976

	M	R	Pts	BP	TPts	Ave	F	P	Total
§Gordon Kennett	39	168	399.0	8.0	407.0	9.690	10	1	11
Dag Lovaas	36	149	271.0	18.0	289.0	7.758	2	1	3
§Richard Greer	**40**	**163**	**265.0**	**23.0**	**288.0**	**7.067**		**1**	**1**
§Trevor Geer	39	144	194.0	46.0	240.0	6.667			
Steve Weatherley	26	98	119.0	28.0	147.0	6.000			
§Paul Gachet	**40**	**127**	**150.5**	**19.0**	**169.5**	**5.339**	**1**	**1**	**2**
§Brian Clark	7	19	19.0	5.0	24.0	5.053			
§Rob Hollingworth	3	8	9.0	1.0	10.0	5.000			
§§Kai Niemi	29	99	94.0	26.0	120.0	4.848			
§§Steve Lawson	1	3	2.0	1.0	3.0	4.000			
§Richard Hellsén	10	34	24.0	5.0	29.0	3.412			
§Neil Cameron	1	2	0.0	0.0	0.0	0.000			
§Jack Millen	1	2	0.0	0.0	0.0	0.000			

1977...1977...1977...1977...1977...1977

	M	R	Pts	BP	TPts	Ave	F	P	Total
Gordon Kennett	**42**	**207**	**524.0**	**15.0**	**539.0**	**10.415**	**10**	**3**	**13**
Paul Gachet	3	10	18.0	1.0	19.0	7.600			
§Mike Sampson	15	62	105.0	9.0	114.0	7.355			
Steve Weatherley	38	170	251.0	60.0	311.0	7.318		2	2
§§Marek Cieslak	34	151	238.0	32.0	270.0	7.152	3	2	5
Kai Niemi	39	164	234.0	47.0	281.0	6.854			
Trevor Geer	**42**	**194**	**288.0**	**44.0**	**332.0**	**6.845**		**2**	**2**
§Ian Clark	6	15	13.0	6.0	19.0	5.067			
§David Kennett	20	63	59.0	15.0	74.0	4.698			
§Kevin Hawkins	3	6	6.0	0.0	6.0	4.000			
§Eric Dugard	2	3	2.0	1.0	3.0	4.000			
§Phil Collins	1	2	2.0	0.0	2.0	4.000			
Brian Clark	5	9	4.0	1.0	5.0	2.222			
§Roger Abel	1	2	1.0	0.0	1.0	2.000			
§§Paul Woods	1	1	0.0	0.0	0.0	0.000			

1978...1978...1978...1978...1978...1978

	M	R	Pts	BP	TPts	Ave	F	P	Total
Gordon Kennett	38	166	392.0	3.0	395.0	9.518	9		9
Kai Niemi	34	137	227.5	18.0	245.5	7.168			
Steve Weatherley	39	163	237.0	35.0	272.0	6.675			
David Kennett	13	46	46.0	17.0	63.0	5.478			
§§John Barker	4	11	12.0	3.0	15.0	5.455			
Marek Cieslak	25	90	106.0	10.0	116.0	5.156			
§§Andrzej Jurczynski	20	61	65.0	12.0	77.0	5.049			
Trevor Geer	**40**	**155**	**167.0**	**25.0**	**192.0**	**4.955**			
Paul Gachet	36	127	129.0	19.0	148.0	4.661			
Mike Sampson	5	15	15.0	1.0	16.0	4.267			
Ian Clark	1	2	1.0	1.0	2.0	4.000			
§Dave Gooderham	6	18	15.0	0.0	15.0	3.333			
§Nigel Couzens	3	10	6.0	1.0	7.0	2.800			
§Sean Willmott	1	6	3.0	0.0	3.0	2.000			
Kevin Hawkins	1	2	1.0	0.0	1.0	2.000			

ETERNA WATCH CHAMPIONSHIP

1976	1 Ivan Mauger	2 Martin Ashby	3 Gordon Kennett

ITEX 100 TROPHY

1977	1 Ole Olsen	2 Peter Collins	3 John Davis
1978	1 Malcolm Simmons	2 Dave Jessup	3 Dave Morton

WIMBLEDON

WIMBLEDON is the second most famous speedway club in the world after Belle Vue.

But sadly the British League chronicled the downfall of a track that had been operating in the very highest plain ever since speedway was first introduced to Britain in 1928.

And for many years Ronnie Greene, the patriarch of Plough Lane, ruled with an iron hand but also used the flair that saw him become an international Charleston dancer between the two wars, to make sure the turnstiles continued clicking away merrily.

At one stage the Dons were the finest cup side in Britain as they beat Wolverhampton, Sheffield and Belle Vue in successive seasons to become the only side to make it a hat-trick of victories.

But Greene's death heralded the decline of the club until they were forced to drop out of the British League at the end of a financially crippling 1984 season. Plough Lane remained the most luxuriously appointed Stadium in the country but, sadly, with the fall in attendances so it was used less and less frequently for major events havcing, at one time, been the traditional home to the Whit Monday Internationale and the National League Riders' Championship Final.

1965...1965...1965...1965...1965...1965

	M	R	Pts	BP	TPts	Ave	F	P	Total
§§Olle Nygren	**37**	**148**	**386.0**	**15.0**	**401.0**	**10.838**	**8**	**2**	**10**
§§Reg Luckhurst	**37**	**148**	**336.0**	**18.0**	**354.0**	**9.568**	**3**	**2**	**5**
§§Trevor Hedge	33	132	277.0	16.0	293.0	8.879	3	1	4
§Bob Dugard	33	132	194.0	31.0	225.0	6.818			
§§Jim Tebby	**37**	**148**	**182.0**	**36.0**	**218.0**	**5.892**		**1**	**1**
§John Edwards	32	128	106.0	40.0	146.0	4.563		1	1
§§Reg Trott	3	12	8.0	1.0	9.0	3.000			
§§Doug Dearden	1	4	1.0	1.0	2.0	2.000			
§§Keith Whipp	5	20	6.0	3.0	9.0	1.800			
§§Mike Coomber	26	104	29.0	8.0	37.0	1.423			
§§Geoff Hughes	14	56	9.0	4.0	13.0	0.929			
§§Alan Jones	1	2	0.0	0.0	0.0	0.000			

1966...1966...1966...1966...1966...1966

	M	R	Pts	BP	TPts	Ave	F	P	Total
Olle Nygren	41	182	463.0	10.0	473.0	10.396	13	2	15
Trevor Hedge	40	167	370.0	22.0	392.0	9.389	10	2	12
Reg Luckhurst	**42**	**182**	**367.0**	**28.0**	**395.0**	**8.681**	**3**	**3**	**6**
Bobby Dugard	**42**	**172**	**265.0**	**34.0**	**299.0**	**6.953**			
Jim Tebby	39	156	125.0	30.0	155.0	3.974			
§§Tony Childs	40	115	74.0	19.0	93.0	3.235			
§§Peter Jackson	24	70	41.0	15.0	56.0	3.200			
John Edwards	13	50	34.0	2.0	36.0	2.880			
§§Steve Chilman	6	15	6.0	2.0	8.0	2.133			
Mike Coomber	4	7	1.0	0.0	1.0	0.571			

1967...1967...1967...1967...1967...1967

	M	R	Pts	BP	TPts	Ave	F	P	Total
Olle Nygren	36	158	367.0	9.0	376.0	9.519	7	1	8
Trevor Hedge	**37**	**163**	**328.0**	**18.0**	**346.0**	**8.491**	**5**		**5**
Reg Luckhurst	**37**	**155**	**285.0**	**34.0**	**319.0**	**8.232**		**2**	**2**
Boby Dugard	11	30	35.0	10.0	45.0	6.000			
Jim Tebby	35	133	160.0	35.0	195.0	5.865		1	1
§Alan Cowland	35	130	152.0	18.0	170.0	5.231			
§Garry Middleton	11	36	34.0	7.0	41.0	4.556			
§§Leif Soderberg	23	79	50.0	13.0	63.0	3.190			
§§Murray Burt	25	62	26.0	6.0	32.0	2.065			
Steve Chilman	3	7	1.0	1.0	2.0	1.143			
§Alan Stapleton	3	8	0.0	0.0	0.0	0.000			
§§Peter Thorn	2	4	0.0	0.0	0.0	0.000			
§§Peter Murray	1	2	0.0	0.0	0.0	0.000			

1968...1968...1968...1968...1968...1968

	M	R	Pts	BP	TPts	Ave	F	P	Total
Olle Nygren	40	180	408.0	11.0	419.0	9.311	9		9
Trevor Hedge	40	171	361.0	30.0	391.0	9.146	3	2	5
Reg Luckhurst	**41**	**178**	**325.0**	**28.0**	**353.0**	**7.933**	**1**	**1**	**2**
Garry Middleton	38	143	182.0	28.0	210.0	5.874		2	2
JIm Tebby	40	139	159.0	36.0	195.0	5.612			
Alan Cowland	39	137	147.0	41.0	188.0	5.489			
Bobby Dugard	39	125	132.0	30.0	162.0	5.184			
Peter Murray	10	26	19.0	4.0	23.0	3.538			

1969...1969...1969...1969...1969...1969

	M	R	Pts	BP	TPts	Ave	F	P	Total
Trevor Hedge	40	175	433.0	19.0	452.0	10.331	14	3	17
§§Ronnie Moore	31	131	297.0	22.0	319.0	9.740	3	4	7
Reg Luckhurst	24	98	220.0	10.0	230.0	9.388	6	1	7
§Cyril Maidment	**41**	**170**	**234.0**	**45.0**	**279.0**	**6.565**		**1**	**1**
Bobby Dugard	38	135	168.0	46.0	214.0	6.341	1	1	2
Jim Tebby	**41**	**143**	**181.0**	**37.0**	**218.0**	**6.098**			
§Gary Everett	40	134	154.5	32.0	186.5	5.567			
Peter Murray	17	46	34.0	4.0	38.0	3.304			

1970...1970...1970...1970...1970...1970

	M	R	Pts	BP	TPts	Ave	F	P	Total
Trevor Hedge	41	177	419.0	22.0	441.0	9.966	9	3	12
Ronnie Moore	30	127	295.0	21.0	316.0	9.953	7	2	9
Reg Luckhurst	40	168	299.0	26.0	325.0	7.738	1	1	2
Cyril Maidment	37	153	212.0	43.0	255.0	6.667		1	1
Jim Tebby	**42**	**154**	**206.0**	**38.0**	**244.0**	**6.338**		**1**	**1**
Gary Everett	25	87	111.0	18.0	129.0	5.931	1		1
Peter Murray	**42**	**126**	**108.0**	**26.0**	**134.0**	**4.254**			
Bobby Dugard	12	36	29.0	5.0	34.0	3.778			
§§Nigel Rackett	9	24	11.0	3.0	14.0	2.333			
§§Gordon Kennett	5	12	5.0	2.0	7.0	2.333			

1971...1971...1971...1971...1971...1971

	M	R	Pts	BP	TPts	Ave	F	P	Total
Ronnie Moore	35	149	356.5	12.0	368.5	9.893	7	1	8
Trevor Hedge	33	139	309.0	10.0	319.0	9.180	6	3	9
Cyril Maidment	34	135	195.0	16.0	211.0	6.252			
§John Dews	36	139	150.5	34.0	184.5	5.309			
JIm Tebby	36	138	141.0	36.0	177.0	5.130			
Peter Murray	32	104	101.0	21.0	122.0	4.692			
§John Bishop	35	107	95.0	17.0	112.0	4.187			
Nigel Rackett	1	3	2.0	1.0	3.0	4.000			
§§Phil Pratt	1	2	1.0	1.0	2.0	4.000			
§§Graeme Stapleton	6	20	15.0	3.0	18.0	3.600			
§§Bob Abell	2	5	1.0	1.0	2.0	1.600			

1972...1972...1972...1972...1972...1972

	M	R	Pts	BP	TPts	Avc	F	P	Total
Ronnie Moore	34	159	402.0	9.0	411.0	10.340	6	2	8
Trevor Hedge	33	150	295.0	10.0	305.0	8.133	1	2	3
Tommy Jansson	17	73	126.0	10.0	136.0	7.452	2		2
John Dews	11	43	46.0	8.0	54.0	5.023			
Graeme Stapleton	**35**	**133**	**127.0**	**21.0**	**148.0**	**4.451**	**1**		**1**
Nigel Rackett	1	2	2.0	0.0	2.0	4.000			
Peter Murray	29	96	77.0	18.0	95.0	3.958			
Jim Tebby	**35**	**119**	**84.0**	**21.0**	**105.0**	**3.529**			
§§Neil Cameron	34	108	77.0	11.0	88.0	3.259			
§§Pete Wigley	10	21	7.0	2.0	9.0	1.714			
§§Rob Jones	2	6	1.0	0.0	1.0	0.667			
Phil Pratt	1	3	0.0	0.0	0.0	0.000			
§Stan Stevens	1	3	0.0	0.0	0.0	0.000			

1973...1973...1973...1973...1973...1973

	M	R	Pts	BP	TPts	Ave	F	P	Total
Tommy Jansson	20	87	188.0	12.0	200.0	9.195	4		4
Trevor Hedge	34	141	247.0	26.0	273.0	7.745	1		1
§Bert Harkins	35	137	217.0	21.0	238.0	6.949		1	1
Graeme Stapleton	35	138	207.0	26.0	233.0	6.754	1	1	2
Neil Cameron	26	99	108.0	18.0	126.0	5.091			
Tony Clarke	12	44	49.0	7.0	56.0	5.091			
Reg Luckhurst	33	127	128.0	22.0	150.0	4.724			
Peter Murray	2	6	7.0	0.0	7.0	4.667			
Alan Cowland	1	2	2.0	0.0	2.0	4.000			
Rob Jones	25	77	50.0	9.0	59.0	3.065			
§§Roland Duke	9	21	10.0	1.0	11.0	2.095			
§§Ian Fletcher	1	2	0.0	0.0	0.0	0.000			

WIMBLEDON

1975...1975...1975...1975...1975...1975

	M	R	Pts	BP	TPts	Ave	F	P	Total
Tommy Jansson	29	128	321.0	3.0	324.0	10.125	5	1	6
Barry Briggs	26	111	250.0	6.0	256.0	9.225	2	3	5
§Edgar Stangeland	28	121	206.0	13.0	219.0	7.240	1	1	2
Bert Harkins	18	72	103.0	7.0	110.0	6.111			
Barry Crowson	11	37	38.0	8.0	46.0	4.973			
§§Larry Ross	35	131	122.0	37.0	159.0	4.855			
Reg Luckhurst	33	116	110.0	28.0	138.0	4.759			
Roger Johns	**36**	**129**	**112.0**	**30.0**	**142.0**	**4.403**			
§Graham Banks	12	31	12.0	5.0	17.0	2.194			
§Alan Johns	1	4	1.0	0.0	1.0	1.000			
Paul Dowdall	2	4	1.0	0.0	1.0	1.000			

1976...1976...1976...1976...1976...1976

	M	R	Pts	BP	TPts	Ave	F	P	Total
Tommy Jansson	8	40	99.5	3.0	102.5	10.250	1		1
§§Mick Hines	**40**	**183**	**316.0**	**19.0**	**335.0**	**7.322**	**1**	**1**	**2**
Edgar Stangeland	36	158	270.0	17.0	287.0	7.266	1		1
Larry Ross	40	168	259.0	45.0	304.0	7.238		2	2
§§Stefan Salomonsson	25	88	72.0	19.0	91.0	4.136			
§Colin Richardson	22	77	64.0	15.0	79.0	4.104			
Barry Crowson	25	73	58.0	16.0	74.0	4.055			
Roger Johns	28	90	67.0	21.0	88.0	3.911			
§§Brendan Shilleto	7	15	5.0	3.0	8.0	2.133			
Alan Johns	1	3	1.0	0.0	1.0	1.333			

1977...1977...1977...1977...1977...1977

	M	R	Pts	BP	TPts	Ave	F	P	Total
§§Edward Jancarz	28	122	284.0	9.0	293.0	9.607	4		4
Mick Hines	37	178	326.0	21.0	347.0	7.798		1	1
Colin Richardson	20	91	147.0	29.0	176.0	7.736		1	1
Edgar Stangeland	5	21	32.0	8.0	40.0	7.619			
Larry Ross	37	166	283.0	21.0	304.0	7.325	3		3
Stefan Salomonsson	33	117	134.0	26.0	160.0	5.470			
Roger Johns	36	134	150.0	33.0	183.0	5.463			
Graeme Stapleton	9	35	29.0	8.0	37.0	4.229			
Brendan Shilleto	7	24	19.0	3.0	22.0	3.667			
§§Rudy Muts	10	30	17.0	4.0	21.0	2.800			
Rob Jones	11	25	12.0	3.0	15.0	2.400			
§§Ian Williams	2	4	1.0	1.0	2.0	2.000			
§Alan Sage	1	2	0.0	0.0	0.0	0.000			
§§Brian Canning	1	2	0.0	0.0	0.0	0.000			

1978...1978...1978...1978...1978...1978

	M	R	Pts	BP	TPts	Ave	F	P	Total
Larry Ross	**38**	**164**	**367.0**	**14.0**	**381.0**	**9.293**	**9**		**9**
Edward Jancarz	25	91	184.0	12.0	196.0	8.615	2	1	3
Roger Johns	**38**	**154**	**253.0**	**48.0**	**301.0**	**7.818**	**2**	**1**	**3**
Mick Hines	36	141	232.0	24.0	256.0	7.262	1		1
Stefan Salomonsson	28	102	133.0	37.0	170.0	6.667			
Rudy Muts	30	114	146.0	40.0	186.0	6.526			
Colin Richardson	28	114	157.0	27.0	184.0	6.456		1	1
Graeme Stapleton	11	27	19.0	5.0	24.0	3.556			
§John Barker	1	3	1.0	1.0	2.0	2.667			
Ian Williams	1	4	2.0	0.0	2.0	2.000			
§Paul Woods	1	4	2.0	0.0	2.0	2.000			
Brendan Shilleto	4	10	3.0	1.0	4.0	1.600			
§§Brian Canning	1	5	2.0	0.0	2.0	1.600			
§§Steve Naylor	1	4	0.0	0.0	0.0	0.000			
§§Colin Ackroyd	1	3	0.0	0.0	0.0	0.000			
§§Martin Charles	1	2	0.0	0.0	0.0	0.000			

1979...1979...1979...1979...1979...1979

	M	R	Pts	BP	TPts	Ave	F	P	Total
Edward Jancarz	18	73	162.0	7.0	169.0	9.260	2		2
Larry Ross	34	152	324.0	17.0	341.0	8.974	2	1	3
Bert Harkins	1	4	8.0	0.0	8.0	8.000			
Roger Johns	32	142	244.0	36.0	280.0	7.887		4	4
Stefan Salomonsson	31	136	221.0	30.0	251.0	7.382	1	2	3
Rudy Muts	25	99	141.0	30.0	171.0	6.909			
Mick Hines	10	38	49.0	3.0	52.0	5.474			
Colin Richardson	30	119	142.0	18.0	160.0	5.378	1	1	2
§§Richard Knight	8	23	19.0	6.0	25.0	4.348			
§Ian Gledhill	1	4	3.0	0.0	3.0	3.000			
§§Patrick Pawson	19	58	22.0	5.0	27.0	1.862			
§§Ray Griffiths	3	11	4.0	1.0	5.0	1.818			
Graham Knowler	1	5	2.0	0.0	2.0	1.600			
§§Dave Brewer	18	55	18.0	1.0	19.0	1.382			
Brendan Shilleto	1	3	1.0	0.0	1.0	1.333			

1980...1980...1980...1980...1980...1980

	M	R	Pts	BP	TPts	Ave	F	P	Total
Larry Ross	32	143	306.0	20.0	326.0	9.119	2	1	3
Roger Johns	**34**	**144**	**269.0**	**27.0**	**296.0**	**8.222**	**1**	**1**	**2**
Edward Jancarz	23	94	182.0	8.0	190.0	8.085	2		2
Colin Richardson	34	156	220.0	28.0	248.0	6.359			
Stefan Salomonsson	26	110	135.0	25.0	160.0	5.818			
§§Simon Wigg	1	3	3.0	1.0	4.0	5.333			
Mick Hines	12	48	50.0	11.0	61.0	5.083			
Rudy Muts	22	72	46.0	9.0	55.0	3.056			
§§Peter Johns	21	57	30.0	5.0	35.0	2.456			
Dave Brewer	11	25	10.0	4.0	14.0	2.240			
Graham Knowler	5	12	3.0	1.0	4.0	1.333			
Patrick Pawson	1	4	1.0	0.0	1.0	1.000			
Alan Johns	1	3	0.0	0.0	0.0	0.000			
§Sigvart Pedersen	1	2	0.0	0.0	0.0	0.000			

1981...1981...1981...1981...1981...1981

	M	R	Pts	BP	TPts	Ave	F	P	Total
Malcolm Simmons	44	227	461.0	14.0	475.0	8.370	1		1
Edward Jancarz	17	72	134.0	10.0	144.0	8.000			
Roger Johns	44	208	337.0	23.0	360.0	6.923			
Colin Richardson	41	190	283.0	42.0	325.0	6.842			
§Jerzy Rembas	3	10	12.0	2.0	14.0	5.600			
§§Brad Oxley	40	185	211.0	38.0	249.0	5.384			
Alan Sage	2	8	8.0	1.0	9.0	4.500			
§§Anders Eriksson	16	52	51.0	6.0	57.0	4.385			
Rudy Muts	23	96	88.0	11.0	99.0	4.125			
§Steve Finch	7	31	22.0	9.0	31.0	4.000			
§Gene Woods	3	17	13.0	2.0	15.0	3.529			
§Robert Henry	1	5	3.0	1.0	4.0	3.200			
Mick Hines	7	26	16.0	3.0	19.0	2.923			
Dave Brewer	5	11	5.0	3.0	8.0	2.909			
Peter Johns	27	79	40.0	9.0	49.0	2.481			
§Eric Dugard	8	27	11.5	4.0	15.5	2.296			
Graham Knowler	2	4	1.0	1.0	2.0	2.000			
§§Alan Mogridge	16	40	13.0	5.0	18.0	1.800			
Simon Wigg	1	5	2.0	0.0	2.0	1.600			

POETRY IN MOTION...the immense talent of the late Tommy Jansson. He heads another rider who was to die tragically, Christer Löfqvist

WIMBLEDON

1982...1982...1982...1982...1982...1982

	M	R	Pts	BP	TPts	F	PTotal		
§Dave Jessup	35	141	297.0	12.0	309.0	8.766	3	1	4
Malcolm Simmons	43	192	403.0	17.0	420.0	8.750	3	2	5
§Kai Niemi	42	185	329.0	43.0	372.0	8.043	2	2	4
Edward Jancarz	14	57	76.0	7.0	83.0	5.825			
Roger Johns	19	70	81.0	13.0	94.0	5.371			
Anders Eriksson	36	123	141.0	24.0	165.0	5.366			
Brad Oxley	41	162	168.0	38.0	206.0	5.086			
Richard Knight	15	49	42.0	8.0	50.0	4.082			
§Alan Sage	4	13	10.0	3.0	13.0	4.000			
§§Trevor Banks	1	4	2.0	1.0	3.0	3.000			
Alan Mogridge	27	68	32.0	3.0	35.0	2.059			
§§Jamie Luckhurst	6	14	6.0	0.0	6.0	1.714			
Peter Johns	5	14	3.0	0.0	3.0	0.857			
§Paul Bosley	1	3	0.0	0.0	0.0	0.000			
§§Chris Mulvihill	1	2	0.0	0.0	0.0	0.000			

1983...1983...1983...1983...1983...1983

	M	R	Pts	BP	TPts	Ave	F	P	Total
Dave Jessup	43	183	402.0	21.0	423.0	9.246	6	2	8
Malcolm Simmons	48	201	353.0	42.0	395.0	7.861		3	3
Kai Niemi	44	181	320.0	27.0	347.0	7.669	1	1	2
Richard Knight	2	6	9.0	2.0	11.0	7.333			
§Ari Koponen	45	174	241.0	44.0	285.0	6.552			
§§Kelvin Tatum	45	144	205.0	18.0	223.0	6.194			
§Mike Ferreira	46	177	221.5	42.0	263.5	5.955		1	1
Roger Johns	48	152	155.0	42.0	197.0	5.184			
Alan Mogridge	6	13	3.0	1.0	4.0	1.231			
Jamie Luckhurst	1	2	0.0	0.0	0.0	0.000			

1984...1984...1984...1984...1984...1984

	M	R	Pts	BP	TPts	Ave	F	P	Total
Malcolm Simmons	50	218	421.0	36.0	457.0	8.385	2	1	3
§John Davis	49	200	407.0	12.0	419.0	8.380	2		2
Kelvin Tatum	34	137	219.0	27.0	246.0	7.182		2	2
Gordon Kennett	50	190	252.0	35.0	287.0	6.042		1	1
§John Titman	47	187	238.0	34.0	272.0	5.818			
Roger Johns	50	189	218.0	51.0	269.0	5.693		1	1
Mike Ferreira	36	121	139.0	26.0	165.0	5.455			
Jamie Luckhurst	4	13	8.0	2.0	10.0	3.077			
§§Andy Galvin	14	38	23.0	5.0	28.0	2.947			
§§Jay Pleece	6	14	3.0	2.0	5.0	1.429			
§§Paul Whittaker	3	9	1.0	0.0	1.0	0.444			
§Phil Vance	1	3	0.0	0.0	0.0	0.000			
Peter Johns	1	2	0.0	0.0	0.0	0.000			

THE LAURELS

1965	1 Barry Briggs	2 Jimmy Gooch	3 Nigel Boocock
1966	1 Nigel Boocock	2 Olle Nygren	3 Sverre Harrfeldt
1967	1 Ray Wilson	2 Barry Briggs	3 Reg Luckhurst
1968	1 Barry Briggs	2 Nigel Boocock	3 Trevor Hedge
1969	1 Trevor Hedge	2 Barry Briggs	3 Tony Clarke
1970	1 Ray Wilson	2 Martin Ashby	3 Terry Betts
1971	1 Ole Olsen	2 Garry Middleton	3 Bengt Jansson
1972	1 Ole Olsen	2 Dave Jessup	3 Ivan Mauger
1973	1 Ole Olsen	2 Dag Lovaas	3 Ray Wilson
1974	1 Dave Jessup	2 Martin Ashby	3 Dag Lovaas
1975	1 Tommy Jansson	2 Phil Crump	3 Dave Jessup
1976	1 Martin Ashby	2 Edgar Stangeland	3 Mick Hines
1977	1 Colin Richardson	2 Gordon Kennett	3 Chris Morton
1978	1 John Davis	2 Rudy Muts	3 Steve Weatherley
1979	1 Bruce Penhall	2 John Davis	3 Zenon Plech
1980	1 Larry Ross	2 Roger Johns	3 Kenny Carter
1981	1 John Davis	2 Chris Morton	3 Larry Ross
1982	1 Malcolm Simmons	2 Erik Gundersen	3 Kai Niemi
1983	1 Hans Nielsen	2 Dave Jessup	3 Bo Petersen
1985	1 Neil Middleditch	2 Mike Ferreira	3 Kevin Hawkins
1986	1 Nigel Sparshott	2 Roger Johns	3 Malcolm Simmons
1987	1 David Mullett	2 Martin Goodwin	3 Les Collins
1988	1 Steve Schofield	2 Todd Wiltshire	3 Roger Johns
1989	1 Todd Wiltshire	2 Chris Louis	3 Andy Galvin

DAILY EXPRESS SPRING CLASSIC

1976	1 Dave Jessup	2 Tommy Jansson	3 Phil Crump
1977	1 Billy Sanders	2 Peter Collins	3 Dave Jessup
1978	1 Scott Autrey	2 Peter Collins	3 John Davis
1979	1 Scott Autrey	2 Peter Collins	3 Dave Jessup
1980	1 John Davis	2 Dave Jessup	3 John Louis
1981	1 Dave Jessup	2 Ole Olsen	3 Gordon Kennett

TOMMY JANSSON MEMORIAL TROPHY

1977	1 Ole Olsen	2 Edward Jancarz	3 John Davis
1978	1 Peter Collins	2 Larry Ross	3 Roger Johns
1979	1 Edward Jancarz	2 Ron Preston	3 Jim McMillan
1980	1 Richard Hellsén	2 Malcolm Simmons	3 Colin Richardson
1981	1 Bo Petersen	2 John Davis	3 Scott Autrey
1983	1 Kelvin Tatum	2 Phil Crump	3 Gordon Kennett

LEVIS FOR FEET SOUTHERN INTERNATIONAL

1978	1 Gordon Kennett	2 Ole Olsen	3 Colin Richardson

W J CEARNS MEMORIAL TROPHY

1979	1 Larry Ross	2 Zenon Plech	3 Edward Jancarz
1980	1 Bo Petersen	2 John Davis	3 Larry Ross
1981	1 Bobby Schwartz	2 Larry Ross	3 Kai Niemi
1982	1 Larry Ross	2 Ron Preston	3 Lance King
1984	1 Phil Crump	2 Mitch Shirra	3 Malcolm Simmons

DONS' legend Ronnie Moore, on a 1991 visit to England, talks over old times with Editor Peter Oakes

WOLVERHAMPTON

WOLVERHAMPTON had the unenviable record of having competed in 22 seasons of the British League without ever winning a single national trophy! The closest they came was when they finished runners-up in both 1989 and 1990 – the last two seasons of the Division. They held another record – they have used more riders in the British League than any other team that has competed since 1965!

1965...1965...1965...1965...1965...1965

	M	R	Pts	BP	TPts	Ave	F	P	Total
§§Peter Jarman	28	112	233.0	15.0	248.0	8.857	6	1	7
§§Bob Andrews	**37**	**148**	**291.0**	**32.0**	**323.0**	**8.730**		**1**	**1**
§§Jim Airey	35	140	271.0	26.0	297.0	8.486	1	1	2
§§Tommy Sweetman	34	136	216.0	39.0	255.0	7.500		3	3
§§Cyril Francis	**37**	**148**	**228.0**	**35.0**	**263.0**	**7.108**	**1**	**2**	**3**
§§Gordon Guasco	**37**	**148**	**198.0**	**55.0**	**253.0**	**6.838**		**2**	**2**
§§Brian Maxted	25	100	80.0	13.0	93.0	3.720			
§§James Bond	20	80	47.0	20.0	67.0	3.350			
§§Paul Sharples	5	20	5.0	2.0	7.0	1.400			
§§Chris Harrison	1	4	1.0	0.0	1.0	1.000			

1966...1966...1966...1966...1966...1966

	M	R	Pts	BP	TPts	Ave	F	P	Total
§Peter Vandenberg	**37**	**161**	**338.0**	**11.0**	**349.0**	**8.671**	**6**		**6**
Gordon Guasco	34	139	258.0	12.0	270.0	7.770	2		2
Peter Jarman	28	109	161.0	18.0	179.0	6.569		1	1
§Alan Cowland	36	133	146.0	36.0	182.0	5.474			
James Bond	31	112	125.0	28.0	153.0	5.464			
Cyril Francis	32	115	134.0	23.0	157.0	5.461			
Brian Maxted	32	124	143.5	21.0	164.5	5.306			
§§Dave Hemus	24	70	70.0	20.0	90.0	5.143			
§§Mick Handley	1	2	0.0	0.0	0.0	0.000			

1967...1967...1967...1967...1967...1967

	M	R	Pts	BP	TPts	Ave	F	P	Total
§§Hasse Holmkvist	26	112	247.0	13.0	260.0	9.286	1	1	2
Jim Airey	35	156	334.0	20.0	354.0	9.077	1	4	5
Peter Vandenberg	**37**	**169**	**328.0**	**19.0**	**347.0**	**8.213**	**1**		**1**
Peter Jarman	23	98	165.0	29.0	194.0	7.918		2	2
James Bond	27	92	106.0	22.0	128.0	5.565			
Dave Hemus	36	134	135.0	34.0	169.0	5.045			
Brian Maxted	36	127	120.0	30.0	150.0	4.724			
Mick Handley	20	43	18.0	3.0	21.0	1.953			
§§Dave Parry	3	7	3.0	1.0	4.0	2.286			
§Ernie Baker	4	12	6.0	1.0	7.0	2.333			
§§Geoff Ambrose	2	5	2.0	0.0	2.0	1.600			
§§Stuart Riley	1	2	0.0	0.0	0.0	0.000			

1968...1968...1968...1968...1968...1968

	M	R	Pts	BP	TPts	Ave	F	P	Total
Hasse Holmkvist	21	91	208.0	10.0	218.0	9.582	2	3	5
Jim Airey	40	184	412.0	13.0	425.0	9.239	4	3	7
Peter Vandenberg	**41**	**186**	**339.0**	**18.0**	**357.0**	**7.677**	**3**		**3**
James Bond	37	159	237.0	34.0	271.0	6.818		1	1
Peter Jarman	37	150	188.0	36.0	224.0	5.973		1	1
Dave Hemus	28	102	110.0	14.0	124.0	4.863			
Mick Handley	34	121	104.0	26.0	130.0	4.298			
Stuart Riley	2	4	3.0	1.0	4.0	4.000			
§Tony Childs	1	3	2.0	1.0	3.0	4.000			
§§Derek Timms	2	5	3.0	1.0	4.0	3.200			
§Doug White	25	63	36.0	9.0	45.0	2.857			
Geoff Ambrose	7	17	8.0	2.0	10.0	2.353			
Dave Parry	8	21	11.0	1.0	12.0	2.286			

1969...1969...1969...1969...1969...1969

	M	R	Pts	BP	TPts	Ave	F	P	Total
§Norman Hunter	15	68	171.0	5.0	176.0	10.353	5		5
James Bond	**37**	**154**	**248.0**	**36.0**	**284.0**	**7.377**		**1**	**1**
Peter Vandenberg	32	142	244.0	14.0	258.0	7.268	1	1	2
Geoff Ambrose	24	93	128.0	14.0	142.0	6.108	1		1
Mick Handley	32	129	172.0	21.0	193.0	5.984		1	1
Tommy Sweetman	29	113	134.0	27.0	161.0	5.699			
§§Bengt Andersson	27	105	119.0	18.0	137.0	5.219			
§Des Lukehurst	4	15	17.0	2.0	19.0	5.067			
§§George Devonport	1	2	1.0	1.0	2.0	4.000			
§Peter Jackson	31	82	57.0	20.0	77.0	3.756			
Cyril Francis	7	27	19.0	3.0	22.0	3.259			
§§Chris Yeatman	1	5	1.0	1.0	2.0	1.600			
Archie Wilkinson	1	3	1.0	0.0	1.0	1.333			

1970...1970...1970...1970...1970...1970

	M	R	Pts	BP	TPts	Ave	F	P	Total
§Ole Olsen	35	160	408.0	2.0	410.0	10.250	12	1	13
§George Major	1	3	4.0	2.0	6.0	8.000			
§Alan Knapkin	1	1	1.0	1.0	2.0	8.000			
Norman Hunter	30	113	186.0	21.0	207.0	7.327			
Peter Vandenberg	34	136	211.0	14.0	225.0	6.618	1	1	2
James Bond	**37**	**143**	**161.0**	**29.0**	**190.0**	**5.315**			
Mick Handley	**37**	**143**	**158.0**	**31.0**	**189.0**	**5.287**			
Geoff Ambrose	**37**	**150**	**168.0**	**28.0**	**196.0**	**5.227**			
§Jon Erskine	8	25	28.0	4.0	32.0	5.120			
§Gary Peterson	5	17	17.0	1.0	18.0	4.235			
Peter Jackson	22	61	47.0	15.0	62.0	4.066			
Archie Wilkinson	1	3	2.0	1.0	3.0	4.000			
§Malcolm Shakespeare	1	3	1.0	1.0	2.0	2.667			
§Alan Bridgett	3	6	1.0	0.0	1.0	0.667			
§§Robin Adlington	1	2	0.0	0.0	0.0	0.000			
George Devonport	1	2	0.0	0.0	0.0	0.000			

1971...1971...1971...1971...1971...1971

	M	R	Pts	BP	TPts	Ave	F	P	Total
Ole Olsen	35	159	435.0	2.0	437.0	10.994	17	2	36
Norman Hunter	38	156	277.0	20.0	297.0	7.615	2		4
Gary Peterson	23	96	152.0	13.0	165.0	6.875	1		2
§Dave Baugh	6	25	36.0	5.0	41.0	6.560			
Alan Knapkin	3	12	13.0	4.0	17.0	5.667			
Jon Erskine	26	106	122.0	12.0	134.0	5.057			
§Bill Powell	29	120	132.0	17.0	149.0	4.967		1	1
Geoff Ambrose	37	145	150.0	24.0	174.0	4.800			
§§Nils Weiss	9	32	32.0	6.0	38.0	4.750			
Geoff Bouchard	2	8	7.0	2.0	9.0	4.500			
§Terry Shearer	2	6	6.0	0.0	6.0	4.000			
§§Jack Millen	1	4	3.0	1.0	4.0	4.000			
§Dai Evans	5	17	13.0	2.0	15.0	3.529			
§Bengt Brannefors	12	35	28.0	2.0	30.0	3.429			
James Bond	3	11	7.0	2.0	9.0	3.273			
§Tim Swales	3	9	6.0	1.0	7.0	3.111			
§§Clive Noy	1	4	2.0	1.0	3.0	3.000			
George Devonport	7	18	9.0	3.0	12.0	2.667			
Robin Adlington	3	8	5.0	0.0	5.0	2.500			
§Roger Johns	1	5	3.0	0.0	3.0	2.400			
§Phil Crump	3	8	4.0	0.0	4.0	2.000			
§§Roger Knight	2	4	1.0	1.0	2.0	2.000			
§§Johannes Fransden	6	15	3.0	0.0	3.0	0.800			
§Laurie Sims	1	4	0.0	0.0	0.0	0.000			
§§Malcolm Corradine	1	3	0.0	0.0	0.0	0.000			
§§Chris Roynon	1	3	0.0	0.0	0.0	0.000			
§§Ted Howgego	1	1	0.0	0.0	0.0	0.000			

1972...1972...1972...1972...1972...1972

	M	R	Pts	BP	TPts	Ave	F	P	Total
Ole Olsen	31	150	424.0	3.0	427.0	11.387	18		18
Bill Powell	1	3	5.0	1.0	6.0	8.000			
George Hunter	4	19	34.0	3.0	37.0	7.789			
§Jan Simensen	12	50	91.0	6.0	97.0	7.760			
Norman Hunter	10	42	67.0	3.0	70.0	6.667			
§§Dave Mills	2	6	7.0	2.0	9.0	6.000			
§Dave Gifford	33	130	174.0	17.0	191.0	5.877	2	1	3
§Tom Leadbitter	34	129	131.0	17.0	148.0	4.589	1		1
Geoff Bouchard	3	10	10.0	1.0	11.0	4.400			
Jon Erskine	29	111	97.0	15.0	112.0	4.036			
§§Per Hansen	6	25	20.0	5.0	25.0	4.000			
Terry Shearer	3	11	9.0	2.0	11.0	4.000			
Dave Baugh	18	64	50.0	10.0	60.0	3.750			
§Russ Dent	1	5	4.0	0.0	4.0	3.200			
George Devonport	3	8	5.0	1.0	6.0	3.000			
§§Colin Meredith	14	29	10.0	2.0	12.0	1.655			
George Major	1	3	1.0	0.0	1.0	1.333			
§§Tony Freegard	1	3	0.0	0.0	0.0	0.000			
Dai Evans	1	2	0.0	0.0	0.0	0.000			
§Garry Flood	1	2	0.0	0.0	0.0	0.000			
§§Roger Parker	1	2	0.0	0.0	0.0	0.000			

WOLVERHAMPTON

1973...1973...1973...1973...1973...1973

	M	R	Pts	BP	TPts	Ave	F	P	Total
Ole Olsen	29	136	361.0	7.0	368.0	10.824	12	2	14
§Arthur Browning	1	5	8.0	3.0	11.0	8.800			
George Hunter	37	172	326.0	15.0	341.0	7.930	2	2	4
Jon Erskine	10	44	67.0	7.0	74.0	6.727			
Gary Peterson	34	151	198.0	28.0	226.0	5.987	1		1
§Carl Glover	1	5	7.0	0.0	7.0	5.600			
Tom Leadbitter	38	163	189.0	34.0	223.0	5.472			
§§Phil Herne	2	7	8.0	1.0	9.0	5.143			
Dave Baugh	16	51	51.0	8.0	59.0	4.627			
§Tony Clarke	7	29	28.0	5.0	33.0	4.552			
Dave Gifford	13	48	46.0	6.0	52.0	4.333			
George Major	1	5	4.0	1.0	5.0	4.000			
§Ken Eyre	37	131	100.0	25.0	125.0	3.817			
§Tony Featherstone	2	8	5.0	1.0	6.0	3.000			
Tony Freegard	8	19	11.0	3.0	14.0	2.947			
Roger Parker	2	5	2.0	1.0	3.0	2.400			
Colin Meredith	1	2	1.0	0.0	1.0	2.000			
§§Nigel Wasley	2	5	0.0	0.0	0.0	0.000			
Alan Bridgett	1	2	0.0	0.0	0.0	0.000			
Colin Burton	1	2	0.0	0.0	0.0	0.000			
§§Mike Fullerton	1	2	0.0	0.0	0.0	0.000			
§§Alan Guest	1	2	0.0	0.0	0.0	0.000			
Roger Johns	1	2	0.0	0.0	0.0	0.000			

1974...1974...1974...1974...1974...1974

	M	R	Pts	BP	TPts	Ave	F	P	Total
Ole Olsen	27	119	335.0	4.0	339.0	11.395	15	2	17
George Hunter	35	148	281.5	16.0	297.5	8.041		1	1
Phil Herne	2	9	16.0	0.0	16.0	7.111			
§Neil Middleditch	4	17	24.0	5.0	29.0	6.824			
Ken Eyre	9	38	55.0	7.0	62.0	6.526			
§§Ricky Day	2	9	13.0	1.0	14.0	6.222			
§Sid Sheldrick	2	7	7.0	3.0	10.0	5.714			
Tom Leadbitter	34	136	157.0	26.0	183.0	5.382			
Arthur Browning	1	5	6.0	0.0	6.0	4.800			
§Paul Gachet	3	11	11.0	2.0	13.0	4.727			
§§Finn Thomsen	22	87	78.0	15.0	93.0	4.276			
Malcolm Shakespeare	27	103	98.0	6.0	104.0	4.039			
Colin Meredith	25	80	54.0	10.0	64.0	3.200			
Tony Featherstone	1	4	3.0	0.0	3.0	3.000			
Alan Bridgett	2	7	5.0	0.0	5.0	2.857			
Bengt Andersson	7	17	10.0	1.0	11.0	2.588			
Tony Freegard	24	60	26.0	9.0	35.0	2.333			
§§Steve Weatherley	1	4	2.0	0.0	2.0	2.000			
§Dennis Gavros	1	3	1.0	0.0	1.0	1.333			
Alan Molyneux	1	3	1.0	0.0	1.0	1.333			
Nigel Wasley	2	5	1.0	0.0	1.0	0.800			
§Colin Goad	1	2	0.0	0.0	0.0	0.000			

1975...1975...1975...1975...1975...1975

	M	R	Pts	BP	TPts	Ave	F	P	Total
Ole Olsen	22	99	267.0	0.0	267.0	10.788	7		7
Arthur Browning	1	5	11.0	0.0	11.0	8.800			
George Hunter	34	146	236.0	19.0	255.0	6.986		3	3
§Keith Anderson	2	6	8.0	2.0	10.0	6.667			
Finn Thomsen	30	126	174.0	24.0	198.0	6.286			
§Alan Grahame	2	8	10.0	2.0	12.0	6.000			
Gary Peterson	30	123	166.0	14.0	180.0	5.854			
Malcolm Shakespeare	29	102	95.0	21.0	116.0	4.549			
Sid Sheldrick	1	4	3.0	1.0	4.0	4.000			
§Alan Emerson	1	3	2.0	1.0	3.0	4.000			
§Rob Holllingworth	1	3	3.0	0.0	3.0	4.000			
Tony Featherstone	1	2	1.0	1.0	2.0	4.000			
§§Carl Askew	3	7	5.0	1.0	6.0	3.429			
Colin Meredith	21	69	48.0	7.0	55.0	3.188			
Tony Clarke	26	86	55.0	13.0	68.0	3.163			
Tom Leadbitter	2	9	6.0	1.0	7.0	3.111			
Nigel Wasley	7	23	15.0	2.0	17.0	2.957			
§§Leif Berlin	4	13	8.0	1.0	9.0	2.769			
§Tony Boyle	1	3	2.0	0.0	2.0	2.667			
§§Dave Trownson	1	2	1.0	0.0	1.0	2.000			
Ricky Day	1	3	1.0	0.0	1.0	1.333			
§Eric Dugard	1	3	1.0	0.0	1.0	1.333			
§§Phil Michelidies	1	4	1.0	0.0	1.0	1.000			
Alan Knapkin	2	6	0.0	0.0	0.0	0.000			

1976...1976...1976...1976...1976...1976

	M	R	Pts	BP	TPts	Ave	F	P	Total
§Jim McMillan	**38**	**174**	**365.0**	**25.0**	**390.0**	**8.966**	**3**	**1**	**4**
Finn Thomsen	30	161	269.0	36.0	305.0	7.578			
George Hunter	37	169	297.0	22.0	319.0	7.550	1		1
Colin Meredith	5	12	12.0	5.0	17.0	5.667			
§§Colin Farquharson	1	3	4.0	0.0	4.0	5.333			
Phil Michelides	3	7	7.0	2.0	9.0	5.143			
John Jackson	21	88	93.0	16.0	109.0	4.955			
Rob Hollingworth	5	18	18.0	4.0	22.0	4.889			
Dave Trownson	3	8	7.0	1.0	8.0	4.000			
Tony Featherstone	1	3	2.0	1.0	3.0	4.000			
Leif Berlin	30	100	78.0	18.0	96.0	3.840			
Malcolm Shakespeare	4	12	9.0	1.0	10.0	3.333			
§§Guiseppe Marzotto	11	36	25.0	4.0	29.0	3.222			
§§Robbie Blackadder	1	3	1.0	0.0	1.0	1.333			
§§Steve McDermott	3	6	0.0	0.0	0.0	0.000			
§§Mark Stokes	1	2	0.0	0.0	0.0	0.000			
Jack Millen	1	2	0.0	0.0	0.0	0.000			

1977...1977...1977...1977...1977...1977

	M	R	Pts	BP	TPts	Ave	F	P	Total
Jim McMillan	36	159	320.0	25.0	345.0	8.679	1	1	2
Finn Thomsen	33	145	275.0	21.0	296.0	8.166	1	1	2
§§Hans Nielsen	32	144	230.o	31.0	261.0	7.250			
§Kelvin Mullarkey	1	5	9.0	0.0	9.0	7.200			
George Hunter	31	101	123.0	21.0	144.0	5.703			
§Sören Sjösten	32	114	140.0	12.0	152.0	5.333	1		1
§Robbie Gardner	1	3	4.0	0.0	4.0	5.333			
§Bert Harkins	2	7	6.0	3.0	9.0	5.143			
§Phil Collins	1	5	5.0	1.0	6.0	4.800			
Rob Hollingworth	29	105	106.0	17.0	123.0	4.686			
Steve McDermott	4	8	7.0	1.0	8.0	4.000			
§Alan Sage	3	12	9.0	1.0	10.0	3.333			
§Steve Lomas	15	45	26.0	5.0	31.0	2.756			
§§Markku Helminen	1	3	2.0	0.0	2.0	2.667			
§Brian Havelock	1	2	1.0	0.0	1.0	2.000			
§§Preben Eriksen	1	2	1.0	0.0	1.0	2.000			
Robbie Blackadder	1	2	1.0	0.0	1.0	2.000			
Phil Michelides	1	3	1.0	0.0	1.0	1.333			
Dave Trownson	3	8	1.0	0.0	1.0	0.500			
Mark Stokes	3	6	0.0	0.0	0.0	0.000			
§Tim Nunan	1	2	0.0	0.0	0.0	0.000			

1979...1979...1979...1979...1979...1979

	M	R	Pts	BP	TPts	Ave	F	P	Total
Hans Nielsen	34	157	392.0	12.0	404.0	10.293	9	1	10
Jim McMillan	25	111	205.0	15.0	220.0	7.928		1	1
Dave Morton	23	101	162.0	10.0	172.0	6.812			
George Hunter	16	63	87.0	19.0	106.0	6.730			
Hasse Danielsson	30	124	182.0	16.0	198.0	6.387			
Bruce Cribb	35	150	183.0	36.0	219.0	5.840			
Edgar Stangeland	35	133	146.0	35.0	181.0	5.444			
Dave Trownson	7	26	29.0	5.0	34.0	5.231			
Malcolm Corradine	1	2	2.0	0.0	2.0	4.000			
§§Trond Skretting	30	83	63.0	10.0	73.0	3.518			
Knud Ellegard	2	7	5.0	1.0	6.0	3.429			
§§Terry Tulloch	2	7	3.0	2.0	5.0	2.857			
Carl Askew	1	3	1.0	1.0	2.0	2.667			
§§Wayne Brown	1	4	2.0	0.0	2.0	2.000			
§John Goodall	1	4	2.0	0.0	2.0	2.000			
Ivan Blacka	3	10	4.0	0.0	4.0	1.600			
§Ian Gledhill	1	3	1.0	0.0	1.0	1.333			
§§Steve Crockett	6	13	2.0	0.0	2.0	0.615			
§Kris Berrigan	1	2	0.0	0.0	0.0	0.000			
§Tim Curnock	1	2	0.0	0.0	0.0	0.000			

WOLVERHAMPTON'S Peter Jarman probably had the strangest accident of any speedway rider...he broke three toes as an extra in the old ITV soap opera Crossroads! The series, filmed in Birmingham, had a running story line based around a speedway team staying at the Motel and it required action shots to add to the authenticity. Jarman volunteered to race – and crashed during filming!

WOLVERHAMPTON

■ *YOUNG New Zealander Gary Peterson, one of the first discoveries of the Second Division, died while riding for Wolverhampton against Coventry in the 1975 Midland Cup Final.*

■ *Gary (pictured above with his team-mate Ken Eyre) was one of the most exciting discoveries of the late sixties and had established himself in the Wolverhampton team at the time of the accident.*

■ *A measure of his esteem was that Ole Olsen withdrew from the follwing evening's British League Riders' Final as a tribute to his team-mate and Ivan Mauger donated all his BLRC earnings to Gary's widow Val and their 18-month-old son.*

1980...1980...1980...1980...1980...1980

	M	R	Pts	BP	TPts	Ave	F	P	Total
Hans Nielsen	29	137	359.0	7.0	366.0	10.686	11	2	13
§Reidar Eide	20	78	124.0	14.0	138.0	7.077		1	1
Jim McMillan	33	142	230.0	19.0	249.0	7.014		1	1
§David Bargh	1	6	9.0	1.0	10.0	6.667			
§§Petr Ondrasik	19	78	95.0	19.0	114.0	5.846			
Bruce Cribb	24	95	119.0	17.0	136.0	5.726			
Dave Morton	17	50	60.0	7.0	67.0	5.360	1		1
Hasse Danielsson	14	54	61.0	11.0	72.0	5.333		1	1
§Billy Burton	13	41	47.0	5.0	52.0	5.073		1	1
Arthur Browning	2	6	7.0	0.0	7.0	4.667			
Ivan Blacka	17	57	44.0	12.0	56.0	3.930			
Wayne Brown	8	25	21.0	2.0	23.0	3.680			
Dave Trownson	3	8	7.0	0.0	7.0	3.500			
§Neil Evitts	1	6	4.0	1.0	5.0	3.333			
§§Hans Christensen	11	29	13.0	6.0	19.0	2.621			
George Hunter	1	4	1.0	1.0	2.0	2.000			
Steve Crockett	2	5	1.0	1.0	2.0	1.600			
§§Paul Evitts	1	5	1.0	0.0	1.0	0.800			

PETER ADAMS quit as manager of Black Country rivals Cradley Heath – he had led them to the 1983 British League championship – to relaunch First Division speedway at Monmore Green.

He built up an attractive side by signing American Dennis Sigalos and, a year later, brought in Bobby Schwartz and subsequently Sam Ermolenko.

But Adams' big spending was his downfall and in July, 1986, he quit leaving the track's future in limbo.

After several weeks of uncertainty Chris Van Straaten picked up the pieces and Wolverhampton survived.

1984...1984...1984...1984...1984...1984

	M	R	Pts	BP	TPts	Ave	F	P	Total
§Dennis Sigalos	17	77	187.0	3.0	190.0	9.870	3		3
§Kerry Gray	1	3	5.0	2.0	7.0	9.333			
Preben Eriksen	33	141	278.0	20.0	298.0	8.454	2	1	3
§Peter Ravn	40	162	276.5	26.0	302.5	7.469	2	1	3
§Andy Grahame	41	171	277.0	32.0	309.0	7.228		1	1
§Tom Owen	2	5	3.0	3.0	6.0	4.800			
§Steve Lucero	13	46	45.0	8.0	53.0	4.609			
§Louis Carr	7	23	23.0	3.0	26.0	4.522			
§§Robert Pfetzing	47	179	175.0	27.0	202.0	4.514			
§Trevor Banks	1	3	3.0	0.0	3.0	4.000			
§Kent Noer	24	78	60.0	12.0	72.0	3.692			
§David Cheshire	23	62	43.0	7.0	50.0	3.226			
Dave Trownson	3	10	6.0	2.0	8.0	3.200			
§Steve Schofield	7	24	13.0	5.0	18.0	3.000			
§Colin Cook	1	4	2.0	1.0	3.0	3.000			
§Paul Thorp	13	40	27.0	2.0	29.0	2.900			
§Andrew Silver	1	3	1.0	1.0	2.0	2.667			
§§Flemming Pedersen	6	18	11.0	0.0	11.0	2.444			
§Kevin Teager	2	5	2.0	1.0	3.0	2.400			
§Alan Mogridge	1	4	1.0	0.0	1.0	1.000			
§Mark Fiora	2	4	0.0	0.0	0.0	0.000			
§§Paul Price	1	3	0.0	0.0	0.0	0.000			
§Brett Saunders	1	3	0.0	0.0	0.0	0.000			
§Paul Stead	1	3	0.0	0.0	0.0	0.000			
Mike Spink	1	2	0.0	0.0	0.0	0.000			

1985...1985...1985...1985...1985...1985

	M	R	Pts	BP	TPts	Ave	F	P	Total
§Bobby Schwartz	35	149	349.0	16.0	365.0	9.799	2		2
Peter Ravn	22	86	149.0	17.0	166.0	7.721			
Preben Eriksen	43	183	327.0	25.0	352.0	7.694	2	1	3
John Eskildsen	33	139	223.0	35.0	258.0	7.424		1	1
§Martin Goodwin	1	3	3.0	1.0	4.0	5.333			
Steve Schofield	43	144	157.0	22.0	179.0	4.972			
§Martin Scarisbrick	23	72	73.0	15.0	88.0	4.889			
§Brian Jakobsen	24	81	82.0	15.0	97.0	4.790			
§Roger Johns	3	11	10.0	3.0	13.0	4.727			
§Stan Bear	7	24	18.0	9.0	27.0	4.500			
§Gerd Riss	11	34	29.0	4.0	33.0	3.882			
David Cheshire	14	51	31.0	6.0	37.0	2.902			
§§Jan Staechmann	11	38	15.0	4.0	19.0	2.000			
Paul Thorp	5	16	5.0	0.0	5.0	1.250			
Dave Trownson	2	7	2.0	0.0	2.0	1.143			
§Gary Havelock	1	4	0.0	0.0	0.0	0.000			
Kevin Teager	1	3	0.0	0.0	0.0	0.000			

1986...1986...1986...1986...1986...1986

	M	R	Pts	BP	TPts	Ave	F	P	Total
§Sam Ermolenko	39	184	407.0	40.0	447.0	9.717	3	8	11
§Paul Whittaker	1	4	5.0	3.0	8.0	8.000			
Preben Eriksen	25	95	177.0	6.0	183.0	7.705	1	1	2
John Eskildsen	**41**	**176**	**275.0**	**35.0**	**310.0**	**7.045**	**1**	**1**	**2**
Peter Ravn	34	128	179.0	23.0	202.0	6.313			
§Gordon Kennett	3	11	16.0	1.0	17.0	6.182			
§Sam Nikolajsen	37	136	189.0	21.0	210.0	6.176		1	1
§Andy Buck	2	9	11.0	1.0	12.0	5.333			
Jan Staechmann	38	137	159.0	20.0	179.0	5.226		1	1
Paul Evitts	1	4	4.0	0.0	4.0	4.000			
§§Andy Phillips	37	117	71.0	16.0	87.0	2.974			
§§Chris Cobby	5	15	3.0	1.0	4.0	1.067			

BRITISH LEAGUE AVERAGES...BRITISH LEAGUE AVERAGES...BRITISH LEAGUE AVERAGES

WOLVERHAMPTON

1987...1987...1987...1987...1987...1987

	M	R	Pts	BP	TPts	Ave	F	P	Total
Sam Ermolenko	27	127	292.0	21.0	313.0	9.858	2	2	4
John Eskildsen	5	20	41.0	4.0	45.0	9.000			
Preben Eriksen	44	188	317.0	25.0	342.0	7.277	3		
§§Ronnie Correy	42	187	269.0	27.0	296.0	6.332			
Robert Pfetzing	5	20	26.0	5.0	31.0	6.200			
Jan Staechmann	40	173	216.0	44.0	260.0	6.012			
§§Lars Munkedal	32	135	168.0	17.0	185.0	5.481			
David Blackburn	2	9	10.0	1.0	11.0	4.889			
Andy Phillips	25	97	101.0	14.0	115.0	4.742			
§§Dean Standing	4	14	12.0	4.0	16.0	4.571			
Chris Cobby	21	55	30.0	14.0	44.0	3.200			
Paul Evitts	1	4	2.0	0.0	2.0	2.000			
§§Carl Bodley	4	9	3.0	1.0	4.0	1.778			
§§Richard Smith	5	11	3.0	1.0	4.0	1.455			
§§Andy Sumner	16	38	9.0	3.0	12.0	1.263			
§Peter Schroeck	5	12	2.0	1.0	3.0	1.000			
§§Torben Hansen	7	20	2.0	0.0	2.0	0.400			
Steve McDermott	1	3	0.0	0.0	0.0	0.000			

1988...1988...1988...1988...1988...1988

	M	R	Pts	BP	TPts	Ave	F	P	Total
Sam Ermolenko	41	226	504.0	27.0	531.0	9.398	2	3	5
§Graham Jones	1	5	11.0	0.0	11.0	8.800			
§§Chris Louis	1	3	4.0	2.0	6.0	8.000			
§Bo Petersen	8	36	64.0	5.0	69.0	7.667			
Ronnie Correy	33	158	259.0	27.0	286.0	7.241	1		1
Jan Staechmann	**42**	**178**	**224.0**	**48.0**	**272.0**	**6.112**		**1**	**1**
Louis Carr	1	4	4.0	2.0	6.0	6.000			
Preben Eriksen	**42**	**183**	**237.0**	**35.0**	**272.0**	**5.945**			
Andy Grahame	40	162	213.0	19.0	232.0	5.728	1		1
§Kenny McKinna	3	14	18.0	2.0	20.0	5.714			
Andy Phillips	41	151	175.0	33.0	208.0	5.510			
Lars Munkedal	15	52	64.0	7.0	71.0	5.462			
§Steve Bastable	2	8	7.0	3.0	10.0	5.000			
§Peter Glanz	18	67	63.0	11.0	74.0	4.418			
§Ian Barney	1	3	2.0	0.0	2.0	2.667			
§§Ade Hoole	2	4	0.0	0.0	0.0	0.000			
§Lee Edwards	1	1	0.0	0.0	0.0	0.000			

1989...1989...1989...1989...1989...1989

	M	R	Pts	BP	TPts	Ave	F	P	Total
Sam Ermolenko	16	80	179.0	18.0	197.0	9.850	1	3	4
Ronnie Correy	31	147	264.0	25.0	289.0	7.864	1	2	3
§Neil Collins	36	154	230.0	35.0	265.0	6.883		1	1
Robert Pfetzing	37	147	211.0	32.0	243.0	6.612		2	2
Graham Jones	37	163	245.0	24.0	269.0	6.601		1	1
Jan Staechmann	37	153	207.0	43.0	250.0	6.536		1	1
Andy Phillips	36	134	161.0	31.0	192.0	5.731			
§§Wayne Carter	1	3	0.0	0.0	0.0	0.000			
Ade Hoole	1	3	0.0	0.0	0.0	0.000			

1990...19890...1990...1990...1990...1990

	M	R	Pts	BP	TPts	Ave	F	P	Total
Sam Ermolenko	24	133	269.0	26.0	295.0	8.872		3	3
Ronnie Correy	32	175	366.0	21.0	387.0	8.846	4	1	5
Graham Jones	17	79	112.0	10.0	122.0	6.177			
Neil Collins	30	127	157.0	24.0	181.0	5.701			
Jan Staechmann	22	84	94.0	23.0	117.0	5.571			
§Carl Stonehewer	23	107	125.0	20.0	145.0	5.421			
§§Peter Karlsson	14	55	58.0	7.0	65.0	4.727			
Lars Munkedal	6	21	18.0	5.0	23.0	4.381			
Wayne Carter	20	66	48.0	9.0	57.0	3.455			
Bo Petersen	4	14	8.0	1.0	9.0	2.571			
Ade Hoole	1	3	0.0	0.0	0.0	0.000			

PRIDE OF THE MIDLANDS

1965	1 Barry Briggs	2 Peter Jarman	3 Martin Ashby
1966	1 Martin Ashby	2 Gordon Guasco	3 Rick France
1967	1 Barry Briggs	2 Ray Wilson	3 Jim Airey
1968	1 Peter Jarman	2 Jim Airey	3 Bob Andrews
1969	1 Barry Briggs	2 Peter Vandenberg	3 Nigel Boocock
1970	1 Ole Olsen	2 Barry Briggs	3 Bob Kilby
1971	1 Ole Olsen	2 Terry Betts	3 Ivan Mauger
1972	1 Ole Olsen	2 Ivan Mauger	3 George Hunter
1974	1 Martin Ashby	2 Eric Broadbelt	3 Chris Pusey
1975	1 Billy Sanders	2 Dag Lovaas	3 Jim McMillan
1977	1 Gordon Kennett	2 Steve Bastable	3 Hans Nielsen

CHAMPION OF CHAMPIONS

1965	1 Brian Brett	2 Ivan Mauger	3 Mike Broadbank
1966	1 Barry Briggs	2 Martin Ashby	3 Roy Trigg
1967	1 Barry Briggs	2 Eric Boocock	3 Nigel Boocock
1970	1 Ole Olsen	2 Anders Michanek	3 Bernt Persson
1971	1 Sören Sjösten	2 Terry Betts	3 John Louis
1972	1 Ole Olsen	2 Anders Michanek	3 Peter Collins
1972	1 Anders Michanek	2 Ole Olsen	3 Peter Collins
1974	1 Ole Olsen	2 Martin Ashby	3 Edgar Stangeland, Billy Sanders
1975	1 John Louis	2 Peter Collins and Dave Jessup	
1977	1 Peter Collins	2 Ole Olsen	3 Michael Lee
1979	1 Les Collins	2 Phil Collins	3 Chris Morton
1980	1 Bobby Schwartz	2 Alan Grahame	3 Erik Gundersen

CROSSROADS TV TROPHY

1968	1 Barry Briggs	2 Hasse Holmkvist	3 Malcolm Simmons

MONMORE JUNIOR CHAMPIONSHIP

1969	1 Dai Evans	2 Geoff Ambrose	3 George Devonport

FESTIVAL OF SPEEDWAY

1971	1 Ole Olsen	2 Doug Wyer	3 Michael Lee
1972	1 Ole Olsen	2 Bernt Persson	3 Martin Ashby
1975	1 Ivan Mauger	2 Malcolm Simmons	3 Ole Olsen and Billy Sanders

BREW XI TROPHY

1973	1 Anders Michanek	2 Terry Betts	3 Dag Lovaas

CHAMPIONS TROPHY

1974	1 Ole Olsen	2 Peter Collins	3 Martin Ashby

GARY PETERSON MEMORIAL TROPHY

1976	1 Gordon Kennett	2 Ole Olsen	3 Jim McMillan

WHOLESALE MARKETS MARATHON

1984	1 Peter Ravn	2 Simon Wigg	3 Simon Cross
1985	1 Chris Morton	2 Jan O. Pedersen	3 Hans Nielsen

WORDS OF ADVICE...former promoter Peter Adams returned to Monmore Green as team manager and passes on a few words of wisdom to Ronnie Correy

INDIVIDUAL MEETS

Anglia Junior League Riders' Championship

1978	1 Kevin Smith	2 Richard Knight	3 Graham Steward
1979	1 Nigel Sparshott	2 Mark Baldwin	3 Alan Leaver
1980	1 Rob Lightfoot	2 Andy Fines	3 Mark Cornish
1981	1 Marvyn Cox	2 Chris Cole	3 Keven Dye
1982	1 Chris Pidcock	2 Paul Clarke	3 Andy Harris
1984	1 Rob Wall	2 Michael Keepe	3 Lawrie Bloomfield

Venues: Mildenhall, 1978-81; Milton Keynes, 1982-84.

British Speedway Supporters Club Trophy

1965	1 Peter Jackson	2 Tony Clarke	3 George Marsh
1966	1 Ray Cousins	2 Joe Weichlbauer	3 Colin Clark
1967	1 Graham Edmunds	2 Peter Murray	3 Dave Callington
1972	1 Keith White	2 Bob Jennings	3 Jack Walker
1973	1 Andy Sims	2 Brian Emery	3 Brian Paddington
1974	1 Rob Mouncer	2 Richard Davey	3 Ashley Pullen
1975	1 William Spiers	2 Andy Bales	3 Phil Garneys
1976	1 Derek Harrison	2 Nigel Crabtree	3 Andy Fisher

Venues: Rye House, 1965-66; King's Lynn, 1967-76.

British Junior League Riders' Championship

1984	1 Lawrie Bloomfield	2 Michael Keepe	3 Gary Chessell
1985	1 Jamie Habbin	2 Robbie Fuller	3 Mike Bacon
1986	1 Sean Wilson	2 Andy Phillips	3 Jon Stokes
1987	1 Mark Loram	2 Ray Morton	3 Ian Stead
1989	1 Carl Stonehewer	2 Joe Screen	3 Mike Lewthwaite
1990	1 Richie Musson	2 Troy Smith	3 Ade Hoole

Venues: King's Lynn, 1984-87; Belle Vue, 1989-90.

Central Junior League Riders' Championship

1982	1 Steve Bishop	2 Steve Mildoon	3 Kevin Smart
1983	1 David Smart	2 Rob Price	3 Russell Birks

Venues: Long Eaton, 1982; Leicester, 1983.

Central Riders' Championship

1987	1 Dave Jessup	2 Melvyn Taylor	3 David Jackson
1988	1 Paul Thorp	2 Eric Monaghan	3 Dave Jessup

Venues: Mildenhall, 1987; Milton Keynes, 1988.

Championship of Kent

1968	1 Peter Murray	2 Barry Crowson	3 Eric Broadbelt
1969	1 Martyn Piddock	2 Geoff Ambrose	3 Graham Miles
1969	1 Martyn Piddock	2 Graham Miles	3 Tony Childs
†1969	***1 Martyn Piddock***	***2 Graham Miles***	***3 Peter Murray***

Venues: Canterbury, 1968-69; Crayford, 1969. †In 1969 the competition was held over two meetings. Overall result.

Cheshire Open Championship

1969	1 Geoff Curtis	2 Ian Bottomley	3 Colin Tucker
1972	1 Phil Crump	2 Robin Adlington	3 Robbie Gardner
1973	1 Geoff Ambrose	2 Paul O'Neal	3 Colin Goad
1974	1 John Jackson	2 Colin Goad	3 Graham Drury
1975	1 John Jackson	2 Alan Molyneux	3 Tom Owen
1979	1 John Jackson	2 Louis Carr	3 Steve Finch

Venues: Crewe, 1969 ; Ellesmere Port, 1972-79.

Geoff Curtis Memorial Trophy

1974	1 John Jackson	2 Cliff Anderson	3 Keith White
1975	1 Alan Molyneux	2 Stuart Cope	3 John Jackson

Venue: Crewe, 1974-75.

East Midlands Championship

1967	1 Anders Michanek	2 Barry Briggs	3 Nigel Boocock
1968	1 Ray Wilson	2 James Bond	3 Charlie Monk
1969	1 Barry Briggs	2 Ivan Mauger	3 Ray Wilson
1970	1 Ray Wilson	2 Martin Ashby	3 Garry Middleton
1971	1 Anders Michanek	2 Ray Wilson	3 John Boulger
1978	1 Steve Bastable	2 Michael Lee	3 Keith White
1989	1 Eric Monaghan	2 Gordon Kennett	3 Mick Poole
1990	1 Nigel Crabtree	2 Eric Monaghan	3 Paul Fry

Venues: Long Eaton, 1967-1968, 1989-90; Leicester, 1968-1978.

In some instances no official decision was given on rostrum placings although awards may have been made on the night.

London Riders' Championship

1965	1 Sverre Harrfeldt	2 Mike Broadbank	3 Colin Pratt
1966	1 Norman Hunter	2 Olle Nygren	3 Brian Leonard
1967	1 Colin Pratt	2 Malcolm Simmons	3 Colin McKee
1968	1 Colin Pratt	2 Trevor Hedge	3 Reg Luckhurst
1969	1 Trevor Hedge	2 Garry Middleton	3 Cyril Maidment
1970	1 Trevor Hedge	2 Reidar Eide	3 Garry Middleton
1971	1 Bengt Jansson	2 Garry Middleton	3 Ronnie Moore
1972	1 Ronnie Moore	2 Geoff Maloney	3 Barry Thomas
1973	1 Barry Thomas	2 Dave Jessup	3 Hugh Saunders
1974	1 Barry Thomas	2 Colin Gooddy	3 Graeme Stapleton
1975	1 Dave Jessup	2 Tommy Jansson	3 Dave Morton
1976	1 Gordon Kennett	2 Trevor Hedge	3 Barry Thomas
1977	1 Larry Ross	2 Gordon Kennett	3 Keith White
1978	1 Keith White	2 Barry Thomas	3 Kai Niemi
1979	1 Larry Ross	2 Colin Richardson	3 Zenon Plech
1980	1 Finn Thomsen	2 Zenon Plech	3 Larry Ross
1982	1 Kai Niemi	2 Finn Thomsen	3 Bo Petersen
1983	1 Bo Petersen	2 Dave Jessup	3 Kelvin Tatum

Venues: Hackney, 1965-83; Wimbledon, 1982-83. The 1983 Championship was held over two meetings.

London Riders' Championship Division Two

1970	1 Dave Jessup	2 Phil Woodock	3 Brian Foote
1971	1 Hugh Saunders	2 Kevin Holden	3 Bob Coles
1988	1 Andy Galvin	2 Mark Loram	3 Jens Rasmussen

Venues: Romford, 1970-71; Wimbledon, 1988.

Midland Junior Riders' Championship

1966	1 Ian Champion	2 Peter Seaton	3 Joe Weichlbauer
1971	1 Dave Baugh	2 George Major	3 John Jackson
1979	1 Andy Buck	2 Paul Evitts	3 Nigel Sparshott
1980	1 Neil Evitts	2 Mike Wilding	3 Guy Robson
1981	1 Ritchie Owen	2 Gary O'Hare	3 Paul Holdbrook
1982	1 Gary Johnson	2 Jim Burdfield	3 Glenn Parrott
1982	1 Mitchell Barker	2 Jim Burdfield	3 Gary O'Hare
1987	1 Chris Cobby	2 Wayne Elliott	3 Wayne Garratt

Venues: Brafield, 1966; Wolverhampton, 1971, 1987; Stoke, 1979-1982. In 1981 the competition was known as the Potteries Open Junior Championship.

Midland Riders Championship

1966	1 Barry Briggs	2 Jim Lightfoot	3 Arne Pander
1967	1 Barry Briggs	2 Rick France	3 Ray Wilson
1968	1 Nigel Boocock	2 Ray Wilson	3 James Bond
1969	1 Norman Hunter	2 Barry Briggs	3 Nigel Boocock
1970	1 Barry Briggs	2 Ole Olsen	3 Nigel Boocock
1971	1 Ole Olsen	2 Nigel Boocock	3 Ray Wilson
1972	1 Ole Olsen	2 Ray Wilson	3 Barry Briggs
1973	1 John Boulger	2 Bernt Persson	3 Garry Middleton
1974	1 Dave Jessup	2 Ray Wilson	3 Martin Ashby
1975	1 Ole Olsen	2 Ray Wilson	3 Tony Lomas
1976	1 Ole Olsen	2 Martin Ashby	3 Alan Molyneux
1978	1 Ole Olsen	2 Alan Molyneux	3 Jan Andersson
1979	1 Hans Nielsen	2 Bobby Schwartz	3 Phil Collins
1980	1 Scott Autrey	2 Bruce Penhall	3 Ole Olsen
1981	1 Erik Gundersen	2 Tommy Knudsen	3 Andy Grahame
1982	1 Erik Gundersen	2 Gary Guglielmi	3 Tommy Knudsen
1983	1 Erik Gundersen	2 Hans Nielsen	3 Andy Grahame
1984	1 Lance King	2 Phil Collins	3 Tommy Knudsen
1985	1 Hans Nielsen	2 Erik Gundersen	3 Jan Andersson
1986	1 Tommy Knudsen	2 Hans Nielsen	3 Marvyn Cox

Venues: Coventy, 1966-1985; Oxford, 1986.

Northern Riders' Championship

1967	1 Ivan Mauger	2 Tommy Roper	3 Billy Bales
1968	1 Ivan Mauger	2 Eric Boocock	3 Charlie Monk
1969	1 Ivan Mauger	2 Jim Airey	3 Eric Boocock
1970	1 Eric Boocock	2 Jim Airey	3 Jim McMillan
1971	1 Jim Airey	2 Sören Sjösten	3 Eric Broadbelt
1972	1 Ivan Mauger	2 Arnie Haley	3 George Hunter
1973	1 Bob Valentine	2 Arnie Haley	3 Bengt Larsson
1974	1 Peter Collins	2 Sören Sjösten	3 Reg Wilson
1975	1 Peter Collins	2 Doug Wyer	3 Sören Sjösten
1976	1 Doug Wyer	2 Peter Collins	3 Chris Pusey
1977	1 Alan Wilkinson	2 Graham Drury	3 Bobby Beaton
1978	1 Reg Wilson	2 Ian Cartwright	3 Ivan Mauger
1979	1 Doug Wyer	2 Chris Morton	3 Joe Owen
1980	1 Ivan Mauger	2 Kenny Carter	3 Dennis Sigalos

1981	1 Kenny Carter	2 Billy Sanders	3 Chris Morton
1982	1 Shawn Moran	2 Doug Wyer	3 Chris Morton
1983	1 Chris Morton	2 Peter Collins	3 Peter Carr
1984	1 Peter Collins	2 Les Collins	3 Shawn Moran
1985	1 Shawn Moran	2 Peter Carr	3 Chris Morton
1987	1 Chris Morton	2 Shawn Moran	3 Gary Havelock

Northern Riders' Championship (Division Two)

1970	1 Gary Peterson	2 Alan Knapkin	3 Eric Broadbelt
1975	1.Tom Owen	2 Joe Owen	3 Colin Meredith
1976	1 Joe Owen	2 Tom Owen	3 Steve Finch
1986	1 Martin Dixon	2 Mark Courtney	3 David Blackburn
1987	1 Les Collins	2 Mark Courtney	3 Martin Dixon

Venues: Bradford, 1970; Newcastle, 1975; Middlesbrough, 1976-87.

Northern Star Trophy

1965	1 Ivan Mauger	2 Charlie Monk	3 Eric Boocock
1971	1 Dave Baugh	2 Doug Wyer	3 George Barclay
1972	1 Dave Baugh	2 Graeme Smith	3 Peter Reading
1973	1 Russ Dent	2 Dave Mills	3 Dave Gatenby

Venues: Newcastle, 1965; Sunderland, 1971-73.

Olympiad

1970	1 Dave Jessup	2 Graeme Smith	3 Barry Thomas
1971	1 Alan Knapkin	2 Russ Dent	3 Geoff Maloney
1972	1 Phil Crump	2 Paul Tyrer	3 Andy Meldrum
1973	1 Dave Baugh	2 Alan Knapkin	3 Carl Glover
1974	1 Colin Meredith	2 Robin Adlington	3 Tom Owen
1975	1 Arthur Browning	2 Brian Havelock	3 Colin Meredith
1976	1 John Jackson	2 Les Collins	3 Chris Turner
1977	1 Martin Yeates	2 Arthur Browning	3 Tom Owen
1978	1 Tom Owen	2 Martin Dixon	3 Dave Trownson
1980	1 Steve Wilcock	2 George Hunter	3 Wayne Brown

Venues: Crayford, 1970; Bradford, 1971-75; Stoke, 1976; Edinburgh, 1977-80.

Olympique

1966	1 Barry Briggs	2 Peter Kelly	3 Nigel Boocock
1967	1 Anders Michanek	2 Ivan Mauger	3 Nigel Boocock
1970	1 Ole Olsen	2 Ivan Mauger	3 Ronnie Moore
1971	1 Ole Olsen	2 Barry Briggs	3 Bernt Persson
1972	1 Ole Olsen	2 Terry Betts	3 Ivan Mauger
1973	1 Ole Olsen	2 Peter Collins and Chris Pusey	
1974	1 Ole Olsen	2 Peter Collins	3 Terry Betts
1975	1 Ole Olsen	2 Billy Sanders	3 Sören Sjösten
1976	1 Peter Collins	2 Ole Olsen	3 Chris Morton
1977	1 Billy Sanders	2 Gordon Kennett	3 Dave Jessup
1978	1 Gordon Kennett	2 Ole Olsen	3 Ila Teromaa
1979	1 Phil Crump	2 Bruce Penhall	3 Jan Andersson
1980	1 Les Collins	2 Bobby Schwartz	3 Tommy Knudsen
1981	1 Mitch Shirra	2 Hans Nielsen	3 Dave Jessup
1982	1 Hans Nielsen	2 Alan Grahame	3 Tommy Knudsen
1984	1 Hans Nielsen	2 Shawn Moran	3 Preben Eriksen
1987	1 Sam Ermolenko	2 Hans Nielsen	3 Jan O. Pedersen
1988	1 Hans Nielsen	2 Sam Ermolenko	3 Mike Faria
1989	1 Jan O. Pedersen	2 Ronnie Correy	3 Hans Nielsen
1990	1 Ronnie Correy	2 Billy Hamill	3 John Jørgensen

Venues: Newcastle, 1966-67; Wolverhampton, 1970-1980; 1984-1990; Birmingham, 1981-82.

Pride of the North

1971	1 George Hunter	2 Jim McMillan	3 Eric Broadbelt
1974	1 Sid Sheldrick	2 Tom Owen	3 Robin Adlington
1980	1 Louis Carr	2 Nigel Close	3 Steve Finch

Venues: Belle Vue, 1971; Barrow, 1974; Newcastle, 1980.

Scotianapolis

1969	1 Ivan Mauger	2 Nigel Boocock	3 Jim Airey
1970	1 Ivan Mauger	2 Jim McMillan	3 Arnie Haley
1972	1 Ivan Mauger	2 Chris Pusey	3 Ray Wilson
1973	1 Peter Collins	2 Jim McMillan	3 Ray Wilson
1974	1 Phil Herne	2 Robin Adlington	3 Tom Owen
1975	1 Jim Gallacher	2 Brian Collins	3 Grahame Dawson, Graham Drury
1976	1 Brian Collins	2 Graham Jones	3 Grahame Dawson

Venue: Glasgow, 1969-1972; Coatbridge, 1973-76.

Scottish Open Championship

1965	1 Arne Pander	2 George Hunter	3 Ivan Mauger
1966	1 Bill Landels	2 Charlie Monk	3 Ivan Mauger
1967	1 Barry Briggs	2 Ray Wilson	3 Bernt Persson
1968	1 Martin Ashby	2 Charlie Monk	3 Reidar Eide
1969	1 Reidar Eide	2 Ole Olsen	3 Ray Wilson
1970	1 Ivan Mauger	2 Reidar Eide	3 Olle Nygren
1971	1 Ivan Mauger	2 Jim McMillan	3 Anders Michanek
1972	1 Ivan Mauger	2 Jim McMillan	3 Reidar Eide
1973	1 Ivan Mauger	2 Jim McMillan	3 Anders Michanek
1975	1 Brian Collins	2 Mitch Shirra	3 Graham Drury
1976	1 Peter Collins	2 Bobby Beaton	3 Kjell Gimre
1977	1 Bert Harkins	2 Jack Millen	3 Phil Kynman
1981	1 Wayne Brown	2 Bobby Beaton	3 Les Collins
1983	1 Phil Collins	2 Mitch Shirra	3 Jim McMillan
1984	1 Mitch Shirra	2 Martin Hagon	3.Alun Rossiter
1985	1 Jamie Luckhurst	2 Jim McMillan	3 Martin Dixon
1986	1 Les Collins	2 Steve Schofield	3 Martin Dixon
1987	1 Neville Tatum	2 Steve Lawson	3 Les Collins
1988	1 Steve Lawson	2 Les Collins	3 Kenny McKinna
1989	1 Todd Wiltshire	2 Kenny McKinna	3 Brett Saunders

Venues: Old Meadowbank, Edinburgh, 1965-67; Coatbridge, 1968-69, 1973-76; Hampden Park, Glasgow, 1970-72; Blantyre, 1977; Powderhall, Edinburgh, 1981-90. In 1981 the Championship was incorporated in the Carlo Biagi Testimonial and in 1983 the George Hunter Testimonial.

Scottish Junior Championship

1965	1 Bill McMillan	2 Red Monteith	3 Ross Nickisson
1967	1 Brian Collins		
1968	1 Alastair Brady		
1969	1 Kenny Omand		
1970	1 Alastair Brady		
1972	1 Allan Mackie		
1973	1 George Wells		
1975	1 Frank Hall	2 Fred Caffrey	3 Colin Caffrey
1976	1 Benny Rourke		
1977	1 Peter Waite		
1978	1 Bill Logan		
1979	1 Kenny McKinna		
1980	1 Will Mirtle	2 Ronnie Craig	3 Ian Anderson
1983	1 Dennis Gallagher	2 Kenny Brailsford	3 Tam Baggley
1987	1 George Wells	2 Ian Atkinson	3 Andy Buck
1988	1 Colin Smith	2 Tony Rizzo	3 Mike Long

Scottish Junior League Riders' Championship

1979	1 Alan Stansfield	2 Rob Grant	3 Tam Nichol
1982	1 Ronnie Craig	2 Gary Riddall	3 Niven Munro

Venues: Workington, 1979; Edinburgh, 1982.

Scottish Superbike Championship

1966	1 George Hunter	2 Bluey Scott	3 Charlie Monk
1966	1 George Hunter	2 Charlie Monk	3 Willie Templeton

Meetings run at Edinburgh and Glasgow.

Southern Riders' Championship

1969	1 Colin Pratt	2 Terry Betts	3 Malcolm Simmons
1970	1 Terry Betts	2 Garry Middleton	3 Howard Cole
1971	1 Terry Betts	2 Bengt Jansson	3 Bruce Cribb
1975	1 Tommy Jansson	2 Scott Autrey	3 John Louis
1976	1 John Louis	2 Malcolm Simmons	3 John Davis
1984	1 Jamie Luckhurst	2 Steve Naylor	3 Bob Garrad
1985	1 Jamie Luckhurst	2 Martin Goodwin	3 Neil Middleditch
1986	1 Martin Dugard	2 Kevin Smith	3 Steve Schofield
1987	1 Andy Buck	2 Andrew Silver	3 Kevin Jolly
1988	1 Andy Galvin	2 Steve Schofield	3 Gordon Kennett
1989	1 Andy Galvin	2 Steve Schofield	3 Mark Loram
1990	1 Steve Schofield	2 Chris Louis	3 Tony Langdon

Venues: King's Lynn, 1969; Wimbledon, 1970-75; Reading, 1976; Arena Essex, 1984-85; Poole, 1986-87; Hackney, 1988-90.

Stars of Tomorrow

1966	1 Hasty Humphries	2 Colin Clarke	3 Dennis Mannion
1969	1 Neville Brice	2 Nigel Rackett	3 Charlie Coleman
1971	1 Mike Lanham	2 Dave Slatford	3 Trevor Jones
1982	1 Rob Mather – *Final abandoned, Mather declared winner*		
1988	1 Shawn Venables		
1989	1 Darren Grayling	2 Michael Warren	3 Shawn Venables

Venues: King's Lynn, 1966, 1971; Canterbury, 1969; Weymouth, 1982; Hackney, 1988-89.
See also Berwick, Division Two Averages.

INDIVIDUAL MEETS

Suffolk Open Championship

1970	1 Richard May	2 Geoff Maloney	3 Eric Broadbelt
1976	1 Tom Owen	2 Steve Weatherley	3 Colin Cook
1977	1 Bob Coles	2 Kelvin Mullarkey	3 Colin Richardson

Venues: Ipswich, 1970; Mildenhall, 1976-77.

Yorkshire Open Championship

1969	1 Barry Briggs	2 Arnie Haley	3 Eric Boocock
1970	1 Jim Airey	2 Anders Michanek	3 Gary Middleton
1971	1 John Boulger	2 Jim Airey	3 Doug Wyer
1972	1 Göte Nordin	2 Eric Boocock	3 John Boulger
1973	1 Bengt Larsson	2 Bob Valentine	3 Peter Collins, Reidar Eide, Sören Sjösten
1974	1 Peter Collins	2 Sören Sjösten	3 Dave Jessup
1975	1 Peter Collins	2 Ivan Mauger	3 Ole Olsen
1976	1 Dave Jessup	2 Ole Olsen	3 Peter Collins
1977	1 John Davis	2 Dave Jessup	3 Doug Wyer
1978	1 Dave Jessup	2 Peter Collins	3 Chris Morton
1982	1 John Louis	2 Steve Baker	3 Merv Janke

Venues: Sheffield, 1969-1978; Halifax, 1982.

Yorkshire Television Trophy

1974	1 Phil Crump	2 Ole Olsen	3 Peter Collins, Scott Autrey
1976	1 Dave Jessup	2 Bobby Beaton	3 Terry Betts
1977	1 Ole Olsen	2 Martin Ashby	3 Alan Wilkinson
1978	1 Vaclav Verner	2 Michael Lee	3 Bruce Penhall
1979	1 Ivan Mauger	2 Michael Lee	3 Kelly Moran
1980	1 Ivan Mauger	2 Michael Lee	3 Dennis Sigalos
1981	1 Bruce Penhall	2 Bobby Schwartz	3 Shawn Moran
1982	1 Bruce Penhall	2 Kenny Carter	3 Doug Wyer

Venues: Hull, 1974-81; Sheffield, 1982.

▲ *DESERT KINGS...Reg Wilson, John Davis and Ian Cartwright on the rostrum after the Craven A Premier Award meet in Abu Dhabi*

■ *ONE of the most ambitious projects to extend the boundaries of world speedway came in November, 1978, when a party of 16 riders set out for the Middle East and a Rothmans sponsored two-day tournament organised by Speedway Racing Developments Limited, a company formed by then BSPA chairman Reg Fearman and his Poole clerk of the course Terry Chandler.*

■ *A second visit was made a year later, this time to three Middle East countries, but despite reported crowds of 50,000 at Kuwait City the project fizzled out quickly.*

ROTHMANS MIDDLE EAST SPECTACULAR
Kuwait City, Kuwait, Thursday-Friday, November 23-24, 1978
Peter Collins 28, Les Collins 25, John Louis 14, Chris Morton 21, Dave Jessup 18, Tom Owen 18, Barry Thomas 17, Jim McMillan 15, Bernie Leigh 14, John Davis 13, Craig Pendlebury 13, Reg Wilson 12, Ian Cartwright 12, Dave Morton 5, Richard Greer 3, Neil Middleditch 3.

CAIRO CHAMPIONSHIP
Cairo, Egypt, Wednesday, November 7, 1979
1 Chris Morton 2 Peter Collins 3 Jim McMillan 11, Dave Morton 10, Phil Collins 10, Joe Owen 9, Dave Jessup 9, Les Collins 9, Bernie Leigh 9, John Davis 6, Barry Thomas 4, Richard Greer 4, Craig Pendlebury 3, Ian Cartwright 3, Reg Wilson 2, Neil Middleditch 2).

CRAVEN A PREMIER AWARD
Kuwait City, Kuwait, Tuesday, November 13
1 Peter Collins 2 Dave Morton 3 John Davis
Abu Dhabi, United Arab Emirates, Tuesday, November 20
1 Reg Wilson 2 Ian Cartwright 3 John Davis

CRAVEN A MIDDLE EAST MASTERS
Round 1, Cairo, Egypt, Thursday, 8, 1979
Chris Morton 14, Phil Collins 13, Dave Morton 13, Bernie Leigh 11, Jim McMillan 11, Joe Owen 10, Richard Greer 9, Peter Collins 8, Dave Jessup 6, Les Collins 6, John Davis 5, Reg Wilson 5, Ian Cartwright 3, Barry Thomas 3, Craig Pendlebury 3, Neil Middleditch 1.
Round 2, Kuwait City, Kuwait, Friday,November 16, 1979
Chris Morton 14, Dave Morton 13, Dave Jessup 13, Peter Collins 12, Phil Collins 10, Bernie Leigh 9, Les Collins 9, John Davis 9, Joe Owen 7, Jim McMillan 7, Craig Pendlebury 4, Richard Greer 4, Reg Wilson 4, Neil Middleditch 2, Barry Thomas 2, Ian Cartwright 1.
Round 3, Abu Dhabi, United Arab Emirates, Thursday, November 22, 1979
Chris Morton 14, Phil Collins 13, Dave Morton 13, Bernie Leigh 11, Jim McMillan 11, Joe Owen 10,Richard Greer 9, Peter Collins 8, Dave Jessup 6, Les Collins 6, John Davis 5, Reg Wilson 5, Craig Pendlebury 3, Barry Thomas 3, Ian Cartwright 2, Neil Middleditch 1.

1968 BRITISH LEAGUE DIVISION TWO

	P	W	D	L	PtsF	PtsA	W	D	L	PtsF	PtsA	Pts
1 BELLE VUE	**18**	**9**	**0**	**0**	**464**	**236**	**5**	**0**	**4**	**348**	**346**	**28**
2 Nelson	18	9	0	0	426	271	2	0	7	309	391	22
3 Middlesbrough	18	8	0	1	399	299	2	1	6	312	388	21
4 Plymouth	18	9	0	0	421	280	1	0	8	283	413	20
5 Rayleigh	18	8	0	1	399	294	1	1	7	301	397	19
6 Crayford	18	8	0	1	435	260	0	1	8	278	420	17
7 Canterbury	18	7	1	1	377	322	1	0	8	268	432	17
8 Reading	18	6	1	2	388	313	0	1	8	287	412	14
9 Weymouth	18	5	2	2	379	319	0	0	9	275	421	12
10 Berwick	18	5	0	4	367	328	0	0	9	261	435	10

BELLE VUE, who competed in the first-ever British League Division Two match were able to call themselves champions as early as the evening of Wednesday, August 21, when they defeated nearest challengers Nelson 42-36.

It meant that even if Nelson and Plymouth won their remaining League matches they could only collect a maximum of 24 match points – a tally Belle Vue had already reached with a superior race points difference.

Mathematically, though, the title was clinched beyond any doubt whatever the following Wednesday (August 28) when the Colts beat Weymouth 63-15 (the most convincing victory of the season) and they were presented with the trophy by Johnnie Hoskins.

1968 Division Two Riders' Championship Final

Friday, September 27, Hackney:
1 Graham Plant 13 2 Ken Eyre 12 3 Graeme Smith 11 4 Mick Handley 11 5 Murray Burt 11 6 Allan Brown 10 7 Mike Cake 10 8 Tony Lomas 7 9 John Poyser 6 10 Barry Crowson 5, 11 Martyn Piddock 5, 12 Phil Woodcock 5, 13 Dave Schofield 5, 14 Chris Bailey 3, 15 Roy Williams 2, 16 Taffy Owen 1. *Reserves: Barry Duke 2, Mike Vernam 2.*

1968 KNOCK OUT CUP

Round 1
Reading 52 Rayleigh 44
Round 2
CANTERBURY 56 Crayford 37
Middlesbrough 53 Nelson 41
Berwick 45 Belle Vue 51
Reading 52 Plymouth 44
Semi Finals
CANTERBURY 64 Middlesbrough 31
Reading 56 Belle Vue 40
FINAL
First leg, October 12:
CANTERBURY 60 (Peter Murray 14, Barry Crowson 14, Martyn Piddock 13, John Hibben 10, Graham Miles 7, Ken Vale 2, Pat Flanagan 0) *Reading 36* (Vic White 11, John Poyser 8, Ian Champion 6, Stuart Wallace 4, Phil Pratt 3, Ted Spittles 2, Dene Davies 2).

Second leg, October 14:
Reading 44 (Poyser 17, White 11, Spittles 9, Wallace 3, Davies 2, Champion 1, Pratt 1)
CANTERBURY 52 (Murray 14, Crowson 12, Hibben 8, Miles 6, Vale 6, Piddock 5, Dave Grimley 1).

❑ CANTERBURY win 112-80 on aggregate.

■ The first-ever Division Two Cup match was not, as might have been expected, the First Round tie between Reading and Rayleigh (which took place on Monday, August 26).

■ It was Canterbury's Second Round match against their Kent rivals Crayford which was held at Kingsmead on Saturday, August 10. So Canterbury took part in both the first League and first Cup match in Division Two.

ROOKIE OF THE YEAR...teenager Martyn Piddock, in his first speedway season, qualified for the Division Two Riders' Championship Final and helped Canterbury win the first-ever Knock Out Cup

1968 ALL THE RESULTS

	BELLE VUE	BERWICK	CANTERBURY	CRAYFORD	MIDDLESBRO	NELSON	PLYMOUTH	RAYLEIGH	READING	WEYMOUTH
BELLE VUE		54-24	55-23	57-21	46-31	42-36	48-30	46-31	53-25	63-15
BERWICK	28-49		52-26	44-33	38-40	37-41	37-41	47-31	41-34	43-33
CANTERBURY	38-39	40-37		40-37	42-36	46-32	43-35	39-39	45-33	44-34
CRAYFORD	43-33	57-21	57-21		37-41	50-27	51-27	49-28	50-28	41-34
MIDDLESBROUGH	40-37	43-34	51-27	48-30		35-42	47-31	40-37	45-33	50-28
NELSON	46-32	54-23	40-37	46-32	43-35		55-21	46-31	53-25	43-35
PLYMOUTH	43-35	43-35	47-31	54-24	53-25	50-28		48-30	42-36	41-36
RAYLEIGH	37-40	51-26	45-33	46-30	41-36	48-30	40-34		44-34	47-31
READING	37-40	45-33	37-41	46-32	39-39	41-37	50-28	44--34		49-29
WEYMOUTH	34-43	48-28	48-29	39-39	49-29	42-36	42-36	38-40	39-39	

1969 BRITISH LEAGUE DIVISION TWO

	P	W	D	L	PtsF	PtsA	W	D	L	PtsF	PtsA	Pts
1 BELLE VUE	**30**	**14**	**0**	**1**	**785**	**380**	**9**	**1**	**5**	**609**	**558**	**47**
2 Reading	30	13	1	1	678	481	6	0	9	543	622	39
3 Romford	30	11	0	4	649	517	8	1	6	573	592	39
4 Crayford	30	15	0	0	730	434	4	0	11	544.5	621.5	38
5 Rayleigh	30	12	1	2	671	495	4	1	10	540	625	34
6 Canterbury	30	13	2	0	695	471	2	0	13	529	634	32
7 Crewe	30	14	0	1	754	377	1	0	14	503	662	30
8 Eastbourne	30	13	0	2	651.5	505.5	1	2	12	483	680	30
9 Middlesbrough	30	10	1	4	661	509	4	0	11	493	674	29
10 Long Eaton	30	11	0	4	622	539	3	1	11	475.5	651.5	29
11 Ipswich	30	12	0	3	625	539	1	1	13	491	672	27
12 Doncaster	30	9	0	6	602	558	3	0	12	463	700	24
13 Nelson	30	10	2	3	604.5	560.5	1	0	14	459	704	24
14 Berwick	30	10	0	5	630.5	528.5	1	1	13	484.5	676.5	23
15 Plymouth	30	9	0	6	629	534	0	0	15	371	783	18
16 King's Lynn	30	6	1	8	576	582	2	0	13	449	708	17

NEWCOMERS Romford became the first team to win an official match at Belle Vue when they took both League points with a 40-38 victory on Wednesday, September 3. It ended a run of 24 successive Hyde Road wins for the Colts.

KING'S LYNN claimed an unwanted record in their debut season in Division Two as the first club to finish bottom in both British League Divisions!

1969 Division Two Riders' Championship Final

Friday, September 26, Hackney:
1 Geoff Ambrose 14, 2 Mick Bell 13, 3 Ross Gilbertson 13, 4 Maurie Robinson 11, 5 Peter Murray 6 Reg Trott 9, 7 Geoff Curtis 6, 8 Peter Wrathall 5, 9 Colin Sanders 5, 10 Ted Spittles 4, 12 Ian Turner 3, 11 Dave Schofield 4, 13 Terry Lee 2, 14 Eric Broadbelt 0, Dingle Brown 0, George Devonport 0. *Reserves: Martyn Piddock 8, Phil Woodcock 7, Paul O'Neal 6.*

1969 KNOCK OUT CUP

Round 1
Eastbourne 37 Rayleigh 40
Crewe 49 Doncaster 29
Ipswich 55 Plymouth 23
Long Eaton 48 Berwick 29
Middlesbrough 49 Nelson 29
Romford 38 Reading 38
Canterbury 51 Crayford 26

Round 1 Replay
Reading 44 Romford 34

Round 2
Crewe 44 Canterbury 33
BELLE VUE 58 Ipswich 20
Long Eaton 42 Reading 35
Rayleigh 43 Middlesbrough 34

Semi Finals
BELLE VUE 55 Rayleigh 23
Crewe 58 Long Eaton 20

FINAL
First leg, September 22:
Crewe 42 (Geoff Curtis 10, Colin Tucker 9, Barry Meeks 8, Ian Bottomley 8, Paul O'Neal 6, Peter Saunders 1, Dave Parry 0) BELLE VUE 36 (Ken Moss 10, Chris Bailey 10, Steve Waplington 5, Taffy Owen 4, Mike Hiftle 4, Eric Broadbelt 3).

Second leg, September 24:
BELLE VUE 55 (Broadbelt 14, Bailey 11, Hiftle 11, Moss 8, Waplington 6, Owen 5) *Crewe 23* (O'Neal 9, Curtis 9, Parry 2, Saunders 1, Tucker 1, Bottomley 1, Meeks 0).

❑ BELLE VUE win 91-65 on aggregate.

■ *Belle Vue became the first Division Two team to complete the Cup and League double.*

■ *Reading and Romford were involved in the first Knock Out Cup draw.*

1969 ALL THE RESULTS

	BELLE VUE	BERWICK	CANTERBURY	CRAYFORD	CREWE	DONCASTER	EASTBOURNE	IPSWICH	KING'S LYNN	LONG EATON	MIDDLESBRO	NELSON	PLYMOUTH	RAYLEIGH	READING	ROMFORD
BELLE VUE		53-24	52-26	45-33	57-21	48-30	60-18	57-21	52-25	61-17	58-20	49-29	57-20	45-32	53-24	38-40
BERWICK	34-44		50-28	22-54	43-35	45-32	41-36	40-38	53-25	33.5 41.5	42-36	55-22	55-22	37-41	36-41	44-33
CANTERBURY	41-36	51-27		46-32	45-33	49-29	39-39	39-39	55-22	52-26	46-32	51-27	52-26	44-33	43-35	42-35
CRAYFORD	44-34	42-35	39-38		44-34	53-24	51-26	55-22	54-24	52-26	53-25	41-37	56-21	51-27	50-28	45-33
CREWE	34-44	51-26	48-30	53-24		56-22	57-21	52-26	56-21	32-10§	42-36	54-24	61-17	43-35	62-16	53-25
DONCASTER	36-41	39-38	45-32	42-36	47-31		43-35	41-36	40-36	38-40	35-42	43-32	51-27	37-41	36-42	29-49
EASTBOURNE	44-34	52-24	35-40	49.5 28.5	43-34	47-30		40-36	39-37	47-31	45-33	41-37	47-30	41-36	45-33	36-42
IPSWICH	42-36	40-38	40-37	41-37	42-36	50-28	39-38		38-39	41-36	36-41	41-37	57-21	41-37	41-36	36-42
KING'S LYNN	33-45	48-29	41-37	38-40	29-48	34-43	38-38	41-35		43-34	36-42	37-40	46-31	43-34	31-46	38-40
LONG EATON	34-44	43-35	40-38	43-35	47-31	47-30	48-30	45-33	50-26		36-42	48-29	38-35†	43-35	28-50	32-46
MIDDLESBROUGH	37-41	39-39	55-23	42-36	48-30	52-26	45-33	42-36	45-33	38-40		49-29	54-24	36-42	37-41	42-36
NELSON	24-54	39.5 37.5	24-54±	36-42	41-37	45-33	45-33	43-35	50-27	38-38	52-25		43-35	39-39	41-37	44-34
PLYMOUTH	36-42	34-44	40-38	40-38	49-28	37-40	38-40	42-35	35-42	51-27	45-33	55-23		49-29	42-36	36-39
RAYLEIGH	36-42	55-23	39-38	36-41	47-31	46-31	42-36	52-26	52-25	43-35	42-36	43-35	57-21		42-36	39-39
READING	39-39	43-35	43-35	47-31	40-36	53-25	49-27	45-33	46-32	41-37	49-29	54-23	51-21	40-38		38-40
ROMFORD	44-33	47-30	43-35	41-37	40-38	38-40	45-33	38-40	43-35	41-37	57-21	43-35	58-20	36-41	35-42	

†Amended result. Was 47-29 on track.

±Raced at Canterbury because of lack of dates

§Abandoned after seven races because of fog, result to stand.

1970 BRITISH LEAGUE DIVISION TWO

	P	W	D	L	PtsF	PtsA	W	D	L	PtsF	PtsA	Pts
1 CANTERBURY	**32**	**16**	**0**	**0**	**774**	**472**	**7**	**1**	**8**	**610**	**636**	**47**
2 Eastbourne	32	16	0	0	788	458	6	1	9	576.5	667.5	45
3 Rochdale	32	16	0	0	842	395	5	2	9	618	625	44
4 Bradford	32	16	0	0	826	418	2	1	13	529	716	37
5 Teesside	32	15	0	1	752	492	3	0	13	552	694	36
6 Ipswich	32	13	2	1	717	529	4	0	12	537	707	36
7 Crewe	32	16	0	0	800	445	1	1	14	505	741	35
8 Romford	32	12	0	4	702.5	541.5	5	1	10	551	690	35
9 Reading	32	14	0	2	723	521	3	0	13	555.5	690.5	34
10 Peterborough	32	13	1	2	681	567	1	1	14	510	734	30
11 Workington	32	12	0	4	690	555	1	1	14	555	681	27
12 Rayleigh	32	12	1	3	666	577	1	0	15	489.5	752.5	27
13 Boston	32	10	1	5	658.5	585.5	2	1	13	485.5	756.5	26
14 Crayford	32	11	1	4	682	561	0	0	16	471	777	23
15 Doncaster	32	8	1	7	621.5	616.5	3	0	13	502	745	23
16 Berwick	32	10	0	6	661	584	0	0	16	428	816	20
17 Long Eaton	32	8	3	5	613.5	631.5	0	0	16	474	769	19

KING'S LYNN and Nelson moved home tracks midway through the season – the Starlets switched to nearby Boston while the Admirals moved out of Seed Hill and re-launched speedway at Odsal Stadium, Bradford. They are listed as Boston and Bradford in the table above.

1970 Division Two Riders' Championship Final

Friday, September 25, Hackney:
1 Dave Jessup 14, 2 Barry Crowson 12, 3 Gary Peterson 12, 4 Eric Broadbelt 11, 5 Tom Leadbitter 10, 6 John Harrhy 9, 7 Bob Valentine 9, 8 Paul O'Neal 8, 9 Ross Gilbertson 7, 10 Richard May 7, 11 Arthur Price 5, 12 Andy Ross 5, 13 Geoff Maloney 4, 14 Maurie Robinson 3, 15 Tony Childs 3, 16 Gordon McGregor 1. *Reserves: Ken Vale 0, Alan Knapkin, did not ride.*

1970 KNOCK OUT CUP

Round 1
Middlesbrough 54 King's Lynn 24
Crewe 49 Nelson 29
Romford 48 Reading 30
Rayleigh 48 Peterborough 30
Rochdale 43 Long Eaton 35
Eastbourne 34 Canterbury 44
***Berwick 53* Doncaster 25**
IPSWICH 51 Crayford 27

Round 2
***Berwick 40* Middlesbrough 36**
Rochdale 50 Romford 28
Canterbury 52 Crewe 26
IPSWICH 46 Rayleigh 31

Semi Finals
IPSWICH 42 Rochdale 36
***Berwick 44* Canterbury 34**

FINAL

First leg, September 24:
IPSWICH 47 (John Louis 12, John Harrhy 11, Peter Bailey 9, Ron Bagley 6, Stan Pepper 5, Ted Spittles 4, Tony Davey 0) *Berwick 31* (Doug Wyer 11, Maurie Robinson 6, Peter Kelly 6, Lex Milloy 4, Alistair Brady 2, Roy Williams 1, Kenny Omand 1).

Second leg, September 26:
***Berwick 43* (Wyer 10, Robinson 9, Brady 7, Kelly 5, Milloy 5, Williams 5, Omand 2) IPSWICH 35 (Louis 15, Bailey 12, Pepper 4, Bagley 2, Spittles 2, Davey 0).**

❑ **IPSWICH win 82-74 on aggregate.**

1970 ALL THE RESULTS

	BERWICK	CANTERBURY	CRAYFORD	CREWE	DONCASTER	EASTBOURNE	IPSWICH	KING'S LYNN/ BOSTON	LONG EATON	NELSON/ BRADFORD	PETERBOROUGH	RAYLEIGH	READING	ROCHDALE	ROMFORD	TEESSIDE	WORKINGTON
BERWICK		38-40	52-26	43-35	36-42	42-34	41-37	46-32	47-31	45-33	47-31	49-29	38-40	26-51	34-44	42-36	35-43
CANTERBURY	57-21		46-32	50-28	49-29	42-36	51-27	51-26	55-22	53-25	44-34	48-30	47-31	45-33	43-35	42-36	51-27
CRAYFORD	51-26	28-50		47-31	45-33	37-41	42-36	43-35	44-34	52-25	40-38	54-24	46-32	39-39	33-42	38-40	43-35
CREWE	56-22	47-31	54-24		49-29	53-25	52-26	53-25	52-26	43-35	58-20	49-27	47-31	47-31	53-24	46-32	41-37
DONCASTER	48-30	35-43	40-38	42-35		44-34	38-40	36-40	40-37	30-47	39-39	36.5 39.5	43-35	36-42	36-42	40-38	38-37
EASTBOURNE	55-23	45-33	51-27	58-20	50-28		53-25	44-34	56-22	52-26	44-33	56-22	41-37	42-35	50-28	47-31	44-34
IPSWICH	57-21	34-44	50-28	48-30	47-31	51-27		44-34	43-35	39-39	47-30	42-36	44-34	39-39	41-36	40-38	51-27
KING'S LYNN/ BOSTON	*43-34*	*40-37*	51-27	47-31	*35-43*	*38-40*	*40-38*		47-30	*49-29*	37-41	*43-35*	44.5 32.5	*26-52*	42-36	*37-41*	*39-39*
LONG EATON	40-38	31-47	47-31	43-35	36-42	38.5 38.5	29-49	39-39		40-38	41-37	40-38	34-44	44-33	39-39	33-45	39-38
NELSON/BRADFORD	52-26	50-28	*55-23*	55-23	58-19	44-34	52-25	59-19	*55-22*		*56-22*	46-32	*49-29*	*46-31*	50-28	59-19	40-38
PETERBOROUGH	46-32	39-39	45-33	42-36	50-28	33-45	43-35	40-38	42-36	47-31		51-27	42-36	30-48	48-30	41-37	42-36
RAYLEIGH	45-32	37-40	47-31	39-39	41-37	31-47	51-27	49-29	40-38	40-38	42-35		45-33	43-35	34-43	40-37	42-36
READING	59-19	37-41	42-36	49-29	47-31	45-33	36-41	55-23	45-33	44-34	43-34	50-27		43-35	40-38	44-34	44-33
ROCHDALE	58-20	51-27	63-15	41-37	52-26	53-25	54-23	61-15	57-21	51-27	45-33	57-20	53-24		50-28	49-29	47-25
ROMFORD	44-33	41-37	46-32	48-30	51-27	38-40	36-41	46.5 31.5	49-29	36-41	54-24	41-37	35-43	47-30		50-28	40-38
TEESSIDE	53-25	42-36	46-32	38-39	44-34	45-32	42-36	53-25	53-25	49-29	49-29	46-32	42-36	43-35	62-15		45-32
WORKINGTON	52-26	41-37	42-36	51-27	55-23	33-45	47-31	37-40	44-33	46-32	48-30	44-34	40-38	29-49	35-43	46-31	

◆ Results in italics indicate Boston racing at King's Lynn and Bradford racing at Nelson.

1971 BRITISH LEAGUE DIVISION TWO

	P	W	D	L	PtsF	PtsA	W	D	L	PtsF	PtsA	Pts
1 EASTBOURNE	**32**	**15**	**0**	**1**	**800**	**438**	**7**	**3**	**6**	**594**	**649**	**47**
2 Bradford	32	16	0	0	778	468	5	1	10	592	651	43
3 Ipswich	32	14	1	1	746	495	6	2	8	599	646	43
4 Boston	32	15	0	1	744	503	3	3	10	568	670	39
5 Rayleigh	32	12	2	2	688	555	6	0	10	589	654	38
6 Hull	32	12	2	2	703	542	4	0	12	589	657	34
7 Crewe	32	15	1	0	826	418	1	0	15	475	766	33
8 Berwick	32	16	0	0	784.5	461.5	0	0	16	500	747	32
9 Rochdale	32	14	0	2	700	544	2	0	14	477	767	32
10 Long Eaton	32	13	2	1	690	555	0	1	15	505	735	29
11 Birmingham	32	13	1	2	704	541	0	2	14	477	771	29
12 Romford	32	12	0	4	700	542	1	0	15	522.5	721.5	26
13 Teesside	32	12	0	4	707.5	536.5	1	0	15	483.5	762.5	26
14 Canterbury	32	12	2	2	702	543	0	0	16	458	789	26
15 Workington	32	11	0	5	701	547	1	1	14	533	703	25
16 Peterborough	32	11	1	4	691	553	0	0	16	482	764	23
17 Sunderland	32	9	1	6	635	600	0	0	16	398	847	19

BERWICK created a slice of history when they became the first Division Two team to go through the entire season without losing a home match – and not gaining a single point on their travels. They lost all 16 away matches but took maximum points from their home programme to finish eighth in the table.

1971 Division Two Riders' Championship Final

Saturday, October 2, Hackney:
1 John Louis 14, 2 Malcolm Shakespeare 13, 3 Hugh Saunders 12, 4 Peter Collins 11, 5 Phil Crump 11, 6 Arthur Price 10, 7 George Major 8, 8 Russ Dent 6, 9 Reg Wilson 6, 10 Doug Wyer 5, 11 Ross Gilbertson 5, 12 Dave Baugh 5, 13 Malcolm Mackay 4, 14 Bruce Forrester 3, 15 Kevin Holden 2, 16 Malcolm Ballard 1. *Reserves: Roger Mills 2, Richard Greer 0.*

1971 KNOCK OUT CUP

Round 1
Long Eaton 46 39 85 Birmingham 31 39 70
Rochdale 47 39 86 Hull 31 38 69

Round 2
Crewe 54 28 82 Berwick 24 50 74
Peterborough 33 21 53 IPSWICH 45 57 102
Long Eaton 43 33 76 Rochdale 35 45 80
Sunderland 37 31 68 Workington 41 46 87
Boston 49 42 91 Romford 28 36 64
Eastbourne 47 39 86 Canterbury 31 39 70
Bradford 47 40 87 Middlesbrough 31 38 69
Rayleigh bye after Crayford withdrew from the League.

Round 3
Crewe 47 32 79 Bradford 31 46 77
Rayleigh 37 35 72 IPSWICH 41 43 84
Boston 40 37 77 Rochdale 38 41 79
Workington 51 31 82 Eastbourne 27 45 72

Semi Finals
Workington 38 28 66 IPSWICH 40 50 90
Crewe 49 Rochdale 29†
†Rochdale forfeited second leg

FINAL
First leg, October 11:
Crewe 41 (Phil Crump 10, John Jackson 6, Jack Millen 6, Dai Evans 6, Garry Moore 5, Barry Meeks 4, Dave Parry 4) IPSWICH 37 (John Louis 14, Tony Davey 11, Peter Prinsloo 9, Peter Bailey 2, Clive Noy 1, Ted Howgego 0, Ray Watkins 0).

Second leg, October 14:
IPSWICH 55 (Davey 12, Louis 12, Prinsloo 9, Bailey 8, Noy 7, Howgego 5, Watkins 2) *Crewe 23* (Evans 7, Jackson 7, Crump 6, Meeks 2, Moore 1, Millen 0, Parry 0).

❑ IPSWICH win 92-64 on aggregate.

Sponsors: Speedway Express.

1971 ALL THE RESULTS

	BERWICK	BIRMINGHAM	BOSTON	NELSON/ BRADFORD	CANTERBURY	CREWE	EASTBOURNE	HULL	IPSWICH	LONG EATON	PETERBOROUGH	RAYLEIGH	ROCHDALE	ROMFORD	SUNDERLAND	TEESSIDE	WORKINGTON
BERWICK		58-20	41-36	42-36	46-32	56-21	49-29	45-33	46-32	45-33	49-29	49-29	60-18	56-22	51-27	45.5 32.5	46-32
BIRMINGHAM	42-36		43-35	42-35	44-34	50-28	39-39	41-37	47-30	44-34	52-26	36-42	36-42	43-35	52-26	51-27	42-35
BOSTON	52-26	50-28		44-33	47-31	53-25	45-33	42-36	37-41	43-35	45-33	41-37	44-34	45-33	56-22	55-23	45-33
BRADFORD	45-33	54-24	54-24		57-21	54-24	52-26	41-37	47-31	53-25	41-37	43-35	46-32	46-32	54-23	48-30	43-34
CANTERBURY	45-33	54-24	39-39	42-36		48-30	36-41	35-42	39-39	45-33	47-31	40-38	46-32	41-37	56-22	47-30	42-36
CREWE	48-30	62-16	50-28	43-35	55-23		54-24	46-32	46-32	55-19	56-22	49-29	55-23	54-24	61-17	53-25	39-39
EASTBOURNE	49-29	57-21	49-28	42-33	58-20	54-23		46-32	46-31	54-23	53-25	36-40	44-34	50-28	59-19	58-20	45-32
HULL	42-36	39-39	35-43	39-39	45-33	47-31	41-37		34-44	46-32	43-35	45-33	51-27	47-30	51-27	55-23	43-33
IPSWICH	55-22	42-36	43-34	37-41	48-29	45-32	39-39	42-35		49-29	49-29	40-38	58-19	45-33	55-22	44-34	55-23
LONG EATON	45-33	39-39	39-39	40-38	47-31	50-27	36-41	42-36	41-37		45-33	40-38	48-29	40-38	53-25	40-38	45-33
PETERBOROUGH	44-34	50-28	39-39	37-41	54-24	47-30	38-39	35-43	29-48	41-37		43-35	48-30	42-36	57-21	44-33	43-35
RAYLEIGH	44-34	42-36	36-42	43-35	43-35	38-39	39-39	45-33	39-39	44-34	41-37		53-25	45-30	44-34	49-29	43-34
ROCHDALE	45-33†	43-35	40-38	52-26	44-34	41-37	41-37	40-38	41-37	50-28	56-22	37-40		41-37†	50-28	38-40	41-34
ROMFORD	43-35	46-32	44-34	33-45	49-29	48-30	37-40	40-38	36-42	45-33	41-36	37-40	50-28		51-27	51-27	49-26
SUNDERLAND	46-32	40-38	32-39	42-36	42-36	40-38	31-46	38-40	43-35	38-38	49-28	36-41	37-40	42-36		41-37	38-40
TEESSIDE	54-24	45-33	44-34	37-41	58-20	42-35	35-43	43-35	38-40	43-34	48-30	36-42	44-33	47.5 30.5	49-28		44-34
WORKINGTON	48-30	50-28	42-36	36-42	52-26	53-25	37-41	36-42	37-41	40-38	49-29	46-32	47-31	37-41	48-30	43-35	

† Matches raced at Belle Vue.

1972 BRITISH LEAGUE DIVISION TWO

	P	W	D	L	PtsF	PtsA	W	D	L	PtsF	PtsA	Pts
1 CREWE	**32**	**15**	**0**	**1**	**834**	**413**	**7**	**1**	**8**	**610**	**628**	**45**
2 Boston	32	16	0	0	785	461	5	1	10	580	666	43
3 Peterborough	32	14	0	2	738	508	7	0	9	574	671	42
4 Rayleigh	32	15	1	0	771	474	2	3	11	562	686	38
5 Eastbourne	32	15	1	0	771	469	3	1	12	552.5	691.5	38
6 Birmingham	32	15	1	0	782	462	3	0	13	547	695	37
7 Workington	32	15	0	1	777	468	3	0	13	531	715	36
8 Hull	32	12	0	4	673	574	4	0	12	550	695	32
9 Barrow	32	13	0	3	712	532	2	1	13	548	698	31
10 Teesside	32	14	1	1	728	516	0	2	14	490	754	31
11 Bradford	32	13	0	3	710	530	2	0	14	517	729	30
12 Sunderland	32	13	1	2	702	541	0	1	15	478	765	28
13 Canterbury	32	11	0	5	717	526	2	1	13	512	734	27
14 Berwick	32	11	3	2	671	575	1	0	15	485	755	27
15 Ellesmere Port	32	11	0	5	667	575	1	0	15	489	754	24
16 Long Eaton	32	10	2	4	655	589	1	0	15	449	796	24
17 Scunthorpe	32	5	1	10	580.5	663.5	0	0	16	402	841	11

CREWE completed a remarkable Second Division treble. They won the League, the Knock Out Cup and provided the winner of the Riders' Championship Final.

1972 Division Two Riders' Championship Final

Saturday, October 14, Wimbledon:
1 Phil Crump 12, 2 Arthur Price 12, 3 Bob Coles 11, 4 Ross Gilbertson 11, 5 Roger Mills 10, 6 Malcolm Ballard 9, 7 Bob Young 9, 8 George Major 8, 9 Doug Templeton 8, 10 Dave Baugh 7, 11 Paul Tyrer 5, 12 Richard Greer 4, 13 Taffy Owen 4, 14 Dave Durham 4, 15 Russ Dent 3, 16 Tony Childs 2. *Reserves: John Jackson 1, Ray Watkins 0.*

1972 KNOCK OUT CUP

Round 1
CREWE 49 45 94 Ellesmere Port 29 33 62
Round 2
Boston 46 35 81 Rayleigh 32 43 75
Eastbourne 50 40 90 Long Eaton 28 38 66
Sunderland 55 31 86 Workington 23 46 69
Scunthorpe 19 19 38 CREWE 59 59 118
Birmingham 43 37 80 Canterbury 35 41 76
Hull 46 34 80 Middlesbrough 32 44 76
Peterborough 52 42 94 Barrow 26 36 62
Bradford 52 38 90 Berwick 26 39 65
Round 3
Boston 40 33 73 Eastbourne 38 45 83
Birmingham 48 37 85 Middlesbrough 30 41 71
CREWE 53 36 89 Sunderland 25 42 67
Bradford 45 14 59 *Peterborough 33 36 69*
Semi Finals
Eastbourne 44 31 75 CREWE 34 47 81
Peterborough 43 36 79 Birmingham 35 42 77
FINAL
First leg, September 4:
CREWE 51 (John Jackson 12, Garry Flood 10, Phil Crump 9, Dave Parry 7, Dai Evans 6, Garry Moore 4, Peter Nicholas 3) *Peterborough 27* (Roy Carter 11, Brian Clark 6, John Davis 4, John Amies 3, David Ashby 1, Ted Howgego 1, Frank Smith 1).
Second leg, September 10:
Peterborough 40 (Richard Greer 11, Carter 10, Clark 6, Davis 5, Howgego 4, Ashby 3, Amies 1) CREWE 38 (Crump 12, Jackson 10, Flood 8, Moore 6, Evans 2, Nicholas 0, Parry 0).

❑ CREWE win 89-67 on aggregate.

Sponsors: Speedway Express.

1972 ALL THE RESULTS

	BARROW/ WEST HAM	BERWICK	BIRMINGHAM	BOSTON	BRADFORD	CANTERBURY	CREWE	EASTBOURNE	ELLESMERE PORT	HULL	LONG EATON	PETERBOROUGH	RAYLEIGH	SCUNTHORPE	SUNDERLAND	TEESSIDE	WORKINGTON
BARROW/ WEST HAM		*42-36*	43-35	43-35	48-29	42-36	44-33	*45-32*	*55-23*	*38-40*	53-25	*37-41*	43-35	43-34	*45-33*	51-27	36-42
BERWICK	46-32		31-46	45-33	49-29	39-39	39-39	40-37	42-36	40-38	55-23	37-41	39-39	40-38	46-32	46-32	41-37
BIRMINGHAM	42-36	48-29		39-39	51-27	48-30	43-35	48-30	52-26	44-34	62-15	57-21	43-35	57-20	54-24	45-32	49-29
BOSTON	55-23	54-24	46-32		53-25	55-23	47-31	43-35	44-33	45-33	46-32	51-27	42-36	51-26	50-28	55-23	48-30
BRADFORD	42-36	46-31	36-41	43-35		52-26	34-40	38-40	44-34	44-34	48-30	42-35	42-36	56-22	58-20	43-34	42-36
CANTERBURY	48-30	51-26	34-44	46-32	44-34		36-40	40-38	44-34	35-43	50-27	37-41	36-42	63-15	45-32	49-29	59-19
CREWE	51-27	45-33	61-17	54-24	49-29	58-19		59-19	44-34	51-27	56-22	37-41	58-20	61-17	50-28	51-27	49-29
EASTBOURNE	46-32	51-26	40-36	47-31	58-20	46-32	41-37		56-21	53-24	42-36	48-30	39-39	55-22	55-23	43-34	51-26
ELLESMERE PORT	41-37	39-36†	46-32	31-46	45-33	38-40	38-40	36-42		38-40	45-32	42-36	40-38	54-24	46-31	47-31	41-37
HULL	48-30	50-28	43-35	29-49	36-42	41-37	41-36	40-38	44-34		50-28	35-43	44-34	48-30	40-38	46-32	38-40
LONG EATON	34-43	44-33	39-38	38-40	41-37	43-35	31-47	43-35	44-34	45-33		35-43	39-39	45-33	51-26	39-39	44-34
PETERBOROUGH	43-35	43-35	49-29	37-41	46-32	44-34	45-33	52-25	52-26	51-27	48-30		37-41	49-29	46-31	47-31	49-29
RAYLEIGH	50-28	57-21	51-27	49-28	46-32	47-30	40-38	39-39	51-27	41-36	52-26	45-33		59-19	40-38	53-25	51-27
SCUNTHORPE	32-46	35-43	43-35	28-50	35-43	34-44	30-48	39.5 37.5	31-46	32-46	36-42	39-38	42-36		39-39	49-28	36-42
SUNDERLAND	42-35	42-36	41-36	43-35	44-34	44-34	34-43	36-42	49-28	47-30	51-27	48-30	43-35	57-21		39-39	42-36
TEESSIDE	39-39	49-29	42-36	44-34	40-38	45-33	37-40	46-32	55-22	47-31	51-27	47-31	48-30	52-26	47-30		39-38
WORKINGTON	43-35	55-23	50-28	50-28	44-33	58-20	48-30	47-31	47-31	44-34	51-27	34-43	51-27	51-26	53-25	51-27	

◆ Barrow fixtures in italics were when they were at West Ham.

†Amended result. On track Ellesmere Port 44 Berwick 34. Cyril Francis ruled ineligible to ride for Ellesmere Port. Subsequently amended to 39-36 when it was found Alastair Brady was ineligible to ride for Berwick

1973 BRITISH LEAGUE DIVISION TWO

	P	W	D	L	PtsF	PtsA	W	D	L	PtsF	PtsA	Pts
1 BOSTON	**33**	**17**	**0**	**0**	**853**	**471**	**12**	**0**	**4**	**653**	**590**	**58**
2 Workington	34	16	1	0	841	481	5	1	11	634	690	44
3 Eastbourne	34	17	0	0	791	532	2	2	13	558	762	40
4 Peterborough	34	16	0	1	813	509	3	1	13	592	731	39
5 Birmingham	34	16	0	1	867	456	3	0	14	585	734	38
6 Teesside	34	16	0	1	827	499	3	0	14	562	763	38
7 Bradford	34	16	0	1	805	519	2	0	15	553	770	36
8 Crewe	34	17	0	0	785.5	538.5	0	1	16	503	820	35
9 Long Eaton	33	14	0	2	743	499	2	1	14	493	831	33
10 Barrow	34	15	0	2	822	499	0	2	15	553	769	32
11 Sunderland	34	15	1	1	777	548	0	1	16	499	824	32
12 Hull	34	10	3	4	707	613	3	2	12	550	775	31
13 Chesterton	34	11	1	5	711	611	3	0	14	540	784	29
14 Ellesmere Port	34	11	0	6	737	586	3	0	14	543	781	28
15 Canterbury	34	11	1	5	718	603	2	1	14	526	797	28
16 Scunthorpe	34	12	1	4	727	598	0	0	17	485	837	25
17 Berwick	34	11	1	5	713	609	0	0	17	435	890	23
18 Rayleigh	34	9	3	5	733.5	592.5	0	0	17	500	823	21

FOR THE second successive season one team dominated the Second Division with Boston winning all three major trophies – as Crewe had done in 1972.

1973 Division Two Riders' Championship Final

Saturday, October 6, Wimbledon:
1 Arthur Price 12, 2 Bobby McNeil 12, 3 Lou Sansom 12, 4 Dave Baugh 11, 5 Bruce Forrester 11, 6 Mike Broadbank 10, 7 Richard Greer 10, 8 Graham Drury 9, 9 Arthur Browning 7, 10 Geoff Bouchard 5, 11 Barney Kennett 5, 12 Ken McKinlay 4, 13 Dave Morton 3, 14 Jim Wells 3, 15 Dave Mills 1, Tom Owen 1. *Reserves: Willie Templeton 3, Bob Young 1.*

1973 KNOCK OUT CUP

Round 1

Eastbourne 37 34 71 Canterbury 41 44 85

Round 2

Hull 43 32 75 Rayleigh 34 46 80
Middlesbrough 48 40 88 Sunderland 30 38 68
BOSTON 58 34 92 Crewe 20 44 64
Scunthorpe 38 32 70 Birmingham 40 46 86
Barrow 45 22 67 Peterborough 32 56 88
Long Eaton 48 36 84 Canterbury 30 42 72
Berwick 42 33 75 *Workington 36 45 81*
Ellesmere Port 42 29 71 Bradford 35 48 83

Round 3

BOSTON 50 41 91 Peterborough 28 37 65
Birmingham 47 30 77 Bradford 31 48 79
Rayleigh 49 42 91 Long Eaton 29 36 65
Middlesbrough 44 25 69 *Workington 33 53 86*

Semi Finals

BOSTON 46 35 81 Bradford 32 43 75
Rayleigh 43 18 61 *Workington 35 60 95*

FINAL

First leg, September 23:
BOSTON 58 (Carl Glover 15, Ray Bales 13, Russ Osborne 10, Arthur Price 10, David Gagen 5, David Piddock 5) *Workington 19* (Lou Sansom 7, Malcolm Mackay 5, Kym Amundson 4, Steve Watson 3, Taffy Owen 0, Mitch Graham 0, Bernie Hornby 0).
Second leg, September 28:
Workington 47 (Sansom 12, Mackay 9, Graham 7, Owen 6, Amundson 6, Watson 6, Hornby 1) BOSTON 31 (Glover 16, Price 6, Bales 4, Piddock 2, Les Glover 1, Gagen 1, Osborne 1).

❑ BOSTON win 89-66 on aggregate.

1973 ALL THE RESULTS

	BARROW	BERWICK	BIRMINGHAM	BOSTON	BRADFORD	CANTERBURY	CHESTERTON	CREWE	EASTBOURNE	ELLESMERE PORT	HULL	LONG EATON	PETERBOROUGH	RAYLEIGH	SCUNTHORPE	SUNDERLAND	TEESSIDE	WORKINGTON
BARROW		46-32	47-31	27-49	45-33	55-23	44-34	58-20	54-24	52-25	57-20	58-20	39-38	56-22	60-18	41-37	49-29	34-44
BERWICK	41-37		42-35	37-41	43-35	39-38	51-27	48-29	37-41	38-40	37-41	43-35	49-29	50-28	41-37	42-35	36-42	39-39
BIRMINGHAM	56-22	53-25		36-42	48-30	55-23	49-28	52-26	41-37	48-30	55-23	57-21	47-30	55-22	56-22	63-15	40-38	56-22
BOSTON	55-22	47-31	57-21		49-28	49-29	55-23	44-34	48-30	57-21	45-33	56-22	42-36	50-28	56-22	50-28	46-32	47-31
BRADFORD	45-33	60-18	46-32	38-40		49-29	40-37	54-24	43-35	44-34	53-25	45-33	46-32	56-22	44-34	49-29	51-27	42-35
CANTERBURY	39-38	47-30	37-41	32-46	36-42		37-41	51-27	42-35	42-36	50-28	50-28	39-39	49-29	40-37	49-29	38-39	40-38
CHESTERTON	45-33	52-26	41-37	38-40	43-35	45-33		41-36	47-31	37-40	39-39	37-40	37-41	40-38	43-34	49-29	44-34	33-45
CREWE	42-36	48-30	39-38	42-36	46.5 31.5	52-26	53-25		48-30	42-36	48-30	53-25	43-35	48-30	42-36	50-27	46-32	43-35
EASTBOURNE	40-37	55-23	42-35	40-38	49-29	43-35	43-35	48-29		51-27	52-26	51-27	50-28	42-36	47-31	53-25	45-33	40-38
ELLESMERE PORT	49-28	46-32	38-40	38-39	52-26	31-47	35-43	41-37	49-29		36-42	54-24	46-32	41-37	57-20	48-30	41-37	35-43
HULL	39-39	60-18	38-40	43-34	42-35	39-39	37-41	48-30	39-39	41-37		46-32	32-45	40-37	40-37	43-35	38-40	42-35
LONG EATON	47-31	55-23	44-34	Void	54-24	41-37	56-22	41-37	51-22	34-44	36-42		45-33	50-27	49-29	58-20	41-37	41-37
PETERBOROUGH	44-34	49-29	39-36	37-41	49-29	51-27	51-27	41-37	49-29	44-34	51-27	52-26		58-20	53-25	47-30	55-23	43-35
RAYLEIGH	43-35	52-26	45-33	38-40	36.5 41.5	36-42	41-37	39-39	34-44	56-22	39-39	39-39	50-28		52-26	47-31	48-30	38-40
SCUNTHORPE	48-30	54-24	42-36	34-43	45-33	51-27	51-27	55-23	44-34	44-34	43-35	36-42	19-59	40-38		39-39	49-29	33-45
SUNDERLAND	44-34	54-24	40-37	31-47	40-38	59-19	43-35	53-25	39-39	51-27	45-33	56-22	45-33	45-33	49-29		42-36	41-37
TEESSIDE	53-25	58-20	44-34	38-40	47-31	45-33	48-30	56-22	51-27	49-29	44-34	45-33	56-22	56-22	53-25	41-37		43-35
WORKINGTON	39-39	54-24	53-25	41-37	45-32	57-19	50-28	50-28	46-32	51-27	45-33	53-24	46-32	47-31	55-23	55-23	54-24	

†Long Eaton v Boston was eventually declared void after a series of protests and counter protests. Original match result 39-36.

1974 BRITISH LEAGUE DIVISION TWO

	P	W	D	L	PtsF	PtsA	W	D	L	PtsF	PtsA	Pts
1 BIRMINGHAM	**35**	**17**	**1**	**0**	**917**	**485**	**9**	**2**	**6**	**711**	**611**	**55**
2 Eastbourne	36	17	0	1	927.5	474.5	7	3	8	709	692	51
3 Boston	36	18	0	0	841	560	5	2	11	667.5	734.5	48
4 Workington	36	17	1	0	856	546	5	2	11	626	778	47
5 Crewe	36	17	0	1	919.5	482.5	5	0	13	616	784	44
6 Teesside	36	15	1	2	834	568	4	0	14	614	788	39
7 Bradford	36	17	0	1	787	614	2	1	15	552	849	39
8 Peterborough	34	14	0	2	740	507	4	1	13	579	822	37
9 Coatbridge	36	17	0	1	879	521	1	0	17	559	814	36
10 Canterbury	36	14	0	4	796	578	4	0	14	606	794	36
11 Berwick	36	14	1	3	762	640	2	0	16	522	879	33
12 Barrow	36	12	2	4	810	589	3	0	15	592.5	807.5	32
13 Stoke	36	15	0	3	815	588	1	0	17	574	830	32
14 Ellesmere Port	35	13	2	3	784	616	1	1	15	547	778	31
15 Long Eaton	36	14	2	2	772	630	0	0	18	530	872	30
16 Rye House	36	12	0	6	745	651	1	0	17	484	915	26
17 Scunthorpe	36	9	2	7	760	640	1	0	17	573	827	22
18 Sunderland	36	10	0	8	755	647	1	0	17	476	923	22
19 Weymouth	36	10	0	8	711.5	687.5	0	0	18	486.5	913.5	20

1974 KNOCK OUT CUP

Round 1

Barrow 36 31 67 Stoke 42 46 88
Crewe 43 32 75 Workington 35 46 81
Sunderland 37 22 59 Middlesbrough 41 55 96

Round 2

Weymouth 44 28 72 Boston 34 49 83
Rye House 36 26 62 Peterborough 42 52 94
Stoke 51 45 96 Middlesbrough 27 32 59
Canterbury 44 31 75 *Eastbourne 34 47 81*
Workington 50 49 99 Berwick 28 29 57
Ellesmere Port 52 34 86 Bradford 26 43 69
BIRMINGHAM 47 40 87 Long Eaton 31 37 68
Coatbridge 55 34 89 Scunthorpe 23 44 67

Round 3

Eastbourne 50 35 85 Workington 28 43 71
Ellesmere Port 40 31 71 Peterborough 38 46 84
BIRMINGHAM 48 39 87 Boston 30 39 69
Stoke 40 30 70 Coatbridge 38 48 86

Semi Finals

Peterborough 41 20 61 BIRMINGHAM 37 58 95
Coatbridge 48 21 69 *Eastbourne 29 56 85*

FINAL

First leg, October 20:
Eastbourne 47 (Paul Gachet 12, Martin Yeates 9, Neil Middleditch 8, Bobby McNeil 7, Peter Jarman 7, Trevor Geer 2, Mike Sampson 2) BIRMINGHAM 31 (Arthur Browning 11, Phil Herne 10, John Hart 4, George Major 4, Carl Askew 2, Keith Anderson 0).
Second leg, October 21:
BIRMINGHAM 50 (Herne 12, Browning 11, Major 10, Hart 7, Anderson 7, Ricky Day 2, Askew 1)
Eastbourne 27 (Jarman 9, Middleditch 8, Gachet 7, Geer 2, Yeates 1, McNeil 0, Sampson 0).

❑ BIRMINGHAM win 81-74 on aggregate.

†The first leg of the Final also counted as a British League Division Two match.

1974 Division Two Riders' Championship Final

Saturday, September 28, Wimbledon:
1 Carl Glover 13, 2 Ted Hubbard 13, 3 Phil Herne 12, 4 John Jackson 10, 5 Geoff Bouchard 10, 6 Mike Lanham 10, 7 Colin Meredith 9, 8 Mike Broadbank 7, 9 Graham Drury 6, 10 Dave Gifford 5, 11 Ken McKinlay 4, 12 Bobby McNeil 4, 13 Bruce Forrester 3, 14 Taffy Owen 3, 15 Brian Foote 3, 16 Mitch Graham 0. *Reserves: Brian Havelock 4, Bob Hughes 2, Willie Templeton 1.*

1974 ALL THE RESULTS

	BARROW	BERWICK	BIRMINGHAM	BOSTON	BRADFORD	CANTERBURY	COATBRIDGE	CREWE	EASTBOURNE	ELLESMERE PORT	LONG EATON	PETERBOROUGH	RYE HOUSE	SCUNTHORPE	STOKE	SUNDERLAND	TEESSIDE	WEYMOUTH	WORKINGTON
BARROW		50-28	39-39	35-43	30-48	40-38	47-31	48-30	38-39	42-35	52-26	53-25	56-21	45-32	48-30	55-23	44-34	49-28	39-39
BERWICK	39-38		32-46	37-41	39-39	42-36	44-34	49-28	40-38	42-36	44-34	38-40	46-32	42-36	51-27	46-32	44-34	44-34	43-35
BIRMINGHAM	52-25	53-25		43-35	54-24	52-26	47-31	49-29	39-39	57-21	56-22	56-22	57-21	51-27	42-36	60-17	43-35	48-30	58-20
BOSTON	49-29	49-29	44-34		58-20	43-34	41-37	50-28	40-38	45-33	47-31	41-36	50-28	46-31	43-35	57-21	46-32	49-29	43-35
BRADFORD	42-36	43-35	26-51	48-30		48-30	49-28	42-36	40-38	42-36	40-37	49-29	50-28	41-37	41-37	44-34	44-34	54-24	44-34
CANTERBURY	49-29	49-29	29-48	42-36	55-23		†41-9	46-32	34-44	59-19	50-28	32-46	48-30	44-34	45-33	46-31	46-32	43-35	38-40
COATBRIDGE	41-37	36-41	45-33	48-30	41-36	58-20		57-20	42-36	49-29	50-28	55-23	59-19	44-34	47-31	61-16	43-35	54-24	49-29
CREWE	61-17	61-17	40-37	52-26	52-26	52-26	51-27		55-23	54-24	49-29	55-23	48-30	46-32	54-24	49-29	52-26	50.5-26.5	38-40
EASTBOURNE	47-31	58-20	47-31	41.5-36.5	58-20	38-39	51-27	54-24		49-29	55-23	57-21	59-19	54-23	51-27	55-23	44-34	52-26	57-21
ELLESMERE PORT	48-29	48-29	39-39	30-47	49-29	44-34	40-38	37-41	39-39		45-32	41-37	56-22	42-36	38-40	47-31	49-29	52-26	40-38
LONG EATON	44-34	39-38	33-45	37-41	47-30	44-34	40-38	41-37	40-38	39-39		39-39	52-26	47-31	48-30	53-25	43-35	42-36	44-34
PETERBOROUGH	47-31	49-29	Not raced	42-36	45-33	29-49	50-28	37-41	43-35	Not raced	47-31		55-23	50-28	44-34	60-18	41-36	55-23	46-32
RYE HOUSE	42-36	50-28	31-46	40-38	50-28	44-33	41-36	37-40	28-49	48-30	40-38	33-44		47-30	47-31	42-35	37-41	50-28	38-40
SCUNTHORPE	38-40	37-41	31-47	39-39	53-24	43-35	58-20	35-43	32-46	31-47	44-34	42-35	52-25		48-30	56-22	32-46	50-27	39-39
STOKE	40-38	51-27	38-40	34-44	41-37	46-32	49-29	41-37	36-42	49-29	50-28	46-32	50-27	43-35		56-22	51-27	50-28	44-34
SUNDERLAND	37-40	56-22	33-45	42-36	44-34	36-42	33-45	32-46	40-38	43-35	51-27	54-24	38-39	44-34	41-37		37-41	60-18	34-44
TEESSIDE	54-24	58-20	40-38	39-39	34-44	47-31	51-27	46-31	37-40	41-37	44-34	50-28	44-34	50-28	44-34	52-26		52-26	51-27
WEYMOUTH	36.5-41.5	47-31	20-58	41-36	41-37	35-42	41-36	41-37	30-48	44-34	50-28	34-44	50-27	45-33	48-30	38-39	37-41		33-45
WORKINGTON	41-37	45-33	44-34	44-34	58-20	53-25	40-38	42-36	39-39	44-34	58-20	47-31	45-33	46-32	50-28	46-32	55-22	59-18	

†Coatbridge riders refused to compete after heat five. Four races were held with Canterbury riders only to establish a winning lead after nine heats.

1975 NEW NATIONAL LEAGUE

	P	W	D	L	PtsF	PtsA	W	D	L	PtsF	PtsA	Pts
1 BIRMINGHAM	**38**	**19**	**0**	**0**	**963**	**515**	**10**	**1**	**8**	**738**	**737**	**59**
2 Newcastle	38	18	0	1	915	565	9	0	10	720	758	54
3 Stoke	38	18	0	1	936	545	8	0	11	714.5	764.5	52
4 Eastbourne	38	18	0	1	982	497	7	0	12	694	783	50
5 Boston	38	17	0	2	932	549	7	2	10	699	776	50
6 Workington	38	17	1	1	881.5	598.5	6	1	12	682	798	48
7 Berwick	38	18	1	0	890	586	3	2	14	596	886	45
8 Crayford	38	17	0	2	930	546	3	2	14	619	860	42
9 Ellesmere Port	38	17	1	1	868	612	2	0	17	587	889	39
10 Canterbury	38	17	0	2	917	560	2	0	17	616	862	38
11 Bradford	38	16	2	1	883	597	1	0	18	523	955	36
12 Coatbridge	38	15	0	4	861	615	2	1	16	594	883	35
13 Scunthorpe	38	14	0	5	801	680	3	0	16	572.5	904.5	34
14 Rye House	38	13	1	5	813	659	0	1	18	574	904	28
15 Paisley	38	14	0	5	809	666	0	0	19	504	973	28
16 Crewe	37	12	1	6	837	640	1	0	17	558	844	27
17 Teesside	38	13	0	6	841	637	0	0	19	590	889	26
18 Peterborough	37	12	0	6	735	665	1	0	18	540	940	26
19 Mildenhall	38	11	1	7	758.5	718.5	0	0	19	515	963	23
20 Weymouth	38	8	2	9	756	723	0	0	19	538	940	18

1975 New National League Riders' Championship Final

Saturday, September 27, Wimbledon.
1 Laurie Etheridge 13, 2 Brian Collins 13, 3 Arthur Browning 10, 4 Les Rumsey 10, 5 Michael Lee 10, 6 John Jackson 9, 7 Paul Gachet 8, 8 Joe Owen 8, 9 Tom Leadbitter 8, 10 Bob Coles 7, 11 Brian Clark 6, 12 Brian Foote 5, 13 Alan Molyneux 5, 14 Colin Meredith 4, 15 Lou Sansom 3, 16 Tony Childs 1. *Reserves: Sid Sheldrick, Dave Gifford, Graham Drury, Martin Yeates, did not ride. Sponsors: Gauloises.*

1975 KNOCK OUT CUP

Round 1
Coatbridge 50 35 85 Ellesmere Port 28 43 71
Birmingham 51 40 91 Crayford 27 37 64
Berwick 40 34 74 Newcastle 38 44 82
Boston 40 36 76 Peterborough 38 42 80
Round 2
Newcastle 50 39 89 Coatbridge 27 39 66
Paisley 43 33 76 *Workington 34 45 79*
Crewe 38 30 68 Bradford 40 48 88
Birmingham 60 46 106 Rye House 18 31 49
Canterbury 40 29 69 EASTBOURNE 37 49 86
Weymouth 50 29 79 Peterborough 28 49 77
Middlesbrough 45 40 85 Scunthorpe 32 38 70
Round 3
Workington 47 36 83 Stoke 31 42 73
Newcastle 54 46 100 Middlesbrough 24 32 56
EASTBOURNE 45 37 82 Birmingham 33 41 74
Weymouth 50 31 81 Bradford 28 47 75
Semi Finals
EASTBOURNE 60 36 96 Weymouth 18 42 60
Newcastle 48 30 78 *Workington 30 48 78*
Semi Final Replay
Workington 51 41 92 Newcastle 27 37 64
FINAL
First leg, October 17:
Workington 47 (Taffy Owen 11, Mick Newton 11, Lou Sansom 10, Roger Wright 8, Robbie Gardner 5, Terry Kelly 1, Steve Lawson 1) EASTBOURNE 31 (Neil Middleditch 12, Paul Gachet 7, Mike Sampson 5, Eric Dugard 3, Peter Jarman 2, Colin Richardson 2, Mick Pither 0).
Second leg, October 19:
EASTBOURNE 52 (Middleditch 10, Jarman 10, Sampson 10, Gachet 8, Dugard 7, Pither 4, Richardson 3) *Workington 25* (Sansom 13, Gardner 6, Owen 4, Kelly 1, Lawson 1, Newton 0, Wright 0).
❑ EASTBOURNE win 83-72 on aggregate.

1975 ALL THE RESULTS

	BERWICK	BIRMINGHAM	BOSTON	BRADFORD	CANTERBURY	COATBRIDGE	CRAYFORD	CREWE	EASTBOURNE	ELLESMERE PORT	MILDENHALL	NEWCASTLE	PAISLEY	PETERBOROUGH	RYE HOUSE	SCUNTHORPE	STOKE	TEESSIDE	WEYMOUTH	WORKINGTON
BERWICK		42-35	41-37	47-31	50-27	39-39	56-22	43-35	47-31	48-30	52-26	43-35	52-26	53-25	47-31	47-30	50-27	48-29	41-36	44-34
BIRMINGHAM	54-24		41-36	55-22	45-33	52-25	49-29	55-23	45-33	51-27	57-20	46-32	53-25	59-19	52-26	56-22	44-34	49-29	53-25	47-31
BOSTON	48-30	45-33		47-31	47-31	52-26	54-24	49-29	48-30	60-18	50-28	42-36	56-22	54-24	39-38	64-14	34-44	45-33	61-17	37-41
BRADFORD	51-27	36-42	39-39		43-35	48-30	49-29	48-30	42-36	47-29	51-27	45-33	40-38	47-31	54-24	53-25	45-33	43-35	63-15	39-39
CANTERBURY	61-17	49-28	45-32	55-23		52-26	49-29	42-36	40-37	43-35	53-23	38-40	59-19	60-18	44-34	55-23	43-35	49-29	43-35	37-41
COATBRIDGE	50-28	34-43	37-41	50-27	45-32		53-25	41-37	38-40	46-31	58-20	43-35	54-24	43-35	43-34	49-29	38-40	45-32	51-27	43-35
CRAYFORD	58-20	43-35	46-30	59-19	47-31	45-31		48-30	38-40	57-20	50-28	37-41	55-23	53-25	46-32	43-35	50-28	48-30	50-27	57-21
CREWE	50-28	32-46	39-39	54-24	50-28	51-26	37-41		31-46	47-31	47-31	38-39	42-36	46-32	58-20	36-40	37-41	41-37	59-19	42-36
EASTBOURNE	50-28	45-33	52-26	63-15	48-30	55-23	41-37	55-23		53-24	61-17	37-40	60-18	59-19	52-26	57-21	52-26	53-25	43-34	46-32
ELLESMERE PORT	45-33	39-39	46-32	51-27	46-32	46-32	55-23	44-33	48-30		54-24	41-37	40-38	45-32	51-27	45-33	34-44	44-34	51-27	43-35
MILDENHALL	46-32	26-52	31-47	49-29	44-34	40-38	39-38	36-41	37-41	41-37		41-37	57-20	37-41	39-39	37-41	21.5 55.5	51-27	46-32	40-37
NEWCASTLE	54-24	38-40	47-31	62-16	49-29	49-29	46-32	50-28	44-34	40-38	49-29		46-32	52-26	52-26	47-29	44-34	50-28	54-24	42-36
PAISLEY	33-45	45-32	47-31	35-43	43-35	38-40	44-33	46-32	45-32	47-31	41-37	46-30		48-30	48-29	47-31	36-41	41-37	42-36	37-41
PETERBOROUGH	35-43	38-40	31-46	43-34	30-48	40-38	45-33	Not raced	44-34	41-37	42-36	37-41	47-29		47-31	40-38	40-38	47-31	50-28	38-40
RYE HOUSE	46-32	33-45	38-39	49-29	39-38	46-32	39-39	53-25	31-45	47-30	47-30	36-42	49-28	47-31		44-34	32-46	48-29	44-33	45-32
SCUNTHORPE	48-30	32-46	34-44	41-37	41-37	52-26	38-40	41-37	40-38	46-32	47-31	38-40	41-37	42-36	43-34		44-34	51-27	45-33	37-41
STOKE	42-36	48-30	44-34	49-29	53-25	48-30	36-42	54-24	54-24	53-25	51-27	41-37	58-20	56-21	44-34	58-20		49-29	46-32	52-26
TEESSIDE	37-41	33-44	37-40	49-29	52-26	50-28	42-35	52-26	38-40	37-41	45-33	35-43	47-30	48-30	48-30	49-29	42-36		58-20	42-36
WEYMOUTH	39-39	38-39	28-50	50-28	35-42	34-43	39-39	43-35	33-45	37-41	50-28	34-44	53-25	48-30	43-35	41-37	37-41	44-34		30-48
WORKINGTON	39-39	41-36	53-25	47-30	55-23	46-32	49-29	44-34	40-38	48-30	58-20	40-38	64-14	43-35	54-24	36.5 41.5	41-37	43-35	40-38	

†Peterborough v Crewe was never raced. Crewe originally refused to ride when Peterborough planned to operate rider replacement for Russell Osbourne.

1976 NATIONAL LEAGUE

	P	W	D	L	PtsF	PtsA	W	D	L	PtsF	PtsA	Pts
1 NEWCASTLE	**34**	**17**	**0**	**0**	**906**	**419**	**13**	**1**	**3**	**736**	**588**	**61**
2 Ellesmere Port	34	16	1	0	830.5	492.5	8	0	9	616	704	49
3 Workington	34	16	0	1	818	505	4	1	12	587.5	730.5	41
4 Canterbury	34	15	0	2	815	507	5	0	12	529	795	40
5 Rye House	34	14	1	2	818.5	500.5	3	1	13	539	705	36
6 Crayford	34	15	1	1	810	508	2	0	15	544	778	35
7 Coatbridge	34	15	0	2	795	522	2	1	14	521	798	35
8 Eastbourne	34	16	0	1	836	484	1	0	16	525	797	34
9 Peterborough	34	14	1	2	785	501	2	1	14	566	759	34
10 Berwick	34	16	0	1	772	548	1	0	16	506	812	34
11 Stoke	34	14	0	3	736	588	1	1	15	568	752	31
12 Boston	34	14	1	2	749	573	1	0	16	549	772	31
13 Mildenhall	34	14	0	3	746	578	1	1	15	524	800	31
14 Oxford	34	14	1	2	760	564	0	0	17	497	786	29
15 Weymouth	34	10	1	6	709	611	1	1	15	477.5	843.5	24
16 Paisley	34	12	0	5	723	598	0	0	17	429	894	24
17 Scunthorpe	34	10	1	6	678	564	1	0	16	506	815	23
18 Teesside	34	10	0	7	690	630	0	0	17	473	848	20

1976 KNOCK OUT CUP

Round 1

Middlesbrough 46 25 71 Coatbridge 32 52 84
Weymouth 40 30 70 Oxford 38 48 86

Round 2

Coatbridge 33 32 65 Workington 45 46 91
Boston 48 32 80 Crayford 30 46 76
Oxford 47 37 84 Eastbourne 31 41 72
Berwick 45 35 80 Scunthorpe 32 43 75
Newcastle 59 41 100 Stoke 19 37 56
Peterborough 42 40 82 Mildenhall 36 38 74
Canterbury 44 32 76 Rye House 34 45 79
Paisley 36 32 68 Ellesmere Port 42 46 88

Round 3

Boston 48 31 79 Workington 29 46 75
Oxford 40 30 70 Berwick 38 48 86
Peterborough 39 31 70 Newcastle 39 47 86
Rye House 38 28 66 Ellesmere Port 39 50 89

Semi Finals

Berwick 49 35 84 Boston 29 42 71
Newcastle 46 37 83 Ellesmere Port 31 41 72

FINAL

First leg, Sptember 18:
Berwick 43 (Graham Jones 10, Mike Hiftle 10, Dave Gifford 9, Willie Templeton 5, Eddie Argall 5, Robin Adlington 4, Wayne Brown 0) NEWCASTLE 35 (Joe Owen 15, Tom Owen 14, Robbie Blackadder 3, Tim Swales 1, Phil Michelides 1, Andy Cusworth 1, Malcolm Davies, number 8, did not ride).
Second leg, September 27:
NEWCASTLE 48 (T. Owen 12, J. Owen 12, Ron Henderson 6, Cusworth 5, Swales 5, Michelides 4, Blackadder 4) *Berwick 29* (Argall 11, Wright 6, Gifford 6, Jones 4, Templeton 2, Peter Waite 0).

❑ NEWCASTLE win 83-72 on aggregate.

1976 National League Riders' Championship Final

Saturday, October 2, Wimbledon:
1 Joe Owen 14, 2 John Jackson 12, 3 Ted Hubbard 12, 4 Steve Weatherley 10, 5 Brian Clark 10, 6 Alan Emerson 10, 7 Lou Sansom 9, 8 Robert Hollingworth 8, 9 Les Rumsey 7, 10 Bob Coles 7, 11 Brian Collins 6, 12 Laurie Etheridge 6, 13 Martin Yeates 4, 14 Graham Jones 2, 15 Keith Evans 1, 16 Les Collins 0. *Reserves: Carl Askew 2, Ian Williams 0.*
Sponsors: Gauloises.

1976 ALL THE RESULTS

	BERWICK	BOSTON	CANTERBURY	COATBRIDGE	CRAYFORD	EASTBOURNE	ELLESMERE PORT	MILDENHALL	NEWCASTLE	OXFORD	PAISLEY	PETERBOROUGH	RYE HOUSE	SCUNTHORPE	STOKE	TEESSIDE	WEYMOUTH	WORKINGTON
BERWICK		47-31	39-38	44-33	52-25	45-33	41-37	48-30	36-40	46-32	48-29	46-32	44-34	48-30	46-32	51-27	42-36	49-29
BOSTON	52-26		57-21	47-31	41-37	54-24	38-40	41-37	34-44	40-37	46-32	40-38	40-38	43-32	39-39	52-26	43-35	42-36
CANTERBURY	51-27	46-31		54-24	38-40	45-32	58-20	46-32	38-40	53-25	57-21	46-32	44-34	47-31	40-37	63-14	49-29	40-38
COATBRIDGE	48-29	51-26	56-22		60-18	45-32	40-37	56-22	32-46	40-38	43-35	47-31	42-35	47-31	41-37	53-24	56-19	38-40
CRAYFORD	62-16	44-34	48-30	51-25		36-42	51-27	45-33	40-38	49-27	51-27	39-39±	40-38	58-20	46-32	50-27	54-24	46-29
EASTBOURNE	50-26	42-36	53-24	59-19	57-21		50-28	45-33	38-40	49-29	54-24	41-36	45-33	59-19	52-26	46-32	55-23	41-35
ELLESMERE PORT	40-38	43-35	57-21	57-21	47-31	42-35		55-23	42-36	51-27	52-26	46-32	56-22	45-32	55-23	49-29	55-23	38.5 38.5
MILDENHALL	42-36	38-40	55-23	41-37	40-37	50-28	34-44		41-37	48-30	50-28	38-40	48-30	43-35	40-38	49-28	48-30	41-37
NEWCASTLE	43-35	53-25	62-16	52-26	53-25	55-23	48-30	54-24		54-24	55-22	47-31	57-21	57-21	53-25	60-18	57-21	46-32
OXFORD	56-22	42-36	41-37	49-29	42-36	53-25	47-30	41-37	30-48		56-22	44-34	39-39	41-37	50-27	43-35	51-27	35-43
PAISLEY	35-43	52-25	38-40	29-49	43-35	41-37	32-46	53-24	25-53	48-30		49-29	43-35	48-29	40-37	50-27	48-30	49-29
PETERBOROUGH	47-31	44-33	47-31	39-39	60-18	49-29	36-42	49-29	36-42	†40-0	60-18		47-30	45-33	42-36	46-32	52-26	46-32
RYE HOUSE	59-19	48-30	38-40	53-23	40-38	44-33	36-39	49-29	39-39	46-32	59-19	53-25		53-25	42-35	50-28	54.5 23.5	55-23
SCUNTHORPE	41-36	50-28	38-40	48-29	41-37	48-30	38-40	47-31	25-53	43-35	46-31	37-41	16-14§		49-27	54-24	39-39	34-43
STOKE	53-25	43-35	43-35	42-36	43-33	43-35	40-38	45-33	29-49	45-33	57-21	41-37	42-36	38-40		40-38	37-41	55-23
TEESSIDE	45-32	40-38	37-41	45-33	36-42	41-37	33-45	37-40	36-42	43-34	60-18	43-35	32-45	40-38	40-38		48-29	34-43
WEYMOUTH	42-33	43-34	38-40	38-40	41-37	49-29	38-40	39-39	33-45	41-36	55-23	46-32	34-43	50-28	37-41	44-34		41-37
WORKINGTON	46-32	46-32	48-30	50-27	44-34	57-21	44-33	50-28	34-44	50-28	45-33	56-22	52-26	53-25	40-38	48-30	55-22	

†Oxford refused to ride and Peterborough sent two riders to the tapes to complete four laps and eight races. ±Match finished 37-41 on track but Peterborough successfully appealed against a decision to award Mike Broadbank (Crayford) two points when he used a machine without a satisfactory silencer in heat three. §Scunthorpe riders refused to compete after heat six. Match points awarded to Rye House.

1977 NATIONAL LEAGUE

	P	*W*	*D*	*L*	*PtsF*	*PtsA*	*W*	*D*	*L*	*PtsF*	*PtsA*	*Pts*
1 EASTBOURNE	**36**	**18**	**0**	**0**	**999**	**403**	**11**	**0**	**7**	**753**	**649**	**58**
2 Rye House	36	16	0	2	857	542	8	3	7	667	731	51
3 Ellesmere Port	36	16	1	1	818	582	6	1	11	675	721	46
4 Canterbury	36	18	0	0	866	532	5	0	13	628	775	46
5 Peterborough	36	18	0	0	873	531	4	0	14	601	801	44
6 Newcastle	36	16	0	2	856	544	5	1	12	666	730	43
7 Boston	36	17	0	1	866	533	3	0	15	596	778	40
8 Mildenhall	36	14	1	3	801	599	2	3	13	582	822	36
9 Teesside	36	15	1	2	763	638	2	0	16	501	900	35
10 Crayford	36	16	0	2	828	567	1	0	17	588	808	34
11 Glasgow	36	14	0	4	794	582	2	0	16	539	860	32
12 Newport	36	16	0	2	808	584	0	0	18	503	898	32
13 Oxford	36	15	1	2	825	572	0	0	18	574	818	31
14 Scunthorpe	36	12	1	5	740	660	3	0	15	552	849	31
15 Edinburgh	36	13	0	5	766	633	2	0	16	578	824	30
16 Workington	36	13	0	5	766	632	1	1	16	522	880	29
17 Weymouth	36	10	3	5	742.5	659.5	1	0	17	583.5	816.5	25
18 Berwick	36	11	1	6	751	652	0	0	18	443	954	23
19 Stoke	36	8	0	10	700	701	1	0	17	595	805	18

Coatbridge moved mid-season to a newly constructed track at Blantyre and rode as Glasgow.

1977 National League Riders' Championship Final

Saturday, September 24, Wimbledon:
1 Colin Richardson 15, 2 Martin Yeates 13, 3 Tom Owen 13, 4 Kelvin Mullarkey 12, 5 Robert Hollingworth 11, 6 John Jackson 10, 7 Steve Koppe 9, 8 Laurie Etheridge 7, 9 Stuart Mountford 5, 10 Bert Harkins 5, 11 Alan Emerson 4, 12 Danny Kennedy 4, 13 Brian Woodward 4, 14 Brian Collins 3, 15 Bob Coles 3, 16 Steve Lawson 2.
Reserves: Ian Clark 0, Graham Jones, did not ride. Sponsors: Gauloises.

1977 KNOCK OUT CUP

Round 1
EASTBOURNE 55 52 107 Canterbury 23 26 49
Edinburgh 48 34 82 Scunthorpe 30 43 73
Oxford 44 34 78 Rye House 34 44 78

Round 1 Replay
Rye House 42 32 74 Oxford 36 45 81

Round 2
Crayford 35 23 58 EASTBOURNE 43 54 97
Coatbridge 47 29 76 Newcastle 30 49 79
Ellesmere Port 46 36 82 Workington 32 42 74
Oxford 50 37 87 Newport 28 41 69
Boston 43 43 86 Weymouth 34 35 69
Peterborough 44 40 84 Mildenhall 34 38 72
Stoke 40 34 74 Edinburgh 38 44 82
Berwick 46 34 80 Middlesbrough 32 44 76

Round 3
EASTBOURNE 54 43 97 Newcastle 24 34 58
Oxford 37 31.5 68.5 Ellesmere Port 41 46.5 87.5
Boston 45 38 83 Peterborough 33 40 73
Berwick 46 37 83 Edinburgh 32 41 73

Semi Finals
Ellesmere Port 50 21 71 EASTBOURNE 28 57 85
Boston 38 33 71 *Berwick 40 45 85*

FINAL
First leg, October 8:
Berwick 41 (Willie Templeton 9, Graham Jones 9, Dave Gifford 7, Mike Hiftle 6, Wayne Brown 5, Robin Adlington 4, Colin Caffrey 1) EASTBOURNE 37 (Colin Richardson 13, Mike Sampson 11, Steve Naylor 7, Eric Dugard 5, Paul Woods 1, David Kennett 0, Roger Abel 0).
Second leg, date to come:
EASTBOURNE 61 (Richardson 12, Sampson 11, Dugard 9, Naylor 9, Abel 7, Kennett 7, Woods 6) *Berwick 16* (Brendan Shilleto 6, Jones 5, Hftle 2, Templeton 2, Ian Darling 1, Gifford 0, Caffrey 0).

❑ EASTBOURNE win 98-57 on aggregate.

1977 ALL THE RESULTS

	BERWICK	BOSTON	CANTERBURY	CRAYFORD	EASTBOURNE	EDINBURGH	ELLESMERE PORT	GLASGOW	MILDENHALL	NEWCASTLE	NEWPORT	OXFORD	PETERBORO	RYE HOUSE	SCUNTHORPE	STOKE	TEESSIDE	WEYMOUTH	WORKINGTON
BERWICK		47-31	36-42	44-34	31-47	43-35	36-42	37-41	39-39	41-37	42-36	44-34	54-24	35-43	38-40	46-31	51-27	40-38	47-31
BOSTON	60-17		53-25	47-31	42-36	52-26	45-32	48-28	54-24	41-37	44-34	58-20	41-36	38-40	57-21	46-32	49-29	45-33	46-32
CANTERBURY	59-19	41-37		43-34	41-37	57-21	42-35	50-27	49-29	47-31	45-32	50-28	40-38	52-26	44-33	45-33	58-20	57-21	46-31
CRAYFORD	47-31	43-34	44-34		29-49	52-26	46-30	54-23	50-28	40-36	47-31	49-29	48-30	37-38	48-30	41-37	52-26	45-33	56-22
EASTBOURNE	62-16	57-20	49-29	51-26		49-29	49-29	60-18	61-17	52-26	59-19	53-25	54-24	51-27	57-21	59-19	59-19	54-24	63-15
EDINBURGH	53-25	45-33	37-41	44-34	30-48		31-47	42-36	40-38	35-42	52-26	43-33	54-24	38-40	40-38	40-37	52-25	45-33	45-33
ELLESMERE PORT	47-31	40-37	44-34	51-24	43-35	45-33		48-30	39-39	42-36	61-17	46-32	36-42	50-28	43-35	41-37	55-23	43-35	44-34
GLASGOW	*45-33*	*43-11*	*49-29*	39-37	*32-46*	44-34	38-40		54-24	37-41	47-31	42-36	48-29	38-40	45-33	46-32	*52-25*	45-33	*50-28*
MILDENHALL	64-14	43-35	42-35	45-33	38-40	48-30	39-39	50-28		45-32	43-34	44-34	34-44	42-36	44-33	46-32	52-26	45-33	37-41
NEWCASTLE	53-25	50-28	47-31	48-30	39-37	45-33	46-32	50-28	51-27		52-26	47-31	56-22	36-42	53-25	43-35	38-40	43-34	59-18
NEWPORT	49-26	40-37	34-44	41-37	36-42	46-32	43-35	59-19	44-34	50-28		41-31	45-33	42-36	48-30	42-35	59-19	43-34	46-32
OXFORD	53-24	38-40	41-37	47-31	44-34	42-35	43-35	60-18	39-39	41-37	58-19		51-27	38-37	38-40	44-34	53-25	44-33	51-27
PETERBOROUGH	60-18	42-36	43-35	53-25	42-36	47-31	42-36	56-22	53-25	40-38	52-26	51-27		44-34	57-21	44-34	43-35	55-23	49-29
RYE HOUSE	63-14	38-40	43-35	45-33	31-47	56-22	39-38	44-34	46-32	44-34	59-19	45-30	49-29		51-27	49-29	50-28	49-29	56-22
SCUNTHORPE	53-25	42-35	47-31	49-29	33-45	32-46	29-49	40-37	44-34	30-47	51-27	40-37	22-56	39-39		40-38	49-29	42-36	58-20
STOKE	52-26	40.5 37.5	38-40	38-40	24-54	37-41	38-40	42-36	34-44	33-45	47-31	41-37	33-45	38-40	48-29		32-45	43.5 33.5	41-37
TEESSIDE	41-36	46-31	35-43	42-36	40-38	40-38	35-43	41-37	42-36	42-35	45-33	40-38	49-29	39-39	51-27	44-34		44-34	47-31
WEYMOUTH	47-31	34.5 43.5	49-29	40-38	37-41	41-37	40-36	38-40	38-40	39-39	45-33	41-37	41-37	39-39	53-25	35-43	46-32		39-39
WORKINGTON	46-32	48-30	44-34	41-36	37-41	48-29	40-37	41-37	45-33	31-45	49-29	43-35	46-32	35-43	34-44	54-23	50-28	34-44	

Glasgow figures in italics indicate raced when they were Coatbridge.

1978 NATIONAL LEAGUE

	P	W	D	L	PtsF	PtsA	W	D	L	PtsF	PtsA	Pts
1 CANTERBURY	**38**	**18**	**0**	**1**	**933**	**547**	**12**	**0**	**7**	**786**	**693**	**60**
2 Newcastle	38	17	0	2	912	567	12	2	5	786	694	60
3 Rye House	38	19	0	0	955	526	8	0	11	695.5	782.5	54
4 Eastbourne	38	19	0	0	992	479	6	1	12	712	769	51
5 Ellesmere Port	38	19	0	0	896	560	5	0	14	680	799	48
6 Peterborough	38	16	1	2	905	576	6	0	13	673	807	45
7 Oxford	38	16	2	1	933.5	545.5	4	2	13	666	813	44
8 Stoke	38	17	0	2	892	590	4	1	14	635	843	43
9 Glasgow	38	17	0	2	850	625	2	1	16	547	931	39
10 Crayford	38	15	1	3	864	612	1	1	17	573	907	34
11 Berwick	38	17	0	2	908	572	0	0	19	481	993	34
12 Mildenhall	38	13	0	6	858	622	3	1	15	680	798	33
13 Weymouth	38	14	0	5	835	643	2	0	17	625	847	32
14 Workington	38	15	0	4	849	630	1	0	18	575	905	32
15 Edinburgh	38	12	0	7	800	677	3	1	15	600	880	31
16 Milton Keynes	38	9	5	5	759	721	3	1	15	591	887	30
17 Boston	38	12	1	6	767	709	1	1	17	541	935	28
18 Teesside	38	11	0	8	769	710	1	0	18	528	952	24
19 Scunthorpe	38	9	1	9	747	732	0	1	18	544	913	20
20 Barrow	38	8	2	9	709.5	769.5	0	0	19	494.5	985.5	18

1978 National League Riders' Championship Final

Saturday, September 23, Wimbledon:
1 Steve Koppe 14, 2 John Jackson 13, 3 Ted Hubbard 12, 4 Dave Gooderham 12, 5 Ray Bales 11, 6 Tom Owen 9, 7 Arthur Price 9, 8 Danny Kennedy 8, 9 Laurie Etheridge 7, 10 Tony Lomas 6, 11 Graham Jones 5, 12 Robert Hollingworth 4, 13 George Hunter 3, 14 Nicky Allott 2, Mike Sampson 2, 16 Steve Lawson 0. *Reserves: Steve Wilcock 4, Dave Allen, Derek Harrison, did not ride. Sponsors: Gauloises.*

1978 KNOCK OUT CUP

Round 1
Workington 40 27 67 Stoke 38 51 89
Newcastle 43 39 82 Middlesbrough 33 39 72
Ellesmere Port 47 42 89 Berwick 31 35 66
Rye House 58 52 110 Milton Keynes 20 26 46

Round 2
EASTBOURNE 57 47 104 Scunthorpe 21 28 49
Barrow 33 35 68 Peterborough 45 43 88
Oxford 47 35 82 Stoke 31 43 74
Mildenhall 56 38 94 Newcastle 21 40 61
Boston 36 23 59 Ellesmere Port 42 54 96
Canterbury 48 41 89 Weymouth 27 37 64
Edinburgh 40 32 72 Crayford 38 46 84
Rye House 52 39 91 Glassgow 26 39 65

Round 3
EASTBOURNE 45 38 83 Peterborough 30 39 69
Mildenhall 40 34 74 Oxford 38 43 81
Ellesmere Port 48 23 71 Canterbury 30 55 85
Rye House 44 39 83 Crayford 34 39 73

Semi Finals
EASTBOURNE 56 45 101 Oxford 22 32 54
Rye House 57 37 94 Canterbury 20 41 61

FINAL
First leg, October 22:
EASTBOURNE 46 (David Kennett 10, Mike Sampson 9, Steve Naylor 9, Eric Dugard 8, Roger Abel 6, Paul Woods 4, Ian Fletcher 0) *Rye House 32* (Bob Garrad 11, Ted Hubbard 7, Ashley Pullen 6, Kelvin Mullarkey 4, Kevin Smith 2, Karl Fiala 1, Hugh Saunders 1).
Second leg, October 29:
Rye House 41 (Hubbard 10, Garrad 9, Mullarkey 9, Saunders 5, Fiala 4, Smith 4, Pullen 0) EASTBOURNE 37 (Dugard 11, Kennett 7, Sampson 6, Woods 4, Abel 4, Naylor 3, Fletcher 2).
❑ EASTBOURNE win 83-73 on aggregate.

1978 ALL THE RESULTS

	BARROW	BERWICK	BOSTON	CANTERBURY	CRAYFORD	EASTBOURNE	EDINBURGH	ELLESMERE PORT	GLASGOW	MILDENHALL	MILTON KEYNES	NEWCASTLE	OXFORD	PETERBOROUGH	RYE HOUSE	SCUNTHORPE	STOKE	TEESSIDE	WEYMOUTH	WORKINGTON
BARROW		52-25	41-37	28-50	43-35	39-39	33-45	35-43	40-37	20-58	39-39	24-54	34-44	35-43	36.5 41.5	48-30	34-43	44-34	43-35	41-37
BERWICK	45-33		52-26	42-36	50-28	46-32	54-24	46-31	53-25	44-34	37-41	37-41	48-29	56-22	40-38	57-21	55-23	54-24	47-31	45-33
BOSTON	48-29	45-32		35-42	42-35	40-38	34-44	37-41	40-37	42-36	40-38	41-37	39-39	26-51	37-41	46-32	43-35	49-29	45-33	38-40
CANTERBURY	53-25	59-19	53-25		56-22	45-33	51-27	47-31	53-25	48-30	47-31	36-42	44-34	49-29	59-17	48-30	40-38	48-30	50-28	47-31
CRAYFORD	53-25	52-25	47-31	37-41		34-44	44-34	47-31	55-23	48-29	42-36	39-39	41-37	45-33	32-44	54-24	52-25	44-34	49-28	49-29
EASTBOURNE	54-24	61-17	42-35	48-29	58-20		46-31	46-32	57-21	54-24	61-17	42-35	51-27	46-32	54-24	56-22	56-20	57-20	49-26	54-23
EDINBURGH	50-28	55-22	63-14	36-42	40-38	32-46		29-49	41-37	35-43	37-40	32-46	41-37	43-35	36-42	45-33	46-32	46-32	40-36	53-25
ELLESMERE PORT	61-17	53-25	50-28	40-38	44-34	48-30	46-31		48-30	45-32	46-32	43-35	50-28	40-38	43-35	†38-16	52-26	53-25	50-28	46-32
GLASGOW	45-33	49-27	53-22	33-45	42-36	45-33	48-30	37-40		49-28	45-33	40-38	41-37	51-27	41-37	49-29	44-34	50-28	42-36	46-32
MILDENHALL	50-28	50-28	47-30	35-43	56-22	38-40	38-40	37-41	55-23		54-24	36-42	45-33	48-30	45-33	41-36	410-37	38-40	51-27	53-25
MILTON KEYNES	57-20	41-37	39-39	31-47	43-35	42-35	39-39	43-35	39-39	44-34		26-52	39-39	38-40	37-41	39-39	33-45	48-30	41-37	40-38
NEWCASTLE	52-26	57-21	50-28	42-36	52-25	40-38	61-17	41-37	62-16	40-38	47-31		32-45	49-29	37-41	48-30	53-25	56-22	45-32	48-30
OXFORD	62.5 15.5	61-17	55-23	41-37	57-21	42-36	51-27	50-28	58-19	39-39	58-20	39-39		38-40	43-35	47-31	43-35	50-27	42-35	57-21
PETERBOROUGH	56-22	51-27	44-34	36-42	54-24	47-31	51-27	51-27	51-27	43-35	47-30	33-45	56-22		41-37	44-34	39-39	50-28	55-23	56-22
RYE HOUSE	59-19	54-24	60-18	42-36	48-30	42-36	54-24	40-38	58-20	40-38	59-19	45-33	46-31	46-32		50-28	52-26	58-20	45-33	57-21
SCUNTHORPE	45-33	48-30	43-35	31-47	39-39	37-41	50-28	40-38	38-40	35-43	46-30	35-43	28-50	42-36	36-42		35-43	42-36	34-43	43-35
STOKE	53-25	57-21	56-22	29-49	57-21	48-30	51-27	42-36	54-24	42-36	41-37	38-40	45-33	44-34	47-31	47-31		55-23	43-35	43-35
TEESSIDE	48-30	50-28	36-42	42-36	34-44	33-45	41-37	40-38	46-31	40-37	38-40	36-41	38-40	44-34	36-42	42-36	47-31		34-44	44-34
WEYMOUTH	54-24	49-28	51-27	32-45	41-37	28-50	41-37	50-28	46-32	42-36	54-24	34-44	43-35	32-45	42-36	56-22	38-40	57-21		45-32
WORKINGTON	40-38	49-28	53-25	33-45	51-27	43-35	47-31	41-36	37-41	48-30	49-29	38-40	52-26	35-43	40-38	58-20	40-38	53-25	42-35	

†Abandoned after heat nine. Result to stand.

1979 NATIONAL LEAGUE

	P	W	D	L	PtsF	PtsA	W	D	L	PtsF	PtsA	Pts
1 MILDENHALL	**36**	**18**	**0**	**0**	**935**	**465**	**12**	**0**	**6**	**723.5**	**674.5**	**60**
2 Rye House	36	18	0	0	947	453	11	1	6	737	663	59
3 Oxford	36	16	0	2	886	513	8	1	9	661	737	49
4 Berwick	36	17	1	0	910	492	4	2	12	630.5	769.5	45
5 Milton Keynes	36	15	0	3	798	598	6	0	12	643	760	42
6 Newcastle	36	13	0	5	822	579	7	0	11	658	742	40
7 Glasgow	36	18	0	0	877	521	1	0	17	555	847	38
8 Peterborough	36	15	1	2	819	584	3	1	14	603	797	38
9 Ellesmere Port	36	15	1	2	845	555	3	0	15	590	811	37
10 Canterbury	36	14	1	3	821	582	3	1	14	580	822	36
11Middlesbrough	36	14	0	4	768	633	3	1	14	577	824	35
12 Crayford	36	14	0	4	764	636	2	0	16	559	843	32
13 Stoke	36	12	1	5	763	638	3	1	14	558.5	839.5	32
14 Nottingham	36	12	1	5	774.5	628.5	2	0	16	577	824	29
15 Workington	36	14	1	3	787	615	0	0	18	532	871	29
16 Boston	36	12	1	5	776	624	1	1	16	541	857	28
17 Edinburgh	36	11	0	7	747.5	653.5	2	1	15	526	871	27
18 Weymouth	36	9	1	8	718.5	683.5	0	0	18	525	877	19
19 Scunthorpe	36	4	1	13	658	733	0	0	18	410	987	9

1980 National League Riders' Championship Final

Saturday, September 29, Wimbledon:
1 Ian Gledhill 14, 2 Steve Wilcock 12, 3 Andy Grahame 11, 4 Nigel Boocock 11, 5 Alan Emerson 9, 6 Karl Fiala 9, 7 Ray Bales 8, 8 Robert Hollingworth 8, 9 Les Rumsey 8, 10 John Jackson 8, 11 Nigel Flatman 8, 12 Dave Perks 7, 13 Steve Lawson 3, 14 Steve Naylor 3, 15 Brian Woodward 1, 16 Graham Jones 0. *Meeting Reserves: Dave Brewer 0, Ray Griffiths, did not ride.*
Sponsors: Gauloises.

1979 KNOCK OUT CUP

Round 1
RYE HOUSE 56 44 100 Weymouth 22 34 56
Edinburgh 46 34 80 Boston 32 44 76

Round 2
RYE HOUSE 54 31 85 Glasgow 24 47 71
Middlesbrough 45 30 75 Workington 32 46 78
Crayford 44 39 83 Edinburgh 34 39 73
Ellesmere Port 41 25 66 Mildenhall 37 53 90
Canterbury 39 21 60 Newcastle 39 57 96
Stoke 42 28 70 Milton Keynes 36 50 86
Peterborough 34 33 67 Oxford 44 45 89
Scunthorpe 38 18 56 *Berwick 40 60 100*

Round 3
Workington 49 19 68 RYE HOUSE 29 59 88
Crayford 39 22 61 Mildenhall 39 56 95
Newcastle 53 42 95 Milton Keynes 25 35 60
Oxford 44 27 71 *Berwick 34 51 85*

Semi Finals
Mildenhall 38 34 72 RYE HOUSE 40 44 84
Newcastle 46 31 77 *Berwick 32 47 79*

FINAL
First leg, October 14:
RYE HOUSE 54 (Karl Fiala 10, Kelvin Mullarkey 10, Bob Garrad 10, Ashley Pullen 9, Ted Hubbard 8, Peter Tarrant 6, Simon Aindow 1) *Berwick 24* (Wayne Brown 8, Nigel Close 6, Mike Fullerton 3, Graham Jones 3, Roger Wright 2, Phil Kynman 2, Rob Grant 0).
Second leg, October 27:
Berwick 40 (Wright 10, Brown 10, Close 8, Mike Caroline 4, Grant 4, Jones 4, Kynman 0)RYE HOUSE 38 (Fiala 11, Garrad 7, Mullarkey 7, Hubbard 5, Pullen 5, Tarrant 3, Aindow 0).
†The original first leg staging, scheduled for October 123, was postponed because of rain.

❑ RYE HOUSE win 92-64 on aggregate.

1979 ALL THE RESULTS

	BERWICK	BOSTON	CANTERBURY	CRAYFORD	EDINBURGH	ELLESMERE PORT	GLASGOW	MIDDLESBRO'	MILDENHALL	MILTON KEYNES	NEWCASTLE	NOTTINGHAM	OXFORD	PETERBORO'	RYE HOUSE	SCUNTHORPE	STOKE	WEYMOUTH	WORKINGTON
BERWICK		52-25	57-21	45-33	55-23	44-34	40-38	52-26	45-33	50-28	46-32	54-24	60-18	53-25	39-39	57-21	48-30	57-20	56-22
BOSTON	36-42		39-39	59-19	51-26	31-46	43-35	33-45	50-28	53-25	38-40	37-41	42-36	44-34	39-38	48-30	42-35	45-33	46-32
CANTERBURY	34-44	45-33		43-35	55-23	46-32	49-29	45-33	42-36	42-36	47-31	53-25	38-39	39-39	35-43	63-15	43-35	43-35	59-19
CRAYFORD	42-36	53-25	41-37		40-38	45-33	49-29	40-37	30-47	40-38	33-45	48-29	34-44	46-31	31-47	60-18	47-31	40-38	45-33
EDINBURGH	40.5 37.5	49-28	48-30	41-37		46-31	41-37	40-38	29-49	35-43	36-41	47-31	36-42	35-43	33-45	59-19	38-40	46-32	48-30
ELLESMERE PORT	39-39	45-33	46-32	43-35	51-26		49-29	48-30	36-42	45-33	43-35	40-38	45-32	56-22	38-40	60-16	56-22	56-22	49-29
GLASGOW	45-33	52-25	52-26	46-30	51-27	51-27		62-16	47-31	41-37	43-35	52-26	41-37	44-33	45-32	51-27	50-27	51-27	53-25
MIDDLESBROUGH	42-36	41-37	40-38	38-40	33-44	43-35	50-27		34-43	48-30	44-34	46-32	45-33	43-35	34-44	42-36	56-22	42-36	47-31
MILDENHALL	59-18	48-30	46-32	60-18	49-29	50-28	55-23	55-23		50-27	54-24	55-23	52-26	42-35	43-34	60-18	49-29	52-26	56-22
MILTON KEYNES	52-26	47-31	46-32	46-32	45-32	49-29	54-24	46-32	36-41		35-42	46-31	38-39	41-37	41-36	51-26	43-35	43-35	39-38
NEWCASTLE	41-37	54-24	51-26	54-24	57-21	41-37	45-33	43-35	37-41	38-40		38-40	37-41	55-23	36-42	59-18	50-28	46-31	40-38
NOTTINGHAM	39-39	45-33	35-43	45-33	47-31	48-30	52-26	49-28	36.5 41.5	37-41	40-38		33-45	44-34	36-42	46-32	48-30	43-35	51-27
OXFORD	49-29	53-24	46-32	48-30	54-23	53-24	52-26	52-26	40-37	38-40	41-37	43-34		50-28	37-41	57-21	58-20	58-20	57-21
PETERBOROUGH	45-33	39-39	49-29	51-27	55-23	46-32	46-32	46-32	35-43	43-35	37-41	41-37	41-36		41-37	57-21	49-29	52-26	46-32
RYE HOUSE	49-27	60-18	53-25	60-18	55-22	61-17	54-24	57-21	46-32	40-38	51-27	47-31	45-33	45-33		59-18	58-20	60-18	47-31
SCUNTHORPE	38-39	36-40	37-40	37-41	39-39	38-40	36-42	36-42	32-45	37-41	37-40	41-37	31-45	41-36	25-53		32-42	44-34	41-37
STOKE	40-38	41-37	49-29	42-36	42-36	40-38	42-36	39-39	32-45	38-40	33-44	44-34	38-40	36-42	47-31	58-19		52-26	50-28
WEYMOUTH	37-41	53-25	37-41	42-36	66-21	37-41	41-36	38-40	29-49	40-38	41-37	46-32	39-39	36-42	26-52	46-32	33.5 44.5		41-37
WORKINGTON	42-36	44-34	50-28	43-35	36-42	42-36	49-29	43-34	38-40	45-33	43-35	46-32	42-36	47-31	37-41	54-23	39-39	47-31	

1980 NATIONAL LEAGUE

	P	W	D	L	PtsF	PtsA	W	D	L	PtsF	PtsA	Pts
1 RYE HOUSE	**38**	**19**	**0**	**0**	**986**	**490**	**12**	**0**	**7**	**749**	**729**	**62**
2 Newcastle	38	18	0	1	932	548	12	1	6	782	690	61
3 Middlesbrough	38	18	0	1	914.5	561.5	9	2	8	751	727	56
4 Berwick	38	18	0	1	948	526	6	1	12	690.5	780.5	49
5 Boston	38	16	1	2	883	595	7	1	11	722	753	48
6 Edinburgh	38	17	1	1	850	627	6	1	12	649	830	48
7 Mildenhall	38	15	1	3	853.5	626.5	6	1	12	690	789	44
8 Peterborough	38	15	0	4	848	633	6	0	13	619	861	42
9 Crayford	37	15	0	3	841	556	5	1	13	701	778	41
10 Ellesmere Port	38	17	0	2	901	580	3	1	15	660	816	41
11 Glasgow	38	17	1	1	906	572	2	1	16	632	844	40
12 Exeter	38	15	0	4	882	597	2	1	16	571	908	35
13 Scunthorpe	38	12	0	7	781	697	3	1	15	582	875	31
14 Nottingham	38	12	1	6	798	682	2	1	16	617	863	30
15 Oxford	38	11	1	7	766	708	3	0	16	573	900	29
16 Stoke	38	11	0	8	749	724	3	0	16	585	891	28
17 Weymouth	37	11	1	7	786	670	2	0	16	586.5	813.5	27
18 Canterbury	38	8	4	7	768	707	2	0	17	629	848	24
19 Milton Keynes	38	8	2	9	737	740	0	0	19	553	928	18
20 Workington	38	2	0	17	600	871	0	0	19	369	1106	4

1980 National League Riders' Championship Final

Saturday, September 27, Wimbledon:
1 Wayne Brown 14, 2 Martin Yeates 12, 3 Steve Finch 12, 4 Gary Guglielmi 10, 5 Paul Woods 10, 6 Mike Sampson 10, 7 Mike Ferreira 10, 8 Robert Maxfield 8, 9 Rod Hunter 6, 10 Kelvin Mullarkey 6, 11 Steve Wilcock 5, 12 Andy Hines 5, 13 Phil White 5, 14 Ray Bales 4, 15 Derek Harrison 2. *Track Reserves:* Graham Knowler 1, Keith Yorke 0. *Sponsors:* Toshiba.

1980 KNOCK OUT CUP

Round 1

Newcastle 41 26 67 BERWICK 37 52 89
Mildenhall 45 34 79 Rye House 33 44 77
Boston 54 51 105 Stoke 24 27 51

Round 2

BERWICK 46 36 82 Ellesmere Port 32 42 74
Edinburgh 42 37 79 Glasgow 34 40 74
Canterbury 44 38 82 Milton Keynes 33 40 73
Mildenhall 46 41 87 Long Eaton 32 37 69
Boston 59 52 111 Workington 19 26 45
Peterborough 42 37 79 Crayford 25 41 66
Oxford 40 38 78 Weymouth 37 40 77
Middlesbrough 51 40 91 Scunthorpe 27 37 64

Round 3

Edinburgh 39 31 70 BERWICK 39 47 86
Mildenhall 51 34 85 Canterbury 27 44 71
Boston 50 39 89 Peterborough 27 39 66
Middlesbrough 45 46 91 Oxford 33 32 65

Semi Finals

BERWICK 52 37 89 Mildenhall 26 41 67
Middlesbrough 54 36 90 Boston 24 42 66

FINAL

First leg, October 26:
Middlesbrough 42 (Brian Havelock 10, Mike Spink 10, Steve Wilcock 9, Mark Courtney 6, Geoff Pusey 4, Martin Dixon 3, John Clegg 0) BERWICK 36 (Mike Fullerton 11, Steve McDermott 9, Brett Saunders 6, Mike Caroline 5, Rob Grant 3, Nigel Close 2, Paul Henderson, number 8, did not ride).

Second leg, October 29:
† BERWICK 43 (McDermott 15, Fullerton 9, Close 8, Grant 8, Saunders 3, Caroline 0, Paul Henderson, number 8, did not ride) *Middlesbrough 34* (Courtney 11, Wilcock 9, Dixon 6, Pusey 6, Spink 2, Alan Armstrong 0, Clegg 0).
The original staging of the first leg, scheduled for October 24 was rained off. †Berwick raced the home leg of the Final at Newcastle.

❑ BERWICK win 79-76 on aggregate.

1980 ALL THE RESULTS

	BERWICK	BOSTON	CANTERBURY	CRAYFORD	EDINBURGH	ELLESMERE PORT	EXETER	GLASGOW	MIDDLESBRO'	MILDENHALL	MILTON KEYNES	NEWCASTLE	NOTTINGHAM	OXFORD	PETERBORO'	RYE HOUSE	SCUNTHORPE	STOKE	WEYMOUTH	WORKINGTON
BERWICK		33-45	47-31	51-27	51-27	52-26	56-22	40-37	47-31	52-26	56-22	39-36	45-33	62-16	49-29	47-30	54-24	54-23	54-23	59-18
BOSTON	58-20		52-26	50-28	46-32	39-39	40-37	52-26	38-40	45-33	56-22	33-44	51-27	52-26	41-37	41-37	44-33	41-37	44-34	60-17
CANTERBURY	37-39	39-39		34-44	40-38	48-29	37-41	45-32	39-39	36-41	48-30	39-39	36-42	46-31	42-36	36-42	39-39	47-31	36-41	44-34
CRAYFORD	41-34	41-37	55-22		38-39	54-24	58-20	40-38	41-37	41-37	45-33	37-41	46-32	43-35	59-19	35-43	50-28	52-25	Not raced	65-12
EDINBURGH	39-39	41-37	41-36	40-38		45-33	47-30	50-28	43-35	45-33	43-35	32-45	52-26	51-26	42-36	45-33	42-36	50-27	41-37	61-17
ELLESMERE PORT	52-26	38-40	38-40	43-35	50-28		53-25	46-32	41-37	42-36	52-26	41-37	50-28	44-33	53-25	42-36	55-23	50-28	49-29	62-16
EXETER	37-41	43-35	54-24	43-34	51-27	42-35		48-30	34-43	44-34	52-26	38-40	51-27	53-25	51-27	36-42	63-15	44-34	40-38	58-20
GLASGOW	40-37	43-34	41-37	39-39	48-30	47-31	54-24		51-27	46-32	54-24	40-38	47-31	37-40	52-26	57-21	57-21	42-36	49-28	62-16
MIDDLESBROUGH	42.5 34.5	58-18	47-31	42-36	49-28	40-38	52-26	44-34		47-31	43-35	48-29	50-28	44-34	55-23	38-40	44-33	63-15	51-27	57-21
MILDENHALL	41-37	42-36	40-38	41-37	45-33	43-34	46-32	49-29	39-39		46-32	33-45	40-38	52-25	38-40	38-40	50-28	53-25	55.5 22.5	62-16
MILTON KEYNES	38-40	28-49	40-38	38-40	35-43	40-38	39-39	39-39	31-47	48-29		30-47	41-37	45-33	36-42	26-52	33-44	43-35	50-28	57-20
NEWCASTLE	42-36	47-31	42-36	47-31	48-30	45-33	48-30	53-25	38-40	53-25	56-22		49-29	60-17	48-29	49-29	53-25	54-24	41-37	59-19
NOTTINGHAM	42-36	33-45	48-30	36-42	36-42	33-45	43-34	44-34	36-42	39-39	44-34	43-35		46-32	54-24	40-38	44-34	35-42	43-35	59-19
OXFORD	45-33	36-41	39-38	40-38	39-39	50-28	49-29	45-32	34-44	28-49	51-27	32-45	43-34		31-47	34-43	43-35	37-40	40-38	50-28
PETERBOROUGH	44-34	41-37	48-30	44-34	52-26	38-40	45-33	43-35	42-36	38-40	47-30	37-41	48-30	53-25		37-41	42-36	40-38	49-29	60-18
RYE HOUSE	50-28	47-29	56-22	40-38	52-26	48-30	58-20	59-19	43-35	47-31	57-21	45-32	52-26	50-27	56-22		53-25	56-22	54-24	63-13
SCUNTHORPE	34-44	42-36	46-32	35-43	35-42	46-32	50-28	44-34	42-36	29-49	44-34	35-43	42-36	37-40	45-33	34-44		46-31	43-35	52-25
STOKE	29-48	41-37	35-43	39-38	35-43	40-38	50-28	39-36	29-49	42-36	49-29	37-40	43-34	43-34	38-39	27-51	38-40		41-37	54-24
WEYMOUTH	41-37	37-41	39-38	41-36	50-28	40-38	48-30	38-40	32-45	37-41	45-33	31-47	39-39	47-31	37-41	36-41	38-18	48-30		62-16
WORKINGTON	28-47	23-55	40-37	35-43	30-48	26-49	35-43	26-52	27-49	30-48	40-38	20-58	38-40	35-43	34-44	31-46	33-45	36-42	33-44	

1981 NATIONAL LEAGUE

	P	W	D	L	PtsF	PtsA	W	D	L	PtsF	PtsA	Pts
1 MIDDLESBROUGH	**36**	**18**	**0**	**0**	**922**	**479**	**12**	**1**	**5**	**770**	**630**	**61**
2 Weymouth	36	17	1	0	879	525	9	0	9	691	711	53
3 Newcastle	36	17	1	0	890	511	8	0	10	676.5	721.5	51
4 Edinburgh	36	16	0	2	850.5	531.5	9	0	9	685	715	50
5 Glasgow	36	18	0	0	870.5	525.5	6	0	12	630	769	48
6 Boston	36	18	0	0	878	525	4	0	14	625.5	776.5	44
7 Exeter	36	18	0	0	893	508	4	0	14	604	797	44
8 Mildenhall	36	14	0	4	809.5	591.5	6	0	12	608	792	40
9 Peterborough	36	17	0	1	852	549	2	1	15	581	819	39
10 Crayford	36	16	0	2	820.5	577.5	3	0	15	541	855	38
11 Ellesmere Port	36	14	1	3	869	531	4	0	14	577	823	37
12 Oxford	36	13	0	5	760	639	5	1	12	632	768	37
13 Wolverhampton	36	10	0	8	752	646	4	1	13	593	806	29
14 Canterbury	36	10	0	8	723	678	4	1	13	617	782	29
15 Stoke	36	9	0	9	728	670	5	0	13	615	782	28
16 Rye House	36	10	0	8	773	625	1	0	17	555	847	22
17 Scunthorpe	36	5	1	12	647	754	1	0	17	467	928	13
18 Workington	36	6	1	11	670	728	0	0	18	377	1024	13
19 Milton Keynes	36	3	0	15	659	741	1	0	17	490	900	8

■ *Berwick withdrew from the League on September 6, 1981, after the Speedway Control Board upheld a protest from Edinburgh promoter Mike Parker when they attempted to complete their fixtures at Glasgow. Their record was expunged from the League table as above but, at the time, their own League record was:*

Berwick	*26*	*6*	*0*	*2*	*366*	*257*	*2*	*0*	*16*	*632*	*769*	*16*

1981 KNOCK OUT CUP

Round 1

Mildenhall 58 44 102 Canterbury 38 52 90
Ellesmere Port 47 53 100 Wolverhampton 49 43 92
Middlesbrough 69 40 109 Glasgow 27 55 82
Milton Keynes 38 45 83 Stoke 58 51 109

Round 2

EDINBURGH 65 40 105 Exeter 31 56 87
Scunthorpe 46 34 80 Oxford 49 59 108
Ellesmere Port 30 20 50 Mildenhall 64 76 140
Peterborough 70 64 134 Rye House 26 32 58
Stoke 48 41 89 Middlesbrough 48 55 103
Crayford 42 27 69 Boston 51 69 120
Workington 31 20 51 Weymouth 59 74 133
†Berwick 53 44 97 Newcastle 42 52 94

Round 3

Oxford 41 31 72 EDINBURGH 54 65 119
Peterborough 49 35 84 Mildenhall 47 61 108
Boston 57 51 108 Middlesbrough 39 45 84
Weymouth 48 45 93 *†Berwick 48 51 99*

Semi Finals

EDINBURGH 64 50 114 Mildenhall 32 46 78
Boston 58.5 32 90.5 *†Berwick 37.5 64 101.5*

FINAL

First leg, October 21
Berwick 49 (Steve McDermott 13, Wayne Brown 11, Mike Caroline 9, Rob Grant 6, Brett Saunders 5, Brian Collins 3, Jim Beaton 2) EDINBURGH 46 (Dave Trownson 10, Ivan Blacka 9, Neil Collins 9, Chris Turner 8, George Hunter 7, Guy Robson 3, Ian Westwell 0)
Second leg, November 6:
EDINBURGH 55 (Hunter 13, Trownson 11, Blacka 11, Collins 7, Turner 7, Roger Lambert 6, Westwell 0) *Berwick 40* (Charlie McKinna 14, McDermott 9, Caroline 7, Grant 5, Saunders 3, Collins 2, Beaton 0)

❑ EDINBURGH win 101-89 on aggregate.

† Berwick raced all their HOME meetings on neutral tracks. Round 2 v Newcastle at Barrow; Round 3 v Weymouth at Workington; semi final v Boston at Glasgow; Final v Edinburgh at Newcastle.

1981 ALL THE RESULTS

	BOSTON	CANTERBURY	CRAYFORD	EDINBURGH	ELLESMERE PORT	EXETER	GLASGOW	MIDDLESBRO'	MILDENHALL	MILTON KEYNES	NEWCASTLE	OXFORD	PETERBORO'	RYE HOUSE	SCUNTHORPE	STOKE	WEYMOUTH	WOLVES	WORKINGTON	BERWICK
BOSTON		47-30	57-21	47-31	51-27	48-30	53-25	40-38	50-28	53-25	43-35	51-27	42-36	47-31	52-26	51-27	51-27	40-38	55-23	*45-33*
CANTERBURY	36-42		40-38	39-38	35-43	43-35	41-37	31-46	35-43	43-35	34-44	41-37	44-34	45-33	53-25	36-42	35-43	32-45	60-18	*38-40*
CRAYFORD	44-34	47-31		37-40	47-30	54-24	40-38	25-52	50-28	44-34	39-38	42-36	43-35	55-23	60-18	39-38	40-37	51.5 26.5	63-15	*42-36*
EDINBURGH	50.5 27.5	41-35	47-30		49-29	47-31	48-29	37-41	58-20	53-13	36-42	42-36	51-27	50-27	43-30	41-37	46-32	49-29	62-16	*42-36*
ELLESMERE PORT	40-38	48-30	56-22	45-33		51-26	37-41	30-48	55-23	60-18	50-28	39-39	43-34	51-27	57-21	52-26	37-41	55-22	63-14	*44-34*
EXETER	44-34	48-30	62-16	45-33	43-35		47-31	49-29	47-31	58-20	44-34	51-27	53-25	57-21	59-19	40-35	43-35	51-27	52-26	*47-31*
GLASGOW	44-34	46-32	58-20	52-25	58-20	50-28		40-38	41-34	47-31	41-35	41-37	47-30	46-32	55-23	55-22	40-38	54.5 23.5	55-23	*46-32*
MIDDLESBROUGH	57-21	55-23	51-27	51-27	55-22	45-33	48-29		42-36	58-19	43-35	54-24	55-23	44-34	59-19	41-37	46-32	55-23	63-15	*48-30*
MILDENHALL	38-40	41-37	50-28	34-44	44-34	46-32	53-25	38-40		45-33	38.5 39.5	40-38	48-28	41-37	47-31	48-30	53-25	57-20	48-30	*42-36*
MILTON KEYNES	38-40	41-37	35-43	34-44	37-41	38-40	38-40	32-46	34-44		36-42	37-41	33-45	40-38	34-41	37-40	27-51	36-42	52-26	*43-35*
NEWCASTLE	45-32	44-34	55-23	44-34	58-20	50-27	51-27	39-39	60-18	53-24		49-29	50-28	52-26	54-24	47-31	44-34	42-36	53-25	*45-32*
OXFORD	42-36	37-40	44-34	43-35	46-30	41-37	42-36	33-45	35-43	49-29	36-42		42-36	43-35	43-35	44-34	34-43	44-34	62-15	*44-34*
PETERBOROUGH	52-26	44-33	54-24	34-44	44-34	43-35	48-30	48-29	44-34	56-22	43-35	52-26		42-36	47-31	54-24	45-33	44-33	58-20	*40-38*
RYE HOUSE	42-35	48-30	43-35	33-44	45-33	34-44	31-46	37-41	38-39	51-27	45-33	37-41	59-19		55-22	41-36	34-44	37-41	63-15	*42-36*
SCUNTHORPE	24-54	38-40	36-42	35-43	42-36	35-43	44-34	31-47	40-38	49-29	38-40	34-43	39-39	28-49		31-47	26-52	33-45	44-33	
STOKE	43-35	38-40	35-39	38-40	37-41	40-37	37-41	23-54	28-50	48-30	40-38	41-37	37-41	48-30	56-22		37-41	45-33	57-21	*42-36*
WEYMOUTH	49-29	44-34	43-35	40-38	52-26	50-28	51-27	45-33	54-24	56-22	48-30	44-34	47-31	54-24	47-31	53-25		39-39	63-15	*42-36*
WOLVERHAMPTON	42-36	36-42	48-29	35-43	44-34	46-32	32-45	28-50	48-30	41-37	31-46	36-39	44-34	55-23	60-18	38-40	37-41		51-27	*45-32*
WORKINGTON	46-32	39-39	41-36	29-49	36-42	36-42	28-49	24-54	33-45	36-42	36-40	37-41	42-36	49-29	47-31	34-44	36-42	41-36		*32-45*
BERWICK			*B44-34*			*B44-34*				*G46-32*	*G37-41*		*G46-31*	*B55-23*	*B57-21*		*B37-41*			

Berwick rode all their home matches on neutral tracks: B - Barrow; G - Glasgow Blantyre.

1982 NATIONAL LEAGUE

	P	W	D	L	PtsF	PtsA	W	D	L	PtsF	PtsA	Pts
1 NEWCASTLE	**36**	**18**	**0**	**0**	**1165**	**562**	**12**	**0**	**6**	**941**	**783**	**60**
2 Mildenhall	36	18	0	0	1130	596	8	1	9	837	891	53
3 Ellesmere Port	36	17	0	1	1069	659	8	0	10	779	947	50
4 Middlesbrough	36	17	0	1	1053	670	7	1	10	787	935	49
5 Weymouth	36	17	0	1	1030	697	5	1	12	791	934	45
6 Rye House	36	18	0	0	1037	682	4	0	14	726	953	44
7 Long Eaton	36	15	0	3	1039	688	5	1	12	785.5	938.5	41
8 Boston	36	16	0	2	1005	719	3	1	14	771	955	39
9 Berwick	36	15	0	3	1048	674	3	1	14	736	988	37
10 Exeter	36	16	0	2	1006.5	676.5	1	0	17	668	1054	34
11 Glasgow	36	16	0	2	954	762	0	0	18	638	1086	32
12 Milton Keynes	36	12	0	6	906	815	2	1	15	692	1028	29
13 Peterborough	36	13	1	4	948	777	0	1	17	735	991	28
14 Edinburgh	36	11	0	7	897	814	3	0	15	734	986	28
15 Crayford	36	12	0	6	974	744	1	0	17	651	1070	26
16 Canterbury	36	10	1	7	883	841	2	0	16	728	992	25
17 Scunthorpe	36	9	2	7	884	843	2	0	16	681	1036	24
18 Stoke	36	10	1	7	853	870	1	0	17	657	1067	23
19 Oxford	36	5	3	10	837	886	2	0	16	638	1084	17

1982 National League Riders' Championship Final

Saturday, August 28, Wimbledon
1 Joe Owen 14, 2 Steve Lomas 12, 3 Bob Garrad 11, 4 Andy Hines 10, 5 Keith White 9, 6 Derek Harrison 9, 7 Steve Lawson 8, 8 Andy Campbell 8, 9 Dave Trownson 7, 10 Alan Molyneux 6, 11 Martin Yeates 5, 12 Barry Thomas 5, 13 Steve Wilcock 5, 14 Barney Kennett 5, 15 John Jackson 4, 16 Steve McDermott 2.
Sponsors: Daily Mirror.

1982 KNOCK OUT CUP

Round 1
Stoke 42 37 79 Boston 54 59 113
Canterbury 54 36 90 Weymouth 42 60 102
Oxford 54 49 103 Milton Keynes 42 47 89
Glasgow did not compete.

Round 2
Middlesbrough 53 41 94 NEWCASTLE 43 55 98
Exeter 60 34 94 Weymouth 36 62 98
Peterborough 58 45 103 Scunthorpe 38 51 89
Ellesmere Port 60 43 103 Edinburgh 36 53 89
Berwick 67 29 96 Long Eaton 29 67 96
Rye House 35 62 97 Crayford 25 33 58
Mildenhall 62 56 118 Oxford 34 39 73
Boston - bye.

Round 2 Replay
Berwick 67 34 101 Long Eaton 29 62 91

Round 3
Boston 47 34 81 NEWCASTLE 49 62 111
Peterborough 48 43 91 Weymouth 48 53 101
Ellesmere Port 69 32 101 Berwick 26 64 90
Mildenhall 56 35 91 Rye House 39 60 99

Semi Finals
NEWCASTLE 63 61 124 Weymouth 32 35 67
Ellesmere Port 71 37 108 Rye House 25 59 84

FINAL
First leg, October 10:
Ellesmere Port 51 (John Jackson 13, Steve Finch 12, Eric Monaghan 11, Phil Alderman 6, Robert Maxfield 4, Billy Burton 4, Glenn Parrott 1)
NEWCASTLE 45 (Joe Owen 15, Rod Hunter 14, Bobby Beaton 8, Tom Owen 5, Keith Bloxsome 2, Alan Emerson 1, Robbie Foy 0).
Second leg, October 11:
NEWCASTLE 73 (J. Owen 15, Hunter 14, Emersion 12, T. Owen 11, Bloxsome 11, Beaton 10, Foy 0)
Ellesmere Port 23 (Monaghan 7, Finch 5, Jackson 3, Alderman 3, Parrott 2, Burton 2, Maxfield 1).

❑ NEWCASTLE win 118-74 on aggregate.

1982 ALL THE RESULTS

	BERWICK	BOSTON	CANTERBURY	CRAYFORD	EDINBURGH	ELLESMERE PORT	EXETER	GLASGOW	LONG EATON	MIDDLESBRO'	MILDENHALL	MILTON KEYNES	NEWCASTLE	OXFORD	PETERBORO'	RYE HOUSE	SCUNTHORPE	STOKE	WEYMOUTH
BERWICK		55-41	64-32	55-40	63-33	43-53	65-31	54-42	73-23	42-53	67-29	55-40	50-45	72-24	61-35	64-31	63-33	55-40	47-49
BOSTON	53-40		57-39	66-30	59-37	47-49	64-32	57-39	47-48	49-47	49-47	62-34	50-46	66-30	50-46	50-46	60-36	●61-35	58-38
CANTERBURY	41-55	62-34		52-43	44-52	47-49	53-43	62-34	52-44	48-48	45-51	†49-45	38-58	36-60	49-47	53-43	57-39	53-43	42-53
CRAYFORD	55-41	49-46	45-51		53-43	69-26	49-47	56-38	46-50	41-54	46-50	76-20	43-52	*65-29	51-44	47-49	55-41	70-26	58-37
EDINBURGH	43-53	44-52	52-41	50-45		54-42	53-41	51-44	47-49	52-44	34-62	46-50	51-45	73-23	53-42	44-51	41-47	57-39	52-44
ELLESMERE PORT	61-35	60-36	56-40	68-28	57-39		57-39	70-26	58-38	67-29	46-50	58-38	51-45	60-36	55-41	59-37	71-25	57-39	58-38
EXETER	55-41	57-39	57-39	66-30	59-37	58-38		73-23	52.5 43.5	52-44	45-51	58-38	45-50	67-28	64-32	34-19	51-45	61-35	52-44
GLASGOW	53-43	53-43	60-36	46-49	51-44	50-46	52-43		63-32	55-40	52-44	50-42	38-58	50-45	50-46	54-41	62-34	64-31	51-45
LONG EATON	60-36	47-49	52-44	59-37	60-36	58-38	61-35	63-33		63-33	52-44	60-36	40-56	70-26	61-35	47-49	68-28	57-38	61-35
MIDDLESBROUGH	62-34	56-39	56-39	56-40	58-35	56-40	70-26	59-37	51-45		55-41	71-25	44-52	67-29	60-36	57-39	64-32	54-42	57-39
MILDENHALL	72-24	53-43	±57-38	72-24	66-30	55-41	74-22	68-28	60-36	60-35		60-36	49-47	63-33	62-34	61-35	62-34	75-21	61-35
MILTON KEYNES	53-42	55-41	39-57	62-34	43-53	47-48	50-45	56-40	51-45	44-52	47-49		42-53	58-37	50-46	52-43	49-46	59-37	49-47
NEWCASTLE	60-36	63-33	71-25	72-24	59-37	70-26	61-35	69-27	55-41	66-30	61-35	63-33		74-22	72-24	67-28	64-32	52-44	66-30
OXFORD	50-46	39-57	49-46	$50-45	47-48	45-51	47-48	53-43	48-48	47-49	43-53	48-48	32-64		48-48	47-49	44-51	55-41	45-51
PETERBOROUGH	56-40	53-43	54-42	64-32	50-44	47-49	55-41	64-32	51-45	46-50	48-48	62-34	41-55	56-40		54-42	60-36	53-42	34-62
RYE HOUSE	64-32	59-37	55-40	64-31	57-38	56-40	61-34	63-33	52-43	53-41	49-47	54-41	49-47	64-32	52-44		58-38	73-23	54-41
SCUNTHORPE	48-48	48-48	58-37	57-39	49-47	44-52	59-37	63-33	39-57	43-53	50-46	47-49	40-56	50-46	50-46	51-45		47-49	41-55
STOKE	43-53	49-47	49-47	§50-45	54-42	45-51	61-35	49-47	37-58	46-50	44-52	54-42	35-61	31-64	50-46	53-42	55-40		48-48
WEYMOUTH	59-37	53-43	61-35	61-35	57-39	56-40	62-34	56-39	56-40	61-35	58-38	55-41	45-51	62-34	53-43	59-37	52-44	64-32	

†Amended: original score 52-43. ±Amended: original score 56-39. Jamie Luckhurst ineligible for both meetings. *Amended: original score 62-34. $ Amended: original score 58-38. Graham Drury ineligible for both meetings. §Amended: original score 55-41.● Amended: original score 57-39. Mark Collins ineligible for both meetings.

1983 NATIONAL LEAGUE

	P	W	D	L	PtsF	PtsA	W	D	L	PtsF	PtsA	Pts
1 NEWCASTLE	**34**	**17**	**0**	**0**	**976**	**651**	**8**	**1**	**8**	**820**	**811**	**51**
2 Mildenhall	34	17	0	0	942	672	6	2	9	786	844	48
3 Crayford	34	17	0	0	1043	585	6	0	11	768.5	858.5	46
4 Weymouth	34	14	2	1	940	688	5	0	12	771	858	40
5 Scunthorpe	34	17	0	0	935.5	685.5	2	2	13	733	895	40
6 Milton Keynes	34	15	0	2	931.5	697.5	4	1	12	720.5	906.5	39
7 Middlesbrough	34	15	2	0	935	694	3	1	13	717	913	39
8 Berwick	34	16	0	1	935	696	1	0	16	710	919	34
9 Edinburgh	34	14	1	2	948	680	2	0	15	666	957	33
10 Exeter	34	15	0	2	998	630	1	0	16	661.5	969.5	32
11 Rye House	34	14	1	2	934	689	1	0	16	709	916	31
12 Peterborough	34	14	1	2	945	686	0	1	16	640	990	30
13 Glasgow	34	14	0	3	943	684	0	1	16	700	925	29
14 Oxford	34	13	0	4	851	781	1	1	15	678	949	29
15 Canterbury	34	12	1	4	886	740	0	1	16	668	959	26
16 Boston	34	12	1	4	848.5	782.5	0	0	17	585	1044	25
17 Stoke	34	10	1	6	879	751	0	0	17	611	1016	21
18 Long Eaton	34	9	1	7	835	794	0	0	17	642	975	19

NEWCASTLE became the first club to win the Second Division Championship for a third time having previous title success in 1976 and 1982.

1983 National League Riders' Championship Final

Saturday, September 24, Wimbledon
1 Steve McDermott 13, 2 Richard Knight 13, 3 Martin Yeates 12, 4 Marvyn Cox 11, 5 Steve Wilcock 10, 6 Dave Perks 8, 7 Joe Owen 7, 8 Keith Millard 7, 9 Dave Trownson 7, 10 Nigel Crabtree 7, 11 Barney Kennett 6, 12 Jim McMillan 5, 13 Tom Owen 4, 14 Barry Thomas 4, 15 Keith White 3, 16 Nigel Sparshott 1.
Sponsors: F.S.O. Cars.

1983 KNOCK OUT CUP

Round 1

Milton Keynes 47 45 92 Oxford 49 51 100
Mildenhall 55 50 105 Crayford 41 46 87

Round 2

EXETER 70 51 121 Canterbury 26 45 71
Weymouth 58 51 109 Boston 38 45 83
Mildenhall 58 39 97 Peterborough 38 57 95
Scunthorpe 43 35 78 Newcastle 53 61 114
Rye House 51 51 102 Oxford 45 45 90
Stoke 55 34 89 Glasgow 41 62 103
Berwick 61 38 99 Long Eaton 35 58 93
Middlesbrough 55 46 101 Edinburgh 41 50 91

Round 3

Rye House 55 32 87 EXETER 41 64 105
Newcastle 53 50 103 Berwick 42 45 87
Middlesbrough 47 29 76 Mildenhall 49 67 116
Glasgow 41 31 72 *Weymouth 54 65 119*

Semi Finals

EXETER 74 30 104 Mildenhall 21 66 87
Weymouth 55 42 97 Newcastle 41 54 95

FINAL

First leg, October 10:
EXETER 52 (Kevin Price 10, Keith Millard 9, Robert Maxfield 9, Steve Bishop 8, Rob Ashton 7, Bob Coles 6, Alun Rossiter 3) *Weymouth 43* (Martin Yeates 13, Steve Schofield 10, Stan Bear 9, Simon Cross 9, Gordon Humphreys 1, Chris Martin 1, David Biles 0).
Second leg, October 11:
Weymouth 52 (Schofield 15, Yeates 12, Cross 11, Bear 6, Humphreys 3, Biles 3, Martin 2) EXETER 44 (Rossiter 10, Ashton 10, Millard 9, Coles 7, Maxfield 5, Price 2, Bishop 1).

❑ EXETER win 96-95 on aggregate.

1983 ALL THE RESULTS

	BERWICK	BOSTON	CANTERBURY	CRAYFORD	EDINBURGH	EXETER	GLASGOW	LONG EATON	MIDDLESBRO'	MILDENHALL	MILTON KEYNES	NEWCASTLE	OXFORD	PETERBORO'	RYE HOUSE	SCUNTHORPE	STOKE	WEYMOUTH
BERWICK		55-41	55-41	44-52	62-34	51-45	55-41	53-43	51-45	57-39	61-34	50-46	65-31	60-36	57-39	52-44	54-42	53-43
BOSTON	50-46		59-37	61-35	54-42	59.5 36.5	50-46	50-46	50-46	48-48	36-60	44-52	46-50	49-47	50-45	44-52	49-47	49-47
CANTERBURY	50-46	56-40		47-48	55-41	46-50	59-37	51-45	56-40	43-53	45-51	49-47	49-44	55-41	58-37	48-48	67-29	52-43
CRAYFORD	58-38	75-21	61-34		59-37	62-34	59-36	71-25	60-36	60-36	64-32	58-38	61-35	66-30	50-44	52-44	73-23	54-42
EDINBURGH	57-38	74-22	57-39	46-50		61-35	48-48	50-46	66-30	49-47	49-47	34-62	72-23	59-37	53-43	59-36	64-31	50-46
EXETER	46-49	68-28	70-25	56-39	53-43		54-42	67-29	64-32	45-51	50-46	54-42	64-31	74-22	55-41	55-41	62-34	61-35
GLASGOW	49-47	64-32	57-37	47-49	67-29	55-41		68-28	46-50	50-46	61-35	50-45	51-45	49-45	59-37	65-31	59-37	46-50
LONG EATON	51-45	54-42	68-28	39-57	42-54	49-47	53-42		53-42	42-54	37-59	46-50	48-48	57-39	47-49	54-41	54-42	41-55
MIDDLESBROUGH	64-32	63-33	48-48	50-46	54-41	56-40	55-40	51-45		63-33	48-48	51-45	56-40	60-36	56-40	52-44	56-39	52-44
MILDENHALL	53-42	59-37	53-43	62-34	59-37	60-36	54-42	†58-25	53-43		51-44	49-47	53-43	58-38	55-40	55-40	59-37	51-44
MILTON KEYNES	61-35	60-35	50-46	53.5 42.5	55-41	58-38	52-44	63-33	59-37	47-49		43-53	57-39	55-41	51-44	52-43	66-30	49-47
NEWCASTLE	57-39	61-33	49-47	54-41	66-30	63-33	62-34	56-40	57-39	49-46	64-32		63-33	60-36	50-45	55-41	54-42	56-40
OXFORD	53-43	49-47	53-43	53-43	41-55	52-44	49-47	53-43	51-45	46-50	56-40	47-49		50-46	49-47	51-45	55-41	43-53
PETERBOROUGH	61-35	60-36	5343	51-45	56-39	67-29	63-33	49-47	48-48	51-45	64-32	47-49	51-45		60-36	52-44	65-31	47-49
RYE HOUSE	52-44	58-38	59-37	49-46	54-42	60-35	58-36	62-34	47-49	51-45	59-36	45-51	54-42	64-32		48-48	59-34	55-40
SCUNTHORPE	55-41	56-40	56-39	49-47	68-21	56-40	51-44	59-36	49-47	50-45	58.5 37.5	49-47	50-46	61-35	56-40		58-38	54-42
STOKE	49-47	68-28	60-36	46-50	63-33	53-43	55-41	48-47	42-53	45-51	59-37	±47-49	55-41	48-48	50-46	46-50		45-51
WEYMOUTH	53-43	64-32	51-45	51-44	49-47	61-35	48-47	66-30	61-35	48-48	44-50	48-48	54-42	65-31	60-36	55-41	62-34	

†Abandoned after 14 heats, result to stand. ±Amended score. Original result 49-47.

1984 NATIONAL LEAGUE

	P	W	D	L	PtsF	PtsA	W	D	L	PtsF	PtsA	Pts
1 LONG EATON	**30**	**14**	**0**	**1**	**710**	**455**	**7**	**1**	**7**	**575**	**593**	**43**
2 Mildenhall	30	12	3	0	683	486	7	1	7	571	596	42
3 Stoke	30	14	0	1	694	474	3	3	9	559	611	37
4 Hackney	30	14	0	1	688	481	2	0	13	518	643	32
5 Berwick	30	13	0	2	658	510	2	1	12	523	642	31
6 Boston	30	14	0	1	696	468	1	1	13	460	707	31
7 Milton Keynes	30	13	0	2	665	502	1	1	13	507	660	29
8 Rye House	30	14	0	1	672	481	0	0	15	487	679	28
9 Middlesbrough	30	11	2	2	649	517	2	0	13	503	664	28
10 Scunthorpe	30	13	1	1	649	515	0	1	14	495	666	28
11 Glasgow	30	12	1	2	662	506	1	1	13	480	687	28
12 Canterbury	30	13	1	1	672	496	0	0	15	494	668	27
13 Weymouth	30	12	0	3	655.5	511.5	1	0	14	461	705	26
14 Arena Essex	30	10	2	3	607	551	1	1	13	497.5	670.5	25
15 Peterborough	30	12	0	3	645	521	0	0	15	397	756	24
16 Edinburgh	30	9	1	5	623	540	1	0	14	487	681	21

1984 National League Riders' Championship Final

Sunday, September 23, Wimbledon:
Dave Perks 6, Carl Baldwin 5, Tom Owen 5, Bruce Cribb 4, Steve Wilcock 4, Andy Buck 3, Colin Cook 3, Mark Fiora 3, Steve Lawson 3, Barry Thomas 3, Jamie Luckhurst 2, Martin Yeates 2, Bob Garrad 1, Alan Sage 1, Keith White 1, Ian Barney 0. *Track reserve: Paul Muchene 0.*
Meeting abandoned after eight heats because of heavy rain.

1984 National League Riders' Championship Re-staged Final

Saturday, October 13, Peterborough
1 Ian Barney 14, 2 Dave Perks 14, 3 Martin Yeates 12, 4 Andy Buck 12, 5 Steve Wilcock 10, 6 Colin Cook 8, 7 Tom Owen 8, 8 Keith White 7, 9 Alan Sage 7, 10 Steve Lawson 7, 11 Mark Fiora 7, 12 Bruce Cribb 4, 13 Jamie Luckhurst 4, 14 Bob Garrad 3, 15 Barry Thomas 3, 16 Carl Baldwin 0. *Track Reserves: Rob Fortune 0, Ian Gutteridge 0.*

1984 KNOCK OUT CUP

Round 1

HACKNEY 53 42 95 Rye House 25 36 61
Glasgow 33 34 67 *Berwick 44 44 88*
Scunthorpe 43 26 69 Middlesbrough 35 52 87
Canterbury 39 44 83 Weymouth 39 34 73
Edinburgh 46 38 84 Boston 32 40 72
Long Eaton 45 38 83 Stoke 33 39 72
Milton Keynes 41 34 75 Mildenhall 37 44 81
Arena Essex 42 36 78 Peterborough 36 42 78

Round 1 Replay

Arena Essex 41 30 71 Peterborough 37 48 85

Round 2

Peterborough 47 34 81 Canterbury 30 44 74
***Berwick 43 43 86* Edinburgh 35 35 70**
Long Eaton 48 23 71 Middlesbrough 30 55 85
Mildenhall 45 27 72 HACKNEY 33 51 84

Semi Finals

***Berwick 46 37 83* Middlesbrough 31 41 72**
HACKNEY 54 25 79 Peterborough 24 53 77

FINAL

First leg, September 21:
HACKNEY 46 (Trevor Banks 11, Barry Thomas 11, Paul Bosley 7, Andy Galvin 6, Kevin Teager 5, Paul Whittaker 5, Lindon Warner 1) *Berwick 32* (Jim McMillan 13, Bruce Cribb 12, David Walsh 3, Dennis Gallagher 3, Eric Broadbelt 1, Mike Caroline 0, Paul Cooper, number eight, did not ride).

Second leg, September 29:
***Berwick 40* (Cribb 12, McMillan 12, Walsh 10, Gallagher 3, Craig Pendlebury 3, Caroline 0, Cooper, number eight, did not ride) HACKNEY 37 (Thomas 11, Banks 7, Teager 6, Bosley 5, Galvin 5, Whittaker 3, Warner 0).**

❑ **HACKNEY win 83-72 on aggregate.**

1984 ALL THE RESULTS

	ARENA ESSEX	BERWICK	BOSTON	CANTERBURY	EDINBURGH	GLASGOW	HACKNEY	LONG EATON	MIDDLESBRO	MILDENHALL	MILTON KEYNES	PETERBORO'	RYE HOUSE	SCUNTHORPE	STOKE	WEYMOUTH
ARENA ESSEX		51-27	37-41	42-32	41-37	40-38	41-36	41-36	40-38	39-39	31-47	46-31	41-36	37-37	32-46	48-30
BERWICK	38-40		49-29	44-34	40-38	48-30	47-31	41-37	46-32	40-37	46-32	44-34	43-34	44-34	37-41	51-27
BOSTON	51-27	50-28		40-36	54-24	47-31	40-34	41-37	49-29	38-40	40-38	60-18	47-31	41-37	41-37	57-21
CANTERBURY	49-29	47-31	54-24		45-32	39-39	42-36	35-43	44-34	40-37	45-33	51-27	45-33	42-36	44-34	50-28
EDINBURGH	47-31	40-38	45-32	42-34		36-41	44-34	37-41	34-43	38-40	39-38	54-24	41-37	51-26	39-39	36-42
GLASGOW	39-39	40-38	47-31	48-30	34-44		45-33	38-39	47-31	41-37	49-29	57-21	43-35	41-36	45-33	48-30
HACKNEY	44-34	44-34	46-32	47-31	47-31	43-35		42-36	46-32	37-41	46-32	53-25	48-30	55-23	45-33	45-32
LONG EATON	48-30	45-32	57-21	44-34	47-31	49-29	41-37		50-28	36-42	50-28	50-25	47-31	58-20	47-31	41-36
MIDDLESBROUGH	46-31	36-42	43-35	50-28	40-37	45-32	42-36	39-39		37-41	40-38	51-27	52-26	41-36	39-39	48-30
MILDENHALL	48-30	39-39	39-39	50-28	45-33	52-26	54-24	44-34	47-31		39-39	48-30	44-34	41-36	42-36	51-27
MILTON KEYNES	40-38	38-40	55-23	40-38	49-29	51-27	47-30	37-41	41-37	42-36		55-22	41-37	43-35	40-38	46-31
PETERBOROUGH	44-34	41-37	43-34	45-33	44-34	53-25	42-34	38-40	43-35	36-42	44-34		52-25	41-37	38-40	41-37
RYE HOUSE	43-34	44-32	52-26	42-36	58-20	43-35	42-36	44-34	37-40	44-34	44-33	†44-22		45-33	43-35	47-31
SCUNTHORPE	46-32	41-36	50-27	43-35	43-35	43-35	36-41	42-36	41-37	41-36	52-26	49-29	42-35		39-39	41-36
STOKE	48-30	44-34	44-34	44-34	50-28	53-25	42-36	36-42	47-30	49-29	44-33	53-25	43-35	42-36		55-23
WEYMOUTH	39.5 38.5	42-35	46-32	47-31	44-34	45-32	38-40	38-40	52-26	38-40	51-27	41-37	50-28	44-33	40-38	

†Abandoned after 11 heats. Result to stand.

1985 NATIONAL LEAGUE

	P	W	D	L	PtsF	PtsA	W	D	L	PtsF	PtsA	Pts
1 Ellesmere Port	**36**	**17**	**0**	**1**	**882**	**517**	**8**	**2**	**8**	**697**	**700**	**52**
2 Poole	36	17	1	0	900	502	8	0	10	676	724	51
3 Middlesbrough	36	18	0	0	849	552	7	1	10	652	744	51
4 Wimbledon	36	17	0	1	852	549	6	1	11	644.5	756.5	47
5 Hackney	36	17	0	1	899	502	5	0	13	645	749	44
6 Arena Essex	36	16	0	2	806	593	4	2	12	614	788	42
7 Peterborough	36	17	1	0	798	513	2	1	15	560	822	40
8 Stoke	36	15	0	3	780	603	5	0	13	605	792	40
9 Berwick	36	15	1	2	869	530	4	0	14	605	793	39
10 Eastbourne	36	15	1	2	794	608	3	1	14	630	766	38
11 Milton Keynes	36	15	0	3	762.5	636.5	1	1	16	566	834	33
12 Exeter	36	16	0	2	889	514	0	0	18	532	871	32
13 Rye House	36	13	0	5	781	603	2	0	16	549	851	30
14 Birmingham	36	11	1	6	753	642	3	0	15	556	833	29
15 Mildenhall	36	12	0	6	778	623	2	0	16	548	776	28
16 Canterbury	36	11	0	7	758	645	3	0	15	569	820	28
17 Glasgow	36	10	2	6	749	649	0	0	18	439	963	22
18 Long Eaton	36	7	2	9	726	673	2	0	16	526	875	20
19 Edinburgh	36	8	0	10	730	665	1	0	17	506	898	18
The following team records were expunged:												
Scunthorpe	*9*	*2*	*0*	*2*	*162*	*148*	*0*	*0*	*5*	*163*	*225*	*4*
Barrow	*3*	*0*	*0*	*0*	*0*	*0*	*0*	*0*	*3*	*65*	*168*	*0*

1985 National League Riders' Championship Final

Saturday, August 10, Coventry:
1 Neil Middleditch 14, 2 Kevin Hawkins 13, 3 Trevor Banks 12, 4 Stan Bear 10, 5 Doug Wyer 9, 6 Gordon Kennett 8, David Mullett 8, 8 Nigel De'ath 7, 9 Louis Carr 7, 10 Dave Perks 6, 11 Mike Ferreira 5, 12 Carl Baldwin 5, Steve McDermott 5, Tom Owen 5, 15 Steve Lawson 4, 16 Steve Wilcock 2. *Track Reserve: Mike Bacon 0.*

1985 KNOCK OUT CUP

Round 1

Arena Essex 55 33 88 Peterborough 23 45 68
Glasgow 42 28 70 Birmingham 36 50 86
Exeter 58 24 82 Barrow 20 18 38
Poole 38 16 54 Wimbledon 40 62 102
*Ellesmere Port 43 38.5 81.5*Edinburgh 35 38.5 73.5
EASTBOURNE 47 33 80 Canterbury 31 45 76

Round 2

Middlesbrough 48 45 93 Stoke 30 33 63
Hackney 44 35 79 Mildenhall 34 42 76
†Birmingham 38 *Ellesmere Port 39*
Milton Keynes 35 28 63 EASTBOURNE 42 50 92
Berwick 57 27.5 84.5 Exeter 21 50.5 71.5
Arena Essex 40 35 75 Wimbledon 38 43 81
†Second leg never race. Tie awarded to Ellesmere Port.

Round 3

Rye House 37 33 70 Middlesbrough 41 45 86
Long Eaton 33 31 64 Hackney 45 47 92
Wimbledon 39 33 72 EASTBOURNE 39 44 83
Ellesmere Port 56 45 101 Berwick 22 33 55

Semi Finals

EASTBOURNE 49 30 79 Middlesbrough 29 48 77
Ellesmere Port 50 29 79 Hackney 28 49 77

FINAL

First leg, October 13:
EASTBOURNE 46 (Colin Richardson 10, Gordon Kennett 10, Martin Dugard 8, Andy Buck 7, Paul Clarke 6, Chris Mulvihill 4, Keith Pritchard 1)
Ellesmere Port 32 (Louis Carr 9, Joe Owen 9, Dave Morton 8, David Walsh 4, Miles Evans 1, Phil Alderman 1, Richie Owen 0).
Second leg, October 18:
Ellesmere Port 41 (Carr 13, Morton 9, J. Owen 9, Walsh 4, Gary O'Hare 2, R. Owen 2, Alderman 2)
EASTBOURNE 37 (Kennett 12, Buck 9, Richardson 7, Dugard 4, Clarke 2, Mulvihill 2, Pritchard 1).

❑ EASTBOURNE win 83-73 on aggregate.

1985 ALL THE RESULTS

	ARENA ESSEX	BERWICK	BIRMINGHAM	CANTERBURY	EASTBOURNE	EDINBURGH	ELLESMERE PORT	EXETER	GLASGOW	HACKNEY	LONG EATON	MIDDLESBRO'	MILDENHALL	MILTON KEYNES	PETERBORO'	POOLE	RYE HOUSE	STOKE	WIMBLEDON	SCUNTHORPE *BARROW*
ARENA ESSEX		40-38	44-34	38-40	41-37	52-26	40-38	48-29	55-23	44-34	53-25	38-39	46-32	40-37	54-24	43-35	44-34	44-33	42-35	
BERWICK	55-23		50-28	49-28	38-39	53-25	38-40	56-22	53-24	41-37	44-34	39-39	46-32	49-29	55-23	53-24	57-21	43-34	50-28	
BIRMINGHAM	46-32	52-26		43-35	39-39	40-38	41-36	47-31	49-29	36-38	37-40	35-43	46-32	44-34	34-43	44-34	44-33	38-40	38-39	40-38
CANTERBURY	36-41	33-45	37-41		43-35	49-29	34-44	42-36	52-26	44-34	54-24	32-46	40-38	43-35	53-25	36-42	51-27	37-41	42-36	
EASTBOURNE	42-36	47-31	41-37	43-35		58-20	39-39	52-26	50-28	44-34	43-35	47-31	46-31	43-35	41-37	42-35	38-40	41-37	37-41	Barrow 51-27
EDINBURGH	35-43	37-41	52-26	40-38	36-41		36-41	50-28	48-29	30-45	37-41	37-41	42-36	37-41	46-31	37-41	43-34	50-27	37-41	Barrow 59-19
ELLESMERE PORT	54-24	±34-41	58-20	55-22	50-28	52-26		43-35	54-24	41-37	52-26	48-29	43-35	54-24	46-32	45-33	56-22	44-34	53-25	40-37
EXETER	49-29	57-21	37-41	43-35	42-35	48-30	49-29		56-22	50-28	50-28	48-30	51-27	58-20	55-23	38-40	48-30	59-19	51-27	
GLASGOW	39-39	32-46	35-43	50-28	38-39	42-36	*37-38	46-32		47-31	48-30	41-37	35-43	46-32	41-37	46-32	49-28	38-39	39-39	
HACKNEY	45-33	50-27	56-22	54-24	50-28	58-20	39-38	43-35	62-16		57-21	48-29	55-23	55-23	53-25	37-41	49-29	44-34	44-34	
LONG EATON	39-39	52-26	41-36	37-41	43-35	38-40	36-42	44-34	56-22	37-40		38-39	48-30	39-39	46-32	27-51	33-44	37-40	35-43	
MIDDLESBROUGH	41-37	40-38	46-32	57-21	45-33	50-28	40-38	52-26	54-24	50-28	52-26		43-34	46-30	47-31	45-33	49-29	51-27	41-37	Barrow 58-19
MILDENHALL	38-40	51-27	40-38	42-36	45-33	53-25	34-44	53-25	51-27	44-34	52-26	49-28		41-37	36-41	32-45	47-31	35-43	35-43	53-24
MILTON KEYNES	39-38	46-32	41-37	41-36	39-37	45-33	35-43	47-31	51-27	37-41	47-31	47-31	49-29		44-34	40-37	42-36	42-36	30.5 47.5	
PETERBOROUGH	50-28	48-30	§65-0	42-35	43-35	50-28	39-39	40-38	55-23	49-28	52-26	44-34	†Won	41-37		44-34	54-24	42-36	40-38	
POOLE	49-29	45-32	50-27	51-27	51-27	56-22	40-38	53-25	53-25	43-35	56-22	40-38	51-27	57-21	39-39		55-23	55-23	56-22	
RYE HOUSE	43-35	42-36	49-29	$32-36	39-37	57-21	43-35	57-21	54-24	23-54	47-30	36-41	38-40	51-26	41-36	38-40		51-25	40-37	
STOKE	37-41	43-35	48-30	51-26	40-38	45-33	36-41	51-27	47-31	44-34	46-32	37-40	42-36	43-35	§§39-21	40-38	45-33		46-32	49-29
WIMBLEDON	51-27	44-33	43-35	52-26	44-34	52-26	44-34	47-31	63-15	45-33	48-29	40-37	55-23	47-31	52-26	37-41	47-31	41-37		45-33
SCUNTHORPE											36-41			52-26	40-37				34-44	

§Birmingham refused to race. Peterborough tracked two riders in all 13 heats. §§Match abandoned after 10 heats, results to stand. † Match awarded, Mildenhall failed to arrive. ± After SCB appeal. Original result 50-28. * After SCB appeal. Original result 39-38. $ After SCB apeal. Original result 42-36.

1986 NATIONAL LEAGUE

	P	W	D	L	PtsF	PtsA	W	D	L	PtsF	PtsA	Pts
1 EASTBOURNE	**38**	**18**	**1**	**0**	**930**	**551**	**10**	**0**	**9**	**758**	**721**	**57**
2 Poole	38	19	0	0	911	568	6	1	12	703	773	51
3 Middlesbrough	38	19	0	0	880	598	6	1	12	694	779	51
4 Arena Essex	38	17	1	1	839.5	633.5	6	0	13	687	790	47
5 Stoke	38	18	0	1	922	554	5	0	14	706	773	46
6 Wimbledon	38	17	0	2	860	615	4	1	14	664	816	43
7 Mildenhall	37	18	0	1	853	623	3	1	14	618	771	43
8 Milton Keynes	37	15	1	2	788	614	5	0	14	639	839	41
9 Edinburgh	38	16	0	3	845	632	3	0	16	675	804	38
10 Peterborough	38	17	0	2	797	606	1	2	16	644.5	830.5	38
11 Rye House	38	15	0	4	778	681	3	0	16	608	862	36
12 Boston	38	14	0	5	833	648	3	1	15	666	810	35
13 Hackney	38	13	0	6	816	657	3	0	16	617	860	32
14 Berwick	38	14	0	5	853	621	1	1	17	628	850	31
15 Canterbury	38	12	1	6	788	692	3	0	16	617	865	31
16 Exeter	38	13	0	6	838	639	2	0	17	553	909	30
17 Birmingham	38	14	1	4	785	695	0	0	19	508	888	29
18 Glasgow	38	14	0	5	788	686	0	0	19	510	968	28
19 Newcastle	38	13	1	5	808	671	0	0	19	610.5	867.5	27
20 Long Eaton	38	11	2	6	778.5	683.5	0	0	19	562	915	24

1986 National League Riders' Championship Final

Saturday, August 30, Coventry:
1 Paul Thorp 15, 2 Steve Schofield 13, 3 Les Collins 12, 4 Malcolm Simmons 10, 5 Andrew Silver 10, 6 Jamie Luckhurst 9, 7 Kevin Jolly 9, 8 Gordon Kennett 8, 9 Mark Fiora 6, 10 Mark Courtney 6, 11 Steve McDermott 5, 12 David Mullett 5, 13 Dave Jessup 4, 14 Paul Woods 4, 15 Steve Lawson 2, 16 Kevin Hawkins 1.
Reserve: Bruce Cribb 1.

1986 KNOCK OUT CUP

Round 1
Edinburgh 53 41 94 Glasgow 25 37 62
Exeter 37 23 60 Rye House 41 55 96
Boston 37 35 72 Newcastle 41 43 84
Birmingham 48 25 73 Canterbury 30 53 83

Round 2
Poole 36 33 69 Arena Essex 42 45 87
Berwick 50 42 92 Newcastle 28 36 64
Hackney 48 35 83 Rye House 30 42 72
Stoke 40 29 69 Middlesbrough 37 49 86
Mildenhall 49 35 84 Milton Keynes 29 43 72
Wimbledon 36 30 66 EASTBOURNE 42 48 90
Peterborough 49 39 88 Canterbury 29 39 68
Edinburgh 50 35 85 Long Eaton 28 43 71

Round 3
Berwick 42 33 75 Peterborough 36 45 81
Arena Essex 43 39 82 Hackney 35 39 74
Mildenhall 43 42 85 Middlesbrough 35 36 71
EASTBOURNE 48 40 88 Edinburgh 28 38 66

Semi Finals
Arena Essex 43 34 77 *Mildenhall 35 44 79*
EASTBOURNE 49.5 41 90.5 Peterborough 28.5 37 65.5

FINAL
First leg, October 26:
EASTBOURNE 51 (Gordon Kennett 13, Martin Dugard 12, Dean Standing 11, Keith Pritchard 9, Andy Buck 6, Chris Mulvihill, number eight, did not ride) *Mildenhall 25* (Melvyn Taylor 11, Dave Jessup 7, Kelvin Mullarkey 3, Eric Monaghan 2, Lee Potter 2, Rob Parish 0, Peter McNamara 0).
Second leg, November 2:
MILDENHALL 39 (Taylor 12, Monaghan 8, Mullarkey 7, Potter 6, Parish 4, McNamara 1, Wayne Dunworth 1) Eastbourne 39 (Dugard 8, Standing 8, Kennett 7, Buck 6, Pritchard 5, Steve Chambers 3, Dean Barker 2).

❑ EASTBOURNE win 90-64 on aggregate.

1986 ALL THE RESULTS

	ARENA ESSEX	BERWICK	BIRMINGHAM	BOSTON	CANTERBURY	EASTBOURNE	EDINBURGH	EXETER	GLASGOW	HACKNEY	LONG EATON	MIDDLESBRO'	MILDENHALL	MILTON KEYNES	NEWCASTLE		PETERBORO'	RYE HOUSE	STOKE	
ARENA ESSEX		42-34	57-21	40-38	46-32	40-37	41-37	46-32	44-34	50-28	44-34	36-41	45-33	42-36	51.5 25.5	44-34	45-32	44-33	43-33	39-39
BERWICK	36-42		50-27	37-40	51-27	40-38	35-43	52-26	54-24	50-27	53-25	45-31	36-42	47-31	41-36	50-28	42-34	51-27	45-33	38-40
BIRMINGHAM	43-35	38-39		43-35	37-41	30-48	41-37	46-32	49-29	38-39	40-38	41-37	39-39	48-30	42-36	45-33	40-38	42-36	40-38	43-35
BOSTON	49-29	50-28	48-30		45-33	45-33	37-41	48-30	43-35	38-39	47-31	36-42	38-40	36-42	47-31	41-37	42-36	47-31	45-33	51-27
CANTERBURY	44-34	40-38	53-25	35-43		33-45	42-36	38-40	51-27	40-38	49-29	40-38	43-35	35-42	45-33	39-39	36-42	36-41	40-38	49-29
EASTBOURNE	47-31	58-20	47-31	50-28	46-32		47-31	59-19	54-24	46-32	57-21	39-39	44-34	54-24	52-26	54-23	51-27	41-37	42-36	42-36
EDINBURGH	41-36	42-36	57-21	45-33	46-32	37-40		55-23	47-31	45-33	52-26	39-37	40-38	50-28	42-36	42-36	37-41	48-29	36-42	44-34
EXETER	37-41	48-29	53-25	50-28	37-41	38-40	40-38		59-19	45-33	54-23	46-32	39-38	40-37	51-27	36-42	38-40	50-28	37-41	40-37
GLASGOW	42-35	40-38	48-30	39-37	45-33	37-41	40-38	50-28		44-34	44-33	35-42	41-37	47-31	43-34	40-36	36-42	36-42	44-34	37-41
HACKNEY	33-44	43-35	54-23	44-33	51-27	37-41	37-40	52-25	49-28		44-34	42-36	39-38	38-40	45-33	41-37	37-40	43-35	38-40	49-28
LONG EATON	41-36	39-39	40-38	44-33	37-41	32-46	43-35	45-32	53-24	35-42		34-44	±65-0	41-37	41-37	39.5 37.5	39-39	37-40	40-38	33-45
MIDDLESBROUGH	41-37	44-34	47-31	44-33	48-30	44-33	49-29	50-28	43-35	56-22	39-38		45-33	56-22	40-37	50-28	41-37	50-28	43-35	50-28
MILDENHALL	40-38	48-30	49-28	42-36	47-31	42-36	44-34	50-28	53-25	43-35	47-31	42-35		44-34	47-31	40-38	38-39	51-24	42-36	44-34
MILTON KEYNES	37-41	40-38	47-31	39-39	52-26	30-48	48-28	44-34	51-27	46-32	46-32	40-38	Not Raced		50-28	44-34	40-38	42-36	45-33	47-31
NEWCASTLE	41-37	52-26	43-35	43-35	44-34	28-50	41-37	38-40	52-26	51-27	45-33	54-23	44-34	38-40		38-38	41-37	48-30	34-44	33-45
PETERBOROUGH	49-29	41-37	§12-5	37-41	43-35	42-36	40-38	56-22	57-21	41-37	51-27	41-37	43-35	38-40	54-24		41-37	41-36	40-38	42-36
POOLE	46-32	47-31	46-32	42-36	55-23	44-34	46-32	46-32	58-20	51-27	52-26	53-25	44-34	51-26	44-34	44-34		60-17	41-36	41-37
RYE HOUSE	37-41	42-36	44-31	45-33	40-38	36-42	42-36	†37-24	42-36	41-37	45-31	38-40	34-44	45-33	40-38	46-32	42-35		42-36	40-38
STOKE	49-28	49-29	58-19	44-34	50-28	43-35	46-32	53-25	55-22	51-26	49-29	38-40	45-33	45-33	48-30	49-28	45-33	51-26		54-24
WIMBLEDON	37-41	47-31	47-30	47-31	45-33	43-35	45-33	44-33	54-23	49-29	57-21	40-37	47-31	44-33	44-34	48-30	42-36	44-32	36-42	

37-41 On track result was 41-37 but it was changed on appeal by Edinburgh against Boston's use of Gary O'Hare as a guest. His points were deducted from the revised score.

†Match abandoned after 11 heats because of darkness. Result to stand. ±Mildenhall refused to race and all 13 heats were completed with two Long Eaton riders only. §Match abandoned by referee Les Morrell after three heats after complaints of an overwatered track by Birmingham. Never re-staged, match points awarded to Peterborough.

1987 NATIONAL LEAGUE

	P	W	D	L	PtsF	PtsA	W	D	L	PtsF	PtsA	Pts
1 EASTBOURNE	**30**	**15**	**0**	**0**	**771**	**397**	**7**	**0**	**8**	**577**	**590**	**44**
2 Mildenhall	30	14	0	1	692	478	6	1	8	570	594	41
3 Milton Keynes	30	14	0	1	671	498	5	1	9	582	587	39
4 Stoke	30	13	1	1	677	488	5	0	10	533	636	37
5 Peterborough	30	15	0	0	733	437	3	0	12	522	643	36
6 Berwick	30	15	0	0	744	420	2	1	12	497	671	35
7 Wimbledon	30	12	0	3	662.5	505.5	2	2	11	540	625	30
8 Poole	30	14	0	1	670	498	1	0	14	489	674	30
9 Middlesbrough	30	12	1	2	643	523	1	2	12	481	683	29
10 Edinburgh	30	12	1	2	664	502	1	1	13	488.5	678.5	28
11 Newcastle	30	10	2	3	624	544	2	0	13	504	662	26
12 Arena Essex	30	7	1	7	606	555	5	0	10	552	612	25
13 Canterbury	30	10	1	4	631	536	1	0	14	440	729	23
14 Exeter	30	11	1	3	631	536	0	0	15	421	746	23
15 Long Eaton	30	8	1	6	613	553	0	0	15	447	716	17
16 Rye House	30	7	0	8	571	584	1	1	13	411	757	17

The following records were expunged from the League table:

†Workington	*23*	*3*	*1*	*6*	*374*	*402*	*0*	*0*	*13*	*319*	*692*	*7*
Boston	*16*	*0*	*1*	*7*	*261*	*363*	*0*	*0*	*8*	*195*	*426*	*1*

1987 National League Riders' Championship Final

Saturday, September 12, Coventry:
1 Andrew Silver 15, 2 Nigel Crabtree 14, 3 David Blackburn 10, 4 Les Collins 10, 5 David Biles 10, 6 David Mullett 9, 7 Dave Jessup 8, 8 Martin Dixon 8, 9 Martin Dugard 7, 10 Kevin Jolly 7, 11 Trevor Banks 6, 12 Paul Woods 6, 13 Steve Lawson 4, 14 Ian Barney 2, 14 Nigel Sparshott 2, 14 Rob Woffinden 2. ***Track Reserve: Wayne Broadhurst 0.***
Sponsors: Jawa-Barum.

1987 KNOCK OUT CUP

Round 1

Newcastle 51 32 83 Berwick 44 64 108
Mildenhall 66 48 114 Rye House 30 47 77

Round 2

Boston 50 35 85 Canterbury 46 61 107
Milton Keynes 50 36 86 Stoke 46 60 106
Wimbledon 48 44 92 Arena Essex 48 52 100
EASTBOURNE 62 45 107 Poole 33 51 84
Exeter 51 31 82 *Mildenhall 45 64 109*
Long Eaton 51 31 82 Berwick 45 65 110
Middlesbrough 56 39 95 Peterborough 40 57 97
Edinburgh 65 49 114 †Glasgow 31 47 78
†Glasgow's home match was staged at Workington.

Round 3

Mildenhall 61 50 111 Berwick 35 46 81
Arena Essex 60 42 102 Canterbury 36 54 90
Peterborough 50 29 79 Stoke 46 49 95
EASTBOURNE 56 50 106 Edinburgh 40 45 85

Semi Finals

Stoke 53 39 92 EASTBOURNE 42 57 99
Arena Essex 51 36 87 *Mildenhall 45 60 105*

FINAL

First leg, September 27:
Mildenhall 50 (Melvyn Taylor 12, Dave Jessup 11, David Jackson 10, Glen Baxter 8, Eric Monaghan 5, Richard Green 4, Lee Farthing 0) EASTBOURNE 46 (Martin Dugard 14, Gordon Kennett 13, Andy Buck 9, Dean Standing 5, Keith Pritchard 2, Dean Barker 2, Darren Standing 1).
Second leg, October 4:
EASTBOURNE 54 (Dean Standing 11, Buck 11, Kennett 10, Dugard 9, Barker 6, Pritchard 5, Darren Standing 2) *Mildenhall 41* (Taylor 12, Jackson 11, Jessup 11, Green 5, Monaghan 1, Paul Blackbird 1, Baxter 0).

❑ EASTBURNE win 100-91 on aggregate.

1987 ALL THE RESULTS

	ARENA ESSEX	BERWICK	CANTERBURY	EASTBOURNE	EDINBURGH	EXETER	LONG EATON	MIDDLESBRO'	MILDENHALL	MILTON KEYNES	NEWCASTLE	PETERBORO'	POOLE	RYE HOUSE	STOKE	WIMBLEDON	*BOSTON*	*GLASGOW/ WORKINGTON*
ARENA ESSEX		37-41	41-36	38-40	39-38	49-27	53-25	41-36	36-42	34-44	37-40	38-40	41-35	39-39	37-41	46-31	*41-36*	*53-24*
BERWICK	42-36		48-30	42-35	51-27	60-18	63-14	52-26	43-35	45-33	47-30	50-28	57-21	60-18	44-33	40-36	*60-18*	*55-23*
CANTERBURY	34-43	55-23		43-35	40-38	44-34	52-26	35-41	35-43	42-36	50-28	44-34	42-36	42-36	34-44	39-39		*42-36*
EASTBOURNE	50-28	53-25	57-21		55-22	56-22	54-23	53-25	40-38	43-35	50-28	52-26	54-24	55-23	57-21	42-36	*57-21*	*60-18*
EDINBURGH	40-38	43-34	59-19	38-39		54-24	46-32	49-29	39-39	34-44	44-34	44-34	43-35	46-31	43-35	42-35		*53-25*
EXETER	34-44	45-33	54-24	41-37	39-39		43-35	41-37	36-42	47-31	41-37	37-41	39-36	49-29	41-37	44-34	*50-27*	*54-24*
LONG EATON	37-41	46-31	37-41	42-35	50-28	44-34		39-39	38-40	34-44	35-43	42-36	43-34	37-41	47-31	42-35	*47-30*	*54-24*
MIDDLESBROUGH	39-38	44-34	47-31	33-45	49-29	52-26	40-37		37-41	39-39	41-36	44-33	40-38	55-23	40-38	43-35		*48-30*
MILDENHALL	47-31	50-28	48-30	45-33	47-31	44-34	48-30	54-24		38-40	43-35	51-27	47-31	49-29	40-38	41-37	*57-21*	*48-30*
MILTON KEYNES	40-38	46-32	49-29	36-42	50-28	48-30	42-35	42-36	44-34		43-35	43-35	43-35	57-21	45-33	43-35		*59-19*
NEWCASTLE	42-36	47-31	43-35	34-44	37-41	44-33	55-23	39-39	44-34	41-37		41-37	40-38	43-34	35-43	39-39		*59-19*
PETERBOROUGH	47-31	54-24	51-27	40-38	44-34	55-23	51-27	54-24	44-34	40-38	44-34		48-30	59-19	55-23	47-31		*57-21*
POOLE	43-34	40-38	51-27	44-34	47-31	47-31	42-36	45-33	42-36	42-36	47-31	41-36		54-24	48-30	37-41	*59-19*	
RYE HOUSE	36-39	29-49	43-35	33-45	41-36	46-32	43-34	40-36	†33-39	43-34	46-31	34-44	36-42		32-46	36-42		
STOKE	43-35	39-39	50-28	43-35	46-32	62-16	43-34	47-30	43-35	23-55	45-33	40-35	53-25	56-22		44-34		
WIMBLEDON	38-40	43-35	51-27	38-40	43.5 34.5	41-37	41-36	52-26	40-38	42-36	49-29	42-36	48-29	56-22	38-40			*50-26*
BOSTON				*23-55*			*37-41*	*35-43*	*31-47*		*32-46*	*39-39*			*32-46*	*32-46*		
GLASGOW/ WORKINGTON	*40-38*		*33-44*		*39-39*	*36-42*	*44-34*	*23-53*		*33-44*	*34-44*					*37-41*	*55-23*	

†Abandoned after 12 heats, result to stand. BOSTON withdrew from the National League on August 11, 1987. GLASGOW rode home matches at Derwent Park, Workington, and changed their name to Workington on August 1. They were expelled from the National League on September 17, 1987, for failing to comply with National League rules and regulations in respect of the administration of the club and the Derwent Park track on September 17, 1987.

1988 NATIONAL LEAGUE

	P	W	D	L	PtsF	PtsA	W	D	L	PtsF	PtsA	Pts
1 HACKNEY	**30**	**15**	**0**	**0**	**914**	**522**	**11**	**2**	**2**	**768**	**670**	**54**
2 Poole	30	13	1	1	838.5	600.5	7	0	8	699	736	41
3 Eastbourne	30	13	1	1	860	574	4	1	10	686.5	748.5	36
4 Wimbledon	30	13	1	1	861	577	4	1	10	670	761	36
5 Berwick	30	14	1	0	855	583	3	1	11	633	802	36
6 Milton Keynes	30	13	0	2	812	619	4	2	9	616	822	36
7 Stoke	30	15	0	0	872	567	1	0	14	627	809	32
8 Peterborough	30	12	1	2	876	545	3	0	12	670	769	31
9 Arena Essex	30	13	1	1	819	615	2	0	13	592.5	829.5	31
10 Glasgow	30	10	2	3	794	643	3	0	12	618	817	28
11 Edinburgh	30	12	0	3	781	658	2	0	13	623	810	28
12 Exeter	30	12	0	3	774	665	0	0	15	480	957	24
13 Mildenhall	30	8	0	7	780.5	656.5	2	1	12	606	831	21
14 Rye House	30	7	1	7	704	726	1	0	14	576	862	17
15 Middlesbrough	30	6	0	9	736	700	1	1	13	616	822	15
16 Long Eaton	30	7	0	8	700	738	0	0	15	508	931	14

1988 KNOCK OUT CUP

Round 1

Edinburgh 55 45 100 Stoke 41 50 91
Berwick 56 49 105 Glasgow 40 47 87
Hackney 70 40 110 Poole 26 56 82
Peterborough 58 39 97 Rye House 38 56 94
Arena Essex 54 39 93 Mildenhall 42 57 99
Eastbourne 66 50 116 Exeter 29 46 75
Milton Keynes 44 41 85 Wimbledon 52 55 107
Long Eaton 51 33 84 Middlesbrough 45 63 108

Round 2

Edinburgh 51 46 97 Peterborough 45 49 94
Berwick 56 45 101 Eastbourne 40 51 91
Mildenhall 59 37 96 Wimbledon 37 59 96
Hackney 56 51 107 Middlesbrough 40 45 85

Round 2 Replay

Wimbledon 50 50 100 Mildenhall 45 46 91

Semi Finals

Berwick 58 33 91 Wimbledon 38 63 101
Edinburgh 45 25 70 Hackney 51 71 122

FINAL

First leg, October 7:
HACKNEY 60 (Andy Galvin 13, Alan Mogridge 11, Mark Loram 10, Paul Whittaker 9, Barry Thomas 7, Gary Rolls 5, Chris Louis 5) *Wimbledon 36* (Todd Wiltshire 15, Ray Morton 12, Kevin Jolly 8, Nathan Simpson 1, Andy Campbell 0, Rodney Payne 0, Roger Johns 0).
Second leg, October 12:
Wimbledon 46 (Morton 13, Johns 10, Wiltshire 8, Jolly 7, Simpson 5, Campbell 3, Payne 0) HACKNEY 50 (Whittaker 11, Mogridge 9, Galvin 8, Loram 8, Louis 8, Rolls 4, Thomas 2).

❑ HACKNEY win 110-82 on aggregate.

1988 ALL THE RESULTS

	ARENA ESSEX	BERWICK				GLASGOW	HACKNEY	LONG EATON	MIDDLESBRO	MILDENHALL	MILTON KEYNES	PETERBORO'			STOKE	
ARENA ESSEX		49-47	48-48	53-41	73-22	53-43	45-51	65-31	53-42	55-40	54-42	59-37	50-46	51-45	54-42	57-38
BERWICK	60-36		52-44	51-45	65-30	54-42	48-48	60-36	59-37	56-40	67-29	55-41	48-47	68-28	56-40	56-40
EASTBOURNE	58-38	64-32		60-36	67-29	57-38	41-55	66-30	51-45	58-36	62-34	52-44	56-40	60-34	60-35	48-48
EDINBURGH	50-46	46-50	47-49		60-36	53-43	40-56	62-34	56-40	61-35	51-45	52-44	51-45	55-41	49-47	48-47
EXETER	52-44	62-34	49-47	49-47		57-39	47-49	59-37	62-34	32-64	57-39	52-44	50-45	52-44	54-42	40-56
GLASGOW	63-33	48-48	50-46	51-44	65-31		46-50	63-33	54-42	48-48	63-33	50-46	38-57	58-38	51-45	46-49
HACKNEY	58-38	59-37	50-44	60-36	68-28	60-36		73-23	50-46	69-27	74-22	55-41	60-36	62-34	58-38	58-36
LONG EATON	46-50	50-45	51-45	50-45	49-47	47-49	44-52		42-54	62-34	39-57	46-50	40-56	36-60	49-47	49-47
MIDDLESBROUGH	55-41	46-48	46-49	46-50	61-35	47-49	41-55	56-40		55-41	46-50	47-49	47-48	50-46	50-46	43-53
MILDENHALL		58-38	45-51	58-37	63-33	57-39	47-49	63-33	53-43		46-50	46-50	45-51	56-40	47-48	44-51
MILTON KEYNES	45-51	49-47	51-45	51-44	63-33	49-44	46-50	55-40	60-35	73-23		50-46	51-44	60-36	54-42	55-39
PETERBOROUGH	60-18	65-31	57-39	73-23	61-35	59-37	46-50	68-28	56-40	49-47	48-48		46-50	67-29	59-36	62-34
POOLE	66-30	60-36		52-44	64-32	62-34	49-47	62-34	65-31	47-49	48-48	52-44		60-36	52-44	49-46
RYE HOUSE	50-46	42-53	47-48	37-58	61-34	44-52	33-61	55-41	48-48	49-47	39-55	51-44	47-49		50-45	51-45
STOKE	59-37	55-41	52-43	59-37	67-29	60-36	49-47	64-32	54-42	55-41	69-27	50-46	61-35	63-33		55-41
WIMBLEDON	55-41	49-46	53-43	60-36	70-26	58-37	48-48	60-36	59-37	62-34	59-37	52-44	46-50	64-32	66-30	

1989 NATIONAL LEAGUE

	P	W	D	L	PtsF	PtsA	W	D	L	PtsF	PtsA	Pts
1 POOLE	**34**	**16**	**0**	**1**	**1000**	**629**	**10**	**1**	**6**	**843**	**783**	**53**
2 Wimbledon	34	16	1	0	992	639	7	1	9	805	820	48
3 Berwick	34	17	0	0	1097	528	6	0	11	785	843	46
4 Ipswich	34	16	0	1	956	656	7	0	10	782.5	837.5	46
5 Exeter	34	17	0	0	1071	557	2	1	14	674	953	39
6 Hackney	34	17	0	0	967	661	2	1	14	734	896	39
7 Eastbourne	34	15	0	2	969	658	4	0	13	698	929	38
8 Edinburgh	34	13	0	4	932	693	6	0	11	703	906	38
9 Glasgow	34	16	0	1	951	676	1	0	16	673	950	34
10 Stoke	34	12	0	5	932	699	4	1	12	730	900	33
11 Peterborough	34	13	0	4	932	688	3	0	14	752	874	32
12 Arena Essex	34	11	2	4	866	751	3	0	14	609	1015	30
13 Middlesbrough	34	11	0	6	856	768	3	0	14	609	1016	28
14 Rye House	34	12	0	5	864.5	753.5	1	0	16	700	929	26
15 Newcastle	34	9	1	7	793	834	2	1	14	675	950	24
16 Mildenhall	34	9	0	8	813	812	1	1	15	657	974	21
17 Long Eaton	34	8	1	8	823	807	2	0	15	635	989	21
18 Milton Keynes	34	7	2	8	799	830	0	0	17	575	1049	16

LONG EATON finished in the bottom two for the fifth successive season – having finished with the wooden spoon in 1986 and 1988 and next to bottom in the other three years.

1989 National League Riders' Championship Final

Saturday, September 9, Coventry:
1 Mark Loram 14, 2 Kenny McKinna 12, 3 David Blackburn 11, 4 Steve Schofield 10, 5 Martin Goodwin 10, 6 Richard Hellsén 10, 7 Mick Poole 9, 8 Todd Wiltshire 8, 9 Les Collins 8, 10 Nigel Crabtree 7, 11 Jens Rasmussen 5, 12 Gordon Kennett 5, 13 Steve Regeling 5, 14 Preben Eriksen 4, 15 Rod Hunter 2, 16 Leigh Adams 0.
Sponsors: Jawa-Barum.

1989 KNOCK OUT CUP

Round 1
BERWICK 65 52 117 Newcastle 30 43 73
Rye House 57 34 91 Exeter 39 62 101
Round 2
Ipswich 60 49 109 Middlesbrough 36 47 83
Edinburgh 60 39 99 Arena Essex 36 57 93
Long Eaton 43 27 70 BERWICK 53 69 122
Glasgow 48 32 80 Eastbourne 48 64 112
Peterborough 63 51 114 Mildenhall 33 45 78
Stoke 51 44 95 Exeter 45 52 97
Milton Keynes 43 37 90 Wimbledon 53 59 112
Poole 63 54 117 Hackney 33 42 75
Round 3
Ipswich 48 44 92 Wimbledon 48 52 100
Peterborough 64 33 97 Edinburgh 32 63 95
BERWICK 58 38 96 Exeter 38 58 96
Eastbourne 43 36 79 *Poole 53 60 113*
Round 3 Replay
BERWICK 58 43 101 Exeter 38 52 90
Semi Finals
BERWICK 61 37 98 Peterborough 35 59 94
Wimbledon 48 33 81 *Poole 48 62 110*
FINAL
First leg, September 12:
Poole 50 (Leigh Adams 14, Alun Rossiter 11, Alastair Stevens 8, Tony Langdon 6, Craig Boyce 5, Gary Allan 4, Mike Lewthwaite 2) BERWICK 46 (Mark Courtney 14, David Blackburn 14, Andy Campbell 5, David Walsh 4, Rob Grant 4, Scott Robson 3, Sean Courtney 2).
Second leg, September 16
BERWICK 63 (Blackburn 14, Courtney 13, Walsh 9, Grant 9, Campbell 8, Robson 6, Courtney 4) Poole 33 (Adams 12, Rossiter 9, Boyce 6, Allan 3, Langdon 3, Stevens 0, Lewthwaite 0).

❏ BERWICK win 109-83 on aggregate.

1989 ALL THE RESULTS

	ARENA ESSEX	BERWICK	EASTBOURNE	EDINBURGH	EXETER	GLASGOW	HACKNEY	IPSWICH	LONG EATON	MIDDLESBRO'	MILDENHALL	MILTON KEYNES	NEWCASTLE	PETERBORO'	POOLE	RYE HOUSE	STOKE	WIMBLEDON
ARENA ESSEX		46-49	50-45	51-45	50-44	52-44	48-48	54-40	†43-51	47-48	55-40	67-28	49-46	54-41	56-39	51-45	45-50	48-48
BERWICK	70-26		62-32	61-34	78-18	68-28	60-36	61-35	71-25	72-24	65-31	65-31	59-35	57-39	59-37	72-23	66-30	51-44
EASTBOURNE	62-34	49-47		66-30	67-29	55-39	52-44	55-41	61-35	62-34	47-49	65-30	67-28	43-53	52-44	59-37	59-37	48-47
EDINBURGH	43-51	50-45	53-43		62-34	56-39	51-45	47-49	61-34	64-32	69-27	59-36	59-37	51-45	42-54	55-41	68-28	42-53
EXETER	76-20	59-37	72-24	71-25		61-34	57-39	60-36	63-33	76-20	71-25	62-33	61-35	53-42	57-38	59-37	49-47	64-32
GLASGOW	64-32	50-46	56-40	52-43	64-32		53-43	43-51	61-35	53-43	68-28	61-35	59-36	58-38	50-45	50-46	59-37	50-46
HACKNEY	60-36	50-46	67-29	53-43	55-40	62-33		51-44	53-43	59-37	55-41	63-33	64-32	54-41	50-46	61-35	58-38	52-44
IPSWICH	65-31	69-27	66-30	±49-29	53-43	52-44	64-32		59-37	58-37	53-43	58-38	56-40	51-45	47-48	55-41	49-47	52-44
LONG EATON	63-33	50-46	59-37	42-54	44-52	50-46	46-50	50-45		44-52	48-48	57-39	43-53	51-45	42-53	59-37	38-58	37-59
MIDDLESBROUGH	46-47	44-52	45-50	45-50	52-44	54-42	49-47	55-40	57-39		52-44	61-34	57-39	49-47	40-56	51-44	53-43	46-50
MILDENHALL	49-47	37-59	43-53	42-53	47-49	48-46	49-47	42-54	65-30	63-33		66-28	41-55	41-54	30-66	50-46	50-46	50-46
MILTON KEYNES	57-39	49-47	45-51	46-50	48-48	55-41	56-40	37-59	51-44	53-42	53-43		48-48	35-61	38-58	43-52	41-55	44-52
NEWCASTLE	45-51	36-60	49-47	44-52	49-46	42-54	51-45	53-43	50-45	44-51	49-47	50-46		50-44	44-52	50-46	48-48	39-57
PETERBOROUGH	55-40	65-30	45-50	60-36	59-37	61-33	55-41	36-57	60-36	59-36	62-34	61-35	56-40		42-54	52-44	58-38	46-47
POOLE	71-24	44-52	59-37	61-35	55-41	68-28	51-44	50-46	66-30	66-30	59-37	68-28	59-36	51-45		55-41	58-38	59-37
RYE HOUSE	53-42	38-57	51-45	49-46	53-42	52-44	45-50	43.5 50.5	60-35	61-34	55-41	61-34	49-46	52-44	44-51		47-48	51-44
STOKE	68-28	54-42	56-40	47-49	60-36	60-36	52-44	47-49	46-49	64-32	56-40	63-33	53-43	67-29	42-54	56-40		41-55
WIMBLEDON	68-28	53-43	51-45	67-29	57-39	54-42	57-39	53-43	62-34	71-24	57-39	62-34	70-26	57-39	48-48	51-45	54-42	

†Result amended after protest over the use of rider replacement for Malcolm Simmons (Arena Essex). On track score was Arena Essex 49 Long Eaton 46. ±Abandoned after 13 heats, result to stand.

1990 NATIONAL LEAGUE

	P	W	D	L	PtsF	PtsA	W	D	L	PtsF	PtsA	Pts
1 POOLE	**32**	**16**	**0**	**0**	**970**	**564**	**13**	**0**	**3**	**809**	**720**	**58**
2 Middlesbrough	32	16	0	0	966	567	6	2	8	735	800	46
3 Ipswich	32	13	2	1	906	626	9	0	7	768	761	46
4 Glasgow	32	13	0	3	934.5	598.5	6	0	10	709	821	38
5 Hackney	32	13	0	3	887	644	6	0	10	721	807	38
6 Berwick	32	15	0	1	941	584	3	1	12	634.5	899.5	37
7 Wimbledon	32	12	1	3	872	656	4	2	10	720	813	35
8 Stoke	32	11	0	5	839	691	5	1	10	734	798	33
9 Exeter	32	14	0	2	951	582	1	1	14	625	907	31
10 Peterborough	32	13	0	3	878	657	2	0	14	578	956	30
11 Eastbourne	32	12	0	4	828	702	3	0	13	598	934	30
12 Newcastle	32	11	0	5	802	731	3	0	13	676.5	855.5	28
13 Edinburgh	32	10	1	5	854.5	678.5	2	0	14	666	861	25
14 Arena Essex	32	9	1	6	797	729	3	0	13	583	945	25
15 Rye House	32	7	0	9	778	749	1	0	15	608	923	16
16 Long Eaton	32	7	2	7	778	758	0	0	16	594	939	16
17 Milton Keynes	32	5	0	11	724	804	1	0	15	562	966	12

POOLE equalled Hackney's 1988 record of going through a full National League season dropping only six points, having ridden in two meetings more than Londoners.

1990 National League Riders' Championship Final

Saturday, September 15, Coventry:
1 Andy Grahame 14, 2 Chris Louis 13, 3 Craig Boyce 11, 4 David Bargh 11, 5 Steve Regeling 10, 6 Steve Schofield 9, 7 Les Collins 8, 8 Eric Monaghan 8, 9 Martin Goodwin 8, 10 Rod Hunter 6, 11 Shane Bowes 6, 12 Richard Hellsén 6, 13 David Walsh 5, 14 Gordon Kennett 4, 15 Mick Poole 1, 16 Jens Rasmussen 0.
Track Reserves: Andy Meredith 0, Lee Coleman 0.
Sponsors: Jawa-Barum.

1990 KNOCK OUT CUP

Round 1
Long Eaton 57 33 90 Berwick 39 62 101
Round 2
Ipswich 60 41 101 Glasgow 36 54 90
Peterborough 48 31 79 Stoke 48 65 113
Arena Essex 41 35 76 Newcastle 55 61 116
Edinburgh 51 44 95 Middlesbrough 45 51 96
Exeter 61 33 94 Wimbledon 35 62 97
Poole 56 44 100 Berwick 40 50 90
Milton Keynes 56 45 101 Rye House 39 51 90
Eastbourne 40 32 72 Hackney 56 64 120
Round 3
Milton Keynes 40 27 67 Middlesbrough 56 69 125
Wimbledon 57 45 102 Stoke 37 51 88
Ipswich 61 41 102 Newcastle 35 54 89
Hackney 47 33 80 Poole 48 62 110
Semi Finals
Wimbledon 36 27 63 Middlesbrough 59 69 128
POOLE 60 49 109 Ipswich 36 47 83
FINAL
First leg, September 18:
POOLE 62 (Craig Boyce 19, Alun Rossiter 13, Gary Allan 11, Tony Langdon 10, Rod Colquhoun 6, Gary Chessell 3, Justin Elkins, number eight, did not ride) *Middlesbrough 34* (Rod Hunter 11, Jamie Luckhurst 7, Darren Sumner 5, Paul Bentley 5, David Cheshire 3, Dave Edwards 2, Steve Wilcock 1).
Second leg, September 20
Middlesbrough 51 (Sumner 9, Bentley 9, Hunter 9, Wilcock 9, Cheshire 7, Luckhurst 7, Edwards 1) POOLE 45 (Boyce 16, Allan 11, T. Langdon 10, Colquhoun 4, Rossiter 3, Elkins 1, Steve Leigh, number eight, did not ride).

❑ POOLE win 107-85 on aggregate.

1990 ALL THE RESULTS

	ARENA ESSEX	BERWICK	EASTBOURNE	EDINBURGH	EXETER	GLASGOW	HACKNEY	IPSWICH	LONG EATON	MIDDLESBRO'	MILTON KEYNES	NEWCASTLE	PETERBORO'	POOLE	RYE HOUSE	STOKE	WIMBLEDON
ARENA ESSEX		58-38	38-58	57-36	62-34	44-52	54-42	47-49	51-43	48-48	47-49	47-49	52-43	41-51	51-45	50-46	50-46
BERWICK	71-25		61-35	48-45	63-32	51-44	46-47	49-47	54-42	51-45	68-27	68-27	73-23	61-35	68-28	56-40	53-42
EASTBOURNE	39-56	58-38		62-34	66-30	53-42	51-45	46-49	49-47	42-54	56-39	49-46	53-43	35-61	61-34	54-42	54-42
EDINBURGH	67-29	46.5 49.5	60-36		66-29	43-52	40-56	31-64	71-25	45-51	66-30	56-40	62-34	53-43	51-45	49-47	48-48
EXETER	76-20	56-40	63-32	56-39		60-35	45-51	53-43	65-31	67-29	64-32	55-41	68-28	44-52	64-32	53-43	62-34
GLASGOW	74-22	60-36	66-30	53-43	61-35		54-42	62-33	74-22	57-39	63-32	51.5 44.5	64-32	46-49	60-36	45-51	44-52
HACKNEY	44-50	61-35	62-33	52-44	51-45	50-46		53-42	62-34	43-53	67-29	60-35	59-37	47-49	68-28	57-39	51-45
IPSWICH	70-25	48-48	63-33	56-40	50-46	56-40	48-47		55-41	60-36	65-31	60-36	63-33	44-51	67-28	48-48	53-43
LONG EATON	54-42	46-50	41-55	52-44	48-48	40-56	49-47	43-53		40-56	56-40	54-42	69-27	45-51	49-47	44-52	48-48
MIDDLESBROUGH	53-43	71-25	61-35	65-31	61-34	60-36	58-38	53-43	62-34		68-28	55-41	70-26	59-37	58-37	52-44	60-35
MILTON KEYNES	53-42	46-49	41-55	46-50	40-56	40-56	45-51	44-49	59-37	39-57		49-46	51-45	44-52	48-47	37-59	42-53
NEWCASTLE	55-41	50-46	51-45	54-42	55-41	45-50	44-52	47-49	50-46	48-47	63-33		55-41	45-51	51-44	50-46	39-57
PETERBOROUGH	67-29	64-32	74-22	53-43	50-46	67-29	61-35	41-55	52-44	50-46	59-37	51-45		29-67	57-39	46-49	57-39
POOLE	61-35	70-26	71-25	52-43	57-39	62-34	63-32	59-37	56-40	58-38	56-40	63-33	58-38		73-23	57-39	54-42
RYE HOUSE	46-49	52-43	62-33	43-52	55-40	46-49	50-46	44-52	56-39	59-37	51-45	39-57	47-49	36-60		45-49	47-49
STOKE	54-40	58-38	54-42	62-34	61-35	50-46	47-49	40-56	61-35	45-51	55-37	41-55	66-30	44-52	50-46		51-45
WIMBLEDON	61-35	55-41	66-29	50-46	61-35	54-42	52-41	49-47	62-34	48-48	62-33	57-39	46-49	47-48	47-49	55-40	

MILDENHALL had entered the 1990 National League but were expelled on March 22, 1990, by the National League Management Committee when their declared team failed to meet the minimum 42 point limit.

AT THE DOUBLE...the 1990 Poole squad that completed the League and Cup double but then surprisingly went out of the National Series in the first round

1982 ◆ SUPERNATIONAL ◆ 1983

Round 1

Long Eaton 56 34 90 Ellesmere Port 40 62 102
Middlesbrough 56 52 108 Rye House 40 44 84
NEWCASTLE 69 65 134 Boston 27 31 58
Weymouth 50 44 94 Mildenhall 46 51 97

Semi Finals

Ellesmere Port 63 46 109 Mildenhall 33 49 82
NEWCASTLE 64 49 113 Middlesbrough 32 43 75

FINAL

First leg, October 22:
Ellesmere Port 47 (Robert Maxfield 13, Eric Monaghan 13, Billy Burton 9, Steve Finch 7, John Jackson 3, Glenn Parrott 2, Phil Alderman 0) NEWCASTLE 49 (Joe Owen 14, Bobby Beaton 12, Rod Hunter 10, Alan Emerson 7, Tom Owen 3, Keith Bloxsome 2, Robbie Foy 1).

Second leg, October 25:
NEWCASTLE 72 (J. Owen 15, Hunter 13, Beaton 13, T. Owen 11, Emerson 10, Bloxsome 8, Foy 2) Ellesmere Port 24 (Finch 10, Monaghan 5, Maxfield 4, Burton 3, Alderman 1, Jackson 1, Parrott 0).

❑ NEWCASTLE win 121-71 on aggregate.

◆ *The competition was contested by the top eight clubs in the National League table as of Sunday, September 19, 1982.*

Round 1

Edinburgh 42 21 63 Newcastle 54 75 129
Middlesbrough 52 44 96 Mildenhall 42 52 94
Milton Keynes 54 26 80 Crayford 42 70 112
Scunthorpe 54 34 88 Weymouth 42 62 104

Semi Finals

Crayford 68 49 117 Middlesbrough 38 47 75
Newcastle 55 44 99 Weymouth 41 52 93

FINAL

First leg, October 26:
Crayford 48 (Barry Thomas 10, Paul Bosley 9, Alan Mogridge 9, Alan Sage 6, Trevor Banks 5, Andy Galvin 5, Kevin Teager 4) NEWCASTLE 47 (Joe Owen 14, Rod Hunter 12, Alan Emerson 9, Martin Scarisbrick 8, Bernie Collier 4, John Place 0, rider replacement for Bobby Beaton).

Second leg, October 24:
NEWCASTLE 53 (Hunter 15, Owen 11, Scarisbrick 9, Beaton 8, Collier 8, Emerson 1, Place 1) Crayford 43 (Thomas 13, Banks 12, Bosley 6, Galvin 6, Mogridge 5, Sage 1, rider replacement for Kevin Teager).

❑ NEWCASTLE win 100-91 on aggregate.

◆ *The competition was contested by the top eight clubs in the National League table as of Sunday, September 25, 1983. Edinburgh took eighth place on race points as they, Exeter and Berwick all had 32 points.*

1990 NATIONAL SERIES

Qualifying Rounds

First leg
Exeter 39 Poole 35 Wimbledon 34
Middlesbrough 50 Glasgow 31 Berwick 27
Stoke 47 Ipswich 32 Hackney 29

Second leg
Poole 42 Exeter 33 Wimbledon 33
Glasgow 50 Berwick 33 Middlesbrough 25
Ipswich 44 Stoke 35 Hackney 29

Third leg
Wimbledon 52 Poole 29 Exeter 27
Berwick 40 Glasgow 35 Middlesbrough 33
Ipswich 38 Hackney 35 Stoke 34

Aggregate scores
Wimbledon 119 Poole 106 Exeter 99
Glasgow 116 Middlesbrough 108 Berwick 100
Stoke 116 Ipswich 114 Hackney 93

◆ *The competition was contested by the top nine clubs in the National League table as of Sunday, September 23, 1990.*

FINAL

Round 1
Wimbledon, October 24:
Wimbledon 31 (Andy Grahame 9, Nathan Simpson 7, Neville Tatum 6, Nigel Leaver 6, Peter Chapman 3, Ray Morton 0, Peter Schroeck, did not ride) Glasgow 25 (Steve Lawson 6, Charlie McKinna 5, Kenny McKinna 5, Shane Bowes 4, Jason Lyons 3, Sean Courtney 2, Phil Jeffrey, did not ride) Stoke 15 (Chris Cobby 6, Louis Carr 4, Garry Stead 2, Eric Monaghan 1, Mark Carlson 1, David Clarke 1, Jason Reed did not ride).
■ *Abandoned after 12 races. Scores to count.*

Round 2
Stoke, October 26:
Glasgow 42 (Bowes 10, K. McKinna 10, Lawson 8, Lyons 8, C. McKinna 4, Jeffrey 2, Courtney 0) Wimbledon 38 (Grahame 12, Morton 8, Tatum 7, Leaver 6, Simpson 4, Chapman 1, Schroeck, did not ride) Stoke 28 (Carr 8, Cobby 8, Monaghan 5, Clarke 3, Carlson 3, Jonathan Hughes 1, Stead 0).

Round 3
Glasgow, October 27:
Glasgow 40 (K. McKinna 12, Bowes 9, Lawson 7, Courtney 6, Lyons 5, C. McKinna 1, Jeffrey, did not ride) Wimbledon 35 (Simpson 10, Grahame 7, Morton 6, Leaver 6, Tatum 4, Chapman 1, Schroeck 1) Stoke 32 (Monaghan 10, Carr 8, Cobby 6, Stead 4, Clarke 3, Carlson 1).

❑ GLASGOW 107 Wimbledon 104 Stoke 75.

ARENA ESSEX

1984...1984...1984...1984...1984...1984

	M	R	Pts	BP	TPts	Ave	F	P	Total
§Bob Humphreys	**34**	**143**	**242.0**	**15.0**	**257.0**	**7.189**		**2**	**2**
§Alan Sage	**34**	**138**	**221.0**	**27.0**	**248.0**	**7.188**	**1**		**1**
§§Martin Goodwin	33	134	222.0	16.0	238.0	7.104	1		1
§§David Smart	**34**	**137**	**187.0**	**27.0**	**214.0**	**6.248**			
§Bill Barrett	30	113	146.0	24.0	170.0	6.018			
§§David Cheshire	15	52	61.0	12.0	73.0	5.615			
§§Paul Fry	1	3	3.0	1.0	4.0	5.333			
§John Grahame	1	4	3.0	2.0	5.0	5.000			
§§Jeremy Luckhurst	18	54	54.0	11.0	65.0	4.815		1	1
§Peter Johns	31	107	105.5	22.0	127.5	4.766			
§Ian Humphreys	2	4	4.0	0.0	4.0	4.000			
§Keith Pritchard	1	4	2.0	0.0	2.0	2.000			
§§Steve Collins	4	9	3.0	0.0	3.0	1.333			

1985...1985...1985...1985...1985...1985

	M	R	Pts	BP	TPts	Ave	F	P	Total
§Neil Middleditch	**40**	**171**	**360.0**	**45.0**	**405.0**	**9.474**	**1**	**6**	**7**
Martin Goodwin	40	172	287.0	32.0	319.0	7.419	2	1	3
Bob Humphreys	**40**	**158**	**252.0**	**23.0**	**275.0**	**6.962**		**2**	**2**
David Cheshire	33	127	197.0	22.0	219.0	6.898		2	2
David Smart	35	126	173.0	25.0	198.0	6.286		1	1
Alan Sage	**40**	**157**	**183.0**	**38.0**	**221.0**	**5.631**		**1**	**1**
§Gary Chessell	33	99	101.0	17.0	118.0	4.768			
Ian Humphreys	6	18	11.0	0.0	11.0	2.444			
§§Sean Barker	9	17	8.0	1.0	9.0	2.118			
§Paul Muchene	1	2	0.0	0.0	0.0	0.000			

1986...1986...1986...1986...1986...1986

	M	R	Pts	BP	TPts	Ave	F	P	Total
§Andrew Silver	36	155	389.0	14.0	403.0	10.400	6	6	12
Neil Middleditch	36	151	342.0	19.0	361.0	9.563	6	3	9
Martin Goodwin	43	190	395.5	26.0	421.5	8.874	5	2	7
David Smart	32	130	184.0	26.0	210.0	6.462			
§Peter Chapman	5	22	27.0	2.0	29.0	5.273			
Gary Chessell	36	144	148.0	38.0	186.0	5.167			
§Lawrie Bloomfield	43	167	165.0	31.0	196.0	4.695			
§Russell Paine	3	6	2.0	2.0	4.0	2.667			
Sean Barker	37	97	51.0	12.0	63.0	2.598			
Paul Muchene	19	50	21.0	6.0	27.0	2.160			
§Andy Fisher	3	11	3.0	1.0	4.0	1.455			
§§Lee Paine	1	3	0.0	0.0	0.0	0.000			

1987...1987...1987...1987...1987...1987

	M	R	Pts	BP	TPts	Ave	F	P	Total
Andrew Silver	31	146	378.0	11.0	389.0	10.658	11	2	13
Martin Goodwin	32	145	312.0	11.0	323.0	8.910	4	1	5
§Nigel Leaver	**36**	**161**	**249.0**	**23.0**	**272.0**	**6.758**	**1**	**2**	**3**
Gary Chessell	31	130	180.0	21.0	201.0	6.185			
Ian Humphreys	32	116	108.0	24.0	132.0	4.552			
§Steve Bishop	34	126	121.0	7.0	128.0	4.063			
§Mark Chessell	28	90	50.0	17.0	67.0	2.978			
Lawrie Bloomfield	9	22	12.0	3.0	15.0	2.727			
§§Simon Wolstenholme	7	26	11.0	2.0	13.0	2.000			
Paul Muchene	3	5	1.0	1.0	2.0	1.600			

1988...1988...1988...1988...1988...1988

	M	R	Pts	BP	TPts	Ave	F	P	Total
Martin Goodwin	31	169	402.0	7.0	409.0	9.680	6	1	7
David Smart	30	157	260.5	25.0	285.5	7.274		1	1
§Rob Tilbury	32	169	274.0	11.0	285.0	6.746			
Nigel Leaver	32	162	183.0	52.0	235.0	5.802		1	1
§Chris Cobby	32	147	180.0	30.0	210.0	5.714		1	1
Ian Humphreys	32	115	114.0	23.0	137.0	4.765			
Simon Wolstenholme	32	98	90.0	23.0	113.0	4.612			
Lawrie Bloomfield	2	2	1.0	0.0	1.0	2.000			

1989...1989...1989...1989...1989...1989

	M	R	Pts	BP	TPts	Ave	F	P	Total
Martin Goodwin	34	180	371.0	10.0	381.0	8.467	3		3
Rob Tilbury	32	182	349.0	20.0	369.0	8.110	2	1	3
§Malcolm Simmons	16	76	136.0	10.0	146.0	7.684			
§§Wayne Garratt	32	153	198.0	25.0	223.0	5.830			
Simon Wolstenholme	36	190	210.0	32.0	242.0	5.095		1	1
Troy Pratt	36	180	181.0	23.0	204.0	4.533			
Ian Humphreys	**36**	**138**	**100.0**	**23.0**	**123.0**	**3.565**			
§§Robert Ledwith	1	5	3.0	1.0	4.0	3.200			
§§Nick Floyd	12	36	19.0	7.0	26.0	2.889			
§§Chris Young	2	7	1.0	0.0	1.0	0.571			
§§Russell Etherington	1	4	0.0	0.0	0.0	0.000			

1990...1990...1990...1990...1990...1990

	M	R	PTs	BP	TPts	Ave	F	P	Total
Martin Goodwin	22	123	260.0	12.0	272.0	8.846		1	1
Rob Tilbury	**34**	**187**	**362.0**	**16.0**	**378.0**	**8.086**	**1**	**1**	**2**
Wayne Garratt	**34**	**176**	**217.0**	**37.0**	**254.0**	**5.773**			
Troy Pratt	25	119	150.0	18.0	168.0	5.647	1		1
§Kevin Brice	**34**	**155**	**166.0**	**26.0**	**192.0**	**4.955**			
§§Adrian Stevens	**34**	**126**	**120.0**	**21.0**	**141.0**	**4.476**			
Simon Wolstenholme	**34**	**154**	**143.0**	**23.0**	**166.0**	**4.312**			
§Kevin Teager	7	34	28.0	5.0	33.0	3.882			
Robert Ledwith	5	14	9.0	1.0	10.0	2.857			
Chris Young	1	2	1.0	0.0	1.0	2.000			

NATIONAL SUPER MARATHON

1984	1 Andrew Silver	2 Keith White	3 Martin Goodwin
1985	1 Gordon Kennett	2 Trevor Banks	3 David Mullett
1986	1 Martin Goodwin	2 Andrew Silver	3 Gordon Kennett
1987	1 Andrew Silver	2 Gordon Kennett	3 Neville Tatum
1988	1 Martin Goodwin	2 Gordon Kennett	3 Rob Tilbury
1989	1 Martin Goodwin	2 Jens Rasmussen	3 Steve Schofield
1990	1 Alan Mogridge	2 Nigel Leaver	3 Dean Standing

RADIO ESSEX CHAMPIONSHIP

1984	1 Bob Garrad	2 Alan Sage	3 Brian Kennett
1985	1 Mike Ferreira	2 Neil Middleditch	3 Bob Humphreys
1986	1 Malcolm Simmons	2 Neil Middleditch	3 David Mullett
1987	1 Gordon Kennett	2 Melvyn Taylor	3 Steve Schofield
1988	1 Mark Loram	2 Andy Galvin	3 Andy Buck
1990	1 Jens Rasmussen	2 Steve Schofield	3 Rob Tilbury

EVENING ECHO ESSEX CHAMPIONSHIP

1988	1 Martin Goodwin	2 Neil Middleditch	3 Jamie Luckhurst

■ *STOCK CAR promoter Chick Woodroffe, who was already staging banger racing at his Motorsport Complex just off the Arterial Road alongside Dartford Tunnel, and multi-track boss Wally Mawdsley teamed up to bring National League racing to the Purfleet track at the beginning of 1984.*

■ *Peter Thorogood was appointed manager and remained in that rôle even when Mawdsley left the promoting company, leaving Woodroffe in sole charge until he put the track and team up for sale at the end of the 1990 season because of ill-health.*

■ *One feature of the track was that it became the first League track to be licensed even though it didn't have a safety fence.*

■ *Instead the width of the stock cartrack acted as a run-off area for riders – a feature that provoked considerable criticism from some riders, notably the then Hackney captain Barry Thomas.*

■ *Even though team honours eluded the Hammers (they took their nickname from the defunct West Ham) they enjoyed considerable individual success with Neil Middleditch winning the National League Riders' Championship in 1985 and Andrew Silver taking the same title in 1987.*

■ *Silver was also capped by England at senior level while with the club (only the second rider to be honoured that way) and became the first National League rider to qualify for successive British Finals.*

BARROW

1972...1972...1972...1972...1972...1972

	M	R	Pts	BP	TPts	Ave	F	P	Total
§WBrian Foote	12	50	104.0	6.0	110.0	8.800	1		1
§WBBob Coles	**34**	**145**	**287.0**	**25.0**	**312.0**	**8.607**		**1**	**1**
§WBMike Sampson	30	124	239.0	20.0	259.0	8.355	3	1	4
§WKevin Holden	12	46	89.0	5.0	94.0	8.174	2	1	3
§WBStan Stevens	17	66	106.0	13.0	119.0	7.212			
§§BMike Watkin	20	80	126.0	9.0	135.0	6.750			
§§BTom Owen	22	85	91.0	23.0	114.0	5.365			
§WMike Lanham	8	33	36.0	6.0	42.0	5.091			
§BIan Hindle	22	80	90.0	9.0	99.0	4.950			
§BChris Roynon	14	42	39.0	9.0	48.0	4.571			
§BBobby Campbell	4	11	11.0	1.0	12.0	4.364			
§BGeoff Lyon	3	12	10.0	3.0	13.0	4.333			
§§BKeith Evans	14	49	42.0	11.0	53.0	4.327			
§WTed Howgego	1	4	3.0	1.0	4.0	4.000			
§WIan Gills	7	22	18.0	3.0	21.0	3.818			
§WCharlie Benham	6	15	12.0	2.0	14.0	3.733			
§BAllan Mackie	6	13	9.0	3.0	12.0	3.692			
§WVic Cross	4	11	8.0	1.0	9.0	3.273			
§§BHarry Maclean	1	3	2.0	0.0	2.0	2.667			
§§BClive Buckler	1	2	0.0	0.0	0.0	0.000			

BARROW took over from West Ham on the track's closure because of the redevelopment of their Custom House Lane track. The first six home League matches were held at West Ham and the remainder at Barrow. In the legend above W indicates West Ham and B indicates Barrow.
The first Division Two match at Holker Street was on Tuesday, June 20, when Workington won 42-36. A Knock Out Cup match had been held the previous week, Barrow losing 36-42 to Peterborough.

1973...1973...1973...1973...1973...1973

	M	R	Pts	BP	TPts	Ave	F	P	Total
Tom Owen	30	125	225.0	35.0	260.0	8.320	2	4	6
Mike Sampson	35	156	300.0	24.0	324.0	8.308	1	1	2
§Terry Kelly	31	126	208.0	25.0	233.0	7.397		2	2
§Sid Sheldrick	**36**	**137**	**195.0**	**44.0**	**239.0**	**6.978**	**1**	**3**	**4**
§Joe Owen	27	107	142.0	24.0	166.0	6.206	1		1
§Chris Bailey	9	35	52.0	9.0	61.0	6.971			
§Craig Pendlebury	9	24	33.0	6.0	39.0	6.500			
Chris Roynon	35	109	133.0	22.0	155.0	5.688			
Keith Evans	27	105	133.0	14.0	147.0	5.600		1	1
Ian Hindle	1	3	4.0	0.0	4.0	5.333			
§§Don Howison	2	6	4.0	2.0	6.0	4.000			

1974...1974...1974...1974...1974...1974

	M	R	Pts	BP	TPts	Ave	F	P	Total
Tom Owen	37	166	322.5	32.0	354.5	8.542		2	2
§Dave Baugh	6	26	54.0	1.0	55.0	8.462			
Terry Kelly	34	136	246.0	26.0	272.0	8.000	3		3
Sid Sheldrick	26	103	184,0	16.0	200.0	7.767	1		1
Joe Owen	36	151	248.0	30.0	278.0	7.364	1	3	4
§Paul O'Neal	8	32	55.0	4.0	59.0	7.375	2		2
Chris Roynon	**38**	**160**	**211.0**	**324.0**	**245.0**	**6.125**		**1**	**1**
§Mick Sheldrick	32	113	821.0	14.0	96.0	3.398			
§Graham Tattersall	33	95	53.0	12.0	65.0	2.737			
§§Charlie McCormack	2	4	0.0	0.0	0.0	0.000			

BARROW withdrew at the beginning of March, 1975, following the breakdown of lease talks between promoter George Graham and landlords Barrow A.F.C.

1978...1978...1978...1978...1978...1978

	M	R	Pts	BP	TPts	AVe	F	P	Total
§Charlie Monk	38	156	306.0	14.0	320.0	8.205	1		1
§Geoff Pusey	**40**	**182**	**304.5**	**24.0**	**328.5**	**7.220**	**1**		**1**
§Chris Bevan	16	61	92.0	12.0	104.0	6.820		1	1
Andy Reid	38	163	208.5	17.0	225.5	5.534			
Chris Roynon	**40**	**147**	**154.0**	**30.0**	**184.0**	**5.007**			
§Malcolm Bedkober	4	14	15.0	1.0	16.0	4.571			
§§Ken Murray	6	17	13.0	5.0	18.0	4.235			
§Bob Watts	1	2	1.0	1.0	2.0	4.000			
§§Mark Courtney	38	134	102.0	19.0	121.0	3.612			
§Chris Robins	11	37	24.0	5.0	29.0	3.135			
§Malcolm Chambers	6	14	7.0	1.0	8.0	2.286			
§§Gary Pottenger	7	14	6.0	2.0	8.0	2.286			
§§Wayne Muddle	2	6	2.0	1.0	3.0	2.000			
§Keith Williams	1	2	1.0	0.0	1.0	2.000			
§§Les Race	7	23	9.0	1.0	10.0	1.739			
§§David Butt	14	44	17.0	2.0	19.0	1.727			
§Des Wilson	5	16	3.0	2.0	5.0	1.250			
§§Andy Heyes	2	4	0.0	0.0	0.0	0.000			

ON THE re-opening of National League speedway in Barrow the sport moved from Holker Street Stadium, where Barrow AFC were the landlords, to a purpose built speedway and stock-car stadium at Park Road on the outskirts of the town here there was non-League racing in 1977 and 1984. The venue never attracted good crowds.

1985...1985...1985...1985...1985...1985

	M	R	Pts	BP	TPts	Ave	F	P	Total
Kevin Armitage	**5**	**18**	**15.0**	**3.0**	**18.0**	**4.000**			
Eric Broadbelt	**5**	**19**	**16.0**	**0.0**	**16.0**	**3.368**			
Garry Clegg	2	6	2.0	0.0	2.0	1.333			
Bob Coles	2	7	3.0	0.0	3.0	1.714			
Bernie Collier	3	14	23.0	2.0	25.0	7.143			
Wayne Jackson	2	4	1.0	0.0	1.0	1.000			
Terry Kelly	**5**	**15**	**7.0**	**0.0**	**7.0**	**1.867**			
Gary O'Hare	**5**	**17**	**14.0**	**2.0**	**16.0**	**3.765**			
Paul Price	**5**	**20**	**18.0**	**4.0**	**22.0**	**4.400**			

Barrow were expelled from the League on May 16, 1985, for failing to reach the 43 point minimum limit. At the time they had ridden three League and two Knock Out matches.

EDDIE CROOKS TROPHY

1972	1 Jack Millen	2 Mike Sampson	3 Lou Sansom
1973	1 Lou Sansom	2 Carl Glover	3 Graham Drury
1974	1 Joe Owen	2 Phil Herne	3 Robin Adlington, Mick Sheldrick and Brian Clark
1977	1 Tom Owen	2 Mick McKeon	3 Nigel Close

DUCKHAMS ROSEBOWL

1972	1 Mike Sampson	2 Bob Coles	3 Alan Knapkin

HUGHIE GREEN TROPHY

1973	1 Chris Roynon	2 Joe Owen	3 Sid Sheldrick

CHARLIE WILLIAMS GOLD CUP

1973	1 Lou Sansom	2 Tom Owen, Alan Knapkin and Dave Baugh	

AUTUMN CLASSIC

1974	1 Tom Owen	2 Joe Owen	3 Colin Meredith and Robin Adlington

MISTER JUNIOR OF THE NORTH

1977	1 Mark Dickinson	2 Andy Reid	3 Gary Pottenger

CUMBRIA OPEN CHAMPIONSHIP

1984	1 Eric Broadbelt	2 Paul Thorp	3 Steve Lawson

■ ***WORLD CHAMPION Ivan Mauger and his business partner Peter Oakes were barred from becoming promoters at Barrow in 1972 by the British Speedway Promoters' Association. The promoting licence was issued in the name of a third partner Wally Mawdsley although Mauger continued to play an active rôle at the track.***
■ ***SOCCER star George Best was booked to officially open Barrow but failed to turn up and was replaced, at late notice, by actress Julie Goodyear, who was playing barmaid Bet Lynch in the ITV soap opera Coronation Street.***

BELLE VUE

1968...1968...1968...1968...1968...1968

	M	R	Pts	BP	TPts	Ave	F	P	Total
§§Taffy Owen	18	74	161.0	12.0	173.0	9.351	5	1	6
§§Ken Eyre	**20**	**85**	**170.0**	**20.0**	**190.0**	**8.941**		**3**	**3**
§§John Woodcock	**20**	**81**	**153.0**	**12.0**	**165.0**	**8.148**	**1**	**2**	**3**
§§Eric Broadbelt	13	54	98.0	12.0	110.0	8.148	1	1	2
§§Chris Bailey	19	78	139.0	12.0	151.0	7.744	1	1	2
§§Ken Moss	15	43	59.0	9.0	68.0	6.326			
§§Peter Thompson	17	60	70.0	19.0	89.0	5.933			
§§Brian Bentley	14	43	46.0	13.0	59.0	5.488			
§§Dave Brockbank	3	12	7.0	1.0	8.0	2.667			
§§Terry Holmes	1	2	0.0	0.0	0.0	0.000			

1969...1969...1969...1969...1969...1969

	M	R	Pts	BP	TPts	Ave	F	P	Total
Ken Eyre	23	89	213.0	6.0	219.0	9.843	7	1	8
Eric Broadbelt	32	129	298.0	16.0	314.0	9.736	6	1	7
§§Phil Whitaker	1	3	6.0	1.0	7.0	9.333			
Chris Bailey	33	127	217.0	45.0	262.0	8.252		7	7
§§Bill Moulin	28	104	188.0	25.0	213.0	8.192		2	2
§Mike Hiftle	7	27	47.0	7.0	54.0	8.000			
§§Steve Waplington	**35**	**142**	**254.0**	**28.0**	**282.0**	**7.944**	**2**	**2**	**4**
Ken Moss	34	130	204.0	54.0	258.0	7.938		1	1
Taffy Owen	27	96	153.0	17.0	170.0	7.083	1	2	3
Peter Thompson	10	33	42.0	13.0	55.0	6.667			
§§Colin Goad	7	24	23.0	8.0	31.0	5.167			

■ *BELLE VUE, under the direction of former World Finalist and ex-England Test star Dent Oliver, agreed to enter a second team in the newly formed British League Division Two.*

■ *After being refused permission to call them the Belle Vue Babes, the team raced as the Colts and dominated the lower Division in its first two seasons winning the League title in 1968 and completing the Cup and League double the following year.*

■ *In their first season they lost only five matches all season and the following year won 27 out of 35 matches in the two major competitions.*

■ *The majority of the riders used by the Colts in their two seasons went on to First Division status with the club.*

■ *The team, still under the promotion of Belle Vue, moved to nearby Rochdale at the beginning of the 1970 season.*

For a list of Belle Vue individual meetings see Belle Vue, Division One Averages

TAFFY OWEN (left) created his own slice of speedway history when he won the first-ever race in the British League Division Two as captain of Belle Vue Colts.

Owen, one of the few speedway riders born in Wales, led the Belle Vue second team into action against Canterbury at Hyde Road on Wednesday, May 8, 1968.

He won the opening race and then went on to record a four-ride maximum, the first unbeaten performance in Division Two. The meeting also provided a number of other firsts.

Belle Vue's Chris Bailey recorded the first paid maximum, Tyburn Gallows (heat one) was the first rider to fail to finish a race; and Dave Brockbank (heat 5) was the first faller.

Barry Crowson (heat two) was the first visiting rider to win a race; Lex Milloy (Berwick) was the first guest rider to compete in the Second Division; and Tyburn Gallows (real name Ray Humphries) was the first rider to use an assumed name in the competition.

The full scores from the match:

BELLE VUE 55 (Taffy Owen 12, Chris Bailey 11, John Woodcock 11, Ken Eyre 9, Brian Bentley 6, Dave Brockbank 3, Ken Moss 3) CANTERBURY 23 (Barry Crowson 9, Tyburn Gallows 5, Martyn Piddock 4, Les Milloy 3, Neville Slee 1, Barry Lee 1, Chris Raines 0).

BERWICK

BERWICK were founder members of the British League Second Division and raced their first home League match on Saturday, May 25, 1968, losing 28-49 to Belle Vue Colts.
They had opened at Shielfield Park a week earlier with a challenge match against a B team from British League Newcastle, losing 37-41.

1968...1968...1968...1968...1968...1968

	M	R	Pts	BP	TPts	Ave	F	P	Total
§§Bill McMillan	6	25	56.0	1.0	57.0	9.120	3		3
§§Roy Williams	**19**	**82**	**157.0**	**4.0**	**161.0**	**7.854**	**2**		**2**
§§Brian Whaley	11	51	93.0	5.0	98.0	7.686	2		2
§§Brian Black	9	37	57.0	6.0	63.0	6.811		1	1
§§Mark Hall	17	71	105.0	12.0	117.0	6.592	1	1	2
§§Lex Milloy	9	36	50.0	3.0	53.0	5.889			
§§Grieves Davidson	5	15	15.0	2.0	17.0	4.533			
§§Mike Hiftle	3	7	5.0	2.0	7.0	4.000			
§§Alex Nichol	13	49	39.0	4.0	43.0	3.510			
§§Brian Oliver	3	8	5.0	2.0	7.0	3.500			
§§Tom Blackwood	12	38	24.0	8.0	32.0	3.368			
§§Wayne Barry	4	9	7.0	0.0	7.0	3.111			
§§Colin Robertson	9	28	16.0	3.0	19.0	2.714			
§§Alan Hartley	4	12	5.0	1.0	6.0	2.000			

1969...1969...1969...1969...1969...1969

	M	R	Pts	BP	TPts	Ave	F	P	Total
§§Maurie Robinson	28	120	270.5	9.0	279.5	9.317	3	1	4
Mark Hall	30	127	238.0	17.0	255.0	8.031	1	1	2
§§Peter Kelly	14	54	100.0	7.0	107.0	7.926	3	1	4
Roy Williams	30	119	185.0	20.0	205.0	6.891	1	1	2
Lex Milloy	3	10	17.0	0.0	17.0	6.800			
Brian Black	26	99	127.5	24.0	151.5	6.121		1	1
§§Ken Omand	13	49	49.0	9.0	58.0	4.735			
§§Andy Meldrum	5	20	19.0	4.0	23.0	4.600			
§§Ian Paterson	14	41	36.0	7.0	43.0	4.195			
§§Terry Holmes	5	17	13.0	2.0	15.0	3.529			
Alex Nicol	18	49	37.0	5.0	42.0	3.429			
§§Mick Beaton	1	5	4.0	0.0	4.0	3.200			
Grieves Davidson	6	17	13.0	0.0	13.0	3.059			
§Malcolm Bruce	2	7	4.0	1.0	5.0	2.857			
Colin Robertson	12	38	21.0	5.0	26.0	2.737			
Tom Blackwood	4	14	6.0	0.0	6.0	1.714			
§§Bill Maxwell	5	12	4.0	1.0	5.0	1.667			

1970...1970...1970...1970...1970...1970

	M	R	Pts	BP	TPts	Ave	F	P	Total
§Doug Wyer	7	31	62.0	3.0	65.0	8.387	1		1
Maurie Robinson	36	153	294.0	17.0	311.0	8.131	1	3	4
Peter Kelly	28	111	180.0	22.0	202.0	7.279	1		1
Roy Williams	34	134	183.0	18.0	201.0	6.000			
Ken Omand	35	128	138.0	35.0	173.0	5.406			
Alan Paynter	33	117	135.0	19.0	154.0	5.265			
§§Peter Baldock	7	28	27.0	9.0	36.0	5.143			
Ian Paterson	13	35	37.0	7.0	44.0	5.029			
§§Alistair Brady	30	108	119.0	13.0	132.0	4.889			
Andy Meldrum	21	85	91.0	11.0	102.0	4.800			
Lex Milloy	4	16	12.0	3.0	15.0	3.750			
§§Jim Gallacher	6	17	12.0	3.0	15.0	3.529			
§§Brian Murray	1	4	2.0	0.0	2.0	2.000			
§§Derek Greaves	1	2	1.0	0.0	1.0	2.000			
Mick Beaton	1	2	0.0	0.0	0.0	0.000			

1971...1971...1971...1971...1971...1971

	M	R	Pts	BP	TPts	Ave	F	P	Total
Doug Wyer	33	149	359.0	2.0	361.0	9.691	12		12
Maurie Robinson	30	127	228.0	25.0	253.0	7.969		2	2
Andy Meldrum	32	121	186.0	33.0	219.0	7.240		2	2
Alistair Brady	33	130	212.5	16.0	228.5	7.031	3	1	4
Peter Kelly	26	88	107.0	20.0	127.0	5.773			
Alan Paynter	13	45	52.0	9.0	61.0	5.422		1	1
§§Bobby Campbell	33	112	119.0	14.0	133.0	4.750			
§§Jim Beaton	24	85	67.0	21.0	88.0	4.141			
§George Beaton	9	25	18.0	3.0	21.0	3.360			
§§Geoff Davies	2	3	0.0	0.0	0.0	0.000			

1972...1972...1972...1972...1972...1972

	M	R	Pts	BP	TPts	Ave	F	P	Total
Andy Meldrum	**34**	**148**	**279.0**	**30.0**	**309.0**	**8.351**	**3**	**1**	**4**
Jim Gallacher	13	57	114.0	5.0	119.0	8.351		2	2
§§Doug Templeton	**34**	**143**	**290.0**	**7.0**	**297.0**	**8.308**	**3**		**3**
§§Willie Templeton	32	138	234.0	17.0	251.0	7.275	1		1
Jim Beaton	11	41	53.0	12.0	65.0	6.341			
§Graham Jones	22	78	68.0	15.0	83.0	4.256			
George Beaton	11	35	28.0	7.0	35.0	4.000			
Geoff Davies	28	92	72.0	17.0	89.0	3.870			
§§Dennis Jackson	21	69	44.0	9.0	53.0	3.072			
Alistair Brady	18	60	33.0	5.0	38.0	2.533			
§John Lynch	4	10	2.0	1.0	3.0	1.200			
§§Mark Perram	6	18	4.0	1.0	5.0	1.111			

1973...1973...1973...1973...1973...1973

	M	R	Pts	BP	TPts	Ave	F	P	Total
Doug Templeton	30	129	258.0	4.0	262.0	8.124		1	1
Willie Templeton	34	149	263.0	12.0	275.0	7.383	1	2	3
Andy Meldrum	34	149	250.0	14.0	264.0	7.087		2	2
Alistair Brady	1	4	4.0	2.0	6.0	6.000			
Graham Jones	**36**	**133**	**134.0**	**26.0**	**160.0**	**4.812**		**2**	**2**
§§Chris Quigley	28	101	93.0	22.0	115.0	4.554			
§§Denny Morter	18	69	58.0	14.0	72.0	4.174			
§§Ettienne Olivier	8	27	24.0	4.0	28.0	4.148			
§§Robert Hollingworth	28	99	90.0	9.0	99.0	4.000			
Geoff Davies	14	43	28.0	4.0	32.0	2.977			
§John Wilson	4	11	7.0	0.0	7.0	2.545			
Dennis Jackson	11	28	12.0	3.0	15.0	2.143			

AUSTRALIAN Chris Quigley is the only rider in British League history (either Division) whose surname begins with a Q!

1974...1974...1974...1974...1974...1974

	M	R	Pts	BP	TPts	Ave	F	P	Total
§Brian Havelock	6	27	51.0	1.0	52.0	7.704	1		1
Willie Templeton	**38**	**154**	**266.0**	**14.0**	**280.0**	**7.273**	**3**		**3**
Graham Jones	**38**	**160**	**241.0**	**31.0**	**272.0**	**6.800**	**1**		**1**
§Jim Wells	7	21	32.0	3.0	35.0	6.667			
DougTempleton	22	88	137.0	8.0	145.0	6.591			
Denny Morter	30	132	164.0	34.0	198.0	6.000			
§Alf Wells	10	37	50.0	4.0	54.0	5.838			
§§Colin Farquharson	37	139	180.0	17.0	197.0	5.669			
§Dave Trownson	21	71	77.0	10.0	87.0	4.901	1		1
§Ian Wilson	26	83	69.0	9.0	78.0	3.759			
§Robin Dixon	25	72	51.0	12.0	63.0	3.500			

1975...1975...1975...1975...1975...1975

	M	R	Pts	BP	TPts	Ave	F	P	Total
§Dave Gifford	**40**	**172**	**338.0**	**31.0**	**369.0**	**8.581**	**3**	**3**	**6**
Graham Jones	**40**	**159**	**284.0**	**20.0**	**304.0**	**7.648**	**1**	**2**	**3**
Colin Farquharson	30	123	204.0	24.0	228.0	7.415	1	1	2
§Steve Finch	33	138	191.0	42.0	233.0	6.754		1	1
Willie Templeton	38	142	203.0	22.0	225.0	6.338	1		1
Denny Morter	14	54	50.0	16.0	66.0	4.889			
Dave Trownson	**40**	**140**	**152.0**	**18.0**	**170.0**	**4.857**			
§Bernie Hornby	36	118	125.0	18.0	143.0	4.847	1		1
§Jon Bower	5	12	5.0	3.0	8.0	2.667			
§§Frank Hall	1	1	0.0	0.0	0.0	0.000			

1976...1976...1976...1976...1976...1976

	M	R	Pts	BP	TPts	Ave	F	P	Total
Graham Jones	**42**	**172**	**332.0**	**17.0**	**349.0**	**8.116**	**5**	**1**	**6**
Dave Gifford	**42**	**179**	**314.0**	**40.0**	**354.0**	**7.911**	**2**	**4**	**6**
Mike Hiftle	34	130	203.0	30.0	233.0	7.169		3	3
§Robin Adlington	33	138	196.0	40.0	236.0	6.841	1	2	3
Willie Templeton	39	149	215.0	32.0	247.0	6.631	1	1	2
§Eddie Argall	41	165	249.0	21.0	270.0	6.545			
§§Malcolm Chambers	1	4	2.0	1.0	3.0	3.000			
§§Keith Williams	10	34	17.0	0.0	17.0	2.000			
§§Peter Waite	27	80	33.0	3.0	36.0	1.800			
§§Wayne Brown	10	21	8.0	1.0	9.0	1.714			
Frank Hall	3	8	1.0	0.0	1.0	0.500			
§§Ian Darling	1	2	0.0	0.0	0.0	0.000			

BERWICK

1977...1977...1977...1977...1977...1977

	M	R	Pts	BP	TPts	Ave	F	P	Total
Graham Jones	**44**	**192**	**355.0**	**22.0**	**377.0**	**7.854**	**1**	**4**	**5**
Robin Adlington	34	150	244.0	19.0	263.0	7.013	3		3
Mike Hiftle	37	95	142.0	16.0	158.0	6.653	1		1
Willie Templeton	43	168	218.0	24.0	242.0	5.762		1	1
Dave Gifford	43	173	216.0	30.0	246.0	5.688		1	1
§Terry Kelly	15	54	56.0	4.0	60.0	4.444			
Keith Williams	14	45	38.0	7.0	45.0	4.000			
§§Noel Suckling	30	112	88.0	20.0	108.0	3.857			
Wayne Brown	32	106	93.0	9.0	102.0	3.849			
Eddie Argall	3	10	9.0	0.0	9.0	3.600			
§Colin Caffrey	11	30	20.0	6.0	26.0	3.467			
Ian Darling	3	7	5.0	1.0	6.0	3.429			

1978...1978...1978...1978...1978...1978

	M	R	Pts	BP	TPts	Ave	F	P	Total
Graham Jones	37	167	343.0	24.0	367.0	8.790	3	5	8
§Roger Wright	30	117	206.0	18.0	224.0	7.658		2	2
§Jack Millen	5	21	33.0	5.0	38.0	7.238			
Mike Hiftle	32	130	195.0	13.0	208.0	6.400	1	2	3
Willie Templeton	37	136	177.0	31.0	208.0	6.118		2	2
§Mike Fullerton	33	119	160.0	19.0	179.0	6.017			
Dave Gifford	35	136	170.0	21.0	191.0	5.618		2	2
Colin Caffrey	31	111	95.0	23.0	118.0	4.252		1	1
Wayne Brown	18	70	62.0	7.0	69.0	3.943			
Ian Darling	11	25	13.0	4.0	17.0	2.720			
§§David Foot	4	8	0.0	0.0	0.0	0.000			
§§Rob Grant	1	2	0.0	0.0	0.0	0.000			

1979...1979...1979...1979...1979...1979

	M	R	Pts	BP	TPts	Ave	F	P	Total
§Steve McDermott	15	62	128.5	13.0	141.5	9.129		4	4
Wayne Brown	43	192	408.0	24.0	432.0	9.000	4	3	
Mike Fullerton	41	168	293.0	31.0	324.0	7.714	1	5	6
Graham Jones	43	181	297.0	46.0	343.0	7.580	1	4	5
Nigel Close	43	179	277.0	47.0	324.0	7.240	1	3	4
Phil Kynman	**44**	**167**	**231.0**	**28.0**	**259.0**	**6.204**			
Roger Wright	39	122	161.0	27.0	188.0	6.164		1	1
Mike Hiftle	1	4	3.0	2.0	5.0	5.000			
§Mike Caroline	11	33	27.0	9.0	36.0	4.364			
Rob Grant	12	31	26.0	5.0	31.0	4.000			
Ian Darling	1	2	0.0	0.0	0.0	0.000			

1980...1980...1980...1980...1980...1980

	M	R	Pts	BP	TPts	Ave	F	P	Total
Wayne Brown	45	207	469.0	22.0	491.0	9.488	4	10	14
Steve McDermott	45	200	416.0	37.0	453.0	9.060	6	6	12
Mike Fullerton	38	161	264.0	43.0	307.0	7.627	3		3
Roger Wright	25	85	133.0	25.0	158.0	7.435		2	2
Nigel Close	44	188	303.0	41.0	344.0	7.319	1	3	4
Graham Jones	13	56	76.0	13.0	89.0	6.357			
Mike Caroline	46	143	166.0	38.0	204.0	5.706			
§§Brett Saunders	19	51	60.0	11.0	71.0	5.569			
Rob Grant	46	155	173.5	36.0	209.5	5.406			
§§Paul Henderson	2	6	3.0	0.0	3.0	2.000			

BERWICK were forced to leave Shielfield Park after their match against Peterborough on September 7, and raced their last two League matches and one leg of the Cup Final at Brough Park, Newcastle. They completed nine matches without a home base.

◆ ***BERWICK were the first club in British League history to have a lady promoter when Mrs. Elizabeth Taylor and her husband Danny introduced speedway to the Border Country track in 1968.***

◆ ***On her husband's death shortly after that initial season she continued running the track with her son Ken and was still actively involved relinquishing family control at the end of 1984.***

1981...1981...1981...1981...1981...1981

	M	R	Pts	BP	TPts	Ave	F	P	Total
Wayne Brown	*33*	*155*	*342.0*	*16.0*	*358.0*	*9.239*		*2*	*2*
Steve McDermott	*30*	*139*	*274.0*	*18.0*	*292.0*	*8.403*			
Rob Grant	***35***	***148***	***230.0***	***27.0***	***257.0***	***6.946***	***2***	***3***	***5***
Mike Caroline	***35***	***142***	***172.0***	***39.0***	***211.0***	***5.944***			
§Brian Collins	*29*	*123*	*143.5*	*22.0*	*165.5*	*5.382*			
Brett Saunders	*31*	*107*	*113.0*	*22.0*	*135.0*	*5.047*			
Roger Wright	*23*	*74*	*81.0*	*10.0*	*91.0*	*4.919*		*1*	*1*
Graham Jones	*12*	*39*	*36.0*	*9.0*	*45.0*	*4.615*			
Jim Beaton	*6*	*15*	*13.0*	*2.0*	*15.0*	*4.000*			
§§Ian Anderson	*8*	*19*	*5.0*	*1.0*	*6.0*	*1.263*			

Berwick withdrew from the League after their match at Edinburgh on September 4, following a protest from Edinburgh at their use of Glasgow's Blantyre track for home meetings. They continued in the Knock Out Cup. All home matches were raced at neutral tracks Barrow, Workington, Glasgow and Newcastle. The official Knock Out Cup averages were:

	M	R	Pts	BP	TPts	Ave	F	P	Total
Wayne Brown	7	35	83.0	4.0	87.0	9.943		1	1
Steve McDermott	8	40	85.0	10.0	95.0	9.500			
Rob Grant	8	41	6.07	7.0	74.0	7.220			
Mike Caroline	8	42	53.0	10.0	63.0	6.000			
Brett Saunders	8	40	44.0	10.0	54.0	5.400			
Roger Wright	3	9	11.0	0.0	11.0	4.889			
Jim Beaton	1	2	2.0	0.0	2.00	4.000			
§Brian Collins	7	33	26.5	3.0	29.5	3.576			
§§Ian Anderson	4	10	1.0	0.0	1.0	0.400			

1982...1982...1982...1982...1982...1982

	M	R	Pts	BP	TPts	Ave	F	P	Total
Steve McDermott	40	212	454.0	14.0	468.0	8.830	8	1	9
Bruce Cribb	41	216	400.0	24.0	424.0	7.852	2		2
§Brian Collins	**42**	**212**	**325.0**	**59.0**	**384.0**	**7.245**		**2**	**2**
§George Hunter	36	166	270.0	30.0	300.0	7.229			
§Paul Thorp	34	139	190.0	35.0	225.0	6.475		2	2
Rob Grant	39	177	220.0	51.0	271.0	6.124		2	2
Mike Caroline	40	168	182.0	47.0	229.0	5.452		1	1
§§Phil Jeffrey	4	13	8.0	2.0	10.0	3.077			
§Rob Carter	11	32	17.0	5.0	22.0	2.750			
§§Ian Anderson	2	4	1.0	1.0	2.0	2.000			
§§Stephen Brown	2	5	2.0	0.0	2.0	1.600			
§Dennis Gallagher	1	5	2.0	0.0	2.0	1.600			

BERWICK re-opened at a new venue at Berrington Lough in a purpose-built speedway stadium in the countryside.

The new track is actually situated at the village of Ancroft and was built on virgin farmland by the promotion and helpers.

The Bandits had previously raced at Shielfield Park, home of Berwick Rangers soccer club, the only English club competing in the Scottish Football League.

1983...1983...1983...1983...1983...1983

	M	R	Pts	BP	TPts	Ave	F	P	Total
Steve McDermott	37	204	464.0	17.0	481.0	9.431	2		2
Bruce Cribb	**38**	**215**	**426.0**	**20.0**	**446.0**	**8.298**	**1**	**1**	**2**
Brian Collins	**38**	**187**	**246.0**	**50.0**	**296.0**	**6.332**			
Paul Thorp	**38**	**191**	**259.0**	**37.0**	**296.0**	**6.199**			
Rob Grant	30	137	170.0	31.0	201.0	5.869			
Mike Caroline	35	154	167.0	48.0	215.0	5.584			
Phil Jeffrey	18	56	53.0	8.0	61.0	4.357			
§§Robin Hampton	17	49	35.0	7.0	42.0	3.429			
Roger Wright	2	5	3.0	1.0	4.0	3.200			
§Peter Erskine	4	11	5.0	1.0	6.0	2.182			
§§Paul Cooper	3	9	3.0	1.0	4.0	1.778			

BERWICK

1984...1984...1984...1984...1984...1984

	M	R	Pts	BP	TPts	Ave	F	P	Total
Steve McDermott	16	67	165.0	2.0	167.0	9.970	3		3
Bruce Cribb	**38**	**168**	**375.0**	**13.0**	**388.0**	**9.238**	**6**	**1**	**7**
§Jim McMillan	**38**	**170**	**342.0**	**29.0**	**371.0**	**8.729**	**1**	**1**	**2**
§Charlie McKinna	20	77	110.0	18.0	128.0	6.649	1		1
Phil Kynman	21	87	111.0	24.0	135.0	6.207			
§Craig Pendlebury	19	74	88.0	12.0	100.0	5.405			
§David Walsh	33	137	146.0	37.0	183.0	5.343			
Rob Grant	15	58	68.0	6.0	74.0	5.103			
Dennis Gallagher	21	55	42.0	8.0	50.0	3.636			
Mike Caroline	7	22	17.0	3.0	20.0	3.636			
Paul Cooper	14	38	27.0	7.0	34.0	3.579			
§Jackson Irving	12	32	17.0	3.0	20.0	2.500			
§Eric Broadbelt	1	4	1.0	1.0	2.0	2.000			
§Bernie Collier	3	6	1.0	0.0	1.0	0.667			

1985...1985...1985...1985...1985...1985

	M	R	Pts	BP	TPts	Ave	F	P	Total
Jim McMillan	**40**	**167**	**318.0**	**26.0**	**344.0**	**8.240**	**2**	**5**	**7**
Steve McDermott	34	138	233.5	32.0	265.5	7.696	1	1	2
Bruce Cribb	**40**	**173**	**299.0**	**28.0**	**327.0**	**7.561**	**2**	**1**	**3**
Charlie McKinna	38	162	275.0	31.0	306.0	7.556	3	2	5
Rob Grant	39	153	224.0	46.0	270.0	7.059		2	2
§Sean Courtney	28	96	117.0	24.0	141.0	5.875		1	1
Phil Kynman	37	104	110.0	27.0	137.0	5.269			
Jackson Irving	7	21	17.0	4.0	21.0	4.000			
Dennis Gallagher	6	16	12.0	2.0	14.0	3.500			
§Kym Mauger	5	13	8.0	3.0	11.0	3.385			
§Scott Lamb	1	3	0.0	0.0	0.0	0.000			

1986...1986...1986...1986...1986...1986

	M	R	PTs	BP	TPts	Ave	F	P	Total
Charlie McKinna	41	175	349.0	15.0	364.0	8.320	2	2	4
Steve McDermott	38	157	302.0	18.0	320.0	8.153	2		2
Jim McMillan	**42**	**173**	**296.0**	**36.0**	**332.0**	**7.676**	**1**		**1**
Steve Finch	13	53	86.0	13.0	99.0	7.472			
Rob Grant	**42**	**171**	**235.0**	**50.0**	**285.0**	**6.667**			
Sean Courtney	39	149	187.0	33.0	220.0	5.906		1	1
§Roger Lambert	36	108	118.0	25.0	143.0	5.296			
§Paul McHale	16	52	42.0	6.0	48.0	3.692			
§Wayne Ross	10	31	20.0	7.0	27.0	3.484			
Paul Cooper	3	8	4.0	2.0	6.0	3.000			
Barrie Dixon	5	10	5.0	2.0	7.0	2.800			
§Tony Rizzo	6	11	4.0	0.0	4.0	1.455			

1987...1987...1987...1987...1987...1987

	M	R	Pts	BP	TPts	Ave	F	P	Total
Charlie McKinna	34	143	251.0	38.0	289.0	8.084	3	2	5
Steve McDermott	**36**	**156**	**298.0**	**14.0**	**312.0**	**8.000**	**1**	**2**	**3**
§Phil White	16	66	104.0	26.0	130.0	7.879		3	3
§Rob Woffinden	31	127	230.0	14.0	244.0	7.685		1	1
Rob Grant	**36**	**149**	**223.0**	**35.0**	**258.0**	**6.926**		**2**	**2**
§Ian Stead	25	87	123.0	26.0	149.0	6.851		1	1
Wayne Ross	24	75	99.0	22.0	121.0	6.453			
Sean Courtney	34	138	174.0	35.0	209.0	6.058	1		1
Paul McHale	11	28	26.0	6.0	32.0	4.571			
Steve Finch	3	13	12.0	1.0	13.0	4.000			
§§Scott Robson	1	1	0.0	0.0	0.0	0.000			

1988...1988...1988...1988...1988...1988

	M	R	Pts	BP	TPts	Ave	F	P	Total
§Mark Courtney	**36**	**191**	**465.0**	**16.0**	**481.0**	**10.073**	**6**	**2**	**8**
Charlie McKinna	**36**	**191**	**370.0**	**31.0**	**401.0**	**8.398**	**3**		**3**
Steve McDermott	35	182	273.0	30.0	303.0	6.659	1		1
Rob Grant	**36**	**179**	**244.0**	**49.0**	**293.0**	**6.547**			
Sean Courtney	**36**	**177**	**232.0**	**39.0**	**271.0**	**6.124**			
Phil Kynman	15	43	45.0	12.0	57.0	5.302			
Rob Woffinden	10	48	45.0	12.0	57.0	4.750			
Wayne Ross	7	26	26.0	4.0	30.0	4.615			
Ian Stead	21	85	74.0	23.0	97.0	4.565			
Scott Robson	13	26	11.0	3.0	14.0	2.154			
§Steve Wicks	3	7	0.0	0.0	0.0	0.000			

BLACKBURN AND PRICE VAUXHALL-BEDFORD CLASSIC

1985	1 Bruce Cribb	2 Steve Wilcock	3 Martin Dixon

BERWICK £3,500 BONANZA

1990	1 David Walsh	2 Steve Regeling	3 Frede Schøtt

1989...1989...1989...1989...1989...1989

	M	R	Pts	BP	TPts	Ave	F	P	Total
§David Blackburn	**46**	**249**	**575.0**	**34.0**	**609.0**	**9.783**	**3**	**6**	**9**
Mark Courtney	**46**	**240**	**543.0**	**28.0**	**571.0**	**9.517**	**6**	**4**	**10**
Sean Courtney	35	157	238.0	58.0	296.0	7.541		3	3
David Walsh	**46**	**245**	**377.0**	**72.0**	**449.0**	**7.331**		**4**	**4**
§Andy Campbell	**46**	**239**	**362.0**	**63.0**	**425.0**	**7.113**	**1**	**1**	**2**
Rob Grant	43	186	265.0	59.0	324.0	6.968		2	2
Scott Robson	38	124	149.0	25.0	174.0	5.613			
Jason Straughan	1	3	2.0	1.0	3.0	4.000			
§Kevin Little	11	31	13.0	2.0	15.0	1.935			
§§Colin Smith	3	6	1.0	0.0	1.0	0.667			

1990...1990...1990...1990...1990...1990

	M	R	Pts	BP	TPts	Ave	F	P	Total
Mark Courtney	36	196	386.0	39.0	425.0	8.673	4	1	5
David Walsh	27	135	265.0	26.0	291.0	8.622	1	2	3
David Blackburn	29	150	286.0	9.0	295.0	7.867	2		2
Andy Campbell	35	190	265.5	38.0	303.5	6.389		1	1
§Alan Rivett	35	161	206.0	37.0	243.0	6.037			
Rob Grant	32	140	170.0	36.0	206.0	5.886		1	1
Scott Robson	25	106	136.0	17.0	153.0	5.774			
Kevin Little	20	59	41.0	15.0	56.0	3.797			
§Steve Widt	6	15	11.0	2.0	13.0	3.467			
Jason Straughan	1	2	0.0	0.0	0.0	0.000			

BERWICK FESTIVAL TROPHY

1968	1 Brian Whaley	2 Terry Lee	3 Mark Hall
1969	1 Geoff Curtis	2 Steve Waplington	3 Bill Moulin
1970	1 Alan Knapkin	2 Alf Wells	3 Tim Swales
1971	1 Doug Wyer	2 Lou Sansom	3 Russ Dent

TWEEDMOUTH FEAST TROPHY

1968	1 Mark Hall	2 Chris Bailey	3 Roy Williams
1969	1 Maurie Robinson	2 Ron Bagley	3 Peter Kelly
1970	1 Graeme Smith	2 Andy Ross	3 Maurie Robinson, Hec Haslinger
1971	1 Bruce Forrester	2 Maurie Robinson	3 Reg Wilson, Frank Auffret

DANNY TAYLOR MEMORIAL TROPHY

1969	1 Alf Wells	2 Maurie Robinson	3 Mark Hall
1970	1 Ian Turner	2 Tom Leadbitter	3 Alf Wells
1971	1 Lou Sansom	2 Tony Davey	3 George Major
1972	1 Willie Templeton	2 Arthur Browning	3 Dave Durham
1973	1 Willie Templeton	2 Lou Sansom	3 Alan Knapkin
1974	1 Mitch Graham	2 Terry Kelly	3 Malcolm Mackay
1975	1 Colin Farquharson	2 Brian Havelock	3 Dave Gifford
1976	1 Robert Hollingworth	2 Willie Templeton	3 Dave Gifford
1977	1 Robin Adlington	2 Noel Suckling	3 Nicky Hollingworth
1978	1 Graham Jones	2 Dave Gifford	3 Steve McDermott
1979	1 Steve McDermott	2 Mike Fullerton	3 Ivan Blacka
1980	1 Steve McDermott	2 Wayne Brown	3 Kelvin Mullarkey

STARS OF TOMORROW

1970	1 Jim Gallacher	2 Mick Beaton	3 Frank Auffret
1971	1 Malcolm McPhie	2 Frank Skinner	3 Gordon Case
1972	1 Wattie Robertson	2 Derek Allen	3 Jim Beresford
1973	1 Robin Dixon	2 Jim Beresford	3 Wattie Robertson
1974	1 Vic Harding	2 Wattie Robertson	3 Alan Legge
1975	1 Peter Waite	2 Jim Beaton	3 Jon Bower
1976	1 Jon Bower	2 Greg Clark	3 –
1977	1 Ian Darling	2 Alan MacLean	3 Mick McCoy
1978	1 Rob Grant	2 Mark Dekok	3 Barry Simpson
1979	1 Neil Farnish	2 Martin Hewlett	3 Rob Grant
1980	1 Paul Henderson	2 Ronnie Craig	3 Ian Anderson
1982	1 Martin McKinna	2 Phil Jeffrey	3 Jackson Irving
1983	1 Peter Erskine	2 David Cassells	3 Dennis Gallagher
1984	1 Jackson Irving	2 Scott Lamb	3.Gary Havelock
1985	1 Jackson Irving	2 Paul Heyes	3 Garry Clegg
1986	1 Scott Lamb	2 Tony Rizzo	3 Paul Heyes
1987	1 Steve Wicks	2 Andrew Buck	3 David Holliday
1990	1 Mike McLuskey	2 Jason Straughan	3 Frank Smart

BORDERNAPOLIS

1972	1 Doug Templeton	2 Robin Adlington	3 Andy Meldrum
1973	1 Robin Adlington	2 Doug Templeton	3 Graham Drury
1974	1 Andy Meldrum	2 Willie Templeton	3 Tom Owen
1975	1 Joe Owen	2 Lou Sansom	3 Dave Gifford
1976	1 Joe Owen	2 Dave Gifford	3 Tom Owen
1977	1 Graham Jones	2 Robin Adlington	3.Sid Sheldrick
1978	1 Bernie Rourke	2 Mike Hiftle	3 Dave Trownson
1979	1 Steve McDermott	2 Mike Fullerton	3 Wayne Brown

BIRMINGHAM

1971...1971...1971...1971...1971...1971

	M	R	Pts	BP	TPts	Ave	F	P	Total
§George Major	**34**	**146**	**312.0**	**13.0**	**325.0**	**8.904**	**1**	**1**	**2**
§Terry Shearer	24	101	201.0	11.0	212.0	8.396			
§Archie Wilkinson	32	127	172.0	27.0	199.0	6.268	1		1
§Chris Harrison	**34**	**121**	**162.0**	**22.0**	**184.0**	**6.083**			
§Malcolm Corradine	29	114	131.0	25.0	156.0	5.474		1	1
§Cliff Emms	26	105	119.0	24.0	143.0	5.448			
§Ian Wilson	13	49	49.0	8.0	57.0	4.653			
§Gunter Haslinger	31	107	99.0	19.0	118.0	4.411			
§§Rob Homer	5	14	5.0	2.0	7.0	2.000			
§Gordon McGregor	2	3	1.0	0.0	1.0	1.333			
§Clark Facey	2	4	0.0	0.0	0.0	0.000			

1972...1972...1972...1972...1972...1972

	M	R	Pts	BP	TPts	Ave	F	P	Total
§Peter Bailey	13	56	129.0	5.0	134.0	9.571	4	1	5
§§Arthur Browning	31	138	304.0	21.0	325.0	9.420	5		5
George Major	**38**	**158**	**279.0**	**32.0**	**311.0**	**7.873**	**1**	**4**	**5**
Terry Shearer	37	150	259.0	24.0	283.0	7.547	1	3	4
§§Mick Hines	34	139	207.0	48.0	255.0	7.338		3	3
Malcolm Corradine	18	60	81.0	9.0	90.0	6.000	1		1
§Mike Lanham	24	97	122.0	22.0	144.0	5.938		1	1
Cliff Emms	10	35	40.0	11.0	51.0	5.829			
Archie Wilkinson	19	60	63.0	12.0	75.0	5.000			
§Mike Gardner	8	25	25.0	2.0	27.0	4.320			
§§Steve Wilson	18	50	38.0	10.0	48.0	3.840			
Rob Homer	5	12	5.0	2.0	7.0	2.333			

1973...1973...1973...1973...1973...1973

	M	R	Pts	BP	TPts	Ave	F	P	Total
Arthur Browning	30	122	243.0	27.0	270.0	8.852	3	6	9
§Ted Howgego	12	45	86.0	11.0	97.0	8.622	2		2
§§John Hart	10	41	72.0	13.0	85.0	8.293		1	1
George Major	37	151	282.0	31.0	313.0	8.291		3	3
§§Phil Herne	37	147	249.0	30.0	279.0	7.592	3	2	5
Mike Lanham	36	141	219.0	36.0	255.0	7.234	2	3	5
Malcolm Corradine	35	131	215.0	21.0	236.0	7.206	2		2
Steve Wilson	23	74	95.0	12.0	107.0	5.784			
Terry Shearer	27	92	104.0	17.0	121.0	5.261			
§§Alan Grahame	8	28	20.0	3.0	23.0	3.286			
§§Richard Eslick	1	2	1.0	0.0	1.0	2.000			
§§Martin Hitch	1	3	0.0	0.0	0.0	0.000			

1974...1974...1974...1974...1974...1974

	M	R	Pts	BP	TPts	Ave	F	P	Total
Phil Herne	37	153	391.0	10.0	401.0	10.484	14	3	17
Arthur Browning	38	161	366.0	42.0	408.0	10.137	5	7	12
John Hart	**42**	**174**	**350.0**	**41.0**	**391.0**	**8.989**	**6**	**2**	**8**
Georger Major	39	160	334.0	25.0	359.0	8.975	5	5	10
Steve Wilson	2	7	10.0	3.0	13.0	7.429			
§§Ricky Day	39	146	187.0	52.0	239.0	6.548		3	3
§§Carl Askew	41	133	139.0	32.0	171.0	5.143			
§§Keith Anderson	34	114	122.0	21.0	143.0	5.018			
Alan Grahame	12	31	28.0	4.0	32.0	4.129			
§§Martin Sumsion	1	2	2.0	0.0	2.0	4.000			

1975...1975...1975...1975...1975...1975

	M	R	Pts	BP	TPts	Ave	F	P	Total
Arthur Browning	38	151	333.0	20.0	353.0	9.351	8	6	1
Alan Grahame	40	157	291.0	38.0	329.0	8.382	4	5	
§Keith White	**44**	**179**	**329.0**	**39.0**	**368.0**	**8.223**	**2**	**5**	**7**
John Hart	43	170	303.0	37.0	340.0	8.000		2	2
Keith Anderson	20	76	125.0	19.0	144.0	7.579	1	1	2
Ricky Day	27	97	155.0	23.0	178.0	7.340		1	1
George Major	42	144	220.0	43.0	263.0	7.306		3	3
Carl Askew	42	158	211.0	62.0	273.0	6.911	1	2	3
§Bobby Baker	3	8	1.0	1.0	2.0	1.000			
§§John Priest	2	5	1.0	0.0	1.0	0.800			

SECOND CITY TROPHY

1971	1 John Louis	2 Arthur Price	3 Tony Davey
1972	1 Malcolm Ballard	2 Tony Childs	3 George Major
1973	1 Ian Hindle	2 Carl Glover and Mike Lanham	
1974	1 Bruce Forrester	2 Steve Bastable	3 Phil Herne
1975	1 Alan Grahame	2 Arthur Browning	3 Dave Gooderham
1985	1 Reg Wilson	2 Keith White	3 Dave Perks
1986	1 Paul Thorp	2 Gary Havelock	3 Jamie Luckhurst

See also Birmingham First Division averages

■ *BIRMINGHAM were accepted into the 1976 British League after winning the previous season's National League championship, an impressive five points ahead of their nearest challengers Newcastle.*

■ *They raced in the First Division for eight seasons before the closure of Perry Barr for re-development.*

■ *After initially being promised a new home at Bordesley Green for the 1984 season there was no speedway in the Second City. Promoter Dan McCormick announced there would be no re-opening in 1985 because of the lack of facilities at the new World of Wheels Motor Sports centre but shortly before the start of the season local businessman Les Powell and Tom Evitts, father of riders Paul and Neil, agreed to buy the promoting rights from McCormick and re-launched the Brummies in the National League in 1985.*

1985...1985...1985...1985...1985...1985

	M	R	Pts	BP	TPts	Ave	F	P	Total
§Doug Wyer	**39**	**160**	**329.0**	**14.0**	**343.0**	**8.575**	**3**	**1**	**4**
§Reg Wilson	37	159	281.0	17.0	298.0	7.497	3	2	5
§Phil White	**39**	**158**	**257.0**	**35.0**	**292.0**	**7.392**	**2**	**1**	**3**
§Paul Evitts	**3**	**154**	**199.0**	**33.0**	**232.0**	**6.026**	**1**		**1**
§§Gary Court	1	2	2.0	1.0	3.0	6.000			
§Paul Stead	22	82	112.0	9.0	121.0	5.902	1		1
§Linden Warner	**39**	**136**	**135.0**	**18.0**	**153.0**	**4.500**			
§Mark Stevenson	16	46	45.0	6.0	51.0	4.435			
§John Hough	6	16	14.0	2.0	16.0	4.000			
§§Ian M. Stead	16	44	30.0	8.0	38.0	3.455			
§Steve Collins	3	5	4.0	0.0	4.0	3.200			
§Julian Parr	14	40	25.0	3.0	28.0	2.800			

1986...1986...1986...1986...1986...1986

	M	R	Pts	BP	TPts	Ave	F	P	Total
Paul Evitts	14	64	138.0	8.0	146.0	9.125	1		1
§David Cheshire	22	98	172.0	14.0	186.0	7.592		2	2
Reg Wilson	32	137	244.0	14.0	258.0	7.533	1		1
Phil White	38	163	227.0	36.0	263.0	6.454			
§Rob Woffinden	18	82	106.0	14.0	120.0	5.854			
§Ian Stead	22	89	106.0	20.0	126.0	5.663			
Ian M. Stead	**39**	**149**	**184.0**	**20.0**	**204.0**	**5.477**			
Mark Stevenson	**39**	**133**	**129.0**	**29.0**	**158.0**	**4.752**			
§Steve Finch	7	28	27.0	2.0	29.0	4.143			
§§Wayne Elliott	13	33	17.0	3.0	20.0	2.424			
§§David Rose	13	37	16.0	2.0	18.0	1.946			
§§ Chris Lockyer	3	5	0.0	0.0	0.0	0.000			

REG WILSON (left) and Sheffield and England team-mate Doug Wyer were the two big name signings on speedway's return to Birmingham in 1985

NATIONAL LEAGUE AVERAGES...NATIONAL LEAGUE AVERAGES...NATIONAL

BOSTON

SPEEDWAY was introduced to Boston in 1970 when the King's Lynn British League Division Two side moved mid-season.
Details of the 1970 campaign are included under King's Lynn.

1971...1971...1971...1971...1971...1971

	M	R	Pts	BP	TPts	Ave	F	P	Total
Arthur Price	35	148	318.0	12.0	330.0	8.919	6	1	7
§§Jim Ryman	**36**	**148**	**273.0**	**35.0**	**308.0**	**8.324**		**2**	**2**
§§Carl Glover	**36**	**143**	**243.0**	**17.0**	**260.0**	**7.273**			
Brian Osborn	1	3	4.0	1.0	5.0	6.667			
Russell Osborne	35	127	183.0	28.0	211.0	6.646			
Jack Bywater	**36**	**126**	**177.0**	**27.0**	**204.0**	**6.476**		**1**	**1**
Tony Featherstone	**36**	**135**	**169.0**	**35.0**	**204.0**	**6.044**		**1**	**1**
§§Vic Cross	21	66	74.0	15.0	89.0	5.394			
§§Ray Bales	9	25	29.0	4.0	33.0	5.280			
§Graham Edmunds	2	4	2.0	2.0	4.0	4.000			
§§Graham Jones	5	16	8.0	2.0	10.0	2.500			

1972...1972...1972...1972...1972...1972

	M	R	Pts	BP	TPts	Ave	F	P	Total
Arthur Price	32	142	307.0	16.0	323.0	9.099	4	2	6
Jim Ryman	27	111	224.0	14.0	238.0	8.577	2	1	3
Russell Osborne	35	141	255.0	17.0	272.0	7.716	2	1	3
Carl Glover	**36**	**143**	**218.0**	**46.0**	**264.0**	**7.385**		**3**	**3**
§§Ted Laessing	3	12	17.0	5.0	22.0	7.333			
Tony Featherstone	**36**	**138**	**184.0**	**36.0**	**220.0**	**6.377**			
Ray Bales	34	118	161.0	24.0	185.0	6.272	1		1
Vic Cross	14	47	61.0	8.0	69.0	5.872			
Jack Bywater	20	65	77.0	8.0	85.0	5.231			
§Lindsay Davies	5	10	9.0	1.0	10.0	4.000			
§§Les Glover	1	2	1.0	1.0	2.0	4.000			
§§Geoff Carnell	3	6	3.0	1.0	4.0	2.667			

1973...1973...1973...1973...1973...1973

	M	R	Pts	BP	TPts	Ave	F	P	Total
Carl Glover	40	168	381.0	23.0	404.0	9.619	6	7	13
Arthur Price	40	162	348.0	22.0	370.0	9.136	4	3	7
Jim Ryman	29	115	204.0	38.0	242.0	8.417	1	3	4
Russell Osborne	40	157	264.0	44.0	308.0	7.847	2	3	5
§David Piddock	12	42	77.0	5.0	82.0	7.810			
Ray Bales	39	151	246.0	29.0	275.0	7.285	1	4	5
§§David Gagen	40	151	215.0	47.0	262.0	6.940			
Tony Featherstone	14	50	70.0	16.0	86.0	6.880		1	1
Geoff Carnell	5	16	11.0	3.0	14.0	3.500			
Les Glover	22	53	39.0	6.0	45.0	3.396			
§§Dave Trownson	2	6	4.0	1.0	5.0	3.333			

1974...1974...1974...1974...1974...1974

	M	R	Pts	BP	TPts	Ave	F	P	Total
Carl Glover	39	173	436.0	9.0	445.0	10.289	11	3	14
Jim Ryman	31	118	205.0	33.0	238.0	8.068		2	2
Russell Osborne	35	144	272.0	16.0	288.0	8.000	2		2
David Gagen	33	137	207.0	38.0	245.0	7.153	1	1	2
§Robert Hollingworth	**40**	**168**	**217.5**	**42.0**	**259.5**	**6.179**		**2**	**2**
David Piddock	31	112	153.0	12.0	165.0	5.893		2	2
Les Glover	26	90	97.0	17.0	114.0	5.067			
§§Rob Mouncer	14	38	32.0	4.0	36.0	3.789			
§Billy Burton	24	62	35.0	11.0	46.0	2.968			
§§Trevor Whiting	2	6	3.0	1.0	4.0	2.667			
Dave Trownson	1	4	1.0	0.0	1.0	1.000			

1975...1975...1975...1975...1975...1975

	M	R	Pts	BP	TPts	Ave	F	P	Total
§§Michael Lee	39	162	352.0	14.0	366.0	9.037	8	2	10
§Bruce Forrester	23	90	161.0	24.0	185.0	8.222	2	2	4
David Gagen	**40**	**164**	**272.0**	**49.0**	**321.0**	**7.829**	**1**	**4**	**5**
Robert Hollingworth	**40**	**155**	**249.0**	**34.0**	**283.0**	**7.303**	**2**	**1**	**3**
Billy Burton	**40**	**158**	**251.0**	**33.0**	**284.0**	**7.190**		**3**	**3**
Les Glover	38	122	183.0	29.0	212.0	6.951		1	1
§§Ron Cooper	1	3	3.0	2.0	5.0	6.667			
David Piddock	14	48	66.0	8.0	74.0	6.167			
Rob Mouncer	29	92	122.0	19.0	141.0	6.130		1	1
Trevor Whiting	12	38	35.0	8.0	43.0	4.526			
§§Brian Emery	2	7	5.0	2.0	7.0	4.000			

1976...1976...1976...1976...1976...1976

	M	R	Pts	BP	TPts	Ave	F	P	Total
Robert Hollingworth	**40**	**186**	**436.0**	**12.0**	**448.0**	**9.634**	**6**	**3**	**9**
Billy Burton	24	107	210.0	11.0	221.0	8.262	3		3
Paul Gilbert	26	90	125.0	23.0	148.0	6.578		1	1
§Stuart Cope	35	136	182.0	16.0	198.0	5.824		2	2
Trevor Whiting	35	130	164.0	17.0	181.0	5.569	1		1
§Chris Emery	11	41	52.0	5.0	57.0	5.561			
§Steve Clarke	35	134	153.0	24.0	177.0	5.284			
Ron Cooper	33	124	135.0	20.0	155.0	5.000			
§Andy Sims	5	17	17.0	3.0	20.0	4.706			
§§Nicky Hollingworth	4	14	13.0	3.0	16.0	4.571			
§§Derek Harrison	4	9	7.0	2.0	9.0	4.000			
§§Dave Allen	14	37	27.0	5.0	32.0	3.459			
§§Chris Sully	5	10	4.0	3.0	7.0	2.800			
§§Andy Bales	1	2	1.0	0.0	1.0	2.000			

1977...1977...1977...1977...1977...1977

	M	R	Pts	BP	TPts	Ave	F	P	Total
Robert Hollingworth	**42**	**181**	**430.0**	**18.0**	**448.0**	**9.901**	**5**	**4**	**9**
Carl Glover	13	51	92.0	8.0	100.0	7.843	2		2
§Colin Cook	**42**	**173**	**304.0**	**28.0**	**332.0**	**7.676**		**3**	**3**
Paul Gilbert	31	108	175.0	15.0	190.0	7.037	2	1	3
Steve Clarke	38	151	212.5	32.0	244.5	6.477	2	1	3
Billy Burton	13	44	58.0	11.0	69.0	6.273			
David Piddock	8	24	30.5	4.0	34.5	5.750			
Dave Allen	35	127	148.0	25.0	173.0	5.449			
Stuart Cope	39	137	159.0	25.0	184.0	5.372			
Ron Cooper	22	64	72.0	12.0	84.0	5.250		1	1
§§Andy Fisher	6	18	16.0	3.0	19.0	4.222			
Chris Emery	2	6	5.0	1.0	6.0	4.000			
Nicky Hollingworth	1	2	0.0	0.0	0.0	0.000			

1978...1978...1978...1978...1978...1978

	M	R	Pts	BP	TPts	Ave	F	P	Total
§§Gary Gulgielmi	26	115	227.0	14.0	241.0	8.383	2	2	4
§Tony Boyle	19	81	157.0	4.0	161.0	7.951	2		2
Steve Clarke	9	36	59.0	5.0	64.0	7.111	1		1
Dave Allen	33	127	208.0	15.0	223.0	7.024		2	2
Paul Gilbert	18	72	107.0	10.0	117.0	6.500	1		1
Stuart Cope	32	126	153.0	16.0	169.0	5.365			
Andy Fisher	34	144	177.0	15.0	192.0	5.333			
§§Craig Featherby	17	57	61.0	14.0	75.0	5.263			
§§Andy Hibbs	3	12	14.0	1.0	15.0	5.000			
§David Mortiboys	15	51	50.0	13.0	63.0	4.941			
Ron Cooper	8	30	31.0	0.0	31.0	4.133			
§§Roger Lambert	8	23	20.0	3.0	23.0	4.000			
§§Keith Bloxsome	26	95	69.0	21.0	90.0	3.789			
§§Dennis Mallett	10	30	20.0	2.0	22.0	2.933			
§§Alan Louth	3	7	3.0	1.0	4.0	2.286			
§§Eddie Reeves	6	18	8.0	2.0	10.0	2.222			
§§Steve Kulwicki	4	10	2.0	1.0	3.0	1.200			

1979...1979...1979...1979...1979...1979

	M	R	Pts	BP	TPts	Ave	F	P	Total
David Gagen	15	60	130.0	9.0	139.0	9.267		3	3
Robert Hollingworth	**38**	**172**	**368.0**	**15.0**	**383.0**	**8.907**	**4**	**1**	**5**
Dave Allen	36	155	308.0	11.0	319.0	8.232	3		3
Tony Featherstone	37	151	192.0	39.0	231.0	6.119		2	2
Dennis Mallett	**38**	**141**	**142.0**	**29.0**	**171.0**	**4.851**			
Andy Fisher	37	133	128.0	21.0	149.0	4.481			
Dave Mortiboys	14	40	33.0	5.0	38.0	3.800			
Andy Hibbs	26	72	56.0	10.0	66.0	3.667			
§§Ian Peel	4	7	4.0	2.0	6.0	3.429			
§Peter Tarrant	5	16	9.0	4.0	13.0	3.250			
Stuart Cope	5	13	8.0	2.0	10.0	3.077			
§Colin Ackroyd	7	20	11.0	2.0	13.0	2.600			
§§Phil Vance	2	8	4.0	1.0	5.0	2.500			

BOSTON provided the winners of the Division Two Riders' Championship Finals in 1973 and 1974 with Arthur Price and Carl Glover.
It is the only instance where riders from the same club have won the crown in successive seasons.

BOSTON

1980...1980...1980...1980...1980...1980

	M	R	Pts	BP	TPts	Ave	F	P	Total
David Gagen	27	113	262.0	15.0	277.0	9.805	3	5	8
Gary Guglielmi	41	175	377.0	31.0	408.0	9.326	4	9	13
Robert Hollingworth	**46**	**203**	**410.0**	**25.0**	**435.0**	**8.571**	**4**	**2**	**6**
§Steve Lomas	41	162	286.0	42.0	328.0	8.099	2	6	8
Dennis Mallett	35	140	207.0	41.0	248.0	7.086		2	2
§Chris Turner	32	128	188.0	32.0	220.0	6.875			
Tony Featherstone	9	31	40.0	8.0	48.0	6.194			
Andy Fisher	1	3	4.0	0.0	4.0	5.333			
§Michael Holding	23	62	53.0	17.0	70.0	4.516			
Ian Turner	11	41	40.0	6.0	46.0	4.488		1	1
§§Michael Spinks	33	104	95.0	10.0	105.0	4.038			
§Chris Cole	9	25	10.0	4.0	14.0	2.240			
§§Keven Dye	4	11	4.0	0.0	4.0	1.455			

1981...1981...1981...1981...1981...1981

	M	R	Pts	BP	TPts	Ave	F	P	Total
Steve Lomas	41	157	335.5	11.5	347.0	8.841	6	1	7
David Gagen	37	155	307.5	35.0	342.5	8.839		3	3
§Steve Regeling	42	179	341.0	38.0	379.0	8.469	2	1	3
Robert Hollingworth	43	185	353.0	38.0	391.0	8.454	2	2	4
Dennis Mallett	41	169	233.5	35.0	268.5	6.355	1	3	4
Mike Spinks	13	43	56.0	8.0	64.0	5.953			
Michael Holding	34	120	135.5	21.5	157.0	5.233			
Keven Dye	10	39	37.0	5.0	42.0	4.308			
§Peter Framingham	3	15	13.0	0.0	13.0	3.467			
Chris Cole	21	65	46.0	10.0	56.0	3.446			
§§Gary Marsters	5	11	7.0	2.0	9.0	3.273			
§§Steve Parker	2	4	1.0	0.0	1.0	1.000			
§§Mitchell Barker	3	9	1.0	1.0	2.0	0.889			
§Robbie McGregor	2	6	0.0	0.0	0.0	0.000			
§§Steve L. Baker	1	2	0.0	0.0	0.0	0.000			

1982...1982...1982...1982...1982...1982

	M	R	Pts	BP	TPts	Ave	F	P	Total
Steve Lomas	**40**	**211**	**464.0**	**20.0**	**484.0**	**9.175**	**4**	**1**	**5**
David Gagen	37	195	426.0	17.0	443.0	9.087	2	1	3
Robert Hollingworth	39	209	419.0	44.0	463.0	8.861	1	5	6
Dennis Mallett	**40**	**198**	**241.0**	**53.0**	**294.0**	**5.939**			
§David Blackburn	17	79	73.0	20.0	93.0	4.709			
§Guy Wilson	39	171	169.0	31.0	200.0	4.678		1	1
Peter Framingham	34	126	114.0	18.0	132.0	4.190			
Robbie MacGregor	9	30	23.0	4.0	27.0	3.600			
Chris Cole	18	58	36.0	7.0	43.0	2.966			
§§Peter Chapman	5	11	5.0	1.0	6.0	2.182			

LINCOLNSHIRE TROPHY

1971	1 Tony Davey	2 Arthur Price	3 Tony Featherstone
1972	1 Russ Osborne	2 Brian Foote	3 John Harrhy
1973	1 Lou Sansom	2 Jack Bywater	3 Dave Mills
1974	1 Graham Jones	2 Steve Taylor	3 Jim Ryman
1975	1 Michael Lee	2 Les Glover	3 Phil Bass
1976	1 Joe Owen	2 Robert Hollingworth	3 Stuart Cope
1977	1 Robert Hollingworth	2 Steve Koppe	3 Billy Burton
1978	1 Les Rumsey	2 Steve Koppe	3 Nicky Allott
1979	1 Tom Owen	2 Dave Allen	3 Mike Sampson
1980	1 Paul Woods	2 Gary Guglielmi	3 Nicky Allott
1981	1 Robert Hollingworth	2 Steve Lomas	3 Mick Bates
1982	1 Robert Hollingworth	2 Alan Molyneux	3 Dennis Mallett
1984	1 Billy Burton	2 Guy Wilson	3 Keith White

SUPPORTERS' CLUB TROPHY

1971	1 Arthur Price	2 Reg Wilson	3 Carl Glover
1972	1 Mick Hines	2 Jim Ryman	3 Tony Childs
1973	1 Carl Glover	2 Arthur Browning	3 Brian Clark
1974	1 Carl Glover	2 Ted Hubbard	3 Arthur Browning
1975	1 Michael Lee	2 David Gagen	3 Laurie Etheridge

MILLENIUM TROPHY

1974	1 Carl Glover	2 Tony Featherstone and Bruce Forrester	
1975	1 Alan Molyneux	2 Laurie Etheridge	3 Michael Lee
1976	1 Joe Owen	2 Robert Hollingworth	3 Paul Gilbert

CUDAS SOCIAL CLUB SPEEDERAMA

1979	1 John Jackson	2 Bob Humphreys	3 Tom Owen

NORPRINT £100 TROPHY

1972	1 Ray Bales	2 Arthur Price	3 Jim Ryman

EAST MIDLANDS LINCOLNSHIRE TROPHY

1983	1 Steve Lomas	2 David Gagen	3 Steve McDermott

1983...1983...1983...1983...1983...1983

	M	R	Pts	BP	TPts	Ave	F	P	Total
Steve Lomas	22	116	222.0	8.0	230.0	7.931			
David Gagen	32	176	319.0	22.0	341.0	7.750		2	2
Billy Burton	33	176	261.5	20.0	281.5	6.398		2	2
§Alan Mason	4	18	21.0	6.0	27.0	6.000			
§Phil Alderman	31	156	188.0	33.0	221.0	5.667			
David Blackburn	**36**	**188**	**220.0**	**25.0**	**245.0**	**5.213**			
Dennis Mallett	10	47	50.0	8.0	58.0	4.936			
Peter Framingham	20	75	74.0	8.0	82.0	4.373			
Peter Chapman	23	91	89.0	9.0	98.0	4.308	1		1
Guy Wilson	12	51	38.0	12.0	50.0	3.922			
Michael Holding	15	48	31.0	3.0	34.0	2.833			
§Eric Broadbelt	2	7	3.0	1.0	4.0	2.286			
§§Chris Schmidt	2	3	0.0	0.0	0.0	0.000			
§§David Lee	1	2	0.0	0.0	0.0	0.000			

1984...1984...1984...1984...1984...1984

	M	R	Pts	BP	TPts	Ave	F	P	Total
Colin Cook	30	130	214.0	22.0	236.0	7.262	1	1	2
Robert Hollingworth	**32**	**143**	**233.0**	**23.0**	**256.0**	**7.161**		**1**	**1**
Guy Wilson	**32**	**117**	**193.0**	**15.0**	**208.0**	**7.111**			
David Gagen	8	37	58.0	7.0	65.0	7.027		1	1
Dennis Mallett	26	105	154.0	21.0	175.0	6.667	2		2
Billy Burton	31	128	184.0	22.0	206.0	6.438			
§Paul Clarke	15	59	72.0	11.0	83.0	5.627			
Steve Lomas	15	49	53.0	10.0	63.0	5.143			
Peter Chapman	28	70	63.0	14.0	77.0	4.400			
§§Wayne Dunworth	3	5	4.0	1.0	5.0	4.000			

1986...1986...1986...1986...1986...1986

	M	R	Pts	BP	TPts	Ave	F	P	Total
§Kevin Jolly	39	177	420.0	18.0	438.0	9.898	6	3	9
§Andy Hines	36	155	317.0	14.0	331.0	8.542	2	1	3
Paul Clarke	36	148	242.0	27.0	269.0	7.270	1	1	2
§Rob Woffinden	21	82	110.0	17.0	127.0	6.195			
§David Jackson	32	128	156.0	25.0	181.0	5.656			
§Wally Hill	4	14	14.0	5.0	19.0	5.429			
§§Jon Cooper	4	12	9.0	6.0	15.0	5.000			
Andy Fisher	26	82	89.0	11.0	100.0	4.878			
Peter Framingham	23	78	79.0	12.0	91.0	4.667			
Robert Hollingworth	1	4	4.0	0.0	4.0	4.000			
§Wayne Ross	27	74	58.0	14.0	72.0	3.892			
§Derrol Keats	7	22	15.0	5.0	20.0	3.636			
§Jamie Young	2	9	7.0	1.0	8.0	3.556			
§§Gary Clegg	16	44	31.0	6.0	37.0	3.364			
Colin Cook	1	2	0.0	0.0	0.0	0.000			

1987...1987...1987...1987...1987...1987

	M	R	Pts	BP	TPts	Ave	F	P	Total
Andy Hines	*13*	*70*	*141.0*	*2.0*	*143.0*	*8.171*			
§Carl Baldwin	*17*	*85*	*124.0*	*11.0*	*135.0*	*6.353*			
§Phil White	*17*	*84*	*109.0*	*13.0*	*122.0*	*5.810*			
Andy Fisher	*12*	*46*	*47.0*	*10.0*	*57.0*	*4.957*			
§Mark Lyndon	*1*	*4*	*3.0*	*1.0*	*4.0*	*4.000*			
§§Nigel Greenhalgh	*2*	*2*	*1.0*	*1.0*	*2.0*	*4.000*			
§Kenny Young	*1*	*2*	*1.0*	*1.0*	*2.0*	*4.000*			
Wally Hill	*6*	*20*	*14.0*	*4.0*	*18.0*	*3.600*			
Jon Cooper	*15*	*53*	*39.0*	*5.0*	*44.0*	*3.321*			
Gary Clegg	***18***	***56***	***36.0***	***10.0***	***46.0***	***3.286***			
Jamie Young	*6*	*22*	*14.0*	*4.0*	*18.0*	*3.273*			
Dave Allen	*2*	*7*	*4.0*	*1.0*	*5.0*	*2.857*			
Wayne Dunworth	*1*	*3*	*1.0*	*1.0*	*2.0*	*2.667*			
§Chris Mulvihill	*6*	*16*	*6.0*	*1.0*	*7.0*	*1.750*			
§Rob Parish	*2*	*6*	*1.0*	*0.0*	*1.0*	*0.667*			
§§Anthony Hulme	*2*	*4*	*0.0*	*0.0*	*0.0*	*0.000*			

BOSTON resigned from the League because of financial problems on Monday, August 9, 1987, after 16 League matches and two Knock Out Cup matches.
Several abortive attempts were made in the following years to resurrect the sport at New Hammond Beck Roads but no formal application was ever considered by the National League.

BRADFORD

1971...1971...1971...1971...1971...1971

	M	R	Pts	BP	TPts	Ave	F	P	Total
Alan Knapkin	35	153	371.0	18.0	389.0	10.170	8	4	12
Alf Wells	26	106	215.0	24.0	239.0	9.019	2	1	3
§Dave Baugh	**36**	**156**	**312.0**	**19.0**	**331.0**	**8.487**	**2**	**3**	**5**
Dave Schofield	18	69	113.0	17.0	130.0	7.536	1		1
Robin Adlington	34	152	239.0	32.0	271.0	7.132		2	2
Sid Sheldrick	25	87	91.0	21.0	112.0	5.149			
§§Rod Chessell	4	17	17.0	4.0	21.0	4.941			
Alan Bridgett	31	102	101.0	22.0	123.0	4.824			
§Brian Murray	12	46	42.0	9.0	51.0	4.435			
Peter Thompson	8	23	19.0	6.0	25.0	4.348			
§§Stan Dewhurst	8	23	10.0	1.0	11.0	1.913			
§Mick Fielding	4	11	1.0	0.0	1.0	0.364			
Barry Fitzgerald	1	1	0.0	0.0	0.0	0.000			

1972...1972...1972...1972...1972...1972

	M	R	Pts	BP	TPts	Ave	F	P	Total
Dave Baugh	**36**	**157**	**318.0**	**23.0**	**341.0**	**8.688**	**2**	**4**	**6**
Alan Knapkin	29	112	218.0	9.0	227.0	8.107	3	2	5
Robin Adlington	34	146	276.0	12.0	288.0	7.890	4	1	5
§§Colin Meredith	13	50	64.0	10.0	74.0	5.920			
Alf Wells	13	48	63.0	8.0	71.0	5.917			
Alan Bridgett	**36**	**134**	**170.0**	**25.0**	**195.0**	**5.821**		**1**	**1**
§§Barry Meeks	17	59	65.0	6.0	71.0	4.814			
Sid Sheldrick	**36**	**143**	**139.0**	**30.0**	**169.0**	**4.727**			
Mick Fielding	12	33	25.0	7.0	32.0	3.879			
Mick Fairbairn	15	52	35.0	11.0	46.0	3.538			
Stan Dewhurst	2	6	1.0	1.0	2.0	1.333			
§§Graham Tattersall	1	4	1.0	0.0	1.0	1.000			

1973...1973...1973...1973...1973...1973

	M	R	Pts	BP	TPts	Ave	F	P	Total
§§Mike Fishwick	3	9	17.0	6.0	23.0	10.222		1	1
Alan Knapkin	14	57	136.0	7.0	143.0	10.035	1	1	2
Dave Baugh	34	145	317.5	17.0	334.5	9.228	2	3	5
Robin Adlington	38	164	304.0	21.0	325.0	7.927	1	3	4
§Tony Featherstone	24	107	199.0	8.0	207.0	7.738	3		3
§§Brenton Langlois	38	145	179.0	28.0	207.0	5.710			
Mick Fairbairn	17	58	68.0	14.0	82.0	5.655			
Colin Meredith	32	121	132.5	30.0	162.5	5.372			
§§Mike Fullerton	36	128	129.0	23.0	152.0	4.750			
§§Tony Freegard	18	60	60.0	10.0	70.0	4.667			
§§Robert Maxfield	12	30	30.0	3.0	33.0	4.400			
Mick Fielding	3	7	5.0	2.0	7.0	4.000			
Rod Chessell	7	22	18.0	1.0	19.0	3.455			

1974...1974...1974...1974...1974...1974

	M	R	Pts	BP	TPts	Ave	F	P	Total
Alan Knapkin	12	45	92.0	13.0	105.0	9.333	2	1	3
Tony Featherstone	**38**	**163**	**336.0**	**17.0**	**353.0**	**8.663**	**3**	**3**	**6**
Colin Meredith	**38**	**156**	**313.0**	**12.0**	**325.0**	**8.333**	**4**	**1**	**5**
Mick Fairbairn	30	117	154.0	21.0	175.0	5.983	2		2
Mike Fishwick	25	98	114.0	24.0	138.0	5.633			
§Eddie Argall	15	55	58.0	13.0	71.0	5.164			
§§Steve Wilcock	26	94	93.0	28.0	121.0	5.149			
§Roger Austin	27	105	110.0	15.0	125.0	4.762			
Mick Fielding	31	103	106.0	16.0	122.0	4.738			
§§Brian Chaldercott	4	11	8.0	3.0	11.0	4.000			
§Dave Parkin	14	43	23.0	6.0	29.0	2.698			
§§Brian Donovan	3	8	1.0	0.0	1.0	0.500			

1975...1975...1975...1975...1975...1975

	M	R	Pts	BP	TPts	Ave	F	P	Total
Tony Featherstone	41	174	345.0	18.0	363.0	8.345	3		3
Colin Meredith	39	151	270.0	29.0	299.0	7.921	3	1	4
Dave Baugh	**42**	**174**	**294.0**	**29.0**	**323.0**	**7.425**		**3**	**3**
§Tony Boyle	21	85	134.0	17.0	151.0	7.106	1	1	2
Steve Wilcock	**42**	**158**	**197.0**	**30.0**	**227.0**	**5.747**			
§Andy Cowan	10	31	39.0	4.0	43.0	5.548			
Alan Knapkin	21	84	94.0	21.0	115.0	5.476		1	1
Eddie Argall	5	17	18.0	4.0	22.0	5.176			
Mick Fielding	21	73	72.0	10.0	82.0	4.493			
Brenton Langlois	30	95	83.0	20.0	103.0	4.337			
Dave Parkin	7	17	9.0	4.0	13.0	3.059			
§§John Wilkins	4	10	5.0	1.0	6.0	2.400			
§§Barry Weaver	8	22	8.0	2.0	10.0	1.818			
Mick Fairbairn	2	5	1.0	1.0	2.0	1.600			

SPEEDWAY was re-introduced to Bradford in 1970 when the Nelson British League Division Two side moved mid-season from Lancashire across the Pennines to Odsal Stadium.

Details of the 1970 campaign are included under Nelson.

Racing finished at Odsal at the end of the 1975 season but was revived in 1986 when Halifax moved to Odsal as a British League First Division club.

Full details of Bradford's Division One averages are given in that section.

INTERNATIONAL SPEEDWAY CLUB TROPHY

1970 1 Gary Peterson 2 Maurie Robinson 3 Doug WyerODSAL TROPHY

1970 1 Gary Peterson 2 Malcolm Mackay 3 Maurie Robinson
1971 1 Dave Baugh 2 Alan Knapkin 3 Doug Wyer
1972 1 Robin Adlington 2 Jack Millen 3 Mick Hines

BRADFORD OPEN CHAMPIONSHIP

1971 1 Dai Evans 2 Phil Crump 3 Doug Wyer
1972 1 Mick Hines 2 Robin Adlington 3 Alan Knapkin

SPONSORS CLUB TROPHY

1971 1 Dave Baugh 2 John Louis 3 Malcolm Mackay

PRIDE OF ENGLAND CHAMPIONSHIP

1972 1 Lou Sansom 2 Paul Tyrer 3 Dave Baugh
1973 1 Mitch Graham 2 Tony Freegard 3 Colin Meredith

See also Bradford Division One averages

DOUBLE TOP...Gary Peterson won the first two Odsal individual meets

CANTERBURY

1968...1968...1968...1968...1968...1968

	M	R	Pts	BP	TPts	Ave	F	P	Total
§§Peter Murray	9	41	97.0	6.0	103.0	10.049		2	2
§§Barry Crowson	18	82	162.0	11.0	173.0	8.439	1	1	2
§§Ken Vale	19	82	154.0	10.0	164.0	8.000	1		1
§§Martyn Piddock	**22**	**97**	**182.0**	**11.0**	**193.0**	**7.959**	**1**		**1**
§§John Hibben	13	52	69.0	20.0	89.0	6.846			
§§Judd Drew	2	4	4.0	1.0	5.0	5.000			
§§Tyburn Gallows	6	22	25.0	2.0	27.0	4.909			
§§Pat Adaway	1	5	5.0	1.0	6.0	4.800			
§§Bob Warner	2	6	6.0	1.0	7.0	4.667			
§§Pat Flanagan	14	39	40.0	5.0	45.0	4.615			
§§Chris Raines	10	28	26.0	6.0	32.0	4.571			
§§Graham Miles	4	17	18.0	1.0	19.0	4.471			
§§Frank Wendon	17	67	62.0	10.0	72.0	4.299			
§§Charlie Coleman	1	5	2.0	2.0	4.0	3.200			
§§Barry Lee	9	33	20.0	6.0	26.0	3.152			
§§Neville Slee	3	9	1.0	0.0	1.0	0.444			

CANTERBURY competed in the first-ever Second Division meeting at Belle Vue on Wednesday, May 8, 1968. The riders were Crowson, Gallows, Piddock, guest Lex Milloy, Slee, Lee and Raines.

1969...1969...1969...1969...1969...1969

	M	R	Pts	BP	TPts	Ave	F	P	Total
Peter Murray	25	107	272.0	5.0	277.0	10.355	9	2	11
Martyn Piddock	30	129	302.0	14.0	316.0	9.798	7	3	10
Ken Vale	16	62	124.0	11.0	135.0	8.710	3		3
Graham Miles	21	79	123.0	13.0	136.0	6.886			
John Hibben	25	101	143.0	23.0	166.0	6.574			
§§Barry Thomas	16	65	89.0	9.0	98.0	6.031		1	1
§§Jake Rennison	7	24	29.0	3.0	32.0	5.333		1	1
Pat Flanagan	2	7	7.0	2.0	9.0	5.143			
§§Dave Percy	12	35	31.0	10.0	41.0	4.686			
§§Graham Banks	4	13	15.0	0.0	15.0	4.615			
§§Jim Crowhurst	18	64	64.0	9.0	73.0	4.563			
§Brian Foote	7	23	18.0	5.0	23.0	4.000			
§§Alan Kite	4	14	9.0	4.0	13.0	3.714			
§§Gerald Reardon	8	27	20.0	5.0	25.0	3.704			
§§Neville Brice	12	39	30.0	6.0	36.0	3.692			
Chris Raines	4	16	8.0	4.0	12.0	3.000			
Frank Wendon	1	4	3.0	0.0	3.0	3.000			
§§Roy Bridges	2	7	1.0	1.0	2.0	1.143			

1970...1970...1970...1970...1970...1970

	M	R	Pts	BP	TPts	Ave	F	P	Total
§Graeme Smith	27	111	284.0	7.0	291.0	10.486	7		7
Barry Crowson	32	133	277.0	28.0	305.0	9.173	1	5	6
Barry Thomas	33	137	285.0	27.0	312.0	9.109	2	5	7
Graham Banks	33	128	219.0	22.0	241.0	7.531	2	4	6
Graham Miles	23	93	147.0	26.0	173.0	7.441	1		1
Alan Kite	29	89	93.0	13.0	106.0	4.764			
Jake Rennison	23	79	64.0	21.0	85.0	4.304			
§§Ted Hubbard	5	18	18.0	1.0	19.0	4.222			
§§Dave Smith	17	56	47.0	10.0	57.0	4.071			
§§Mike Barkaway	11	35	26.0	7.0	33.0	3.771			
§Joe Robson	3	10	3.0	1.0	4.0	1.600			
Dave Percy	1	2	0.0	0.0	0.0	0.000			

1971...1971...1971...1971...1971...1971

	M	R	Pts	BP	TPts	Ave	F	P	Total
§Ross Gilbertson	29	133	286.0	11.0	297.0	8.932	3	2	5
Graham Banks	31	128	242.0	15.0	257.0	8.031	2		2
§§Dave Piddock	10	32	49.0	5.0	54.0	6.750		1	1
Graeme Smith	28	114	163.0	17.0	180.0	6.316	1	1	2
§§Graeme Stapleton	9	35	48.0	7.0	55.0	6.286			
§Phil Pratt	12	42	58.0	6.0	64.0	6.095		1	1
Ted Hubbard	32	142	169.0	24.0	193.0	5.437			
§Bob Tabet	18	63	62.0	13.0	75.0	4.762	1		1
§§Barney Kennett	29	91	80.0	13.0	93.0	4.088			
§John Hammond	10	33	27.0	6.0	33.0	4.000			
Dave Smith	3	9	7.0	1.0	8.0	3.556			
Mike Barkaway	10	31	19.0	3.0	22.0	2.839			
§Trevor Barnwell	2	5	2.0	1.0	3.0	2.400			
§Laurie Guilfoyle	2	8	3.0	1.0	4.0	2.000			
§§Colin Perry	2	6	0.0	0.0	0.0	0.000			

1972...1972...1972...1972...1972...1972

	M	R	Pts	BP	TPts	Ave	F	P	Total
Ross Gilbertson	29	129	281.0	24.0	305.0	9.457	1	7	8
Graham Banks	29	117	212.0	11.0	223.0	7.624	3		3
Ted Hubbard	31	125	200.0	27.0	227.0	7.264	1	1	2
David Piddock	23	91	149.0	11.0	160.0	7.033	3	2	5
Trevor Barnwell	3	10	14.0	3.0	17.0	6.800			
§§Frank Smith	1	3	5.0	0.0	5.0	6.667			
§§Bob Hughes	29	78	114.0	12.0	126.0	6.462	1	1	2
Barney Kennett	29	110	150.0	22.0	172.0	6.255	1		1
§§Les Rumsey	15	55	50.0	17.0	67.0	4.873			
Phil Pratt	2	7	7.0	1.0	8.0	4.571			
§§Trevor Jones	11	39	37.0	5.0	42.0	4.308			
§Charlie Benham	11	39	29.0	5.0	34.0	3.487			
§Mike Vernam	8	24	18.0	2.0	20.0	3.333			
§§Gary Cottham	8	25	17.0	3.0	20.0	3.200			
§§Steve Davies	3	8	5.0	1.0	6.0	3.000			
§§Ian Silk	4	11	4.0	0.0	4.0	1.455			
§§Peter Compson	1	2	0.0	0.0	0.0	0.000			
§§Terry Spain	1	2	0.0	0.0	0.0	0.000			

1973...1973...1973...1973...1973...1973

	M	R	Pts	BP	TPts	Ave	F	P	Total
Ross Gilbertson	1	5	11.0	1.0	12.0	9.600			
Barney Kennett	29	116	189.0	25.0	214.0	7.379		3	3
Peter Murray	20	73	114.0	12.0	126.0	6.904		1	1
Ted Hubbard	36	157	244.0	21.0	265.0	6.752		1	1
§Derek Cook	27	98	141.0	16.0	157.0	6.408		1	1
Trevor Jones	**38**	**165**	**233.0**	**28.0**	**261.0**	**6.327**			
Graham Banks	35	139	189.0	18.0	207.0	5.957			
David Piddock	17	63	82.0	8.0	90.0	5.714			
Les Rumsey	34	110	136.0	21.0	157.0	5.709		1	1
Gary Cottham	6	13	14.0	1.0	15.0	4.615			
§§Dave Gooderham	11	27	26.0	3.0	29.0	4.296			
§Paul Scanlon	2	6	2.0	1.0	3.0	2.000			
Bob Hughes	2	4	1.0	0.0	1.0	1.000			

1974...1974...1974...1974...1974...1974

	M	R	Pts	BP	TPts	Ave	F	P	Total
Trevor Jones	24	100	208.0	13.0	221.0	8.840	3	3	6
Ted Hubbard	36	158	297.0	24.0	321.0	8.127	1	1	2
§George Barclay	1	2	4.0	0.0	4.0	8.000			
Dave Gooderham	37	150	248.0	25.0	273.0	7.280		2	2
§Roger Johns	13	56	91.0	6.0	97.0	6.929	1		1
Barney Kennett	36	149	217.0	38.0	255.0	6.846		1	1
Derek Cook	29	94	126.0	25.0	151.0	6.426		1	1
Les Rumsey	29	116	162.0	23.0	185.0	6.379			
Graham Clifton	11	38	35.0	10.0	45.0	4.737			
§§Rob Jones	6	22	22.0	3.0	25.0	4.545			
§§Dave Mackay	2	6	3.0	2.0	5.0	3.333			
Peter Murray	9	22	13.0	4.0	17.0	3.091			
§Jimmy Squibb	9	26	16.0	4.0	20.0	3.077			
§§David Emery	5	11	6.0	2.0	8.0	2.909			
§Ian Fletcher	6	14	8.0	2.0	10.0	2.857			
§§Merv Salt	1	2	1.0	0.0	1.0	2.000			
§Terry Barclay	3	5	1.0	0.0	1.0	0.800			

1975...1975...1975...1975...1975...1975

	M	R	Pts	BP	TPts	Ave	F	P	Total
Les Rumsey	38	162	390.0	11.0	401.0	9.901	10	3	13
David Piddock	3	12	23.0	5.0	28.0	9.333			
Dave Gooderham	**40**	**170**	**349.0**	**18.0**	**367.0**	**8.635**	**5**	**4**	**9**
Barney Kennett	39	155	302.0	17.0	319.0	8.232	1	6	7
Graham Clifton	32	122	130.0	32.0	162.0	5.311		1	1
§§Bob Spelta	36	115	129.0	18.0	147.0	5.113			
Jimmy Squibb	8	24	22.0	8.0	30.0	5.000			
§§Gerald Purkiss	34	122	124.0	24.0	148.0	4.852			
§§Peter Mittell	5	17	14.0	4.0	18.0	4.235			
§§Alan Diprose	1	4	4.0	0.0	4.0	4.000			
§§Terry Casserly	32	105	84.0	15.0	99.0	3.771			
§Alan Johns	2	6	3.0	1.0	4.0	2.667			
Derek Cook	1	3	2.0	0.0	2.0	2.667			
§Steve Gibson	4	12	6.0	1.0	7.0	2.333			
§§Garry Keown	1	3	0.0	0.0	0.0	0.000			

CANTERBURY

1976...1976...1976...1976...1976...1976

	M	R	Pts	BP	TPts	Ave	F	P	Total
Graham Banks	33	133	254.0	14.0	268.0	8.060	2	2	4
§§Steve Koppe	**36**	**158**	**278.0**	**32.0**	**310.0**	**7.848**	**1**	**3**	**4**
Les Rumsey	24	97	163.0	19.0	182.0	7.505	1	2	3
Barney Kennett	35	138	214.0	22.0	236.0	6.841	1	2	3
Graham Clifton	29	105	150.0	22.0	172.0	6.552			
§§Reg Luckhurst	24	83	117.0	18.0	135.0	6.506		2	2
§§Brendan Shilleto	3	10	11.0	3.0	14.0	5.600			
Bob Spelta	25	87	102.0	17.0	119.0	5.471		1	1
Terry Casserly	35	106	114.0	22.0	136.0	5.132			
Alan Diprose	4	9	6.0	2.0	8.0	3.556			
§§Danny Kennedy	2	6	5.0	0.0	5.0	3.333			

1977...1977...1977...1977...1977...1977

	M	R	Pts	BP	TPts	Ave	F	P	Total
Dave Johnson	1	4	9.0	0.0	9.0	9.000			
Steve Koppe	**38**	**163**	**328.0**	**32.0**	**360.0**	**8.834**	**4**	**6**	**10**
Graham Banks	31	122	248.0	5.0	253.0	8.295	3		3
Les Rumsey	23	88	167.0	13.0	180.0	8.182	1	2	3
Bob Spelta	34	139	226.0	30.0	256.0	7.367	1	3	4
Barney Kennett	**38**	**149**	**201.0**	**39.0**	**240.0**	**6.443**	**1**	**2**	**3**
Brendan Shilleto	37	140	193.0	20.0	213.0	6.086	1	1	2
Terry Casserly	20	62	67.0	19.0	86.0	5.548			
Graham Clifton	23	79	73.0	19.0	92.0	4.658			
§§Brian Canning	7	25	21.0	6.0	27.0	4.320			
Alan Diprose	4	9	4.0	1.0	5.0	2.222			
§§Bob Watts	4	9	5.0	0.0	5.0	2.222			
§§Mick Adlington	1	3	1.0	0.0	1.0	1.333			

1978...1978...1978...1978...1978...1978

	M	R	Pts	BP	TPts	Ave	F	P	Total
Les Rumsey	42	175	403.0	26.0	429.0	9.806	11	4	15
Steve Koppe	42	176	383.0	43.0	426.0	9.682	3	8	11
Graham Banks	10	35	69.0	2.0	71.0	8.114	1		1
§Tony Garard	1	3	4.0	2.0	6.0	8.000			
§Mike Ferreira	36	137	229.0	33.0	262.0	7.650	2	1	3
Bob Spelta	7	26	43.0	6.0	49.0	7.538			
Graham Clifton	42	161	257.0	44.0	301.0	7.478		2	2
Brendan Shilleto	41	141	209.0	23.0	232.0	6.582			
Barney Kennett	**44**	**176**	**237.0**	**48.0**	**285.0**	**6.477**			
David Piddock	21	63	76.0	13.0	89.0	5.651			
Dave Johnson	3	8	8.0	3.0	11.0	5.500			
§Derek Hole	10	28	19.0	7.0	26.0	3.714			
§§Graham Knowler	1	5	2.0	0.0	2.0	1.600			

1979...1979...1979...1979...1979...1979

	M	R	Pts	BP	TPts	Ave	F	P	Total
Mike Ferreira	36	158	307.0	23.0	330.0	8.354	2	1	3
§§Nigel Boocock	35	148	284.0	24.0	308.0	8.324	2	1	3
Brendan Shilleto	4	14	24.0	2.0	26.0	7.429		1	1
Barney Kennett	37	160	245.0	42.0	287.0	7.175		1	1
David Piddock	27	92	148.0	13.0	161.0	7.000	1	2	3
§Tim Hunt	29	123	193.0	20.0	213.0	6.927	1	1	2
§Paul Woods	1	3	3.0	2.0	5.0	6.667			
§Roger Abel	20	78	81.0	18.0	99.0	5.077			
§§Mick Wilde	10	30	26.0	5.0	31.0	4.133			
Graham Clifton	22	71	65.0	8.0	73.0	4.113			
§§Peter Christopher	6	17	14.0	3.0	17.0	4.000			
§§Neil Farnish	15	49	36.0	12.0	48.0	3.918			
§§Tony Reynolds	7	18	11.0	1.0	12.0	2.667			
§§Rob Dolman	5	14	6.0	3.0	9.0	2.571			
§§Barry Etherington	2	5	0.0	0.0	0.0	0.000			

1980...1980...1980...1980...1980...1980

	M	R	Pts	BP	TPts	Ave	F	P	Total
Mike Ferreira	40	183	466.0	6.0	472.0	10.317	12	2	14
Barney Kennett	38	165	302.0	24.0	326.0	7.903			
Ted Hubbard	31	130	229.0	20.0	249.0	7.662	1	1	2
§Denzil Kent	**42**	**179**	**261.0**	**36.0**	**297.0**	**6.637**			
David Piddock	9	29	28.0	7.0	35.0	4.828		1	1
§Kevin Brice	34	114	90.0	14.0	104.0	3.649			
Rob Dolman	30	103	79.0	9.0	88.0	3.417			
Tony Reynolds	12	39	23.0	4.0	27.0	2.769			
§§Kevin Howland	29	83	39.0	7.0	46.0	2.217			
§§Duncan Tolhurst	4	13	5.0	1.0	6.0	1.846			
§§Ray Griffiths	5	14	6.0	0.0	6.0	1.714			
§Simon Franks	8	16	4.0	1.0	5.0	1.250			
§§Peter Framingham	5	10	2.0	1.0	3.0	1.200			
§§Mark Summerfield	2	5	0.0	0.0	0.0	0.000			

1981...1981...1981...1981...1981...1981

	M	R	Pts	BP	TPts	Ave	F	P	Total
Mike Ferreira	31	138	373.0	2.0	375.0	10.870	13	2	15
§Ian Clark	5	20	37.0	3.0	40.0	8.000			
Denzil Kent	36	161	297.0	15.0	312.0	7.752	4		4
Barney Kennett	**38**	**162**	**245.0**	**31.0**	**276.0**	**6.815**			
§Nigel Couzens	5	20	31.0	3.0	34.0	6.800			
Kevin Howland	1	3	3.0	2.0	5.0	6.667			
§§Mark Martin	26	87	82.0	20.0	102.0	4.690			
§§Darryl Simpson	22	74	69.0	13.0	82.0	4.432			
Kevin Brice	28	97	87.0	15.0	102.0	4.206	1		1
Brendan Shilleto	32	113	101.0	14.0	115.0	4.071			
§§David Mullett	1	2	1.0	1.0	2.0	4.000			
§§Kevin Smart	1	2	1.0	1.0	2.0	4.000			
§§Jamie Luckhurst	13	36	27.0	7.0	34.0	3.778			
Rob Dolman	14	46	33.0	5.0	38.0	3.304			
Graham Knowler	7	24	16.0	0.0	16.0	2.667			
§§Steve Bishop	2	6	2.0	0.0	2.0	1.333			

1982...1982...1982...1982...1982...1982

	M	R	Pts	BP	TPts	Ave	F	P	Total
Les Rumsey	4	23	48.0	3.0	51.0	8.870			
Barney Kennett	37	201	404.0	31.0	435.0	8.657		2	2
Denzil Kent	32	170	308.0	21.0	329.0	7.741		1	1
Ian Clark	37	199	356.0	24.0	380.0	7.638			
Darryl Simpson	36	159	171.0	35.0	206.0	5.182			
§Keith Pritchard	37	156	150.0	24.0	174.0	4.462			
Nigel Couzens	33	122	121.0	12.0	133.0	4.361			
Kevin Brice	29	122	105.0	28.0	133.0	4.361			
Mark Martin	8	31	25.0	4.0	29.0	3.742			
§§Rob Tilbury	4	10	4.0	1.0	5.0	2.000			

1983...1983...1983...1983...1983...1983

	M	R	Pts	BP	TPts	Ave	F	P	Total
Denzil Kent	20	98	190.0	11.0	201.0	8.204	2	2	4
Barney Kennett	**36**	**183**	**309.0**	**37.0**	**346.0**	**7.563**	**1**		**1**
§Kelvin Mullarkey	33	162	274.0	27.0	301.0	7.432			
§Andy Hibbs	15	77	117.0	12.0	129.0	6.701			
Rob Tilbury	4	14	18.0	4.0	22.0	6.286			
Jamie Luckhurst	32	143	194.0	30.0	224.0	6.266			
David Mullett	25	111	135.0	22.0	157.0	5.658			
§Laurie Etheridge	24	104	113.0	31.0	144.0	5.538			
Kevin Brice	27	109	125.0	24.0	149.0	5.468			
Keith Pritchard	32	140	145.0	27.0	172.0	4.914			
§§Terry Broadbank	3	8	5.0	1.0	6.0	3.000			
Les Rumsey	1	4	0.0	0.0	0.0	0.000			

JOHNNIE HOSKINS, the founder of speedway, opened Canterbury, the last track he promoted, on Saturday, May 18, 1968, in the British League Division Two match. He retained an interest in the club and was a regular spectator, health permitting, until his death (only two weeks before his 95th birthday) on April 4, 1987.

Wally Mawdsley joined him as a co-promoter at Kingsmead Stadium at the end of 1976 and they continued in partnership until the promoting rights were awarded to Chris Galvin (father of rider Andy) and his partner Terry Waller on August 2, 1986.

Despite speculation about the possible construction of a new stadium in Canterbury there has been no speedway in the city since 1987 although Wally Mawdsley remained at Kingsmead Stadium as chief executive and consultant to the owners who continued to operate dog racing.

CANTERBURY

1984...1984...1984...1984...1984...1984

	M	R	Pts	BP	TPts	Ave	F	P	Total
Kelvin Mullarkey	1	4	7.0	3.0	10.0	10.000			
Jamie Luckhurst	33	147	272.0	26.0	298.0	8.109			
§Alan Mogridge	25	104	184.0	16.0	200.0	7.692			
David Mullett	32	135	233.0	24.0	257.0	7.615	2		2
§Jeremy Luckhurst	5	14	17.0	7.0	24.0	6.857			
Barney Kennett	29	123	173.0	34.0	207.0	6.732		1	1
Rob Tilbury	**34**	**121**	**153.0**	**20.0**	**173.0**	**5.719**			
Kevin Brice	28	93	117.0	13.0	130.0	5.591			
§Andy Fines	13	38	44.0	5.0	49.0	5.158			
Keith Pritchard	13	39	38.0	12.0	50.0	5.128			
§§Neville Tatum	19	61	67.0	6.0	73.0	4.787			

1985...1985...1985...1985...1985...1985

	M	R	Pts	BP	TPts	Ave	F	P	Total
David Mullett	33	143	294.0	20.0	314.0	8.783	1	1	2
§Mike Spink	37	161	301.0	20.0	321.0	7.975	1		1
Rob Tilbury	**38**	**156**	**221.0**	**30.0**	**251.0**	**6.436**			
Neville Tatum	37	142	179.0	24.0	203.0	5.718	1	2	3
§Bill Barrett	32	112	135.0	23.0	158.0	5.643			
§Steve Bryenton	**38**	**131**	**143.0**	**26.0**	**169.0**	**5.160**			
§Mick Hines	16	50	47.0	12.0	59.0	4.720			
§Lawrie Bloomfield	20	62	54.0	12.0	66.0	4.258			
§Mark Terry	6	15	8.0	0.0	8.0	2.133			
Tony Hansford	1	2	1.0	0.0	1.0	2.000			
Kevin Brice	2	3	0.0	0.0	0.0	0.000			

1986...1986...1986...1986...1986...1986

	M	R	Pts	BP	TPts	Ave	F	P	Total
§Paul Evitts	14	60	129.0	4.0	133.0	8.867	2	1	3
David Mullett	**42**	**190**	**378.0**	**35.0**	**413.0**	**8.695**	**1**	**1**	
Mike Spink	39	170	302.0	21.0	323.0	7.600	2	1	
Alan Mogridge	19	79	132.0	13.0	145.0	7.342	1	1	
Rob Tilbury	**42**	**177**	**243.0**	**25.0**	**268.0**	**6.056**	**2**	**1**	
§Alan Sage	**42**	**163**	**162.0**	**37.0**	**199.0**	**4.883**			
Steve Bryenton	41	155	153.0	22.0	175.0	4.516			
§§Steve Hone	5	13	9.0	2.0	11.0	3.385			
Tony Hansford	19	40	25.0	6.0	31.0	3.100			
§Paul Hilton	13	28	14.0	6.0	20.0	2.857			
§§Gary Hopkins	7	15	4.0	2.0	6.0	1.600			

1987...1987...1987...1987...1987...1987

	M	R	Pts	BP	TPts	Ave	F	P	Total
David Mullett	30	135	258.0	33.0	291.0	8.622		2	2
Mike Spink	**34**	**155**	**262.0**	**29.0**	**291.0**	**7.510**	**1**	**1**	**2**
Rob Tilbury	31	137	231.0	14.0	245.0	7.153	2		2
§Paul Whittaker	22	90	138.0	18.0	156.0	6.933	1	2	3
Paul Evitts	31	127	178.0	23.0	201.0	6.331			
§Mark Lyndon	8	27	31.0	7.0	38.0	5.630			
§Richard Pettman	23	83	70.0	12.0	82.0	3.952			
§Carl Chalcraft	32	99	77.0	16.0	93.0	3.758			
§§Warren Mowat	3	7	3.0	2.0	5.0	2.857			
§§Jimmy Goodsell	8	18	7.0	2.0	9.0	2.000			
Steve Hone	6	19	7.0	0.0	7.0	1.474			

KENT MESSENGER TROPHY

1969	1 Martyn Piddock	2 Geoff Ambrose	3 Graeme Smith
1970	1 Des Lukehurst	2 Reg Trott	3 Pete Bailey
1971	1 John Louis	2 Tony Davey	3 Pete Bailey
1973	1 Brian Foote	2 Trevor Barnwell	3 Bobby McNeil

KENT OPEN CHAMPIONSHIP

1969	1 Geoff Ambrose	2 Pete Bailey	3 Ron Bagley
1972	1 Richard Greer	2 Allen Emmett	3 George Major

CHAMPAGNE DERBY

1969	1 Martyn Piddock	2 Richard May	3 Dave Jessup

MARTYN PIDDOCK MEMORIAL TROPHY

1971	1 Ross Gilbertson	2 Graeme Stapleton	3 Malcolm Balland
1972	1 Ross Gilbertson	2 Arthur Price	3 Ted Hubbard

GOLDEN PINNACLE

1971	1 Graham Banks	2 Graeme Smith	3 Dave Smith

CRUSADERAMA

1971	1 Tony Davey	2 Brian Foote	3 Graham Banks

EASTER CUP

1972	1 Dave Piddock	2 Barney Kennett	3 Graeme Smith

KING OF KENT

1973	1 Roger Mills	2 Graham Banks	3 Ted Hubbard and Trevor Jones

INVICTA LUDORUM

1973	1 Peter Murray	2 Derek Cook	3 Bobby McNeil
1976	1 Steve Koppe	2 Les Rumsey	3 Alan Cowland
1984	1 Jamie Luckhurst	2 Bob Garrad	3 Kelvin Mullarkey

KENT GOLDEN TROPHY

1976	1 Brian Leonard	2 Steve Koppe	3 Les Rumsey

JESUS CHRIST SUPERSTAR TROPHY

1976	1 Les Rumsey	2 Steve Weatherley	3 Ted Hubbard

GRAHAM BANKS MEMORIAL TROPHY

1978	1 Ted Hubbard	2 Barney Kennett	3 Les Rumsey

BRIAN KENNETT TESTIMONIAL

1980	1 Tim Hunt	2 Barry Thomas	3 Gordon Kennett

BBC RADIO KENT CLASSIC

1984	1 David Mullett	2 Neville Tatum	3 Kevin Brice
1985	1 David Mullett	2 Rob Tilbury	3 Mike Spink

CRUSADER CHALLENGE TROPHY

1985	1 Trevor Banks	2 Rob Tilbury	3 Kevin Teager

MANNESMANN DEMAG HAMILTON TROPHY

1985	1 Neil Middleditch	2 David Mullett	3 Jamie Luckhurst

CANTERBURY, founder members of the British League Division Two closed down when Canterbury City Council refused to renew promoter Chris Galvin's licence at the Kingsmead Stadium for the 1988 season.

Their final home meeting was the second leg of the Kent-Herts Trophy against Rye House on Saturday, October 31, 1987, and the Crusaders' last home League match was on Saturday, September 26, 1987, when they beat Poole 42-36.

WELCOME...Canterbury's first major discovery Martyn Piddock greets Czechoslovakian skipper Miloslav Verner before the Test series against England

COATBRIDGE

1974...1974...1974...1974...1974...1974

	M	R	Pts	BP	TPts	Ave	F	P	Total
§§Dave Gifford	**42**	**165**	**330.0**	**34.0**	**364.0**	**8.824**	**4**	**7**	**11**
§§Brian Collins	40	164	337.0	18.0	355.0	8.659	4	5	9
§§Robin Adlington	34	139	233.0	31.0	264.0	7.597	1	4	5
§Jimmy Gallacher	**42**	**168**	**277.0**	**33.0**	**310.0**	**7.381**	**1**	**4**	**5**
§Grahame Dawson	**42**	**157**	**204.0**	**25.0**	**229.0**	**5.834**			
§John Wilson	**42**	**150**	**169.0**	**24.0**	**193.0**	**5.147**		**2**	**2**
§Eddie Argall	18	62	54.0	10.0	64.0	4.129			
§Chris Quigley	11	39	31.0	8.0	39.0	4.000			
§§Mike Ferreira	11	36	27.0	3.0	30.0	3.333			
§§Jim Beresford	7	19	10.0	3.0	13.0	2.737			
§Norman Strachan	2	5	3.0	0.0	3.0	2.400			
§§Ali Devine	1	2	1.0	0.0	1.0	2.000			

MITCH SHIRRA, the New Zealand born son of former rider Tom, competed successfully in second half races at Coatbridge in 1974 until the authorities discovered that he was only 14! He was restricted to interval and after the meeting demonstration rides only.

1975...1975...1975...1975...1975...1975

	M	R	Pts	BP	TPts	Ave	F	P	Total
Brian Collins	**42**	**197**	**442.0**	**24.0**	**466.0**	**9.462**	**8**	**4**	**12**
§§Mitch Shirra	41	193	390.0	14.0	404.0	8.373	6	1	7
Jimmy Gallacher	21	87	150.0	14.0	164.0	7.540	2	3	5
Grahame Dawson	40	174	241.0	37.0	278.0	6.391		2	2
§§Mick McKeon	9	39	50.0	5.0	55.0	5.641			
§Doug Templeton	13	51	56.0	7.0	63.0	4.941			
§Russell Foot	3	9	9.0	2.0	11.0	4.889			
John Wilson	15	55	54.0	11.0	65.0	4.727			
§§Paul Heller	10	33	29.0	4.0	33.0	4.000			
Eddie Argall	22	84	73.0	9.0	82.0	3.905		1	1
§§Derek Richardson	28	96	75.0	14.0	89.0	3.708			
§Robin Dixon	2	7	5.0	1.0	6.0	3.429			
§Mick Fairbairn	2	7	4.0	2.0	6.0	3.429			
§Harry Maclean	3	6	3.0	2.0	5.0	3.333			
§§Norrie Allan	1	2	1.0	0.0	1.0	2.000			
§§Billy Rae	5	11	4.0	1.0	5.0	1.818			
§§Alan Grimshaw	2	7	3.0	0.0	3.0	1.714			
§Barry Booth	7	19	6.0	2.0	8.0	1.684			
§Jim Beaton	6	17	6.0	1.0	7.0	1.647			
Jim Beresford	2	8	1.0	1.0	2.0	1.000			
§§Ken Jarvie	2	3	0.0	0.0	0.0	0.000			
§§Dave Mortiboys	1	2	0.0	0.0	0.0	0.000			
§§Paul Dowdall	1	1	0.0	0.0	0.0	0.000			
§Geoff Jones	1	1	0.0	0.0	0.0	0.000			

TEAM manager Neil Macfarlane quit Coatbridge during the 1974-75 winter so that he could take up a new appointment in charge of rival Scottish Division Two track Paisley. The post was then awarded to former Berwick manager John Doherty – to the consternation of diehard Coatbridge fans who deplored the shock appointment of a man from one of their chief rivals.

1976...1976...1976...1976...1976...1976

	M	R	Pts	BP	TPts	Ave	F	P	Total
Brian Collins	37	169	375.0	9.0	384.0	9.089	3	1	4
Grahame Dawson	34	141	268.0	11.0	279.0	7.915	2	3	5
Mick McKeon	31	142	219.0	22.0	241.0	6.789	1	1	2
Jimmy Gallacher	26	88	105.0	20.0	125.0	5.682			
Derek Richardson	**38**	**155**	**179.0**	**40.0**	**219.0**	**5.652**		**2**	**2**
§Max Brown	15	54	59.0	11.0	70.0	5.185			
Doug Templeton	8	27	33.0	2.0	35.0	5.185			
§Robert Maxfield	26	102	104.0	24.0	128.0	5.020			
§§Bernie Rourke	28	91	86.0	24.0	110.0	4.835			
John Wilson	11	30	19.0	3.0	22.0	2.933			
§Chris Roynon	1	1	0.0	0.0	0.0	0.000			
§§Peter Wordingham	1	2	0.0	0.0	0.0	0.000			

CALEDONIAN OPEN CHAMPIONSHIP

1975 1 Brian Collins 2 Mitch Shirra 3 Graham Drury

See also Glasgow and Edinburgh, Division One Averages and Division Two Averages.

HOME FROM HOME...Kent-born New Zealander Dave Gifford stayed at Coatbridge even though he was offered the opportunity to continue his First Division career at Hull. He remained at Cliftonhill to finish top of the Tigers' averages before moving to Berwick at the beginning of the following season

■ ***COATBRIDGE began the 1977 season – their fourth year – at the Albion Rovers Football Club ground in Cliftonhill, Coatbridge, but at the beginning of June the landlords gave the speedway tenants 14 days' notice to quit as they intended to utilise the speedway circuit to build a greyhound track. The club raced their last League match at Coatbridge on Friday, June 17, 1977, when they lost 32-46 to Eastbourne. The entire operation was moved to a newly-constructed track at Blantyre and resumed their home League programme against Crayford on Friday, July 8. In the intervening period the Tigers raced two away League matches in England, at Rye House and Crayford when they were, in effect, without a home base. For details of the 1977 campaign see under Glasgow.***

■ ***Coatbridge operated as a First Division track in 1973 (following the closure of Hampden Park) but during the winter it was announced that the licence and top riders Jim McMillan (who was seeking a transfer to an English track), Bobby Beaton and New Zealander Dave Gifford (eventually to stay at Coatbridge) had been sold to Ian Thomas to launch First Division racing at Hull. Coatbridge applied, and were accepted, into the 1974 Second Division, retaining Gifford, Jim Gallacher and Robin Adlington.***

CRAYFORD

1968...1968...1968...1968...1968...1968

	M	R	Pts	BP	TPts	Ave	F	P	Total
§§Archie Wilkinson	3	12	30.0	4.0	34.0	11.333	1	1	2
§§Mick Handley	16	66	171.0	2.0	173.0	10.485	7	1	8
§§Tony Childs	**19**	**75**	**136.0**	**8.0**	**144.0**	**7.680**	**2**	**1**	**3**
§§Derek Timms	14	52	76.0	9.0	85.0	6.538			
§§Colin Clark	11	41	53.0	9.0	62.0	6.049			
§§Dai Evans	18	68	81.0	19.0	100.0	5.882			
§§Geoff Ambrose	**19**	**77**	**107.0**	**6.0**	**113.0**	**5.870**	**1**		**1**
§§Stuart Riley	18	68	73.0	14.0	87.0	5.118			
§§Tony Armstrong	6	13	11.0	3.0	14.0	4.308			
§§Dave Parry	4	12	7.0	1.0	8.0	2.667			
§Arthur Price	3	9	5.0	1.0	6.0	2.667			
§§Peter Gay	1	2	0.0	0.0	0.0	0.000			

1969...1969...1969...1969...1969...1969

	M	R	Pts	BP	TPts	Ave	F	P	Total
Geoff Ambrose	30	120	297.0	4.0	301.0	10.033	6		6
Derek Timms	4	13	24.0	5.0	29.0	8.923			
Archie Wilkinson	22	89	173.5	17.0	190.5	8.562		3	3
Tony Childs	**31**	**131**	**255.0**	**15.0**	**270.0**	**8.244**	**1**	**3**	**4**
§§Chris Harrison	**31**	**118**	**161.0**	**31.0**	**192.0**	**6.508**			**0**
§Mick Steel	24	87	117.0	23.0	140.0	6.437	1	1	2
Colin Clark	**31**	**116**	**149.0**	**30.0**	**179.0**	**6.172**			**0**
Tony Armstrong	30	98	99.0	30.0	129.0	5.265		1	1
§Judd Drew	9	24	20.0	6.0	26.0	4.333			
Dai Evans	2	3	2.0	0.0	2.0	2.667			
Stuart Riley	1	5	2.0	0.0	2.0	1.600			

1970...1970...1970...1970...1970...1970

	M	R	Pts	BP	TPts	Ave	F	P	Total
Archie Wilkinson	10	44	100.0	5.0	105.0	9.545	1	1	2
Tony Childs	**33**	**149**	**277.0**	**20.0**	**297.0**	**7.973**	**1**	**2**	**3**
§George Devonport	32	136	220.0	18.0	238.0	7.000	1	1	2
Derek Timms	32	111	129.0	15.0	144.0	5.189	1		1
Mick Steel	29	106	112.0	20.0	132.0	4.981			
Tony Armstrong	31	109	101.0	23.0	124.0	4.550			
§Chris Hawkins	18	63	59.0	12.0	71.0	4.508		1	1
Colin Clark	13	39	31.0	8.0	39.0	4.000			
Judd Drew	16	45	37.0	7.0	44.0	3.911			
§§Ian Spencer	2	4	1.0	1.0	2.0	2.000			
§Cyril Hathaway	1	2	0.0	0.0	0.0	0.000			

CRAYFORD, founder members of the British League Division Two when they rode under the nickname The Highwaymen, closed down at the end of 1970 because of poor attendances at their London Road track but continued to operate as a motor-sports venue with regular banger and stock car racing. There was no speedway at the greyhound track until the beginning of 1975 when promoters Allied Presentations Limited rejoined the Second Division and operated under the general managership of Peter Thorogood who remained at the track until its eventual closure for redevelopment at the end of the 1983 season.

1975...1975...1975...1975...1975...1975

	M	R	Pts	BP	TPts	Ave	F	P	Total
§Laurie Etheridge	**40**	**175**	**412.0**	**14.0**	**426.0**	**9.737**	**7**	**4**	**11**
§Alan Sage	**40**	**180**	**366.0**	**17.0**	**383.0**	**8.511**	**5**	**3**	**8**
§Trevor Barnwell	25	102	181.0	16.0	197.0	7.725	3	2	5
§Peter Wigley	39	159	203.0	46.0	249.0	6.264		3	3
§Bob Young	7	28	35.0	6.0	41.0	5.857			
§Les Ott	8	27	36.0	3.0	39.0	5.778			
§Alan Johns	24	88	110.0	15.0	125.0	5.682		1	1
§George Barclay	37	122	140.0	23.0	163.0	5.344			
§§Dave Shepherd	9	26	28.0	4.0	32.0	4.923			
§§Bill Archer	38	108	89.0	22.0	111.0	4.111			
§§Roy Barwick	5	14	11.0	2.0	13.0	3.714			
§§Richard Willis	2	6	2.0	1.0	3.0	2.000			
§§Dave Howard	2	4	0.0	0.0	0.0	0.000			
§Terry Barclay	1	3	0.0	0.0	0.0	0.000			

1976...1976...1976...1976...1976...1976

	M	R	Pts	BP	TPts	Ave	F	P	Total
Laurie Etheridge	35	154	361.0	19.0	380.0	9.870	11	2	13
Alan Sage	**36**	**163**	**340.0**	**18.0**	**358.0**	**8.785**	**3**	**1**	**4**
§Mike Broadbank	**36**	**143**	**224.0**	**38.0**	**262.0**	**7.329**	**2**	**3**	**5**
Peter Wigley	10	36	52.0	13.0	65.0	7.222		1	1
Alan Johns	34	145	207.0	30.0	237.0	6.538	2	1	3
Trevor Barnwell	6	21	28.0	2.0	30.0	5.714			
Bill Archer	10	33	40.0	5.0	45.0	5.455			
§§Richard Davey	14	45	47.0	6.0	53.0	4.711			
§§Gary Spencer	24	76	61.0	17.0	78.0	4.105			
§§John Hooper	17	57	32.0	12.0	44.0	3.088			
Dave Shepherd	18	52	33.0	3.0	36.0	2.769			
§§Colin Archer	4	8	4.0	0.0	4.0	2.000			
Roy Barwick	1	3	1.0	0.0	1.0	1.333			

1977...1977...1977...1977...1977...1977

	M	R	Pts	BP	TPts	Ave	F	P	Total
Laurie Etheridge	37	162	363.0	18.0	381.0	9.407	4	4	8
Alan Sage	**38**	**172**	**351.0**	**21.0**	**372.0**	**8.651**	**5**	**3**	**8**
§§Colin Gooddy	30	128	257.0	16.0	273.0	8.531	2		2
§Vic Harding	3	13	23.0	1.0	24.0	7.385	1		1
§§Jack Bibby	2	5	7.0	1.0	8.0	6.400			
Alan Johns	34	133	149.0	33.0	182.0	5.474			
John Hooper	33	108	110.0	15.0	125.0	4.630			
Mike Bessent	30	91	72.0	23.0	95.0	4.176			
Richard Davey	36	115	95.0	25.0	120.0	4.174			
§Garry May	17	54	43.0	8.0	51.0	3.778			
§Dingle Brown	3	8	4.0	0.0	4.0	2.000			

1978...1978...1978...1978...1978...1978

	M	R	Pts	BP	TPts	Ave	F	P	Total
Laurie Etheridge	**42**	**185**	**413.0**	**19.0**	**432.0**	**9.341**	**7**	**3**	**10**
Alan Sage	**42**	**183**	**379.0**	**16.0**	**395.0**	**8.634**	**5**		**5**
Garry May	1	2	3.0	1.0	4.0	8.000			
Alan Johns	**42**	**172**	**231.0**	**39.0**	**270.0**	**6.279**	**2**	**2**	**4**
Peter Wigley	40	138	150.0	29.0	179.0	5.188		1	1
Richard Davey	**42**	**142**	**147.0**	**37.0**	**184.0**	**5.183**			
§Tony Featherstone	35	126	143.0	15.0	158.0	5.016	1		1
John Hooper	**42**	**121**	**109.0**	**23.0**	**132.0**	**4.364**			
§Tony Garard	4	12	11.0	1.0	12.0	4.000			
Jack Bibby	3	10	7.0	2.0	9.0	3.600			
§§Nigel Sparshott	1	3	1.0	0.0	1.0	1.333			

1979...1979...1979...1979...1979...1979

	M	R	Pts	BP	TPts	Ave	F	P	Total
§Steve Naylor	36	163	361.0	7.0	368.0	9.031	6		6
Alan Sage	20	86	170.0	5.0	175.0	8.140	2	1	3
Laurie Etheridge	36	154	284.0	24.0	308.0	8.000	1	2	3
§Paul Woods	39	182	315.0	32.0	347.0	7.626	3		3
Alan Johns	3	14	14.0	2.0	16.0	4.571			
Richard Davey	**40**	**153**	**135.0**	**28.0**	**163.0**	**4.261**			
§Paul Gilbert	**40**	**129**	**92.0**	**22.0**	**114.0**	**3.535**			
§§Paul Hollingsbee	7	19	13.0	3.0	16.0	3.368			
John Hooper	33	104	73.0	13.0	86.0	3.308			
§Mick Pither	4	10	6.0	2.0	8.0	3.200			
Jack Bibby	7	17	3.0	1.0	4.0	0.941			
Peter Wigley	4	9	1.0	1.0	2.0	0.889			

1980...1980...1980...1980...1980...1980

	M	R	Pts	BP	TPts	Ave	F	P	Total
Paul Woods	38	165	411.0	21.0	432.0	10.473	10	3	13
Steve Naylor	**39**	**165**	**319.0**	**12.0**	**331.0**	**8.024**	**3**	**1**	**4**
§Tony Brooks	1	3	5.0	1.0	6.0	8.000			
§Les Rumsey	38	158	287.0	18.0	305.0	7.722	5	2	7
Alan Sage	27	108	156.0	30.0	186.0	6.889		1	1
Laurie Etheridge	28	104	133.0	23.0	156.0	6.000	1	1	2
Mick Pither	34	111	123.0	24.0	147.0	5.297			
Alan Johns	38	143	141.0	42.0	183.0	5.119			
Paul Hollingsbee	2	5	3.0	3.0	6.0	4.800			
Paul Gilbert	14	37	30.0	4.0	34.0	3.676			
Trevor Barnwell	2	8	6.0	1.0	7.0	3.500			
Jack Bibby	3	8	4.0	3.0	7.0	3.500			
§Chris Tritton	1	1	0.0	0.0	0.0	0.000			

PETER THOROGOOD never missed a single meeting, home or away, during his x years at Crayford.

CRAYFORD

1981...1981...1981...1981...1981...1981

	M	R	Pts	BP	TPts	Ave	F	P	Total
§Barry Thomas	**38**	**173**	**374.0**	**16.0**	**390.0**	**9.017**	**3**	**3**	**6**
Alan Sage	**38**	**168**	**304.0**	**27.0**	**331.0**	**7.881**	**1**	**2**	**3**
Laurie Etheridge	37	142	219.0	26.0	245.0	6.901		2	2
Mick Pither	**38**	**136**	**152.5**	**42.0**	**194.5**	**5.721**	**1**	**2**	**3**
Trevor Barnwell	32	106	129.0	22.0	151.0	5.698			
§Mike Spinks	25	91	100.0	10.0	110.0	4.835	2		2
Paul Hollingsbee	5	17	17.0	2.0	19.0	4.471			
§§Keith Pritchard	**38**	**133**	**121.0**	**17.0**	**138.0**	**4.150**			
§Paul Bosley	10	25	12.0	2.0	14.0	2.240			
§Ian Fletcher	1	4	1.0	0.0	1.0	1.000			
Tony Brooks	2	4	0.0	0.0	0.0	0.000			
§§Keith Cornell	1	2	0.0	0.0	0.0	0.000			

1982...1982...1982...1982...1982...1982

	M	R	Pts	BP	TPts	Ave	F	P	Total
Barry Thomas	37	208	429.0	26.0	455.0	8.750	4		4
Trevor Banks	10	42	75.0	5.0	80.0	7.619			
Mike Spinks	30	137	214.0	20.0	234.0	6.832		1	1
Alan Sage	**38**	**200**	**298.0**	**26.0**	**324.0**	**6.480**	**2**	**1**	**3**
§§Alan Mogridge	19	94	110.0	30.0	140.0	5.957		2	2
Laurie Etheridge	**38**	**175**	**208.0**	**40.0**	**248.0**	**5.669**			
Paul Bosley	**38**	**177**	**195.0**	**36.0**	**231.0**	**5.220**		**2**	**2**
Mike Pitcher	20	86	84.0	24.0	108.0	5.023			
Trevor Barnwell	6	17	14.0	1.0	15.0	3.529			
Chris Tritton	17	52	34.0	8.0	42.0	3.231			
§§Andy Galvin	6	15	8.0	1.0	9.0	2.400			
Keith Cornell	1	2	0.0	0.0	0.0	0.000			
§Richard Newnham	2	2	0.0	0.0	0.0	0.000			

1983...1983...1983...1983...1983...1983

	M	R	Pts	BP	TPts	Ave	F	P	Total
Barry Thomas	**36**	**185**	**429.0**	**19.0**	**448.0**	**9.686**	**4**	**5**	**9**
Paul Bosley	**36**	**179**	**317.5**	**35.0**	**352.5**	**7.877**	**1**	**3**	**4**
§Kevin Teager	**36**	**172**	**282.0**	**43.0**	**325.0**	**7.558**	**2**	**3**	**5**
Andy Galvin	**36**	**141**	**203.0**	**34.0**	**237.0**	**6.723**			
Alan Sage	**36**	**166**	**227.0**	**48.0**	**275.0**	**6.627**	**1**		**1**
Alan Mogridge	**36**	**168**	**233.0**	**44.0**	**277.0**	**6.595**		**1**	**1**
Trevor Banks	32	130	191.0	19.0	210.0	6.462			
§§Mark Terry	4	14	15.0	3.0	18.0	5.143			

CRAYFORD closed down, for the second time, at the end of the 1983 season and the entire operation moved to Hackney to ride as the Hackney Kestrels. The Stadium was redeveloped incorporating a new smaller greyhound track but speedway has not been staged there since it's re-opening.

CRAYFORD OPEN CHAMPIONSHIP

1969 1 Martyn Piddock — 2 Graham Miles — 3 Geoff Maloney

KENTISH TIMES TROPHY

1975	1 Tom Owen	2 Laurie Etheridge	3 Kelvin Mullarkey, Alan Sage and Les Rumsey
1976	1 Tom Owen	2 Ted Hubbard	3 Hugh Saunders
1977	1 Tom Owen	2 Colin Richardson	3 Martin Yeates
1978	1 Tom Owen	2 Eric Dugard	3 Steve Koppe
1979	1 Tom Owen	2 Les Rumsey	3 Mick Hines

SOUTHERN JUNIOR LEAGUE RIDERS' CHAMPIONSHIP

1983 1 Nigel De'ath — 2 David Smart — 3 Ian Humphreys

CHEERS...Long-serving Crayford skipper Barry Thomas enjoys the sweet taste of success during his days as the Kestrels' top points scorer

CREWE

1969...1969...1969...1969...1969...1969

	M	R	Pts	BP	TPts	Ave	F	P	Total
§§Geoff Curtis	33	135	329.5	11.5	341.0	10.104	6	3	9
§Paul O'Neal	32	123	260.0	13.0	273.0	8.878	5	2	7
§Barry Meeks	24	92	147.0	27.0	174.0	7.565		3	3
§Ian Bottomley	28	103	161.0	20.0	181.0	7.029	1	2	3
§Dave Parry	**35**	**132**	**189.0**	**34.0**	**223.0**	**6.758**		**4**	**4**
§Pete Seaton	7	26	37.0	5.0	42.0	6.462			
§Colin Tucker	34	123	174.5	20.5	195.0	6.341		1	1
§Peter Saunders	34	119	146.0	30.0	176.0	5.916		2	2
§§Glyn Blackburn	9	28	24.0	5.0	29.0	4.143			
§§Rob Jackson	2	4	2.0	0.0	2.0	2.000			
§Freddie Sweet	1	3	0.0	0.0	0.0	0.000			

1970...1970...1970...1970...1970...1970

	M	R	Pts	BP	TPts	Ave	F	P	Total
Colin Tucker	3	11	23.0	4.0	27.0	9.818			
Paul O'Neal	27	118	280.0	6.0	286.0	9.695	7	2	9
§§John Jackson	32	139	250.0	26.0	276.0	7.942		1	1
Barry Meeks	33	134	221.0	18.0	239.0	7.134	3	1	4
Dai Evans	31	135	181.0	33.0	214.0	6.341		1	1
§§Warren Hawkins	23	78	103.0	16.0	119.0	6.103			
Ian Bottomley	28	94	123.0	16.0	139.0	5.915	2	1	3
Dave Parry	17	63	75.0	14.0	89.0	5.651			
Glyn Blackburn	15	47	49.0	13.0	62.0	5.277			
Rob Jackson	8	23	24.0	5.0	29.0	5.043			
§§Ray Cousins	2	7	2.0	1.0	3.0	1.714			
§§John Mulligan	5	13	2.0	0.0	2.0	0.615			

1971...1971...1971...1971...1971...1971

	M	R	Pts	BP	TPts	Ave	F	P	Total
§§Phil Crump	38	164	349.0	19.0	368.0	8.976	6	6	12
John Jackson	37	149	294.0	16.0	310.0	8.322	4	3	7
§§Ray Hassall	1	4	6.0	2.0	8.0	8.000			
Dai Evans	39	160	284.0	25.0	309.0	7.725	2	4	6
§Jack Millen	31	109	155.0	25.0	180.0	6.606	1	2	3
Ian Bottomley	6	21	27.0	7.0	34.0	6.476			
Barry Meeks	**39**	**138**	**165.0**	**32.0**	**197.0**	**5.710**		**2**	**2**
§Gary Moore	**39**	**143**	**160.0**	**30.0**	**190.0**	**5.315**			
Dave Parry	34	112	128.0	18.0	146.0	5.214		1	1
§§Dave Morton	2	6	3.0	2.0	5.0	3.333			
§§Charlie Scarborough	1	2	1.0	0.0	1.0	2.000			
§Stuart Riley	2	5	2.0	0.0	2.0	1.600			
§§Don Beecroft	3	6	0.0	0.0	0.0	0.000			
§§Barrie Smitherman	1	2	0.0	0.0	0.0	0.000			

1972...1972...1972...1972...1972...1972

	M	R	Pts	BP	TPts	Ave	F	P	Total
Phil Crump	41	175	481.0	6.0	487.0	11.131	21	4	25
John Jackson	**42**	**171**	**422.0**	**7.0**	**429.0**	**10.035**	**17**	**3**	**20**
§§Garry Flood	41	170	330.0	27.0	357.0	8.400		10	10
Dai Evans	38	141	202.0	49.0	251.0	7.121		5	5
Dave Morton	27	94	125.0	30.0	155.0	6.596		3	3
Dave Parry	40	136	159.0	37.0	196.0	5.765		2	2
§§Peter Nicholas	12	32	32.0	8.0	40.0	5.000		1	1
Gary Moore	**42**	**149**	**151.0**	**19.0**	**170.0**	**4.564**			
§§Barry Booth	2	6	2.0	0.0	2.0	1.333			
§Reg Brassington	2	6	2.0	0.0	2.0	1.333			
Ray Hassall	5	14	7.0	3.0	10.0	2.857			

PETER NICHOLAS made his debut at home to Canterbury on July 24, 1972, and by the end of the evening had scored a paid maximum. He came home behind partner Garry Flood in heats three, five and nine and John Jackson in heat 13. That was the only maximum of his career.

CHESTER VASE HANDICAP

1970	1 John Jackson	2 Chris Bailey	3 Bob Valentine
1971	1 Phil Crump	2 John Louis	3 Peter Collins
1972	1 Dave Parry	2 Allen Emmett	3 John Jackson

LITTLECHILD £100 TROPHY

1973	1 John Jackson	2 Tom Owen	3 Dave Baugh
1975	1 Paul Gachet	2 Keith White	3 Robert Hollingworth

1973...1973...1973...1973...1973...1973

	M	R	Pts	BP	TPts	Ave	F	P	Total
John Jackson	32	145	301.0	9.0	310.0	8.552	5	1	6
§Geoff Ambrose	31	133	266.5	16.0	282.5	8.496	4	2	6
Dave Morton	24	101	202.0	11.0	213.0	8.436	2	2	4
§§Wayne Forrest	27	111	135.0	16.0	151.0	5.441			
§Glyn Taylor	31	121	140.0	20.0	160.0	5.289		1	1
§Dave O'Connor	2	7	7.0	2.0	9.0	5.143			
§§Ian Cartwright	29	95	95.0	21.0	116.0	4.884			
§Keith White	35	146	155.0	16.0	171.0	4.685			
§§Stuart Cope	1	2	2.0	0.0	2.0	4.000			
§Peter Thompson	7	18	13.0	4.0	17.0	3.778			
§Cliff Anderson	7	27	18.0	4.0	22.0	3.259			
Reg Brassington	4	10	3.0	1.0	4.0	1.600			
Dave Parry	3	7	2.0	0.0	2.0	1.143			
Kelvin Mullarkey	1	1	0.0	0.0	0.0	0.000			

1974...1974...1974...1974...1974...1974

	M	R	Pts	BP	TPts	Ave	F	P	Total
John Jackson	36	160	386.0	12.0	398.0	9.950	11	6	17
Jack Millen	10	29	62.0	4.0	66.0	9.103	1	2	3
Dave Morton	37	167	348.5	22.0	370.5	8.874	6	3	9
Keith White	**38**	**162**	**264.0**	**37.0**	**301.0**	**7.432**		**4**	**4**
Ian Cartwright	36	145	204.0	29.0	233.0	6.428		4	4
§Les Ott	36	62	79.0	15.0	94.0	6.065		1	1
Cliff Anderson	32	114	139.0	24.0	163.0	5.719			
Wayne Forrest	22	68	63.0	15.0	78.0	4.588			
§Mike Gardner	9	28	27.0	5.0	32.0	4.571			
Barry Meeks	3	7	5.0	1.0	6.0	3.429			
Stuart Cope	9	22	15.0	1.0	16.0	2.909			
§§Paul Wells	6	17	8.0	1.0	9.0	2.118			
§§Andy Reid	3	7	2.0	1.0	3.0	1.714			

1975...1975...1975...1975...1975...1975

	M	R	Pts	BP	TPts	Ave	F	P	Total
§Graham Drury	38	166	345.0	16.0	361.0	8.699	2	2	4
§§Chris Turner	28	122	222.0	26.0	248.0	8.131	1	2	3
§Nigel Wasley	30	126	236.0	8.0	244.0	7.746	1	2	3
§Chris Emery	10	43	55.0	13.0	68.0	6.326		1	1
§Ricky Day	9	35	46.0	7.0	53.0	6.057		2	2
Stuart Cope	28	94	125.0	12.0	137.0	5.830	1	1	2
§§Mick Mellor	2	6	5.0	3.0	8.0	5.333			
§§Les Collins	36	131	139.0	33.0	172.0	5.252		1	1
§Max Brown	32	117	116.0	30.0	146.0	4.991		1	1
Geoff Ambrose	7	25	27.0	4.0	31.0	4.960			
Cliff Anderson	24	80	87.0	9.0	96.0	4.800			
Ray Hassall	2	5	4.0	1.0	5.0	4.000			
§§Graham Crook	5	12	7.0	3.0	10.0	3.333			
§Ian Robertson	7	22	16.0	2.0	18.0	3.273			
§Mick Fielding	3	7	4.0	0.0	4.0	2.286			
§§Terry Owen	1	5	2.0	0.0	2.0	1.600			
§§Stuart Roberts	3	6	2.0	0.0	2.0	1.333			
Andy Reid	1	1	0.0	0.0	0.0	0.000			

■ *CREWE – at 429 metres (470 yards) – was both the biggest and fastest track in the country until winter alterations before the opening of the 1971 season saw the length reduced by around 27 metres (30 yards).*

■ *Barry Meeks set a track record of 70.4 seconds on Friday, March 27, 1970, which was credited by the Guinness Book of Records as being the fastest recorded speed on a British speedway track at 87.90 kilometres per hour (54.62 m.p.h.).*

■ *The London and Midlands Railway Sports Ground, was owned by British Rail and originally used by a local cricket club. Since its closure for speedway it has continued to stage monthly stock car meetings although it has only operated on a season to season basis because of impending re-development.*

DONCASTER

PROMOTERS Mike Parker and Bill Bridgett opened the short speedway life of Doncaster Greyhound Stadium in York Road, with the visit of British League Second Division Eastbourne on Sunday, April 17, 1969, amidst a storm of complaints about the bumpiness of the track circuit.
The home side, known as the Stallions, won 43-35 but the visitors threatened to walk-out at one stage because of track conditions. Alan Bridgett, nephew of promoter Bill was one of the new faces introduced in the debut season.

1969...1969...1969...1969...1969...1969

	M	R	Pts	BP	TPts	Ave	F	P	Total
§Terry Shearer	19	76	181.0	3.0	184.0	9.684	3		3
§§David Baugh	16	68	142.0	7.0	149.0	8.765	1	1	2
§§Guy Hawkes	17	72	117.0	9.0	126.0	7.000			
§§Chris Hawkins	9	37	57.0	2.0	59.0	6.378			
§Derek Timms	29	115	149.0	17.0	166.0	5.774	1		1
§§Alan Bridgett	**31**	**123**	**149.0**	**27.0**	**176.0**	**5.724**	**1**		**1**
§§George Devonport	21	72	82.0	12.0	94.0	5.222			
§§Reg Wilson	1	2	2.0	0.0	2.0	4.000			
§§Doug Wyer	12	45	32.0	11.0	43.0	3.822			
§§Stuart Ulph	29	103	85.0	11.0	96.0	3.728			
§§Stuart Jay	5	9	5.0	2.0	7.0	3.111			
§§Neil Glover	8	22	9.0	3.0	12.0	2.182			
§§Cyril Hathaway	1	2	0.0	0.0	0.0	0.000			
§§Dave Kumeta	1	2	0.0	0.0	0.0	0.000			
§§Peter Maxted	1	2	0.0	0.0	0.0	0.000			

1970...1970...1970...1970...1970...1970

	M	R	Pts	BP	TPts	Ave	F	P	Total
§§George Major	23	99	226.0	11.0	237.0	9.576	4		4
§Gordon McGregor	29	118	267.0	9.0	276.0	9.356	6		6
§Clark Facey	1	3	5.0	2.0	7.0	9.333			
§Chris Harrison	30	112	180.0	11.0	191.0	6.821	1		1
§§Mike Holmes	1	3	3.0	1.0	4.0	5.333			
§§Gunther Haslinger	31	125	138.0	18.0	156.0	4.992			
§Chris Roynon	23	88	87.0	9.0	96.0	4.364			
§Dennis Wasden	22	75	67.0	6.0	73.0	3.893			
§§Ian Wilson	27	99	80.0	12.0	92.0	3.717			
§§Malcolm Corradine	6	22	15.0	5.0	20.0	3.636			
§§Cliff Emms	28	104	73.5	15.0	88.5	3.404			
§Jack Lee	4	13	7.0	0.0	7.0	2.154			

■ *JOHN BERRY and Joe Thurley bought the promoting rights at Doncaster early in 1970 but within a year had announced the track's closure and transfer of the speedway licence to Birmingham Perry Barr.*
■ *In all there were only 36 meetings staged at York Road, the final one being the Ronnie Cliffe Trophy on Sunday, September 27, 1970.*
■ *Speedway has never returned to the Yorkshire town although there was a planning application – turned down – to launch the sport at Tattersfield, home of the Doncaster Rugby League Club in 1972.*

SPEEDWAY ST LEGER

1970 1 John Harrhy 2 Gordon McGregor 3 Alan Bridgett

RONNIE CLIFFE TROPHY

1970 1 George Major 2 John Louis 3 John Harrhy

THE STALLIONS...the 1969 squad Derek Timms, Alan Bridgett, Stuart Ulph, Neil Glover, Terry Shearer, George Devonport and (on bike) Chris Hawkins

NATIONAL LEAGUE AVERAGES...NATIONAL LEAGUE AVERAGES...NATIONAL

EASTBOURNE

1969...1969...1969...1969...1969...1969

	M	R	Pts	BP	TPts	Ave	F	P	Total
§Barry Crowson	15	59	145.5	1.0	146.5	9.932	3		3
§§Reg Trott	30	142	290.0	19.0	309.0	8.704	1	2	3
§§Alby Golden	14	68	126.0	8.0	134.0	7.882	1	1	2
§§Hugh Saunders	13	52	78.0	13.0	91.0	7.000			
§§Dave Jessup	**31**	**136**	**201.0**	**24.0**	**225.0**	**6.618**			
§§Derek Cook	28	103	113.0	24.0	137.0	5.320			
§§Mac Woolford	4	13	14.0	3.0	17.0	5.231			
§§Laurie Sims	26	101	102.0	24.0	126.0	4.990			
§§Graeme Johnston	2	6	5.0	2.0	7.0	4.667			
§§Cec Platt	7	20	18.0	5.0	23.0	4.600			
§§John Heddrick	8	26	23.0	4.0	27.0	4.154			
§Tony Hall	11	29	22.0	7.0	29.0	4.000			
§§Joe Robson	7	17	12.0	4.0	16.0	3.765			
§§Ray Boughtflower	7	15	9.0	1.0	10.0	2.667			
§§Tony Smith	4	7	1.0	1.0	2.0	1.143			
§§Garry Hay	1	5	0.0	0.0	0.0	0.000			

1970...1970...1970...1970...1970...1970

	M	R	Pts	BP	TPts	Ave	F	P	Total
Dave Jessup	30	123	285.0	12.0	297.0	9.659	5	2	7
Derek Cook	23	90	169.0	21.0	190.0	8.444	3		3
Reg Trott	**33**	**142**	**242.0**	**25.0**	**267.0**	**7.521**	**2**		**2**
Alby Golden	18	73	112.0	18.0	130.0	7.123		1	1
§Phil Pratt	13	48	73.0	12.0	85.0	7.083		1	1
§§Gordon Kennett	29	116	166.0	31.0	197.0	6.793		2	2
Mac Woolford	29	103	140.5	22.0	162.5	6.311			
Laurie Sims	32	111	147.0	19.0	166.0	5.982			
Hugh Saunders	5	14	12.0	3.0	15.0	4.286			
§§Roger Johns	1	2	2.0	0.0	2.0	4.000			
§§David Kennett	8	25	17.0	4.0	21.0	3.360			

1971...1971...1971...1971...1971...1971

	M	R	Pts	BP	TPts	Ave	F	P	Total
Derek Cook	4	16	37.0	4.0	41.0	10.250	1		1
§§Malcolm Ballard	28	113	235.0	12.0	247.0	8.743	1	2	3
Gordon Kennett	35	148	294.0	28.0	322.0	8.703	3	3	6
§Bobby Dugard	2	6	12.0	1.0	13.0	8.667			
David Kennett	**36**	**141**	**234.0**	**30.0**	**264.0**	**7.489**	**1**	**2**	**3**
Laurie Sims	28	93	148.0	17.0	165.0	7.097			
Reg Trott	**36**	**135**	**184.0**	**52.0**	**236.0**	**6.993**		**2**	**2**
Roger Johns	34	126	183.0	34.0	217.0	6.889		2	2
§§Bobby McNeil	21	78	114.0	19.0	133.0	6.821		1	1
Mac Woolford	18	57	78.0	17.0	95.0	6.667			
Phil Pratt	1	4	5.0	1.0	6.0	6.000			
§§Trevor Geer	4	11	11.0	2.0	13.0	4.727			
§§Simon Bruce	1	4	3.0	1.0	4.0	4.000			

1972...1972...1972...1972...1972...1972

	M	R	Pts	BP	TPts	Ave	F	P	Total
Malcolm Ballard	32	134	322.0	11.0	333.0	9.940	5	2	7
Gordon Kennett	**38**	**164**	**324.0**	**32.0**	**356.0**	**8.683**		**6**	**6**
Bobby McNeil	37	154	268.0	34.0	302.0	7.844		2	2
§§Eric Dugard	3	7	9.0	4.0	13.0	7.429			
Roger Johns	37	148	236.0	32.0	268.0	7.243		1	1
Reg Trott	21	75	88.0	17.0	105.0	5.600	1	1	2
Trevor Geer	36	118	131.5	31.0	162.5	5.508		1	1
Derek Cook	22	73	86.0	13.0	99.0	5.425			
§§Paul Gachet	19	63	67.0	14.0	81.0	5.143			
§§Timmy Ballard	2	7	6.0	2.0	8.0	4.571			
Simon Bruce	16	43	34.0	8.0	42.0	3.907			

1973...1973...1973...1973...1973...1973

	M	R	Pts	BP	TPts	Ave	F	P	Total
Bobby McNeil	34	140	311.0	16.0	327.0	9.343	1	1	2
§Ross Gilbertson	11	41	81.0	10.0	91.0	8.878	1	2	3
Roger Johns	32	135	274.0	16.0	290.0	8.593	3	4	7
Paul Gachet	**36**	**141**	**239.0**	**19.0**	**258.0**	**7.319**	**1**	**2**	**3**
Trevor Geer	36	131	169.0	36.0	205.0	6.260	2	1	3
§Mike Vernam	**14**	**47**	**59.0**	**7.0**	**66.0**	**5.617**			
§§Neil Middleditch	22	83	89.0	11.0	100.0	4.819			
§§Martin Yeates	2	11	13.0	0.0	13.0	4.727			
Eric Dugard	26	81	75.0	17.0	92.0	4.543			
§§Jimmy Squibb	28	92	79.0	17.0	96.0	4.174			
Simon Bruce	1	1	1.0	0.0	1.0	4.000			
§§Alan Johns	5	13	5.0	1.0	6.0	1.846			
Timmy Ballard	1	2	0.0	0.0	0.0	0.000			

1974...1974...1974...1974...1974...1974

	M	R	Pts	BP	TPts	Ave	F	P	Total
Bobby McNeil	33	124	254.0	18.0	272.0	8.774	4	3	7
Trevor Geer	**43**	**174**	**346.0**	**22.0**	**368.0**	**8.460**	**8**	**1**	**9**
Paul Gachet	**43**	**176**	**317.0**	**48.0**	**365.0**	**8.295**	**2**	**8**	**10**
§Mike Sampson	35	134	242.0	19.0	261.0	7.791	2	2	4
Neil Middleditch	**43**	**169**	**280.0**	**46.0**	**326.0**	**7.716**		**3**	**3**
§§Pete Jarman	41	139	200.0	43.0	243.0	6.993		2	2
§§Steve Weatherley	20	59	78.5	16.0	94.5	6.407		1	1
Martin Yeates	34	122	170.0	21.0	191.0	6.262			
Eric Dugard	9	25	27.0	6.0	33.0	5.280			

1975...1975...1975...1975...1975...1975

	M	R	Pts	BP	TPts	Ave	F	P	Total
Paul Gachet	44	184	431.0	23.0	454.0	9.870	8	7	15
Neil Middleditch	44	185	422.0	23.0	445.0	9.622	8	3	11
Steve Weatherley	42	173	294.0	55.0	349.0	8.069	1	5	6
Pete Jarman	45	177	286.0	38.0	324.0	7.322	1	4	5
Mike Sampson	42	166	261.0	41.0	302.0	7.277	2	4	
Trevor Geer	2	6	9.0	0.0	9.0	6.000			
Eric Dugard	**46**	**148**	**163.0**	**40.0**	**203.0**	**5.486**			
§§Colin Richardson	40	123	133.0	28.0	161.0	5.236			
§Mike Bessent	3	7	7.0	1.0	8.0	4.571			
§Terry Barclay	6	18	13.0	4.0	17.0	3.778			
§Mick Pither	3	7	4.0	2.0	6.0	3.429			
§Ian Fletcher	2	5	0.0	0.0	0.0	0.000			

1976...1976...1976...1976...1976...1976

	M	R	Pts	BP	TPts	Ave	F	P	Total
Steve Weatherley	32	143	362.0	8.0	370.0	10.350	11	3	17
Eric Dugard	**36**	**149**	**231.0**	**31.0**	**262.0**	**7.034**	**1**		**1**
Pete Jarman	35	122	185.0	21.0	206.0	6.754	4		4
Colin Richardson	**36**	**152**	**214.0**	**33.0**	**247.0**	**6.500**			
Mike Sampson	24	101	150.0	14.0	164.0	6.495		1	2
§§Ian Gledhill	15	46	65.0	9.0	74.0	6.435			
§§Steve Naylor	13	47	53.0	11.0	64.0	5.447			
§§Roger Abel	26	88	98.0	18.0	116.0	5.273			
§§Colin Ackroyd	5	10	9.0	4.0	13.0	5.200			
Ian Fletcher	20	62	57.0	10.0	67.0	4.323			
§§Paul Woods	5	16	9.0	2.0	11.0	2.750			
Mick Pither	1	2	0.0	0.0	0.0	0.000			

1977...1977...1977...1977...1977...1977

	M	R	Pts	BP	TPts	Ave	F	P	Total
Colin Richardson	45	187	475.0	22.0	497.0	10.631	21	3	24
Mike Sampson	**46**	**184**	**441.0**	**23.0**	**464.0**	**10.087**	**13**	**8**	**21**
David Kennett	**46**	**182**	**332.0**	**49.0**	**381.0**	**8.374**	**5**	**7**	**12**
Eric Dugard	45	179	321.0	48.0	369.0	8.246	1	6	7
Peter Jarman	19	64	96.0	24.0	120.0	7.500			
Roger Abel	**46**	**164**	**256.0**	**44.0**	**300.0**	**7.317**	**1**		**1**
Paul Woods	30	94	127.0	34.0	161.0	6.851		2	2
Steve Naylor	42	131	178.0	39.0	217.0	6.626			
Ian Fletcher	2	8	8.0	2.0	10.0	5.000			
§§Peter Tarrant	1	3	2.0	0.0	2.0	2.667			

1978...1978...1978...1978...1978...1978

	M	R	Pts	BP	TPts	Ave	F	P	Total
Mike Sampson	**46**	**198**	**455.0**	**27.0**	**482.0**	**9.737**	**9**	**2**	**11**
David Kennett	41	167	350.0	23.0	373.0	8.934	9	4	13
Eric Dugard	45	177	351.0	42.0	393.0	8.881	6	3	9
Roger Abel	45	166	245.0	62.0	307.0	7.398		3	3
Steve Naylor	43	169	276.0	33.0	309.0	7.314	4	3	7
Paul Woods	**45**	**159**	**214.0**	**50.0**	**264.0**	**6.642**		**3**	**3**
Colin Ackroyd	12	33	42.0	7.0	49.0	5.939			
§§John Barker	40	121	140.0	35.0	175.0	5.785			
Ian Fletcher	3	6	2.0	2.0	4.0	2.667			

EASTBOURNE, a long-time Sunday afternoon Training track, won itself a proud reputation for discovering fresh new talent. The Eagles have unearthed more riders during the Second Division era than any other track in the country. Their first 1969 find Dave Jessup went on to win more than 100 England caps.

EASTBOURNE

1985...1985...1985...1985...1985...1985

	M	R	Pts	BP	TPts	Ave	F	P	Total
Gordon Kennett	44	186	480.0	7.0	487.0	10.473	10	1	11
Colin Richardson	45	189	392.0	17.0	409.0	8.656	5	4	9
§Andy Buck	39	163	272.0	24.0	296.0	7.264	2		2
§§Martin Dugard	28	102	120.0	25.0	145.0	5.686			
§Keith Pritchard	**46**	**184**	**227.0**	**32.0**	**259.0**	**5.630**			
§Paul Clarke	38	150	176.0	30.0	206.0	5.493			
§Mick Hines	6	22	25.0	5.0	30.0	5.455			
§§Chris Mulvihill	38	115	100.0	26.0	126.0	4.383			
§Mark Summerfield	5	14	14.0	1.0	15.0	4.286			
§Peter Framingham	3	9	6.0	2.0	8.0	3.556			
§Derek Harrison	11	34	21.0	6.0	27.0	3.176			
§§Dean Standing	14	33	8.0	2.0	10.0	1.212			
§Bob Kinning	3	5	0.0	0.0	0.0	0.000			

1986...1986...1986...1986...1986...1986

	M	R	Pts	BP	TPts	Ave	F	P	Total
Gordon Kennett	**46**	**210**	**487.0**	**31.0**	**518.0**	**9.867**	**4**	**7**	**11**
Martin Dugard	**46**	**212**	**483.0**	**34.0**	**517.0**	**9.755**	**7**	**4**	**11**
Colin Richardson	16	62	102.0	23.0	125.0	8.065		1	1
Keith Pritchard	**46**	**194**	**298.0**	**52.0**	**350.0**	**7.216**	**2**		**2**
Andy Buck	**46**	**199**	**296.5**	**56.0**	**352.5**	**7.085**	**1**		**1**
Dean Standing	44	178	274.0	40.0	314.0	7.056	1	2	3
Chris Mulvihill	32	82	72.0	14.0	86.0	4.195			
§§Colin Smith	1	2	1.0	1.0	2.0	4.000			
§§Dean Barker	14	45	27.0	8.0	35.0	3.111			
§§Steve Chambers	3	8	5.0	1.0	6.0	3.000			
§§Darren Standing	2	4	1.0	0.0	1.0	1.000			
§§Ian Atkinson	1	2	0.0	0.0	0.0	0.000			

1987...1987...1987...1987...1987...1987

	M	R	Pts	BP	TPts	Ave	F	P	Total
Martin Dugard	**38**	**168**	**429.0**	**8.0**	**437.0**	**10.405**	**12**	**3**	**15**
Gordon Kennett	**38**	**166**	**368.0**	**22.0**	**390.0**	**9.398**	**6**	**3**	**9**
Andy Buck	**38**	**163**	**324.0**	**29.0**	**353.0**	**8.663**	**5**	**6**	**11**
Dean Standing	37	156	222.0	64.0	286.0	7.333		4	4
Keith Pritchard	36	143	199.0	52.0	251.0	7.021		3	3
Dean Barker	21	76	85.0	13.0	98.0	5.158			
Darren Standing	33	93	82.0	18.0	100.0	4.301			
Steve Chambers	13	38	31.0	7.0	38.0	4.000			
§§Kevin Pitts	6	20	11.0	2.0	13.0	2.600			
§Jay Pleece	2	4	1.0	0.0	1.0	1.000			
§Jon Cooper	3	7	1.0	0.0	1.0	0.571			

1988...1988...1988...1988...1988...1988

	M	R	Pts	BP	TPts	Ave	F	P	Total
Gordon Kennett	**34**	**178**	**424.5**	**19.0**	**443.5**	**9.966**	**5**	**1**	**6**
Andy Buck	32	161	363.0	22.0	385.0	9.565	2	3	5
Dean Standing	**34**	**166**	**297.0**	**23.0**	**320.0**	**7.711**	**3**		**3**
Dean Barker	32	164	251.0	51.0	302.0	7.366		1	1
Keith Pritchard	31	151	175.0	37.0	212.0	5.616			
§Gary Tagg	5	14	16.0	3.0	19.0	5.429			
§§David Norris	12	48	53.0	7.0	60.0	5.000			
§Jon Surman	22	91	84.0	17.0	101.0	4.440			
Darren Standing	29	99	84.0	23.0	107.0	4.323			
Kevin Pitts	3	11	6.0	2.0	8.0	2.909			
§§Darren Grayling	3	6	0.0	0.0	0.0	0.000			

1989...1989...1989...1989...1989...1989

	M	R	Pts	BP	TPts	Ave	F	P	Total
Gordon Kennett	**38**	**207**	**473.0**	**24.0**	**497.0**	**9.604**	**1**	**3**	**4**
Dean Barker	24	114	238.0	19.0	257.0	9.018	2	2	4
Andy Buck	36	192	375.0	19.0	394.0	8.208	1	2	3
David Norris	**38**	**201**	**284.0**	**70.0**	**354.0**	**7.045**			
Keith Pritchard	**38**	**192**	**233.0**	**47.0**	**280.0**	**5.833**			
Darren Standing	**38**	**166**	**158.0**	**36.0**	**194.0**	**4.675**			
Jon Surman	11	35	34.0	4.0	38.0	4.343			
§§Steve Masters	18	55	33.0	10.0	43.0	3.127			
Darren Grayling	18	56	30.0	6.0	36.0	2.571			
§§Jon Cook	2	3	0.0	0.0	0.0	0.000			

1990...1990...1990...1990...1990...1990

	M	R	Pts	BP	TPts	Ave	F	P	Total
Gordon Kennett	27	140	303.0	10.0	313.0	8.943	1	1	2
Andy Buck	30	154	257.0	12.0	269.0	6.987	1		1
§Tony Primmer	**34**	**177**	**240.0**	**47.0**	**287.0**	**6.486**		**1**	**1**
Paul Woods	**34**	**193**	**262.0**	**39.0**	**301.0**	**6.238**			
Darren Standing	11	41	47.0	12.0	59.0	5.756			
Keith Pritchard	**34**	**168**	**193.0**	**39.0**	**232.0**	**5.524**			
§§Brian Nixon	7	29	34.0	6.0	40.0	5.517			
§Justin Walker	23	73	69.0	19.0	88.0	4.822			
Darren Grayling	27	100	90.0	13.0	103.0	4.120			
Steve Masters	5	10	2.0	1.0	3.0	1.200			
§§Scott Swain	1	4	1.0	0.0	1.0	1.000			
Jon Cook	2	2	0.0	0.0	0.0	0.000			

CHAMPIONSHIP OF SUSSEX

1969	1 Martyn Piddock	2 Graeme Smith	3 Mike Vernam
1970	1 Richard May	2 Gordon Kennett, Alby Golden and Dave Jessup	
1972	1 Allen Emmett	2 Malcolm Ballard	3 Arthur Browning
1973	1 Roger Johns	2 Arthur Browning	3 Trevor Geer and John Davis
1976	1 Steve Weatherly	2 Mike Sampson	3 Les Rumsey
1985	1 Jamie Luckhurst	2 Mike Ferreira	3 Neil Middleditch
1986	1 Neil Middleditch	2 Colin Richardson	3 Gordon Kennett
1987	1 Nigel Crabtree	2 Martin Goodwin	3 Andy Buck
1989	1 Dean Standing	2 Martin Goodwin	3 Todd Wiltshire
1990	1 Alan Mogridge	2 Chris Louis	3 Gordon Kennett

ARLINGTON OPEN CHAMPIONSHIP

1970	1 Malcolm Shakespeare	2 Dave Jessup	3 Arthur Price

EVENING ARGUS TROPHY

1970	1 Richard May	2 Gordon Kennett	3 Alby Golden
1971	1 Malcolm Ballard	2 Kevin Holden	3 Gordon Kennett
1974	1 Phil Herne	2 Paul Gachet	3 Arthur Browning
1977	1 Mike Sampson	2 Martin Yeates	3 Colin Richardson

ARTHUR NUTLEY MEMORIAL

1990	1 Scott Humphries	2 Brian Nixon	3 Scott Swain

See also Eastbourne, Division One Averages

DOUBLE WINNERS...the successful 1987 Eagles – Gordon Kennett, Martin Dugard, Andy Buck, Dean Barker, Darren Standing, Dean Standing, Keith Pritchard, promoter Bob Dugard and manager Russell Lanning

EDINBURGH

RACING returned to Edinburgh (this time at Powderhall Stadium) in 1977 for the first time in a decade.

EDINBURGH'S victory against Berwick in the 1981 National League Cup Final was the first national success for the club since they had lost to Cradley Heath in the 1961 Provincial League Cup Final. There was one survivor from that era – George Hunter who rode in BOTH Cup Finals, 20 seasons apart!

1977...1977...1977...1977...1977...1977

	M	R	Pts	BP	TPts	Ave	F	P	Total
§§Bert Harkins	**42**	**178**	**335.0**	**25.0**	**360.0**	**8.090**	**3**	**1**	**4**
§Jack Millen	41	159	292.0	18.0	310.0	7.799	2	2	4
§§Charlie Monk	36	145	252.0	13.0	265.0	7.310	1	1	2
§Steve McDermott	23	96	136.0	17.0	153.0	6.375	1	1	2
§Dave Trownson	40	151	194.0	38.0	232.0	6.146		2	2
§Colin Farquharson	8	32	40.0	6.0	46.0	5.750			
§Nigel Wasley	20	77	87.0	19.0	106.0	5.506			
§Malcolm Chambers	2	5	5.0	1.0	6.0	4.800			
§Alan Bridgett	40	131	129.0	21.0	150.0	4.580			
§§Alan Morrison	26	92	86.0	17.0	103.0	4.478			
§§Des Allen	7	17	13.0	2.0	15.0	3.529			
§Peter Waite	3	8	5.0	2.0	7.0	3.500			
§Mark Stokes	2	8	6.0	0.0	6.0	3.000			
§Neil Webb	1	2	0.0	0.0	0.0	0.000			

1978...1978...1978...1978...1978...1978

	M	R	Pts	BP	TPts	Ave	F	P	Total
§Robert Hollingworth	**40**	**165**	**285.0**	**20.0**	**305.0**	**7.394**	**2**	**1**	**3**
Bert Harkins	35	149	238.0	29.0	267.0	7.168	2		2
§Steve Lomas	25	105	171.0	11.0	182.0	6.933			
Dave Trownson	**40**	**163**	**233.0**	**34.0**	**267.0**	**6.552**		**2**	**2**
§Brian Collins	38	147	203.0	19.0	222.0	6.041	1	2	3
Steve McDermott	27	106	141.0	18.0	159.0	6.000		1	1
§Ivan Blacka	12	47	53.0	7.0	60.0	5.106			
Alan Bridgett	33	101	101.0	19.0	120.0	4.752	1	1	2
Alan Morrison	13	36	37.0	5.0	42.0	4.667			
Mark Stokes	8	16	7.0	1.0	8.0	2.000			
Malcolm Chambers	2	4	1.0	0.0	1.0	1.000			
§§Terry Freeman	2	5	1.0	0.0	1.0	0.800			

1979...1979...1979...1979...1979...1979

	M	R	Pts	BP	TPts	Ave	F	P	Total
Dave Trownson	37	166	305.0	18.0	323.0	7.783	1		1
Steve Lomas	30	125	202.5	22.0	224.5	7.184		1	1
Bert Harkins	27	116	178.0	17.0	195.0	6.724		2	2
Brian Collins	36	153	229.0	22.0	251.0	6.562	1		1
Alan Bridgett	33	111	138.0	15.0	153.0	5.514			
Ivan Blacka	37	141	163.0	24.0	187.0	5.305			
Benny Rourke	20	67	67.0	21.0	88.0	5.254			
§Rob Mouncer	23	99	109.0	20.0	129.0	5.212			
§Tim Curnock	3	12	11.0	3.0	14.0	4.667			
§Roger Lambert	15	37	22.0	6.0	28.0	3.027			
§§Alan Stansfield	4	10	1.0	0.0	1.0	0.400			

1980...1980...1980...1980...1980...1980

	M	R	Pts	BP	TPts	Ave	F	P	Total
§George Hunter	37	145	300.0	22.0	322.0	8.883	3	3	6
Dave Trownson	41	170	332.0	25.0	357.0	8.400		1	1
§Neil Collins	36	154	291.0	22.0	313.0	8.130	2		2
§Chris Turner	5	18	23.0	7.0	30.0	6.667			
Brian Collins	41	153	195.0	38.0	233.0	6.092			
Benny Rourke	36	134	166.0	34.0	200.0	5.970		1	1
§Harry Maclean	33	108	120.0	20.0	140.0	5.185			
Roger Lambert	39	135	142.0	31.0	173.0	5.126			
§Arnold Haley	12	42	37.0	13.0	50.0	4.762			
Rob Mouncer	2	7	4.0	2.0	6.0	3.429			
§Adrian Pepper	2	4	0.0	0.0	0.0	0.000			
Alan Morrison	1	1	0.0	0.0	0.0	0.000			

1981...1981...1981...1981...1981...1981

	M	R	Pts	BP	TPts	Ave	F	P	Total
Neil Collins	**47**	**207**	**463.0**	**38.0**	**501.0**	**9.681**	**9**	**3**	**12**
Dave Trownson	**47**	**198**	**390.0**	**34.0**	**424.0**	**8.566**	**1**	**3**	**4**
George Hunter	46	185	336.0	55.0	391.0	8.454		6	6
Chris Turner	**47**	**201**	**316.5**	**60.0**	**376.5**	**7.493**		**4**	**4**
Harry Maclean	3	9	13.0	3.0	16.0	7.111			
Ivan Blacka	43	181	288.0	32.0	320.0	7.072	1		1
Benny Rourke	23	78	93.0	21.0	114.0	5.846			
Roger Lambert	37	132	147.0	27.0	174.0	5.273			
§Guy Robson	18	52	28.0	8.0	36.0	2.769			
§§Peter Erskine	3	7	4.0	0.0	4.0	2.286			
§Ian Westwell	11	30	17.0	0.0	17.0	2.267			
§Graham Knowler	2	5	1.0	0.0	1.0	0.800			

1982...1982...1982...1982...1982...1982

	M	R	Pts	BP	TPts	Ave	F	P	Total
Dave Trownson	37	191	420.0	20.0	440.0	9.215	2	1	3
§Eric Broadbelt	19	84	139.0	9.0	148.0	7.048			
§Brett Saunders	37	189	288.0	44.0	332.0	7.026	1		1
Ivan Blacka	30	134	185.0	34.0	219.0	6.537			
Benny Rourke	29	126	170.0	19.0	189.0	6.000		1	1
Chris Turner	34	178	228.0	37.0	265.0	5.955			
§Mark Fiora	22	111	142.0	16.0	158.0	5.694			
Roger Lambert	21	88	74.0	22.0	96.0	4.364			
Ian Westwell	11	39	24.0	4.0	28.0	2.872			
§§Sean Courtney	16	49	25.0	6.0	31.0	2.531			
Peter Erskine	5	15	8.0	1.0	9.0	2.400			
§§Billy Murphy	1	2	0.0	0.0	0.0	0.000			
§§Scott Cook	1	1	0.0	0.0	0.0	0.000			

1983...1983...1983...1983...1983...1983

	M	R	Pts	BP	TPts	Ave	F	P	Total
Dave Trownson	31	156	321.0	20.0	341.0	8.744	1	1	2
Mark Fiora	31	156	278.0	25.0	303.0	7.769	1	1	2
Brett Saunders	33	164	270.0	35.0	305.0	7.439	2	1	3
George Hunter	29	119	179.0	28.0	207.0	6.958		1	1
Chris Turner	31	146	215.0	37.0	252.0	6.904			
Roger Lambert	34	164	212.0	38.0	250.0	6.098		1	1
§Glyn Taylor	19	85	111.0	18.0	129.0	6.071		1	1
Sean Courtney	23	94	93.0	17.0	110.0	4.681			
§§Chris Kelly	6	24	14.0	3.0	17.0	2.833			
Scott Cook	6	17	8.0	2.0	10.0	2.353			
§George Wells	1	3	1.0	0.0	1.0	1.333			
§§Mick Baynham	2	3	0.0	0.0	0.0	0.000			
§§Tony Rizzo	1	3	0.0	0.0	0.0	0.000			
Eric Broadbelt	1	2	0.0	0.0	0.0	0.000			

1984...1984...1984...1984...1984...1984

	M	R	Pts	BP	TPts	Ave	F	P	Total
§Bobby Beaton	27	129	294.0	6.0	300.0	9.302	5		5
Mark Fiora	18	80	174.0	8.0	182.0	9.100	1		1
Dave Trownson	10	36	62.0	7.0	69.0	7.667		1	1
§Craig Pendlebury	13	67	98.0	9.0	107.0	6.388			
Sean Courtney	28	118	151.0	26.0	177.0	6.000			
Roger Lambert	26	110	142.0	19.0	161.0	5.855		1	1
Brett Saunders	15	60	65.0	16.0	81.0	5.400			
§Paul McHale	30	91	87.0	15.0	102.0	4.484			
§Phil Jeffrey	29	116	103.0	22.0	125.0	4.310			
§Rob Grant	6	22	16.0	1.0	17.0	3.091			
§§Martin Johnson	15	46	27.0	5.0	32.0	2.783			
Scott Cook	1	3	1.0	0.0	1.0	1.333			
Tony Rizzo	1	2	0.0	0.0	0.0	0.000			

1985...1985...1985...1985...1985...1985

	M	R	Pts	BP	TPts	Ave	F	P	Total
Brett Saunders	37	156	266.0	25.0	291.0	7.462	2	2	4
Bobby Beaton	**38**	**158**	**280.0**	**12.0**	**292.0**	**7.392**	**3**	**1**	**4**
§Steve Finch	32	139	233.0	11.0	244.0	7.022	1	1	2
Dave Trownson	25	95	139.5	6.0	145.5	6.126			
Phil Jeffrey	17	61	78.0	9.0	87.0	5.705			
§Billy Burton	32	115	120.0	25.0	145.0	5.043			
§Mark Burrows	18	67	52.0	18.0	70.0	4.179			
Sean Courtney	5	14	11.0	3.0	14.0	4.000			
§Gary O'Hare	1	5	5.0	0.0	5.0	4.000			
§§Edward Baldi	1	1	1.0	0.0	1.0	4.000			
§Alan Mason	19	67	52.0	11.0	63.0	3.761			
§§Gordon Whitaker	13	42	28.0	6.0	34.0	3.238			
Roger Lambert	9	31	21.0	2.0	23.0	2.968			
§§Barrie Dixon	3	7	2.0	2.0	4.0	2.286			
§§Tony Forward	6	21	10.0	1.0	11.0	2.095			
§§Scott Lamb	10	25	11.0	1.0	12.0	1.920			

EDINBURGH

1986...1986...1986...1986...1986...1986

	M	R	Pts	BP	TPts	Ave	F	P	Total
§Les Collins	**44**	**198**	**493.0**	**9.0**	**502.0**	**10.141**	**12**	**1**	**13**
§Doug Wyer	35	149	333.0	7.0	340.0	9.128	1		1
Dave Trownson	**44**	**171**	**257.0**	**49.0**	**306.0**	**7.158**		**3**	**3**
Brett Saunders	**44**	**184**	**255.0**	**27.0**	**282.0**	**6.130**	**1**		**1**
Mark Burrows	**44**	**152**	**152.0**	**41.0**	**193.0**	**5.079**			
Phil Jeffrey	**44**	**160**	**143.0**	**44.0**	**187.0**	**4.675**			
Scott Lamb	41	117	113.0	22.0	135.0	4.615			
§§Colin Smith	3	7	6.0	2.0	8.0	4.571			
§§Jamie Young	3	7	8.0	0.0	8.0	4.571			
§§Ray Taaffe	1	2	1.0	0.0	1.0	2.000			

POWDERHALL SPRINT

1978	1 Robert Hollingworth	2 Steve McDermott	3 Nicky Allott
1979	1 Dave Trownson	2 Les Rumsey	3 George Hunter
1980	1 George Hunter	2 Wayne Brown	3 Derek Richardson

FESTIVAL TROPHY

1987	1 Les Collins	2 Neville Tatum	3 Troy Butler

STELRAD GAMES BONANZA

1988	1 Les Collins	2 Gordon Kennett	3 Martin Dugard

FUTURE CHAMPIONS CHASE

1990	1 Dave Edwards	2 Max Schofield	3 Anthony Boyd

See also Edinburgh, Division One averages for Scottish Open Championship

1987...1987...1987...1987...1987...1987

	M	R	PTs	BP	TPts	Ave	F	P	Total
Les Collins	33	162	394.5	9.0	403.5	9.963	6	2	8
Doug Wyer	17	70	145.0	2.0	147.0	8.400	3		3
Brett Saunders	**34**	**159**	**275.0**	**34.0**	**309.0**	**7.774**		**1**	**1**
Dave Trownson	26	102	150.0	26.0	176.0	6.902		1	1
§§Chris Cobby	19	82	105.0	21.0	126.0	6.146			
Scott Lamb	**34**	**150**	**166.0**	**42.0**	**208.0**	**5.547**		**1**	**1**
Phil Jeffrey	20	77	71.0	20.0	91.0	4.727			
Jamie Young	12	39	24.0	4.0	28.0	2.872			
Ray Taaffe	8	17	10.0	2.0	12.0	2.824			
§Barry Ayres	2	4	2.0	0.0	2.0	2.000			
Colin Smith	13	28	7.0	0.0	7.0	1.000			
§§Shaun Bickley	8	17	2.0	1.0	3.0	0.706			
§James Hayhow	1	2	0.0	0.0	0.0	0.000			

1989...1989...1989...1989...1989...1989

	M	R	Pts	BP	TPts	Ave	F	P	Total
Les Collins	36	196	423.0	20.0	443.0	9.041	6	3	9
Brett Saunders	37	186	362.0	21.0	383.0	8.237	2	1	3
Michael Coles	**38**	**202**	**288.0**	**52.0**	**340.0**	**6.733**			
§§Mick Powell	33	150	202.0	38.0	240.0	6.400			
Scott Lamb	**38**	**194**	**260.0**	**39.0**	**299.0**	**6.165**			
§§Lars Munkedal	32	131	173.0	18.0	191.0	5.832			
§Peter McNamara	25	78	68.0	14.0	82.0	4.205			
Tony Rizzo	6	13	9.0	4.0	13.0	4.000			
§Rod Colquhoun	3	11	6.0	3.0	9.0	3.273			
§Mark Pearce	7	21	9.0	3.0	12.0	2.286			
Jamie Luckhurst	2	6	2.0	0.0	2.0	1.333			
§§Mike McLuskey	2	8	0.0	0.0	0.0	0.000			
Ray Taaffe	1	1	0.0	0.0	0.0	0.000			

1988...1988...1988...1988...1988...1988

	M	R	Pts	BP	TPts	Ave	F	P	Total
Les Collins	**36**	**216**	**475.0**	**11.0**	**486.0**	**9.000**	**4**	**1**	**5**
§Jamie Luckhurst	**36**	**201**	**418.0**	**14.0**	**432.0**	**8.597**	**5**		**5**
Doug Wyer	7	33	57.0	3.0	60.0	7.273			
Brett Saunders	**36**	**207**	**298.0**	**42.0**	**340.0**	**6.570**		**1**	**1**
Scott Lamb	**36**	**169**	**162.0**	**36.0**	**198.0**	**4.686**			
§Rob Woffinden	16	74	75.0	10.0	85.0	4.595			
§Jeremy Luckhurst	31	131	114.0	25.0	139.0	4.244			
Tony Rizzo	4	18	13.0	3.0	16.0	3.556			
§Jackson Irving	6	17	11.0	2.0	13.0	3.059			
§§Darrell Branford	17	49	28.0	7.0	35.0	2.857			
§§Mike Long	7	19	11.0	2.0	13.0	2.737			
Ray Taaffe	6	22	9.0	2.0	11.0	2.000			

1990...1990...1990...1990...1990...1990

	M	R	Pts	BP	TPts	Ave	F	P	Total
Les Collins	**34**	**183**	**376.0**	**25.0**	**401.0**	**8.765**	**2**	**1**	**3**
§§Freddy Schøtt	30	144	262.0	19.0	281.0	7.806	1	2	3
Carl Blackbird	31	163	252.0	39.0	291.0	7.141		1	1
Brett Saunders	27	137	210.0	29.0	239.0	6.978		2	2
Michael Coles	**34**	**178**	**237.0**	**34.0**	**271.0**	**6.090**			
Scott Lamb	33	143	176.0	24.0	200.0	5.594		1	1
Mick Powell	25	84	68.5	16.0	84.5	4.024		1	1
Mark Pearce	5	15	11.0	2.0	13.0	3.467			
§§Nigel Alderton	11	32	18.0	4.0	22.0	2.750			
Mike McLuskey	2	5	2.0	1.0	3.0	2.400			
§Anthony Boyd	2	4	2.0	0.0	2.0	2.000			
§§Brian Mercer	1	2	1.0	0.0	1.0	2.000			

PAIR OF KINGS...two all-time Monarchs Powderhall favourites Neil Collins and George Hunter prepare for the start of a race

ELLESMERE PORT

SPEEDWAY returned to Merseyside for the first time since the closure of Liverpool in 1960, with the birth of the Ellesmere Port Gunners at the Joe Mercer Stadium in Thornton Road.

Promoters Bill Carman, Ian Thomas and Wally Mawdsley bought the Rochdale Division Two licence and took over the contracts of the majority of the 1971 Hornets to introduce the sport to the Cheshire town.

1972...1972...1972...1972...1972...1972

	M	R	Pts	BP	TPts	Ave	F	P	Total
§Paul Tyrer	28	127	261.0	8.0	269.0	8.472	3	1	4
§Graham Drury	**34**	**144**	**209.0**	**27.0**	**236.0**	**6.556**		**1**	**1**
§Colin Goad	**34**	**149**	**219.0**	**20.0**	**239.0**	**6.416**	**1**		**1**
§Robbie Gardner	32	135	198.0	18.0	216.0	6.400	1	1	2
§§Cyril Francis	17	58	75.0	7.0	82.0	5.655			
§Terry Kelly	5	11	11.0	4.0	15.0	5.455			
§Ian Gills	15	54	59.0	14.0	73.0	5.407			
§Chris Blythe	33	112	95.0	31.0	126.0	4.500			
§Paul Callaghan	20	62	60.0	9.0	69.0	4.452			
§Clark Facey	1	5	4.0	1.0	5.0	4.000			
§Ken Moss	2	8	3.0	1.0	4.0	2.000			
§§Geoff Pusey	8	21	8.0	2.0	10.0	1.905			
§Phil Pratt	1	1	0.0	0.0	0.0	0.000			

1973...1973...1973...1973...1973...1973

	M	R	Pts	BP	TPts	Ave	F	P	Total
Graham Drury	34	147	318.0	14.0	332.0	9.034	3	3	6
§Paul O'Neal	31	132	252.0	10.0	262.0	7.939	3		3
Robbie Gardner	**36**	**147**	**236.0**	**21.0**	**257.0**	**6.993**	**3**	**1**	**4**
Colin Goad	34	142	205.0	26.0	231.0	6.507		1	1
§§Chris Morton	22	91	128.0	15.0	143.0	6.286			
Ray Hassall	2	6	6.0	2.0	8.0	5.333			
§Barry Booth	25	79	68.0	18.0	86.0	4.354			
§§Gerald Smitherman	10	33	31.0	4.0	35.0	4.242		1	1
§§Roger Austin	9	28	24.0	5.0	29.0	4.143			
§Phil Woodcock	1	3	2.0	1.0	3.0	4.000			
§§Wayne Hughes	21	67	46.0	11.0	57.0	3.403			
Ian Gills	6	18	11.0	3.0	14.0	3.111			
Paul Callaghan	8	21	9.0	3.0	12.0	2.286			
§§Cliff Anderson	6	19	8.0	2.0	10.0	2.105			
Chris Blythe	3	9	3.0	0.0	3.0	1.333			

1974...1974...1974...1974...1974...1974

	M	R	Pts	BP	TPts	Ave	F	P	Total
Graham Drury	35	149	337.0	10.0	347.0	9.315	3		3
Colin Goad	34	138	276.0	11.0	287.0	8.319	5		5
§§Steve Taylor	33	144	242.0	23.0	265.0	7.361	2	1	3
§Nigel Wasley	21	87	115.0	19.0	134.0	6.161	1		1
§Wayne Hughes	38	154	195.0	38.0	233.0	6.052		1	1
§§Duncan Meredith	24	91	116.0	18.0	134.0	5.890	1		1
Gerald Smitherman	8	30	33.0	6.0	39.0	5.200			
§Nicky Allott	29	107	105.0	12.0	117.0	4.374			
§Ken Stafford	11	30	22.0	5.0	27.0	3.600			
§§Steve Casey	13	31	15.0	6.0	21.0	2.710			
Ray Hassall	16	50	23.0	4.0	27.0	2.160			

1975...1975...1975...1975...1975...1975

	M	R	Pts	BP	TPts	Ave	F	P	Total
§John Jackson	39	180	433.0	7.0	440.0	9.778	13	2	15
Steve Taylor	3	9	15.0	2.0	17.0	7.556			
Colin Goad	**40**	**156**	**246.0**	**32.0**	**278.0**	**7.128**		**1**	**1**
Wayne Hughes	37	152	235.0	22.0	257.0	6.763		1	1
Nicky Allott	28	108	160.0	13.0	173.0	6.407			
Duncan Meredith	36	135	153.0	42.0	195.0	5.778		1	1
§Mick McKeon	21	79	84.0	12.0	96.0	4.861			
Steve Casey	9	23	21.0	5.0	26.0	4.522			
Gerald Smitherman	26	98	95.0	12.0	107.0	4.367			
Barry Booth	12	40	32.0	8.0	40.0	4.000			
§Andy Reid	14	37	28.0	6.0	34.0	3.676			
§§Chris Bevan	3	8	5.0	1.0	6.0	3.000			
§§Alan Legge	1	3	1.0	0.0	1.0	1.333			
§§Geoff Jones	3	4	1.0	0.0	1.0	1.000			
§§Ian Robertson	1	2	0.0	0.0	0.0	0.000			

1976...1976...1976...1976...1976...1976

	M	R	Pts	BP	TPts	Ave	F	P	Total
John Jackson	39	169	419.0	7.0	426.0	10.083	19		19
§Chris Turner	33	136	304.0	14.0	318.0	9.353	3	4	7
§Steve Finch	**40**	**172**	**301.0**	**46.0**	**347.0**	**8.070**	**1**	**3**	**4**
Wayne Hughes	4	15	23.0	6.0	29.0	7.733			
Robbie Gardner	33	131	207.0	37.0	244.0	7.450		3	3
§Steve Hartley	6	20	27.0	8.0	35.0	7.000			
Duncan Meredith	25	88	114.0	20.0	134.0	6.091			
Gerald Smitherman	38	137	174.5	24.0	198.5	5.796			
Steve Casey	2	6	5.0	3.0	8.0	5.333			
§§Phil Collins	17	60	55.0	10.0	65.0	4.333			
Geoff Jones	13	41	28.0	10.0	38.0	3.707			
§§Louis Carr	17	49	27.0	7.0	34.0	2.776			
§§Paul Clements	5	13	8.0	1.0	9.0	2.769			
§§Peter Williams	3	8	3.0	1.0	4.0	2.000			

1977...1977...1977...1977...1977...1977

	M	R	Pts	BP	TPts	Ave	F	P	Total
John Jackson	41	197	484.0	12.0	496.0	10.071	15	4	19
Steve Finch	**42**	**197**	**416.0**	**19.0**	**435.0**	**8.832**	**1**	**2**	**3**
§Dave Mortiboys	8	21	31.0	8.0	39.0	7.429			
Phil Collins	41	199	307.5	52.0	359.5	7.226		2	2
Nigel Wasley	5	17	28.0	0.0	28.0	6.588			
Duncan Meredith	37	149	174.0	36.0	210.0	5.638		1	1
Paul Clements	3	11	13.0	2.0	15.0	5.455			
§§James Moore	9	30	32.0	5.0	37.0	4.933			
§§John J. Williams	34	116	120.0	22.0	142.0	4.897		1	1
Louis Carr	39	117	104.0	14.0	118.0	4.034			
§§Paul Sheard	11	35	24.0	4.0	28.0	3.200			
§§Stuart Shirley	1	2	0.0	0.0	0.0	0.000			
§§Bob Steel	1	2	0.0	0.0	0.0	0.000			

1978...1978...1978...1978...1978...1978

	M	R	Pts	BP	TPts	Ave	F	P	Total
§§Robert Craven	1	1	2.0	1.0	3.0	12.000			
John Jackson	37	156	402.0	2.0	404.0	10.359	17	1	18
Steve Finch	42	184	411.0	16.0	427.0	9.283	7	1	8
Phil Collins	42	184	377.0	23.0	400.0	8.696	5	2	7
John J. Williams	35	124	142.0	37.0	179.0	5.774		1	1
Louis Carr	**44**	**155**	**185.0**	**37.0**	**222.0**	**5.729**	**2**	**1**	**3**
Paul Tyrer	22	78	77.0	23.0	100.0	5.128		1	1
§§Paul Embley	3	8	7.0	3.0	10.0	5.000			
§Pete Ellams	41	123	119.0	16.0	135.0	4.390			
Steve Taylor (1)	18	66	54.0	13.0	67.0	4.061			
Paul Sheard	2	5	5.0	0.0	5.0	4.000			
§§Neil Collins	15	46	24.0	9.0	33.0	2.870			

1979...1979...1979...1979...1979...1979

	M	R	Pts	BP	TPts	Ave	F	P	Total
Steve Finch	**38**	**168**	**387.0**	**13.0**	**400.0**	**9.524**	**3**	**3**	**6**
John Jackson	**38**	**160**	**362.0**	**9.0**	**371.0**	**9.275**	**12**		**12**
Louis Carr	**38**	**153**	**248.0**	**18.0**	**266.0**	**6.954**	**1**	**4**	**5**
John J. Williams	37	127	152.0	38.0	190.0	5.984		3	3
Peter Ellams	37	140	151.0	32.0	183.0	5.229			
§§Eric Monaghan	15	52	50.0	11.0	61.0	4.692			
Robert Craven	9	28	27.0	1.0	28.0	4.000			
§§Chris Mason	1	2	1.0	1.0	2.0	4.000			
Paul Tyrer	8	24	21.0	2.0	23.0	3.833			
Paul Embley	30	98	80.0	13.0	93.0	3.796			
§§Peter Carr	14	41	22.0	3.0	25.0	2.439			

1980...1980...1980...1980...1980...1980

	M	R	Pts	BP	TPts	Ave	F	P	Total
Steve Finch	**40**	**171**	**411.0**	**13.0**	**424.0**	**9.918**	**6**	**3**	**9**
Louis Carr	39	161	332.0	13.0	345.0	8.571	7	4	11
John Jackson	**40**	**166**	**338.0**	**13.0**	**351.0**	**8.458**	**7**	**2**	**9**
§§Paul Price	2	9	12.0	3.0	15.0	6.667			
Eric Monaghan	30	103	119.0	16.0	135.0	5.243		1	1
John J. Williams	16	52	51.0	17.0	68.0	5.231		1	1
§§Phil Alderman	11	38	38.0	11.0	49.0	5.158			
Peter Ellams	30	105	114.0	18.0	132.0	5.029			
Peter Carr	37	138	131.0	31.0	162.0	4.696			
Paul Embley	30	90	80.0	13.0	93.0	4.133			
§§Howard Jackson	4	10	8.0	2.0	10.0	4.000			
§§Dean Zaman	1	2	1.0	0.0	1.0	2.000			

ELLESMERE PORT

1981...1981...1981...1981...1981...1981

	M	R	Pts	BP	TPts	Ave	F	P	Total
§Billy Burton	20	83	169.0	10.0	179.0	8.627	1	1	2
Steve Finch	**40**	**169**	**305.0**	**39.0**	**344.0**	**8.142**	**2**	**5**	**7**
Peter Carr	38	150	252.0	29.0	281.0	7.493	1	1	2
John Jackson	38	146	257.0	11.0	268.0	7.342	3	1	4
§§Rob Ashton	37	150	200.0	44.0	244.0	6.507		3	3
Phil Alderman	35	125	163.0	24.0	187.0	5.984			
Eric Monaghan	29	103	133.0	21.0	154.0	5.981		1	1
Peter Ellams	4	12	15.0	1.0	16.0	5.333			
Paul Embley	18	59	60.0	11.0	71.0	4.814			
Paul Price	14	54	35.0	7.0	42.0	3.111			
§§Andrew Reeves	7	19	7.0	1.0	8.0	1.684			

1982...1982...1982...1982...1982...1982

	M	R	Pts	BP	TPts	Ave	F	P	Total
John Jackson	**43**	**219**	**488.0**	**13.0**	**501.0**	**9.151**	**8**	**1**	**9**
Steve Finch	**43**	**230**	**471.0**	**21.0**	**492.0**	**8.557**	**1**	**2**	**3**
§Robert Maxfield	36	168	266.0	39.0	305.0	7.262	1	1	2
Eric Monaghan	**43**	**210**	**317.0**	**49.0**	**366.0**	**6.971**		**3**	**3**
Billy Burton	**43**	**206**	**256.0**	**52.0**	**308.0**	**5.981**		**1**	**1**
Phil Alderman	41	178	223.0	43.0	266.0	5.978		2	2
§§Glen Parrott	41	145	144.0	34.0	178.0	4.910		1	1
§§Rob Tate	8	19	18.0	4.0	22.0	4.632		1	1
§§Brian Lock	1	2	0.0	0.0	0.0	0.000			
Andrew Reeves	1	2	0.0	0.0	0.0	0.000			

1985...1985...1985...1985...1985...1985

	M	R	Pts	BP	TPts	Ave	F	P	Total
§Joe Owen	**45**	**178**	**456.0**	**10.0**	**466.0**	**10.472**	**9**	**4**	**13**
Louis Carr	42	172	387.0	16.0	403.0	9.372	10	3	13
§Dave Morton	44	171	328.5	15.0	343.5	8.035	4	2	6
§David Walsh	**45**	**180**	**243.0**	**60.0**	**303.0**	**6.733**	**1**	**1**	**2**
§Gary O'Hare	28	92	125.0	13.0	138.0	6.000	1		1
§Miles Evans	40	157	188.0	38.0	226.0	5.758			
Phil Alderman	23	82	99.0	11.0	110.0	5.366			
§Richie Owen	**45**	**139**	**124.0**	**42.0**	**166.0**	**4.777**			
§§Paul Heyes	2	5	2.0	1.0	3.0	2.400			

K O TROPHY

1972	1 Robbie Gardner	2 Phil Crump	3 Colin Goad

MAYFAIR OPEN CHAMPIONSHIP

1974	1 Graham Drury	2 Phil Herne	3 John Jackson

SUPPORTERS TROPHY

1974	1 Colin Goad	2 Alan Bridgett	3 Colin Meredith
1978	1 John Jackson	2 Nicky Allott	3 Phil Collins

MICHAEL NESBITT MEMORIAL TROPHY

1975	1 Arthur Browning	2 Graham Drury	3 Lou Sansom

FORWARD CHEMICALS CHAMPIONSHIP

1980	1 Steve Finch	2 Louis Carr	3 John Jackson

JOE OWEN led Ellesmere Port to the 1985 National League Championship...but then was crippled in a track crash at Birmingham which has left him in a wheelchair.

Owen had been the major signing of new promoter Mervyn Porter, a Bolton greengrocer, when he resurrected the Gunners after a two-season absence from racing at the beginning of the year.

In only his first season in charge of a track he built up a title-winning side that also reached the National League Knock Out Cup Final before going down to Eastbourne.

Joe Owen's tragedy was the final blow in a catastrophic season for Porter who was forced to pull out of Thornton Road after losing the majority of his investment because of poor crowds.

His tenure began badly when his first-ever meeting, against Long Eaton, was abandoned because the visiting riders refused to race claiming the track was too dangerous.

And it ended with that horrific accident to his skipper on October 20.

Ellesmere Port had a chequered career under a variety of different promoters.

At the end of the first season of racing (1972) the promoters applied to the British Speedway Promoters' Association to join the British League First Division by taking over Wembley's licence.

The move was vetoed (and subsequently confirmed by a Speedway Control Board Tribunal) and the Gunners remained in the Second Division until eventual closure at the end of 1985.

The track has now been converted to a greyhound circuit although much of the old speedway pits area still remains, almost exactly as it was when Mervyn Porter walked out of the stadium after the last official meeting – a Boxing Day morning charity meeting in aid of former skipper Owen on Thursday, December 26, 1985.

Following the closure of Ellesmere Port the promotion moved to Long Eaton at the beginning of 1986 when, amazingly, they finished bottom of the National League!

EXETER

1980...1980...1980...1980...1980...1980

	M	R	Pts	BP	TPts	Ave	F	P	Total
§Robert Maxfield	34	132	283.0	17.0	300.0	9.091	3	4	7
§Nigel Boocock	37	156	324.0	13.0	337.0	8.641	6	2	8
§John Barker	34	137	273.0	18.0	291.0	8.496	4	2	6
§§Martin Hewlett	**38**	**167**	**223.0**	**44.0**	**267.0**	**6.395**	**1**	**2**	**3**
§John J. Williams	15	62	84.0	13.0	97.0	6.258		1	1
§Arnold Haley	19	81	96.0	22.0	118.0	5.827	1		1
§Tony Garard	8	25	27.0	9.0	36.0	5.760			
§§David Brewer	27	95	79.0	20.0	99.0	4.168		1	1
§§Chris Hunt	1	2	1.0	1.0	2.0	4.000			
§Tony Sanford	16	50	39.0	10.0	49.0	3.920			
§Mike Sanderson	7	20	6.0	3.0	9.0	1.800			
§Phil Vance	16	36	14.0	2.0	16.0	1.778			
§§Patrick Pawson	3	8	2.0	1.0	3.0	1.500			
§Ricky Jones	3	7	1.0	1.0	2.0	1.143			
§§Alan Leaver	2	5	1.0	0.0	1.0	0.800			
§Neil Farnish	1	3	0.0	0.0	0.0	0.000			
§Bob Watts	1	2	0.0	0.0	0.0	0.000			

1981...1981...1981...1981...1981...1981

	M	R	Pts	BP	TPts	Ave	F	P	Total
Robert Maxfield	34	135	286.0	20.0	306.0	9.067	3	4	7
§Bob Coles	9	33	65.0	3.0	68.0	8.242			
Martin Hewlett	36	154	283.0	29.0	312.0	8.104	1	3	4
John Barker	21	83	153.0	10.0	163.0	7.855	3	1	4
§Les Sawyer	37	150	252.0	36.0	288.0	7.680	1		1
Dave Brewer	6	20	29.0	4.0	33.0	6.600		1	1
Andy Campbell	35	147	201.0	39.0	240.0	6.531		1	1
§§Keith Wright	13	38	44.0	13.0	57.0	6.000			
John Williams	**38**	**145**	**190.0**	**27.0**	**217.0**	**5.986**	**1**	**1**	**2**
§§Keith Millard	18	54	47.0	11.0	58.0	4.296			
Tony Sanford	14	35	21.0	7.0	28.0	3.200			
§§Kevin Price	1	3	1.0	0.0	1.0	1.333			

1982...1982...1982...1982...1982...1982

	M	R	Pts	BP	TPts	Ave	F	P	Total
John Barker	16	71	154.0	7.0	161.0	9.070	2	3	5
Les Sawyer	17	79	154.0	15.0	169.0	8.557	1	1	2
Andy Campbell	**38**	**220**	**431.0**	**30.0**	**461.0**	**8.382**	**1**	**1**	**2**
Keith Millard	**38**	**218**	**421.0**	**25.0**	**446.0**	**8.183**	**4**	**2**	**6**
Bob Coles	37	192	263.0	51.0	314.0	6.542		3	3
John J. Williams	1	5	7.0	0.0	7.0	5.600			
Keith Wright	32	144	139.0	29.0	168.0	4.667			
§Steve Bishop	20	87	80.0	15.0	95.0	4.368			
§§Mike Semmonds	14	43	30.0	10.0	40.0	3.721			
Dave Brewer	22	84	62.0	10.0	72.0	3.429			
§§Alun Rossiter	2	11	7.0	2.0	9.0	3.273			
§Mark Reeve	5	16	12.0	1.0	13.0	3.250			
§Kevin Lock	1	3	2.0	0.0	2.0	2.667			
§§Michael Coles	5	14	6.5	2.0	8.5	2.429			
§§Tony Forward	1	2	0.0	0.0	0.0	0.000			
§§John Barclay	3	6	0.0	0.0	0.0	0.000			
§Mitchell Barker	3	6	0.0	0.0	0.0	0.000			
§§Tim Fey	3	5	0.0	0.0	0.0	0.000			
Chris Hunt	1	1	0.0	0.0	0.0	0.000			

1983...1983...1983...1983...1983...1983

	M	R	Pts	BP	TPts	Ave	F	P	Total
Keith Millard	41	214	445.0	22.0	467.0	8.729	2	2	4
Robert Maxfield	36	172	302.0	37.0	339.0	7.884	3	3	6
§Rob Ashton	36	175	281.5	40.0	321.5	7.349		2	2
Alun Rossiter	40	185	299.5	30.0	329.5	7.124	1		1
Steve Bishop	**42**	**199**	**293.0**	**57.0**	**350.0**	**7.035**		**3**	**3**
Kevin Price	40	158	196.0	52.0	248.0	6.278	1		1
Bob Coles	41	192	239.5	36.0	275.5	5.740		1	1
Mike Semmonds	5	16	14.0	5.0	19.0	4.750			
Michael Coles	1	3	2.0	1.0	3.0	4.000			
§Malcolm Bedkober	1	3	2.0	0.0	2.0	2.667			
§Mark Summerfield	4	16	8.0	2.0	10.0	2.500			
§Rob Carter	4	10	3.0	0.0	3.0	1.200			
§§Marcus Williams	1	3	0.0	0.0	0.0	0.000			

EXTER, who had dropped out of Division One at the end of 1979 because of financial worries returned to the British League in 1984 but after one season in the top flight re-applied to join Division Two.

1985...1985...1985...1985...1985...1985

	M	R	Pts	BP	TPts	Ave	F	P	Total
Robert Maxfield	36	140	234.0	37.0	271.0	7.743	1	3	4
§Colin Cook	38	154	280.0	18.0	298.0	7.740	1	2	3
§Nigel Sparshott	**40**	**164**	**268.0**	**35.0**	**303.0**	**7.390**	**2**	**3**	**5**
Steve Bishop	38	158	248.0	34.0	282.0	7.139	2	1	3
Kevin Price	38	142	222.5	23.0	245.5	6.915	2	3	5
Michael Coles	39	137	192.0	23.0	215.0	6.277		1	1
Mike Semmonds	23	71	81.0	13.0	94.0	5.296			
§§Ray Dole	2	7	6.0	2.0	8.0	4.571			
§Bernie Collier	2	10	7.0	3.0	10.0	4.000			
§§Brian Hussey	5	12	6.0	2.0	8.0	2.667			
§§Andy Sell	1	3	1.0	1.0	2.0	2.667			
§Dave Roberts	14	38	22.0	1.0	23.0	2.421			
§§Steve Brennan	2	4	0.0	0.0	0.0	0.000			

1986...1986...1986...1986...1986...1986

	M	R	Pts	BP	TPts	Ave	F	P	Total
§Bruce Cribb	**40**	**177**	**356.0**	**8.0**	**364.0**	**8.226**	**5**		**5**
§Alan Rivett	15	60	106.0	11.0	117.0	7.800	1		1
Colin Cook	33	139	244.0	20.0	264.0	7.597	2	1	3
Steve Bishop	**40**	**169**	**260.0**	**38.0**	**298.0**	**7.053**		**3**	**3**
Kevin Price	26	107	153.0	11.0	164.0	6.131			
§Alan Mason	15	50	52.0	14.0	66.0	5.280			
Michael Coles	39	150	148.0	41.0	189.0	5.040			
§§Tony Mattingley	12	35	31.0	7.0	38.0	4.343			
Andy Sell	14	40	31.0	10.0	41.0	4.100			
§§Martin Chambers	1	2	1.0	1.0	2.0	4.000			
David Roberts	16	49	35.0	6.0	41.0	3.347			
Mike Semmonds	14	41	22.0	9.0	31.0	3.024			
§§Jon Gould	1	2	1.0	0.0	1.0	2.000			
§§Stuart Williams	6	15	5.0	1.0	6.0	1.600			
Steve Brennan	2	4	0.0	0.0	0.0	0.000			
§§John Stokes	1	2	0.0	0.0	0.0	0.000			
§§Alan Theobald	1	2	0.0	0.0	0.0	0.000			

1987...1987...1987...1987...1970...1987

	M	R	Pts	BP	TPts	Ave	F	P	Total
Alan Rivett	**32**	**166**	**307.0**	**8.0**	**315.0**	**7.590**	**1**	**1**	**2**
Colin Cook	**32**	**143**	**249.0**	**17.0**	**266.0**	**7.441**	**2**		**2**
§David Smart	22	105	170.0	25.0	195.0	7.429			
Kevin Price	10	37	48.0	15.0	63.0	6.811			
Michael Coles	26	114	129.0	16.0	145.0	5.088			
Andy Sell	25	85	81.0	18.0	99.0	4.659			
David Gibbs	18	70	67.0	11.0	78.0	4.457			
Bruce Cribb	1	4	2.0	2.0	4.0	4.000			
Tony Mattingley	21	69	57.0	8.0	65.0	3.768			
Tony Garard	4	8	5.0	2.0	7.0	3.500			
Alan Mason	5	19	12.0	3.0	15.0	3.158			
§§Peter Jeffery	3	7	4.0	0.0	4.0	2.286			
Jon Gould	3	9	3.0	0.0	3.0	1.333			
§§Keith Newman	3	5	0.0	0.0	0.0	0.000			
§§Lee Ingham	1	2	0.0	0.0	0.0	0.000			

1988...1988...1988...1988...1988...1988

	M	R	Pts	BP	TPts	Ave	F	P	Total
§Steve Regeling	14	80	144.0	14.0	158.0	7.900			
Colin Cook	23	113	173.0	19.0	192.0	6.796			
§Richard Green	26	148	209.0	30.0	239.0	6.459			
Alan Rivett	31	166	250.0	17.0	267.0	6.434			
§Dave Trownson	14	76	106.0	11.0	117.0	6.158			
Peter Jeffery	29	133	159.0	25.0	184.0	5.534			
Andy Sell	31	124	144.0	21.0	165.0	5.323	1		1
§Rob Fortune	16	50	43.0	16.0	59.0	4.720			
§Paul Evitts	5	21	21.0	2.0	23.0	4.381			
Bruce Cribb	8	37	29.0	1.0	30.0	3.243			
Tony Mattingley	16	58	35.0	7.0	42.0	2.897			
Jon Gould	1	3	2.0	0.0	2.0	2.667			
Steve Brennan	1	2	0.0	0.0	0.0	0.000			
§§Trevor Williams	1	2	0.0	0.0	0.0	0.000			

FESTIVAL K. O. TROPHY

1980	1 Robert Maxfield	2 Mike Ferreira	3 John Barker

TRATHENS RAPIDE

1983	1 Stan Bear	2 Alun Rossiter	3 Rob Ashton

SOUTH WEST JUNIOR CHAMPIONSHIP

1987	1 Peter Jeffery	2 Darren Knapman	3 Brian Hussey
1989	1 Mark Simmonds	2 John Wainwright	3 Mark Pearce
1990	1 Scott Swain	2 Frank Smart	3 Mark Lemon

See also Exeter, Division One averages

EXETER

1989...1989...1989...1989...1989...1989

	M	R	Pts§	BP	TPts	Ave	F	P	Total
Steve Regeling	**42**	**227**	**514.0**	**39.0**	**553.0**	**9.744**	**1**	**6**	**7**
§§Frank Andersen	31	155	265.0	37.0	302.0	7.794	1	3	4
Richard Green	**42**	**218**	**388.0**	**28.0**	**416.0**	**7.633**	**2**	**1**	**3**
Steve Bishop	18	71	112.0	13.0	125.0	7.042	1		1
Peter Jeffery	**42**	**212**	**304.0**	**52.0**	**356.0**	**6.717**		**3**	**3**
Colin Cook	39	176	254.0	39.0	293.0	6.659		1	1
§§Greg Daniels	1	2	2.0	1.0	3.0	6.000			
Andy Sell	39	158	181.0	45.0	226.0	5.722			
Alan Rivett	10	40	49.0	4.0	53.0	5.300			
§Steve Hone	4	13	10.0	3.0	13.0	4.000			
§Wayne Ross	14	44	32.0	4.0	36.0	3.273			
§§Scott Pegler	2	9	6.0	1.0	7.0	3.111			
§§Mark Simmonds	8	21	12.0	2.0	14.0	2.667			

1990...1990...1990...1990...1990...1990

	M	R	Pts	BP	TPts	Ave	F	P	Total
Steve Regeling	**34**	**184**	**458.0**	**11.0**	**469.0**	**10.196**	**6**	**3**	**9**
Peter Jeffery	29	150	265.0	24.0	289.0	7.707	2	2	4
Richard Green	**34**	**174**	**298.0**	**36.0**	**334.0**	**7.678**	**1**	**3**	**4**
Colin Cook	33	164	230.0	41.0	271.0	6.610	1	4	5
Andy Sell	11	37	46.0	7.0	53.0	5.730			
Steve Bishop	**34**	**151**	**173.0**	**23.0**	**196.0**	**5.192**			
Mark Simmonds	**34**	**121**	**121.0**	**24.0**	**145.0**	**4.793**			
§Ian Barney	21	88	72.0	13.0	85.0	3.864			
§Deon Prinsloo	2	6	4.0	1.0	5.0	3.333			
§§Frank Smart	2	5	3.0	0.0	3.0	2.400			
Greg Daniels	3	8	0.0	0.0	0.0	0.000			
Scott Pegler	1	1	0.0	0.0	0.0	0.000			

TREBLE TOP...Australian Robert Maxfield was number one in the Exeter averages for three seasons – in 1980, 1981 and 1985

GLASGOW

COATBRIDGE were given 14 days' notice to quit their Cliftonhill Stadium and moved to a new track at Blantyre midway through the 1977 season. See Coatbridge.
*In the Legend below for the 1977 season **C** indicates Coatbridge and **G** indicates Glasgow.*

1977...1977...1977...1977...1977...1977

	M	R	Pts	BP	TPts	Ave	F	P	Total
§GBrian Collins	**38**	**162**	**353.0**	**9.0**	**362.0**	**8.938**	**7**		**7**
§GMick McKeon	**38**	**164**	**311.0**	**15.0**	**326.0**	**7.951**	**3**		**3**
§GGrahame Dawson	29	113	204.0	12.0	216.0	7.646	2		2
Robert Maxfield	10	37	53.0	13.0	66.0	7.135			
§GDerek Richardson	36	145	161.0	35.0	196.0	5.407			
§GColin Caffrey	3	10	10.0	2.0	12.0	4.800			
§§C§GMerv Janke	28	96	88.0	26.0	114.0	4.750			
§GBenny Rourke	23	84	81.0	15.0	96.0	4.571			
§§GCarl Clarke	2	7	5.0	3.0	8.0	4.571			
§GJimmy Gallacher	35	113	107.0	16.0	123.0	4.354		1	1
§§GJohn Hack	4	16	12.0	3.0	15.0	3.750			
§GNicky Hollingworth	11	32	19.0	4.0	23.0	2.875			
§CRob Hamman	1	2	1.0	0.0	1.0	2.000			
§§GCharlie McKinna	1	3	1.0	0.0	1.0	1.333			
§GKen Jarvie	2	3	0.0	0.0	0.0	0.000			
§§GDoug Poole	1	1	0.0	0.0	0.0	0.000			

1978...1978...1978...1978...1978...1978

	M	R	Pts	BP	TPts	Ave	F	P	Total
§Steve Lawson	**40**	**176**	**343.0**	**6.0**	**349.0**	**7.932**	**8**		**8**
Derek Richardson	**40**	**174**	**304.0**	**23.0**	**327.0**	**7.517**	**2**		2
Mervn Janke	34	140	244.0	19.0	263.0	7.514	3	3	6
Benny Rourke	32	139	213.0	19.0	232.0	6.676	1	2	3
§Colin Farquharson	**40**	**162**	**166.0**	**22.0**	**188.0**	**4.642**			
Jim Beaton	27	82	82.0	10.0	92.0	4.488			
Charlie McKinna	25	79	51.0	19.0	70.0	3.544			
§Keith Bloxsome	7	24	16.0	5.0	21.0	3.500			
Terry Kelly	9	23	19.0	1.0	20.0	3.478			
§Mick Newton	13	39	21.0	8.0	29.0	2.974			
§Rod Hunter	1	3	2.0	0.0	2.0	2.667			
§David Butt	1	1	0.0	0.0	0.0	0.000			

1979...1979...1979...1979...1979...1979

	M	R	Pts	BP	TPts	Ave	F	P	Total
Steve Lawson	37	162	359.0	8.0	367.0	9.062	8	2	10
Merv Janke	21	83	178.0	10.0	188.0	9.060	1	1	2
Derek Richardson	**38**	**160**	**303.0**	**19.0**	**322.0**	**8.050**	**1**	**1**	**2**
§Andy Reid	28	110	142.0	30.0	172.0	6.255		1	1
§Colin Caffrey	31	102	132.0	24.0	156.0	6.118			
Charlie McKinna	34	125	144.0	40.0	184.0	5.888		1	1
Jim Beaton	26	93	108.0	26.0	134.0	5.763		1	1
Keith Bloxsome	28	107	121.0	19.0	140.0	5.234			
§§Roger Commerford	1	4	2.0	1.0	3.0	3.000			
§§Kevin Clapham	1	3	2.0	0.0	2.0	2.667			
§§Kenny McKinna	3	7	3.0	1.0	4.0	2.286			
§Paul Sheard	2	6	2.0	1.0	3.0	2.000			
§§Dave Wheatland	1	4	2.0	0.0	2.0	2.000			
§Barry Allaway	1	3	1.0	0.0	1.0	1.333			
§§Andy Campbell	1	3	1.0	0.0	1.0	1.333			
§Dave Parkin	2	3	1.0	0.0	1.0	1.333			
§Ray Watkins	1	4	1.0	0.0	1.0	1.000			
§Keith Chapman	1	5	1.0	0.0	1.0	0.800			
§§Bernie Collier	1	3	0.0	0.0	0.0	0.000			

1980...1980...1980...1980...1980...1980

	M	R	PTs	BP	TPts	Ave	F	P	Total
Steve Lawson	**40**	**175**	**441.0**	**4.0**	**445.0**	**10.171**	**15**		**15**
Alan Emerson	38	161	330.0	21.0	351.0	8.720	1	2	3
Andy Reid	38	159	302.0	17.0	319.0	8.025	5	3	8
Terry Kelly	1	4	6.0	0.0	6.0	6.000			
Jim Beaton	17	50	54.0	19.0	73.0	5.840		1	1
Charlie McKinna	35	137	147.0	45.0	192.0	5.606		3	3
Kenny McKinna	**40**	**150**	**172.0**	**29.0**	**201.0**	**5.360**		**1**	**1**
Colin Caffrey	19	63	63.0	17.0	80.0	5.079			
§§Ray Palmer	16	54	51.0	15.0	66.0	4.889			
§Ken Hall	4	11	7.0	2.0	9.0	3.273			
Andy Campbell	9	24	15.0	2.0	17.0	2.833			
§§Robbie McGregor	4	10	5.0	2.0	7.0	2.800			
§Adrian Pepper	3	9	4.0	1.0	5.0	2.222			
§§Mark Warren	3	8	2.0	2.0	4.0	2.000			
§§Alistair Craig	1	2	1.0	0.0	1.0	2.000			
§§Steve Mildoon	7	16	5.0	2.0	7.0	1.750			

1981...1981...1981...1981...1981...1981

	M	R	Pts	BP	TPts	Ave	F	P	Total
Steve Lawson	37	160	417.0	5.0	422.0	10.550	15	1	16
Charlie McKinna	36	156	283.5	30.0	313.5	8.038	1	5	6
Kenny McKinna	37	149	262.0	20.0	282.0	7.570	3	1	4
§Nigel Close	**38**	**157**	**229.0**	**49.0**	**278.0**	**7.083**		**4**	**4**
§Harry Maclean	28	99	118.0	31.0	149.0	6.020			
Colin Caffrey	36	131	147.0	43.0	190.0	5.802			
Andy Reid	11	42	48.0	10.0	58.0	5.524			
Ray Palmer	15	45	40.0	10.0	50.0	4.444			
§Willie Mirtle	5	14	10.0	2.0	12.0	3.429			
§§Alan Mason	14	38	21.0	5.0	26.0	2.737			
§§Geoff Powell	3	6	1.0	0.0	1.0	0.667			
Jim Gallacher	1	3	0.0	0.0	0.0	0.000			

1982...1982...1982...1982...1982...1982

	M	R	Pts	BP	TPts	Ave	F	P	Total
Steve Lawson	**36**	**200**	**516.0**	**4.0**	**520.0**	**10.400**	**10**	**2**	**12**
Kenny McKinna	**36**	**194**	**419.0**	**7.0**	**426.0**	**8.784**	**9**	**1**	**10**
Colin Caffrey	31	144	190.0	23.0	213.0	5.917		2	2
Harry Maclean	**36**	**166**	**158.0**	**30.0**	**188.0**	**4.530**			
§Rob Carter	18	57	47.0	8.0	55.0	3.860			
§Kym Mauger	29	135	104.0	20.0	124.0	3.674			
Alan Mason	34	139	103.0	24.0	127.0	3.655			
§§Jackson Irving	3	14	9.0	3.0	12.0	3.429			
§§Martin McKinna	12	44	24.0	5.0	29.0	2.636			
§Roger Lambert	2	7	3.0	1.0	4.0	2.286			
§§David Cassells	1	2	1.0	0.0	1.0	2.000			
§Derek Wilson	13	49	18.0	3.0	21.0	1.714			
Geoff Powell	1	0	0.0	0.0	0.0	n.a.			

■ *GLASGOW moved from Blantyre Stadium to the adjoining Craighead Park, Blantyre, at the end of 1981 season and re-opened at their new venue at the beginning of 1982.*
■ *The switch of home track from Blantyre Greyhound Stadium to Craighead Park (home of Blantyre Celtic F.C.) was the shortest move in speedway history as the two stadia virtually adjoined each other and the riders changing rooms at Blantyre was the Craighead Park Pavilion.*
■ *The old Blantyre track was bulldozed to provide land for East Kilbride Expressway.*

1983...1983...1983...1983...1983...1983

	M	R	Pts	BP	TPts	Ave	F	P	Total
Steve Lawson	37	198	486.0	9.0	495.0	10.000	7	2	9
§§Jim McMillan	**38**	**210**	**505.0**	**12.0**	**517.0**	**9.848**	**8**	**2**	**10**
Kenny McKinna	11	60	133.0	2.0	135.0	9.000	2	1	3
Andy Reid	16	85	160.0	15.0	175.0	8.235			
Colin Caffrey	29	139	158.0	38.0	196.0	5.640			
David Cassells	14	63	62.0	16.0	78.0	4.952			
Jim Beaton	19	78	63.0	15.0	78.0	4.000			
§§Rob Parish	1	2	1.0	1.0	2.0	4.000			
Martin McKinna	24	94	78.0	10.0	88.0	3.745			
Geoff Powell	29	121	86.0	22.0	108.0	3.570			
§§Miles Evans	11	40	27.0	7.0	34.0	3.400			
§§David Walsh	14	61	38.0	6.0	44.0	2.885			
§§Tam Baggley	2	7	4.0	0.0	4.0	2.286			
§§Kenny Brailsford	4	9	4.0	1.0	5.0	2.222			
Jackson Irving	2	9	4.0	1.0	5.0	2.222			
Harry Maclean	1	6	3.0	0.0	3.0	2.000			
§Robin Hampton	1	2	1.0	0.0	1.0	2.000			
§§Gary Reid	2	6	1.0	1.0	2.0	1.333			
§John Walmsley	6	20	4.0	0.0	4.0	0.800			
Rob Carter	1	3	0.0	0.0	0.0	0.000			
§Chris Hunt	1	3	0.0	0.0	0.0	0.000			
§§Mike Warren	1	2	0.0	0.0	0.0	0.000			

GLASGOW

1984...1984...1984...1984...1984...1984

	M	R	Pts	BP	TPts	Ave	F	P	Total
Steve Lawson	**32**	**148**	**374.0**	**10.0**	**384.0**	**10.378**	**9**	**2**	**5**
Andy Reid	**32**	**146**	**260.0**	**19.0**	**279.0**	**7.644**			
Brian Collins	30	121	188.0	11.0	199.0	6.579	1		1
Colin Caffrey	21	87	110.0	23.0	133.0	6.115		1	1
Martin McKinna	25	89	102.0	19.0	121.0	5.438		1	1
Jim Beaton	21	80	79.0	12.0	91.0	4.550			
§Jim Burdfield	2	6	4.0	2.0	6.0	4.000			
David Cassells	17	54	36.0	8.0	44.0	3.259			
Tam Baggley	11	32	18.0	4.0	22.0	2.750			
§§Barry Ayres	12	36	20.0	4.0	24.0	2.667			
Geoff Powell	14	34	16.0	6.0	22.0	2.588			
Kenny Brailsford	4	12	2.0	1.0	3.0	1.000			

1985...1985...1985...1985...1985...1985

	M	R	Pts	BP	TPts	Ave	F	P	Total
Steve Lawson	**38**	**181**	**421.0**	**4.0**	**425.0**	**9.392**	**4**		**4**
Martin McKinna	26	97	143.0	17.0	160.0	6.598	2	1	3
Andy Reid	33	145	206.0	11.0	217.0	5.986			
Kenny Brailsford	30	119	106.0	28.0	134.0	4.504			
David Cassels	**38**	**139**	**127.0**	**20.0**	**147.0**	**4.230**			
JIm Beaton	34	115	94.0	27.0	121.0	4.209			
Brian Collins	24	85	77.0	9.0	86.0	4.047			
Geoff Powell	14	40	34.0	6.0	40.0	4.000			
Colin Caffrey	14	46	29.0	13.0	42.0	3.652			
§Eric Broadbelt	2	5	4.0	0.0	4.0	3.200			
§Mark Crang	3	10	6.0	1.0	7.0	2.800			
§Kevin Armitage	5	19	8.0	0.0	8.0	1.684			
§§Edward Baldi	3	8	3.0	0.0	3.0	1.500			

1986...1986...1986...1986...1986...1986

	M	R	Pts	BP	TPts	Ave	F	P	Total
Steve Lawson	**40**	**180**	**408.0**	**2.0**	**410.0**	**9.111**	**3**		**3**
§Bobby Beaton	36	146	287.0	11.0	298.0	8.164	1		1
Martin McKinna	36	134	191.0	14.0	205.0	6.119			
Jackson Irving	**40**	**157**	**149.0**	**40.0**	**189.0**	**4.815**			
Geoff Powell	**40**	**143**	**140.0**	**21.0**	**161.0**	**4.503**		**1**	**1**
Kym Mauger	7	21	21.0	2.0	23.0	4.381			
§Derek Cooper	22	78	60.0	21.0	81.0	4.154			
Colin Caffrey	30	101	68.0	25.0	93.0	3.683			
Jim Beaton	7	21	11.0	5.0	16.0	3.048			
Kenny Brailsford	9	28	14.0	5.0	19.0	2.714			
Andy Reid	5	18	8.0	1.0	9.0	2.000			
§§Kelvin Jelaca	3	11	3.0	1.0	4.0	1.455			
§§Nathan Murray	2	5	0.0	0.0	0.0	0.000			
Ray Palmer	1	2	0.0	0.0	0.0	0.000			
Derek Wilson	1	2	0.0	0.0	0.0	0.000			

1987...1987...1987...1987...1987...1987

	M	R	Pts	BP	TPts	Ave	F	P	Total
Steve Lawson	*24*	*116*	*240.0*	*6.0*	*246.0*	*8.483*			
§G§WGordon Whitaker	*19*	*81*	*138.0*	*7.0*	*145.0*	*7.160*		*1*	*1*
§WBobby Beaton	*5*	*17*	*26.0*	*2.0*	*28.0*	*6.588*		*1*	*1*
§WMartin McKinna	*22*	*95*	*117.0*	*10.0*	*127.0*	*5.347*			
§WJackson Irving	***25***	***108***	***104.0***	***21.0***	***125.0***	***4.630***			
§WDerek Cooper	***25***	***92***	***60.0***	***17.0***	***77.0***	***3.348***			
§WGeoff Powell	*24*	*76*	*50.0*	*9.0*	*59.0*	*3.105*			
§§G§WJim Graham	*11*	*37*	*20.0*	*4.0*	*24.0*	*2.595*			
§GRoland Tebbs	*3*	*11*	*7.0*	*0.0*	*7.0*	*2.545*			
§GPhil Kynman	*2*	*8*	*3.0*	*1.0*	*4.0*	*2.000*			
Michael Irving	*6*	*12*	*3.0*	*1.0*	*4.0*	*1.333*			
Colin Caffrey	*4*	*7*	*1.0*	*0.0*	*1.0*	*0.571*			
§§GSimon Green	*1*	*3*	*0.0*	*0.0*	*0.0*	*0.000*			

▲GLASGOW began the season staging their home meetings at Workington. Their last meeting of 19 official matches as Glasgow was on July 27, 1987. They took the name Workington from August 7 when the match against Peterborough was abandoned.

▲WORKINGTON were expelled from the League on Tuesday, September 15 for 'failing to promote the track in a satisfactory manner' after six official matches.

1988...1988...1988...1988...1988...1988

	M	R	Pts	BP	TPts	Ave	F	P	Total
Kenny McKinna	30	160	398.0	4.0	402.0	10.050	7		7
Steve Lawson	**32**	**162**	**348.0**	**4.0**	**352.0**	**8.691**	**3**		**3**
§David Blackburn	30	156	263.0	23.0	286.0	7.333		1	1
Phil Jeffrey	20	94	104.0	22.0	126.0	5.362			
§Shane Bowes	28	130	139.0	24.0	163.0	5.015			
Bobby Beaton	1	5	5.0	1.0	6.0	4.800			
§Gordon Whitaker	16	69	61.0	11.0	72.0	4.174			
Martin McKinna	21	94	80.0	18.0	98.0	4.170			
Geoff Powell	18	59	46.0	9.0	55.0	3.729			
Jackson Irving	6	20	12.0	5.0	17.0	3.400			
§Wayne Ross	11	51	32.0	7.0	39.0	3.059			
§Michael Irving	8	20	9.0	2.0	11.0	2.200			
Colin Caffrey	2	5	2.0	0.0	2.0	1.600			
§§Gary Frankum	1	3	0.0	0.0	0.0	0.000			

GLASGOW returned to National League racing in 1988 at a new venue at Shawfield Park.

1989...1989...1989...1989...1989...1989

	M	R	Pts	BP	TPts	Ave	F	P	Total
Kenny McKinna	**36**	**196**	**469.0**	**7.0**	**476.0**	**9.714**	**9**	**1**	**10**
Steve Lawson	33	167	362.0	6.0	368.0	8.814	4		4
Shane Bowes	31	150	200.0	37.0	237.0	6.320			
Charlie McKinna	**36**	**187**	**235.0**	**41.0**	**276.0**	**5.904**			
Phil Jeffrey	32	148	166.0	35.0	201.0	5.432		1	1
Martin McKinna	**36**	**165**	**172.0**	**38.0**	**210.0**	**5.091**			
Nathan Murray	3	10	9.0	2.0	11.0	4.400			
Geoff Powell	29	94	80.0	14.0	94.0	4.000			
Colin Caffrey	1	3	1.0	1.0	2.0	2.667			
Kenny Brailsford	3	7	3.0	1.0	4.0	2.286			
Jackson Irving	3	6	2.0	1.0	3.0	2.000			
§Shaun Bickley	1	5	2.0	0.0	2.0	1.600			
Michael Irving	3	8	3.0	0.0	3.0	1.500			
§§Kevin Little	1	2	0.0	0.0	0.0	0.000			

1990...1990...1990...1990...1990...1990

	M	R	Pts	BP	TPts	Ave	F	P	Total
Steve Lawson	**34**	**169**	**352.0**	**21.0**	**373.0**	**8.828**	**3**	**2**	**5**
Kenny McKinna	30	156	315.0	18.0	333.0	8.538	2	3	5
Shane Bowes	30	154	292.0	32.0	324.0	8.416	1		1
Charlie McKinna	**34**	**173**	**254.0**	**35.0**	**289.0**	**6.682**			
§Sean Courtney	26	124	168.0	36.0	204.0	6.581		1	1
Phil Jeffrey	31	121	140.5	37.0	177.5	5.868			
§§Jason Lyons	**34**	**143**	**174.0**	**33.0**	**207.0**	**5.790**		**1**	**1**
Geoff Powell	10	28	21.0	4.0	25.0	3.571			
Martin McKinna	8	25	17.0	2.0	19.0	3.040			

SVEIN KAASA MEMORIAL TROPHY

1989 1 Todd Wiltshire 2 Kenny McKinna 3 Martin McKinna

RECORDBREAKER... Steve Lawson holds all the Glasgow records

HACKNEY

HACKNEY withdrew from the British League Division One at the end of the 1983 season when promoter Len Silver transferred his assets to Oxford. New promoter Terry Russell moved into Waterden Road with Second Division racing after being forced to move out of Crayford from their London Road Stadium because of re-development. The entire Crayford side moved en bloc to London. Hackney retained their Kestrels team nickname.

1984...1984...1984...1984...1984...1984

	M	R	Pts	BP	TPts	Ave	F	P	Total
§Trevor Banks	37	156	314.0	16.0	330.0	8.462	2	1	3
§Barry Thomas	**38**	**165**	**328.0**	**20.0**	**348.0**	**8.436**	**3**		**3**
§Kevin Teager	**38**	**152**	**239.0**	**40.0**	**279.0**	**7.342**	**2**	**2**	**4**
§Paul Bosley	34	137	217.0	19.0	236.0	6.891	3	1	4
§Andy Galvin	35	139	184.0	25.0	209.0	6.014			
§Mark Terry	16	46	47.0	13.0	60.0	5.217			
§§Linden Warner	26	83	90.0	17.0	107.0	5.157			
§§Paul Whittaker	**38**	**122**	**126.0**	**26.0**	**152.0**	**4.984**			
§§Steve Carter	2	4	2.0	0.0	2.0	2.000			

1985...1985...1985...1985...1985...1985

	M	R	Pts	BP	TPts	Ave	F	P	Total
Trevor Banks	41	171	314.0	36.0	350.0	8.187	2	3	5
Andy Galvin	**42**	**173**	**307.0**	**40.0**	**347.0**	**8.023**	**2**	**6**	**8**
Paul Whittaker	**42**	**150**	**266.0**	**25.0**	**291.0**	**7.760**	**3**		**3**
Paul Bosley	39	151	250.0	34.0	284.0	7.523	1	5	6
§Alan Mogridge	**42**	**165**	**257.0**	**45.0**	**302.0**	**7.321**	**2**	**1**	**3**
Barry Thomas	40	164	274.0	25.0	299.0	7.293		2	2
§§Richard Pettman	**42**	**114**	**115.0**	**27.0**	**142.0**	**4.982**			
§Gary Rolls	4	10	7.0	3.0	10.0	4.000			
Mike Fitzpatrick	1	3	2.0	0.0	2.0	2.667			

1986...1986...1986...1986...1986...1986

	M	R	Pts	BP	TPts	Ave	F	P	Total
§§Malcolm Simmons	38	165	391.0	9.0	400.0	9.697	9	1	10
Andy Galvin	40	168	318.0	16.0	334.0	7.952	2		2
Barry Thomas	**42**	**183**	**314.0**	**24.0**	**338.0**	**7.388**	**1**	**2**	**3**
Alan Mogridge	7	30	42.0	8.0	50.0	6.667			
Paul Whittaker	**42**	**172**	**223.0**	**47.0**	**270.0**	**6.279**		**1**	**1**
Gary Rolls	33	115	91.0	26.0	117.0	4.070			
§§Carl Chalcraft	33	91	72.0	17.0	89.0	3.912			
Richard Pettman	39	128	109.0	12.0	121.0	3.781			
Mike Fitzpatrick	7	21	17.0	2.0	19.0	3.619			
§§Steve Smith	8	18	6.0	1.0	7.0	1.556			
§§Gary Chalcraft	1	2	0.0	0.0	0.0	0.000			

HACKNEY returned to Division One racing in 1987 with disastrous financial implications.

1988...1988...1988...1988...1988...1988

	M	R	Pts	BP	TPts	Ave	F	P	Total
§§Mark Loram	33	166	410.0	19.0	429.0	10.337	7	4	11
Andy Galvin	37	193	426.0	50.0	476.0	9.865	2	5	7
§§Chris Louis	**38**	**182**	**333.0**	**33.0**	**366.0**	**8.044**		**2**	**2**
Alan Mogridge	**38**	**189**	**301.0**	**49.0**	**350.0**	**7.407**		**2**	**2**
Paul Whittaker	**38**	**185**	**283.0**	**54.0**	**337.0**	**7.286**		**4**	**4**
Gary Rolls	36	126	160.0	27.0	187.0	5.937			
Barry Thomas	35	152	189.0	36.0	225.0	5.921		1	1
§§Shawn Venables	4	11	10.0	0.0	10.0	3.636			
Paul Bosley	3	13	10.0	0.0	10.0	3.077			

1989...1989...1989...1989...1989...1989

	M	R	Pts	BP	TPts	Ave	F	P	Total
§Steve Schofield	**36**	**192**	**491.0**	**13.0**	**504.0**	**10.500**	**8**	**4**	**12**
Andy Galvin	**36**	**193**	**463.0**	**17.0**	**480.0**	**9.948**	**7**	**2**	**9**
Paul Whittaker	**36**	**182**	**292.0**	**34.0**	**326.0**	**7.165**			
§Gary Tagg	34	166	184.0	39.0	223.0	5.373			
Barry Thomas	**36**	**164**	**154.0**	**24.0**	**178.0**	**4.341**			
Shawn Venables	5	16	15.0	2.0	17.0	4.250			
Gary Rolls	14	57	49.0	10.0	59.0	4.140			
§§Steve Verge	2	5	4.0	1.0	5.0	4.000			
§Michael Warren	28	108	80.0	14.0	94.0	3.481			
§§Lee Pavitt	13	37	24.0	5.0	29.0	3.135			
Mike Fitzpatrick	3	8	5.0	1.0	6.0	3.000			
§Warren Mowat	9	27	15.0	1.0	16.0	2.370			

1990...1990...1990...1990...1990...1990

	M	R	Pts	BP	TPts	Ave	F	P	Total
Steve Schofield	34	180	467.0	6.0	473.0	10.511	7	3	10
Andy Galvin	27	132	279.0	27.0	306.0	9.273	4	2	6
Paul Whittaker	**36**	**199**	**390.0**	**17.0**	**407.0**	**8.181**	**2**		**2**
Gary Tagg	32	159	193.0	44.0	237.0	5.962			
Michael Warren	**36**	**188**	**222.0**	**34.0**	**256.0**	**5.447**			
§§Dave Hamnett	32	117	114.0	15.0	129.0	4.410			
§§Tim Korneliussen	27	100	88.0	11.0	99.0	3.960			
Shawn Venables	9	40	30.0	8.0	38.0	3.800			
§Roland Pollard	2	4	2.0	1.0	3.0	3.000			
§Ian Humphreys	10	33	22.0	2.0	24.0	2.909			
§§David Wolstenholme	1	2	1.0	0.0	1.0	2.000			

LONDON JUNIOR CHAMPIONSHIP

1967	1 Mike Cake	2 George Barclay	3 Dave Callington
1983	1 Kerry Gray	2 Chris Chaplin	3 Mark Terry

WARNERS' GRAND NATIONAL

1977	1 Martin Yeates	2 Mike Sampson	3 Tom Owen
1978	1 Danny Kennedy	2 Bob Humphreys	3 David Shields
1979	1 Tom Owen	2 Bob Garrad	3 Nigel Boocock
1980	1 David Gagen	2 Paul Woods	3 Mike Ferreira

WARNERS' HOLIDAY CHASE–CHAMPIONS CHASE

1985	1 Mike Ferreira	2 Alan Mogridge	3 Bob Humphreys

VIC HARDING MEMORIAL TROPHY

1985	1 Martin Yeates	2 Bob Garrad	3 Carl Baldwin
1988	1 Steve Schofield	2 Andy Galvin	3 Ray Morton

JOHNNIE HOSKINS MEMORIAL CHASE

1988	1 Mark Loram	2 Rob Tilbury	3 Andy Galvin

See also Hackney, Division One Averages

GLITTERING...the 1988 Hackney double winning side show off their trophies

HULL

1971...1971...1971...1971...1971...1971

	M	R	Pts	BP	TPts	Ave	F	P	Total
§Reg Wilson	33	163	387.0	8.0	395.0	9.693	5	1	6
§Tony Childs	**34**	**167**	**372.0**	**13.0**	**385.0**	**9.222**	**4**		**4**
§George Devonport	6	14	25.0	2.0	27.0	7.714	1		1
§Colin Tucker	32	122	155.0	34.0	189.0	6.197			
§§Robin Amundson	31	126	148.0	39.0	187.0	5.937			
§Dennis Wasden	**34**	**140**	**148.0**	**32.0**	**180.0**	**5.143**			
§§Peter Boston	11	34	31.0	7.0	38.0	4.471			
§Ian Bottomley	21	71	65.0	13.0	78.0	4.394			
§Peter Baldock	12	34	20.0	8.0	28.0	3.294			
§§George Beaton	1	4	0.0	0.0	0.0	0.000			
§Tony Armstrong	1	2	0.0	0.0	0.0	0.000			
§Mick Glover	1	2	0.0	0.0	0.0	0.000			

1972...1972...1972...1972...1972...1972

	M	R	Pts	BP	TPts	Ave	F	P	Total
Tony Childs	**34**	**151**	**322.0**	**19.0**	**341.0**	**9.033**	**3**	**1**	**4**
§§Dave Mills	31	136	274.0	18.0	292.0	8.588	5	2	7
Robin Amundson	27	105	191.0	12.0	203.0	7.733			
§Stan Stevens	11	45	67.0	9.0	76.0	6.756			
§§Dennis Gavros	13	49	64.0	6.0	70.0	5.714			
§§Bryan Loakes	22	94	108.0	19.0	127.0	5.404			
Pete Boston	27	93	92.0	23.0	115.0	4.946			
§Clark Facey	12	52	54.0	5.0	59.0	4.538			
Dennis Wasden	28	89	85.0	11.0	96.0	4.315			
Colin Tucker	9	27	21.0	7.0	28.0	4.148			
§Bernie Hornby	8	22	9.0	1.0	10.0	1.818			
George Devonport	5	12	4.0	0.0	4.0	1.333			
§Nicky Allott	2	6	2.0	0.0	2.0	1.333			
§§Doug Underwood	1	2	0.0	0.0	0.0	0.000			
§§Shane Hearty	1	1	0.0	0.0	0.0	0.000			

1973...1973...1973...1973...1973...1973

	M	R	Pts	BP	TPts	Ave	F	P	Total
Dave Mills	32	152	335.0	18.0	353.0	9.289	4	2	6
Tony Childs	25	114	224.0	18.0	242.0	8.491	1	2	3
§§Alan Cowland	23	107	196.0	9.0	205.0	7.664		1	1
Robin Amundson	16	60	100.0	14.0	114.0	7.600		1	1
Dennis Gavros	34	139	177.0	16.0	193.0	5.554			
Peter Boston	24	83	82.0	13.0	95.0	4.578			
Dennis Wasden	20	66	62.0	11.0	73.0	4.424			
§§Kelvin Mullarkey	10	39	37.0	5.0	42.0	4.308			
Clark Facey	9	28	25.0	3.0	28.0	4.000			
§§Grahame Dawson	14	53	36.0	6.0	42.0	3.170			
§Roger Austin	10	30	19.0	2.0	21.0	2.800			
§Mike Vernam	2	8	4.0	1.0	5.0	2.500			
§§Peter Thompson	2	5	3.0	0.0	3.0	2.400			
§§Eddie Argall	9	33	16.0	0.0	16.0	1.939			
§Chris Blythe	6	14	4.0	1.0	5.0	1.429			
Dave O'Connor	1	2	0.0	0.0	0.0	0.000			

HULL OPEN CHAMPIONSHIP

1971	1 Reg Wilson	2 Malcolm Mackay	3 Doug Wyer
1972	1 Phil Crump	2 Jim Ryman	3 Arthur Browning
1973	1 Dave Mills	2 Tony Childs	3 Carl Glover

SUPREME INDIVIDUAL OPEN TROPHY

1972	1 Jim Ryman	2 Alan Knapkin	3 Mitch Graham and Lou Sansom

COLIN TUCKER FAREWELL

1973	1 Dennis Gavros	2 Alan Cowland	3 Carl Glover

IPSWICH

1969...1969...1969...1969...1969...1969

	M	R	Pts	BP	TPts	Ave	F	P	Total
§§Les Steward	1	1	2	0	2.0	8.000			
§§John Harrhy	30	124	228	16	244.0	7.871	2	1	3
§§Peter Bailey	25	107	181	26	207.0	7.738			
§Ted Spittles	26	104	176	22	198.0	7.615	2	1	3
§§Ron Bagley	**32**	**133**	**229**	**15**	**244.0**	**7.338**	**1**	**1**	**2**
§§Ernie Baker	28	111	157	20	177.0	6.378		1	1
§§Barry Meeks	1	3	4	0	4.0	5.333			
§Dennis Wasden	14	46	46	15	61.0	5.304			
§Neville Slee	24	79	81	14	95.0	4.810			
§§Gil Farmer	7	21	16	6	22.0	4.190			
§§Mike Coomber	15	46	39	8	47.0	4.087			
§§Bernie Aldridge	12	33	25	7	32.0	3.879			
§§Steve Chilman	4	13	5	2	7.0	2.154			
§§Dick Baxter	1	4	1	0	1.0	1.000			

1970...1970...1970...1970...1970...1970

	M	R	Pts	BP	TPts	Ave	F	P	Total
John Harrhy	32	135	300.0	11.0	311.0	9.215	3	5	8
§§John Louis	35	156	325.0	16.0	341.0	8.744	7	1	8
Peter Bailey	35	150	273.0	12.0	285.0	7.600	2	3	5
Ron Bagley	31	132	202.0	30.0	232.0	7.030		1	1
Ted Spittles	27	96	124.0	18.0	142.0	5.917		1	1
Neville Slee	13	44	42.0	8.0	50.0	4.545			
§Dave Whitaker	9	27	25.0	3.0	28.0	4.148			
§Mike Holt	1	3	2.0	1.0	3.0	4.000			
Bernie Aldridge	15	47	36.0	10.0	46.0	3.915			
§§Stan Pepper	31	97	68.0	18.0	86.0	3.546			
§§Tony Davey	4	13	10.0	1.0	11.0	3.385			
§Bob Tabet	5	13	9.0	1.0	10.0	3.077			
Les Steward	3	6	4.0	0.0	4.0	2.667			
§Brian Osborne	2	5	2.0	0.0	2.0	1.600			
§§Clive Noy	2	4	1.0	0.0	1.0	1.000			

1971...1971...1971...1971...1971...1971

	M	R	Pts	BP	Tpts	Ave	F	P	Total
John Louis	38	162	452.0	6.0	458.0	11.309	21	4	25
Tony Davey	**40**	**166**	**400.0**	**12.0**	**412.0**	**9.928**	**9**	**4**	**13**
Peter Bailey	**40**	**162**	**307.0**	**25.0**	**332.0**	**8.198**	**4**	**6**	**10**
§§Peter Prinsloo	15	51	59.0	8.0	67.0	5.255			
Clive Noy	39	146	157.0	29.0	186.0	5.096		1	1
Ron Bagley	20	71	77.0	12.0	89.0	5.014			
§§Rex Garrod	3	8	7.0	3.0	10.0	5.000			
§§Ted Howgego	32	108	106.0	25.0	131.0	4.852			
Ted Spittles	21	75	67.0	14.0	81.0	4.320			
Stan Pepper	23	79	60.0	13.0	73.0	3.696			
§§Ray Watkins	4	9	5.0	2.0	7.0	3.111			
Brian Osborn	1	2	0.0	0.0	0.0	0.000			

GEOFF REVETT TROPHY

1969	1 Ernie Baker	2 John Harrhy	3 Geoff Maloney
1970	1 Ian Turner	2 Peter Bailey	3 John Louis
1971	1 John Louis	2 Malcolm Mackay	3 Arthur Price

NICHOLLS MOTORS TROPHY

1969	1 John Harrhy	2 Ron Bagley	3 Gordon McGregor

STADIUM TROPHY

1970	1 John Harrhy	2 John Louis	3 Arthur Price

See also Ipswich, Division One Averages

1989...1989...1989...1989...1989...1989

	M	R	Pts	BP	TPts	Ave	F	P	Total
§Mark Loram	35	184	422.0	22.0	444.0	9.652	3	2	5
§Chris Louis	35	185	421.0	15.0	436.0	9.427	5	1	6
§Dean Standing	37	199	377.0	31.0	408.0	8.201	1	4	5
§Alan Mogridge	36	189	287.0	69.0	356.0	7.534			
§Robbie Fuller	**38**	**160**	**169.0**	**28.0**	**197.0**	**4.925**			
§Peter Chapman	33	155	166.0	24.0	190.0	4.903			
§Kevin Teager	20	72	62.5	17.0	79.5	4.417			
§§Craig Hyde	18	50	22.0	7.0	29.0	2.320			
§Warren Mowat	4	12	7.0	2.0	9.0	3.000			
§David Steen	1	1	1.0	0.0	1.0	4.000			
§§Steve Widt	3	8	5.0	1.0	6.0	3.000			

1990...1990...1990...1990...1990...1990

	M	R	Pts	BP	TPts	Ave	F	P	Total
Chris Louis	**38**	**211**	**518.0**	**19.0**	**537.0**	**10.180**	**7**	**1**	**8**
Dean Standing	36	179	326.0	33.0	359.0	8.022	2	2	4
§David Norris	27	132	237.0	37.0	274.0	8.303	1	1	2
Alan Mogridge	**38**	**209**	**345.0**	**63.0**	**408.0**	**7.809**		**3**	**3**
§§Shane Parker	**38**	**204**	**286.0**	**43.0**	**329.0**	**6.451**	**1**	**1**	**2**
Robbie Fuller	36	153	176.0	18.0	194.0	5.072		1	1
§§Damon Richardson	1	3	2.0	0.0	2.0	2.667			
§§Darren Fitch	3	6	2.0	2.0	4.0	2.667			
§§Colin White	23	68	38.0	5.0	43.0	2.529			
Craig Hyde	19	55	29.0	5.0	34.0	2.473			

TIGER-IFIC...John Louis, Ipswich's first major discovery, took the Witches' into the First Division as both rider and promoter

■ *IPSWICH was one of the success stories of the British League era...*

■ *When prospective promoters John Berry and Joe Thurley first applied for a licence to run Second Division racing at Foxhall Heath they were turned down because the other promoters didn't believe they could do the job and told them to re-apply if they could find someone with experience to guide them!*

■ *Former rider Howdy Byford was taken on board but there was no doubting the bosses at the East Anglian track as the two schoolfriends transformed a backwater track into a thriving business with crowds flocking to the Thursday night racing.*

■ *The shrewd Berry quickly realised that he needed a local hero and began scouring the East Anglian grass track and scrambles circuits for someone he could turn into a speedway star.*

■ *That man was John Louis who averaged nearly nine points a meeting in his debut season and provided the platform for Ipswich's eventual elevation to the First Division in 1972. How ironic that it was John's son Chris who would provide precisely the same sort of big scoring in 1990 when he also became World Under 21 Champion.*

■ *Strange as it may seem despite all their success, Ipswich have never won the Second Division championship and have never finished higher than third in the League at that level although they were First Division title winners.*

KING'S LYNN

1969...1969...1969...1969...1969...1969

	M	R	Pts	BP	TPts	Ave	F	P	Total
§§Brian Davies	1	4	12.0	0.0	12.0	12.000	1		1
§Allan Brown	1	4	11.0	0.0	11.0	11.000			
§Graham Edmunds	3	13	33.0	1.0	34.0	10.462			
§§George Barclay	6	27	60.0	2.0	62.0	9.185		1	1
§Gordon McGregor	1	5	11.0	0.0	11.0	8.800			
§Dennis Mannion	2	9	15.0	2.0	17.0	7.556			
§§Peter Bradshaw	2	7	13.0	0.0	13.0	7.429			
§Ken Vale	7	30	52.0	3.0	55.0	7.333			
§§Ian Turner	28	124	207.0	15.0	222.0	7.161	1		1
§§Peter Seaton	11	44	69.0	8.0	77.0	7.000	1	1	2
§Arthur Price	28	120	185.0	12.0	197.0	6.567	1	1	2
§§Tony Featherstone	30	124	128.0	36.0	164.0	5.290			
§Peter Maxted	8	30	35.0	3.0	38.0	5.067			
§§John Ingamells	23	82	70.0	13.0	83.0	4.049			
§§Tony Peasland	5	17	14.0	2.0	16.0	3.765			
§§Russell Osborne	18	67	58.0	5.0	63.0	3.761			
§Malcolm Mackay	1	4	2.0	1.0	3.0	3.000			
§§Cyril Crane	1	3	2.0	0.0	2.0	2.667			
§Fred Hodder	1	3	2.0	0.0	2.0	2.667			
§§John Knock	6	15	8.0	1.0	9.0	2.400			
§§Geoff Gale	3	7	3.0	1.0	4.0	2.286			
§§Chris Blythe	6	16	6.0	1.0	7.0	1.750			
§§Nigel Spindler	7	15	3.0	2.0	5.0	1.333			
§§Jack Bywater	3	5	0.0	0.0	0.0	0.000			
§§Alan Appleton	1	3	0.0	0.0	0.0	0.000			
§§Freddie Sweet	1	2	0.0	0.0	0.0	0.000			
§Pat Flanagan	1	1	0.0	0.0	0.0	0.000			

1970...1970...1970...1970...1970...1970

	M	R	Pts	BP	TPts	Ave	F	P	Total
§§BDavid Crane	4	20	42.0	5.0	47.0	9.400			
§BIan Turner	21	95	218.0	4.0	222.0	9.347	8	1	9
§BArthur Price	**33**	**147**	**259.5**	**17.0**	**276.5**	**7.524**	**4**	**1**	**5**
§BGraham Edmonds	16	60	102.0	7.0	109.0	7.267			
§BRuss Osborne	31	120	151.0	20.0	171.0	5.700			
§BJack Bywater	**33**	**124**	**142.0**	**12.0**	**154.0**	**4.968**			
§BTony Featherstone	32	122	115.0	15.0	130.0	4.262			
§KCol Smith	1	5	4.0	1.0	5.0	4.000			
§KNigel Spindler	1	2	2.0	0.0	2.0	4.000			
§BJohn Ingamells	22	67	52.5	10.0	62.5	3.731		1	1
§K§BBrian Osborn	11	32	26.0	3.0	29.0	3.625			
§BAlan Sage	3	7	4.0	2.0	6.0	3.429			
§KJudd Drew	1	4	2.0	0.0	2.0	2.000			
§KTyburn Gallows	1	2	1.0	0.0	1.0	2.000			
§KColin Clark	2	5	1.0	0.0	1.0	0.800			
§§KSteve Josh	1	2	0.0	0.0	0.0	0.000			
§BNeville Slee	1	2	0.0	0.0	0.0	0.000			

KING'S LYNN moved to Boston on date to come, 1970 after ten meetings at Saddlebow Road. The last match there was on August 13, 1970, and the first meeting at Boston was an Inter Counties Challenge Cup against Peterborough on August 16. In the above averages B indicates Boston and K indicates King's Lynn. E.G: Ian Turner made his club debut for Boston; David Crane made his Second Division debut for Boston; Col Smith made his club debut for King's Lynn but did not ride for Boston; Brian Osborn made his club debut for BOTH Boston and King's Lynn.

STAR-BLAZER... Ian 'Tiddler' Turner

LONG EATON

***POSTMASTER** Ivor Brown, whose own racing career had ended in retirement because of an injury, was successful where local businessman Alex Beattie had failed...in persuading the powers-that-be to give a Second Division licence to Long Eaton who had lost their own speedway team when the side moved, en bloc, to Leicester at the end of 1967.*

Mr. Beattie wanted to be in on the ground floor of the new British League Division Two but it was felt he didn't have sufficient speedway background to ensure the success of the venture.

Some months later Brown, who lived locally at Wymeswold, was given the green light to re-introduce the sport at Station Road and had ex-rider Vic White as his promoting lieutenant.

He remained in charge until selling out to Tony Allsop in 1974 and at the end of that season the track closed down again.

Another former rider James Bond applied for an Open licence in 1975 which was refused and the Stadium didn't play host to speedway again until Dan McCormick, then in charge at Cradley Heath, successfully applied for a Division Two licence.

His reign was for five years before another season's closure after stock car promoter Keith Barber and long-time Long Eaton follow Maurice Jones had been refused a promoters' licence.

John Turner came to the fore in 1982, eventually was given the go-ahead to re-open the track, took the club to their first League title in 1984 before moving the championship-winning team to Newcastle.

Mervyn Porter became the latest in a long line of Second Division promoters at Station Road but he didn't last too long before he had pulled out leaving yet another promoting team in charge of the East Midlands club...probably the one track in the country that has experienced more promoters than any other in the Division Two era.

	SHAFTESBURY TROPHY		
1969	1 Geoff Ambrose	2 Murray Burt	3 Geoff Pennikett
	SUPPORTERS' TROPHY		
1970	1 Taffy Owen	2 Eric Broadbelt	3 Ian Turner
1971	1 Malcolm Shakespeare	2 Malcolm Mackay	3 Geoff Bouchard
1972	1 Geoff Bouchard	2 Garry Flood	3 John Jackson
	LUNN POLY TROPHY		
1973	1 Arthur Browning	2 Keith White	3 Richard Greer
1974	1 Keith White	2 Alan Molyneux	3 Ricky Day
	NIGEL WASLEY MEMORIAL TROPHY		
1980	1 Bruce Penhall	2 Phil Crump	3 Phil Collins
	MICK SPIERS MEMORIAL TROPHY		
1983	1 David Baugh	2 Neil Evitts	3 Paul Stead
	EAST MIDLANDS JUNIOR CHAMPIONSHIP		
1989	1 Jon Roberts	2 Scott Smith	3 Craig Hyde

NATIONAL LEAGUE AVERAGES...NATIONAL LEAGUE AVERAGES...NATIONAL

LONG EATON

1969...1969...1969...1969...1969...1969

	M	R	Pts	BP	TPts	Ave	F	P	Total
§Tony Lomas	17	74	191.0	3.0	194.0	10.486	7		7
§§Geoff Penniket	24	107	215.0	6.0	221.0	8.262	3		3
§§Peter Wrathall	26	109	195.0	17.0	212.0	7.780	1		1
§§Malcolm Shakespeare	26	114	178.0	18.0	196.0	6.877	1	1	2
§§Glyn Chandler	16	61	85.0	12.0	97.0	6.361			
§Roy Carter	21	80	96.5	15.0	111.5	5.575			
§Pat Adaway	16	49	55.0	6.0	61.0	4.980			
§Peter Gay	28	83	82.0	18.0	100.0	4.819			
§Gil Farmer	12	46	41.0	11.0	52.0	4.522			
§§Pat Johnson	5	15	9.0	3.0	12.0	3.200			
§§John Chadwick	4	14	7.0	1.0	8.0	2.286			
§§Bernie Hornby	16	47	21.0	4.0	25.0	2.128			
§§Dennis Wasden	1	4	2.0	0.0	2.0	2.000			
§Alan Palmer	3	6	1.0	1.0	2.0	1.333			
§§Eric Hockaday	1	4	1.0	0.0	1.0	1.000			
§Fred Hodder	3	9	2.0	0.0	2.0	0.889			
§Malcolm Mackay	2	6	1.0	0.0	1.0	0.667			

1970...1970...1970...1970...1970...1970

	M	R	Pts	BP	TPts	Ave	F	P	Total
Malcolm Shakespeare	19	87	186.0	6.0	192.0	8.828	4		4
§Ken Vale	30	124	191.0	16.0	207.0	6.677			
§Freddie Sweet	1	2	2.0	1.0	3.0	6.000			
§§Geoff Bouchard	**33**	**148**	**189.5**	**27.0**	**216.5**	**5.851**	**1**		**1**
Roy Carter	32	115	143.0	17.0	160.0	5.565	1		1
Gil Farmer	31	123	147.0	13.0	160.0	5.203	1		1
Peter Wrathall	14	50	60.0	4.0	64.0	5.120			
§Colin Tucker	10	37	38.0	3.0	41.0	4.432			
§§Steve Bass	23	76	49.0	12.0	61.0	3.211			
Peter Gay	8	24	14.0	2.0	16.0	2.667			
§§Geoff Langmaid	1	3	1.0	1.0	2.0	2.667			
§§Gerry Scott	3	8	3.0	2.0	5.0	2.500			
§§Col Smith	2	6	1.0	0.0	1.0	0.667			

1971...1971...1971...1971...1971...1971

	M	R	Pts	BP	TPts	Ave	F	P	Total
Malcolm Shakespeare	31	133	320.0	6.0	326.0	9.805	8	1	9
§Roger Mills	33	136	311.0	9.0	320.0	9.412	8		8
Geoff Bouchard	34	155	304.0	16.0	320.0	8.258	1	2	3
Gil Farmer	17	57	50.0	13.0	63.0	4.421			
Peter Wrathall	24	86	82.0	13.0	95.0	4.419			
§Phil Whittaker	22	77	69.0	15.0	84.0	4.364			
Steve Bass	27	88	69.0	14.0	83.0	3.773			
§Ian Champion	32	116	94.0	6.0	100.0	3.448			
§Stuart Jay	1	4	2.0	1.0	3.0	3.000			
§§Ken Wakefield	1	4	3.0	0.0	3.0	3.000			
Gerry Scott	15	47	28.0	1.0	29.0	2.468			
§§Peter Jarvis	3	8	2.0	2.0	4.0	2.000			
§§Peter Taylor	2	3	1.0	0.0	1.0	1.333			
§§Barry Holdsworth	4	11	1.0	1.0	2.0	0.727			

1972...1972...1972...1972...1972...1972

	M	R	Pts	BP	TPts	Ave	F	P	Total
Geoff Bouchard	31	139	266.0	14.0	280.0	8.058	2	2	4
§Ray Watkins	1	1	2.0	0.0	2.0	8.000			
Roger Mills	**34**	**151**	**289.0**	**11.0**	**300.0**	**7.947**	**1**	**1**	**2**
§Joe Hughes	27	110	151.0	22.0	173.0	6.291		2	2
Steve Bass	**34**	**147**	**195.0**	**17.0**	**212.0**	**5.769**			
Chris Harrison	23	86	80.0	15.0	95.0	4.419			
Peter Jarvis	26	78	63.0	16.0	79.0	4.051			
§Alan Witt	2	6	4.0	2.0	6.0	4.000			
§§Martin Edwards	1	3	2.0	1.0	3.0	4.000			
Peter Taylor	1	3	2.0	1.0	3.0	4.000			
§Cliff Emms	17	60	48.0	6.0	54.0	3.600			
Phil Whittaker	14	46	32.0	7.0	39.0	3.391			
Gil Farmer	6	17	11.0	2.0	13.0	3.059			
Ian Champion	8	27	14.0	4.0	18.0	2.667			
§§Brian Woodhouse	8	18	6.0	1.0	7.0	1.556			

1973...1973...1973...1973...1973...1973

	M	R	Pts	BP	TPts	Ave	F	P	Total
Roger Mills	27	113	218.0	16.0	234.0	8.283	5	2	7
Geoff Bouchard	36	157	305.0	17.0	322.0	8.204	3		3
§Mick Handley	4	18	33.0	1.0	34.0	7.556	1		1
§§Norman Strachan	16	61	101.0	12.0	113.0	7.410		2	2
§Phil Bass	36	153	232.0	33.0	265.0	6.928	1	2	3
§§Dave Harvey	7	22	29.0	5.0	34.0	6.182			
§§Alan Molyneux	35	121	146.0	22.0	168.0	5.554			
Alan Witt	36	129	152.0	27.0	179.0	5.550		1	1
§§John Mills	4	12	12.0	3.0	15.0	5.000			
Joe Hughes	14	55	53.0	9.0	62.0	4.509			
Steve Bass	19	71	63.0	8.0	71.0	4.000			
§Mick Moore	8	23	16.0	5.0	21.0	3.652			
§§Ian Teale	8	21	11.0	2.0	13.0	2.476			
§Ken Stafford	2	6	2.0	1.0	3.0	2.000			
Brian Woodhouse	1	2	0.0	0.0	0.0	0.000			

1974...1974...1974...1974...1974...1974

	M	R	Pts	BP	TPts	Ave	F	P	Total
Geoff Bouchard	36	165	370.0	11.0	381.0	9.236	5	2	7
Alan Molyneux	37	157	315.0	8.0	323.0	8.229	8	1	9
Phil Bass	**38**	**157**	**243.0**	**30.0**	**273.0**	**6.955**		**1**	**1**
Alan Witt	33	118	126.0	23.0	149.0	5.051			
§§Steve Finch	22	86	80.0	13.0	93.0	4.326			
§§James Bond	21	69	57.0	13.0	70.0	4.058		1	1
§Dave Patten	1	2	2.0	0.0	2.0	4.000			
Dave Harvey	12	42	34.0	7.0	41.0	3.905			
§§Max Brown	13	40	35.0	4.0	39.0	3.900			
§§Pip Austen	28	87	65.0	14.0	79.0	3.632			
§Harry Maclean	10	31	18.0	5.0	23.0	2.968			
§Malcolm Corradine	2	6	3.0	1.0	4.0	2.667			
Ian Teale	4	11	4.0	3.0	7.0	2.545			
§Nigel Rackett	5	15	3.0	2.0	5.0	1.333			
§§Mick Durose	1	2	0.0	0.0	0.0	0.000			

WHEN Dan McCormick re-opened Long Eaton in 1979 he changed the long-standing team nickname from Archers to Outlaws – a name kept until 1982.

1979...1979...1979...1979...1979...1979

	M	R	Pts	BP	TPts	Ave	F	P	Total
§Dave Perks	**36**	**150**	**364.0**	**16.0**	**380.0**	**10.133**	**6**	**3**	**9**
§Mike Sampson	22	84	201.0	1.0	202.0	9.619	7		7
§Kevin Hawkins	32	149	281.0	18.0	299.0	8.027	1	2	3
§Tony Garard	1	2	3.0	0.0	3.0	6.000			
§§Glenn McDonald	15	61	74.5	6.0	80.5	5.279			
§Les Sawyer	34	120	128.0	24.0	152.0	5.067			
§Nigel Wasley	25	96	102.0	14.0	116.0	4.833			
§Craig Featherby	**36**	**137**	**132.0**	**33.0**	**165.0**	**4.818**			
§Paul Share	2	5	3.0	2.0	5.0	4.000			
§John Homer	21	74	48.0	11.0	59.0	3.189			
§Neil Collins	2	6	2.0	1.0	3.0	2.000			
§Terry Freeman	5	15	5.0	0.0	5.0	1.333			
§§Mark Williams	17	30	7.0	1.0	8.0	1.067			
§Roger Lambert	1	3	0.0	0.0	0.0	0.000			

1980...1980...1980...1980...1980...1980

	M	R	Pts	BP	TPts	Ave	F	P	Total
Mike Sampson	**40**	**187**	**460.0**	**2.0**	**462.0**	**9.882**	**11**		**11**
§Ivan Blacka	15	52	97.0	5.0	102.0	7.846	1		1
Glenn Macdonald	28	127	217.0	23.0	240.0	7.559		1	1
Craig Featherby	39	159	276.0	20.0	296.0	7.447		2	2
§§Paul Bosley	1	4	6.0	1.0	7.0	7.000			
§§Mark Collins	39	163	179.0	40.0	219.0	5.374			
§Arthur Price	18	62	60.0	15.0	75.0	4.839			
§Steve Sant	34	127	92.0	23.0	115.0	3.622			
Mark Williams	21	50	37.0	8.0	45.0	3.600			
§§Peter Bacon	8	21	11.0	7.0	18.0	3.429			
John Homer	15	59	39.0	5.0	44.0	2.983			
§Steve Mildoon	9	26	10.0	1.0	11.0	1.692			

LONG EATON raced as Nottingham in the 1979 and 1980 seasons but at the same Station Road track.

The records for those two seasons as Nottingham are listed above and all individual records are included as Long Eaton.

LONG EATON

1982...1982...1982...1982...1982...1982

	M	R	Pts	BP	TPts	Ave	F	P	Total
Alan Molyneux	37	191	428.0	19.0	447.0	9.361	2	3	5
§Paul Stead	39	203	398.0	29.0	427.0	8.414	1	3	4
§§Paul Bickley	1	1	1.0	1.0	2.0	8.000			
Dave Perks	28	133	233.0	31.0	264.0	7.940		3	3
§Nigel Close	39	199	290.0	40.0	330.0	6.633		1	1
§Paul Evitts	40	207	276.5	58.0	334.5	6.464		2	2
§Nicky Allott	29	102	151.0	7.0	158.0	6.196			
§Mark Summerfield	**40**	**155**	**163.0**	**32.0**	**195.0**	**5.032**			
§David Blackburn	18	71	65.0	16.0	81.0	4.563			
§§Mark Stevenson	1	5	2.0	1.0	3.0	2.400			
§John Frankland	5	10	2.0	1.0	3.0	1.200			
§§Derek Cooper	2	7	2.0	0.0	2.0	1.143			
§Geoff Powell	1	2	0.0	0.0	0.0	0.000			

1983...1983...1983...1983...1983...1983

	M	R	Pts	BP	TPts	Ave	F	P	Total
Dave Perks	**36**	**195**	**375.0**	**22.0**	**397.0**	**8.144**	**1**	**1**	**2**
Alan Molyneux	27	136	264.0	11.0	275.0	8.088	2		2
Paul Stead	28	142	267.0	12.0	279.0	7.859	3		3
Paul Evitts	**36**	**180**	**218.0**	**36.0**	**254.0**	**5.644**		**1**	**1**
John Frankland	**36**	**178**	**195.0**	**37.0**	**232.0**	**5.213**			
Mark Stevenson	**36**	**147**	**145.0**	**25.0**	**170.0**	**4.626**			
§Tony Featherstone	6	29	30.0	1.0	31.0	4.276			
Nicky Allott	18	64	46.0	10.0	56.0	3.500			
§Eric Broadbelt	2	7	3.0	2.0	5.0	2.857			
§§David Tyler	9	31	14.0	6.0	20.0	2.581			
Glen Parrott	5	19	9.0	2.0	11.0	2.316			
§§John Proctor	6	17	4.0	1.0	5.0	1.176			
Derek Cooper	2	2	0.0	0.0	0.0	0.000			

1984...1984...1984...1984...1984...1984

	M	R	Pts	BP	TPts	Ave	F	P	Total
Dave Perks	**34**	**145**	**285.0**	**41.0**	**326.0**	**8.993**	**3**	**5**	**8**
Paul Stead	24	96	200.0	10.0	210.0	8.750	3	1	4
§Graham Drury	33	136	269.0	20.0	289.0	8.500	3	1	4
David Tyler	24	83	132.0	21.0	153.0	7.373			
§Chris Pidcock	**34**	**142**	**219.0**	**28.0**	**247.0**	**6.958**			
§Miles Evans	**34**	**120**	**152.0**	**23.0**	**175.0**	**5.833**			
Mark Stevenson	26	82	91.0	20.0	111.0	5.415			
John Frankland	24	86	91.0	24.0	115.0	5.349			

1985...1985...1985...1985...1985...1985

	M	R	Pts	BP	TPts	Ave	F	P	Total
Chris Pidcock	12	58	111.0	7.0	118.0	8.138	1		1
Dave Perks	**38**	**169**	**317.0**	**25.0**	**342.0**	**8.095**		**1**	**1**
§Andy Fisher	1	3	5.0	1.0	6.0	8.000			
David Tyler	11	47	76.0	7.0	83.0	7.064		1	1
Paul Stead	12	55	88.0	2.0	90.0	6.545			
Graham Drury	17	67	88.0	12.0	100.0	5.970			
Alan Molyneux	11	44	62.0	3.0	65.0	5.909	1		1
§§Gerald Short	24	104	142.0	10.0	152.0	5.846			
§Alan Mason	13	46	49.0	7.0	56.0	4.870			
§Peter E. Smith	**38**	**144**	**148.0**	**24.0**	**172.0**	**4.778**		**1**	**1**
John Proctor	35	119	118.0	17.0	135.0	4.538			
John Frankland	14	45	48.0	2.0	50.0	4.444	1		1
Mark Stevenson	12	36	33.0	3.0	36.0	4.000			
§§Mick May	2	4	3.0	1.0	4.0	4.000			
Derek Cooper	13	40	23.0	4.0	27.0	2.700			
§§Phil Ricketts	5	10	5.0	1.0	6.0	2.400			

1986...1986...1986...1986...1986...1986

	M	R	Pts	BP	TPts	Ave	F	P	Total
§Mark Fiora	38	169	379.0	9.0	388.0	9.183	8	1	9
§Ray Taaffe	1	2	2.0	2.0	4.0	8.000			
Miles Evans	39	174	278.0	24.0	302.0	6.943		1	1
Gerald Short	36	151	244.0	15.0	259.0	6.861	2	3	5
§Geoff Pusey	39	154	163.0	37.0	200.0	5.195			
John Proctor	33	119	122.0	21.0	143.0	4.807	1	1	2
§Phil Alderman	16	57	51.0	15.0	66.0	4.632		1	1
§§Glenn Doyle	19	63	62.5	5.0	67.5	4.286			
Peter E. Smith	7	17	11.0	4.0	15.0	3.529			
§Mark Ferry	2	6	4.0	1.0	5.0	3.333			
Eric Broadbelt	24	71	42.0	14.0	56.0	3.155			
§Rob Carter	6	17	13.0	0.0	13.0	3.059			
§Kenny Young	14	38	20.0	0.0	20.0	2.105			
Phil Ricketts	1	3	0.0	0.0	0.0	0.000			

1987...1987...1987...1987...1987...1987

	M	R	Pts	BP	TPts	Ave	F	P	Total
Glenn Doyle	28	127	253.0	17.0	270.0	8.504		2	2
§Nigel Sparshott	19	85	158.0	6.0	164.0	7.718	1		1
§Keith White	10	42	70.0	7.0	77.0	7.333			0
Gerald Short	**32**	**147**	**236.0**	**22.0**	**258.0**	**7.020**	**1**	**2**	**3**
§Glyn Taylor	10	43	54.0	12.0	66.0	6.140			
Miles Evans	31	138	184.0	23.0	207.0	6.000			
§Richie Owen	17	46	48.0	7.0	55.0	4.783			
§Ian Stead	9	31	27.0	4.0	31.0	4.000			
Rob Carter	10	25	18.0	4.0	22.0	3.520			
§Kevin Price	21	70	50.0	8.0	58.0	3.314			
§John Stokes	5	15	8.0	1.0	9.0	2.400			
Mark Ferry	13	33	17.0	2.0	19.0	2.303			
§§Mark Hepworth	14	37	14.0	3.0	17.0	1.838			
Kenny Young	1	1	0.0	0.0	0.0	0.000			

1988...1988...1988...1988...1988...1988

	M	R	Pts	BP	TPts	Ave	F	P	Total
Keith White	26	140	275.0	19.0	294.0	8.400	1		1
Glenn Doyle	29	161	298.0	17.0	315.0	7.826	1		1
§Mike Spink	**32**	**187**	**264.0**	**26.0**	**290.0**	**6.203**			
§Gary O'Hare	30	169	207.0	23.0	230.0	5.444		1	1
Richie Owen	20	83	72.0	11.0	83.0	4.000			
Gerald Short	2	11	10.0	0.0	10.0	3.636			
§Darrell Branford	14	62	45.0	9.0	54.0	3.484			
§Dave Morton	8	28	18.0	5.0	23.0	3.286			
§Wayne Elliott	21	61	39.0	10.0	49.0	3.213			
§§Jon Roberts	16	52	30.0	8.0	38.0	2.923			
§Steve Bishop	11	59	32.0	8.0	40.0	2.712			
§§Keith Stanley	1	3	0.0	0.0	0.0	0.000			
§§Peter Green	1	2	0.0	0.0	0.0	0.000			

1989...1989...1989...1989...1989...1989

	M	R	Pts	BP	TPts	Ave	F	P	Total
§§Richard Hellsén	**36**	**200**	**424.0**	**16.0**	**440.0**	**8.800**	**1**	**1**	**2**
Keith White	30	142	216.0	24.0	240.0	6.761		1	1
Paul Fry	33	170	231.0	22.0	253.0	5.953		1	1
Dave Perks	18	82	108.0	14.0	122.0	5.951			
Gary O'Hare	31	165	220.0	24.0	244.0	5.915			
§Nigel Leaver	10	50	58.0	11.0	69.0	5.520			
§Peter Lloyd	32	159	166.0	20.0	186.0	4.679			
Steve Bishop	6	16	13.0	0.0	13.0	3.250			
§Andrew Sumner	3	9	5.0	2.0	7.0	3.111			
§Mark Blackbird	24	83	52.0	12.0	64.0	3.084			
Jon Roberts	8	21	12.0	3.0	15.0	2.857			
§Alan Rivett	4	16	9.0	1.0	10.0	2.500			
§Bernie Collier	1	4	1.0	1.0	2.0	2.000			
§§Michael Howe	1	2	1.0	0.0	1.0	2.000			
§§Thierry Hilaire	10	35	12.0	0.0	12.0	1.371			
§§Clinton Butler	1	3	0.0	0.0	0.0	0.000			

1990...1990...1990...1990...1990...1990

	M	R	Pts	BP	TPts	Ave	F	P	Total
Richard Hellsén	30	157	322.0	9.0	331.0	8.433			
§Nigel De'ath	25	125	194.0	22.0	216.0	6.912			
§Kevin Smart	34	173	238.0	23.0	261.0	6.035	1		1
Paul Fry	**34**	**176**	**236.0**	**29.0**	**265.0**	**6.023**			
§Jamie Habbin	30	136	179.0	19.0	198.0	5.824		1	1
§Jon Surman	19	76	70.0	18.0	88.0	4.632			
Gary O'Hare	33	140	141.0	20.0	161.0	4.600			
Mark Blackbird	2	8	6.0	3.0	9.0	4.500			
Peter Lloyd	16	61	54.0	10.0	64.0	4.197			
§Duncan Chapman	4	15	12.0	2.0	14.0	3.733			
Michael Howe	5	8	5.0	1.0	6.0	3.000			
Jon Roberts	2	6	3.0	1.0	4.0	2.667			
§§Jon Bell	1	4	1.0	0.0	1.0	1.000			
Keith White	1	4	1.0	0.0	1.0	1.000			

● *LONG EATON finished bottom of the National League in 1983, were champions in 1984, finished next to bottom in 1985 and were wooden spoonists in 1986!*
It is the most dramatic roller-coaster record of any club in the history of the Second Division.

MIDDLESBROUGH

1968...1968...1968...1968...1968...1968

	M	R	Pts	BP	TPts	Ave	F	P	Total
§§Allan Brown	13	54	125.0	5.0	130.0	9.630	4	1	5
§§Graham Plant	**20**	**89**	**186.0**	**4.0**	**190.0**	**8.539**	**5**		**5**
§§Graham Edmunds	3	13	27.0	0.0	27.0	8.308			
§§Tom Leadbitter	**20**	**85**	**137.0**	**8.0**	**145.0**	**6.824**		**1**	**1**
§§Terry Lee	**20**	**85**	**115.0**	**29.0**	**144.0**	**6.776**			
§§Paul O'Neal	**20**	**81**	**105.0**	**18.0**	**123.0**	**6.074**			
§§Lex Fielding	1	2	2.0	1.0	3.0	6.000			
§§Peter Reading	17	64	64.0	12.0	76.0	4.750			
§§Dave Durham	1	2	2.0	0.0	2.0	4.000			
§§Dave Hardy	2	6	4.0	1.0	5.0	3.333			
§§Alan Palmer	7	16	10.0	3.0	13.0	3.250			
§§Brian Foote	2	6	3.0	1.0	4.0	2.667			
§§John Spilsbury	10	21	8.0	3.0	11.0	2.095			
§§Tim Swales	1	3	1.0	0.0	1.0	1.333			

1969...1969...1969...1969...1969...1969

	M	R	Pts	BP	TPts	Ave	F	P	Total
Terry Lee	31	131	301.0	3.0	304.0	9.282	6	1	7
Tom Leadbitter	29	124	269.0	9.0	278.0	8.968	3		3
§§Roger Mills	31	114	182.0	23.0	205.0	7.193	1	2	3
Pete Reading	**32**	**113**	**135.0**	**35.0**	**170.0**	**6.018**			
Dave Durham	29	112	121.0	31.0	152.0	5.429			
§§Bruce Forrester	21	67	68.0	18.0	86.0	5.134			
§§Tim Swales	**32**	**112**	**113.0**	**20.0**	**133.0**	**4.750**			
Paul O'Neal	6	21	16.0	8.0	24.0	4.571			
John Spilsbury	5	16	12.0	2.0	14.0	3.500			
§§Fred Greenwell	2	5	2.0	0.0	2.0	1.600			
§Peter Thompson	1	3	0.0	0.0	0.0	0.000			
§§Gerry Richardson	1	2	0.0	0.0	0.0	0.000			

1970...1970...1970...1970...1970...1970

	M	R	Pts	BP	TPts	Ave	F	P	Total
Tom Leadbitter	**34**	**147**	**334.0**	**17.0**	**351.0**	**9.551**	**4**	**1**	**5**
§§Mick Moore	1	3	5.0	1.0	6.0	8.000			
Roger Mills	**34**	**133**	**231.0**	**16.0**	**247.0**	**7.429**	**1**	**3**	**4**
Bruce Forrester	25	94	146.0	25.0	171.0	7.277	1	3	4
Tim Swales	32	129	208.0	22.0	230.0	7.132	1	1	2
§§Bob Jameson	**34**	**131**	**187.0**	**30.0**	**217.0**	**6.626**			
Dave Durham	33	118	141.0	25.0	166.0	5.627			
Pete Reading	33	108	121.0	25.0	146.0	5.407			
§Tony Swales	5	15	14.0	4.0	18.0	4.800			
§Brian Whaley	3	6	3.0	1.0	4.0	2.667			
§John Knock	2	7	4.0	0.0	4.0	2.286			
§§Malcolm McPhie	2	4	0.0	0.0	0.0	0.000			

1971...1971...1971...1971...1971...1971

	M	R	Pts	BP	TPts	Ave	F	P	Total
Bruce Forrester	28	120	244.0	6.0	250.0	8.333	3	2	5
Tim Swales	31	125	207.0	13.0	220.0	7.040	3		3
Dave Durham	**34**	**144**	**225.0**	**27.0**	**252.0**	**7.000**	**1**	**1**	**2**
Bob Jameson	23	91	124.5	19.0	143.5	6.308		1	1
Terry Lee	11	42	57.0	7.0	64.0	6.095			
§§Frank Auffret	27	104	125.0	29.0	154.0	5.923		1	1
Pete Reading	24	76	86.5	17.0	103.5	5.447			
Tony Swales	33	111	115.0	23.0	138.0	4.973			
§Dene Davies	12	45	47.0	5.0	52.0	4.622			
Mick Moore	13	35	29.0	10.0	39.0	4.457			

1972...1972...1972...1972...1972...1972

	M	R	Pts	BP	TPts	Ave	F	P	Total
§Roger Wright	22	93	191.0	8.0	199.0	8.559	2		2
Dave Durham	**36**	**160**	**290.0**	**26.0**	**316.0**	**7.900**	**3**		**3**
Bruce Forrester	19	74	124.0	12.0	136.0	7.351	2		2
Frank Auffret	35	153	238.0	27.0	265.0	6.928		4	4
Pete Reading	**36**	**153**	**224.0**	**26.0**	**250.0**	**6.536**	**1**		**1**
Tim Swales	22	81	103.0	18.0	121.0	5.975		1	1
Mick Moore	27	87	103.0	23.0	126.0	5.793			
Tony Swales	34	101	85.0	24.0	109.0	4.317			
§§Maxwell Clift	8	20	11.0	4.0	15.0	3.000			
§§Brian Havelock	3	8	4.0	2.0	6.0	3.000			
§§Dave Wilson	3	7	0.0	0.0	0.0	0.000			

1973...1973...1973...1973...1973...1973

	M	R	Pts	BP	TPts	Ave	F	P	Total
Bruce Forrester	32	129	278.0	17.0	295.0	9.147	3	2	5
Frank Auffret	37	156	327.0	9.0	336.0	8.615	5	2	7
Roger Wright	33	129	196.0	45.0	241.0	7.473		3	3
Peter Reading	37	146	223.0	27.0	250.0	6.849	3		3
Dave Durham	32	119	161.0	28.0	189.0	6.353			
Tim Swales	**38**	**147**	**190.0**	**35.0**	**225.0**	**6.122**	**1**	**2**	**3**
§§Colin Rogerson	4	16	22.0	1.0	23.0	5.750			
§Russ Hodgson	29	90	94.0	27.0	121.0	5.378		1	1
Mick Moore	7	22	20.0	2.0	22.0	4.000			
§§Tom Black	7	21	23.0	3.0	26.0	4.952			
§§Alan Emerson	4	9	2.0	1.0	3.0	1.333			

1974...1974...1974...1974...1974...1974

	M	R	Pts	BP	TPts	Ave	F	P	Total
Tim Swales	1	4	9.0	2.0	11.0	11.000			
Tom Black	1	2	3.0	2.0	5.0	10.000			
Bruce Forrester	36	144	326.0	12.0	338.0	9.389	5	2	7
Dave Durham	39	154	282.0	21.0	303.0	7.870	6	2	8
Peter Reading	**40**	**164**	**286.0**	**31.0**	**317.0**	**7.732**	**3**	**2**	**5**
Roger Wright	38	141	217.0	34.0	251.0	7.121	1	1	2
Russ Hodgson	37	139	198.0	25.0	223.0	6.417		1	1
Malcolm Davis	1	3	2.0	2.0	4.0	5.333			
Alan Emerson	**40**	**154**	**177.0**	**21.0**	**198.0**	**5.143**			
Colin Pestell	2	6	5.0	1.0	6.0	4.000			
Tony Swales	26	75	56.0	12.0	68.0	3.627			
§Merv Salt	15	45	28.0	9.0	37.0	3.289			

1975...1975...1975...1975...1975...1975

	M	R	Pts	BP	TPts	Ave	F	P	Total
Tom Leadbitter	33	154	346.0	16.0	362.0	9.403	5	3	8
Bruce Forrester	6	22	45.0	4.0	49.0	8.909		1	1
Doug Underwood	41	189	360.0	34.0	394.0	8.339	2	2	4
Alan Emerson	26	110	219.0	10.0	229.0	8.327	3	2	5
Roger Wright	11	38	67.0	6.0	73.0	7.684			
Dave Durham	12	43	56.0	9.0	65.0	6.047		2	2
Peter Reading	41	173	212.0	34.0	246.0	5.688	1	2	3
§Harry Maclean	13	48	47.0	16.0	63.0	5.250			
§§Trevor Stead	14	43	30.0	7.0	37.0	3.442			
§§David Levings	23	78	52.0	8.0	60.0	3.077			
§§Peter E. Smith	6	18	12.0	1.0	13.0	2.889			
Colin Pestell	29	89	54.0	9.0	63.0	2.831			
§Brian Johnson	2	6	4.0	0.0	4.0	2.667			
§Ian Silk	8	28	15.0	1.0	16.0	2.286			
§§Andy Cowan	1	4	1.0	0.0	1.0	1.000			
§Graham Tattersall	3	11	1.0	0.0	1.0	0.364			
§§Graham Hartley	1	1	0.0	0.0	0.0	0.000			

1976...1976...1976...1976...1976...1976

	M	R	Pts	BP	TPts	Ave	F	P	Total
Alan Emerson	30	127	260.0	7.0	267.0	8.409	3		3
Tom Leadbitter	25	108	189.0	18.0	207.0	7.667	1	3	4
§Steve Wilcock	**36**	**145**	**191.0**	**21.0**	**212.0**	**5.848**		**1**	**1**
Peter Reading	35	140	172.0	22.0	194.0	5.543	2		2
Andy Cowan	34	132	150.0	24.0	174.0	5.273	1	1	2
Peter E. Smith	35	135	150.0	16.0	166.0	4.919	1		1
§§Nigel Close	23	77	81.0	11.0	92.0	4.779			
David Levings	6	18	14.0	1.0	15.0	3.333			
§John Robson	7	19	11.0	3.0	14.0	2.947			
§§Mike Beaumont	5	14	6.0	4.0	10.0	2.857			
§Martin Cusworth	7	16	8.0	2.0	10.0	2.500			
Trevor Stead	3	6	1.0	0.0	1.0	0.667			

■ *STEVE WILCOCK made his debut for Middlesbrough in the opening Division Two match of 1976 against Workington on Thursday, April 1, and didn't miss a fixture until injury forced him out of the match at Rye House on August 15, 1982. He rode in a total of 267 consecutive League and Cup matches for the club.*

MIDDLESBROUGH raced as Teesside from 1968 until 1978 at the Cleveland Park track.

The records for those 11 seasons as Teesside are listed above and all individual records are included as Middlesbrough.

NATIONAL LEAGUE AVERAGES...NATIONAL LEAGUE AVERAGES...NATIONAL

MIDDLESBROUGH

1977...1977...1977...1977...1977...1977

	M	R	Pts	BP	TPts	Ave	F	P	Total
Alan Emerson	36	142	295.0	9.0	304.0	8.563	3		3
Steve Wilcock	38	159	254.0	18.0	272.0	6.843	1	1	2
Peter Reading	38	152	199.0	35.0	234.0	6.158		1	1
Peter E. Smith	38	157	218.0	21.0	239.0	6.089		1	1
Nigel Close	37	137	157.0	19.0	176.0	5.139			
Martin Cusworth	38	143	146.0	31.0	177.0	4.951			
John Robson	8	20	20.0	4.0	24.0	4.800			
Mike Beaumont	12	30	24.0	11.0	35.0	4.667			
Andy Cowan	3	11	7.0	2.0	9.0	3.273			
Harry MacLean	15	36	20.0	3.0	23.0	2.556			
§§Mike Sanderson	4	6	0.0	0.0	0.0	0.000			

1978...1978...1978...1978...1978...1978

	M	R	Pts	BP	TPts	Ave	F	P	Total
Steve Wilcock	40	192	367.0	14.0	381.0	7.938		1	1
Nigel Close	12	59	104.0	5.0	109.0	7.390			
Peter E. Smith	38	176	296.0	22.0	318.0	7.227	1		1
Peter Reading	28	124	173.0	17.0	190.0	6.129		1	1
Martyn Cusworth	40	159	161.0	28.0	189.0	4.755			
§Peter Spink	21	70	64.0	14.0	78.0	4.457			
§Martin Dixon	40	140	122.0	21.0	143.0	4.086			
§Bob Watts	12	39	35.0	2.0	37.0	3.795			
John Robson	6	14	9.0	2.0	11.0	3.143			
§Dave Gatenby	22	58	35.0	7.0	42.0	2.897			
Mike Sanderson	4	5	0.0	0.0	0.0	0.000			

1979...1979...1979...1979...1979...1979

	M	R	Pts	BP	TPts	Ave	F	P	Total
Steve Wilcock	38	169	341.0	38.0	379.0	8.970	3	3	6
§Malcolm Corradine	28	107	201.0	10.0	211.0	7.888	3		3
§Geoff Pusey	38	161	258.0	22.0	280.0	6.957		1	1
§Mark Courtney	38	159	261.0	14.0	275.0	6.918	1	2	3
Martin Dixon	38	153	165.0	27.0	192.0	5.020			
Martyn Cusworth	29	105	104.0	21.0	125.0	4.762			
John Robson	1	1	1.0	0.0	1.0	4.000			
§§Paul Stead	28	87	73.0	9.0	82.0	3.770	1		1
Mike Sanderson	9	21	9.0	1.0	10.0	1.905			
Peter Reading	6	15	4.0	0.0	4.0	1.067			
§Mick Conroy	5	12	3.0	0.0	3.0	1.000			

1980...1980...1980...1980...1980...1980

	M	R	Pts	BP	TPts	Ave	F	P	Total
Steve Wilcock	46	193	447.0	49.0	496.0	10.280	6	6	12
Mark Courtney	46	190	406.0	30.0	436.0	9.179	9	4	13
Brian Havelock	36	136	227.0	35.0	262.0	7.706	1		1
§Mike Spink	44	182	302.5	38.0	340.5	7.484		3	3
Geoff Pusey	46	185	284.0	39.0	323.0	6.984		2	2
Martin Dixon	46	176	239.0	55.0	294.0	6.682	1	3	4
Peter Reading	4	12	14.0	5.0	19.0	6.333			
§Bernie Collier	39	104	90.0	23.0	113.0	4.346			
§David Butt	4	11	4.0	0.0	4.0	1.455			
§§John Clegg	3	6	0.0	0.0	0.0	0.000			
§Alan Armstrong	1	2	0.0	0.0	0.0	0.000			

1981...1981...1981...1981...1981...1981

	M	R	Pts	BP	TPts	Ave	F	P	Total
Mark Courtney	42	174	437.0	17.0	454.0	10.437	10	1	11
Steve Wilcock	43	185	409.0	51.0	460.0	9.946	7	8	15
Martin Dixon	42	171	309.0	45.0	354.0	8.281	1	4	5
Brian Havelock	41	160	254.0	34.0	288.0	7.200	1		1
Mike Spink	43	176	260.0	56.0	316.0	7.182		2	2
Geoff Pusey	43	177	250.0	47.0	297.0	6.712	1	2	3
Bernie Collier	22	61	64.0	13.0	77.0	5.049			
§Peter Tarrant	7	20	13.0	5.0	18.0	3.600			
Alan Armstrong	11	26	20.0	3.0	23.0	3.538			
§§John Place	4	10	4.0	1.0	5.0	2.000			

MDDLESBROUGH became the third founder member of the British League Division Two to win the Championship when they took the crown in 1981. Belle Vue had been successful in 1968 and 1969 and then Canterbury won the League title in 1970. None of the other seven founder members were ever crowned League champions...

1982...1982...1982...1982...1982...1982

	M	R	Pts	BP	TPts	Ave	F	P	Total
Martin Dixon	38	201	440.0	32.0	472.0	9.393		4	4
Steve Wilcock	37	201	423.0	43.0	466.0	9.274	3	4	7
§§Brian Manning	1	1	2.0	0.0	2.0	8.000			
Mike Spink	38	205	361.0	32.0	393.0	7.668	1	2	3
Geoff Pusey	38	193	316.0	38.0	354.0	7.337		4	4
Frank Auffret	3	13	19.0	1.0	20.0	6.154			
§Paul Price	37	158	172.0	34.0	206.0	5.215			
§Rob Woffinden	24	116	115.0	26.0	141.0	4.862			
Alan Armstrong	16	48	45.0	7.0	52.0	4.333			
§Peter Spink	10	31	23.0	5.0	28.0	3.613			
§§Ashley Norton	4	13	9.0	2.0	11.0	3.385			
Bernie Collier	10	22	6.0	3.0	9.0	1.636			
John Place	6	14	3.0	0.0	3.0	0.857			

1983...1983...1983...1983...1983...1983

	M	R	PTs	BP	TPts	Ave	F	P	Total
Steve Wilcock	36	187	412.0	31.0	443.0	9.476	1	1	2
Mike Spink	38	207	421.0	27.0	448.0	8.657		3	3
Geoff Pusey	34	162	240.0	32.0	272.0	6.716	1	2	3
Brian Havelock	36	165	231.0	23.0	254.0	6.158			
Rob Woffinden	38	188	244.0	34.0	278.0	5.915			
Paul Price	16	65	73.0	16.0	89.0	5.477			
Ashley Norton	38	150	152.0	27.0	179.0	4.773		1	1
Alan Armstrong	4	9	5.0	3.0	8.0	3.556			
§§Peter Nightingale	15	51	32.0	6.0	38.0	2.980			
§§Mark Crang	7	25	15.0	3.0	18.0	2.880			
Miles Evans	2	8	4.0	1.0	5.0	2.500			

1984...1984...1984...1984...1984...1984

	M	R	Pts	BP	TPts	Ave	F	P	Total
Steve Wilcock	36	154	362.0	12.0	374.0	9.714	7	2	9
Mike Spink	36	153	308.0	17.0	325.0	8.497		3	3
Geoff Pusey	36	156	247.0	36.0	283.0	7.256	1	3	4
Paul Price	32	115	144.0	20.0	164.0	5.704	1		1
Peter E. Smith	29	106	111.0	18.0	129.0	4.868			
Mark Crang	25	85	79.0	22.0	101.0	4.753		1	1
§Jim Burdfield	11	47	44.0	11.0	55.0	4.681			
Ashley Norton	15	50	49.0	4.0	53.0	4.240			
§Rob Carter	19	51	37.0	4.0	41.0	3.216			
John Place	13	31	15.0	1.0	16.0	2.065			

GARAGE owner Tim Swales, who had ridden for the Teessiders from 1968 until 1974, took over as sole promoter from Leicestershire-based Wally Martin at the beginning of the 1985 season and led the club to third place in the League.

1985...1985...1985...1985...1985...1985

	M	R	Pts	BP	TPts	Ave	F	P	Total
Steve Wilcock	42	182	401.0	19.0	420.0	9.231	5	2	7
Martin Dixon	42	177	358.0	37.0	395.0	8.927	4	5	9
§Mark Fiora	33	133	263.0	22.0	285.0	8.571	2	1	3
§§Gary Havelock	38	150	239.0	36.0	275.0	7.333		2	2
Jim Burdfield	39	150	215.0	37.0	252.0	6.720		1	1
Geoff Pusey	42	165	199.0	50.0	249.0	6.036		1	1
Mark Crang	16	46	38.0	6.0	44.0	3.826			
§§Ian Wedgwood	18	45	25.0	9.0	34.0	3.022			
Bernie Collier	4	12	7.0	2.0	9.0	3.000			
§§Vic Gollagher	1	2	1.0	0.0	1.0	2.000			
§§Roland Tebbs	11	26	10.0	0.0	10.0	1.538			
§§Wayne Ross	2	6	1.0	0.0	1.0	0.667			

1986...1986...1986...1986...1986...1986

	M	R	Pts	BP	TPts	Ave	F	P	Total
Martin Dixon	42	169	371.0	22.0	393.0	9.302	8	5	13
Mark Courtney	41	172	380.0	16.0	396.0	9.209	7	2	9
Gary Havelock	35	131	253.0	30.0	283.0	8.641	1	5	6
Steve Wilcock	42	179	324.0	33.0	357.0	7.978	5	2	7
Jim Burdfield	42	160	170.0	41.0	211.0	5.275	1		1
§Tony Forward	18	53	48.0	9.0	57.0	4.302			
Roland Tebbs	30	107	103.0	12.0	115.0	4.299			
§§Glenn Hornby	28	94	74.0	14.0	88.0	3.745			
§Paul Heyes	3	9	5.0	1.0	6.0	2.667			
§§David Holiday	6	15	3.0	0.0	3.0	0.800			

MIDDLESBROUGH

1987...1987...1987...1987...1970...1987

	M	R	Pts	BP	TPts	Ave	F	P	Total
Martin Dixon	**32**	**151**	**369.0**	**9.0**	**378.0**	**10.013**	**4**	**2**	**6**
Mark Fiora	10	45	97.0	3.0	100.0	8.889	1		1
Steve Wilcokk	27	126	221.0	17.0	238.0	7.556		3	3
§Ian Atkinson	3	7	8.0	2.0	10.0	5.714			
§Peter McNamara	30	134	163.0	18.0	181.0	5.403			
Ashley Norton	31	135	146.0	29.0	175.0	5.185			
§§Andrew Buck	9	33	32.0	9.0	41.0	4.970			
§Mark Burrows	23	73	65.0	15.0	80.0	4.384			
Geoff Pusey	**32**	**123**	**112.0**	**13.0**	**125.0**	**4.065**			
David Holiday	3	7	2.0	2.0	4.0	2.286			
§§Tracy Bray	6	14	4.0	2.0	6.0	1.714			

1988...1988...1988...1988...1988...1988

	M	R	Pts	BP	TPts	Ave	F	P	Total
Mark Fiora	32	182	414.0	16.0	430.0	9.451	3	2	5
§Darren Sumner	**34**	**191**	**363.0**	**24.0**	**387.0**	**8.105**			
Martin Dixon	23	124	236.0	12.0	248.0	8.000			
Peter McNamara	32	164	201.0	37.0	238.0	5.805			
Ashley Norton	17	85	83.0	14.0	97.0	4.565			
§Nigel Sparshott	12	61	59.0	10.0	69.0	4.525			
Geoff Pusey	12	41	35.0	4.0	39.0	3.805			
§Andrew Sumner	21	76	60.0	11.0	71.0	3.737			
Andrew Buck	14	54	35.0	6.0	41.0	3.037			
§§David Clay	7	21	15.0	0.0	15.0	2.857			
§§Max Schofield	16	42	21.0	4.0	25.0	2.381			
§Paul Bentley	13	43	21.0	4.0	25.0	2.326			
§David Blackburn	1	3	1.0	0.0	1.0	1.333			
Ian Atkinson	2	4	1.0	0.0	1.0	1.000			

1989...1989...1989...1989...1989...1989

	M	R	Pts	BP	TPts	Ave	F	P	Total
Darren Sumner	**36**	**197**	**377.0**	**17.0**	**394.0**	**8.000**		**2**	**2**
§Jamie Luckhurst	16	82	147.0	9.0	156.0	7.610			
Martin Dixon	**36**	**195**	**351.0**	**17.0**	**368.0**	**7.549**		**1**	**1**
Paul Bentley	**36**	**180**	**221.0**	**34.0**	**255.0**	**5.667**			
Steve Wilcock	**36**	**169**	**182.0**	**39.0**	**221.0**	**5.231**			
Nigel Sparshott	35	163	156.0	26.0	182.0	4.466			
Peter McNamara	10	42	34.0	11.0	45.0	4.286			
Andrew Sumner	15	46	35.0	5.0	40.0	3.478			
Max Schofield	7	22	16.0	3.0	19.0	3.455			
§§David Edwards	14	41	27.0	6.0	33.0	3.220			
Ian Atkinson	2	4	2.0	0.0	2.0	2.000			
§§Duncan Chapman	5	13	0.0	0.0	0.0	0.000			

KNOCK-OUT... 1989 top scorer Daz Sumner and World boxing champion Barry McGuigan

1990...1990...1990...1990...1990...1990

	M	R	Pts	BP	TPts	Ave	F	P	Total
§Rod Hunter	40	205	486.0	23.0	509.0	9.932	8	2	10
Darren Sumner	**40**	**206**	**415.0**	**29.0**	**444.0**	**8.621**	**4**	**1**	**5**
§David Cheshire	**40**	**200**	**334.0**	**37.0**	**371.0**	**7.420**			
Jamie Luckhurst	**33**	**151**	**245.0**	**33.0**	**278.0**	**7.364**		**3**	**3**
Steve Wilcock	38	170	248.0	63.0	311.0	7.318		4	4
Paul Bentley	38	194	294.0	58.0	352.0	7.258			
Max Schofield	1	3	4.0	0.0	4.0	5.333			
Mark Crang	5	17	12.0	4.0	16.0	3.765			
Duncan Chapman	26	85	64.0	13.0	77.0	3.624			
David Edwards	12	34	26.0	3.0	29.0	3.412			
§§Paul Smith	1	4	2.0	0.0	2.0	2.000			
Andy Sumner	3	8	3.0	1.0	4.0	2.000			
§§Martin Jones	3	9	2.0	1.0	3.0	1.333			

EASTER TROPHY

1965	1 George Hunter	2 Dave Younghusband	3 Eric Boocock

STADIUM SILVER HELMET

1968	1 Dave Schofield	2 Tom Leadbitter	3 Mick Handley
1969	1 Geoff Ambrose	2 Maurie Robinson	3 Mark Hall
1970	1 Graeme Smith	2 Taffy Owen	3 Bob Jameson
1971	1 Bruce Forrester	2 Phil Crump	3 Dave Durham
1972	1 John Jackson	2 Dave Durham	3 Bruce Forrester
1973	1 Lou Sansom	2 Peter Reading	3 Bruce Forrester
1974	1 Dave Durham	2 John Jackson	3 Roger Wright
1975	1 Alan Emerson	2 Doug Underwood	3 Tom Owen and Lou Sansom
1976	1 Joe Owen	2 Tom Owen	3 Steve Finch
1977	1 Nigel Close	2 Steve Finch	3 Tom Owen
1978	1 Brian Havelock	2 John McNeill	3 Steve Wilcock
1979	1 Steve Wilcock	2 Bob Humphreys	3 Bob Garrad
1980	1 Steve Wilcock	2 Brian Havelock	3 Steve Lomas
1981	1 Steve Wilcock	2 Mark Courtney	3 Martin Dixon
1985	1 Steve Wilcock	2 Gary Havelock	3 Mark Fiora
1989	1 Darren Sumner	2 Martin Dixon	3 Peter Carr

MIDDLESBROUGH OPEN CHAMPIONSHIP

1968	1 Allan Brown	2 Tom Leadbitter	3 Taffy Owen
1969	1 Terry Lee	2 Geoff Ambrose	3 Maurie Robinson
1970	1 Geoff Maloney	2 Taffy Owen	3 Tim Swales
1971	1 Tim Swales	2 Alan Knapkin	3 John Jackson
1972	1 Phil Crump	2 Arthur Price	3 Ross Dent and Tony Childs
1973	1 Arthur Price	2 Peter Reading	3 Frank Auffret
1974	1 Arthur Browning	2 Bruce Forrester	3 Peter Reading
1975	1 John Jackson	2 Brian Havelock	3 Alan Emerson
1976	1 John Jackson	2 Lou Sansom	3 Tom Owen
1977	1 Alan Emerson	2 Steve Finch	3 John Jackson
1978	1 Mike Sampson	2 Steve Finch	3 Arthur Browning
1979	1 Mike Sampson	2 Steve Finch	3 Tom Owen
1980	1 Mark Courtney	2 Steve Wilcock	3 Mike Sampson

FAREWELL TROPHY

1971	1 Russ Dent	2 Bruce Forrester	3 Malcolm Shakespeare
1972	1 Frank Auffret	2 Russ Dent	3 Peter Reading
1973	1 Frank Auffret	2 Alan Cowland	3 Bruce Forrester
1975	1 Doug Underwood	2 Brian Havelock	3 Graham Jones
1976	1 Pete Smith	2 Andy Cusworth	3 Graham Jones
1977	1 Kelvin Mullarkey	2 Alan Emerson	3 Nigel Close
1979	1 Mark Courtney	2 Brian Havelock	3 Kevin Hawkins
1980	1 Geoff Pusey	2 Brian Havelock	3 Steve Wilcock
1981	1 Mark Courtney	2 Wayne Brown	3 Mike Spink
1983	1 Joe Owen	2 Rod Hunter	3 Brian Havelock
1984	1 Geoff Pusey	2 Paul Price	3 Mike Spink
1985	1 Martin Dixon	2 Geoff Pusey	3 Steve Wilcock

JUBILEE TROPHY

1978	1 Pete Smith	2 Phil Collins	3 Harry MacLean

NORTHERN JUNIOR CHAMPIONSHIP

1978	1 Paul Stead	2 Mike Sanderson	3 Mike Caroline

MIDDLESBROUGH are the only founder members of the 1968 British League Division Two who ran every season in the same League and at the same track – Cleveland Park – until the amalgamation of the two Leagues at the end of the 1990 season.

MILDENHALL

MILDENHALL joined the Second Division in 1975 after operating throughout the winter as a Training track and their initial squad included their own discoveries Paul Clipstone, Paul Gilbert, Fred Mills and Graham Kerry and long distance commuter Chris Julian from Cornwall.

1975...1975...1975...1975...1975...1975

	M	R	Pts	BP	TPts	Ave	F	P	Total
§Bob Coles	36	169	361.5	11.0	372.5	8.817	7	1	8
§§Chris Julian	27	114	181.0	11.0	192.0	6.737			
§Stan Stevens	25	97	126.0	20.0	146.0	6.021			
§John Gibbons	20	81	106.0	14.0	120.0	5.926		1	1
§§Kevin Jolly	**38**	**168**	**208.0**	**34.0**	**242.0**	**5.762**		**1**	**1**
§John McNeill	34	130	141.0	14.0	155.0	4.769			
§Roger Austin	3	11	10.0	2.0	12.0	4.364			
§Roger Pascall	3	5	4.0	1.0	5.0	4.000			
§§Paul Clipstone	16	49	34.0	10.0	44.0	3.592			
§§Paul Gilbert	15	35	27.0	3.0	30.0	3.429			
§§Fred Mills	28	89	53.0	13.0	66.0	2.966			
§§Graham Kerry	6	21	11.0	1.0	12.0	2.286			
§Alan Witt	5	14	8.0	0.0	8.0	2.286			
§§Trevor Harvey	1	3	1.0	0.0	1.0	1.333			

1976...1976...1976...1976...1976...1976

	M	R	Pts	BP	TPts	Ave	F	P	Total
Bob Coles	34	155	348.0	9.0	357.0	9.213	4		4
Kevin Jolly	24	98	195.0	11.0	206.0	8.408	3	1	4
§Trevor Jones	7	33	60.0	5.0	65.0	7.879		1	1
§Alan Cowland	24	93	136.0	9.0	145.0	6.237			
Fred Mills	34	132	152.0	35.0	187.0	5.667			
Stan Stevens	19	60	65.0	12.0	77.0	5.133			
§§Robert Henry	35	121	134.0	15.0	149.0	4.926	1		1
§§Mike Spink	5	14	14.0	3.0	17.0	4.857			
§§Mick Bates	19	59	54.0	17.0	71.0	4.814			
§§Neil Leeks	8	26	22.0	1.0	23.0	3.538			
Paul Clipstone	3	8	2.0	1.0	3.0	1.500			
John McNeill	1	2	0.0	0.0	0.0	0.000			

1977...1977...1977...1977...1977...1977

	M	R	Pts	BP	TPts	Ave	F	P	Total
Bob Coles	37	168	358.0	12.0	370.0	8.810	4	2	6
Trevor Jones	29	109	179.0	13.0	192.0	7.046	1	1	2
Robert Henry	**38**	**158**	**238.0**	**25.0**	**263.0**	**6.658**		**2**	**2**
Mike Spink	13	40	56.0	8.0	64.0	6.400			
Mick Bates	36	137	175.0	38.0	213.0	6.219		1	1
Neil Leeks	34	129	152.0	36.0	188.0	5.829		1	1
John Gibbons	18	65	87.0	5.0	92.0	5.662			
Fred Mills	37	132	152.0	34.0	186.0	5.636			
§§Melvyn Taylor	19	57	58.0	8.0	66.0	4.632			

1978...1978...1978...1978...1978...1978

	M	R	Pts	BP	TPts	Ave	F	P	Total
§Ray Bales	**42**	**179**	**377.0**	**31.0**	**408.0**	**9.117**	**3**	**4**	**7**
Melvyn Taylor	39	160	300.0	34.0	334.0	8.350		2	2
Bob Coles	25	103	209.0	6.0	215.0	8.350	3	1	4
§Paul Gachet	6	26	38.0	8.0	46.0	7.077			
Robert Henry	**42**	**167**	**243.0**	**27.0**	**270.0**	**6.467**		**2**	**2**
Neil Leeks	29	104	129.0	35.0	164.0	6.308		1	1
Mike Spink	39	145	200.0	27.0	227.0	6.262			
Mick Bates	41	137	155.0	31.0	186.0	5.431		1	1
§§Graham Steward	5	14	14.0	4.0	18.0	5.143			
§§Richard Knight	17	51	39.0	16.0	55.0	4.314			
§§Mark Baldwin	2	4	2.0	0.0	2.0	2.000			

1979...1979...1979...1979...1979...1979

	M	R	Pts	BP	TPts	Ave	F	P	Total
Ray Bales	35	143	310.0	30.0	340.0	9.510	2	4	6
§Mick Hines	40	162	344.0	33.0	377.0	9.309	2	6	8
Melvyn Taylor	40	169	358.0	25.0	383.0	9.065	5	2	7
Robert Henry	41	160	326.0	29.0	355.0	8.875	2	3	5
Mike Spink	**42**	**163**	**227.0**	**41.0**	**268.0**	**6.577**	**1**		**1**
Mick Bates	36	123	165.5	35.0	200.5	6.520		1	1
Richard Knight	38	130	147.0	37.0	184.0	5.662			
Mark Baldwin	9	25	26.0	5.0	31.0	4.960			
§§Mark Bilner	6	16	11.0	2.0	13.0	3.250			
§§Andy Warne	2	3	1.0	1.0	2.0	2.667			

1980...1980...1980...1980...1980...1980

	M	R	Pts	BP	TPts	Ave	F	P	Total
Ray Bales	**46**	**190**	**399.0**	**27.0**	**426.0**	**8.968**	**4**	**3**	**7**
Robert Henry	**46**	**193**	**387.0**	**30.0**	**417.0**	**8.642**	**2**	**1**	**3**
Mick Bates	41	161	274.0	32.0	306.0	7.602		1	1
§Ian Gledhill	**46**	**179**	**280.0**	**35.0**	**315.0**	**7.039**	**1**	**2**	**3**
Richard Knight	41	158	193.5	51.0	244.5	6.190			
Andy Warne	25	78	85.0	19.0	104.0	5.333			
Mark Bilner	27	87	101.0	13.0	114.0	5.241			
Mark Baldwin	29	93	88.0	16.0	104.0	4.473			
§§Carl Baldwin	17	51	46.0	11.0	57.0	4.471			
§§Mark Cornish	3	9	8.0	2.0	10.0	4.444			

1981...1981...1981...1981...1981...1981

	M	R	Pts	BP	TPts	Ave	F	P	Total
Robert Henry	42	185	365.5	32.0	397.5	8.595	3	3	6
Ray Bales	43	182	358.0	22.0	380.0	8.352	3	4	7
Mick Bates	38	175	316.0	45.0	361.0	8.251	1	3	4
Ian Gledhill	36	149	276.0	18.0	294.0	7.893	3	4	7
Richard Knight	44	190	299.0	45.0	344.0	7.242		2	2
Carl Baldwin	34	116	102.0	28.0	130.0	4.483			
Andy Warne	37	125	95.0	23.0	118.0	3.776			
Mark Bilner	22	74	57.0	12.0	69.0	3.730			
§§Carl Blackbird	10	26	13.0	5.0	18.0	2.769			

1982...1982...1982...1982...1982...1982

	M	R	Pts	BP	TPts	Ave	F	P	Total
§Derek Harrison	**40**	**198**	**411.0**	**51.0**	**462.0**	**9.333**		**6**	**6**
Ray Bales	39	199	387.0	50.0	437.0	8.784		7	7
Richard Knight	33	164	302.0	39.0	341.0	8.317		3	3
Mick Bates	39	193	322.0	47.0	369.0	7.648	2	1	3
Robert Henry	40	201	326.0	57.0	383.0	7.622		4	4
Carl Baldwin	**40**	**174**	**294.0**	**36.0**	**330.0**	**7.586**		**2**	**2**
Andy Warne	25	84	78.0	16.0	94.0	4.476			
Carl Blackbird	22	64	56.0	15.0	71.0	4.438			
§§Greg DeKok	1	2	0.0	0.0	0.0	0.000			

1983...1983...1983...1983...1983...1983

	M	R	Pts	BP	TPts	Ave	F	P	Total
Derek Harrison	**42**	**217**	**457.0**	**43.0**	**500.0**	**9.217**	**2**	**1**	**3**
Richard Knight	**42**	**220**	**457.0**	**37.0**	**494.0**	**8.982**	**2**	**4**	**6**
Carl Baldwin	39	201	362.0	46.0	408.0	8.119		2	2
Robert Henry	**42**	**220**	**337.0**	**48.0**	**385.0**	**7.000**	**2**	**1**	**3**
Carl Blackbird	39	177	252.0	32.0	284.0	6.418		1	1
§§David Jackson	39	139	143.0	23.0	166.0	4.777			
Andy Warne	28	111	97.0	17.0	114.0	4.108			
§§Chris Felgate	3	9	5.0	1.0	6.0	2.667			
§§Ian Farnham	11	29	16.0	1.0	17.0	2.345			
§Rob Parish	7	20	6.0	3.0	9.0	1.800			

1984...1984...1984...1984...1984...1984

	M	R	Pts	BP	TPts	Ave	F	P	Total
Carl Baldwin	31	133	282.0	21.0	303.0	9.113	2	2	4
Carl Blackbird	**34**	**145**	**312.0**	**13.0**	**325.0**	**8.966**	**6**		**6**
Robert Henry	**34**	**144**	**275.0**	**28.0**	**303.0**	**8.417**		**1**	**1**
Ray Bales	**34**	**141**	**237.0**	**41.0**	**278.0**	**7.887**	**1**	**5**	**6**
David Jackson	32	112	130.0	18.0	148.0	5.286			
§§Wally Hill	26	87	80.0	21.0	101.0	4.644			
§§Nick Doncaster	4	11	9.0	2.0	11.0	4.000			
Rob Parish	17	54	41.0	9.0	50.0	3.704			
Ian Farnham	18	48	29.0	3.0	32.0	2.667			
§Lawrie Bloomfield	1	3	2.0	0.0	2.0	2.667			
§§Richard Green	1	3	2.0	0.0	2.0	2.667			
Chris Felgate	2	5	3.0	0.0	3.0	2.400			

WHEN the Fen Tigers finished runners-up in the 1984 Second Division for the third time in succession they created a new record. No other Second Division team before (or since) had been second three years in a row and the only other side in British League history to have gone so close to winning the title in three successive seasons was First Division Belle Vue who were runners-up in 1974, 1975 and 1976. Coincidentally Mildenhall and Belle Vue both finished second two years later.

MILDENHALL

1985...1985...1985...1985...1985...1985

	M	R	Pts	BP	TPts	Ave	F	P	Total
Carl Blackbird	9	39	92.0	2.0	94.0	9.641	1	1	2
Melvyn Taylor	18	75	140.0	7.0	147.0	7.840	1	1	2
Carl Baldwin	36	156	284.0	21.0	305.0	7.821			
Robert Henry	**37**	**155**	**264.0**	**25.0**	**289.0**	**7.458**		**2**	**2**
§Andy Hines	31	125	213.0	12.0	225.0	7.200	2	1	3
§Robert Hollingworth	27	98	126.0	17.0	143.0	5.837	1		1
David Jackson	33	124	140.0	29.0	169.0	5.452			
Richard Green	34	99	80.0	17.0	97.0	3.919			
Rob Parish	23	70	45.0	12.0	57.0	3.257			
Wally Hill	8	22	11.0	3.0	14.0	2.545			
§§Stuart Thompson	1	2	0.0	0.0	0.0	0.000			

1986...1986...1986...1986...1986...1986

	M	R	Pts	BP	TPts	Ave	F	P	Total
§Dave Jessup	44	193	509.0	7.0	516.0	10.694	16	3	19
Melvyn Taylor	43	184	393.0	26.0	419.0	9.109	4	1	5
§Eric Monaghan	43	177	291.0	46.0	337.0	7.616		3	3
Robert Henry	37	150	228.0	36.0	264.0	7.040	2		2
Richard Green	41	148	162.0	30.0	192.0	5.189			
Rob Parish	**45**	**139**	**125.0**	**16.0**	**141.0**	**4.058**			
§Kelvin Mullarkey	7	30	25.0	3.0	28.0	3.733			
§§Lee Potter	14	34	22.0	4.0	26.0	3.059			
§Gary Reid	4	9	4.0	2.0	6.0	2.667			
§Peter McNamara	4	18	6.0	3.0	9.0	2.000			
§Wayne Dunworth	15	31	9.0	3.0	12.0	1.548			
§Andy Steward	14	34	9.0	3.0	12.0	1.412			

Statistics include match at Long Eaton on Wednesday, June 11, 1986, when the Mildenhall team refused to ride claiming the track was unfit. Subsequently the Speedway Control Board fined the promoting consortium £1,000 with £1,000 costs. All programmed riders and officials were fined as follows: Robert Henry, Dave Jessup and Melvyn Taylor (£250 each), Eric Monaghan, Rob Parish, Richard Green, Wayne Dunworth and team manager Maurice Everett (£200 each). All parties were banned for six montrhs, the penalty suspended for two years.

In the above figures the programmed riders have been credited with an appearance but no rides or points.

1987...1987...1987...1987...1987...1987

	M	R	Pts	BP	TPts	Ave	F	P	Total
Melvyn Taylor	38	170	435.0	6.0	441.0	10.376	10	1	11
Dave Jessup	35	160	382.0	15.0	397.0	9.925	7	2	9
Eric Monaghan	35	154	266.0	38.0	304.0	7.896		3	3
David Jackson	38	170	234.0	39.0	273.0	6.424		1	1
Richard Green	39	157	188.0	44.0	232.0	5.911		1	1
§§Glen Baxter	**40**	**153**	**173.0**	**29.0**	**202.0**	**5.281**			
§§Lee Farthing	36	102	83.0	21.0	104.0	4.078			
Rob Parish	7	20	15.0	2.0	17.0	3.400			
§§Paul Blackbird	2	4	2.0	1.0	3.0	3.000			
§§Mark Blackbird	1	3	0.0	0.0	0.0	0.000			

1988...1988...1988...1988...1988...1988

	M	R	Pts	BP	TPts	Ave	F	P	Total
Melvyn Taylor	32	176	431.0	14.0	445.0	10.114	2	5	7
David Jackson	15	77	132.0	17.0	149.0	7.740			
Andy Hines	**36**	**192**	**312.0**	**28.0**	**340.0**	**7.083**		**1**	**1**
Dave Jessup	1	7	12.0	0.0	12.0	6.857			
Eric Monaghan	35	180	273.0	25.0	298.0	6.622			
Glen Baxter	**36**	**177**	**219.5**	**31.0**	**250.5**	**5.661**			
§Michael Coles	**36**	**174**	**208.0**	**35.0**	**243.0**	**5.586**			
§Kelvin Mullarkey	5	21	12.0	4.0	16.0	3.048			
Paul Blackbird	15	42	24.0	3.0	27.0	2.571			
§§Simon Green	29	92	46.0	13.0	59.0	2.565			
§Paul Evitts	1	4	1.0	0.0	1.0	1.000			
Lee Farthing	6	12	2.0	0.0	2.0	0.667			
§§Colin Thorpe	1	1	0.0	0.0	0.0	0.000			

1989...1989...1989...1989...1989...1989

	M	R	Pts	BP	TPts	Ave	F	P	Total
§§Preben Eriksen	27	146	308.0	16.0	324.0	8.877	1	2	3
§§Peter Glanz	32	177	334.0	19.0	353.0	7.977		1	1
§Malcolm Holloway	12	61	94.0	6.0	100.0	6.557			
§Jamie Habbin	**36**	**187**	**278.0**	**17.0**	**295.0**	**6.310**			
David Jackson	35	174	232.0	42.0	274.0	6.299		1	1
§§Spencer Timmo	12	51	57.0	3.0	60.0	4.706			
§Derrol Keats	28	110	97.0	17.0	114.0	4.145			
§Jonathon Cooper	24	112	72.0	14.0	86.0	3.071			
§§Wayne Bridgeford	24	81	52.0	10.0	62.0	3.062			
§§Wayne Carter	1	2	0.0	0.0	0.0	0.000			
Lee Farthing	1	2	1.0	1.0	2.0	4.000			
§§Mark Jolly	1	2	0.0	0.0	0.0	0.000			
§§Andrew Mountain	3	7	2.0	0.0	2.0	1.143			
Rob Parish	4	10	7.0	4.0	11.0	4.400			
§Rodney Payne	3	12	7.0	1.0	8.0	2.667			
§§Alan Spencer	1	4	0.0	0.0	0.0	0.000			
§John Wainwright	3	8	2.0	1.0	3.0	1.500			

MILDENHALL intended competing in the 1990 National League under the promotion of Skid Parish but they were expelled from the League on March 22, 1990, seven days after the official start to the season because their declared line-up did not reach the 42 point minimum.

They immediately signed Danish international Bo Petersen and appealed to the National League Management Committee but were turned down and had to sit out the season. Even before the decision to expel the club there had been considerable doubt about the track's future as promoter Parish put the club on the market during a troubles winter.

The decision brought to an end a run of 15 successive League seasons during which time the Fen Tigers had won the League once, finished in the top three five times, and appeared in two Knock Out Cup Finals.

But they had also won themselves a reputation of being one of the most troublesome teams on away tracks, mainly through the repeated complaints of their team manager Maurice Everett who had been relieved of his duties before the planned start to 1990.

	SUFFOLK OPEN JUNIOR CHAMPIONSHIP		
1975	1 Robert Henry	2 Gerarde Ellis	3 Phil Garneys
1976	1 Graham Steward	2 Nigel Flatman	3 Richard Knight
1977	1 Graham Davidson	2 Craig Featherby	3 Richard Knight
1978	1 Tim Hunt	2 Mark Baldwin	3 Robert Woodruff
1979	1 Mark Baldwin	2 Linden Warner	3 Andy Warne
1981	1 Phil Vance	2 Steve Bryenton	3 Ian Barney
1982	1 Carl Blackbird	2 Paul Clark	3 Mitchell Baxter
	JOE COBBOLD TROPHY		
1976	1 John Gibbons	2 Carl Askew	3 Colin Cook
1977	1 Bob Coles	2 Steve Finch	3 Robert Henry
1978	1 Gary Guglielmi	2 Ray Bales	3 Steve Wilcock
1979	1 Melvyn Taylor	2 Ray Bales	3 Mick Hines
1981	1 Neil Collins	2 Derek Harrison	3 Mick Hines
1982	1 Carl Baldwin	2 Richard Knight	3 Mike Spink
	PALMER TROPHY		
1978	1 Melvyn Taylor	2 Tom Owen	3 Nicky Allott
1979	1 Melvyn Taylor	2 Nigel Flatman	3 Bob Garrad
1980	1 Bob Garrad	2 Robert Henry	3 Ian Gledhill
1981	1 Ray Bales	2 Wayne Brown	3 Richard Knight
	RTS MARATHON		
1985	1 Jamie Luckhurst	2 David Mullett	3 Robert Henry
	CRM TROPHY		
1986	1 Dave Jessup	2 Eric Monaghan	3 Paul Thorp
1987	1 Melvyn Taylor	2 Richard Green	3 Andy Hines

MILTON KEYNES

1978...1978...1978...1978...1978...1978

	M	R	Pts	BP	TPts	Ave	F	P	Total
§§Bob Humphreys	23	102	262.0	8.0	270.0	10.588	6	2	8
§Derek Harrison	**40**	**167**	**264.0**	**23.0**	**287.0**	**6.874**		**1**	**1**
§Chris Robins	7	27	35.0	9.0	44.0	6.519			
§Andy Grahame	39	164	231.0	22.0	253.0	6.171			
§Malcolm Holloway	34	127	151.0	20.0	171.0	5.386		1	1
§Cliff Anderson	38	137	150.0	19.0	169.0	4.934	1		1
§Phil BASS	30	117	130.0	11.0	141.0	4.821			
§Harry Maclean	38	133	132.0	20.0	152.0	4.571			
§Richard Evans	15	46	30.0	5.0	35.0	3.043			
§§Derek Hole	1	3	1.0	1.0	2.0	2.667			
§§Keith Eastwood	1	2	1.0	0.0	1.0	2.000			
§§Alan Maclean	1	3	1.0	0.0	1.0	1.333			
§Roy Carter	2	4	1.0	0.0	1.0	1.000			
§§Kevin Cox	4	9	2.0	0.0	2.0	0.889			
§§Kevin Pope	1	2	0.0	0.0	0.0	0.000			

1979...1979...1979...1979...1979...1979

	M	R	Pts	BP	TPts	Ave	F	P	Total
Andy Grahame	31	135	303.0	20.0	323.0	9.570	8	1	9
Bob Humphreys	**40**	**183**	**406.0**	**19.0**	**425.0**	**9.290**	**6**	**2**	**8**
Derek Harrison	**40**	**176**	**333.0**	**21.0**	**354.0**	**8.045**	**3**	**1**	**4**
Malcolm Holloway	24	100	134.0	15.0	149.0	5.960	1		1
§David Ashby	30	109	124.0	24.0	148.0	5.431		1	1
§Nigel Sparshott	5	17	16.0	4.0	20.0	4.706			
Harry Maclean	35	116	112.0	16.0	128.0	4.414			
§Mick Conroy	1	2	1.0	1.0	2.0	4.000			
§§Greg McNeill	38	119	95.0	22.0	117.0	3.933			
Chris Robins	23	78	62.0	8.0	70.0	3.590	1		1
Keith Eastwood	4	8	1.0	1.0	2.0	1.000			

ANDY GRAHAME became the first and only rider to qualify for both the First and Second Division Riders' Championship Finals in the same season as the Knights' top-scorer and also as number one in the Birmingham averages. He was third in the NLRC and 15th in the British League Riders' Championship.

1980...1980...1980...1980...1980...1980

	M	R	Pts	BP	TPts	Ave	F	P	Total
Bob Humphreys	39	172	371.0	8.0	379.0	8.814	4	1	5
§Graham Plant	26	101	154.0	6.0	160.0	6.337		1	1
Nigel Sparshott	8	35	51.0	2.0	53.0	6.057			
§Andy Hibbs	33	135	174.0	27.0	201.0	5.956	1		1
§Bert Harkins	37	153	203.0	21.0	224.0	5.856	1		1
§Mick Blaynee	33	123	137.0	37.0	174.0	5.659		1	1
§Barry Allaway	38	133	133.0	21.0	154.0	4.632			
§Nigel Davis	16	51	48.0	8.0	56.0	4.392			
§§Ray Wood	4	12	9.0	3.0	12.0	4.000			
§§Robbie Vigus	18	58	43.0	12.0	55.0	3.793			
§Graham Clifton	11	36	26.0	6.0	32.0	3.556			
Chris Robins	1	3	2.0	0.0	2.0	2.667			
§§Steve Payne	9	24	10.0	3.0	13.0	2.167			
§Barry Etherington	2	3	0.0	0.0	0.0	0.000			

1981...1981...1981...1981...1981...1981

	M	R	Pts	BP	TPts	Ave	F	P	Total
Bob Humphreys	35	161	354.0	14.0	368.0	9.143	1	2	3
§Craig Featherby	1	5	11.0	0.0	11.0	8.800			
§John Barker	1	5	8.0	1.0	9.0	7.200			
Graham Plant	17	69	104.0	6.0	110.0	6.377			
Andy Hibbs	37	160	215.0	25.0	240.0	6.000		1	1
Mick Blaynee	13	47	45.0	11.0	56.0	4.766			
Barry Allaway	35	128	132.0	9.0	141.0	4.406			
§Mark Baldwin	37	134	125.0	21.0	146.0	4.358			
Steve Payne	36	133	118.0	25.0	143.0	4.301			
Nigel Davis	7	20	16.0	5.0	21.0	4.200			
§§Brett Alderton	32	103	88.0	19.0	107.0	4.155			
§§Mark Reeve	3	15	12.0	0.0	12.0	3.200			
Robbie Vigus	1	2	1.0	0.0	1.0	2.000			
§§Paul Turner	2	7	2.0	1.0	3.0	1.714			
§§Bob Kinning	2	5	1.0	0.0	1.0	0.800			
§§Martin Rayner	1	2	0.0	0.0	0.0	0.000			
§§Mark Astley	1	2	0.0	0.0	0.0	0.000			

1982...1982...1982...1982...1982...1982

	M	R	Pts	BP	TPts	Ave	F	P	Total
§Keith White	36	181	343.0	23.0	366.0	8.088	3	1	4
Andy Hibbs	11	51	94.0	8.0	102.0	8.000			
Craig Featherby	35	166	281.0	20.0	301.0	7.253	1		1
Nigel Sparshott	37	203	327.0	30.0	357.0	7.034			
Brett Alderton	2	11	17.0	1.0	18.0	6.545			
Steve Payne	35	178	239.0	41.0	280.0	6.292	1		1
§Tony Featherstone	35	172	211.0	30.0	241.0	5.605			
Paul Clarke	24	102	88.0	16.0	104.0	4.078			
§§Kevin Lock	1	1	1.0	0.0	1.0	4.000			
Mark Reeve	7	23	20.0	1.0	21.0	3.652			
Mark Baldwin	16	62	46.0	9.0	55.0	3.548			
§§Nigel Garrad	1	3	2.0	0.0	2.0	2.667			
§§Tony Abson	6	20	7.0	2.0	9.0	1.800			
§§Mike Hintz	2	7	2.0	1.0	3.0	1.714			
§Kevin Young	1	5	2.0	0.0	2.0	1.600			
§Chris Hunt	2	6	2.0	0.0	2.0	1.333			
§§Adrian Squirrell	1	4	1.0	0.0	1.0	1.000			
§Chris Cole	5	11	1.0	1.0	2.0	0.727			
§§Rob Price	1	4	0.0	0.0	0.0	0.000			
§§Dave Gentry	1	1	0.0	0.0	0.0	0.000			
§§Glen Ratcliffe	1	1	0.0	0.0	0.0	0.000			
§§Robert Wall	1	1	0.0	0.0	0.0	0.000			

1983...1983...1983...1983...1983...1983

	M	R	Pts	BP	TPts	Ave	F	P	Total
Craig Featherby	31	152	313.0	16.0	329.0	8.658	1	1	2
Keith White	**36**	**193**	**395.0**	**18.0**	**413.0**	**8.560**	**2**		2
Steve Payne	13	63	120.0	14.0	134.0	8.508		1	1
§Charlie McKinna	33	176	303.0	42.0	345.0	7.841			
§Craig Pendlebury	5	26	33.0	11.0	44.0	6.769			
§§Chris Pidcock	30	128	167.0	28.0	195.0	6.094			
Paul Clarke	**36**	**175**	**212.5**	**31.0**	**243.5**	**5.566**			
§Dennis Mallett	23	114	115.0	28.0	143.0	5.018			
§Peter Framingham	10	34	36.5	6.0	42.5	5.000			
§§Greg Williamson	3	6	4.0	2.0	6.0	4.000			
§Steve Mildoon	9	23	12.0	4.0	16.0	2.783			
Graham Plant	3	9	4.0	2.0	6.0	2.667			
Robert Wall	9	27	12.0	4.0	16.0	2.370			
Chris Hunt	1	4	0.0	0.0	0.0	0.000			

1984...1984...1984...1984...1984...1984

	M	R	Pts	BP	TPts	Ave	F	P	Total
Keith White	30	129	274.0	11.0	285.0	8.837	4	1	5
§Kevin Smart	15	62	121.0	9.0	130.0	8.387			
§David Blackburn	**32**	**138**	**216.0**	**38.0**	**254.0**	**7.362**		**1**	**1**
Paul Clarke	20	77	114.0	16.0	130.0	6.753		1	1
§Nigel De'ath	31	121	162.0	31.0	193.0	6.380			
Steve Payne	30	114	147.0	21.0	168.0	5.895		1	1
Peter Framingham	31	112	120.0	25.0	145.0	5.179			
Rob Wall	19	72	77.0	12.0	89.0	4.944			
Chris Hunt	9	15	10.0	1.0	11.0	2.933			

1985...1985...1985...1985...1985...1985

	M	R	Pts	BP	TPts	Ave	F	P	Total
Keith White	**38**	**159**	**322.0**	**18.0**	**340.0**	**8.553**	**5**	**3**	**8**
Nigel De'ath	**38**	**168**	**337.0**	**19.0**	**356.0**	**8.476**	**3**	**1**	**4**
§§Gary Tagg	1	1	1.0	1.0	2.0	8.000			
David Blackburn	35	142	199.0	24.0	223.0	6.282	1	1	2
§Derek Richardson	26	101	126.0	24.0	150.0	5.941			
Kevin Smart	**38**	**154**	**189.5**	**30.0**	**219.5**	**5.701**	**1**		**1**
§Mark Chessell	13	49	57.0	11.0	68.0	5.551			
§Ashley Pullen	14	43	39.0	4.0	43.0	4.000			
Rob Wall	24	77	61.0	8.0	69.0	3.584			
§§Peter McNamara	20	60	44.0	9.0	53.0	3.533			
§§Paul Pratt	2	4	2.0	0.0	2.0	2.000			
§§Robbie Price	14	35	14.0	3.0	17.0	1.943			

MILTON KEYNES had the tragic misfortune to lose two young riders in less than 18 months. Australian Brett Alderton died four days after a track crash at King's Lynn on Saturday, April 17, 1982, and Craig Featherby was killed in a heat six track crash during the Knights' National League match at Peterborough on Friday, September 16, 1983.

NATIONAL LEAGUE AVERAGES...NATIONAL LEAGUE AVERAGES...NATIONAL

MILTON KEYNES

1986...1986...1986...1986...1986...1986

	M	R	Pts	BP	TPts	Ave	F	P	Total
Keith White	**39**	**150**	**291.0**	**24.0**	**315.0**	**8.400**	**3**	**4**	**7**
§Trevor Banks	**39**	**162**	**301.0**	**24.0**	**325.0**	**8.025**		**4**	**4**
Kevin Smart	**39**	**162**	**272.0**	**38.0**	**310.0**	**7.654**		**1**	**1**
§Ian Clark	36	145	217.0	18.0	235.0	6.483			
§§Mark Carlson	**39**	**133**	**153.0**	**24.0**	**177.0**	**5.323**			
Derek Richardson	22	70	79.0	14.0	93.0	5.314			
Mark Chessell	32	100	101.0	15.0	116.0	4.640			
§§Peter Lloyd	19	80	79.0	11.0	90.0	4.500			
Paul Pratt	5	10	4.0	1.0	5.0	2.000			
§§Martin Chessell	3	8	2.0	0.0	2.0	1.000			

1987...1987...1987...1987...1987...1987

	M	R	Pts	BP	TPts	Ave	F	P	Total
§§John Bostin	2	7	12.0	4.0	16.0	9.143			
Kevin Smart	31	132	261.0	20.0	281.0	8.515	1	3	4
Trevor Banks	30	134	257.0	27.0	284.0	8.478		2	2
Keith White	11	43	86.0	2.0	88.0	8.186	2		
§Andy Hines	14	55	86.0	14.0	100.0	7.273			
Mark Carlson	**32**	**123**	**186.0**	**28.0**	**214.0**	**6.959**		**2**	**2**
§§Troy Butler	28	116	174.0	24.0	198.0	6.828		1	1
Peter Lloyd	**32**	**114**	**154.0**	**30.0**	**184.0**	**6.456**			
§Keith Millard	2	6	6.0	2.0	8.0	5.333			
Ian Clark	31	103	110.0	21.0	131.0	5.087			
§§Paul Atkins	6	15	7.0	1.0	8.0	2.133			

1988...1988...1988...1988...1988...1988

	M	R	Pts	BP	TPts	Ave	F	P	Total
Troy Butler	28	144	297.0	17.0	314.0	8.722	1	1	2
§Alastair Stevens	11	60	100.0	15.0	115.0	7.667		1	1
§Carl Baldwin	23	114	191.0	23.0	214.0	7.509			
Trevor Banks	31	165	272.0	25.0	297.0	7.200	1	1	2
Peter Lloyd	5	26	34.0	9.0	43.0	6.615		1	1
Ian Clark	27	133	189.0	25.0	214.0	6.436	2		2
Mark Carlson	**32**	**152**	**194.0**	**38.0**	**232.0**	**6.105**		**1**	**1**
§Tony Primmer	15	56	70.0	15.0	85.0	6.071		1	1
Nigel Sparshott	16	82	102.0	13.0	115.0	5.610			
§Jon Cooper	1	4	3.0	2.0	5.0	5.000			
John Bostin	7	22	21.0	5.0	26.0	4.727			
Paul Atkins	12	34	21.0	10.0	31.0	3.647			
§Tony Mattingley	4	11	5.0	2.0	7.0	2.545			
§Trevor Williams	3	11	3.0	0.0	3.0	1.091			
§§Mike Wilson	2	4	0.0	0.0	0.0	0.000			

MILTON KEYNES moved from the Groveway Greyhound Stadium to Elfield Park at the end of 1988. The new venue had previously been used as a training track by the Knights' Australian skipper Bob Humphreys.

1989...1989...1989...1989...1989...1989

	M	R	Pts	BP	TPts	Ave	F	P	Total
§Andy Hines	34	195	313.0	16.0	329.0	6.749			
Trevor Banks	31	172	251.0	22.0	273.0	6.349			
§David Clarke	19	92	118.0	19.0	137.0	5.957			
Tony Primmer	26	124	153.0	31.0	184.0	5.935			
Nigel De'ath	29	145	196.0	17.0	213.0	5.876			
§Mark Lyndon	33	153	176.0	33.0	209.0	5.464			
§Paul Evitts	11	44	47.0	6.0	53.0	4.818			
Paul Atkins	24	92	87.0	18.0	105.0	4.565			
§Rob Fortune	13	68	69.0	7.0	76.0	4.471			
Carl Baldwin	10	44	37.0	8.0	45.0	4.091			
§§Glenn Allan	7	16	3.0	2.0	5.0	1.250			
§Mark Fordham	2	2	0.0	0.0	0.0	0.000			
Mike Wilson	4	6	1.0	0.0	1.0	0.667			

1990...1990...1990...1990...1990...1990

	M	R	Pts	BP	TPts	Ave	F	P	Total
§Kevin Jolly	35	177	290.0	32.0	322.0	7.277			
§Peter Glanz	34	184	309.0	24.0	333.0	7.239			
Jon Cooper	8	38	47.0	10.0	57.0	6.000			
§Mark Blackbird	27	142	182.0	14.0	196.0	5.521			
David Clarke	28	144	171.0	26.0	197.0	5.472			
Trevor Banks	14	69	86.0	8.0	94.0	5.449			
Mark Lyndon	17	72	86.0	10.0	96.0	5.333			
Andy Hines	30	136	145.0	26.0	171.0	5.029			
§Rob Woffinden	8	34	37.0	2.0	39.0	4.588			
§Thierry Hilaire	27	102	83.0	11.0	94.0	3.686			
§§Kieran McCullagh	6	16	7.0	3.0	10.0	2.500			
Paul Atkins	5	13	8.0	0.0	8.0	2.462			
§§Glenn Allan	7	16	3.0	2.0	5.0	1.250			
§§Peter Byrne	5	10	2.0	0.0	2.0	0.800			
§Michael Howe	4	11	1.0	0.0	1.0	0.364			
Rob Fortune	2	5	0.0	0.0	0.0	0.000			

KNIGHT OF THE TRACK CLASSIC

1978	1 Bob Humphreys	2 Bert Harkins	3 George Hunter
1979	1 Bob Garrad	2 Derek Harrison	3 Tom Owen

SWORD OF HONOUR

1978	1 Mike Sampson	2 Tom Owen	3 Bob Coles
1979	1 Bob Humphreys	2 Mike Sampson	3 Tom Owen
1980	1 Bob Humphreys	2 Mike Ferreira	3 Robert Henry

BRETT ALDERTON MEMORIAL TROPHY

1982	1 Bo Petersen	2 Kenny Carter	3 Hans Nielsen
1985	1 Carl Blackbird	2 Barry Thomas	3 Dave Perks
1987	1 Trevor Banks	2 Martin Dugard	3 Andrew Silver
1988	1 Mark Loram	2 Nigel De'ath	3 Nigel Sparshott
1990	1 Paul Blackbird	2 Robert Ledwith	3 Kieran McCullagh

CRAIG FEATHERBY MEMORIAL

1983	1 Kenny Carter	2 Bo Petersen	3 Simon Wigg
1984	1 Keith White	2 Carl Blackbird	3 Dave Perks and Carl Baldwin
1985	1 Neil Middleditch	2 Jamie Luckhurst	3 Martin Goodwin
1986	1 Alastair Stevens	2 Andrew Silver	3 Nigel De'ath
1988	1 Andy Galvin	2 Troy Butler	3 Steve Regeling
1989	1 Les Collins	2 Rob Tilbury	3 Andy Galvin
1990	1 Steve Regeling	2 Steve Schofield	3 Peter Glanz

NATIONAL JUNIOR LEAGUE CHAMPIONSHIP

1987	1 John Bostin	2 Kevin Pitts	3 Mick May

ROTARY CLUB CHARITY CHAMPIONSHIP

1988	1 Mark Loram	2 Trevor Banks	3 Mick Poole

ANDY HINES TESTIMONIAL

1989	1 Troy Butler	2 Jeremy Doncaster	3 Alan Grahame

READY-TEDDY-GO...Derek Harrison was a popular Knight until injury ended his racing career

NELSON

■ *NEW ZEALANDER Gordon 'Goog' Allan – whose son Gary was to join Poole some years later – celebrated the opening of a new track at the Lancashire cotton town of Nelson by winning the Olympiad on Saturday, August 5, 1967, with a 15 point maximum.*

■ *And promoter Mike Parker was satisfied enough with crowds for five open meetings (three wins against B sides from Wolverhampton, Sheffield and Glasgow) to enter the 1968 Second Division.*

■ *But, sadly, the track, backing onto the cricket field where West Indian Learie Constantine had been the club professional, closed down on June 20, 1970, and the League team moved across the Pennines to Bradford's Odsal Stadium for the remainder of the season. A Motorway now runs across the old site of the track.*

1968...1968...1968...1968...1968...1968

	M	R	Pts	BP	TPts	Ave	F	P	Total
§§Dave Schofield	**19**	**83**	**178.0**	**20.0**	**198.0**	**9.542**	**2**	**5**	**7**
§§Alan Paynter	7	29	60.0	6.0	66.0	9.103		3	3
§§Murray Burt	15	63	131.0	7.0	138.0	8.762	2	2	4
§§Gary Peterson	14	56	109.0	5.0	114.0	8.143	1		1
§§Fred Powell	4	16	30.0	2.0	32.0	8.000			
§§Terry Shearer	7	29	47.0	2.0	49.0	6.759		1	1
§§Dave Beacon	13	49	59.0	12.0	71.0	5.[illegible]96			
§§Jack Winstanley	12	45	53.0	9.0	62.0	5.[illegible]11			
§§Alan Knapkin	6	17	16.0	6.0	22.0	5.176			
§§Arthur Price	1	4	4.0	1.0	5.0	5.000			
§§Jack Lee	4	17	16.0	5.0	21.0	4.9[illegible]1			
§§Paul Sharples	17	54	47.0	9.0	56.0	4.148			
§§Laszlo Munkasci	4	15	13.0	2.0	15.0	4.000			
§§Sid Sheldrick	1	2	2.0	0.0	2.0	4.000			
§§Ian Terrar	1	3	1.0	0.0	1.0	1.333			
§§Gerry Birtwell	5	10	1.0	0.0	1.0	0.400			

1969...1969...1969...1969...1969...1969

	M	R	Pts	BP	TPts	Ave	F	P	Total
Gary Peterson	4	17	41.0	0.0	41.0	9.647	1		1
Dave Schofield	24	99	191.0	7.0	198.0	8.000	1		1
Murray Burt	11	45	88.0	2.0	90.0	8.000			
Alan Knapkin	29	126	214.5	14.0	228.5	7.254	3		3
§§Chris Baybutt	4	12	19.0	2.0	21.0	7.000			
§Stuart Riley	22	77	91.0	19.0	110.0	5.714		1	1
Sid Sheldrick	28	100	115.0	14.0	129.0	5.160	1		1
§Dai Evans	16	69	69.0	11.0	80.0	4.638			
§Peter Thompson	16	56	47.0	13.0	60.0	4.286			
Paul Sharples	14	49	38.0	2.0	40.0	3.265			
§§John Lynch	2	7	4.0	1.0	5.0	2.857			
Jack Lee	21	58	35.0	5.0	40.0	2.759			
Dave Beacon	8	24	10.0	1.0	11.0	1.833			
§§Norman Truman	1	2	0.0	0.0	0.0	0.000			

1970...1970...1970...1970...1970...1970

	M	R	Pts	BP	TPts	Ave	F	P	Total
§BGary Peterson	22	94	250.0	3.0	253.0	10.766	11	1	12
§§N§BAlf Wells	21	79	171.0	13.0	184.0	9.316	2	4	6
§BAlan Knapkin	28	131	293.0	11.0	304.0	9.282	5	3	8
§BDave Schofield	32	132	168.0	35.0	203.0	6.152		4	4
§BSid Sheldrick	29	108	132.0	28.0	160.0	5.926		2	2
§NBAlan Bridgett	29	121	154.0	23.0	177.0	5.851	1	2	3
§NStuart Riley	1	3	3.0	1.0	4.0	5.333			
§BPeter Thompson	16	49	55.0	9.0	64.0	5.224			
§§N§BRobin Adlington	19	79	74.0	12.0	86.0	4.354			
§BJack Lee	2	6	3.0	0.0	3.0	2.000			
§BJohn Lynch	1	4	2.0	0.0	2.0	2.000			
§§BAlan Druggett	1	3	1.0	0.0	1.0	1.333			
§§BMick Fairbairn	1	3	1.0	0.0	1.0	1.333			
§§BBarry Fitzgerald	3	7	2.0	0.0	2.0	1.143			
§§BStan Holey	1	2	0.0	0.0	0.0	0.000			

THE SEED HILL TROPHY

1967	1 Bruce Cribb	2 John Dews	3 Mick Handley

NELSON TROPHY

1968	1 John Poyser	2 Murray Burt	3 Terry Lee

NELSON'S Murray Burt and Middlesbrough's Tom Leadbitter share a joke before facing each other on track

NEWCASTLE

■ *AFTER a four season absence speedway returned to Newcastle's Brough Park Stadium under the control of promoter Ian Thomas and Brian Larner and they quickly built a National League team around the Owen brothers.*

1975...1975...1975...1975...1975...1975

	M	R	Pts	BP	TPts	Ave	F	P	Total
§Tom Owen	47	199	507.0	23.0	530.0	10.653	11	8	19
§Joe Owen	44	187	491.0	7.0	498.0	10.652	21		21
§Brian Havelock	41	166	254.0	25.0	279.0	6.723		1	1
§§Ron Hendersen	46	179	215.0	45.0	260.0	5.810		2	2
§Mike Watkin	37	126	146.0	30.0	176.0	5.587		1	1
§Robbie Blackadder	35	124	140.0	29.0	169.0	5.452			
§Tim Swales	39	140	155.0	28.0	183.0	5.229			
§§Phil Michelides	36	126	133.0	26.0	159.0	5.048			
§John Robson	4	13	7.0	1.0	8.0	2.462			
§Tony Boyle	1	2	0.0	0.0	0.0	0.000			

1976...1976...1976...1976...1976...1976

	M	R	Pts	BP	TPts	Ave	F	P	Total
Joe Owen	39	167	482.0	0.0	482.0	11.545	28		28
Tom Owen	**42**	**176**	**432.0**	**27.0**	**459.0**	**10.432**	**9**	**7**	**16**
Ron Henderson	27	109	196.0	31.0	227.0	8.330		6	6
Phil Michelides	40	158	252.0	46.0	298.0	7.544		2	2
Brian Havelock	10	41	65.0	12.0	77.0	7.512			
§Andy Cusworth	**42**	**174**	**279.0**	**43.0**	**322.0**	**7.402**	**2**	**2**	**4**
Robbie Blackadder	36	120	149.0	37.0	186.0	6.200			
Tim Swales	34	111	133.0	31.0	164.0	5.910			
§§Greg Clarke	1	3	1.0	1.0	2.0	2.667			
Martin Cusworth	2	5	2.0	0.0	2.0	1.600			
§Malcolm Davies	3	9	1.0	0.0	1.0	0.444			
§§Gerarde Ellis	4	11	1.0	0.0	1.0	0.364			
Robin Dixon	5	13	1.0	0.0	1.0	0.308			

1977...1977...1977...1977...1977...1977

	M	R	Pts	BP	TPts	Ave	F	P	Total
Tom Owen	39	190	504.0	10.0	514.0	10.821	13	6	19
Robbie Blackadder	33	137	259.0	36.0	295.0	8.613	1	1	2
Ron Henderson	17	71	130.0	7.0	137.0	7.718	2	1	3
§Phil Kynman	38	175	289.0	27.0	316.0	7.223		3	3
§Robbie Gardner	36	155	212.0	34.0	246.0	6.348		1	1
§§Neil Coddington	18	72	75.0	16.0	91.0	5.056			
Phil Michelides	28	96	98.0	16.0	114.0	4.750			
§Eddie Argall	11	37	37.0	4.0	41.0	4.432			
§Taffy Owen	3	10	8.0	1.0	9.0	3.600			
§Robert Maxfield	10	36	21.0	4.0	25.0	2.778			
Robin Dixon	10	31	16.0	1.0	17.0	2.194			
§§Nigel Crabtree	13	30	9.0	2.0	11.0	1.467			
§§Mark Bullivant	1	5	1.0	0.0	1.0	0.800			
§§Chris Prime	2	3	0.0	0.0	0.0	0.000			

1978...1978...1978...1978...1978...1978

	M	R	Pts	BP	TPts	Ave	F	P	Total
Tom Owen	38	169	450.0	7.0	457.0	10.817	12	3	15
Robbie Blackadder	32	120	259.0	14.0	273.0	9.100	2	3	5
§§Kenny Carter	41	181	296.0	47.0	343.0	7.580	1	5	6
Robbie Gardner	39	159	261.0	33.0	294.0	7.396	1	5	6
§Graeme Stapleton	37	155	212.0	42.0	254.0	6.555		2	2
§§Kevin McDonald	3	11	15.0	3.0	18.0	6.545			
§§Rod Hunter	38	151	219.0	28.0	247.0	6.543		1	1
§§David Bargh	5	12	15.0	0.0	15.0	5.000			
Robert Maxfield	3	12	10.0	3.0	13.0	4.333			
Neil Coddington	34	97	86.0	15.0	101.0	4.165		1	1
Nigel Crabtree	9	27	18.0	6.0	24.0	3.556			
Chris Prime	1	1	0.0	0.0	0.0	0.000			

1979...1979...1979...1979...1979...1979

	M	R	Pts	BP	TPts	Ave	F	P	Total
Tom Owen	30	146	400.0	8.0	408.0	11.178	16	1	17
Robbie Blackadder	37	168	315.0	18.0	333.0	7.929	1	1	2
Rod Hunter	**42**	**200**	**364.0**	**29.0**	**393.0**	**7.860**	**1**	**4**	**5**
Graeme Stapleton	32	140	197.0	33.0	230.0	6.571		1	1
David Bargh	**42**	**161**	**202.0**	**36.0**	**238.0**	**5.913**			
Neil Coddington	31	121	145.0	29.0	174.0	5.752			
Nigel Crabtree	34	116	110.0	27.0	137.0	4.724			
§§Paul Brown	9	21	7.0	3.0	10.0	1.905			
§§Michael Easton	8	25	8.0	2.0	10.0	1.600			

1980...1980...1980...1980...1980...1980

	M	R	Pts	BP	TPts	Ave	F	P	Total
Tom Owen	2	8	23.0	0.0	23.0	11.500	1		1
Rod Hunter	**40**	**188**	**398.0**	**38.0**	**436.0**	**9.277**	**1**	**4**	**5**
Robbie Blackadder	39	170	330.0	33.0	363.0	8.541	4	2	6
David Bargh	**40**	**190**	**350.0**	**45.0**	**395.0**	**8.316**	**2**	**2**	**4**
§Derek Richardson	39	176	288.0	47.0	335.0	7.614		1	1
Nigel Crabtree	**40**	**139**	**170.0**	**56.0**	**226.0**	**6.504**	**1**	**1**	**2**
§Keith Bloxsome	**40**	**148**	**212.0**	**28.0**	**240.0**	**6.486**	**1**		**1**
Paul Brown	7	17	8.0	4.0	12.0	2.824			
Michael Easton	2	5	2.0	1.0	3.0	2.400			

1981...1981...1981...1981...1981...1981

	M	R	Pts	BP	TPts	Ave	F	P	Total
David Bargh	35	160	340.5	21.0	361.5	9.038	5	1	6
Derek Richardson	1	4	6.0	3.0	9.0	9.000			
Rod Hunter	**39**	**170**	**336.0**	**33.0**	**369.0**	**8.682**	**7**	**3**	**10**
Robbie Blackadder	38	140	273.0	21.0	294.0	8.400	4	1	5
§Alan Emerson	**39**	**171**	**294.0**	**51.0**	**345.0**	**8.070**	**1**	**5**	**6**
Keith Bloxsome	**39**	**166**	**253.0**	**32.0**	**285.0**	**6.867**			
§Glenn McDonald	**39**	**135**	**151.0**	**36.0**	**187.0**	**5.541**			
Tom Owen	1	3	2.0	2.0	4.0	5.333			
§§Kym Mauger	25	67	39.0	10.0	49.0	2.925			
§§Paul McHale	5	12	5.0	2.0	7.0	2.333			
§§Dennis Gallagher	3	6	1.0	1.0	2.0	1.333			

1982...1982...1982...1982...1982...1982

	M	R	Pts	BP	TPts	Ave	F	P	Total
Joe Owen	42	211	569.0	12.0	581.0	11.014	13	2	15
Rod Hunter	40	198	473.0	28.0	501.0	10.121	5	3	8
§§Bobby Beaton	**43**	**225**	**449.0**	**58.0**	**507.0**	**9.013**		**4**	**4**
Alan Emerson	40	191	293.0	80.0	373.0	7.812		1	1
Keith Bloxsome	**43**	**215**	**337.0**	**58.0**	**395.0**	**7.349**		**3**	**3**
Tom Owen	43	210	310.0	64.0	374.0	7.124	1	3	4
Kym Mauger	3	16	15.0	2.0	17.0	4.250			
§§Robbie Foy	33	80	55.0	18.0	73.0	3.650			
§§Barry Shearer	8	19	5.0	2.0	7.0	1.474			
§§Richard Newnham	1	3	0.0	0.0	0.0	0.000			
§§Gary Riddell	1	3	0.0	0.0	0.0	0.000			

1983...1983...1983...1983...1983...1983

	M	R	Pts	BP	TPts	Ave	F	P	Total
Joe Owen	**40**	**217**	**595.0**	**7.0**	**602.0**	**11.097**	**15**	**5**	**20**
Rod Hunter	**40**	**217**	**548.0**	**22.0**	**570.0**	**10.507**	**7**	**6**	**13**
Bobby Beaton	28	142	332.0	30.0	362.0	10.197	3	4	7
Alan Emerson	35	175	242.0	73.0	315.0	7.200		2	2
§John Place	1	4	5.0	2.0	7.0	7.000			
§§Clayton Isbel	1	2	2.0	1.0	3.0	6.000			
§§Martin Scarisbrick	25	131	163.0	25.0	188.0	5.740			
§§Steven Duckworth	2	5	3.0	2.0	5.0	4.000			
§Bernie Collier	21	91	78.0	4.0	82.0	3.604			
§David Walsh	4	18	12.0	4.0	16.0	3.556			
§§David Wild	11	42	27.0	5.0	32.0	3.048			
Gary Riddell	3	9	4.0	2.0	6.0	2.667			
§§Lawrie Bloomfield	6	27	15.0	2.0	17.0	2.519			
Paul McHale	14	55	33.0	1.0	34.0	2.473			
§§Neil Barnsley	23	100	36.0	9.0	45.0	1.800			
§§Chris Pailor	3	7	2.0	1.0	3.0	1.714			
§Greg DeKok	9	27	10.0	1.0	11.0	1.630			
§§Kenny Young	2	7	1.0	0.0	1.0	0.571			
§§Andy Nightingale	1	2	0.0	0.0	0.0	0.000			
§§Phil Ranson	1	1	0.0	0.0	0.0	0.000			

■*SUCCESSIVE National League championship victories in 1982 and 1983 tempted the Brough Park management to join several other new clubs in the 1984 British League.*

It was to be a disastrous decision as the Diamonds retained the cream of their Division Two squad but still finished bottom of the League and were forced into eventual closure.

See also Newcastle, Division One averages

NEWCASTLE

■ *NEWCASTLE returned to National League racing, after a dormant year, with new promoter John Turner virtually moving the 1985 Long Eaton side to Brough Park.*

1986...1986...1986...1986...1986...1986

	M	R	Pts	BP	TPts	Ave	F	P	Total
§Dave Morton	**42**	**174**	**340.5**	**18.0**	**358.5**	**8.241**	**1**	**1**	**2**
§Paul Stead	41	176	316.0	12.0	328.0	7.455	1	2	3
§David Blackburn	**42**	**186**	**298.0**	**31.0**	**329.0**	**7.075**		**1**	**1**
§Dave Perks	41	157	201.0	45.0	246.0	6.268	2		2
§Gary O'Hare	**42**	**166**	**219.0**	**28.0**	**247.0**	**5.952**	**1**	**1**	**2**
Bernie Collier	**42**	**131**	**126.0**	**28.0**	**154.0**	**4.702**		**1**	**1**
§Paul Cooper	17	47	36.0	15.0	51.0	4.340			
Keith Bloxsome	11	32	17.0	2.0	19.0	2.375			
§§Derrol Keats	1	4	2.0	0.0	2.0	2.000			
§§Steve Wicks	10	22	9.0	2.0	11.0	2.000			
§§Mark Ferry	3	8	2.0	0.0	2.0	1.000			

1987...1987...1987...1987...1970...1987

	M	R	Pts	BP	TPts	Ave	F	P	Total
David Blackburn	**32**	**142**	**283.0**	**33.0**	**316.0**	**8.901**	**2**	**2**	**4**
Tom Owen	24	99	166.0	15.0	181.0	7.313			
Dave Morton	**32**	**139**	**236.0**	**15.0**	**251.0**	**7.223**	**1**	**1**	**2**
§Mark Courtney	27	107	174.0	18.0	192.0	7.178			
Gary O'Hare	31	121	146.0	18.0	164.0	5.421			
§§Shane Bowes	29	121	121.0	21.0	142.0	4.694			
Bernie Collier	20	60	58.0	12.0	70.0	4.667			
Steve Wicks	5	10	7.0	1.0	8.0	3.200			
§§Paul Bentley	5	12	6.0	2.0	8.0	2.667			
Bobby Duncan	1	2	1.0	0.0	1.0	2.000			
Paul Cooper	10	26	10.0	1.0	11.0	1.692			
§Roland Tebbs	5	12	3.0	2.0	5.0	1.667			

NEWCASTLE fans, bred on the success of the Thomas-Larner years, turned their back on the Diamonds as they settled into a comfortable mid-table position and it was no surprise when they announced their decision not to compete in the 1988 National League.

1989...1989...1989...1989...1989...1989

	M	R	Pts	BP	TPts	Ave	F	P	Total
Rod Hunter	35	195	439.0	7.0	446.0	9.149	3		3
§Peter Carr	35	193	409.0	9.0	418.0	8.663		1	1
§§David Clarke	17	86	106.0	11.0	117.0	5.442			
§§Mark Thorpe	**36**	**175**	**199.0**	**27.0**	**226.0**	**5.166**			
§Simon Green	29	131	138.0	11.0	149.0	4.550			
Derek Richardson	27	120	108.0	23.0	131.0	4.367			
§§Bryan Larner	3	9	7.0	1.0	8.0	3.556			
§Gordon Whitaker	16	59	40.0	10.0	50.0	3.390			
§§Anthony Hulme	25	97	61.0	12.0	73.0	3.010			
Steve Wicks	12	38	18.0	5.0	23.0	2.421			
Bernie Collier	6	24	11.0	1.0	12.0	2.000			
§§Derek Green	4	16	4.0	3.0	7.0	1.750			
§§Phil Daley	3	8	1.0	0.0	1.0	0.500			
§§Roland Pollard	1	2	0.0	0.0	0.0	0.000			

1990...1990...1990...1990...1990...1990

	M	R	Pts	BP	TPts	Ave	F	P	Total
David Bargh	32	170	406.0	7.0	413.0	9.718	6		6
Peter Carr	35	185	370.0	16.0	386.0	8.346	1	2	3
§Martin Dixon	31	160	264.0	32.0	296.0	7.400			
Simon Green	34	177	227.0	37.0	264.0	5.966			
Mark Thorpe	33	155	179.0	29.0	208.0	5.368			
§Ian Stead	18	66	63.0	10.0	73.0	4.424			
§§Jack Stevens	1	3	2.0	1.0	3.0	4.000			
§Paul Smith	34	148	125.0	21.0	146.0	3.946			
Gordon Whitaker	1	3	2.0	0.0	2.0	2.667			
§Spencer Timmo	15	43	24.0	4.0	28.0	2.605			
§John Wainwright	13	39	19.0	5.0	24.0	2.462			
Steve Wicks	2	6	2.0	1.0	3.0	2.000			

GOLDEN JUBILEE

1979 1 Tom Owen 2 Ivan Mauger 3 Peter Collins

TYNE TEES TELEVISION TROPHY

1980 1 Wayne Brown 2 Mike Ferreira 3 Rod Hunter

TYNE TEES TELEVISION CLASSIC

1983 1 Joe Owen 2 Steve McDermott 3 Jim McMillan

CHRIS PRIME MEMORIAL TROPHY

1989 1 Duncan Chapman 2 Jon Roberts 3 Derek Green

See also Newcastle, Division One Averages

NEWPORT

WHEN the nucleus of the 1976 Newport British League side was moved across the Severn Bridge for the opening of speedway at Bristol's Eastville Stadium the Somerton Park promoters Wally Mawdsley and Pat Tapson decided to gamble on introducing Second Division racing to Wales.

They retained Brian Woodward as a spearhead and built up an attractive looking side with the signing of the talented Jim Brett and New Zealand international John Goodall.

But operating on the same race-night as Bristol (a Friday), it was a losing battle for manager Maurice Morley as a high percentage of the Newport fans decided to travel across the Bristol Channel to support their former heroes Phil Crump, Phil Herne, Steve Gresham and Tormod Langli in the new red, white and blue colours of the Bulldogs.

It was, therefore, no great surprise when the announcement came that speedway would end at the Gwent track once the domestic season was over.

Since then there have been a number of vain attempts to revive the sport at Somerton Park but redevelopment work to satisfy soccer safety standards saw the old track built on at one end and that appeared to deter any prospective promoters – including former announcer Gareth Rogers – from pursuing their interest beyond the inquiry stage.

1977...1977...1977...1977...1977...1977

	M	R	Pts	BP	TPts	Ave	F	P	Total
§Jim Brett	25	105	218.0	14.0	232.0	8.838			
§Brian Woodward	35	155	310.0	12.0	322.0	8.310	7		7
§John Goodall	32	144	256.0	18.0	274.0	7.611	2	2	4
§Mike Broadbank	30	122	167.0	32.0	199.0	6.525		1	1
§Cliff Anderson	35	140	154.0	30.0	184.0	5.257			
§Chris Robins	26	102	115.0	17.0	132.0	5.176	1		1
§§Malcolm Bedkober	20	68	74.0	11.0	85.0	5.000			
§§John Williams (Aus)	1	4	2.0	2.0	4.0	4.000			
§Terry Casserly	4	14	9.0	3.0	12.0	3.429			
§Dave Shepherd	25	75	45.0	9.0	54.0	2.880			
§Steve Casey	6	13	9.0	0.0	9.0	2.769			
§Tony Childs	3	9	6.0	0.0	6.0	2.667			
§§Rob Hamman	5	21	8.0	3.0	11.0	2.095			
§§Tony Garard	4	11	3.0	1.0	4.0	1.455			

OXFORD

■ *BOB DUGARD moved Oxford's British League franchise to London White City at the beginning of 1976 and opened the way for new promoters Harry Bastable and Tony Allsop to introduce National League racing to Cowley.*

1976...1976...1976...1976...1976...1976

	M	R	Pts	BP	TPts	Ave	F	P	Total
§Carl Askew	39	153	279.0	28.0	307.0	8.026		5	5
§§Brian Leonard	39	150	251.0	24.0	275.0	7.333	1	2	3
§Phil Bass	38	153	238.0	35.0	273.0	7.137		3	3
§Mick Handley	33	123	202.0	14.0	216.0	7.024			
§Malcolm Corradine	16	61	86.0	7.0	93.0	6.098			
§§Pip Lamb	2	4	4.0	2.0	6.0	6.000			
§Roy Sizmore	34	111	137.0	27.0	164.0	5.910			
§Jim Wells	25	83	108.0	14.0	122.0	5.880		2	2
§Kevin Young	35	131	150.0	29.0	179.0	5.466			
§Harry Maclean	5	17	17.0	2.0	19.0	4.471			
§Steve Holden	9	26	20.0	4.0	24.0	3.692			
§Colin Meredith	2	7	4.0	0.0	4.0	2.286			

1977...1977...1977...1977...1977...1977

	M	R	Pts	BP	TPts	Ave	F	P	Total
§Martin Yeates	43	187	479.5	13.0	492.5	10.535	12	4	16
Phil Bass	43	175	284.0	28.0	312.0	7.131		3	3
Kevin Young	32	132	203.0	22.0	225.0	6.818	1	2	3
Colin Meredith	39	149	221.0	29.0	250.0	6.711		1	1
Brian Leonard	10	38	56.0	6.0	62.0	6.526			
Mick Handley	38	148	185.0	37.0	222.0	6.000	1	1	2
§§Malcolm Holloway	11	40	49.0	10.0	59.0	5.900			
Pip Lamb	39	142	148.0	29.0	177.0	4.986		1	1
§Gerald Smitherman	16	48	39.0	7.0	46.0	3.833			
§Paul Share	2	8	5.0	2.0	7.0	3.500			
§§Richie Caulwell	18	52	36.0	7.0	43.0	3.308			
Roy Sizmore	3	9	3.0	1.0	4.0	1.778			
§§Greg Joynt	3	8	1.0	1.0	2.0	1.000			
§§Kevin Poole	2	4	0.0	0.0	0.0	0.000			

1978...1978...1978...1978...1978...1978

	M	R	Pts	BP	TPts	Ave	F	P	Total
§§George Hunter	41	172	381.0	29.0	410.0	9.535	3	7	10
§§David Shields	42	171	353.0	21.0	374.0	8.749	4	2	6
§John Hack	36	139	210.0	46.0	256.0	7.367		2	2
Carl Askew	**44**	**170**	**251.0**	**50.0**	**301.0**	**7.082**	**1**	**4**	**5**
Colin Meredith	36	134	194.0	36.0	230.0	6.866			
Pip Lamb	**44**	**180**	**250.5**	**37.0**	**287.5**	**6.389**			
§James Moore	23	75	89.0	20.0	109.0	5.813			
Mick Handley	18	49	54.0	13.0	67.0	5.469		1	1
§§Les Sawyer	12	38	28.0	3.0	31.0	3.263			
Brian Leonard	2	7	3.0	2.0	5.0	2.857			
§§John Homer	3	5	2.0	1.0	3.0	2.400			
§§Mick Blaynee	1	3	1.0	0.0	1.0	1.333			

1979...1979...1979...1979...1979...1979

	M	R	Pts	BP	TPts	Ave	F	P	Total
George Hunter	32	133	345.0	16.0	361.0	10.857	7	5	2
§Les Rumsey	**40**	**186**	**440.0**	**15.0**	**455.0**	**9.785**	**8**	**4**	**4**
Pip Lamb	11	44	89.0	13.0	102.0	9.273		1	1
John Hack	33	141	206.0	34.0	240.0	6.809	1		1
Carl Askew	**40**	**174**	**248.0**	**40.0**	**288.0**	**6.621**		**1**	**1**
§John Barker	36	133	184.0	31.0	215.0	6.466		1	1
Mick Handley	31	112	127.0	22.0	149.0	5.321		1	1
§§John Grahame	1	3	3.0	0.0	3.0	4.000			
§Colin Ackroyd	13	47	33.0	4.0	37.0	3.149			
§Rob Dole	7	20	12.0	1.0	13.0	2.600			
Colin Meredith	5	17	8.0	1.0	9.0	2.118			
§Keith Chapman	5	11	3.0	1.0	4.0	1.455			
§§Denzil Kent	2	6	1.0	1.0	2.0	1.333			

SUPER NATIONAL

1976 1 Les Collins — 2 Ted Hubbard — 3 Colin Richardson
1977 1 Martin Yeates — 2 Phil Collins — 3 Laurie Etheridge

OXFORD STADIUM TROPHY

1978 1 Steve Koppe — 2 Melvyn Taylor — 3 James Moore

See also Oxford, Division One Averages

1980...1980...1980...1980...1980...1980

	M	R	Pts	BP	TPts	Ave	F	P	Total
§Dave Perks	23	95	256.0	1.0	257.0	10.821	10	1	11
§Derek Harrison	34	150	314.0	14.0	328.0	8.747	3		3
§§Bruce Cribb	9	48	82.0	7.0	89.0	7.417			
John Hack	24	99	160.0	10.0	170.0	6.869	1		1
Colin Ackroyd	**42**	**183**	**226.0**	**31.0**	**257.0**	**5.617**	**1**		**1**
§Trevor Geer	6	30	35.0	4.0	39.0	5.200			
§§Steve Crockett	39	148	147.0	26.0	173.0	4.676	1		1
Mick Fletcher	30	100	92.0	17.0	109.0	4.360			
§Kevin Bowen	21	69	65.0	9.0	74.0	4.290			
Mick Handley	18	65	55.0	10.0	65.0	4.000			
John Grahame	15	46	35.0	10.0	45.0	3.913			
§Paul Evitts	3	10	4.0	1.0	5.0	2.000			
§§Alan Williams	1	2	1.0	0.0	1.0	2.000			
§Andy Passey	8	21	7.0	1.0	8.0	1.524			
§Chris Sully	4	9	2.0	0.0	2.0	0.889			
§§Ray Caruana	2	7	1.0	0.0	1.0	0.571			
§Billy Spiers	2	6	0.0	0.0	0.0	0.000			

1981...1981...1981...1981...1981...1981

	M	R	Pts	BP	TPts	Ave	F	P	Total
Dave Perks	38	165	406.0	12.0	418.0	10.133	10	3	13
Derek Harrison	36	160	361.0	15.0	376.0	9.400	4	1	5
Colin Ackroyd	31	132	250.0	18.0	268.0	8.121	2		2
§Ashley Pullen	3	13	22.0	1.0	23.0	7.077			
Paul Evitts	33	137	159.0	23.0	182.0	5.314	1		1
§Arthur Price	23	79	79.0	10.0	89.0	4.506			
John Grahame	30	110	94.0	20.0	114.0	4.145		1	1
Mick Handley	27	90	72.0	19.0	91.0	4.044			
Mick Fletcher	38	140	120.0	18.0	138.0	3.943			
§Arnold Haley	1	2	1.0	0.0	1.0	2.000			
§Alan Maclean	13	36	9.0	4.0	13.0	1.444			
Andy Passey	1	2	0.0	0.0	0.0	0.000			

1982...1982...1982...1982...1982...1982

	M	R	Pts	BP	TPts	Ave	F	P	Total
Ashley Pullen	39	224	419.0	14.0	433.0	7.732	1		1
§Graham Drury	27	148	260.0	19.0	279.0	7.541			
Colin Ackroyd	26	132	227.0	18.0	245.0	7.424		1	1
§§Simon Cross	22	111	168.0	23.0	191.0	6.883			
§Kevin Smart	23	117	127.0	23.0	150.0	5.128			
§Wayne Jackson	29	145	167.0	18.0	185.0	5.103			
§Brian Woodward	7	29	28.0	7.0	35.0	4.828			
§John Frankland	12	48	44.0	10.0	54.0	4.500			
§Ian Gledhill	17	70	72.0	6.0	78.0	4.457			
§§Gary Chessell	11	41	36.0	4.0	40.0	3.902			
§§Bill Barrett	22	84	57.0	9.0	66.0	3.143			
Mick Handley	9	34	20.0	6.0	26.0	3.059			
§Kevin Lock	1	4	3.0	0.0	3.0	3.000			
Mitck Fletcher	9	39	18.0	3.0	21.0	2.154			
§§Paul Cooper	1	2	1.0	0.0	1.0	2.000			
§§Keith Booth	2	8	2.0	0.0	2.0	1.000			
Andy Passey	2	8	1.0	1.0	2.0	1.000			
§§Martin Satchell	4	9	1.0	1.0	2.0	0.889			
§Peter Erskine	1	4	0.0	0.0	0.0	0.000			
§§Scott Cook	1	3	0.0	0.0	0.0	0.000			
§George Wells	1	3	0.0	0.0	0.0	0.000			

1983...1983...1983...1983...1983...1983

	M	R	Pts	BP	TPts	Ave	F	P	Total
§Nigel Sparshott	**38**	**201**	**370.0**	**35.0**	**405.0**	**8.060**		**1**	**1**
Graham Drury	32	173	320.0	17.0	337.0	7.792	1		1
§Ian Clark	22	116	187.0	24.0	211.0	7.276			
§Mike Wilding	23	115	188.0	17.0	205.0	7.130			
Kevin Smart	**38**	**191**	**258.0**	**45.0**	**303.0**	**6.346**			
Wayne Jackson	29	120	143.0	19.0	162.0	5.400			
§§Nigel De'ath	11	50	54.0	13.0	67.0	5.360			
Steve Crockett	34	129	125.0	27.0	152.0	4.713			
§Mark Summerfield	12	48	38.0	12.0	50.0	4.167			
Gary Chessell	5	19	12.0	7.0	19.0	4.000			
Keith Booth	5	19	11.0	5.0	16.0	3.368			
§§Mark Chessell	12	34	13.0	1.0	14.0	1.647			
§Mark Minett	1	2	0.0	0.0	0.0	0.000			

■ *NORTHERN SPORTS took over Len Silver's Hackney licence to bring First Division racing back to Oxford.*

PAISLEY

■ *PAISLEY had a short-lived speedway life at the home of Scottish soccer club St. Mirren.*
Neil Macfarlane and Joe Thurley launched a massive fund-raising exercise at the end of a disastrous 1976 season but were unable to wipe out operating losses and announced their withdrawal from the 1977 National League early in the New Year .

1975...1975...1975...1975...1975...1975

	M	R	Pts	BP	TPts	Ave	F	P	Total
§Sid Sheldrick	37	153	286.0	20.0	306.0	8.000	2		2
§Mike Fullerton	**40**	**166**	**286.0**	**13.0**	**299.0**	**7.205**		**2**	**2**
§Alan Bridgett	23	95	149.0	20.0	169.0	7.116			
§Chris Roynon	36	144	198.0	18.0	216.0	6.000		1	1
§§Bryan Townsend	1	3	4.0	0.0	4.0	5.333			
§§Tom Davie	24	89	97.0	20.0	117.0	5.258			
§§Bernie Foot	37	113	123.0	24.0	147.0	5.204			
§§Stuart Mountford	27	101	99.0	14.0	113.0	4.475			
§Mick Sheldrick	35	123	108.0	15.0	123.0	4.000			
§§Geoff Snider	12	47	35.0	12.0	47.0	4.000			
§Fred Caffrey	3	9	3.0	0.0	3.0	1.333			

1976...1976...1976...1976...1976...1976

	M	R	Pts	BP	TPts	Ave	F	P	Total
§Colin Farquharson	32	147	287.0	15.0	302.0	8.218	3	3	6
§Mike Fishwick	22	99	164.0	9.0	173.0	6.990	1	1	2
Stuart Mountford	34	145	226.0	20.0	246.0	6.786	3	2	5
Sid Sheldrick	13	54	79.0	6.0	85.0	6.296			
Mike Fullerton	17	70	78.0	16.0	94.0	5.371	1	1	2
Alan Bridgett	33	137	151.0	26.0	177.0	5.168			
§Mal Chambers	32	98	85.0	12.0	97.0	3.959			
Chris Roynon	12	44	40.0	3.0	43.0	3.909			
Mick Sheldrick	21	69	57.0	9.0	66.0	3.826			
§§Colin Caffrey	13	43	29.0	5.0	34.0	3.163			
Bernie Foot	3	10	5.0	1.0	6.0	2.400			
Tom Davie	8	29	15.0	2.0	17.0	2.345			
Fred Caffrey	2	6	3.0	0.0	3.0	2.000			

CHAMPIONSHIP OF STRATHCLYDE

1975	1 Mick Sheldrick	2 Lou Sansom	3 Brian Collins
1976	1 Tom Owen	2 Colin Farquharson	3 Grahame Dawson

FESTIVAL OF PAISLEY TROPHY

1975	1 Brian Collins	2 Peter Jarman	3 Alan Bridgett and Mike Fullerton

SCOTTISH YOUTH CHAMPIONSHIP

1976	1 Colin Caffrey	2 Peter Waite	3 Frank Hall

PETERBOROUGH

DANNY DUNTON somewhat surprisingly persuaded the registered charity running the East of England Showground into allowing him to build a shale track around their main showring.
And Peterborough became one of the unexpected success stories of the Second Division with it's big fast track, 2,300 seat grandstand and home-grown policy.

1970...1970...1970...1970...1970...1970

	M	R	Pts	BP	TPts	Ave	F	P	Total
§Andy Ross	28	118	260.0	8.0	268.0	9.085	3	1	4
§John Poyser	8	34	63.0	2.0	65.0	7.647			
§§Richard Greer	**33**	**140**	**233.0**	**29.0**	**262.0**	**7.486**			
§Pete Seaton	31	125	204.0	19.0	223.0	7.136	2		2
§Brian Davies	15	59	98.0	4.0	102.0	6.915			
§§Joe Hughes	22	87	101.0	27.0	128.0	5.885			
§§John Stayte	22	70	71.0	17.0	88.0	5.029			
§Peter Saunders	30	105	95.0	26.0	121.0	4.610			
§§Mervyn Hill	28	91	86.0	17.0	103.0	4.527			
§John Knock	1	2	1.0	1.0	2.0	4.000			
§Alan Palmer	1	2	2.0	0.0	2.0	4.000			
§§Alan Witt	1	3	1.0	1.0	2.0	2.667			
§§Colin Smalley	3	7	2.0	2.0	4.0	2.286			
§§Brian Clark	2	4	0.0	0.0	0.0	0.000			
§§Pat Johnson	2	3	0.0	0.0	0.0	0.000			
§§Barrie Smith	1	3	0.0	0.0	0.0	0.000			
§§Alan Sage	1	2	0.0	0.0	0.0	0.000			
§§Harry Thompson	1	2	0.0	0.0	0.0	0.000			

1971...1971...1971...1971...1971...1971

	M	R	Pts	BP	TPts	Ave	F	P	Total
Andy Ross	9	43	97.0	0.0	97.0	9.023	2		2
Richard Greer	33	153	285.0	19.0	304.0	7.948	4	1	5
§Roy Carter	30	120	177.0	25.0	202.0	6.733			
§John Davis	13	39	53.0	4.0	57.0	5.846			
Joe Hughes	**34**	**135**	**174.0**	**22.0**	**196.0**	**5.807**	**1**		**1**
John Stayte	26	88	102.0	21.0	123.0	5.591		1	1
Alan Witt	13	45	52.0	10.0	62.0	5.511			
Peter Saunders	**34**	**117**	**133.0**	**27.0**	**160.0**	**5.470**			
Brian Clark	33	113	127.0	18.0	145.0	5.133		1	1
Pete Seaton	8	29	24.0	2.0	26.0	3.586			
§§Kevin Reynolds	1	3	1.0	1.0	2.0	2.667			
Colin Smalley	1	3	2.0	0.0	2.0	2.667			

1972...1972...1972...1972...1972...1972

	M	R	Pts	BP	TPts	Ave	F	P	Total
Richard Greer	35	144	336.0	25.0	361.0	10.028	1	6	7
§John Harrhy	7	29	70.0	2.0	72.0	9.931	2		2
John Davis	38	156	299.5	17.5	317.0	8.128	3	1	4
Roy Carter	**40**	**164**	**294.5**	**38.5**	**333.0**	**8.122**	**3**	**1**	**4**
§Clive Noy	18	67	100.0	11.0	111.0	6.627			
§Ted Howgego	30	120	171.0	26.0	197.0	6.567		1	1
Alan Witt	25	84	93.0	14.0	107.0	5.095			
Brian Clark	37	129	140.0	23.0	163.0	5.054			
Peter Saunders	9	27	25.0	9.0	34.0	5.037			
§Frank Smith	11	30	30.0	5.0	35.0	4.667			
§Chris Harrison	2	6	5.0	1.0	6.0	4.000			
§§John Amies	10	35	26.0	8.0	34.0	3.886			
§§David Ashby	10	35	26.0	8.0	34.0	3.886			
§§Ralph Waller	1	4	3.0	0.0	3.0	3.000			
§§Keith White	1	3	0.0	0.0	0.0	0.000			
§§Steve Osborne	1	2	0.0	0.0	0.0	0.000			
Kevin Reynolds	1	2	0.0	0.0	0.0	0.000			

1973...1973...1973...1973...1973...1973

	M	R	Pts	BP	TPts	Ave	F	P	Total
Richard Greer	36	158	332.0	22.0	354.0	8.962	5	3	8
John Davis	31	125	265.0	12.0	277.0	8.864	3	2	5
Frank Smith	**38**	**156**	**246.0**	**39.0**	**285.0**	**7.308**	**1**	**4**	**5**
Brian Clark	**38**	**149**	**245.0**	**26.0**	**271.0**	**7.275**	**3**	**2**	**5**
Ted Howgego	21	85	115.0	21.0	136.0	6.400		1	1
Roy Carter	33	112	138.0	32.0	170.0	6.071		3	3
§§Jack Walker	**38**	**123**	**151.0**	**25.0**	**176.0**	**5.724**			
Steve Osbourne	3	9	10.0	2.0	12.0	5.333			
§§Roy Sizmore	8	21	18.0	3.0	21.0	4.000			
§§Glyn Taylor	1	3	3.0	0.0	3.0	4.000			
§§Ken Matthews	12	35	20.0	3.0	23.0	2.629			

1974...1974...1974...1974...1974...1974

	M	R	Pts	BP	TPts	Ave	F	P	Total
§Mike Lanham	35	148	313.0	24.0	337.0	9.108	2	7	9
Brian Clark	39	170	347.0	24.0	371.0	8.729	3	4	7
Jack Walker	17	67	98.0	15.0	113.0	6.746			
§Mike Cake	7	25	37.0	5.0	42.0	6.720			
Ken Matthews	22	83	119.5	11.5	131.0	6.313			
Roy Carter	38	143	199.5	25.5	225.0	6.294	1	2	3
Steve Osborn	**40**	**153**	**207.0**	**27.0**	**234.0**	**6.118**		**1**	**1**
Roy Sizmore	19	69	80.0	19.0	99.0	5.739			
§Peter Thompson	15	47	47.0	10.0	57.0	4.851			
§Eric Dugard	12	45	43.0	7.0	50.0	4.444			
§Chris Drewett	20	58	51.0	9.0	60.0	4.138			
§Peter Cairns	6	17	7.0	3.0	10.0	2.353			
§§Phil Cornwell	4	13	5.0	1.0	6.0	1.846			

PETERBOROUGH

1975...1975...1975...1975...1975...1975

	M	R	Pts	BP	TPts	Ave	F	P	Total
Brian Clark	**41**	**184**	**394.0**	**20.0**	**414.0**	**9.000**	**3**	**5**	**8**
§Russell Osborne	13	51	79.0	12.0	91.0	7.137			
Roy Carter	38	147	216.0	29.0	245.0	6.667	3	1	4
Ken Matthews	**41**	**173**	**269.0**	**19.0**	**288.0**	**6.659**		**1**	**1**
Mike Cake	19	73	89.0	12.0	101.0	5.534			
Steve Osborn	2	7	9.0	0.0	9.0	5.143			
Jack Walker	34	114	113.0	21.0	134.0	4.702			
§§Ian Clark	15	44	42.0	6.0	48.0	4.364			
Roy Sizmore	35	121	115.0	16.0	131.0	4.331			
§§Steve Taylor (2)	35	124	94.0	15.0	109.0	3.516			
§§Paul Cooper	3	8	6.0	0.0	6.0	3.000			
Phil Cornwell	8	15	4.0	1.0	5.0	1.333			

1976...1976...1976...1976...1976...1976

	M	R	Pts	BP	TPts	Ave	F	P	Total
Brian Clark	32	131	290.0	17.0	307.0	9.374	4	4	8
§Tony Featherstone	34	141	264.0	22.0	286.0	8.113		2	2
§§Paul Tapp	2	7	11.0	3.0	14.0	8.000			
Phil Cornwell	1	2	3.0	1.0	4.0	8.000			
Ian Clark	20	82	124.0	18.0	142.0	6.927		2	2
Roy Carter	32	122	187.0	22.0	209.0	6.852		1	1
Ken Matthews	34	131	190.0	24.0	214.0	6.534	1	3	4
Steve Taylor (2)	27	91	118.0	28.0	146.0	6.418	1		1
§§Kevin Hawkins	18	60	68.0	12.0	80.0	5.333			
§Nigel Couzens	26	97	111.0	13.0	124.0	5.113			
§Alan Cowland	9	33	32.0	3.0	35.0	4.242			
Paul Cooper	7	21	20.0	2.0	22.0	4.190			
Russell Osborne	8	27	24.0	4.0	28.0	4.148			
§§Peter Spink	3	8	4.0	1.0	5.0	2.500			
§John McNeill	1	2	0.0	0.0	0.0	0.000			

1977...1977...1977...1977...1977...1977

	M	R	Pts	BP	TPts	Ave	F	P	Total
§Andy Hines	39	163	295.0	24.0	319.0	7.828	1	1	2
Ian Clark	39	165	279.0	29.0	308.0	7.467	1	5	6
Kevin Hawkins	**40**	**165**	**265.0**	**39.0**	**304.0**	**7.370**		**4**	**4**
§§Nigel Flatman	26	88	130.0	24.0	154.0	7.000			
Brian Clark	34	131	200.0	29.0	229.0	6.992			
Nigel Couzens	**40**	**153**	**223.0**	**24.0**	**247.0**	**6.458**		**1**	**1**
Ken Matthews	**40**	**145**	**207.0**	**20.0**	**227.0**	**6.262**	**1**	**1**	**2**
Roy Carter	2	8	8.0	2.0	10.0	5.000			
Peter Spink	9	24	21.0	5.0	26.0	4.333			
Steve Taylor (2)	1	3	2.0	1.0	3.0	4.000			

1978...1978...1978...1978...1978...1978

	M	R	Pts	BP	TPts	Ave	F	P	Total
§Dave Gooderham	36	144	287.0	14.0	301.0	8.361	3	2	5
Ian Clark	36	144	247.0	42.0	289.0	8.028		3	3
Andy Hines	36	159	301.0	16.0	317.0	7.975	1	1	2
Nigel Flatman	**42**	**168**	**271.0**	**43.0**	**314.0**	**7.476**	**2**	**1**	**3**
Kevin Hawkins	20	84	121.0	19.0	140.0	6.667		1	1
§§Tim Hunt	13	52	67.0	18.0	85.0	6.538			
Brian Clark	41	151	212.0	29.0	241.0	6.384		1	1
Nigel Couzens	**42**	**135**	**182.0**	**23.0**	**205.0**	**6.074**			
Steve Taylor (2)	2	6	6.0	3.0	9.0	6.000			
Peter Spink	13	38	37.0	8.0	45.0	4.737			
§§Andy Buck	1	3	2.0	1.0	3.0	4.000			
§§Steve Popely	5	10	2.0	1.0	3.0	1.200			

1979...1979...1979...1979...1979...1979

	M	R	Pts	BP	TPts	Ave	F	P	Total
Nigel Flatman	**38**	**162**	**322.0**	**23.0**	**345.0**	**8.519**	**3**	**1**	**4**
Richard Greer	17	72	122.0	13.0	135.0	7.500	2		2
Dave Gooderham	36	150	250.0	25.0	275.0	7.333			
Andy Hines	35	140	236.0	18.0	254.0	7.257		1	1
Ian Clark	29	121	178.0	25.0	203.0	6.711		2	2
Nigel Couzens	12	31	42.0	5.0	47.0	6.065			
Brian Clark	32	113	142.0	21.0	163.0	5.770			
Peter Spink	28	94	109.0	25.0	134.0	5.702			
Steve Popely	16	49	45.0	9.0	54.0	4.408			
Paul Tapp	10	26	19.0	7.0	26.0	4.000			
Ken Matthews	8	26	21.0	3.0	24.0	3.692			
Andy Buck	2	5	3.0	1.0	4.0	3.200			

1980...1980...1980...1980...1980...1980

	M	R	Pts	BP	TPts	Ave	F	P	Total
Andy Hines	37	157	336.0	10.0	346.0	8.815	4	1	5
Nigel Flatman	35	142	298.0	12.0	310.0	8.732	3		3
Richard Greer	41	170	309.0	39.0	348.0	8.188	2	6	8
§Mick Hines	30	131	223.0	28.0	251.0	7.664		2	2
Peter Spink	4	16	16.0	7.0	23.0	5.750			
§§Adrian Pepper	12	34	36.0	3.0	39.0	4.588			
§Andy Fisher	37	127	125.0	20.0	145.0	4.567			
Nigel Couzens	39	135	122.0	27.0	149.0	4.415			
Andy Buck	31	101	86.0	23.0	109.0	4.317			
Dave Gooderham	5	19	15.0	1.0	16.0	3.368			
§§Ian Barney	11	33	10.0	3.0	13.0	1.576			
§§David Ashby (2)	2	5	1.0	0.0	1.0	0.800			
§§Adrian Smith	2	5	0.0	0.0	0.0	0.000			
§Steve Bryenton	1	2	0.0	0.0	0.0	0.000			

1981...1981...1981...1981...1981...1981

	M	R	Pts	BP	TPts	Ave	F	P	Total
Richard Greer	39	158	281.0	43.0	324.0	8.203	1	4	5
Andy Hines	**43**	**191**	**357.0**	**27.0**	**384.0**	**8.042**	**1**	**1**	**2**
§Dave Allen	41	169	294.0	31.0	325.0	7.692	2	2	4
Mick Hines	**43**	**181**	**309.0**	**34.0**	**343.0**	**7.580**	**2**	**1**	**3**
Andy Fisher	**43**	**169**	**214.0**	**43.0**	**257.0**	**6.083**			
Nigel Couzens	22	67	84.0	16.0	100.0	5.970			
§§Peter Lloyd	2	6	6.0	2.0	8.0	5.333			
Adrian Pepper	1	3	3.0	1.0	4.0	5.333			
Andy Buck	**43**	**151**	**157.0**	**44.0**	**201.0**	**5.325**			
Ian Barney	22	66	67.0	14.0	81.0	4.909			

1982...1982...1982...1982...1982...1982

	M	R	Pts	BP	TPts	Ave	F	P	Total
Andy Hines	38	207	429.0	18.0	447.0	8.638	2	1	3
Dave Allen	**40**	**198**	**388.0**	**21.0**	**409.0**	**8.263**		**4**	**4**
Mick Hines	36	174	291.0	28.0	319.0	7.333		1	1
Andy Buck	**40**	**207**	**279.0**	**51.0**	**330.0**	**6.377**			
Andy Fisher	36	175	200.0	40.0	240.0	5.486			
Ian Barney	**40**	**183**	**216.0**	**30.0**	**246.0**	**5.377**	**2**	**1**	**3**
§§Ron Schliebs	6	20	15.0	2.0	17.0	3.400			
§§Neil Cotton	24	72	45.0	10.0	55.0	3.056			
Steve Popeley	2	5	3.0	0.0	3.0	2.400			
§§Adrian Hume	5	12	5.0	1.0	6.0	2.000			
Adrian Pepper	6	17	5.0	1.0	6.0	1.412			
§§Wayne Lorymer	5	12	1.0	1.0	2.0	0.667			
§§David Main	1	2	0.0	0.0	0.0	0.000			

1983...1983...1983...1983...1983...1983

	M	R	Pts	BP	TPts	Ave	F	P	Total
§Ashley Pullen	28	146	296.0	23.0	319.0	8.740			
Dave Allen	25	130	243.0	20.0	263.0	8.092			
Mick Hines	30	153	257.0	19.0	276.0	7.216			
Ian Barney	**36**	**190**	**282.0**	**28.0**	**310.0**	**6.526**	**1**	**1**	**2**
Andy Buck	31	159	216.0	40.0	256.0	6.440			
§Mike Spinks	35	163	189.0	30.0	219.0	5.374		1	1
Neil Cotton	36	162	172.0	26.0	198.0	4.889			
§§Dale Watson	9	22	11.0	2.0	13.0	2.364			
Adrian Hume	4	15	6.0	2.0	8.0	2.133			
§§Mike Smart	4	11	4.0	1.0	5.0	1.818			
§§Andy Steward	1	3	0.0	0.0	0.0	0.000			

1984...1984...1984...1984...1984...1984

	M	R	Pts	BP	TPts	Ave	F	P	Total
§Derek Harrison	6	25	49.0	4.0	53.0	8.480			
Mick Hines	33	131	226.0	20.0	246.0	7.511	5	2	7
Dave Allen	11	43	66.0	9.0	75.0	6.977			
Ian Barney	**38**	**166**	**269.0**	**20.0**	**289.0**	**6.964**	**1**		**1**
Andy Fisher	**38**	**161**	**222.0**	**34.0**	**256.0**	**6.360**			
§Keith Millard	22	94	135.0	12.0	147.0	6.255		1	1
Adrian Hume	32	112	144.0	20.0	164.0	5.857			
Mike Spinks	15	55	59.0	5.0	64.0	4.655			
Neil Cotton	36	124	120.0	14.0	134.0	4.323			
§Lawrie Bloomfield	12	39	36.0	2.0	38.0	3.897			
Mike Smart	11	25	14.0	2.0	16.0	2.560			
§§Alan Rivett	2	5	2.0	0.0	2.0	1.600			

◆ *MARTIN ROGERS began his first full season as Peterborough at the beginning of the 1985 season.*

PETERBOROUGH

1985...1985...1985...1985...1985...1985

	M	R	Pts	BP	TPts	Ave	F	P	Total
Kevin Hawkins	**37**	**160**	**343.0**	**22.0**	**365.0**	**9.125**	**3**	**4**	**7**
§§Mick Poole	29	124	211.0	22.0	233.0	7.516	2	1	3
Dave Allen	**37**	**131**	**203.0**	**35.0**	**238.0**	**7.267**		**4**	**4**
Ian Clark	**37**	**148**	**219.0**	**30.0**	**249.0**	**6.730**		**1**	**1**
Ian Barney	37	144	197.0	19.0	216.0	6.000		1	1
§Keith Bloxsome	31	106	125.0	32.0	157.0	5.925			
Adrian Hume	22	69	71.0	12.0	83.0	4.812			
Andy Fisher	11	35	31.0	10.0	41.0	4.686			
§Michael Keepe	1	2	1.0	1.0	2.0	4.000			
§§Rob Fortune	1	4	2.0	1.0	3.0	3.000			
§Peter Chapman	13	34	22.0	2.0	24.0	2.824			
§Mark Summerfield	1	2	1.0	0.0	1.0	2.000			

1986...1986...1986...1986...1986...1986

	M	R	Pts	BP	TPts	Ave	F	P	Total
Kevin Hawkins	**43**	**189**	**384.5**	**29.0**	**413.5**	**8.751**	**3**	**1**	**4**
Nigel Flatman	**43**	**187**	**341.5**	**40.0**	**381.5**	**8.160**		**1**	**1**
Dave Allen	19	76	116.0	17.0	133.0	7.000		1	1
§Carl Baldwin	35	140	217.0	28.0	245.0	7.000		1	1
Ian Barney	**43**	**168**	**251.0**	**19.0**	**270.0**	**6.429**			
Peter Chapman	23	58	72.0	12.0	84.0	5.793			
Rob Fortune	4	14	16.0	3.0	19.0	5.429			
§§Jamie Habbin	**43**	**123**	**125.0**	**29.0**	**154.0**	**5.008**			
Adrian Hume	29	107	104.0	22.0	126.0	4.710			
§John Stokes	18	52	47.0	9.0	56.0	4.308			
§Stuart Thompson	2	5	2.0	1.0	3.0	2.400			

1987...1987...1987...1987...1987...1987

	M	R	Pts	BP	TPts	Ave	F	P	Total
Ian Barney	33	135	298.0	11.0	309.0	9.156	7	1	8
Kevin Hawkins	**34**	**144**	**291.0**	**22.0**	**313.0**	**8.694**	**1**	**1**	**2**
§§Jason Straughan	1	1	1.0	1.0	2.0	8.000			
Nigel Flatman	**34**	**140**	**238.0**	**29.0**	**267.0**	**7.629**		**2**	**2**
Carl Baldwin	17	68	104.0	21.0	125.0	7.353			
§§Craig Hodgson	30	115	143.0	36.0	179.0	6.226			
Jamie Habbin	29	96	123.0	25.0	148.0	6.167			
Peter Chapman	**34**	**130**	**170.0**	**28.0**	**198.0**	**6.092**			
Rob Fortune	16	52	51.0	15.0	66.0	5.077			
Stuart Thompson	3	8	5.0	3.0	8.0	4.000			
§Mick May	1	3	3.0	0.0	3.0	4.000			
§§Harvey Bell	1	2	1.0	1.0	2.0	4.000			
John Stokes	5	11	3.0	1.0	4.0	1.455			

OLD BOY...long-time Alwalton favourite Brian Clark, who spent 10 seasons with the club as a rider later took over as the Panthers' team manager

1988...1988...1988...1988...1988...1988

	M	R	Pts	BP	TPts	Ave	F	P	Total
§§Mick Poole	32	163	361.0	27.0	388.0	9.521	1	4	5
Ian Barney	33	167	338.0	13.0	351.0	8.407	4	4	8
Kevin Hawkins	**34**	**175**	**299.0**	**50.0**	**349.0**	**7.977**	**1**	**2**	**3**
Craig Hodgson	33	165	296.0	26.0	322.0	7.806	3	1	4
§§Scott Norman	6	27	32.0	8.0	40.0	5.926			
Jamie Habbin	32	144	181.0	25.0	206.0	5.722		1	1
Rob Fortune	2	9	11.0	1.0	12.0	5.333			
John Stokes	27	99	98.0	25.0	123.0	4.970			
Peter Chapman	32	117	112.0	21.0	133.0	4.547			
§§Rod Colquhoun	2	6	4.0	2.0	6.0	4.000			
§Sean Barker	3	10	5.0	1.0	6.0	2.400			
§§Andrew Giddings	1	1	0.0	0.0	0.0	0.000			

1989...1989...1989...1989...1989...1989

	M	R	Pts	BP	TPts	Ave	F	P	Total
Mick Poole	31	168	338.0	32.0	370.0	8.810	1	1	2
§Kevin Jolly	37	193	372.0	39.0	411.0	8.518	1	1	2
Peter Chapman	1	5	10.0	0.0	10.0	8.000			
Craig Hodgson	34	179	298.0	40.0	338.0	7.553		3	3
Ian Barney	35	182	302.0	29.0	331.0	7.275	1		1
Scott Norman	31	159	246.0	38.0	284.0	7.145		1	1
Nigel Flatman	32	132	160.0	39.0	199.0	6.030			
§§Justin Walker	29	110	123.0	25.0	148.0	5.382			
Rod Colquhoun	7	25	21.0	5.0	26.0	4.160			
§Jon Cooper	11	34	26.0	6.0	32.0	3.765			
Paul Blackbird	6	22	17.0	2.0	19.0	3.455			
§John Wainwright	7	25	15.0	5.0	20.0	3.200			
§Matthew Cross	2	5	0.0	0.0	0.0	0.000			

1990...1990...1990...1990...1990...1990

	M	R	Pts	BP	TPts	Ave	F	P	Total
Mick Poole	13	71	154.0	16.0	170.0	9.577		4	4
Craig Hodgson	33	196	379.0	15.0	394.0	8.041	1	1	2
§Frank Andersen	29	163	289.0	30.0	319.0	7.828	1	2	3
Scott Norman	31	177	285.0	21.0	306.0	6.915	1	1	2
Ian Barney	11	53	76.0	13.0	89.0	6.717			
Nigel Flatman	27	113	131.0	32.0	163.0	5.770		2	2
§Peter Chapman	25	93	106.0	10.0	116.0	4.989			
§Mark Lyndon	16	78	75.0	12.0	87.0	4.462			
§§Robert Fisher	1	1	1.0	0.0	1.0	4.000			
§Wayne Bridgeford	12	54	44.0	6.0	50.0	3.704			
Sean Barker	34	130	80.0	17.0	97.0	2.985			
§§Phil Disney	5	18	11.0	2.0	13.0	2.889			
Paul Blackbird	3	6	2.0	1.0	3.0	2.000			
§Mark Crang	4	14	5.0	0.0	5.0	1.429			
§Mark Jolly	1	3	1.0	0.0	1.0	1.333			
§§Darren Tupper	3	10	2.0	1.0	3.0	1.200			
§§Matthew Poole	1	1	0.0	0.0	0.0	0.000			

PETERBOROUGH OPEN CHAMPIONSHIP

1971	1 Arthur Price	2 Tony Davey	3 Geoff Bouchard
1972	1 Roy Carter	2 Roger Mills	3 Geoff Bouchard

KRC TROPHY

1973	1 Dave Morton	2 Carl Glover	3 Bobby McNeil
1974	1 Brian Clark	2 Phil Herne	3 Jack Millen
1975	1 Dave Gooderham	2 Ken Matthews	3 Roy Carter
1976	1 Roy Carter	2 Brian Clark	3 Tony Featherstone
1977	1 Colin Richardson	2 Phil Bass	3 Kelvin Mullarkey
1978	1 Dave Gooderham	2 Ray Bales	3 Brian Clark

SUPPORTERS' TROPHY

1976	1 Andy Cusworth	2 Robert Hollingworth	3 Ken Matthews

TOLLCOTE BUILDERS OPEN CHAMPIONSHIP

1983	1 Richard Knight	2 Dave Allen	3 Mike Spink
1985	1 Kevin Hawkins	2 Martin Dixon	3 Carl Blackbird

KING OF THE SHOWGROUND

1983	1 Joe Owen	2 Richard Knight	3 Bob Garrad

HEXAGON TROPHY

1986	1 Les Collins	2 Kevin Hawkins	3 Steve Schofield
1987	1 Les Collins	2 Ray Morton	3 Ian Barney
1988	1 Ian Barney	2 Kevin Hawkins	3 Ray Morton

SMITHS MOTORS SPECTACULAR

1988	1 Eric Monaghan	2 Melvyn Taylor	3 Mick Poole
1989	1 Richard Hellsén	2 Mick Poole	3 Craig Hodgson

HILLSIDE TROPHY

1989	1 Richard Hellsén	2 Melvyn Taylor	3 Chris Louis
1990	1 Steve Regeling	2 Neville Tatum	3 Craig Hodgson

NENE TROPHY

1990	1 Mark Blackbird	2 Les Collins	3 Alan Mogridge

FRANK BARNEY MEMORIAL TROPHY

1990	1 Wayne Bridgeford	2 John Wainwright	3 Roger Horspool

PLYMOUTH

■ *PLYMOUTH were founder members of the Second Division in 1968 but after one season promoters Wally Mawdsley and Pete Lansdale sold out to local businessman Fred Osaborne who, after only one season, sold his League licence to Peterborough. The old Pennycross Stadium has since been redeveloped as an industrial site.*

1968...1968...1968...1968...1968...1968

	M	R	Pts	BP	TPts	Ave	F	P	Total
§§Mike Cake	17	74	187.0	2.0	189.0	10.216	6	1	7
§§Chris Bass	10	41	101.0	3.0	104.0	10.146	2		2
§§Phil Woodcock	14	60	96.0	4.0	100.0	6.667			
§§Tony George	**19**	**75**	**98.0**	**17.0**	**115.0**	**6.133**		**1**	**1**
§§Dave Whitaker	18	73	97.0	14.0	111.0	6.082		1	1
§§Keith Marks	9	26	31.0	6.0	37.0	5.692			
§§Frank Payne	10	30	32.0	6.0	38.0	5.067			
§§Chris Roynon	14	48	48.0	9.0	57.0	4.750			
§§Bob Coles	3	12	10.0	2.0	12.0	4.000			
§§Ian Gills	8	31	24.0	1.0	25.0	3.226			
§§Dan Jewell	3	7	5.0	0.0	5.0	2.857			
§§Eric Howe	1	4	2.0	0.0	2.0	2.000			
§§Mike Gimlett	1	3	0.0	0.0	0.0	0.000			

1969...1969...1969...1969...1969...1969

	M	R	Pts	BP	TPts	Ave	F	P	Total
§§Colin Sanders	30	135	236.0	6.0	242.0	7.170	3		3
Bob Coles	30	125	187.0	12.0	199.0	6.368			
Dave Whitaker	28	121	176.0	11.0	187.0	6.182	1	1	2
Chris Roynon	26	110	149.0	19.0	168.0	6.109			
§§Tony Smith	4	9	8.0	4.0	12.0	5.333			
Keith Marks	22	74	77.0	20.0	97.0	5.243			
Frank Payne	4	10	12.0	0.0	12.0	4.800			
§§John Ellis	6	19	19.0	2.0	21.0	4.421			
§John Hammond	22	73	69.0	10.0	79.0	4.329			
Ian Gills	10	38	32.0	8.0	40.0	4.211			
§§Cliff Cox	6	19	18.0	2.0	20.0	4.211			
§Phil Arnold	2	6	5.0	1.0	6.0	4.000			
§§Paul Sly	2	5	3.0	1.0	4.0	3.200			
§Stuart Wallace	1	4	2.0	1.0	3.0	3.000			
§§Clark Facey	10	33	16.0	4.0	20.0	2.424			
§§Russ Skinner	4	8	1.0	1.0	2.0	1.000			
§Adrian Degan	2	5	0.0	0.0	0.0	0.000			

PLYMOUTH CITY F.C. TROPHY

1969 1 Mike Vernam 2 Dave Jessup 3 Bob Coles

GUARDS TROPHY

1968 1 Mike Cake 2 Martyn Piddock 3 Phil Woodcock

POOLE

■ ***THE DECISION to move National League Weymouth along the South Coast to Poole at the beginning of 1985 following the liquidation of the old British League Pirates proved to be one of speedway's inspired switches.***

1985...1985...1985...1985...1985...1985

	M	R	Pts	BP	TPts	Ave	F	P	Total
§Stan Bear	34	132	303.0	20.0	323.0	9.788	5	10	15
§Kevin Smith	**38**	**161**	**364.0**	**11.0**	**375.0**	**9.317**	**6**	**4**	**10**
§Martin Yeates	37	150	305.0	10.0	315.0	8.400	8	2	10
§David Biles	**38**	**154**	**197.0**	**49.0**	**246.0**	**6.390**		**3**	**3**
§Marcus Bisson	28	88	116.0	18.0	134.0	6.091		1	1
§Guy Wilson	28	89	105.0	28.0	133.0	5.978			
§Ray Dole	24	102	135.0	17.0	152.0	5.961			
§Gordon Humphreys	4	13	13.0	3.0	16.0	4.923			
§David Gibbs	21	76	67.0	8.0	75.0	3.947			
§Rob Mather	5	18	10.0	3.0	13.0	2.889			
§Dave Roberts	4	15	5.0	1.0	6.0	1.600			

1986...1986...1986...1986...1986...1986

	M	R	Pts	BP	TPts	Ave	F	P	Total
§Steve Schofield	**40**	**185**	**459.0**	**20.0**	**479.0**	**10.357**	**8**	**3**	**11**
Kevin Smith	23	94	209.0	13.0	222.0	9.447	3	1	4
Martin Yeates	39	172	361.0	13.0	374.0	8.698	3	2	5
David Biles	39	174	288.0	49.0	337.0	7.747	1	4	5
Marcus Bisson	37	155	166.0	30.0	196.0	5.058			
David Gibbs	36	116	108.0	24.0	132.0	4.552			
§Wayne Barrett	18	55	46.0	11.0	57.0	4.145			
§§Will James	26	76	42.0	4.0	46.0	2.421			
Gordon Humphreys	4	11	3.0	1.0	4.0	1.455			
§§Peter Read	2	4	1.0	0.0	1.0	1.000			

1987...1987...1987...1987...1987...1987

	M	R	Pts	BP	TPts	Ave	F	P	Total
Steve Schofield	25	112	257.0	10.0	267.0	9.536	3	2	5
David Biles	31	141	284.0	39.0	323.0	9.163	1	4	5
Martin Yeates	**32**	**143**	**265.0**	**9.0**	**274.0**	**7.664**	**2**	**1**	**3**
Kevin Smith	28	120	195.0	25.0	220.0	7.333	2	2	4
§Wayne Barrett	30	103	87.0	18.0	105.0	4.078			
§§Jonathan Blake	1	3	3.0	0.0	3.0	4.000			
Peter Read	25	77	59.0	9.0	68.0	3.532			
Will James	28	99	72.0	12.0	84.0	3.394			
§§Nigel Newman	8	29	19.0	2.0	21.0	2.897			
§Brian Hussey	5	12	2.0	2.0	4.0	1.333			
§§Gary Brown	1	1	0.0	0.0	0.0	0.000			
§§Nigel Tremeling	1	1	0.0	0.0	0.0	0.000			

For details of the Blue Riband see Poole, Division One Averages.

1988...1988...1988...1988...1988...1988

	M	R	Pts	BP	TPts	Ave	F	P	Total
Steve Schofield	29	152	380.5	8.0	388.5	10.224	2	1	3
David Biles	**32**	**167**	**332.0**	**22.0**	**354.0**	**8.479**	**1**	**1**	**2**
§§Craig Boyce	29	147	251.0	30.0	281.0	7.646		1	1
§Kevin Smart	29	139	203.0	29.0	232.0	6.676			
§§Tony Langdon	18	81	119.0	16.0	135.0	6.667			
§§Gary Allan	15	66	78.0	14.0	92.0	5.576			
§§Robbie Fuller	20	82	92.0	10.0	102.0	4.976			
§Nigel Flatman	20	80	81.0	17.0	98.0	4.900			
§Steve Bishop	10	42	38.0	9.0	47.0	4.476			
§§Steve Langdon	15	56	41.0	8.0	49.0	3.500			
§§Matthew Cross	1	3	2.0	0.0	2.0	2.667			
§Mark Chessell	2	5	0.0	0.0	0.0	0.000			
Jonathan Blake	2	3	0.0	0.0	0.0	0.000			

1989...1989...1989...1989...1989...1989

	M	R	Pts	BP	TPts	Ave	F	P	Total
Craig Boyce	40	198	419.0	43.0	462.0	9.333		6	6
§§Leigh Adams	40	202	429.0	36.0	465.0	9.208	3	4	7
§Alun Rossiter	**42**	**200**	**353.0**	**43.0**	**396.0**	**7.920**			
§Alastair Stevens	**42**	**206**	**324.0**	**48.0**	**372.0**	**7.223**		**1**	**1**
Gary Allan	**42**	**186**	**283.0**	**48.0**	**331.0**	**7.118**			
Tony Langdon	33	153	229.0	30.0	259.0	6.771		1	1
Kevin Smart	23	88	107.0	25.0	132.0	6.000			
§§Mike Lewthwaite	7	19	20.0	3.0	23.0	4.842			
§Jon Surman	11	44	39.0	8.0	47.0	4.273			
§§Steve Leigh	10	29	18.0	5.0	23.0	3.172			

1990...1990...1990...1990...1990...1990

	M	R	Pts	BP	TPts	Ave	F	P	Total
Craig Boyce	**40**	**229**	**579.0**	**19.0**	**598.0**	**10.445**	**4**	**5**	**9**
§§Tom Knudsen	13	61	117.0	16.0	133.0	8.721			
Alun Rossiter	39	194	380.0	39.0	419.0	8.639	3		3
Tony Langdon	37	204	351.0	69.0	420.0	8.235		3	3
Gary Allan	**40**	**220**	**355.0**	**58.0**	**413.0**	**7.509**	**1**		**1**
§Gary Chessell	29	131	196.0	29.0	225.0	6.870		1	1
§Rod Colquhoun	36	141	160.0	42.0	202.0	5.730			
Steve Langdon	12	42	37.0	9.0	46.0	4.381			
§§Mark Lemon	5	16	8.0	6.0	14.0	3.500			
§§Justin Elkins	6	15	12.0	1.0	13.0	3.467			
Steve Leigh	3	9	5.0	2.0	7.0	3.111			
§Peter Schroeck	1	2	1.0	0.0	1.0	2.000			
§John Gould	4	13	4.0	1.0	5.0	1.538			

RAYLEIGH

■ *RAYLEIGH was a natural venue to launch Second Division racing.*

■ *The Weir Stadium itself was ideally situated on the outskirts of the Essex market town, slap bang on the main trunk road linking London and the holiday resort of Southend-on-Sea.*

■ *Promoter Len Silver, who lived at nearby Ilford, decided to re-open the track after a two-season closure (open meetings had been run there in 1965) and it was an immediate success with a raw and wild young side, led by the one veteran in the ranks, locally-based Terry Stone, improving almost weekly and providing exciting entertainment.*

■ *The major discovery was New Zealander Graeme Smith who began in the second half at their opening meeting against Plymouth on Saturday, May 11, forced his way into the side and was appointed captain.*

■ *He made such rapid progress that he qualified for and then finished third in the end of season Division Two Riders' Championship Final at Hackney!*

1968...1968...1968...1968...1968...1968

	M	R	Pts	BP	TPts	Ave	F	P	Total
§Barry Lee	5	16	27.0	4.0	31.0	7.750		1	1
§§Graeme Smith	**19**	**80**	**140.0**	**11.0**	**151.0**	**7.550**	**1**		**1**
§§Mike Gardner	**19**	**78**	**129.0**	**17.0**	**146.0**	**7.487**	**1**		**1**
§§Dennis Mannion	14	50	87.0	6.0	93.0	7.440	2		2
§§Dingle Brown	15	63	91.0	11.0	102.0	6.476			
§§Laurie Etheridge	18	69	99.0	8.0	107.0	6.203			
§§Geoff Maloney	16	62	83.0	11.0	94.0	6.065			
§§Terry Stone	15	59	71.0	18.0	89.0	6.034		1	1
§§Colin Tucker	11	22	17.0	0.0	17.0	3.091			

1969...1969...1969...1969...1969...1969

	M	R	Pts	BP	TPts	Ave	F	P	Total
Graeme Smith	13	57	152.0	1.0	153.0	10.737	4		4
Laurie Etheridge	17	68	125.0	20.0	145.0	8.529	2		2
Mike Gardner	16	63	114.0	9.0	123.0	7.810	2		2
Geoff Maloney	**33**	**133**	**216.0**	**31.0**	**247.0**	**7.429**	**2**	**2**	**4**
§§Roger Wright	28	111	173.0	29.0	202.0	7.279		1	1
Dingle Brown	30	121	195.0	22.0	217.0	7.174	1	2	3
Terry Stone	32	120	170.0	15.0	185.0	6.167	1	1	2
Dennis Mannion	17	56	65.0	12.0	77.0	5.500			
§§Andy Ross	1	3	2.0	2.0	4.0	5.333			
Barry Lee	13	41	37.0	8.0	45.0	4.390			
§Ian Champion	9	32	30.0	4.0	34.0	4.250			
§Bob Newman	13	39	28.0	10.0	38.0	3.897			
§Bernie Leigh	1	5	4.0	0.0	4.0	3.200			
§§Charlie Mugford	1	3	2.0	0.0	2.0	2.667			
§Cyril Hathaway	1	2	1.0	0.0	1.0	2.000			
§Malcolm Mackay	1	2	1.0	0.0	1.0	2.000			

1970...1970...1970...1970...1970...1970

	M	R	Pts	BP	TPts	Ave	F	P	Total
Geoff Maloney	**34**	**162**	**337.0**	**17.0**	**354.0**	**8.741**	**3**	**1**	**4**
§Hugh Saunders	19	86	145.0	18.0	163.0	7.581			
§Alan Jackson	32	136	224.0	16.0	240.0	7.059		1	1
Terry Stone	23	104	153.0	25.0	178.0	6.846	1		1
§§Nigel Rackett	9	37	48.0	11.0	59.0	6.378			
Dingle Brown	7	27	34.0	2.0	36.0	5.333			
§§Garry Moore	33	125	124.0	23.0	147.0	4.704			
§§Allan Emmett	10	25	25.5	2.0	27.5	4.400			
§George Barclay	13	44	42.0	4.0	46.0	4.182			
§Tony Hall	22	77	59.0	12.0	71.0	3.688			
Ian Champion	12	36	28.0	3.0	31.0	3.444			
§§Laurie Guilfoyle	7	23	11.0	3.0	14.0	2.435			
§§Dave Heritage	1	2	1.0	0.0	1.0	2.000			
§Colin Clark	1	1	0.0	0.0	0.0	0.000			
Barry Lee	1	1	0.0	0.0	0.0	0.000			

1971...1971...1971...1971...1971...1971

	M	R	Pts	BP	TPts	Ave	F	P	Total
Alan Jackson	1	5	12.0	1.0	13.0	10.400			
Hugh Saunders	33	164	358.0	28.0	386.0	9.415	1	4	5
Geoff Maloney	29	130	205.0	35.0	240.0	7.385	1		1
§Bob Young	**34**	**151**	**217.0**	**35.0**	**252.0**	**6.675**		**1**	**1**
Allan Emmett	28	123	178.0	20.0	198.0	6.439			
Nigel Rackett	17	69	100.0	10.0	110.0	6.377			
Dingle Brown	28	110	158.0	5.0	163.0	5.927	2		2
Terry Stone	24	68	66.0	13.0	79.0	4.647			
§§David Beech	14	48	49.0	3.0	52.0	4.333			
§Peter Claridge	2	3	1.0	1.0	2.0	2.667			
§Mike Weston	1	2	1.0	0.0	1.0	2.000			
§§Dave Slatford	3	7	1.0	0.0	1.0	0.571			
§Brian Osborn	1	3	0.0	0.0	0.0	0.000			

1972...1972...1972...1972...1972...1972

	M	R	Pts	BP	TPts	Ave	F	P	Total
Geoff Maloney	15	65	163.0	5.0	168.0	10.338	4	1	5
Bob Young	**34**	**146**	**302.0**	**17.0**	**319.0**	**8.740**	**6**	**4**	**10**
§Brian Foote	20	84	171.0	11.0	182.0	8.667	1	2	3
Allen Emmett	33	135	253.0	24.0	277.0	8.207	4	2	6
§§Peter Wigley	1	5	9.0	0.0	9.0	7.200			
§Trevor Barnwell	21	81	104.0	22.0	126.0	6.222		1	1
Dingle Brown	18	68	90.0	14.0	104.0	6.118			
David Beech	18	126	155.0	31.0	186.0	5.905		1	1
Nigel Rackett	10	32	34.0	7.0	41.0	5.125			
§§Ivan Miller	8	23	28.0	1.0	29.0	5.043			
Peter Claridge	18	53	50.0	8.0	58.0	4.377			
Terry Stone	21	58	45.0	10.0	55.0	3.793			
§Les Ott	3	8	2.0	0.0	2.0	1.000			

1973...1973...1973...1973...1973...1973

	M	R	Pts	BP	TPts	Ave	F	P	Total
Allen Emmett	1	4	9.0	2.0	11.0	11.000			
§§Peter Moore	31	148	289.0	18.0	307.0	8.297	1	1	2
Peter Claridge	1	1	2.0	0.0	2.0	8.000			
Bob Young	**40**	**187**	**297.0**	**32.0**	**329.0**	**7.037**	**1**	**2**	**3**
Trevor Barnwell	27	116	165.0	26.0	191.0	6.586		1	1
David Beech	**40**	**168**	**244.0**	**13.0**	**257.0**	**6.119**	**3**		**3**
Les Ott	33	128	164.0	24.0	188.0	5.875			
Brian Foote	11	48	59.0	10.0	69.0	5.750			
Terry Stone	17	52	59.5	9.0	68.5	5.269			
§Peter Cairns	27	83	88.0	15.0	103.0	4.964	1		1
Peter Wigley	14	36	33.0	8.0	41.0	4.556			
Dingle Brown	7	28	27.0	3.0	30.0	4.286			
§§John Gibbons	6	19	15.0	4.0	19.0	4.000			
§§Steve Clarke	8	19	13.0	4.0	17.0	3.579			

EASTER TROPHY

1965	1 Jim Heard	2 Terry Stone	3 Malcolm Brown

EASTERN COUNTIES CHAMPIONSHIP

1968	1 Vic White	2 Peter Seaton	3 Mike Gardner
1969	1 Laurie Etheridge	2 Geoff Ambrose	3 Roger Wright
1971	1 John Louis	2 Peter Bailey	3 Mike Vernam
1972	1 Brian Foote	2 Bob Young	3 Allen Emmett

ESSEX OPEN CHAMPIONSHIP

1972	1 Gordon Kennett	2 Bob Young	3 Dingle Brown

HOOVER CHALLENGE TROPHY

1973	1 John Davis	2 Mike Broadbank	3 Peter Moore

EVENING ECHO EASTER TROPHY

1973	1 Roger Johns	2 Bob Young	3 Jack Millen

■ *INDUSTRIAL development of the valuable site with easy access to both London and the coast, forced the eventual closure of Rayleigh at the end of the 1973 season.*

■ *It had been inevitable for some years and in their latter seasons the Rockets knew they were living on borrowed time.*

■ *The side was moved, en bloc, across the county border to Hertfordshire where they set up new home at Hoddesdon and became the Rye House Rockets from the opening of the 1974 campaign.*

READING

■ *ALLIED PRESENTATIONS LIMITED – a consortium of leading promoters – brought speedway to Royal Berkshire where the Reading Racers staged their opening Division Two match against Nelson on Monday, June 17, 1968.*

Led by former Hackney star John Poyser, the Racers, adopting as winged wheel as their emblem, reached the Knock Out Cup Final and a reported 6,000 crowd saw them go down to Canterbury. An early discovery, in 1969, was grass tracker Bernie Leigh who went on to become one of the most popular riders in the club's history.

After three highly successful seasons Reading stepped up into the First Division but after six seasons at Tilehurst – a greyhound stadium – they were forced to look for a new virgin site on which to build a new stadium because of redevelopment at their old track.

1968...1968...1968...1968...1968...1968

	M	R	Pts	BP	TPts	Ave	F	P	Total
§§John Poyser	**23**	**102**	**230.0**	**7.0**	**237.0**	**9.294**	**5**	**1**	**6**
§§Vic White	5	27	54.0	4.0	58.0	8.593	1		1
§§Ian Champion	14	59	94.0	8.0	102.0	6.915			
§§Joe Wiechlbauer	13	50	74.0	12.0	86.0	6.880			
§§Ted Spittles	**23**	**94**	**146.0**	**11.0**	**157.0**	**6.681**		**1**	**1**
§§Stuart Wallace	20	78	103.0	18.0	121.0	6.205			
§§Dene Davies	18	69	81.0	12.0	93.0	5.391			
§§Ian Bottomley	10	35	38.0	5.0	43.0	4.914			
§§Phil Pratt	22	74	65.0	20.0	85.0	4.595			
§§Paul Walch	6	21	19.0	5.0	24.0	4.571			
§§Pete Saunders	5	11	9.0	3.0	12.0	4.364			
§§Danny Dennis	1	3	1.0	1.0	2.0	2.667			
§§Fred Hodder	1	3	1.0	0.0	1.0	1.333			

READING OPEN CHAMPIONSHIP

1968	1 Graham Plant	2 John Poyser	3 Allan Brown
1970	1 Richard May	2 John Louis	3 Bernie Leigh

STADIUM TROPHY

1968	1 Graham Plant	2 Dene Davies	3 Mick Handley
1969	1 Barry Crowson	2 Peter Bradshaw	3 Dene Davies
1970	1 Richard May	2 Mike Vernam	3 Alan Knapkin

PETER ARNOLD MEMORIAL TROPHY

1969	1 John Harrhy	2 Martyn Piddock	3 Mick Bell
1970	1 Richard May	2 Arthur Price	3 John Harrhy

See also Reading, Division One Averages

1969...1969...1969...1969...1969...1969

	M	R	Pts	BP	TPts	Ave	F	P	Total
§§Mick Bell	32	131	277.0	19.0	296.0	9.038	2	1	3
§§Richard May	24	97	181.0	12.0	193.0	7.959			
§Mike Vernam	32	131	233.0	22.0	255.0	7.786	2		2
§§Alan Jackson	17	60	94.0	18.0	112.0	7.467	1	1	2
Ian Champion	16	62	91.0	12.0	103.0	6.645			
Phil Pratt	22	79	109.0	16.0	125.0	6.329		1	1
Dene Davies	32	119	157.0	27.0	184.0	6.185		1	1
§§Bob Tabet	**33**	**107**	**119.0**	**27.0**	**146.0**	**5.458**			
§§Bernie Leigh	18	61	70.0	7.0	77.0	5.049			
§§Dave Grimley	1	3	3.0	0.0	3.0	4.000			

1970...1970...1970...1970...1970...1970

	M	R	Pts	BP	TPts	Ave	F	P	Total
Richard May	30	127	302.0	2.0	304.0	9.575	6	1	7
Mike Vernam	30	123	265.0	12.0	277.0	9.008	6		6
Bernie Leigh	**33**	**130**	**186.5**	**38.0**	**224.5**	**6.908**		**1**	**1**
Bob Tabet	5	21	31.0	2.0	33.0	6.286			
§§Bob Young	26	104	141.0	18.0	159.0	6.115			
§Phil Pratt	14	44	51.0	8.0	59.0	5.364			
Dene Davies	32	122	142.0	19.0	161.0	5.279			
§John Hammond	28	99	106.0	19.0	125.0	5.051			
§Cec Platt	20	59	52.0	10.0	62.0	4.203			
§Neil Glover	2	4	3.0	1.0	4.0	4.000			
§§Mike Holt	1	3	3.0	0.0	3.0	4.000			
§Dave Whitaker	3	10	7.0	1.0	8.0	3.200			
§Roger Knight	1	3	1.0	1.0	2.0	2.667			
Dave Grimley	1	3	0.0	0.0	0.0	0.000			
§John Knock	1	3	0.0	0.0	0.0	0.000			

ROCHDALE

■ *BELLE VUE turned to the Athletics Grounds in Rochdale home at that time of the local Rugby League club – when they searched for a new home base for the Second Division Colts.*

■ *A big, fast 427 yard track, it was an ideal proving ground for the Belle Vue youngsters but the crowds didn't respond and after two seasons of operating in Division Two the track closed down and remained so staging regular stock car racing although eventually the Rugby League club moved in with their soccer club neighbours and the stadium was designated for redevelopment.*

1970...1970...1970...1970...1970...1970

	M	R	Pts	BP	TPts	Ave	F	P	Total
§Eric Broadbelt	32	139	344.0	6.0	350.0	10.072	11	1	12
§Taffy Owen	25	101	222.0	16.0	238.0	9.426	3	3	6
§Chris Bailey	22	89	158.0	25.0	183.0	8.225	1	4	5
§Steve Waplington	26	107	198.0	17.0	215.0	8.037	3	2	5
§§Alan Wilkinson	31	124	209.0	39.0	248.0	8.000		4	4
§§Paul Tyrer	28	111	156.0	33.0	189.0	6.811		3	3
§Ken Moss	31	112	150.0	25.0	175.0	6.250	1		1
§Gerry Richardson	21	65	65.0	14.0	79.0	4.862		1	1
§Colin Goad	8	26	23.0	6.0	29.0	4.462			
§Phil Whitaker	3	10	8.0	0.0	8.0	3.200			
§§Robbie Gardner	5	13	5.0	1.0	6.0	1.846			
§§Gerry James	1	3	1.0	0.0	1.0	1.333			
§§Paul Callaghan	1	2	0.0	0.0	0.0	0.000			

1971...1971...1971...1971...1971...1971

	M	R	Pts	BP	TPts	Ave	F	P	Total
Alan Wilkinson	19	79	193.0	6.0	199.0	10.076	2	3	5
§§Peter Collins	30	140	323.0	20.0	343.0	9.800	4	2	6
Paul Tyrer	37	158	297.0	16.0	313.0	7.924	2	1	3
Ken Moss	37	145	172.0	24.0	196.0	5.407			
§§Graham Drury	26	100	108.0	27.0	135.0	5.400			
Colin Goad	37	128	127.0	23.0	150.0	4.688			
Robbie Gardner	34	122	117.0	25.0	142.0	4.656			
§Terry Kelly	12	45	41.0	7.0	48.0	4.267			
Paul Callaghan	11	35	18.0	4.0	22.0	2.514			
§§Clive Johnson	11	29	14.0	3.0	17.0	2.345			
§§Ian Hindle	5	13	7.0	0.0	7.0	2.154			
§§Craig Pendlebury	1	4	2.0	0.0	2.0	2.000			
§§Colin Meredith	2	8	3.0	0.0	3.0	1.500			
§§Mitch Graham	1	3	0.0	0.0	0.0	0.000			
Gerry Richardson	1	3	0.0	0.0	0.0	0.000			
§§Geoff Lyon	1	2	0.0	0.0	0.0	0.000			

■ *ROCHDALE will always deserve a place in any history of British speedway because it was the track that saw the debut season of England's 1976 World Champion Peter Collins.*

His enormous and exciting potential was there to see in the statistics of his first season when, as a 16-year-old, he averaged nearly 10 points a meeting, scoring nearly 350 points in a highly competitive 1971 Second Division.

ROMFORD

1969...1969...1969...1969...1969...1969

	M	R	Pts	BP	TPts	Ave	F	P	Total
§Barry Duke	2	8	24.0	0.0	24.0	12.000	2		2
§§Des Lukehurst	11	42	120.5	0.5	121.0	11.524	6	1	7
§§Ross Gilbertson	31	137	334.0	12.0	346.0	10.102	5	4	9
§Phil Woodcock	30	133	285.5	19.5	305.0	9.173	4	2	6
§§Brian Davies	15	61	105.0	6.0	111.0	7.279	1		1
§Tony George	7	27	37.0	3.0	40.0	5.926			
§Brian Foote	23	84	99.0	16.0	115.0	5.476		1	1
§Mick Steel	2	8	9.0	1.0	10.0	5.000			
§Frank Wendon	25	93	99.0	17.0	116.0	4.989			
§§Brian Curtis	7	13	14.0	2.0	16.0	4.923			
§Ian Gills	16	56	57.0	8.0	65.0	4.643		1	1
§§Charlie Benham	28	94	68.0	12.0	80.0	3.404			
§Chris Yeatman	8	30	20.0	4.0	24.0	3.200			
§§Roland Schofield	7	22	10.0	2.0	12.0	2.182			
§§Adrian Baker	2	7	2.0	0.0	2.0	1.143			
§§Roger Knight	2	6	1.0	0.0	1.0	0.667			
§§Brian Read	1	1	0.0	0.0	0.0	0.000			

1970...1970...1970...1970...1970...1970

	M	R	Pts	BP	TPts	Ave	F	P	Total
Phil Woodcock	29	124	267.0	8.0	275.0	8.871	7		7
Ross Gilbertson	**33**	**142**	**288.0**	**21.0**	**309.0**	**8.704**	**1**	**3**	**4**
Des Lukehurst	7	31	63.0	1.0	64.0	8.258	1		1
§Geoff Penniket	7	28	57.0	2.0	59.0	8.429			
Brian Foote	32	122	182.0	27.0	209.0	6.852	1		1
§Colin Sanders	**33**	**126**	**161.5**	**33.0**	**194.5**	**6.175**			
Ian Gills	20	71	84.0	17.0	101.0	5.690	1		1
Charlie Benham	26	74	81.0	18.0	99.0	5.351			
§§Kevin Holden	28	92	87.0	20.0	107.0	4.652			
Tony George	5	15	10.0	1.0	11.0	2.933			
§John Hibben	7	24	15.0	2.0	17.0	2.833			
§Mike Holt	1	3	1.0	0.0	1.0	1.333			
§§Dave O'Connor	1	2	0.0	0.0	0.0	0.000			
Frank Wendon	1	2	1.0	1.0	2.0	4.000			

1971...1971...1971...1971...1971...1971

	M	R	Pts	BP	TPts	Ave	F	P	Total
Phil Woodcock	2	8	19.0	1.0	20.0	10.000	1		1
Kevin Holden	33	152	317.0	23.0	340.0	8.947	4		4
§Bob Coles	14	62	119.0	6.0	125.0	8.065	2	1	3
Brian Foote	25	99	185.0	13.0	198.0	8.000			
§Dave Percy	1	1	1.0	1.0	2.0	8.000			
§§Stan Stevens	14	63	94.0	10.0	104.0	6.603			
§§Mike Sampson	12	43	53.0	13.0	66.0	6.140			
§Mike Vernam	24	87	119.0	14.0	133.0	6.115			
Colin Sanders	21	72	89.0	15.0	104.0	5.778			
Charlie Benham	**34**	**129**	**144.5**	**24.0**	**168.5**	**5.225**			
Ian Gills	20	72	66.0	20.0	86.0	4.778			
§Clark Facey	5	18	20.0	1.0	21.0	4.667			
§Terry Shearer	8	27	25.0	6.0	31.0	4.593			
§§Bruce Edgar	9	24	13.0	5.0	18.0	3.000			
§Dene Davies	6	15	7.0	1.0	8.0	2.133			
§Ted Spittles	1	2	1.0	0.0	1.0	2.000			
§Ron Edwards	1	2	0.0	0.0	0.0	0.000			
§Colin Clark	1	1	0.0	0.0	0.0	0.000			

BORO INDIVIDUAL TROPHY

1969	1 Geoff Ambrose	2 Phil Woodcock	3 Martyn Piddock

BATTLE OF BRITAIN TROPHY

1969	1 Ross Gilbertson	2 Mick Bell	3 Geoff Maloney
1970	1 Phil Woodcock	2 Ross Gilbertson	3 Alan Jackson

CARNIVAL ROSEBOWL TROPHY

1970	1 Phil Woodcock	2 John Louis	3 Ross Gilbertson
1971	1 Kevin Holden	2 Tony Childs	3 Colin Sanders

RECORDER TROPHY

1970	1 Dave Jessup	2 Ross Gilbertson	3 Des Lukehurst
1971	1 George Major	2 Tony Childs	3 Stan Stevens

SPRING CUP CLASSIC

1971	1 Kevin Holden	2 Brian Foote	3 Colin Sanders, Tony Childs, Hugh Saunders

BOMBERS ON PARADE...The 1969 Romford team, Phil Woodcock, Judd Drew, Ross Gilbertson (on bike), Chris Yeatman, Frank Wendon. Kneeling: Tony George and Charlie Benham

RYE HOUSE

■ *RYE HOUSE, a long-time Sunday afternoon training track, finally welcomed genuine League racing to their Hoddesdon circuit when Len Silver moved his Rayleigh team to the Lea Valley arena. Former England rider Colin Pratt, who began as manager, became a co-promoter in 1976 and introduced a hugely successful youth policy which ensured the track's viability.*

1974...1974...1974...1974...1974...1974

	M	R	Pts	BP	TPts	Ave	F	P	Total
§Brian Foote	**38**	**183**	**352.0**	**11.0**	**363.0**	**7.934**	**4**		**4**
§Steve Clarke	8	29	43.0	11.0	54.0	7.448		1	1
§§Clive Hitch	13	61	92.0	13.0	105.0	6.885		1	1
§Trevor Barnwell	24	96	147.0	14.0	161.0	6.708			
§George Barclay	10	48	65.0	2.0	67.0	5.583			
§Peter Moore	15	49	58.0	8.0	66.0	5.388			
§Bob Young	**38**	**147**	**163.0**	**32.0**	**195.0**	**5.306**			
§John Gibbons	34	127	149.0	19.0	168.0	5.291			
§§Bob Cooper	27	82	78.0	20.0	98.0	4.780			
§Peter Wigley	37	122	115.0	18.0	133.0	4.361			
§Les Ott	5	14	11.0	4.0	15.0	4.286			
§Stan Stevens	12	27	17.0	4.0	21.0	3.111			
§Allen Emmett	3	6	1.0	0.0	1.0	0.667			

1975...1975...1975...1975...1975...1975

	M	R	Pts	BP	TPts	Ave	F	P	Total
Brian Foote	**40**	**185**	**371.0**	**17.0**	**388.0**	**8.389**	**3**	**2**	**5**
§Hugh Saunders	24	97	161.0	20.0	181.0	7.464			
Bob Cooper	39	166	240.0	40.0	280.0	6.747		1	1
§§Chris Mackett	1	3	3.0	2.0	5.0	6.667			
§Kelvin Mullarkey	32	126	176.0	21.0	197.0	6.254			
§David Beech	36	128	164.0	18.0	182.0	5.688		1	1
John Gibbons	10	32	36.0	6.0	42.0	5.250			
Bob Young	19	60	56.0	15.0	71.0	4.733			
§Dingle Brown	27	84	83.0	14.0	97.0	4.619			
§§Karl Fiala	30	96	92.0	18.0	110.0	4.583			
§John Waldrab	2	8	7.0	2.0	9.0	4.500			
§Barry Duke	8	24	22.0	4.0	26.0	4.333			
Steve Clarke	10	31	25.0	5.0	30.0	3.871			

1976...1976...1976...1976...1976...1976

	M	R	Pts	BP	TPts	Ave	F	P	Total
§Ted Hubbard	35	154	340.0	13.0	353.0	9.169	4	4	8
Kelvin Mullarkey	**37**	**160**	**263.0**	**39.0**	**302.0**	**7.550**	**2**	**1**	**3**
Hugh Saunders	**37**	**144**	**229.0**	**40.0**	**269.0**	**7.472**	**1**	**4**	**5**
Brian Foote	17	66	105.0	11.0	116.0	7.030		1	1
Karl Fiala	32	132	198.0	24.0	222.0	6.727		1	1
David Beech	1	3	4.0	1.0	5.0	6.667			
§§Bob Garrad	36	135	186.0	21.0	207.0	6.133		1	1
Bob Cooper	16	54	61.0	8.0	69.0	5.111			
§§Ashley Pullen	30	94	100.5	15.0	115.5	4.915			
John Waldrab	6	16	8.0	3.0	11.0	2.750			

1977...1977...1977...1977...1977...1977

	M	R	Pts	BP	TPts	Ave	F	P	Total
Kelvin Mullarkey	**40**	**176**	**373.0**	**29.0**	**402.0**	**9.136**	**5**	**5**	**10**
Ted Hubbard	30	121	245.0	28.0	273.0	9.025	2	4	6
Bob Garrad	**40**	**165**	**301.0**	**32.0**	**333.0**	**8.073**	**2**	**3**	**5**
Hugh Saunders	39	158	249.0	40.0	289.0	7.316		4	4
Karl Fiala	30	110	151.0	20.0	171.0	6.218		2	2
Ashley Pullen	**40**	**144**	**194.0**	**26.0**	**220.0**	**6.111**		**2**	**2**
§Peter Tarrant	6	18	22.0	5.0	27.0	6.000			
Bob Cooper	39	132	135.0	23.0	158.0	4.788			
§Alan Diprose	4	10	5.0	2.0	7.0	2.800			

1978...1978...1978...1978...1978...1978

	M	R	Pts	BP	TPts	Ave	F	P	Total
Ted Hubbard	46	190	409.5	33.0	442.5	9.316	2	10	12
Kelvin Mullarkey	**48**	**201**	**413.0**	**45.0**	**458.0**	**9.114**	**2**	**5**	**7**
Karl Fiala	**48**	**187**	**326.0**	**39.0**	**365.0**	**7.807**	**3**	**4**	**7**
Hugh Saunders	36	137	215.0	50.0	265.0	7.737		3	3
Bob Garrad	46	177	294.0	39.0	333.0	7.525	1	3	4
Ashley Pullen	**48**	**168**	**256.0**	**32.0**	**288.0**	**6.857**	**2**	**1**	**3**
Peter Tarrant	34	103	100.0	25.0	125.0	4.854			
Bob Cooper	7	19	17.0	6.0	23.0	4.842			
§Kevin Smith	22	68	71.0	11.0	82.0	4.824			

1979...1979...1979...1979...1979...1979

	M	R	Pts	BP	TPts	Ave	F	P	Total
Karl Fiala	**46**	**187**	**387.0**	**43.0**	**430.0**	**9.198**	**6**	**5**	**11**
Bob Garrad	**46**	**188**	**404.0**	**24.0**	**428.0**	**9.106**	**4**	**5**	**9**
Kelvin Mullarkey	**46**	**191**	**332.0**	**84.0**	**416.0**	**8.712**		**7**	**7**
Kevin Smith	42	164	311.0	25.0	336.0	8.195	4	1	5
Ted Hubbard	31	126	236.0	21.0	257.0	8.159	3	1	4
Ashley Pullen	44	152	239.0	40.0	279.0	7.342		2	2
Hugh Saunders	39	129	171.0	41.0	212.0	6.574		1	1
Peter Tarrant	18	52	49.0	19.0	68.0	5.231			
§§Simon Aindow	4	7	4.0	0.0	4.0	2.286			

1980...1980...1980...1980...1980...1980

	M	R	Pts	BP	TPts	Ave	F	P	Total
Bob Garrad	**40**	**169**	**410.0**	**6.0**	**416.0**	**9.846**	**11**	**2**	**13**
Karl Fiala	**40**	**163**	**360.0**	**25.0**	**385.0**	**9.448**	**6**	**5**	**11**
Kelvin Mullarkey	**40**	**161**	**305.0**	**69.0**	**374.0**	**9.292**	**2**	**8**	**10**
Kevin Smith	**40**	**157**	**292.0**	**39.0**	**331.0**	**8.433**		**7**	**7**
Ashley Pullen	**40**	**152**	**225.0**	**35.0**	**260.0**	**6.842**	**1**	**1**	**2**
Peter Tarrant	35	117	131.0	38.0	169.0	5.778		1	1
Simon Aindow	1	3	3.0	1.0	4.0	5.333			
§§Andy Fines	21	61	50.0	12.0	62.0	4.066			
§§Carl Squirrell	12	33	22.0	3.0	25.0	3.030			
§§Barry King	11	25	14.0	1.0	15.0	2.400			

1981...1981...1981...1981...1981...1981

	M	R	Pts	BP	TPts	Ave	F	P	Total
Andy Fines	2	8	18.0	4.0	22.0	11.000		1	1
Bob Garrad	25	113	232.0	18.0	250.0	8.850	4	1	5
Kelvin Mullarkey	**39**	**179**	**345.0**	**25.0**	**370.0**	**8.268**	**1**	**2**	**3**
§Steve Naylor	**39**	**168**	**307.0**	**15.0**	**322.0**	**7.667**	**1**	**1**	**2**
§Kevin Bowen	34	114	123.0	21.0	144.0	5.053		1	1
§§Peter Johns	18	51	49.0	11.0	60.0	4.706			
Peter Tarrant	14	58	61.0	6.0	67.0	4.621		1	1
§§Marvyn Cox	37	148	136.0	33.0	169.0	4.568	1	1	2
Garry Monk	20	47	45.0	8.0	53.0	4.511			
Carl Squirrell	4	10	11.0	0.0	11.0	4.400			
Barry King	15	59	50.0	12.0	62.0	4.203			
Simon Aindow	4	15	10.0	1.0	11.0	2.933			
§Phil Vance	5	17	11.0	0.0	11.0	2.588			
§Tony Garard	15	44	21.0	3.0	24.0	2.182			
§§Martin Hagon	1	2	1.0	0.0	1.0	2.000			
§§Colin Tarrant	1	1	0.0	0.0	0.0	0.000			

1982...1982...1982...1982...1982...1982

	M	R	Pts	BP	TPts	Ave	F	P	Total
Bob Garrad	**42**	**229**	**536.0**	**28.0**	**564.0**	**9.852**	**7**	**2**	**9**
Marvyn Cox	27	143	287.0	30.0	317.0	8.867	1	2	3
Kelvin Mullarkey	**42**	**220**	**391.0**	**37.0**	**428.0**	**7.782**	**1**	**4**	**5**
Steve Naylor	41	212	384.0	25.0	409.0	7.717	4	2	6
Peter Johns	37	134	130.0	36.0	166.0	4.955		1	1
§John Barclay	6	19	18.0	5.0	23.0	4.842			
Andy Fines	33	136	134.0	25.0	159.0	4.676			
§Steve Bryenton	35	144	123.0	32.0	155.0	4.306		1	1
Garry Monk	13	46	31.0	4.0	35.0	3.043			
§§Paul Hilton	6	17	6.0	1.0	7.0	1.647			
Kevin Bowen	7	17	3.0	1.0	4.0	0.941			
§§Lee Edwards	1	1	0.0	0.0	0.0	0.000			

1983...1983...1983...1983...1983...1983

	M	R	Pts	BP	TPts	Ave	F	P	Total
Marvyn Cox	37	210	509.0	7.0	516.0	9.829	8	1	9
Bob Garrad	**38**	**213**	**483.0**	**11.0**	**494.0**	**9.277**	**8**	**1**	**9**
Steve Naylor	22	106	188.0	24.0	212.0	8.000	1	2	3
Peter Johns	8	37	57.0	8.0	65.0	7.027			
§§Kerry Gray	23	120	152.0	20.0	172.0	5.733			
Steve Bryenton	**38**	**200**	**243.0**	**42.0**	**285.0**	**5.700**		**1**	**1**
§§Andrew Silver	9	29	28.0	6.0	34.0	4.690			
Kevin Bowen	15	60	59.0	10.0	69.0	4.600			
§§Chris Chaplin	24	90	53.0	12.0	65.0	2.889			
§Terry Broadbank	11	39	24.0	4.0	28.0	2.872			
§§Mark Sales	5	13	6.0	2.0	8.0	2.462			
§§Mike Fitzpatrick	3	6	2.0	1.0	3.0	2.000			
John Barclay	16	61	15.0	4.0	19.0	1.246			
§§Cliff Ottewell	5	11	2.0	1.0	3.0	1.091			
Garry Monk	4	12	1.0	0.0	1.0	0.333			

RYE HOUSE

1984...1984...1984...1984...1984...1984

	M	R	Pts	BP	TPts	Ave	F	P	Total
Bob Garrad	**32**	**150**	**309.0**	**17.0**	**326.0**	**8.693**		**5**	**5**
§§Peter Turle	1	1	1.0	1.0	2.0	8.000			
Andrew Silver	27	117	203.0	25.0	228.0	7.795		1	1
Steve Naylor	19	77	144.0	4.0	148.0	7.688			
Kevlin Mullarkey	24	111	173.0	24.0	197.0	7.099			
Kerry Gray	26	112	141.0	19.0	160.0	5.714		1	1
Steve Bryenton	19	74	82.0	19.0	101.0	5.459			
Chris Chaplin	30	95	96.0	21.0	117.0	4.926			
§§Michael Keepe	10	28	24.0	3.0	27.0	3.857			
§Mark Chessell	8	27	24.0	1.0	25.0	3.704			
§§Gary Rolls	11	29	17.0	7.0	24.0	3.310			
Peter Johns	2	8	5.0	1.0	6.0	3.000			
§§Richard Harris	1	3	1.0	0.0	1.0	1.333			
§Andy Steward	2	5	0.0	0.0	0.0	0.000			

1985...1985...1985...1985...1985...1985

	M	R	Pts	BP	TPts	Ave	F	P	Total
§Julian Parr	3	13	25.0	5.0	30.0	9.231			
Andrew Silver	**38**	**191**	**385.0**	**26.0**	**411.0**	**8.607**	**4**	**2**	**6**
§§Rob Allen	1	2	2.0	2.0	4.0	8.000			
§§Alastair Stevens	37	166	274.0	32.0	306.0	7.373	1	2	3
§Rob Woffinden	22	100	155.0	16.0	171.0	6.840			
Bob Garrad	34	154	216.0	28.0	244.0	6.338	1	2	3
Kelvin Mullarkey	34	149	184.0	36.0	220.0	5.906		1	1
Steve Naylor	2	8	9.0	2.0	11.0	5.500			
§Kevin Brice	23	69	70.0	6.0	76.0	4.406			
§Neil Cotton	10	24	20.0	6.0	26.0	4.333			
§Paul Coward	1	2	1.0	1.0	2.0	4.000			
Chris Chaplin	4	11	8.0	2.0	10.0	3.636			
§Keith Millard	13	36	25.0	3.0	28.0	3.111			
Gary Rolls	10	27	17.0	4.0	21.0	3.111			
§§Nigel Leaver	8	19	8.0	2.0	10.0	2.105			
§§Russell Paine	1	2	0.0	0.0	0.0	0.000			

1986...1986...1986...1986...1986...1986

	M	R	Pts	BP	TPts	Ave	F	P	Total
§Paul Woods	41	177	391.0	6.0	397.0	8.972	5	1	6
§Alan Mogridge	18	77	123.0	22.0	145.0	7.532	1		1
Alastair Stevens	**42**	**173**	**301.0**	**22.0**	**323.0**	**7.468**	**3**		**3**
§Paul Bosley	32	125	176.0	12.0	188.0	6.016			
Kevin Brice	39	150	173.0	32.0	205.0	5.467			
Bob Garrad	**42**	**155**	**180.0**	**30.0**	**210.0**	**5.419**	**1**		**1**
Julian Parr	30	94	101.0	17.0	118.0	5.021			
§Linden Warner	35	99	96.0	18.0	114.0	4.606			
Mike Fitzpatrick	3	9	7.0	1.0	8.0	3.556			
Chris Chaplin	2	6	4.0	1.0	5.0	3.333			
§§Colin Lambkin	9	19	2.0	1.0	3.0	0.632			

1987...1987...1987...1987...1987...1987

	M	R	Pts	BP	TPts	Ave	F	P	Total
Paul Woods	31	146	288.0	8.0	296.0	8.110	1	1	2
Barry Thomas	31	142	228.0	18.0	246.0	6.930		2	2
§Jame Luckhurst	7	30	45.0	3.0	48.0	6.400			
§Gary Brown	1	3	4.0	0.0	4.0	5.333			
Kevin Brice	31	124	147.0	11.0	158.0	5.097			
Linden Warner	19	69	71.0	15.0	86.0	4.986			
§Kevin Teager	31	128	123.0	31.0	154.0	4.813			
Gary Rolls	21	63	56.0	14.0	70.0	4.444			
§Rob Parish	8	27	25.0	3.0	28.0	4.148			
Steve Bryenton	10	23	19.0	4.0	23.0	4.000			
§Rob Fortune	5	21	19.0	1.0	20.0	3.810			
Julian Parr	13	41	27.0	9.0	36.0	3.512			
§James Hayhow	1	2	1.0	0.0	1.0	2.000			
§§John Wainwright	2	7	2.0	0.0	2.0	1.143			
§§Gary Thompson	4	8	1.0	0.0	1.0	0.500			
§§Martin Cobbin	1	3	0.0	0.0	0.0	0.000			
§Paul Coward	1	2	0.0	0.0	0.0	0.000			
§Jason Straughan	1	2	0.0	0.0	0.0	0.000			

HERTS GOLD CUP

1975	1 Brian Clark	2 Arthur Browning and Alan Sage	
1976	1 Joe Owen	2 Mike Broadbank	3 Vic Harding
1979	1 Andy Grahame	2 Tom Owen	3 Bob Garrad
1981	1 Bob Garrad	2 Kelvin Mullarkey	3 Kevin Bowen
1983	1 Martin Yeates	2 Marvyn Cox	3 Bob Garrad

FAREWELL TROPHY

1976	1 Kelvin Mullarkey	2 Bob Garrad	3 Karl Fiala

HARTSMAN LAGER CHASE

1984	1 Barry Thomas	2 Bob Garrad	3 Kevin Teager

SUPPORTERS' CLUB TROPHY

1984	1 Bob Garrad	2 Andrew Silver	3 Steve Naylor

HARTSMAN LAGER CHALLENGE CUP

1984	1 Andrew Silver	2 Keith White	3 Jamie Luckhurst and Steve Naylor

MERCURY INVITATION CHAMPIONSHIP

1990	1 Steve Schofield	2 Jens Rasmussen	3 Andy Galvin

1988...1988...1988...1988...1988...1988

	M	R	Pts	BP	TPts	Ave	F	P	Total
§§Jens Rasmussen	30	162	367.0	9.0	376.0	9.284	5	1	6
Paul Woods	24	133	254.0	16.0	270.0	8.120		1	1
§Steve Wilcock	**32**	**173**	**235.0**	**36.0**	**271.0**	**6.266**		**1**	**1**
§Mark Lyndon	27	136	171.0	19.0	190.0	5.588			
Kevin Brice	28	127	126.0	18.0	144.0	4.535		1	1
§Carl Chalcraft	28	119	110.0	24.0	134.0	4.504			
§§Peter Schroeck	19	82	62.0	9.0	71.0	3.463			
John Wainwright	18	45	27.0	3.0	30.0	2.667			
Kevin Teager	12	42	20.0	5.0	25.0	2.381			
§Sean Barker	2	6	2.0	0.0	2.0	1.333			
§Wally Hill	1	3	0.0	0.0	0.0	0.000			

1989...1989...1989...1989...1989...1989

	M	R	Pts	BP	TPts	Ave	F	P	Total
Jens Rasmussen	**36**	**192**	**416.0**	**30.0**	**446.0**	**9.292**	**3**	**3**	**6**
Glen Baxter	35	192	363.0	20.0	383.0	7.979	1	1	2
§Melvyn Taylor	33	171	326.0	6.0	332.0	7.766	1		1
Paul Woods	6	28	34.0	10.0	44.0	6.286			
Martin Cobbin	3	6	5.0	4.0	9.0	6.000			
Kelvin Mullarkey	11	54	58.0	18.0	76.0	5.630			
Kevin Brice	31	145	145.0	22.0	167.0	4.607			
Jamie Fagg	25	103	91.0	16.0	107.0	4.155			
Peter Schroeck	22	93	76.0	18.0	94.0	4.043			
Carl Chalcraft	32	109	86.0	22.0	108.0	3.963			
§§Trevor O'Brien	13	53	41.5	6.0	47.5	3.585			
§Colin Thorpe	3	6	3.0	2.0	5.0	3.333			

1990...1990...1990...1990...1990...1990

	M	R	Pts	BP	TPts	Ave	F	P	Total
Jens Rasmussen	33	191	441.0	6.0	447.0	9.361	2	1	3
Melvyn Taylor	11	56	119.0	5.0	124.0	8.857			
Glen Baxter	28	160	293.0	15.0	308.0	7.700	1		1
§Roger Johns	13	75	103.0	11.0	114.0	6.080			
Jamie Fagg	9	42	49.0	11.0	60.0	5.714			
Trevor O'Brien	**34**	**187**	**218.0**	**34.0**	**252.0**	**5.390**			
§Scott Humphries	11	58	57.0	11.0	68.0	4.690			
§§Wayne Baxter	24	91	72.0	9.0	81.0	3.560			
§Nigel Sparshott	14	56	34.0	10.0	44.0	3.143			
Kevin Teager	6	27	16.0	3.0	19.0	2.815			
Kelvin Mullarkey	13	47	25.0	8.0	33.0	2.809			
Linden Warner	14	69	32.0	7.0	39.0	2.261			
Colin Thorpe	2	4	1.0	0.0	1.0	1.000			

RYE HOUSE CHAMPIONSHIP

1965	1 Clive Hitch	2 Brian Davies	3 Ken Adams
1972	1 Gordon Kennett	2 Peter Wigley	3 Tony Childs
1972	1 Lou Sansom	2 Malcolm Bedkober	3 Peter Claridge
1983	1 Bob Garrad	2 Chris Chaplin	3 Steve Naylor

PROMOTORS TROPHY

1965	1 Malcolm Simmons	2 Clive Hitch	3 Geoff Pennikett

CAVALCADE TROPHY

1965	1 Malcolm Brown	2 Peter Jackson	3 Tyburn Gallows

GERRY HUSSEY MEMORIAL TROPHY

1965	1 Bob Andrews	2 Pete Sampson	3 Brian Leonard
1966	1 Alan Cowland	2 Clive Hitch	3 Ray Wilson
1969	1 Dave Jessup	2 Ron Bagley	3 Geoff Maloney
1970	1 Brian Foote	2 Nigel Rackett	3 Barry Thomas
1971	1 Brian Foote	2 Geoff Maloney	3 Bob Young

RAYMENTS ROSE BOWL

1965	1 Howard Cole	2 Sandor Levai	3 Clive Hitch
1966	1 Clive Hitch	2 David Crane	3 Sandor Levai
1969	1 Ted Spittles	2 Mick Steel	3 Nigel Rackett

SKOL LAGER TROPHY

1965	1 Roy Trigg	2 Clive Hitch	3 Eric Hockaday
1966	1 Peter Seaton	2 Eddie Reeves	3 Tony Clarke
1970	1 Dave Jessup	2 Barry Thomas	3 Derek Cook
1971	1 Kevin Holden	2 Tony Davey	3 Nigel Rackett

ACE OF HERTS TROPHY

1965	1 Malcolm Simmons	2 Gordon Guasco	3 Ken Adams
1966	1 Brian Leonard	2 Malcolm Simmons	3 Sandor Levai
1969	1 John Hibben	2 Frank Wendon	3 Pat Adaway
1970	1 Nigel Rackett	2 Barry Thomas	3 Judd Drew
1972	1 Stan Stevens	2 Brian Clark	3 Jack Walker

RONNIE MOORE TROPHY

1969	1 Maurie Robinson	2 Ted Spittles	3 Dave Jessup
1970	1 Tony Childs	2 Colin Sanders	3 Alan Jackson
1971	1 Tony Childs	2 Bruce Forrester	3 Stan Stevens and Bob Young

LEA VALLEY PARK TROPHY

1970	1 Nigel Rackett	2 Barry Thomas	3 John Hibben
1971	1 Bob Young	2 Nigel Rackett	3 Colin Sanders
1972	1 Allan Emmett	2 Bob Young	3 Dingle Brown
1973	1 Barney Kennett	2 Peter Moore	3 George Barclay

MIKE LETCH TROPHY

1970	1 John Louis	2 Brian Foote	3 Barry Thomas

SCUNTHORPE

■ SPEEDWAY was introduced to the Steel town of Scunthorpe on Monday, May 13, 1971 and after a series of open meetings a Second Division licence was granted at Quibel Park, an athletics and cycling stadium in the middle of Brumby Woods.

1972...1972...1972...1972...1972...1972

	M	R	Pts	BP	TPts	Ave	F	P	Total
§§Jim Irvine	1	2	2.0	2.0	4.0	8.000			
§§Chris Emery	1	5	8.0	1.0	9.0	7.200			
§§Brian Maxted	25	100	148.0	11.0	159.0	6.360			
§Terry Kelly	10	46	66.0	3.0	69.0	6.000			
§Ray Watkins	20	90	120.5	10.0	130.5	5.800			
§§Phil Bass	33	139	192.0	9.0	201.0	5.784			
§Doug Underwood	19	74	79.0	15.0	94.0	5.081			
§Ian Wilson	33	120	137.0	13.0	150.0	5.000	1		1
§§Rod Haynes	20	76	83.0	8.0	91.0	4.789			
§Brian Osborn	18	60	55.0	6.0	61.0	4.067			
§§Alan Bellham	10	40	33.0	4.0	37.0	3.700			
§Rex Garrod	7	26	20.0	4.0	24.0	3.692			
§§John Bowerman	14	48	35.0	9.0	44.0	3.667			
§Pete Taylor	9	34	19.0	5.0	24.0	2.824			
§Phil Whittaker	3	10	6.0	1.0	7.0	2.800			
§Barry Holdsworth	5	11	4.0	0.0	4.0	1.455			
§§Chris Doyle	1	3	1.0	0.0	1.0	1.333			
§§Dave Johnson	1	2	0.0	0.0	0.0	0.000			
§§Dave Perks	1	2	0.0	0.0	0.0	0.000			
§§Mike Ryan	1	2	0.0	0.0	0.0	0.000			

1973...1973...1973...1973...1973...1973

	M	R	Pts	BP	TPts	Ave	F	P	Total
§§Ken McKinlay	31	111	254.0	15.0	269.0	9.694	6	5	11
§Ian Hindle	31	130	251.0	15.0	266.0	8.185		3	3
§Dingle Brown	26	99	142.0	11.0	153.0	6.182		1	1
Rod Haynes	33	135	175.0	23.0	198.0	5.867	2		2
§Jack Bywater	33	123	148.0	18.0	166.0	5.398			
Doug Underwood	27	100	102.0	14.0	116.0	4.640		1	1
Rex Garrod	31	123	134.0	7.0	141.0	4.585			
Chris Emery	20	69	47.0	10.0	57.0	3.304			
John Bowerman	4	14	11.0	0.0	11.0	3.143			
§Rob Homer	1	3	1.0	1.0	2.0	2.667			
Ian Wilson	2	3	1.0	1.0	2.0	2.667			
§§Roger Pascall	2	11	6.0	1.0	7.0	2.545			
Ray Watkins	5	12	5.0	1.0	6.0	2.000			
§§Ken Stafford	3	6	3.0	0.0	3.0	2.000			
§§Cliff Hindle	2	5	1.0	0.0	1.0	0.800			

1974...1974...1974...1974...1974...1974

	M	R	Pts	BP	TPts	Ave	F	P	Total
§Tony Childs	10	44	92.0	5.0	97.0	8.818		1	1
Ken McKinlay	33	124	243.0	9.0	252.0	8.129	3	2	5
Doug Underwood	**38**	**150**	**219.0**	**27.0**	**246.0**	**6.560**		**2**	**2**
§§Andy Sims	37	153	214.0	36.0	250.0	6.536	1		1
§Keith Evans	30	112	152.0	18.0	170.0	6.071		2	2
Dingle Brown	**38**	**149**	**204.0**	**21.0**	**225.0**	**6.040**		**1**	**1**
Chris Emery	18	65	83.0	15.0	98.0	6.031			
Jack Bywater	21	80	102.0	10.0	112.0	5.600	1		1
§Tim Swales	8	24	23.0	4.0	27.0	4.500			
Chris Doyle	9	28	24.0	5.0	29.0	4.143			
Rex Garrod	1	1	1.0	0.0	1.0	4.000			
Roger Pascall	9	28	17.0	3.0	20.0	2.857			
Ray Watkins	2	7	4.0	1.0	5.0	2.857			
§§Andy Hines	7	24	12.0	2.0	14.0	2.333			

1975...1975...1975...1975...1975...1975

	M	R	Pts	BP	TPts	Ave	F	P	Total
Tony Childs	35	150	302.0	11.0	313.0	8.347		2	2
Keith Evans	36	153	272.5	15.0	287.5	7.516	2		2
Ken McKinlay	26	86	131.0	8.0	139.0	6.465	1		1
Andy Hines	**40**	**161**	**212.0**	**29.0**	**241.0**	**5.988**			
§§Colin Cook	23	90	112.0	21.0	133.0	5.911			
§§Tony Gillias	16	49	56.0	12.0	68.0	5.551			
Andy Sims	39	145	170.0	25.0	195.0	5.379			
Ray Watkins	28	100	93.0	13.0	106.0	4.240			
Chris Emery	25	93	85.0	11.0	96.0	4.129			
§Ian Silk	8	23	10.0	2.0	12.0	2.087			

1976...1976...1976...1976...1976...1976

	M	R	Pts	BP	TPts	Ave	F	P	Total
Keith Evans	32	148	331.0	12.0	343.0	9.270	4		4
Andy Hines	**35**	**159**	**248.0**	**21.0**	**269.0**	**6.767**	**2**		**2**
§Tony Boyle	15	61	82.0	9.0	91.0	5.967			
§§Phil Kynman	28	109	139.0	17.0	156.0	5.725		1	1
Colin Cook	29	125	142.0	25.0	167.0	5.344		1	1
Sid Sheldrick	17	58	67.0	7.0	74.0	5.103			
Ray Watkins	33	110	117.0	20.0	137.0	4.982			
Tony Gillias	20	64	66.0	10.0	76.0	4.750			
§§Danny Boyle	7	18	11.0	1.0	12.0	2.667			
§§Ian Jeffcoate	5	18	10.0	1.0	11.0	2.444			
§Dick Partridge	2	8	1.0	0.0	1.0	0.500			
Ian Silk	2	3	0.0	0.0	0.0	0.000			

1977...1977...1977...1977...1977...1977

	M	R	Pts	BP	TPts	Ave	F	P	Total
§Nicky Allott	36	163	324.0	14.0	338.0	8.294	4	2	6
§Arthur Browning	25	103	180.0	18.0	198.0	7.689		2	2
§John McNeill	24	102	178.0	6.0	184.0	7.216	1	1	2
Sid Sheldrick	37	142	178.0	30.0	208.0	5.859			
§Dave Baugh	**38**	**143**	**178.0**	**28.0**	**206.0**	**5.762**		**2**	**2**
§Trevor Whiting	24	84	91.0	16.0	107.0	5.095			
§Paul Cooper	13	50	47.0	13.0	60.0	4.800			
§§Phil White	27	106	106.0	20.0	126.0	4.755			
§§Danny Young	28	77	66.0	15.0	81.0	4.208			
Ray Watkins	6	21	15.0	0.0	15.0	2.857			
§Mick Sheldrick	1	1	0.0	0.0	0.0	0.000			

1978...1978...1978...1978...1978...1978

	M	R	Pts	BP	TPts	Ave	F	P	Total
Nicky Allott	**40**	**186**	**416.0**	**4.0**	**420.0**	**9.032**	**10**		**10**
John McNeill	22	100	188.0	11.0	199.0	7.960	2		2
Arthur Browning	20	77	107.0	9.0	116.0	6.026			
Phil White	**40**	**177**	**219.0**	**30.0**	**249.0**	**5.627**			
§Mick Handley	14	55	52.0	7.0	59.0	4.291			
Trevor Whiting	37	140	122.0	18.0	140.0	4.000			
Danny Boyle	18	49	40.0	9.0	49.0	4.000			
Danny Young	23	75	59.0	6.0	65.0	3.467			
§§Kevin Teager	3	10	5.0	2.0	7.0	2.800			
Paul Cooper	23	62	40.0	3.0	43.0	2.774			
§Rob Woffinden	4	9	5.0	1.0	6.0	2.667			
§John Priest	14	41	20.0	3.0	23.0	2.244			
§Doug Poole	6	12	3.0	2.0	5.0	1.667			

1979...1979...1979...1979...1979...1979

	M	R	Pts	BP	TPts	Ave	F	P	Total
Phil White	37	168	311.0	8.0	319.0	7.595	1	1	2
Arthur Browning	28	123	215.0	9.0	224.0	7.285	1	1	2
§Robert Maxfield	10	39	65.0	1.0	66.0	6.769			
§Arthur Price	28	104	106.0	17.0	123.0	4.731			
Kevin Teager	34	136	119.0	23.0	142.0	4.176			
Trevor Whiting	**38**	**143**	**110.0**	**25.0**	**135.0**	**3.776**			
§Stuart Cope	16	64	48.0	4.0	52.0	3.250			
John Priest	5	10	6.0	2.0	8.0	3.200			
Ian Jeffcoate	18	64	46.0	5.0	51.0	3.188			
§§Phil Cain	7	23	14.0	2.0	16.0	2.783			
Rob Woffinden	14	48	27.0	3.0	30.0	2.500			
§David Coles	6	16	8.0	1.0	9.0	2.250			
§Graham Tattersall	7	17	5.0	1.0	6.0	1.412			
§Peter Wordingham	2	3	0.0	0.0	0.0	0.000			

SCUNTHORPE moved home track from Quibell Park during the 1978-79 winter after complaints about the damage bikes were causing to the shared athletics track.

They switched to a new purpose built circuit at Ashby Ville but crowds were always on the lean side and after only four matches promoter Tony Nicholls – the track had a variety of bosses over the years, including Ivor Brown, Vic White, Brian Osborne, Jim Streets, Ted Hornsby and Richard Judge – officially withdrew from the 1985 National League because of poor crowds. The last meeting was on Monday, May 13, 1985.

SCUNTHORPE

1980...1980...1980...1980...1980...1980

	M	R	Pts	BP	TPts	Ave	F	P	Total
Phil White	35	153	330.0	17.0	347.0	9.072	5	5	10
Arthur Browning	34	142	287.0	18.0	305.0	8.592		3	3
Nicky Allott	37	157	266.0	12.0	278.0	7.083	3	1	4
Kevin Teager	35	143	169.0	21.0	190.0	5.315		1	1
Rob Woffinden	**40**	**146**	**128.0**	**19.0**	**147.0**	**4.027**	**1**		**1**
John Priest	8	20	18.0	2.0	20.0	4.000			
Ian Jeffcoate	38	137	116.0	19.0	135.0	3.942			
§Ian Westwell	13	34	26.0	7.0	33.0	3.882			
§§Kevin Paxton	5	15	8.0	5.0	13.0	3.467			
§Mark Stokes	4	9	6.0	1.0	7.0	3.111			
§§Graham Mortimer	9	23	12.0	5.0	17.0	2.957			
§Mike Beaumont	7	17	10.0	2.0	12.0	2.824			
§§Steve Bryenton	1	2	1.0	0.0	1.0	2.000			
§Andy Sims	1	2	1.0	0.0	1.0	2.000			
§Robert Craven	2	4	1.0	0.0	1.0	1.000			
§§Graham Barker	2	6	0.0	0.0	0.0	0.000			
§Phil Vance	1	2	0.0	0.0	0.0	0.000			

1981...1981...1981...1981...1981...1981

	M	R	Pts	BP	TPts	Ave	F	P	Total
Kevin Teager	37	173	310.0	17.0	327.0	7.561	3		3
Nicky Allott	22	99	179.0	7.0	186.0	7.515		1	1
§Mark DeKok	33	136	171.0	23.0	194.0	5.706			
§Tony Featherstone	37	156	175.0	33.0	208.0	5.333			
Rob Woffinden	36	154	183.0	17.0	200.0	5.195			
Tony Childs	10	42	35.0	3.0	38.0	3.619			
§§Graeme Beardsley	24	66	46.0	11.0	57.0	3.455			
§§Julian Parr	27	71	40.0	13.0	53.0	2.986			
Phil Kynman	12	41	24.0	4.0	28.0	2.732			
§§Mark Fiora	5	17	8.0	3.0	11.0	2.588			
§§Paul Thorp	4	13	8.0	0.0	8.0	2.462			
Graham Mortimer	1	2	1.0	0.0	1.0	2.000			
§Peter Framingham	7	20	8.0	1.0	9.0	1.800			
§§Guy Wilson	2	5	1.0	0.0	1.0	0.800			
Kevin Paxton	2	6	1.0	0.0	1.0	0.667			

1982...1982...1982...1982...1982...1982

	M	R	Pts	BP	TPts	Ave	F	P	Total
§Mike Wilding	31	172	311.0	28.0	339.0	7.884	1		1
Kevin Teager	**38**	**209**	**339.0**	**36.0**	**375.0**	**7.177**			
§Nigel Crabtree	37	185	287.0	40.0	327.0	7.070			
Rob Woffinden	14	71	97.0	9.0	106.0	5.972			
§Derek Richardson	31	140	171.0	30.0	201.0	5.743			
Julian Parr	35	143	161.0	34.0	195.0	5.455			
Terry Kelly	26	112	134.0	9.0	143.0	5.107			
§§Ian Gibson	20	63	55.0	10.0	65.0	4.127			
Mark DeKok	24	93	78.0	17.0	95.0	4.086			
Nicky Allott	6	29	21.0	3.0	24.0	3.310			

1983...1983...1983...1983...1983...1983

	M	R	Pts	BP	TPts	Ave	F	P	Total
Nigel Crabtree	35	186	403.0	20.0	423.0	9.097	3		3
§Andy Fisher	30	146	258.0	19.0	277.0	7.589		1	1
§Rob Hollingworth	34	170	275.0	29.0	304.0	7.153			
§Craig Pendlebury	12	55	85.0	10.0	95.0	6.909			
Julian Parr	34	167	234.0	40.0	274.0	6.563			
Derek Richardson	31	149	203.0	31.0	234.0	6.282	1		1
Ian Gibson	32	126	152.0	27.0	179.0	5.683			
§§Kevin Armitage	16	51	58.5	9.0	67.5	5.294			
Mark DeKok	21	85	71.0	14.0	85.0	4.000			
§§Jamie Hildreth	6	17	7.0	3.0	10.0	2.353			

MANSFIELD ALES TROPHY

1972	1 Tony Childs	2 Phil Bass	3 Malcolm Mackay

SUPPORTERS TROPHY

1973	1 Ian Hindle	2 Dave Baugh	3 Carl Glover

STADIUM INDIVIDUAL CHAMPIONSHIP

1974	1 Andy Hines	2 Tony Childs	3 Doug Underwood
1975	1 Doug Underwood	2 Dave Gooderham	3 Colin Cook

SOUTH HUMBERSIDE CHAMPIONSHIP

1978	1 Dave Allen	2 John McNeill	3 Arthur Browning
1979	1 Steve Wilcock	2 Andy Hines	3 Steve Finch
1980	1 Steve Lomas	2 Steve Wilcock	3 Kelvin Mullarkey
1981	1 Steve Stomas	2 Neil Collins	3 Billy Burton

SCUNTHORPE JUNIOR OPEN

1982	1 Jim Burdfield	2 Gary O'Hare	3 Ritchie Owen

1984...1984...1984...1984...1984...1984

	M	R	Pts	BP	TPts	Ave	F	P	Total
Julian Parr	18	70	133.0	9.0	142.0	8.114	1		1
§Andy Buck	**32**	**139**	**246.0**	**25.0**	**271.0**	**7.799**	**1**	**1**	**2**
Rob Woffinden	**32**	**139**	**247.0**	**19.0**	**266.0**	**7.655**		**1**	**1**
Derek Richardson	29	120	192.0	33.0	225.0	7.500	1	3	4
§Paul Evitts	12	44	64.0	9.0	73.0	6.636			
Mike Wilding	8	33	46.0	4.0	50.0	6.061			
Kevin Armitage	31	117	140.0	22.0	162.0	5.538			
Ian Gibson	18	60	60.0	11.0	71.0	4.733			
§Kenny Young	2	4	3.0	1.0	4.0	4.000			
§§Mark Burrows	23	71	56.0	14.0	70.0	3.944			
Nicky Allott	5	15	12.0	1.0	13.0	3.467			
§Richie Owen	8	23	13.0	1.0	14.0	2.435			
§§Paul Muchene	1	2	1.0	0.0	1.0	2.000			

1985...1985...1985...1985...1985...1985

	M	R	Pts	BP	TPTs	Ave	F	P	Total
Andy Buck	***9***	***39***	***88.0***	***6.0***	***94.0***	***9.641***	***2***		***2***
Mark Burrows	***9***	***30***	***27.0***	***6.0***	***33.0***	***4.400***			
Steve Finch	***9***	***40***	***67.0***	***8.0***	***75.0***	***7.500***		***1***	***1***
Peter McNamara	***9***	***27***	***12.0***	***1.0***	***13.0***	***1.926***			
Julian Parr	***9***	***35***	***38.0***	***2.0***	***40.0***	***4.571***			
Derek Richardson	***9***	***36***	***47.0***	***5.0***	***52.0***	***5.778***			
Rob Woffinden	*6*	*26*	*46.0*	*3.0*	*49.0*	*7.538*			
Kenny Young	*2*	*3*	*0.0*	*0.0*	*0.0*	*0.000*			

Scunthorpe withdrew from the League because of financial problems on Friday, May 17, 1985, after completing nine National League matches. All results were expunged from official records.

PHRILLER...1980 Stags' top gun was the experienced Phil White

STOKE

■ *VETERAN Mike Broadbank scored a 12 point maximum as speedway returned to the Potteries on Thursday, April 12, 1973, when the reborn Potters defeated Birmingham in a challenge match at the opening of a new stadium at Chesterton. The track had been well bedded down by a series of training schools run by World Champions Ivan Mauger and Ole Olsen during the build up to the Five Towns' first speedway meeting since the closure of Stoke's Sun Street Stadium at the end of the 1963 Provincial League campaign.*

1973...1973...1973...1973...1973...1973

	M	R	Pts	BP	TPts	Ave	F	P	Total
§§Mike Broadbank	33	145	323.0	12.0	335.0	9.241	5	5	10
§Mick Handley	22	83	133.0	6.0	139.0	6.699	1		1
§Geoff Pusey	**34**	**151**	**216.0**	**18.0**	**234.0**	**6.199**			
§Alan Bridgett	32	120	159.0	18.0	177.0	5.900			
§§Roger Parker	13	54	71.0	6.0	77.0	5.704			
§§Brian Woodward	**34**	**137**	**159.0**	**30.0**	**189.0**	**5.518**		**1**	**1**
§§Steve Holden	6	20	22.0	5.0	27.0	5.400			
§Cyril Francis	14	47	50.0	10.0	60.0	5.106			
§§Martin Yeates	7	21	21.0	4.0	25.0	4.762			
§§Nigel Wasley	26	82	75.0	10.0	85.0	4.146			
§§Andy Cusworth	4	9	6.0	3.0	9.0	4.000			
§Stan Stevens	1	3	2.0	0.0	2.0	2.667			
§George Devonport	2	4	2.0	0.0	2.0	2.000			
§Ray Hassall	3	7	2.0	0.0	2.0	1.143			

1974...1974...1974...1974...1974...1974

	M	R	Pts	BP	TPts	Ave	F	P	Total
Mike Broadbank	38	161	355.0	22.0	377.0	9.366	3	6	9
Geoff Pusey	40	171	300.0	19.0	319.0	7.462	1	2	3
Brian Woodward	30	117	186.0	24.0	210.0	7.179	1	1	2
§§Steve Bastable	33	136	189.0	15.0	204.0	6.000	2		2
Alan Bridgett	38	140	186.0	23.0	209.0	5.971		1	1
Steve Holden	35	120	159.0	17.0	176.0	5.867		2	2
Nigel Wasley	14	56	70.0	9.0	79.0	5.643			
Andy Cusworth	33	121	136.0	22.0	158.0	5.223	1		1
Roger Parker	4	12	10.0	4.0	14.0	4.667			
§Tony Freegard	5	15	11.0	4.0	15.0	4.000			
§§Mick Newton	14	39	23.0	3.0	26.0	2.667			
§Barry Duke	2	5	2.0	1.0	3.0	2.400			

1975...1975...1975...1975...1975...1975

	M	R	Pts	BP	TPts	Ave	F	P	Total
§Alan Molyneux	**40**	**183**	**444.0**	**20.0**	**464.0**	**10.142**	**5**	**5**	**10**
Steve Bastable	**40**	**163**	**296.5**	**31.0**	**327.5**	**8.037**	**1**	**3**	**4**
Steve Holden	14	50	87.0	12.0	99.0	7.920	2		2
Andy Cusworth	29	100	160.0	28.0	188.0	7.520	1	2	3
§Jack Millen	13	50	80.0	7.0	87.0	6.960	1		1
§Phil Bass	37	142	211.0	35.0	246.0	6.930	1		1
§Jim Wells	35	127	175.0	33.0	208.0	6.551	1	2	3
Mick Handley	37	136	177.0	30.0	207.0	6.088		2	2
§Harry Maclean	3	9	10.0	3.0	13.0	5.778			
Alan Bridgett	12	45	46.0	6.0	52.0	4.622			
§§Kevin Young	4	10	5.0	1.0	6.0	2.400			
§§Martin Cusworth	2	6	3.0	0.0	3.0	2.000			
§§Trevor Charley†	1	1	0.0	0.0	0.0	0.000			

†Rode under the name of Trevor Vincent.

1976...1976...1976...1976...1976...1976

	M	R	Pts	BP	TPts	Ave	F	P	Total
§Les Collins	35	165	368.0	16.0	384.0	9.309	4	4	8
Jack Millen	28	116	218.0	11.0	229.0	7.897	3		3
§Malcolm Corradine	8	31	49.0	8.0	57.0	7.355			
§Ricky Day	24	85	121.0	8.0	129.0	6.071			
§Dave Trownson	1	4	6.0	0.0	6.0	6.000			
§§Jim Brett	34	138	174.0	24.0	198.0	5.739		1	1
Mick Newton	25	104	130.0	18.0	148.0	5.692			
§§Steve McDermott	23	72	81.0	15.0	96.0	5.333			
§§Mick Howard	1	3	4.0	0.0	4.0	5.333			
§§Tim Nunan	34	127	129.0	30.0	159.0	5.008			
§§Neil Webb	2	8	7.0	3.0	10.0	5.000			
§Andy Reid	6	14	13.0	4.0	17.0	4.857			
Colin Meredith	9	34	35.0	6.0	41.0	4.824			
§Mike Gardner	4	12	10.0	4.0	14.0	4.667			
§Malcolm Shakespeare	2	6	6.0	0.0	6.0	4.000			
§§Gerry Hintz	1	2	1.0	1.0	2.0	4.000			
§§Paul Share	1	3	2.0	0.0	2.0	2.667			
§§Mark Stokes	6	11	4.0	3.0	7.0	2.545			
§Ian Robertson	4	7	2.0	0.0	2.0	1.143			

1977...1977...1977...1977...1977...1977

	M	R	Pts	BP	TPts	Ave	F	P	Total
§Stuart Mountford	37	164	308.0	26.0	334.0	8.146		1	1
Tim Nunan	36	154	265.5	18.0	283.5	7.364		1	1
§Ian Gledhill	32	138	213.0	17.0	230.0	6.667	1		1
§Carl Askew	15	61	87.0	12.0	99.0	6.492			
Ian Robertson	32	122	161.0	30.0	191.0	6.262		1	1
§Mick Fishwick	15	58	70.0	12.0	82.0	5.655			
Steve McDermott	8	31	35.0	6.0	41.0	5.290			
§§Stephen Barr	5	15	16.0	2.0	18.0	4.800			
§§Rob Dole	22	72	69.0	12.0	81.0	4.500			
§Colin Farquharson	20	73	67.0	8.0	75.0	4.110			
§Ian Jeffcoate	19	59	46.0	11.0	57.0	3.864			
§Stewart Collin	6	12	9.5	1.0	10.5	3.500			
Trevor Charley	7	19	15.0	1.0	16.0	3.368			
Gerry Hintz	4	8	3.0	0.0	3.0	1.500			
§§Des Allen	1	3	1.0	0.0	1.0	1.333			
§§Tim Curnock	1	1	0.0	0.0	0.0	0.000			

1978...1978...1978...1978...1978...1978

	M	R	Pts	BP	TPts	Ave	F	P	Total
§Tony Lomas	40	161	355.0	10.0	365.0	9.068	10	1	11
Ian Gledhill	41	166	285.0	24.0	309.0	7.446	1	3	4
§John Harrhy	41	161	256.0	25.0	281.0	6.981	3	2	5
Stuart Mountford	40	150	220.0	40.0	260.0	6.933			
Ian Robertson	**42**	**166**	**255.0**	**31.0**	**286.0**	**6.892**		**2**	**2**
Tim Nunan	40	153	199.0	38.0	237.0	6.196		1	1
§Frank Smith	12	39	54.0	5.0	59.0	6.051			
Ian Jeffcoate	15	40	37.0	5.0	42.0	4.200			
§§Steve Sant	1	3	2.0	1.0	3.0	4.000			
§Rod North	2	4	2.0	1.0	3.0	3.000			
Stewart Collin	7	15	9.0	0.0	9.0	2.400			
§§Chris Sully	4	14	4.0	3.0	7.0	2.000			
§§Ivan Blacka	2	5	1.0	1.0	2.0	1.600			
Tim Curnock	4	11	4.0	0.0	4.0	1.455			

1979...1979...1979...1979...1979...1979

	M	R	Pts	BP	TPts	Ave	F	P	Total
Ian Gledhill	37	150	290.0	18.0	308.0	8.213		1	1
§Billy Burton	**38**	**161**	**272.0**	**12.0**	**284.0**	**7.056**	**2**		**2**
Tony Lomas	31	119	174.0	27.0	201.0	6.756		2	2
Tim Curnock	1	3	3.0	2.0	5.0	6.667			
§Chris Turner	32	129	184.0	23.0	207.0	6.419		1	1
Ian Robertson	8	31	41.0	7.0	48.0	6.194		1	1
Stuart Mountford	**38**	**156**	**211.5**	**29.0**	**240.5**	**6.167**		**1**	**1**
§Nicky Allott	8	28	38.0	1.0	39.0	5.571	1		1
Frank Smith	21	68	83.0	11.0	94.0	5.529			
§Mitch Graham	4	14	14.0	0.0	14.0	4.000			
§Alan Maclean	24	72	46.0	14.0	60.0	3.333			
Ian Jeffcoate	13	34	22.0	3.0	25.0	2.941			
§§Paul Evitts	9	26	13.0	2.0	15.0	2.308			
§Roger Commerford	1	2	0.0	0.0	0.0	0.000			

1980...1980...1980...1980...1980...1980

	M	R	Pts	BP	TPts	Ave	F	P	Total
Billy Burton	**40**	**166**	**315.0**	**18.0**	**333.0**	**8.024**		**4**	**4**
Tony Boyle	35	140	237.0	17.0	254.0	7.257	1		1
§Paul Stead	**40**	**162**	**241.0**	**21.0**	**262.0**	**6.469**	**1**	**1**	**2**
§Les Sawyer	**40**	**155**	**208.0**	**24.0**	**232.0**	**5.987**			
Alan Maclean	13	47	55.0	12.0	67.0	5.702			
§§Neil Evitts	26	92	89.0	21.0	110.0	4.783			
Ian Robertson	10	31	26.0	10.0	36.0	4.645			
Rod North	30	104	106.0	13.0	119.0	4.577			
Paul Evitts	7	20	16.0	4.0	20.0	4.000			
§§Mike Wilding	9	29	23.0	5.0	28.0	3.862			
§John Homer	5	16	12.0	3.0	15.0	3.750			
§§Rob Lightfoot	20	73	53.0	8.0	61.0	3.342			
§Paul Holdbrook	1	2	1.0	0.0	1.0	2.000			
§§John Hough	3	7	3.0	0.0	3.0	1.714			
§§Kris Berrigan	1	3	0.0	0.0	0.0	0.000			

STOKE raced as Chesterton in the 1973 season at Loomer Road track. The records for that one season as Chesterton are listed above and all individual records are included as Stoke.

STOKE

1981...1981...1981...1981...1981...1981

	M	R	Pts	BP	TPts	Ave	F	P	Total
§Peter E. Smith	17	72	136.0	13.0	149.0	8.278		1	1
§Mike Sampson	37	145	268.0	21.0	289.0	7.972	1	4	5
§Arthur Browning	36	143	216.0	23.0	239.0	6.685	1		1
Rob Lightfoot	39	155	224.0	30.0	254.0	6.555		1	1
§Mark Collins	37	147	210.0	21.0	231.0	6.286			
Rod North	38	146	193.0	30.0	223.0	6.110			
Steve Sant	**40**	**157**	**198.0**	**40.0**	**238.0**	**6.064**		**2**	**2**
Ian Robertson	19	61	51.0	8.0	59.0	3.869			
Paul Holdbrook	2	7	3.0	1.0	4.0	2.286			
§§Russ Birks	6	16	4.0	2.0	6.0	1.500			
§Mark Summerfield	1	2	0.0	0.0	0.0	0.000			

■ *EVERPRESENT Steve Sant later became team manager of the Potters when his father Ray took over as promoter.*

1982...1982...1982...1982...1982...1982

	M	R	Pts	BP	TPts	Ave	F	P	Total
Rod North	29	157	260.0	24.0	284.0	7.236	1		1
Peter E. Smith	**38**	**202**	**325.0**	**24.0**	**349.0**	**6.911**		**1**	**1**
Mark Collins	17	95	134.0	21.0	155.0	6.526		1	1
Mike Sampson	27	127	174.0	18.0	192.0	6.047			
Ian Robertson	38	177	238.0	28.0	266.0	6.011			
§Brian Havelock	12	64	85.0	6.0	91.0	5.688			
Arthur Browning	23	97	115.0	15.0	130.0	5.361	1		1
§Peter Ellams	16	70	84.0	9.0	93.0	5.314			
Rob Lightfoot	3	13	15.0	0.0	15.0	4.615			
§§Jim Burdfield	20	78	73.0	13.0	86.0	4.410			
§§Garry Johnson	3	7	5.0	2.0	7.0	4.000			
Russell Birks	3	7	5.0	1.0	6.0	3.429			
Steve Sant	22	88	61.0	12.0	73.0	3.318			
§§Gary O'Hare	5	18	13.0	1.0	14.0	3.111			
§§Ritchie Owen	4	11	2.0	1.0	3.0	1.091			

1983...1983...1983...1983...1983...1983

	M	R	Pts	BP	TPts	Ave	F	P	Total
§Tom Owen	35	191	418.0	11.0	429.0	8.984	4		4
Peter E. Smith	**36**	**186**	**321.0**	**21.0**	**342.0**	**7.355**		**1**	**1**
§John Jackson	33	161	252.0	16.0	268.0	6.658	2	1	3
Ian Robertson	**36**	**165**	**173.0**	**40.0**	**213.0**	**5.164**			
Gary O'Hare	25	118	128.0	17.0	145.0	4.915			
Jim Burdfield	35	169	169.0	34.0	203.0	4.805		1	1
Steve Sant	22	74	60.0	13.0	73.0	3.946			
§John Grahame	6	26	21.0	4.0	25.0	3.846			
Russell Birks	4	13	11.0	1.0	12.0	3.692			
Garry Johnson	7	20	13.0	2.0	15.0	3.000			
Richie Owen	7	20	11.0	2.0	13.0	2.600			
§§Ian Stead	3	9	2.0	2.0	4.0	1.778			
§David Butt	1	3	0.0	0.0	0.0	0.000			

1984...1984...1984...1984...1984...1984

	M	R	Pts	BP	TPts	Ave	F	P	Total
Tom Owen	31	129	305.0	13.0	318.0	9.860	4	1	5
§Nigel Crabtree	**32**	**136**	**313.0**	**12.0**	**325.0**	**9.559**	**3**	**3**	**6**
§Paul Thorp	**32**	**130**	**215.0**	**21.0**	**236.0**	**7.262**	**2**		**2**
Paul Evitts	18	68	89.0	21.0	110.0	6.471			
§Steve Bishop	**32**	**125**	**144.0**	**27.0**	**171.0**	**5.472**			
§Ashley Pullen	11	41	53.0	3.0	56.0	5.463			
§§Graham Jones	27	92	107.0	10.0	117.0	5.087			
§Phil Alderman	10	32	30.0	10.0	40.0	5.000			
Ian Stead	20	63	54.0	13.0	67.0	4.254			
Russell Birks	5	16	12.0	3.0	15.0	3.750			
Gary O'Hare	3	6	3.0	0.0	3.0	2.000			
Jim Burdfield	1	2	0.0	0.0	0.0	0.000			

1985...1985...1985...1985...1985...1985

	M	R	Pts	BP	TPts	Ave	F	P	Total
Nigel Crabtree	28	116	239.0	13.0	252.0	8.690	4	1	5
Tom Owen	**38**	**168**	**327.0**	**24.0**	**351.0**	**8.357**	**1**		**1**
Paul Thorp	**38**	**168**	**302.0**	**8.0**	**310.0**	**7.381**	**1**		**1**
Graham Jones	37	141	168.0	33.0	201.0	5.702			
Mike Wilding	36	133	154.0	30.0	184.0	5.534	1		1
Ian Stead	31	96	108.0	20.0	128.0	5.333			
§§Darren Sumner	**38**	**137**	**136.0**	**29.0**	**165.0**	**4.818**			
§§Nigel Harrhy	9	22	14.0	5.0	19.0	3.455			
§§Richard Smith	2	2	0.0	0.0	0.0	0.000			
Gary O'Hare	1	1	0.0	0.0	0.0	0.000			

1986...1986...1986...1986...1986...1986

	M	R	Pts	BP	TPts	Ave	F	P	Total
Paul Thorp	39	162	408.0	15.0	423.0	10.444	16	5	21
Nigel Crabtree	**40**	**172**	**405.0**	**24.0**	**429.0**	**9.977**	**3**	**6**	**9**
Tom Owen	37	151	239.0	38.0	277.0	7.338		4	4
Mike Wilding	**40**	**157**	**245.0**	**33.0**	**278.0**	**7.083**		**1**	**1**
Darren Sumner	37	144	196.0	58.0	254.0	7.056		5	5
Graham Jones	15	54	65.0	12.0	77.0	5.704		1	1
Nigel Harrhy	27	73	61.0	17.0	78.0	4.274			
§Carl Chalcraft	1	2	2.0	0.0	2.0	4.000			
§Mark Crang	19	61	52.0	8.0	60.0	3.934			
§Jamie Young	9	25	11.0	3.0	14.0	2.240			
§§Andy Sumner	4	13	4.0	3.0	7.0	2.154			
§Mark Ferry	5	11	4.0	1.0	5.0	1.818			
Peter E. Smith	3	11	4.0	0.0	4.0	1.455			
§§Trevor Eadon	2	4	1.0	0.0	1.0	1.000			
§§Tony Atkins	1	2	0.0	0.0	0.0	0.000			

1987...1987...1987...1987...1987...1987

	M	R	Pts	BP	TPts	Ave	F	P	Total
Nigel Crabtree	31	138	340.0	12.0	352.0	10.203	7	4	11
Darren Sumner	30	126	237.0	16.0	253.0	8.032	3	1	4
Graham Jones	29	131	237.0	23.0	260.0	7.939		1	1
Paul Stead	32	136	224.0	27.0	251.0	7.382	1	4	5
Mike Wilding	**36**	**152**	**207.0**	**34.0**	**241.0**	**6.342**			
§Derek Richardson	**36**	**127**	**141.0**	**23.0**	**164.0**	**5.165**			
§Dave Perks	7	25	23.0	7.0	30.0	4.800			
§§Bobby Duncan	35	96	72.0	17.0	89.0	3.708			
§Derrol Keats	4	16	8.0	0.0	8.0	2.000			
§§David Stanford	5	12	3.0	2.0	5.0	1.667			
Andrew Sumner	1	1	0.0	0.0	0.0	0.000			

1988...1988...1988...1988...1988...1988

	M	R	Pts	BP	TPts	Ave	F	P	Total
Nigel Crabtree	30	155	328.0	27.0	355.0	9.161	2	1	3
Graham Jones	27	143	293.0	26.0	319.0	8.923	1	1	2
§Louis Carr	**32**	**171**	**323.0**	**20.0**	**343.0**	**8.023**		**1**	**1**
Steve Bastable	**32**	**165**	**235.0**	**52.0**	**287.0**	**6.958**		**1**	**1**
Derek Richardson	28	117	179.0	22.0	201.0	6.872		1	1
§Paul Fry	31	139	159.0	21.0	180.0	5.180			
Bobby Duncan	7	21	18.0	2.0	20.0	3.810			
§§Wayne Broadhurst	20	71	40.0	4.0	44.0	2.479			
§§Jon Hughes	9	25	9.0	4.0	13.0	2.080			
§§Anthony Boyd	4	13	6.0	0.0	6.0	1.846			
David Stanford	2	6	0.0	0.0	0.0	0.000			

STEVE BASTABLE announced his retirement at the end of a career that started and finished at Stoke. He had made his debut for the Potters in 1974.

1989...1989...1989...1989...1989...1989

	M	R	Pts	BP	TPts	Ave	F	P	Total
Nigel Crabtree	**36**	**194**	**456.0**	**18.0**	**474.0**	**9.773**	**6**	**5**	**11**
§Eric Monaghan	**36**	**187**	**375.0**	**34.0**	**409.0**	**8.749**	**2**	**1**	**3**
Louis Carr	**36**	**181**	**302.0**	**28.0**	**330.0**	**7.293**			
§Chris Cobby	34	172	213.0	39.0	252.0	5.860			
§Rob Woffinden	**36**	**150**	**157.0**	**24.0**	**181.0**	**4.827**			
§Ian M. Stead	**36**	**153**	**159.0**	**21.0**	**180.0**	**4.706**		1	1
§Ian Stead	31	96	88.0	20.0	108.0	4.500			
§§Mark Pearce	4	12	6.0	2.0	8.0	2.667			
§§Richard Davidson	1	3	1.0	0.0	1.0	1.333			
Anthony Boyd	2	6	0.0	0.0	0.0	0.000			

1990...1990...1990...1990...1990...1990

	M	R	Pts	BP	TPts	Ave	F	P	Total
Eric Monaghan	35	187	400.0	21.0	421.0	9.005	1	3	4
Nigel Crabtree	34	180	381.0	14.0	395.0	8.778	3		3
Louis Carr	35	186	353.0	32.0	385.0	8.280		2	2
Chris Cobby	35	165	201.0	36.0	237.0	5.745			
§Mark Carlson	**36**	**169**	**201.0**	**40.0**	**241.0**	**5.704**			
Mark Pearce	26	87	82.0	23.0	105.0	4.828			
Rob Woffinden	21	91	95.0	10.0	105.0	4.615			
Ian Stead	5	15	11.0	4.0	15.0	4.000			
§David Clarke	11	50	42.0	8.0	50.0	4.000			
§§Garry Stead	1	3	2.0	0.0	2.0	2.667			
Richard Davidson	7	17	5.0	3.0	8.0	1.882			
Jonathan Hughes	2	4	1.0	0.0	1.0	1.000			

STOKE

	STAFFORDSHIRE OPEN		
1973	1 Mike Broadbank	2 Jack Millen	3 Geoff Pusey
1974	1 Peter Jarman	2 Joe Owen	3 Geoff Bouchard
	STAR OF STARS CHAMPIONSHIP		
1975	1 Joe Owen	2 John Jackson	3 Alan Molyneux
	PRIDE OF THE POTTERIES		
1976	1 Joe Owen	2 Les Collins	3 Tom Owen
1977	1 John Jackson	2 Robert Hollingworth	3 Nicky Allott
1978	1 Steve Finch	2 Tim Nunan	3 Stuart Mountford
1979	1 Andy Grahame	2 Ian Gledhill	3 Billy Burton
1980	1 Billy Burton	2 Mark Courtney	3 Paul Stead
1981	1 Rob Lightfoot	2 John Jackson	3 Robert Maxfield
1982	1 Steve Lawson	2 Paul Stead	3 Steve Lomas
1983	1 Alan Molyneux	2 Steve Lawson	3 Dave Trownson
1984	1 Martin Yeates	2 Barry Thomas	3 Paul Thorp
1985	1 Gary Havelock	2 Reg Wilson	3 Keith White
1986	1 Paul Thorp	2 Nigel Crabtree	3 Jamie Luckhurst
1987	1 Nigel Crabtree	2 Mark Carlson	3 Mike Wilding
1988	1 Mick Poole	2 Steve Schofield	3 Nigel Crabtree
1989	1 Mick Poole	2 Mark Loram	3 Les Collins
	EASTER VASE		
1977	1 John Jackson	2 Mick Handley	3 Phil Collins

POTTERING ON...Nigel Crabtree, who joined Stoke from Scunthorpe at the beginning of 1984, set up new appearance and points-scoring records for the Potters.

SUNDERLAND

■ *SEVEN years after a fateful 1964 Provincial League campaign, speedway returned to the Sunderland Greyhound Stadium under the Allied Presentations banner on Sunday, May 2, 1971, when the Stars defeated North East rivals Middlesbrough by two points in a challenge. It was always a struggle to attract crowds to the out of town track and the final meeting was held on Friday the 13th - the 13th of September, 1974, against Stoke.*

1971...1971...1971...1971...1971...1971

	M	R	Pts	BP	TPts	Ave	F	P	Total
§§Russ Dent	**34**	**153**	**304.0**	**8.0**	**312.0**	**8.157**	**6**	**1**	**7**
§George Barclay	**34**	**142**	**245.0**	**11.0**	**256.0**	**7.211**	**4**	**1**	**5**
§§John Goodall	19	74	117.0	2.0	119.0	6.432			
§Peter Wrathall	9	39	41.0	7.0	48.0	4.923			
§§Alan Mackie	27	95	90.0	15.0	105.0	4.421			
§Brian Whaley	18	63	57.0	8.0	65.0	4.127			
§John Lynch	20	73	65.0	9.0	74.0	4.055			
§Gerry Richardson	22	77	72.0	5.0	77.0	4.000			
§John Knock	27	92	70.0	18.0	88.0	3.826			
§Bernie Aldridge	6	15	10.0	2.0	12.0	3.200			
§§Paul Scanlan	4	12	8.0	1.0	9.0	3.000			
§§Jack Millen	2	7	5.0	0.0	5.0	2.857			
§§Peter Claridge	2	8	5.0	0.0	5.0	2.500			
§Brian Murray	1	5	3.0	0.0	3.0	2.400			
§§Dave Gatenby	4	13	2.0	1.0	3.0	0.923			
§Colin Robertson	2	4	0.0	0.0	0.0	0.000			
§§John Wilson	1	1	0.0	0.0	0.0	0.000			

1972...1972...1972...1972...1972...1972

	M	R	Pts	BP	TPts	Ave	F	P	Total
Jack Millen	30	127	265.0	11.0	276.0	8.693	2	2	4
§Graeme Smith	**36**	**151**	**297.0**	**16.0**	**313.0**	**8.291**		**2**	**2**
Russ Dent	35	139	240.0	12.0	252.0	7.252	3	1	4
George Barclay	27	107	158.0	26.0	184.0	6.879		2	2
Dave Gatenby	35	139	159.0	24.0	183.0	5.266		1	1
Peter Wrathall	**36**	**127**	**109.0**	**23.0**	**132.0**	**4.157**			
§§Jim Wells	32	106	89.0	12.0	101.0	3.811			
Brian Whaley	1	2	1.0	0.0	1.0	2.000			
§§John Robson	6	20	7.0	2.0	9.0	1.800			
§§Russ Hodgson	3	11	3.0	1.0	4.0	1.455			
Gerry Richardson	4	9	3.0	0.0	3.0	1.333			
§§John Alexander	1	1	0.0	0.0	0.0	0.000			
§§Peter Cairns	1	1	0.0	0.0	0.0	0.000			

1973...1973...1973...1973...1973...1973

	M	R	Pts	BP	TPts	Ave	F	P	Total
Jack Millen	23	85	204.0	3.0	207.0	9.741	7	1	8
Dave Gatenby	35	155	263.0	30.0	293.0	7.561	3	1	4
Jim Wells	**36**	**157**	**258.0**	**34.0**	**292.0**	**7.439**	**1**	**1**	**2**
Russ Dent	34	134	191.0	17.0	208.0	6.209	1		1
George Barclay	34	135	182.0	24.0	206.0	6.104		2	2
§§Terry Barclay	31	103	107.0	13.0	120.0	4.660			
§Brian Havelock	22	81	82.0	12.0	94.0	4.642			
Peter Wrathall	18	58	48.0	11.0	59.0	4.069			
§§Brian Johnston	1	3	2.0	1.0	3.0	4.000			
John Robson	8	21	6.0	0.0	6.0	1.143			
§§Lloyd Dobson	1	4	1.0	0.0	1.0	1.000			
§§Steve Pearce	2	2	0.0	0.0	0.0	0.000			

■ *GEORGE and Terry Barclay became the first father and son to ride together in the British League at Boston on March 25, 1973, after which they were regular team-mates.*

1974...1974...1974...1974...1974...1974

	M	R	Pts	BP	TPts	Ave	F	P	Total
Jim Wells	36	144	266.0	19.0	285.0	7.917	3	1	4
Brian Havelock	**38**	**166**	**271.0**	**29.0**	**300.0**	**7.229**		**3**	**3**
§Tim Swales	18	75	115.0	12.0	127.0	6.773			
George Barclay	25	102	151.0	13.0	164.0	6.431			
Russ Dent	36	143	196.0	24.0	220.0	6.154	2		2
§Andy Meldrum	15	56	78.0	7.0	85.0	6.071			
§Dennis Gavros	9	28	32.0	3.0	35.0	5.000			
Brian Johnson	20	60	46.0	14.0	60.0	4.000			
§Stewart Collin	1	3	3.0	0.0	3.0	4.000			
§§Vic Harding	25	82	59.0	17.0	76.0	3.707			
§Garry Moore	5	17	13.0	2.0	15.0	3.529			
John Robson	21	71	44.0	6.0	50.0	2.817			
§§Derek Fell	9	24	14.0	1.0	15.0	2.500			
§§Jon Bower	4	11	1.0	1.0	2.0	0.727			
§Paul Callaghan	4	11	1.0	0.0	1.0	0.364			

WEYMOUTH

■ *WEYMOUTH experienced a rocky existence almost from day one as a Second Division track.*

■ *Former rider Howdy Byford was installed as manager by promoters Wally Mawdsley and Pete Lansdale but a regular Sunday afternoon race-day failed to tempt either the locals or holiday-makers off the beach and after only ten home meetings throughout 1968 the track closed down and remained closed until Cyril Crane re-opened the venue in 1974.*

■ *The long-term future of the sport was never really secure with a succession of promoters until local property tycoon Mervyn Stewkesbury was persuaded by former track manager Phil Lock to step in and save the track from another closure at the end of the 1979 season.*

1968...1968...1968...1968...1968...1968

	M	R	Pts	BP	TPts	Ave	F	P	Total
§§Tony Lomas	17	72	163.0	6.0	169.0	9.389	4	3	7
§§Mike Vernam	17	70	129.0	10.0	139.0	7.943	3		3
§§Barry Duke	13	56	102.0	6.0	108.0	7.714	1		1
§§Chris Yeatman	**18**	**69**	**97.0**	**9.0**	**106.0**	**6.145**			
§§Mick Steel	14	52	56.0	10.0	66.0	5.077			
§§Roy Carter	12	41	39.0	8.0	47.0	4.585			
§§John Hammond	4	16	15.0	2.0	17.0	4.250			
§§Tony Hall	1	4	2.0	2.0	4.0	4.000			
§§Ian Warren	2	5	2.0	2.0	4.0	3.200			
§§Adrian Degan	7	21	13.0	3.0	16.0	3.048			
§§Phil Arnold	17	53	31.0	5.0	36.0	2.717			

1974...1974...1974...1974...1974...1974

	M	R	Pts	BP	TPts	Ave	F	P	Total
§Kelvin Mullarkey	37	158	258.0	26.0	284.0	7.190		2	2
§Bob Hughes	29	107	166.0	15.0	181.0	6.766	2	1	3
§§Steve Lomas	27	111	161.5	15.0	176.5	6.360			
§§Nigel Couzens	36	140	180.5	17.0	197.5	5.643			
§§Geoff Swindells	**38**	**151**	**186.0**	**22.0**	**208.0**	**5.510**			
§§Russell Foot	32	109	117.0	16.0	133.0	4.881	1		1
§Clark Facey	12	41	47.0	3.0	50.0	4.878		1	1
§§Glyn Facey	10	35	34.0	8.0	42.0	4.800			
§§Brian Paddington	32	115	104.0	19.0	123.0	4.278			
§§Mark Sawyers	7	15	12.0	1.0	13.0	3.467			

1975...1975...1975...1975...1975...1975

	M	R	Pts	BP	TPts	Ave	F	P	Total
§Martin Yeates	40	179	355.0	17.0	372.0	8.313	4	2	6
§Brian Woodward	32	138	252.0	16.0	268.0	7.768	1	1	2
§Vic Harding	**44**	**200**	**306.0**	**35.0**	**341.0**	**6.820**		**2**	**2**
§§Chris Robins	41	157	180.0	22.0	202.0	5.146			
Geoff Swindells	13	47	49.0	7.0	56.0	4.766			
Nigel Couzens	42	154	162.0	20.0	182.0	4.727		1	1
§§Melvin Soffe	30	98	96.0	8.0	104.0	4.245			
Frank Harvey	1	1	1.0	0.0	1.0	4.000			
Tony Freegard	19	69	55.0	7.0	62.0	3.594			
§§Ricky Owen	22	57	34.0	10.0	44.0	3.088			
§§Roger Stratton	14	35	20.0	5.0	25.0	2.857			
Glyn Facey	5	11	4.0	2.0	6.0	2.182			

1976...1976...1976...1976...1976...1976

	M	R	Pts	BP	TPts	Ave	F	P	Total
Martin Yeates	33	139	292.0	10.0	302.0	8.691	8	1	9
§§Dennis Cavill	1	2	2.0	2.0	4.0	8.000			
Vic Harding	30	127	211.0	17.0	228.0	7.181		2	2
Chris Robins	30	121	203.0	11.0	214.0	7.074	1		1
§Gerald Purkiss	27	103	134.0	27.0	161.0	6.252		1	1
§Danny Kennedy	19	77	103.0	9.0	112.0	5.818			
§§Billy Spiers	13	53	63.5	7.0	70.5	5.321			
§Trevor Charley	21	68	53.0	14.0	67.0	3.941			
§Jack Walker	27	87	68.0	9.0	77.0	3.540			
§§Garry May	20	66	48.0	10.0	58.0	3.515			
Roger Stratton	19	60	40.0	12.0	52.0	3.467			
§§Gary Wade	1	3	2.0	0.0	2.0	2.667			
Ricky Owen	2	6	1.0	0.0	1.0	0.667			
§§Rod Small	1	2	0.0	0.0	0.0	0.000			
§§Kevin May	1	1	0.0	0.0	0.0	0.000			

1977...1977...1977...1977...1977...1977

	M	R	Pts	BP	TPts	Ave	F	P	Total
Danny Kennedy	37	164	345.5	9.0	354.5	8.646	4		4
Vic Harding	20	84	143.0	24.0	167.0	7.952		2	2
§Malcolm Corradine	34	127	234.0	17.0	251.0	7.906			
Chris Robins	12	43	60.0	6.0	66.0	6.140			
§§Sean Willmott	28	126	157.0	21.0	178.0	5.651	1		1
§§Rob Jones	10	34	42.5	5.0	47.5	5.588			
Geoff Swindells	32	110	133.0	12.0	145.0	5.273			
§§Richard Evans	22	74	81.0	16.0	97.0	5.243			
§§Bruce Spargo	2	5	6.0	0.0	6.0	4.800			
§Chris Julian	9	31	35.0	2.0	37.0	4.774			
Roger Stratton	33	117	109.0	25.0	134.0	4.581			
Gerald Purkiss	3	9	8.0	2.0	10.0	4.444			
Richard Owen	6	20	14.0	3.0	17.0	3.400			
§Roy Sizmore	6	20	15.0	2.0	17.0	3.400			
Melvin Soffe	4	11	7.0	2.0	9.0	3.273			
§Dick Partridge	2	6	2.0	0.0	2.0	1.333			
§§Keith Pilcher	2	7	2.0	0.0	2.0	1.143			
§§Phil Baker	2	4	1.0	0.0	1.0	1.000			

1978...1978...1978...1978...1978...1978

	M	R	Pts	BP	TPts	Ave	F	P	Total
Danny Kennedy	38	172	381.0	13.0	394.0	9.163	7	4	11
§Malcolm Shakespeare	36	150	260.0	21.0	281.0	7.493	1	3	4
Sean Willmott	33	143	210.0	39.0	249.0	6.965		2	2
Malcolm Corradine	39	155	238.0	24.0	262.0	6.761	1		1
Geoff Swindells	35	131	187.0	28.0	215.0	6.565	1	1	2
§§Gary Ford	35	129	149.0	27.0	176.0	5.457		1	1
§§Mike Conroy	19	52	44.0	5.0	49.0	3.769			
§§Chris Lane	4	12	7.0	2.0	9.0	3.000			
§§Nigel Davis	21	65	39.0	7.0	46.0	2.831			
Richard Evans	3	8	3.0	1.0	4.0	2.000			
§§Mark Leslie	3	8	3.0	1.0	4.0	2.000			
§§Kevin Smith	2	4	2.0	0.0	2.0	2.000			

1979...1979...1979...1979...1979...1979

	M	R	Pts	BP	TPts	Ave	F	P	Total
Geoff Swindells	1	4	10.0	1.0	11.0	11.000			
Brian Woodward	**38**	**161**	**300.5**	**22.0**	**322.5**	**8.012**	**2**	**2**	**4**
§Doug Underwood	35	149	242.0	26.0	268.0	7.195	1	2	3
§Bob Coles	33	149	245.0	19.0	264.0	7.087		1	1
Malcolm Shakespeare	22	86	124.0	10.0	134.0	6.233	2		2
§§Terry Tulloch	**38**	**156**	**166.0**	**19.0**	**185.0**	**4.744**			
§Derek Hole	2	7	8.0	0.0	8.0	4.571			
Garry May	36	117	96.0	27.0	123.0	4.205			
Greg Joynt	5	11	10.0	1.0	11.0	4.000			
§Kevin Bowen	32	93	71.0	15.0	86.0	3.699			
Nigel Davis	7	21	15.0	2.0	17.0	3.238			
Mick Fletcher	3	8	5.0	1.0	6.0	3.000			
§§Mark DeKok	6	13	5.0	2.0	7.0	2.154			
§Barry Allaway	2	5	1.0	1.0	2.0	1.600			
Billy Spiers	1	3	0.0	0.0	0.0	0.000			
§§Andy Nichols	1	2	0.0	0.0	0.0	0.000			

1980...1980...1980...1980...1980...1980

	M	R	Pts	BP	TPts	Ave	F	P	Total
Martin Yeates	**39**	**175**	**399.0**	**8.0**	**407.0**	**9.303**	**7**		**7**
Brian Woodward	38	157	273.5	28.0	301.5	7.682		1	1
§§Simon Wigg	27	106	159.0	16.0	175.0	6.604			
Bob Coles	25	103	138.0	23.0	161.0	6.252		1	1
§§Chris Pusey	37	142	169.0	42.0	211.0	5.944			
Malcolm Corradine	11	40	49.0	6.0	55.0	5.500			
Mark DeKok	38	125	130.0	24.0	154.0	4.928			
Terry Tulloch	32	108	105.0	9.0	114.0	4.222			
Geoff Swindells	7	23	14.0	2.0	16.0	2.783			
§§George Toth	3	9	5.0	1.0	6.0	2.667			
§§Steve Schofield	1	3	2.0	0.0	2.0	2.667			
§Chris Sully	1	3	2.0	0.0	2.0	2.667			
Garry May	3	8	2.0	2.0	4.0	2.000			
§§Mark Minett	2	6	2.0	0.0	2.0	1.333			

WEYMOUTH share a rare distinction with Hackney. They were the only National League tracks to provide TWO different British Finalists throughout the British League era.
Simon Wigg (1982) and Martin Yeates (1984) represented the Wildcats while Hackney's two British Finalists were Malcolm Simmons (1986) and Andy Galvin (1988).

WEYMOUTH

1981...1981...1981...1981...1981...1981

	M	R	Pts	BP	TPts	Ave	F	P	Total
§Les Rumsey	20	82	194.0	15.0	209.0	10.195	3	6	9
Martin Yeates	**40**	**166**	**407.0**	**13.0**	**420.0**	**10.120**	**12**	**2**	**14**
Simon Wigg	34	141	338.0	17.0	355.0	10.071	7	5	12
Brian Woodward	**40**	**161**	**235.0**	**51.0**	**286.0**	**7.106**		**1**	**1**
Malcolm Shakespeare	36	131	190.0	40.0	230.0	7.023		2	2
Terry Tulloch	34	115	150.0	20.0	170.0	5.913			
§Steve Crockett	10	31	37.0	7.0	44.0	5.677			
Steve Schofield	31	112	133.0	25.0	158.0	5.643			
Bob Coles	19	72	75.0	19.0	94.0	5.222			
Mark DeKok	4	11	14.0	0.0	14.0	5.091			
§Kevin Young	5	18	10.0	3.0	13.0	2.889			
§§Geoff Reid	1	5	1.0	1.0	2.0	1.600			
Mark Minett	4	10	1.0	1.0	2.0	0.800			

1982...1982...1982...1982...1982...1982

	M	R	Pts	BP	TPts	Ave	F	P	Total
Simon Wigg	40	219	549.0	18.0	567.0	10.356	11	8	19
Martin Yeates	43	228	445.0	37.0	482.0	8.456	5	3	8
Steve Schofield	**44**	**230**	**366.0**	**42.0**	**408.0**	**7.096**	**1**	**2**	**3**
Terry Tulloch	5	25	36.0	6.0	42.0	6.720			
Les Rumsey	27	119	185.0	5.0	190.0	6.387			
§§Stan Bear	**44**	**200**	**267.0**	**33.0**	**300.0**	**6.000**	**1**		**1**
§John McNeill	30	144	176.0	29.0	205.0	5.694			
Steve Crockett	33	127	96.0	17.0	113.0	3.559			
Mark Minett	17	63	39.0	6.0	45.0	2.857			
§§Rob Mather	17	52	30.0	7.0	37.0	2.846			

WESSEX CHAMPIONSHIP

1965	1 Peter Swain	2 John McGill	3 Norman Brown

SEYCO SOFT DRINKS TROPHY

1974	1 Carl Glover	2 Nigel Couzens	3 Kelvin Mullarkey
1975	1 Vic Harding	2 Brian Woodward	3 Mike Sampson
1976	1 Les Collins	2 Kevin Young	3 Phil Bass
1977	1 Malcolm Corradine	2 Danny Kennedy	3 Mike Sampson
1978	1 Malcolm Shakespeare	2 Steve Koppe	3 Danny Kennedy
1979	1 George Hunter	2 Melvyn Taylor	3 Ashley Pullen
1980	1 John Hack	2 Robert Henry	3 Martin Yeates
1981	1 Martin Yeates	2 Les Sawyer	3 Robert Maxfield

WESSEX ROSEBOWL

1976	1 Chris Robins	2 Vic Harding	3 Martin Yeates

GOLDEN JUBILEE CELEBRATION TROPHY

1978	1 Vic Harding	2 Sean Willmott	3 Nigel Boocock

1983...1983...1983...1983...1983...1983

	M	R	Pts	BP	TPts	Ave	F	P	Total
Martin Yeates	41	219	555.0	14.0	569.0	10.393	9	3	12
Steve Schofield	38	197	417.0	25.0	442.0	8.975	7	1	8
§Simon Cross	**42**	**219**	**401.0**	**56.0**	**457.0**	**8.347**	**2**	**1**	**3**
Stan Bear	39	200	320.0	39.0	359.0	7.180		1	1
Rob Mather	14	59	67.0	19.0	86.0	5.831		1	1
§Kym Mauger	2	5	5.0	1.0	6.0	4.800			
§§Gordon Humphreys	34	148	140.0	23.0	163.0	4.405			
§§Chris Martin	**42**	**177**	**165.0**	**17.0**	**182.0**	**4.113**			
§§David Biles	20	67	38.0	10.0	48.0	2.866			
§§Ian Humphreys	12	35	15.0	4.0	19.0	2.171			
§Martin Satchell	6	16	7.0	1.0	8.0	2.000			
§§David Gibbs	1	3	1.0	0.0	1.0	1.333			

1984...1984...1984...1984...1984...1984

	M	R	Pts	BP	TPts	Ave	F	P	Total
Martin Yeates	20	85	218.0	2.0	220.0	10.353	8	1	9
§Alun Rossiter	31	136	302.0	12.0	314.0	9.235	1	1	2
David Biles	**32**	**141**	**223.0**	**26.0**	**249.0**	**7.064**			
§John Barker	21	86	131.0	16.0	147.0	6.837			
§Kevin Price	23	86	99.0	13.0	112.0	5.209		1	1
Gordon Humphreys	8	29	26.0	5.0	31.0	4.276			
§Mike Semmonds	17	58	53.5	6.0	59.5	4.103			
§Michael Coles	6	18	15.0	2.0	17.0	3.778			
Ian Humphreys	7	21	14.0	5.0	19.0	3.619			
David Gibbs	16	53	38.0	9.0	47.0	3.547			
Chris Martin	5	14	10.0	1.0	11.0	3.143			
§Colin Ackroyd	5	19	14.0	0.0	14.0	2.947			
§§Terry Mussett	9	26	16.0	3.0	19.0	2.923			
Rob Mather	5	17	10.0	2.0	12.0	2.824			
§§Wayne Barrett	8	22	5.0	1.0	6.0	1.091			
§§Marcus Bisson	2	5	1.0	0.0	1.0	0.800			
§§Dave Roberts	3	6	0.0	0.0	0.0	0.000			

POOR crowds over the years and mounting losses persuaded promoter Mervyn Stewkesbury to pull out of Weymouth – where his business empire was rooted – and move the entire operation to Poole during the 1984-85 closed season. He took the full Wildcats team with him and immediately hit a rich seam of support with the happy mix of old and new fans providing bumper gates.

- ***MARTIN YEATES developed into one of the finest riders in the National League during his years with Weymouth.***
- ***He had started slowly while on loan to Stoke in 1973 but once he moved to Radipole Lane at the beginning of 1975 he dramatically developed into a strong-scoring heat leader, averaging more than eight points a match.***
- ***He moved away to Oxford in 1977 – where he had his best ever seasons in terms of statistics – but he was glad to return to Dorset the following year when, for the second season in a row, he finished runner-up in the National League Riders' Championship Final.***
- ***He later led Weymouth to the 1983 Knock Out Cup Final and finally retired after three seasons with Poole when the Wildcats team moved along the sunny South Coast after the end of regular speedway at the Wessex Stadium.***
- ***Only a lack of confidence in his own ability prevented Yeates, the first Second Division rider to qualify beyond the World Championship British Final when he reached the 1984 Overseas Final, from achieving far more out of his career.***

WIMBLEDON

WIMBLEDON applied and were accepted in the 1985 National League because of the financial problems of competing in the British League Division One.

1985...1985...1985...1985...1985...1985

	M	R	Pts	BP	TPts	AVe	F	P	Total
§Mike Ferreira	40	169	405.0	10.0	415.0	9.822	6	4	10
§Roger Johns	37	163	370.0	23.0	393.0	9.644	3	4	7
§Jamie Luckhurst	40	175	344.0	21.0	365.0	8.343	2	3	5
§Kevin Teager	**42**	**170**	**229.0**	**45.0**	**274.0**	**6.447**		**3**	**3**
§Peter Johns	**42**	**139**	**144.0**	**33.0**	**177.0**	**5.094**			
§Mark Baldwin	**42**	**148**	**145.0**	**30.0**	**175.0**	**4.730**		**1**	**1**
§Jeremy Luckhurst	**42**	**136**	**114.5**	**27.0**	**141.5**	**4.943**		**1**	**1**

1986...1986...1986...1986...1986...1986

	M	R	Pts	BP	TPts	Ave	F	P	Total
Jamie Luckhurst	38	168	403.0	10.0	413.0	9.833	7	1	8
Roger Johns	**40**	**173**	**372.0**	**28.0**	**400.0**	**9.249**	**3**	**4**	**7**
§Nigel Sparshott	26	104	157.0	23.0	180.0	6.923		1	1
§Neville Tatum	36	156	236.0	27.0	263.0	6.744	1	1	2
Jeremy Luckhurst	39	149	182.0	43.0	225.0	6.040			
Kevin Teager	5	21	23.0	2.0	25.0	4.762			
§Terry Mussett	32	103	102.0	14.0	116.0	4.505			
§§Mark Fordham	19	52	38.0	8.0	46.0	3.538			
Mark Baldwin	29	94	68.0	10.0	78.0	3.319			
§§Jay Pleece	8	19	4.0	2.0	6.0	1.263			

1987...1987...1987...1987...1987...1987

	M	R	Pts	BP	TPts	Ave	F	P	Total
§Kevin Jolly	29	120	274.5	10.0	284.5	9.483	2	2	4
Roger Johns	**32**	**137**	**285.0**	**24.0**	**309.0**	**9.022**	**3**	**3**	**6**
Neville Tatum	**32**	**143**	**295.0**	**11.0**	**306.0**	**8.559**	**3**		**3**
§§Chris Standen	1	2	3.0	1.0	4.0	8.000			
Jeremy Luckhurst	27	105	125.0	34.0	159.0	6.057		1	1
§§Alan Farmer	18	63	63.0	20.0	83.0	5.270			
Terry Mussett	31	104	110.0	20.0	130.0	5.000			
§§Nathan Simpson	13	45	39.0	10.0	49.0	4.356			
Mark Fordham	17	56	47.0	6.0	53.0	3.786			
§David Gibbs	5	18	15.0	2.0	17.0	3.778			
§§Mark Lyndon	17	52	38.0	7.0	45.0	3.462			

1988...1988...1988...1988...1988...1988

	M	R	Pts	BP	TPts	Ave	F	P	Total
Kevin Jolly	39	198	410.0	38.0	448.0	9.051	3	4	7
§§Ray Morton	23	106	206.0	14.0	220.0	8.302		1	1
§§Todd Wiltshire	28	140	253.0	15.0	268.0	7.657	1		1
Roger Johns	37	174	264.0	53.0	317.0	7.287		2	2
§Alastair Stevens	25	130	209.0	25.0	234.0	7.200			
§Mark Chessell	1	3	4.0	1.0	5.0	6.667			
§Andy Campbell	38	190	283.0	30.0	313.0	6.589			
Nathan Simpson	**40**	**193**	**255.0**	**47.0**	**302.0**	**6.259**	**1**		**1**
Terry Mussett	26	93	93.0	17.0	110.0	4.731			
§§Tony Primmer	5	16	14.0	4.0	18.0	4.500			
§§Rodney Payne	14	37	26.0	11.0	37.0	4.000			
§Warren Mowat	1	3	0.0	0.0	0.0	0.000			

1989...1989...1989...1989...1989...1989

	M	R	Pts	BP	TPts	Ave	F	P	Total
Todd Wiltshire	37	198	478.0	14.0	492.0	9.939	7	4	11
Ray Morton	34	172	338.0	19.0	357.0	8.302	3		3
Neville Tatum	33	180	332.0	31.0	363.0	8.067	1	1	2
Roger Johns	36	183	295.0	49.0	344.0	7.519			
Nathan Simpson	33	177	259.0	52.0	311.0	7.028		1	1
§§Jerry Glendenning	1	2	3.0	0.0	3.0	6.000			
§Nigel Leaver	23	110	134.0	28.0	162.0	5.891			
Rodney Payne	30	119	135.0	21.0	156.0	5.244			
§§Scott Humphries	33	100	88.0	29.0	117.0	4.680		1	1
§§Jim Dormer	11	32	25.0	4.0	29.0	3.625			
§Tony Forward	4	11	3.0	0.0	3.0	1.091			

1990...1990...1990...1990...1990...1990

	M	R	Pts	BP	TPts	Ave	F	P	Total
§Andy Grahame	35	180	404.0	19.0	423.0	9.400	3	3	6
Nathan Simpson	**38**	**210**	**374.0**	**46.0**	**420.0**	**8.000**		**1**	**1**
Ray Morton	37	176	311.0	20.0	331.0	7.523	1	2	3
Neville Tatum	**38**	**199**	**325.0**	**42.0**	**367.0**	**7.377**		**2**	**2**
Nigel Leaver	**38**	**198**	**218.0**	**50.0**	**268.0**	**5.414**			
§§Deon Prinsloo	21	77	55.0	12.0	67.0	3.481			
§§Justin Pryor	23	61	41.0	10.0	51.0	3.344			
§Peter Schroeck	5	17	9.0	3.0	12.0	2.824			
Jim Dormer	2	5	0.0	0.0	0.0	0.000			

MARLBORO SOUTHERN

1985	1 Jamie Luckhurst	2 Mike Ferreira	3 Colin Richardson

See also Wimbledon, Division One Averages

SPRING CLASSIC

1987	1 Trevor Banks	2 Andrew Silver	3 Paul Woods
1988	1 Andy Galvin	2 Gordon Kennett	3 Steve Schofield
1989	1 Andy Galvin	2 Neville Tatum	3 Steve Schofield
1990	1 Andy Grahame	2 Jens Rasmussen	3 Chris Louis

DONS '89...the most talked about squad in British speedway! Back row, Rodney Payne, Neville Tatum, Jim Dormer, Tony Forward, Scott Humphries, Todd Wiltshire, Ray Morton. Front: Nigel Leaver, skipper Roger Johns and Nathan Simpson

WOLVERHAMPTON

■*WOLVERHAMPTON'S sole season in Division Two began with the major boost of a team sponsorship...but ended with the promotion hurriedly arranging a series of double headers so that they could close the doors on racing as early as Sunday, August 30, when they lost their final match to Middlesbrough.*
By then some of their star assets had already been sold off to try and recoup some of the money lost in trying to tempt the Black Country public with Division Two fare.

GOODYEAR AIRSHIP TROPHY

1981 1 Martin Yeates 2 Billy Burton 3 Les Rumsey

See also Wolverhampton, Division One Averages

1981...1981...1981...1981...1981...1981

	M	R	Pts	BP	TPts	Ave	F	P	Total
§Bruce Cribb	36	156	369.5	20.0	389.5	9.987	9	2	11
§Les Rumsey	13	52	108.0	6.0	114.0	8.769	2		2
§Neil Evitts	33	139	253.0	18.0	271.0	7.799	2		2
§Billy Burton	23	92	142.0	13.0	155.0	6.739	3		3
§Tony Boyle	34	119	166.0	11.0	177.0	5.950	1		1
§Paul Stead	33	130	162.0	17.0	179.0	5.508		2	2
§Mike Wilding	37	139	123.0	20.0	143.0	4.115			
§Paul Embley	12	52	38.5	11.0	49.5	3.808			
§John Hough	15	47	30.0	11.0	41.0	3.489			
§§Rob Carter	15	53	44.0	3.0	47.0	3.547			
§§Alan Jones	1	5	2.0	0.0	2.0	1.600			
§Steve Crockett	7	17	5.0	1.0	6.0	1.412			
§§Paul Simons	3	7	0.0	0.0	0.0	0.000			
§§Keiron Boyle	1	2	0.0	0.0	0.0	0.000			

WORKINGTON

WORKINGTON, an isolated outpost in far flung Cumbria, owed its surprise success to the willingness of a stream of Aussies to make Derwent Park their home base.

Their first genuine superstar discovery was the stylish Lou Sansom (pictured right talking to Comets' team-mates Malcolm Mackay (3) and Lindsay Davies) who modelled his whole approach on Ivan Mauger – even down to a chequered helmet.

There were some glorious days at Derwent Park – home of the local Rugby League team – and Workington's victories included successive wins over First Division Ipswich and King's Lynn in the 1976 Inter League Knock Out Cup when they reached the semi-final before going out to Hull.

1970...1970...1970...1970...1970...1970

	M	R	Pts	BP	TPts	Ave	F	P	Total
§Taffy Owen	7	33	79.0	3.0	82.0	9.939		1	1
§§Bob Valentine	27	120	264.0	17.0	281.0	9.367	4	6	10
§Malcolm Mackay	30	126	216.0	22.0	238.0	7.556	2	1	3
§Geoff Penniket	28	119	195.0	20.0	215.0	7.227	1	1	2
§Reg Wilson	30	121	171.0	26.0	197.0	6.512			
§§Lou Sansom	23	92	124.0	17.0	141.0	6.130		1	1
§§Ian Armstrong	14	40	37.0	13.0	50.0	5.000			
§Chris Blythe	29	92	79.0	18.0	97.0	4.217			
§Dave Kumeta	15	50	41.0	7.0	48.0	3.840			
§§Vic Lonsdale	10	27	21.0	4.0	25.0	3.704			
§Ray Cousins	1	2	1.0	0.0	1.0	2.000			

1971...1971...1971...1971...1971...1971

	M	R	Pts	BP	TPts	Ave	F	P	Total
Malcolm Mackay	36	161	383.0	12.0	395.0	9.814	8	3	11
Taffy Owen	27	114	241.0	4.0	245.0	8.596	3		3
Lou Sansom	36	157	283.0	26.0	309.0	7.873	3	3	6
§Ken Vale	29	108	130.0	29.0	159.0	5.889		1	1
Dave Kumeta	36	148	159.0	23.0	182.0	4.919			
§§Kym Amundson	30	113	112.0	21.0	133.0	4.708			
§Bernie Hornby	10	38	36.0	5.0	41.0	4.316			
Geoff Penniket	7	27	26.0	2.0	28.0	4.148			
Chris Blythe	21	58	41.0	16.0	57.0	3.931			
§§Steve Watson	19	56	41.0	9.0	50.0	3.571			
§§Roy Young	2	3	1.0	1.0	2.0	2.667			

1972...1972...1972...1972...1972...1972

	M	R	Pts	BP	TPts	Ave	F	P	Total
Taffy Owen	29	113	232.0	18.0	250.0	8.850	3		3
Lou Sansom	**34**	**151**	**301.0**	**21.0**	**322.0**	**8.530**	**5**	**4**	**9**
Malcolm Mackay	33	146	291.0	18.0	309.0	8.466	5	1	6
§Mitch Graham	21	79	107.0	20.0	127.0	6.430		2	2
Kym Amundson	**34**	**133**	**171.0**	**25.0**	**196.0**	**5.895**	**1**	**1**	**2**
Steve Watson	**34**	**124**	**141.0**	**18.0**	**159.0**	**5.129**			
Dave Kumeta	28	94	87.0	8.0	95.0	4.043			
§§Darrell Stobbart	8	23	17.0	6.0	23.0	4.000			
§§Lindsay Davies	13	42	29.0	10.0	39.0	3.714			

1973...1973...1973...1973...1973...1973

	M	R	Pts	BP	TPts	Ave	F	P	Total
Lou Sansom	**42**	**182**	**469.0**	**9.0**	**478.0**	**10.505**	**20**	**2**	**22**
Malcolm Mackay	**42**	**178**	**349.0**	**46.0**	**395.0**	**8.876**	**1**	**9**	**10**
Mitch Graham	41	166	299.0	36.0	335.0	8.072	2	3	5
Taffy Owen	**42**	**164**	**267.0**	**38.0**	**305.0**	**7.439**		**3**	**3**
Kym Amundson	37	132	150.0	32.0	182.0	5.515		1	1
Steve Watson	**42**	**145**	**167.0**	**29.0**	**196.0**	**5.407**			
Bernie Hornby	33	102	74.0	17.0	91.0	3.569			
Darrell Stobbart	13	34	23.0	7.0	30.0	3.529			

1974...1974...1974...1974...1974...1974

	M	R	Pts	BP	TPts	Ave	F	P	Total
Mitch Graham	40	174	413.0	22.0	435.0	10.000	9	5	14
Malcolm Mackay	31	129	272.0	11.0	283.0	8.775	5	1	6
Taffy Owen	41	173	321.0	43.0	364.0	8.416		8	8
§Alan Cowland	39	167	280.0	24.0	304.0	7.281		1	1
Steve Watson	**42**	**151**	**171.0**	**38.0**	**209.0**	**5.536**		**2**	**2**
Darrell Stobbart	37	131	135.0	28.0	163.0	4.977			
Bernie Hornby	41	140	121.0	24.0	145.0	4.143		1	1
§§Steve Lawson	12	38	13.0	3.0	16.0	1.684			

1975...1975...1975...1975...1975...1975

	M	R	Pts	BP	TPts	Ave	F	P	Total
Lou Sansom	47	232	482.0	29.0	511.0	8.810	3	1	4
Taffy Owen	37	171	340.0	18.0	358.0	8.374	2	2	4
Malcolm Mackay	2	9	17.0	0.0	17.0	7.556			
§Robbie Gardner	45	213	345.0	48.0	393.0	7.380		1	1
Kym Amundson	16	68	108.0	10.0	118.0	6.941		2	2
§Mick Newton	37	148	215.5	30.0	245.5	6.635		1	1
§Roger Wright	25	91	123.0	19.0	142.0	6.242		1	1
Terry Kelly	38	151	197.0	32.0	229.0	6.066			
Steve Watson	12	38	36.0	6.0	42.0	4.421			
Steve Lawson	29	99	78.0	12.0	90.0	3.636		1	1
§Brian Johnson	1	3	2.0	0.0	2.0	2.667			
§§Andy Walker	6	18	7.0	3.0	10.0	2.222			
§Graham Tattersall	2	6	2.0	0.0	2.0	1.333			
§Stewart Collin	2	6	1.0	0.0	1.0	0.667			

WORKINGTON

1976...1976...1976...1976...1976...1976

	M	R	Pts	BP	TPts	Ave	F	P	Total
Lou Sansom	28	125	268.0	6.0	274.0	8.768	5		5
Steve Lawson	29	133	276.0	14.0	290.0	8.722	1	3	4
Taffy Owen	16	57	111.0	4.0	115.0	8.070	1		1
§Colin Goad	**38**	**163**	**276.0**	**38.0**	**314.0**	**7.706**		**3**	**3**
§Brian Havelock	28	122	220.0	14.0	234.0	7.672	2	2	4
Roger Wright	31	110	150.0	30.0	180.0	6.545		1	1
Terry Kelly	37	146	165.5	38.0	203.5	5.575		1	1
§§Derek Wilson	2	5	5.0	1.0	6.0	4.800			
§Chris Bevan	25	81	61.0	16.0	77.0	3.802			
Stewart Collin	13	38	24.0	6.0	30.0	3.158			
§§Mark Dickinson	1	2	0.0	0.0	0.0	0.000			

1977...1977...1977...1977...1977...1977

	M	R	Pts	BP	TPts	Ave	F	P	Total
Steve Lawson	37	164	327.0	9.0	336.0	8.195	6	3	9
§§Mike Stewart	1	1	1.0	1.0	2.0	8.000			
Brian Havelock	27	111	204.0	13.0	217.0	7.820	2		2
Mick Newton	27	123	177.0	22.0	199.0	6.472			
§Ian Hindle	**38**	**155**	**224.0**	**23.0**	**247.0**	**6.374**	**1**	**2**	**3**
Roger Wright	26	82	96.0	19.0	115.0	5.610			
Colin Goad	35	142	173.0	22.0	195.0	5.493		2	2
Terry Kelly	14	55	54.0	10.0	64.0	4.655			
Mark Dickinson	8	28	19.0	3.0	22.0	3.143			
Chris Bevan	21	67	45.0	6.0	51.0	3.045			
§Andy Reid	15	46	32.0	3.0	35.0	3.043			
§Rob Hamman	2	7	3.0	0.0	3.0	1.714			
Des Wilson	5	13	3.0	0.0	3.0	0.923			
§§Trevor Oldham	2	5	0.0	0.0	0.0	0.000			

1978...1978...1978...1978...1978...1978

	M	R	Pts	BP	TPts	Ave	F	P	Total
§Arthur Price	31	133	272.0	15.0	287.0	8.632	2	1	3
Brian Havelock	39	174	339.0	26.0	365.0	8.391	2	2	4
§Robert Maxfield	31	128	215.0	30.0	245.0	7.656	2		2
§Dave Baugh	3	9	16.0	0.0	16.0	7.111			
Ian Hindle	38	160	238.0	18.0	256.0	6.400	3	2	5
Mick Newton	4	12	11.0	7.0	18.0	6.000			
Mark Dickinson	25	95	103.0	19.0	122.0	5.137			
§§David Coles	24	83	79.0	21.0	100.0	4.819			
§§Andy Margarson	30	106	114.0	13.0	127.0	4.792			
Des Wilson	20	65	56.0	16.0	72.0	4.431			
§Tony Childs	7	22	15.0	3.0	18.0	3.273			
§§Rod North	4	12	6.0	2.0	8.0	2.667			
§§Neil Abrahams	2	4	1.0	1.0	2.0	2.000			
§Les Race	6	17	7.0	1.0	8.0	1.882			
§Richie Caulwell	2	4	1.0	0.0	1.0	1.000			
Trevor Oldham	3	9	1.0	0.0	1.0	0.444			
§§Mike Caroline	1	3	0.0	0.0	0.0	0.000			
§§Ken Hall	1	2	0.0	0.0	0.0	0.000			

1979...1979...1979...1979...1979...1979

	M	R	Pts	BP	TPts	Ave	F	P	Total
§Alan Emerson	35	150	321.0	16.0	337.0	8.987	3	2	5
Brian Havelock	36	154	271.0	21.0	292.0	7.584		1	1
§§Arnold Haley	11	39	62.0	5.0	67.0	6.872			
Ian Hindle	39	156	249.0	16.0	265.0	6.795	1	2	3
Mark Dickinson	32	112	162.0	21.0	183.0	6.536		1	1
§Neil Collins	28	126	163.0	30.0	193.0	6.127			
§§Dave McKenzie	1	3	3.0	1.0	4.0	5.333			
Andy Margarson	15	51	55.0	9.0	64.0	5.020			
§§Gary Forscutt	1	2	1.0	1.0	2.0	4.000			
§Mick Blaynee	29	102	86.0	13.0	99.0	3.882			
Des Wilson	22	81	62.0	11.0	73.0	3.605			
Stewart Collin	1	3	2.0	0.0	2.0	2.667			
§Terry Freeman	2	3	1.0	1.0	2.0	2.667			
Les Race	2	5	2.0	1.0	3.0	2.400			
§§Keith Starkey	3	10	3.0	2.0	5.0	2.000			
§§Tim Nichol	8	23	11.0	0.0	11.0	1.913			
§§Kym McConnell	3	9	3.0	0.0	3.0	1.333			

1980...1980...1980...1980...1980...1980

	M	R	Pts	BP	TPts	Ave	F	P	Total
Ian Hindle	23	89	147.0	1.0	148.0	6.652	2		2
§Ian Robertson	30	135	162.0	12.0	174.0	5.156			
Des Wilson	35	140	137.0	21.0	158.0	4.514			
§§Steve Regeling	13	39	40.0	4.0	44.0	4.513			
§§Wayne Jackson	35	139	146.0	8.0	154.0	4.432			
Mark Dickinson	33	130	122.0	10.0	132.0	4.062			
Terry Kelly	17	62	53.0	4.0	57.0	3.677			
Chris Roynon	11	40	35.0	0.0	35.0	3.500			
§Kevin Clapham	**40**	**152**	**115.0**	**16.0**	**131.0**	**3.447**			
§§Ian Westwell	1	5	4.0	0.0	4.0	3.200			
Les Race	3	11	8.0	0.0	8.0	2.909			
Andy Margarson	7	29	18.0	2.0	20.0	2.759			
Chris Bevan	4	14	6.0	3.0	9.0	2.571			
§Greg Joynt	3	10	6.0	0.0	6.0	2.400			
§§Bob Hitchcock	1	3	1.0	0.0	1.0	1.333			
§Brett Saunders	1	3	1.0	0.0	1.0	1.333			
Tim Nichol	6	12	2.0	1.0	3.0	1.000			
§Greg Irving	6	11	1.0	0.0	1.0	0.364			
§§Alan Armstrong	1	4	0.0	0.0	0.0	0.000			
§Dave Parkin	1	2	0.0	0.0	0.0	0.000			
§§Guy Robson	1	2	0.0	0.0	0.0	0.000			

1981...1981...1981...1981...1981...1981

	M	R	Pts	BP	TPts	Ave	F	P	Total
Terry Kelly	36	175	299.0	6.0	305.0	6.971	1	1	2
Ian Hindle	3	12	19.0	1.0	20.0	6.667			
Wayne Jackson	**38**	**198**	**299.0**	**9.0**	**308.0**	**6.222**			
Mark Dickinson	13	60	78.0	7.0	85.0	5.667	1		1
§Guy Wilson	28	118	114.0	18.0	132.0	4.475			
Des Wilson	21	76	72.0	12.0	84.0	4.421			
Kevin Clapham	12	49	38.0	7.0	45.0	3.673			
§§David Price	4	12	7.0	4.0	11.0	3.667			
§§David Blackburn	29	130	92.0	22.0	114.0	3.508			
Mick Newton	6	22	15.0	3.0	18.0	3.273			
§Howard Jackson	7	26	19.0	0.0	19.0	2.923			
§§John Frankland	18	67	39.0	6.0	45.0	2.687			
§Chris Pusey	3	6	2.0	1.0	3.0	2.000			
§Dean Zaman	6	19	5.0	1.0	6.0	1.263			
§§Andy Elliott	2	4	1.0	0.0	1.0	1.000			
§§Michael Irving	7	18	3.0	1.0	4.0	0.889			
§§John Walmsley	1	5	1.0	0.0	1.0	0.800			
Ian Westwell	1	3	0.0	0.0	0.0	0.000			
§Mike Hiftle	1	2	0.0	0.0	0.0	0.000			
§Paul Thorp	1	1	0.0	0.0	0.0	0.000			

GRAHAM'S HANDICAP TROPHY

1970	1 John Jackson	2 Bob Valentine	3 Taffy Owen

CUMBERLAND OPEN CHAMPIONSHIP

1970	1 Alan Knapkin	2 Taffy Owen	3 Malcolm Mackay
1971	1 Doug Wyer	2 Taffy Owen	3 Malcolm Mackay and Lou Sansom
1972	1 John Jackson	2 Dennis Gavros	3 Malcolm Mackay and Lou Sansom
1973	1 Lou Sansom	2 Malcolm Mackay	3 Graham Drury

NORTHERN COUNTIES CHAMPIONSHIP

1970	1 Lou Sansom	2 Geoff Pennikett	3 Malcolm Mackay
1971	1 Dave Kumeta	2 Reg Wilson	3 Doug Wyer
1972	1 Malcolm Mackay	2 Paul Tyrer	3 Lou Sansom
1973	1 Lou Sansom	2 Sid Sheldrick	3 Taffy Owen

CUMBRIA KO TROPHY

1972	1 John Jackson	2 Lou Sansom	3 Tom Owen
1973	1 Mitch Graham	2 Malcolm Mackay	3 Steve Watson

STARS OF THE LEAGUE SUPPORTERS' TROPHY

1976	1 Tom Owen	2 Robbie Gardner	3 Steve Lawson

CUMBRIAN APOLLO CUP

1981	1 Alan Emerson	2 Terry Kelly	3 Wayne Jackson

LEAGUE racing returned to Derwent Park in 1987 when Glasgow promoter Jim Beaton, without a home base, decided to start the National League season by travelling the Tigers to Cumbria for home meetings. They took the name of Workington from August 7 but were expelled from the League on Tuesday, September 15, after only six official matches. See Glasgow Division Two Averages for full details.

NOBODY could accuse the authorities of being over ambitious when they launched the Junior Championship of the British Isles.

For the Speedway Control Board, who inaugurated and retained control of the competition throughout its 22-year history, decided that the initial competition, restricted to British-born riders under the age of 21, should be run as a second half event during the Western Zone semi-final of the 1969 World Pairs Championship.

Nelson Mills Baldwin, chairman of the Speedway Control Board, said: "I have always felt that for speedway in this country to be really healthy there must be a plentiful supply of native riders and it is as an encouragement to this end that the Board have instituted the new competition."

Nine riders were selected for the initial staging and the plan was to have six qualifying races (with three riders in each race) with the top four scorers meeting in a sudden death final after they had all had two races each. But that first staging, at Wimbledon on Thursday, August 14, never even got underway with referee Gordon Little being forced to abandon the meeting because of heavy rain before Graham Plant, Roger Mills and Geoff Ambrose got onto the Plough Lane track for the opening heat. It was eventually re-staged six weeks later over three heats, a semi-final and a final.

But the powers-that-be saw enough good in the concept that the following year it was promoted to a full-scale 20-heat championship at Swindon with tracks being asked to nominate contenders and the final 16 being based on averages.

At that time the competition was also open to anyone born in the British Commonwealth (excluding Canada and Northern Ireland) but in subsequent years this was amended to English-born riders only.

Another early rule was that irrespective of his age the previous season's winner could not defend his championship! This helps to explain why in 22 years of competition there were 22 different names on the roll of honour although Mark Loram, who won the crown in 1988, was allowed to challenge again two years later when he finished runner-up!

In 1972 the competition was moved from Swindon to Canterbury and it remained at Kingsmead until 1986 when it was staged at Stoke and, subsequently, at both Eastbourne and Wimbledon. In 1981 it became accepted practice that the best placed riders from the previous season's Junior Championship of Great Britain would be nominated for the European Junior Championship which later developed into the World Junior Championship.

Over the years the British event provided a mixed bag of talent.

Some – like Peter Collins and Michael Lee – enjoyed the sweet taste of victory in a World Final. Others – like Chris Morton, Les Collins, Phil Collins, Kenny Carter, Marvyn Cox, Gary Havelock and Martin Dugard – went on to become World Finalists.

And some, like Rayleigh's Allen Emmett, Stoke's Robert Lightfoot and Exeter's Keith Millard, disappeared from the scene through injury or a lack of application.

The Collins family provided three winners (Peter, Les and Phil) and Belle Vue provided even more.

Peter Collins, Chris Morton, Les Collins, Peter Carr, Mark Blackbird and Joe Screen were all attached to the Aces when they won.

The unluckiest rider of all?

That, surely, has to be Simon Cross who figured in a run-off for the championship on three successive occasions and was beaten each time!

By and large though, the competition has rewarded rich talent with Peter Collins, Chris Morton, Michael Lee, Les Collins, Phil Collins, Kenny Carter and Gary Havelock all going on to greater things with World Championship success in major title rounds.

And there can be little doubt that recent champions Mark Loram, Martin Dugard and the last winner Joe Screen have the potential to extend the impressive records of some of their predecessors.

FIRST-TIMER...1969 Champion Graham Plant

HAPPY...1975 title-winner Neil Middleditch

FAMILY WAY...Les Collins, champ in 1977

MEMORIES...happier times for 1983 British Junior Champion Keith Millard

THE Golden Helmet was one of the oldest competitions in speedway history having evolved from the old British Match Race Championship.

On the amalgamation of the old National League (First Division) and the Provincial League it was agreed to continue the competition but also to run alongside it the Silver Sash, a match-race competition that had been staged successfully in the Provincial League.

Barry Briggs (pictured right) dominated in the early stages and was unbeaten when the competition was suspended at the end of the 1967 season. At that time all defences were on neutral tracks and this proved to have a big appeal.

As a monthly event it had a certain crowd appeal but much of this was lost when it was agreed that it should be defended on a match-by-match basis against the opposing side's top scorer.

That took away much of the glamour and sometimes fans would turn up at a meeting unaware that there was to be a Golden Helmet challenge or, conversely, expecting one when the holder had lost the title the previous evening.

At the beginning of 1974, after four years of match-by-match challenges, the competition reverted to a monthly challenge although this time it was to be on a home and away basis.

It remained that until May 7, 1987, when it was announced that the competition was being suspended while the British League Management Committee studied and recommended a new method of operation.

Despite assurances that the competition would continue that season there was never another Golden Helmet challenge....

1965

*Nominated holder: **Barry Briggs**.*

Barry Briggs defeated Charlie Monk (0-2 Poole, 2-0 Sheffield, 2-0 West Ham), Ken McKinlay (2-0 Wolverhampton, 2-0 Newport), George Hunter (2-0 Newcastle, 2-0 Oxford), Nigel Boocock (2-1 Glasgow, 2-1 Hackney), Sverre Harrfeldt (2-0 Wimbledon, 2-0 Coventry), Olle Nygren (2-0 Edinburgh, 2-1 Halifax).

1966

*Winter holder: **Barry Briggs**.*

Barry Briggs defeated Nigel Boocock (2-0 Long Eaton), Gote Nordin (2-1 Oxford), Arne Pander (2-0 Poole), Mike Broadbank (2-1 Swindon), Ivan Mauger (2-1 Sheffield), Sverre Harrfeldt (2-0 Wimbledon).

1967

Not contested. Holder: Barry Briggs.

1968

Not contested. Holder: Barry Briggs.

1969

Not Contested. Holder: Barry Briggs.

1970

***Ivan Mauger** as winter holder of the now defunct Silver Sash was nominated as the new Golden Helmet holder.*

Ivan Mauger defeated Jim McMillan, Roy Trigg, Ray Wilson, Colin Pratt, Olle Nygren, Rick France, Barry Briggs, Trevor Hedge, Howard Cole. Lost to Martin Ashby.

Martin Ashby defeated Terry Betts, Olle Nygren, Mike Cake. Lost to Arnold Haley.

Arnold Haley defeated Eric Boocock, Sandor Levai. Lost to Howard Cole.

Howard Cole defeated Chris Julian. Lost to Eric Boocock.

Eric Boocock defeated Peter Jarman. Lost to Garry Middleton.

Garry Middleton lost to Anders Michanek.

Anders Michanek defeated Eric Boocock, Ray Wilson, Geoff Mudge, Eric Boocock. Lost to Ivan Mauger by default.

Ivan Mauger lost to Garry Middleton.

Garry Middleton lost to Nigel Boocock.

Nigel Boocock lost to Ole Olsen.

Ole Olsen defeated Bengt Jansson, Roy Trigg, Pete Smith, Hasse Holmkvist, Graham Plant, Bill Andrew. Lost to Ivan Mauger.

Ivan Mauger defeated Ronnie Moore.

1971

*Winter holder: **Ivan Mauger**.*

Ivan Mauger lost to Ole Olsen.

Ole Olsen defeated Brian Leonard, Sandor Levai, Edgar Stangeland, Eric Boocock, Reidar Eide, Bengt Jansson, Trevor Hedge, Bernt Persson, Ray Wilson, Ivan Mauger, lost by default to Ken McKinlay.

Ken McKinlay lost to Richard May.

Richard May lost to Ronnie Moore.

Ronnie Moore defeated Pete Smith, lost to Ray Wilson.

Ray Wilson lost to Anders Michanek.

Anders Michanek defeated Malcolm Simmons, Bobby Beaton, Jim Airey, lost to Garry Middleton.

Garry Middleton defeated Sandor Levai, Eric Boocock, lost to Nigel Boocock.

Nigel Boocock lost to Ray Wilson.

Ray Wilson beat Eric Boocock, Jim Airey, lost by default to Ole Olsen.

1972

*Winter holder: **Ole Olsen**.*

Ole Olsen lost by default to Bobby Beaton.

Bobby Beaton defeated Eric Boocock, lost to Nigel Boocock.

Nigel Boocock lost to Garry Middleton.

Garry Middleton lost to Dave Younghusband.

Dave Younghusband lost to Bengt Jansson.

Bengt Jansson lost to Chris Pusey.

Chris Pusey defeated Ronnie Moore, lost to Reidar Eide.

Reidar Eide defeated Olle Nygren, lost to Terry Betts.

Terry Betts defeated Dave Younghusband, Alan Wilkinson, Neil Street, Laurie Etheridge, Reidar Eide, Garry Middleton, lost to Jim McMillan.

Jim McMillan defeated Edgar Stangeland, Geoff Curtis, lost to Christer Löfqvist.

Christer Löfqvist lost to Ole Olsen.

Ole Olsen defeated David Kennett, Edgar Stangeland, Sandor Levai, Martin Ashby, John Langfield, Bobby Beaton, Sandor Levai, Oyvind Berg, Graham Plant, Martin Ashby, Ivan Mauger, Graham Plant, Terry Betts.

1973

*Winter holder: **Ole Olsen.***

Ole Olsen defeated Nigel Boocock, Bernt Persson, Tommy Jansson, Graham Plant, Malcolm Shakespeare. Lost to Reidar Eide.

Reidar Eide defeated Tommy Jansson, John Boulger, Bob Valentine. Lost to John Louis.

John Louis lost to Reidar Eide.

Reidar Eide lost to Barry Thomas.

Barry Thomas lost to Roy Trigg.

Roy Trigg defeated Bob Kilby. Lost to Tony Davey.

Tony Davey lost to Chris Pusey.

Chris Pusey lost to Martin Ashby.

Martin Ashby lost to Barry Thomas.

Barry Thomas lost to Eric Boocock.

Eric Boocock defeated Sören Sjösten (twice), Anders Michanek, Trevor Hedge, Garry Middleton. Lost to Ivan Mauger.

Ivan Mauger defeated Bob Valentine, Bobby Beaton. Lost to Terry Betts.

Terry Betts defeated Eric Broadbelt, Charlie Monk. Lost to Graham Plant.

Graham Plant lost to Arnold Haley.

Arnold Haley lost to John Louis.

John Louis defeated Pete Smith, Edgar Stangeland, John Titman, Malcolm Simmons, Ulf Lovaas.

1974

*Winter holder: **John Louis.***

John Louis defeated Ray Wilson (2-1 Leicester, 2-0 Ipswich); Peter Collins (2-1 Ipswich, 2-0 Belle Vue), Malcolm Simmons (1-2 Ipswich, 2-1 King's Lynn, 2-0 Hackney), Dag Lovaas (2-0 Hackney, 2-0 Ipswich), Ole Olsen (2-0 Ipswich, 0-2 Wolverhampton, 2-0 Swindon). Lost to Phil Crump (1-2 Ipswich, 0-2 Newport).

Phil Crump defeated John Boulger (2-1 Cradley Heath, 1-2 Newport, 2-1 Wimbledon).

Sponsor: Speedway Star.

1975

*Winter holder: **Phil Crump.***

Phil Crump defeated Peter Collins (2-0 Newport, 1-2 Belle Vue, 2-0 Leicester), Anders Michanek (2-0 Newport, 1-2 Reading, 2-1 Poole). Lost to Ole Olsen (2-0 Newport, 0-2 Wolverhampton, 1-2 King's Lynn).

Ole Olsen lost to Dave Jessup (0-2 Wolverhampton, 0-2 Leicester).

Dave Jessup lost to John Louis (1-2 Leicester, 1-2 Ipswich).

John Louis defeated Malcolm Simmons (2-1 Ipswich, 0-2 Poole, 2-1 Wimbledon). Lost to Martin Ashby (2-0 †Belle Vue, 1-2 Ipswich, 0-2 Hackney).

† Martin Ashby opted to race his home leg at Belle Vue as his club Swindon had completed their home fixtures.

Sponsor: Speedway Star.

✪ **OLE OLSEN holds the all-time record for successful Golden Helmet defences. He won the titfer off Poole's Christer Löfqvist on July 5, 1972, and then successfully defended it on EIGHTEEN occasions against 14 different opponents (he met Graham Plant three times) before losing it to Reidar Eide on April 25, 1973.**

✪ **BARRY BRIGGS and PETER COLLINS both successfully defended the Golden Helmet on 12 occasions when it was run as a monthly challenge. Briggo began the 1965 season as the nominated holder and was still the holder when the competition was suspended at the end of the 1966 season. As the competition was not reintroduced until the beginning of the 1970 season he technically was Golden Helmet Match-Race Champion for the first five years of the British League. Peter Collins won the crown off Gordon Kennett in the last monthly challenge of 1977, retained it with seven successful defences in 1979 before finally losing it to Phil Crump in the final defence of 1979!**

✪ **MICHAEL LEE is the only rider in history to have been stripped of the Golden Helmet TWICE. He forfeited the title when he failed to turn up for the second leg at Eastbourne on June 7, 1981, and again when he was a non-arrival at Sheffield on May 26, 1984.**

✪ **TOMMY JANSSON was the Golden Helmet holder when he was killed while riding in a World Championship qualifying round in Sweden on Thursday, May 20, 1976. The Golden Helmet was presented to Tommy's parents in a mark of respect and a new Golden Helmet was forged for the subsequent challenge.**

✪ **MITCH SHIRRA is the only rider who can honestly claim to have been the undefeated Golden Helmet holder. He took the title off Jeremy Doncaster early in the 1987 season and the competition was discontinued before he had a chance to defend the title. In theory he held the title from May 7, 1987, until the amalgamation of the British League and the National League – a total of nearly four years even though he never figured in another challenge!**

1976

Winter holder: ***Martin Ashby.***

Martin Ashby defeated Malcolm Simmons (2-0 Swindon, 2-0 Poole). Lost to Tommy Jansson (0-2 Wimbledon, 2-0 Swindon, 1-2 Cradley Heath).
Tommy Jansson defeated Dave Jessup (2-1 Reading, 2-1 Wimbledon).
Peter Collins and Malcolm Simmons were nominated to race-off for the title after Tommy Jansson's death in a track crash. Peter Collins withdrew from the competition and Dave Morton was nominated as challenger.
Malcolm Simmons defeated Dave Morton (2-0 Poole, 2-0 Hackney), Chris Morton (2-0 Poole, 1-2 Belle Vue, 2-0 Hull).
Malcolm Simmons *forfeited the title when he was unable to defend the crown because of illness. Phil Crump, his challenger, was asked to race against Ivan Mauger for the title.*
Phil Crump defeated Ivan Mauger (2-0 Newport, 2-0 Exeter), Peter Collins (2-0 Belle Vue, 2-0 Newport).
Sponsor: Standard Motorists Centres.

1977

Winter holder: ***Phil Crump.***

Phil Crump defeated John Louis (2-1 Ipswich, 2-1 Bristol), Michael Lee (2-1 Bristol, 2-1 King's Lynn), Edward Jancarz (2-0 Wimbledon, 2-0 Bristol). Lost to Billy Sanders (0-2 Bristol, 0-2 Ipswich).
Billy Sanders defeated Peter Collins who was unfit to race either leg. Lost to Gordon Kennett (0-2 Ipswich, 0-2 White City).
Gordon Kennett lost to Peter Collins (1-2 White City, 0-2 Belle Vue).
Sponsor: Standard Motorists Centres.

1978

Winter holder: ***Peter Collins.***

Peter Collins defeated John Davis (2-0 Belle Vue, 0-2 Reading, 2-1 Leicester), Scott Autrey (2-0 Belle Vue, 1-2 Exeter, 2-0 Swindon), Michael Lee (2-0 King's Lynn, 2-1 Belle Vue), Tony Davey (2-0 Belle Vue, 0-2 Ipswich, 2-0 Hackney), Malcolm Simmons (2-1 Poole, walked over Belle Vue, Simmons unfit to challenge), John Titman (2-1 Leicester, 2-0 Belle Vue), Dave Jessup (2-0 Belle Vue, 2-1 Reading).
Sponsor: Standard Motorists Centres.

1979

Winter holder: ***Peter Collins.***

Peter Collins defeated Gordon Kennett (2-0 Eastbourne, 2-0 Belle Vue), Scott Autrey (2-1 Belle Vue, 1-2 Exeter, 2-0 Hackney), Hans Nielsen (2-1 Wolverhampton, 2-0 Belle Vue), Michael Lee (0-2 Belle Vue, 2-0 King's Lynn, 2-0 Leicester), Ian Cartwright (2-0 Belle Vue, 2-0 Halifax). Lost to Phil Crump (1-2 Swindon, 1-2 Belle Vue).
Phil Crump lost to Bruce Penhall (0-2 Cradley Heath, 0-2 Swindon)
Sponsor: Standard Motorists Centres.

1980

Winter holder: ***Bruce Penhall.***

Bruce Penhall defeated John Louis (2-0 Ipswich, 2-0 Cradley Heath), John Davis (2-0 Reading, walkover Cradley Heath, Davis unfit to challenge). Lost to Hans Nielsen (0-2 Wolverhampton, 2-0 Cradley Heath, 0-2 Birmingham).
Hans Nielsen lost to Dave Jessup (1-2 Wolverhampton, 0-2 King's Lynn).
Dave Jessup lost to Chris Morton (0-2 Belle Vue, 1-2 King's Lynn).
Chris Morton lost to Bo Petersen (2-0 Belle Vue, .5-1.5 Hackney, 0-2 Leicester).
Sponsor: Motor Cycle News.

1981

Winter holder: ***Bo Petersen.***

Bo Petersen lost to Michael Lee (0-2 King's Lynn, 0-2 Hackney)
Michael Lee defeated Les Collins (2-0 King's Lynn, 2-0 Leicester).
Michael Lee defeated Gordon Kennett (2-0 King's Kynn) but failed to turn up for the leg at Eastbourne and was stripped of the title. Gordon Kennett was nominated to meet a new challenger.
Gordon Kennett defeated Steve Bastable (2-0 Eastbourne, 0-2 Swindon, 2-0 Wimbledon). Lost to Kenny Carter (1-2 Halifax, 2-1 Eastbourne, 1-2 Reading).
Kenny Carter defeated Bruce Penhall (2-1 Cradley Heath, 2-1 Halifax).
Sponsor: Motor Cycle News.

1982

Winter holder: ***Kenny Carter.***

Kenny Carter defeated Chris Morton (0-2 Belle Vue, 2-0 Halifax, 2-0 Sheffield), Bo Petersen (2-0 Hackney, 2-0 Halifax)). Lost to Shawn Moran (2-1 Halifax, 1-2 Sheffield, 1-2 Birmingham).
Shawn Moran defeated Phil Crump (1-2 Swindon, 2-1 Sheffield, walk-over, Crump unfit to challenge), Les Collins (2-0 Leicester, 2-1 Sheffield).
Sponsor: Motor Cycle News

1983

Winter holder: ***Shawn Moran.***

Shawn Moran *forfeited title with a broken arm. Kenny Carter and Dennis Sigalos nominated to challenge for the vacant title.*
Kenny Carter defeated Dennis Sigalos (0-2 Ipswich, 2-1 Halifax, 2-0 Cradley Heath), Shawn Moran (2-0 Sheffield, 2-0 Halifax), Hans Nielsen (2-0 Halifax, 0-2 Birmingham, 2-1 Coventry). Lost to Michael Lee (0-2 Poole, 0-2 Halifax).
Michael Lee defeated Chris Morton (2-0 Poole, 2-1 Belle Vue), Erik Gundersen (2-0 Cradley Heath, 2-0 Poole).

1984

Winter holder: ***Michael Lee.***

Michael Lee defeated Phil Crump (2-1 Swindon, 2-0 Poole). *Forfeited the title after failing to turn up at Sheffield for the second leg against Shawn Moran having lost the first leg 0-2 at Poole. Shawn Moran and Chris Morton nominated to challenge for the vacant title.*
Shawn Moran defeated Chris Morton (2-0 Sheffield, 2-0 Belle Vue). Lost to Hans Nielsen (1-2 Sheffield, 0-2 Oxford).
Hans Nielsen defeated Jan Andersson (2-1 Reading, 2-1 Oxford). Lost to Erik Gundersen (1-2 Cradley Heath, 0-2 Oxford).
Erik Gundersen defeated Peter Collins (2-0 Cradley Heath, 2-0 Belle Vue).

1985

Winter holder: ***Erik Gundersen.***

Erik Gundersen defeated Malcolm Simmons, Richard Knight, Billy Sanders, Kelvin Tatum, lost to Bobby Schwartz.
Bobby Schwartz defeated Per Jonsson, Malcolm Simmons, lost to Chris Morton.
Chris Morton lost to Billy Sanders.
Billy Sanders lost to Bo Petersen.
Bo Petersen defeated Jeremy Doncaster, lost to Shawn Moran.
Shawn Moran defeated John Davis, lost to Erik Gundersen.
Erik Gundersen defeated Chris Morton, Per Jonsson, Hans Nielsen, lost to Jeremy Doncaster.
Jeremy Doncaster lost to Kenny Carter.
Kenny Carter lost to Jan Andersson.
Jan Andersson defeated Hans Nielsen, lost to John Cook.
John Cook lost to Bo Petersen.
Bo Petersen lost to Shawn Moran.
Shawn Moran defeated Jan Andersson (twice), Hans Nielsen, lost to Tommy Knudsen.
Tommy Knudsen defeated Kenny Carter, lost to Hans Nielsen.
Hans Nielsen defeated Kelvin Tatum, Jan Andersson (twice), Larry Ross, Bobby Schwartz. Lost to Bobby Schwartz.
Bobby Schwartz defeated Larry Ross, lost to Bo Petersen.
Bo Petersen defeated Bobby Schwartz, lost to Hans Nielsen.
Hans Nielsen defeated Jan Andersson, Malcolm Simmons, John Cook, Preben Eriksen, Jan Andersson, Tommy Knudsen, Kelvin Tatum, John Cook.

1986

Winter holder: ***Hans Nielsen.***

Hans Nielsen lost to Carl Blackbird
Carl Blackbird lost to Erik Gundersen.
Erik Gundersen lost to Kenny Carter.
Kenny Carter lost to Jeremy Doncaster,
Jeremy Doncaster defeated Sam Ermolenko, Kelly Moran, Bobby Schwartz. Lost to Sam Ermolenko.
Sam Ermolenko defeated Alan Grahame. Lost to John Jorgensen.
John Jorgensen lost to Neil Evitts.
Neil Evitts defeated Steve Regeling. Lost to Sam Ermolenko.
Sam Ermolenko lost to Erik Gundersen
Erik Gundersen defeated Steve Regeling, Hans Nielsen, Ray Morton. Lost to Jeremy Doncaster.
Jeremy Doncaster lost to Marvyn Cox
Marvyn Cox defeated Simon Cross, Kenny McKinna, Chris Morton, Erik Gundersen, Bobby Schwartz. Lost to Carl Blackbird.
Carl Blackbird defeated Jan Andersson (unable to challenge because of injury). Lost to John Jorgensen.
John Jorgensen defeated Erik Gundersen, Bobby Schwartz. Lost to Erik Gundersen.
Erik Gundersen defeated Phil Crump (twice), Jan Andersson. Lost to Jeremy Doncaster.
Jeremy Doncaster lost to Phil Crump.
Phil Crump defeated Shawn Moran, Peter Glanz. Lost to Peter Carr.
Peter Carr lost to Hans Nielsen.
Hans Nielsen defeated Brian Karger. Lost to Shawn Moran.

1987

Winter holder: ***Shawn Moran.***

Shawn Moran lost to Simon Wigg.
Simon Wigg lost to Jan O. Pedersen.
Jan O. Pedersen defeated Steve Regeling, lost by default to John Jorgensen.
John Jorgensen lost to Jeremy Doncaster.
Jeremy Doncaster defeated Chris Morton, Kelly Moran, lost to Mitch Shirra.
Competition discontinued after May 7, 1987, with ***Mitch Shirra*** *as holder.*

1988-1990

Not contested.
Holder: Mitch Shirra.

See also Silver Sash & Silver Helmet.

IVAN MAUGER'S 1965 season started disastrously and painfully as he broke his ankle in his second ride of the British League – and had to forfeit the Silver Sash, a match-race championship inherited from the Provincial League.

As holder of the 1964 title, the Kiwi was nominated to start the new era as the Silver Sash Champion and would defend it against the opposition's top scorer after every official fixture.

It left Wolverhampton's Peter Jarman having a walk over challenge and another new competition was underway.

By the end of the first season the Silver Sash had been worn by only six riders even though it was up for grabs more than 30 times during the summer. Colin Pratt (pictured left) ended the season as the winter holder but, like Mauger, lost the crown in his opening challenge of the new season.

Unlike the Golden Helmet, the Silver Sash did the rounds although Barry Briggs, who had such a dominant grip on the monthly-match race title had his fair share of Silver Sash success and actually spent three winters as the close season champion.

The competition was finally merged with the Golden Helmet in 1971, a year after the British League Second Division launched its own Silver Helmet championship.

Like the Silver Sash it was initially up for grabs after every official meeting although, in 1974, it adopted a monthly status with Jack Millen and Carl Glover nominated as the contenders.

Only three riders – Newcastle's Joe Owen, his elder brother Tom and Steve Lawson – were able to go through a full season as Silver Helmet holder. Joe defeated seven challengers, including his own brother Tom, during 1976 before giving up the title on his move up into the British League in 1977.

And then, two years later, Tom was nominated to face Bob Coles for the crown made vacant by Martin Yeates' elevation and he went through a further six successful defences that year and five the following season before losing the title by default after breaking his leg on August 27, 1979.

Lawson, like Owen, won the title in a race-off (this time against Steve Wilcock following Mark Courtney's move to the First Division) and beat off challenges from Steve Naylor, John Barker and Simon Wigg during the subsequent months.

Ironically he then forfeited the Silver Helmet because of illness when it reverted to a match-by-match championship at the beginning of 1983. It remained in that form until the end of the 1990 season when Andy Grahame was the final holder.

John Louis holds the record for the most consecutive successful defences. He took the Silver Helmet off champion Reg Wilson on July 7, 1971 and defended it TWENTY times before finally losing out to Phil Crump on October 11, 1971, in the penultimate defence of the season. Ironically Louis had an immediate chance to regain the helmet in Crump's first defence three days later but failed in what was his 29th challenge of the season!

SILVER SASH

Staged in the 1964 Provincial League as one-race challenge between the holder and the opposing team's top scorer.

1965

*Nominated holder: **Ivan Mauger.***

Ivan Mauger lost on default, injured, to Peter Jarman.

Peter Jarman defeated Jack Biggs, Eric Boocock, Cyril Maidment. Lost to Olle Nygren.

Olle Nygren defeated Ronnie Genz, Alan Cowland. Lost to Jim Lightfoot.

Jim Lightfoot defeated Peter Vandenberg. Lost to Ken McKinlay.

Ken McKinlay defeated Eric Boocock, Dave Younghusband, Jack Geran, Reg Luckhurst, Cyril Maidment, Jack Biggs (twice). Lost to Bob Andrews.

Bob Andrews defeated Nils Paulsen, Colin Gooddy, John Hart. Lost to Eric Boocock.

Eric Boocock defeated Gordon McGregor, Colin Pratt, Colin Gooddy, Bill Andrew, Brian Craven, Alf Wells. Lost to Jimmy Gooch.

Jimmy Gooch lost to Colin Pratt.

Colin Pratt defeated Nigel Boocock, Charlie Monk, Tommy Sweetman.

1966

*Winter holder: **Colin Pratt.***

Colin Pratt lost to Gote Nordin.

Gote Nordin defeated John Dews, Chum Taylor. Lost to Cyril Maidment.

Cyril Maidment lost to Arne Pander.

Arne Pander lost to Barry Briggs.

Barry Briggs defeated John Dews, Reg Luckhurst, Brian Brett, Ivor Hughes, Sverre Harrfeldt, Arne Pander, Ray Wilson, Doug Templeton. Lost to Olle Nygren.

Olle Nygren defeated Nigel Boocock. Lost to Tommy Sweetman.

Tommy Sweetman lost to Chris Julian.

Chris Julian lost to Olle Nygren.

Olle Nygren lost to Barry Briggs.

Barry Briggs defeated Ray Wilson, Terry Betts. Lost to Eric Boocock.

Eric Boocock lost to Olle Nygren.

Olle Nygren defeated Nigel Boocock, Terry Betts, Ronnie Genz, Brian Brett, Peter Kelly, Ray Wilson. Lost to Charlie Monk.

Charlie Monk lost to Peter Vandenberg.

Peter Vandenberg lost to Barry Briggs.

1967

*Winter holder: **Barry Briggs.***

Barry Briggs defeated Eric Boocock, Trevor Hedge, Hasse Holmkvist, Sverre Harrfeldt, Olle Nygren, Göte Nordin, Nigel Boocock, Arne Pander. Lost to Ray Wilson.

Ray Wilson lost to Arne Pander.

***Arne Pander** forfeited title to Mike Broadbank when he was unfit to defend.*

Mike Broadbank lost to Ray Wilson.

Ray Wilson defeated Charlie Monk, Cyril Maidment, Arnold Haley, Ken McKinlay, Arnold Haley, Eddie Reeves. Lost to Graham Coombes.

Graham Coombes lost to Jim Airey.

Jim Airey defeated Øyvind Berg, Ivan Mauger. Lost to Göte Nordin.

Göte Nordin beat Bo Josefsson. Lost to Gunnar Malmqvist.

Gunnar Malmqvist defeated Olle Nygren, Terry Betts. Lost to Malcolm Simmons.

Malcolm Simmons defeated Olle Nygren, Tommy Bergqvist. Lost to Barry Briggs.

Barry Briggs defeated Charlie Monk (unable to challenge), Nigel Boocock, Jim Airey, David Crane, Alan Jay, John Hart, Reidar Eide, Wayne Briggs, Bengt Jansson, Cyril Maidment, Jon Erskine, Wayne Briggs, Charlie Monk, Allan Butterfield, Norman Hunter, Terry Betts.

1968

*Winter holder: **Barry Briggs.***

Barry Briggs defeated Eric Boocock, Ronnie Genz, Nigel Boocock, Dave Younghusband. Lost to Bengt Jansson.

Bengt Jansson defeated Trevor Hedge, Eddie Reeves, Malcolm Simmons, Anders Michanek. Lost to Neil Street.

Neil Street lost to Soren Sjosten.

Sören Sjösten lost to Sverre Harrfeldt.

Sverre Harrfeldt lost to Ivan Mauger.

Ivan Mauger defeated Ronnie Genz, Anders Michanek, Pete Smith, Roy Trigg. Lost to Trevor Hedge.

Trevor Hedge defeated Torbjörn Harrysson, Mike Keen. Lost to Eric Boocock.

Eric Boocock defeated Rick Timmo. Lost to Ivan Mauger.

Ivan Mauger defeated Brian Leonard, Nigel Boocock. Lost to Hasse Holmkvist.

Hasse Holmkvist lost to Jimmy Gooch on default.

Jimmy Gooch lost to Ted Laessing.

Ted Laessing lost to Ray Wilson.

Ray Wilson lost to Reidar Eide.

Reidar Eide defeated Willie Templeton, Anders Michanek. Lost to Barry Briggs.

Barry Briggs defeated Ivan Mauger.

1969

*Winter holder: **Barry Briggs.***

Barry Briggs lost to Eric Boocock.

Eric Boocock defeated Norman Hunter. Lost to Colin Gooddy.

Colin Gooddy lost to Eric Boocock.

Eric Boocock lost to Norman Hunter.

Norman Hunter defeated Chris Julian. Lost to Ivan Mauger.

Ivan Mauger defeated Bernt Persson, Malcolm Simmons, Pete Smith, Jim Airey, Ole Olsen (twice), Greg Kentwell. Lost to Nigel Boocock.

Nigel Boocock defeated Pete Smith, Tony Clarke. Lost to Eric Boocock.

Eric Boocock lost to Jim Airey.

Jim Airey lost to James Bond.

James Bond lost to Barry Briggs.

Barry Briggs defeated Chris Bass. Lost to John Boulger by default.

John Boulger lost to Ivan Mauger.

Ivan Mauger defeated Geoff Mudge. Lost to Arnold Haley.

Arnold Haley defeated Eddie Reeves, Eric Boocock. Lost to Terry Betts.

Terry Betts lost to Peter Vandenberg.

Peter Vandenberg lost to Malcolm Simmons.

Malcolm Simmons defeated Geoff Mudge. Lost to Colin Pratt.

Colin Pratt lost to Rick France.

Rick France lost to Ole Olsen.

Ole Olsen lost to Ivan Mauger.

1970

*Winter holder: **Ivan Mauger.***

SILVER HELMET

Launched in the British League Division Two.
Ross Gilbertson was declared holder on the strength of his 1969 Division Two Riders' Championship placing.

1970

Ross Gilbertson defeated Ron Bagley. Lost to Ron Bagley.
Ron Bagley lost to Malcolm Shakespeare.
Malcolm Shakespeare lost to Phil Woodcock.
Phil Woodcock defeated Lou Sansom. Lost to Mike Vernam.
Mike Vernam lost to Alan Bridgett.
Alan Bridgett defeated Gordon McGregor by default, Archie Wilkinson. Lost to Malcolm Shakespeare.
Malcolm Shakespeare defeated Gordon McGregor, Archie Wilkinson, Bob Valentine. Lost to Paul O'Neal by default through injury.
Paul O'Neal defeated Andy Ross, Alan Paynter, Graeme Smith, Taffy Owen. Lost to George Major.
George Major defeated Taffy Owen, Phil Pratt, Geoff Bouchard. Lost to Maurie Robinson.
Maurie Robinson defeated Alan Knapkin. Lost to Eric Broadbelt.
Eric Broadbelt defeated Maurie Robinson. Lost to John Louis.
John Louis defeated Geoff Maloney, Gil Farmer, Arthur Price, Doug Wyer, Maurie Robinson, Eric Broadbelt, Reg Wilson.

1971
Winter holder: ***John Louis.***

John Louis defeated Colin Sanders, Brian Foote, Hugh Saunders, Dave Baugh, Tony Childs. Lost to Graham Banks.
Graham Banks defeated Alan Wilkinson, Jim Ryman, George Major. Lost to Bruce Forrester.
Bruce Forrester lost to Alan Wilkinson by default.
Alan Wilkinson defeated Russ Dent, George Major. Lost to Malcolm Shakespeare.
Malcolm Shakespeare lost to Alan Wilkinson.
Alan Wilkinson defeated George Barclay. Lost to Reg Wilson by default.
Reg Wilson lost to John Louis.
John Louis defeated Arthur Price, Alan Wilkinson, Cliff Emms, Hugh Saunders (twice), Gordon Kennett, Bobby McNeil, Lou Sansom, Richard Greer, Frank Auffret, Bruce Forrester, Taffy Owen, Malcolm Mackay, Richard Greer, Paul Tyrer, Russ Dent, Ross Gilbertson, Arthur Price, Phil Crump, Lou Sansom. Lost to Phil Crump.
Phil Crump defeated John Louis.

1972
Winter holder: ***Phil Crump.***

Phil Crump defeated Peter Bailey. Lost to Richard Greer.
Richard Greer lost to Brian Foote.
Brian Foote lost to Peter Bailey.
Peter Bailey lost to Roger Mills.
Roger Mills defeated Russ Osborne, Arthur Price, Phil Bass, Lou Sansom. Lost to Gordon Kennett.
Gordon Kennett lost to John Davis.
John Davis defeated Bob Coles, Geoff Bouchard. Lost to Dave Baugh.
Dave Baugh lost to Roy Carter by default.
Roy Carter defeated Paul Tyrer, Peter Reading, Lou Sansom, Arthur Browning. Lost to Rodney Haynes.
Rodney Haynes lost to Paul Tyrer.
Paul Tyrer lost to Dave Mills by default.
Dave Mills lost to Arthur Browning.
Arthur Browning defeated Graham Banks, Graeme Smith. Lost to Richard Greer by default.
Richard Greer lost to George Major by default.

1973
Winter holder: ***George Major.***

George Major defeated Graham Drury, Colin Meredith, Mitch Graham. Lost to Roger Mills.
Roger Mills defeated Jim Ryman, Robin Amundson. Lost to Mike Broadbank.
Mike Broadbank defeated Barry Booth, John Davis, Dave Baugh. Lost to Tony Childs.
Tony Childs lost to Peter Moore.
Peter Moore lost to George Major.
George Major lost to Sid Sheldrick.
Sid Sheldrick lost to Derek Cook.
Derek Cook lost to Lou Sansom.
Lou Sansom lost to Bobby McNeil.
Bobby McNeil lost to Mike Broadbank.
Mike Broadbank defeated Bob Young, George Major, Mike Lanham. Lost to Geoff Ambrose.
Geoff Ambrose lost to Peter Moore.
Peter Moore defeated Brian Kennett. Lost to Mitch Graham.
Mitch Graham defeated Graham Jones. Lost to Andy Meldrum.
Andy Meldrum lost to Mike Broadbank.
Mike Broadbank lost to Brian Clark.
Brian Clark lost to Trevor Barnwell.
Trevor Barnwell defeated Dave Morton. Lost to Carl Glover by default when he failed to turn up for meeting.
Carl Glover defeated Lou Sansom. Lost to Lou Sansom.
Lou Sansom defeated Trevor Geer, Dave Gatenby. Lost to Ted Howgego.

1974
Winter holder: ***Ted Howgego.***
Title declared vacant on Howgego's move into the British League.

Jack Millen defeated Carl Glover (2-0, 2-1). Forfeited title through injury.
Bobby McNeill defeated Malcolm Mackay (2-0, 2-0). Lost to Jack Millen (0-2, 0-2).
Jack Millen forfeited title to Bruce Forrester (2-0, unfit to compete in second leg through injury).
Bruce Forrester lost to Arthur Browning (2-0, 0-2, 1-2).
Arthur Browning defeated Bobby McNeil (2-0, 2-0).

1975
Winter holder: ***Arthur Browning.***

Arthur Browning lost to John Jackson (2-1, 0-2, 0-2).
John Jackson defeated Les Rumsey (1-2, 2-0, 2-0). Lost to Tom Owen (0-2, 0-2).
Tom Owen defeated Laurie Etheridge (2-0, 0-2, 2-0), Alan Molyneux (2-0, 1-2, 2-0). Lost to Joe Owen (1-2, 0-2).
Joe Owen defeated Paul Gachet (2-1, 2-0).

1976
Winter holder: ***Joe Owen.***

Joe Owen defeated Laurie Etheridge (0-2 Newcastle, 2-0 Crayford, 2-0 Workington), Steve Weatherley (2-0 Eastbourne, 2-0 Newcastle), John Jackson (2-0 Newcastle, 0-2 Ellesmere Port, 2-0 Stoke), Brian Collins (2-1 Coatbridge, 2-1 Newcastle), Robert Hollingworth (2-1 Boston, 2-0 Newcastle), Tom Owen (2-1 Teesside, 2-0 Berwick), Brian Clark (2-0 Newcastle).
†Joe Owen was unable to complete the second leg at Peterborough because of injury but Brian Clark declined to take the title by default.
Sponsor: Speedway Star.

1977
Winter holder: ***Joe Owen.***
Title declared vacant on Owen's move into the British League.

Brian Clark defeated Ted Hubbard (2-0 Peterborough, 0-1 Rye House, Hubbard unable to compete in second race through injury). Lost to Colin Richardson (2-0 Peterborough, 0-2 Eastbourne, 1-2 Weymouth).
Colin Richardson defeated Tom Owen (2-1 Eastbourne, 1-2 Newcastle, 2-1 Workington), Ted Hubbard (2-1 Peterborough), Steve Koppe (2-1 Hackney). Lost to Martin Yeates (0-2 Oxford, 2-0 Eastbourne, 0-2 Newcastle).
Martin Yeates defeated John Jackson (0-2 Ellesmere Port, 2-0 Oxford, 2-0 Mildenhall).
Sponsor: Speedway Star.

1978
Winter holder: ***Martin Yeates.***
Title declared vacant on Yeates' move into the British League.

Tom Owen defeated Bob Coles (2-0 Mildenhall, 2-0 Newcastle), Steve Finch (2-0 Newcastle, 0-2 Ellesmere Port, 2-0 Teesside), Mike Sampson (2-0 Eastbourne, 2-0 Newcastle), Les Rumsey (2-0 Canterbury, 2-0 Newcastle), Kelvin Mullarkey (2-0 Rye House, by default Newcastle when Mullarkey notified the authorities he would be unable to attend second leg because of mechanical problems), Nicky Allott (2-0 Newcastle, 1-2 Scunthorpe, 2-0 Milton Keynes), Steve Koppe (2-0 Newcastle, 2-0 Canterbury).
Sponsor: Gulf Oil.

1979
Winter holder: ***Tom Owen.***

Tom Owen defeated Bob Humphreys (2-1 Newcastle, 2-1 Milton Keynes), John Jackson (2-0 Newcastle, 2-0 Ellesmere Port), Mick Hines (2-1 Newcastle, 2-0 Mildenhall), Dave Perks (2-0 Newcastle, 2-1 Nottingham), Steve Lawson (2-0 Glasgow, 2-0 Newcastle). Forfeited title after breaking his leg on August 27. Andy Grahame and Karl Fiala nominated for vacant title.
Karl Fiala defeated Andy Grahame (2-0 Milton Keynes, 2-0 Rye House), Ian Gledhill (2-0 Stoke, 2-0 Rye House).

1980
Winter holder: ***Karl Fiala.***

Karl Fiala lost to Les Rumsey (1-2 Crayford, 2-0 Rye House, 1-2 Peterborough).
Les Rumsey defeated Steve Wilcock (2-1 Crayford, 0-2 Middlesbrough, 2-0 Glasgow). *June challenger David Gagen withdrew after breaking his leg.* Lost to Dave Perks (0-2 Oxford, 0-2 Crayford).
***Dave Perks** forfeited the title through injury. Mike Ferreira and Bob Garrad nominated for the vacant crown.*
Mike Ferreira defeated Bob Garrad (2-0 Canterbury, 2-0 Rye House). Lost to Paul Woods (2-1 Crayford, 0-2 Canterbury, 0-2 Milton Keynes).
Paul Woods defeated David Gagen (2-0 Crayford, 2-0 Boston).

1981
Winter holder: ***Paul Woods.***
Title declared vacant on Woods' move into the British League.

Martin Yeates defeated Dave Perks (2-0 Weymouth, 2-0 Oxford). Lost to Steve Lawson (1-2 Weymouth, 1-2 Glasgow).
Steve Lawson lost to Mike Ferreira (0-2 Canterbury, 2-0 Glasgow, 1-2 Stoke).
Mike Ferreira defeated Neil Collins (2-0 Edinburgh, 2-0 Canterbury). *Relinquished title after winning the National League Riders' Championship Final and opting to move into the British League.*
Mark Courtney defeated Wayne Brown (0-2 Newcastle, 2-0 Middlesbrough, 2-0 Stoke).

1982
Winter holder: ***Mark Courtney.***
Title declared vacant on Courtney's move into the British League.

Steve Lawson defeated Steve Wilcock (0-2 Middlesbrough, 2-1 Glasgow, 2-0 Scunthorpe (April), Steve Naylor (2-0 Glasgow, 2-1 Rye House), John Barker (0-2 Exeter, 2-0 Glasgow, 2-0 Oxford), Simon Wigg (2-0 Weymouth, 2-1 Glasgow).

1983
Winter holder: ***Steve Lawson.***

Steve Lawson forfeited the title through illness to Paul Price.
Paul Price lost to Mark Fiora.
Mark Fiora lost to Bob Garrad.
Bob Garrad lost to Steve McDermott.
Steve McDermott defeated Steve Wilcock. Lost to Barry Thomas.
Barry Thomas defeated Rod Hunter, Mark Fiora, Dave Perks, Billy Burton, Paul Stead, Bruce Cribb. Lost to Julian Parr.
Julian Parr lost to Kevin Teager.
Kevin Teager defeated Bob Garrad. Lost to Steve Wilcock.
Steve Wilcock defeated Ashley Pullen, Graham Drury. Lost to Ashley Pullen.
Ashley Pullen lost to Jim McMillan.
Jim McMillan lost to Bruce Cribb.
Bruce Cribb lost to Keith Millard.
Keith Millard defeated David Mullett, Joe

Owen. Lost to Marvyn Cox.
Marvyn Cox defeated Keith Millard, John Jackson, Chris Turner lost to Jim McMillan.
Jim McMillan lost to Barry Thomas.
Barry Thomas defeated Rod Hunter. Lost to Nigel Sparshott.
Nigel Sparshott defeated Marvyn Cox. Lost to Barry Thomas.
Barry Thomas defeated Peter E. Smith, Keith White. Lost to Steve Lomas.
Steve Lomas defeated Ian Barney. Lost to Mick Hines.
Mick Hines defeated Chris Pidcock. Lost to Robert Henry.

1984
*Winter holder: **Robert Henry.***

Robert Henry lost to Kevin Smart.
Kevin Smart defeated Jim McMillan. Lost to Bob Garrad.
Bob Garrad defeated Kevin Smart, Jamie Luckhurst. Lost to Dave Perks.
Dave Perks lost to Mike Spink.
Mike Spink lost to Paul Stead.
Paul Stead lost to Kevin Smart.
Kevin Smart lost to Andy Buck.
Andy Buck defeated Jamie Luckhurst. Lost to Peter E. Smith.
Peter E. Smith lost to Kevin Teager.
Kevin Teager lost to Graham Drury.
Graham Drury lost to Alan Sage.
Alan Sage lost to Nigel Crabtree.
Nigel Crabtree defeated Adrian Hume. Lost to Steve Lawson.
Steve Lawson lost to Mark Fiora.
Mark Fiora lost to Carl Blackbird.
Carl Blackbird defeated Bruce Cribb (twice). Lost to Paul Thorp.
Paul Thorp lost to David Blackburn.
David Blackburn lost to Mick Hines. .
Mick Hines lost to Colin Cook.
Colin Cook defeated Trevor Banks. Lost to Keith White.

1985
*Winter holder: **Keith White.***

Keith White lost to Nigel Sparshott.
Nigel Sparshott lost to Trevor Banks.
Trevor Banks lost to Steve Finch
Steve Finch lost to Tom Owen.
Tom Owen lost to Steve Wilcock.
Steve Wilcock lost to Paul Thorp.
Paul Thorp lost to Nigel Sparshott.
Nigel Sparshott lost to Dave Morton.
Dave Morton lost to Stan Bear.
Stan Bear defeated Phil White, Paul Evitts, Gordon Kennett, Martin Dixon, Tom Owen, Andy Hines, Alastair Stevens, Trevor Banks, Steve Lawson. Lost to Mike Ferreira.
Mike Ferreira lost to Steve Wilcock.
Steve Wilcock lost to Andrew Silver.
Andrew Silver defeated Jim McMillan, Paul Stead, Martin Dixon. Lost to Martin Dixon.
Martin Dixon defeated Kevin Hawkins. Lost to Alan Mogridge.
Alan Mogridge defeated Paul Evitts. Lost to Neil Middleditch.
Neil Middleditch lost to Paul Thorp.
Paul Thorp defeated Andy Galvin. Lost to Carl Baldwin.
Carl Baldwin defeated Steve McDermott, Gordon Kennett, Colin Richardson. Lost to Doug Wyer.
Doug Wyer lost to Ian Barney by default.
Ian Barney defeated Louis Carr. Lost to Jim McMillan.
Jim McMillan defeated Mike Spink, Gordon Kennett.

1986
*Winter holder: **Jim McMillan.***

Jim McMillan lost to Colin Richardson.
Colin Richardson lost to Paul Evitts.
Paul Evitts defeated Gerald Short, Miles Evans. Lost to Dave Jessup.
Dave Jessup lost to Kevin Smart.
Kevin Smart lost to Steve McDermott by default.
Steve McDermott lost to Les Collins by default.
Les Collins defeated Trevor Banks. Lost to Dave Perks.
Dave Perks lost to Les Collins.
Les Collins defeated Dave Jessup. Lost to Andrew Silver.
Andrew Silver defeated Mike Spink. Lost to Andy Hines.
Andy Hines lost to Martin Dixon.
Martin Dixon defeated Paul Woods. Lost to Keith White.
Keith White lost to David Cheshire.
David Cheshire lost to Eric Monaghan by default, injured.
Eric Monaghan lost to Andy Hines.
Andy Hines lost to Gordon Kennett.
Gordon Kennett lost to David Mullett.
David Mullett defeated Martin Dugard. Lost to Nigel Crabtree.
Nigel Crabtree lost to Mark Fiora.
Mark Fiora lost to Paul Thorp.
Paul Thorp defeated Kevin Jolly, Kevin Smith. Lost to Trevor Banks by default, injured.
Trevor Banks defeated Gerald Short. Lost to Malcolm Simmons.
Malcolm Simmons lost to Les Collins.
Les Collins lost to Martin Dugard.
Martin Dugard defeated Alan Mogridge (twice), David Blackburn, Kevin Smith, Steve Schofield. Lost to Nigel Flatman.

FLAT-OUT FLATTERS: Nigel Flatman was the 1986-87 winter title holder

1987
*Winter holder: **Nigel Flatman.***
Nigel Flatman defeated Kevin Smart, Martin McKinna. Lost to Steve Schofield.
Steve Schofield defeated Gary Rolls. Lost to Gerald Short by default.
Gerald Short lost to Paul Woods.
Paul Woods lost to Steve Wilcock.
Steve Wilcock lost to David Blackburn.
David Blackburn defeated Paul Woods, Ian Barney, Gordon Whitaker, Colin Cook, Martin Goodwin, Kevin Smart, Steve Lawson, Martin Dixon, Gerald Short, Trevor Banks, Glenn Doyle. Lost to Charlie McKinna.
Charlie McKinna lost to Neville Tatum.
Neville Tatum defeated Steve Schofield, Dave Morton. Lost to Martin Dixon.
Martin Dixon lost to David Mullett.
David Mullett defeated Melvyn Taylor. Lost to Nigel Leaver.
Nigel Leaver lost to Keith Pritchard.
Keith Pritchard lost to David Blackburn.
David Blackburn lost to Darren Sumner.
Darren Sumner lost to Trevor Banks.
Trevor Banks defeated Kevin Jolly.

1988
*Winter holder: **Trevor Banks.***

Trevor Banks defeated Keith White. Lost to Nigel Crabtree.
Nigel Crabtree lost to Andy Galvin.
Andy Galvin defeated Keith White, Richard Green, Nigel Sparshott, Darren Sumner, Craig Boyce, Ian Clark, Jens Rasmussen. Lost to Todd Wiltshire.
Todd Wiltshire lost to Melvyn Taylor.
Melvyn Taylor defeated Kevin Jolly, Keith White. Lost to Martin Goodwin.
Martin Goodwin lost to Kevin Jolly.
Kevin Jolly lost to Martin Goodwin.
Martin Goodwin defeated Steve Schofield, Kenny McKinna, Glenn Doyle. Lost to Nigel Crabtree.
Nigel Crabtree defeated Mark Lyndon (twice). Lost to Andy Galvin.
Andy Galvin lost to Kevin Hawkins.
Kevin Hawkins lost to Louis Carr.
Louis Carr lost to Steve Schofield.

1989
*Winter holder: **Steve Schofield.***

Steve Schofield defeated Charlie McKinna. Lost to Jens Rasmussen.
Jens Rasmussen defeated Malcolm Simmons, Ray Morton, Craig Hodgson, Darren Sumner, Nigel Flatman, Tony Primmer, Malcolm Simmons. Lost to David Norris.
David Norris defeated Trevor Banks. Lost to Preben Eriksen.
Preben Eriksen defeated Nigel Crabtree. Lost to Andy Galvin.
Andy Galvin defeated Todd Wiltshire, Andy Hines, Neville Tatum. Lost to Mick Poole.
Mick Poole defeated Todd Wiltshire. Lost to Mark Courtney.
Mark Courtney defeated Glen Baxter. Lost to Richard Green.
Richard Green defeated Steve Schofield. Lost to Martin Dixon.
Martin Dixon lost to Steve Schofield.
Steve Schofield defeated Michael Coles. Lost to Les Collins.
Les Collins defeated Nigel Crabtree, Peter Glanz, Jens Rasmussen, Nigel De'ath. Lost to Kenny McKinna.
Kenny McKinna defeated Mick Poole, Richard Hellsén.

1990
*Winter holder: **Kenny McKinna.***

Kenny McKinna lost to Craig Boyce.
Craig Boyce defeated David Blackburn. Lost to Kenny McKinna.
Kenny McKinna defeated Nigel Crabtree, Steve Regeling, Rob Tilbury, David Norris. Lost to Dean Standing.
Dean Standing defeated Craig Hodgson, Andy Buck. Forfeited title at Exeter through injury.
Chris Louis defeated Steve Regeling. Lost to Craig Boyce.
Craig Boyce defeated Jens Rasmussen, Eric Monaghan. Lost to David Bargh.
David Bargh lost to Rob Tilbury.
Rob Tilbury defeated Steve Lawson. Lost to Jens Rasmussen.
Jens Rasmussen forfeited title at Eastbourne through injury.
Paul Woods defeated Scott Humphries. Lost to Steve Lawson.
Steve Lawson lost to Nigel De'ath.
Nigel De'ath defeated Jonathon Cooper. Lost to Darren Sumner.
Darren Sumner lost to David Bargh.
David Bargh defeated Peter Glanz, Gordon Kennett, Steve Lawson, Chris Louis. Lost to Andy Grahame.
*Winter holder: **Andy Grahame.***

✪ Five riders have forfeited the Silver Helmet because they moved up into the British League during the winter – Ted Howgego, Joe Owen, Martin Yeates, Paul Woods and Mark Courtney.

✪ Brian Clark refused to claim the Silver Helmet by default when champion Joe Owen (who had already won the first leg) was unable to defend the title at Peterborough in October, 1976, and when Owen joined British League Hull the following season Clark was nominated as one of the challengers for the vacant title. Clark won the first leg at Peterborough but in the second leg at challenger Ted Hubbard's home track Rye House on Sunday, April 24, 1977, both riders fell going into the first turn of the second race. Referee Laurie Pike ordered a re-run but Hubbard, who had won the first race, was unfit to compete and the tie was awarded to Clark!

1969

Wimbledon, Thursday, October 2
1 Graham Plant, 2 Geoff Ambrose, 3 Mick Bell, 4 Martyn Piddock. ***Semi Final:*** Piddock, Bobby Beaton, Ian Turner, Phil Pratt.
The competition was staged over three heats with the heat winners going through to the Final to be joined by the semi final winner. Eliminated in qualifying heat: Roy Carter and Malcolm Shakespeare.
Shakespeare replaced Roger Mills in competition.
Originally scheduled to be staged as a second half to the World Pairs Western Zone semi-final at Wimbledon on August 14. Postponed because of rain. The programmed competitors were: Graham Plant, Bobby Beaton, Mick Bell, Martyn Piddock, Ian Turner, Roger Mills, Phil Pratt, Roy Carter, Geoff Ambrose.

1970

Swindon, Wednesday, September 2
1 Barry Thomas 14, 2 Dave Jessup 14, 3 Mick Bell 13, 4 Bobby Beaton 11, 5 John Jackson 11, 6 Malcolm Shakespeare 10, 7 Graham Miles 8, 8 Graham Banks 7, 9 Ian Turner 7, 10 Gordon Kennett 6, 11 Paul Tyrer 4, 12 Sid Sheldrick 3, 13 Alan Bridgett 3, 14 George Devonport 2, 15 Barry Duke 0, Steve Waplington 0. *Reserve:* Malcolm Mackay 3. *Track reserves:* Shawn Murtagh 2, Mac Woolford 1.
Original staging on August 19 was postponed because of a waterlogged track.

1971

Swindon, Wednesday, July 14
1 Ian Turner 15, 2 Dave Jessup 14, 3 Peter Ingram 11, 4 Malcolm Shakespeare 10, 5 Tony Davey 9, 6 Malcolm Ballard 8, Doug Wyer 8, Jim Gallacher 8, 9 Geoff Bouchard 7, Gordon Kennett 7, 11 John Jackson 5, Peter Collins 5, 13 Alan Wilkinson 4, 14 Malcolm Mackay 3, 15 Paul Tyrer 2, Graham Banks 2. *Reserves:* Richard Greer 1, Alastair Brady 0.
Sponsors: Sunday Mirror.

1972

Canterbury, Saturday, June 24
1 Allen Emmett 13, 2 Gordon Kennett 12, 3 Tony Davey 11, 4 Trevor Barnwell 11, 5 David Piddock 10, 6 Alan Sage 9, 7 David Kennett 9, 8 Brian Kennett 8, 9 John Davis 7, 10 Roger Johns 7, 11 Robbie Gardner 6, 12 Bobby McNeil 5, 13 Frank Auffret 4, 14 Carl Glover 4, 15 Trevor Geer 3, 16 Phil Bass 0. *Reserves:* Mike Lanham 1, Rodney Haynes 0.
Sponsors: Sunday Mirror.

1973

Canterbury, Saturday, June 16
1 Peter Collins 14 2 Brian Kennett 13 3 David Gagen 12, 4 David Piddock 11, 5 Ian Hindle 9, 6 Paul Gachet 8, 7 Bobby McNeil 8, 8 Carl Glover 7, 9 John Davis 7, 10 Trevor Geer 6, 11 Colin Meredith 6, 12 Les Rumsey 5, 13 Tim Ballard 4, 14 Terry Barclay 4, 15 Peter Cairns 3, 16 Eric Dugard 2. *Reserve:* Keith White 0.
Sponsors: Sunday Mirror.

1974

Canterbury, Saturday, June 29
1 Chris Morton 15 2 Steve Bastable 13 3 Neil Middleditch 12, 4 Keith White 10, 5 Andy Sims 10, 6 Ian Cartwright 9, 7 Eric Dugard 7, 8 Robert Hollingworth 7, 9 Wayne Hughes 7, 10 Joe Owen 6, 11 Les Rumsey 6, 12 Ian Hindle 5, 13 Steve Weatherley 5, 14 Nigel Wasley 4, 15 Martin Yeates 3, 16 Paul Gachet 1. *Reserve:* Russell Foot 0.
Sponsors: Sunday Mirror.

1975

Canterbury, Saturday, June 28
1 Neil Middleditch 13, 2 Steve Weatherley 13, 3 Joe Owen 12, 4 Michael Lee 12, 5 Andy Hines 12, 6 Billy Burton 8, 7 Robert Hollingworth 8, 8 Kevin Jolly 8, 9 Duncan Meredith 7, 10 Steve Finch 5, 11 Andy Sims 5, 12 Steve Bastable 4, 13 Ian Silk 4, 14 Gerald Purkiss 4, 15 Tom Davie 2, 16 Mike Bessant 1. *Track Reserves:* Steve Gibson 1, Mike Hooper 0.
Sponsors: Sunday Mirror.

1976

Canterbury, Saturday, September 25
1 Michael Lee 15, 2 Steve Weatherley 14, 3 Colin Richardson 12, 4 Graham Clifton 12, 5 Steve Finch 11, 6 Les Collins 10, 7 Karl Fiala 8, 8 Kevin Jolly 8, 9 Andy Hines 7, 10 Andy Cusworth 6, 11 Jim Brett 3, Paul Gilbert 3, Gerald Purkiss 3, 14 Mick Bates 3, 15 Bob Garrad 3, 16 Trevor Whiting 2.
Track reserve: Alan Diprose 0.
Sponsors: Sunday Mirror.
Original staging on September 11 was abandoned after three heats because of heavy rain. Scorers at the time were: Michael Lee 3, Colin Richardson 3, Steve Weatherley 3,Graham Clifton 2, Steve Finch 2, Kevin Jolly 2, Les Collins 1, Andy Hines 1, Gerald Purkiss 1, Mick Bates 0, Andy Cusworth 0, Paul Gilbert 0, Bob Garrad, Karl Fiala, Chris Turner and Trevor Whiting, did not ride.

1977

Canterbury, Saturday, June 25
1 Les Collins 15, 2 Phil Collins 12, 3 Colin Richardson 11, 4 Brendan Shilleto 10, 5 Ian Gledhill 10, 6 Paul Gilbert 9, 7 Ian Clark 8, 8 Bob Garrad 8, 9 Neil Leeks 8, 10 Dave Allen 8, 11 Steve Naylor 5, 12 Kevin Young 5, 13 Peter E. Smith 4, 14 Nigel Close 3, 15 Chris Bevan 2. Derek Richardson did not ride. *Track reserves:* Dave Johnson 2, Kevin Brice 0.
Sponsors: Sunday Mirror.

1978

Canterbury, Saturday, June 24
1 Phil Collins 15, 2 Ian Gledhill 10, 3 Bob Garrad 10, 4 Melvyn Taylor 10, 5 Steve Naylor 9, 6 Pip Lamb 9, 7 John Hack 9, 8 Brendan Shilleto 8, 9 Nigel Flatman 8, 10 Kenny Carter 7, 11 Louis Carr 5, 12 Paul Woods 5, 13 Sean Willmott 5, 14 Neil Leeks 5, 15 Derek Harrison 3, 16 Mike Spink 2. *Track reserve:* Dave Shepherd 0.
Sponsors: Sunday Mirror.

1979

Canterbury, Saturday, June 23
1 Kenny Carter 12, 2 Nigel Flatman 12, 3 Melvyn Taylor 12, 4 Peter Ellams 11, 5 Mark Courtney 9, 6 John Barker 9, 7 Tim Hunt 8, 8 Paul Embley 7, 9 Kevin Smith 7, 10 Richard Knight 6, 11 Dennis Mallett 5, 12 Keith Bloxsome 5, 13 Charlie McKinna 5, 14 Martin Dixon 4, 15 Peter Tarrant 3. John Hack did not ride. *Track reserve:* Rob Dolman 4.
Sponsors: Sunday Mirror.

1980

Canterbury, Saturday, July 12
1 Mark Courtney 14, 2 Kevin Smith 12, 3 John Barker 11, 4 Bob Garrad 11, 5 Tim Hunt 10, 6 Neil Collins 9, 7 Nigel Sparshott 8, 8 Nigel Flatman 8, 9 Paul Stead 7, 10 Peter Carr 7, 11 Mark Baldwin 6, 12 Dennis Mallett 6, 13 Steve Crockett 5, 14 Charlie McKinna 3, 15 Martin Hewlett 3, 16 Mark Bilner 1.
Sponsors: Sunday Mirror.

1981

Canterbury, Saturday, July 4
1 Robert Lightfoot 14, 2 Peter Carr 13, 3 Neil Evitts 11, 4 Martin Hewlett 10, Charlie McKinna 10, Dennis Mallett 10, 7 Simon Wigg 9, 8 Wayne Jackson 7, 9 Andy Hibbs 7, 10 Martin Dixon 6, 11 Paul Evitts 5, 12 Paul Stead 5, 13 Jamie Luckhurst 4, 14 Andy Buck 3, 15 Peter Tarrant 2, 16 Nigel Sparshott 0. *Track reserves:* David Mullett 3, Rob Tilbury 1.
Sponsors: Sunday Mirror.

1982

Canterbury, Saturday, July 31
1 Peter Carr 12, 2 Martin Hagon 12, 3 Simon Cross 12, 4 Paul Stead 11, 5 Neil Evitts 11, 6 Carl Baldwin 10, 7 Martin Hewlett 8, 8 Nigel Sparshott 8, 9 Glen Parrott 6, 10 Rob Woffinden 6, 11 Paul Price 6, 12 Kenny McKinna 5, 13 Paul Bosley 4, 15 Keith Millard 3, 16 Rob Tilbury 3. *Track reserves:* Kevin Howland 1, David Mullett 0.
Sponsors: Sunday Mirror.

1983

Canterbury, Saturday, July 30
1 Keith Millard 13, 2 Simon Cross 13, 3 Kenny McKinna 12, 4 Paul Stead 11, 5 Kelvin Tatum 9, 6 Marvyn Cox 9, 7 Alun Rossiter 7, 8 Paul Clarke 7, 9 Jamie Luckhurst 7, 10 Kevin Price 7, 11 Carl Baldwin 6, 12 Carl Blackbird 6, 13 Andy Smith 5, 14 Julian Parr 3, 15 John Frankland 0, Gary O'Hare 0.
Track reserves: Jeremy Luckhurst 3, Jay Pleece 0.
Sponsors: Sunday Mirror.

1984

Canterbury, Saturday, June 2
1 Marvyn Cox 13, 2 Simon Cross 13, 3 Andy Smith 12, 4 Alun Rossiter 12, 5 Kevin Smart 11, 6 Steve Bishop 9, 7 David Mullett 9, 8 Carl Blackbird 7, 9 David Smart 6, 10 Paul Clarke 6, 11 Jamie Luckhurst 5, 12 Carl Baldwin 5, 13 Guy Wilson 4, 14 Andy Galvin 3, 15 Julian Parr 2, 16 Paul Price 2.
Sponsors: Sunday Mirror.

1985

Canterbury, Saturday, June 15
1 Carl Blackbird 15, 2 David Mullett 12, 3 Andy Smith 12, 4 Jamie Luckhurst 10, 5 Nigel De'ath 10, 6 Gary Havelock 9, 7 Simon Cross 9, 8 Andy Galvin 7, 9 Paul Whittaker 7, 10 Andrew Silver 6, 11 Paul Clarke 6, 12 Carl Baldwin 4, 13 David Smart 4, 14 Kevin Price 3, 15 Neville Tatum 2, 16 Jeremy Luckhurst 1. *Track reserves:* Lawrie Bloomfield 2, Mark Terry 1.

1986

Stoke, Saturday, May 17
1 Gary Havelock 15, 2 Andrew Silver 14, 3 Darren Sumner 13, 4 Michael Coles 9, 5 Andy Galvin 8, 6 Paul Whittaker 8, 7 Gordon Whitaker 8, 8 Mark Chessell 7, 9 Alastair Stevens 7, 10 David Biles 6, 11 Richard Green 6, 12 Paul Clarke 5, 13 Ian Stead 4, 14 David Smart 4, 15 Andy Phillips 4, 16 Jon Surman 1.

1987

Stoke, Saturday, September 5
1 Darren Sumner 14, 2 David Biles 13, 3 Mark Loram 12, 4 Sean Wilson 11, 5 Chris Cobby 9, 6 Alastair Stevens 9, 7 Bobby Duncan 8, 8 Peter McNamara 8, 9 Ian M. Stead 8, 10 Andrew Sumner 7, 11 Scott Lamb 7, 12 Adrian Stevens 6, 13 Jon Surman 4, 14 Will James 3, 15 Lee Farthing 1, 16 Steve Wicks 0.

1988

Eastbourne, Sunday, June 12
1 Mark Loram 15, 2 Andy Phillips 14, 3 Martin Dugard 13, 4 Chris Cobby 10, 5 Dean Standing 10, 6 Alastair Stevens 10, 7 Wayne Garratt 9, 8 Paul Whittaker 7, 9 Chris Louis 7, 10 Kevin Pitts 6, 11 Rodney Payne 4, 12 Gary Tagg 4, 13 Darren Standing 4, 14 Nathan Simpson 4, 15 Adrian Stevens 3, 16 Simon Wolstenholme 0.

1989

Eastbourne, Saturday, June 11
1 Martin Dugard 15, 2 Chris Louis 13, 3 Dean Barker 13, 4 Dean Standing 12 5 Andy Hackett 12, 6 Alastair Stevens 8, 7 Joe Screen 7, 8 David Norris 7, 9 Justin Walker 6, 10 Wayne Garratt 5, 11 Simon Wolstenholme 5, 12 Nathan Simpson 4, 13 Steve Masters 3, Darren Standing 3, Adrian Stevens 3, 16 Paul Dugard 3. *Track reserve:* Darren Grayling 1.

1990

Wimbledon, Saturday, July 11
1 Joe Screen 14, 2 Mark Loram 14, 3 Chris Louis 13, 4 Nathan Simpson 13, 5 Dean Standing 8, 6 Carl Stonehewer 7, 7 Gary Tagg 7, 8 Richard Musson 7, 9 David Clarke 6, 10 Simon Wolstenholme 6, 11 Chris Cobby 6, 12 Simon Green 5, 13 Darren Grayling 5, 14 Scott Robson 4, 15 Kevin Little 2, 16 Mark Simmonds 2.
Sponsors: Coastal Windows.

The Grand Slam

▲ MARTIN GOODWIN was honest enough to admit after the first major success of his career: "I didn't expect to win it."
▲ And neither did anyone else as second season rider Goodwin became the first winner of the Grand Slam, an individual competition that began life as the aperitif to the traditional National League Four Team Championships.
▲ The first staging was part of a two-day festival of racing at Peterborough but it subsequently developed into a competition in its own right even though the qualification system changed on a regular basis.

1985

Peterborough, Saturday, July 20
1 Martin Goodwin 14, 2 Andy Galvin 12, 3 Neil Middleditch 11, 4 Andrew Silver 11, 5 Robert Henry 9, 6 Ian Clark 9, 7 Dave Morton 9, 8 Kevin Hawkins 8, 9 Martin Dixon 7, 10 Stan Bear 7, 11 Tom Owen 6, 12 Andy Buck 6, 13 Mike Spink 5, 14 Steve Finch 4, 15 Joe Owen 0, Mike Ferreira 0. *Track Reserves:* Peter Chapman 1, Adrian Hume 0.
Semi Final 1: Andrew Silver 12, Andy Galvin 11, Mike Ferreira 10, Martin Goodwin 10, Martin Dixon 10, Andy Buck 9, Tom Owen 8, Ian Clark 8, Colin Cook 8, Mark Fiora 7 Carl Baldwin 7, Nigel De'ath 7, Charlie McKinna 6, Miles Evans 4, Phil White 2, Bob Humphreys 0. *Track reserve:* Adrian Hume 1.
Semi Final 2: Dave Morton 14, Robert Henry 12, Mike Spink 11, Kevin Hawkins 10, Stan Bear 9, Joe Owen 8, Neil Middleditch 8, Steve Finch 7, Bob Garrad 6, Paul Bosley 6, Jim McMillan 6, Nigel Sparshott 6, Nigel Crabtree 5, Colin Richardson 4, Steve Wilcock 4, Dave Perks 3. *Track reserve:* Peter Chapman 0.
The 32 semi-finalists were based on performances in rider of the night qualifying races in second half events.

1986

Arena Essex, Sunday, June 22
Final (10 laps): 1 Gary Havelock, 2 Gordon Kennett, 3 Nigel Crabtree, 4 Martin Goodwin, 5 Paul Thorp, 6 Dave Jessup, 7 Steve Schofield, 8 Roger Johns.
Eliminated semi-finalists (8 laps): Kevin Hawkins, Andrew Silver, David Mullett, David Biles, Steve Lawson, Alan Mogridge, Martin Dugard, Malcolm Simmons.
Semi Final 1: Kennett 9, Crabtree 9, Jessup 8, Schofield 8, Simmons 6, Biles 5, Hawkins 5, Lawson 5, Ian Stead 5, Les Collins 5, Mark Fiora 4, Bob Garrad 4, Dave Perks 4, David Smart 4, David Cheshire 2, Kevin Smart 2, Bobby Beaton 2, John Proctor 1, Doug Wyer 1, Colin Cook 0. *Track reserves:* Sean Barker 1, Lee Paine 0.
Semi Final 2: Thorp 9, Goodwin 8, Silver 8, Johns 7, Mullett 7, Havelock 6, Dugard 6, Mogridge 5, Bruce Cribb 5, Paul Woods 5, Rob Woffinden 4, Martin Dixon 3, Robert Henry 3, Andy Galvin 3, Mark Carlson 3, Nigel Flatman 2, Paul Stead 1, Lawrie Bloomfield 1, Paul Clarke 0, Jamie Luckhurst 0. *Track reserves:* Lee Paine 1, Sean Barker 0.
The 40 qualifiers were voted for by supporters at all National League tracks.

1987

Oxford, Sunday, June 28
1 Andrew Silver 14, 2 Nigel Crabtree 12, 3 Martin Dugard 11, 4 Andy Buck 11, 5 Martin Dixon 10, 6 Keith White 9, 7 Gordon Kennett 8, 8 Kevin Hawkins 7, 9 David Biles 7, 10 Les Collins 6, 11 Mark Fiora 6, 12 Kevin Jolly 6, 13 David Blackburn 5, 14 Mark Courtney 4, 15 Roger Johns 3, 16 Colin Cook 1.
Qualifying scorers: Andrew Silver 56, Gordon Kennett 55, Nigel Crabtree 48, David Biles 47, Kevin Jolly 47, Les Collins 46, Mark Fiora 46, David Blackburn 45, Martin Dixon 43, Andy Buck 42, Keith White 41, Martin Dugard 40, Roger Johns 40, Kevin Hawkins 40, Colin Cook 39, Mark Courtney 38, Steve Lawson 38, Melvyn Taylor 38, Paul Woods 37, Ian Barney 35, Darren Sumner 35, Neville Tatum 35, Gary Chessell 32, Dave Jessup 32, Trevor Banks 31, Miles Evans 31, Dave Morton 31, Kevin Smart 30, Doug Wyer 30, Keith Pritchard 29, Alan Rivett 29, Rob Grant 28, Richard Green 28, Gerald Short 27, Phil White 27, David Jackson 26, Mike Wilding 26, Paul Evitts 25, Jeremy Luckhurst 25, Steve McDermott 25, David Smart 25, Paul Stead 25, Steve Wilcock 24, Sean Courtney 23, Charlie McKinna 23, Andy Hines 22, Mike Spink 22, Martin Yeates 22, Kevin Brice 21 Mark Burrows 20, Nigel Leaver 19, David Mullett 19, Kevin Price 18, Brett Saunders 18, Ian Clark 17, Bruce Cribb 16, Kevin Teager 16, Dave Trownson 16, Bobby Beaton 15, Peter Chapman 15, Nigel Flatman 15, Geoff Powell 15, Rob Tilbury 15, Rob Woffinden 15, Kevin Smith 14, Graham Jones 13, Carl Baldwin 12, Mark Chessell 12, Barry Thomas 12, Shane Bowes 9, Andy Fisher 9, Ashley Norton 9, Carl Chalcraft 8, Steve Schofield 8, Steve Bishop 7, Craig Hodgson 7, Gary O'Hare 7, Jonathon Cooper 6, Ritchie Owen 6, Paul Cooper 5, Glenn Doyle 5, Wayne Ross 5, Mark Carlson 4, Steve Finch 4, Jimmy Goodsell 4, Steve Hone 4, Jackson Irving 4, Nigel Newman 4, Linden Warner 4, Derek Cooper 3, Alan Farmer 3, Martin Chessell 2, Ian Humphreys 2, Terry Mussett 2, Roland Tebbs 2, Richard Pettman 1, Steve Wicks 1, Martin McKinna 0, Eric Monaghan 0. *Track Reserves:* Andy Sumner 5, Steve Masters 2, Warren Mowatt 2, Harvey Bell 1, Rob Carter 1, Bobby Duncan 1, Peter McNamara 1, Gary Thompson 1, Glen Baxter 0, Mark Ferry 0, Scott Lamb 0.
Qualifying rounds at Middlesbrough, Peterborough, Berwick, Canterbury, Stoke, Edinburgh, Rye House and Long Eaton.
Sponsor: Tee Mill Tours.

1988

Oxford, Sunday, June 19
1 Jens Rasmussen 14, 2 Nigel Crabtree 13, 3 Ian Barney 11, 4 Andy Buck 11, 5 Andy Galvin 9, 6 Melvyn Taylor 9, 7 Steve Schofield 9, 8 Mark Fiora 7, 9 Mark Loram 7, 10 Darren Sumner 6, 11 Steve Bastable 5, 12 Martin Goodwin 5, 13 Les Collins 4, 14 Paul Woods 4, 15 Kenny McKinna 3, 16 Nigel Sparshott 3. *Track reserves:* Spencer Timmo 0, Ian Batley 0.
Qualifying scorers: Mark Loram 35, Melvyn Taylor 33, Nigel Crabtree 32, Ian Barney 32, Martin Goodwin 32, Jens Rasmussen 31, Andy Buck 31, Mark Fiora 31, Steve Schofield 30, Darren Sumner 28, Steve Bastable 27, Andy Galvin 27, Les Collins 26, Nigel Sparshott 25, Kenny McKinna 23, Paul Woods 21, Glenn Doyle 19, Roger Johns 18, Steve Lawson 17, Keith White 17, Rob Grant 16, Eric Monaghan 15, Kevin Jolly 14, Brett Saunders 13, Sean Courtney 13, Trevor Banks 12, Alan Rivett 12, David Smart 12, Kevin Hawkins 11, Mick Poole 10, Craig Hodgson 9, Dean Standing 9, Bruce Cribb 7, David Biles 7, Scott Robson 6, Nigel Flatman 5, Ian Stead 3, Andrew Buck 2, Mark Courtney 0.
Qualifying rounds at Mildenhall, Middlesbrough, Peterborough, Arena Essex, Rye House and Berwick. Riders had three qualifying rounds.

1989

Oxford, Sunday, June 18
1 Mick Poole 12, 2 Preben Eriksen 12, 3 Dean Barker 11, 4 Alastair Stevens 10, 5 Gordon Kennett 9, 6 Rod Hunter 7, 7 Jens Rasmussen 7, 8 Richard Hellsén 7, 9 Martin Goodwin 6, 10 Andy Galvin 6, 11 Melvyn Taylor 5, 12 Peter Carr 5, 13 David Blackburn 4, 14 Steve Schofield 4, 15 Colin Cook 4, 16 Alun Rossiter 4. *Reserve:* Neville Tatum 5.
Qualifying scorers: Steve Schofield 29, Melvyn Taylor 24, David Blackburn 24, Rod Hunter 24, Preben Eriksen 23, Chris Louis 22, Martin Goodwin 21, Gordon Kennett 21, Andy Galvin 20, Richard Hellsén 20, Peter Carr 20, Colin Cook 19, Dean Standing 19, Dean Barker 18, Mick Poole 18, Jens Rasmussen 18, Alastair Stevens 18, Alun Rossiter 17, Neville Tatum 17, Ray Morton 17, David Clarke 17, Andy Hines 16, Brett Saunders 15, Kevin Jolly 14, Les Collins 13, Darren Sumner 13, Mark Loram 13, Craig Boyce 13, Martin Dixon 12, Richard Green 12, Nigel Crabtree 12, Steve Regeling 11, Malcolm Holloway 10, Kenny McKinna 10, Charlie McKinna 10, David Walsh 10, Andy Buck 9, Keith White 9, Paul Whittaker 9, Ian Barney 8, Trevor Banks 8, Louis Carr 8, Steve Lawson 7, Mark Courtney 7, David Jackson 6, Spencer Timmo 6, Andy Sell 6, Simon Green 5, Phil Jeffrey 4, Anthony Hulme 4, Nigel Flatman 2, Ian Stead 2, Peter Boast 2, Ian M. Stead 2, Wayne Bridgeford 1.
Qualifying rounds at Ipswich, Peterborough, Glasgow, Mildenhall, Exeter and Newcastle. Riders had two qualifying rounds.

Su-pair-b

THEY sold out of programmes for the first semi-final of the Gauloises British League Pairs Championship.

And, little more than two years later, the competition was laid to rest after referee Graham Brodie tried to keep the meeting going in thick fog by officiating from the centre green rather than the box at Ipswich's Foxhall Heath Stadium.

But even he had to give up the ghost and then stumble back to the pits as the East Anglian stadium was enveloped in thick fog which made it impossible to separate the two leading clubs Coventry and Cradley Heath who were announced as joint winners after both had scored 18 points as they were preparing to meet each other in the abandoned heat 15!

There had been, though, during the three seasons of the competition's life plenty to enthrall and infuriate. John Louis almost missed the first final on his home track when, as he was pushed off in the pits before the parade, his throttle stuck open and he crashed into another machine and had to go into the meeting with a badly grazed hand.

The following year Michael Lee was unbeaten in both semi-final and final but led a one-man King's Lynn challenge.

Partner Ian Turner failed to arrive until the later stages of the Sheffield semi and then, in the final, he was again missing after team-mate Terry Betts had stepped down insisting: "He rode in the semi – he should ride in the final!"

By the time Turner notified the authorities he wouldn't be going to Ipswich it was too late to contact Betts and instead Lee lined up alongside the Stars' number four David Gagen.

Those two maximums were the best of Lee – the worst came in 1978 when he didn't turn up for the final until the 14th and last heat after he'd been delayed practising for the Superbike Six at Donington Park!

1976

SEMI FINALS

Hackney, Friday, September 24
Ipswich 24 (John Louis 13 Billy Sanders 11) Belle Vue 24 (Chris Morton 14 Peter Collins 10) Poole 21 (Malcolm Simmons 16 Eric Broadbelt 5) Hackney 19 (Zenon Plech 10 Dave Morton 9) Swindon 13 (Martin Ashby 12 Bobby McNeil 1) White City 13 (Gordon Kennett 12 Dag Lovaas 1) Exeter 11 (Ivan Mauger 6 Scott Autrey 5).
John Louis beat Chris Morton in run-off for first place.

Sheffield, Thursday, October 7
Coventry 26 (Ole Olsen 17 Mitch Shirra 9) Reading 23 (John Davis 12 Dave Jessup 11) Cradley Heath 22 (John Boulger 11 Bruce Cribb 11) Sheffield 18 (Reg Wilson 11 Doug Wyer 7) Wolverhampton 15 (George Hunter 9 Jim McMillan 6) King's Lynn 11 (Terry Betts 11 Ian Turner 0) Newport 11 (Phil Crump 7 Phil Herne 4).

FINAL

Ipswich, Tuesday, October 19
Ipswich 22 (Louis 12 Sanders 10) Coventry 21 (Olsen 14 Shirra 7) Belle Vue 21 (Collins 15 Morton 6) Cradley Heath 21 (Boulger 11 Cribb 10) Poole 18 (Simmons 15 Broadbelt 3) Hackney 12 (Plech 6 Morton 6) Sheffield 8 (Wyer 5 Wilson 3). *Meeting reserves: Tony Davey 3, Ted Howgego 0.*
Sponsors: Gauloises.

1977

SEMI FINALS

Hackney, Friday, September 9
White City 26 (Gordon Kennett 15 Steve Weatherley 11) Ipswich 24 (John Louis 14 Billy Sanders 10) Reading 21 (Dave Jessup 13 John Davis 8) Wimbledon 19 (Larry Ross 12 Mick Hines 7) Coventry 16 (Mitch Shirra 13 Alf Busk 3) Cradley Heath 13 (Steve Bastable 8 Colin Gooddy 5) Hull 7 (Graham Drury 6 Bobby Beaton 1). *Meeting reserves: Tony Featherstone 0, Vic Harding 0.*

Sheffield, Thursday, September 15
Sheffield 23 (Doug Wyer 15 Craig Pendlebury 8) Wolverhampton 22 (Jim McMillan 13 Finn Thomsen 9) Belle Vue 21 (Chris Morton 16 Alan Wilkinson 5) King's Lynn 20 (Michael Lee 18 Ian Turner 2) Bristol 16 (Phil Herne 14 Phil Crump 2) Swindon 13 (Martin Ashby 8 Geoff Bouchard 5) Exeter 8 (Scott Autrey 6 Ivan Mauger 2). *Meeting reserves: Tony Boyle 2, Carl Glover 0.*

FINAL

Ipswich, Thursday, September 29
Ipswich 26 (Sanders 14 Louis 12) King's Lynn 23 (Lee 18 David Gagen 5) White City 20 (Kennett 13 Weatherley 7) Reading 17 (Jessup 10 Davis 7) Wolverhampton 17 (McMillan 10 Thomsen 7) Belle Vue 12 (Wilkinson 8 Morton 4) Sheffield 11 (Pendlebury 6 Wyer 5). *Meeting reserve: Kevin Jolly.*
Sponsors: Gauloises.

1978

FINAL

Ipswich, Thursday, October 12
Coventry 18 (Ole Olsen 10 Mitch Shirra 8) Cradley Heath 18 (Steve Bastable 10 Bruce Penhall 8) Belle Vue 12 (Peter Collins 10 Chris Morton 2) Ipswich 11 (Billy Sanders 8 Tony Davey 3) Exeter 10 (Scott Autrey 5 Reidar Eide 5) Reading 8 (Dave Jessup 5 John Davis 3) King's Lynn 7 (Terry Betts 4 Michael Lee 3). *Meeting reserves: Kevin Jolly 0, Mike Lanham 0.*

Meeting abandoned after 14 heats because of thick fog. Result to stand with tied winners.
Sponsors: Gauloises.

The Grand National

■ *NEIL COLLINS provided a fitting finale to the Grand National – with a typical last to first burst that brought him the £200 first prize at Boston.*

■ *He had fought his way through a series of complicated qualifying rounds, a quarter final, and a semi-final and then came from the back to pip Mike Ferreira on the line.*

■ *The Grand National, launched by sponsors Warners Holidays in 1977, only survived for five years and was scrapped after just one stab at running it without a cash backer.*

1977

Hackney, Saturday, August 20
1 Martin Yeates 15, 2 Mike Sampson 13, 3 Tom Owen 12, 4 Ted Hubbard 12, 5 Laurie Etheridge 9, Brian Havelock 9, Stuart Mountford 9, 8 Steve Finch 8, 9 Nicky Allott 7, Robert Hollingworth 7, Alan Sage 7, 12 Robbie Blackadder 4, Paul Gilbert 4, 14 Robbie Gardner 2, 15 Danny Kennedy 1, Bert Harkins 1. ***Track reserves: Garry Monk 0, Peter Tarrant 0.***
Sponsors: Warners Holidays.

1978

Hackney, Saturday, September 9
1 Danny Kennedy 13, 2 Bob Humphreys 13, 3 David Shields 12, 4 David Kennett 11, 5 Tony Lomas 11, 6 Tom Owen 9, 7 Graeme Stapleton 8, 8 Tim Nunan 7, 9 Kenny Carter 6, 10 Malcolm Shakespeare 6, 11 Graham Clifton 6, 12 Ian Robertson 5, 13 Nicky Allott 5, 14 Arthur Price 5, 15 Melvyn Taylor 1, Steve Wilcock 1. ***Track reserves: Ray Griffiths 1, Martin Charles 0.***
Sponsors: Warners Holidays.

1979

Hackney, Saturday, August 18
1 Tom Owen 14, 2 Bob Garrad 12, 3 Nigel Boocock 11, 4 Steve Wilcock 11, 5 Melvyn Taylor 10, 6 Mick Hines 10, 7 Kevin Smith 9, 8 Robbie Blackadder 7, 9 Mike Ferreira 6, 10 Robert Henry 6, 11 Billy Burton 6, 12 Bob Humphreys 5, 13 Brian Woodward 4, 14 Nigel Flatman 4, 15 Dave Trownson 3, 16 Nigel Close 2.
Sponsors: Warners Holidays.

1980

King's Lynn, Saturday, June 21
1 David Gagen, 2 Paul Woods, 3 Mike Ferreira, 4 Billy Burton.
Defeated semi-finalists: **Ray Bales, Nigel Boocock, Nigel Flatman, Dave Perks.** ***Defeated quarter finalists:*** **Robbie Blackadder, Wayne Brown, Arthur Browning, Karl Fiala, Steve Finch, Bob Garrad, Kelvin Mullarkey, Martin Yeates.** ***Defeated repechage:*** **Peter Framingham, Andy Hines, Dennis Mallett, Robert Maxfield, Mike Sampson, Dave Trownson, Steve Wilcock.** ***Eliminated first round:*** **Bob Humphreys.**
Sponsors: Warners Holidays.

1981

Boston, Saturday, August 15
1 Neil Collins, 2 Mike Ferreira, 3 Steve Lomas, 4 Les Rumsey.
Defeated semi finalists: **David Gagen, Robert Hollingworth, Denzil Kent, Dave Perks.** ***Defeated quarter finalists:*** **Bruce Cribb, Steve Finch, Derek Harrison, Andy Hines, Bob Humphreys, Steve Lawson, Barry Thomas, Steve Wilcock.** ***Defeated repechage:*** **Wayne Brown, Peter Carr, Nigel Close, Alan Emerson, Ian Gledhill, Robert Henry, Martin Hewlett, Martin Yeates.**

YANKEE DOODLE DANDY...Californian Scott Autrey made the big breakthrough with victory in 1979 and was succeeded by his fellow American Dennis Sigalos the following year

Freddie's Starr tur

TV STAR Freddie Starr won a fan for life when he ready about Tony Davey's Grand Prix financial plight.

Davey, one of the 16 qualifiers for the 1978 final, admitted that he was considering selling his car to survive as a rider.

Starr, appearing in a summer season at Paignton, Devon, immediately posted off a £1,000 cheque for a new engine – and was at London White City to see Shrimp finish fourth overall.

Another rider to find a pot of gold at the end of the Grand Prix rainbow was Exeter's Scott Autrey who not only picked up the £1,250 winner's cheque in 1979 but also had his own quiet revenge on the American authorities who had refused to let him compete in that season's World Championship!

The competition ran successfully for five seasons and owing to the qualifying system managed to avoid the major problem of the winner being known before the last rounds.

The first ever Grand Prix meeting was staged at Wimbledon on July 1, 1976, and after a series of qualifying rounds the 16 top-scorers took part in a Final where the points formula was so weighted that the Grand Prix champion *had* to come from that Final.

The Daily Mirror provided valuable backing throughout the competition's life, initially as sole sponsors and, later, in conjunction with Volkswagen cars and Berger Paints.

GRAND PRIX – All the Results Year by Year

1976

1 Peter Collins 99, 2 Gordon Kennett 84, 3 Ole Olsen 84, 4 Malcolm Simmons 80, 5 Dave Jessup 61, 6 John Boulger 59, 7 Dave Morton 48, 8 John Davis 46, 9 Jim McMillan 43, 10 Phil Crump 43.

FINAL

White City, Wednesday, August 4

1 Peter Collins, 2 Gordon Kennett, 3 Malcolm Simmons, 4 Ole Olsen, 5 Dave Jessup, 6 John Boulger, 7 John Davis, 8 Dave Morton, 9 Jim McMillan, 10 Chris Morton, 11 Billy Sanders, 12 Kevin Holden, 13 Scott Autrey, 14 Terry Betts, 15 Bruce Cribb, 16 Phil Crump.

Round Winners

Wimbledon: Malcolm Simmons; Belle Vue: Peter Collins; Cradley Heath: Malcolm Simmons; King's Lynn: Phil Crump; Reading: Peter Collins; Hull: Peter Collins; Poole: Malcolm Simmons; White City: Chris Morton; Ipswich: Billy Sanders; Hackney: Dave Morton; Newport: Phil Herne; Wolverhampton: Peter Collins; Coventry: Ole Olsen; Halifax: Graham Plant; Swindon: Malcolm Simmons; Birmingham: Ole Olsen; Exeter: Phil Crump; Leicester: Ole Olsen; Sheffield: Ole Olsen.

Sponsors: Daily Mirror.

1977

1 Ole Olsen 88, 2 John Louis 85, 3 Malcolm Simmons 83, 4 Dave Jessup 66, 5 John Davis 65, 6 Gordon Kennett 63, 7 Michael Lee 58, 8 Steve Bastable 53, 9 Doug Wyer 42, 10 Larry Ross 35.5.

FINAL

White City, Wednesday, October 5

1 Ole Olsen, 2 John Louis, 3 Malcolm Simmons, 4 John Davis, 5 Dave Jessup, 6 Gordon Kennett, 7 Michael Lee, 8 Steve Bastable, 9 Ivan Mauger, 10 Ila Teromaa, 11 Finn Thomsen, 12 Ray Wilson, 13 Larry Ross, 14 Eric Broadbelt, 15 Tony Davey, 16 Doug Wyer.

Round Winners

Belle Vue: Larry Ross; King's Lynn: Michael Lee; Swindon: Malcolm Simmons; White City: Michael Lee; Ipswich: John Louis; Sheffield: Doug Wyer. Wimbledon: Gordon Kennett; Bristol: Phil Crump; Cradley Heath: Ray Wilson; Leicester: Michael Lee; Hackney: John Louis; Wolverhampton: Bob Valentine; Coventry: Ole Olsen; Halifax: Doug Wyer; Birmingham: Ole Olsen; Exeter: Scott Autrey; Reading: Dave Jessup; Hull: Ole Olsen; Poole: Dave Jessup.

Sponsors: Volkswagen and Daily Mirror.

1978

1 Chris Morton 71, 2 John Louis 65.5, Malcolm Simmons 65.5, 4 Tony Davey 60, 5 Dave Jessup 55, 6 John Titman 46, 7 Bob Kilby 44, 8 Reg Wilson 37, 9 Keith White 32, 10 Gordon Kennett 29.

FINAL

White City, Sunday, July 9

1 Chris Morton 2 John Louis, Malcolm Simmons, 4 Tony Davey, 5 Dave Jessup, 6 Bob Kilby, 7 John Titman, 8 Reg Wilson, 9 Keith White, 10 Bobby Beaton, 11 Billy Sanders, 12 Finn Thomsen, 13 John Davis, Gordon Kennett, 15 Ivan Mauger, 16 Steve Bastable.

Round Winners

Sheffield: Ivan Mauger; Wimbledon: Peter Collins; Hackney: Dave Jessup; Belle Vue: Peter Collins; Coventry: Alan Molyneux; King's Lynn: Michael Lee; Birmingham: Ray Wilson; Exeter: Phil Crump; Reading: Gordon Kennett; Leicester: Scott Autrey; Hull: Ivan Mauger; Poole: Tony Davey; White City: Kai Niemi; Ipswich: John Louis; Swindon: Peter Collins; Bristol: Joe Owen; Wolverhampton: Gordon Kennett; Cradley Heath: Alan Grahame; Halifax: Eric Broadbelt.

Sponsors: Volkswagen and Daily Mirror.

1979

1 Scott Autrey 77.5, 2 Bruce Penhall 71, 3 John Davis 66.5, 4 Michael Lee 58.5, 5 John Louis 54, 6 Phil Crump 51, 7 Joe Owen 40, 8 Roger Johns 36, 9 Kenny Carter 32, 10 Ivan Mauger 31.

FINAL

Wimbledon, Thursday, August 23

1 Scott Autrey, 2 Bruce Penhall, 3 John Davis, 4 Michael Lee, 5 John Louis, 6 Phil Crump, 7 Joe Owen, 8 Roger Johns, 9 Kenny Carter, 10 Ivan Mauger, 11 Alan Grahame, 12 Bruce Cribb, 13 Colin Richardson, 14 Steve Bastable, 15 Trevor Geer, 16 Doug Wyer.

Round Winners

Coventry: Mitch Shirra; Halifax: Ivan Mauger; Swindon: Phil Crump; Birmingham: Peter Collins; Exeter: Scott Autrey; Reading: Jan Andersson; Hull: Ivan Mauger; Poole: Ole Olsen; Sheffield: Doug Wyer; Wimbledon: Colin Richardson; Eastbourne: Roger Johns; Hackney: John Davis and Mitch Shirra; Wolverhampton: Kenny Carter; Belle Vue: Doug Wyer and Larry Ross; Cradley Heath: Bruce Penhall; King's Lynn: Michael Lee and Gordon Kennett; Leicester: Michael Lee; Ipswich: Steve Bastable.

Sponsors: Berger Paints and Daily Mirror.

1980

1 Dennis Sigalos 69, 2 Dave Jessup 64, 3 Michael Lee 57, 4 John Davis 44, 5 Bobby Schwartz 42, 6 Alan Grahame 35, 7 Kenny Carter 33, 8 Scott Autrey 27, Bruce Penhall 27, 10 Chris Morton 25.

FINAL

Wimbledon,Thursday, August 14

1 Michael Lee, 2 Dennis Sigalos, 3 Dave Jessup, 4 Bobby Schwartz, 5 Alan Grahame, 6 John Davis, 7 Kenny Carter, 8 Scott Autrey, 9 Chris Morton, 10 Malcolm Simmons, Phil White, 12 Kai Niemi, 13 Steve Bastable, 14 Phil Crump, 15 Andy Grahame, 16 Larry Ross.

Round Winners

Reading: Dennis Sigalos; Eastbourne: Dave Jessup; Birmingham: Bruce Penhall; Sheffield: Chris Morton.

Sponsors: Berger Paints and Daily Mirror.

Riders scored points in qualifying rounds and Final based on finishing positions in the meeting. In the qualifiying rounds the Grand Prix points were 10-9-8-7-6-5-4-3-2-1-0-0-0-0-0-0. In the Final Grand Prix points were: 50-45-40-35-30-25-20-15-10-5-0-0-0-0-0-0.

1965

Wimbledon, Monday, June 7

1 Charlie Monk 13, 2 Göte Nordin 11, 2 Björn Knutsson 11, 4 Barry Briggs 9, 5 Jimmy Gooch 9, 6 Ken McKinlay 9, 7 Nigel Boocock 8, 8 Sverre Harrfeldt 7, 9 Peter Jarman 7, 10 Ove Fundin 6, 11 Mike Broadbank 5, 12 Ronnie Genz 5, 13 Reg Luckhurst 4, 14 Arne Pander 4, 15 Ivor Brown 0, Ron How 0. *Reserves:* Olle Nygren 6, Trevor Hedge 4.

Sponsor: W.D. & H. O. Wills.

1966

Wimbledon, Monday, May 30

1 Göte Nordin 15, 2 Barry Briggs 14, 3 Ove Fundin 13, 4 Trevor Hedge 11, 5 Ken McKinlay 8, Olle Nygren 8, Cyril Maidment 8, 8 Bill Andrew 7, 9 Sverre Harrfeldt 7, 10 Ron Mountford 7, 11 Arne Pander 7, 12 Colin Pratt 4, 13 Bob Paulson 3, 14 Nigel Boocock 3, 15 Charlie Monk 3, 16 Peter Moore 1.

Sponsor: W.D. & H. O. Wills.

1967

Wimbledon, Monday, May 29

1 Göte Nordin 15, 2 Torbjörn Harrysson 11, 3 Ivan Mauger 11, 4 Eric Boocock 11, 5 Olle Nygren 10, 6 Nigel Boocock 9, 7 Trevor Hedge 8, 8 Sverre Harrfeldt 7, 9 Bengt Jansson 7, 10 Hasse Holmkvist 6, 11 Barry Briggs 5, 12 Roy Trigg 5, 13 Norman Hunter 4, 14 Ray Wilson 4, 15 Charlie Monk 3, 16 Jack Scott 0. *Reserves:* Reg Luckhurst 3, Terry Betts 1.

Sponsor: W.D. & H. O. Wills.

1968

Wimbledon, Monday, June 3

1 Nigel Boocock 15, 2 Bengt Jansson 14, 3 Barry Briggs 11, 4 Olle Nygren 11, 5 Sverre Harrfeldt 10, 6 Trevor Hedge 10, 7 Ole Olsen 10, 8 Terry Betts 7, 9 Ken McKinlay 7, 10 Ivan Mauger 4, 11 Jim Airey 4, 12 Ray Wilson 3, 13 Eric Boocock 3, 14 Roy Trigg 3, 15 Torbjörn Harrysson 2, Antonin Kasper 0. *Reserves:* Martin Ashby 4, Reg Luckhurst 2.

Sponsor: W.D. & H.O. Wills.

1969

Wimbledon, Monday, May 26

1 Trevor Hedge 13, 2 Ivan Mauger 13, 3 Barry Briggs 12, 4 Ray Wilson 10, 5 Eric Boocock 9, 6 Nigel Boocock 8, 7 Reg Luckhurst 8, 8 Ronnie Moore 7, 9 Terry Betts 7,10 Göte Nordin 7, 11 Bernt Persson 6, 12 Martin Ashby 5, 13 Olle Nygren 4, 14 Ole Olsen 4, 15 Norman Hunter 4, 16 Jim Airey 3. *Reserve:* Roy Trigg 0.

Sponsor: W.D. & H.O. Wills.

1970

Wimbledon, Monday, May 25

1 Ivan Mauger 15, 2 Trevor Hedge 13, 3 Ronnie Moore 11, 4 Terry Betts 11, 5 Ole Olsen 8, 6 Bengt Jansson 8, 7 Jim Airey 8, 8 Ray Wilson 8, 9 Barry Briggs 6, 10 Martin Ashby 6, 11 Eric Boocock 6, 12 Reidar Eide 5, 13 Bernt Persson 4, 14 Nigel Boocock 4, 15 Jimmy Ogisu 1, 16 Tony Clarke 0. *Reserves:* Christer Löfqvist 3, Reg Luckhurst 2.

Sponsor: W.D. & H.O. Wills.

OLLE NYGREN, the Internationale and controversy went hand-in-glove throughout the British League era.

The Internationale, sponsored throughout it's life by cigarette manufacturers W.D. & H.O. Wills, was another of the meetings which was retained on the merger of the old National League and the Provincial League.

It had first been staged in 1961 at Harringay and was ranked as the most important individual meeting outside the World Championship.

Nygren first hit the headlines a few days before the 1965 Whit Monday event when he was barred from competing by the Swedish authorities even though he had been programmed at number three.

He was replaced in the meeting proper by his Wimbledon team-mate Reg Luckhurst but, to some extent, the organisers got round that by nominating him as a track reserve – and the rider who shouldn't have ridden actually came out in four races!

Three years later Nygren was again the central figure in a drama when he looked over his shoulder and then slowed to allow Swedish team-mate Bengt Jansson to claim his third successive heat win, a victory he needed to stay in contention for the title.

Nygren, who had dropped three points at that stage, was given a public warning by referee Alan Day, booed by the big crowd when he came out for his next two rides and reported to the Speedway Control Board.

He claimed he was having fuel problems which caused him to slow but a Speedway Control Board Tribunual found him guilty of failing to make a bona fide attempt to race and he was fined £50.

Other highlights of the International, which sadly ran out of steam over the years and was finally axed from the FIM calendar when the sponsors withdrew their support, included a remarkable win by Charlie Monk in 1965 when he rode at Exeter in the morning (he dropped only one point) travelled onto London straight after his last race; a stormy run-off in 1969 which saw home hero Trevor Hedge get the better of a fallen, angry Ivan Mauger; a disproved protest that the New Zealander was using a banned additive in his fuel on his way to victory in 1972 by runner-up Garry Middleton.

1971

Wimbledon, Monday, May 31

1 Ivan Mauger 13, 2 Garry Middleton 12, 3 Ronnie Moore 12, 4 Ray Wilson 11, 5 Terry Betts 10 6 Barry Briggs 10, 7 Ole Olsen 9, 8 Jim Airey 8, 9 Nigel Boocock 8 10 Anders Michanek 8, 11 Trevor Hedge 5, 12 Jim McMillan 4, 13 Bert Harkins 4, 14 Eric Boocock 3, 15 Antonin Woryna 2, 16 Pawel Waloszek 0. *Reserve:* Christer Löfqvist 0.

Sponsor: W.D. & H. O. Wills.

1972

Wimbledon, Monday, May 29

1 Ivan Mauger 13, 2 Ronnie Moore 13, 3 Bengt Jansson 12, 4 Ole Olsen 11, 5 Ray Wilson 10, 6 Anders Michanek 9, 7 Terry Betts 9, 8 Christer Löfqvist 8, 9 Garry Middleton 7, 10 Martin Ashby 7, 11 Barry Briggs 4, 12 Eric Boocock 4, Reidar Eide 4, Trevor Hedge 4, 15 Bernt Persson 3, 16 Nigel Boocock 2. *Reserve:* Bob Kilby 0.

Sponsor: W.D. & H.O. Wills.

1973

Wimbledon, Monday, May 28

1 Ole Olsen 14, 2 Anders Michanek 14, 3 Tommy Jansson 11, 4 Ivan Mauger 11, 5 Bernt Persson 10, 6 Terry Betts 9, 7 Bengt Jansson 8, 8 Christer Löfqvist 7, 9 Garry Middleton 7, 10 Reidar Eide 6, 11 Reg Wilson 5, 12 Ray Wilson 5, 13 John Boulger 4, 14 Chris Pusey 3, 15 JIm McMillan 3, 16 Scott Autrey 3.

Sponsors: W.D. & H.O. Wills.

1974

Wimbledon, Monday, May 27

1 Peter Collins 14, 2 Ray Wilson 12, 3 Ole Olsen 12, 4 John Louis 12, 5 Bob Valentine 10, 6 Terry Betts 10, 7 Martin Ashby 8, 8 Dave Jessup 7, 9 Barry Briggs 6, 10 Anders Michanek 6, 11 Phil Crump 6, 12 Malcolm Simmons 5, 13 Dag Lovaas 4, 14 Tommy Jansson 2, 15 John Boulger 0, Ivan Mauger 0. *Reserves:* Billy Sanders 3, Reidar Eide 3, George Hunter 0.

Sponsor: W.D. & H.O. Wills.

1975

Wimbledon, Monday, May 26

1 Ole Olsen 14, 2 Phil Crump 13, 3 Ray Wilson 12, 4 Malcolm Simmons 12, 5 Tommy Jansson 10, 6 John Louis 9, 7 Anders Michanek 7, 8 John Boulger 7, 9 Peter Collins 7, 10 Ivan Mauger 7, 11 Jim McMillan 5, 12 Martin Ashby 5, 13 Dag Lovaas 4, 14 Barry Thomas 4, 15 Terry Betts 2, 16 Sören Sjösten 0. *Reserves:* Chris Pusey 2, Bob Humphreys 0.

Sponsor: W.D. & H.O. Wills.

1976

Wimbledon, Monday, May 31

1 Malcolm Simmons 15, 2 Chris Morton 13, 3 Michael Lee 11, 4 Dave Jessup 11, 5 Phil Crump 10, 6 Dave Morton 9, 7 Peter Collins 9, 8 Ivan Mauger 7, 9 John Boulger 6, 10 John Davis 4, 11 Martin Ashby 4, 12 Terry Betts 4,13 Gordon Kennett 4, 14 Zenon Plech 3, 15 Billy Sanders 3, 16 Chris Pusey 2. *Reserves:* Mick Hines 2, Barry Thomas 2.

Sponsor: W.D. & H.O. Wills.

1977

Wimbledon, Monday, June 6

1 Edward Jancarz 13, 2 Larry Ross 11, 3 Phil Crump 11, 4 Dave Jessup 9, 5 Gordon Kennett 9, 6 Billy Sanders 9, 6 7 John Davis 9, 8 Jim McMillan 8, 9 Chris Morton 8, 10 Peter Collins 7, 11 Martin Ashby 7, 12 Malcolm Simmons 7, 13 John Louis 5, 14 John Boulger 4, 15 Doug Wyer 2, 16 Michael Lee 1. *Reserve:* Neil Middleditch 0.

Sponsor: W.D. & H.O. Wills.

1978

Wimbledon, Monday, May 29

1 Peter Collins 13, 2 Malcolm Simmons 13, 3 John Davis 13, 4 Michael Lee 12, 5 Ole Olsen 10, 6 Larry Ross 10, 7 Edward Jancarz 9, 8 Billy Sanders 7, 9 Dave Jessup 5, 10 Colin Richardson 5, 11 Steve Bastable 4, Phil Crump 4, Mitch Shirra 4, Finn Thomsen 4, 15 Bruce Penhall 3, 16 Gordon Kennett 2. *Reserve:* Roger Johns 1.

Sponsor: W.D. & H.O. Wills.

1979

Wimbledon, Monday, May 28

1 Michael Lee 14, 2 John Davis 13, 3 Edward Jancarz 11, 4 Bruce Penhall 9, 5 Gordon Kennett 9, 6 Malcolm Simmons 8, 7 Phil Crump 7, 8 John Louis 6, 9 Ole Olsen 6, 10 Billy Sanders 6, 11 Larry Ross 6, 12 Kai Niemi 6, 13 Hans Nielsen 5, 14 Dave Jessup 4, 15 Jan Andersson 3, 16 Peter Collins 3. *Reserve:* Roger Johns 4.

Sponsor: W.D. & H.O. Wills.

1980

Wimbledon, Monday, May 26

1 Dave Jessup 15, 2 Bruce Penhall 12, 3 Hans Nielsen 11, 4 Chris Morton 9, 5 Michael Lee 9, 6 Scott Autrey 9, 7 Zenon Plech 9, 8 Bobby Schwartz 9, 9 Bo Petersen 8, 10 Gordon Kennett 8, 11 Kai Niemi 5, 12 Edward Jancarz 5, 13 Peter Collins 5, 14 Larry Ross 4, 15 Billy Sanders 1, 16 Rudy Muts 0. *Reserve:* Colin Richardson 1.

Sponsor: W.D. & H.O. Wills.

1981

Wimbledon, Sunday, August 9

1 Hans Nielsen 15, 2 Kenny Carter 12, 3 Jan Andersson 12, 4 Chris Morton 10, 5 Dave Jessup 9, 6 Larry Ross 9, 7 Kelly Moran 9, 8 Erik Gundersen 9, 9 Ole Olsen 9, 10 Gordon Kennett 8, 11 Edward Jancarz 6, 12 Phil Crump 5, 13 Billy Sanders 3, 14 Malcolm Simmons 2, 15 Les Collins 2, 16 Shawn Moran 0. *Reserve:* Roger Johns 0.

Original staging on Monday, May 25 was postponed because of a waterlogged track.

Sponsor: W.D. & H.O. Wills.

● *The event was known as the Internationale from 1961 until 1967; the Wills International from 1968 until 1974; and the Embassy Internationale from 1975 until 1981.*

INTER LEAGUE TEAM CHAMPIONSHIP – All the Results

1979

Qualifying Rounds

Belle Vue 10 16 17 35 **78** Cradley Heath 35 34 30 35 **134** *Ellesmere Port 4 7 18 8* ***37*** Wolverhampton 38 39 31 18 **126**.

Exeter 38 35 26 31 **130** *Oxford 7 12 19 4* ***42*** Poole 31 26 32 22 **111** Swindon 20 23 19 38 **100**.

Ipswich 13 23 29 29 **94** King's Lynn 24 30 31 34 **119** Reading 37 38 25 29 **129** *Rye House 22 5 11 4 42*.

Birmingham 36 28 28 27 **119** Coventry 31 36 38 23 **128** Leicester 19 29 26 28 **102** *Peterborough 10 3 4 18* ***35***.

Halifax 26 32 29 22 **109** Hull 47 28 21 41 **137** *Newcastle 9 7 17 25* ***58*** Sheffield 14 35 30 8 **87**.

Canterbury 22 3 11 4 ***40*** Eastbourne 27 36 22 27 **112** Hackney 25 28 39 23 **115** Wimbledon 21 29 18 42 **110**.

The round at Hackney was abandoned after 15 races following the fatal crash involving Vic Harding. Results to stand.

SEMI FINALS

Sheffield, Sunday, June 24

Semi Final 1: Exeter 28 (Scott Autrey 11, Vaclav Verner 8, Zdenek Kudrna 5, Steve Koppe 4) Hull 24 (Bobby Beaton 10, Joe Owen 5, Frank Auffret 5, Dennis Sigalos 2, Graham Drury 2) King's Lynn 22 (Dave Jessup 12, Pete Smith 5, Craig Featherby 3, Richard Hellsén 2) Reading 22 (John Davis 8, Jan Andersson 7, Bernie Leigh 6, Doug Underwood 1).

Semi Final 2: Cradley Heath 32 (Bobby Schwartz 11, Alan Grahame 10, Phil Collins 7, Dave Perks 3, Nigel Wasley 1) Coventry 19 (Mitch Shirra 8, Gary Guglielmi 6, Alf Busk 2, Tommy Knudsen 2, Alan Molyneux 1) Hackney 24 (Finn Thomsen 12, Zenon Plech 6, Bo Petersen 5, Bobby McNeil 1, Barry Thomas 0) Wolverhampton 21 (Jim McMillan 8, Bruce Cribb 8, Trond Skretting 4, Edgar Stangeland 1).

FINAL

Sheffield, Sunday, June 24

Hull 36 (Beaton 12, Sigalos 12, Auffret 6, Drury 5, Owen 1) Exeter 30 (Verner 9, Kudrna 8, Autrey 7, Koppe 3, Peter Prinsloo 3) Cradley Heath 21 (Schwartz 8, Collins 6, Grahame 4, Perks 2, Wasley 1) Hackney 8 (Thomsen 5, Keith White 1, Petersen 1, Plech 1, McNeil 0).

1980

Qualifying Rounds

Belle Vue 26 21 28 36 **111** Birmingham 24 36 32 40 **132** *Milton Keynes 10 10 6 4* ***30*** Wolverhampton 35 29 30 16 **110**.

Coventry 28 30 35 8 **101** Cradley Heath 26 28 20 33 **107** Hackney 23 18 23 27 **91** *Rye House 19 20 18 28* ***85***.

Berwick 7 23 9 15 ***54*** Halifax 26 27 22 42 **117** Hull 38 31 44 18 **131** Sheffield 25 15 21 21 **82**.

Eastbourne 37 31 14 33 **115** *Oxford 12 20 15 9* ***56*** Poole 25 32 29 35 **121** Wimbledon 22 13 38 19 **92**.

Ipswich 28 38 27 32 **125** King's Lynn 35 35 40 33 **143** Leicester 27 20 15 13 **75** *Mildenhall 6 2 14 18* **40**.

SEMI FINALS

Wolverhampton, Sunday, July 20

Semi Final 1: King's Lynn 28 (Dave Jessup 12, Micahel Lee 6, Richard Hellsén 5, Melvyn Taylor 4, Bent Rasmussen 1) Cradley Heath 26 (Bruce Penhall 8, Alan Grahame 8, Ila Teromaa 5, Dave Perks 5) Ipswich 22 (Billy Sanders 7, Mike Lanham 6, Tim Hunt 5, John Louis 4) Poole 20 (Malcolm Simmons 10, Peter Prinsloo 5, Neil Middleditch 5, Danny Kennedy 0, John McNeill 0).

Semi Final 2: Birmingham 28 (Steve Bastable 11, Andy Grahame 8, Kelly Moran 7, Phil Herne 2, Zdenek Kudrna 0) Halifax 28 (Kenny Carter 10, Merv Janke 9, Ian Cartwright 5, Piotr Pyszny 4, Craig Pendlebury 0) Eastbourne 23 (Gordon Kennett 11, Paul Woods 6, David Kennett 4, Veijo Tuorieniemi 2, Jan Davidsson 0) Hull 16 (Joe Owen 5, John Cook 5, Frank Auffret 3, David Bargh 3).

FINAL

Wolverhampton, Sunday, July 20

Cradley Heath 33 (Grahame 11, Penhall 10, Perks 7, Teromaa 5) King's Lynn 32 (Jessup 8, Taylor 8, Lee 6, Hellsén 6, Rasmussen 4) Birmingham 18 (Moran 9, Grahame 4, Bastable 4, Neil Evitts 1) Halifax 13 (Carter 6, Pyszny 3, Janke 3, Pendlebury 1).

National League teams are indicated in italics. Figures in bold indicate qualifying totals.

NATIONAL LEAGUE TEAM CHAMPIONSHIP – All the Results

1976

Qualifying rounds

Canterbury 26 21 21 6 **74** Crayford 21 18 27 30 **96** Eastbourne 24 36 18 26 **104** RYE HOUSE 24 21 30 33 **108**.

Coatbridge 10 24 32 24 **90** NEWCASTLE 41 37 31 34 **143** Paisley 20 8 20 28 **76** Teesside 25 26 12 10 **73**.

Berwick 14 10 21 24 **69** Ellesmere Port 20 32 29 19 **100** Scunthorpe 23 14 13 21 71 WORKINGTON 39 40 33 32 **144**.

Boston 22 20 23 31 **96** Mildenhall 18 14 18 18 **68** Peterborough 31 30 35 31 **127** Weymouth 25 30 20 16 **91**.

SEMI FINALS

King's Lynn, Sunday, July 17

Semi Final 1: Ellesmere Port 17 (John Jackson 6, Steve Finch 5, Chris Turner 3, Robbie Gardner 3) Workington 15 (Brian Havelock 4, Colin Goad 4, Steve Lawson 4, Terry Kelly 3) Rye House 10 (Ted Hubbard 3, Hugh Saunders 3, Kelvin Mullarkey 2, Bob Garrad 2, Karl Fiala 0) Peterborough 5 (Roy Carter 4, Ken Matthews 1, Brian Clark 0, Tony Featherstone 0).

Semi Final 2: Newcastle 17 (Joe Owen 6, Andy Cusworth 4, Phil Michelides 3, Tom Owen 3, Robbie Blackadder 1) Eastbourne 13 (Mike Sampson 5, Steve Weatherley 4, Eric Dugard 3, Colin Richardson 1, Peter Jarman 0) Boston 9 (Robert Hollingworth 4, Billy Burton 3, Paul Gilbert 1, Ron Cooper 1, Stuart Cope 0) Coatbridge 9 (Brian Collins 5, Mick McKeon 4, Grahame Dawson 0, Derek Richardson 0, Max Brown 0).

FINAL

King's Lynn, Sunday, July 17

Newcastle 18 (T. Owen 6, J. Owen 6, Cusworth 3, Michelides 3) Eastbourne 13 (Weatherley 5, Sampson 4, Richardson 4, Dugard 0, Jarman 0) Ellesmere Port 12 (Jackson 6, Gardner 3, Turner 2, Finch 1) Workington 5 (Lawson 4, Goad 1, Kelly 0, Havelock 0).

1977

Qualifying rounds

Canterbury 29 29 24 20 **102** Crayford 17 22 13 12 **64** Eastbourne 35 31 34 36.5 **136 .5** Rye House 15 14 24 27.5 **80.5**.

Newport 10 23 15 10 **58** Oxford 26 22 33 23 **104** Stoke 32 35 25 36 **128** Weymouth 28 16 23 26 **93**.

Berwick 20 9 21 5 **55** Ellesmere Port 29 37 44 36 **146** Teesside 26 19 24 21 **90** Workington 21 31 7 34 **93**.

Boston 37 34 32 31 **134** Mildenhall 19 27 17 21 **84** Peterborough 27 18 28 30 **103** Scunthorpe 13 17 19 14 **63**.

Barrow 7 7 4 **18** Coatbridge 34 26 18 **78** Edinburgh 27 27 28 **82** Newcastle 28 36 46 **110**.

Barrow never staged a home leg.

SEMI FINALS

Peterborough, Sunday, August 7

Semi Final 1: Eastbourne 21 (Colin Richardson 6, Mike Sampson 6, Eric Dugard 5, Roger Abel 4) Stoke 12 (Ian Robertson 4, Tim Nunan 3, Stuart Mountford 3, Ian Gledhill 2) Ellesmere Port 8 (John Jackson 5, Phil Collins 1, Duncan Meredith 1, Louis Carr 1) Boston 7 (Robert Hollingworth 4, Dave Allen 3, Billy Burton 0, Paul Gilbert 0, Steve Clarke 0).

Semi Final 2: Canterbury 18 (Bob Spelta 6, Steve Koppe 5, Graham Banks 5, Brian Kennett 2) Peterborough 14 (Nigel Flatman 5, Ian Clark 4, Kevin Hawkins 3, Brian Clark 1, Andy Hines 1) Newcastle 9 (Tom Owen 6, Robbie Gardner 2, Phil Kynman 1, Robbie Blackadder 0, Phil Michelides 0) Oxford 7 (Martin Yeates 4, Phil Bass 2, Mick Handley 1, Kevin Young 0, Colin Meredith 0).

FINAL

Peterborough, Sunday, August 7

Peterborough 17 (I. Clark 6, Hawkins 5, Hines 5, Flatman 1, B. Clark 0) Canterbury 14 (Banks 6, Koppe 3, Spelta 3, Kennett 2) Eastbourne 13 (Richardson 5, Sampson 5, Dugard 2, Abel 1) Stoke 4 (Mountford 2, Nunan 1, Gledhill 1, Robertson 0).

1978

Qualifying rounds

Mildenhall 42 26 20 17 **105** Milton Keynes 13 20 9 12 **54** Oxford 14 34 27 31 **106** Weymouth 27 16 40 34 **117**.

Ellesmere Port 32 32 38 21 **123** Newcastle 40 26 28 25 **119** Teesside 15 25 17 27 **84** Workington 9 12 13 23 **57**.

Barrow 33 16 25 23 **97** Berwick 19 11 34 4 **68** Edinburgh 34 36 22 23 **125** Glasgow 10 33 15 36 **94**.

Canterbury 34 29 26 20 **109** Crayford 20 4 16 19 **59** Eastbourne 22 37 31 34 **124** Rye House 20 26 23 23 **92**.

Boston 29 13 19 23 **84** Peterborough 25 36 25 38 **124** Scunthorpe 11 14 26 12 **63** Stoke 31 33 26 22 **112**.

SEMI FINALS

Peterborough, Sunday, July 30

Semi Final 1: Stoke 13 (John Harrhy 6, Stuart Mountford 3, Tony Lomas 2, Ian Robertson 2) Peterborough 12 (Nigel Couzens 6, Nigel Flatman 3, Dave Gooderham 2, Tim Hunt 1, Brian Clark 0) Newcastle 12 (Tom Owen 5, Robbie Gardner 5, Robbie Blackadder 2, Kenny Carter 0) Edinburgh 10 (Robert Hollingworth 5, Steve Lomas 2, Dave Trownson 2, Steve McDermott 1).

Semi Final 2: Canterbury 16 (Steve Koppe 5, Les Rumsey 4, Mike Ferreira 4, Graham Clifton 3) Ellesmere Port 12 (Phil Collins 6, Steve Finch 4, John Jackson 1, Louis Carr 1) Weymouth 12 (Malcolm Shakespeare 5, Danny Kennedy 4, Sean Willmott 2, Geoff Swindells 1) Eastbourne 8 (Mike Sampson 3, David Kennett 3, Steve Naylor 2, Eric Dugard 0).

Peterborough and Ellesmere Port qualified for Final on race wins.

FINAL

Peterborough, Sunday, July 30

Peterborough 18 (Couzens 6, Flatman 5, Hunt 4, Gooderham 3) Stoke 12 (Robertson 4, Harrhy 3, Lomas 3, Mountford 2) Canterbury 9 (Koppe 4, Clifton 3, Ferreira 2, Rumsey 0) Ellesmere Port 9 (Peter Ellams 4, Collins 3, Carr 2, Finch 0, Jackson 0).

1979

Qualifying Rounds

Berwick 24 23 36 30 **113** Edinburgh

15 27 22 13 **77** Glasgow 21 24 16 26 **87** Newcastle 34 21 22 26 **103**.

Ellesmere Port 31 32 22 42 **127** Oxford 34 32 39 34 **136** Stoke 20 11 26 12 **69** Workington 11 20 9 11 **51**.

Boston 28 25 22 22 **97** Milton Keynes 17 24 20 32 **93** Peterborough 37 31 31 27 **126** Weymouth 14 16 23 15 **68**.

Canterbury 21 19 18 10 **68** Crayford 14 9 11 22 **56** Mildenhall 32 42 31 28 **133** Rye House 29 26 35 36 **126**.

SEMI FINALS

Peterborough, Sunday, July 29

Semi Final 1: Peterborough 18 (Nigel Flatman 5, Peter Spink 5, Dave Gooderham 4, Andy Hines 4) Ellesmere Port 14 (Steve Finch 5, John Jackson 4, Peter Ellams 3, Louis Carr 2) Rye House 12 (Karl Fiala 4, Kevin Smith 3, Kelvin Mullarkey 3, Ashley Pullen 2, Bob Garrad 0) Oxford 4 (Les Rumsey 3, John Barker 1, Carl Askew 0, Keith Chapman 0).

Semi Final 2: Mildenhall 18 (Ray Bales 5, Melvyn Taylor 5, Mick Hines 4, Robert Henry 4) Berwick 11 (Wayne Brown 5, Nigel Close 4, Graham Jones 2, Phil Kynman 0) Newcastle 10 (Tom Owen 5, Robbie Blackadder 3, Rod Hunter 2, Graeme Stapleton 0, Neil Coddington 0) Boston 9 (Dave Allen 5, Dennis Mallett 3, Robert Hollingworth 1, Andy Fisher 0, Tony Featherstone 0).

FINAL

Peterborough, Sunday, July 29)

Ellesmere Port 17 (Jackson 6, Carr 6, Finch 5, Ellams 0, Eric Monaghan 0) Mildenhall 15 (Hines 5, Bales 4, Taylor 3, Henry 3) Peterborough 9 (Gooderham 4, Flatman 2, Hines 1, Spink 1, Brian Clark 1) Berwick 7 (Brown 5, Close 2, Jones 0, Kynman 0).

1980

Qualifying Rounds

Canterbury 27 20 24 25 **96** Crayford 27 28 28 28 **111** Mildenhall 16 20 11 15 **62** Rye House 26 28 33 28 **115**.

Boston 32 33 30 28 **123** Milton Keynes 17 12 13 11 **53** Oxford 30 31 21 28 **110** Peterborough 17 20 32 29 **98**.

Berwick 20 24 31 23 **98** Glasgow 22 34 20 24 **100** Middlesbrough 39 16 8 28 **91** Newcastle 15 20 27 21 **93**.

Ellesmere Port 30 37 42 36 **145** Nottingham 20 30 18 25 **93** Stoke 20 24 32 29 **105** Workington 25 5 4 6 **40**.

SEMI FINALS

Peterborough, Sunday, July 27

Semi Final 1: Crayford 17 (Paul Woods 6, Les Rumsey 6, Steve Naylor 5, Laurie Etheridge 0, Alan Sage 0) Ellesmere Port 16 (Steve Finch 5, Louis Carr 5, John Jackson 4, Peter Carr 2, Peter Ellams 0) Berwick 8 (Wayne Brown 3, Mike Fullerton 3, Steve McDermott 2, Nigel Close 0) Boston 7 (Steve Lomas 3, Gary Guglielmi 2, Robert Hollingworth 1, Dennis Mallett 1).

Semi Final 2: Rye House 18 (Kevin Smith 6, Bob Garrad 5, Kelvin Mullarkey 4, Karl Fiala 3) Stoke 15 (Paul Stead 6, Billy Burton 4, Neil Evitts 3, Tony Boyle 2) Glasgow 8 (Alan Emerson 4, Steve Lawson 2, Andy Reid 2, Kenny McKinna 0) Oxford 7 (John Hack 4, Dave Perks 2, Colin Ackroyd 1, Steve Crockett 0, Derek Harrison 0).

FINAL

Peterborough, Sunday, July 27

Crayford 14 (Rumsey 7, Woods 4, Naylor 3, Sage 0, Etheridge 0) Rye House 13 (Mullarkey 4, Garrad 4, Smith 3, Ashley Pullen 2, Fiala 0) Ellesmere Port 12 (L. Carr 5, Jackson 3, P. Carr 2, Finch 2, Ellams 0) Stoke 9 (Burton 6, Les Sawyer 2, Boyle 1, Stead 0, Evitts 0).

1981

Qualifying rounds

Berwick 16 24 18 21 **79** Edinburgh 28 24 33 41 **126** Glasgow 12 14 12 23 **61** Newcastle 40 34 33 8 **115**

Crayford 28 28 21 22 **99** Exeter 25 17 33 20 **95** Rye House 17 20 7 35 **79** Weymouth 25 31 34 19 **109**

Ellesmere Port 21 35 19 14 **89** Middlesbrough 32 17 31 31 **111** Scunthorpe 14 16 17 24 **71** Wolverhampton 29 27 29 27 **112**

Boston 24 18 23 28 **93** Mildenhall 26 27 24 33 **110** Oxford 18 22 14 6 **60** Peterborough 28 29 35 29 **121**

SEMI FINALS

Peterborough, Sunday, July 26

Semi Final 1: Middlesbrough 16 (Mark Courtney 6, Steve Wilcock 4, Brian Havelock 4, Geoff Pusey 2) Newcastle 16 (Alan Emerson 5, Robbie Blackadder 4, Rod Hunter 4, David Bargh 3) Peterborough 11 (Richard Greer 4, Mick Hines 3, Andy Hines 2, Dave Allen 2) Weymouth 4 (Les Rumsey 3, Brian Woodward 1, Martin Yeates 0, Malcolm Shakespeare 0).

Semi Final 2: Edinburgh 16 (Neil Collins 6, Dave Trownson 6, Ivan Blacka 3, Chris Turner 1) Wolverhampton 16 (Billy Burton 5, Bruce Cribb 4, Neil Evitts 4, Paul Stead 3) Mildenhall 13 (Ray Bales 5, Ian Gledhill 2, Mick Bates 2, Robert Henry 2, Richard Knight 2) Crayford 3 (Alan Sage 2, Laurie Etheridge 1, Barry Thomas 0, Michael Spinks 0).

FINAL

Peterborough, Sunday, July 26

Edinburgh 15 (Collins 4, Turner 4, Trownson 4, Blacka 3) Newcastle 13 (Bargh 5, Hunter 3, Emerson 3, Blackadder 2) Middlesbrough 11 (Courtney 5, Pusey 3, Wilcock 2, Havelock 1) Wolverhampton 9 (Burton 5, Stead 2, Evitts 2, Cribb 0).

1982

Qualifying Rounds

Ellesmere Port 41 21 30 34 **126** Oxford 8 34 30 31 **103** Scunthorpe 21 25 11 23 **80** Stoke 26 15 25 8 **74**.

Edinburgh 20 18 17 16 **71** Glasgow 16 10 25 11 **62** Middlesbrough 24 37 18 28 **107** Newcastle 36 31 36 41 **144**.

Canterbury 25 22 16 25 **88** Crayford 11 13 15 15 **54** Peterborough 29 33 26 19 **107** Rye House 31 28 39 34 **132**.

Boston 24 28 8 6 **66** Exeter 18 23 36 32 **109** Mildenhall 35 35 25 23 **118** Weymouth 19 10 27 35 **91**.

SEMI FINALS

Peterborough, Sunday, July 25

Semi Final 1: Mildenhall 15 (Ray Bales 5, Derek Harrison 5, Richard Knight 3, Robert Henry 2) Rye House 14 (Kelvin Mullarkey 5, Steve Naylor 5, Bob Garrad 4, Steve Bryenton 0, Andy Fines 0) Oxford 12 (Graham Drury 5, Ashley Pullen 4, Colin Ackroyd 2, Wayne Jackson 1, Ian Gledhill 0) Exeter 7 (Andy Campbell 3, Les Sawyer 2, Bob Coles 1. Mark Reeve 1, Dave Brewer 0).

Semi Final 2: Newcastle 16 (Bobby Beaton 6, Joe Owen 4, Rod Hunter 4, Alan Emerson 2) Middlesbrough 12 (Martin Dixon 5, Mike Spink 4, Steve Wilcock 2, Geoff Pusey 1) Peterborough 10 (Andy Hines 5, Dave Allen 4, Mick Hines 1, Ian Barney 0) Ellesmere Port 10 (Steve Finch 5, Eric Monaghan 3, John Jackson 1, Robert Maxfield 1, Billy Burton 0).

FINAL

Peterborough, Sunday, July 25)

Newcastle 17 (Owen 6, Beaton 4, Hunter 4, Emerson 3) Mildenhall 15 (Knight 5, Henry 5, Bales 4, Harrison 1) Middlesbrough 13 (Dixon 5, Wilcock 4, Pusey 2, Spink 2) Rye House 3 (Mullarkey 2, Naylor 1, Garrad 0, Bryenton 0).

1983

Qualifying Rounds

Boston 18 24 13 19 **65** Long Eaton 31 24 28 19 **102** Middlesbrough 30 25 29 45 **129** Scunthorpe 17 23 26 22 **88**.

Berwick 17 19 11 17 **64** Edinburgh 29 24 23 19 **95** Glasgow 15 21 25 23 **84** Newcastle 35 32 17 37 **141**.

Crayford 11 28 33 20 **92** Mildenhall 29 18 28 39 **114** Peterborough 37 18 13 20 **88** Rye House 19 29 22 17 **87**.

Canterbury 29 26 20 26 **101** Exeter 12 18 34 13 **77** Milton Keynes 29 33 17 24 **103** Weymouth 26 19 25 33 **103**.

SEMI FINALS

Peterborough, Sunday, July 24

Semi Final 1: Newcastle 15 (Joe Owen 5, Rod Hunter 4, Bobby Beaton 4 Alan Emerson 2) Milton Keynes 13 (Craig Pendlebury 6, Keith White 4, Paul Clarke 3, Charlie McKinna 0) Middlesbrough 13 (Mike Spink 6, Steve Wilcock 4, Rob Woffinden 2, Brian Havelock 1) Crayford 7 (Barry Thomas 3, Trevor Banks 3, Kevin Teager 1, Alan Mogridge 0).

Semi Final 2: Mildenhall 21 (Richard Knight 6, Robert Henry 6, Carl Baldwin 5, Derek Harrison 4) Long Eaton 11 (Dave Perks 5, Paul Stead 3, Alan Molyneux 2, Paul Evitts 1, John Frankland 0) Edinburgh 8 (Dave Trownson 5, Mark Fiora 2, Brett Saunders 1, Chris Turner 0, Glyn Taylor 0) Weymouth 7 (Stan Bear 4, Martin Yeates 3, Chris Martin 0, Rob Mather 0, Gordon Humphreys 0).

FINAL

Peterborough, Sunday, July 24

Newcastle 21 (Emerson 6, Hunter 5, Owen 5, Martin Scarisbrick 3, Beaton 2) Mildenhall 17 (Knight 5, Harrison 5, Baldwin 4, Henry 3) Milton Keynes 6 (Pendlebury 2, White 1, Clarke 1, McKinna 1, Dennis Mallett 1) Long Eaton 4 (Perks 2, Molyneux 1, Stead 1, Frankland 0, Evitts 0).

1984

Qualifying Rounds

Mildenhall 28 35 27 24 **114** Milton Keynes 30 22 22 30 **104** Peterborough 13 23 34 7 77 Rye House 25 16 13 35 **89**.

Boston 23 27 34 25 **109** Long Eaton 33 22 16 12 **83** Scunthorpe 20 16 24 26 **86** Stoke 20 31 22 32 **105**.

Arena Essex 19 29 16 20 **84** Canterbury 31 16 30 19 **96** Hackney 29 32 25 22 **108** Weymouth 16 19 25 35 **95**.

Berwick 34 31 32 40 137 Edinburgh 17 23 16 8 64 Glasgow 12 23 28 27 90 Middlesbrough 33 18 20 21 92

SEMI FINALS

Peterborough, Sunday, July 22

Semi Final 1: Boston 16 (Colin Cook 4, Robert Hollingworth 4, Billy Burton 4, Guy Wilson 4) Stoke 13 (Tom Owen 5, Paul Thorp 3, Nigel Crabtree 3, Graham Jones 2, Paul Evitts 0) Canterbury 10 (David Mullett 3, Brian Kennett 3, Jamie Luckhurst 2, Alan Mogridge 2) Berwick 9 (Bruce Cribb 5, David Walsh 2, Craig Pendlebury 1, Jim McMillan 1, Steve McDermott 0).

Semi Final 2: Mildenhall 23 (Carl Baldwin 6, Carl Blackbird 6, Ray Bales 6, Robert Henry 5) Milton Keynes 10 (Keith White 3, David Blackburn 3, Nigel De'ath 3, Peter Framingham 1) Middlesbrough 8 (Geoff Pusey 3, Steve Wilcock 2, Paul Price 2, Mike Spink 1) Hackney 7 (Barry Thomas 3, Paul Bosley 3, Andy Galvin 1, Trevor Banks 0, Kevin Teager 0).

FINAL

Peterborough, Sunday, July 22

Mildenhall 19 (Bales 6, Blackbird 5, Henry 5, Baldwin 3) Stoke 15 (Crabtree 5, Thorp 4, Owen 4, Evitts 2) Milton Keynes 11 (White 4, Blackburn 4, Steve Payne 2, De'ath 1, Framingham 0) Boston 3 (Burton 2, Wilson 1, Cook 0, Hollingworth 0).

1985

Qualifying Rounds

Arena Essex 25 29 37 **91** Mildenhall 21 30 16 **67** Rye House 7 17 11 **35** Wimbledon 43 19 30 **92**.

Rye House leg was never staged.

Berwick 35 28 33 **96** Edinburgh 32 21 14 **67** Glasgfow 4 12 13 **29** Middlesbrough 25 35 36 **96**.

Glasgow leg was never staged.

Long Eaton 20 19 26 17 **82** Milton Keynes 21 32 14 15 **82** Peterborough 31 20 25 31 **107** Stoke 24 25 31 33 **113**.

Canterbury 22 23 11 **56** Eastbourne 26 18 23 **67** Hackney 24 27 23 **74** Poole 24 28 39 **91**.

Hackney leg was never staged.

SEMI FINALS

Peterborough, Sunday, July 21

Semi Final 1: Hackney 18 (Alan Mogridge 6, Trevor Banks 5, Andy Galvin 4, Paul Bosley 3) Stoke 12 (Tom Owen 4, Nigel Crabtree 4, Paul Thorp 4, Mike Wilding 0, Darren Sumner 0) Berwick 10 (Jim McMillan 5, Bruce Cribb 3, Steve McDermott 1, Charlie McKinna 1) Wimbledon 8 (Roger Johns 4, Mark Baldwin 2, Kevin Teager 2, Peter Johns 0).

Semi Final 2: Middlesbrough 17 (Gary Havelock 6, Steve Wilcock 5, Martin Dixon 5, Geoff Pusey 1, Mark Fiora 0) Peterborough 12 (Dave Allen 5, Kevin Hawkins 3, Ian Clark 3, Ian Barney 1) Poole 11 (Kevin Smith 5, Martin Yeates 3, David Biles 2, Stan Bear 1) Arena Essex 8 (Neil Middleditch 4, David Cheshire 3, Martin Goodwin 1, Bob Humphreys 0).

FINAL

Peterborough, Sunday, July 21

Middlesbrough 17 (Havelock 7, Pusey 4, Dixon 3, Wilcock 3) Peterborough 12 (Barney 8, Hawkins 2, Allen 2, Clark 0) Hackney 10 (Banks 5, Mogridge 3, Galvin 2, Bosley 0) Stoke 9 (Crabtree 6, Thorp 2, Owen 1, Wilding 0, Sumner 0).

1986

Qualifying Rounds

Arena Essex 26.5 32 38 **27** 123.5

Hackney 28 34 21 31 **114** Rye House 12 15 21 13 **61** Wimbledon 29.5 15 15 24 **83.5**.

Birmingham 10.5 15 19 15 **59.5** Long Eaton 20.5 24 22 14 **80.5** Newcastle 32 26 19 23 **100** Stoke 33 31 36 44 **144**.

Boston 20 34 25 27 **106** Mildenhall 38 35 34 37 **144** Milton Keynes 14 9 23 11 **57** Peterborough 24 18 14 21 **77**.

Canterbury 20 17 16 19 **72** Eastbourne 36 42 24 24 **126** Exeter 13 15 27 13 **68** Poole 27 21 29 40 **117**.

Berwick 22 26 23 28 **99** Edinburgh 25 29 22 36 **112** Glasgow 15 12 22 8 **57** Middlesbrough 34 28 29 24 **115**.

SEMI FINALS

Peterborough, Sunday, August 10

Semi Final 1: Arena Essex 18 (Andrew Silver 5, Martin Goodwin 5, Neil Middleditch 4, David Smart 4) Mildenhall 12 (Dave Jessup 5, Robert Henry 3, Eric Monaghan 3, Melvyn Taylor 1) Edinburgh 11 (Les Collins 6, Dave Trownson 3, Mark Burrows 1, Brett Saunders 1) Eastbourne 7 (Gordon Kennett 2, Andy Buck 2, Martin Dugard 2, Keith Pritchard 1, Dean Standing 0).

Semi Final 2: Middlesbrough 15 (Martin Dixon 6, Mark Courtney 4, Jim Burdfield 3, Steve Wilcock 2) Hackney 13 (Andy Galvin 5, Malcolm Simmons 4, Paul Whittaker 2, Gary Rolls 2, Barry Thomas 0) Stoke 11 (Paul Thorp 4, Nigel Crabtree 3, Tom Owen 2, Mike WIlding 2) Poole 9 (Steve Schofield 5, Kevin Smith 2, David Biles 2, Martin Yeates 0).

FINAL

Peterborough, Sunday, August 10

Middlesbrough 15 (Burdfield 5, Courtney 4, Dixon 4, Wilcock 2, Glenn Hornby 0) Arena Essex 14 (Silver 6, Middleditch 4, Goodwin 3, Smart 1) Hackney 11 (Simmons 5, Galvin 4, Whittaker 1, Rolls 1) Mildenhall 8 (Monaghan 3, Henry 2, Taylor 2, Jessup 1).

1987

Qualifying Rounds

Boston 21 16 10 7 **53** Mildenhall 38 31 42 29 **140** Peterborough 16 34 35 23 **108** Stoke 21 15 9 37 **82**.

Arena Essex 25.5 28 23 32 **108.5** Milton Keynes 33.5 26 23 12 **94.5** Rye House 10 8 24 27 **69** Wimbledon 27 34 25 25 **111**.

Berwick 33 27 35 29 **124** Edinburgh 20 34 27 23 **104** Glasgow 6 14 16 8 **44** Middlesbrough 37 21 17 36 **111**.

Canterbury 24 22 16 14 **76** Eastbourne 29 40 28 35 **132** Exeter 22 10 33 21 **86** Poole 21 24 19 26 **90**.

SEMI FINALS

Peterborough, Sunday, August 9

Semi Final 1: Mildenhall 18 (Eric Monaghan 6, Dave Jessup 4, Melvyn Taylor 4, David Jackson 4) Arena Essex 16 (Andrew Silver 6, Martin Goodwin 4, Nigel Leaver 3, Ian Humphreys 3) Berwick 8 (Charlie McKinna 3, Sean Courtney 3, Rob Woffinden 2, Steve McDermott 0, Rob Grant 0) Poole 6 (Kevin Smith 3, David Biles 2, Will James 1, Martin Yeates 0).

Semi Final 2: Eastbourne 13 (Martin Dugard 6, Gordon Kennett 4, Andy Buck 3, Keith Pritchard 0, Dean Standing 0) Wimbledon 11 (Kevin Jolly 4, Jamie Luckhurst 3, Roger Johns 2, Neville Tatum 2) Middlesbrough 9 (Martin Dixon 5, Peter McNamara 2, Steve Wilcock 1, Geoff Pusey 1, Ashley Norton 0) Peterborough 9 (Kevin Hawkins 4, Ian Barney 3, Nigel Flatman 1, Peter Chapman 1, Craig Hodgson 0).

Meeting abandoned after 15 heats leaving one heat remaining in the second semi-final.

SEMI FINAL 2

Milton Keynes, Tuesday, September 8

One race was staged at Milton Keynes to complete the unfinished second semi-final from Peterborough.

Result: Wimbledon 3 (Neville Tatum) Middlesbrough 2 (Geoff Pusey, Peter McNamara, ex, tapes) Peterborough 0 (Ian Barney) Eastbourne 0 (Andy Buck).

Semi Final 2: Wimbledon 14 (Neville Tatum 5, Kevin Jolly 4, Jamie Luckhurst 3, Roger Johns 2) Eastbourne 13 (Martin Dugard 6, Gordon Kennett 4, Andy Buck 3, Keith Pritchard 0, Dean Standing 0) Middlesbrough 11 (Martin Dixon 5, Geoff Pusey 3, Peter McNamara 2, Steve Wilcock 1, Ashley Norton 0) Peterborough 9 (Kevin Hawkins 4, Ian Barney 3, Nigel Flatman 1, Peter Chapman 1, Craig Hodgson 0).

FINAL

Hackney, Friday, October 30

Mildenhall 31 (Melvyn Taylor 10, Eric Monaghan 9, David Jackson 6, Dave Jessup 6) Arena Essex 30 (Andrew Silver 12, Martin Goodwin 10, Gary Chessell 5, Mark Chessell 3) Eastbourne 27 (Andy Buck 8, Gordon Kennett 8, Dean Standing 4, Keith Pritchard 4, Martin Dugard 3) Wimbledon 7 (Neville Tatum 5, Roger Johns 1, Nathan Simpson 1, Terry Mussett 0, Kevin Jolly 0).

1988

Qualifying Rounds

Berwick 23 21 22 15 **81** Edinburgh 25 26 22 22 **95** Glasgow 28 20 22 32 **102** Middlesbrough 20 28 30 27 **105**.

Long Eaton 18 15 22 25 **80** Milton Keynes 19 26 4 16 **65** Peterborough 25 23 33 31 **112** Stoke 34 32 37 24 **127**.

Eastbourne 36 26 25 24 **121** Exeter 12 20 8 6 **46** Poole 25 33 35 27 **120** Wimbledon 23 17 28 29 **97**.

Arena Essex 21 19 30 20 **90** Hackney 28 33 30 21 **112** Mildenhall 23 20 16 38 **97** Rye House 24 24 19 17 **84**.

SEMI FINALS

Peterborough, Sunday, August 7

Semi Final 1: Poole 20 (Steve Schofield 6, Craig Boyce 6, Kevin Smart 5, David Biles 3) Peterborough 18 (Mick Poole 6, Craig Hodgson 5, Kevin Hawkins 4, Ian Barney 3) Stoke 9 (Graham Jones 4, Nigel Crabtree 2, Steve Bastable 2, Louis Carr 1) Glasgow 1 (Steve Lawson 1, Shane Bowes 0, David Blackburn 0, Martin McKinna 0, Geoff Powell 0).

Semi Final 2: Mildenhall 15 (Melvyn Taylor 6, Andy Hines 3, Eric Monaghan 3, Glen Baxter 3, Michael Coles 0) Eastbourne 12 (Andy Buck 5, Gordon Kennett 4, Dean Barker 3, Dean Standing 0) Middlesbrough 11 (Mark Fiora 5, Darren Sumner 4, Martin Dixon 1, Peter McNamara 1) Hackney 10 (Alan Mogridge 4, Chris Louis 2, Andy Galvin 2, Paul Whittaker 1, Gary Rolls 1).

FINAL

Peterborough, Sunday, August 7

Peterborough 14 (Hodgson 5, Poole 4, Hawkins 4, Barney 1) Mildenhall 13 (Taylor 4, Monaghan 4, Hines 4, Baxter 1) Eastbourne 13 (Buck 6, Standing 4, Barker 3, Kennett 0) Poole 8 (Biles 4, Smart 2, Boyce 2, Schofield 0).

1989

Qualifying Rounds

Berwick 30 23 31 40 **124** Edinburgh 35 30 26 31 **122** Glasgow 13 17 27 11 **68** Middlesbrough 17 26 12 14 **69**.

Arena Essex 23 41 29 18 **111** Hackney 35 19 31 26 **111** Mildenhall 17 15 17 22 **71** Rye House 20 21 19 30 **90**.

Long Eaton 18 15 13 19 **65** Milton Keynes 15 20 18 20 **73** Peterborough 29 30 36 22 **117** Stoke 34 31 29 35 **129**.

Eastbourne 38 26 27 24 **115** Exeter 19 41 27 21 **108** Poole 18 18 31 34 **101** Wimbledon 21 11 11 17 **60**.

SEMI FINALS

Peterborough, Sunday, July 23

Semi Final 1: Stoke 22 (Eric Monaghan 6, Nigel Crabtree 5, Chris Cobby 5, Louis Carr 3, Rob Woffinden 3) Eastbourne 11 (Andy Buck 6, Gordon Kennett 2, Dean Barker 2, Keith Pritchard 1, David Norris 0) Edinburgh 10 (Les Collins 3, Michael Coles 3, Brett Saunders 2, Scott Lamb 1, Mick Powell 1) Hackney 5 (Paul Whittaker 3, Andy Galvin 1, Gary Tagg 1, Barry Thomas 0, Michael Warren 0).

Semi Final 2: Peterborough 21 (Kevin Jolly 6, Craig Hodgson 6, Mick Poole 5, Ian Barney 4) Exeter 12 (Richard Green 4, Colin Cook 4, Steve Regeling 3, Frank Andersen 1) Berwick 12 (David Blackburn 5, Mark Courtney 3, David Walsh 3, Andy Campbell 1, Rob Grant 0) Arena Essex 3 (Martin Goodwin 2, Wayne Garratt 1, Rob Tilbury 0, Troy Pratt 0, Simon Wolstenholme 0).

Exeter qualify for final on second places in semi final.

FINAL

Peterborough, Sunday, July 23

Peterborough 15 (Barney 5, Jolly 5, Poole 3, Hodgson 2) Stoke 14 (Monaghan 5, Crabtree 4, Carr 3, Cobby 2) Exeter 12 (Andersen 6, Cook 4, Regeling 1, Green 1) Eastbourne 7 (Buck 3, Norris 2, Barker 1, Kennett 1).

IPSWICH and NEWCASTLE did not compete in the competition.

1990

Qualifying Rounds

Berwick 16 23 26 28 **93** Edinburgh 32 13 23 22 **90** Glasgow 26 38 29 19 **112** Newcastle 22 22 18 27 **89**.

Arena Essex 16 10 13 18 **57** Hackney 31 26 36 29 **122** Ipswich 30 38 32 35 **135** Rye House 19 22 15 13 **69**.

Long Eaton 12 16 23 12 **63** Middlesbrough 15 21 30 42 **108** Peterborough 35 25 13 17 **90** Stoke 34 33 30 25 **122**.

Eastbourne 19 12 13 14 **58** Exeter 24 38 17 22 **101** Poole 25 30 27 39 **121** Wimbledon 28 16 39 21 **104**.

SEMI FINALS

Peterborough, Sunday, August 5)

Ipswich 16 (Chris Louis 6, Shane Parker 4, Dean Standing 3, Alan Mogridge 3) Stoke 11 (Eric Monaghan 4, Louis Carr 3, Mark Carlson 2, Nigel Crabtree 2) Wimbledon 11 (Ray Morton 5, Neville Tatum 3, Andy Grahame 2, NAthan Simpson 1) Glasgow 10 (Shane Bowes 5, Kenny McKinna 4, Steve Lawson 1, Jason Lyons 0, Charlie McKinna 0).

Semi Final 2: Poole 16 (Craig Boyce 5, Tony Langdon 4, Gary Allan 4, Alun Rossiter 3) Hackney 13 (Andy Galvin 5, Steve Schofield 4, Gary Tagg 2, Paul Whittaker 2) Berwick 10 (David Blackburn 6, Alan Rivett 3, Andy Campbell 1, Mark Courtney 0) Middlesbrough 9 (Paul Bentley 3, David Cheshire 2, Rod Hunter 2, Darren Sumner 2).

FINAL

Peterborough, Sunday, August 5

Stoke 16 (Monaghan 6, Carr 5, Crabtree 4, Chris Cobby 1, Carlson 0) Poole 13 (Rossiter 5, Langdon 4, Boyce 3, Allan 1) Hackney 10 (Schofield 5, Galvin 3, Whittaker 2, Tagg 0) Ipswich 9 (Louis 4, Standing 2, Parker 2, Mogridge 1).

ALL THE RECORDS

✪ THE HIGHEST ever team score in a round of the Championship was 46 by Newcastle at home to Edinburgh, Coatbridge and Barrow in 1977. Tom Owen, Robbie Gardner and Robbie Blackadder all scored maximum points and while Ron Henderson dropped two points.

✪ THE LOWEST ever team score in a round was four points – by Barrow (at Newcastle, 1977), Crayford (at Eastbourne, 1978), Glasgow (at Edinburgh, 1985) and Workington (at Ellesmere Port, 1980).

✪ ARENA ESSEX'S Andrew Silver had the most successful Four Team Championship of any rider. In 1987 he scored 63 points out of a total of 66 in 22 rides in the qualifying rounds, the semi-final and the final. He dropped three points in the qualifiers but was unbeaten in six rides from the last two stages.

✪ EASTBOURNE'S Mike Sampson was the highest ever individual scorer in the qualifying rounds. In 1978 he scored 12 point maximums at Canterbury, Eastbourne and Crayford but dropped one point to Ted Hubbard in the final race of the qualifiers at Rye House.

✪ PETERBOROUGH and Rye House were the only two teams to have competed in all 15 seasons of the Four Team Championship.

✪ STOKE and Mildenhall both reached the Final on seven separate occasions. Peterborough were next on six.

✪ PETERBOROUGH won the Four Team Championship on a record four occasions, one more than Newcastle. The only other teams to have won more than once were Middlesbrough and Mildenhall.

NATIONAL LEAGUE PAIRS CHAMPIONSHIP – All the Results

1975

Belle Vue, Saturday, May 17

Section A: Eastbourne 14 (Paul Gachet 9 Neil Middleditch 5) Scunthorpe 10 (Ken McKinlay 6 Tony Childs 4) Workington 8 (Lou Sansom 7 Robbie Gardner 1) Paisley 4 (Sid Sheldrick 4 Chris Roynon 0).

Section B: Crayford 14 (Alan Sage 8 Laurie Etheridge 6) Birmingham 10 (John Hart 8 Arthur Browning 2) Bradford 9 (Tony Featherstone 6 Dave Baugh 3) Rye House 3 (Brian Foote 3 Steve Clarke 0).

Section C: Ellesmere Port 12 (John Jackson 9 Colin Goad 3) Peterborough 11 (Brian Clark 6 Ken Matthews 5) Coatbridge 7 (Brian Collins 6 Jim Gallacher 1) Stoke 6 (Alan Molyneux 4 Jack Millen 2).

Section D: Newcastle 13 (Brian Havelock 8 Tom Owen 5) Crewe 10 (Graham Drury 8 Nigel Wasley 2) Teesside 9 (Peter Reading 5 Dave Durham 4) Berwick 4 (Dave Gifford 4 Willie Templeton 0).

Semi Finals

Ellesmere Port 5 (Jackson 3 Goad 2) beat Eastbourne 1 (Gachet 1 Middleditch 0); Newcastle 3 (Havelock 3 Owen 0) beat Crayford 3 (Etheridge 2 Sage 1).

FINAL

Newcastle 4 (Havelock 3 Owen 1) beat Ellesmere Port 2 (Jackson 2 Goad 0).

1976

Belle Vue, Saturday, June 5

Section A: Ellesmere Port 11 (John Jackson 7 Chris Turner 4) Eastbourne 10 (Steve Weatherley 9 Peter Jarman 1) Peterborough 10 (Brian Clark 7 Tony Featherstone 3) Teesside 5 (Alan Emerson 5 Peter Reading 0).

Section B: Newcastle 15 (Joe Owen 9 Tom Owen 6) Boston 9 (Billy Burton 5 Robert Hollingworth 4) Scunthorpe 8 (Keith Evans 5 Andy Hines 3) Coatbridge 4 (Grahame Dawson 3 Brian Collins 1).

Section C: Workington 11 (Lou Sansom 6 Colin Goad 5) Paisley 9 (Colin Farquharson 9 Sid Sheldrick 0) Berwick 8 (Mike Hiftle 5 Robin Adlington 3) Rye House 8 (Ted Hubbard 7 Brian Foote 1).

Section D: Mildenhall 12 (Bob Coles 8 Kevin Jolly 4) Stoke 10 (Les Collins 8 Jack Millen 2) Weymouth 9 (Martin Yeates 8 Vic Harding 1) Crayford 5 (Laurie Etheridge 4 Alan Johns 1).

Semi Finals

Ellesmere Port 5 (Jackson 3 Turner 2) beat Workington 1 (Sansom 1 Goad) 0; Newcastle 4 (J. Owen 3 T. Owen 1) beat Mildenhall 2 (Coles 2 Jolly 0).

FINAL

Ellesmere Port 3 (Jackson 3 Turner 0) beat Newcastle 3 (J. Owen 2 T. Owen 1).

1977

Belle Vue, Saturday, June 4

Section A: Oxford 10 (Martin Yeates 9 Mick Handley 1) Eastbourne 9 (Colin Richardson 5 Eric Dugard 4) Weymouth 9 (Danny Kennedy 6 Vic Harding 3) Mildenhall 8 (Bob Coles 7 John Gibbons 1).

Section B: Canterbury 12 (Steve Koppe 6 Graham Banks 6) Workington 10 (Steve Lawson 8 Brian Havelock 2) Stoke 10 (Stuart Mountford 6 Tim Nunan 4) Berwick 4 (Graham Jones 3 Dave Gifford 1).

Section C: Newport 13 (Jim Brett 8 Brian Woodward 5) Ellesmere Port 12 (John Jackson 9 Steve Finch 3) Newcastle 8 (Tom Owen 4 Ron Hendersen 4) Edinburgh 3 (Jack Millen 2 Bert Harkins 1).

Section D: Boston 13 (Robert Hollingworth 8 Colin Cook 5) Coatbridge 13 (Brian Collins 8 Grahame Dawson 5) Peterborough 7 (Ian Clark 4 Nigel Couzens 3) Teesside 2 (Steve Wilcock 2 Alan Emerson 0).

Semi Finals

Newport 3 (Woodward 3 Brett 0) beat Oxford 3 (Yeates 2 Handley 1); Boston 5 (Hollingworth 3 Cook 2) beat Canterbury 1 (Koppe 1 Banks 0).

FINAL

Boston 5 (Hollingworth 3 Cook 2) beat Newport 1 (Brett 1 Woodward 0).

1978

Halifax, Saturday, July 15

Section A: Newcastle 15 (Tom Owen 9 Robbie Blackadder 6) Stoke 10 (Tony Lomas 6 John Harrhy 4) Crayford 6 (Laurie Etheridge 3 Alan Sage 3) Oxford 5 (George Hunter 3 John Hack 2).

Section B: Eastbourne 11 (Mike Sampson 9 Steve Naylor 2) Peterborough 10 (Dave Gooderham 8 Andy Hines 2) Workington 9 (Arthur Price 6 Robert Maxfield 3) Berwick 6 (Graham Jones 4 Mike Hiftle 2).

Section C: Canterbury 13 (Les Rumsey 7 Steve Koppe 6) Edinburgh 8 (Robert Hollingworth 4 Steve Lomas 4) Mildenhall 8 (Melvyn Taylor 4 Bob Coles 4) Scunthorpe 7 (Phil White 4 Nicky Allott 3).

Section D: Ellesmere Port 15 (John Jackson 9 Steve Finch 6) Rye House 8 (Karl Fiala 5 Ted Hubbard 3) Glasgow 7 (Steve Lawson 6 Merv Janke 1) Weymouth 5 (Danny Kennedy 4 Malcolm Shakespeare 1).

Meeting reserve: Peter Wilson 1.

Semi Finals

Newcastle 4 (Owen 3 Blackadder 1) beat Canterbury 2 (Koppe 2 Rumsey 0); Ellesmere Port 4 (Jackson 3 Finch 1) beat Eastbourne 2 (Sampson 2 Naylor 0).

FINAL

Ellesmere Port 5 (Jackson 3 Finch 2) beat Newcastle 1 (Owen 1 Blackadder 0).

1979

Halifax, Saturday, July 21

Section A: Milton Keynes 13 (Bob Humphreys 9 Andy Grahame 4) Mildenhall 13 (Mick Hines 8 Melvyn Taylor 5) Crayford 7 (Steve Naylor 5 Laurie Etheridge 2) Edinburgh 3 (Rob Mouncer 2 Alan Stansfield 1).

Section B: Nottingham 15 (Dave Perks 8 Mike Sampson 7) Boston 9 (Dave Allen 6 Tony Featherstone 3) Workington 6 (Brian Havelock 6 Mark Dickinson 0) Rye House 6 (Ashley Pullen 4 Karl Fiala 2).

Section C: Newcastle 12 (Tom Owen 7 Robbie Blackadder 5) Middlesbrough 11 (Steve Wilcock 9 Mark Courtney 2) Glasgow 9 (Derek Richardson 6 Steve Lawson 3) Berwick 4 (Mike Fullerton 3 Graham Jones 1).

Section D: Ellesmere Port 11 (Steve Finch 6 John Jackson 5) Stoke 11 (Billy Burton 6 Ian Gledhill 5) Canterbury 11 (Nigel Boocock 9 Paul Sheard 2) Oxford 1 (Les Rumsey 1 George Hunter 0).

Meeting reserves: Ian Westwell 1, John Jones 1, Mick Warren 0.

Semi Finals

Milton Keynes 5 (Grahame 3 Humphreys 2) beat Newcastle 1 (Blackadder 1 Owen 0); Ellesmere Port 5 (Jackson 3 Finch 2) beat Nottingham 1 (Perks 1 Sampson 0).

FINAL

Milton Keynes 5 (Grahame 3 Humphreys 2) beat Ellesmere Port 1 (Jackson 1 Finch 0).

1980

Halifax, Saturday, July 19

Section A: Middlesbrough 11 (Steve Wilcock 6 Mark Courtney 5) Ellesmere Port 10 (Steve Finch 5 John Jackson 5) Rye House 9 (Bob Garrad 7 Kelvin Mullarkey 2) Weymouth 6 (Brian Woodward 6 Martin Yeates 0).

Section B: Boston 13 (Gary Guglielmi 7 Robert Hollingworth 6) Oxford 9 (Dave Perks 9 John Hack 0) Canterbury 9 (Mike Ferreira 5 Ted Hubbard 4) Edinburgh 5 (Dave Trownson 3 Roger Lambert 2).

Section C: Crayford 12 (Steve Naylor 8 Paul Woods 4) Berwick 9 (Nigel Close 6 Wayne Brown 3) Exeter 9 (Robert Maxfield 7 Nigel Boocock 2) Scunthorpe 6 (Phil White 3 Arthur Browning 3).

Section D: Peterborough 11 (Andy Hines 6 Richard Greer 5) Newcastle 11 (Derek Richardson 6 Robbie Blackadder 5) Glasgow 7 (Steve Lawson 5 Andy Reid 2) Mildenhall 7 (Robert Henry 4 Ian Gledhill 3).

Semi Finals

Middlesbrough 5 (Courtney 3 Wilcock 2) beat Crayford 1 (Woods 1 Naylor 0); Boston 5 (Guglielmi 3 Hollingworth 2) beat Peterborough 1 (Hines 1 Greer 0).

FINAL

Middlesbrough 3 (Courtney 3 Wilcock 0) beat Boston 3 (Hollingworth 2 Guglielmi 1).

1981

Halifax, Saturday, July 18

Section A: Mildenhall 13 (Ian Gledhill 9 Ray Bales 4) Middlesbrough 11 (Steve Wilcock 8 Martin Dixon 3) Rye House 6 (Kelvin Mullarkey 6 Steve Naylor 0) Edinburgh 5 (Chris Turner 4 Neil Collins 1).

Section reserve: Kenny Young 1.

Section B: Wolverhampton 13 (Bruce Cribb 8 Neil Evitts 5) Glasgow 10 (Steve Lawson 8 Charlie McKinna 2) Oxford 7 (Dave Perks 5 Derek Harrison 2) Peterborough 6 (Richard Greer 6 Andy Buck 0).

Section C: Berwick 11 (Wayne Brown 9 Steve McDermott 2) Newcastle 11 (Rod Hunter 7 David Bargh 4) Weymouth 8 (Martin Yeates 5 Simon Wigg 3) Exeter 6 (Robert Maxfield 6 Martin Hewlett 0).

Section D: Canterbury 14 (Mike Ferreira 9 Denzil Kent 5) Crayford 12 (Barry Thomas 7 Alan Sage 5) Boston 7 (David Gagen 4 Steve Lomas 3) Ellesmere Port 3 (John Jackson 2 Steve Finch 1).

Section reserve: Dave Mitchell 0.

Semi Finals

Berwick 4 (Brown 3 McDermott 1) beat Mildenhall 2 (Gledhill 2 Bales 0); Canterbury 3 (Ferreira 3 Kent 0) beat Wolverhampton 3 (Cribb 2 Evitts 1).

FINAL

Canterbury 3 (Ferreira 3 Kent 0) beat Berwick 3 (Brown 2 McDermott 1).

1982

Swindon, Saturday, August 28

Section A: Weymouth 15 (Martin Yeates 8 Simon Wigg 7) Boston 8 (Robert Hollingworth 6 Steve Lomas 2) Glasgow 7 (Steve Lawson 4 Kenny McKinna 3) Crayford 6 (Barry Thomas 3 Alan Sage 3). *Section reserve: Steve Bishop 1.*

Section B: Newcastle 15 (Rod Hunter 9 Joe Owen 6) Mildenhall 9 (Ray Bales 5 Derek Harrison 4) Peterborough 9 (Dave Allen 5 Andy Hines 4) Berwick 0 (Bruce Cribb 0 Steve McDermott 0). *Section reserve: Brian Butterfield 1.*

Section C: Middlesbrough 11 (Martin Dixon 9 Steve Wilcock 2) Milton Keynes 11 (Craig Featherby 8 Keith White 3) Ellesmere Port 8 (John Jackson 5 Steve Finch 3) Canterbury 6 (Brian Kennett 5 Ian Clark 1). *Section reserve: Kevin Smart 0.*

Section D: Long Eaton 13 (Dave Perks 8 Alan Molyneux 5) Rye House 10 (Bob Garrad 6 Marvyn Cox 4) Exeter 7 (Andy Campbell 5 Keith Millard 2) Edinburgh 5 (Dave Trownson 5 Ivan Blacka 0).

Semi Finals

Weymouth 5 (Yeates 3 Wigg 2) beat Middlesbrough 1 (Dixon 1 Wilcock 0); Long Eaton 3 (Molyneux 3 Perks 0) beat Newcastle 3 (Hunter 2 Owen 1).

FINAL

Weymouth 5 (Yeates 3 Wigg 2) beat Long Eaton 1 (Molyneux 1 Perks 0).

1983

Belle Vue, Saturday, June 4

Section A: Newcastle 15 (Joe Owen 8 Rod Hunter 7) Stoke 8 (John Jackson 5 Tom Owen 3) Berwick 7 (Steve McDermott 6 Bruce Cribb 1) Scunthorpe 6 (Nigel Crabtree 6 Robert Hollingworth 0).

Section B: Glasgow 14 (Jim McMillan 9 Steve Lawson 5) Peterborough 10 (Dave Allen 6 Ashley Pullen 4) Middlesbrough 9 (Steve Wilcock 5 Mike Spink 4) Canterbury 3 (Kelvin Mullarkey 3 Brian Kennett 0).

Section C: Weymouth 14 (Martin Yeates 7 Simon Cross 7) Crayford 9 (Paul Bosley 5 Barry Thomas 4) Rye House 6 (Marvyn Cox 4 Bob Garrad 2) Edinburgh 5 (Mark Fiora 5 George Hunter 0).

Section D: Mildenhall 11 (Derek Harrison 6 Richard Knight 5) Boston 9 (Steve Lomas 6 David Gagen 3) Milton Keynes 9 (Charlie McKinna 9 Keith White 0) Long Eaton 6 (Paul Stead 6 Alan Molyneux 0).

WINNERS...1989 champions from Stoke, Nigel Crabtree and Eric Monaghan

Semi Finals

Weymouth 3 (Yeates 3 Cross 0) beat Newcastle 3 (Owen 2 Hunter 1); Glasgow 3 (McMillan 3 Lawson 0) beat Mildenhall 3 (Harrison 2 Knight 1).

FINAL

Weymouth 3 (Yeates 3 Cross 0) beat Glasgow 3 (McMillan 2 Lawson 1).

1984

Hackney, Saturday, June 30

Qualifying scorers:

Stoke 20 (Tom Owen 12 Nigel Crabtree 8) Weymouth 18 (Martin Yeates 12 David Biles 6) Berwick 18 (Bruce Cribb 11 Steve McDermott 7) Mildenhall 18 (Carl Blackbird 11 Ray Bales 7) Hackney 17 (Barry Thomas 11 Trevor Banks 6) Middlesbrough 16 (Steve Wilcock 9 Mike Spink 7) Milton Keynes 14 (Keith White 12 David Blackburn 2) Edinburgh 13 (Bobby Beaton 10 Sean Courtney 3) Scunthorpe 13 (Julian Parr 9 Rob Woffinden 4) Canterbury 13 (Jamie Luckhurst 8 David Mullett 5) Glasgow 12 (Steve Lawson 6 Andy Reid 6) Arena Essex 12 (Bob Humphreys 10 Martin Goodwin 2) Long Eaton 9 (Graham Drury 5 Dave Perks 4) Boston 8 (Robert Hollingworth 6 Steve Lomas 2) Rye House 8 (Bob Garrad 6 Steve Naylor 2) Peterborough 7 (Dave Allen 7 Ian Barney 0).

Semi Finals

Stoke 3 (Owen 2 Crabtree 1) beat Mildenhall 3 (Blackbird 3 Bales 0); Berwick 3 (Cribb 2 McDermott 1) beat Weymouth 3 (Yeates 3 Biles 0).

FINAL

Stoke 4 (Owen 3 Crabtree 1) beat Berwick 2 (Cribb 2 McDermott 0).

Sponsors: Speedway Star.

1985

Hackney, Sunday, September 15

Qualifying Scorers:

Ellesmere Port 20 (Louis Carr 11 Joe Owen 9) Wimbledon 20 (Mike Ferreira 11 Roger Johns 9) Poole 18 (Martin Yeates 12 Stan Bear 6) Peterborough 15 (Kevin Hawkins 11 Mick Poole 4) Middlesbrough 15 (Martin Dixon 9 Steve Wilcock 6) Hackney 15 (Andy Galvin 10 Trevor Banks 5) Rye House 14 (Andrew Silver 8 Alastair Stevens 6) Canterbury 13 (David Mullett 10 Rob Tilbury 3) Arena Essex 13 (Neil Middleditch 11 David Cheshire 2) Exeter 12 (Colin Cook 10 Robert Maxfield 2) Mildenhall 11 (Melvyn Taylor 8 Carl Baldwin 3) Stoke 10 (Paul Thorp 8 Tom Owen 2) Berwick 10 (Steve McDermott 6 Jim McMillan 4) Eastbourne 9 (Gordon Kennett 9 Colin Richardson 0) Birmingham 9 (Doug Wyer 9 Phil White 0) Milton Keynes 8 (Keith White 8 Nigel De'ath 0). *Meeting reserves: Carl Chalcraft 2 Mike Fitzpatrick 2.*

Semi Finals

Ellesamere Port 5 (Owen 3 Carr 2) beat Peterborough 4 (Hawkins 4 Poole 0); Poole 6 (Yeates 4 Bear 2) beat Wimbledon 3 (Johns 3 Ferreira 0).

FINAL

Ellesmere Port 6 (Owen 4 Carr 2) beat Poole 3 (Yeates 3 Bear 0).

Scoring: 4-3-2-0.

Sponsors: Speedway Star.

1986

Hackney, Sunday, July 13

Qualifying scorers:

Stoke 21 (Paul Thorp 12 Nigel Crabtree 9) Mildenhall 21 (Dave Jessup 11 Eric Monaghan 10) Hackney 20 (Andy Galvin 11 Barry Thomas 9) Edinburgh 20 (Les Collins 12 Doug Wyer 8) Arena Essex 18 (Martin Goodwin 11 Neil Middleditch 7) Wimbledon 17 (Jamie Luckhurst 10 Roger Johns 7) Boston 15 (Kevin Jolly 9 Andy Hines 6) Canterbury 11 (Alan Mogridge 6 David Mullett 5) Rye House 11 (Paul Woods 9 Alastair Stevens 2) Eastbourne 10 (Martin Dugard 6 Gordon Kennett 4) Poole 10 (Martin Yeates 6 David Biles 4) Exeter 10 (Colin Cook 7 Bruce Cribb 3) Berwick 9 (Charlie McKinna 7 Steve McDermott 2) Middlesbrough 8 (Steve Wilcock 5 Mark Courtney 3) Newcastle 7 (Dave Perks 4 Dave Morton 3) Peterborough 6 (Kevin Hawkins 4 Nigel Flatman 2).

Semi Finals

Edinburgh 5 (Wyer 3 Collins 2) beat Stoke 4 (Crabtree 4 Thorp 0); Hackney 5 (Thomas 3 Galvin 2) beat Mildenhall 4 (Jessup 4 Monaghan 0).

FINAL

Edinburgh 6 (Collins 4 Wyer 2) beat Hackney 3 (Thomas 3 Galvin 0).

Scoring: 4-3-2-0.

Sponsors: Speedway Star.

1987

Poole, Sunday, July 26

Qualifying Scorers:

Eastbourne 21 (Martin Dugard 12 Gordon Kennett 9) Stoke 20 (Nigel Crabtree 12 Paul Stead 8) Peterborough 19 (Ian Barney 12 Kevin Hawkins 7) Mildenhall 17 (Dave Jessup 10 Melvyn Taylor 7) Poole 16 (Steve Schofield 10 David Biles 6) Wimbledon 16 (Kevin Jolly 10 Roger Johns 6) Edinburgh 15 (Les Collins 11 Brett Saunders 4) Milton Keynes 14 (Kevin Smart 10 Trevor Banks 4) Middlesbrough 13 (Martin Dixon 9 Peter McNamara 4) Arena Essex 12 (Andrew Silver 6 Martin Goodwin 6) Newcastle 12 (David Blackburn 8 Mark Courtney 4) Rye House 9 (Paul Woods 7 Jamie Luckhurst 2) Canterbury 8 (David Mullett 8 Paul Evitts 0) Exeter 8 (Colin Cook 6 Alan Rivett 2) Berwick 7 (Rob Woffinden 7 Sean Courtney 0) Long Eaton 7 (Glenn Doyle 5 Gerald Short 2).

Semi Finals

Mildenhall 6 (Jessup 4 Taylor 2) beat Eastbourne 3 (Kennett 3 Dugard 0); Peterborough 5 (Hawkins 3 Barney 2) beat Stoke 4 (Crabtree 4 Stead 0).

FINAL

Mildenhall 6 (Jessup 4 Taylor 2) Peterborough 3 (Barney 3 Hawkins 0).

Sponsors: Speedway Star.

1988

Poole, Tuesday, August 23

Section A: Stoke 18 (Graham Jones 9 Steve Bastable 9) Middlesbrough 13 (Mark Fiora 11 Martin Dixon 2) Hackney 12 (Andy Galvin 6 Alan Mogridge 6) Rye House 11 (Jens Rasmussen 9 Paul Woods 2).

Section B: Peterborough 18 (Mick Poole 11 Ian Barney 7) Milton Keynes 15 (Troy Butler 10 Carl Baldwin 5) Mildenhall 12 (Melvyn Taylor 8 Eric Monaghan 4) Arena Essex 9 (Martin Goodwin 9 Rob Tilbury 0).

Section C: Poole 19 (Steve Schofield 10 David Biles 9) Edinburgh 14 (Les Collins 9 Jamie Luckhurst 5) Long Eaton 13 (Glenn Doyle 10 Gary O'Hare 3) Glasgow 8 (Kenny McKinna 6 Steve Lawson 2).

Section D: Eastbourne 19 (Gordon Kennett 10 Andy Buck 9) Berwick 17 (Mark Courtney 12 Rob Grant 5) Wimbledon 10 (Kevin Jolly 6 Alastair Stevens 4) Exeter 8 (Steve Regeling 8 Alan Rivett 0).

Semi Finals

Stoke 6 (Jones 3 Bastable 2) beat Eastbourne 4 (Kennett 4 Buck 0); Poole 5 (Biles 3 Schofield 2) beat Peterborough 4 (Poole 4 Barney 0).

FINAL

Stoke 7 (Jones 4 Bastable 3) beat Poole 2 (Schofield 2 Biles 0).

Sponsors: Speedway Star.

1989

Hackney, Saturday, August 19

Section A: Hackney 20 (Paul Whittaker 12 Andy Galvin 8) Wimbledon 13 (Ray Morton 7 Todd Wiltshire 6) Poole 12 (Craig Boyce 6 Leigh Adams 6) Newcastle 9 (Peter Carr 6 Rod Hunter 3).

Section B: Edinburgh 20 (Les Collins 12, Brett Saunders 8) Berwick 12 (David Blackburn 10 Mark Courtney 2) Exeter 12 (Richard Green 7 Steve Regeling 5) Ipswich 10 (Dean Standing 6 Mark Loram 4).

Section C: Stoke 18 (Eric Monaghan 12 Nigel Crabtree 6) Rye House 13 (Jens Rasmussen 9 Glen Baxter 4) Arena Essex 12 (Martin Goodwin 8 Rob Tilbury 4) Peterborough 9 (Mick Poole 9 Kevin Jolly 0). *Section reserves: Mike Fitzpatrick 0, Michael Warren 0.*

Section D: Mildenhall 18 (Preben Eriksen 10 Peter Glanz 8) Middlesbrough 13 (Darren Sumner 10 Martin Dixon 3) Eastbourne 13 (Andy Buck 8 Gordon Kennett 5) Glasgow 8 (Kenny McKinna 8 Steve Lawson 0).

Semi Finals

Mildenhall 6 (Glanz 4 Eriksen 2) beat Hackney 3 (Galvin 3 Whittaker 0); Stoke 6 (Monaghan 4 Crabtree 2) beat Edinburgh 3 (Collins 3 Saunders 0).

FINAL

Stoke 6 (Monaghan 4 Crabtree 2) beat Mildenhall 3 (Eriksen 3 Glanz 0).

Scoring: 4-3-2-0.

Sponsors: Speedway Star.

1990

Glasgow, Sunday, June 17

Section A: Hackney 18 (Steve Schofield 10, Andy Galvin 8) Ipswich 15 (Alan Mogridge 8 Chris Louis 7) Poole 10 (Craig Boyce 6 Gary Chessell 4) Rye House 9 (Jens Rasmussen 9 Glen Baxter 0).

Section B: Newcastle 17 (Peter Carr 11 David Bargh 6) Long Eaton 13 (Richard Hellsén 11 Kevin Smart 2) Wimbledon 12 (Nathan Simpson 7 Andy Grahame 5) Arena Essex 10 (Rob Tilbury 10 Kevin Brice 0).

Section C: Exeter 18 (Steve Regeling 11 Peter Jeffery 7) Stoke 18 (Nigel Crabtree 10 Louis Carr 8) Peterborough 11 (Frank Andersen 7 Craig Hodgson 4) Eastbourne 5 (Gordon Kennett 3 Justin Walker 2).

Section D: Middlesbrough 19 (Rod Hunter 11 Darren Sumner 8) Berwick 14 (Mark Courtney 9 David Walsh 5) Edinburgh 12 (Les Collins 12 Carl Blackbird 0) Glasgow 9 (Kenny McKinna 5 Charlie McKinna 4).

Semi Finals

Hackney 7 (Schofield 4 Galvin 3) Middlesbrough 2 (Sumner 2 Hunter 0); Exeter 5 (Regeling 3 Jeffery 2) Newcastle 4 (Carr 4 Bargh 0).

FINAL

Hackney 6 (Schofield 4 Galvin 2) Exeter 3 (Regeling 3 Jeffery 0).

Scoring: 4-3-2-0.

Sponsors: Speedway Star.

HAUL OF FAME

IT'S THE most glittering collection of speedway paraphernalia in the World...and it now has a resident home in the Speedway Hall of Fame at Donington Park motor-sports complex in the East Midlands.

The Hall of Fame – officially opened Tuesday, March 14, 1989 – was the original brainchild of Barry Briggs, who, during his long racing career, had his own haul of fame with four World titles and a host of other championship wins.

He then contacted Tom Wheatcroft, owner of the sprawling Grand Prix circuit where there was already a stupendous motor-racing museum and he agreed to let Briggo use one of his halls. The Speedway Hall of Fame was born.

Initially 22 people were inducted into the Hall of Fame – the 21 World Champions from 1936 until 1988 and the founder of speedway Johnnie Hoskins – and one of the ground rules of membership was that each year's World Champion would automatically be inducted.

Other members can be voted into the Hall of Fame by the Speedway Writers' and Photographers' Association and the first none World Champion riders to have their portraits go up were Jack Parker and the great Australian Vic Duggan.

The exhibition itself is constantly changing but does have a number of static displays with an overall insurance value in excess of £1,500,000. Six-time World Champion Ivan Mauger's gold-plated bike is one of the prize exhibits along with the tractor that was used at Wembley World Finals!

The original Belle Vue starting gate makes another unusual attraction and there are scores of bikes, leathers, trophies, photographs, programmes and other mementoes and memorabilia from the sport's long history.

Briggs travelled 21,000 miles, made more than 3,000 telephone calls and contacted 103 different riders before setting up the Hall of Fame – and the quest for the unusual and the rare continues.

He admitted: "That day it opened was a dream come true for me. I hope everyone else gets as much enjoyment out of seeing the exhibition as I got in setting it up."

SPEEDWAY HALL OF FAME
Donington Park, Castle Donington, Derbyshire
Junction 24 (M1). Open: 10-5 (week-days), 10-6 (week-ends). Tel: 0332-810048.

Top right: Hall of Fame founder Barry Briggs with the World Championship Trophy. Above: A panoramic view of the main Hall of Fame World Champions' gallery

BARRY BRIGGS was watching television and seeing some of golf's elder statesman still competing when it suddenly struck him: "Why not do the same for speedway!"

And that's how he came to launch Golden Greats of Speedway, a time of nostalgia with riders throwing away the cloak of advancing years to once again race against their old rivals.

Fierce opposition from British League promoters forced the cancellation of the intended launch of the concept at Coventry on Sunday, June 19, 1988 when the British Speedway Promoters' Association vetoed the move because it clashed with the National League's staging of the Grand Slam at Oxford.

Subsequently they dithered over giving permission for it to go ahead on Sunday, August 14, but finally agreed.

And it provided speedway fans with an unforgettable afternoon as their old heroes, mounted on new Jawas took to the track again. Not even heavy morning rain could spoil the fun and enjoyment.

So many of the old time greats were there. Many to ride. Some to watch. Others simply to renew old acquaintances.

World Champions Freddie Williams, Ove Fundin, Anders Michanek, Peter Collins, Ivan Mauger and, of course, the man behind the meeting Barry Briggs, were given a tumultous reception by a big crowd who were stunned into disbelieving silence when, in the opening race, Michanek charged through from the back to defeat Bengt Jansson, John Louis and Pete Smith.

Coventry, Sunday, August 14, 1988
FABULOUS FIFTIES: 1 Ove Fundin, 2 George White, 3 Arthur Forrest, 4 Fred Rogers.
Qualifying scorers: Fundin 6, Forrest 5, White 5, Rogers 4, Ken McKinlay 1, Jim Lightfoot 1, Arthur Wright 1, Sandor Levai 0.
SWINGING SIXTIES & SEVENTIES: 1 Peter Collins, 2 Anders Michanek, 3 Terry Betts, 4 John Louis. ***Qualifying scorers:*** Collins 9, Betts 8, Michanek 7, Louis 7, Barry Briggs 6, Bent Jansson 4, Martin Ashby 4, Ray Wilson 4, Bert Harkins 3, Pete Smith 1, Norman Hunter 1, Edgar Stangeland 0.
PHONESPORT HOTLINE CHAMPION OF CHAMPIONS: Ivan Mauger beat Anders Michanek; Mauger beat Barry Briggs.

Swindon, Saturday, October 8, 1988
SWINDON 1967 32 (Martin Ashby 8, Pete Munday 7, Bob Kilby 6, Barry Briggs 5, Mike Broadbank 4, Frank Shuter 2, Peter Jackson 0, Mike Keen 0) **SWINDON SOFT WATER CENTRE ALL STARS 34** (Terry Betts 8, Ray Wilson 8, James Bond 4, Pete Smith 4, Norman Hunter 4, Barry Duke 4, Edgar Stangeland 2, David Ashby 0).

Swindon, Sunday, September 16, 1990
FABULOUS FIFTIES: 1 Roy Trigg, 2 Barry Briggs, 3 Göte Nordin, 4 Ove Fundin. ***Qualifying scorers:*** Nordin 8, Briggs 7, Fundin 7, Trigg 5, Mike Broadbank 4, Taffy Owen 3, Glyn Chandler 2, Col Smith 0, Barry Duke 0.
SWINGING SIXTIES: 1 Terry Betts, 2 Finn Thomsen 3 Anders Michanek 4 Ray Wilson.
Qualifying scorers: Betts 9, Thomsen 9, Michanek 7, Wilson 7, Bob Coles 5, Graham Plant 5, Alan Cowland 3, Mick Handley 3, Ian Turner 3, Bernie Leigh 2, Bert Harkins 1, Tom Leadbitter 0.
†A Golden Greats meeting was also held at Landshut, West Germany, on the eve of the 1989 World Final.

Indoor Racing

Kings of the

EXCUSE ME...Jim McMillan and Kelly Moran get in a tangle in the inaugural indoor speedway meeting at Wembley in 1979. A bemused Kenny Carter looks and wonders what to do next

THEY'RE OFF...Hans Nielsen, Steve Bastable, Jan Andersson and Kenny Carter streak from the tapes

HARRY BASTABLE was the pioneer of indoor racing in the British League era...but it was hardly recognisable as conventional speedway and went under the name Speedtrack racing.

Wolverhampton's Whispering Wheels Roller Skating Rink was the initial venue – the first meet, a Best Pairs, was won by Arthur Browning and Andy Hunt on Tuesday, December 14, 1971 – but that closed after less than a handful of meetings leaving Leicester's Granby Hall, which opened to Speedtrack on Wednesday January 12, 1972 , to become the only regular winter venue.

Riders used specially built lightweight frames and 175 c.c. engines and meetings were held throughout the 1972 and 1973 off seasons.

THE SPORT of the future...or merely an expensive way for fans to while away some of their winter waiting for the *real thing* to start up again?

That was the huge debate as Indoor Speedway came to Britain with a rush and a flourish.

World Indoor Speedway Championship Presentations Limited – a company formed by Coventry promoter Charles Ochiltree in conjunction with Wally Mawdsley and Peter Oakes – were first to announce the advent of pukka indoor racing with an ambitious three-day show at the £7,000 a day National Exhibition Centre at Birmingham.

Charles Ochiltree claimed: "This is the sport for the 21st century. It is ther biggest breakthrough in motorcycle sport since speedway began more than 50 years ago."

And, as if to emphasise that indoor racing was going to be big business, a consortium of ex-World Champions Barry Briggs and Ivan Mauger and promoting partners Ian Thomas and Brian Larner, had announced they were planning a meeting at Wembley Arena.

Ironically the meeting in London was the last speedway meeting of one decade (the seventies) and the NEC gala the first of the eighties!

Opinions on the entertainment value of the two meeting was divided and varied. But the general concensus was that the Wembley meeting provided a Sunday afternoon of sheer entertainment and enjoyment on a 100 yard concrete track while the NEC show, spread over three days, was far more akin to outdoor racing although the latex surface became something of a nightmare to riders with Michael Lee (back), Jim McMillan (cut leg and chin), Robert Henry (dislocated shoulder in practice) and Joe Owen were all injured as racing became faster and more furious.

Birmingham's ambitions proved to be a handicap as the promotion decided the outlay was far too great to risk the following year although Wembley continued to be staged annually until 1983.

Wally Mawdsley returned to the NEC early in 1984 with speedway forming only part of a Motorsport Gala that also embraced moto-cross, trials, BMX and moto-ball.

Crowds were poor but Mawdsley and his Dutch partner Bob de Jong gambled on a follow-up show the follwing November but over a two day period failed to attract a combined audience of 7,000 and indoor speedway, hailed as the sport of the 21st century, died before it had survived even a decade.

After a five-year gap it was revived at the London Arena but the expected boom in winter speedway simply failed to materialise.

One man, above all, must regret that as Jan Andersson proved, as on the ice, that he was the true master of the tiny indoor circuits, winning six of the eight individual competitions he entered and scoring maximum points in four of the five team events!

Concrete...

All the Results

1979

Wembley Arena, London, Sunday, December 2
LADA INDOOR INTERNATIONAL: Ivan Mauger 13, Jim McMillan 12, John Davis 11, Colin Richardson 11, Joe Owen 10, Finn Thomsen 8, Edward Jancarz 8, Zenon Plech 8, Bobby Schwartz 6, Gordon Kennett 6, Kelly Moran 6, Anders Michanek 5, Bruce Penhall 3, Bruce Cribb 3, Kenny Carter 3, Frank Auffret 3, Dennis Sigalos 1, Roger Johns 1.

1980

National Exhibition Centre, Birmingham, Thursday, Friday, Saturday, January 17-18-19
DAILY MIRROR INTERNATIONAL CHAMPIONSHIP: Jan Andersson 29, Bobby Schwartz 22, Bruce Penhall 22, Finn Thomsen 21, Chris Morton 19, Peter Prinsloo 16, Michael Lee 14, Steve Bastable 12, John Louis 11, Bruce Cribb 11, Colin Richardson 11, John Davis 9, Ole Olsen 8, Peter Collins 8, Joe Owen 6, Tim Hunt 5, Gordon Kennett 5, Steen Mastrup 4, Steve Gresham 2.
SUNDAY MIRROR MATCH RACE CHAMPIONSHIP: Jan Andersson beat Michael Lee.
MIRROR SPORT GRAND PRIX: Michael Lee 9, John Louis 7, Steve Bastable 4, Jim McMillan 4.***Group A:*** Steve Bastable 11, Ole Olsen 6, Steve Gresham 5, Edward Jancarz 2. ***Group B:*** Peter Prinsloo 9, Finn Thomsen 7, Malcolm Simmons 3, Peter Collins 2. ***Group C:*** Michael Lee 10, Jan Andersson 8, Chris Morton 3, Bobby Schwartz 3. ***Group D:*** Bruce Cribb 7, Joe Owen 7, Gordon Kennett 6, Bruce Penhall 4. ***Group E:*** Jim McMillan 10, Colin Richardson 8, Phil Collins 3, Scott Autrey 2. ***Group F:*** John Louis 10, John Davis 8, Steen Mastrup 4, Zenon Plech 2.

Wembley Arena, Sunday, December 14
LADA INDOOR INTERNATIONAL: ***Great Britain 40*** (Kenny Carter 7, Chris Morton 6, Joe Owen 6, Bobby Beaton 6, Malcolm Simmons 6, Colin Richardson 5, Jim McMillan 4) ***Rest of the World 38*** (Jan Andersson 12, Ivan Mauger 7, Tony Briggs 6, Finn Thomsen 5, Brad Oxley 5, Bo Petersen 2, Erik Gundersen 1).
KING OF THE CONCRETE: Carter beat Briggs.

WEMBLEY WIZARDS...the victorious World Select with the spoils of war after the last indoor meeting at the plush Wembley Arena in 1983, Hans Nielsen, Jan Andersson, Kai Niemi, Erik Gundersen, Richard Hellsén and Ari Koponen

1981

Wembley Arena, Sunday, November 29
LADA INDOOR INTERNATIONAL: ***Peter Collins' Lions 32*** (Chris Morton 11, Colin Richardson 8, Steve Bastable 5, Peter Collins 3, Jim McMillan 3, Joe Owen 2, Graham Drury 0) ***Bruce Penhall's Select 45*** (Jan Andersson 12, Kai Niemi 10, Hans Nielsen 8, Finn Thomsen 6, Erik Gundersen 5, Bruce Penhall 3, Bo Petersen 1).
KING OF THE CONCRETE: Andersson beat Bastable.
DEVIL TAKE THE HINDMOST: Thomsen.

1982

Wembley Arena, Sunday, November 28
LADA INDOOR INTERNATIONAL: ***Lions 37*** (Andy Grahame 8, Steve Bastable 8, Joe Owen 6, Kenny Carter 6, Alan Grahame 5, Malcolm Simmons 2, John Davis 2) ***World Select 40*** (Jan Andersson 12, Hans Nielsen 9, Erik Gundersen 6, Ivan Mauger 5, Preben Eriksen 4, Finn Thomsen 3, Kai Niemi 1).
LADA WCSSI CHAMPIONSHIP: Andersson, Carter, Nielsen, Owen.

1983

Wembley Arena, Sunday, November 27
LADA INDOOR INTERNATIONAL: ***Kenny Carter's Lions 38*** (Joe Owen 10, Chris Morton 9, Kenny Carter 7, Steve Bastable 6, Kelvin Tatum 5, Martin Yeates 1, Bobby Beaton 0) ***World Select 40*** (Jan Andersson 15, Hans Nielsen 8, Kai Niemi 5, Erik Gundersen 4, Richard Hellsén 4, Ari Koponen 4)

1984

National Exhibition Centre, Birmingham, Saturday, January 21
DAILY MIRROR INTERNATIONAL: ***England 42*** (Mark Courtney 7, Joe Owen 7, Kelvin Tatum 7, Kenny Carter 6, Steve Bastable 6, Colin Richardson 4, Chris Morton 4, Les Collins 1) ***Europe 52*** (Hans Nielsen 15, Jan Andersson 11, Finn Thomsen 8, Björn Andersson 7, Henk Steman 5, Erik Gundersen 4, Preben Eriksen 1, Ralph Geurtz 1).

National Exhibition Centre, Birmingham, Sunday, January 22
DAILY MIRROR EURO-SUPERSTARS GRAND PRIX: Jan Andersson 15, Hans Nielsen 13, Finn Thomsen 11, Erik Gundersen 9, Björn Andersson 8, Steve Bastable 8, Chris Morton 8, Kenny Carter 7, Joe Owen 5, Kelvin Tatum 2, Henk Steman 2, Mark Courtney 1, Colin Richardson 0.

National Exhibition Centre, Birmingham, Saturday, November 17
INTERNATIONAL: ***England 37*** (Chris Morton 11, Neil Evitts 7, Steve Bastable 7, Simon Wigg 5, Simon Cross 5, John Davis 1, Kelvin Tatum 1, Mark Courtney 0) ***Rest of the World 57*** (Jan Andersson 15, Lance King 12, Hans Nielsen 9, Erik Gundersen 7, Shawn McConnell 5, Henk Steman 6, John Jorgensen 2, Sam Ermolenko 1).

National Exhibition Centre, Birmingham, Sunday, November 18
EUROPA SUPERSTARS GRAND PRIX: Jan Andersson, Hans Nielsen, Shawn McConnell, John Jorgensen.

Ice Racing

Jan's-Tastic

JAN ANDERSSON took to the ice like a duck to water...and skated his way to the title of the unofficial Indoor Ice Speedway Champion.

For there's absolutely no doubt that had there been an official World Championship at the ice-racing spectaculars staged by ex-outdoor promoter Ian Thomas and former rider Graham Drury that the quiet Swede would have been crowned King of the Rink!

He was a class above all others and totally dominated the indoor ice scene from 1986 until his retirement in 1988.

He was tempted back to race again in 1990, won the European Ice Masters but was beaten in the British Open Championship by his heir apparent, Guildford's Andy Campbell.

Andersson had taken it all very seriously. While some of his rivals were treating the annual extravaganza as a bit of harmless winter fun he was out on the frozen lake near his Swedish home honing his indoor skills.

He had already proved to be an expert racing on the tiny indoor tracks by the time he switched to the ice and after giving best to the Dane Hans Nielsen in the inaugural ice meeting at Telford in February, 1986, he returned nine months later to begin his long period of domination.

Ice racing in conventional rinks rather than in outdoor stadia was originally the brainchild of Drury who claims he spent the best part of a decade trying to get rink managers to agree to experiment with speedway on ice.

All feared it could cause irreparable harm to their icing systems until he began talking with the management at Telford, ironically the rink closest to his Shropshire home.

Dave Perks and Mark Stevenson, his then Long Eaton team-mates, helped to prove to Telford that it could work and, more important, would not wreck any of the expensive equipment underneath the ice surface.

He then called on the entrepreneurial showmanship of promoter Ian Thomas and was rewarded with two sell-out shows early in 1986 when fans warmed to the pantomime atmosphere of a post-Christmas show.

Like Andersson, they were back within nine months with improvements and innovations and the appeal of their own brand of entertainment and genuine cut-throat racing had won a winter audience.

For their second show at Telford they pulled off a publicity coup by persuading the Soviet authorities to allow Valeri Gordeev and Igor Marko to make the trip.

They looked superb despite the tightness of the track – until rivals in the England-Rest of the World match complained that they were using conventional ice-speedway tyres and they were ordered to use the hand-made tyres provided by the organisers.

That ended their dominance and opened the way for Jan the Ice-Man to freeze out all his rivals with a 15-point maximum.

Even at that stage it was clear where his main danger would come from as Andy Campbell, down as a reserve only, came into the meeting and dropped his only point to Andersson.

Campbell, like the maestro, had taken it seriously admitting: "I wanted to ride here in February and it coincided with a bit of a freeze-up. I made myself some tyres and went out and practised on the ice. I didn't get the chance to rideTelford but that practice eventually came in handy."

English fans had to wait another 15 months for the third Telford ice-meet and the amazing Andersson was even better! He won all 12 races during the two Sunday sessions and took his overall record to 45 wins from 48 races.

After his 1986 Telford debut – when he lost to Pierre Brannefors in one race and finished third behind Hans Nielsen and Chris Morton in another – he went on to win the Yugo Cars Individual Trophy at the Drury-Thomas 1987 venture in Scotland, where they staged a Four Team

RINKMASTER...Jan Andersson wins his first major ice award

international as well, although he lost his third ice race in the final heat when Campbell forced a run-off, which Andersson duly won.

A continuing highlight of the ice shows was the novelty and, fittingly on St. Valentine's Day, 1988, girls raced against men for the first time.

Simon Cross's sister 21-year-old Julie, an accomplished grass-track while at school, took her place in the line-up and there were also two special races for the ladies in which Maxine Hill, Sarah Cunningham and Lisa Whiberley competed.

After the continuing success of the Telford meetings the promoters looked elsewhere and took their own show across to Northern Ireland where Campbell, determined to take over from the retired Andersson, won 18 out of 18 races over the two-day programme, including the last race of all when he started 20 yards behind five rivals!

He dropped one point at Telford in 1989 – in the last race of the first official British Open Championship to Tony Olsson – to leave the organisers beating a path to Andersson's door with an appeal for him to make a comeback for the ice showdown everyone wanted to see.

That came in 1990 at Telford where Campbell finally confirmed that he had taken over Andersson's mantle with three wins out of their five meetings.

The last in the Inter Nations Championship after which Andersson announced: "That's my last race indoors on ice."

All the Results

Ice 'n Easy

1986

Telford, Sunday, February 16

SKOAL BANDITS TROPHY: Hans Nielsen 15, Pierre Brannefors 14, Jan Andersson 12, Chris Morton 12, Preben Eriksen 10, Ric hard Hellsén 9, Erik Gundersen 8, Louis Carr 8, Phil Collins 8, Kenny McKinna 6, Steve Bastable 5, Jens Rasmussen 4, Kelvin Tatum 3, Mark Courtney 3, Richard Knight 1, Peter Collins 1, Alun Rossiter, reserve, 1.

SKOAL BANDITS TEAM INTERNATIONAL: ***England 25*** (Phil Collins 8, Chris Morton 5, Kelvin Tatum 5, Steve Bastable 3, Mark Courtney 2, Richard Knight 2, Peter Collins 0) ***Rest of the World 52*** (Hans Nielsen 12, Jan Andersson 11, Pierre Brannefors 10, Erik Gundersen 8, Richard Hellsén 5, Preben Eriksen 4, Kenny McKinna 2).

SKOAL BANDITS BEST PAIRS: Chris Morton & Peter Collins 17; Hans Nielsen & Jens Rasmussen 16; Jan Andersson & Pierre Brannefors 11; Erik Gundersen & Preben Eriksen 10; Richard Hellsén & Kenny McKinna 3; Mark Courtney & Richard Knight 2; Kelvin Tatum & Steve Bastable 2; Phil Collins & Louis Carr 2.

Telford, Sunday, November 30

ICE INTERNATIONAL INDIVIDUAL: Jan Andersson 15, Andy Campbell 14, Martin Dugard 11, Erik Stenlund 10, Igor Marko 10, Simon Wigg 9, Jan O. Pedersen 8, Alun Rossiter 8, Preben Eriksen 6, Peter Carr 6, Hans Nielsen 5, Paul Thorp 4, Kenny McKinna 4, Carl Blackbird 4, Les Collins 3, Valeri Gordeev 2.

ICE TEAM INTERNATIONAL: ***England 37*** (Simon Wigg 13, Martin Dugard 11, Alun Rossiter 5, Les Collins 4, Paul Thorp 2, Peter Carr 2, Carl Blackbird 0) ***Rest of the World 40*** (Jan Andersson 12, Kenny McKinna 8, Jan O. Pedersen 7, Igor Marko 5, Valeri Gordeev 3, Hans Nielsen 3, Erik Stenlund, did not ride).

ICE PAIRS INTERNATIONAL: Peter Carr & Andy Campbell 18; Jan Andersson & Erik Stenlund 18; Les Collins & Alun Rossiter 8; Preben Eriksen & Kenny McKinna 7; Simon Wigg & Carl Blackbird 4; Igor Marko & Valeri Gordeev 3; Paul Thorp & Martin Dugard 2; Hans Nielsen & Jan O. Pedersen 2.

1987

Murrayfield, Edinburgh, Sunday, February 15

YUGO CLASSIC: Jan Andersson 14, Andy Campbell 14, Hans Nielsen 12, Kenny McKinna 11, Pierre Brannefors 10, Alun Rossiter 10, Preben Eriksen 9, Steve Lawson 8, Tommy Knudsen 7, Chris Morton 5, John Jørgensen 5, Les Collins 4, Richard Hellsén 4, John Davis 3, Jim McMillan 3, Kenneth Nytröm 1.

YUGO INTERNATIONAL FOUR TEAM TOURNAMENT: ***England 28*** (Andy Campbell 9, Alun Rossiter 8, Chris Morton 6, John Davis 5) ***Sweden 27*** (Jan Andersson 12, Pierre Brannefors 8, Richard Hellsen 5, Kenneth Nyström 2) ***Denmark 23*** (Hans Nielsen 11, Preben Eriksen 7, Tommy Knudsen 3, John Jørgensen 2) ***Scotland 18*** (Steve Lawson 7, Kenny McKinna 4, Jim McMillan 4, Les Collins 3).

Victor Ludorum: Jan Andersson, Andy Campbell, Les Collins, Preben Eriksen.

NICE-SKATER...new Ice King Andy Campbell leads Graham Jones and Richard Hellsén at Telford

1988

Telford, Sunday, February 14

ICE INTERNATIONAL INDIVIDUAL: Jan Andersson 15, Kenny McKinna 14, Andy Campbell 12, Alun Rossiter 12, Steve Lawson 10, Simon Cross 10, Martin Dugard 9, Tommy Knudsen 8, Richard Hellsén 8, Jeremy Doncaster 6, Peter Glanz 5, John Jørgensen 4, Steve Bastable 3, Thierry Hilaire 2, Julie Cross 1, Waldemar Mobus 1.

Ladies Invitation: Maxine Hill 5, Sarah Cunningham 5, Lisa Whiberley 0.

ICE TEAM INTERNATIONAL: ***England 38*** (Andy Campbell 10, Simon Cross 8, Jeremy Doncaster 6, Martin Dugard 6, Julie Cross 4, Alun Rossiter 4, Steve Bastable 0) ***Rest of the World 40*** (Jan Andersson 12, Kenny McKinna 8, Tommy Knudsen 7, Thierry Hilaire 6, Richard Hellsén 5, Peter Glanz 1, John Jørgensen 1).

ICE PAIRS INTERNATIONAL: Andy Campbell & Alun Rossiter 19; Jan Andersson & Richard Hellsén 17; Tommy Knudsen & John Jørgensen 9; Martin Dugard & Steve Lawson 7; Waldemar Mobus & Kenny McKinna 4; Simon Cross & Julie Cross 3; Thierry Hilaire & Peter Glanz 2; Steve Bastable & Jeremy Doncaster 2.

Dundunald, Belfast, Thursday, March 10

PEUGEOT TALBOT ICE SPEEDWAY CLASSIC: Andy Campbell 18, Simon Cross 13, Kenny McKinna 10, Steve Lawson 9, Alun Rossiter 9, Bernie Collier 8, Richard Hellsén 8, Thierry Hilaire 5, Andrew Silver 4, Peter Glanz 3, Rob Steman 2, Allan Johansen 1.

Peugeot Talbot Flying Six: Campbell, Hilaire, Cross, Collier, Hellsén, Rossiter.

Dundunald, Belfast, Friday, March 11

PEUGEOT TALBOT ICE SPEEDWAY CLASSIC: Andy Campbell 18, Steve Lawson 13, Simon Cross 12, Kenny McKinna 9, Andrew Silver 8, Thierry Hilaire 7, Richard Hellsén 6, Allan Johansen 4, Bernie Collier 4, Alun Rossiter 4, Peter Glanz 4, Rob Steman 1.

Peugeot Talbot Flying Six: Campbell, Cross, Lawson, Collier, Hellsén, Silver.

1989

Telford, Sunday, February 19

BRITISH OPEN CHAMPIONSHIP: Andy Campbell 14, Steve Lawson 12, Richard Hellsén 12, Rene Elzinga 10, Tony Olsson 9, Allan Johansen 9, Marvyn Cox 8, Jan O. Pedersen 8, Jan Stæchmann 7, Alun Rossiter 7, John Jorgensen 6, Simon Cross 5, Robert Pfetzing 4, Paul Thorp 3, Julie Cross 2, Chris Morton 2.

INTERNATIONAL: ***England Select 56*** (Steve Lawson 18, Andy Campbell 14, Chris Morton 8, Alun Rossiter 8, Simon Cross 6, Marvyn Cox 1, Julie Cross 1) ***Rest of the World Select 34*** (Tony Olsson 12, Robert Pfetzing 6, Jan Stæchmann 5, Richard Hellsén 5, John Jorgensen 3, Jan O. Pedersen 2, Rene Elzinga 1.

Flying Six: Lawson, Campbell, Pfetzing, Hellsén, Olsson, Rossiter.

1990

Telford, Sunday, February 18

BRITISH OPEN CHAMPIONSHIP: Andy Campbell 15, Richard Hellsén 13, Alun Rossiter 12, Tony Olsson 10, Simon Cross 9, Jan Andersson 9, Steve Lawson 8, Graham Jones 7, Peter Glanz 6, Allan Johansen 5, Zdenek Tesar 5, Keith White 4, Andy Smith 4, Neil Evitts 4, Alastair Stevens 2, Vaclav Milik 2.

EUROPEAN ICE MASTERS: Jan Andersson 13, Andy Campbell 13, Simon Cross 12, Peter Glanz 12, Tony Olsson 10, Steve Lawson 9, Richard Hellsén 9, Keith White 8, Alun Rossiter 7, Graham Jones 7, Allan Johansen 6, Vaclav Milik 6, Zdenek Tesar 3, Alastair Stevens 2, Andy Smith 1, Neil Evitts 0.

INTER NATIONS CHAMPIONSHIP: ***Sweden 8*** (Richard Hellsén 6, Jan Andersson 2) ***England 7*** (Andy Campbell 5, Simon Cross 2) ***Denmark 1*** (Allan Johansen 1, Peter Glanz 0)***Czechoslovakia 1*** (Vaclav Milik 1, Zdenek Tesar 0).

A SERIES of ice meetings were staged by advertising executive-promoter Trevor Hay at Scottish venues Murrayfield (Edinburgh), Ayr, Kircaldy and Aviemore during the early part of 1972 with the first meeting at Edinburgh on January 9, 1972, when the home side beat an Ayr team 42-34. The exercise petered out through lack of support through the turnstiles.

MASTERBLASTERS

BRITAIN'S first-ever purpose-built Long Track circuit was opened with the beating of drums...and closed down again less than two years later with hardly anyone noticing!

Long Track Racing Associates, a company formed by Exeter speedway promoters Wally Mawdsley, John Richards and journalist Peter Oakes, could not have made a bigger splash in their first 12 months of existence.

A 15,000 crowd high on Haldon Moors saw Reidar Eide become a popular winner of the first event at the 800 metre track which had been built in the centre of the Devon and Exeter Racecourse on the main A38.

It looked as if the motor-cycle sport that dominated Germany was ready to establish itself in Britain.

That view was reinforced six months later when the second meeting, in May, 1979, went to Australian Phil Crump and the organisers immediately revealed plans for a second October staging, this time with World Champion Grand Prix rider Kenny Roberts bringing over his big Yamaha sliders from the States for their first British appearance.

But cash problems and apparently never-ending disputes with the Auto-Cycle Union, under whose jurisdiction Long Track came, forced the eventual closure of the track after a financially disastrous national event on June 29, 1979, which clashed with the World Championship Commonwealth Final at London White City which not only robbed the meeting of riders but also speedway supporters who were so vital to the sister sport's British future.

The venture had a further little known sequel with one of the partners, Somerset garage owner Richard being successfully sued in court after he refused to meet his share of the company's losses.

It signalled the end of the fourth unsuccessful attempt to promote Long Track racing in the United Kingdom with earlier attempts at Point of Ayr, Prestatyn, North Wales, and Chasewater in the Midlands also fizzling out.

LTRA had hoped to make their Haldon venture – which also included a mini-speedway track which operated as a training arena – a World Championship venue but those hopes remained unrealised after an inspection by FIM representative Charles Ringblom and an insistence that the circuit be enlarged to 1,000 metres if it was to be allocated a qualifier.

Haldon, Sunday, October 8, 1978
Reidar Eide 29, Phil Crump 28, Peter Collins 25, Vaclav Verner 22, Bernie Leigh 18, Don Godden 17, Scott Autrey 16, Tormod Langli 16, Dave Jessup 15, Doug Wyer 13, Les Collins 11, Mike Beaumont 11, Bruce Cribb 6, Doug Dearden 5, Bob Watts 4, John Davis 2, Graham Hurry 2.

Haldon, Sunday, May 13, 1979
Phil Crump 30, Ole Olsen 25, Bruce Penhall 25, Ales Dryml 22, Scott Autrey 22, Larry Ross 21, Doug Wyer 17, Mitch Shirra 13, Phil Collins 10, Bruce Cribb 9, Bob Watts 5, Terry Rawlinson 3, Ian Barclay 1, Richard Moore 0.

Haldon, Sunday, September 30, 1979
INTERNATIONAL: Phil Crump, Bruce Cribb, Vaclav Verner, Chris Baybutt, Les Collins, Trevor Banks.
NATIONAL: Bernie Leigh, Steve Ryding, Martin Goodwin, Neil Farnish, Bob Watts.

▲ *Pictures show the first Haldon winner Reidar Eide and, inset, the first three Peter Collins, Eide and Phil Crump.*

What a wash-out

TEENAGER Bobby Beaton almost pulled off what would have been the biggest long-tracking upset of all time...a few miles from his Glasgow home.

For the 19-year-old Glaswegian came close to upstaging Long Track giants Ivan Mauger, Barry Briggs and Don Godden in the first-ever Long Track event in Scotland.

Speedway enthusiast Allan Robertson and stadium owner Bob Kennedy teamed up to bring the 100-mile an hour continental sport to a 680-metre pony-trotting arena at Motherwell early in 1972.

They staged three pukka long-track meetings at a venue which also had a short season of non-league speedway racing, on a total separate track.

Mauger, the World Long Track Champion at the time, won the opening meeting with a 15 point maximum but not before kid Beaton provided all the thrills.

He won his first four races – the meeting was run under conventional speedway rules with four riders a race – and then faced Mauger, Briggs and 1969 European Long Track Champion Godden in the last race.

Victory would have given Scotland a home-grown winner but Beaton was pegged back to third by the victorious Mauger and Briggs, who had seen his own chances disappear with a first race seized motor while leading.

Briggs was back for the second meeting, a midweek affair in April, and was again out of luck finishing out of the top three in quite atrocious conditions which took a savage slice out of the potential crowd.

Australian Garry Middleton, who had earlier run a training school at the Scottish venue, was in brilliant form and put together five lightning starts which won him the Duckhams Silver Trophy.

The third and final Long Track meeting was on Sunday, May 7, when, once again, the weather took a hand.

A thunderstorm an hour before the start flooded the circuit and poor preparation which left loose sand on the surface played havoc.

England skipper Ray Wilson was so covered in a sand spray in his second ride that his throttle jammed wide open before he managed to bail out to safety.

Eric Boocock and George Hunter pulled out before the main event even got under way and of the top 12 scorers – the race formula was more akin to the continental programme with six riders a race, qualifying races, two semi-finals and a final – Ray Wilson, Reidar Eide, Bob Valentine and Willie Templeton were unable to start in the semis.

Eventual winner was Jim McMillan after a dramatic final dice with Danish international Preben Rosenkilde.

Motherwell, Sunday, January 2, 1972
GOLDEN EAGLE TROPHY: Ivan Mauger 15, Bobby Beaton 13, Alan Wilkinson 12, Barry Briggs 11, Taffy Owen 10, Don Godden 9, Doug Templeton 8, Eric Broadbelt 8, John Wilson 7, Jim Beaton 7, Dave Gifford 6, Ian Paterson 3, Harry MacLean 2, George Beaton 2, Bobby Duncan 2, Ken Omand 2, Alan Emerson 2, Walter Robertson 1.

Motherwell, Wednesday, April 12, 1972
DUCKHAMS SILVER CUP: Garry Middleton 15, George Hunter 13, Reidar Eide 13, Jim McMillan 11, Barry Briggs 9, Martin Ashby 9, Bert Harkins 7, Willie Templeton 7, Roy Trigg 6, John Wilson 6, Dave Gifford 6, Doug Templeton 6, Bernt Persson 5, Frank Skinner 2, Derek Allan 2, Harry MacLean 2.

Motherwell, Sunday, May 7, 1972
CHAMPION OF CHAMPIONS TROPHY: Jim McMillan, Preben Rosenkilde, Bernt Persson, Graeme Stapleton, Jim Clark, Garry Middleton. ***Beaten semi-finalists:*** Doug Templeton, Bert Harkins, Ronnie Moore, Sandy Cook, Reidar Eide, Willie Templeton. ***Qualifying scorers:*** McMillan 8, Rosenkilde 8, Middleton 7, Moore 4, Persson 4, Eide 3, Harkins 3, Stapleton 3, Doug Templeton 3, Bob Valentine 3, Ray Wilson 3, Cook 2, Clark 1, Willie Templeton 1, Øyvind Berg 0, Tom Blackwood 0, Roy Trigg 0, John Wilson 0.

Their Just Rewards

FIRST OF A KIND...Halifax's Eric Boocock was the trend-setter

SCORES of riders owe a debt of gratitude to Eric Boothroyd. For it was the former World Finalist, then promoter at British League Halifax who persuaded his fellow promoters that loyal club riders should be rewarded...with a Testimonial!

Boothroyd eventually overcame early opposition from some of his fellow track bosses who were aghast at the thought of a rider taking the proceeds from a meeting.

But he finally won the day and, on Sunday, July 14, 1974, his own Halifax rider **ERIC BOOCOCK** became the first speedway rider to have a Testimonial meeting.

A packed house at The Shay paid their own special tribute to the England international who was also the first rider to have a Testimionial brochure produced and put on sale at 40 pence a copy.

The 40-page booklet also included a free, personally signed colour photograph of the rider.

Sweden's **SÖREN SJÖSTEN**, who had initially joined Belle Vue in 1962, spent three seasons there and then returned when foreigners were allowed back into the British League in 1967, became the first overseas rider to receive a Testimonial in 1975 when he had completed 12 seasons with the club.

PETER READING, who joined Middlesbrough on the formation of the British League Division Two in 1968 had his Testimonial in September, 1977, as the first Second Division rider to be honoured.

In 1981 it was agreed to hold a Testimonial meeting for Speedway's Medical Officer **Dr. CARLO BIAGI** and was staged at his home track at Edinburgh, the first time such a meeting had been held for anyone other than a rider.

On November 2nd, 1989, **BARRY THOMAS** carved his own niche in the Testimonial records by having a second meeting – the first and only time anyone has completed 20 seasons riding for the same promotion or club.

Since then it has become relatively commonplace and all those riders who have been given a financial windfall as a reward for their loyalty have benefitted from the foresight and thoughtfulness of Eric Boothroyd.

In the latter years of the British League it was becoming more and more prevalent for tracks to stage Farewell meetings for riders but these are NOT included in the details listed below as they have never constituted Testimonial meetings.

A number of benefit meetings have also been held in aid of charities and or injured riders and these are not included in the list of major Testimonials below.

The Testimonial Beneficiaries

1974
Eric Boocock (Halifax), July 14
1975
Sören Sjösten (Belle Vue), April 13
Terry Betts (King's Lynn), May 4
Nigel Boocock (Coventry), June 22
1976
Mike Keen (Swindon), June 19
Arnold Haley (Sheffield), July 4
Pete Smith (Poole), August 8
1977
Peter Reading (Middlesbrough), September 8
1978
Bobby Beaton (Hull), August 9
1979
Alan Wilkinson (Belle Vue), April 22
Ian Turner (King's Lynn), May 19
Bernie Leigh (Reading), August 12
John Louis (Ipswich), August 19
Martin Ashby (Swindon), September 23
Brian Clark (Peterborough), October 5
Barry Thomas (Hackney), November 4
1980
Tony Davey (Ipswich), August 10
Peter Collins (Belle Vue), August 17
Bob Kilby (Swindon), August 31
Doug Wyer (Sheffield), September 22
Barney Kennett (Canterbury), October 4
Gordon Kennett (Eastbourne), October 19
1981
Dr. Carlo Biagi (Edinburgh), June 5
Billy Sanders (Ipswich), July 7
Reg Wilson (Sheffield), September 28
Trevor Geer (Eastbourne), October 18
1982
§Dave Perks (Cradley Heath), June 26
Tom Owen (Newcastle), July 12
Ian Cartwright (Halifax), July 18
Chris Morton (Belle Vue), August 8
Laurie Etheridge (Crayford), September 14
Mike Lanham (Ipswich), September 19
David Gagen (Boston), October 10
Graham Jones (Berwick), October 31
§Meeting rained off and Dave Perks was a shared beneficiary from a meeting for the injured John Hack.
1983
George Hunter (Edinburgh), June 10
Joe Owen (Newcastle), July 18
Bob Coles (Exeter), September 26
Phil Crump (Swindon), October 2
1984
Roger Johns (Wimbledon), June 14
Robert Hollingworth (Boston), September 9
Neil Middleditch (Poole), September 19
1985
None
1986
Bob Garrad (Rye House), October 5
Dave Trownson (Edinburgh), October 26
1987
Alan Grahame (Cradley Heath), July 26
†Malcolm Simmons (Hackney), August 9
Rob Grant (Berwick), October 4
†Malcolm Simmons (King's Lynn), November 7
1988
Tommy Knudsen (Coventry), April 10
Steve Lawson (Glasgow), May 20
Erik Gundersen (Cradley Heath), June 8
Jan Andersson (Reading), July 24
Keith Pritchard (Eastbourne), October 16
Ian Barney (Peterborough), October 21
Geoff Pusey (Middlesbrough), October 23
1989
Steve McDermott (Berwick), April 16
Andy Hines (Milton Keynes), September 19
Barry Thomas (Hackney), November 2
1990
Peter Ravn (Belle Vue), May 27
Geoff Powell (Glasgow), July 18

†Neither meeting was classed as a Testimonial. Both meetings celebrated his Silver Jubilee having ridden in British speedway from 1963 until 1987.

Tuesday JULY 14 1970

BLACKEST DAY OF ALL

THE flag flew at half mast at West Ham Stadium.

And knots of fans gathered outside the wooden gates at Custom House on the day that a speedway team died.

It was Tuesday, July 14, 1970, and the British League Hammers should have been racing against Wembley that evening.

Instead speedway was mourning the loss of four riders and a legendary team manager after their mini-bus crashed into two lorries, both carrying tree trunks, a petrol tanker and then into the side of a farm-house on the outskirts of Lokeren, a small market town in Belgium.

The dead were:

■ PHIL BISHOP, 61, pioneer racer who had survived a 30 year riding career which brought him the nickname King of Crash. He had been West Ham team manager since 1966 and had organised the ill-fated trip to Holland.

■ PETER BRADSHAW, 23, Australian father of a young son who had joined the Hammers from King's Lynn at the beginning of the season.

■ MARTYN PIDDOCK, 22, one of England's brightest young prospects having been a discovery of the Second Division. Only a few weeks earlier he had been reserve for the full England squad.

■ GARY EVERETT, 29, a Wimbledon team member who was guesting for the Hammers and a rider who had established himself in the tough British League.

■ MALCOLM CARMICHAEL, 26, a protegé of England Test star Roy Trigg who was embarking on a new career having paid his own fare from Australia and a youngster who was on the verge of a team place at Romford.

Piddock and Carmichael died instantly, Bishop (on his 35th wedding anniversary), Bradshaw – who initially walked away from the carnage – and Everett in hospital.

The Dutch driver Henrikus Rommoes was also killed instantly and four other passengers injured.

Most seriously hurt was Cradley Heath skipper Colin Pratt with severe neck injuries, a fractured knee cap, head and internal injuries that ended his racing career.

Stan Stevens had a ruptured spleen, a broken leg, a fractured pelvis, serious facial injuries and was on a life support machine for some days.

Mechanic Roy Sullivan sufferered a broken leg and facial cuts and Aussie Garry Hay severe cuts to his head and face.

Tilburg, Sunday, July 12

DUTCH VIKINGS 66 (Finn Schelde 15, Preben Bollerup 13, B. Jensen 11, Nils Schelde 9, B. Larsen 8, F. Larsen 6, Toni Eggers 2, K. Zwierink 2, D. Medema 0) **WEST HAM 54** (Stan Stevens 13, Peter Bradshaw 10, Gary Everett 8, Frits Koning 8, Gary Hay 6, Martyn Piddock 4, Piet Seur 4, Malcolm Carmichael 1).

Amsterdam, Monday, July 13

DUTCH VIKINGS 57 (Jensen 14, Finn Schelde 10, Nils Schelde 10, Bollerup 8, B. Larsen 7, de Groot 4, F Larsen 3, Eggers 1) **WEST HAM 63** (Colin Pratt 15, Gary Everett 13, Martyn Piddock 10, Peter Bradshaw 8, Stan Stevens 7, Frits Koning 7, Piet Seur 2, Gary Hay 1).

"I owe my life to a miracle. If I'd swapped seats I would have been dead!"

COLIN PRATT will always have a constant reminder of the day four of his friends died in speedway's most devastating accident.

For he has named his house Lokeren – scene of the mini-bus smash which cost Colin his racing career but could, so easily, have ended his life.

He explains: "I bought my first house out of the insurance money I received and because of that I called it Lokeren. And I have taken the house name with me when I have moved and I suppose I always will."

COLIN PRATT relives the Lokeren nightmare

"I had 60 stitches in the top of my head and another 50 in my leg. I had a broken neck and a broken knee cap. We had gone to race at the Olympic Stadium in Amsterdam in a challenge match and I can remember scoring 15 points.

"We all left our cars at Dover, wheeled our bikes on the ferry and put them on a lorry at the other side. All the riders, Phil Bishop and Roy Sullivan were taken by a Volkswagen mini-bus. We went to another meeting the other side of Holland first but I didn't ride in that although I helped the youngsters.

"We were on our way back after the meeting and the last thing I remember is that we stopped at Ghent services and some of the lads got out of the mini-bus. I didn't know it then but it turned out that if I had changed seats after that stop my number would have been up. I was sitting behind the driver and Gary Hay was beside me. I remember pulling away from there and going down a three lane road.

"We were on our way back home and heading for Ostend where we were going to catch the ferry. That's the last I remember really. I woke up three and a half days later and was told the awful news.

"I didn't know I had a broken neck straight away, it was only when I got back to the hospital at Bishops Stortford near my home that it was discovered. I wasn't on a life support at the time and at first I wanted to go and see the others before I was told what had happened.

"Whether you got out or not all depended on where you sat – and why!

"Gary Everett couldn't travel in the back of a vehicle and always had to sit in the front. He got sick if he was in the back.

"Behind the driver there was myself, Phil Bishop and Garry Hay. Malcolm Carmichael lay down beside us. Then Stan Stevens, Roy Sullivan and Martyn Piddock were in the next row.

"We still don't really know what happened. We don't know if the Dutch driver fell asleep or what.

"That's most probably what saved me because I was asleep and fairly relaxed when the crash happened. I went straight out of the van and was found nearly 100 yards down the road. The van split wide open and I went through that gap.

"When I woke up in hospital my neck was as big as my head, it was so swollen and because of that they didn't find out it was broken at first. I shaved myself one morning and if I had turned I could have paralysed me for life.

"I travelled back to England with a broken neck and when they x-rayed me they found I had broken the number five cervical vertebra and they put me in traction within the hour to relieve all the pressure.

"I shouldn't really have even been in the meeting. Terry Betts was the first person that Phil Bishop asked to go along but he got the mumps and couldn't go so I replaced him.

"I remember I had to race at Cradley Heath on the Saturday night and had to be at Dover by 3.30 a.m. I loaned my bike to Colin Gooddy and the countershaft broke. It had been agreed if I had problems I would pass the carney onto Roy Trigg but I drove to my home at Harlow, got Ron Beckett, an engineer, out of bed, he fixed the countershaft and I set off for Dover and just got to the ferry in time.

"It was always an enjoyable weekend going away with Phil Bishop and everyone looked forward to it.

"Malcolm Carmichael was in the second half at West Ham, Peter Bradshaw had just broken into the King's Lynn team, Martyn Piddock was a bright Englishman coming through, Gary Everett was guesting, Garry Hay was coming along and Stan Stevens, a West Ham favourite was also with us along with Roy Sullivan, Dingle Brown's cousin who had come along to help us all as a mechanic.

"I've never ridden a competitive race since. A year after the accident I had 10 after the meeting laps at Cradley Heath and then went to see Dr. Carlo Biagi.

"He told me it was my decision but he told me if the vertebra broke now I would be paralysed from the neck down."

It took nearly three years before Colin, Stan Stevens and Roy Sullivan were paid out after a private and lengthy court battle following the discovery that the mini-bus in which they were travelling had not been insured against an accident.

Colin added: "I bought a bungalow at Takeley, near Bishops Stortford and, because of what happened, I decided to call it Lokeren....

TRACK BY TRACK GUIDE TO LEAGUE RACING

ARENA ESSEX
Arena Essex Raceway, A1306 Arterial Road, Purfleet, Essex.
National League, 1984-1990.

BARROW
The Stadium, Holker Street, Barrow-in-Furness.
National League, 1972-1974.
Park Road, Barrow-in-Furness.
National League, 1978, 1985.

BELLE VUE
Hyde Road, Manchester.
British League, 1965-1987.
National League, 1968-1969.
Greyhound Stadium, Kirkmanshulme Lane, Gorton, Manchester.
British League, 1989-1990.

BERWICK
Shielfield Park, Tweedmouth, Berwick-upon-Tweed.
National League, 1968-1980.
Berrington Lough Stadium, Near Ancroft, Berwick-upon-Tweed.
National League, 1982-1990.

BIRMINGHAM
Perry Barr Greyhound Stadium, Regina Drive, Walsall Road, Birmingham.
British League, 1976-1983.
National League, 1971-1975.
Birmingham Wheels, Bordesley Green Road, Bordesley Green, Birmingham.
National League, 1985-1986.

BOSTON
Boston Sports and Speedway Stadium, New Hammond Beck Road, Boston.
National League, 1970-1984, 1986-1987.

BRADFORD
Odsal Stadium, Rooley Avenue, Bradford.
British League, 1986-1990.
National League, 1970-1975.

BRISTOL
Eastville Stadium, Stapleton Road, Bristol.
British League, 1977-1978.

CANTERBURY
Kingsmead Stadium, Kingsmead Road, Canterbury.
National League, 1968-1987.

COATBRIDGE
Clifton Hill Park, Main Street, Coatbridge, Lanarkshire, Scotland.
British League, 1968-1969, 1973.
National League, 1974-1977.

COVENTRY
Coventry Stadium, Rugby Road, Brandon, Near Coventry.
British League, 1965-1990.

CRADLEY HEATH
Cradley Heath Greyhound Stadium, Dudley Wood Road, Dudley, Worcs.
British League, 1965-1990.

CRAYFORD
Crayford and Bexley Heath Stadium, Crayford Road, Crayford, Kent.
National League, 1968-1970, 1975-1983.

CREWE
L.M.R. Sports Ground, Earle Street, Crewe.
National League, 1969-1975.

DONCASTER
Doncaster Greyhound Stadium, York Road, Doncaster.
National League, 1969-1970.

EASTBOURNE
Arlington Road, Hailsham, Eastbourne.
British League, 1979-1984.
National League, 1969-1978, 1985-1990.

EDINBURGH
Old Meadowbank Stadium, Clockmill Road, Edinburg, Scotland.
British League, 1965-1967.
Powderhall Stadium, Beaverhall Road, Edinburgh.
National League: 1977-1990.

ELLESMERE PORT
Ellesmere Port Stadium, Thornton Road, Ellesmere Port, South Wirral
National League, 1972-1982, 1985.

EXETER
County Ground Stadium, Church Road, St. Thomas', Exeter, Devon.
British League, 1965-1979, 1984.
National League, 1980-1983, 1985-1990.

GLASGOW
White City Stadium, Paisley Road West, Glasgow, Scotland.
British League, 1965-1968.
Hampden Park, Mount Florida, Glasgow.
British League, 1969-1972.
Blantyre Stadium, Glasgow Road, Blantyre, Scotland.
National League, 1977-1981.
Craighead Park, Forrest Street, Blantyre, Scotland.
National League, 1982-1986.
Shawfield Sports Stadium, Rutherglen Road, Glasgow, Scotland.
National League, 1988-1990.

HACKNEY
Hackney Wick Stadium, Waterden Road, London.
British League, 1965-1983, 1987.
National League, 1984-1986, 1988-1990.

HALIFAX
The Shay Grounds, Halifax, Yorkshire.
British League, 1965-1985.

HULL
Boulevard Stadium, Airlie Street, Hull.
British League, 1974-1981.
National League, 1971-1973.

IPSWICH
Ipswich Stadium, Foxhall Road, Ipswich.
British League, 1972-1988.
National League, 1971-1973, 1989-1990.
Open Licence, 1965.

KING'S LYNN
The Stadium, Saddlebow Road, King's Lynn, Norfolk.
British League, 1966-1990.
National League, 1969-1970.
Open Licence: 1965.

LEICESTER
Leicester Stadium, Blackbird Road, Leicester.
British League, 1968-1983.

LONG EATON
Long Eaton Stadium, Station Road, Long Eaton.
British League, 1965-1967.
National League, 1969-1974, 1979-1980, 1982-1990.

MIDDLESBROUGH
Cleveland Park Stadium, Stockton Road, Middlesbrough.
National League, 1968-1990.
Open Licence: 1965-1966.

MILDENHALL
West Row, Mildenhall, Suffolk.
National League, 1975-1989.

MILTON KEYNES
Groveway Stadium, Milton Keynes.
National League, 1978-1988.
Elfield Park Stadium, Elfield Park, Bleak Hall, Milton Keynes.
National League, 1989-1990.

NELSON
Seed Hill Stadium, Carr Road, Nelson.
National League, 1968-1970.
Open Licence, 1967.

NEWCASTLE
Brough Park Stadium, The Fossway, Byker, Newcastle-upon-Tyne.
British League, 1965-1970, 1984.
National League, 1975-1983, 1986-1987, 1989-1990.

NEWPORT
Somerton Park Stadium, Somerton Park, Newport, Gwent, South Wales.
British League, 1965-1976.
National League, 1977.

OXFORD
Cowley Stadium, Sandy Lane, Cowley, Oxford.
British League, 1965-1975, 1984-1990.
National League, 1976-1983.

PAISLEY
Love Street, Paisley, Lanarkshire, Scotland.
National League, 1975-1976.

PETERBOROUGH
East of England Showground, Alwalton, Peterborough.
National League, 1970-1990.

PLYMOUTH
Pennycross Stadium, Pennycross, Plymouth.
National League, 1968-1969.

POOLE
The Stadium, Wimborne Road, Poole, Dorset.
British League, 1965-1984.
National League, 1985-1990.

RAYLEIGH
Rayleigh Weir Stadium, Arterial Road, Rayleigh, Essex.
National League, 1968-1973.
Open Licence: 1965.

READING
Reading Greyhound Stadium, Oxford Road, Tilehurst, Reading, Berks.
British League, 1971-1973.
National League, 1968-1970.
Bennet Road, Smallmead, Reading, Berks.
British League, 1975-1990.

ROCHDALE
Athletic Grounds, Milnrow Road, Rochdale.
National League, 1970-1971.

ROMFORD
Brooklands Stadium, Brooklands Road, Mawneys, Romford.
National League, 1969-1971.

RYE HOUSE
Rye House Stadium, Rye Road, Hoddesdon, Herts.
National League, 1974-1990.

SCUNTHORPE
Quibell Park, Scunthorpe.
National League, 1972-1978.
Ashby Ville Stadium, Ashby Ville, Scunthorpe.
National League, 1979-1985.

SHEFFIELD
Owlerton Sports Stadium, Penistone Road, Sheffield.
British League, 1965-1988.

STOKE
Newcastle-under-Lyme Stadium, Loomer Road, Newcastle-under-Lyme.
National League, 1973-1990.

SUNDERLAND
Sunderland Stadium, Cleadon, County Durham.
National League, 1971-1974.

SWINDON
Abbey Stadium, Blunsdon, near Swindon, Wilts.
British League, 1965-1990.

WEMBLEY
Empire Stadium, Wembley, Middlesex.
British League, 1970-1971.

WEST HAM
West Ham Stadium, Prince Regent Lane, London, E 16.
British League: 1965-1971.
National League: 1972.

WEYMOUTH
Wessex Stadium, Radipole Lane, Weymouth, Dorset.
National League, 1968, 1974-1984.

WHITE CITY
White City Stadium, Wood Lane, London.
British League, 1976-1978.

WIMBLEDON
Wimbledon Stadium, Plough Lane, London, SW17.
British League, 1965-1984.
National League, 1985-1990.

WOLVERHAMPTON
Monmore Green Stadium, Bilston Road, Wolverhampton.
British League, 1965-1980, 1984-1990.
National League, 1981.

WORKINGTON
Derwent Park, Workington.
National League, 1970-1981.
Open Licence: 1985.

OPEN LICENCE TRACKS

The following tracks staged speedway within the auspices of the Speedway Control Board but were never admitted to the British League.

ASHINGTON
Portland Park Stadium, Ashington.
Open Licence: 1972.
Ran two meetings only.

BALLYMENA
Ballymena Showground, Ballymena, Northern Ireland.
Open Licence: 1982.
Ran one meeting only.

BRAFIELD
Brafield Stadium, Brafield-on-the-Green, Northamptonshire.
Open Licence: 1966-1967.

CASTLEFORD
Whitwood Stadium, Altofts Lane, Castleford.
Open Licence: 1979-1980.

COWDENBEATH
Central Park Stadium, Fife, Scotland.
Open Licence: 1965.
Ran eight meetings, including a World Championship qualifying round.

MOTHERWELL
Milton Street, Motherwell, Lanarkshire, Scotland.
Open Licence: 1972.

NEWTONGRANGE
Victoria Park Stadium, NewtonGrange, Midlothian, Scotland.
Open Licence: 1970, 1973.

SUBSCRIBERS

1 Philip Rising
2 Alf Weedon
3 Mike Patrick
4 Peter Gudgeon
5 British Speedway Promoters' Association
6 Speedway Control Board
7 British Newspaper Library
8 Peter White
9 Andrew Skeels
10 Andrew Edwards
11 Richard Clark
12 Tony McDonald
13 Tony Millard
14 Arthur Lamb
15 Gordon Burnett
16 James Gudgeon
17 Sarah Oakes
18 Pamela A. Oakes
19 Mark Frankham

20. Mrs J Porter
21. J Richardson
22. R Payne
23. Paul Carrington
24. Frank Billington
25. Kevin Neil Meynell
26. Kevan Fautley
27. Barry Bowles
28. Geoff Ledger
29. Trevor John Mundon
30. Graham Smith
31. Kevin Johns
32. Terry Hunt
33. Ian McConnell
34. Brian Schofield
35. David Greaves
36. Peter Gardner
37. C G Martin
38. Paul Church
39. Bill Lysaght
40. Simon Wise
41. K R Muir
42. Neil Reynolds
43. R D Whittaker
44. Adrian Howell
45. Mark Browne
46. Tony Ellis (Exeter)
47. Paul and Yolande Gillham
48. David Mainwaring
49. Michael Piggins
50. Geoff Shelton
51. Ben Henshaw
52. H H Howard ("H")
53. John Bonner
54. Joseph Allan Green
55. Steven Clarke
56. Ken Weaver
57. Wayne Nation and Sarah Dunford
58. Dave Baker
59. Sharon J Fisher
60. David Coulson
61. Paul and Rosie Brown
62. Keith James Halliwell
63. Phil Edwards
64. Ray Allen
65. Darren Evans
66. George Sheridan
67. A John Moore
68. Jerry Harrison
69. Patricia A Palmer
70. G Marshall
71. Roger Rose
72. Phillip Marshall
73. Marie Wirdman
74. Brian K Outlaw
75. Alan Hickson
76. Kelvin Thompson
77. David Woodley
78. Mr David Ward
79. Andrew Hibbs
80. N J Palmer
81. Jon Shackel
82. Mick Richardson
83. Kevin Hammond
84. Paul Cureton
85. Adrian Fenwick
86. Mr P A H Longdon
87. G Hingley
88. Kevyn Raymond Jones
89. P J Cuckow
90. Mr W A Giles
91. Huw Jones
92. Russell and Eileen Large
93. A J Bayliss
94. David Macdonald
95. D R Howarth
96. Jack Bailey
97. Michael Stuart Brereton
98. Steve Wilkes
99. Iain and Jennifer Davies
100. Sarah Ashford
101. Terry Foster
102. Gary Hicks
103. Barry Richardson
104. Lisa Jayne Matthews
105. Mark Fulton
106. Mike Wright
107. Ann-Marie McCurdy
108. Rob Lyon
109. Michael "Speedo" C Pannell
110. Ellen M Cronin
111. Mr R K Brading
112. Mr J Hill
113. Jeff Bone
114. J J McCormack
115. David Jones
116. Dave Swanton
117. Colin Marshall
118. Mr J W Riley
119. Bridget Brockman
120. Garry Chance
121. Bryan Eric Newbold
122. Derek Dunnett
123. David Armstrong
124. Sally Prodger
125. Roger Hulbert
126. Ian Smith
127. Moira and Frederick Furness
128. Graham E Andrews
129. Anne and Trevor Kimberley
130. Paul Reynolds
131. Stanley Rowles
132. Mr Alan E Naylor
133. Dave Morrell
134. Stephen 'Pep Talk' Allen
135. Stephen Rowland
136. Mark Harvey
137. Kearley Family
138. Sue and Dave Farthing
139. David Whurr
140. Eilee Aston
141. Mr K Vaughan
142. Peter Foster
143. R A Beaven
144. David Kinvig
145. E V Walder
146. John Oughton
147. Brian John Deakin
148. T A Griffiths
149. Ken Taylor
150. Nigel Hillsdon
151. I R Willis
152. Tracey Knights JA-DE'S No 1 Fan
153. Mike Noble
154. Graham Jarvis
155. Colin Roy Pheasant
156. George W Revill
157. Peter Charles Scaife
158. Mr L Hughes
159. James Charles Purchase
160. John Charles Smith
161. B W Coe
162. D A Donaldson
163. Michael and Dorothy Aris
164. Steve Clark
165. Kevin H Critchley
166. Tony Duncombe
167. Stephen Chaloner
168. Gary Steptoe
169. Hilary Peasley
170. Andrew Shurey
171. Mrs Hurrell
172. Peter Pearson
173. Jeremy Frosdick

SUBSCRIBERS

174. George Crawford
175. J "Bob" McEnroe
176. Marianne Batten
177. Dave Day
178. Gary Thompson
179. Philip John Allen
180. Derek Richardson
181. Julie and Bill Gordon
182. Stan Ward
183. Reginald G Melhuish
184. Trevor W R Smart
185. Stuart Wing
186. Michael Stockham
187. Anonymous
188. T Power
189. Richard Haddow
190. Mark Rendell
191. J L Readman
192. Peter Pickup
193. Keith Stanley
194. Nicholas Jennings
195. Jeff Lukomiak
196. David W Stimpson
197. Roy Nuttall
198. Paul McNess
199. Anthony Taylor
200. Derek J Hosie
201. Jayne Higgins
202. Michael Hodson
203. Peter and Deidre Cuckow
204. Michael and Margaret Colman
205. Craig Saul
206. G F Russell
207. Steve Brown
208. G Wilson
209. R J Norman
210. D J Herbert
211. Kevin S Rutter
212. Vic Butcher
213. Rosemary Mellers
214. Nigel Whitworth
215. B A Pearson
216. Bryan Alan Utley
217. Bob Hipkiss
218. James Edward Gooderham
219. Mike Hunter
220. David Hood
221. Stuart Brownhill
222. Leslie O'Keeffe (Wimbledon Speedway)
223. Lisa Cooper
224. Gail Hood
225. J A Woods
226. Mr W J Playle
227. Brian Burford
228. Bary J wood
229. John Tredwell
230. Paul Frankum
231. Christopher Rowsell
232. Glynn Shailes
233. Malcolm Owen
234. Rebecca Jarvis
235. Richard Smethurst
236. Dr J T R Sharrock
237. Graham and Marion Pigney
238. Mr B E Dolbear
239. Frank Dacey
240. Alan Barwick
241. David Styles
242. Stephen Arthur Hopkins
243. Alan Marriott
244. Dion Kelly
245. Malcolm Preen
246. B E Brown
247. John C Vine
248. Graham S Rowland
249. Roger Airey
250. Claire Elston
251. Graham L Smith
252. Mr Paul M Markham
253. Bob Boardman
254. David J Carter
255. Mr Brewer
256. Sharon
257. Linda and Diane Smith
258. David Shadbolt
259. Robert T Bamford
260. Stanley Simpson
261. Andrew Pinfield
262. Dave Bone
263. Mr S Dixon
264. Neil Howard Southam
265. Clive Aiken (Arena)
266. Aileen Mitchell
267. The Colven Family and Ian
268. Paul Eustace
269. Steve Park
270. Michael John Carr
271. Mr Brian Pears
272. Chiefy Lee
273. Steve Standere
274. Denys Jones
275. Paul L Jeffries
276. G W Quinney
277. Len Webster
278. Christopher M Weston
279. Janet and Gerry Shoesmith
280. Adrian Bell
281. A G Gardner
282. Nigel Platt
283. John Henry Hilton Membership No A453
284. Eric Abbott
285. Mr D Wildman
286. Anthony Brown
287. Alan Jones
288. Eddie Baker
289. Mel Homer
290. P Dodgson
291. John Vaughan
292. Sid Kent
293. Mike Moseley
294. Karen Hughes
295. John Weston
296. Martyn Neil Green
297. G K
298. Adrian and Susanna Bursill
299. T H Rowe
300. Frank Marsh
301. Charles McKay
302. Alan Swift
303. Colin Pratt
304. Peter Alan Scully
305. R G Newton
306. Gordon Wm Rowlatt
307. Bob Edwards (Cradley Heath Statistician)
308. Gary Crapper
309. Michael C Tandy
310. Peter Amass
311. Dawn and Peter Gardner
312. Neil Girdham
313. Tony Webb
314. Kath and Les Burden
315. Sam and Dukie Ermolenko
316. Bernard Le Bargy
317. Alan Beckett
318. Gary Bird
319. Graham Oates
320. Keith Bloater Farman
321. Alan Hickson
322. A Hunt
323. Andy Marlow
324. Andrew Townshend
325. John Speirs
326. Bob Tasker
327. Andrew Bayliss
328. A P Reeder
329. John Paul Humphrey
330. Terry Catley
331. Mr Screamy
332. John William Rolfe
333. D A Watters
334. Mike Treadwell
335. Sarah Booth
336. The Sales Family
337. Mr John Hutton
338. James Southerland
339. John Bone
340. Chris Knights
341. Mr Raymond Vockins
342. Peter and Ann Foster
343. R Houghton
344. Martin and Sharyn Titcombe
345. Colin James Salisbury
346. Raymond James Salisbury
347. Karen Cadman
348. Paul Eggett
349 Mike Berry
350 D. Wright